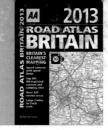

Atlas content

Scale 1:200,000 or 3.16 miles to 1

27th edition June 2012

© AA Media Limited 2012

Original edition printed 1986.

Cartography:
All cartography in this atlas edited, designed and produced by the Mapping Services Department of AA Publishing (A04858).

This atlas contains Ordnance Survey data © Crown copyright and database right 2012 and Royal Mail data © Royal Mail copyright and database right 2012.

 Land & Property Services. This atlas is based upon Crown Copyright and is reproduced with the permission of Land and Property Services under delegated authority from the Controller of Her Majesty's Stationery Office, © Crown copyright and database rights 2012, Licence number 100,363. Permit No. 110085.

 Ordnance Survey Ireland's National Mapping Agency © Ordnance Survey Ireland/Government of Ireland. Permit No. MP000611.

Publisher's Notes:
Published by AA Publishing (a trading name of AA Media Limited, whose registered office is Fanum House, Basing View, Basingstoke, Hampshire RG21 4EA, UK. Registered number 06112600).

All rights reserved. No part of this publication may be reproduced, stored in a retrieval system, or transmitted in any form or by any means – electronic, mechanical, photocopying, recording or otherwise – unless the permission of the publisher has been given beforehand.

ISBN: 978 0 7495 7353 9

A CIP catalogue record for this book is available from The British Library.

Disclaimer:
The contents of this atlas are believed to be correct at the time of the latest revision, it will not contain any subsequent amended, new or temporary information including diversions and traffic control or enforcement systems. The publishers cannot be held responsible or liable for any loss or damage occasioned to any person acting or refraining from action as a result of any use or reliance on material in this atlas, nor for any errors, omissions or changes in such material. This does not affect your statutory rights.

The publishers would welcome information to correct any errors or omissions and to keep this atlas up to date. Please write to the Atlas Editor, AA Publishing, The Automobile Association, Fanum House, Basing View, Basingstoke, Hampshire RG21 4EA, UK.
E-mail: roadatlasfeedback@theaa.com

Acknowledgements:
AA Publishing would like to thank the following for their assistance in producing this atlas:
RoadPilot® Information on fixed speed camera locations provided by and © 2012 RoadPilot® Driving Technology. Crematoria data provided by the Cremation Society of Great Britain. Cadw, English Heritage, Forestry Commission, Historic Scotland, Johnsons, National Trust and National Trust for Scotland, RSPB, The Wildlife Trust, Scottish Natural Heritage, Natural England, The Countryside Council for Wales (road maps).

Road signs are © Crown Copyright 2012. Reproduced under the terms of the Open Government Licence.

Transport for London (Central London Map), Nexus (Newcastle district map).

Printer:
Printed in China by Leo Paper Group on 115gsm paper.

Route planner

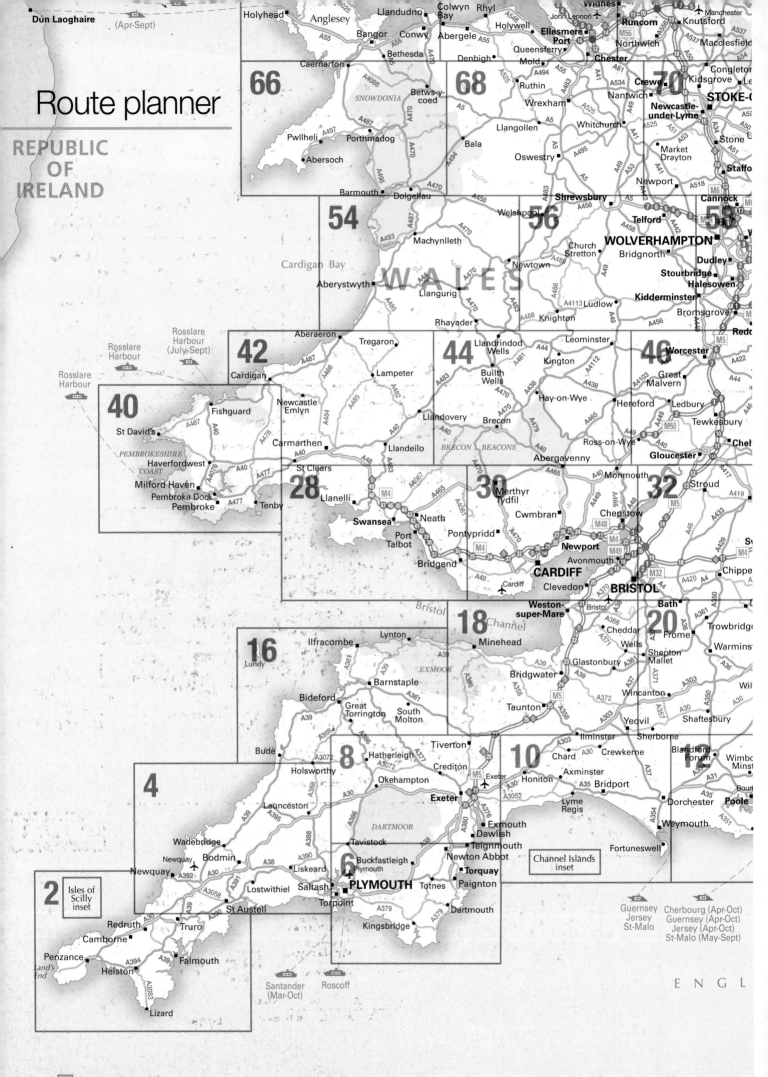

REPUBLIC OF IRELAND

WALES

ENGL

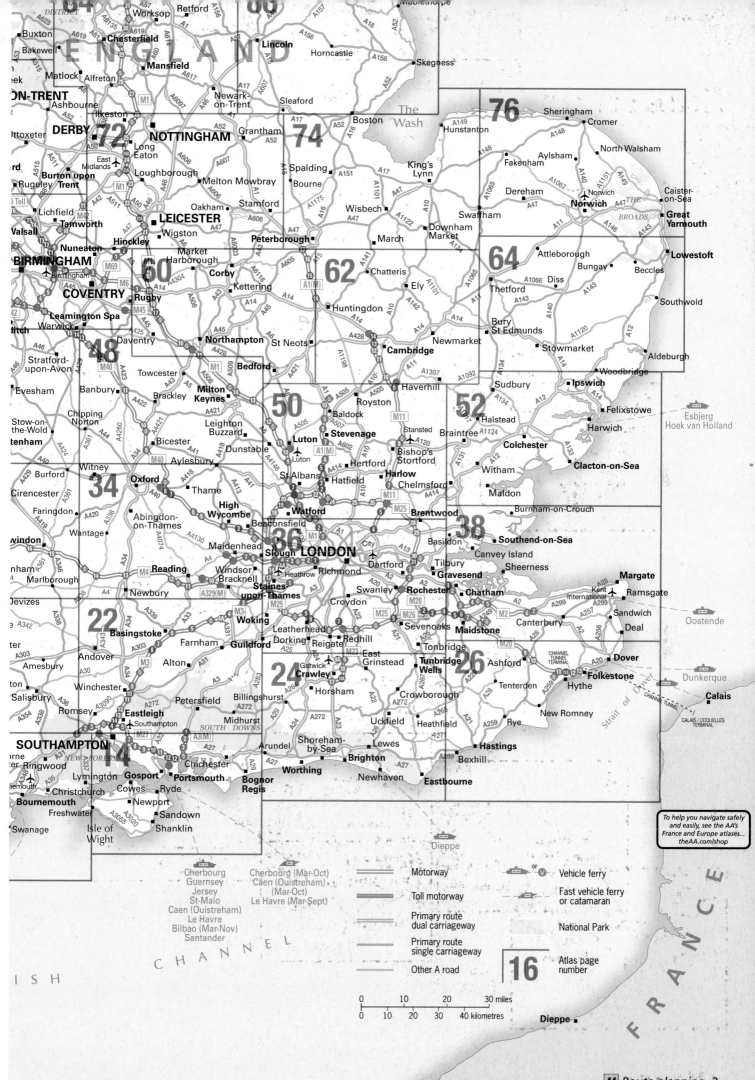

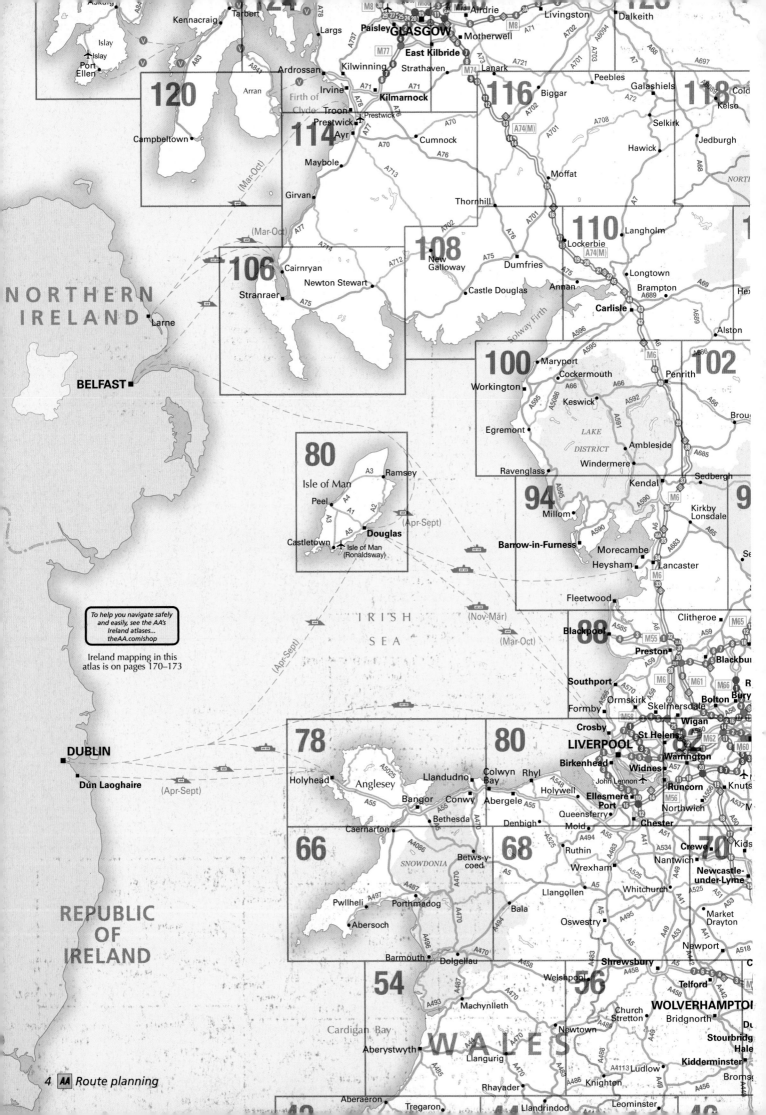

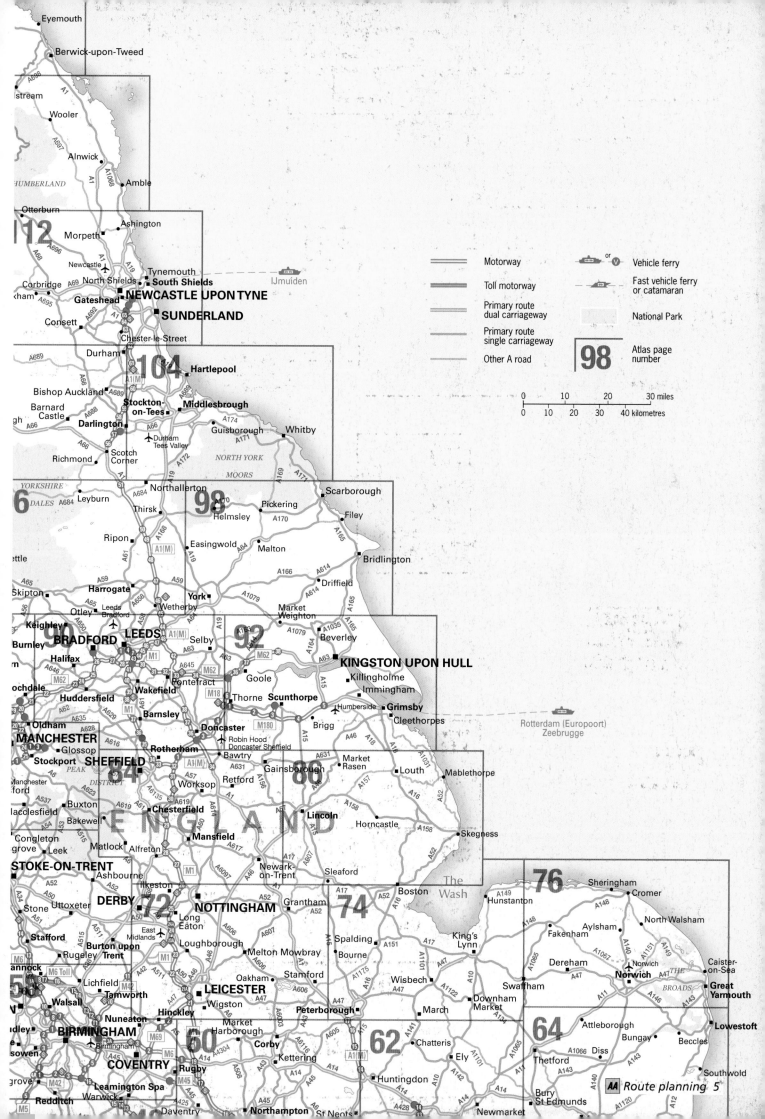

Map Legend

Motorway	
Toll motorway	
Primary route dual carriageway	
Primary route single carriageway	
Other A road	
Vehicle ferry	
Fast vehicle ferry or catamaran	
National Park	
98	Atlas page number

0   10   20   30 miles
0 10 20 30 40 kilometres

AA *Route planning* 5

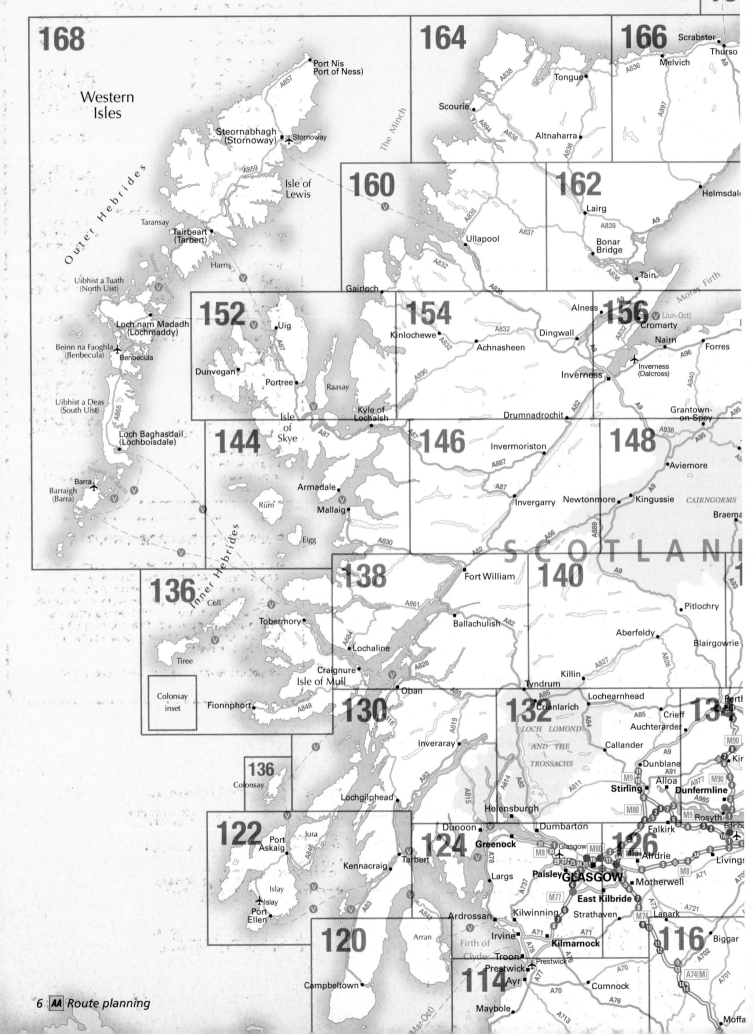

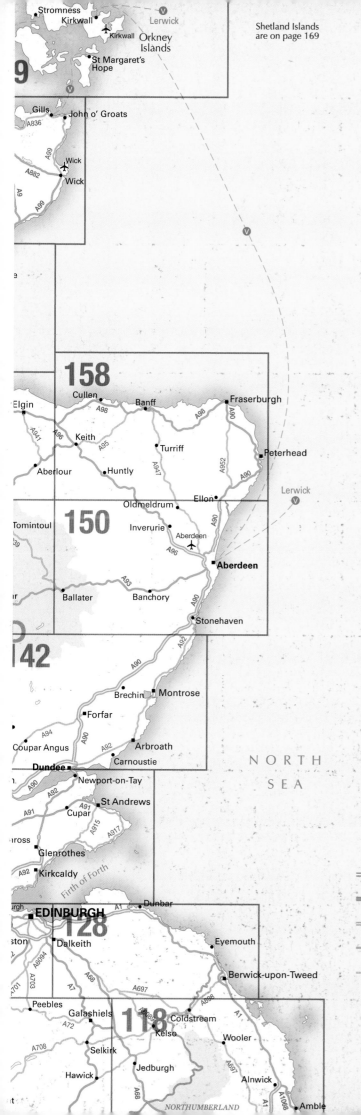

Shetland Islands are on page 169

FERRY INFORMATION

Hebrides and west coast Scotland
calmac.co.uk	0800 066 5000
skyeferry.co.uk	01599 522 756
western-ferries.co.uk	01369 704 452

Orkney and Shetland
northlinkferries.co.uk	0845 6000 449
pentlandferries.co.uk	01856 831 226
orkneyferries.co.uk	01856 872 044
shetland.gov.uk/ferries	01595 693 535

Isle of Man
steam-packet.com	08722 992 992

Ireland
irishferries.com	08717 300 400
poferries.com	08716 642 020
stenaline.co.uk	08447 70 70 70

North Sea (Scandinavia and Benelux)
dfdsseaways.co.uk	08715 229 955
poferries.com	08716 642 020
stenaline.co.uk	08447 70 70 70

Isle of Wight
wightlink.co.uk	0871 376 1000
redfunnel.co.uk	0844 844 9988

Channel Islands
condorferries.co.uk	0845 609 1024

Channel hopping (France and Belgium)
brittany-ferries.co.uk	0871 244 0744
condorferries.co.uk	0845 609 1024
eurotunnel.com	08443 35 35 35
ldlines.co.uk	0844 576 8836
dfdsseaways.co.uk	08715 229 955
poferries.com	08716 642 020
transeuropaferries.com	01843 595 522
transmancheferries.com	0844 576 8836

Northern Spain
brittany-ferries.co.uk	0871 244 0744
poferries.com	08716 642 020

EMERGENCY DIVERSION ROUTES

In an emergency it may be necessary to close a section of motorway or other main road to traffic, so a temporary sign may advise drivers to follow a diversion route. To help drivers navigate the route, black symbols on yellow patches may be permanently displayed on existing direction signs, including motorway signs. Symbols may also be used on separate signs with yellow backgrounds.

For further information see www.highways.gov.uk

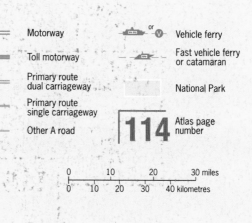

Traffic signs

Signs giving orders

Signs with red circles are mostly prohibitive. Plates below signs qualify their message.

Entry to 20mph zone

End of 20mph zone

Maximum speed

National speed limit applies

School crossing patrol

Stop and give way

Give way to traffic on major road

Manually operated temporary STOP and GO signs

No entry for vehicular traffic

No vehicles except bicycles being pushed

No cycling

No motor vehicles

No buses (over 8 passenger seats)

No overtaking

No towed caravans

No vehicles carrying explosives

No vehicle or combination of vehicles over length shown

No vehicles over height shown

No vehicles over width shown

Give way to oncoming vehicles
Give priority to vehicles from opposite direction

No right turn

No left turn

No U-turns

No goods vehicles over maximum gross weight shown (in tonnes) except for loading and unloading

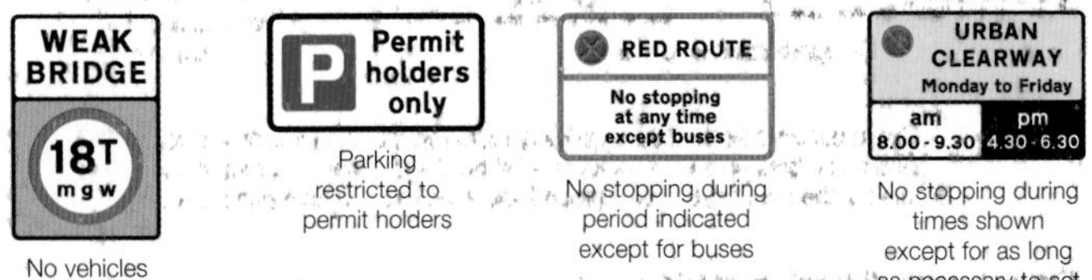

WEAK BRIDGE
No vehicles over maximum gross weight shown (in tonnes)

Permit holders only
Parking restricted to permit holders

RED ROUTE
No stopping at any time except buses
No stopping during period indicated except for buses

URBAN CLEARWAY
Monday to Friday
am 8.00-9.30   pm 4.30-6.30
No stopping during times shown except for as long as necessary to set down or pick up passengers

No waiting

No stopping (Clearway)

Signs with blue circles but no red border mostly give positive instruction.

Ahead only

Turn left ahead (right if symbol reversed)

Turn left (right if symbol reversed)

Keep left (right if symbol reversed)

Vehicles may pass either side to reach same destination

(top right column)

Mini-roundabout (roundabout circulation – give way to vehicles from the immediate right)

Route to be used by pedal cycles only

Segregated pedal cycle and pedestrian route

Minimum speed

End of minimum speed

Only
Buses and cycles only

Only
Trams only

TRAMWAY LOOK BOTH WAYS
Pedestrian crossing point over tramway

One-way traffic (note: compare circular 'Ahead only' sign)

With-flow bus and cycle lane

Contraflow bus lane

With-flow pedal cycle lane

Warning signs

Mostly triangular

STOP 100 yds
Distance to 'STOP' line ahead

Dual carriageway ends

Road narrows on right (left if symbol reversed)

Road narrows on both sides

GIVE WAY 50 yds
Distance to 'Give Way' line ahead

Crossroads

Junction on bend ahead

T-junction with priority over vehicles from the right

Staggered junction

Traffic merging from left ahead

The priority through route is indicated by the broader line.

Double bend first to left (symbol may be reversed)

Bend to right (or left if symbol reversed)

Roundabout

Uneven road

REDUCE SPEED NOW
Plate below some signs

Two-way traffic crosses one-way road

Two-way traffic straight ahead

Opening or swing bridge ahead

Low-flying aircraft or sudden aircraft noise

Falling or fallen rocks

Traffic signals not in use

Traffic signals

Slippery road

10%
Steep hill downwards

20%
Steep hill upwards

Gradients may be shown as a ratio i.e. 20% = 1:5

Tunnel ahead

Trams crossing ahead

Level crossing with barrier or gate ahead

Level crossing without barrier or gate ahead

Level crossing without barrier

Patrol

School crossing patrol ahead (some signs have amber lights which flash when crossings are in use)

Frail (or blind or disabled if shown) pedestrians likely to cross road ahead

No footway for 400 yds

Pedestrians in road ahead

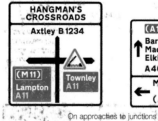
Zebra crossing

Safe height 16'-6"

Overhead electric cable; plate indicates maximum height of vehicles which can pass safely

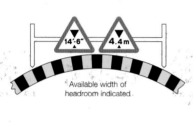
14'-6"   4.4m

Available width of headroom indicated

Sharp deviation of route to left (or right if chevrons reversed)

STOP when lights show

Light signals ahead at level crossing, airfield or bridge

Red | STOP
Green | Clear
IF NO LIGHT - PHONE CROSSING OPERATOR

Miniature warning lights at level crossings

Cattle

Wild animals

Wild horses or ponies

Accompanied horses or ponies

Cycle route ahead

Ice

Risk of ice

Queues likely

Traffic queues likely ahead

Humps for ½ mile

Distance over which road humps extend

Hidden dip

Other danger; plate indicates nature of danger

Soft verges for 2 miles

Soft verges

Side winds

Hump bridge

Ford

Worded warning sign

Quayside or river bank

Risk of grounding

Direction signs

Mostly rectangular

Signs on motorways – blue backgrounds

Nottingham 23 M1

At a junction leading directly into a motorway (junction number may be shown on a black background)

Nottingham A52   25   ½ m

On approaches to junctions (junction number on black background)

M1 The NORTH
Sheffield 32
Leeds 59

Route confirmatory sign after junction

A404 Marlow   Birmingham, Oxford M40
4 ½ m

Downward pointing arrows mean 'Get in lane'
The left-hand lane leads to a different destination from the other lanes.

A46 (M69) Leicester, Coventry (E)
2 ½ m   The NORTH WEST, Birmingham, Coventry (N) M6

The panel with the inclined arrow indicates the destinations which can be reached by leaving the motorway at the next junction

Signs on primary routes - green backgrounds

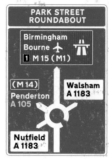
PARK STREET ROUNDABOUT
Birmingham
Bourne
1 M15 (M1)
(M14)
Penderton A105
Walsham A1183
Nutfield A1183

On approaches to junctions

Lampton Axtley A11   14'6"   1 mile

At the junction

A46
The SOUTH
Nottingham 17
Leicester 32
(M1 South) 35

Route confirmatory sign after junction

TURPIN'S CROSSROADS
Biggleswick A11
Lampton (M11)
Dorfield A123
Axtley B1991
Steam railway

On approaches to junctions

Swansea Abertawe A483

On approach to a junction in Wales (bilingual)

Blue panels indicate that the motorway starts at the junction ahead.
Motorways shown in brackets can also be reached along the route indicated.
White panels indicate local or non-primary routes leading from the junction ahead.
Brown panels show the route to tourist attractions.
The name of the junction may be shown at the top of the sign.
The aircraft symbol indicates the route to an airport.
A symbol may be included to warn of a hazard or restriction along that route.

Signs on non-primary and local routes - black borders

HANGMAN'S CROSSROADS
Axtley B1234
(M11)
Lampton A11
Townley A11

On approaches to junctions

(A1(M)) 8
Barnes 10
Mackstone 2½
Elkington 1
A404 (A41)
Millington Green (A4011) 3

Market Walborough B486 7

At the junction

WC

Direction to toilets with access for the disabled

Green panels indicate that the primary route starts at the junction ahead.
Route numbers on a blue background show the direction to a motorway.
Route numbers on a green background show the direction to a primary route.

Emergency diversion routes

In an emergency it may be necessary to close a section of motorway or other main road to traffic, so a temporary sign may advise drivers to follow a diversion route. To help drivers navigate the route, black symbols on yellow patches may be permanently displayed on existing direction signs, including motorway signs. Symbols may also be used on separate signs with yellow backgrounds.

For further information see www.highways.gov.uk

Note: Although this road atlas shows many of the signs commonly in use, a comprehensive explanation of the signing system is given in the AA's handbook *Know Your Road Signs*, which is on sale at theaa.com/shop and booksellers. The booklet also illustrates and explains the vast majority of signs the road user is likely to encounter. The signs illustrated in this road atlas are not all drawn to the same scale. In Wales, bilingual versions of some signs are used including Welsh and English versions of place names. Some older designs of signs may still be seen on the roads.

Channel Hopping

For business or pleasure, hopping on a ferry across to France, Belgium or the Channel Islands has never been easier.

The vehicle ferry routes shown on this map give you all the options, together with detailed port plans to help you navigate to and from the ferry terminals. Simply choose your preferred route, not forgetting the fast sailings; then check the colour-coded table for ferry operators, crossing times and contact details.

Bon voyage!

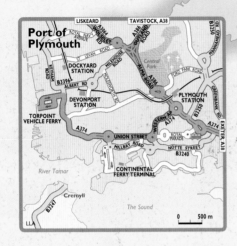

Fast ferry

Conventional ferry

ENGLISH CHANNEL FERRY CROSSINGS AND OPERATORS

To	From	Journey Time	Operator	Telephone	Website
Caen (Ouistreham)	Portsmouth	6 - 7 hrs	Brittany Ferries	0871 244 0744	brittany-ferries.co.uk
Caen (Ouistreham)	Portsmouth	3 hrs 45 mins (Mar-Oct)	Brittany Ferries	0871 244 0744	brittany-ferries.co.uk
Calais (Coquelles)	Folkestone	35 mins	Eurotunnel	08443 35 35 35	eurotunnel.com
Calais	Dover	1 hr 30 mins	P&O Ferries	0871 664 2020	poferries.com
Cherbourg	Poole	2 hrs 30 mins (April-Oct)	Brittany Ferries	0871 244 0744	brittany-ferries.co.uk
Cherbourg	Portsmouth	3 hrs (Mar-Oct)	Brittany Ferries	0871 244 0744	brittany-ferries.co.uk
Cherbourg	Portsmouth	4 hrs 30 mins(day) 8 hrs(o/night)	Brittany Ferries	0871 244 0744	brittany-ferries.co.uk
Cherbourg	Portsmouth	5 hrs 30 mins (May-Sept)	Condor	0845 609 1024	condorferries.co.uk
Dieppe	Newhaven	4 hrs	Transmanche Ferries	0844 576 8836	transmancheferries.co.uk
Dunkerque	Dover	2 hrs	DFDS Seaways	0871 522 9955	dfdsseaways.co.uk
Guernsey	Poole	2 hrs 30 mins (April-Oct)	Condor	0845 609 1024	condorferries.co.uk
Guernsey	Portsmouth	7 hrs	Condor	0845 609 1024	condorferries.co.uk
Guernsey	Weymouth	2 hrs 10 mins	Condor	0845 609 1024	condorferries.co.uk
Jersey	Poole	3 hrs (April-Oct)	Condor	0845 609 1024	condorferries.co.uk
Jersey	Portsmouth	10 hrs 30 mins	Condor	0845 609 1024	condorferries.co.uk
Jersey	Weymouth	3 hrs 25 mins	Condor	0845 609 1024	condorferries.co.uk
Le Havre	Portsmouth	5 hrs 30 mins - 8 hrs	LD Lines	0844 576 8836	ldlines.co.uk
Le Havre	Portsmouth	3 hrs 15 mins (Mar-Sept)	LD Lines	0844 576 8836	ldlines.co.uk
Oostende	Ramsgate	4 hrs - 4 hrs 30 mins	Transeuropa	01843 595 522	transeuropaferries.com
Roscoff	Plymouth	6 - 8 hrs	Brittany Ferries	0871 244 0744	brittany-ferries.co.uk
St-Malo	Poole	4 hrs 35 mins (May-Sept)	Condor	0845 609 1024	condorferries.co.uk
St-Malo	Portsmouth	9 - 10 hrs 45 mins	Brittany Ferries	0871 244 0744	brittany-ferries.co.uk
St-Malo	Weymouth	5 hrs 15 mins	Condor	0845 609 1024	condorferries.co.uk

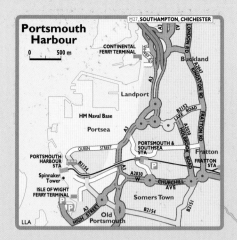

Portsmouth Harbour

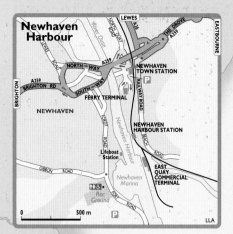

Newhaven Harbour

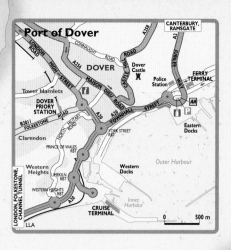

Port of Dover

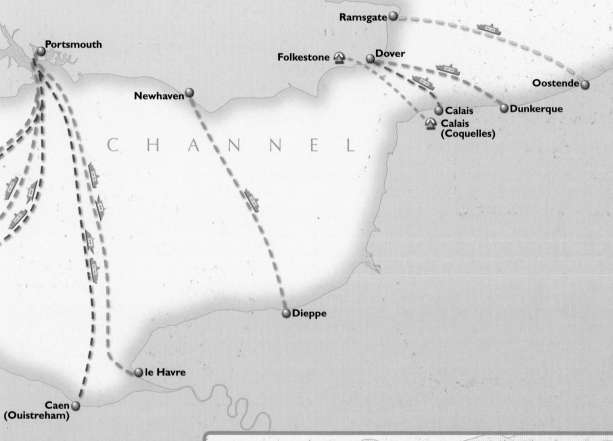

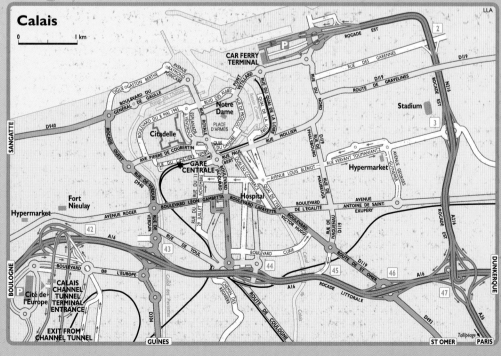

Calais

Ferries to Ireland and the Isle of Man

With so many sea crossings to Ireland and the Isle of Man this map will help you make the right choice.

The vehicle ferry routes shown on this map give you all the options, together with detailed port plans to help you navigate to and from the ferry terminals. Simply choose your preferred route, not forgetting the fast sailings; then check the colour-coded table for ferry operators, crossing times and contact details.

🛳 Fast ferry   🛳 Conventional ferry

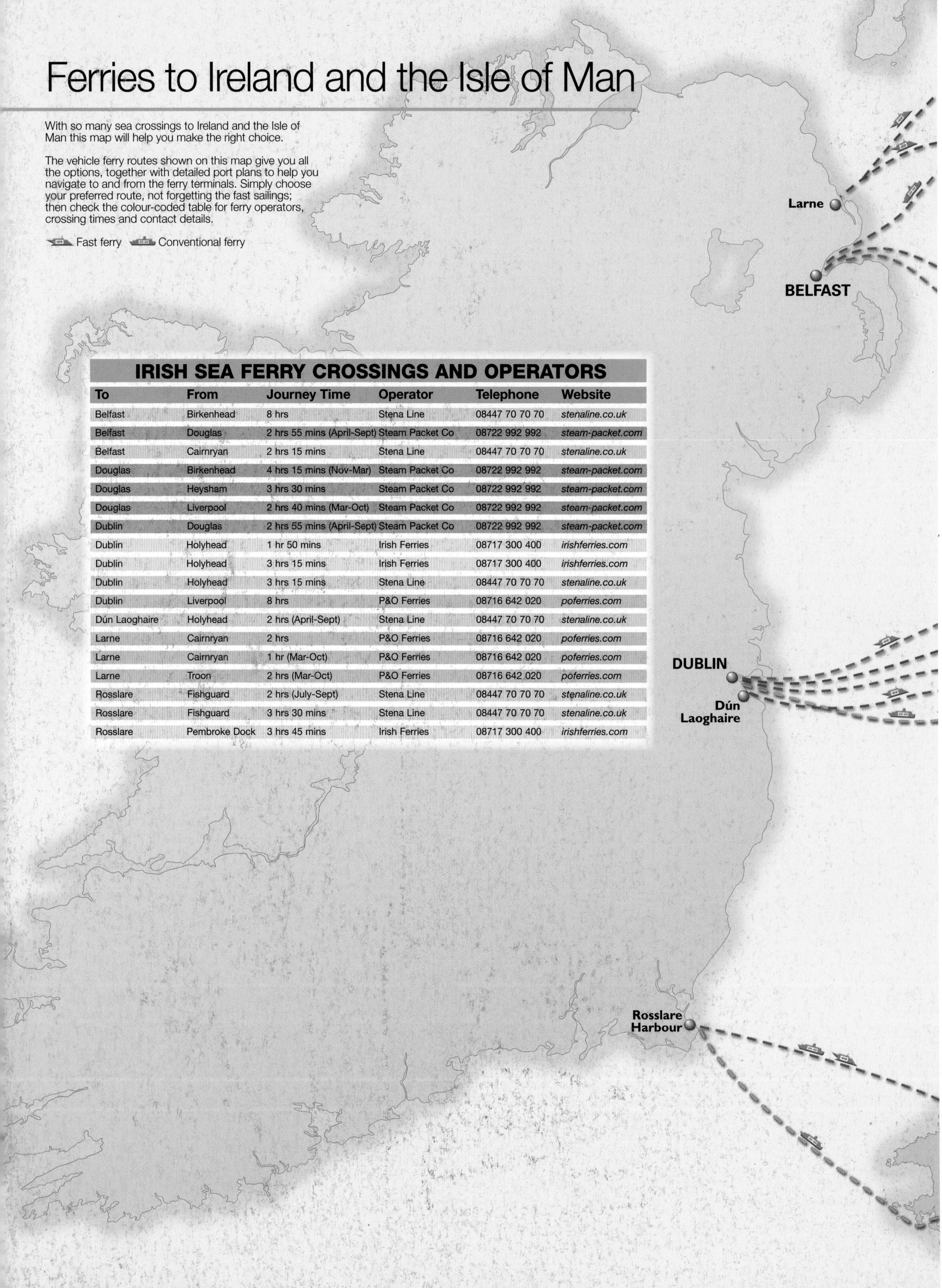

Larne

BELFAST

IRISH SEA FERRY CROSSINGS AND OPERATORS

To	From	Journey Time	Operator	Telephone	Website
Belfast	Birkenhead	8 hrs	Stena Line	08447 70 70 70	stenaline.co.uk
Belfast	Douglas	2 hrs 55 mins (April-Sept)	Steam Packet Co	08722 992 992	steam-packet.com
Belfast	Cairnryan	2 hrs 15 mins	Stena Line	08447 70 70 70	stenaline.co.uk
Douglas	Birkenhead	4 hrs 15 mins (Nov-Mar)	Steam Packet Co	08722 992 992	steam-packet.com
Douglas	Heysham	3 hrs 30 mins	Steam Packet Co	08722 992 992	steam-packet.com
Douglas	Liverpool	2 hrs 40 mins (Mar-Oct)	Steam Packet Co	08722 992 992	steam-packet.com
Dublin	Douglas	2 hrs 55 mins (April-Sept)	Steam Packet Co	08722 992 992	steam-packet.com
Dublin	Holyhead	1 hr 50 mins	Irish Ferries	08717 300 400	irishferries.com
Dublin	Holyhead	3 hrs 15 mins	Irish Ferries	08717 300 400	irishferries.com
Dublin	Holyhead	3 hrs 15 mins	Stena Line	08447 70 70 70	stenaline.co.uk
Dublin	Liverpool	8 hrs	P&O Ferries	08716 642 020	poferries.com
Dún Laoghaire	Holyhead	2 hrs (April-Sept)	Stena Line	08447 70 70 70	stenaline.co.uk
Larne	Cairnryan	2 hrs	P&O Ferries	08716 642 020	poferries.com
Larne	Cairnryan	1 hr (Mar-Oct)	P&O Ferries	08716 642 020	poferries.com
Larne	Troon	2 hrs (Mar-Oct)	P&O Ferries	08716 642 020	poferries.com
Rosslare	Fishguard	2 hrs (July-Sept)	Stena Line	08447 70 70 70	stenaline.co.uk
Rosslare	Fishguard	3 hrs 30 mins	Stena Line	08447 70 70 70	stenaline.co.uk
Rosslare	Pembroke Dock	3 hrs 45 mins	Irish Ferries	08717 300 400	irishferries.com

DUBLIN

Dún Laoghaire

Rosslare Harbour

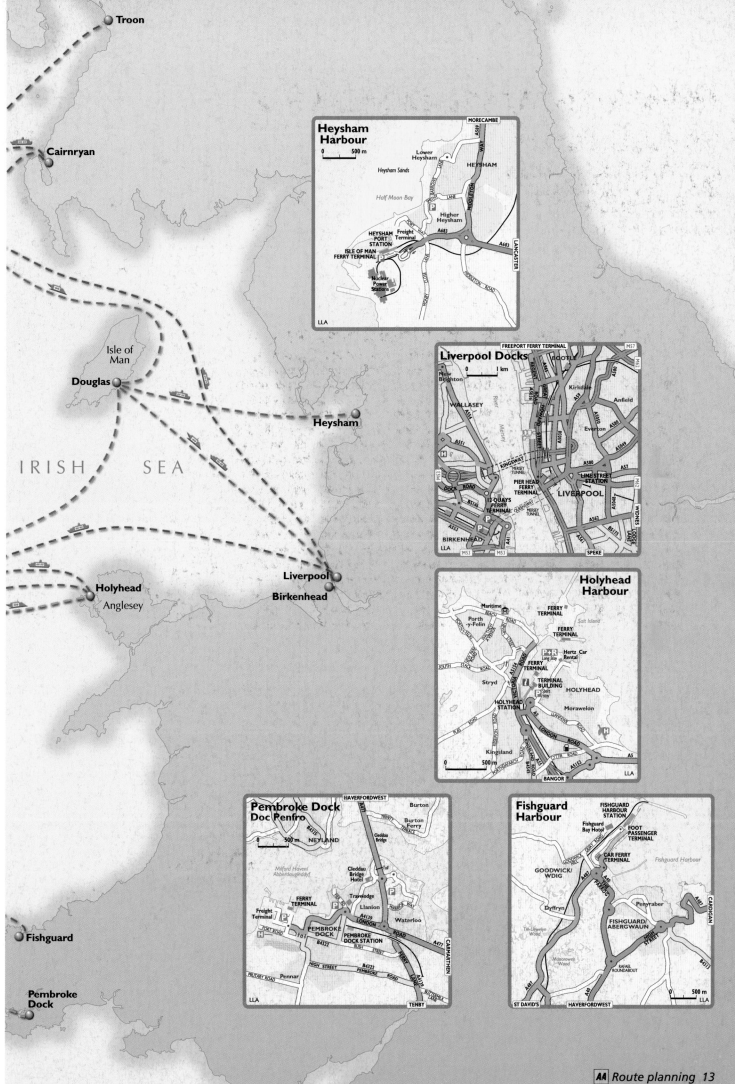

Troon

Cairnryan

Heysham Harbour

0   500 m

MORECAMBE
Lower Heysham
Heysham Sands
HEYSHAM
Half Moon Bay
Higher Heysham
HEYSHAM PORT STATION
Freight Terminal
ISLE OF MAN FERRY TERMINAL
A683
LANCASTER
Nuclear Power Stations
LLA

Isle of Man

Douglas

Heysham

IRISH   SEA

Liverpool Docks

FREEPORT FERRY TERMINAL
0   1 km
New Brighton
WALLASEY
BOOTLE
Kirkdale
Anfield
River Mersey
Everton
KINGSWAY
Mersey Tunnel
PIER HEAD FERRY TERMINAL
LIME STREET STATION
DOCK ROAD
12 QUAYS FERRY TERMINAL
Mersey Tunnel
LIVERPOOL
BIRKENHEAD
LLA
WIDNES LODGE LANE
M53
SPEKE

Liverpool
Birkenhead

Holyhead
Anglesey

Holyhead Harbour

Maritime
FERRY TERMINAL
Porth-y-Felin
Salt Island
FERRY TERMINAL
BEACH ROAD
P+R Long Stay
Hertz Car Rental
FERRY TERMINAL
Stryd
TERMINAL BUILDING
HOLYHEAD
VICTORIA ROAD
HOLYHEAD STATION
Morawelon
LONDON ROAD
A5
Kingsland
0   500 m
A5153
A5
BANGOR
LLA

Fishguard

Pembroke Dock
Doc Penfro

HAVERFORDWEST
0   500 m
Burton
NEYLAND
Burton Ferry
Cleddau Bridge
Milford Haven/Aberdaugleddyf
Cleddau Bridge Hotel
Toll
FERRY TERMINAL
Travelodge
Freight Terminal
Llanion
WARRIOR WAY
Waterloo
PEMBROKE DOCK
A4139 LONDON ROAD
B4322
PEMBROKE DOCK STATION
A477
CARMARTHEN
HIGH STREET
B4322 PEMBROKE ROAD
Military Road   Pennar
LLA
TENBY

Fishguard Harbour

FISHGUARD HARBOUR STATION
Fishguard Bay Hotel
FOOT PASSENGER TERMINAL
GOODWICK/WDIG
CAR FERRY TERMINAL
Fishguard Harbour
GOODWICK HILL
QUAY ROAD
A487
Penyraber
Dyffryn
FISHGUARD/ABERGWAUN
CARDIGAN
Tre-Llewelyn Wood
HIGH STREET
B4313
Manorowen Wood
RAFAEL ROUNDABOUT
A40
A487
0   500 m
ST DAVID'S   HAVERFORDWEST
LLA

Pembroke Dock

Caravan and camping sites in Britain

These pages list the top 300 AA-inspected Caravan and Camping (C & C) sites in the Pennant rating scheme. Five Pennant Premier sites are shown in **green**, Four Pennant sites are shown in blue.

Listings include addresses, telephone numbers and websites together with page and grid references to locate the sites in the atlas. The total number of touring pitches is also included for each site, together with the type of pitch available. The following abbreviations are used: C = Caravan CV = Campervan T = Tent

To find out more about the AA's Pennant rating scheme and other rated caravan and camping sites not included on these pages please visit *theAA.com*

ENGLAND

Abbey Farm Caravan Park
Dark Lane, Ormskirk
L40 5TX
Tel: 01695 572686 **88 E9**
abbeyfarmcaravanpark.co.uk
Total Pitches: 56 (C, CV & T)

Alders Caravan Park
Home Farm, Alne, York
YO61 1RY
Tel: 01347 838722 **97 R7**
alderscaravanpark.co.uk
Total Pitches: 87 (C, CV & T)

Alpine Grove Touring Park
Forton, Chard
TA20 4HD
Tel: 01460 63479 **10 G3**
alpinegrovetouringpark.com
Total Pitches: 40 (C, CV & T)

Andrewshayes Caravan Park
Dalwood, Axminster
EX13 7DY
Tel: 01404 831225 **10 E5**
andrewshayes.co.uk
Total Pitches: 150 (C, CV & T)

Appuldurcombe Gardens Holiday Park
Appuldurcombe Road, Wroxall, Isle of Wight
PO38 3EP
Tel: 01983 852597 **14 F10**
appuldurcombegardens.co.uk
Total Pitches: 100 (C, CV & T)

Ayr Holiday Park
St Ives, Cornwall
TR26 1EJ
Tel: 01736 795855 **2 E5**
ayrholidaypark.co.uk
Total Pitches: 40 (C, CV & T)

Back of Beyond Touring Park
234 Ringwood Rd,
St Leonards, Dorset
BH24 2SB
Tel: 01202 876968 **13 J4**
backofbeyondtouringpark.co.uk
Total Pitches: 80 (C, CV & T)

Bagwell Farm Touring Park
Knights in the Bottom,
Chickerell, Weymouth
DT3 4EA
Tel: 01305 782575 **11 N8**
bagwellfarm.co.uk
Total Pitches: 320 (C, CV & T)

Bardsea Leisure Park
Priory Road, Ulverston
LA12 9QE
Tel: 01229 584712 **94 F5**
bardsealeisure.co.uk
Total Pitches: 83 (C & CV)

Barn Farm Campsite
Barn Farm, Birchover,
Matlock
DE4 2BL
Tel: 01629 650245 **84 B8**
barnfarmcamping.com
Total Pitches: 25 (C, CV & T)

Barnstones C & C Site
Great Bourton, Banbury
OX17 1QU
Tel: 01295 750289 **48 E6**
Total Pitches: 49 (C, CV & T)

Beaconsfield Farm Caravan Park
Battlefield, Shrewsbury
SY4 4AA
Tel: 01939 210370 **69 P11**
beaconsfield-farm.co.uk
Total Pitches: 60 (C & CV)

Bellingham C & C Club Site
Brown Rigg,
Bellingham
NE48 2JY
Tel: 01434 220175 **112 B4**
campingandcaravanningclub.co.uk/bellingham
Total Pitches: 64 (C, CV & T)

Bingham Grange Touring & Camping Park
Melplash, Bridport
DT6 3TT
Tel: 01308 488234 **11 K5**
binghamgrange.co.uk
Total Pitches: 150 (C, CV & T)

Bo Peep Farm Caravan Park
Bo Peep Farm, Aynho Road,
Adderbury, Banbury
OX17 3NP
Tel: 01295 810605 **48 E8**
bo-peep.co.uk
Total Pitches: 104 (C, CV & T)

Briarfields Motel & Touring Park
Gloucester Road,
Cheltenham
GL51 0SX
Tel: 01242 235324 **46 H10**
briarfields.net
Total Pitches: 72 (C, CV & T)

Broadhembury C & C Park
Steeds Lane, Kingsnorth,
Ashford
TN26 1NQ
Tel: 01233 620859 **26 H4**
broadhembury.co.uk
Total Pitches: 110 (C, CV & T)

Brokerswood Country Park
Brokerswood, Westbury
BA13 4EH
Tel: 01373 822238 **20 F4**
brokerswoodcountrypark.co.uk
Total Pitches: 69 (C, CV & T)

Budemeadows Touring Park
Widemouth Bay, Bude
EX23 0NA
Tel: 01288 361646 **16 C11**
budemeadows.com
Total Pitches: 145 (C, CV & T)

Burrowhayes Farm C & C Site
West Luccombe, Porlock,
Minehead
TA24 8HT
Tel: 01643 862463 **18 B5**
burrowhayes.co.uk
Total Pitches: 120 (C, CV & T)

Burton Constable Holiday Park & Arboretum
Old Lodges, Sproatley, Hull
HU11 4LN
Tel: 01964 562508 **93 L3**
burtonconstable.co.uk
Total Pitches: 140 (C, CV & T)

Calloose C & C Park
Leedstown, Hayle
TR27 5ET
Tel: 01736 850431 **2 F7**
calloose.co.uk
Total Pitches: 109 (C, CV & T)

Camping Caradon Touring Park
Trelawne, Looe
PL13 2NA
Tel: 01503 272388 **5 L11**
campingcaradon.co.uk
Total Pitches: 85 (C, CV & T)

Carlton Meres Country Park
Rendham Road, Carlton,
Saxmundham
IP17 2QP
Tel: 01728 603344 **65 M8**
carlton-meres.co.uk
Total Pitches: 96 (C & CV)

Carlyon Bay C & C Park
Bethesda, Cypress Avenue,
Carlyon Bay
PL25 3RE
Tel: 01726 812735 **3 R3**
carlyonbay.net
Total Pitches: 180 (C, CV & T)

Carnevas Holiday Park & Farm Cottages
Carnevas Farm, St Merryn
PL28 8PN
Tel: 01841 520230 **4 D7**
carnevasholidaypark.co.uk
Total Pitches: 195 (C, CV & T)

Carnon Downs C & C Park
Carnon Downs, Truro
TR3 6JJ
Tel: 01872 862283 **3 L5**
carnon-downs-caravanpark.co.uk
Total Pitches: 150 (C, CV & T)

Carvynick Country Club
Summercourt, Newquay
TR8 5AF
Tel: 01872 510716 **4 D10**
carvynick.co.uk
Total Pitches: 47 (CV)

Castlerigg Hall C & C Park
Castlerigg Hall, Keswick
CA12 4TE
Tel: 017687 74499 **101 J6**
castlerigg.co.uk
Total Pitches: 48 (C, CV & T)

Cheddar Bridge Touring Park
Draycott Rd, Cheddar
BS27 3RJ
Tel: 01934 743048 **19 N4**
cheddarbridge.co.uk
Total Pitches: 45 (C, CV & T)

Cheddar C & C Club Site
Townsend, Priddy, Wells
BA5 3BP
Tel: 01749 870241 **19 P4**
campingandcaravanningclub.co.uk/cheddar
Total Pitches: 90 (C, CV & T)

Chiverton Park
East Hill, Blackwater
TR4 8HS
Tel: 01872 560667 **3 J4**
chivertonpark.co.uk
Total Pitches: 12 (C, CV & T)

Church Farm C & C Park
The Bungalow, Church Farm,
High Street, Sixpenny Handley,
Salisbury
SP5 5ND
Tel: 01725 552563 **21 J11**
churchfarmcandcpark.co.uk
Total Pitches: 35 (C, CV & T)

Claylands Caravan Park
Cabus, Garstang
PR3 1AJ
Tel: 01524 791242 **95 K11**
claylands.com
Total Pitches: 30 (C, CV & T)

Clippesby Hall
Hall Lane, Clippesby,
Great Yarmouth
NR29 3BL
Tel: 01493 367800 **77 N9**
clippesby.com
Total Pitches: 120 (C, CV & T)

Cofton Country Holidays
Starcross, Dawlish
EX6 8RP
Tel: 01626 890111 **9 N8**
coftonholidays.co.uk
Total Pitches: 450 (C, CV & T)

Colchester Holiday Park
Cymbeline Way, Lexden,
Colchester
CO3 4AG
Tel: 01206 545551 **52 G6**
colchestercamping.co.uk
Total Pitches: 168 (C, CV & T)

Constable Burton Hall Caravan Park
Constable Burton,
Leyburn
DL8 5LJ
Tel: 01677 450428 **97 J2**
cbcaravanpark.co.uk
Total Pitches: 120 (C & CV)

Coombe Touring Park
Race Plain,
Netherhampton,
Salisbury
SP2 8PN
Tel: 01722 328451 **21 L9**
coombecaravanpark.co.uk
Total Pitches: 50 (C, CV & T)

Corfe Castle C & C Club Site
Bucknowle, Wareham
BH20 5PQ
Tel: 01929 480280 **12 F8**
campingandcaravanningclub.co.uk/corfecastle
Total Pitches: 80 (C, CV & T)

Cornish Farm Touring Park
Shoreditch, Taunton
TA3 7BS
Tel: 01823 327746 **18 H10**
cornishfarm.com
Total Pitches: 50 (C, CV & T)

Cosawes Park
Perranarworthal, Truro
TR3 7QS
Tel: 01872 863724 **3 K6**
cosawestouringandcamping.co.uk
Total Pitches: 40 (C, CV & T)

Cote Ghyll C & C Park
Osmotherley,
Northallerton
DL6 3AH
Tel: 01609 883425 **104 E11**
coteghyll.com
Total Pitches: 77 (C, CV & T)

Cotswold View Touring Park
Enstone Road,
Charlbury
OX7 3JH
Tel: 01608 810314 **48 C10**
cotswoldview.co.uk
Total Pitches: 125 (C, CV & T)

Dell Touring Park
Beyton Road, Thurston,
Bury St Edmunds
IP31 3RB
Tel: 01359 270121 **64 C9**
thedellcaravanpark.co.uk
Total Pitches: 60 (C, CV & T)

Diamond Farm C & C Park
Islip Road, Bletchingdon
OX5 3DR
Tel: 01869 350909 **48 F11**
diamondpark.co.uk
Total Pitches: 37 (C, CV & T)

Dibles Park
Dibles Road, Warsash,
Southampton
SO31 9SA
Tel: 01489 575232 **14 F5**
diblespark.co.uk
Total Pitches: 14 (C, CV & T)

Dolbeare Park C & C
St Ive Road, Landrake,
Saltash
PL12 5AF
Tel: 01752 851332 **5 P9**
dolbeare.co.uk
Total Pitches: 60 (C, CV & T)

Dornafield
Dornafield Farm, Two Mile Oak,
Newton Abbot
TQ12 6DD
Tel: 01803 812732 **7 L5**
dornafield.com
Total Pitches: 135 (C, CV & T)

East Fleet Farm Touring Park
Chickerell, Weymouth
DT3 4DW
Tel: 01305 785768 **11 N9**
eastfleet.co.uk
Total Pitches: 400 (C, CV & T)

Eden Valley Holiday Park
Lanlivery, Nr Lostwithiel
PL30 5BU
Tel: 01208 872277 **4 H10**
edenvalleyholidaypark.co.uk
Total Pitches: 56 (C, CV & T)

Eskdale C & C Club Site
Boot, Holmrook
CA19 1TH
Tel: 019467 23253 **100 G10**
campingandcaravanningclub.co.uk/eskdale
Total Pitches: 80 (CV & T)

Exe Valley Caravan Site
Mill House, Bridgetown,
Dulverton
TA22 9JR
Tel: 01643 851432 **18 B8**
exevalleycamping.co.uk
Total Pitches: 50 (C, CV & T)

Fallbarrow Park
Rayrigg Road, Windermere
LA23 3DL
Tel: 015394 44422 **101 M11**
slholidays.co.uk
Total Pitches: 32 (C & CV)

Fernwood Caravan Park
Lyneal, Ellesmere
SY12 0QF
Tel: 01948 710221 **69 N8**
fernwoodpark.co.uk
Total Pitches: 60 (C & CV)

Fields End Water Caravan Park & Fishery
Benwick Road, Doddington,
March
PE15 0TY
Tel: 01354 740199 **62 E2**
fieldsendcaravans.co.uk
Total Pitches: 52 (C, CV & T)

Fishpool Farm Caravan Park
Fishpool Road, Delamere,
Northwich
CW8 2HP
Tel: 01606 883970 **82 C11**
fishpoolfarmcaravanpark.co.uk
Total Pitches: 50 (C, CV & T)

Flusco Wood
Flusco, Penrith
CA11 0JB
Tel: 017684 80020 **101 N5**
fluscowood.co.uk
Total Pitches: 53 (C & CV)

Forest Glade Holiday Park
Kentisbeare,
Cullompton
EX15 2DT
Tel: 01404 841381 **10 C3**
forest-glade.co.uk
Total Pitches: 80 (C, CV & T)

Globe Vale Holiday Park
Radnor, Redruth
TR16 4BH
Tel: 01209 891183 **3 J5**
globevale.co.uk
Total Pitches: 138 (C, CV & T)

Golden Cap Holiday Park
Seatown, Chideock,
Bridport
DT6 6JX
Tel: 01308 422139 **11 J6**
wdlh.co.uk
Total Pitches: 108 (C, CV & T)

Golden Square Touring Caravan Park
Oswaldkirk, Helmsley
YO62 5YQ
Tel: 01439 788269 **98 C5**
goldensquarecaravanpark.com
Total Pitches: 129 (C, CV & T)

Golden Valley C & C Park
Coach Road, Ripley
DE55 4ES
Tel: 01773 513881 **84 F10**
goldenvalleycaravanpark.co.uk
Total Pitches: 45 (C, CV & T)

Goosewood Caravan Park
Sutton-on-the-Forest, York
YO61 1ET
Tel: 01347 810829 **98 B8**
flowerofmay.com
Total Pitches: 100 (C & CV)

Greenacres Touring Park
Haywards Lane, Chelston,
Wellington
TA21 9PH
Tel: 01823 652844 **18 G10**
greenacres-wellington.co.uk
Total Pitches: 40 (C & CV)

Greenhill Leisure Park
Greenhill Farm, Station Road,
Bletchingdon, Oxford
OX5 3BQ
Tel: 01869 351600 **48 E11**
greenhill-leisure-park.co.uk
Total Pitches: 92 (C, CV & T)

Grouse Hill Caravan Park
Flask Bungalow Farm,
Fylingdales,
Robin Hood's Bay
YO22 4QH
Tel: 01947 880543 **105 P10**
grousehill.co.uk
Total Pitches: 175 (C, CV & T)

Gunvenna Caravan Park
St Minver,
Wadebridge
PL27 6QN
Tel: 01208 862405 **4 F6**
gunvenna.co.uk
Total Pitches: 75 (C, CV & T)

Gwithian Farm Campsite
Gwithian Farm, Gwithian, Hayle
TR27 5BX
Tel: 01736 753127 **2 F5**
gwithianfarm.co.uk
Total Pitches: 87 (C, CV & T)

Harbury Fields
Harbury Fields Farm, Harbury,
Nr Leamington Spa
CV33 9JN
Tel: 01926 612457 **48 C2**
harburyfields.co.uk
Total Pitches: 32 (C & CV)

Hawthorn Farm Caravan Park
Station Road, Martin Mill,
Dover
CT15 5LA
Tel: 01304 852658   **27 P2**
keatfarm.co.uk
Total Pitches: 147 (C, CV & T)

Heathfield Farm Camping
Heathfield Road, Freshwater,
Isle of Wight
PO40 9SH
Tel: 01983 407822   **13 P7**
heathfieldcamping.co.uk
Total Pitches: 60 (C, CV & T)

Heathland Beach Caravan Park
London Road,
Kessingland
NR33 7PJ
Tel: 01502 740337   **65 Q4**
heathlandbeach.co.uk
Total Pitches: 63 (C, CV & T)

Hele Valley Holiday Park
Hele Bay, Ilfracombe,
North Devon
EX34 9RD
Tel: 01271 862460   **17 J2**
helevalley.co.uk
Total Pitches: 50 (C, CV & T)

Heron's Mead
Fishing Lake & Touring Park
Marsh Lane, Orby, Skegness
PE24 5JA
Tel: 01754 811340   **87 P7**
heronsmeadtouringpark.co.uk
Total Pitches: 21 (C, CV & T)

Hidden Valley Park
West Down, Braunton,
Ilfracombe
EX34 8NU
Tel: 01271 813837   **17 J3**
hiddenvalleypark.com
Total Pitches: 115 (C, CV & T)

Highfield Farm Touring Park
Long Road, Comberton,
Cambridge
CB23 7DG
Tel: 01223 262308   **62 E9**
highfieldfarmtouringpark.co.uk
Total Pitches: 120 (C, CV & T)

Highlands End Holiday Park
Eype, Bridport, Dorset
DT6 6AR
Tel: 01308 422139   **11 K6**
wdlh.co.uk
Total Pitches: 195 (C, CV & T)

Hill Cottage Farm C & C Park
Sandleheath Road, Alderholt,
Fordingbridge
SP6 3EG
Tel: 01425 650513   **13 K2**
hillcottagefarmcampingand
caravanpark.com
Total Pitches: 35 (C, CV & T)

Hill Farm Caravan Park
Branches Lane,
Sherfield English,
Romsey
SO51 6FH
Tel: 01794 340402   **21 Q10**
hillfarmpark.com
Total Pitches: 70 (C, CV & T)

Hill of Oaks & Blakeholme
Windermere
LA12 8NR
Tel: 015395 31578   **94 H3**
hillofoaks.co.uk
Total Pitches: 43 (C & CV)

Hillside Caravan Park
Canvas Farm,
Moor Road, Thirsk
YO7 4BR
Tel: 01845 537349   **97 P3**
hillsidecaravanpark.co.uk
Total Pitches: 35 (C & CV)

Hollins Farm C & C
Far Arnside, Carnforth
LA5 0SL
Tel: 01524 701508   **95 J5**
holgates.co.uk
Total Pitches: 12 (C, CV & T)

Homing Park
Church Lane, Seasalter,
Whitstable
CT5 4BU
Tel: 01227 771777   **39 J9**
homingpark.co.uk
Total Pitches: 43 (C, CV & T)

Honeybridge Park
Honeybridge Lane, Dial Post,
Horsham
RH13 8NX
Tel: 01403 710923   **24 E7**
honeybridgepark.co.uk
Total Pitches: 130 (C, CV & T)

Hurley Riverside Park
Park Office, Hurley,
Nr Maidenhead
SL6 5NE
Tel: 01628 824493   **35 M8**
hurleyriversidepark.co.uk
Total Pitches: 200 (C, CV & T)

Hutton-le-Hole Caravan Park
Westfield Lodge,
Hutton-le-Hole
YO62 6UG
Tel: 01751 417261   **98 E3**
westfieldlodge.co.uk
Total Pitches: 42 (C, CV & T)

Hylton Caravan Park
Eden Street, Silloth
CA7 4AY
Tel: 016973 31707   **109 P10**
stanwix.com
Total Pitches: 90 (C, CV & T)

Isle of Avalon
Touring Caravan Park
Godney Road, Glastonbury
BA6 9AF
Tel: 01458 833618   **19 N7**
Total Pitches: 120 (C, CV & T)

Jacobs Mount Caravan Park
Jacobs Mount, Stepney Road,
Scarborough
YO12 5NL
Tel: 01723 361178   **99 L3**
jacobsmount.com
Total Pitches: 156 (C, CV & T)

Jasmine Caravan Park
Cross Lane, Snainton,
Scarborough
YO13 9BE
Tel: 01723 859240   **99 J4**
jasminepark.co.uk
Total Pitches: 94 (C, CV & T)

Juliot's Well Holiday Park
Camelford, North Cornwall
PL32 9RF
Tel: 01840 213302   **4 H5**
juliotswell.com
Total Pitches: 39 (C, CV & T)

Kenneggy Cove Holiday Park
Higher Kenneggy,
Rosudgeon,
Penzance
TR20 9AU
Tel: 01736 763453   **2 F8**
kenneggycove.co.uk
Total Pitches: 45 (C, CV & T)

Kennford International
Caravan Park
Kennford, Exeter
EX6 7YN
Tel: 01392 833046   **9 M7**
kennfordinternational.co.uk
Total Pitches: 96 (C, CV & T)

King's Lynn Caravan &
Camping Park
New Road, North Runcton,
King's Lynn
PE33 0RA
Tel: 01553 840004   **75 M7**
kl-cc.co.uk
Total Pitches: 150 (C, CV & T)

Kloofs Caravan Park
Sandhurst Lane, Bexhill
TN39 4RG
Tel: 01424 842839   **26 B10**
kloofs.com
Total Pitches: 50 (C, CV & T)

Kneps Farm Holiday Park
River Road, Stanah,
Thornton-Cleveleys,
Blackpool
FY5 5LR
Tel: 01253 823632   **88 D2**
knepsfarm.co.uk
Total Pitches: 60 (C & CV)

Knight Stainforth Hall
Caravan & Campsite
Stainforth, Settle
BD24 0DP
Tel: 01729 822200   **96 B7**
knightstainforth.co.uk
Total Pitches: 100 (C, CV & T)

Ladycross Plantation
Caravan Park
Egton, Whitby
YO21 1UA
Tel: 01947 895502   **105 M9**
ladycrossplantation.co.uk
Total Pitches: 130 (C, CV & T)

Lamb Cottage Caravan Park
Dalefords Lane, Whitegate,
Northwich
CW8 2BN
Tel: 01606 882302   **82 D11**
lambcottage.co.uk
Total Pitches: 45 (C & CV)

Langstone Manor C & C Park
Moortown,
Tavistock
PL19 9JZ
Tel: 01822 613371   **6 E4**
langstone-manor.co.uk
Total Pitches: 40 (C, CV & T)

Larches Caravan Park
Mealsgate, Wigton
CA7 1LQ
Tel: 016973 71379   **100 H2**
Total Pitches: 73 (C, CV & T)

Lebberston Touring Park
Filey Road, Lebberston,
Scarborough
YO11 3PE
Tel: 01723 585723   **99 M4**
lebberstontouring.co.uk
Total Pitches: 125 (C & CV)

Lee Valley Campsite
Sewardstone Road, Chingford,
London
E4 7RA
Tel: 020 8529 5689   **51 J11**
Total Pitches: 100 (C, CV & T)

Lemonford Caravan Park
Bickington (near Ashburton),
Newton Abbot
TQ12 6JR
Tel: 01626 821242   **7 K4**
lemonford.co.uk
Total Pitches: 82 (C, CV & T)

Lickpenny Caravan Site
Lickpenny Lane, Tansley, Matlock
DE4 5GF
Tel: 01629 583040   **84 D9**
lickpennycaravanpark.co.uk
Total Pitches: 80 (C & CV)

Lime Tree Park
Dukes Drive, Buxton
SK17 9RP
Tel: 01298 22988   **83 N10**
limetreeparkbuxton.co.uk
Total Pitches: 106 (C, CV & T)

Lincoln Farm Park Oxfordshire
High Street, Standlake
OX29 7RH
Tel: 01865 300239   **34 C4**
lincolnfarmpark.co.uk
Total Pitches: 90 (C, CV & T)

Little Cotton Caravan Park
Little Cotton, Dartmouth
TQ6 0LB
Tel: 01803 832558   **7 M8**
littlecotton.co.uk
Total Pitches: 95 (C, CV & T)

Little Lakeland Caravan Park
Wortwell, Harleston
IP20 0EL
Tel: 01986 788646   **65 K4**
littlelakeland.co.uk
Total Pitches: 38 (C, CV & T)

Little Trevarrack Holiday Park
Laity Lane,
Carbis Bay, St Ives
TR26 3HW
Tel: 01736 797580   **2 E6**
littletrevarrack.co.uk
Total Pitches: 200 (C, CV & T)

Long Acre Caravan Park
Station Road, Old Leake, Boston
PE22 9RF
Tel: 01205 871555   **87 L10**
longacres-caravanpark.co.uk
Total Pitches: 40 (C, CV & T)

Lowther Holiday Park
Eamont Bridge, Penrith
CA10 2JB
Tel: 01768 863631   **101 P5**
lowther-holidaypark.co.uk
Total Pitches: 180 (C, CV & T)

Lytton Lawn Touring Park
Lymore Lane,
Milford on Sea
SO41 0TX
Tel: 01590 648331   **13 N6**
shorefield.co.uk
Total Pitches: 136 (C, CV & T)

Manor Wood
Country Caravan Park
Manor Wood, Coddington,
Chester
CH3 9EN
Tel: 01829 782990   **69 N3**
cheshire-caravan-sites.co.uk
Total Pitches: 45 (C, CV & T)

Maustin Caravan Park
Kearby with Netherby,
Netherby
LS22 4DA
Tel: 0113 288 6234   **97 M11**
maustin.co.uk
Total Pitches: 25 (C, CV & T)

Mayfield Touring Park
Cheltenham Road, Cirencester
GL7 7BH
Tel: 01285 831301   **33 K3**
mayfieldpark.co.uk
Total Pitches: 72 (C, CV & T)

Meadowbank Holidays
Stour Way, Christchurch
BH23 2PQ
Tel: 01202 483597   **13 K6**
meadowbank-holidays.co.uk
Total Pitches: 41 (C & CV)

Merley Court
Merley, Wimborne Minster
BH21 3AA
Tel: 01590 648331   **12 H5**
shorefield.co.uk
Total Pitches: 160 (C, CV & T)

Middlewood Farm
Holiday Park
Middlewood Lane, Fylingthorpe,
Robin Hood's Bay, Whitby
YO22 4UF
Tel: 01947 880414   **105 P10**
middlewoodfarm.com
Total Pitches: 100 (C, CV & T)

Minnows Touring Park
Holbrook Lane, Sampford Peverell
EX16 7EN
Tel: 01884 821770   **18 D11**
ukparks.co.uk/minnows
Total Pitches: 59 (C, CV & T)

Moon & Sixpence
Newbourn Road, Waldringfield,
Woodbridge
IP12 4PP
Tel: 01473 736650   **53 N2**
moonandsixpence.eu
Total Pitches: 65 (C, CV & T)

Moss Wood Caravan Park
Crimbles Lane, Cockerham
LA2 0ES
Tel: 01524 791041   **95 K11**
mosswood.co.uk
Total Pitches: 25 (C, CV & T)

Naburn Lock Caravan Park
Naburn
YO19 4RU
Tel: 01904 728697   **98 C11**
naburnlock.co.uk
Total Pitches: 100 (C, CV & T)

Newberry Valley Park
Woodlands,
Combe Martin
EX34 0AT
Tel: 01271 882334   **17 K2**
newberryvalleypark.co.uk
Total Pitches: 120 (C, CV & T)

New House Caravan Park
Kirkby Lonsdale
LA6 2HR
Tel: 015242 71590   **95 N5**
Total Pitches: 50 (C & CV)

Newlands C & C Park
Charmouth, Bridport
DT6 6RB
Tel: 01297 560259   **10 H6**
newlandsholidays.co.uk
Total Pitches: 240 (C, CV & T)

Newperran Holiday Park
Rejerrah, Newquay
TR8 5QJ
Tel: 01872 572407   **3 K3**
newperran.co.uk
Total Pitches: 357 (C, CV & T)

Newton Mill Holiday Park
Newton Road, Bath
BA2 9JF
Tel: 0844 272 9503   **20 D2**
newtonmillpark.co.uk
Total Pitches: 106 (C, CV & T)

Northam Farm
Caravan & Touring Park
Brean, Burnham-on-Sea
TA8 2SE
Tel: 01278 751244   **19 K3**
northamfarm.co.uk
Total Pitches: 350 (C, CV & T)

North Morte Farm C & C Park
North Morte Road, Mortehoe,
Woolacombe, N Devon
EX34 7EG
Tel: 01271 870381   **16 H2**
northmortefarm.co.uk
Total Pitches: 180 (C, CV & T)

Oakdown
Country Holiday Park
Gatedown Lane,
Sidmouth
EX10 0PT
Tel: 01297 680387   **10 D6**
oakdown.co.uk
Total Pitches: 150 (C, CV & T)

Oathill Farm
Touring & Camping Site
Oathill,
Crewkerne
TA18 8PZ
Tel: 01460 30234   **11 J3**
oathillfarmleisure.co.uk
Total Pitches: 13 (C, CV & T)

Old Barn Touring Park
Cheverton Farm,
Newport Road, Sandown
PO36 9PJ
Tel: 01983 866414   **14 G10**
oldbarntouring.co.uk
Total Pitches: 60 (C, CV & T)

Old Hall Caravan Park
Capernwray,
Carnforth
LA6 1AD
Tel: 01524 733276   **95 L6**
oldhallcaravanpark.co.uk
Total Pitches: 38 (C & CV)

Orchard Farm Holiday Village
Stonegate, Hunmanby
YO14 0PU
Tel: 01723 891582   **99 N5**
orchardfarmholidayvillage.co.uk
Total Pitches: 91 (C, CV & T)

Orchard Park
Frampton Lane,
Hubbert's Bridge, Boston
PE20 3QU
Tel: 01205 290328   **74 E2**
orchardpark.co.uk
Total Pitches: 87 (C, CV & T)

Ord House Country Park
East Ord, Berwick-upon-Tweed
TD15 2NS
Tel: 01289 305288   **129 P9**
ordhouse.co.uk
Total Pitches: 79 (C, CV & T)

Otterington Park
Station Farm,
South Otterington,
Northallerton
DL7 9JB
Tel: 01609 780656   **97 N3**
otteringtonpark.com
Total Pitches: 62 (C & CV)

Oxon Hall Touring Park
Welshpool Road,
Shrewsbury
SY3 5FB
Tel: 01743 340868   **56 H2**
morris-leisure.co.uk
Total Pitches: 105 (C, CV & T)

Padstow Touring Park
Padstow
PL28 8LE
Tel: 01841 532061   **4 E7**
padstowtouringpark.co.uk
Total Pitches: 150 (C, CV & T)

Park Cliffe
Camping & Caravan Estate
Birks Road, Tower Wood,
Windermere
LA23 3PG
Tel: 01539 531344   **94 H2**
parkcliffe.co.uk
Total Pitches: 60 (C, CV & T)

Parkers Farm Holiday Park
Higher Mead Farm,
Ashburton, Devon
TQ13 7LJ
Tel: 01364 654869   **7 K4**
parkersfarmholidays.co.uk
Total Pitches: 100 (C, CV & T)

Pear Tree Holiday Park
Organford Road, Holton Heath,
Organford, Poole
BH16 6LA
Tel: 0844 272 9504   **12 F6**
peartreepark.co.uk
Total Pitches: 154 (C, CV & T)

Penrose Holiday Park
Goonhavern, Truro
TR4 9QF
Tel: 01872 573185   **3 K3**
penroseholidaypark.com
Total Pitches: 110 (C, CV & T)

Polmanter Touring Park
Halsetown,
St Ives
TR26 3LX
Tel: 01736 795640   **2 E6**
polmanter.com
Total Pitches: 270 (C, CV & T)

Porlock Caravan Park
Porlock,
Minehead
TA24 8ND
Tel: 01643 862269   **18 A5**
porlockcaravanpark.co.uk
Total Pitches: 40 (C, CV & T)

Portesham Dairy Farm Campsite
Portesham, Weymouth
DT3 4HG
Tel: 01305 871297 **11 N7**
porteshamdairyfarm.co.uk
Total Pitches: 90 (C, CV & T)

Porth Beach Tourist Park
Porth, Newquay
TR7 3NH
Tel: 01637 876531 **4 C9**
porthbeach.co.uk
Total Pitches: 200 (C, CV & T)

Porthtowan Tourist Park
Mile Hill, Porthtowan, Truro
TR4 8TY
Tel: 01209 890256 **2 H4**
porthtowantouristpark.co.uk
Total Pitches: 80 (C, CV & T)

Quantock Orchard Caravan Park
Flaxpool, Crowcombe,
Taunton
TA4 4AW
Tel: 01984 618618 **18 F7**
quantock-orchard.co.uk
Total Pitches: 69 (C, CV & T)

Ranch Caravan Park
Station Road, Honeybourne,
Evesham
WR11 7PR
Tel: 01386 830744 **47 M6**
ranch.co.uk
Total Pitches: 120 (C & CV)

Ripley Caravan Park
Knaresborough Road, Ripley,
Harrogate
HG3 3AU
Tel: 01423 770050 **97 L8**
ripleycaravanpark.com
Total Pitches: 100 (C, CV & T)

River Dart Country Park
Holne Park, Ashburton
TQ13 7NP
Tel: 01364 652511 **7 J5**
riverdart.co.uk
Total Pitches: 170 (C, CV & T)

Riverside C & C Park
Marsh Lane, North Molton Road,
South Molton
EX36 3HQ
Tel: 01769 579269 **17 N6**
exmoorriverside.co.uk
Total Pitches: 42 (C, CV & T)

Riverside Caravan Park
High Bentham,
Lancaster
LA2 7FJ
Tel: 015242 61272 **95 P7**
riversidecaravanpark.co.uk
Total Pitches: 61 (C & CV)

Riverside Caravan Park
Leigham Manor Drive,
Marsh Mills, Plymouth
PL6 8LL
Tel: 01752 344122 **6 E7**
riversidecaravanpark.com
Total Pitches: 259 (C, CV & T)

Riverside Holidays
21 Compass Point,
Ensign Way, Hamble
SO31 4RA
Tel: 023 8045 3220 **14 E5**
riversideholidays.co.uk
Total Pitches: 77 (C, CV & T)

Riverside Meadows Country Caravan Park
Ure Bank Top, Ripon
HG4 1JD
Tel: 01765 602964 **97 M6**
flowerofmay.com
Total Pitches: 80 (C, CV & T)

River Valley Holiday Park
London Apprentice,
St Austell
PL26 7AP
Tel: 01726 73533 **3 Q3**
rivervalleyholidaypark.co.uk
Total Pitches: 45 (C, CV & T)

Rosedale C & C Park
Rosedale Abbey,
Pickering
YO18 8SA
Tel: 01751 417272 **105 K11**
flowerofmay.com
Total Pitches: 100 (C, CV & T)

Rose Farm Touring & Camping Park
Stepshort, Belton,
Nr Great Yarmouth
NR31 9JS
Tel: 01493 780896 **77 P11**
rosefarmtouringpark.co.uk
Total Pitches: 145 (C, CV & T)

Ross Park
Park Hill Farm, Ipplepen,
Newton Abbot
TQ12 5TT
Tel: 01803 812983 **7 L5**
rossparkcaravanpark.co.uk
Total Pitches: 110 (C, CV & T)

Rudding Holiday Park
Follifoot,
Harrogate
HG3 1JH
Tel: 01423 871350 **97 M10**
ruddingpark.co.uk/
caravans-camping
Total Pitches: 109 (C, CV & T)

Rutland C & C
Park Lane, Greetham, Oakham
LE15 7FN
Tel: 01572 813520 **73 N8**
rutlandcaravanandcamping.co.uk
Total Pitches: 130 (C, CV & T)

Seaview International Holiday Park
Boswinger,
Mevagissey
PL26 6LL
Tel: 01726 843425 **3 P5**
seaviewinternational.com
Total Pitches: 201 (C, CV & T)

Severn Gorge Park
Bridgnorth Road, Tweedale,
Telford
TF7 4JB
Tel: 01952 684789 **57 N3**
severngorgepark.co.uk
Total Pitches: 10 (C & CV)

Shamba Holidays
230 Ringwood Road,
St Leonards,
Ringwood
BH24 2SB
Tel: 01202 873302 **13 K4**
shambaholidays.co.uk
Total Pitches: 150 (C, CV & T)

Shrubbery Touring Park
Rousdon, Lyme Regis
DT7 3XW
Tel: 01297 442227 **10 F6**
shrubberypark.co.uk
Total Pitches: 120 (C, CV & T)

Silverbow Park
Perranwell, Goonhavern,
TR4 9NX
Tel: 01872 572347 **3 K3**
chycor.co.uk/parks/silverbow
Total Pitches: 100 (C, CV & T)

Silverdale Caravan Park
Middlebarrow Plain, Cove Road,
Silverdale, Nr Carnforth
LA5 0SH
Tel: 01524 701508 **95 K5**
holgates.co.uk
Total Pitches: 80 (C, CV & T)

Skelwith Fold Caravan Park
Ambleside, Cumbria
LA22 0HX
Tel: 015394 32277 **101 L10**
skelwith.com
Total Pitches: 150 (C & CV)

Somers Wood Caravan Park
Somers Road, Meriden
CV7 7PL
Tel: 01676 522978 **59 K8**
somerswood.co.uk
Total Pitches: 48 (C & CV)

Southfork Caravan Park
Parrett Works,
Martock
TA12 6AE
Tel: 01935 825661 **19 M11**
southforkcaravans.co.uk
Total Pitches: 27 (C, CV & T)

South Lytchett Manor C & C Park
Dorchester Road,
Lytchett Minster, Poole
BH16 6JB
Tel: 01202 622577 **12 G6**
southlytchettmanor.co.uk
Total Pitches: 150 (C, CV & T)

Springfield Holiday Park
Tedburn St Mary,
Exeter
EX6 6EW
Tel: 01647 24242 **9 K6**
springfieldholidaypark.co.uk
Total Pitches: 48 (C, CV & T)

Stanmore Hall Touring Park
Stourbridge Road,
Bridgnorth
WV15 6DT
Tel: 01746 761761 **57 N6**
morris-leisure.co.uk
Total Pitches: 131 (C, CV & T)

St Helens Caravan Park
Wykeham, Scarborough
YO13 9QD
Tel: 01723 862771 **99 K4**
sthelenscaravanpark.co.uk
Total Pitches: 250 (C, CV & T)

Stowford Farm Meadows
Berry Down, Combe Martin
EX34 0PW
Tel: 01271 882476 **17 K3**
stowford.co.uk
Total Pitches: 700 (C, CV & T)

Stroud Hill Park
Fen Road, Pidley
PE28 3DE
Tel: 01487 741333 **62 D5**
stroudhillpark.co.uk
Total Pitches: 60 (C, CV & T)

Sumners Ponds Fishery & Campsite
Chapel Road, Barns Green,
Horsham
RH13 0PR
Tel: 01403 732539 **24 D5**
sumnersponds.co.uk
Total Pitches: 85 (C, CV & T)

Sun Haven Valley Holiday Park
Mawgan Porth, Newquay
TR8 4BQ
Tel: 01637 860373 **4 D8**
sunhavenvalley.com
Total Pitches: 109 (C, CV & T)

Sun Valley Holiday Park
Pentewan Road, St Austell
PL26 6DJ
Tel: 01726 843266 **3 Q4**
sunvalleyholidays.co.uk
Total Pitches: 29 (C, CV & T)

Swiss Farm Touring & Camping
Marlow Road,
Henley-on-Thames
RG9 2HY
Tel: 01491 573419 **35 L8**
swissfarmcamping.co.uk
Total Pitches: 140 (C, CV & T)

Tanner Farm Touring Caravan & Camping Park
Tanner Farm,
Goudhurst Road,
Marden
TN12 9ND
Tel: 01622 832399 **26 B3**
tannerfarmpark.co.uk
Total Pitches: 100 (C, CV & T)

Tattershall Lakes Country Park
Sleaford Road, Tattershall
LN4 4RL
Tel: 01526 348800 **86 H9**
tattershall-lakes.com
Total Pitches: 186 (C, CV & T)

Teversal C & C Club Site
Silverhill Lane, Teversal
NG17 3JJ
Tel: 01623 551838 **84 G8**
campingandcaravanningclub.co.uk/
teversal
Total Pitches: 126 (C, CV & T)

The Inside Park
Down House Estate,
Blandford Forum
DT11 9AD
Tel: 01258 453719 **12 E4**
theinsidepark.co.uk
Total Pitches: 125 (C, CV & T)

The Old Brick Kilns
Little Barney Lane,
Barney, Fakenham
NR21 0NL
Tel: 01328 878305 **76 E5**
old-brick-kilns.co.uk
Total Pitches: 65 (C, CV & T)

The Old Oaks Touring Park
Wick Farm, Wick,
Glastonbury
BA6 8JS
Tel: 01458 831437 **19 P7**
theoldoaks.co.uk
Total Pitches: 100 (C, CV & T)

The Orchards Holiday Caravan Park
Main Road, Newbridge,
Yarmouth, Isle of Wight
PO41 0TS
Tel: 01983 531331 **14 D9**
orchards-holiday-park.co.uk
Total Pitches: 171 (C, CV & T)

The Quiet Site
Ullswater,
Watermillock
CA11 0LS
Tel: 07768 727016 **101 M6**
thequietsite.co.uk
Total Pitches: 100 (C, CV & T)

Tollgate Farm C & C Park
Budnick Hill, Perranporth
TR6 0AD
Tel: 01872 572130 **3 K3**
tollgatefarm.co.uk
Total Pitches: 102 (C, CV & T)

Townsend Touring Park
Townsend Farm, Pembridge,
Leominster
HR6 9HB
Tel: 01544 388527 **45 M3**
townsendfarm.co.uk
Total Pitches: 60 (C, CV & T)

Treloy Touring Park
Newquay
TR8 4JN
Tel: 01637 872063 **4 D9**
treloy.co.uk
Total Pitches: 223 (C, CV & T)

Trencreek Holiday Park
Hillcrest, Higher Trencreek,
Newquay
TR8 4NS
Tel: 01637 874210 **4 C9**
trencreekholidaypark.co.uk
Total Pitches: 194 (C, CV & T)

Trethem Mill Touring Park
St Just-in-Roseland, Nr St Mawes,
Truro
TR2 5JF
Tel: 01872 580504 **3 M6**
trethem.com
Total Pitches: 84 (C, CV & T)

Trevalgan Touring Park
Trevalgan, St Ives
TR26 3BJ
Tel: 01736 792048 **2 D5**
trevalgantouringpark.co.uk
Total Pitches: 120 (C, CV & T)

Trevarth Holiday Park
Blackwater, Truro
TR4 8HR
Tel: 01872 560266 **3 J4**
trevarth.co.uk
Total Pitches: 30 (C, CV & T)

Trevella Tourist Park
Crantock, Newquay
TR8 5EW
Tel: 01637 830308 **4 C10**
trevella.co.uk
Total Pitches: 313 (C, CV & T)

Troutbeck C & C Club Site
Hutton Moor End, Troutbeck,
Penrith
CA11 0SX
Tel: 017687 79149 **101 L5**
campingandcaravanningclub.co.uk/
troutbeck
Total Pitches: 54 (C, CV & T)

Truro C & C Park
Truro
TR4 8QN
Tel: 01872 560274 **3 K4**
trurocaravanandcampingpark.co.uk
Total Pitches: 51 (C, CV & T)

Tudor C & C
Shepherds Patch, Slimbridge,
Gloucester
GL2 7BP
Tel: 01453 890483 **32 D4**
tudorcaravanpark.com
Total Pitches: 75 (C, CV & T)

Two Mills Touring Park
Yarmouth Road, North Walsham
NR28 9NA
Tel: 01692 405829 **77 K6**
twomills.co.uk
Total Pitches: 81 (C, CV & T)

Ulwell Cottage Caravan Park
Ulwell Cottage, Ulwell, Swanage
BH19 3DG
Tel: 01929 422823 **12 H8**
ulwellcottagepark.co.uk
Total Pitches: 77 (C, CV & T)

Vale of Pickering Caravan Park
Carr House Farm, Allerston,
Pickering
YO18 7PQ
Tel: 01723 859280 **98 H4**
valeofpickering.co.uk
Total Pitches: 120 (C, CV & T)

Warcombe Farm C & C Park
Station Road, Mortehoe
EX34 7EJ
Tel: 01271 870690 **16 H2**
warcombefarm.co.uk
Total Pitches: 250 (C, CV & T)

Wareham Forest Tourist Park
North Trigon, Wareham
BH20 7NZ
Tel: 01929 551393 **12 E6**
warehamforest.co.uk
Total Pitches: 200 (C, CV & T)

Waren Caravan Park
Waren Mill,
Bamburgh
NE70 7EE
Tel: 01668 214366 **119 M4**
meadowhead.co.uk
Total Pitches: 150 (C, CV & T)

Watergate Bay Touring Park
Watergate Bay,
Tregurrian
TR8 4AD
Tel: 01637 860387 **4 C9**
watergatebaytouringpark.co.uk
Total Pitches: 171 (C, CV & T)

Waterrow Touring Park
Wiveliscombe, Taunton
TA4 2AZ
Tel: 01984 623464 **18 E9**
waterrowpark.co.uk
Total Pitches: 45 (C, CV & T)

Wayfarers C & C Park
Relubbus Lane, St Hilary,
Penzance
TR20 9EF
Tel: 01736 763326 **2 F7**
wayfarerspark.co.uk
Total Pitches: 39 (C, CV & T)

Wells Holiday Park
Haybridge, Wells
BA5 1AJ
Tel: 01749 676869 **19 P5**
wellsholidaypark.co.uk
Total Pitches: 72 (C, CV & T)

Westwood Caravan Park
Old Felixstowe Road,
Bucklesham, Ipswich
IP10 0BN
Tel: 01473 659637 **53 N3**
westwoodcaravanpark.co.uk
Total Pitches: 100 (C, CV & T)

Whitefield Forest Touring Park
Brading Road, Ryde,
Isle of Wight
PO33 1QL
Tel: 01983 617069 **14 H9**
whitefieldforest.co.uk
Total Pitches: 80 (C, CV & T)

Whitemead Caravan Park
East Burton Road,
Wool
BH20 6HG
Tel: 01929 462241 **12 D7**
whitemeadcaravanpark.co.uk
Total Pitches: 95 (C, CV & T)

Whitsand Bay Lodge & Touring Park
Millbrook, Torpoint
PL10 1JZ
Tel: 01752 822597 **5 Q11**
whitsandbayholidays.co.uk
Total Pitches: 49 (C, CV & T)

Widdicombe Farm Touring Park
Marldon, Paignton
TQ3 1ST
Tel: 01803 558325 **7 M6**
widdicombefarm.co.uk
Total Pitches: 180 (C, CV & T)

Widemouth Fields C & C Park
Park Farm,
Poundstock, Bude
EX23 0NA
Tel: 01288 361351 **16 C11**
widemouthbaytouring.co.uk
Total Pitches: 156 (C, CV & T)

Widend Touring Park
Berry Pomeroy Road,
Marldon, Paignton
TQ3 1RT
Tel: 01803 550116 **7 M6**
Total Pitches: 207 (C, CV & T)

Wild Rose Park
Ormside,
Appleby-in-Westmorland
CA16 6EJ
Tel: 017683 51077 **102 C7**
wildrose.co.uk
Total Pitches: 226 (C, CV & T)

Wilksworth Farm Caravan Park
Cranborne Road,
Wimborne Minster
BH21 4HW
Tel: 01202 885467 **12 H4**
wilksworthfarmcaravanpark.co.uk
Total Pitches: 85 (C, CV & T)

Wolds Way Caravan and Camping
West Farm, West Knapton,
Malton
YO17 8JE
Tel: 01944 728463 **98 H6**
rydalesbest.co.uk
Total Pitches: 70 (C, CV & T)

Wooda Farm Holiday Park
Poughill, Bude
EX23 9HJ
Tel: 01288 352069   **16 C10**
wooda.co.uk
Total Pitches: 200 (C, CV & T)

Woodclose Caravan Park
High Casterton,
Kirkby Lonsdale
LA6 2SE
Tel: 01524 271597   **95 N5**
woodclosepark.com
Total Pitches: 29 (C, CV & T)

Wood Farm C & C Park
Axminster Road,
Charmouth
DT6 6BT
Tel: 01297 560697   **10 H6**
woodfarm.co.uk
Total Pitches: 216 (C, CV & T)

Woodhall Country Park
Stixwold Road, Woodhall Spa
LN10 6UJ
Tel: 01526 353710   **86 G8**
woodhallcountrypark.co.uk
Total Pitches: 80 (C, CV & T)

Woodlands Grove C & C Park
Blackawton, Dartmouth
TQ9 7DQ
Tel: 01803 712598   **7 L8**
woodlands-caravanpark.com
Total Pitches: 350 (C, CV & T)

**Woodland Springs
Adult Touring Park**
Venton, Drewsteignton
EX6 6PG
Tel: 01647 231695   **8 G6**
woodlandsprings.co.uk
Total Pitches: 81 (C, CV & T)

Woodovis Park
Gulworthy, Tavistock
PL19 8NY
Tel: 01822 832968   **6 C4**
woodovis.com
Total Pitches: 50 (C, CV & T)

**Woolsbridge Manor Farm
Caravan Park**
Three Legged Cross,
Wimborne
BH21 6RA
Tel: 01202 826369   **13 K4**
woolsbridgemanorcaravanpark.
co.uk
Total Pitches: 60 (C, CV & T)

**Yeatheridge Farm
Caravan Park**
East Worlington, Crediton
EX17 4TN
Tel: 01884 860330   **9 J2**
yeatheridge.co.uk
Total Pitches: 85 (C, CV & T)

**Zeacombe House
Caravan Park**
Blackerton Cross,
East Anstey, Tiverton
EX16 9JU
Tel: 01398 341279   **17 R7**
zeacombeadultretreat.com
Total Pitches: 50 (C, CV & T)

SCOTLAND

Aird Donald Caravan Park
London Road, Stranraer
DG9 8RN
Tel: 01776 702025   **106 E5**
aird-donald.com
Total Pitches: 100 (C, CV & T)

Anwoth Caravan Site
Gatehouse of Fleet,
Castle Douglas
DG7 2JU
Tel: 01557 814333   **108 C9**
auchenlarie.co.uk
Total Pitches: 28 (C, CV & T)

Beecraigs C & C Site
Beecraigs Country Park,
The Park Centre, Linlithgow
EH49 6PL
Tel: 01506 844516   **127 J3**
beecraigs.com
Total Pitches: 36 (C, CV & T)

Blair Castle Caravan Park
Blair Atholl, Pitlochry
PH18 5SR
Tel: 01796 481263   **141 L4**
blaircastlecaravanpark.co.uk
Total Pitches: 241 (C, CV & T)

Brighouse Bay Holiday Park
Brighouse Bay, Borgue
DG6 4TS
Tel: 01557 870267   **108 D11**
gillespie-leisure.co.uk
Total Pitches: 190 (C, CV & T)

Cairnsmill Holiday Park
Largo Road,
St Andrews
KY16 8NN
Tel: 01334 473604   **135 M5**
Total Pitches: 62 (C, CV & T)

Castle Cary Holiday Park
Creetown,
Newton Stewart
DG8 7DQ
Tel: 01671 820264   **107 N6**
castlecary-caravans.com
Total Pitches: 50 (C, CV & T)

**Craigtoun Meadows
Holiday Park**
Mount Melville,
St Andrews
KY16 8PQ
Tel: 01334 475959   **135 M4**
craigtounmeadows.co.uk
Total Pitches: 57 (C, CV & T)

Crossburn Caravan Park
Edinburgh Road,
Peebles
EH45 8ED
Tel: 01721 720501   **117 J2**
crossburncaravans.co.uk
Total Pitches: 45 (C, CV & T)

Drum Mohr Caravan Park
Levenhall, Musselburgh
EH21 8JS
Tel: 0131 665 6867   **128 B5**
drummohr.org
Total Pitches: 120 (C, CV & T)

East Bowstrips Caravan Park
St Cyrus, Nr Montrose
DD10 0DE
Tel: 01674 850328   **143 N4**
caravancampingsites.co.uk/
aberdeenshire/eastbowstrips.htm
Total Pitches: 32 (C, CV & T)

Gart Caravan Park
The Gart, Callander
FK17 8LE
Tel: 01877 330002   **133 J6**
theholidaypark.co.uk
Total Pitches: 128 (C & CV)

Glenearly Caravan Park
Dalbeattie
DG5 4NE
Tel: 01556 611393   **108 H8**
glenearlycaravanpark.co.uk
Total Pitches: 39 (C, CV & T)

Glen Nevis C & C Park
Glen Nevis, Fort William
PH33 6SX
Tel: 01397 702191   **139 L3**
glen-nevis.co.uk
Total Pitches: 380 (C, CV & T)

Hoddom Castle Caravan Park
Hoddom, Lockerbie
DG11 1AS
Tel: 01576 300251   **110 C6**
hoddomcastle.co.uk
Total Pitches: 200 (C, CV & T)

Huntly Castle Caravan Park
The Meadow, Huntly
AB54 4UJ
Tel: 01466 794999   **158 D9**
huntlycastle.co.uk
Total Pitches: 90 (C, CV & T)

Invercoe C & C Park
Glencoe, Ballachulish
PH49 4HP
Tel: 01855 811210   **139 K6**
invercoe.co.uk
Total Pitches: 60 (C, CV & T)

Linnhe Lochside Holidays
Corpach, Fort William
PH33 7NL
Tel: 01397 772376   **139 K2**
linnhe-lochside-holidays.co.uk
Total Pitches: 85 (C, CV & T)

Lomond Woods Holiday Park
Old Luss Road, Balloch,
Loch Lomond
G83 8QP
Tel: 01389 755000   **132 D11**
holiday-parks.co.uk
Total Pitches: 100 (C & CV)

Machrihanish Caravan Park
East Trodigal, Machrihanish,
Mull of Kintyre
PA28 6PT
Tel: 01586 810366   **120 B7**
campkintyre.co.uk
Total Pitches: 90 (C, CV & T)

Milton of Fonab Caravan Site
Bridge Road, Pitlochry
PH16 5NA
Tel: 01796 472882   **141 M6**
fonab.co.uk
Total Pitches: 154 (C, CV & T)

River Tilt Caravan Park
Blair Atholl,
Pitlochry
PH18 5TE
Tel: 01796 481467   **141 L4**
rivertilt.co.uk
Total Pitches: 30 (C, CV & T)

Riverview Caravan Park
Marine Drive,
Monifieth
DD5 4NN
Tel: 01382 535471   **143 J11**
riverview.co.uk
Total Pitches: 49 (C & CV)

Sands of Luce Holiday Park
Sands of Luce,
Sandhead,
Stranraer
DG9 9JN
Tel: 01776 830456   **106 F7**
sandsofluceholidaypark.co.uk
Total Pitches: 120 (C, CV & T)

Seaward Caravan Park
Dhoon Bay,
Kirkudbright
DG6 4TJ
Tel: 01557 870267   **108 E11**
gillespie-leisure.co.uk
Total Pitches: 26 (C, CV & T)

Shieling Holidays
Craignure,
Isle of Mull
PA65 6AY
Tel: 01680 812496   **138 C10**
shielingholidays.co.uk
Total Pitches: 90 (C, CV & T)

Silver Sands Leisure Park
Covesea, West Beach,
Lossiemouth
IV31 6SP
Tel: 01343 813262   **157 N3**
silver-sands.co.uk
Total Pitches: 140 (C, CV & T)

Skye C & C Club Site
Loch Greshornish, Borve,
Arnisort, Edinbane,
Isle of Skye
IV51 9PS
Tel: 01470 582230   **152 E7**
campingandcaravanningclub.co.uk/
skye
Total Pitches: 105 (C, CV & T)

Springwood Caravan Park
Kelso
TD5 8LS
Tel: 01573 224596   **118 D4**
springwood.biz
Total Pitches: 20 (C & CV)

Thurston Manor Leisure Park
Innerwick, Dunbar
EH42 1SA
Tel: 01368 840643   **129 J5**
thurstonmanor.co.uk
Total Pitches: 120 (C, CV & T)

Trossachs Holiday Park
Aberfoyle
FK8 3SA
Tel: 01877 382614   **132 G8**
trossachsholidays.co.uk
Total Pitches: 66 (C, CV & T)

Witches Craig C & C Park
Blairlogie, Stirling
FK9 5PX
Tel: 01786 474947   **133 N8**
witchescraig.co.uk
Total Pitches: 60 (C, CV & T)

WALES

Anchorage Caravan Park
Bronllys, Brecon
LD3 0LD
Tel: 01874 711246   **44 G7**
anchoragecp.co.uk
Total Pitches: 110 (C, CV & T)

Barcdy Touring C & C Park
Talsarnau
LL47 6YG
Tel: 01766 770736   **67 L7**
barcdy.co.uk
Total Pitches: 80 (C, CV & T)

Beach View Caravan Park
Bwlchtocyn,
Abersoch
LL53 7BT
Tel: 01758 712956   **66 E9**
Total Pitches: 47 (C, CV & T)

Bodnant Caravan Park
Nebo Road, Llanrwst,
Conwy Valley
LL26 0SD
Tel: 01492 640248   **67 Q2**
bodnant-caravan-park.co.uk
Total Pitches: 54 (C, CV & T)

**Bron Derw
Touring Caravan Park**
Llanrwst
LL26 0YT
Tel: 01492 640494   **67 P2**
bronderw-wales.co.uk
Total Pitches: 43 (C & CV)

Bron-Y-Wendon Caravan Park
Wern Road, Llanddulas,
Colwyn Bay
LL22 8HG
Tel: 01492 512903   **80 C9**
northwales-holidays.co.uk
Total Pitches: 130 (C & CV)

Bryn Gloch C & C Park
Betws Garmon,
Caernarfon
LL54 7YY
Tel: 01286 650216   **67 J3**
campwales.co.uk
Total Pitches: 160 (C, CV & T)

**Caerfai Bay
Caravan & Tent Park**
Caerfai Bay, St David's,
Haverfordwest
SA62 6QT
Tel: 01437 720274   **40 E6**
caerfaibay.co.uk
Total Pitches: 106 (C, CV & T)

Cenarth Falls Holiday Park
Cenarth,
Newcastle Emlyn
SA38 9JS
Tel: 01239 710345   **41 Q2**
cenarth-holipark.co.uk
Total Pitches: 30 (C, CV & T)

**Deucoch
Touring & Camping Park**
Sarn Bach, Abersoch
LL53 7LD
Tel: 01758 713293   **66 E9**
deucoch.com
Total Pitches: 70 (C, CV & T)

Dinlle Caravan Park
Dinas Dinlle, Caernarfon
LL54 5TW
Tel: 01286 830324   **66 G3**
thornleyleisure.co.uk
Total Pitches: 175 (C, CV & T)

Eisteddfa
Eisteddfa Lodge,
Pentrefelin,
Criccieth
LL52 0PT
Tel: 01766 522696   **67 J7**
eisteddfapark.co.uk
Total Pitches: 100 (C, CV & T)

Erwlon C & C Park
Brecon Road,
Llandovery
SA20 0RD
Tel: 01550 721021   **43 Q8**
erwlon.co.uk
Total Pitches: 75 (C, CV & T)

**Hendre Mynach
Touring C & C Park**
Llanaber Road, Barmouth
LL42 1YR
Tel: 01341 280262   **67 L11**
hendremynach.co.uk
Total Pitches: 240 (C, CV & T)

Home Farm Caravan Park
Marian-Glas,
Isle of Anglesey
LL73 8PH
Tel: 01248 410614   **78 H8**
homefarm-anglesey.co.uk
Total Pitches: 98 (C, CV & T)

Hunters Hamlet Caravan Park
Sirior Goch Farm,
Betws-yn-Rhos, Abergele
LL22 8PL
Tel: 01745 832237   **80 C10**
huntershamlet.co.uk
Total Pitches: 23 (C & CV)

Islawrffordd Caravan Park
Tal-y-bont, Barmouth
LL43 2AQ
Tel: 01341 247269   **67 K10**
islawrffordd.co.uk
Total Pitches: 105 (C, CV & T)

Llys Derwen C & C Site
Ffordd Bryngwyn, Llanrug,
Caernarfon
LL55 4RD
Tel: 01286 673322   **67 J2**
llysderwen.co.uk
Total Pitches: 20 (C, CV & T)

Pencelli Castle C & C Park
Pencelli, Brecon
LD3 7LX
Tel: 01874 665451   **44 F10**
pencelli-castle.com
Total Pitches: 80 (C, CV & T)

Penisar Mynydd Caravan Park
Caerwys Road, Rhuallt, St Asaph
LL17 0TY
Tel: 01745 582227   **80 F9**
penisarmynydd.co.uk
Total Pitches: 75 (C, CV & T)

Pen-y-Bont Touring Park
Llangynog Road, Bala
LL23 7PH
Tel: 01678 520549   **68 B8**
penybont-bala.co.uk
Total Pitches: 95 (C, CV & T)

Plas Farm Caravan Park
Betws-yn-Rhos, Abergele
LL22 8AU
Tel: 01492 680254   **80 B10**
plasfarmcaravanpark.co.uk
Total Pitches: 40 (C, CV & T)

Pont Kemys C & C Park
Chainbridge, Abergavenny
NP7 9DS
Tel: 01873 880688   **31 K3**
pontkemys.com
Total Pitches: 65 (C, CV & T)

Riverside Camping
Seiont Nurseries, Pont Rug,
Caernarfon
LL55 2BB
Tel: 01286 678781   **67 J2**
riversidecamping.co.uk
Total Pitches: 60 (C, CV & T)

River View Touring Park
The Dingle, Llanedi, Pontarddulais
SA4 0FH
Tel: 01269 844876   **28 G3**
riverviewtouringpark.com
Total Pitches: 60 (C, CV & T)

The Plassey Leisure Park
The Plassey, Eyton, Wrexham
LL13 0SP
Tel: 01978 780277   **69 L5**
plassey.com
Total Pitches: 90 (C, CV & T)

Trawsdir Touring C & C Park
Llanaber, Barmouth
LL42 1RR
Tel: 01341 280999   **67 K11**
barmouthholidays.co.uk
Total Pitches: 70 (C, CV & T)

Trefalun Park
Devonshire Drive,
St Florence, Tenby
SA70 8RD
Tel: 01646 651514   **41 L10**
trefalunpark.co.uk
Total Pitches: 90 (C, CV & T)

Tyddyn Isaf Caravan Park
Lligwy Bay, Dulas, Isle of Anglesey
LL70 9PQ
Tel: 01248 410203   **78 H7**
tyddynisaf.co.uk
Total Pitches: 30 (C, CV & T)

Tyn Cornel C & C Park
Frongoch, Bala
LL23 7NU
Tel: 01678 520759   **68 A6**
tyncornel.co.uk
Total Pitches: 67 (C, CV & T)

Well Park C & C Site
Tenby
SA70 8TL
Tel: 01834 842179   **41 M10**
wellparkcaravans.co.uk
Total Pitches: 100 (C, CV & T)

**Ynysymaengwyn
Caravan Park**
Tywyn
LL36 9RY
Tel: 01654 710684   **54 E4**
ynysy.co.uk
Total Pitches: 80 (C, CV & T)

CHANNEL ISLANDS

Beuvelande Camp Site
Beuvelande, St Martin, Jersey
JE3 6EZ
Tel: 01534 853575   **11 c1**
campingjersey.com
Total Pitches: 150 (T)

Fauxquets Valley Campsite
Castel, Guernsey
GY5 7QL
Tel: 01481 236951   **10 b2**
fauxquets.co.uk
Total Pitches: 120 (T)

Rozel Camping Park
Summerville Farm,
St Martin, Jersey
JE3 6AX
Tel: 01534 855200   **11 c1**
rozelcamping.co.uk
Total Pitches: 100 (C, CV & T)

Road safety cameras

First, the advice you would expect from the AA - we advise drivers to always follow the signed speed limits – breaking the speed limit is illegal and can cost lives.

Both the AA and the Government believe that safety cameras ('speed cameras') should be operated within a transparent system. By providing information relating to road safety and speed hotspots, the AA believes that the driver is better placed to be aware of speed limits and can ensure adherence to them, thus making the roads safer for all users.

Most fixed cameras are installed at accident 'black spots' where four or more fatal or serious road collisions have occurred over the previous three years. It is the policy of both the police and the Department for Transport to make the location of cameras as well known as possible. By showing camera locations in this atlas the AA is identifying the places where extra care should be taken while driving. Speeding is illegal and dangerous and you MUST keep within the speed limit at all times.

Gatso™   Truvelo™   SPECS™   Traffipax™

There are currently more than 4,000 fixed cameras in Britain and the road mapping in this atlas identifies their on-the-road locations.

 This symbol is used on the mapping to identify **individual** camera locations - with speed limits (mph)

 This symbol is used on the mapping to identify **multiple** cameras on the same stretch of road - with speed limits (mph)

 This symbol is used on the mapping to highlight SPECS™ camera systems which calculate your **average speed** along a stretch of road between two or more sets of cameras - with speed limits (mph)

Mobile cameras are also deployed at other sites where speed is perceived to be a problem and mobile enforcement often takes place at the fixed camera sites shown on the maps in this atlas. Additionally, regular police enforcement can take place on any road.

Speed Limits	Built up areas*	Single carriageways	Dual carriageways	Motorways
Types of vehicle	MPH (km/h)	MPH (km/h)	MPH (km/h)	MPH (km/h)
Cars & motorcycles (including car derived vans up to 2 tonnes maximum laden weight)	30 (48)	60 (96)	70 (112)	70 (112)
Cars towing caravans or trailers (including car derived vans and motorcycles)	30 (48)	50 (80)	60 (96)	60 (96)
Buses, coaches and minibuses (not exceeding 12 metres (39 feet) in overall length)	30 (48)	50 (80)	60 (96)	70 (112)
Goods vehicles (not exceeding 7.5 tonnes maximum laden weight)	30 (48)	50 (80)	60 (96)	70† (112)
Goods vehicles (exceeding 7.5 tonnes maximum laden weight)	30 (48)	40 (64)	50 (80)	60 (96)

* The 30mph (48km/h) limit usually applies to all traffic on all roads with street lighting unless signs show otherwise.
† 60mph (96km/h) if articulated or towing a trailer.

Read this before you use the atlas

Safety cameras and speed limits

The fixed camera symbols on the mapping show the maximum speed in mph that applies to that particular stretch of road and above which the camera is set to activate. The actual road speed limit however will vary for different vehicle types and you must ensure that you drive within the speed limit for your particular class of vehicle at all times.

The chart above details the speed limits applying to the different classes. Don't forget that mobile enforcement can take account of vehicle class at any designated site.

Camera locations

1 The camera locations were correct at the time of finalising the information to go to press.

2 Camera locations are approximate due to limitations in the scale of the road mapping used in this atlas.

3 In towns and urban areas camera locations are shown only on roads that appear on the road maps in this atlas.

4 Where two or more cameras appear close together, a special symbol is used to indicate multiple cameras on the same stretch of road.

5 Our symbols do not indicate the direction in which cameras point.

6 On the mapping we symbolise more than 4,000 fixed camera locations. Mobile laser device locations, roadwork cameras and 'fixed red light' cameras cannot be shown.

Be alert to accident black spots even before seeing the cameras

The AA brings you a Smart Phone app that provides 'real-time' updates of safety camera locations

The AA Safety Camera app brings the latest safety camera location system to your Smart Phone. It improves road safety by alerting you to the location of fixed and mobile camera sites and accident black spots.

The AA Safety Camera app ensures that you will always have the very latest data of fixed and mobile sites on your Smart Phone without having to connect it to your computer. Updates are made available automatically.

Powered by **RoadPilot**®

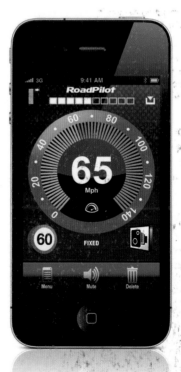

Visual Countdown
To camera location

Your Speed
The speed you are travelling when approaching a camera. Dial turns red as an additional visual alert

Camera Types Located
Includes fixed cameras (Gatso, Specs etc.) and mobile cameras

Speed Limit at Camera

Smart Phone Apps

Map pages

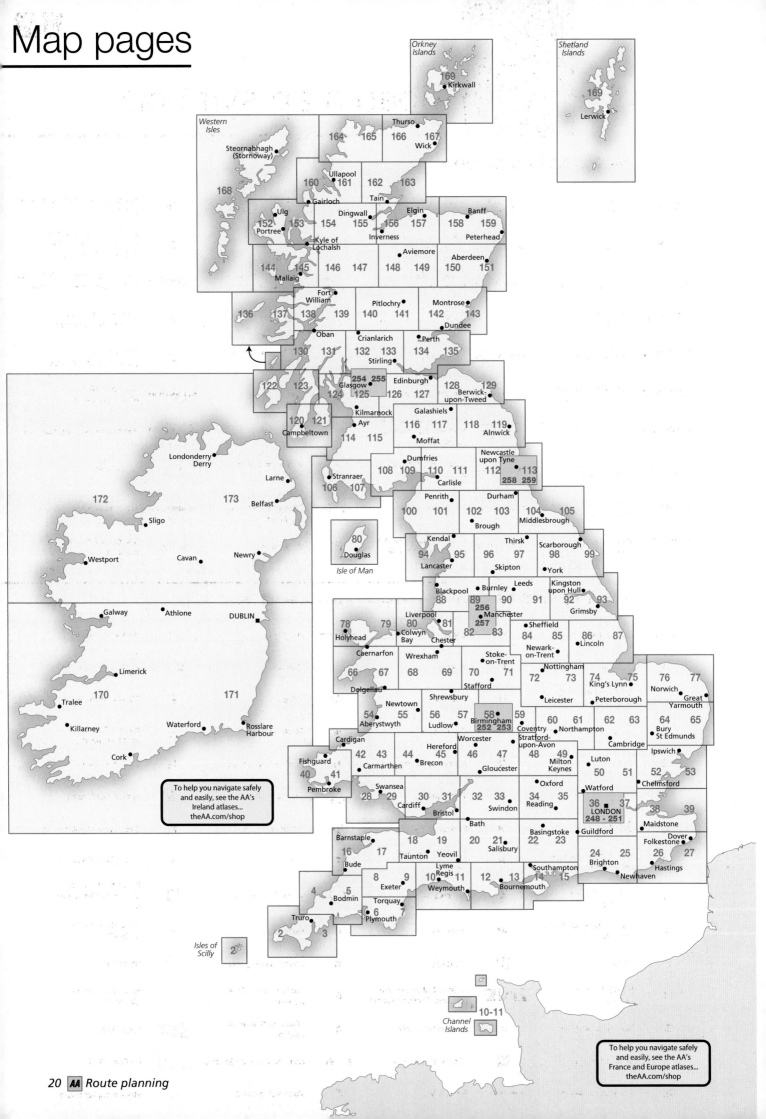

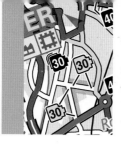

Road map symbols

Motoring information

M4 — Motorway with number	BATH — Primary route destination	Distance in miles between symbols	Speed camera site (fixed location) with speed limit in mph
Toll T4 — Toll motorway with toll station	A1123 — Other A road single/dual carriageway	Vehicle ferry	Section of road with two or more fixed speed cameras, with speed limit in mph
Motorway junction with and without number	B2070 — B road single/dual carriageway	Fast vehicle ferry or catamaran	Average speed (SPECS™) camera system with speed limit in mph
Restricted motorway junctions	Minor road more than 4 metres wide, less than 4 metres wide	Railway line, in tunnel	Fixed speed camera site with variable speed limit
Motorway service area	Roundabout	Railway station and level crossing	Park and Ride (at least 6 days per week)
Motorway and junction under construction	Interchange/junction	Tourist railway	City, town, village or other built-up area
Primary route single/dual carriageway	Narrow primary/other A/B road with passing places (Scotland)	Airport, heliport	Height in metres, mountain pass
Primary route junction with and without number	Road under construction/approved	International freight terminal	Sandy beach
Restricted primary route junctions	Road tunnel	24-hour Accident & Emergency hospital, other hospital	National boundary
Primary route service area	Road toll, steep gradient (arrows point downhill)	Crematorium	County, administrative boundary

Touring information

To avoid disappointment, check opening times before visiting.

Scenic Route	Garden	National trail	Air show venue
Tourist Information Centre	Arboretum	Viewpoint	Ski slope (natural, artificial)
Tourist Information Centre (seasonal)	Vineyard	Hill-fort	National Trust property
Visitor or heritage centre	Country park	Roman antiquity	National Trust for Scotland property
Picnic site	Agricultural showground	Prehistoric monument	English Heritage site
Caravan site (AA inspected)	Theme park	Battle site with year	Historic Scotland site
Camping site (AA inspected)	Farm or animal centre	Steam railway centre	Cadw (Welsh heritage) site
Caravan & camping site (AA inspected)	Zoological or wildlife collection	Cave	Other place of interest
Abbey, cathedral or priory	Bird collection	Windmill, monument	Boxed symbols indicate attractions within urban areas
Ruined abbey, cathedral or priory	Aquarium	Golf course	World Heritage Site (UNESCO)
Castle	RSPB site	County cricket ground	National Park
Historic house or building	National Nature Reserve (England, Scotland, Wales)	Rugby Union national stadium	National Scenic Area (Scotland)
Museum or art gallery	Local nature reserve	International athletics stadium	Forest Park
Industrial interest	Wildlife Trust reserve	Horse racing, show jumping	Heritage coast
Aqueduct or viaduct	Forest drive	Motor-racing circuit	Major shopping centre

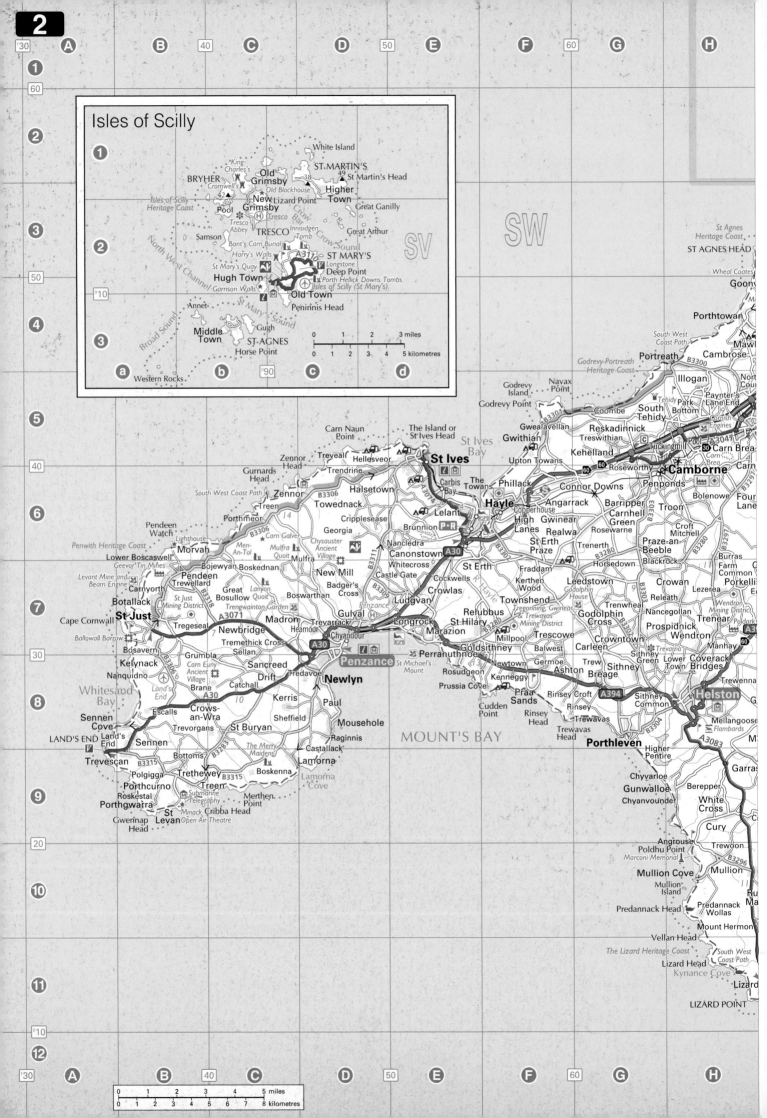

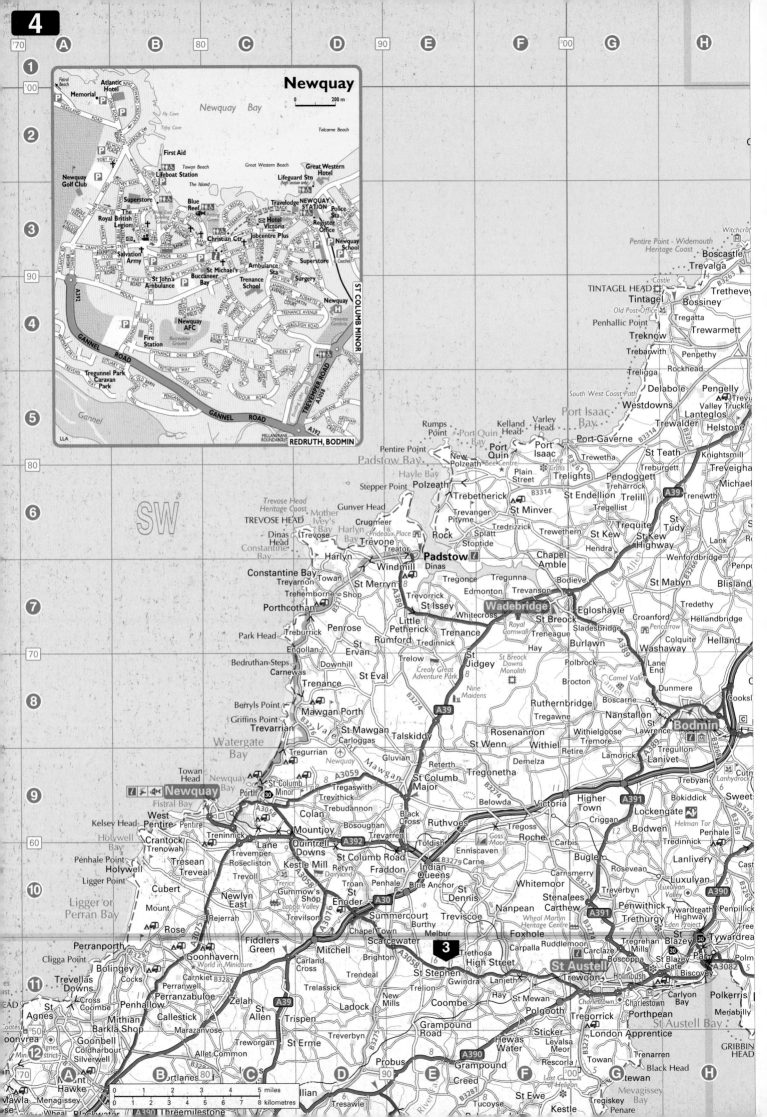

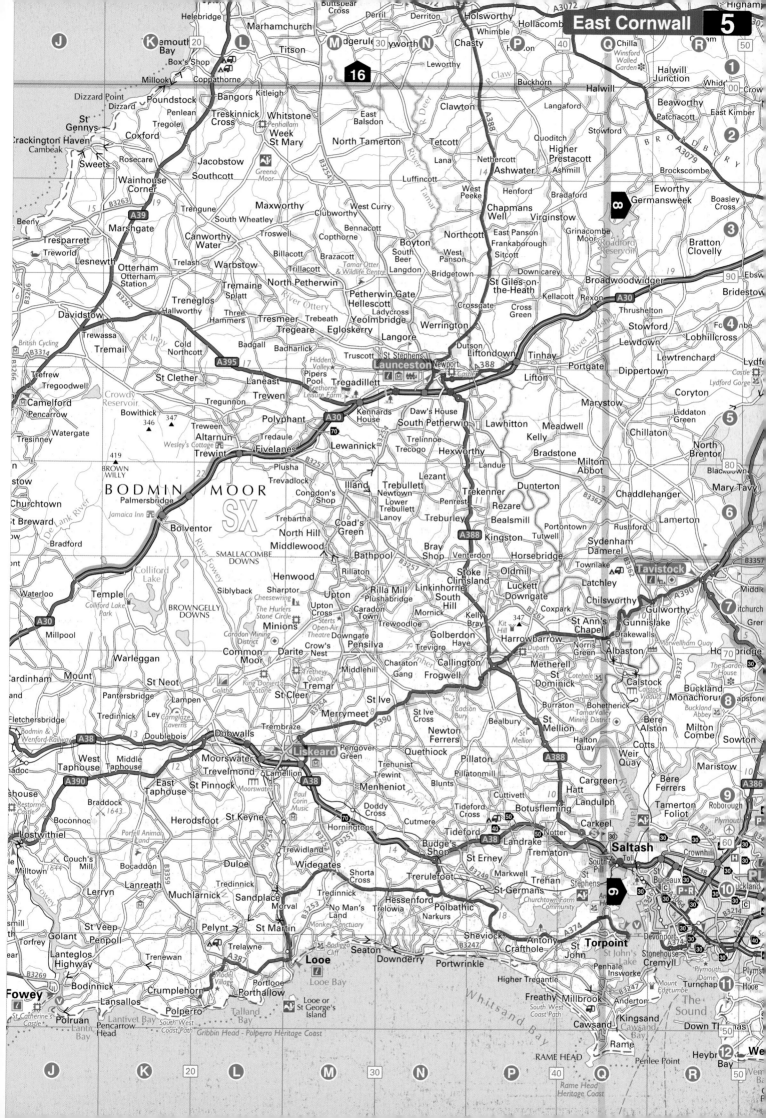

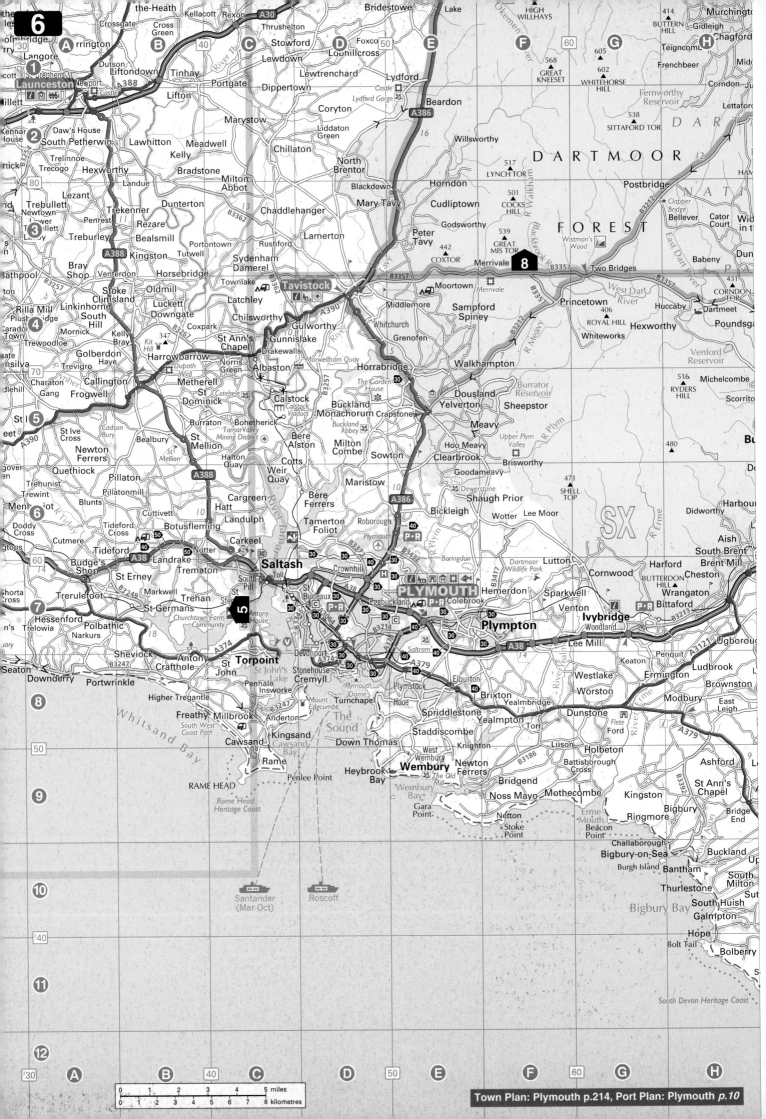

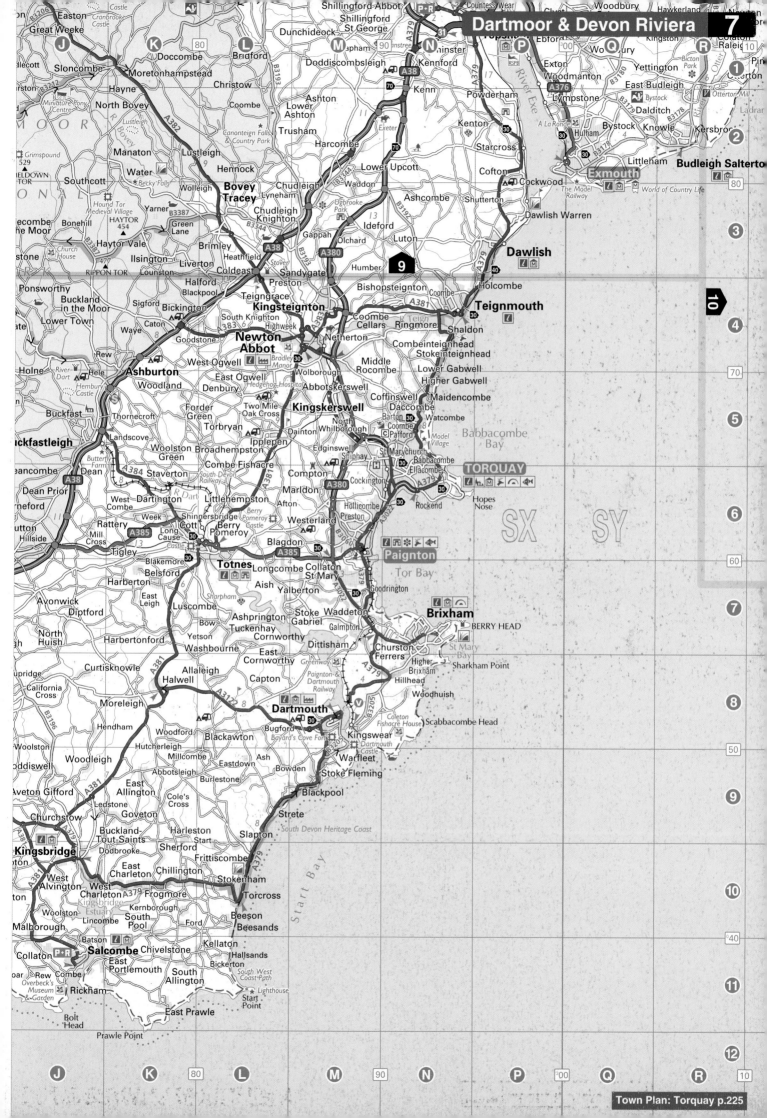

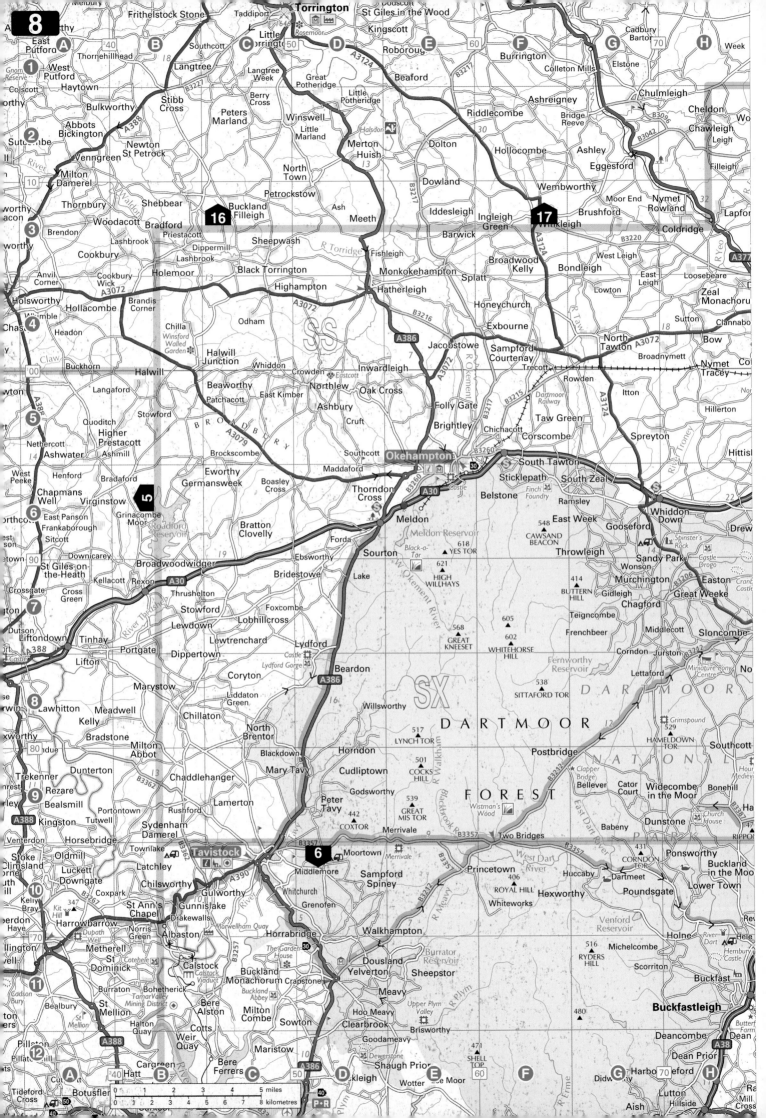

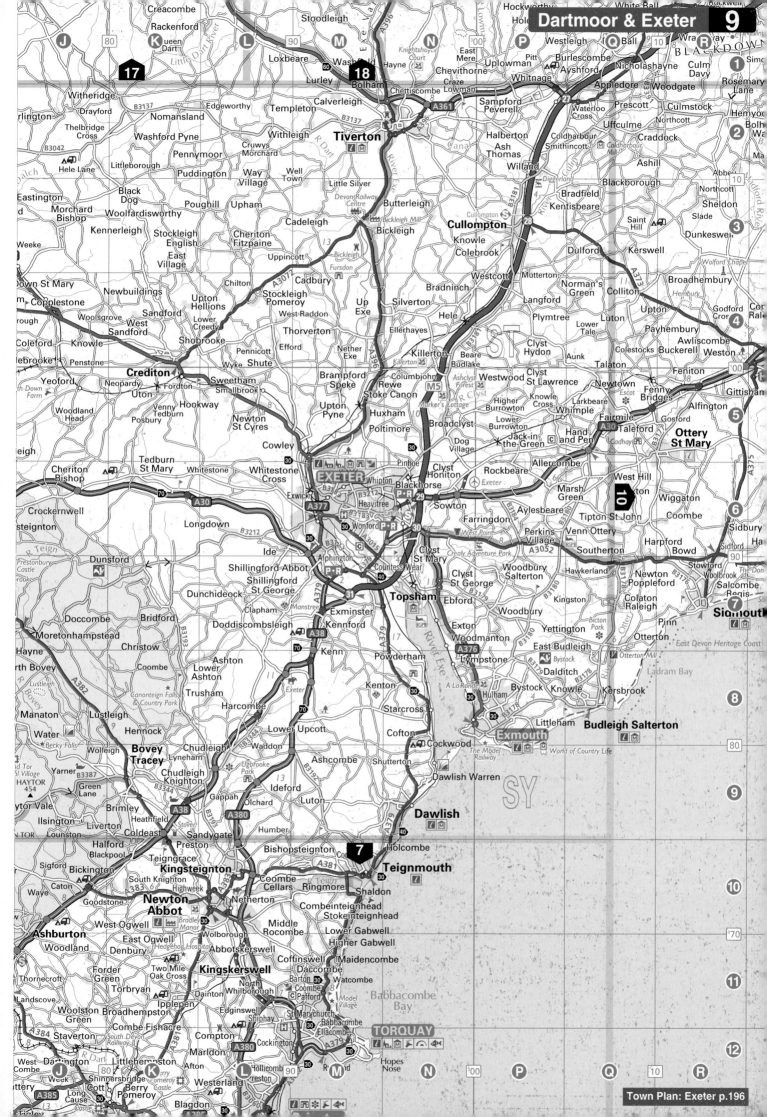

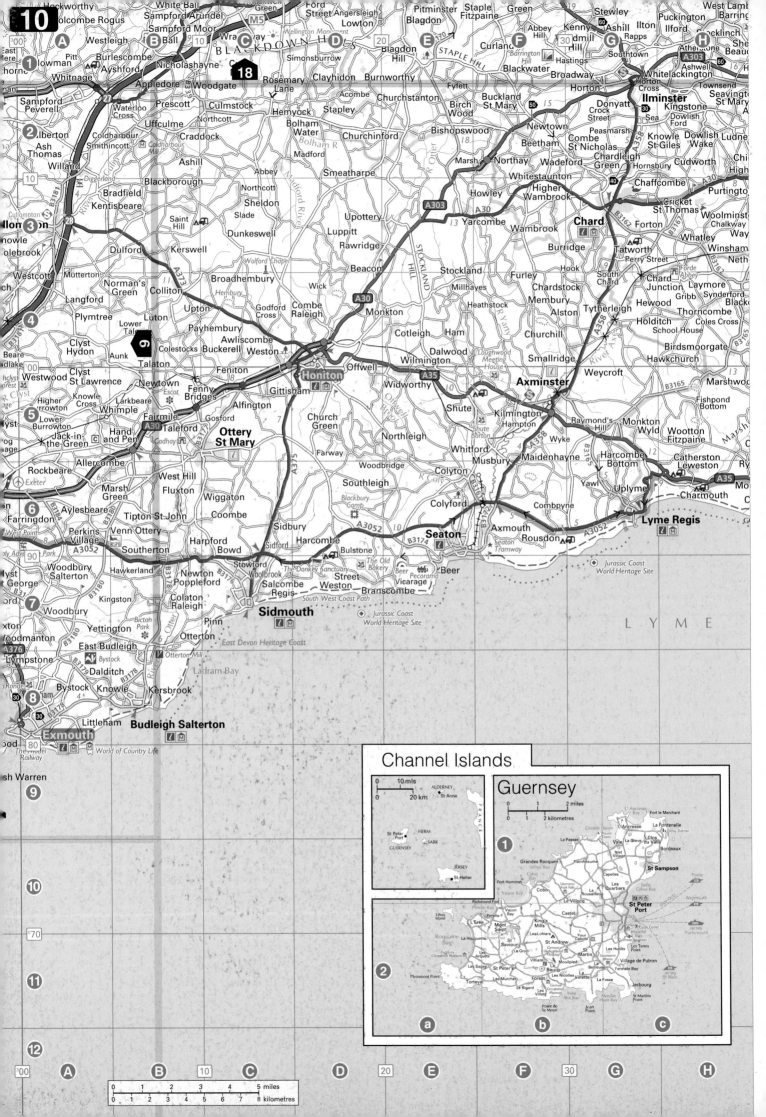

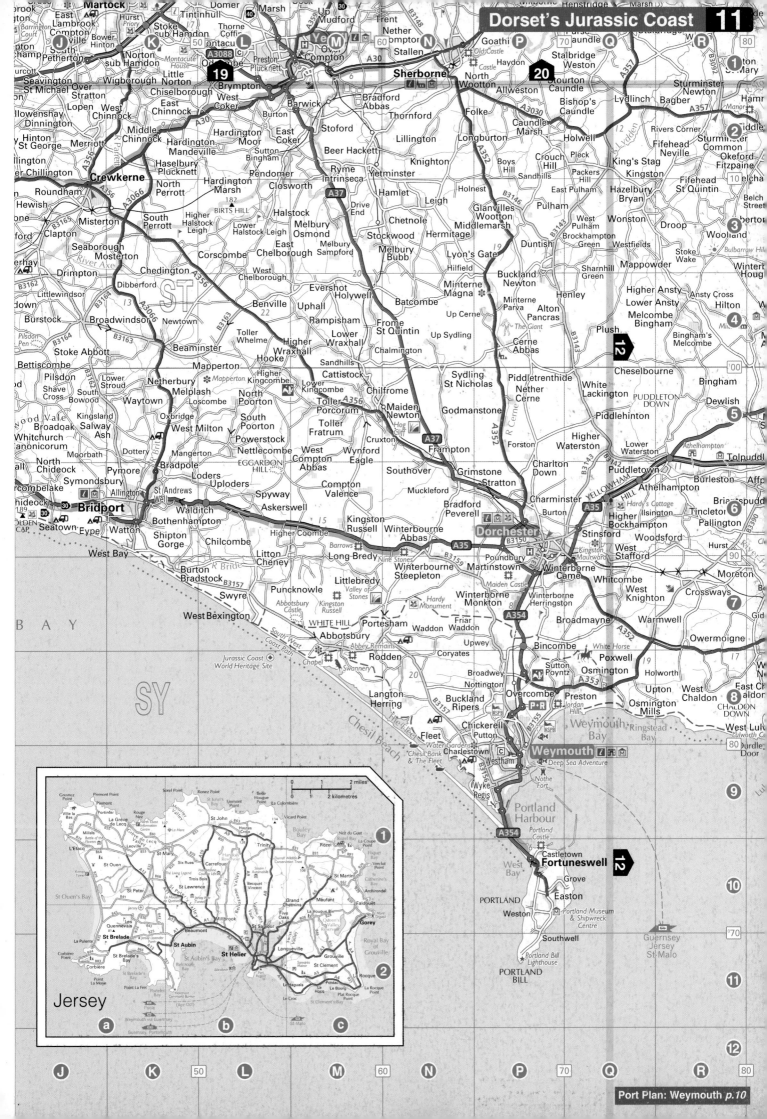

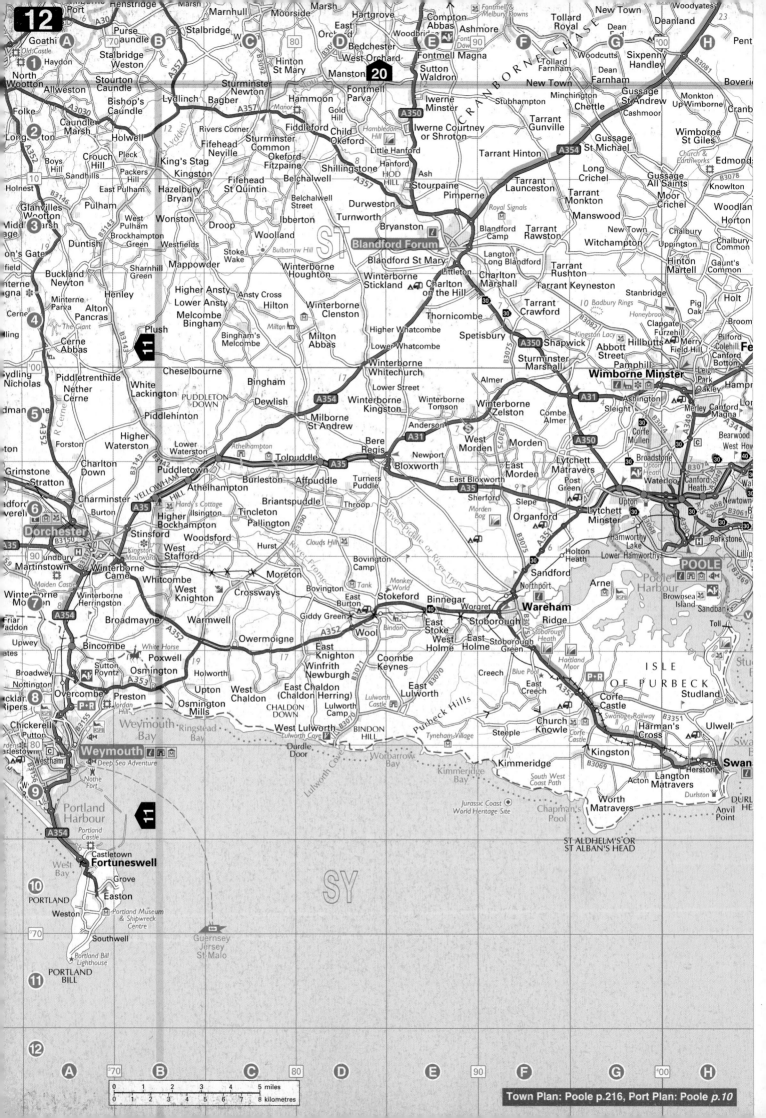

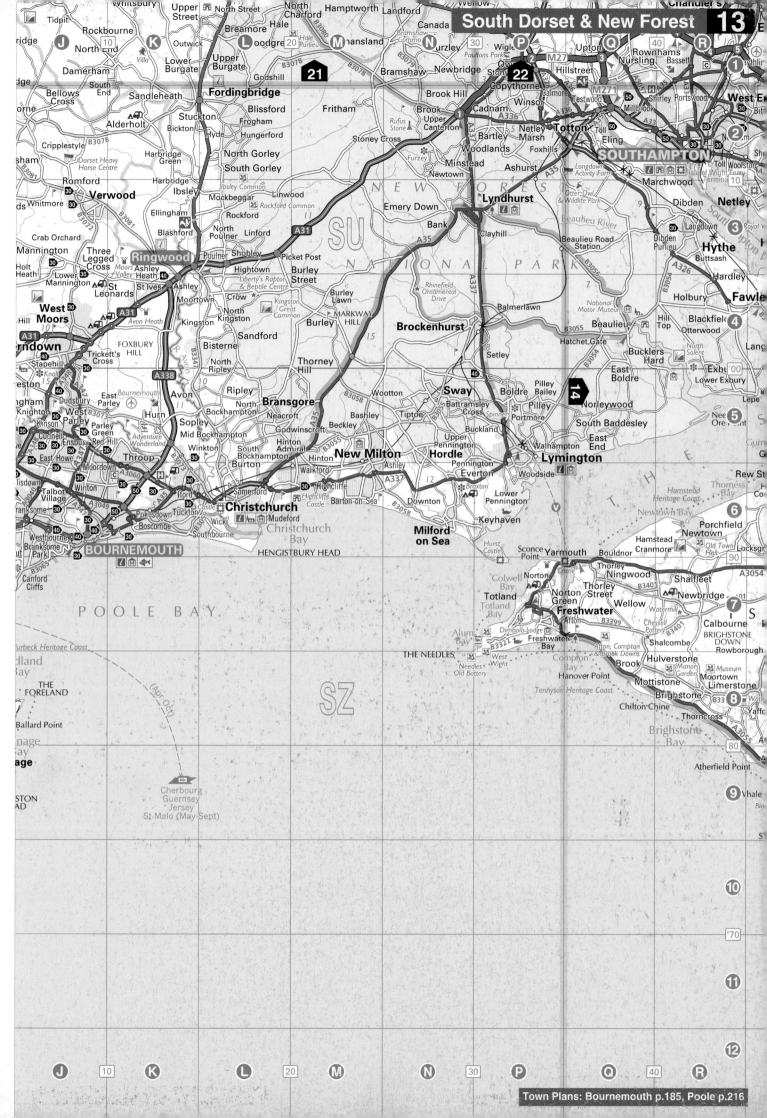

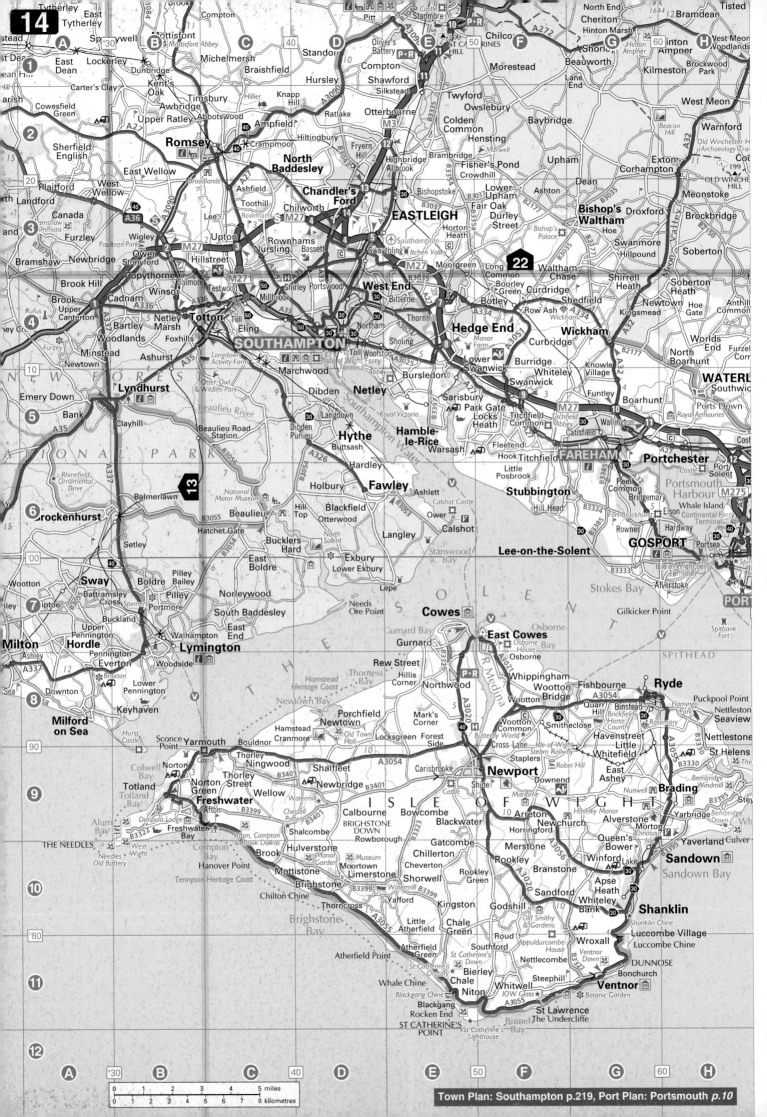

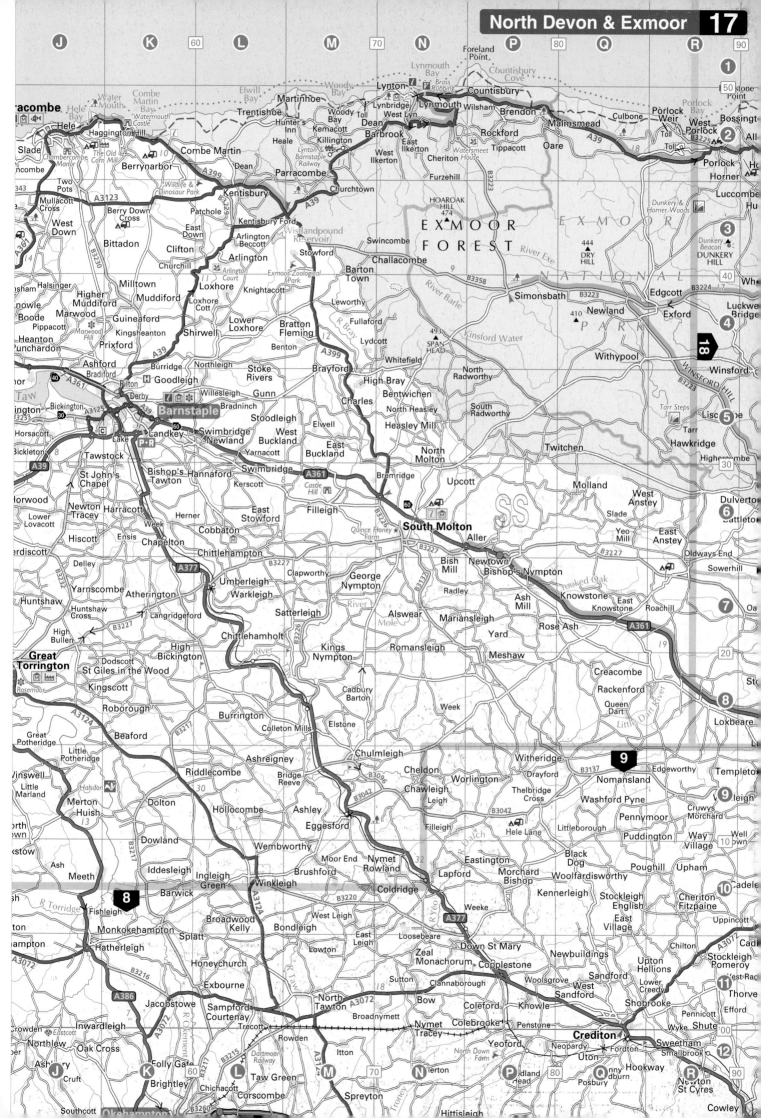

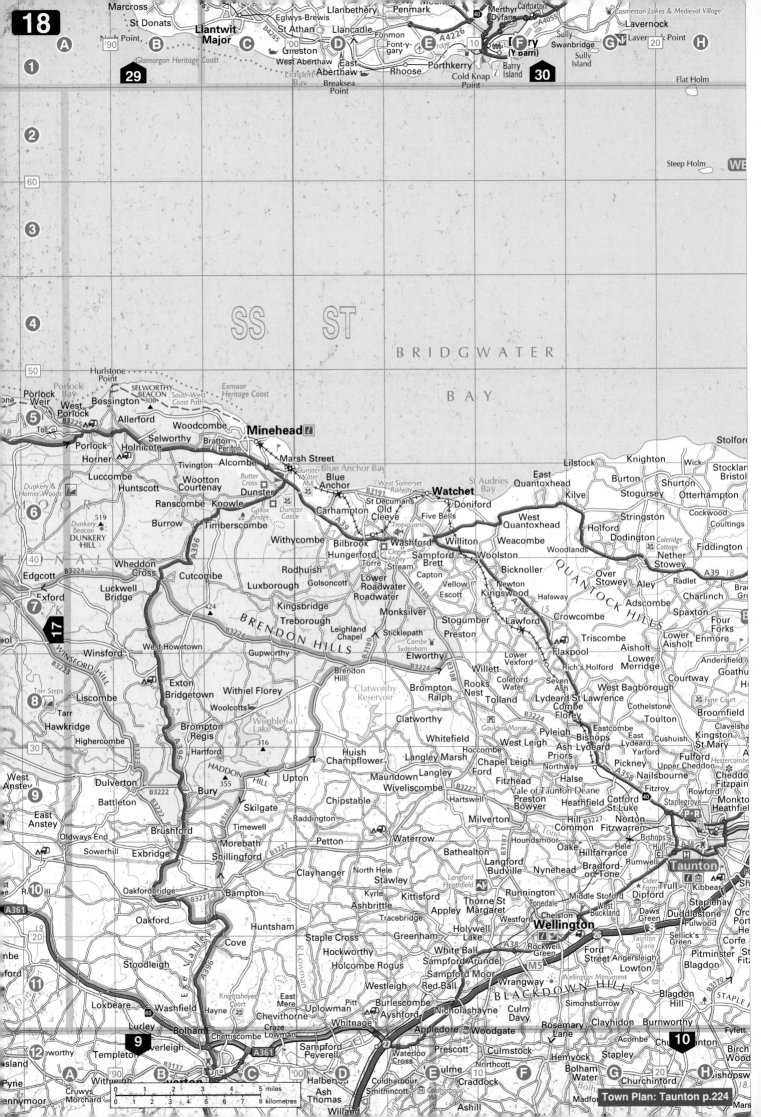

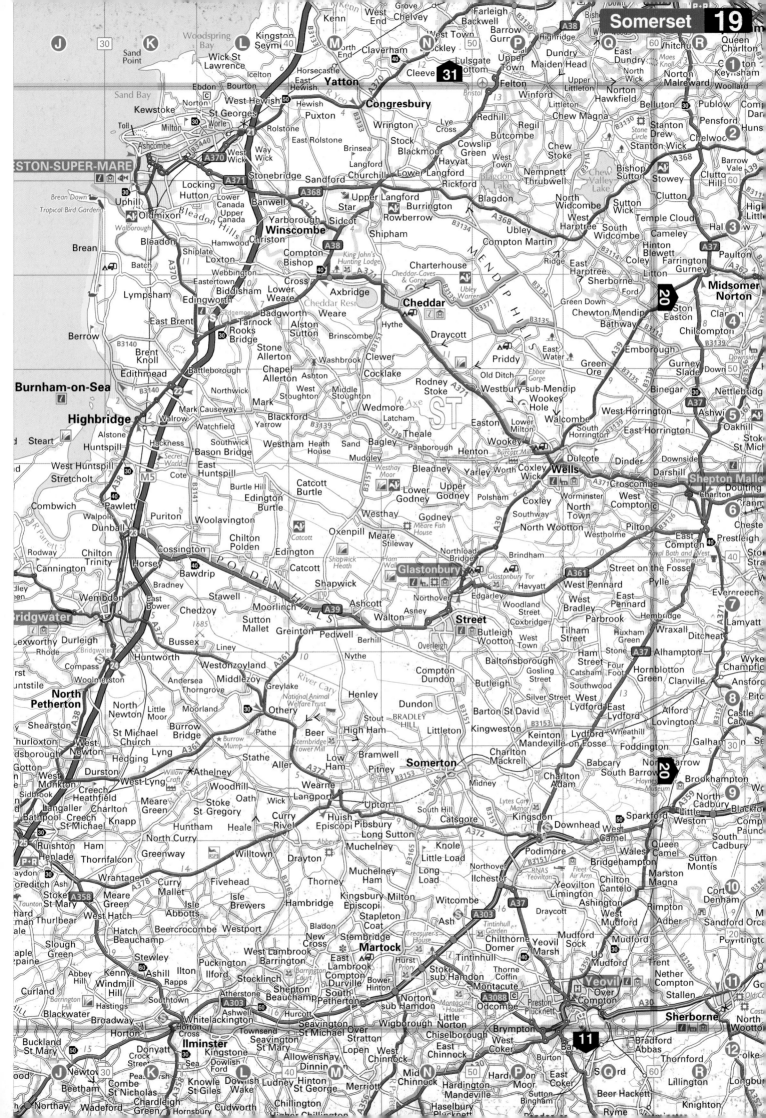

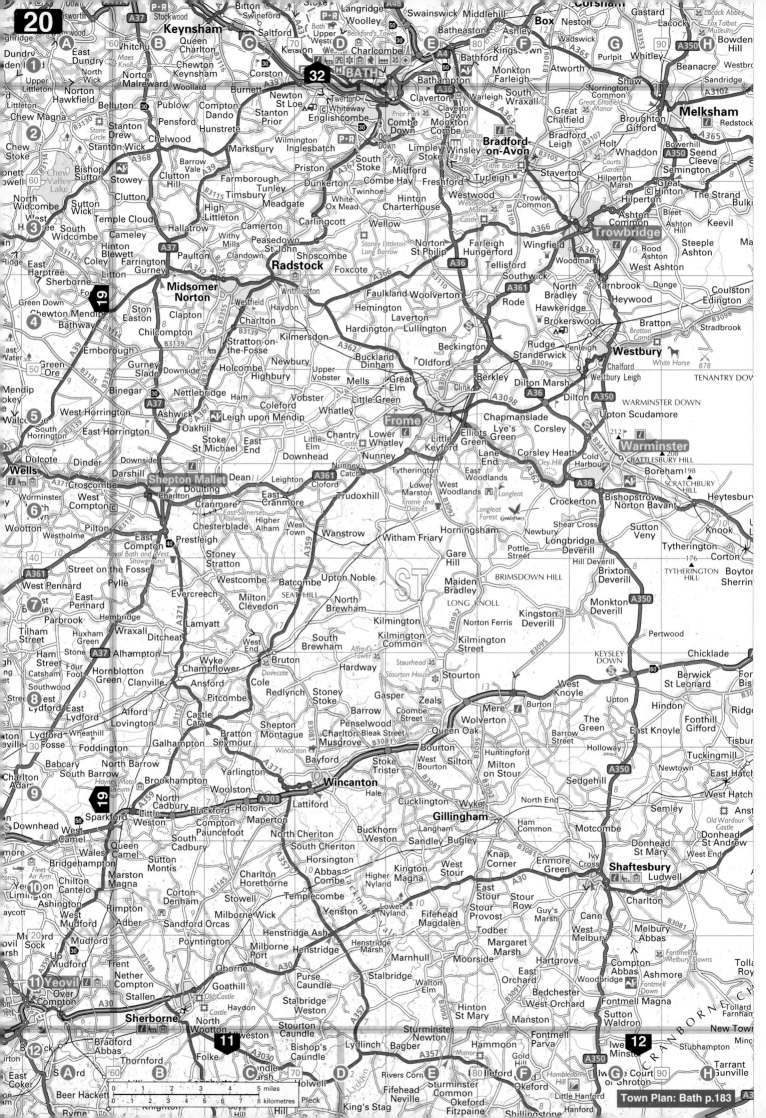

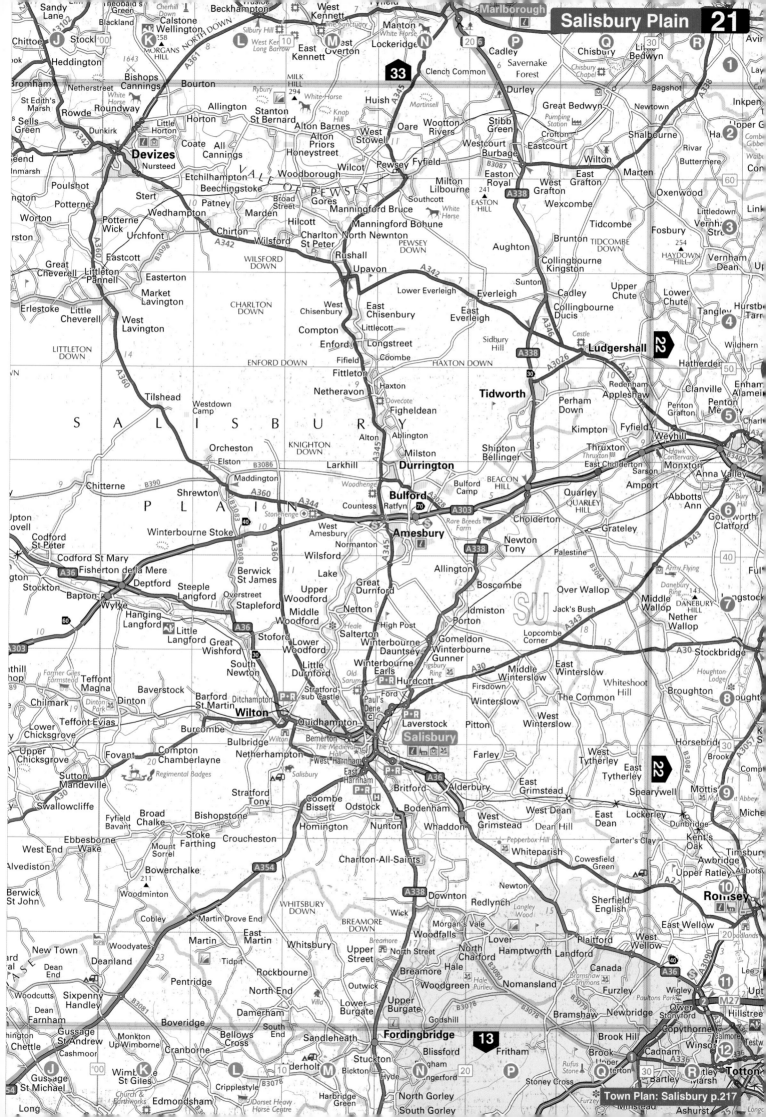

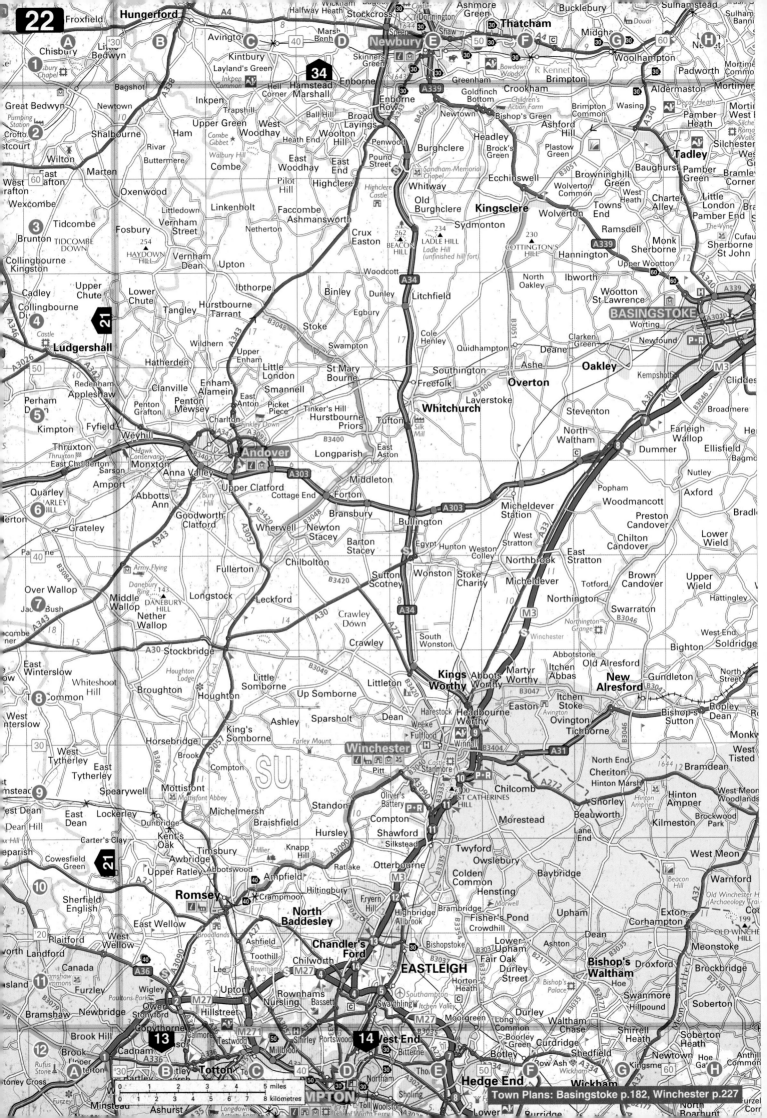

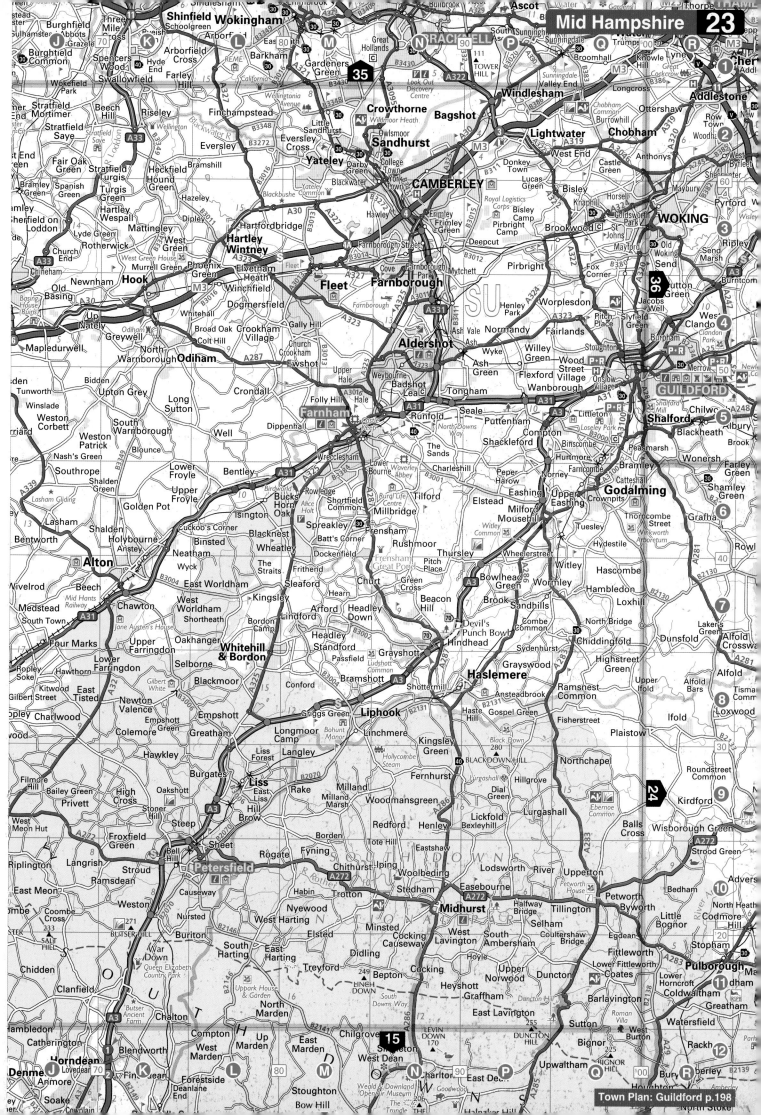

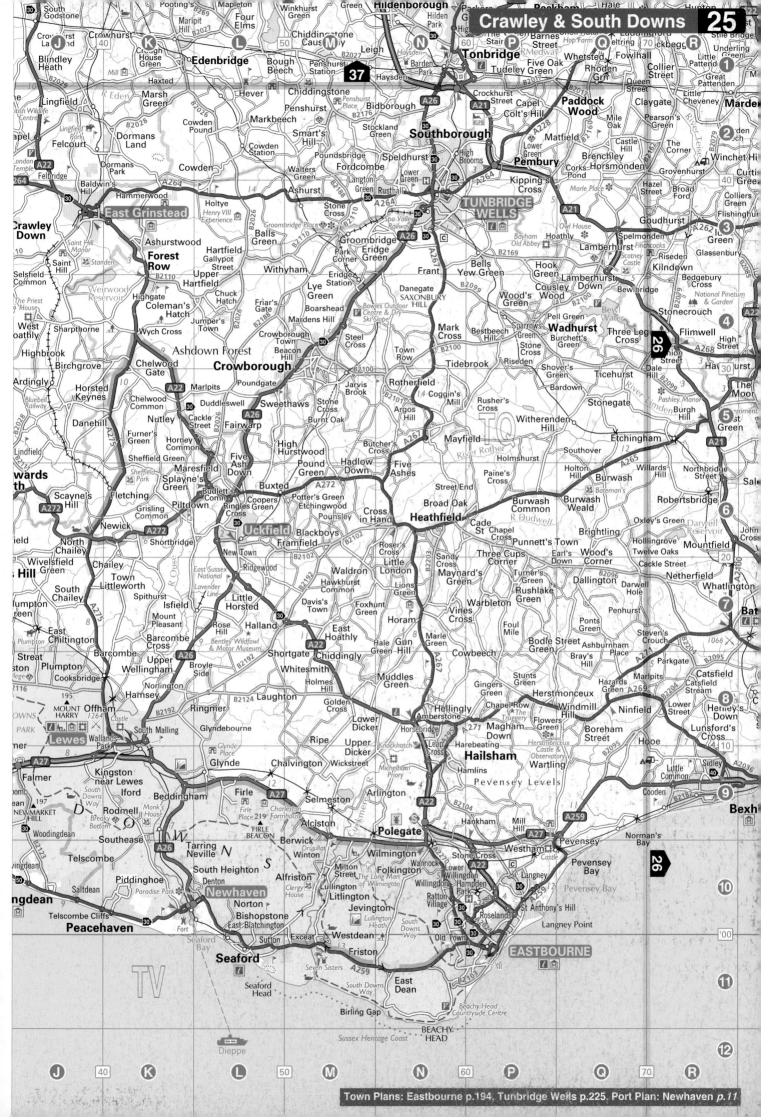

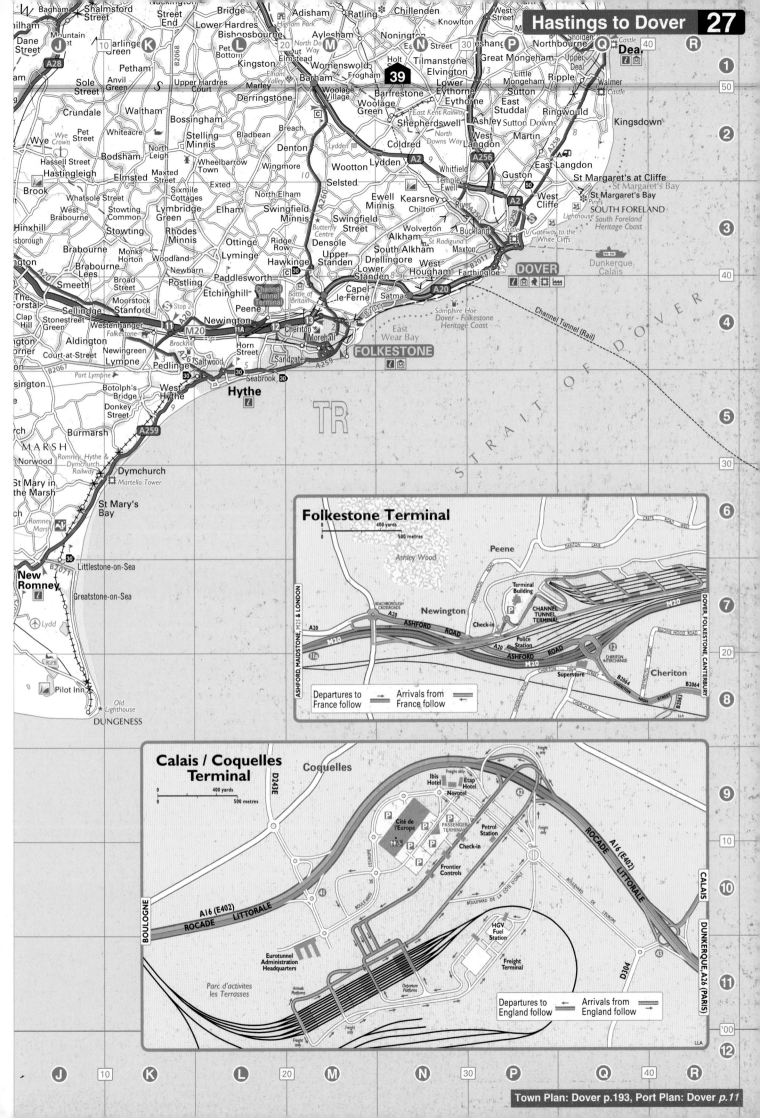

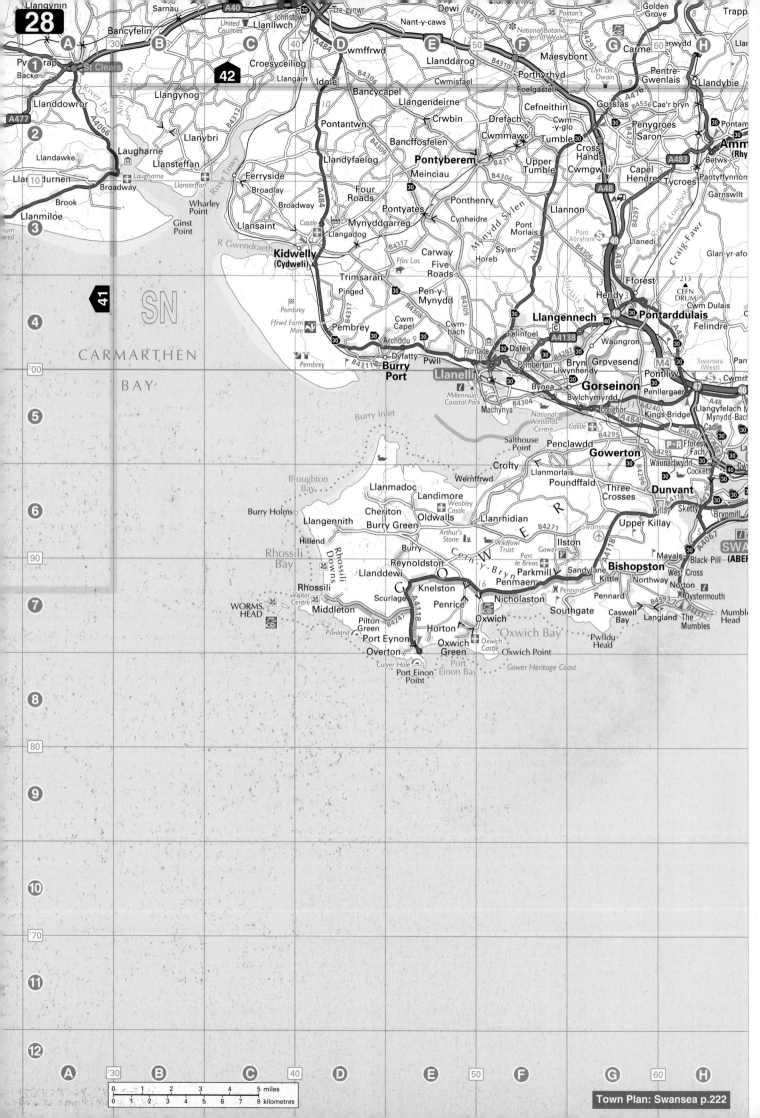

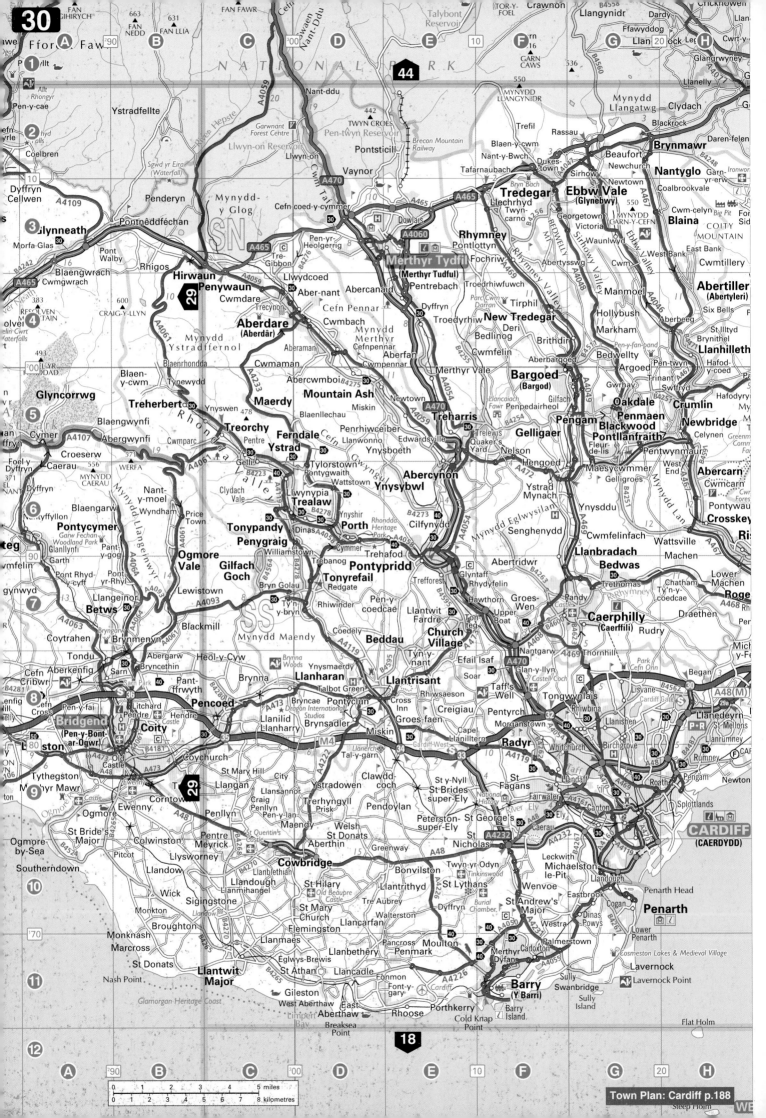

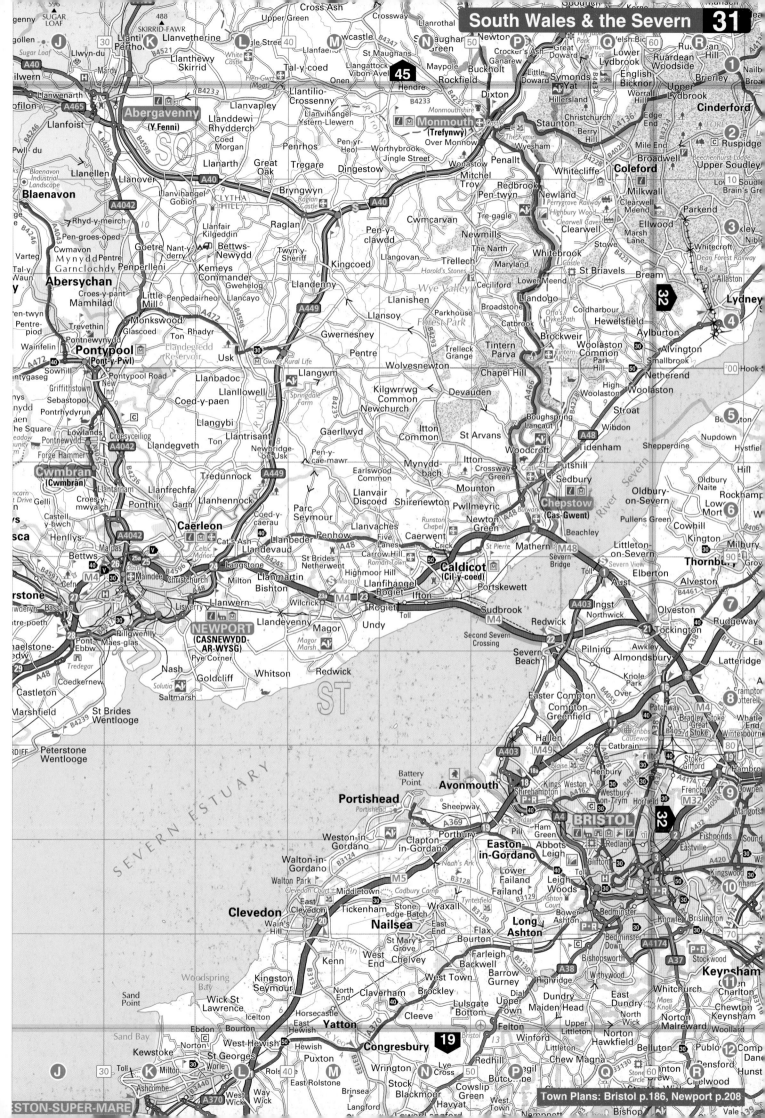

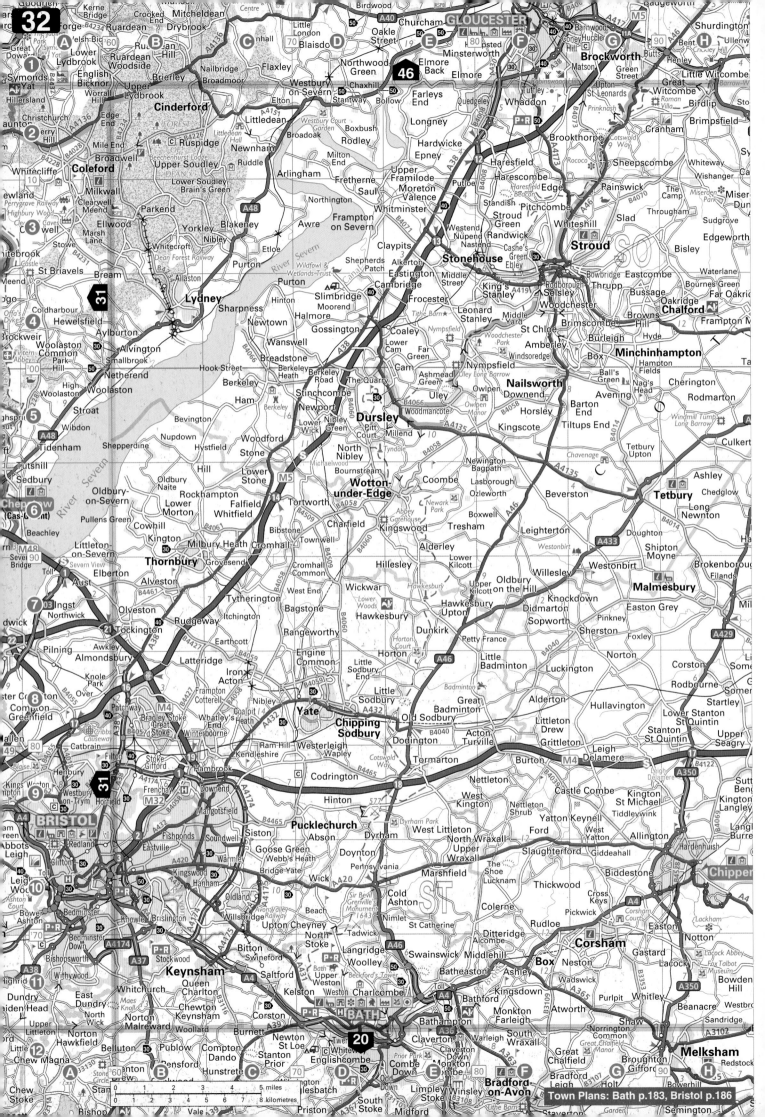

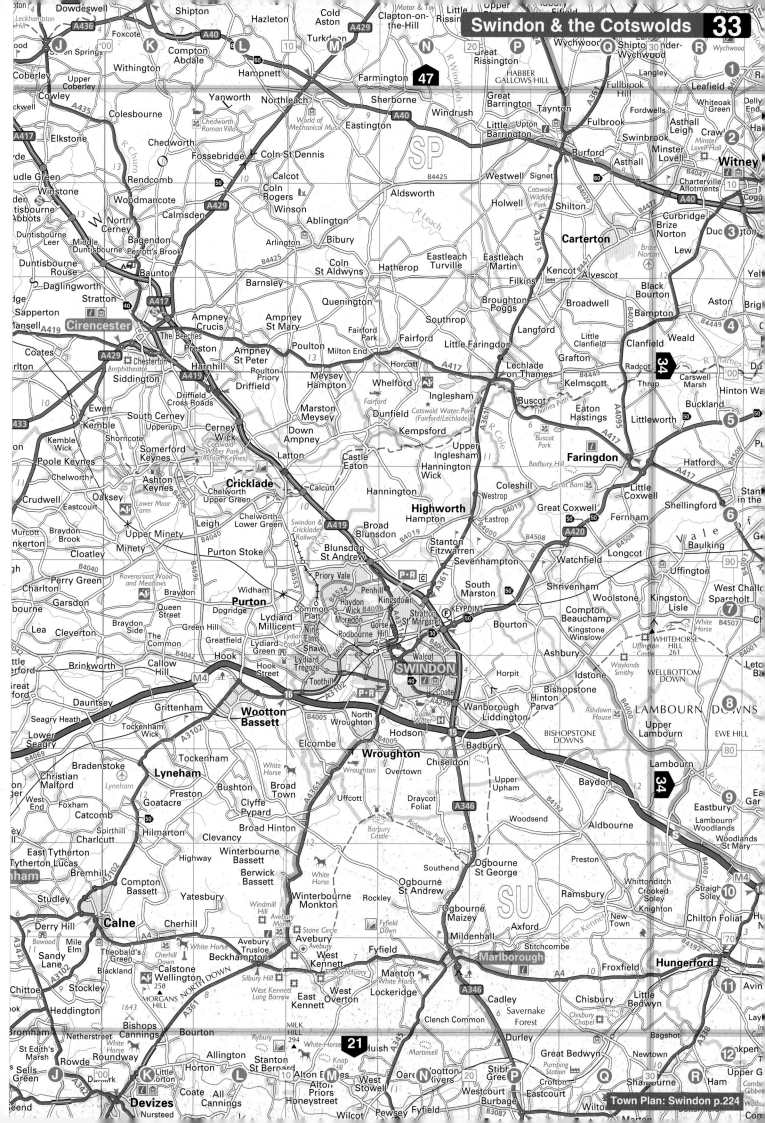

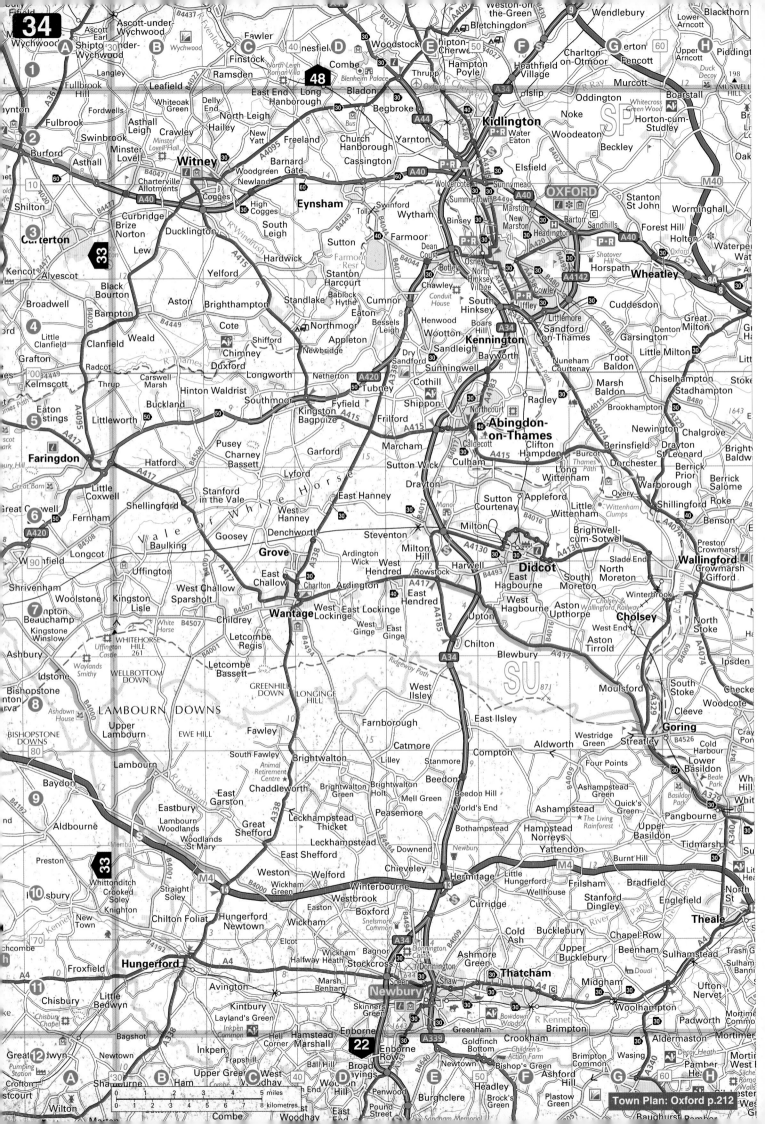

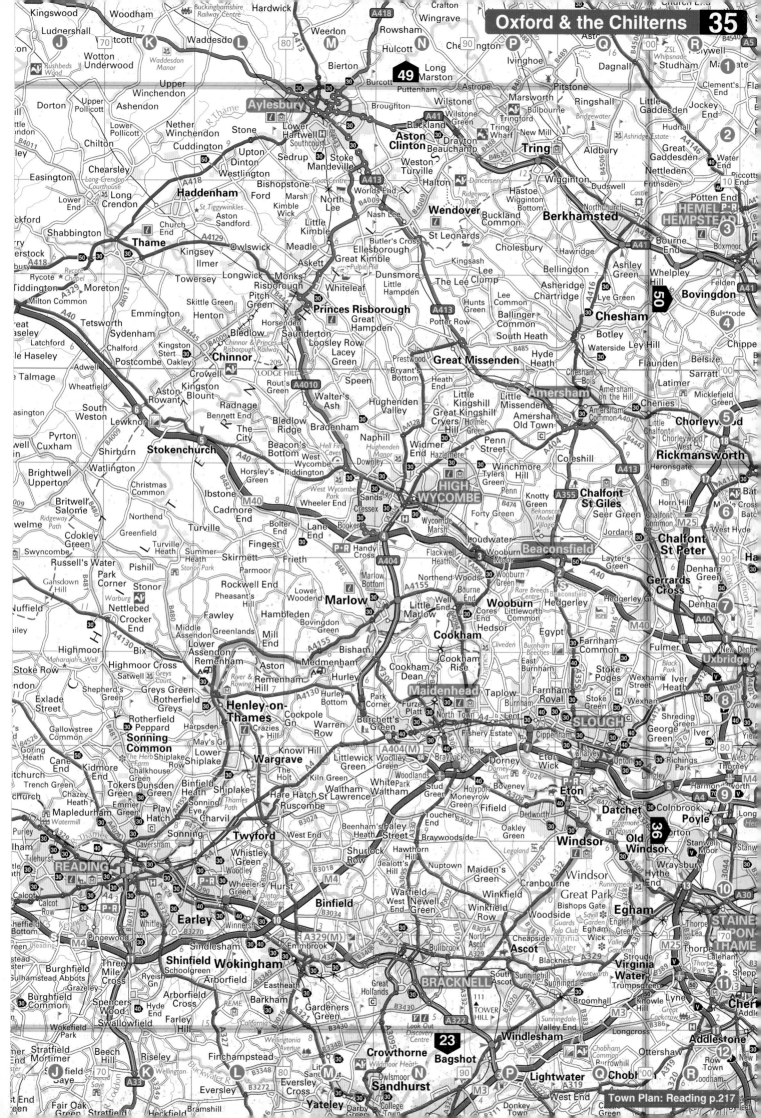

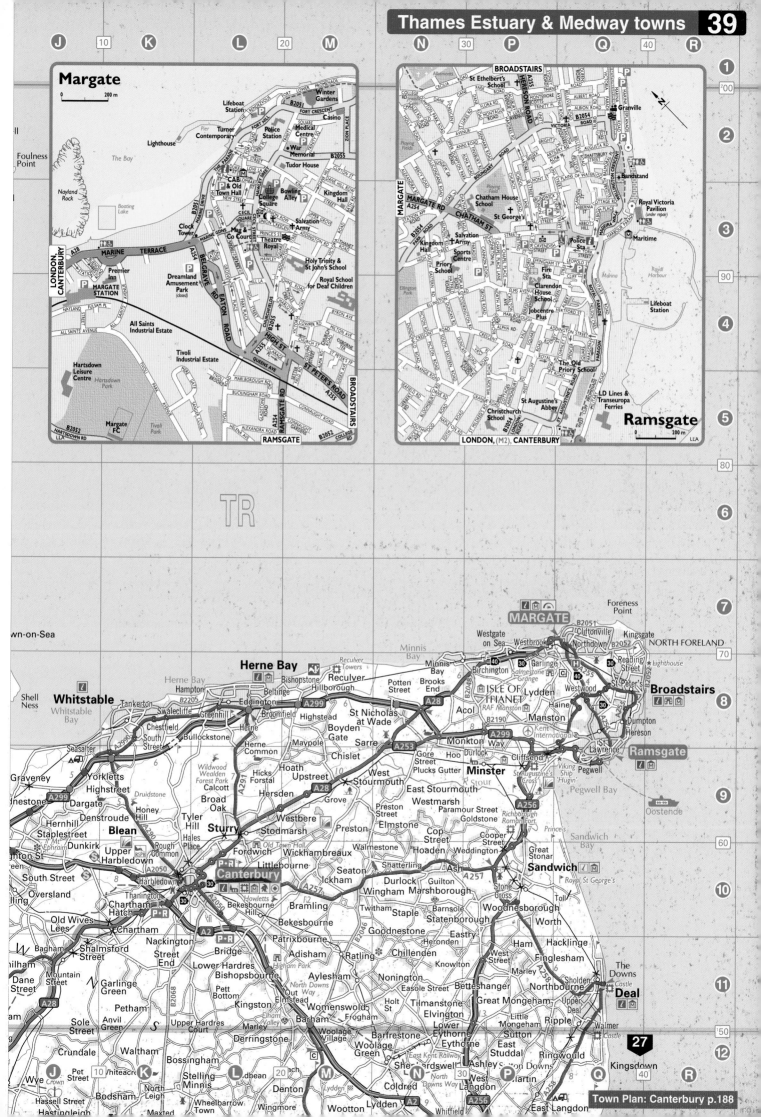

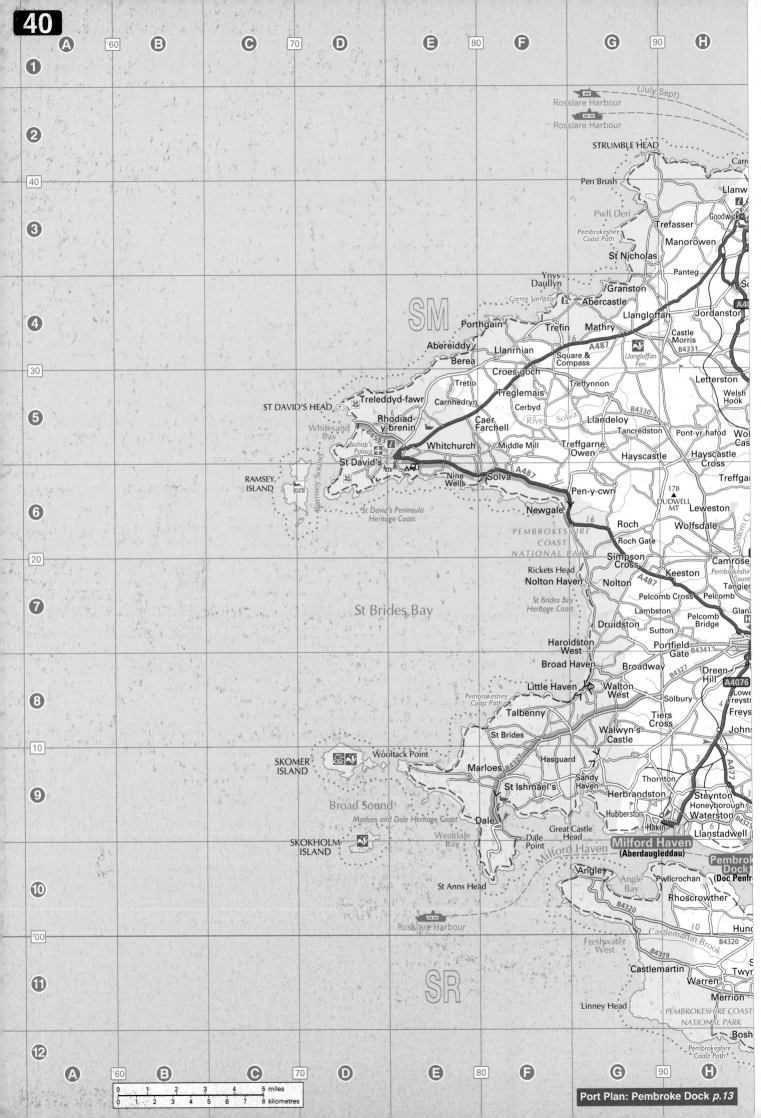

A '60 B C 70 D E 80 F G 90 H

1

2

40

3

4

30

5

6

20

7

8

10

9

10

'00

11

12

A '60 B C 70 D E 80 F G 90 H

Rosslare Harbour (July Sept)
Rosslare Harbour
STRUMBLE HEAD
Pen Brush
Carr
Llanw
Pwll Deri
Goodwick
Trefasser
Pembrokeshire Coast Path
Manorowen
St Nicholas
Panteg
Ynys Daullyn
Granston
Carreg Sampson
Abercastle
SM
Porthgain
Trefin
Mathry
Llangloffan
Jordanston
A487
Castle Morris
B4331
Square & Compass
Letterston
Llanrhian
Croes-goch
Llangloffan Fen
Welsh Hook
Abereiddy
Berea
Tretio
Treffynnon
B4330
Treglemais
Cerbyd
River Solva
Llandeloy
ST DAVID'S HEAD
Treleddyd-fawr
Carnhedryn
Caer Farchell
Tancredston
Pont-yr-hafod
Wol
Cas
Rhodiad-y-brenin
Middle Mill
Treffgarne Owen
Hayscastle
Hayscastle Cross
Treffgar
Whitesand Bay
B1583
Whitchurch
St David's
Nine Wells
Solva
A487
Pen-y-cwn
178
DUDWELL MT
Leweston
RAMSEY ISLAND
RSPB
St David's Peninsula Heritage Coast
Newgale
16
Roch
Wolfsdale
Ramsey Sound
PEMBROKESHIRE COAST NATIONAL PARK
Roch Gate
Simpson Cross
Keeston
Camrose
Pembrokeshire Count
Rickets Head
Nolton Haven
Nolton
A487
Tangier
St Brides Bay Heritage Coast
Pelcomb Cross
Pelcomb
St Brides Bay
Lambston
Pelcomb Bridge
Glana
Druidston
Sutton
Portfield Gate
B4341
Haroldston West
Broadway
Dreen Hill
A4076
Broad Haven
B4327
Little Haven
Walton West
Solbury
Tiers Cross
Lowe Freyst
Pembrokeshire Coast Path
Talbenny
Walwyn's Castle
Freys
Johns
Wooltack Point
St Brides
Hasguard
SKOMER ISLAND
B4327
Thornton
Marloes
Sandy Haven
Herbrandston
Steynton
St Ishmael's
Honeyborough
Waterston
Broad Sound
Hubberston
Hakin
Llanstadwell
Marloes and Dale Heritage Coast
Dale
Great Castle Head
Milford Haven (Aberdaugleddau)
Pembro Dock
Westdale Bay
Dale Point
Milford Haven
SKOKHOLM ISLAND
Angle
Angle Bay
Pwllcrochan
(Doc Penfr
St Anns Head
Rhoscrowther
Rosslare Harbour
Castlemartin Brook
B4320
Hund
Freshwater West
B4319
SR
Castlemartin
Warren
Twyr
Merrion
Linney Head
PEMBROKESHIRE COAST NATIONAL PARK
Bosh
Pembrokeshire Coast Path

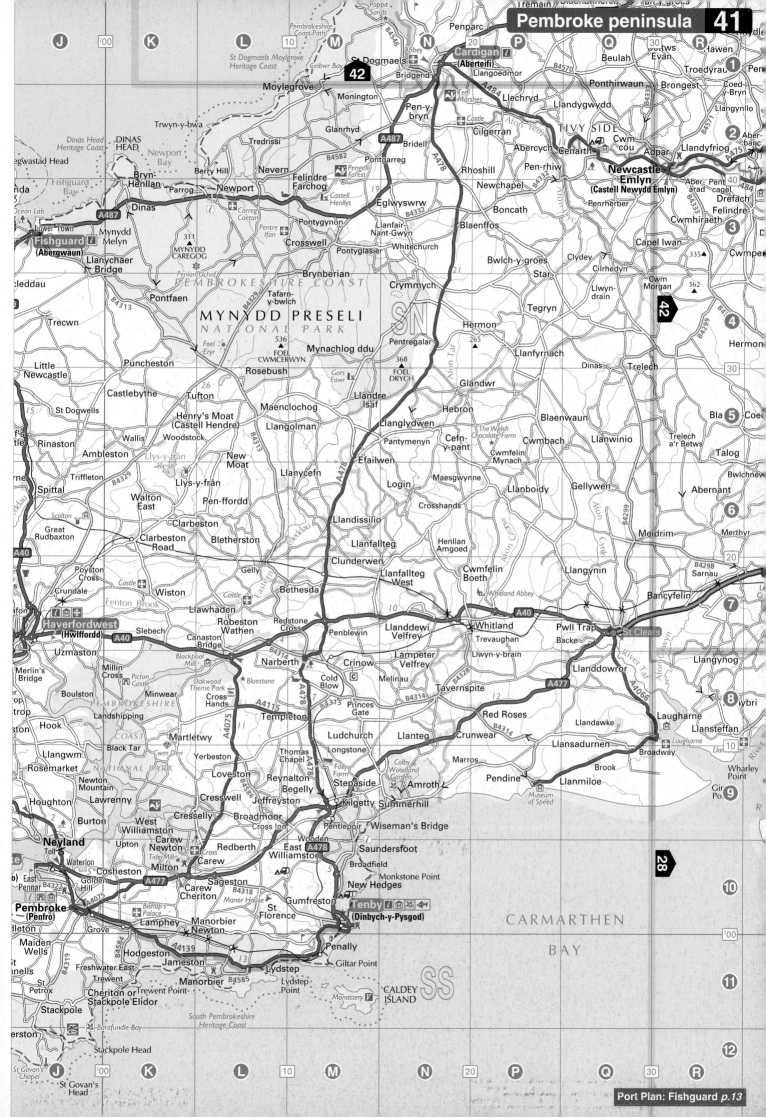

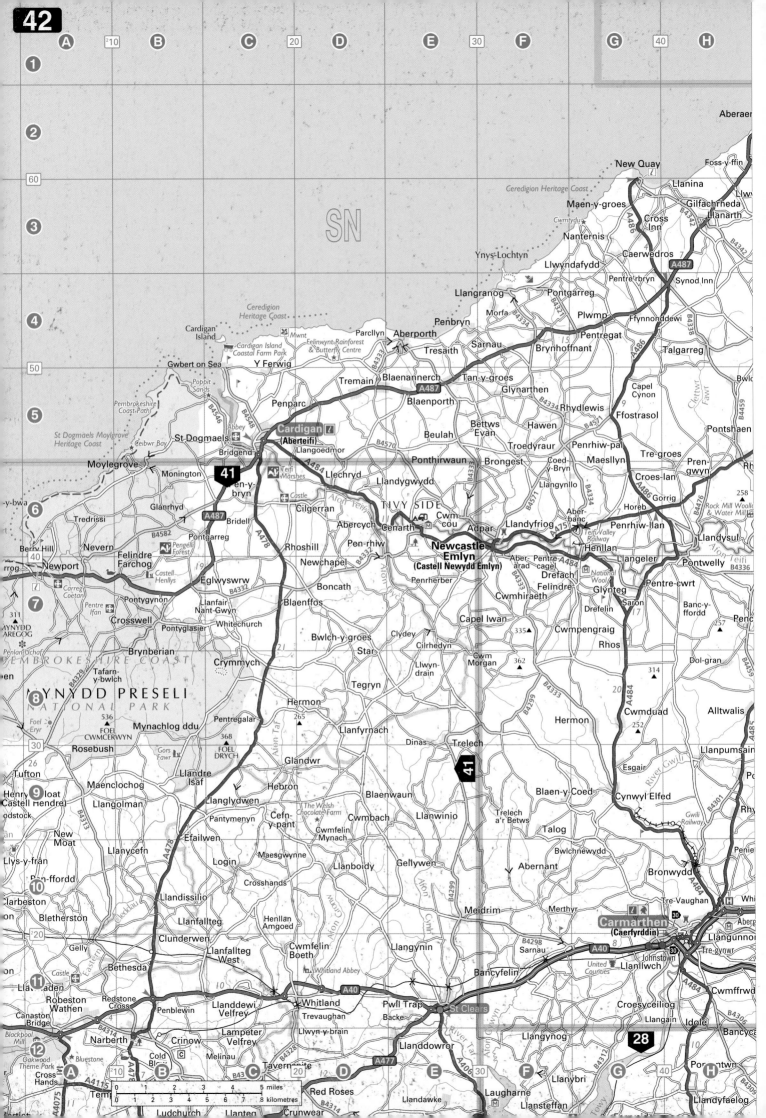

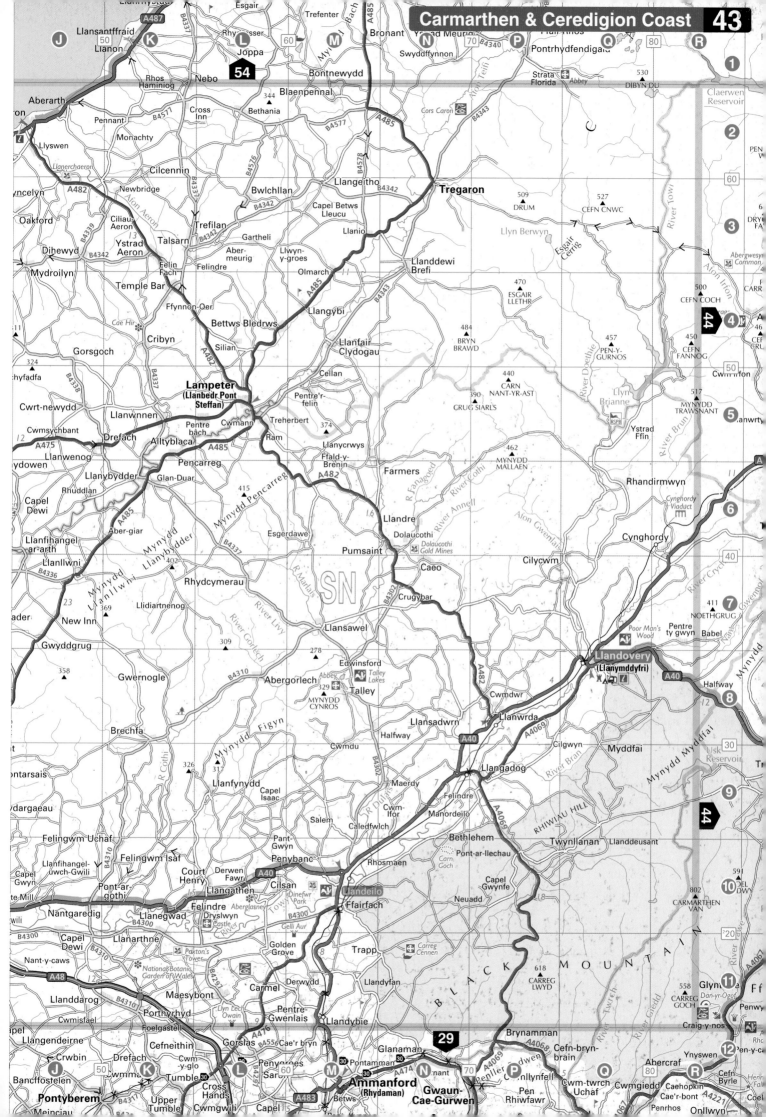

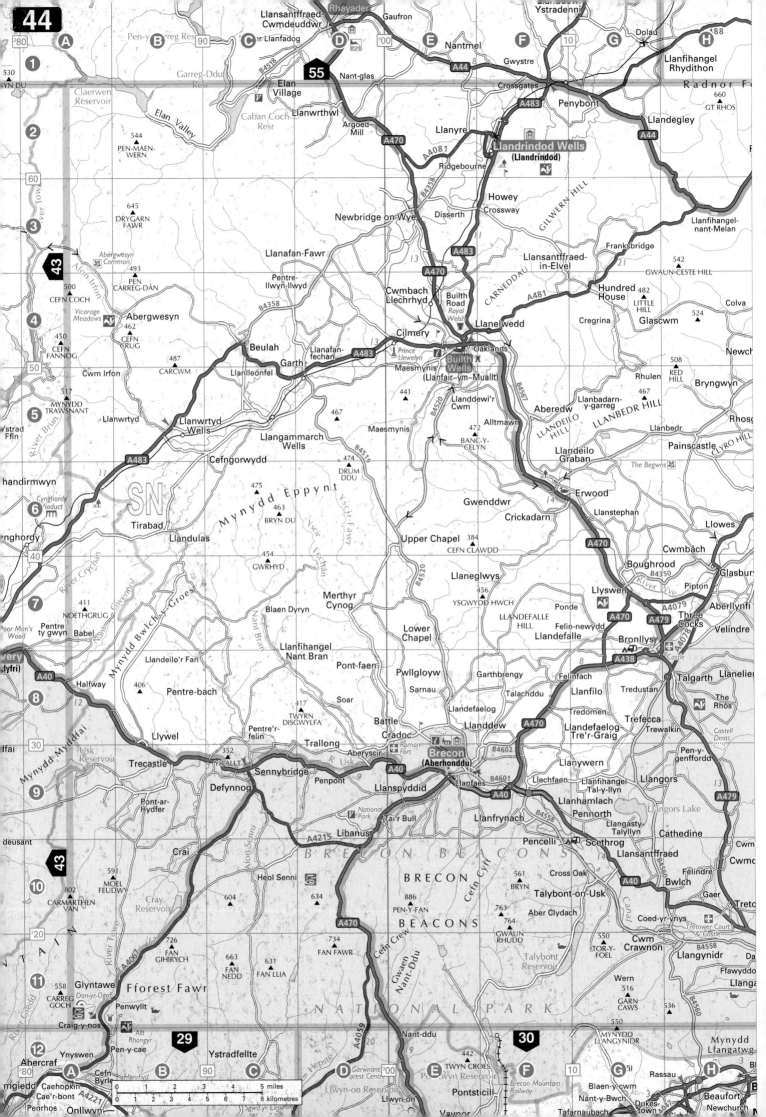

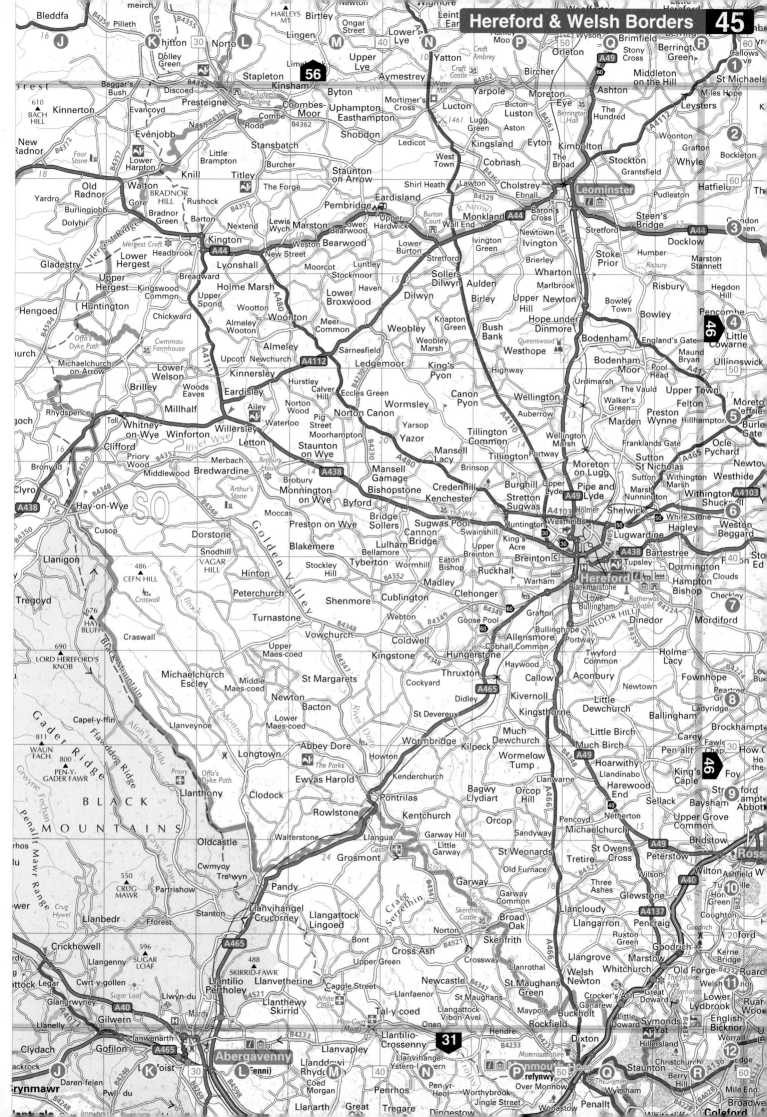

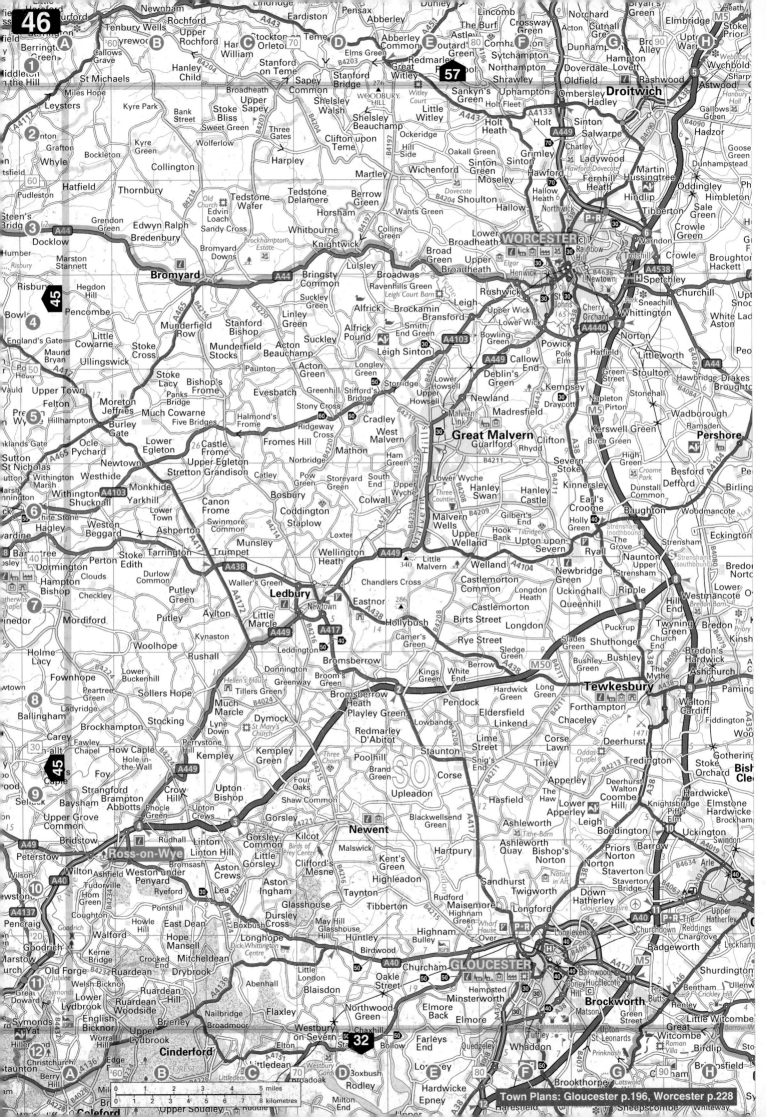

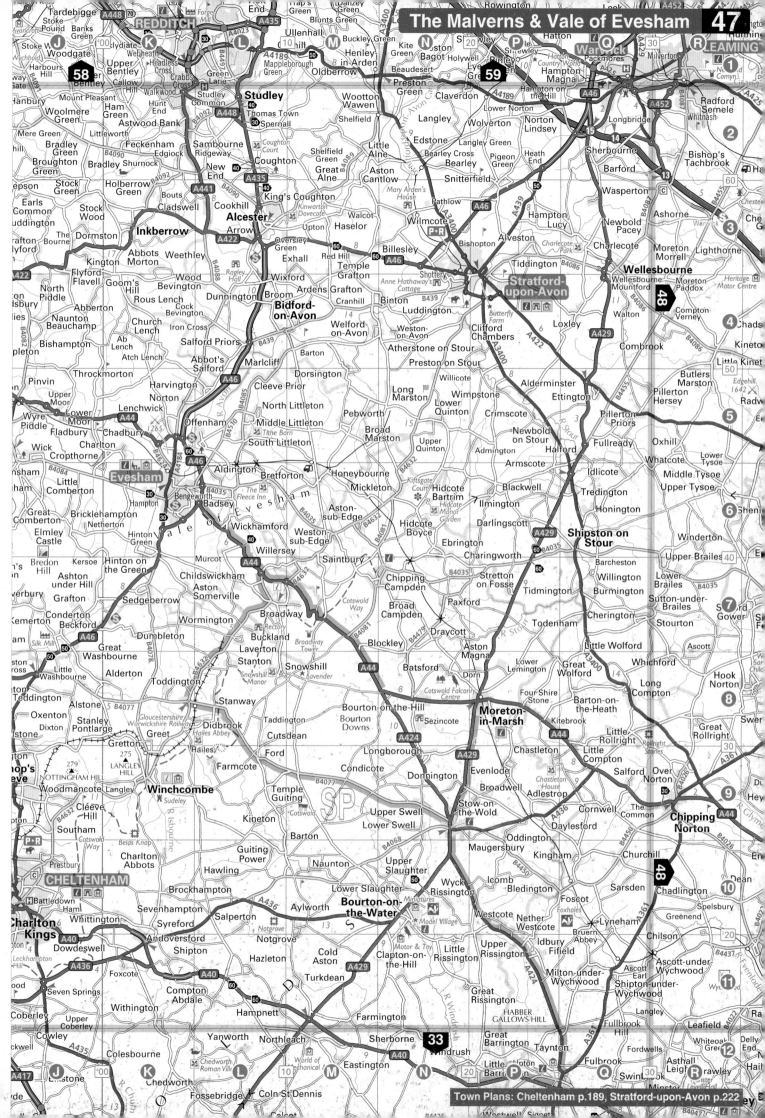

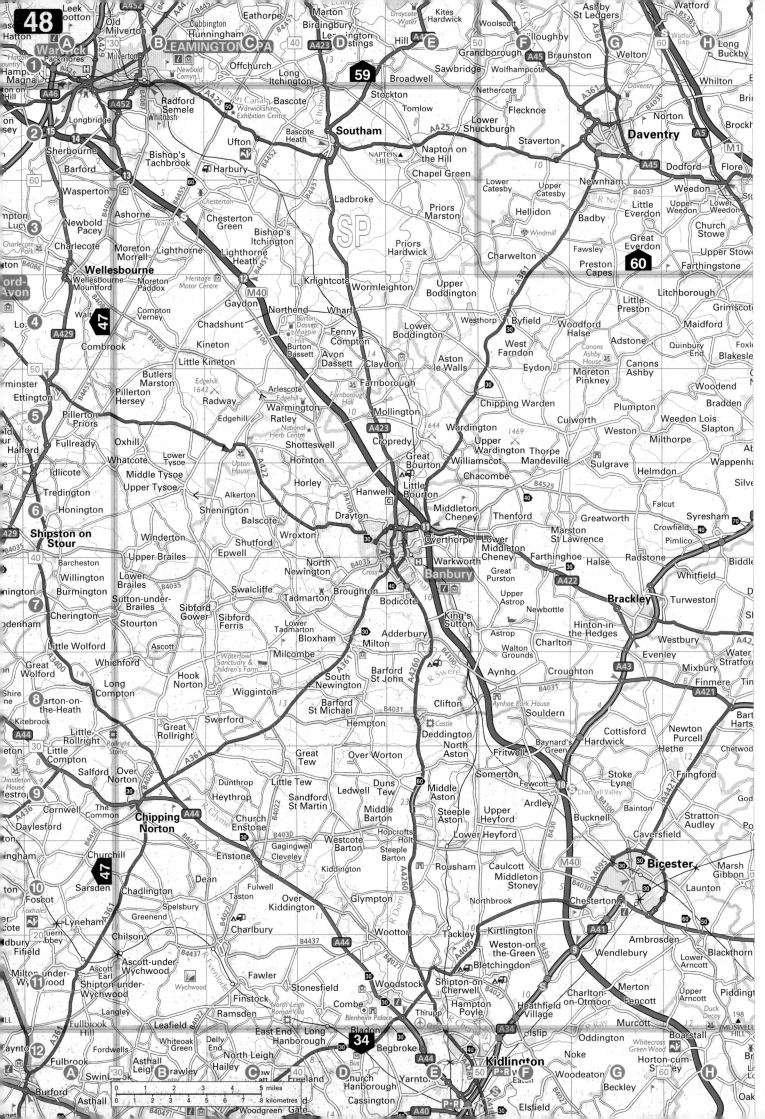

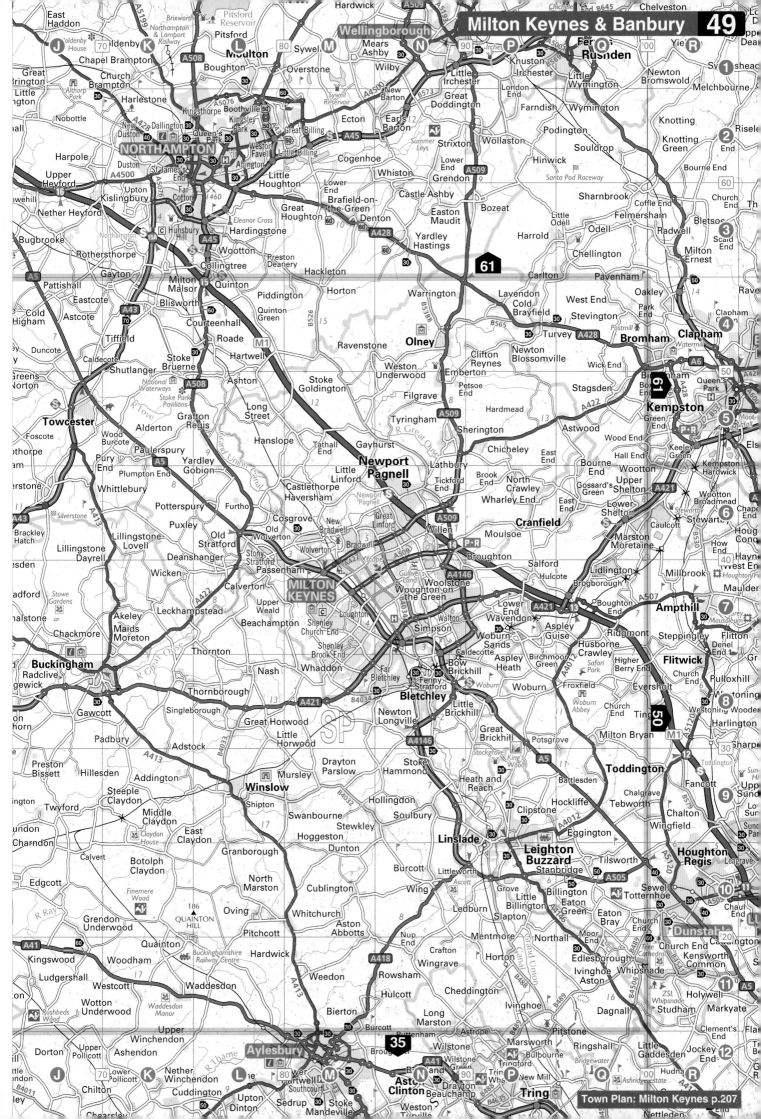

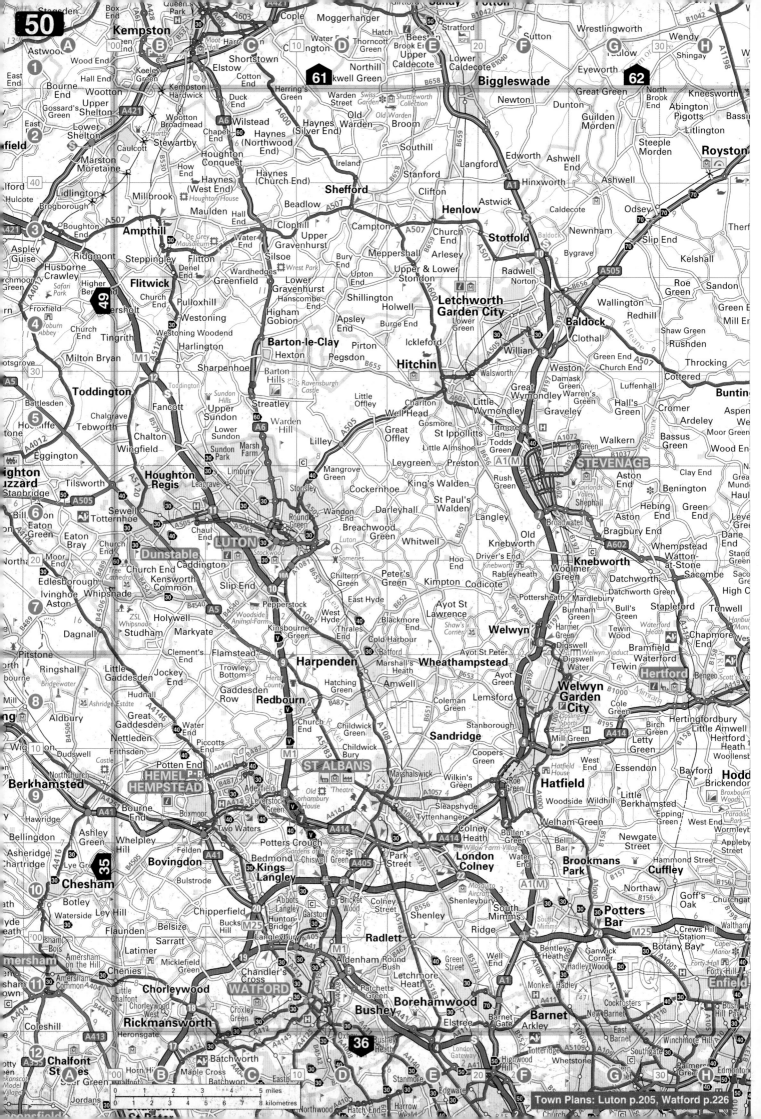

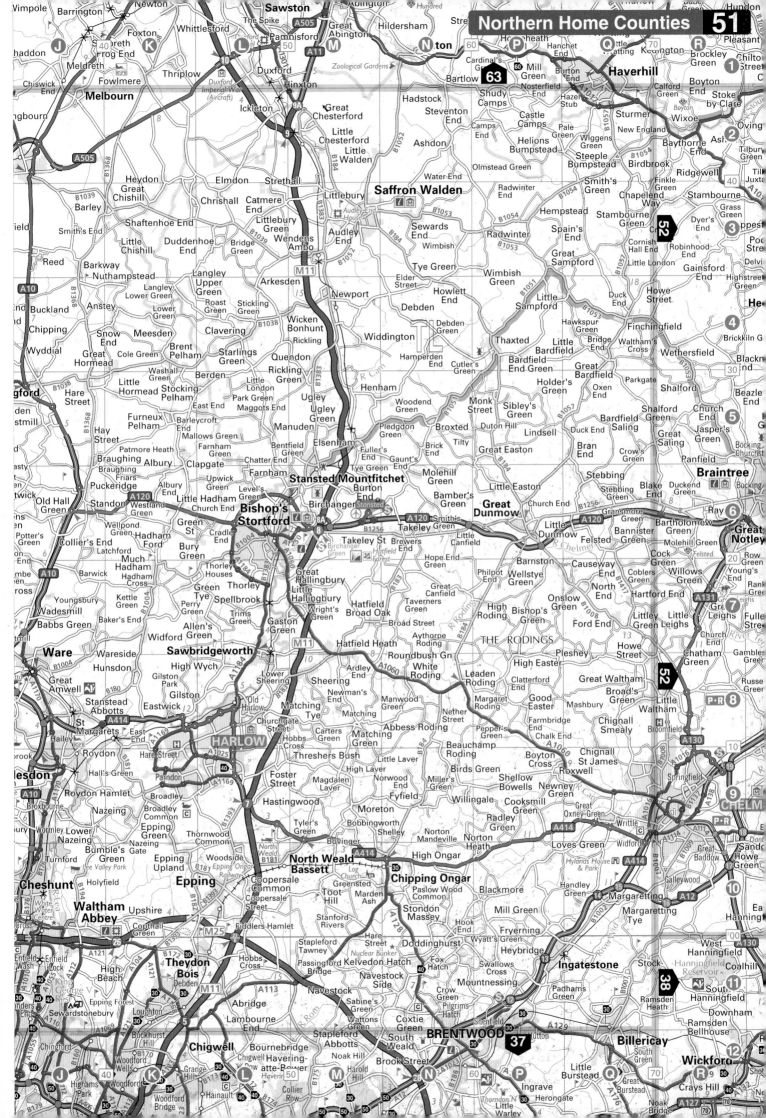

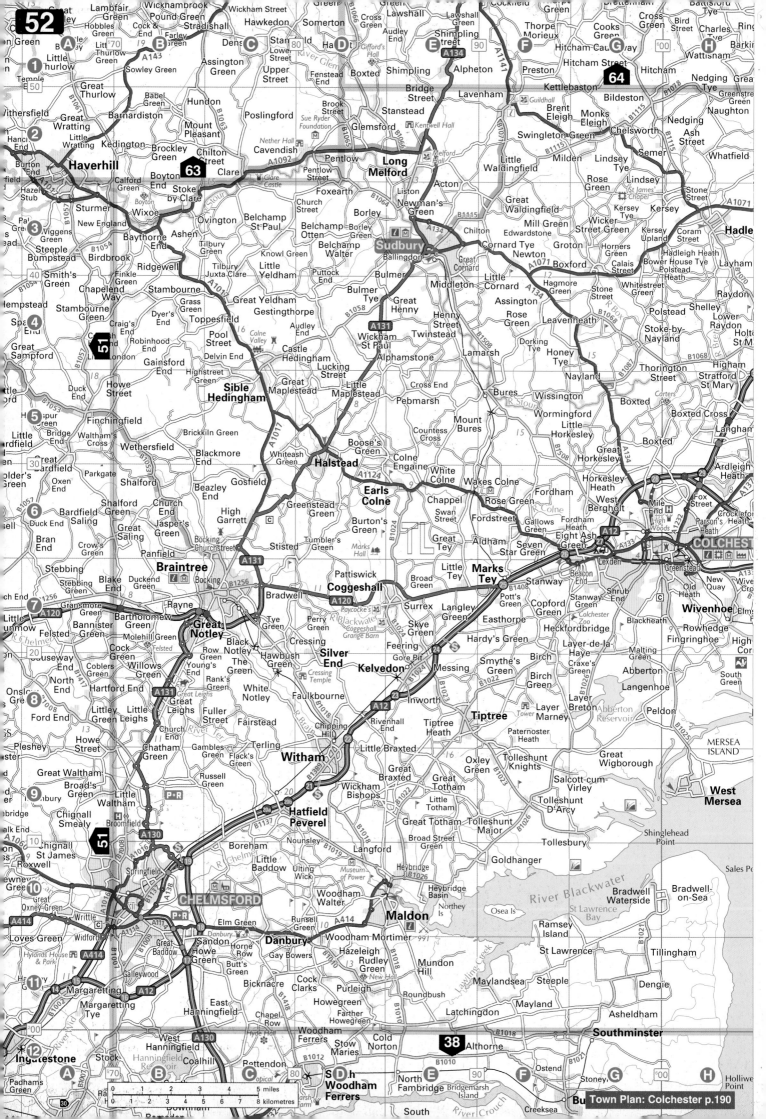

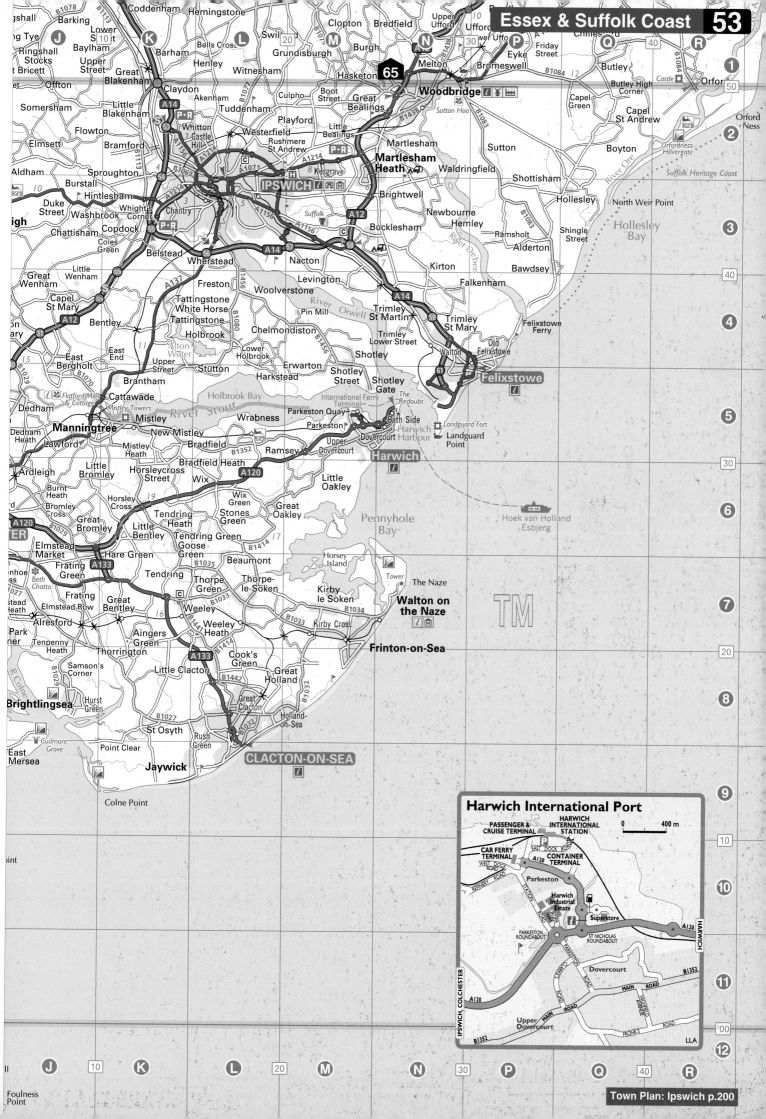

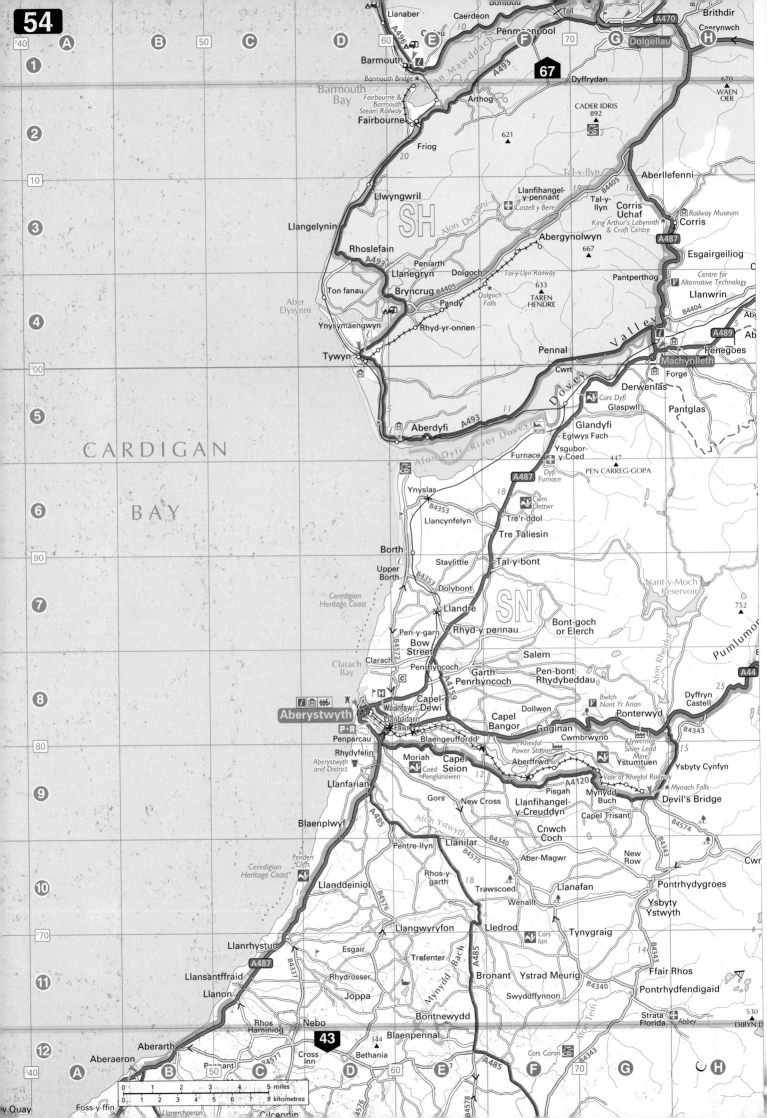

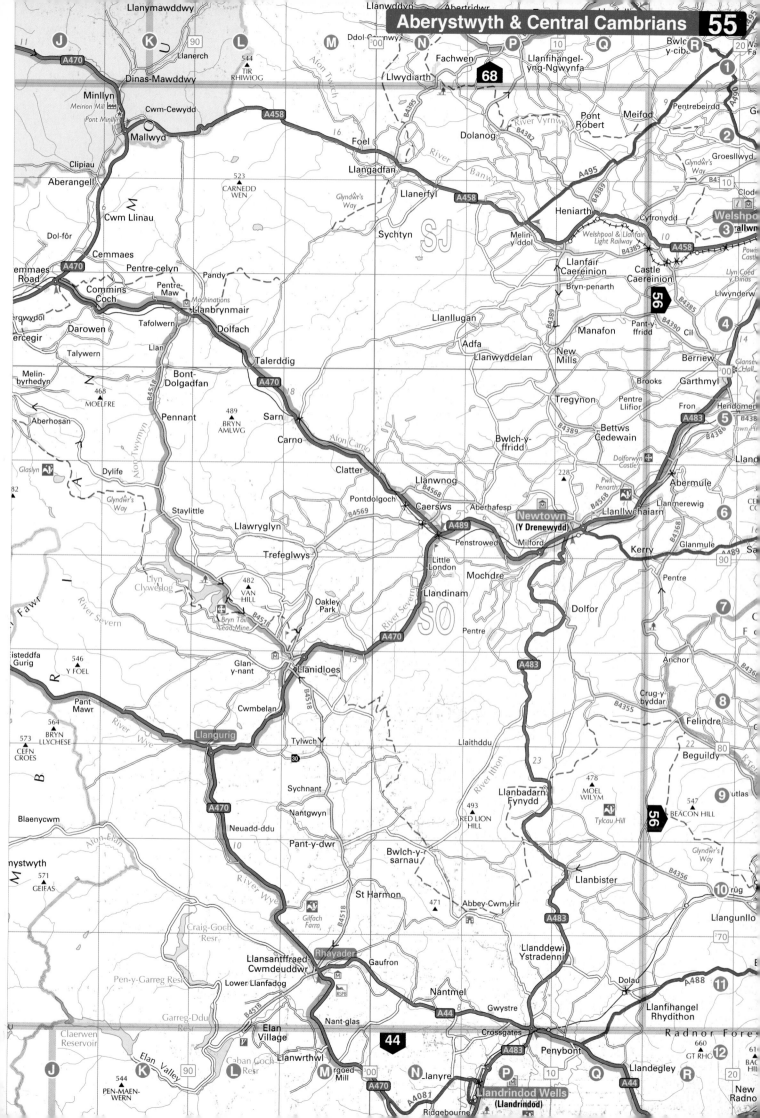

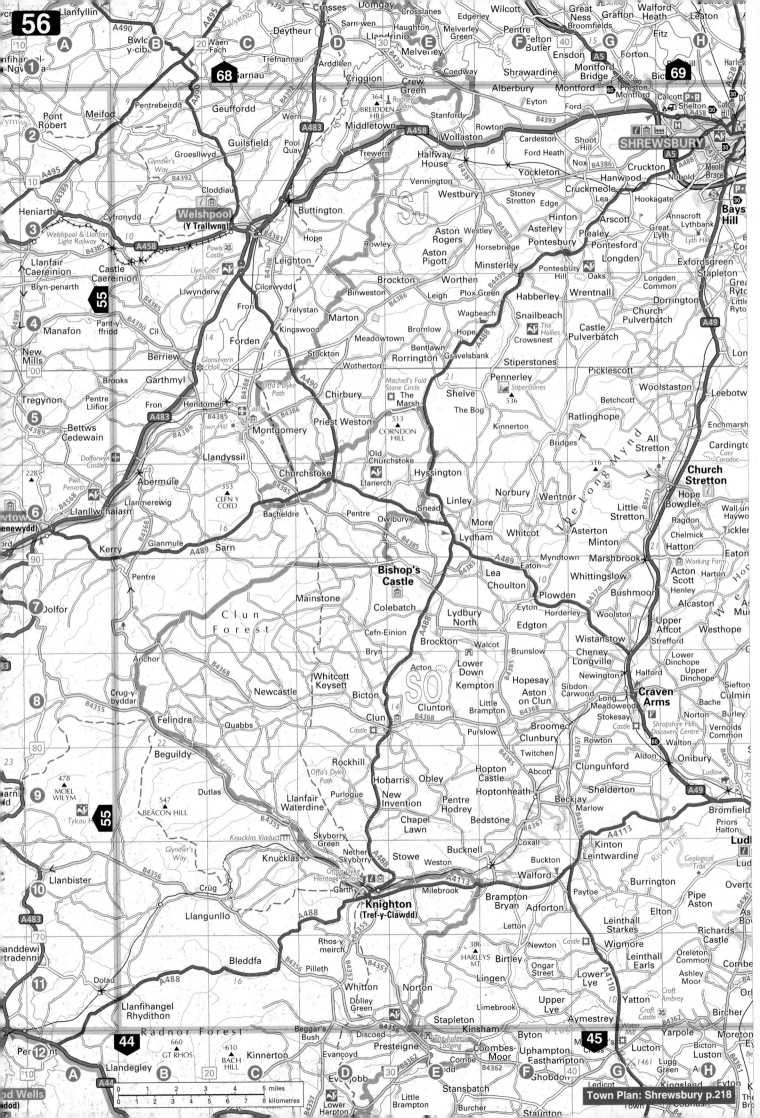

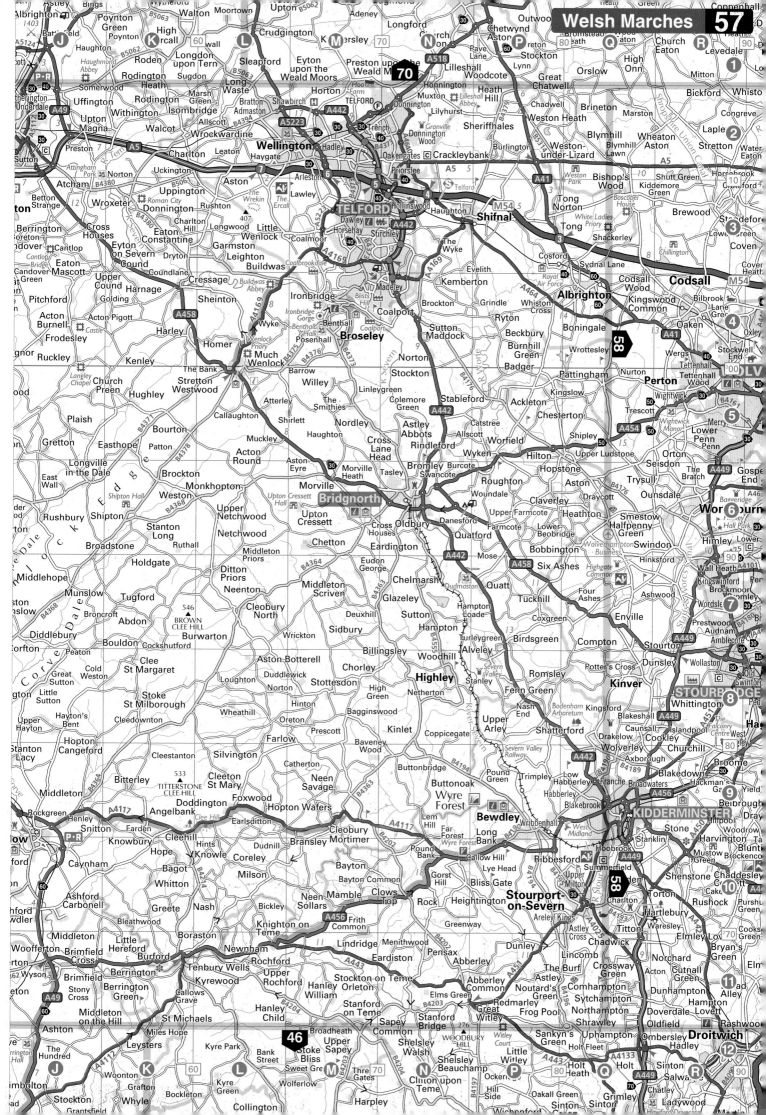

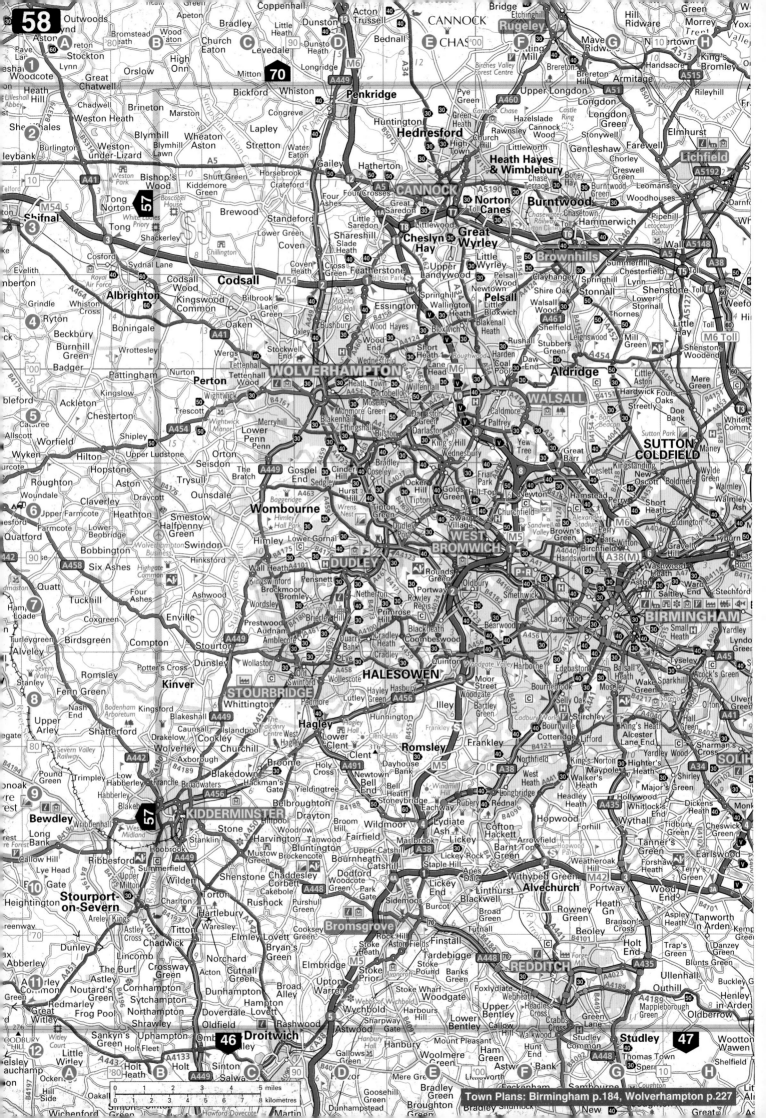

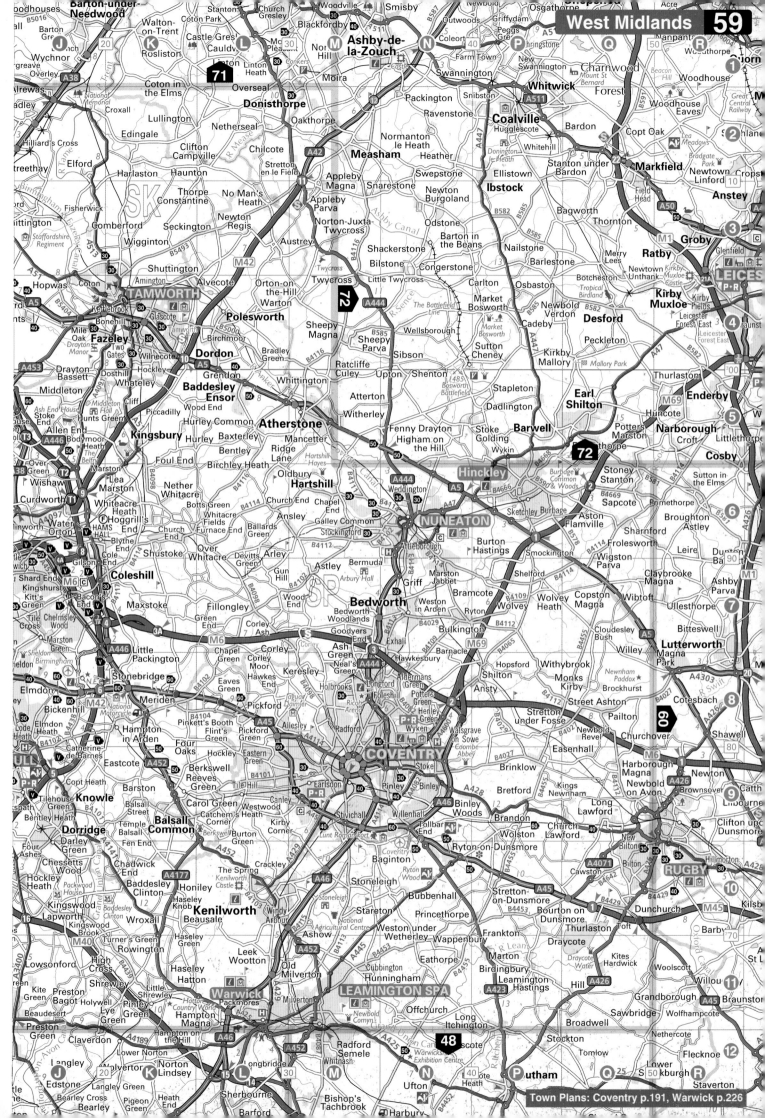

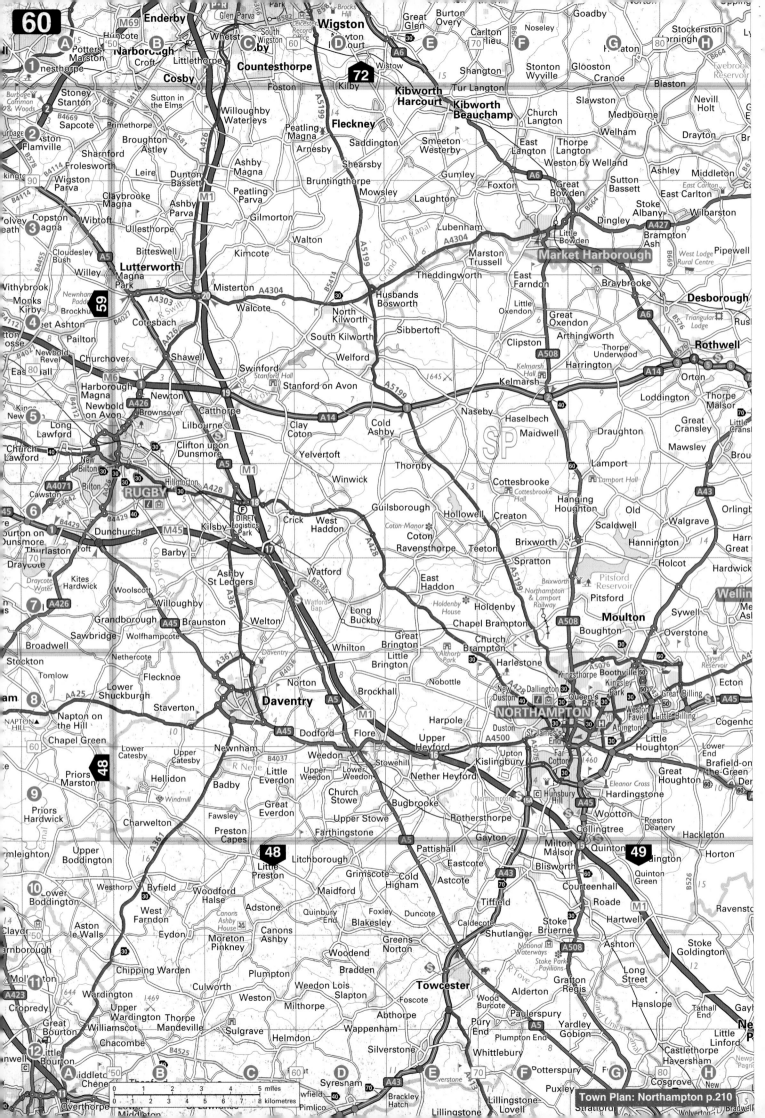

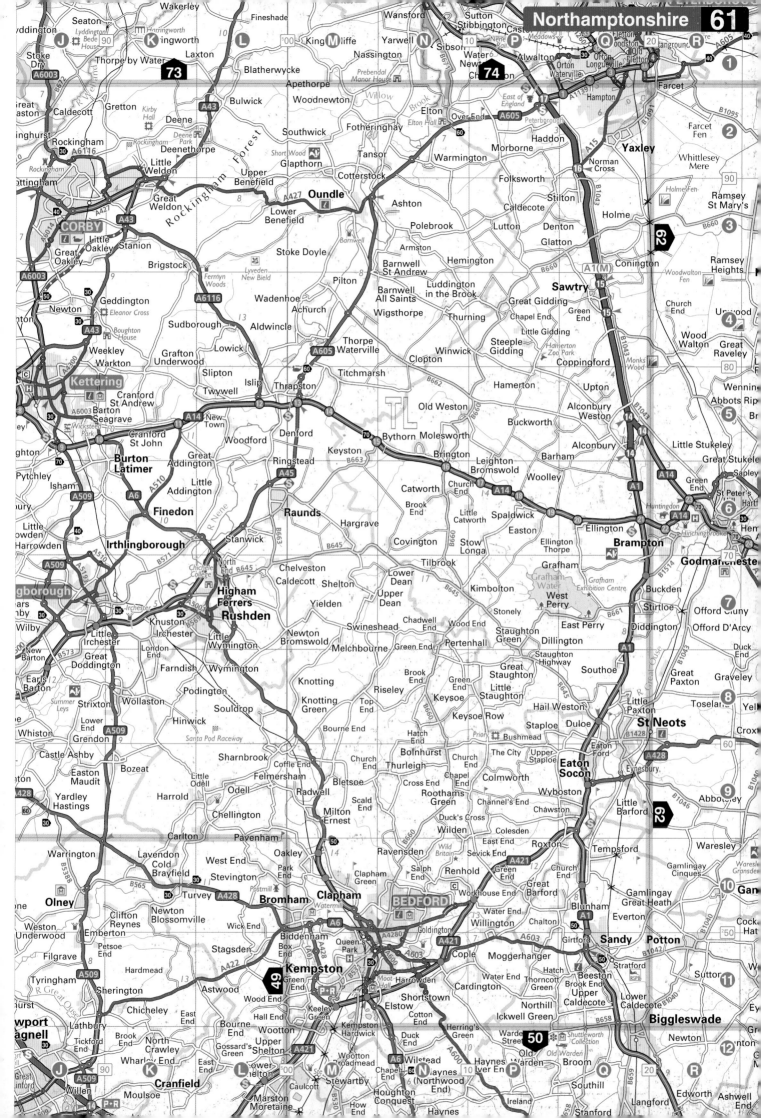

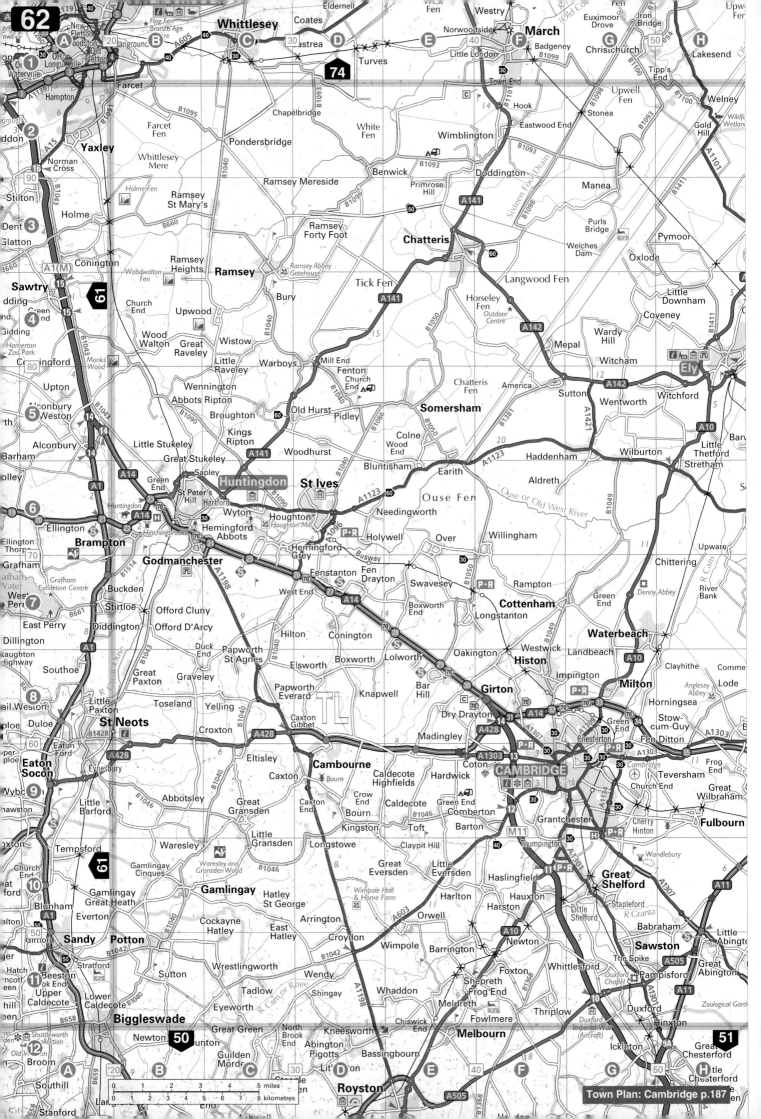

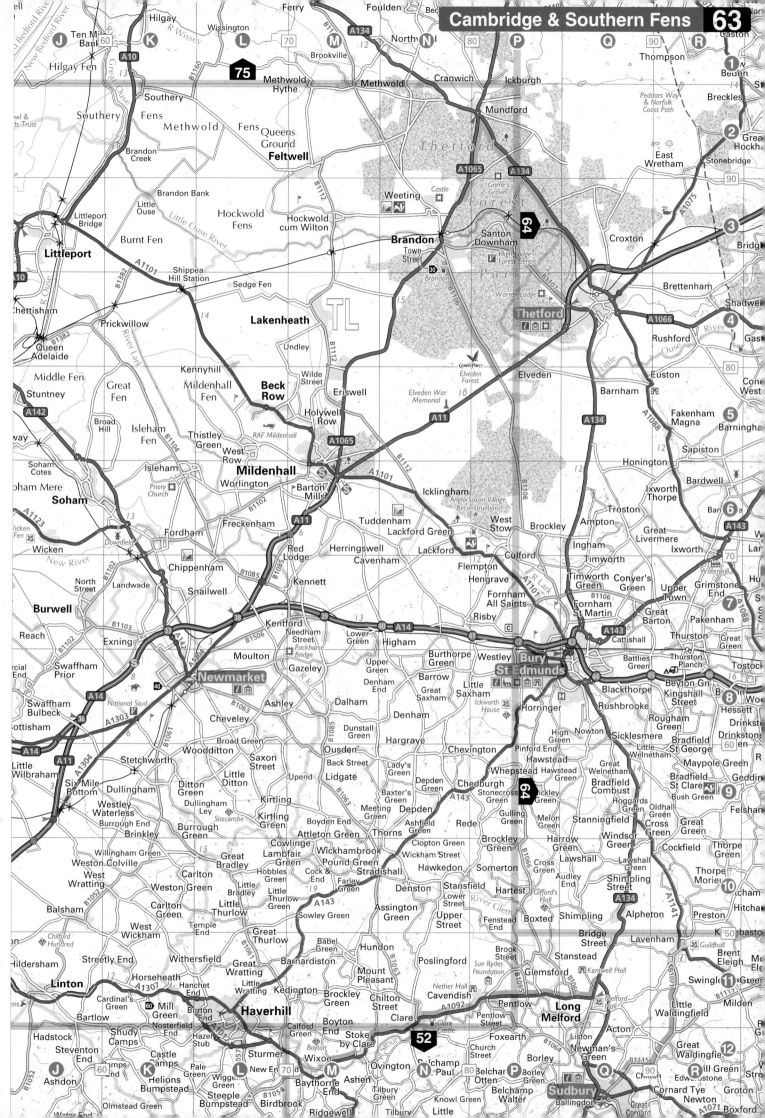

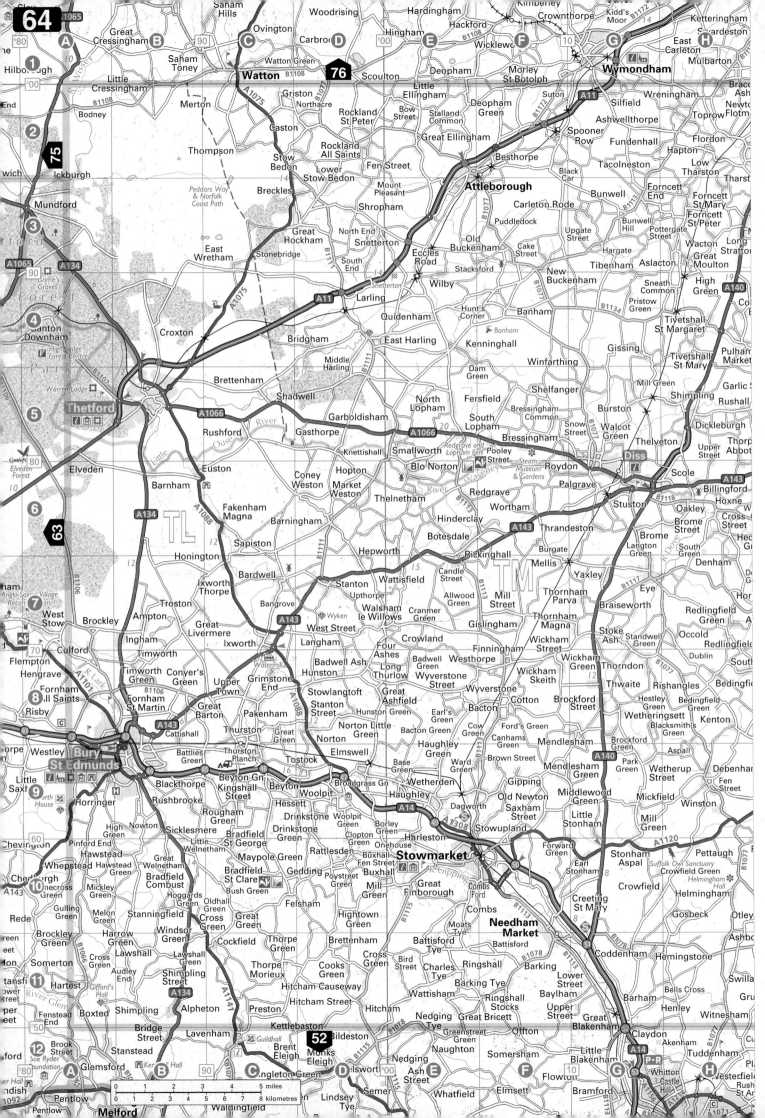

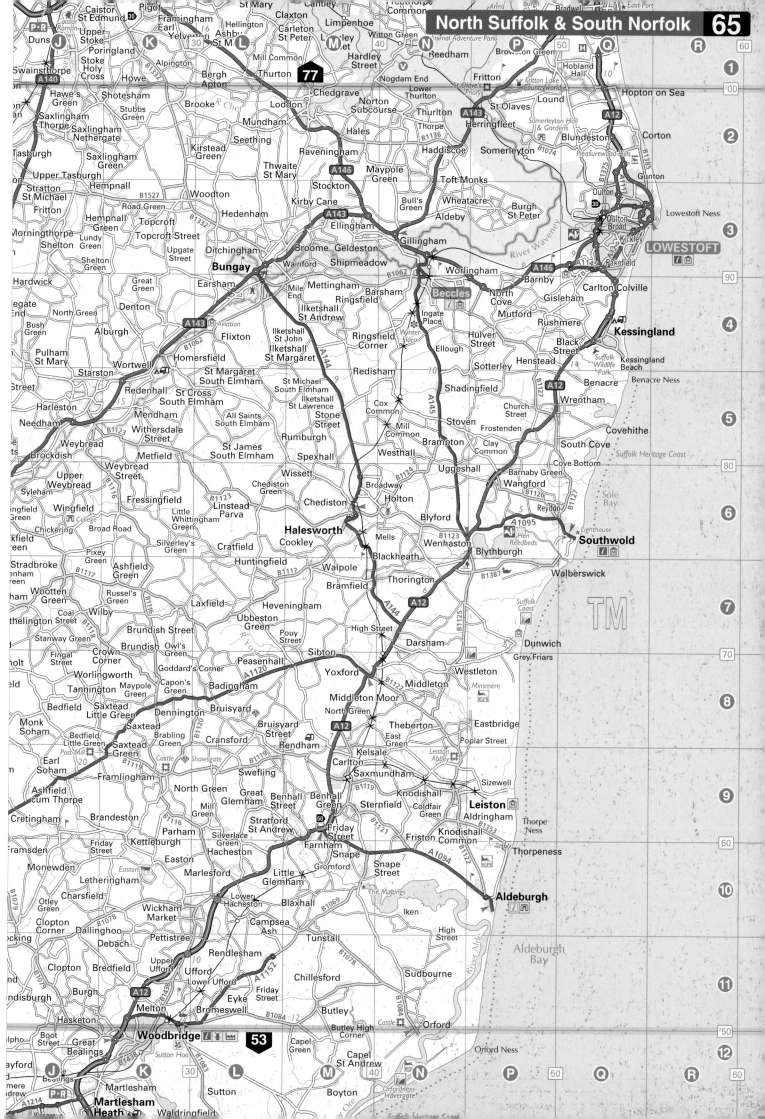

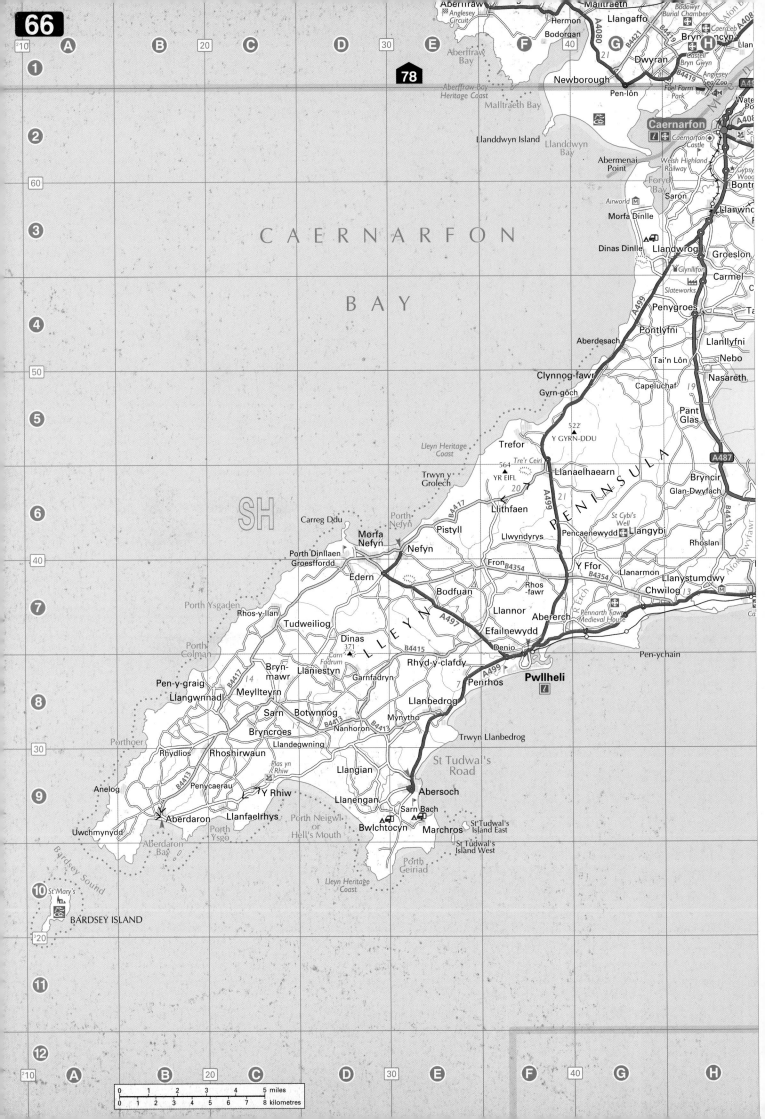

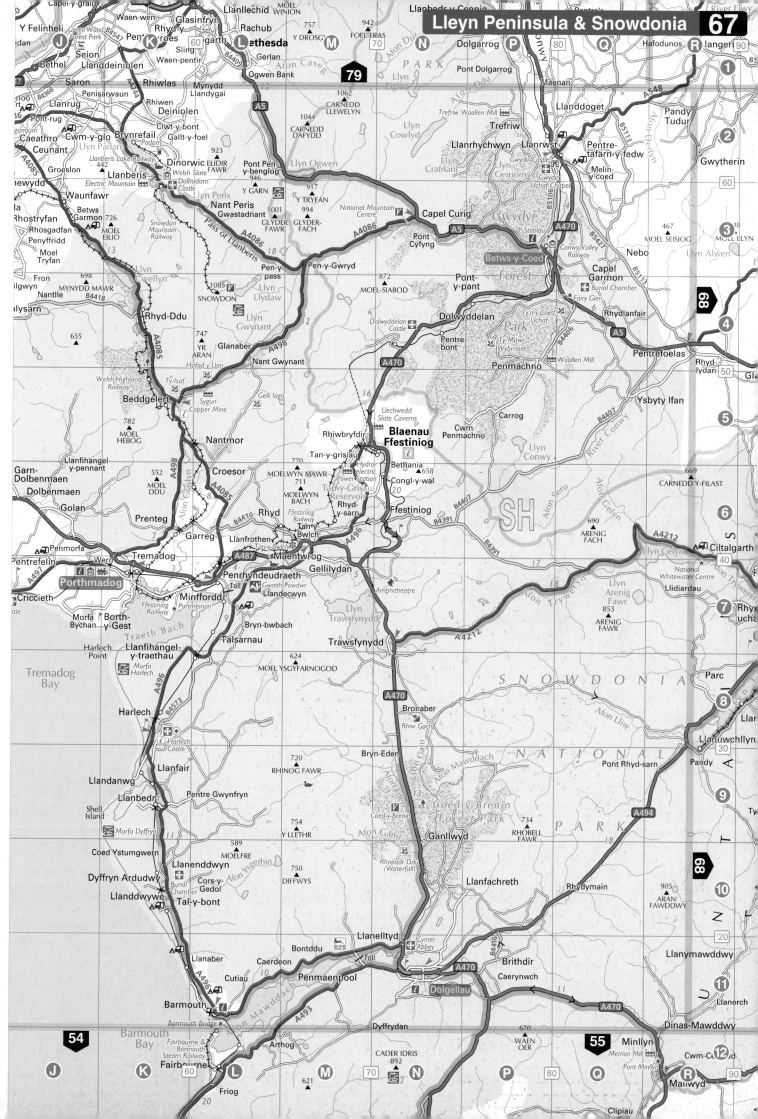

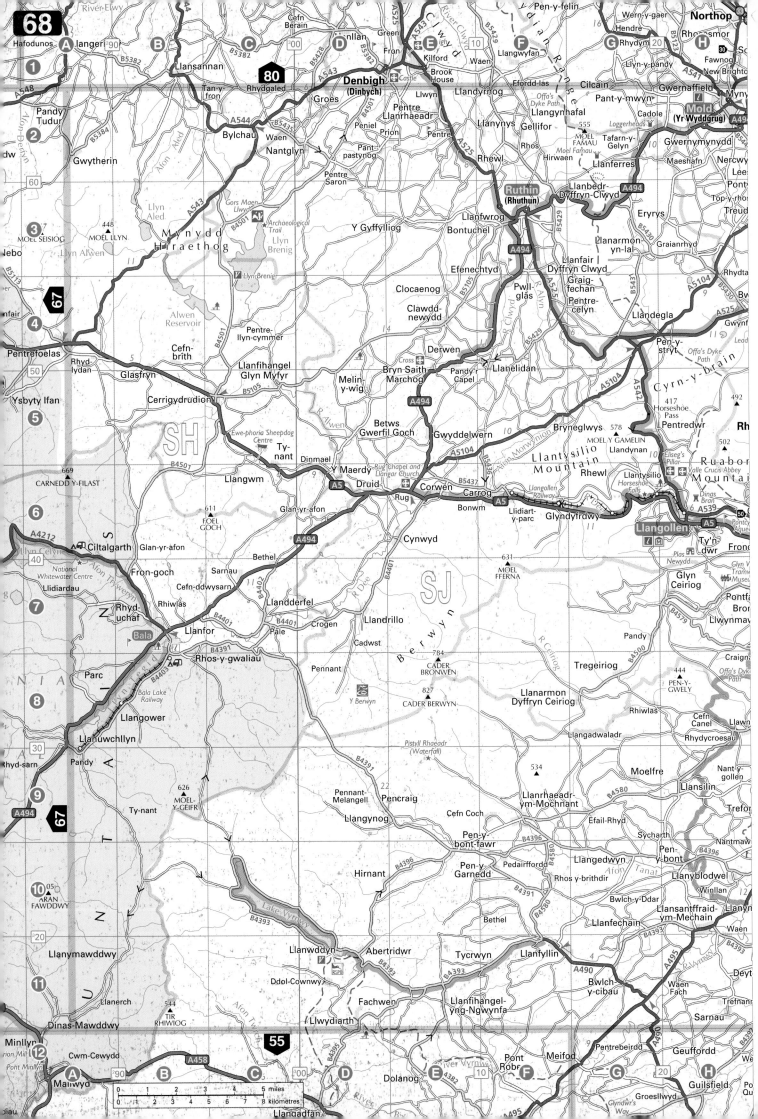

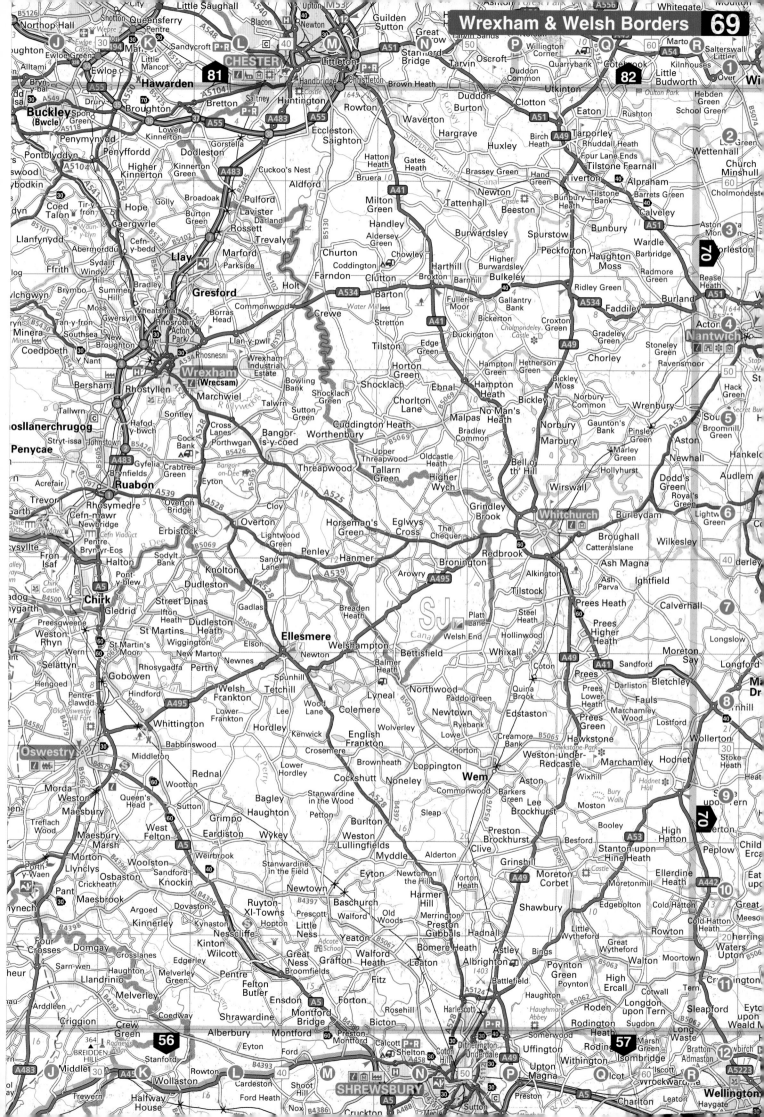

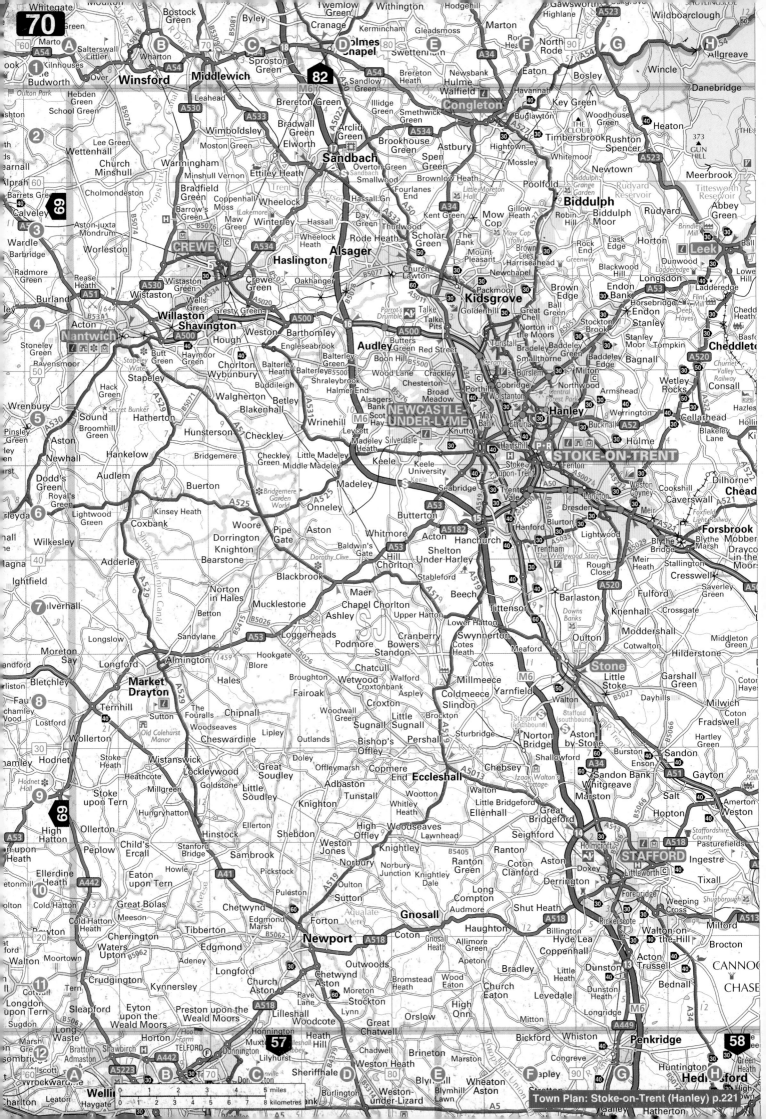

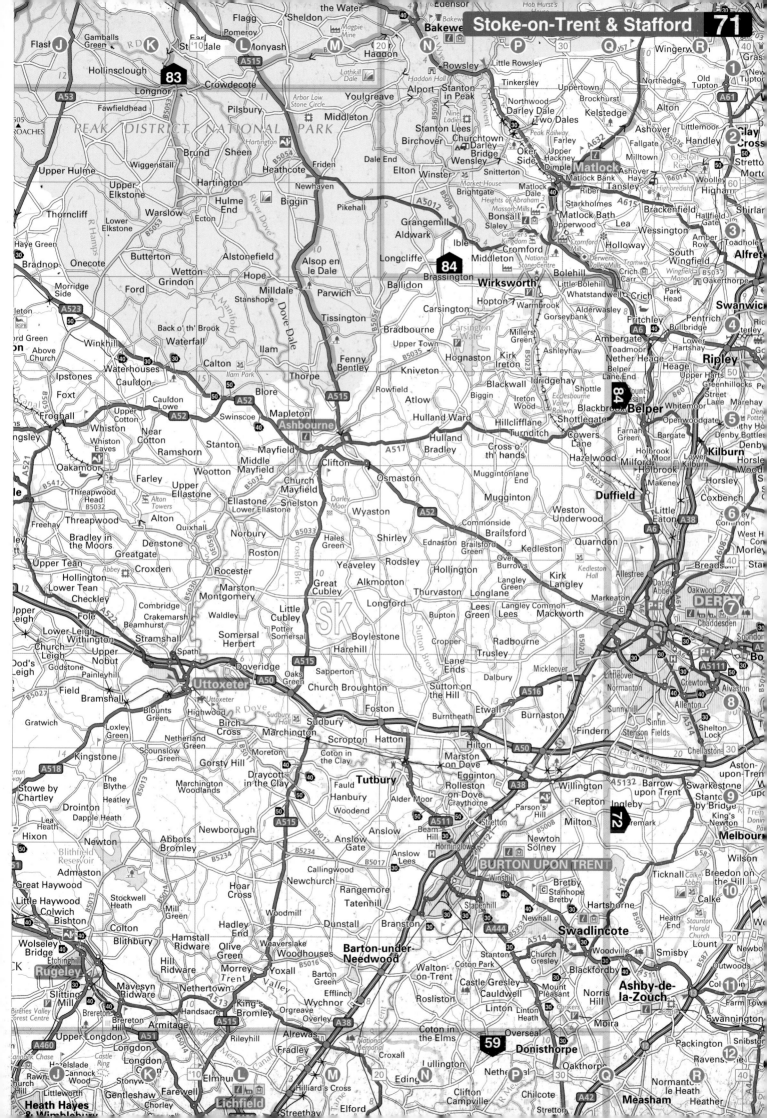

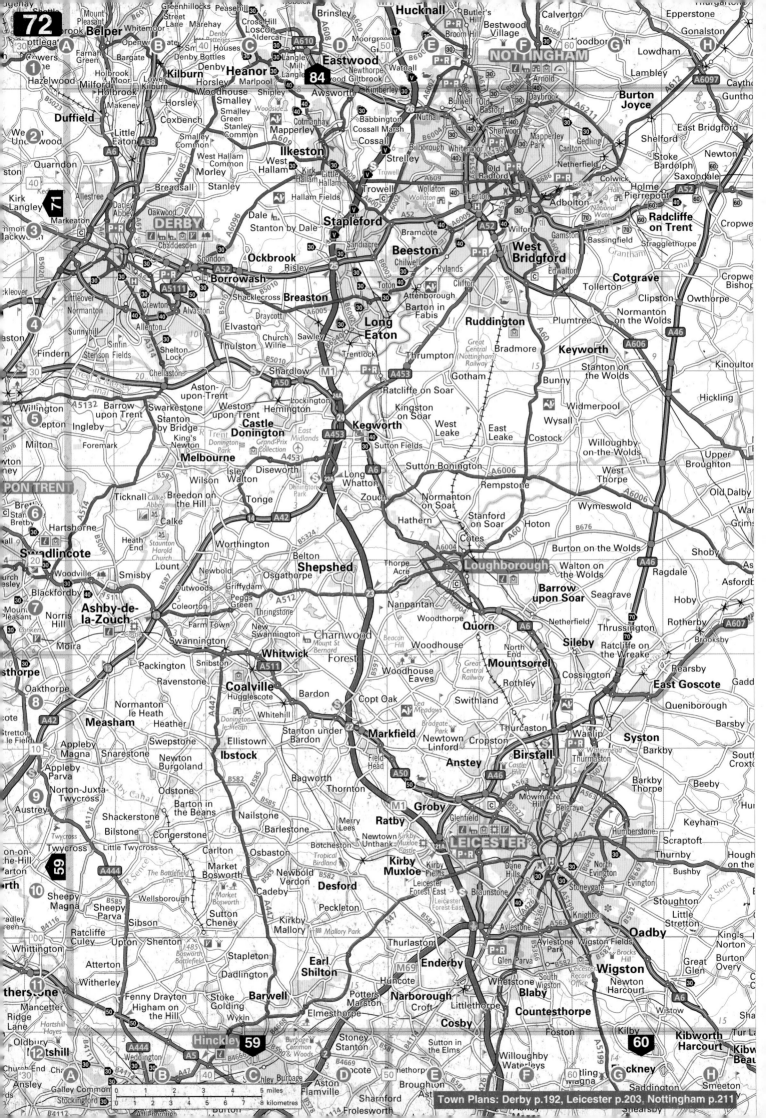

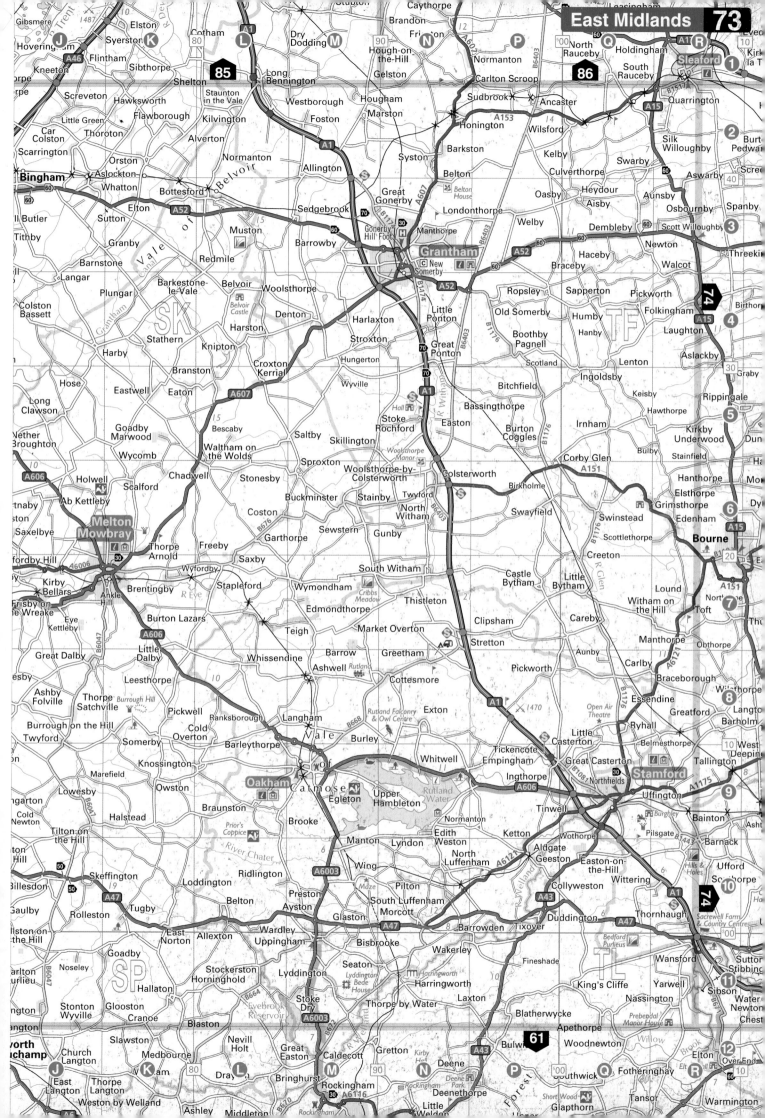

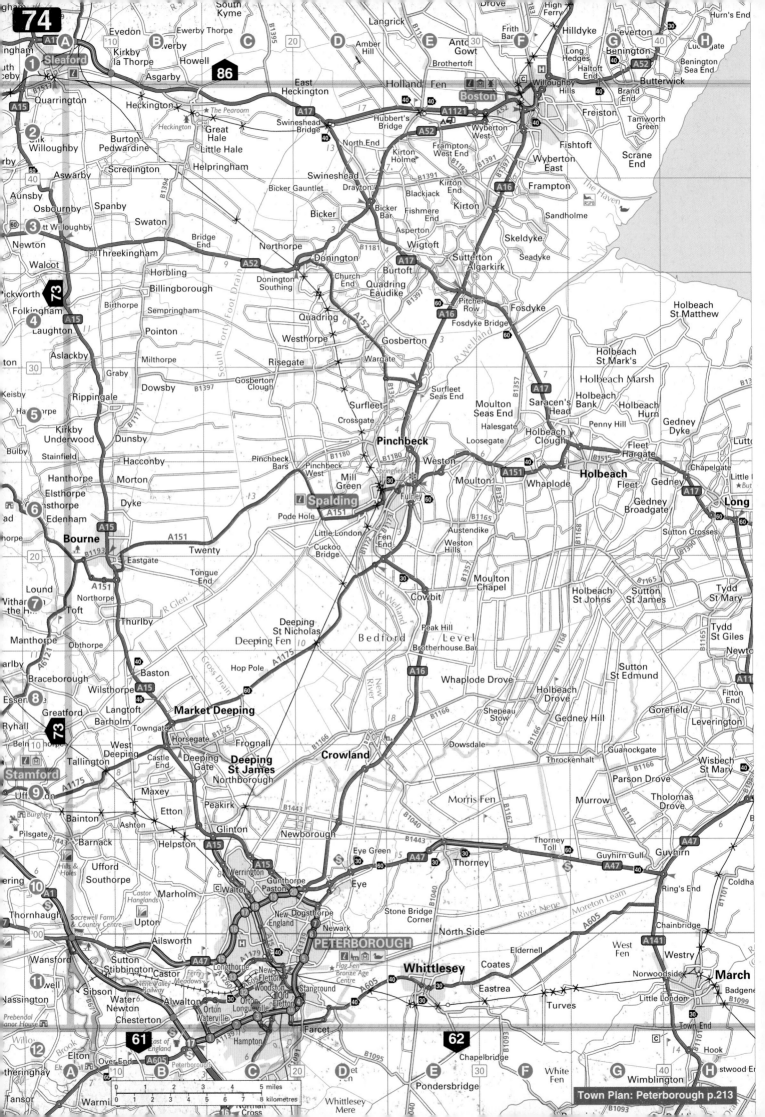

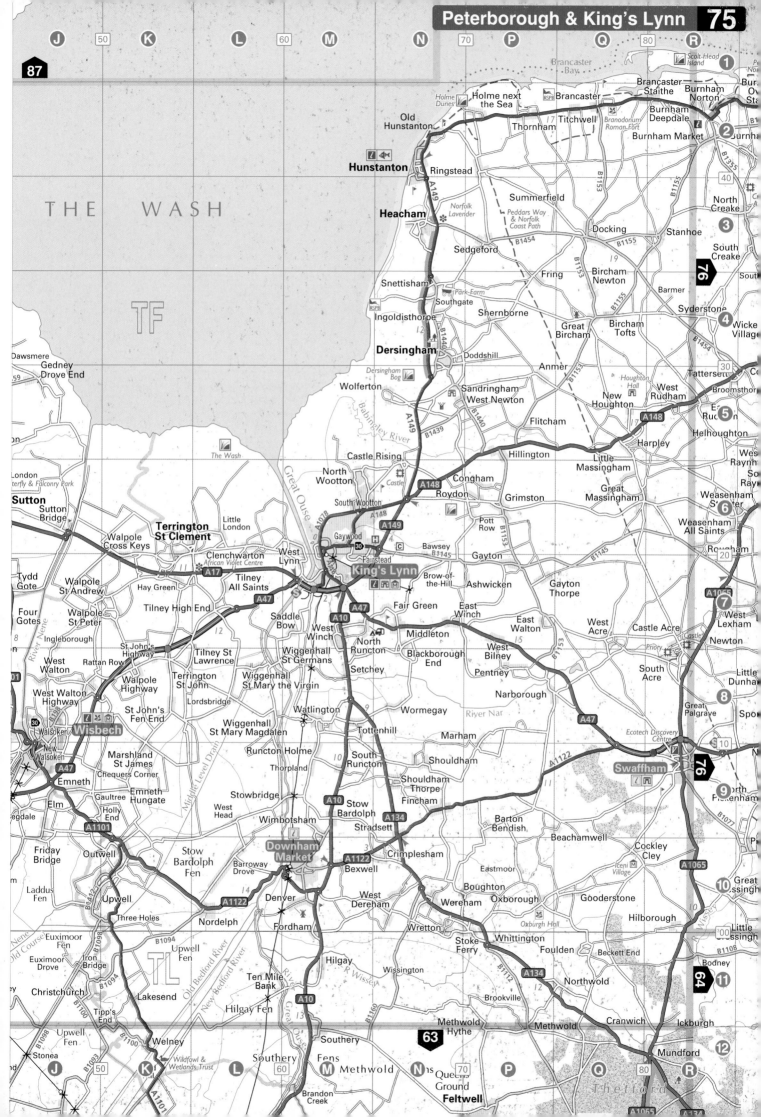

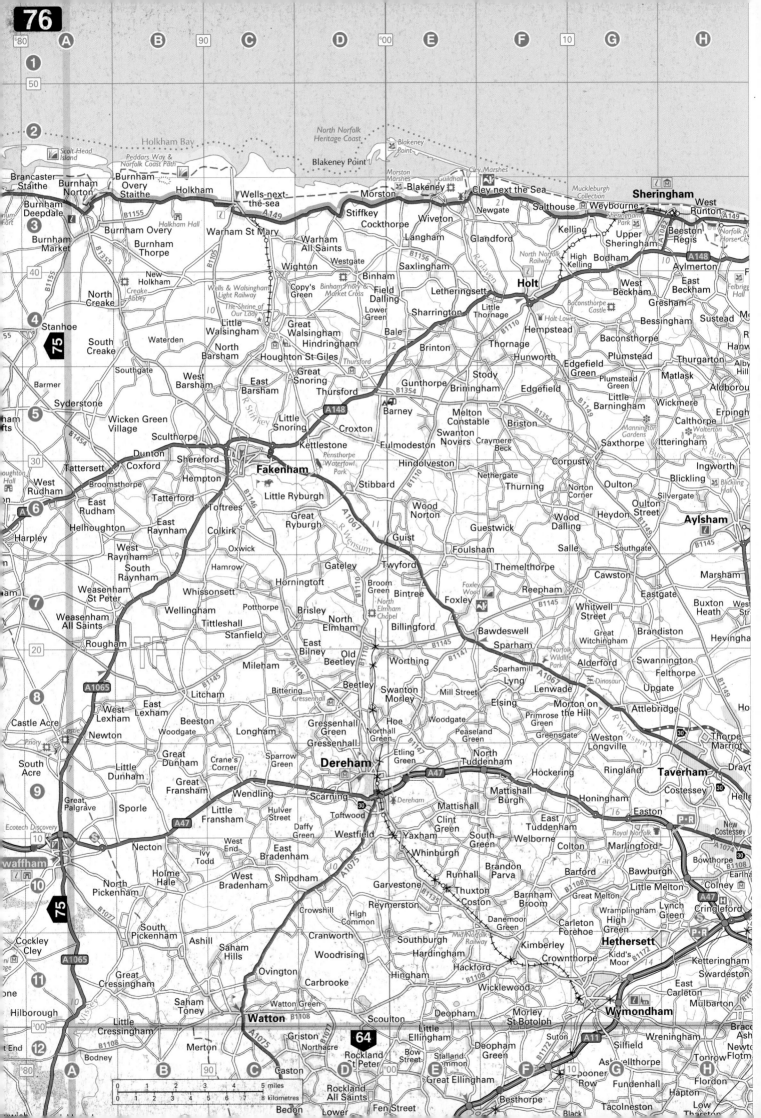

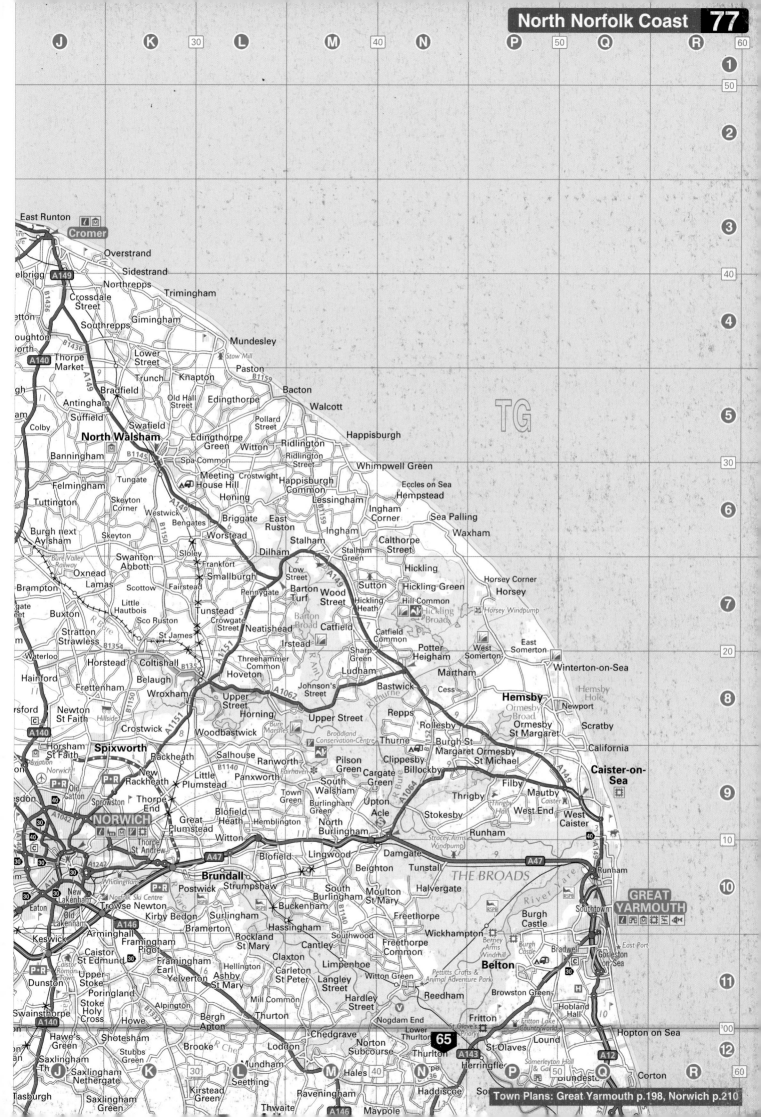

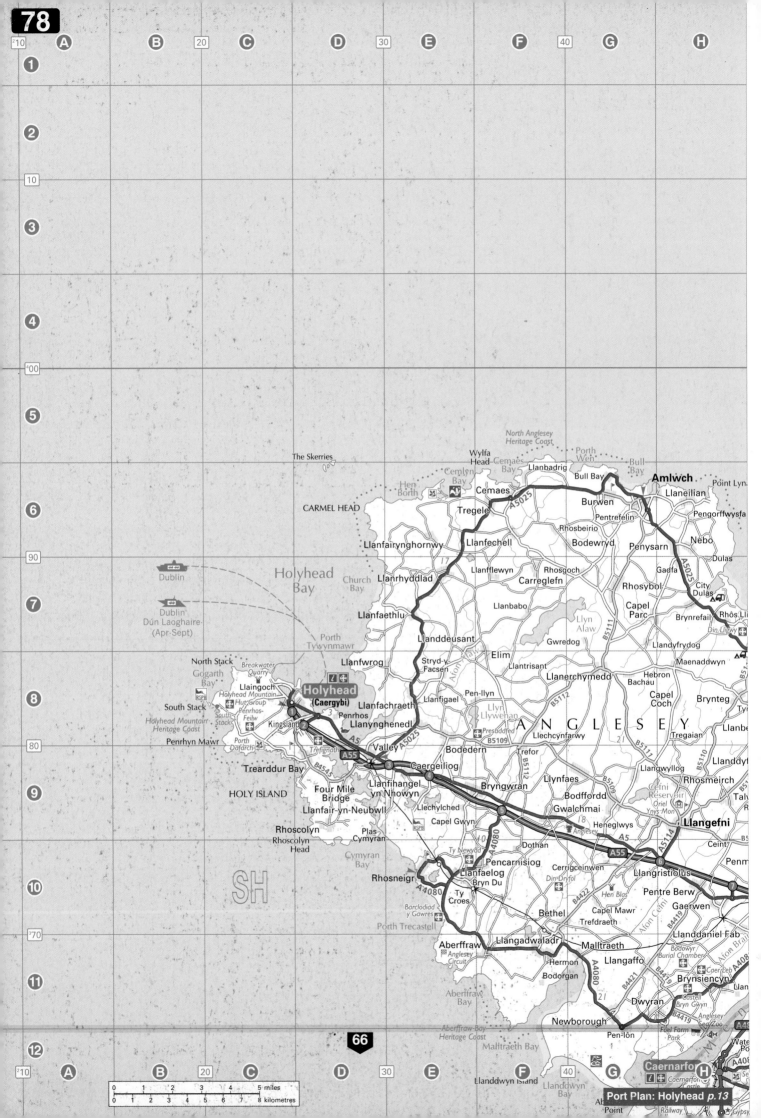

The Skerries

North Anglesey
Heritage Coast

CARMEL HEAD

Holyhead
Bay

Dublin

Dublin
Dún Laoghaire
(Apr-Sept)

North Stack
Gogarth
Bay
Breakwater
Quarry

South Stack
Holyhead Mountain
Heritage Coast

Penrhyn Mawr

Llaingoch
Holyhead Mountain
Hut Group
Penrhos-
Feilw
South
Stack

Kingsland

Holyhead
(Caergybi)

Trefignath

Porth
Dafarch

Trearddur Bay

HOLY ISLAND

Four Mile
Bridge

Llanfair-yn-Neubwll

Rhoscolyn
Rhoscolyn
Head

Porth
Tywynmawr

Llanfwrog

Llanfaethlu

Llanddeusant

Stryd-y-
Facsen

Llanfachraeth

Penrhos

Llanynghenedl

Valley

Bodedern

Caergeiliog

Llanfihangel
yn Nhowyn

Llechylched

Capel Gwyn

Plas
Cymran

Cymyran
Bay

Bryngwran

Gwalchmai

Heneglwys
Anglesey

SH

Rhosneigr

Llanfaelog
Bryn Du

Ty
Croes

Barclodiad
y Gawres

Porth Trecastell

Pencarnisiog

Dothan

Cerrigceinwen

Bethel

Capel Mawr
Trefdraeth

Aberffraw
Anglesey
Circuit

Aberffraw
Bay

Aberffraw Bay
Heritage Coast

Llangadwaladr

Hermon

Bodorgan

Malltraeth

Newborough

Pen-lôn

Malltraeth Bay

Llanddwyn Island

Llanddwyn
Bay

Wylfa
Head

Cemlyn
Bay

Hen
Borth

Cemaes

Tregele

Llanfairynghornwy

Church
Bay

Llanrhyddlad

Llanbabo

Llanfflewyn

Llanfigael

Pen-llyn

Llyn
Llywenan

Presaddfed

Llechcynfarwy

Trefor

Llynfaes

Bodffordd

North Anglesey
Heritage Coast

Porth
Wen

Bull
Bay

Llanbadrig

Bull Bay

Amlwch

Burwen

Point Lyn

Llaneilian

Pengorffwysfa

Pentrefelin

Rhosbeirio

Carreglefn

Rhosgoch

Gwredog

Elim

Llantrisant

Llanerchymedd

Llangwyllog

Cefni
Reservoir
Oriel
Ynys Môn

Rhosmeirch

Bodewryd

Penysarn

Nébo

Dulas

Gadfa

City
Dulas

Rhosybol

Capel
Parc

Brynrefail

Rhôs Lli

Llandyfrydog

Maenaddwyn

Hebron
Bachau

Capel
Coch

Brynteg

Tregaian

A**NGLESEY**

Din-Dryfol

Ty Newydd

Dwyran

Castell
Bryn Gwyn

Anglesey
Sea Zoo

Llangefni

Ceint

Penm

Pentre Berw

Gaerwen

Hen Blas

Llangristiolus

Llanddaniel Fâb

Llangaffo

Brynsiencyn

Caernarfon

0 1 2 3 4 5 miles
0 1 2 3 4 5 6 7 8 kilometres

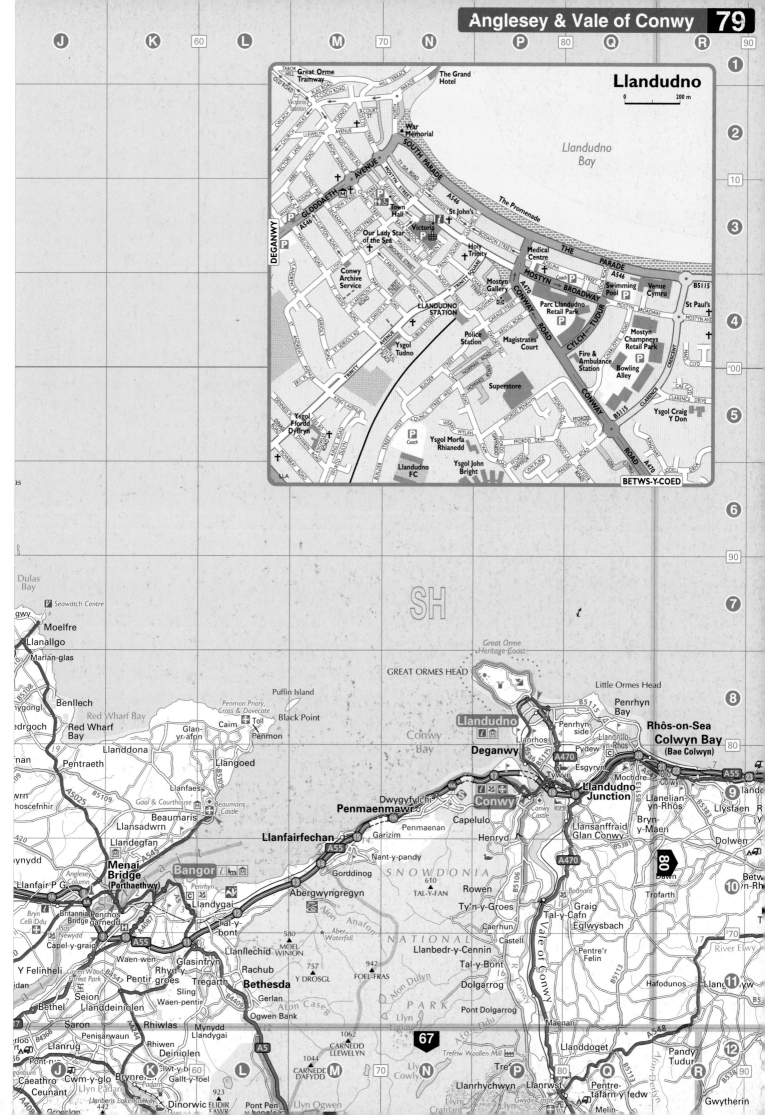

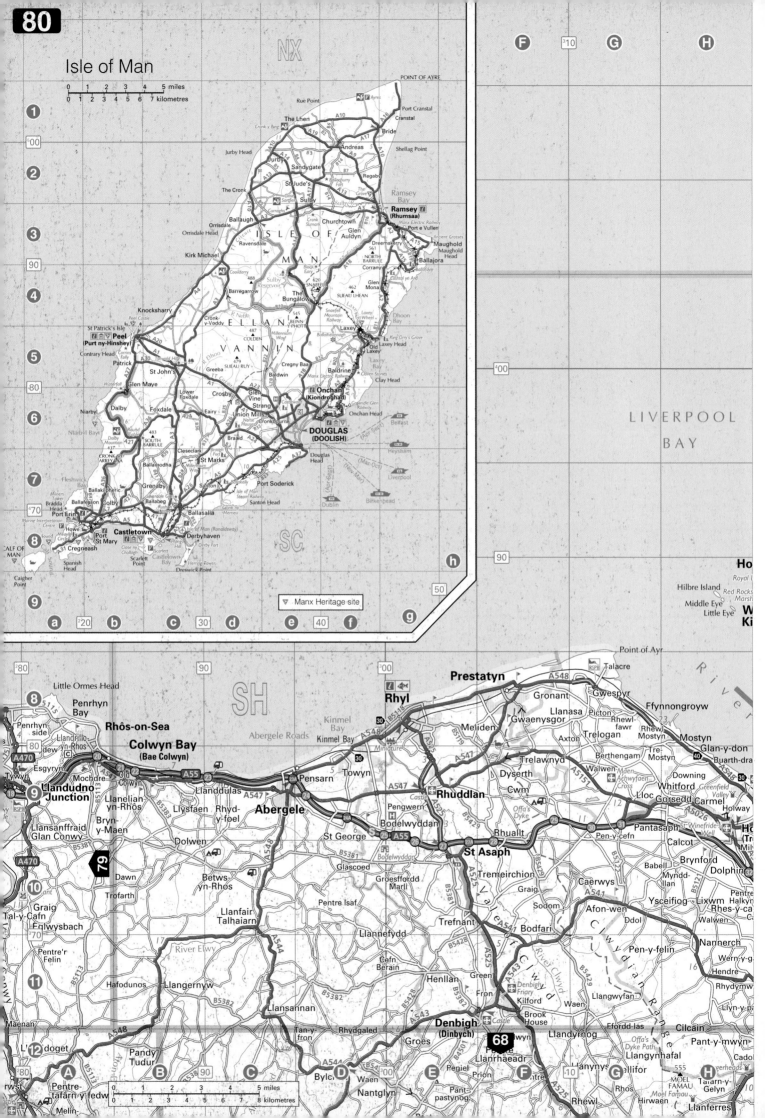

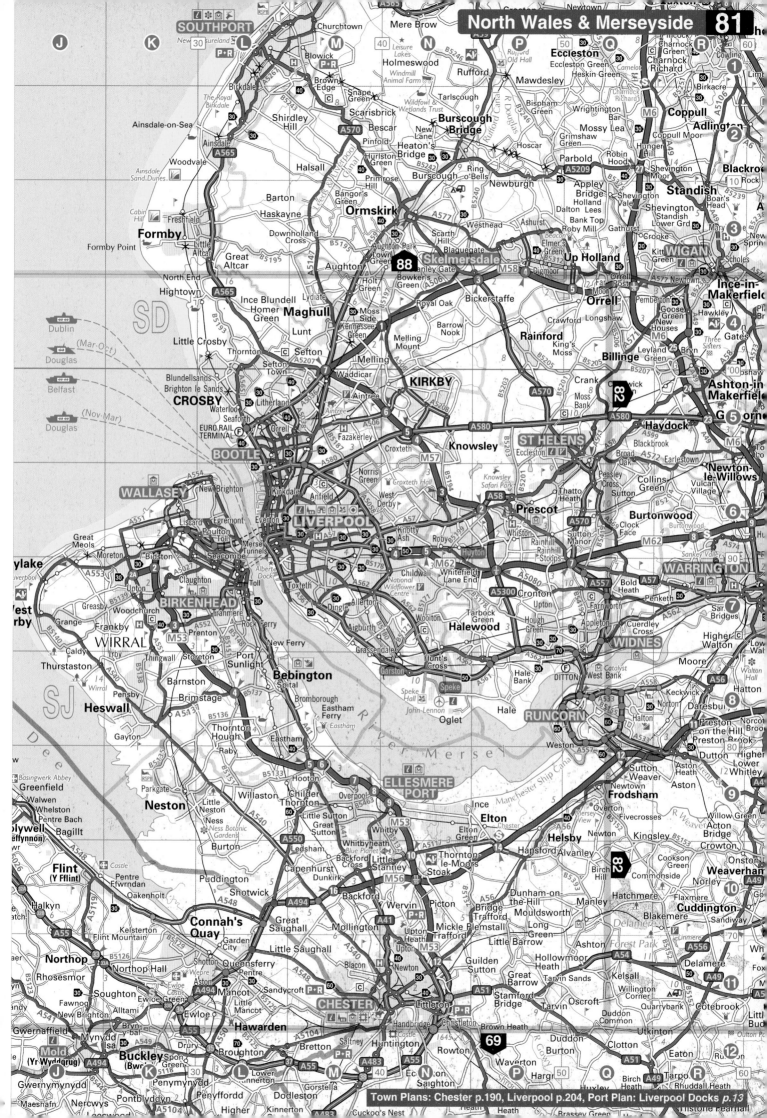

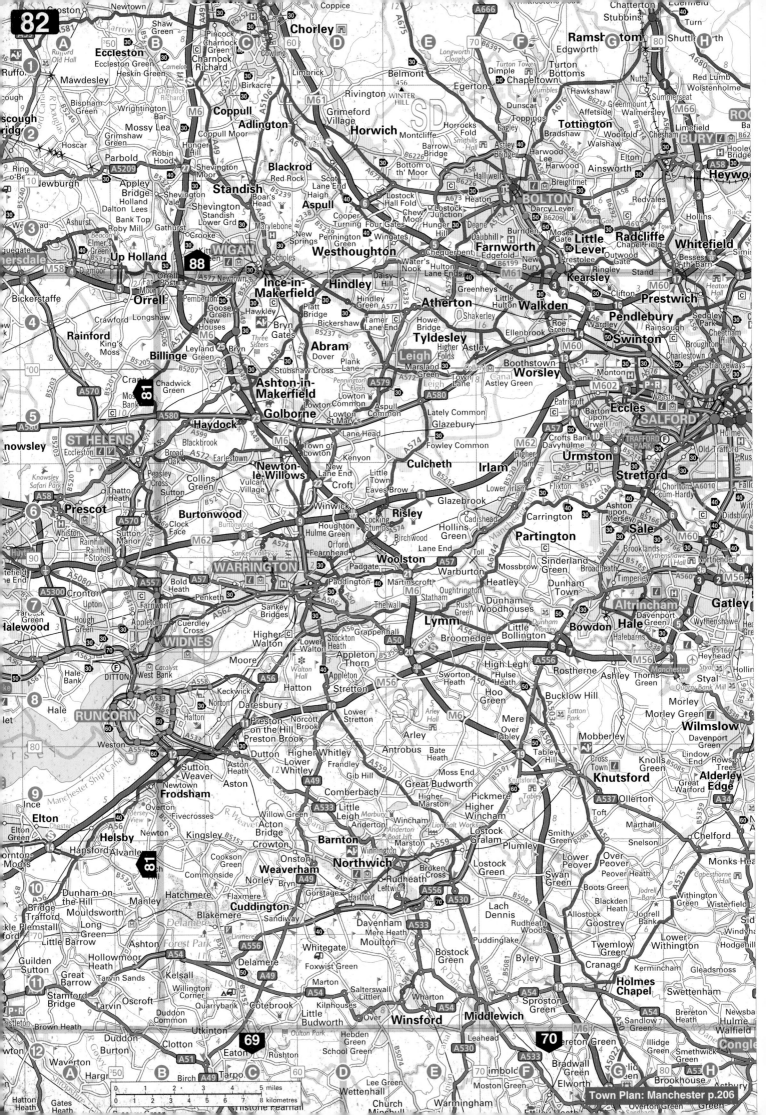

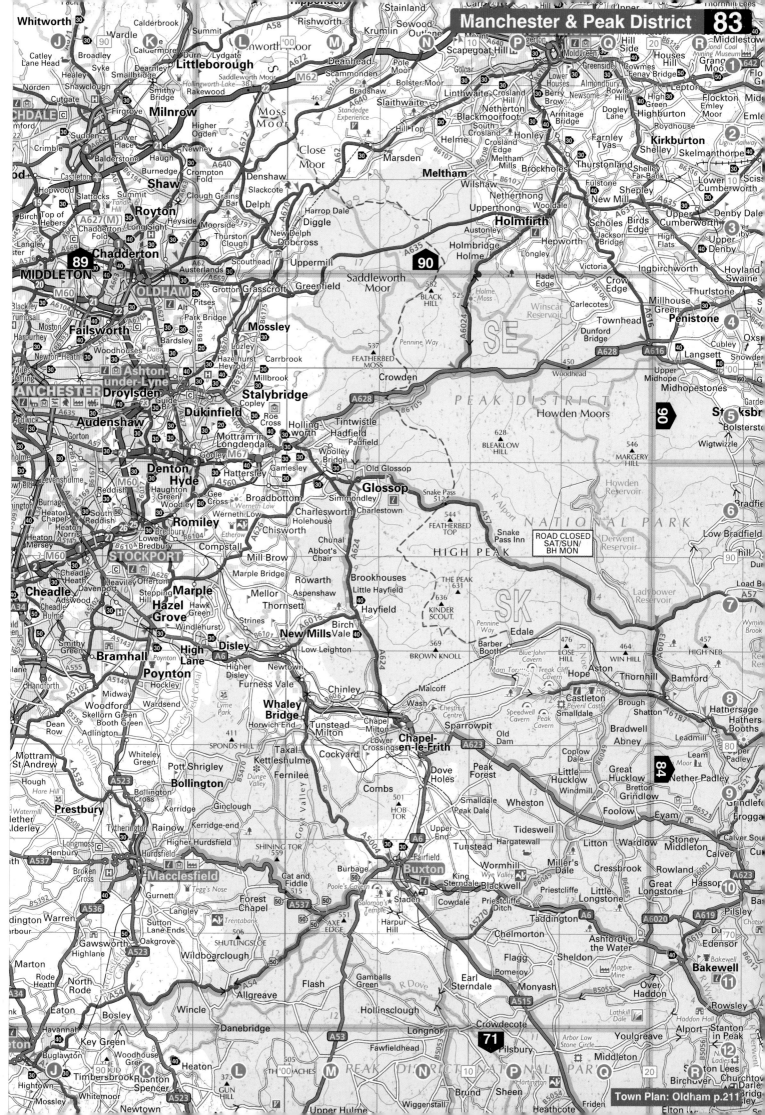

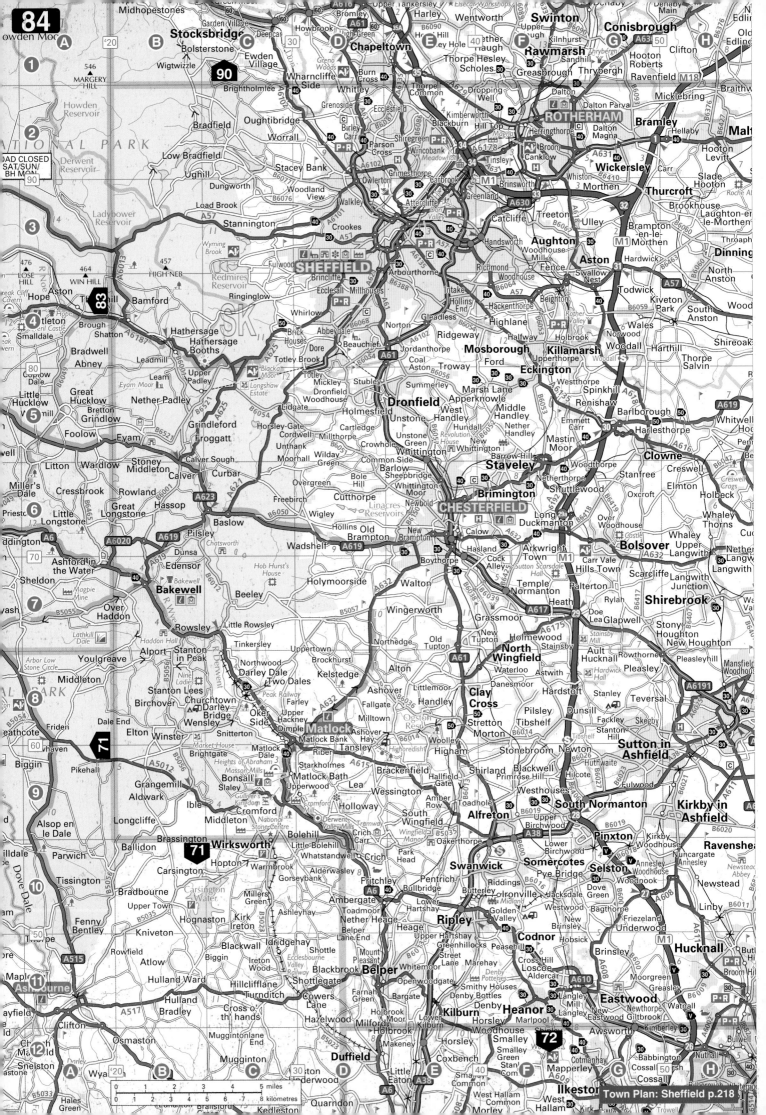

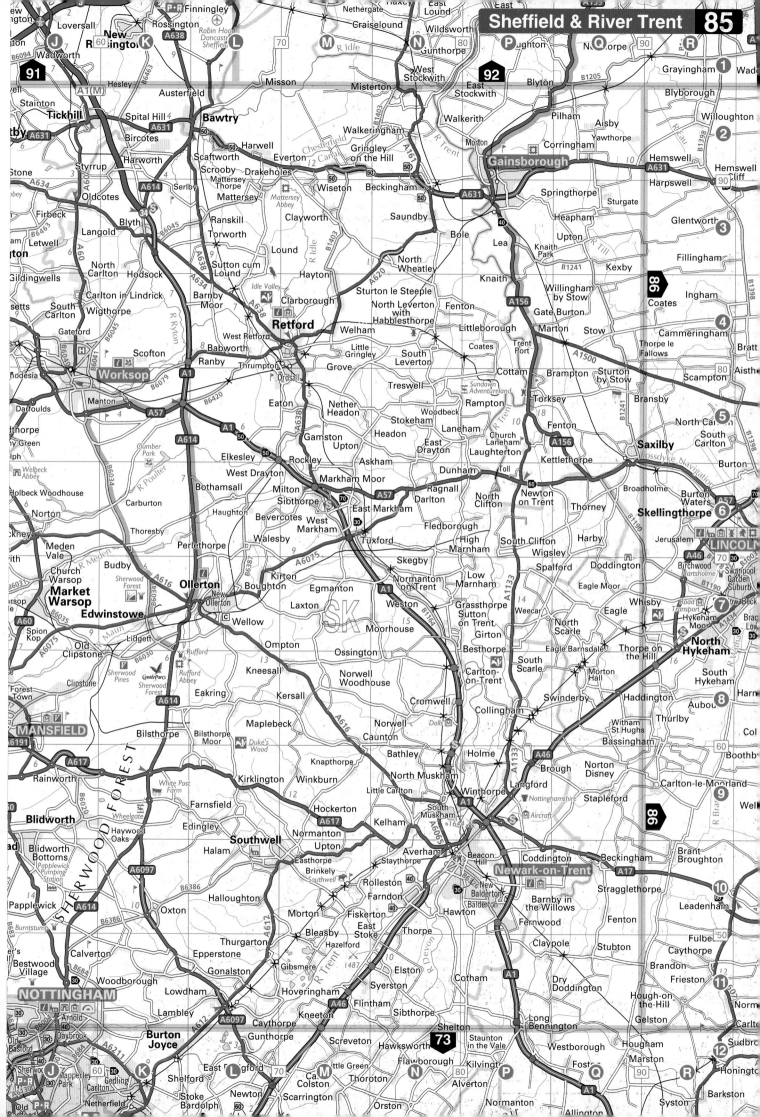

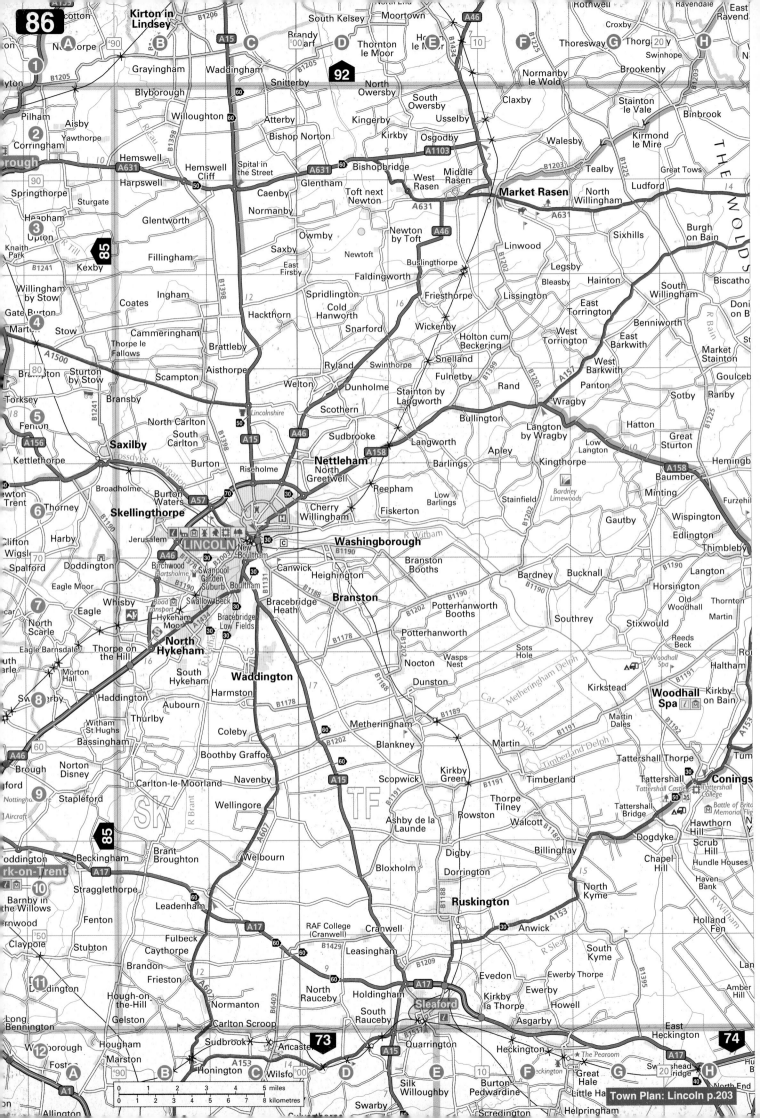

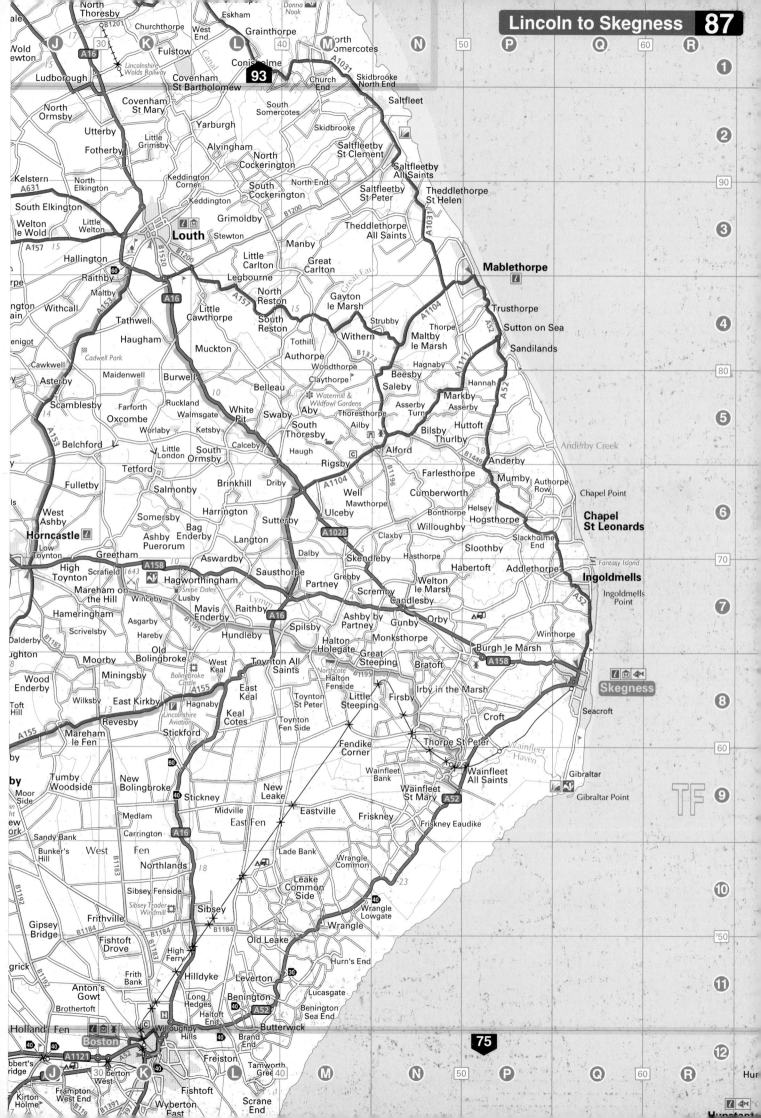

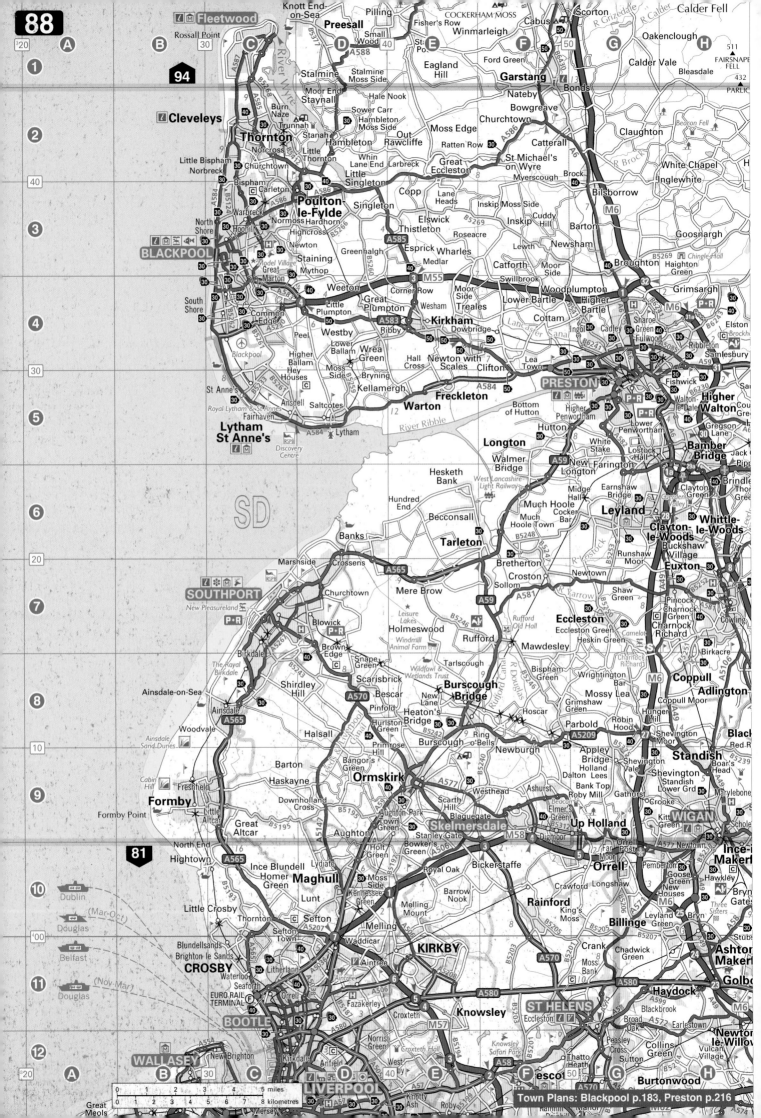

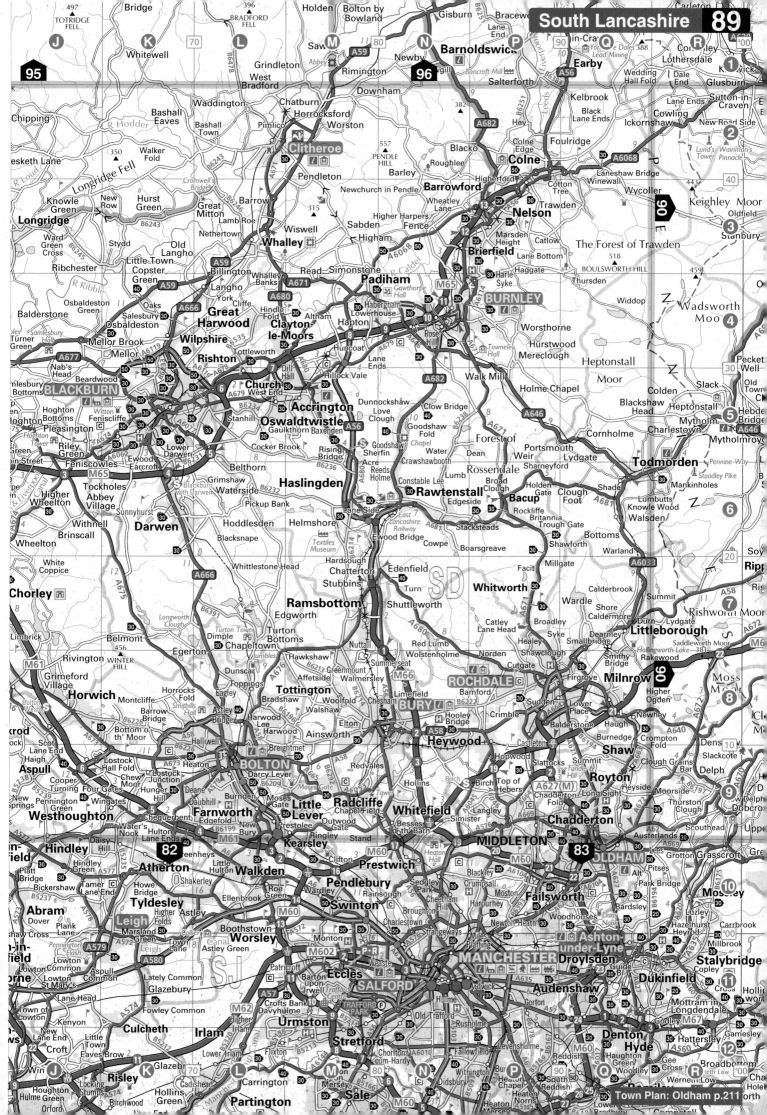

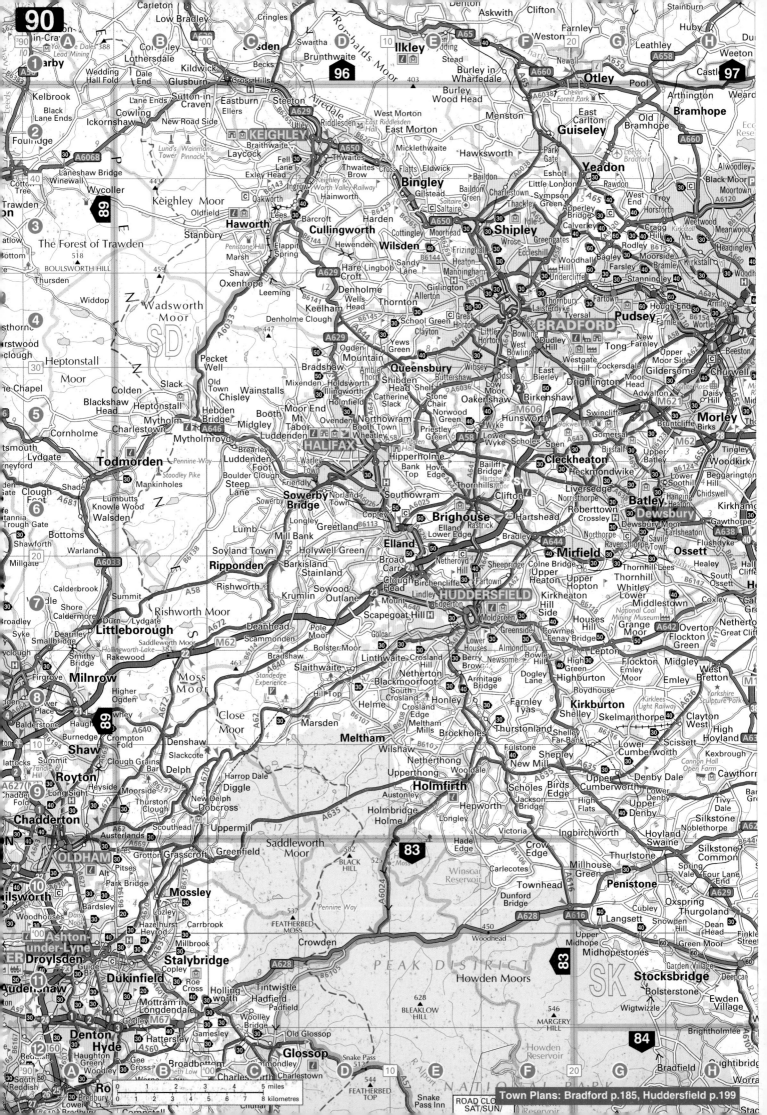

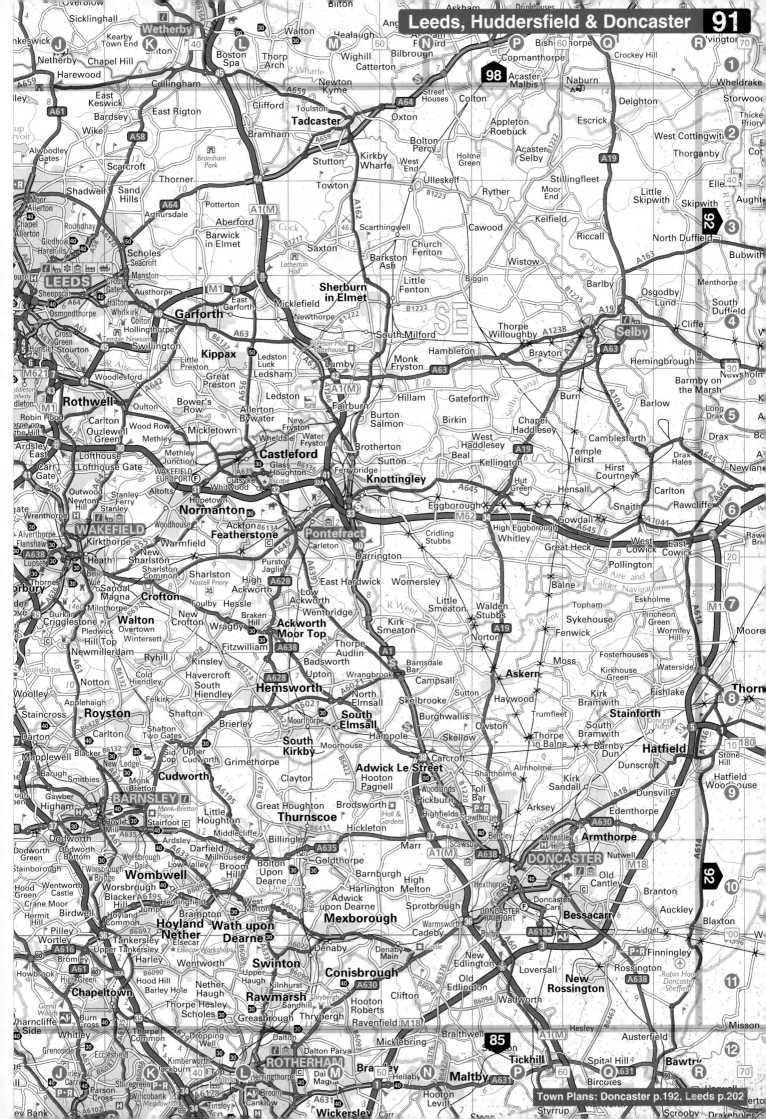

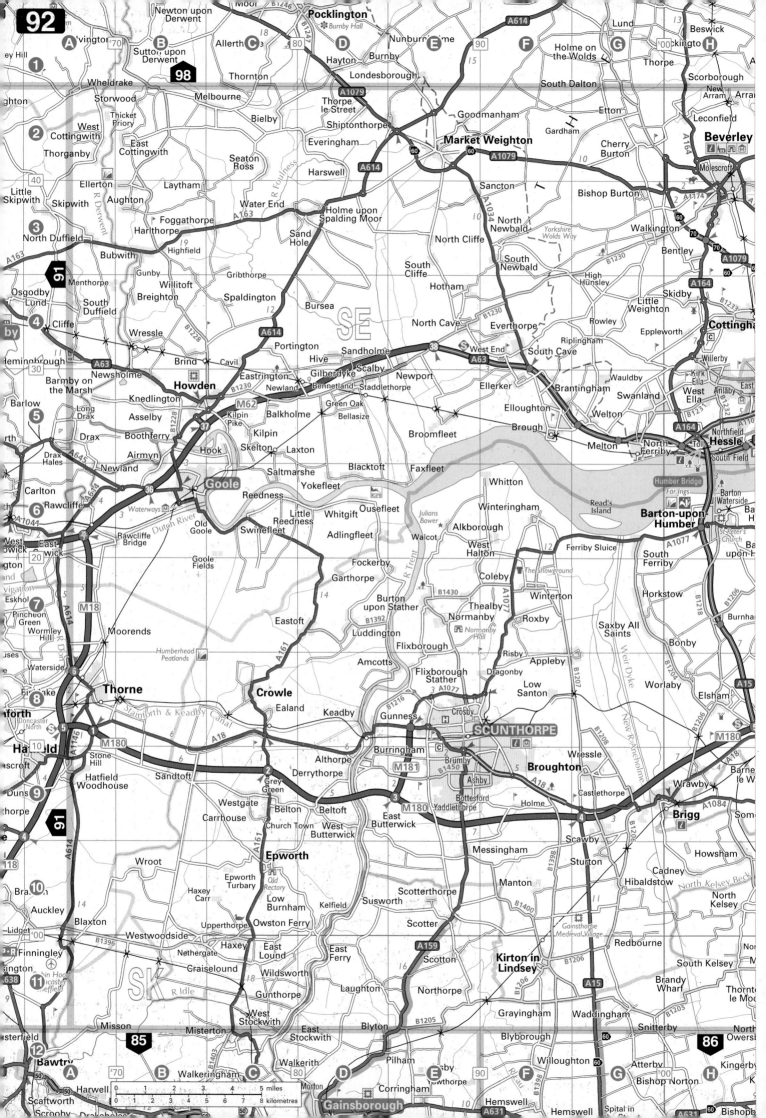

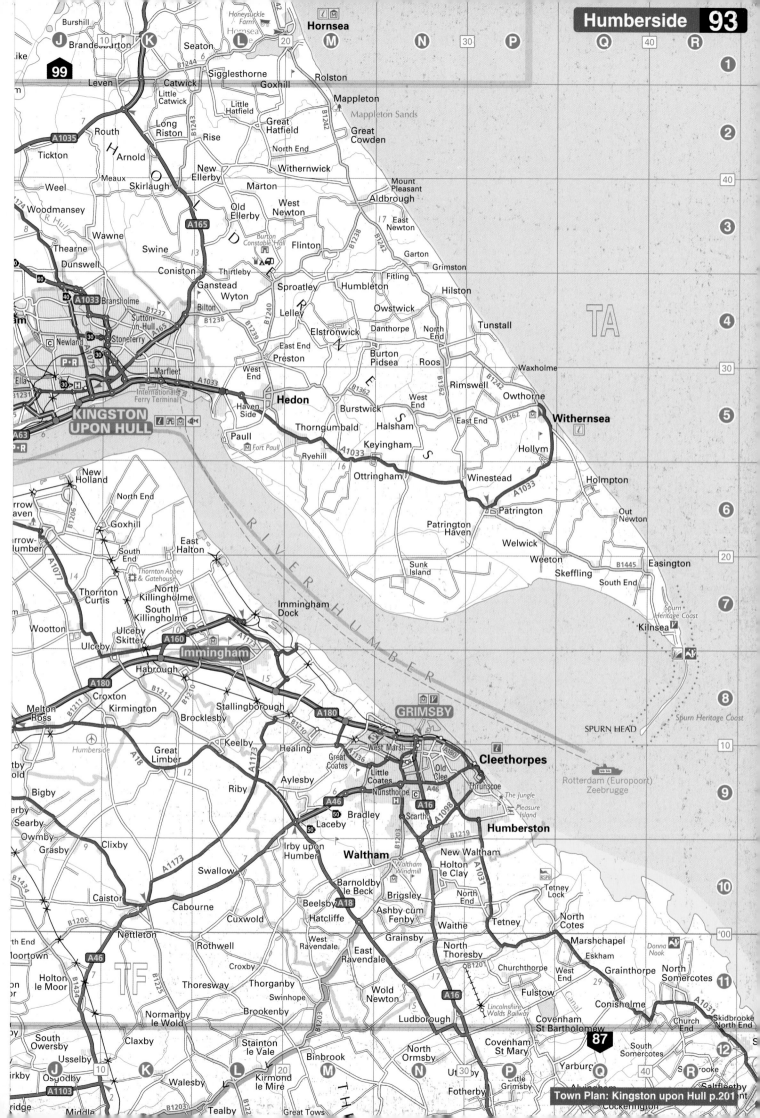

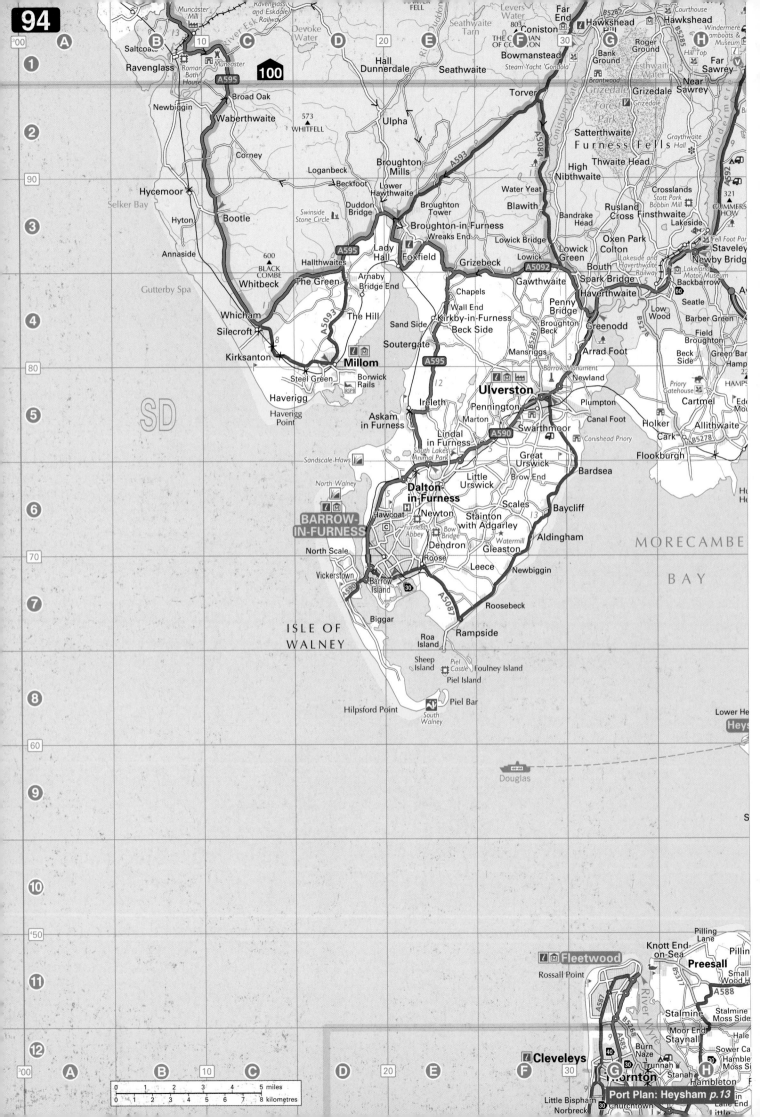

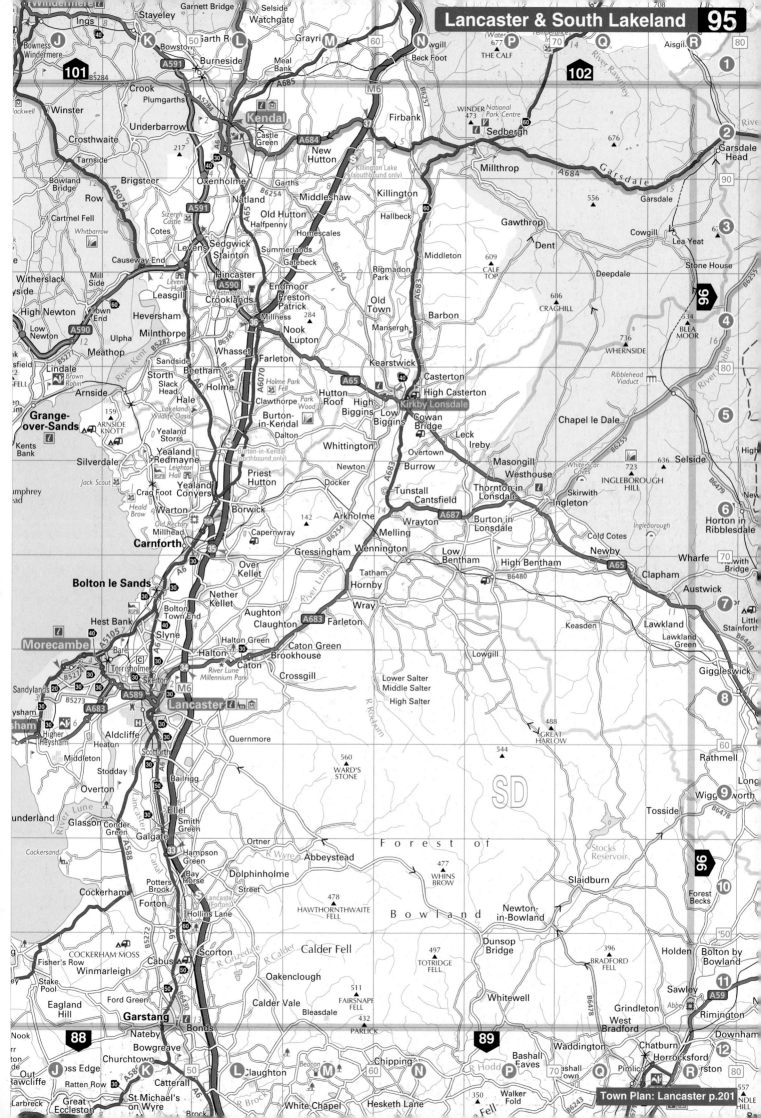

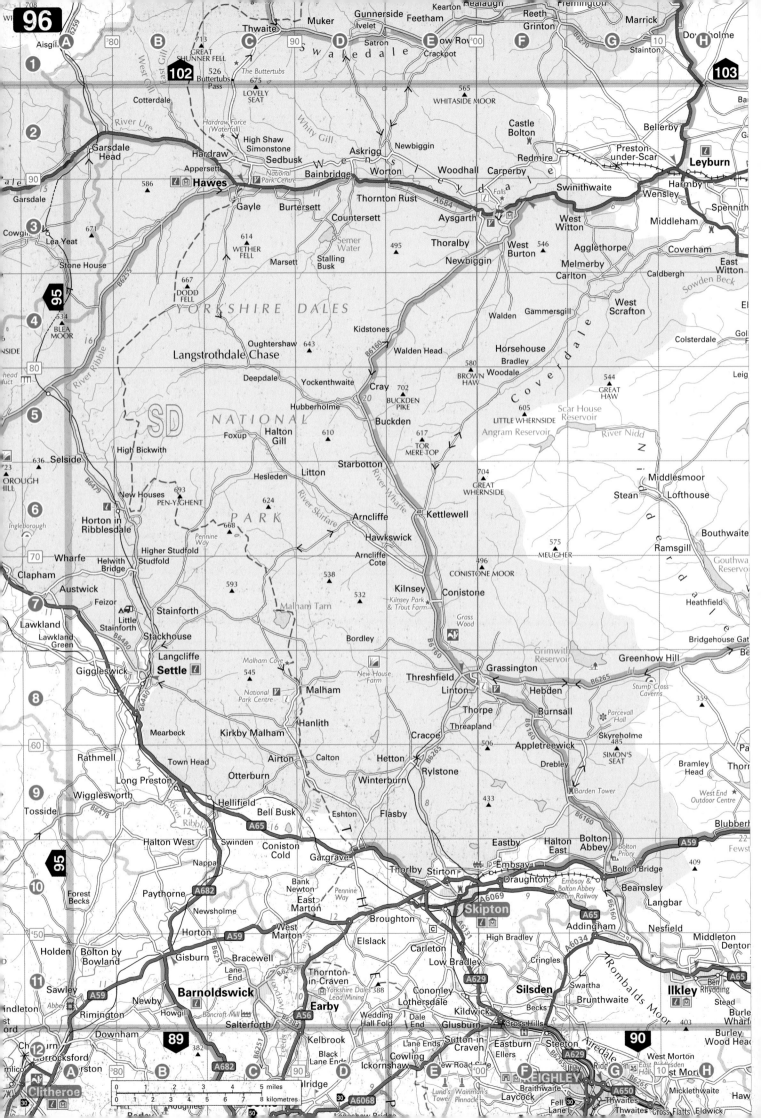

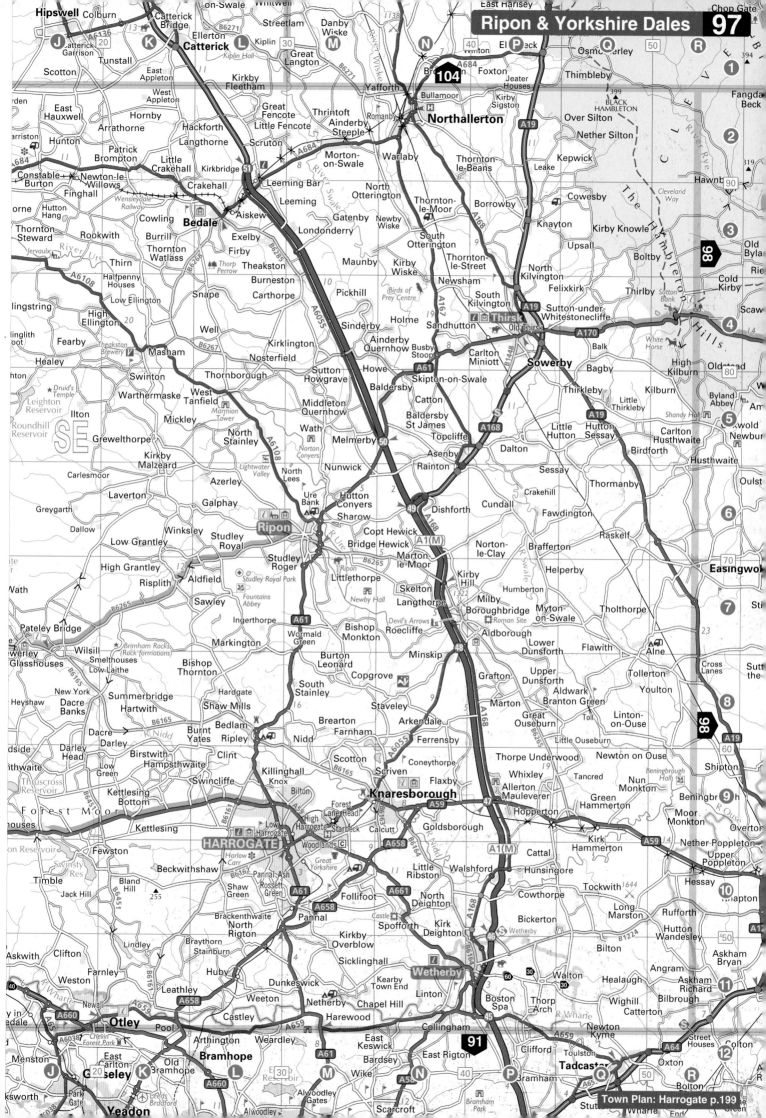

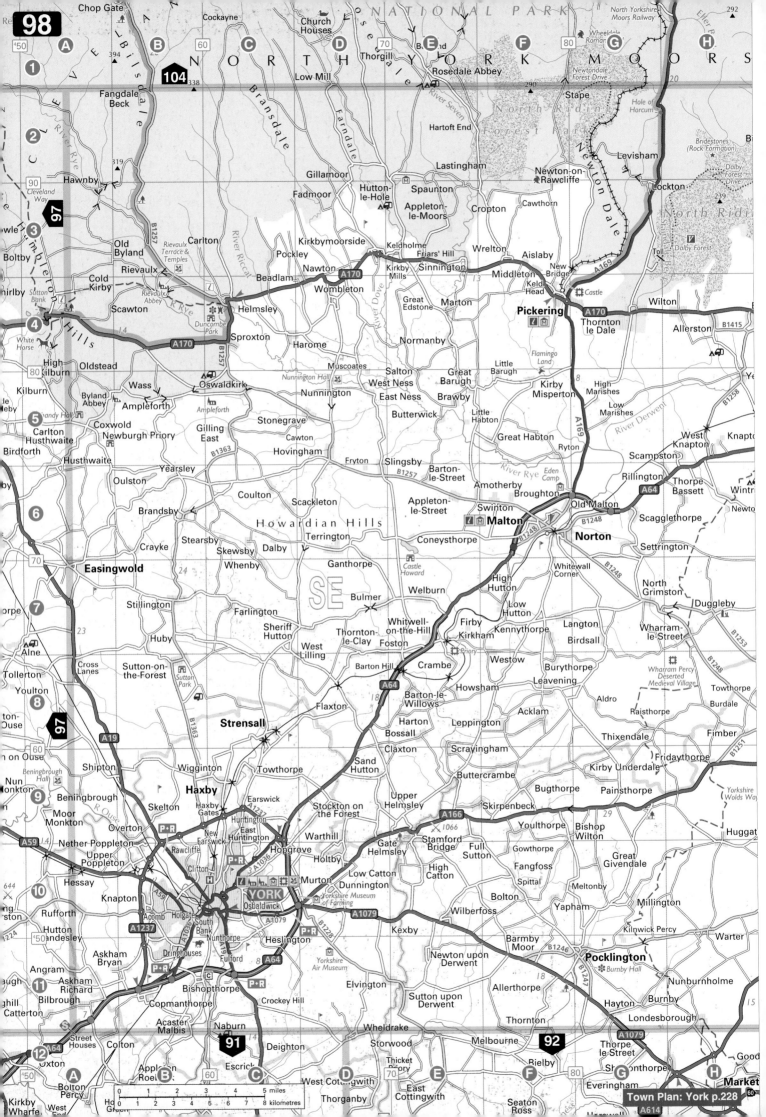

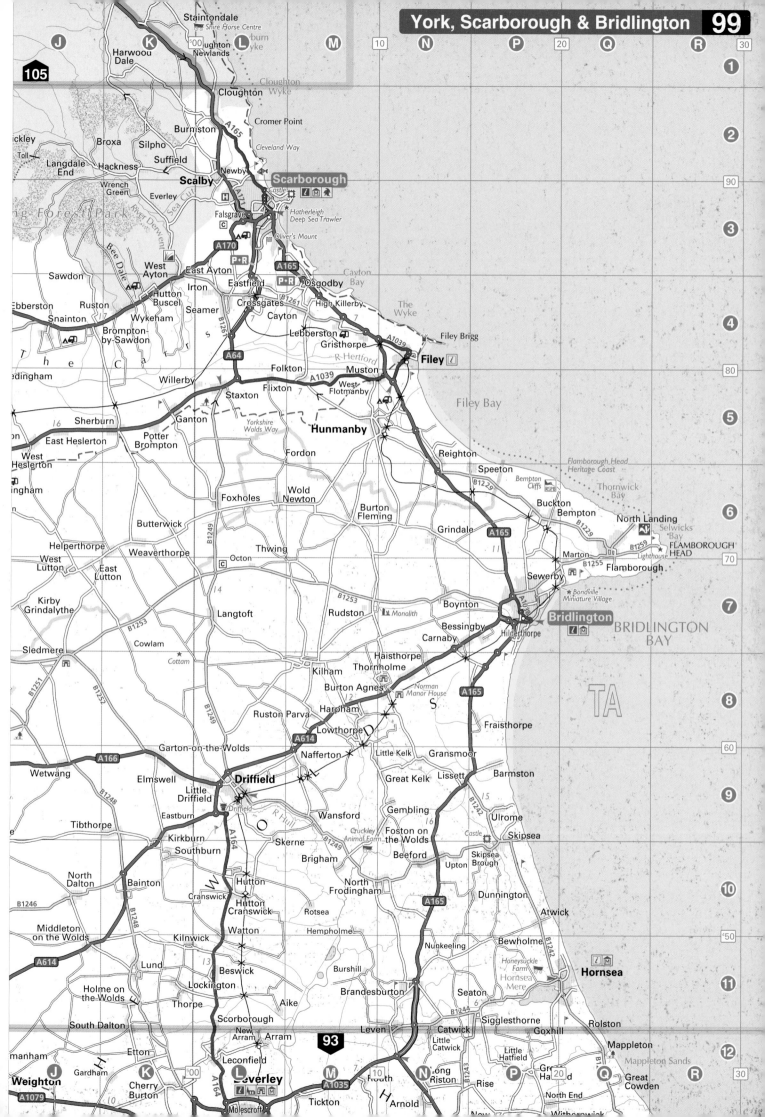

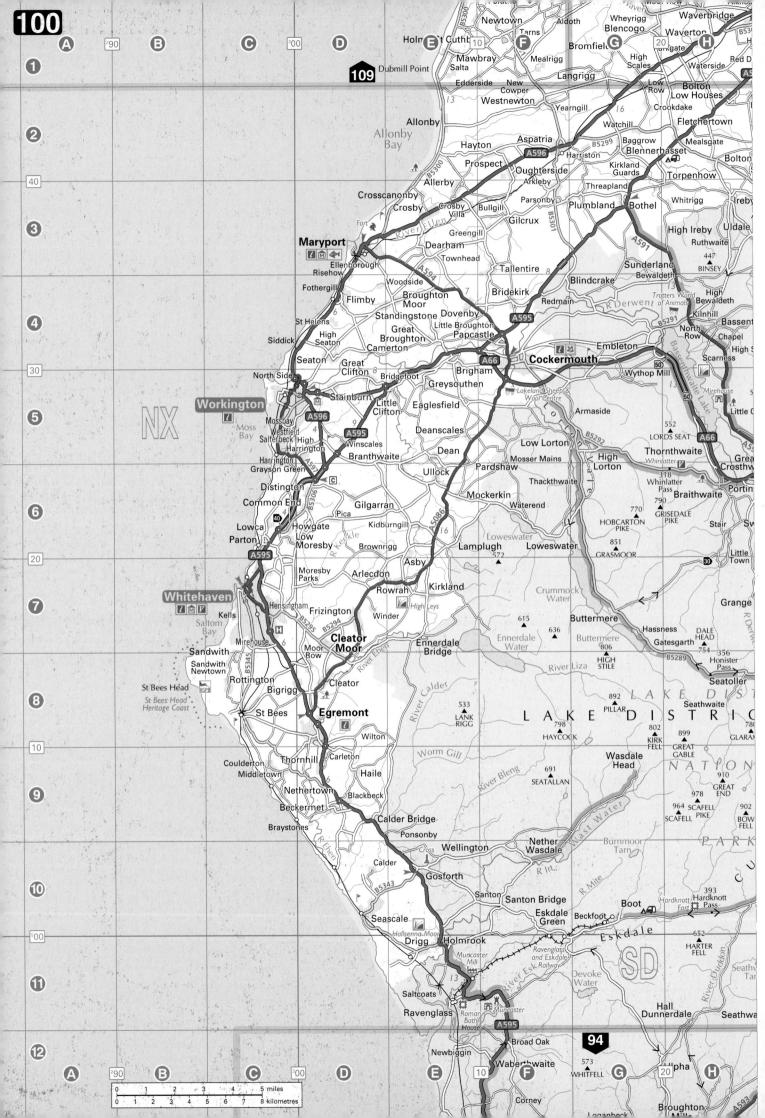

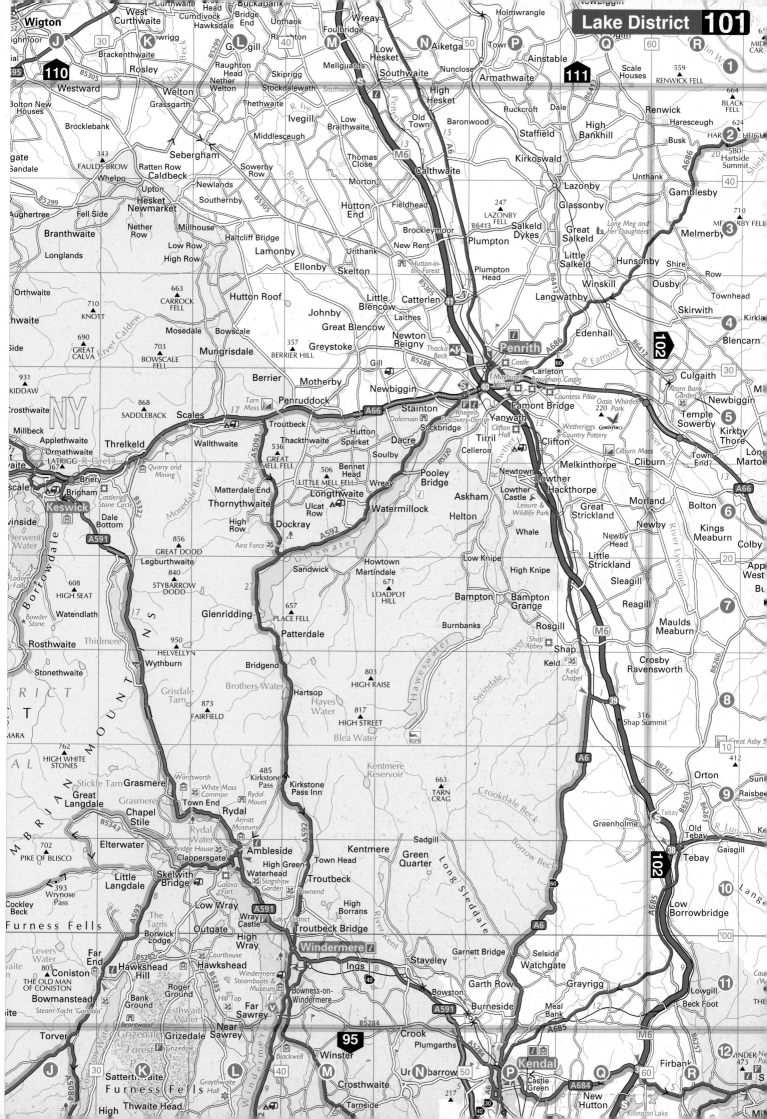

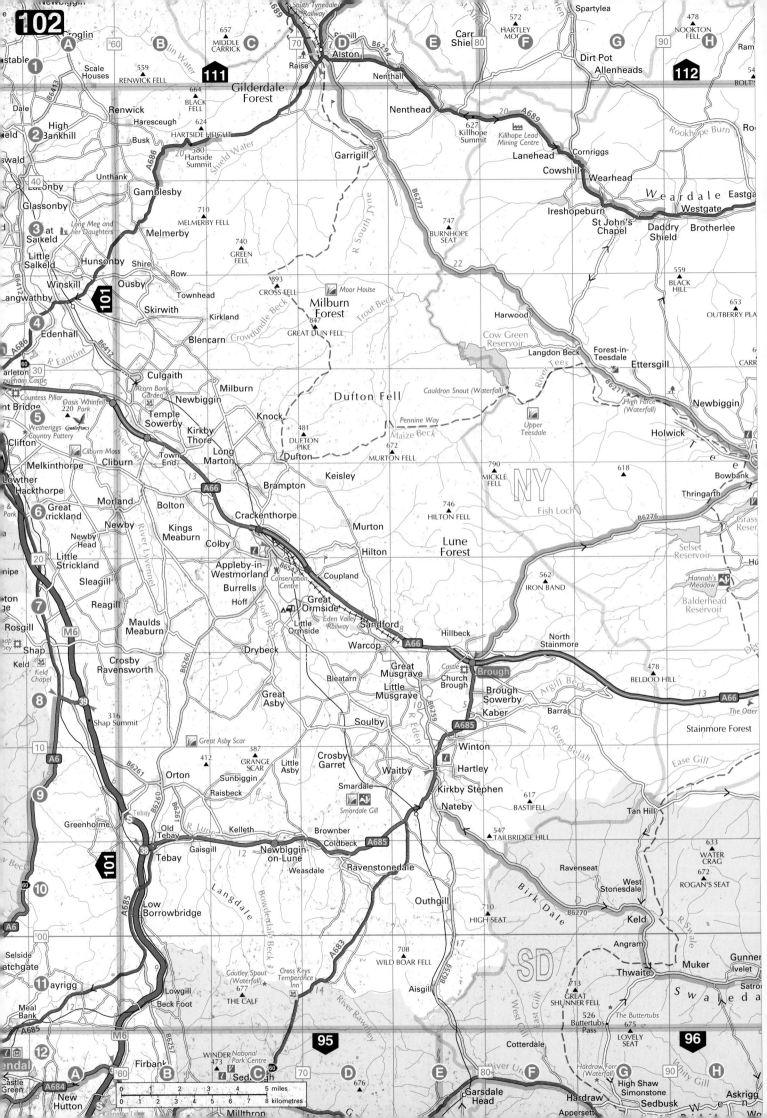

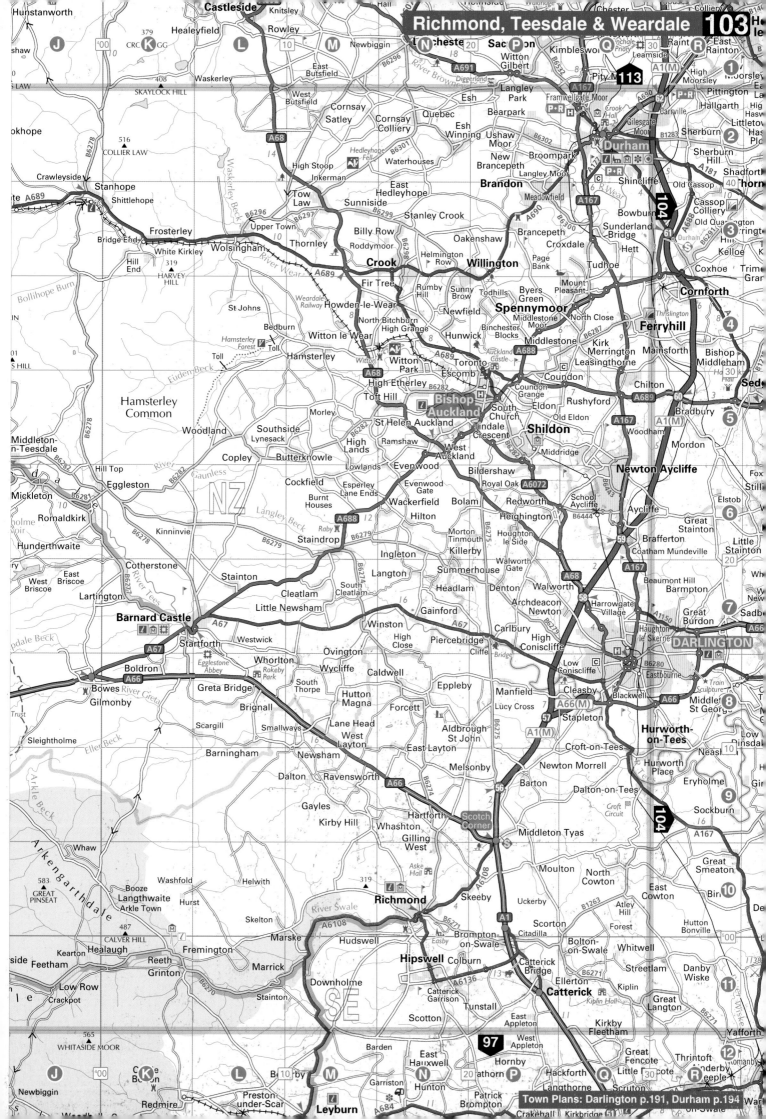

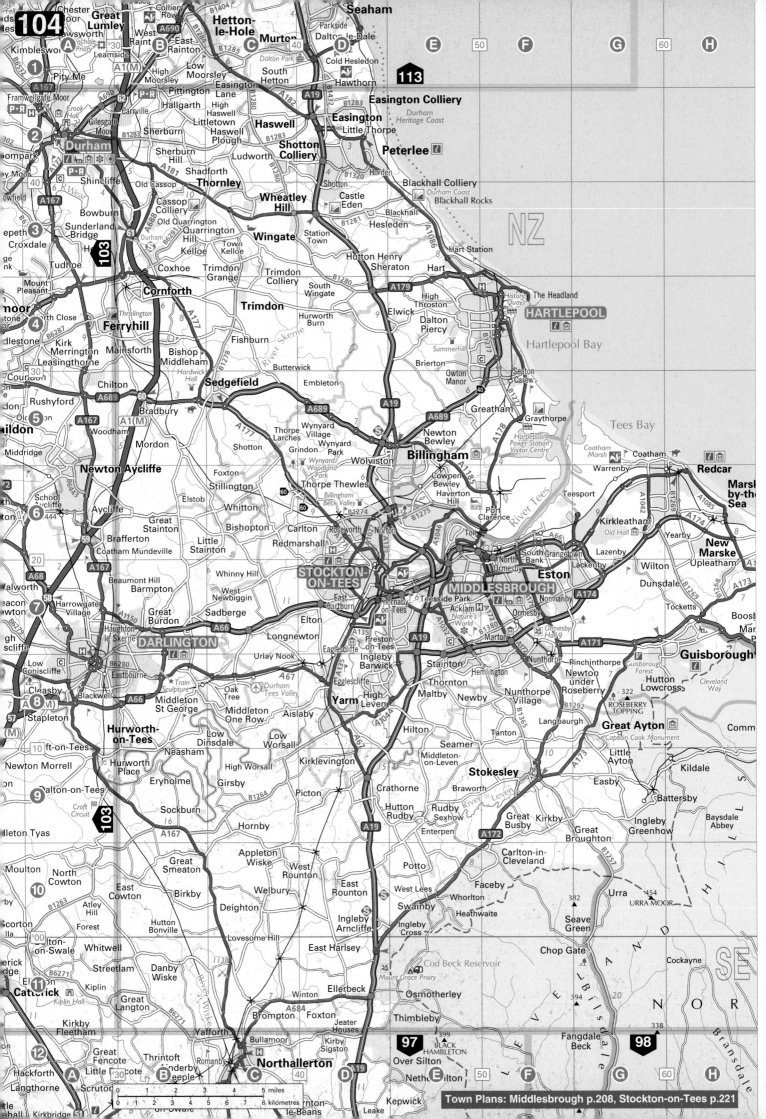

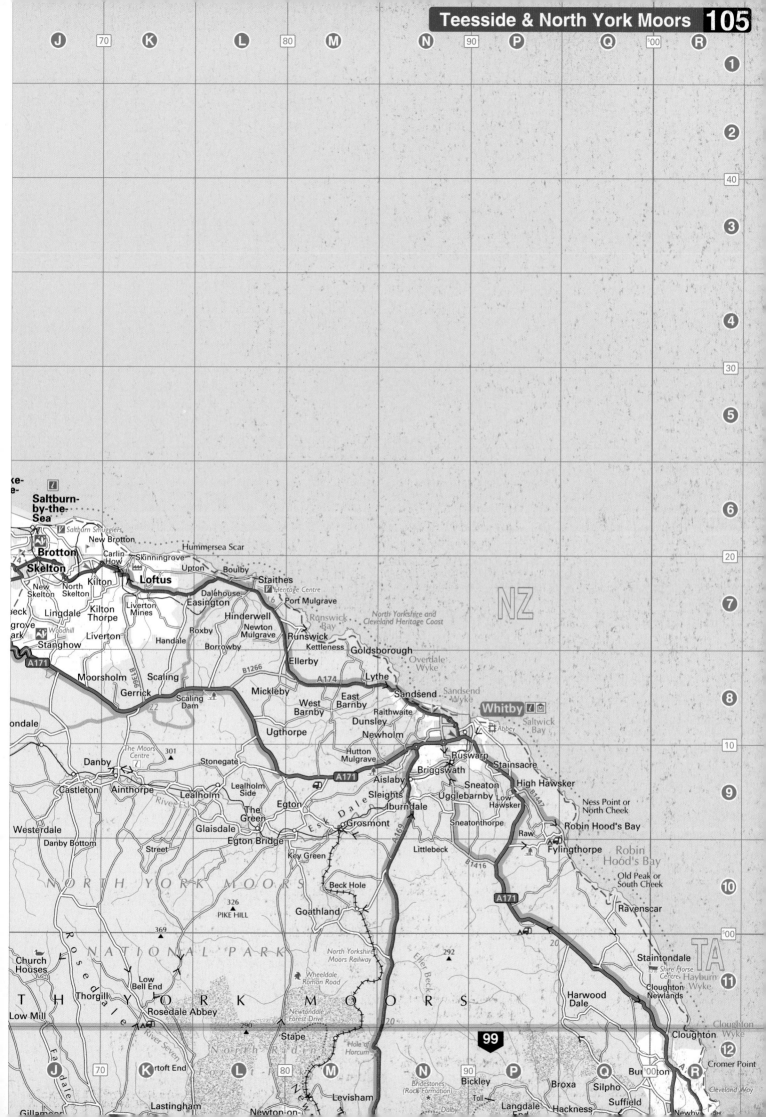

Saltburn-by-the-Sea
Saltburn Smugglers
New Brotton
Brotton
Skelton
Carlin How
New Skelton
North Skelton
Kilton
Loftus
Lingdale
Kilton Thorpe
Stanghow
Woodhill
Liverton
Moorsholm
Gerrick
Scaling
Scaling Dam
Handale
Roxby
Borrowby
Hinderwell
Newton Mulgrave
Easington
Dalehouse
Skinningrove
Upton
Boulby
Staithes
Heritage Centre
Port Mulgrave
Runswick
Kettleness
Goldsborough
Overdale Wyke
North Yorkshire and Cleveland Heritage Coast
Runswick Bay
Hummersea Scar

NZ

A171
B1366
B1266
A174
Mickleby
West Barnby
East Barnby
Raithwaite
Dunsley
Newholm
Hutton Mulgrave
Aislaby
Sleights
Iburndale
Ugthorpe
Stonegate
Lealholm Side
The Green
Egton
Grosmont
Key Green
Glaisdale
Egton Bridge
Street
Danby Bottom
Westerdale
Danby
The Moors Centre
301
Castleton
Ainthorpe
Lealholm
River Esk
Esk Dale

Lythe
Sandsend
Sandsend Wyke
Whitby
Abbey
Saltwick Bay
Ruswarp
Briggswath
Sneaton
Ugglebarnby
Low Hawsker
Sneatonthorpe
Stainsacre
High Hawsker
Ness Point or North Cheek
Robin Hood's Bay
Raw
Fylingthorpe
Robin Hood's Bay
Old Peak or South Cheek
B1447
B1416
A171
A169
Ravenscar

NORTH YORK MOORS
NATIONAL PARK
Church Houses
Low Bell End
Thorgill
Low Mill
Rosedale Abbey
Rosedale
River Seven
326
PIKE HILL
369
290
Wheeldale Roman Road
Newtondale Forest Drive
Stape
Beck Hole
Goathland
North Yorkshire Moors Railway
Eller Beck
292
Littlebeck
Harwood Dale
Staintondale
Shire Horse Centre
Hayburn Wyke
Cloughton Newlands
Cloughton
Cloughton Wyke
TA

T H E   N O R T H   Y O R K   M O O R S
T H E   Y O R K   M O O R S
N O R T H   R i d i n g

99

Fadale
Gillamoor
rtoft End
Lastingham
Newton-on-
Levisham
Bridestones (Rock Formation)
Toll
Dalby
Bickley
Langdale
Broxa
Silpho
Hackness
Suffield
Bur00ton
Cromer Point
Cleveland Way
Newby

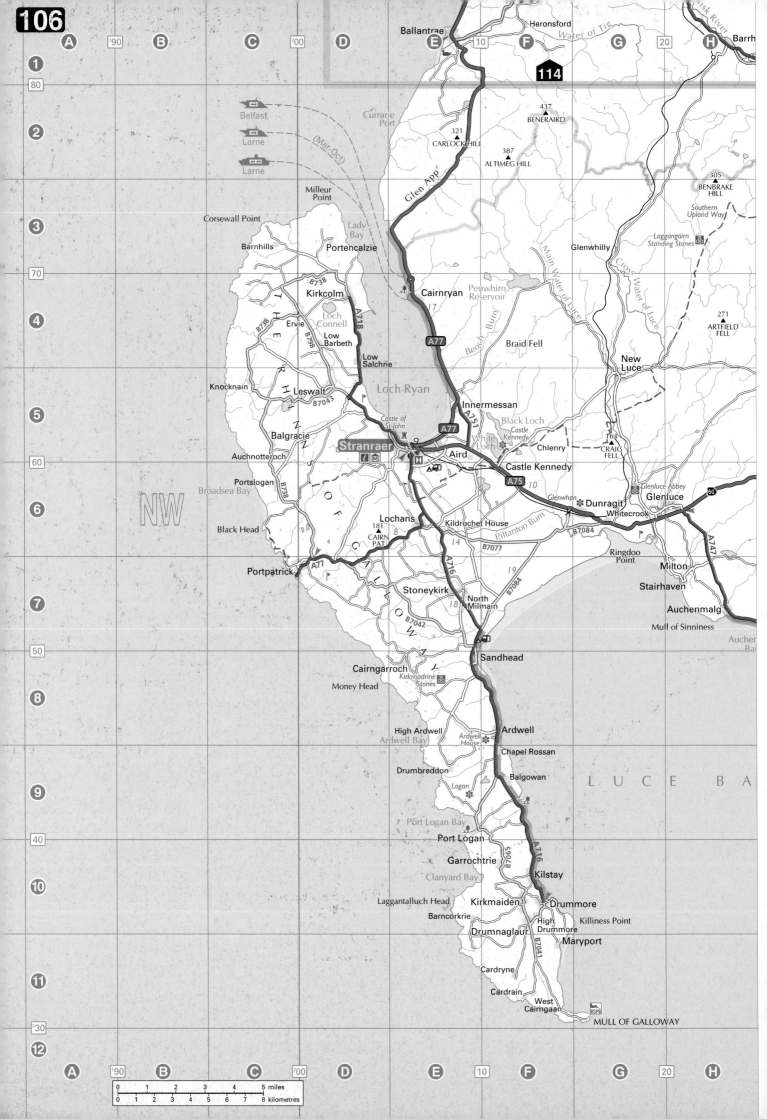

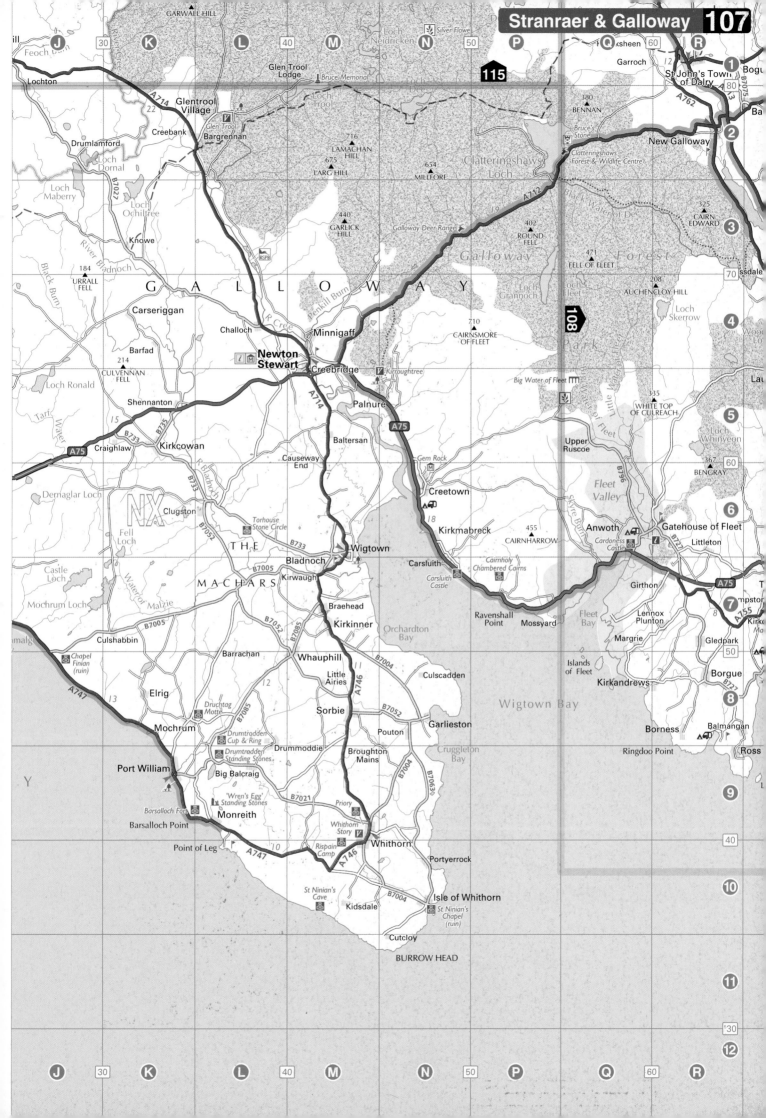

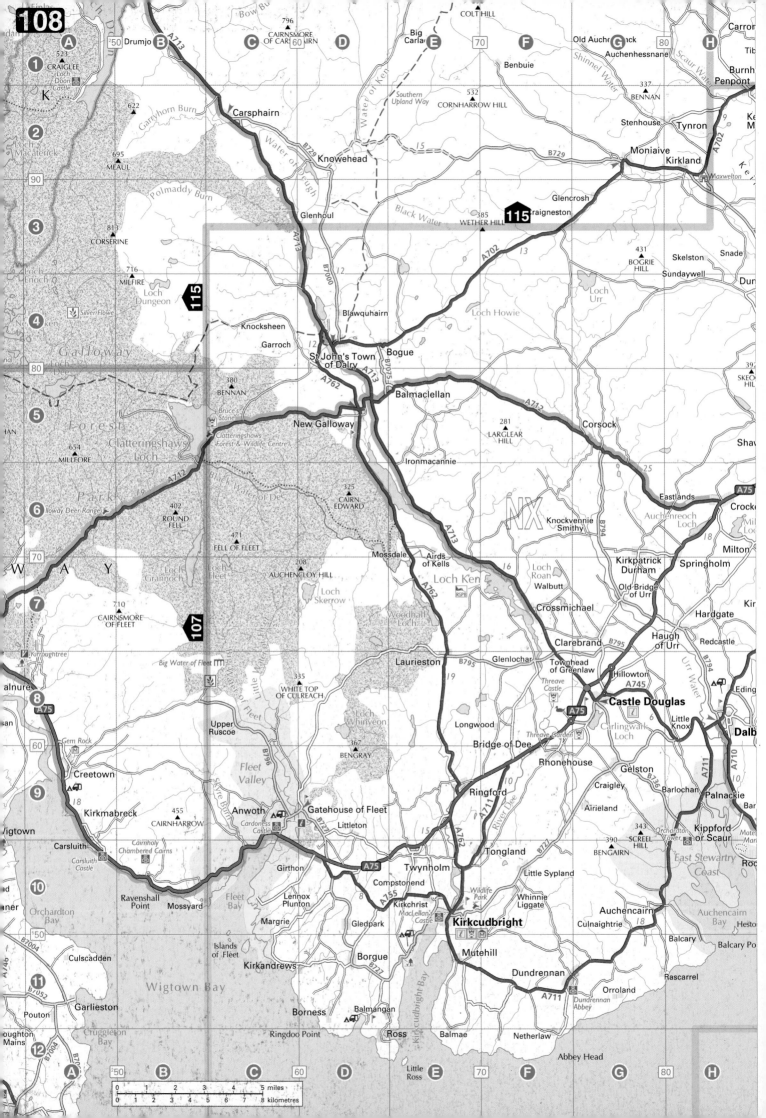

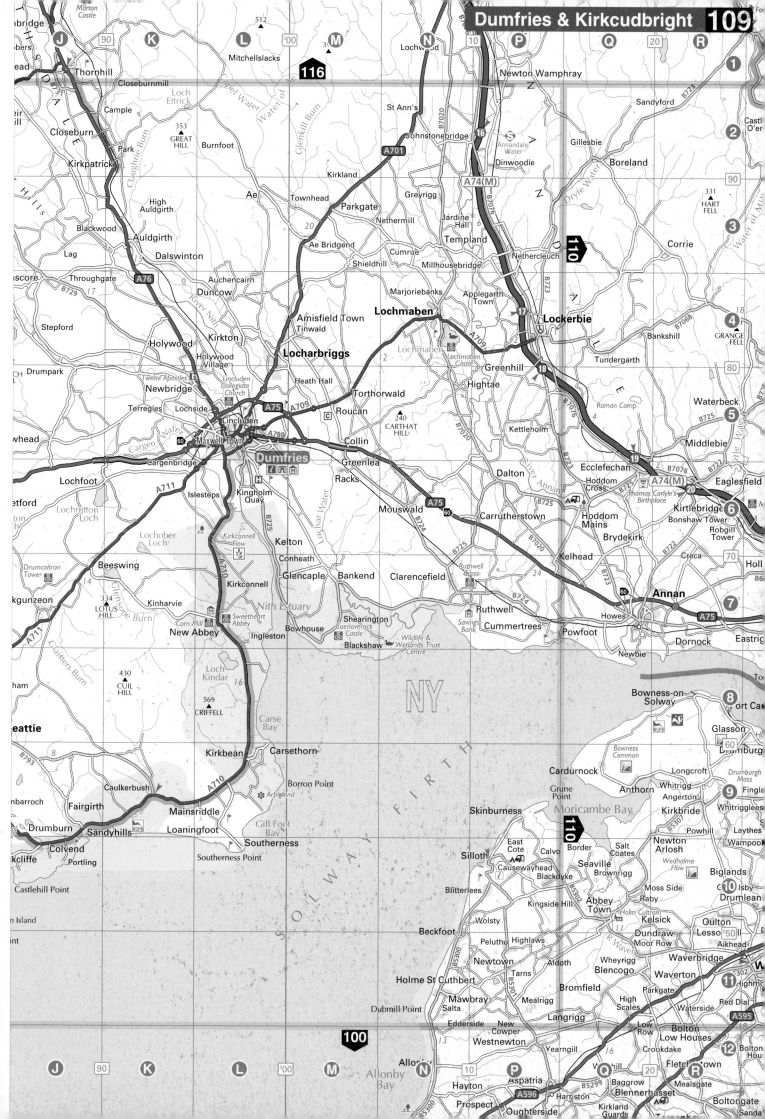

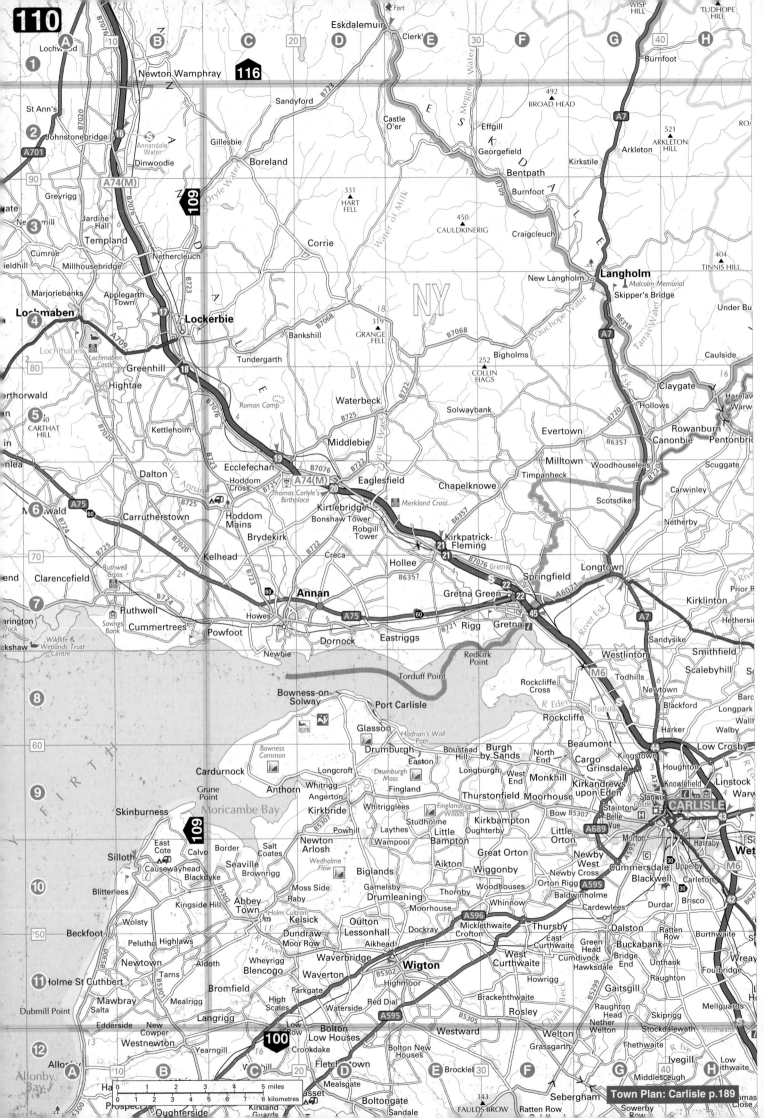

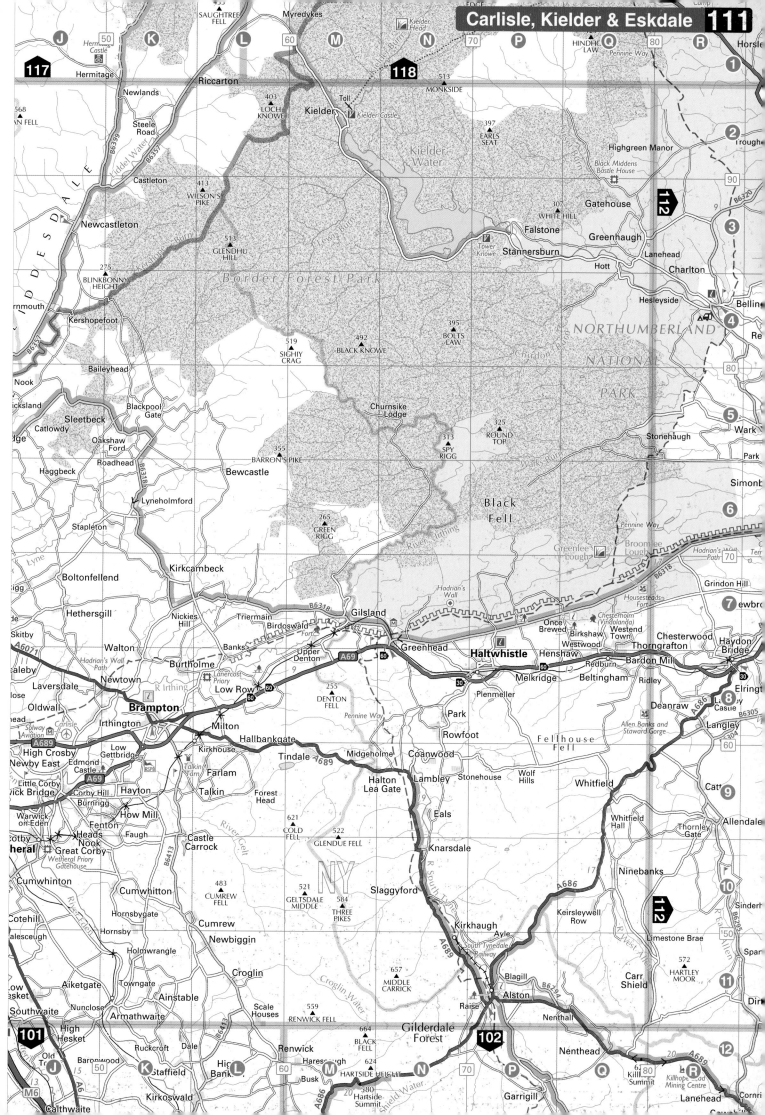

EDGE

Camp

J · K · L · M · N · P · Q · R

`117`

Saughtree Fell ▲
Myredykes

Kielder Head

`118`

1

Hindho Law

Pennine Way

Horsle

Hermitage Castle
Hermitage
Newlands
Riccarton

60

Toll

513
MONKSIDE ▲

70

80

90

2

Trough

568
N FELL

Steele Road

B6399
B6357

Castleton

403
LOCH KNOWE ▲
Kielder

Kielder Castle

397
EARLS SEAT ▲

Highgreen Manor

Black Middens Bastle House

B6320

3

413
WILSON'S PIKE ▲

307
WHITE HILL ▲

Gatehouse

Newcastleton

513
GLENDHU HILL ▲

Falstone

Greenhaugh

Lanehead

Charlton

275
BLINKBONNY HEIGHT ▲

Border Forest Park

Tower Knowe

Stannersburn

Hott

Hesleyside

Bellin

Re

rnmouth
Kershopefoot

B6357

Lewis Burn

395
BOLTS LAW ▲

Chirdon Burn

NORTHUMBERLAND

4

▲

Nook

Baileyhead

519
SIGHIY CRAG ▲

492
BLACK KNOWE ▲

NATIONAL

80

cksland

Blackpool Gate

Churnsike Lodge

325
ROUND TOP ▲

PARK

Stonehaugh

Wark

5

Sleetbeck

Catlowdy

Oakshaw Ford

Roadhead

B6318

355
BARRON'S PIKE ▲

Bewcastle

313
SPY RIGG ▲

Park

Simonb

dge

Haggbeck

Wark Burn

Lyneholmford

Stapleton

265
GREEN RIGG ▲

Black Fell

Greenlee Lough

Pennine Way

6

Broomlee Lough

Lyne

gg

Boltonfellend

Kirkcambeck

River Irthing

Hadrian's Wall

Hadrian's Path

70

Hethersgill

Nickies Hill

Triermain

B6318

Gilsland

B6318

Grindon Hill

7

ewbro

A6071

Walton

Birdoswald Fort

Greenhead

Once Brewed

Chesterholm (Vindolanda)

Birkshaw

Westend Town

Chesterwood

Thorngrafton

Haydon Bridge

Housesteads Fort

aleby

Hadrian's Wall Path

Burtholme

Banks

Upper Denton

A69

60

Haltwhistle

Henshaw

Westwood

30

30

Newtown

Lanercost Priory

Low Row

60

255
DENTON FELL ▲

Melkridge

60

Redburn

Bardon Mill

Elring

Laversdale

R Irthing

Beltingham

Ridley

8

Casue

B6305

Oldwall

Brampton

Milton

Pennine Way

Park

Plenmeller

Deanraw

A686

Langley

head
Solway Aviation

Carlisle

Irthington

Hallbankgate

Rowfoot

Fellhouse Fell

Allen Banks and Staward Gorge

60

L304

High Crosby
Newby East

Low Gettbridge

Kirkhouse

Tindale

A689

Midgeholme

Coanwood

Whitfield

9

Catt

Edmond Castle

A69

RSPB

Talkin Tarn

Farlam

Halton Lea Gate

Lambley

Stonehouse

Wolf Hills

Little Corby
ick Bridge

Corby Hill

Hayton

Talkin

Forest Head

Eals

Whitfield Hall

Thornley Gate

Allendale

Burnrigg

How Mill

621
COLD FELL ▲

Knarsdale

Ninebanks

heral

Heads Nook

Fenton

Faugh

Castle Carrock

522
GLENDUE FELL ▲

R South Tyne

A686

17

Great Corby
Wetheral Priory Gatehouse

NY

Whitfield Row

10

Cumwhinton

Cumwhitton

483
CUMREW FELL ▲

521
GELTSDALE MIDDLE ▲

584
THREE PIKES ▲

Slaggyford

Keirsleywell Row

`112`

Hornsbygate

Cumrew

Kirkhaugh

Ayle

Limestone Brae

Spar

Cotehill

Hornsby

Newbiggin

657
MIDDLE CARRICK ▲

South Tynedale Railway

Blagill

572
HARTLEY MOOR ▲

11

alesceugh

Holmwrangle

Croglin

Carr Shield

Sinder

ow
esket

Aiketgate

Towngate

Ainstable

Scale Houses

559
RENWICK FELL ▲

Croglin Water

Raise

Nenthall

Dir

Southwaite

Nunclose

`101`

High Hesket

J

Baronwood

50

Ruckcroft

K

Staffield

Kirkoswald

Dale

Hig Bank

L

60

Renwick

664
BLACK FELL ▲

Haresceugh

624

Busk

M

HARTSIDE HEIGHT

580
Hartside Summit

20

A686

Gilderdale Forest

Alston

B6294

`102`

Nenthead

Nenthead

Garrigill

N

70

Shield Water

P

Killhope Lead Mining Centre

81

A689

Lanehe

12

Kill Summit

Q

`112`

R

Corn ri

Cawfi

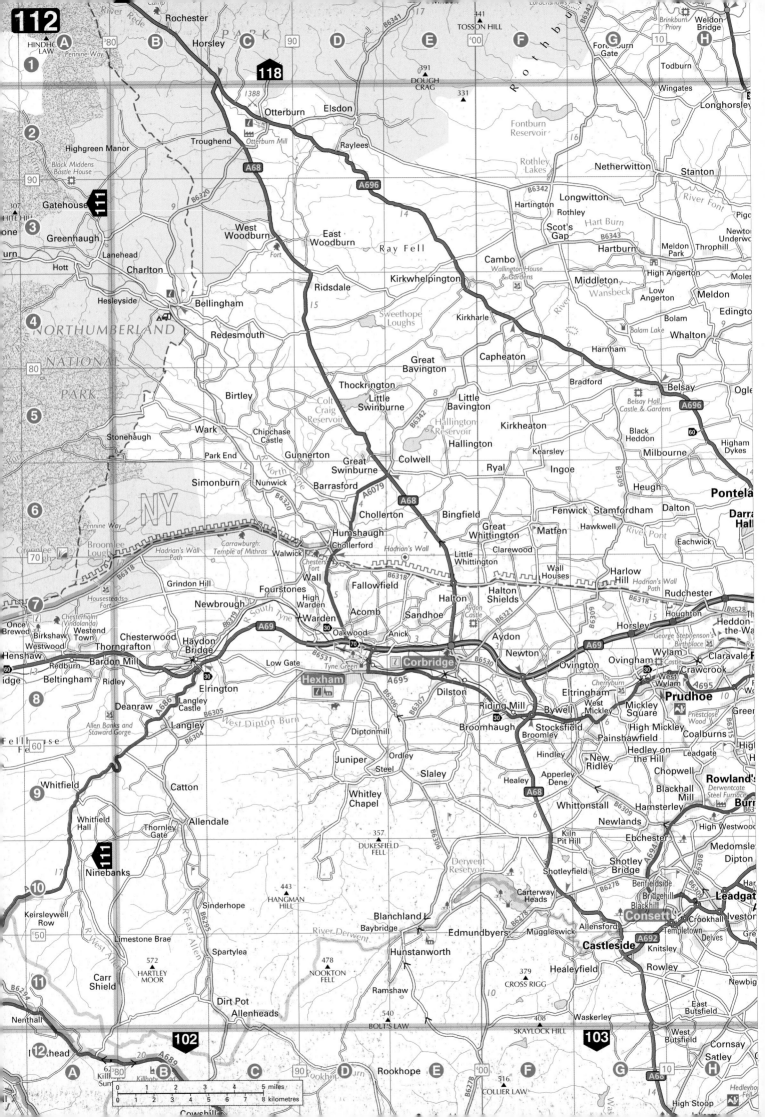

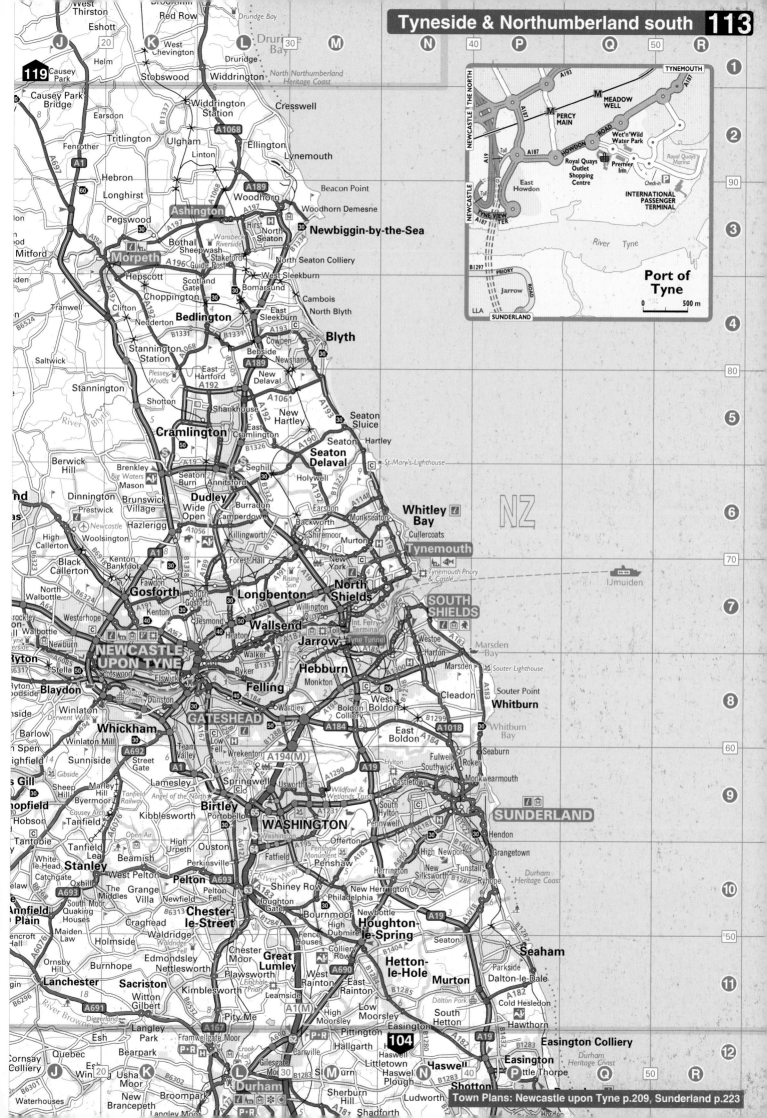

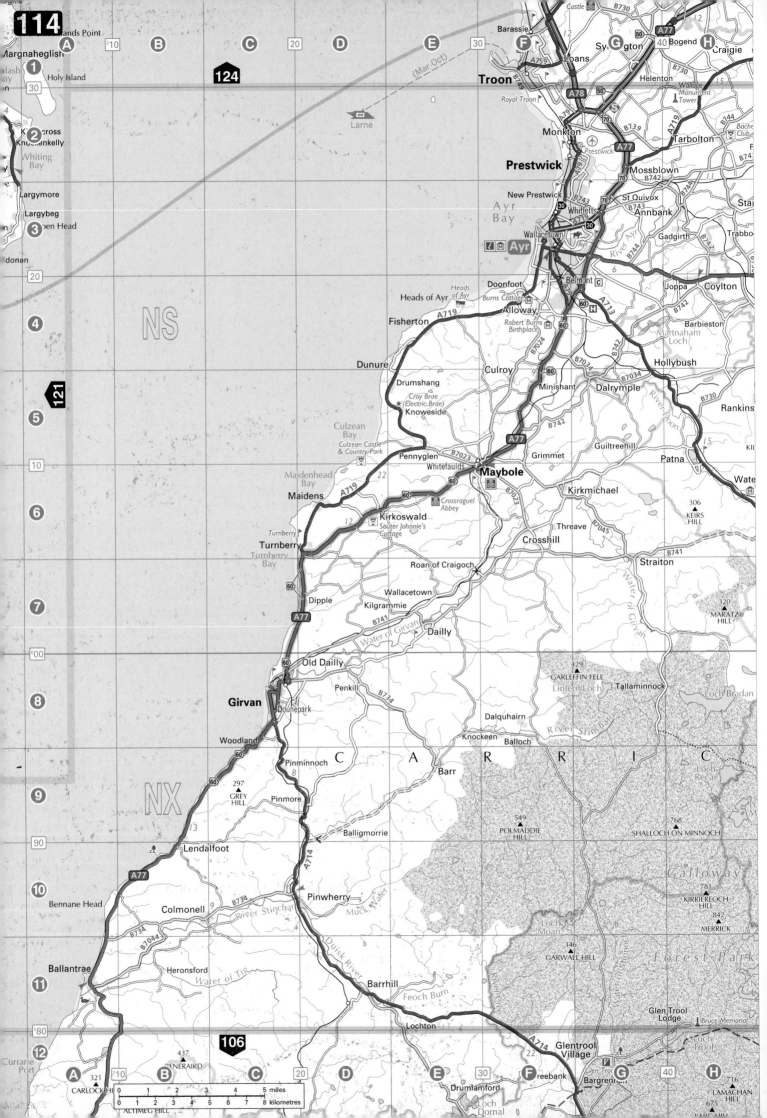

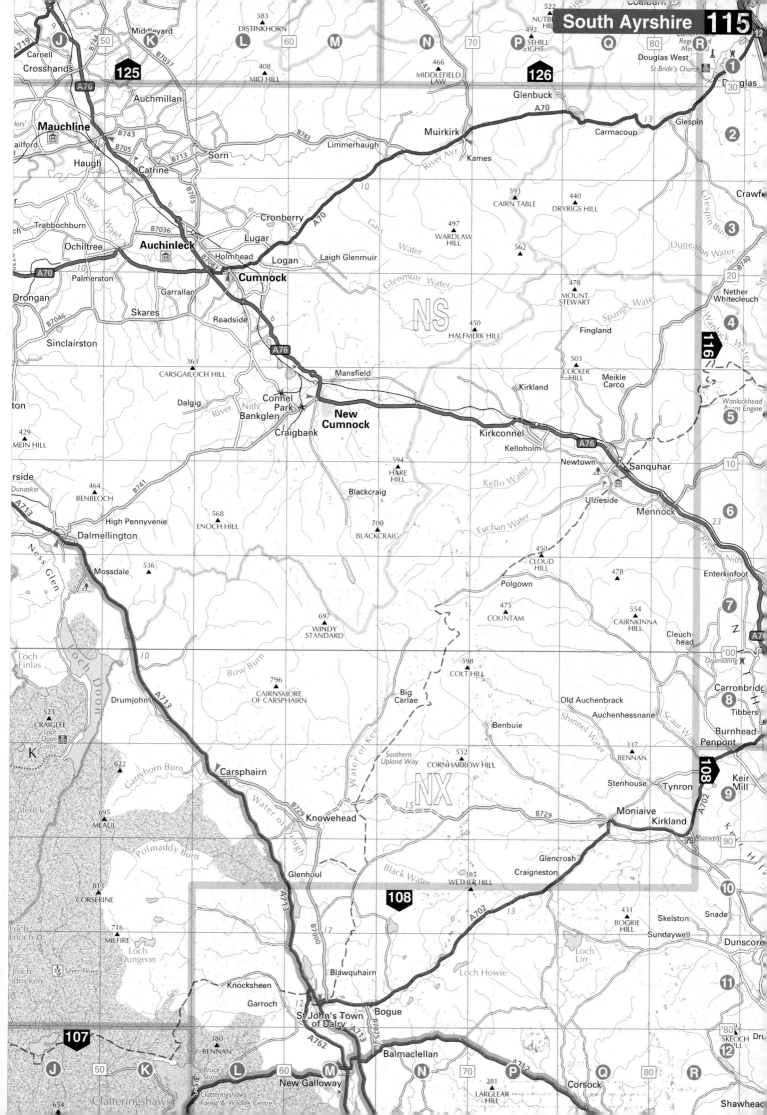

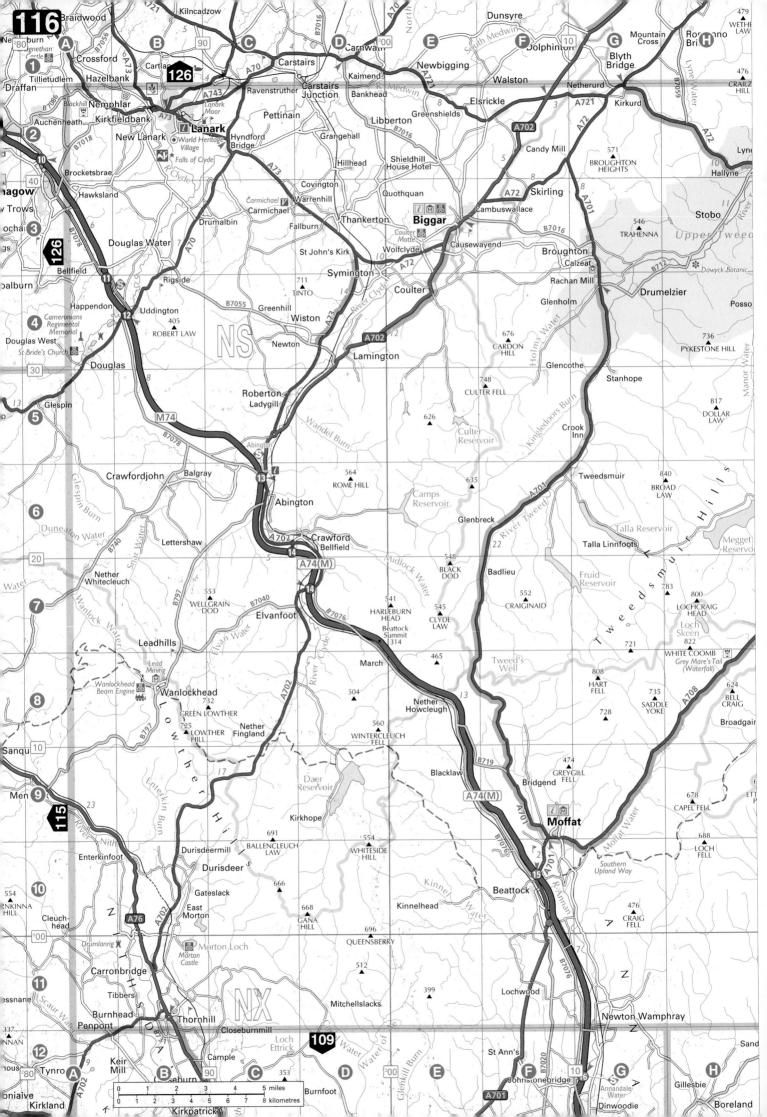

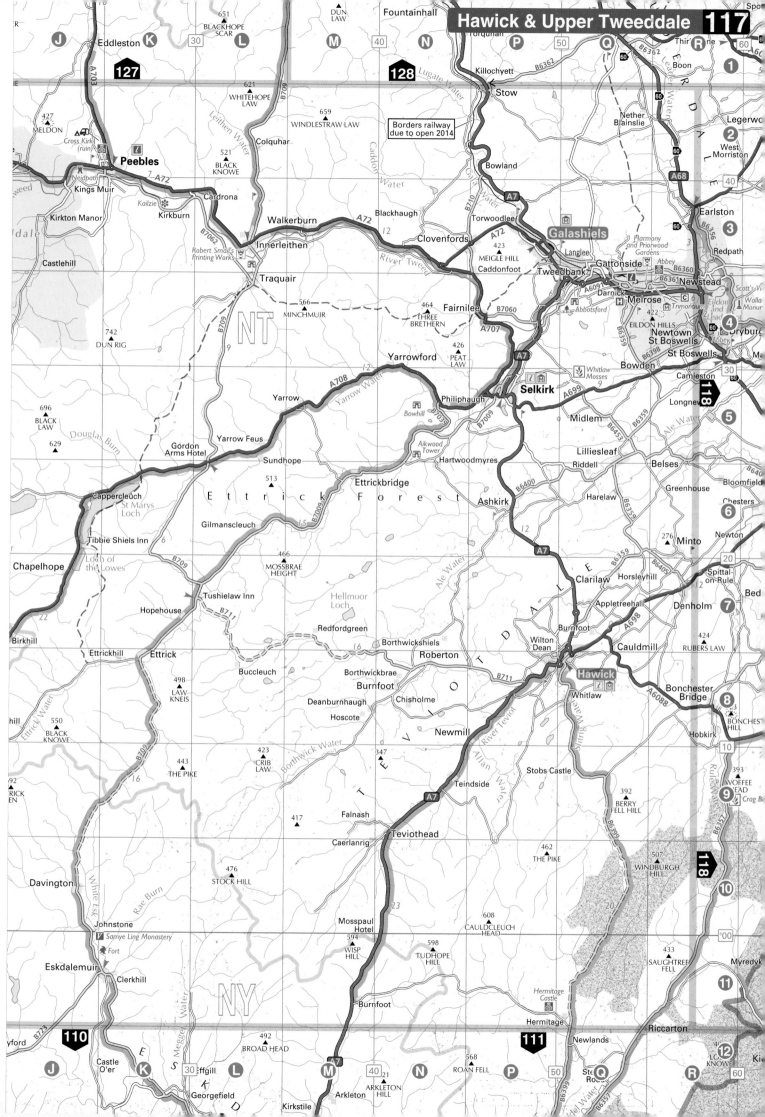

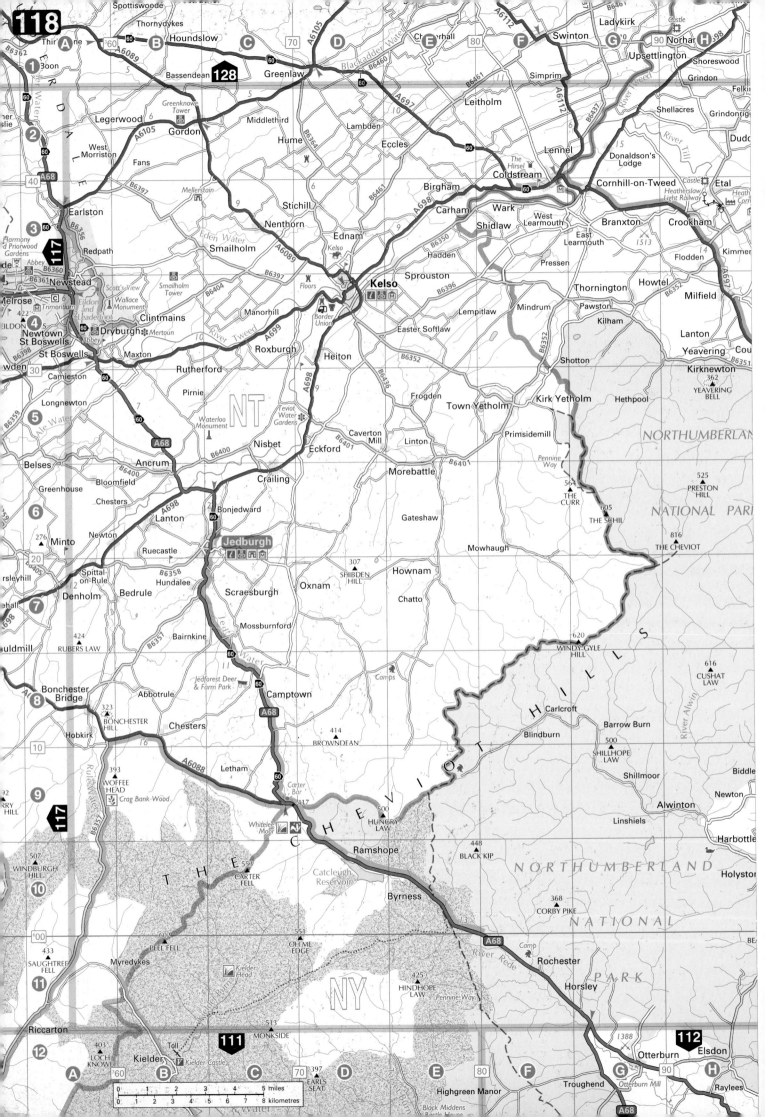

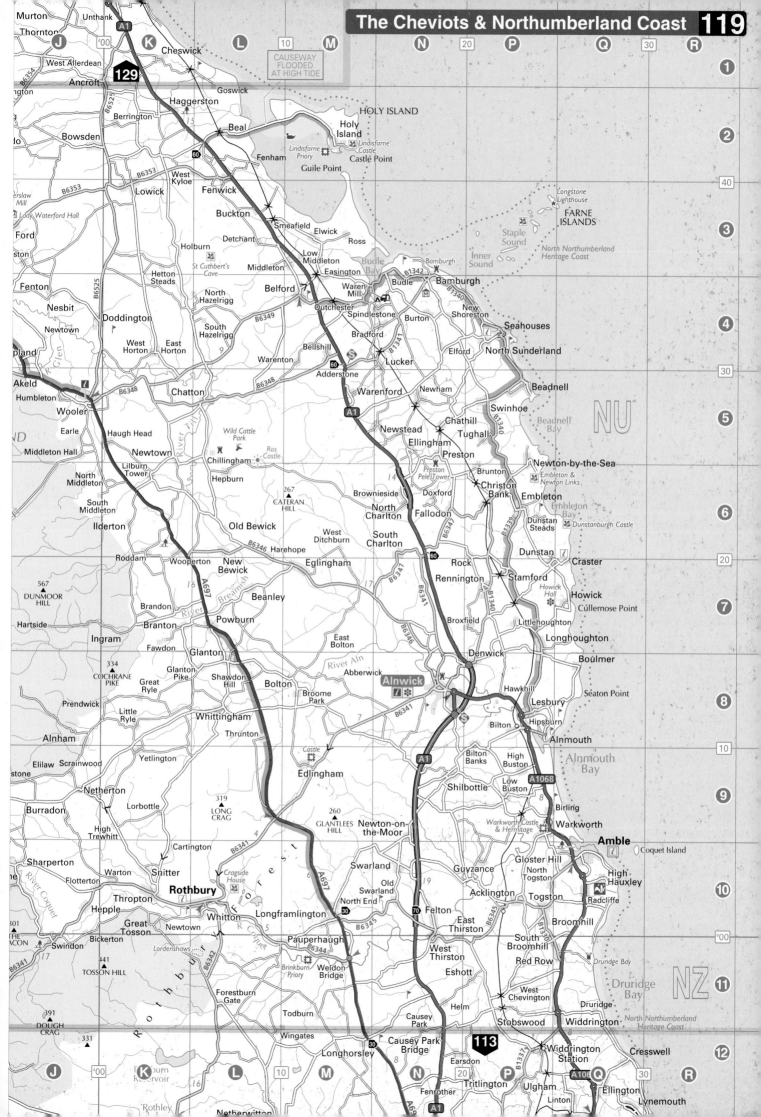

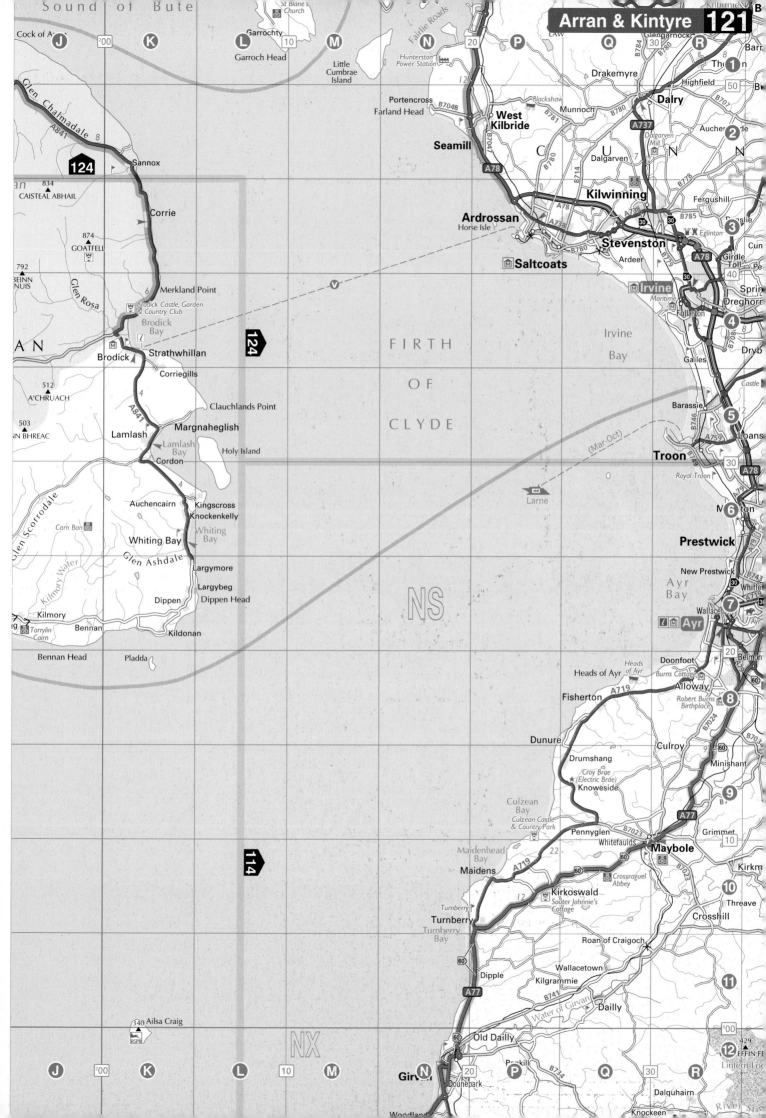

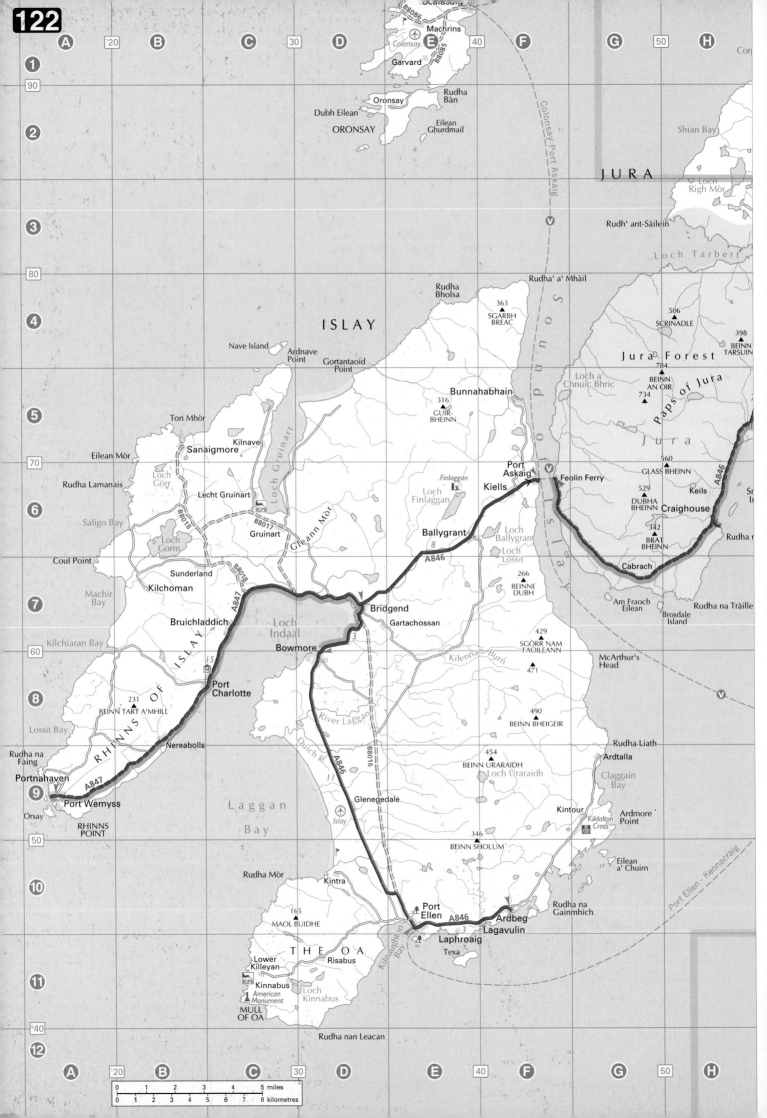

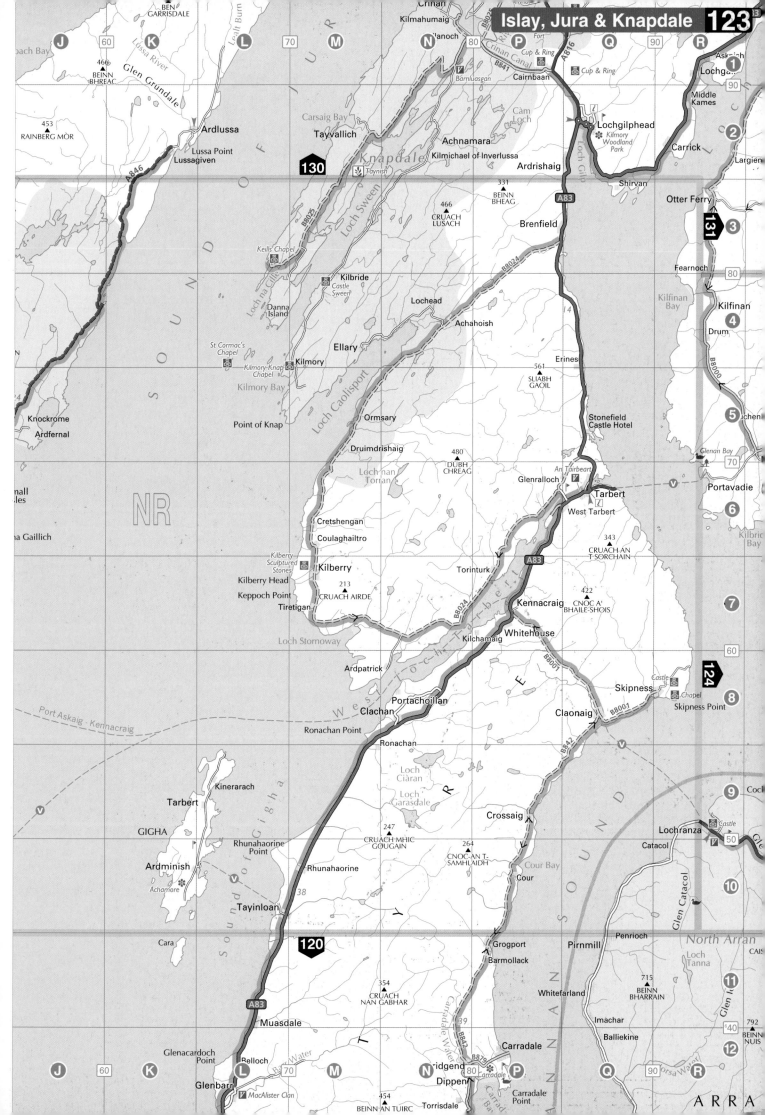

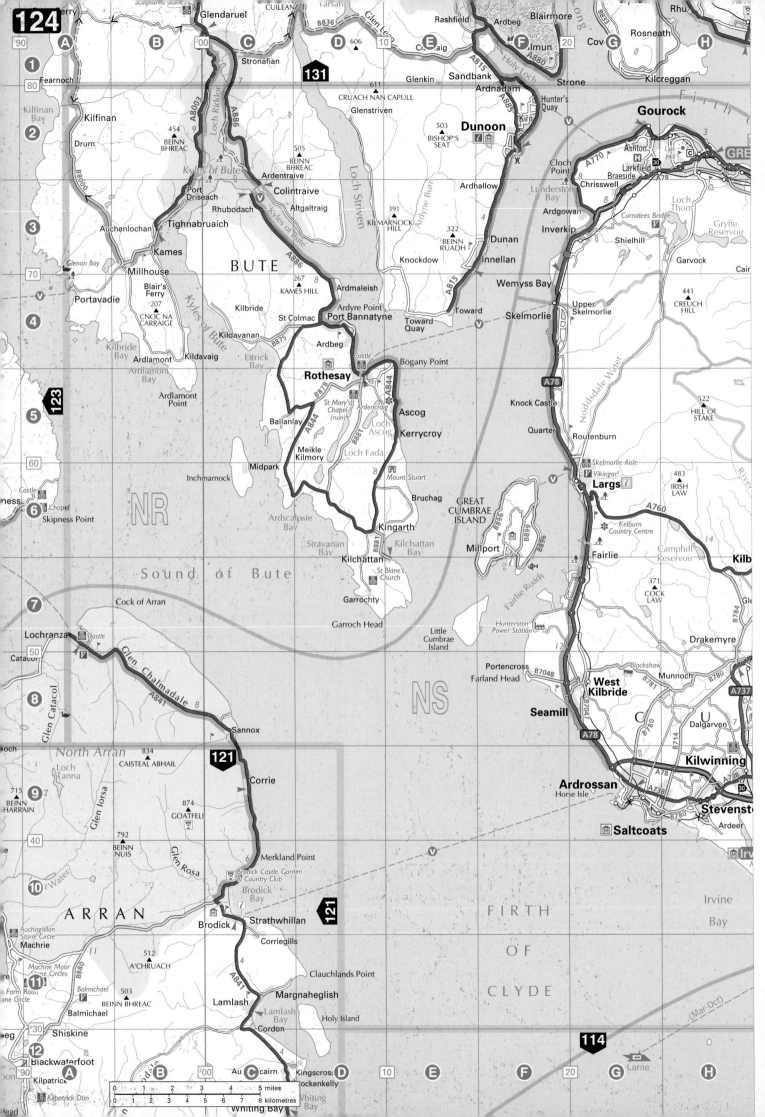

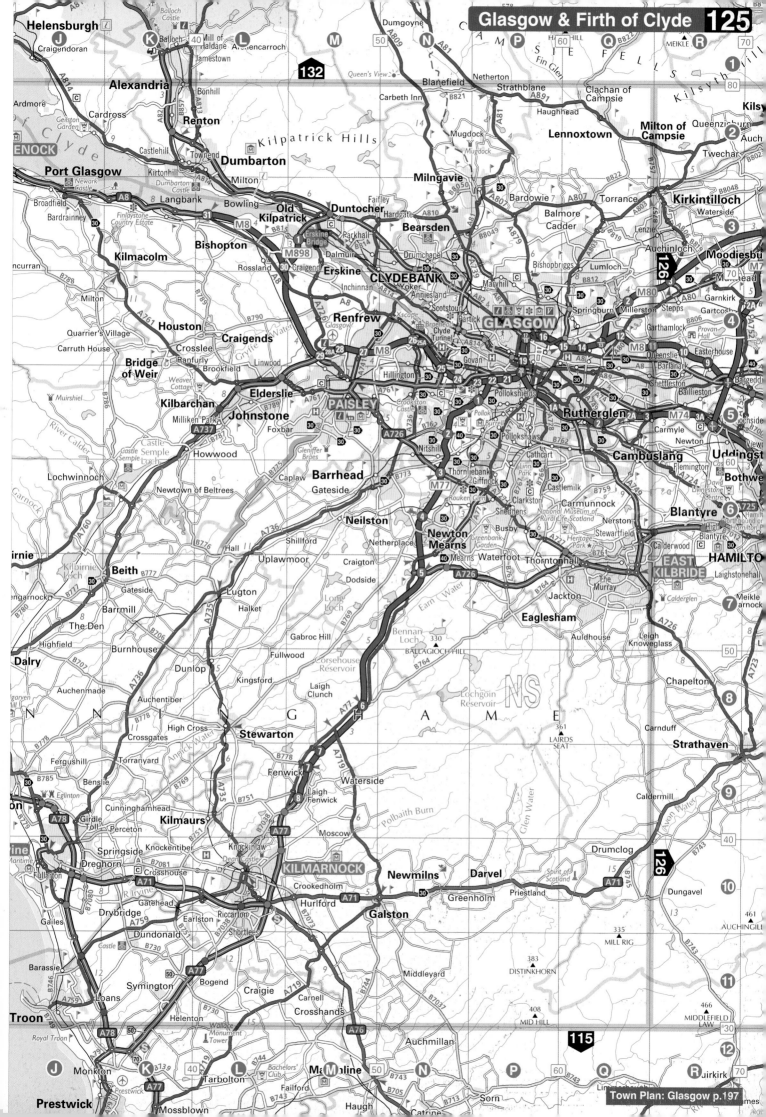

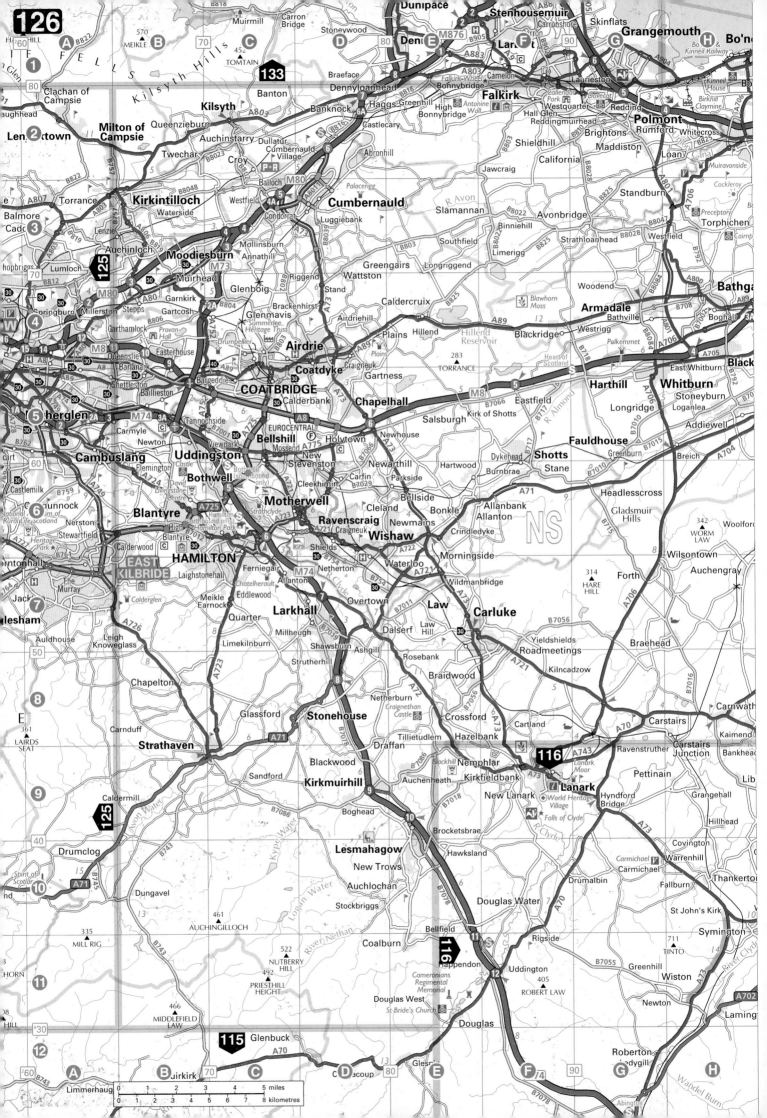

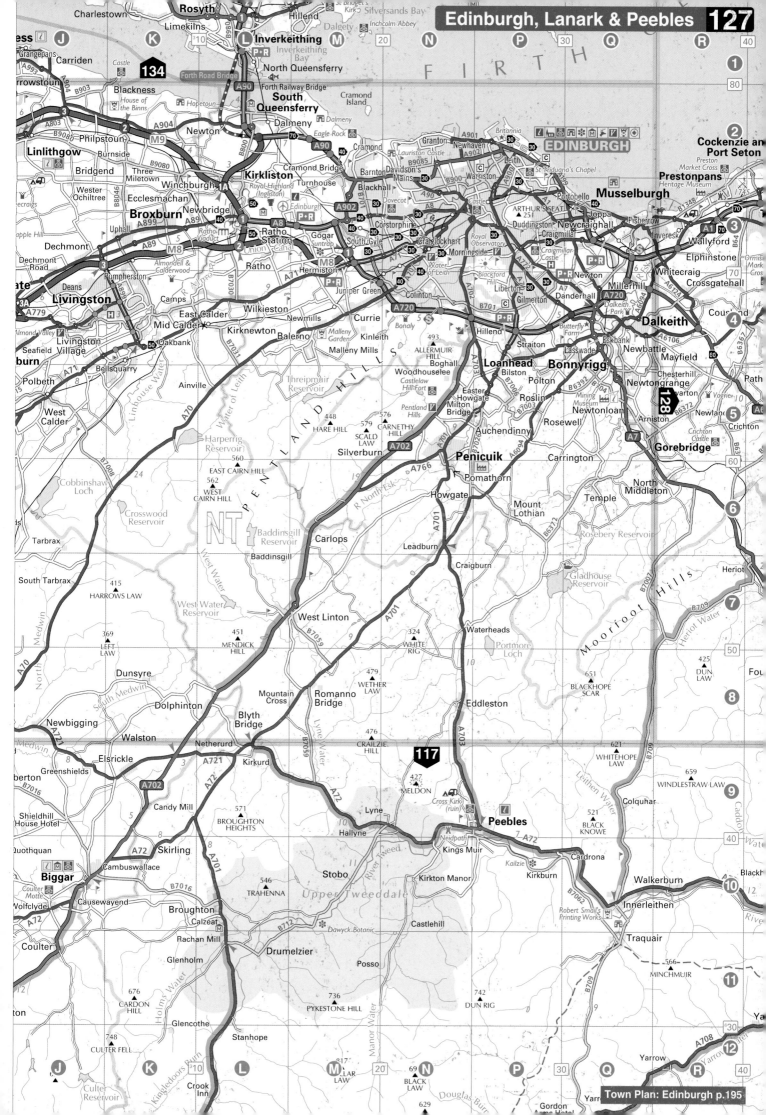

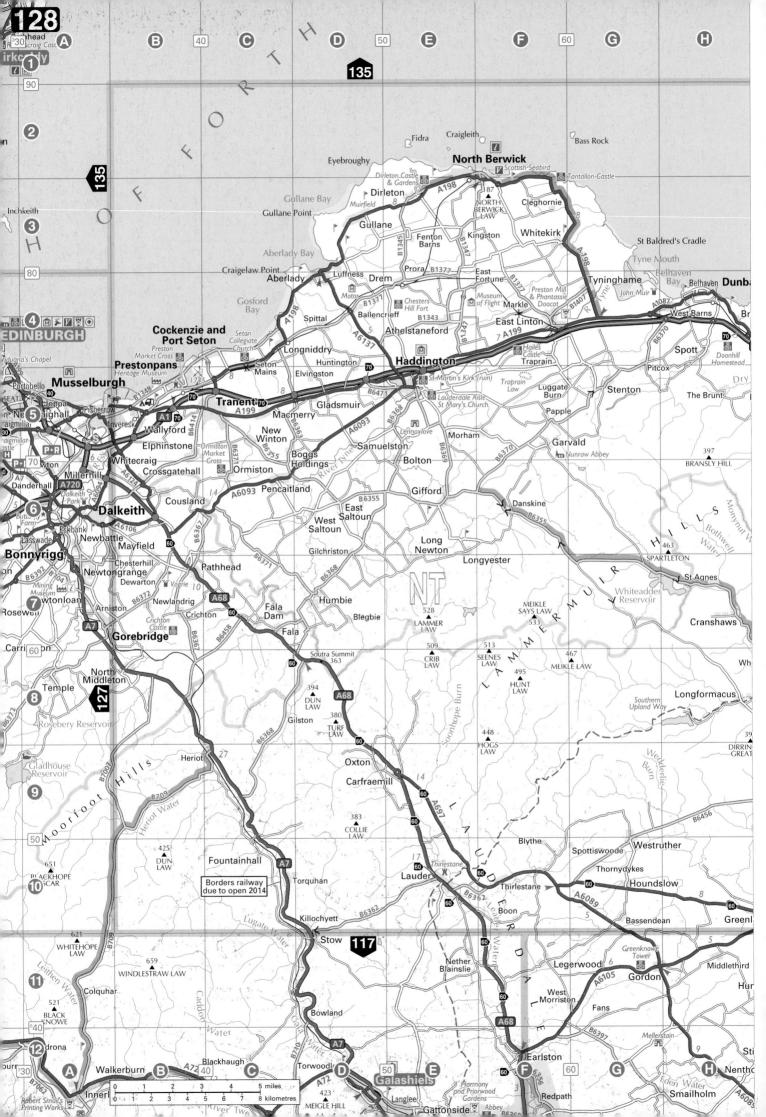

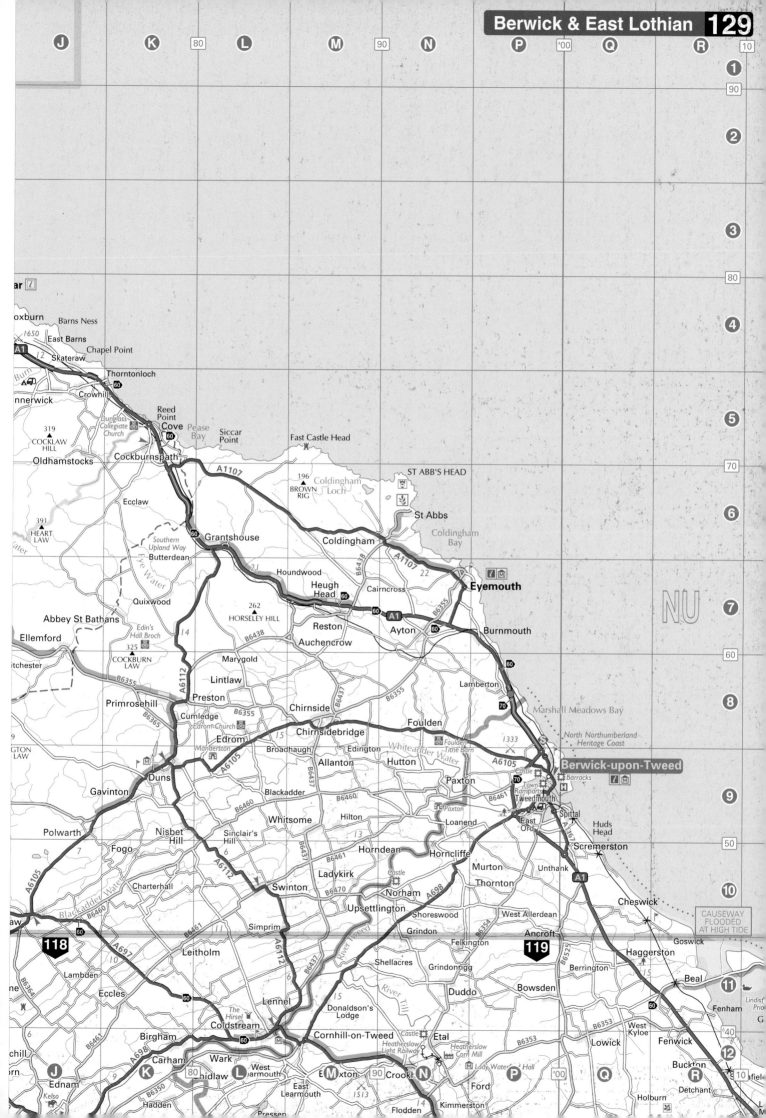

J K 80 L M 90 N P 400 Q R 10

1
90
2
3
80
4
5
70
6
7 NU
60
8
9
50
10

ar

oxburn Barns Ness
1650
A1
East Barns
Skateraw Chapel Point
Thorntonloch
60
nnerwick Crowhill
Dunglass Reed
Collegiate Point Cove Pease Siccar
319 Church 60 Bay Point Fast Castle Head
COCKLAW Cockburnspath
HILL
Oldhamstocks A1107 ST ABB'S HEAD
196
391 BROWN Coldingham
HEART RIG Loch St Abbs
LAW 60 Grantshouse
Ecclaw Coldingham Coldingham
ater Southern Houndwood A1107 22 Bay
Upland Way Butterdean 21
Eye Heugh B6438 Eyemouth
Quixwood 262 Head Cairncross 60
Abbey St Bathans HORSELEY HILL 60 A1 Ayton Burnmouth
Edin's Reston 60
Ellemford Hall Broch 325 Auchencrow 60
itchester COCKBURN B6438 Lamberton
LAW Marygold B6355
B6355 Lintlaw 70
GTON A6112 Preston B6437 Marshall Meadows Bay
LAW Primrosehill Chirnside North Northumberland
Cumledge B6355 Foulden Heritage Coast
Edrom 15 Chirnsidebridge 1333 Berwick-upon-Tweed
Manderston Broadhaugh Edington Foulden Castle
Edom Church A6105 Allanton Hutton Tithe Barn A6105 70 Barracks
M Whiteadder Water Town
9 Duns Blackadder Paxton Ramparts Tweedmouth
Gavinton B6460 Hilton B6460 Paxton Spittal
Polwarth Whitsome Loanend East Huds
Fogo Nisbet Sinclair's 13 Ord Head
7 Hill Hill Horndean Scremerston
Charterhall 6 Horncliffe A167
A6112 Ladykirk Murton Unthank A1 Cheswick
118 Swinton B6470 Norham A698 Thornton
60 B6461 11 Upsettlington West Allerdean Goswick
Leitholm Simprim Shoreswood Ancroft CAUSEWAY
10 Grindon 119 Haggerston FLOODED
Lambden B6461 Felkington Berrington AT HIGH TIDE
Eccles 60 Shellacres Grindonrigg Beal
B636 Lennel 15 Duddo Bowsden 15
The Hirsel Donaldson's River Till 60 West Fenham
Birgham Coldstream Lodge Kyloe Fenwick
chill 60 Cornhill-on-Tweed Castle B6353 Lowick Buckton
Carham Etal Heatherslaw West 12
Ednam Wark West Heatherslaw Corn Mill Ford Allerdean 10
Hadden Learmouth Light Railway Lady Holburn Detchant
East xton 90 Crook Water Q
Learmouth N Ford P
J K 80 L M Kimmerston
Pressen Flodden 14

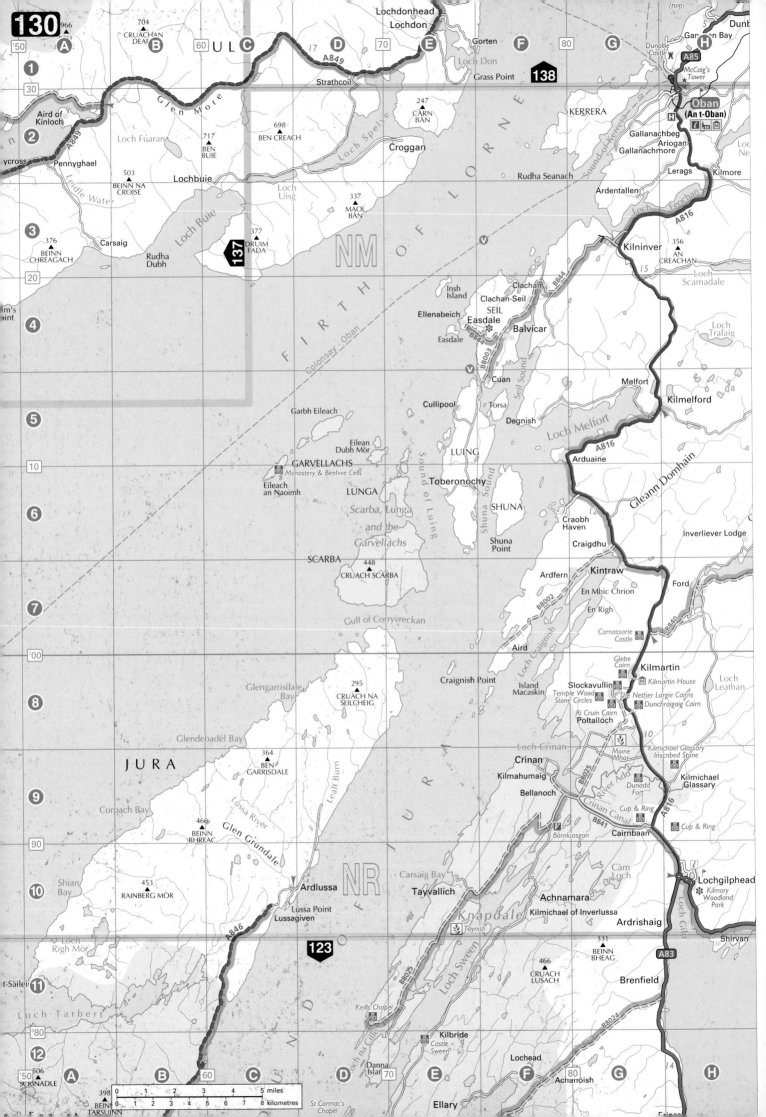

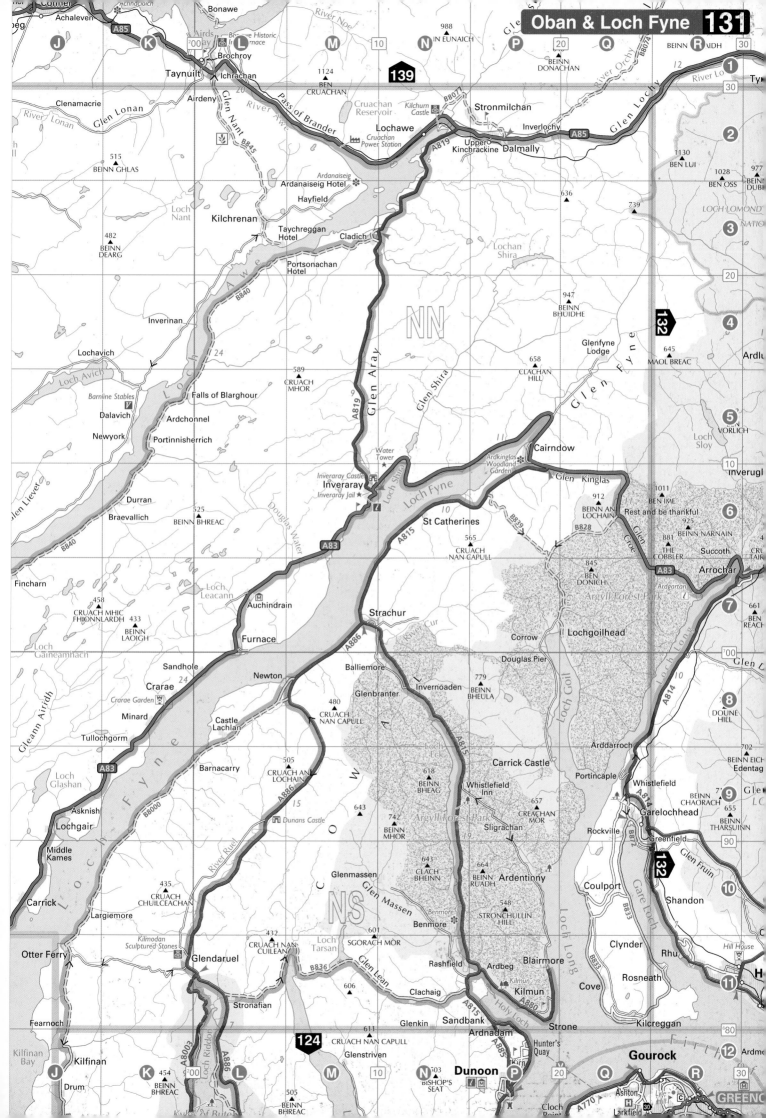

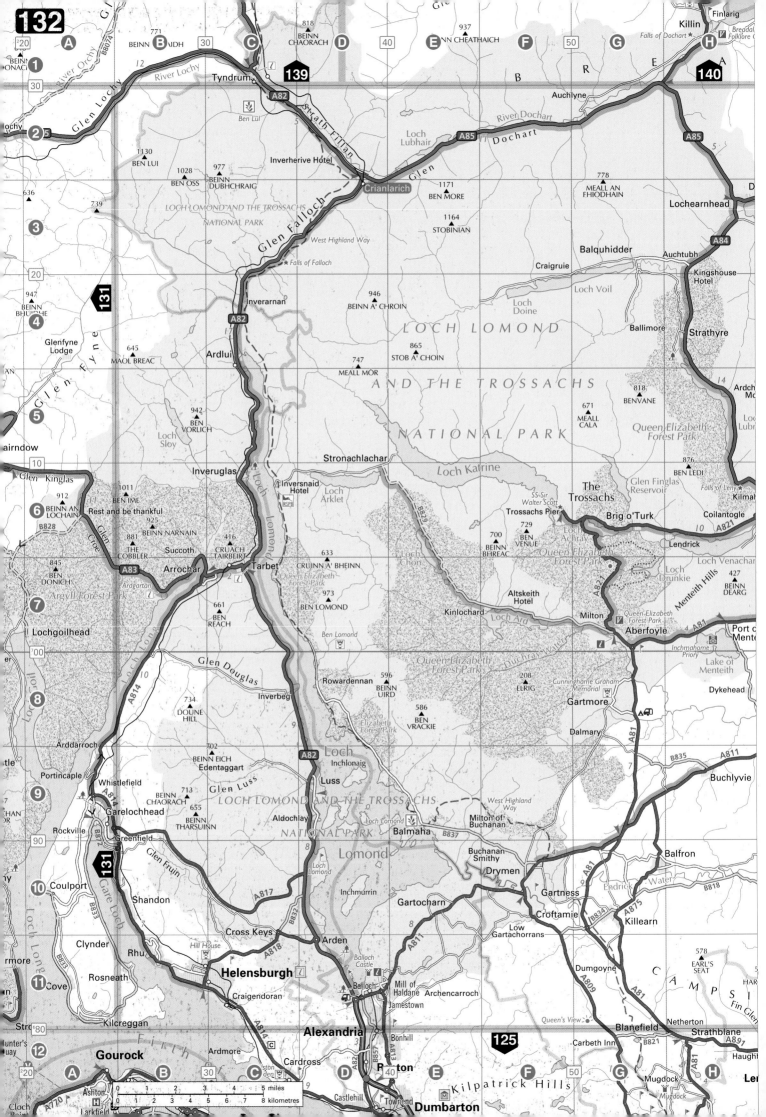

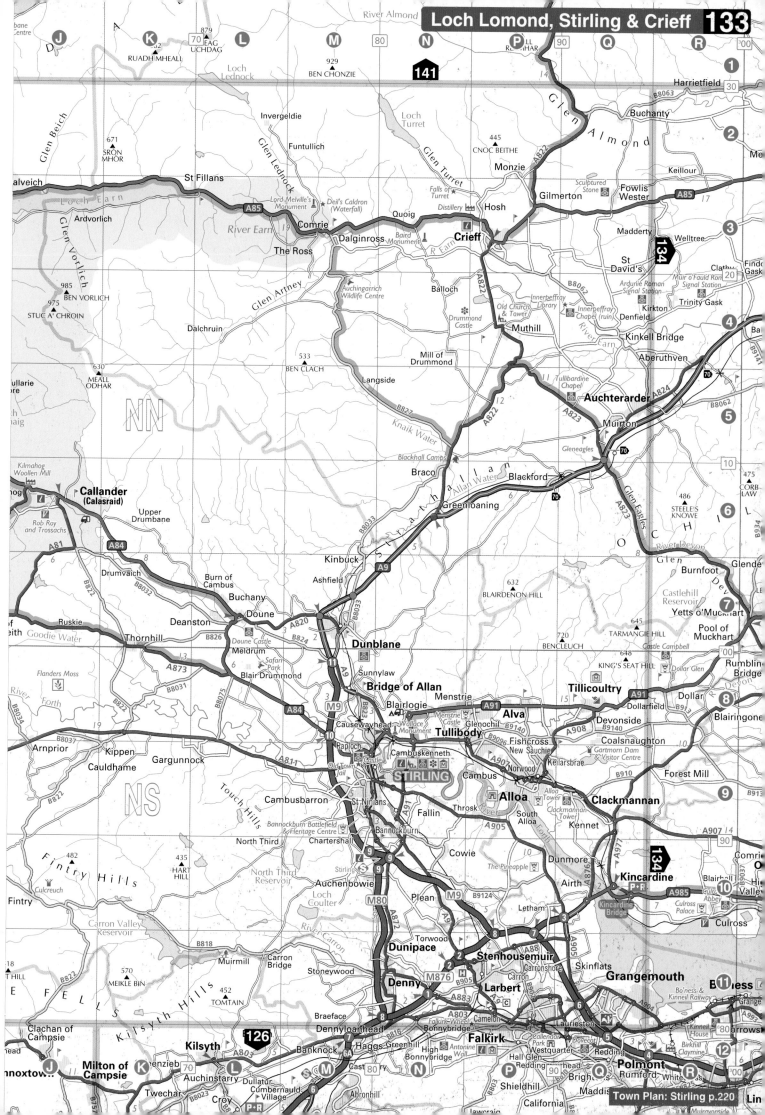

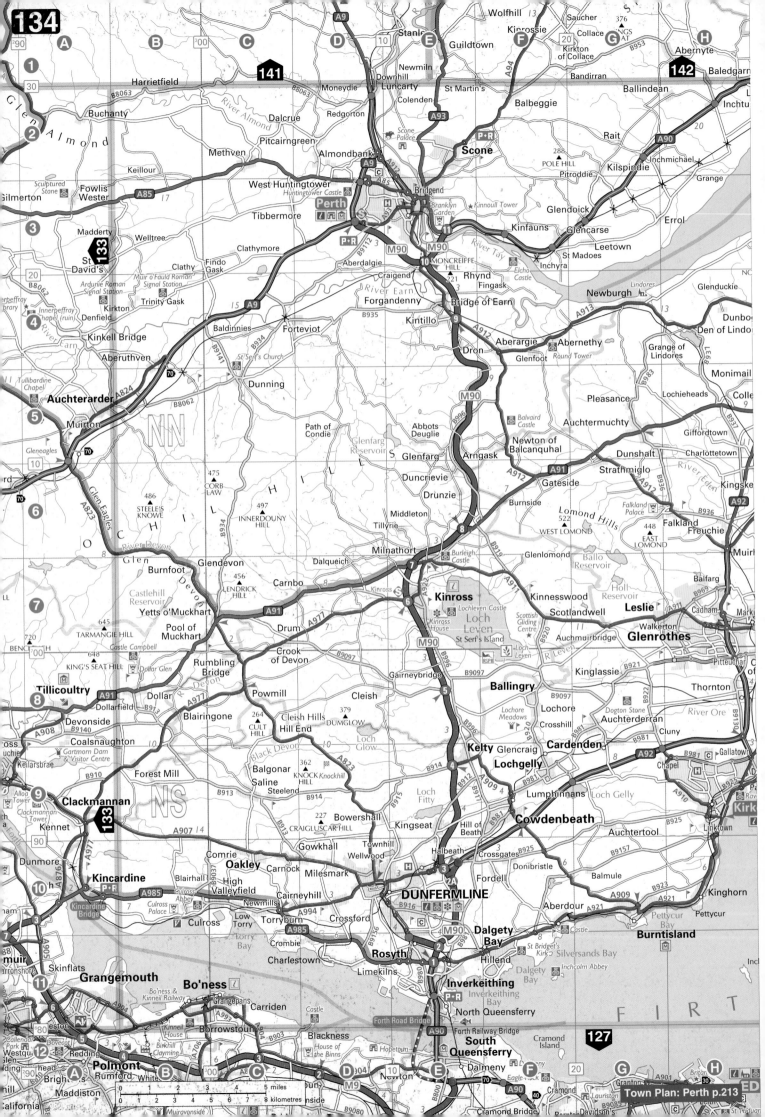

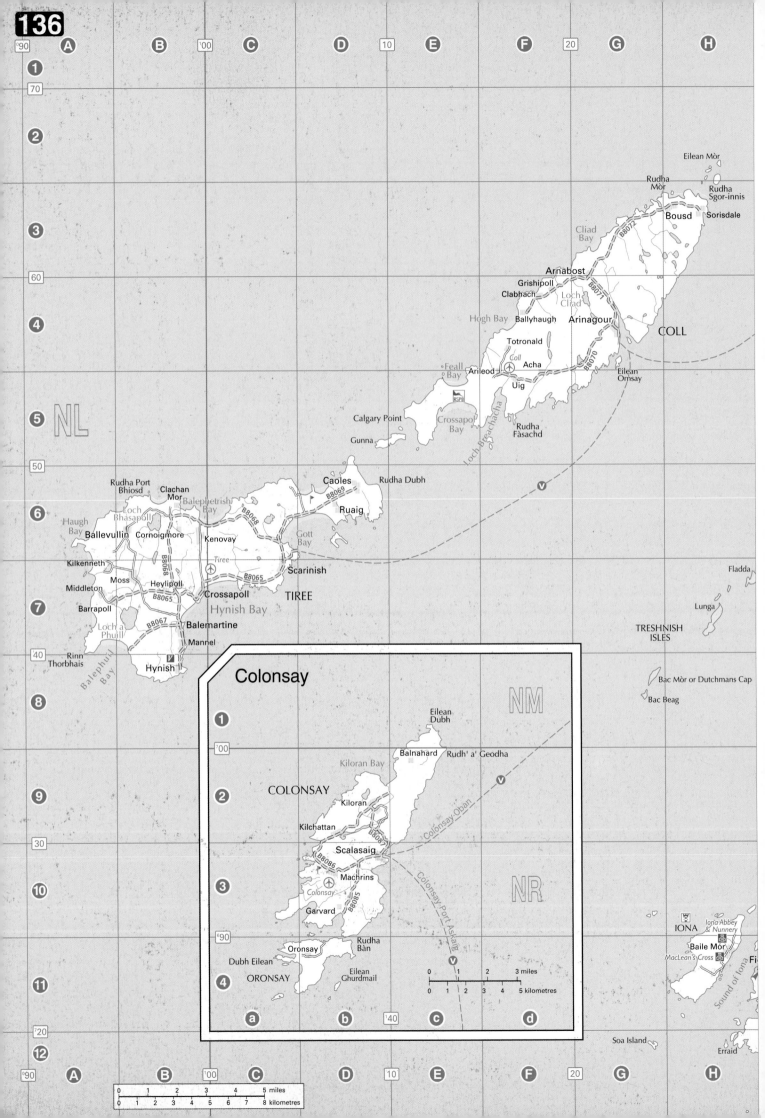

NL

NM

NR

Colonsay

COLL

TIREE

TRESHNISH
ISLES

COLONSAY

ORONSAY

IONA

Eilean Mòr
Rudha
Mòr
Rudha
Sgor-innis
Bousd   Sorisdale
B8072
Cliad
Bay
Arnabost
Grishipoll
Clabhach   Loch
Cliad
Hogh Bay   Ballyhaugh   Arinagour
Totronald
B8071
Coll   Acha
Feall
Bay   Arileod
RSPB   Uig   Eilean
Ornsay
B8070
Calgary Point
Crossapol
Bay
Gunna   Rudha
Fàsachd
Loch Breachacha
V

Rudha Port
Bhiosd   Clachan
Mor
Balephetrish
Bay
Caoles
B8069
Rudha Dubh
Loch
Bhasapoll   Ruaig
Haugh   Ballevullin   Cornoigmore   Kenovay
Bay
Gott
Bay
Kilkenneth   Tiree
B8068
B8068
Moss   Heylipoll
Middleton   B8065   Scarinish
Crossapoll
B8065
Barrapoll   TIREE
Hynish Bay
B8067   Balemartine
Mannel
Rinn   B8067
Thorbhais
V
Balephuil Bay
Hynish

Fladda

Lunga

Bac Mòr or Dutchmans Cap
Bac Beag

Colonsay

Eilean
Dubh
Balnahard   Rudh' a' Geodha
Kiloran Bay
COLONSAY
Kiloran
B8087
Kilchattan
Colonsay-Oban
V
B8086   Scalasaig
Machrins
Colonsay
B8085
Garvard
Oronsay
Rudha
Bàn
Dubh Eilean
Eilean
ORONSAY   Ghurdmail

Colonsay-Port Askaig
V

IONA
Iona Abbey
& Nunnery
Baile Mòr
MacLean's Cross
Sound of Iona
Fi

Soa Island
Erraid

0   1   2   3 miles
0   1   2   3   4   5 kilometres

0   1   2   3   4   5 miles
0   1   2   3   4   5   6   7   8 kilometres

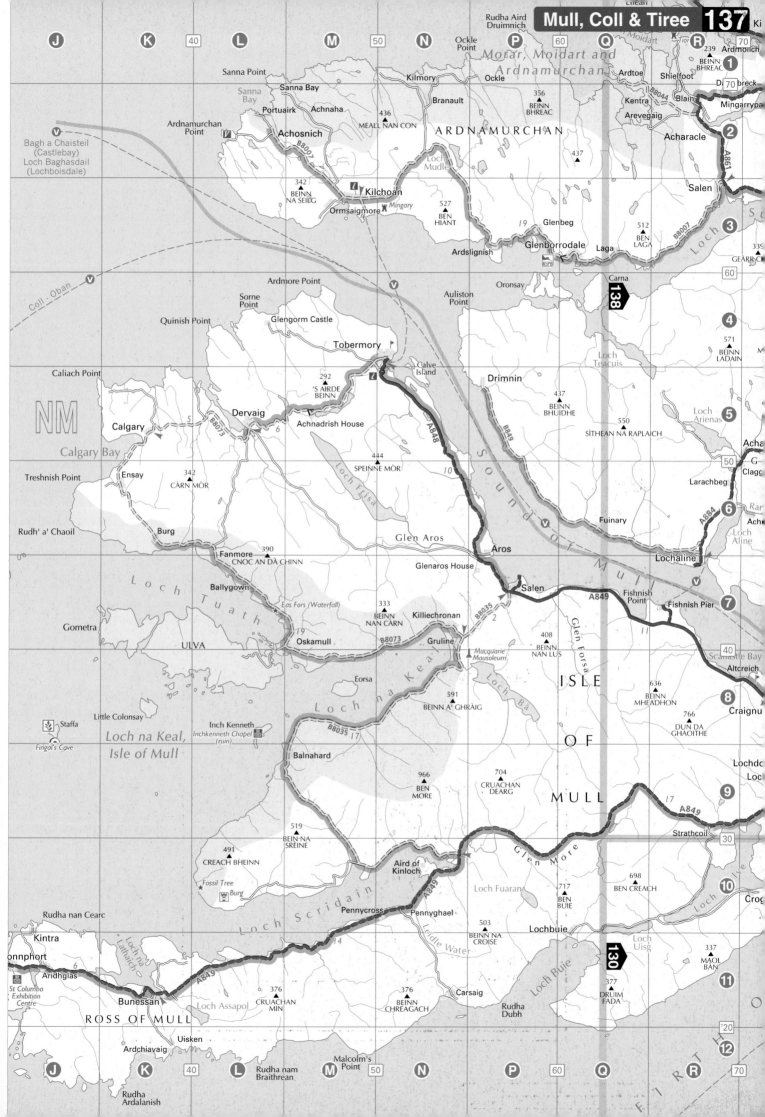

J K 40 L M 50 N P 60 Q R 70

Rudha Aird
Druimnich

① Morar, Moidart and
Ardnamurchan

239 Ardmolich

Ockle
Point

 Kilmory
Ockle
Branault
Sanna Point
Sanna Bay
Sanna Bay
Portuairk
Achnaha
Achosnich
MEALL NAN CON 436
356
BEINN
BHREAC
ARDNAMURCHAN
BEINN
BHREAC ①
breck 70

Ardnamurchan
Point
Ardtoe Shielfoot
Kentra
Arevegaig
Acharacle
Mingarrypa
Blain

437
② Salen

B8007
Kilchoan
342
BEINN
NA SEILG
Ormsaigmore Mingary
527
BEN
HIANT
19 Glenbeg
Ardslignish Glenborrodale Laga
512
BEN
LAGA
③ GEARR C
339

Carna
138 ④ 60

Ardmore Point
Sorne
Point
Glengorm Castle
Oronsay
Auliston
Point
Loch
Teacuis
571
BEINN
LADAIN

Caliach Point
Quinish Point
Tobermory Calve
Island
Drimnin
437
BEINN
BHUIDHE
550
SÌTHEAN NA RAPLAICH
Loch
Arienas
⑤

NM 292
'S AIRDE
BEINN
Achnadrish House
Acha
50 G
Clagg

Calgary
Dervaig
B8073
5 6
444
SPEINNE MÒR
10
Larachbeg
A884
⑥
Loch
Aline

Treshnish Point
Ensay
342
CÀRN MÒR
Loch Frisa
Fuinary
Rar

Rudh' a' Chaoil
Burg
Glen Aros
Aros
Lochaline
v
⑦

Fanmore 390
CNOC AN DÀ CHINN
Glenaros House
Fishnish
Point
Fishnish Pier

Gometra
Ballygown
Eas Fors (Waterfall)
333
BEINN
NAN CÀRN
Killiechronan
Salen A849
⑦

ULVA
Oskamull B8073
Gruline
B8035 2
408
BEINN
NAN LUS
Glen Forsa
11
40
Scanastle Bay
Altcreich

Eorsa Macquarie
Mausoleum
Loch Bà
ISLE
636
BEINN
MHEADHON
766
DUN DA
GHAOITHE
⑧
Craignu

Little Colonsay
Staffa
Inch Kenneth
Inchkenneth Chapel
(ruin)
B8035 17
591
BEINN A' GHRÀIG
OF
Lochd
Loc

Fingal's Cave
Loch na Keal,
Isle of Mull
Balnahard
966
BEN
MORE
704
CRUACHAN
DEARG
MULL
17 A849
⑨

519
BEIN NA
SRÈINE
Strathcoil
30

491
CREACH BHEINN
Aird of
Kinloch
Glen More
717
BEN
BUIE
698
BEN CREACH
⑩

Fossil Tree
Burg
Loch Scridain
Pennycross
Pennyghael
Loch Fuaran
Lochbuie
Loch
Uisg
130

Rudha nan Cearc
Kintra
Loch na
Lathaich
503
BEINN NA
CROISE
337
MAOL
BÀN
⑪

onnphort
Aridhglas
A849
4
Leidle Water
Carsaig
377
DRUIM
FADA

St Columba
Exhibition
Centre
Bunessan
376
CRUACHAN
MIN
376
BEINN
CHREAGACH
Rudha
Dubh
Loch
Buie
⑫

ROSS OF MULL
Loch Assapol
Malcolm's
Point

Uisken
Ardchiavaig
Rudha nam
Braithrean

Rudha
Ardalanish
J K 40 L M 50 N P 60 Q R 70

Bagh a Chaisteil
(Castlebay)
Loch Baghasdail
(Lochboisdale)
v

Coll - Oban v

Calgary Bay

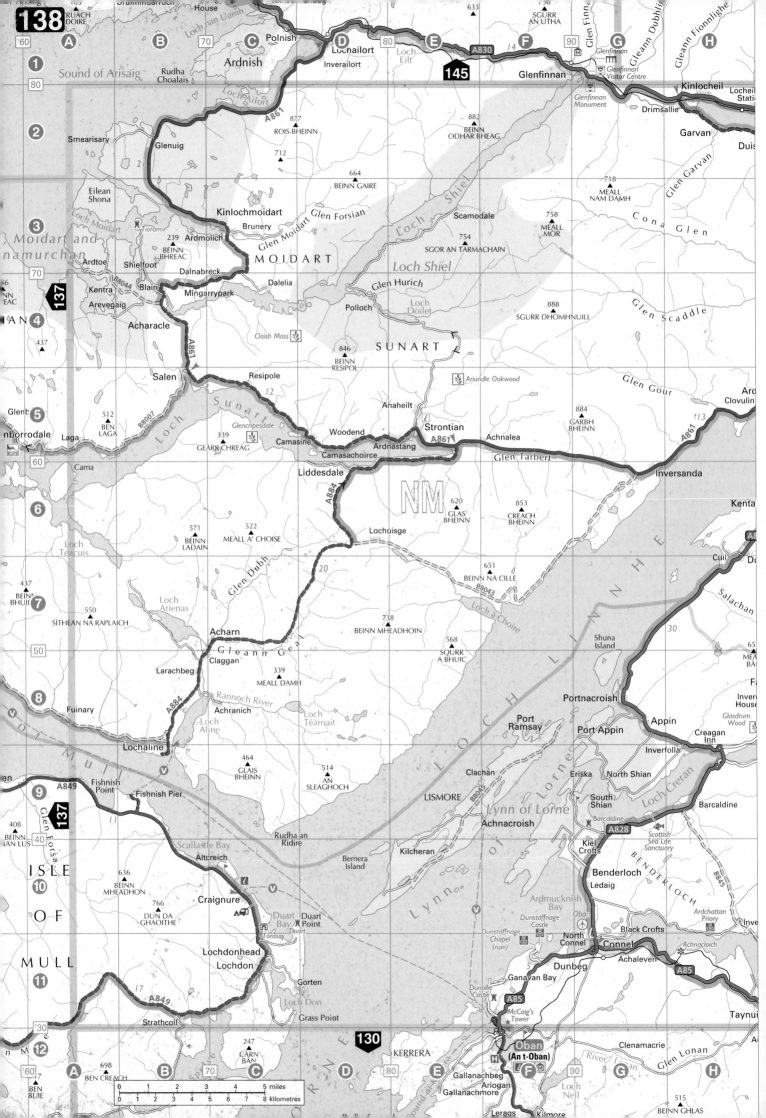

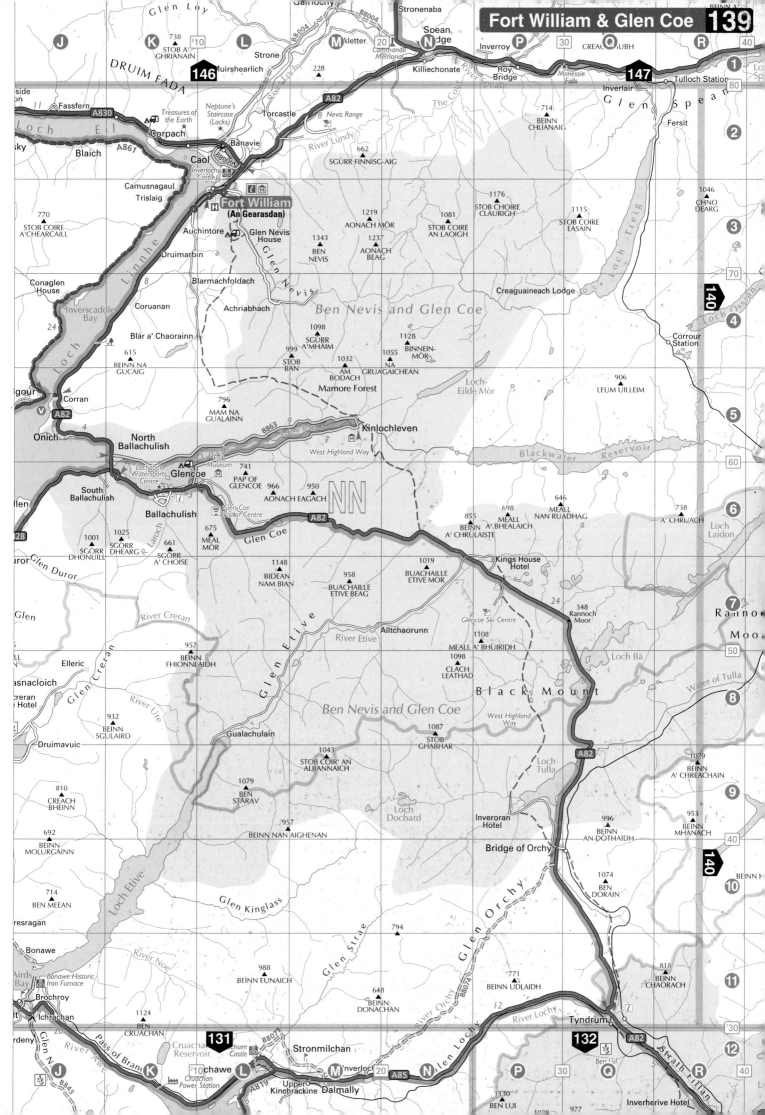

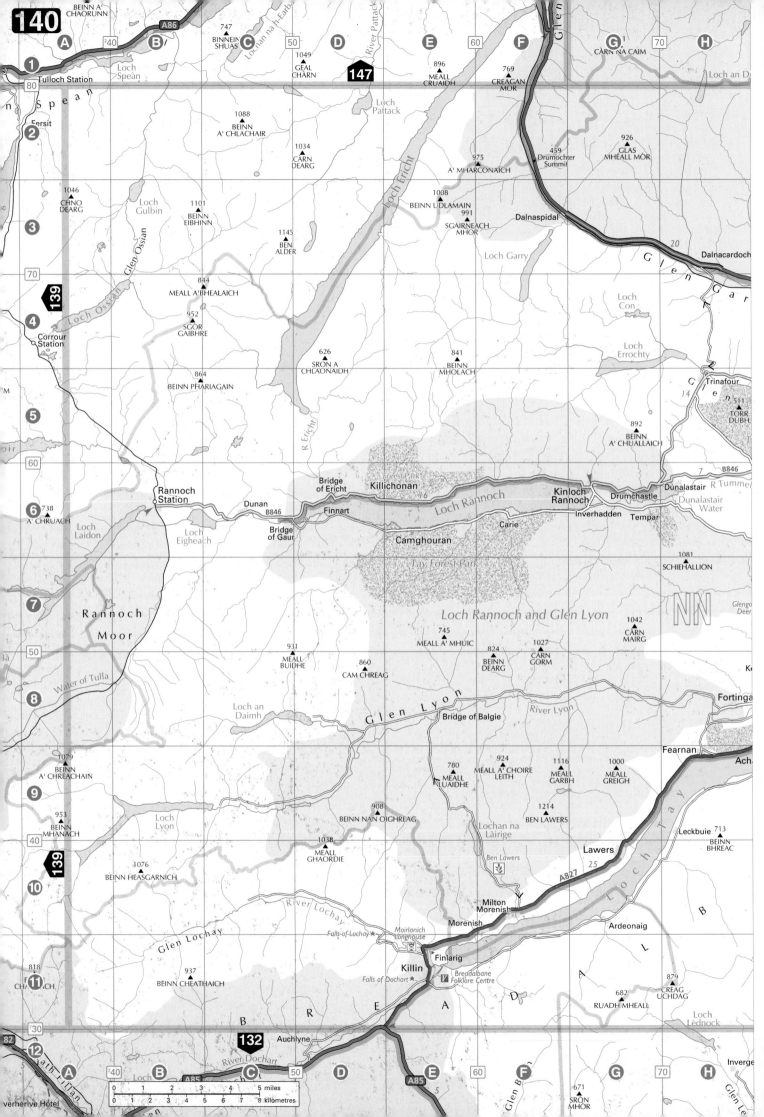

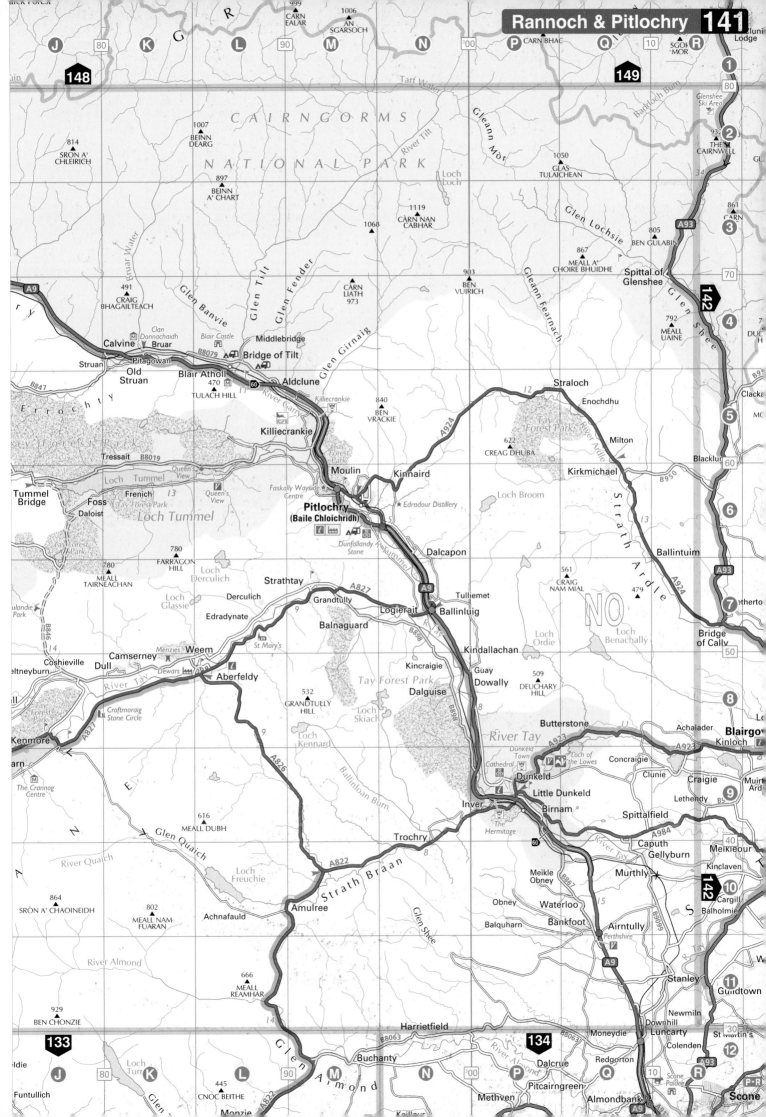

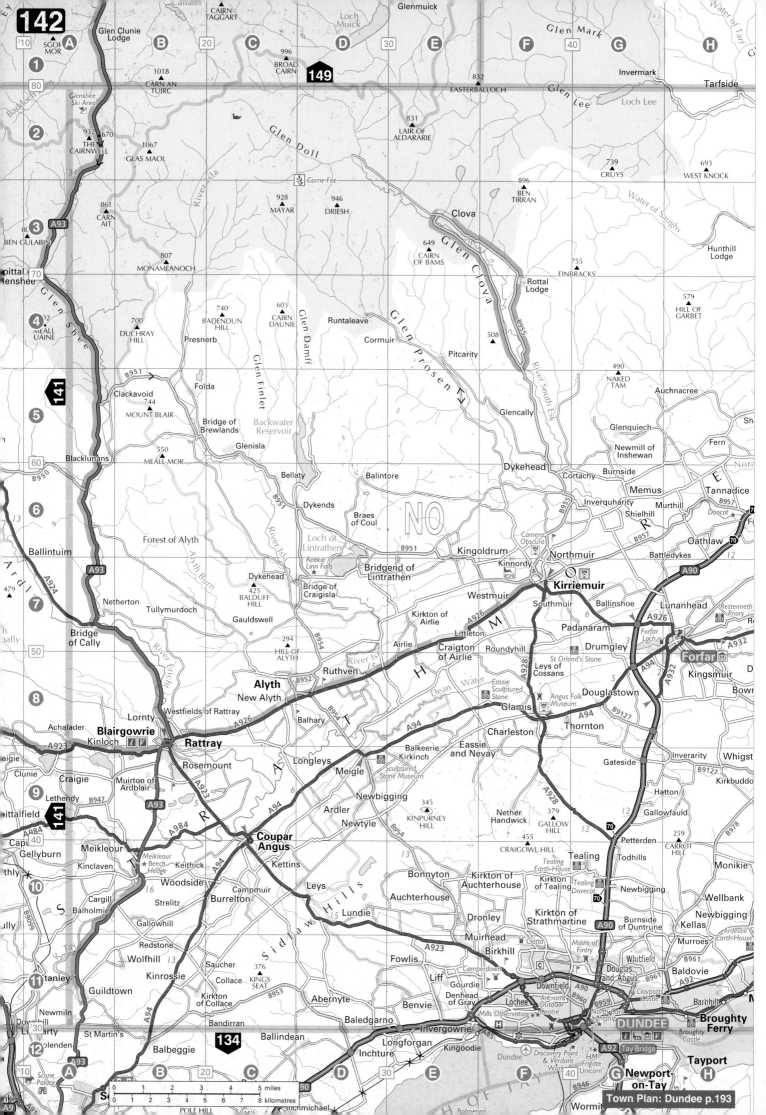

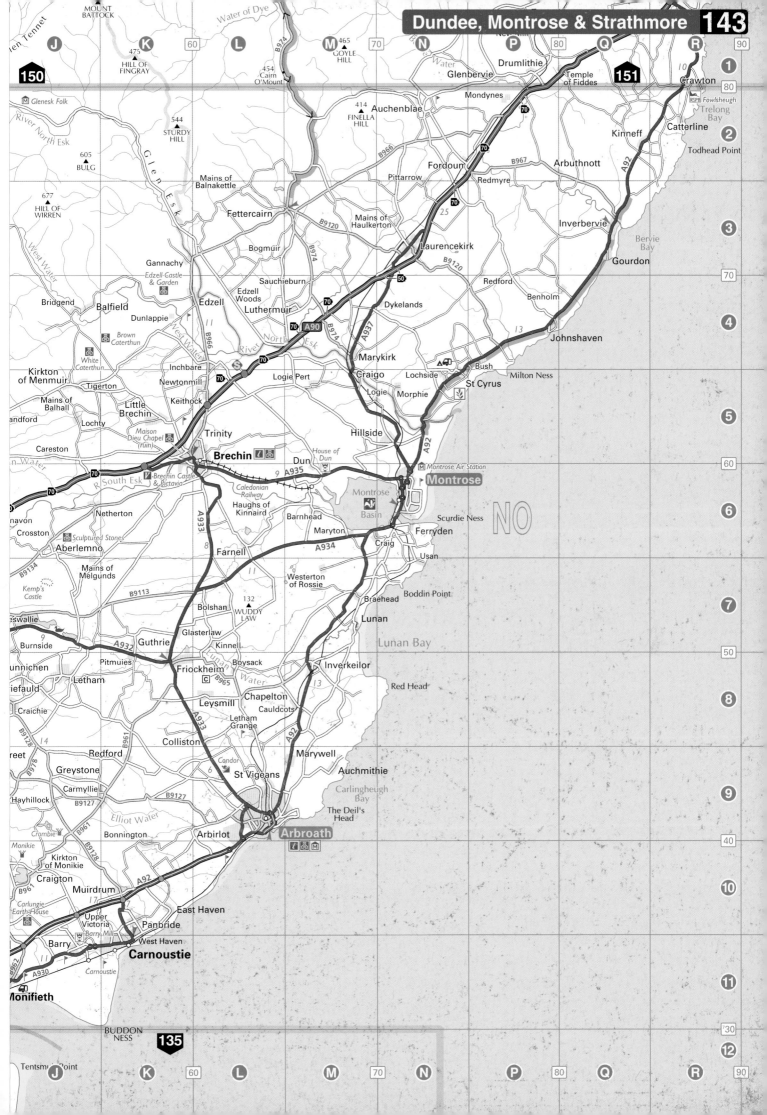

A '20 B C 30 D E Dryno 40 F S G 50 conser H V

Rudha nan Clach

444
BEN LEE
Peinchorra

B8009 Fernilea
369
ARNAVAL
Carbost
Merkadale
Glen Drynoch
A863

1 152 Talisker Bay
Talisker
Glen Eynort
Sligachan
773
GLAMAIG

A87

2 447
BEINN BHREAC
Grula
369
BEINN BHREAC
GL

965
SGURR NAN GILLEAN
The Cuillin Hills

Loch Eynort

3 434
AN CRUACHIN
Glenbrittle House
Bualintur
974
SGURR A' GHEADAIDH
Cuillin Hills
1009
SGURR ALASDAIR
Loch Coruisk
927
BLAVEN
Loch na Crèitheach

894
GARS BHEINN
Kirkibost

4 225
CEANN NA BEINNE
Rudh' an Dùnain
Soay Sound
139
BEINN BHREAC
Loch Scavaig
344
BEN MEABOST

Loch Brittle
Mol-chlach
Elgol
Glasr

5 SOAY
Rudh' Aonghais
Strathaird Point

10 CUILLIN SOUND

6 NG
CANNA
210
CÀRN A' GHAILL
Garrisdale Point
A'Chill
Canna Harbour
Rudha Shamhnan Insir

7 Sanday
Sound of Canna
302
MULLACH MÓR
Rudha na Roinne

'00 A Bhrideanach
Kinloch
Loch Scresort

8 Oigh-sgeir
570
ORVAL
RÙM

810
ASKIVAL

9 763
SGURR NAN GILLEAN
The Small Isles
Sound of Rum
NM

90 Rudha nam Meirleach

Bay of Laig
Cleadale

10 Rudha an Fhasaidh
Laig
299
AN CRUACHAN
EIGG
Kildonnan

393
AN SGURR
Sandavore

11 Eilean nan Each
Eilean Chathastail

'80 MUCK
Sound of Eigg

12 Port Mor

A '20 B C 30 D E 40 F G 50 H

0 1 2 3 4 5 miles
0 1 2 3 4 5 6 7 8 kilometres

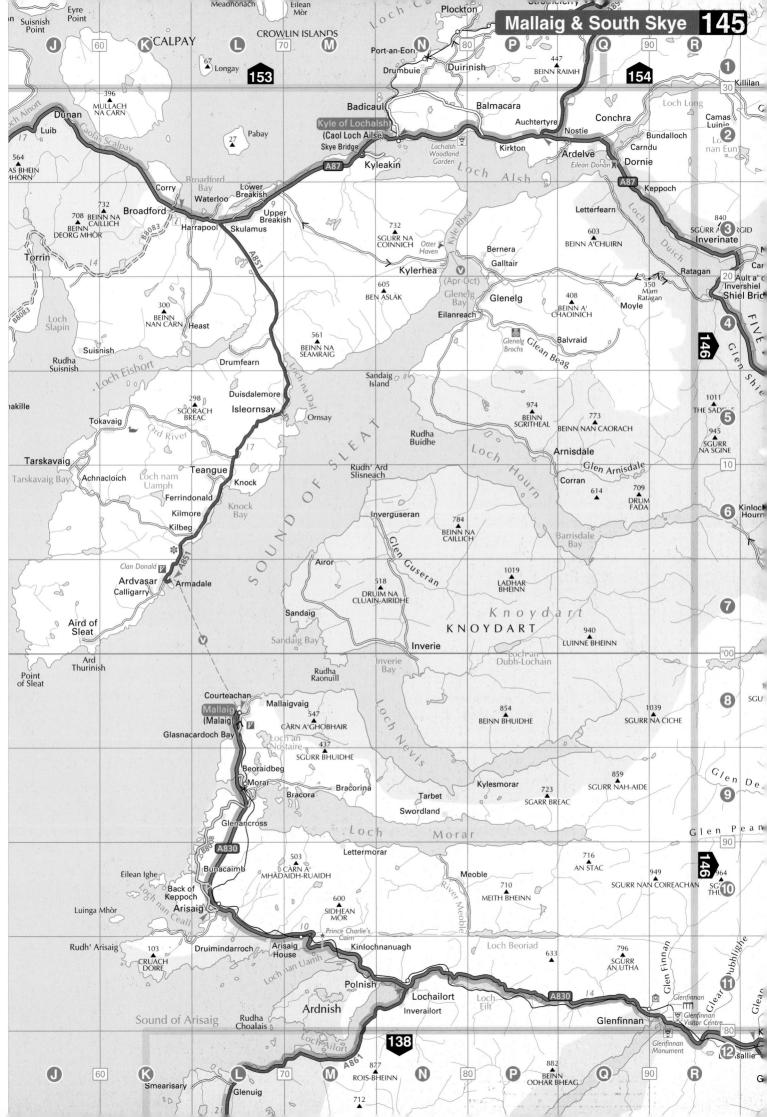

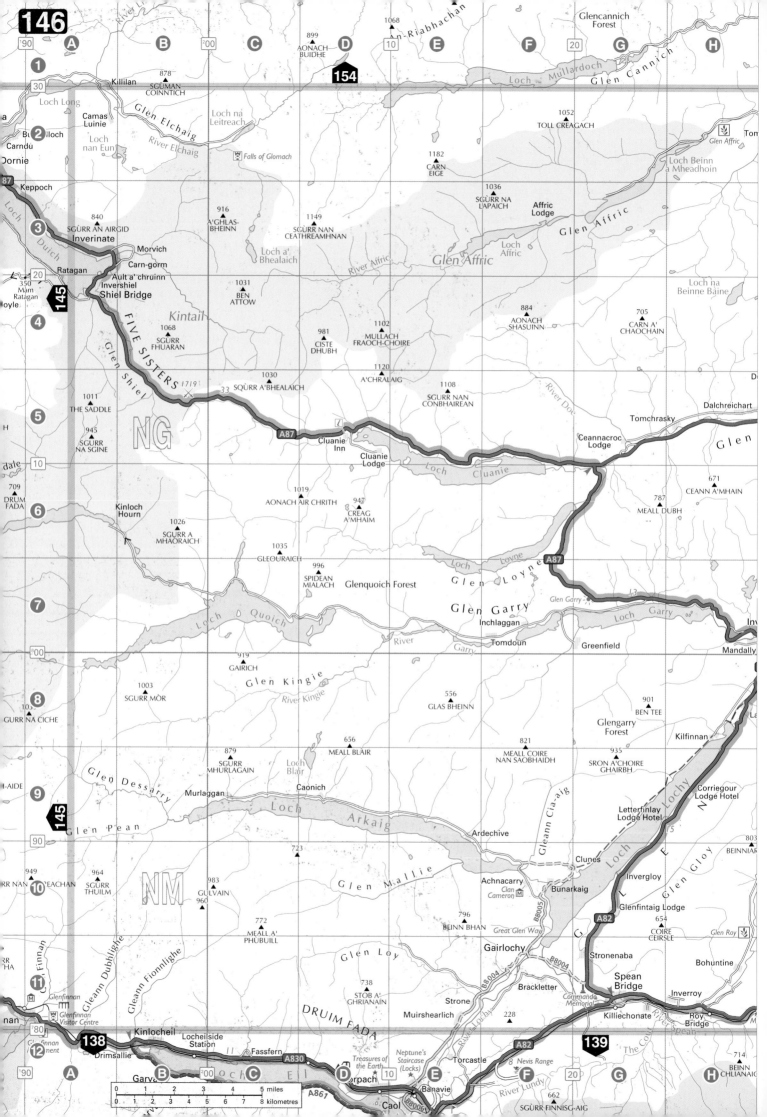

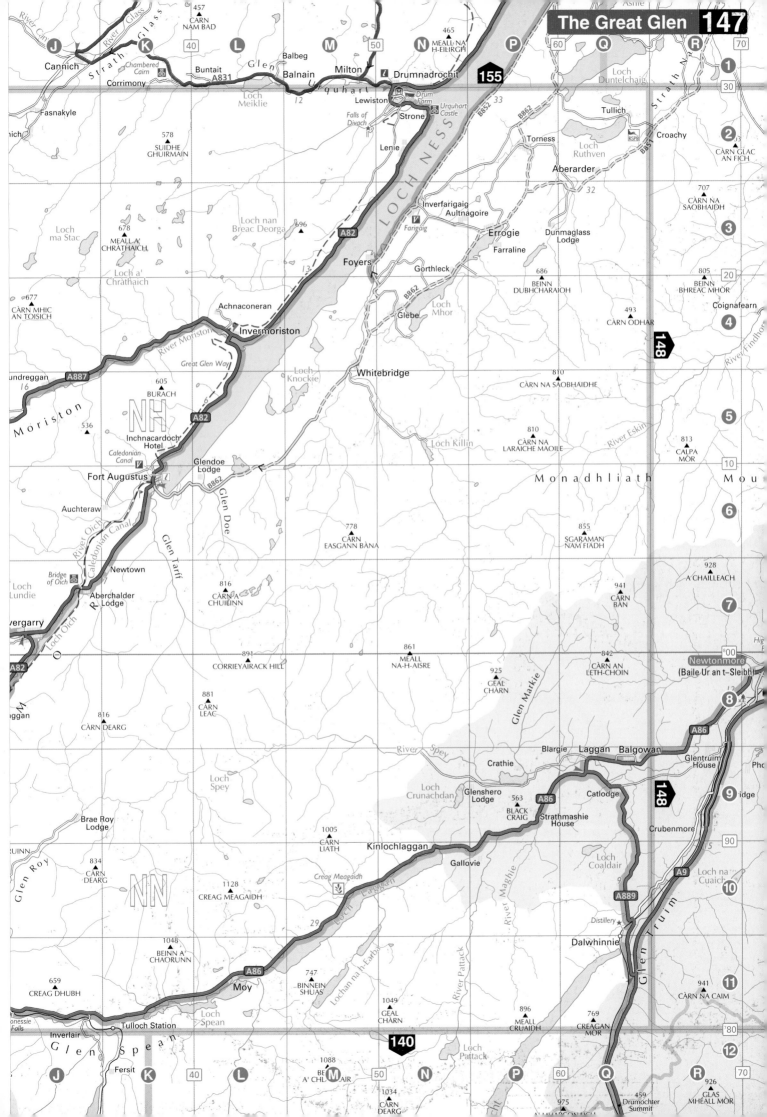

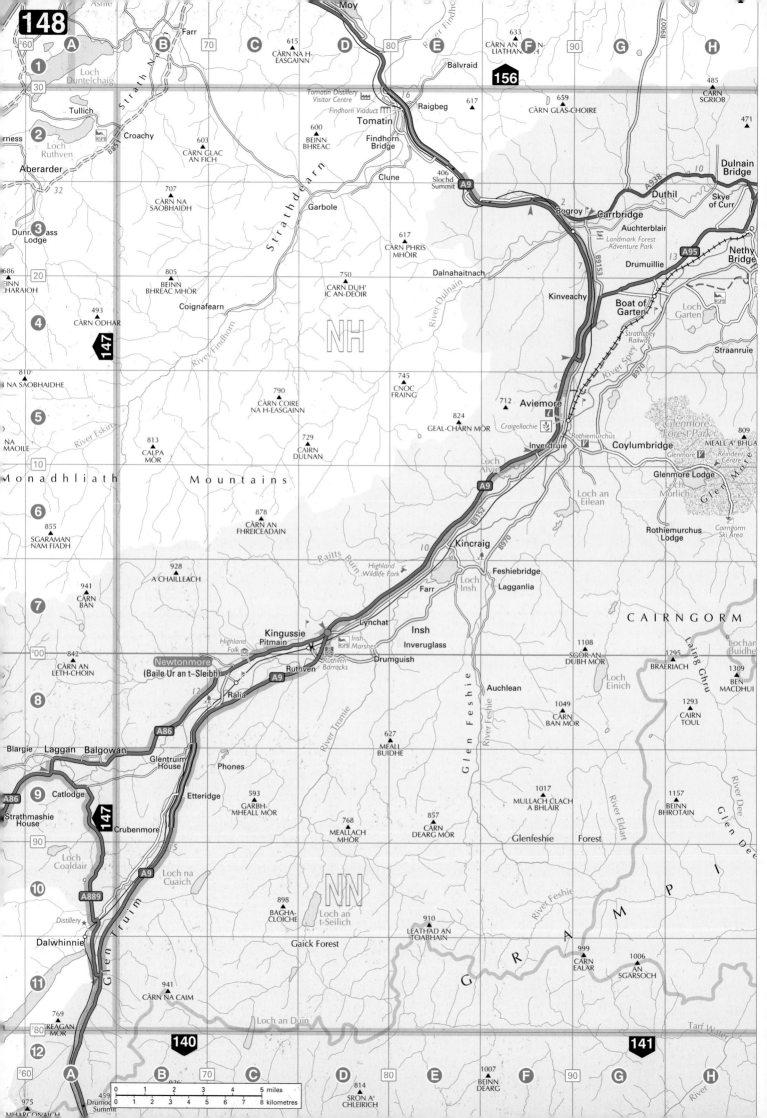

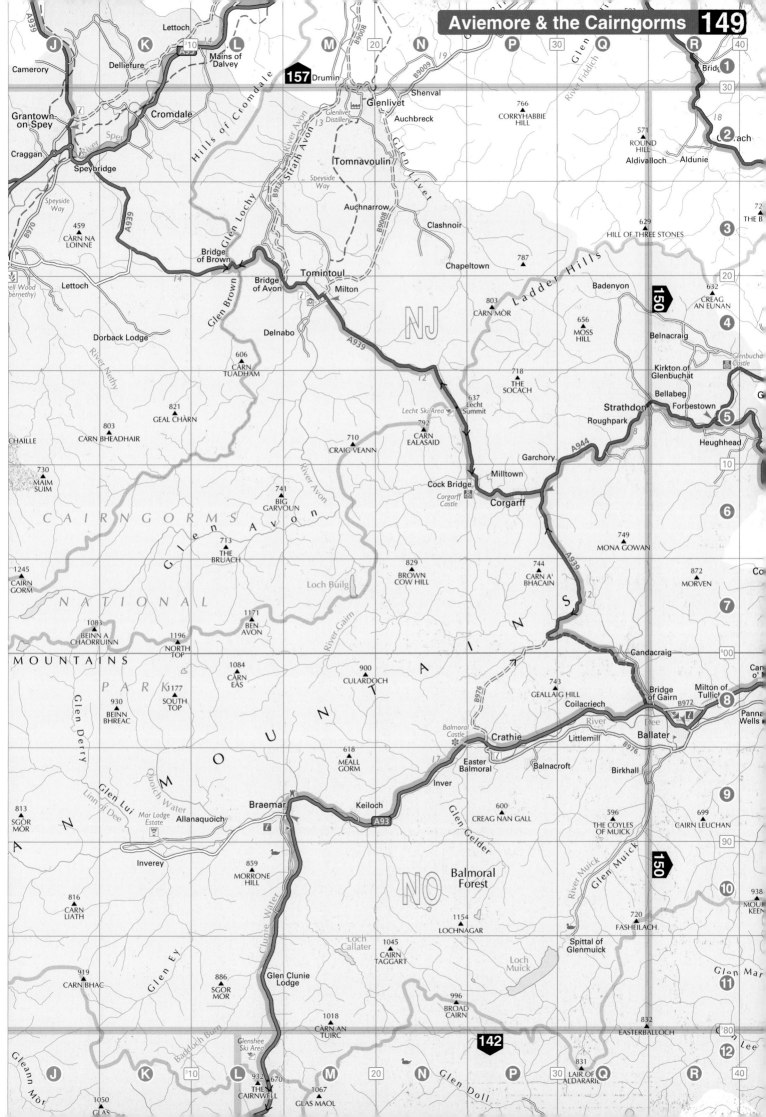

J K L M N P Q R

Camerory
Lettoch
Mains of Dalvey

157 Drumin
Shenval

B9008
B9009

Grantown-on-Spey
Dellifure
Cromdale
Glenlivet
Glenlivet Distillery
Auchbreck

766
CORRYHABBIE HILL

571
ROUND HILL

...ach
Aldivalloch Aldunie

Craggan
Speybridge
River Spey
Hills of Cromdale
River Avon
Strath Avon
Tomnavoulin
Speyside Way
Auchnarrow
Clashnoir

72
THE B...

629
HILL OF THREE STONES

459
CÀRN NA LOINNE

Lettoch
Bridge of Brown
Glen Brown
Glen Lochy
B938
Tomintoul
Bridge of Avon
Milton
Chapeltown

787

803
CÀRN MÒR

632
CREAG AN EUNAN

150

Speyside Way
B970
ell Wood (bernethy)
Dorback Lodge
Delnabo

A939

NJ

Badenyon

656
MOSS HILL

Belnacraig

Kirkton of Glenbuchat
Glenbucha... Castle

CHAILLE

606
CÀRN TUADHAM

718
THE SOCACH

Bellabeg
Strathdon
Forbestown

821
GEAL CHÀRN

637
Lecht Summit

Roughpark

Heughhead

803
CARN BHEADHAIR

Lecht Ski Area
792
CARN EALASAID

A944
Garchory
Milltown

710
CRAIG VEANN

730
MAIM SUIM

Cock Bridge
Corgarff Castle
Corgarff

749
MONA GOWAN

C A I R N G O R M S

741
BIG GARVOUN

Glen Avon
Loch Builg
829
BROWN COW HILL

744
CARN A' BHACAIN

872
MORVEN

1245
CAIRN GORM

713
THE BRUACH

N A T I O N A L

1083
BEINN A CHAORRUINN

1171
BEN AVON

River Gairn

A939

1196
NORTH TOP

Candacraig

'00

M O U N T A I N S

1084
CÀRN EAS

900
CULARDOCH

743
GEALLAIG HILL

Bridge of Gairn
Milton of Tullich

Car... o'...

B976
B972

P A R K

K
1177
SOUTH TOP

930
BEINN BHREAC

Coilacriech

River Dee

Panna... Wells

Glen Derry

Balmoral Castle
Crathie
Littlemill
Ballater

813
SGOR MÒR

Glen Lui
Quoich Water
618
MEALL GORM

Easter Balmoral
Balnacroft
Birkhall

Mar Lodge Estate
Allanaquoich
Inver

600
CREAG NAN GALL

596
THE COYLES OF MUICK

699
CAIRN LEUCHAN

Braemar
Keiloch

A93

Glen Gelder

90

Inverey
Linn of Dee

859
MORRONE HILL

NO
Balmoral Forest

River Muick
Glen Muick

150

816
CARN LIATH

1154
LOCHNAGAR

720
FASHEILACH

938
MOU... KEEN

919
CARN BHAC

Clunie Water
Glen Ey
886
SGOR MÒR

1045
CAIRN TAGGART

Spittal of Glenmuick
Loch Muick

832
EASTERBALLOCH

Glenshee Ski Area
Glen Clunie Lodge

996
BROAD CAIRN

1050
GLAS...

Gleann Mòr
1018
CARN AN TUIRC

142

831
LAIR OF ALDARARIE

Glen... Lee

J K L M N P Q R

932
670
THE CAIRNWELL

1067
GLAS MAOL

Glen Doll

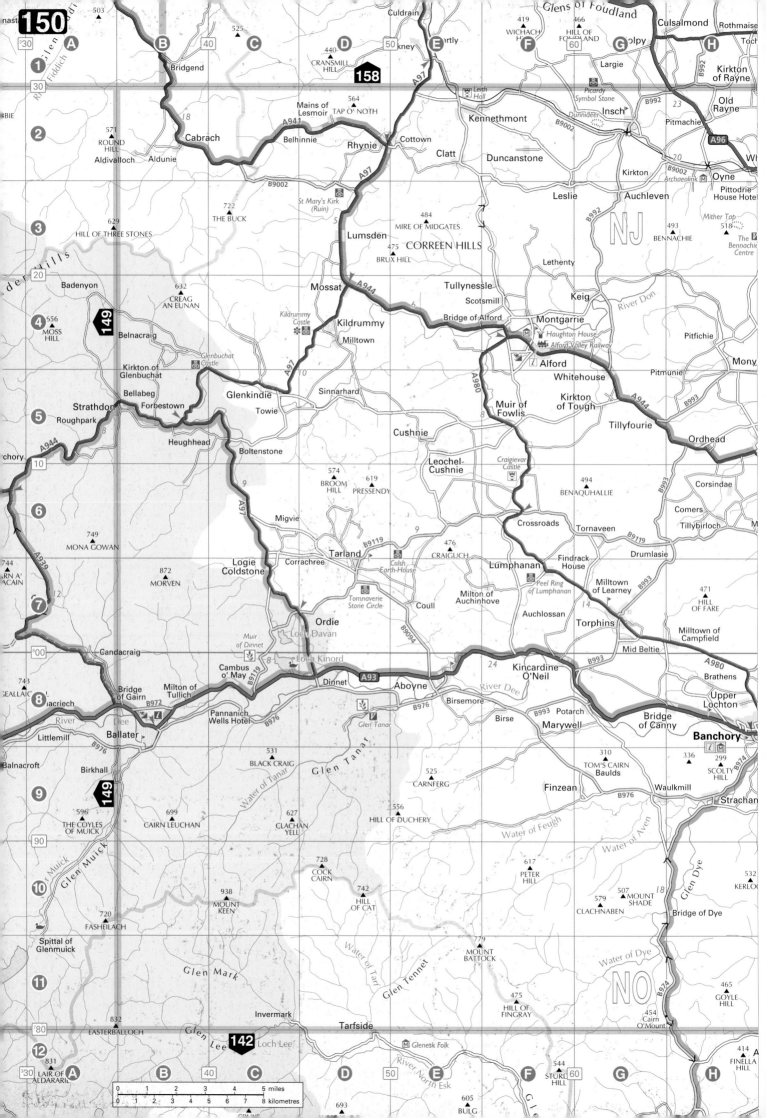

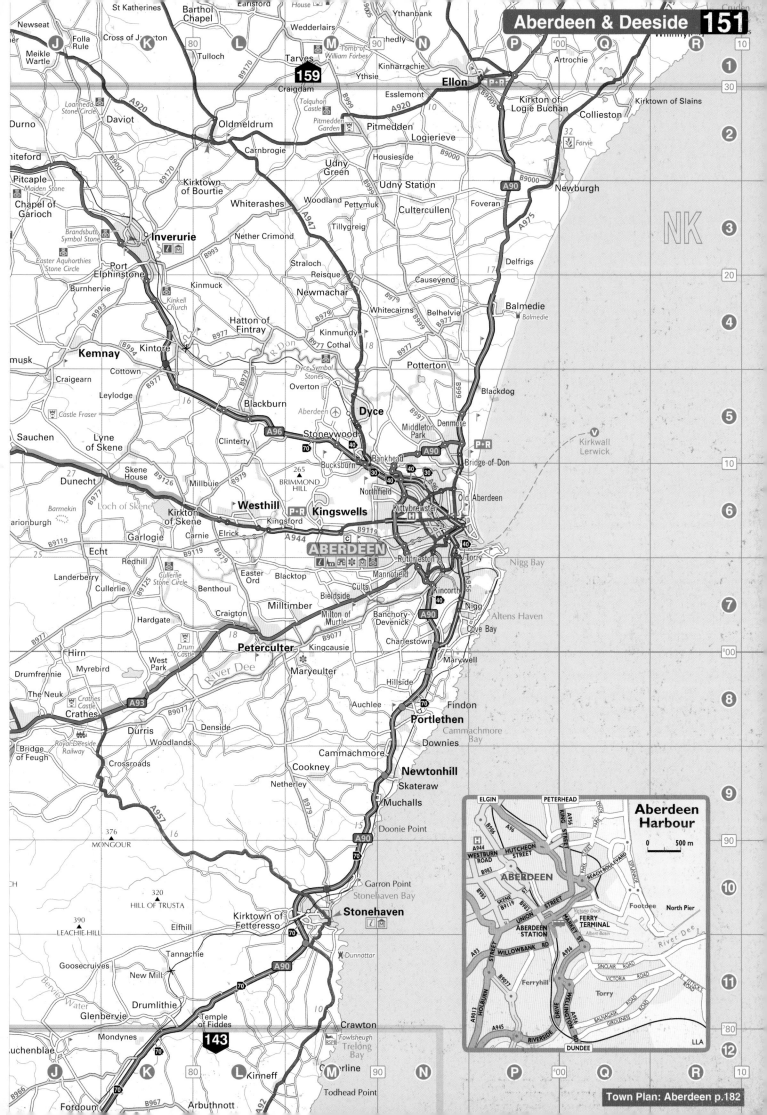

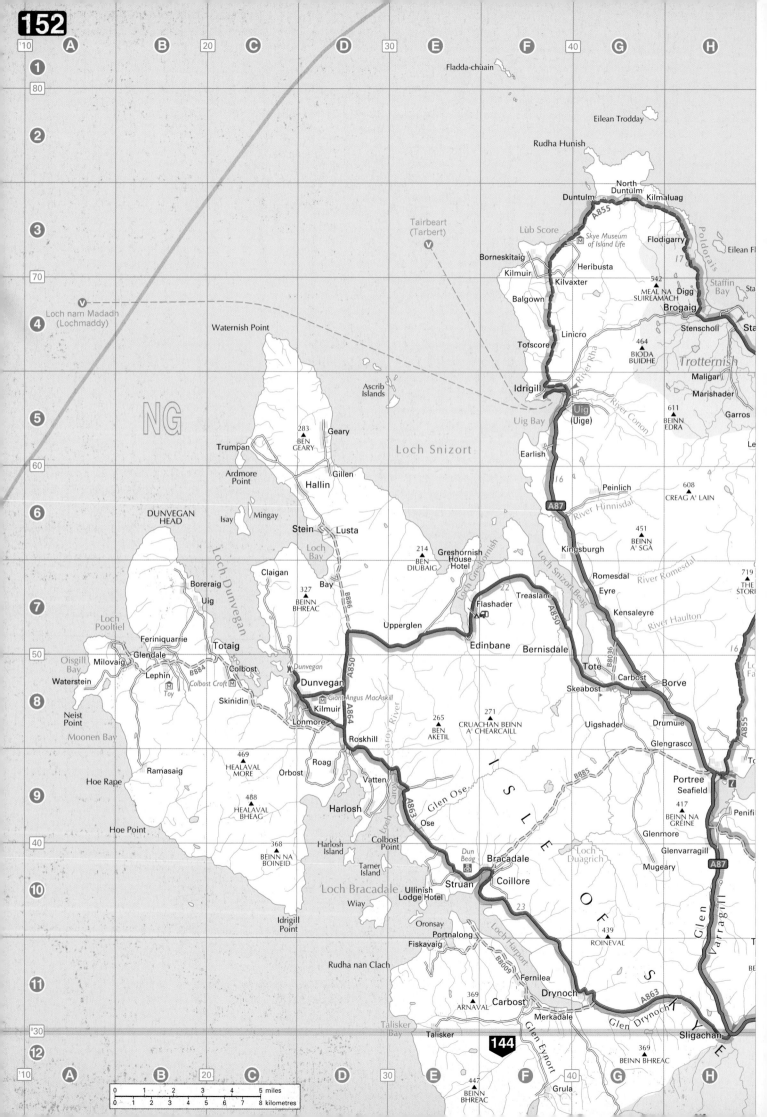

J   K   60   L   M   70   N   B8021   P   80   Q   R   90   250

CNOC
BREAC

Garden   13   ALL NA

1

North Erradale   Poolewe   Londubh   80

Big Sand   **160**   Strath   A832   **2**

Longa   Smithstown   Lonemore   Auchtercairn
Island   Loch   Gairloch   Heritage   Charlestown   421   MEALL AN   Loch
Gairloch   Eilean   DOIREIN
Horrisdale   **3**

Port   B8056   Loch Bad
Henderson   an Sgalaig

Badachro   70   Talla   19
Opinan

South Erradale   Loch Ghaineamhach   **154**   Loch na
A-Oidhe   **4**

Redpoint   Loch a'   875   855
Ghobhainn   BAOSBHEINN   BEINN
AN EOIN
Red   619
Point   BEINN BHREAC   Loch a'   **5**
Bhealaich
985
Loch   **NG**   BEINN   914
Torridon   ALLIGIN   BEINN DEARG
Rudha   Lower   60
na Fearn   Diabaig
Fearnmore   Loch Diabaig   Inveralligin   **6**
Loch a' Bhrage   Ob   Fearnbeg   Alligin Shuas
Chuaig   Kenmore   Torridon   LIATH
RONA   Arrina   House   Torr
Cuaig   Ardheslaig   Upper Loch Torridon
Loch
Eilean   Callakille   Shieldaig   Shieldaig   Annat   **7**
Tigh   An
492   Wester Ross
Lonbain   AN GARBH-   902
MHEALL   Loch   B50
Eilean   493   Damph   DAMPH
Fladday   CROIC-   Glenshieldaig   **8**
BHEINN   Forest
Manish   Loch   Loch Lundie
Point   Arnish   Torran
Arnish   Loch   **9**
Coultrie
SOUND OF RAASAY   Brochel   A896   730
895   SGURR A
INNER SOUND   BEINN BHAN   GHARAIDH
Applecross-Bay   14
RAASAY   Applecross   Rassal Ashwood
Milton   626
Pass of the   Kirkton   40
444   Cattle   774   A896   **9**
DUN CAAN   Camusteel   SGURR A'CHAORACHAIN   Kishorn   Lochcarron
312
Camusterrach   Ardarroch   Achintraid   **154**
BEN   Aird Dhubh   Bealach-   Slumbay
TIANAVAIG   Culduie   No-Ba   394
Oskaig   Rudha na' Leac   Kishorn   BAD A   **10**
Camastianavaig   Island   CHREAMHA   Strome
Tianavaig   310   Toscaig   Ardaneaskan   Ardnarff
Bay   BEINN NA LEAC   Stromeferry   Ardelve
Ollach   Loch Carron   Achmore   A890   **11**
Clachan   Loch Kishorn   Plockton
Inverarish   Eilean   Eilean   Port-an-Eorna
The Braes   Meadhonach   Mòr   Duirinish   **12**
444   Peinchorran   Suisnish   Eyre   **CROWLIN ISLANDS**   Drumbuie   447
N LEE   Point   Point   BEINN RAIMH   30
Sconser   **SCALPAY**   67   Longay   Port-Loch Ailse   Balmacara
773   **145**   Badicaul   Auchtertyre   Conchra   R
GLAMAIG   A87   Dunan   L   60   L   M   Pabay   70   N   Kyle of Lochalsh   P   Kirkton   Q   Nostie   90
564   Skye Bridge   Ardelve   Carndu
Loch Ainort   Kyleakin   Loch   Dornie
A87   MULLACH   396   Eilean Donan
NA CARN   Caolas Scalpay

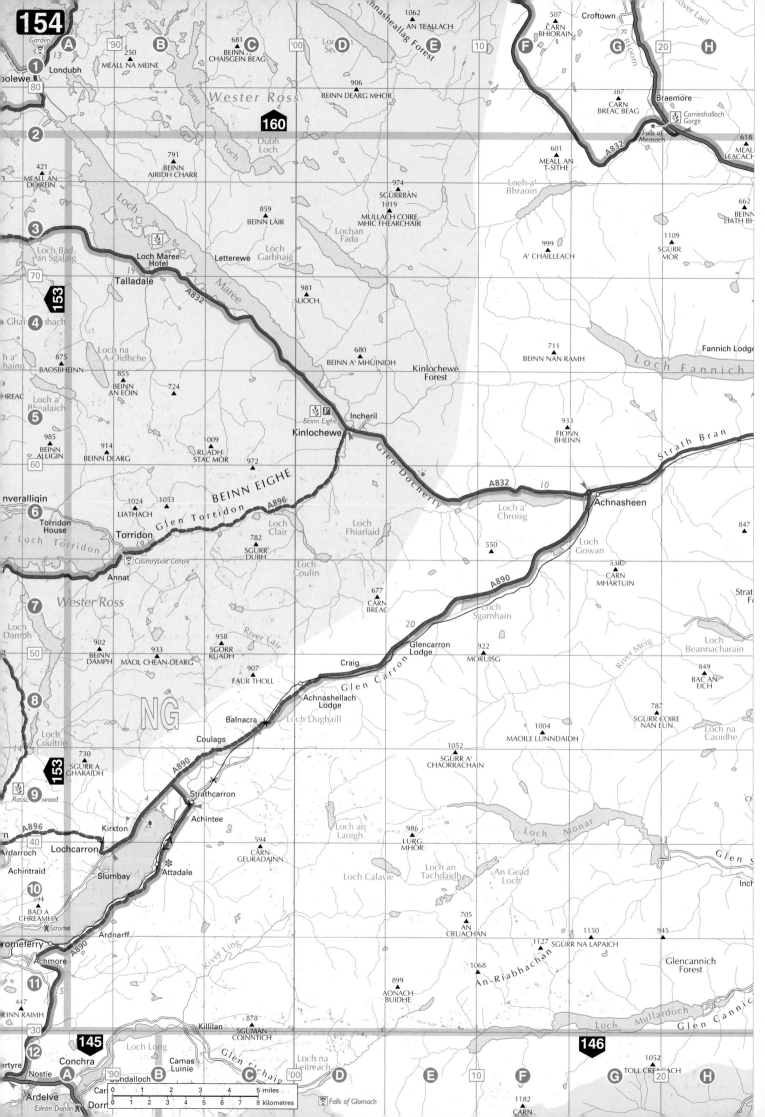

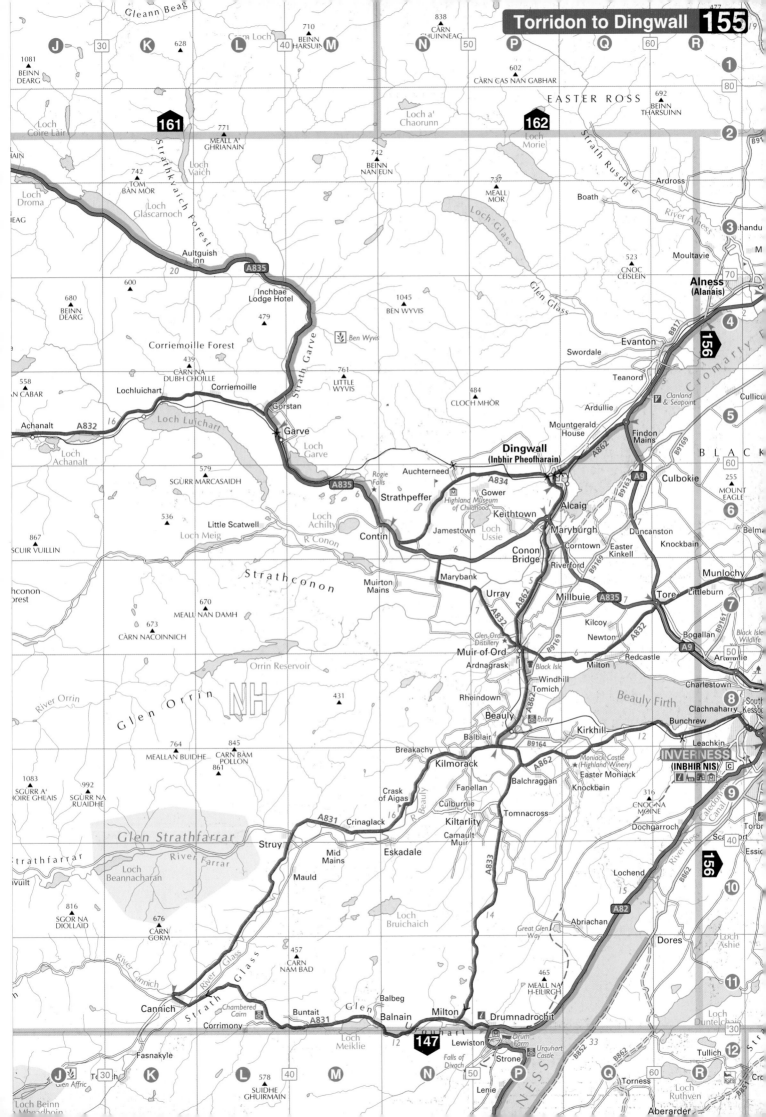

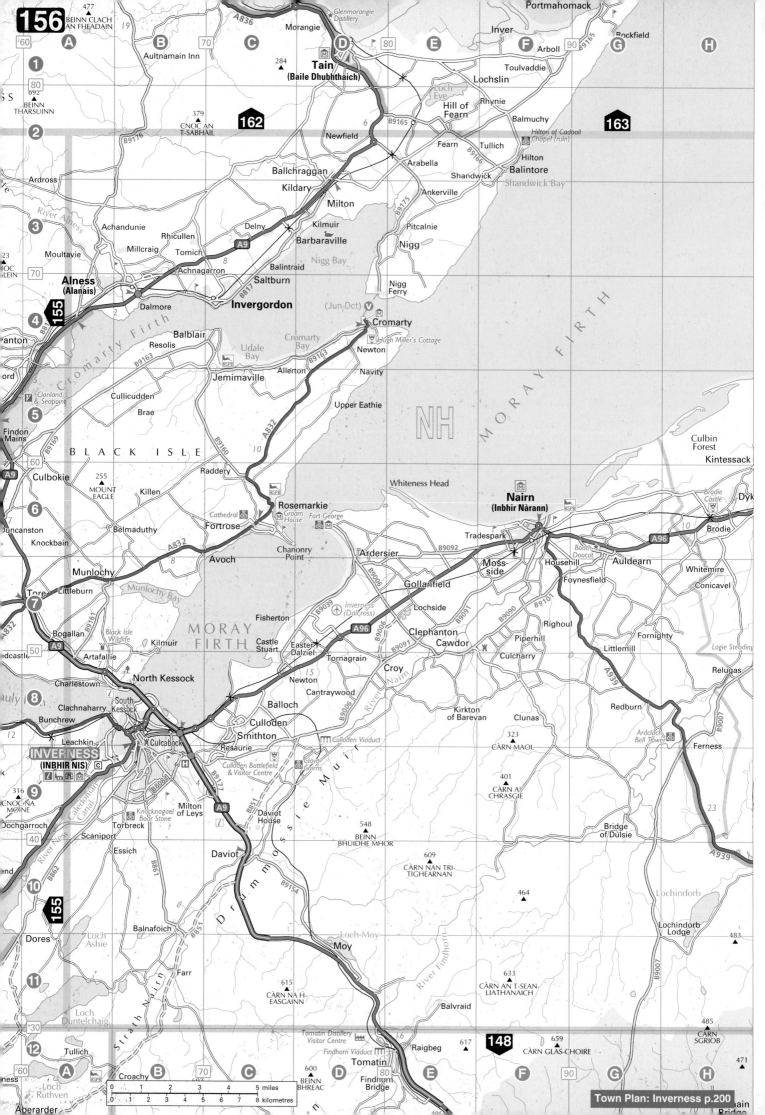

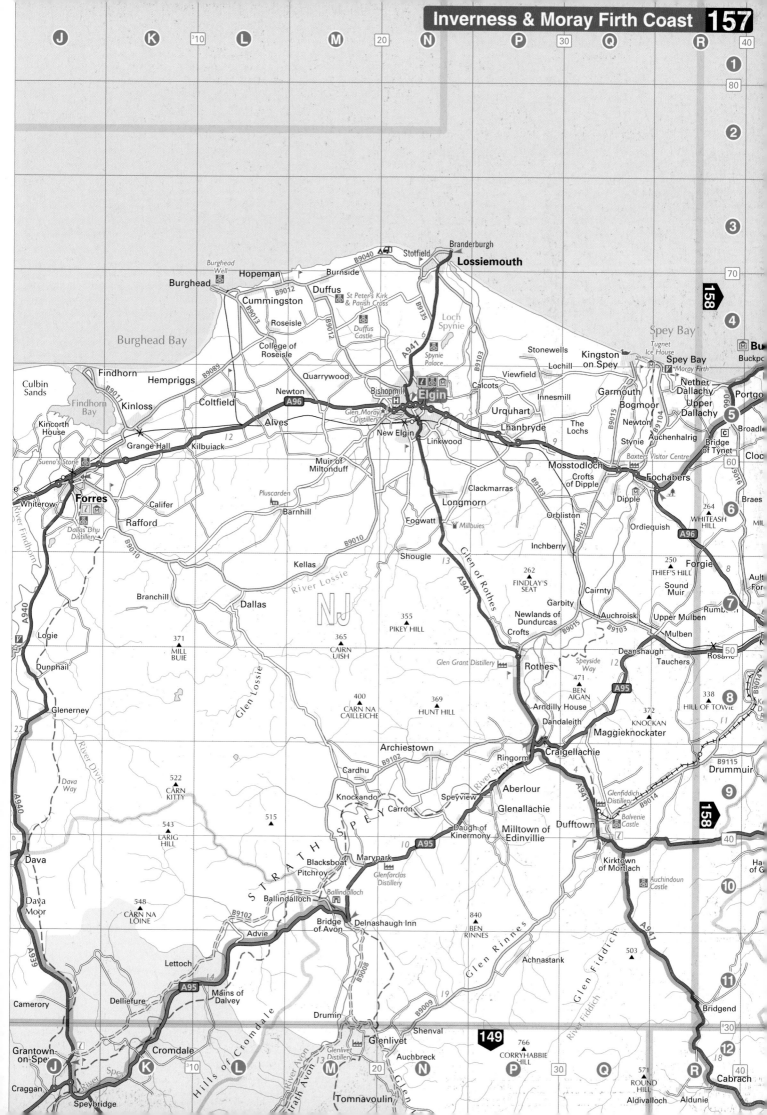

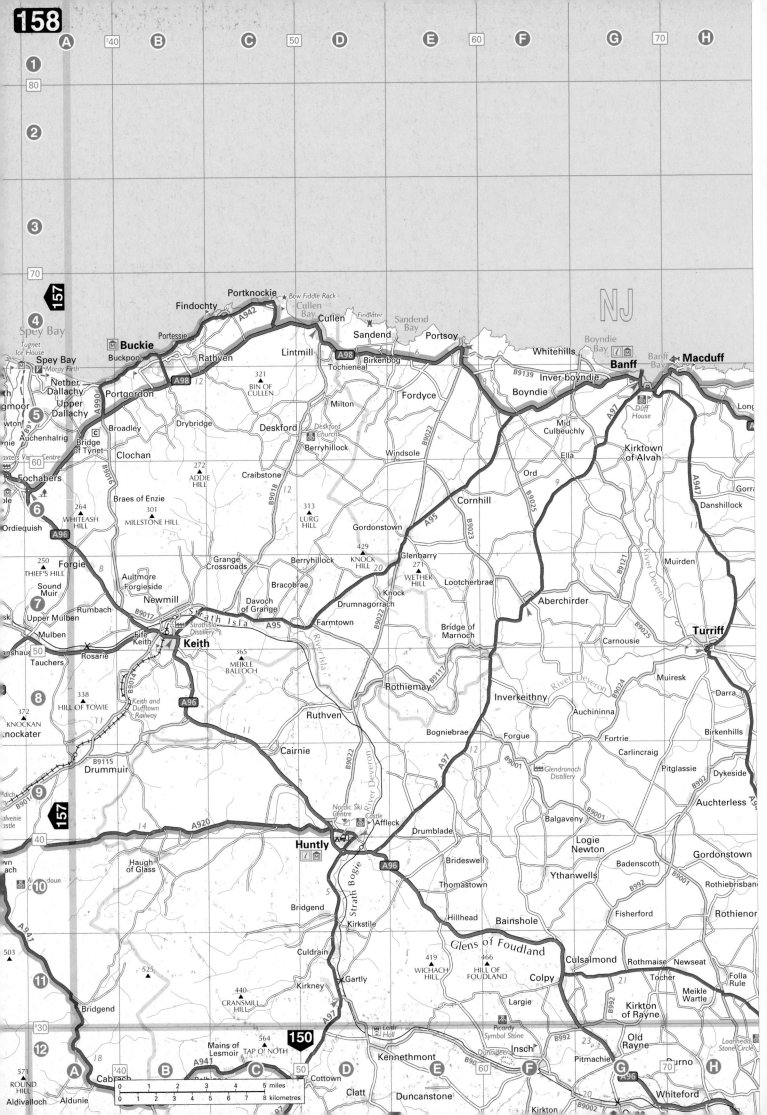

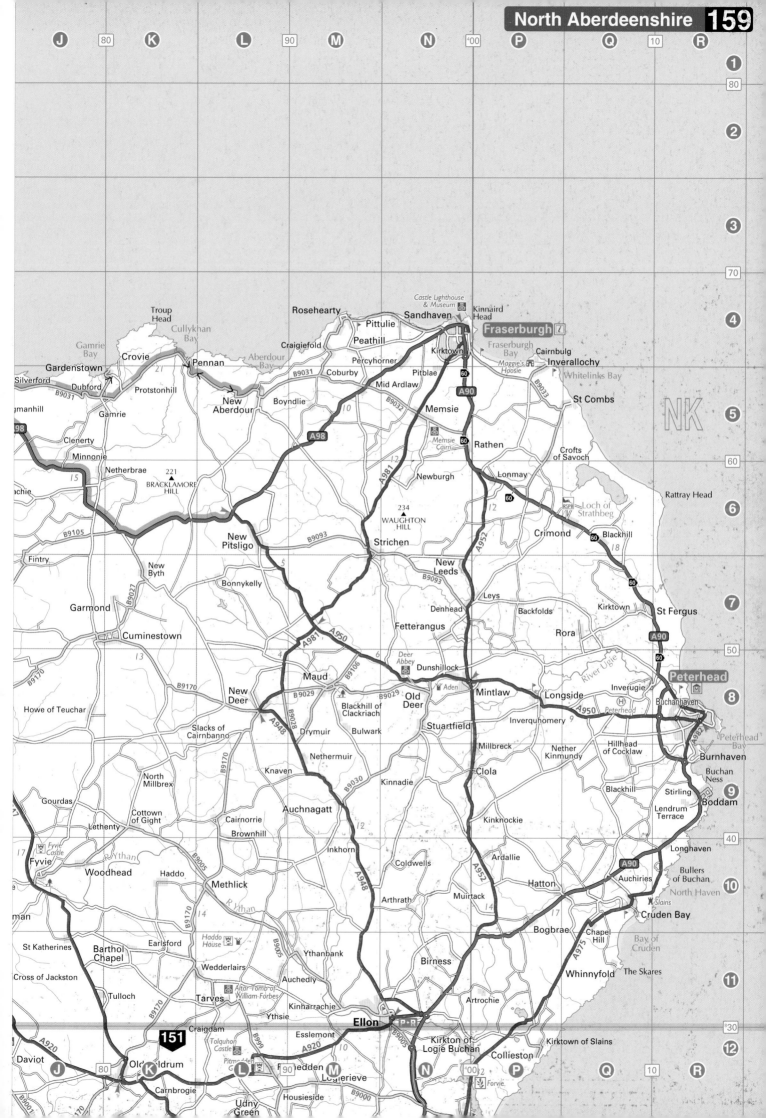

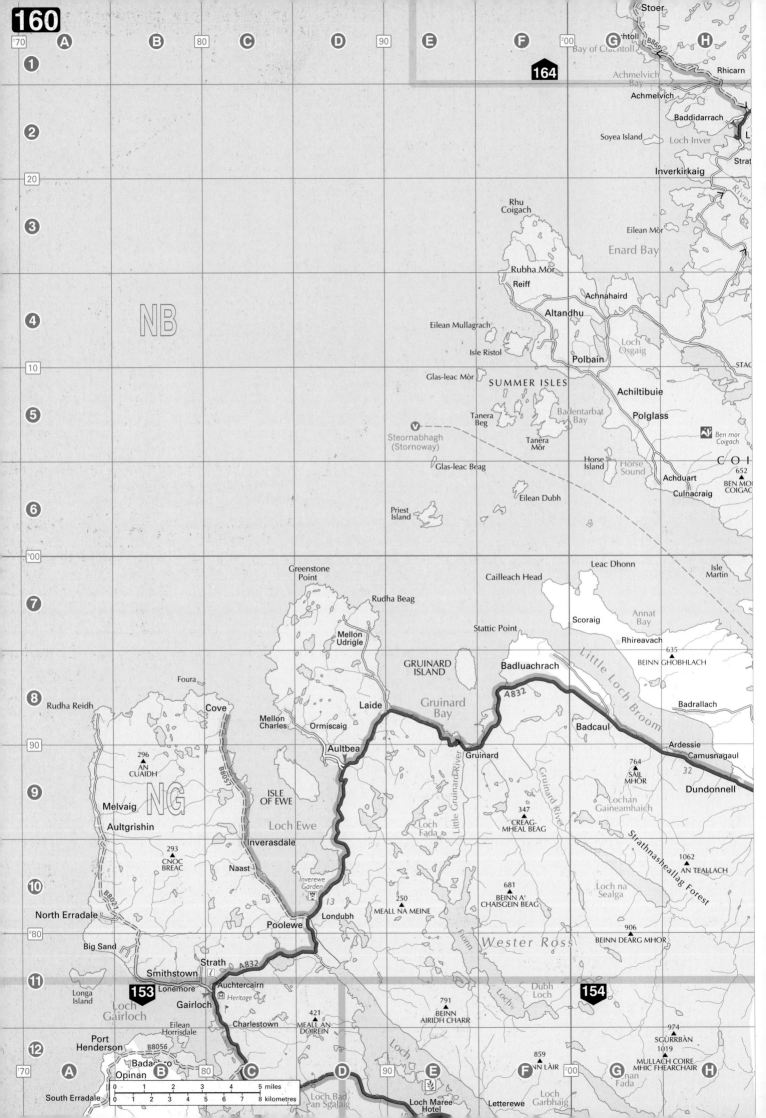

153

154

NB

NG

Stoer
htoll
Bay of Clachtoll
Achmelvich
Bay
Achmelvich
Rhicarn
Baddidarrach
Soyea Island
Loch Inver
Inverkirkaig
Strat
River

Rhu
Coigach
Eilean Mòr
Enard Bay

Rubha Mòr
Reiff
Achnahaird
Altandhu

Eilean Mullagrach
Loch
Osgaig
Isle Ristol
Polbain
Achiltibuie

Glas-leac Mòr
SUMMER ISLES
Badentarbat
Bay
Polglass
Ben mor
Coigach

Tanera
Beg
Steornabhagh
(Stornoway)
Tanera
Mòr
Horse
Island
Horse
Sound
COI
Achduart
652
BEN MO
COIGAC

Glas-leac Beag

Priest
Island
Eilean Dubh

Culnacraig

Greenstone
Point
Leac Dhonn
Isle
Martin

Rudha Beag
Cailleach Head
Scoraig
Annat
Bay

Mellon
Udrigle
Stattic Point
Rhireavach
635
BEINN GHOBHLACH

Foura
GRUINARD
ISLAND
Badluachrach
Little Loch Broom

Rudha Reidh
Cove
Gruinard
Bay
A832
Badrallach

Laide
Badcaul

Mellon
Charles
Ormiscaig
Little Gruinard River
Gruinard
Ardessie
Camusnagaul

Aultbea
764
SAIL
MHOR
32

296
AN
CUAIDH
B8057
Gruinard River
Dundonnell

Melvaig
347
CREAG-
MHEAL BEAG
Lochan
Gaineamhaich

Aultgrishin
Loch Ewe
ISLE
OF EWE
Loch
Fada

293
CNOC
BREAC
Inverasdale
1062
AN TEALLACH

Naast
Strathnasheallag Forest

Inverewe
Garden
250
MEALL NA MEINE
681
BEINN A'
CHAISGEIN BEAG
Loch na
Sealga

North Erradale
B8021
13
906
BEINN DEARG MHOR

Big Sand
Londubh
from
Wester Ross

Longa
Island
Poolewe
Dubh
Loch

Strath
A832
Smithstown
Auchtercairn
791
BEINN
AIRIDH CHARR

Lonemore
Heritage
974
SGÙRR BÀN
1019

Gairloch
421
MEALL AN
DOIREIN
Loch
MULLACH COIRE
MHIC FHEARCHAIR

Eilean
Horrisdale
Charlestown

Port
Henderson
B8056
859
NN LÀIR
nan
Fada

Badachro
Opinan
Loch Maree
Hotel
Letterewe
Loch
Garbhaig

South Erradale
Loch Bad
an Sgalaig

0   1   2   3   4   5 miles
0 1 2 3 4 5 6 7 8 kilometres

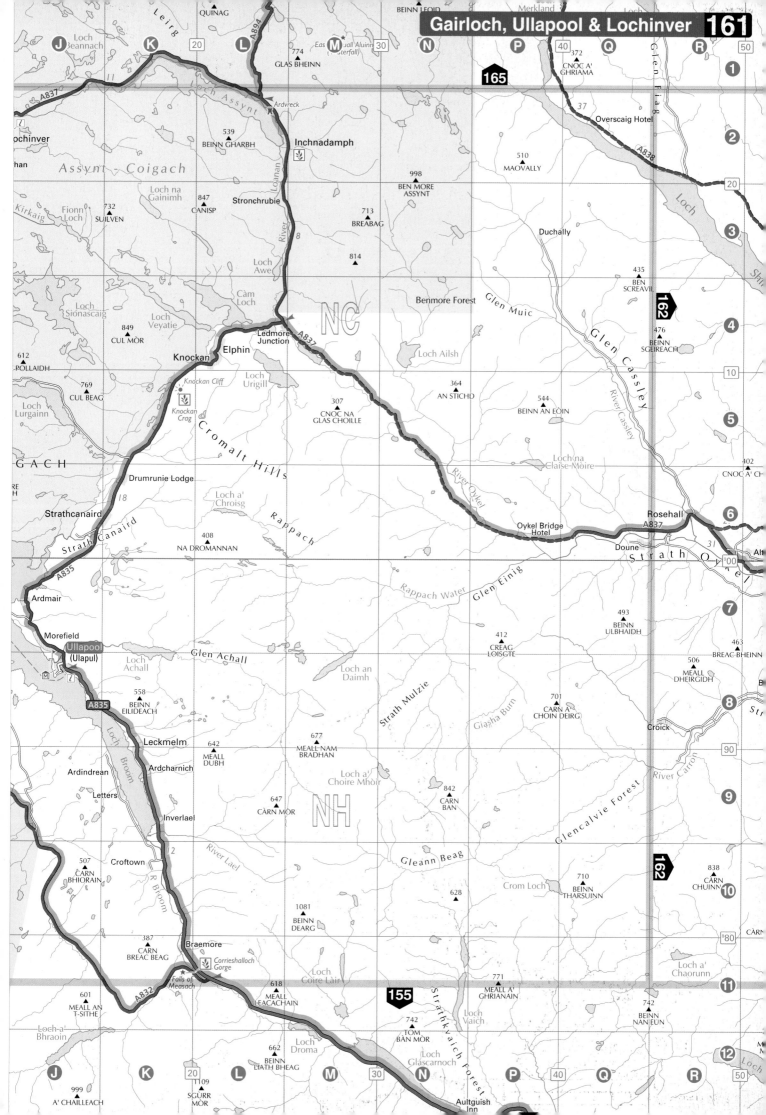

QUINAG

BEINN LEOID

Merkland

Leirg

Loch Beannach

J

K

20

L

A894

M

Eas a' Chual Aluinn (Waterfall)

30

N

P

40

372

Q

Glen Fiag

R

50

774
GLAS BHEINN

165

CNOC A' GHRIAMA

1

A837

Loch Assynt

Ardvreck

37

Overscaig Hotel

A838

2

539
BEINN GHARBH

Inchnadamph

Loch

510
MAOVALLY

Loch

20

Assynt - Coigach

Loanan

998
BEN MORE ASSYNT

Duchally

3

847
CANISP

Stronchrubie

River

Benmore Forest

Glen Muic

Glen Cassley

435
BEN SCREAVIL

732
SUILVEN

Fionn Loch

Loch na Gainimh

713
BREABAG

Loch Awe

8

162

Kirkaig

Càm Loch

814

364
AN STICHD

Loch Ailsh

476
BEINN SGEIREACH

4

Loch Sìonascaig

Loch Veyatie

849
CUL MÒR

Ledmore Junction

A837

NC

544
BEINN AN EÒIN

River Cassley

10

612
POLLAIDH

Knockan

Elphin

Loch Urigill

Knockan Cliff

307
CNOC NA GLAS CHOILLE

5

769
CUL BEAG

Knockan Crag

Loch na Claise-Mòire

402
CNOC A' CH

Loch Lurgainn

Cromalt Hills

River Oykel

Rosehall
A837

6

GACH

Drumrunie Lodge

Loch a' Chroisg

Rappach

Oykel Bridge Hotel

Doune

Strath Oykel

Alt

18

Strathcanaird

Strath Canaird

408
NA DROMANNAN

31

00

7

A835

Rappach Water

Glen Einig

493
BEINN ULBHAIDH

463
BREAC-BHEINN

Ardmair

Loch an Daimh

412
CREAG LOISGTE

506
MEALL DHEIRGIDH

Morefield

Ullapool (Ulapul)

Glen Achall

Loch Achall

701
CARN A' CHOIN DEIRG

8

M

A835

558
BEINN EILIDEACH

Strath Mulzie

Giusha Burn

Croick

90

Leckmelm

642
MEALL DUBH

677
MEALL-NAM BRADHAN

River Carron

Ardcharnich

Loch a' Choire Mhòir

842
CARN BAN

Glencalvie Forest

9

Ardindrean

Letters

647
CÀRN MÒR

NH

Inverlael

River Lael

Gleann Beag

Strathkvaich Forest

162

838
CÀRN CHUINN

10

507
CÀRN BHIORAIN

Croftown

710
BEINN THARSUINN

Crom Loch

628

R Broom

1081
BEINN DEARG

11

387
CARN BREAC BEAG

Braemore

Corrieshalloch Gorge

771
MEALL A' GHRIANAIN

Loch a' Chaorunn

11

Falls of Measach

618
MEALL LEACACHAIN

Loch Coire Làir

155

742
BEINN NAN EUN

601
MEALL AN T-SITHE

A832

Loch Glascarnoch

12

Loch-a' Bhraoin

Loch Droma

742
TOM BÀN MÒR

Loch Vaich

999
A' CHAILLEACH

SGÙRR MÒR

662
BEINN LIATH BHEAG

Aultguish Inn

CÀR

J

K

20

1109

L

M

30

N

P

40

Q

R

50

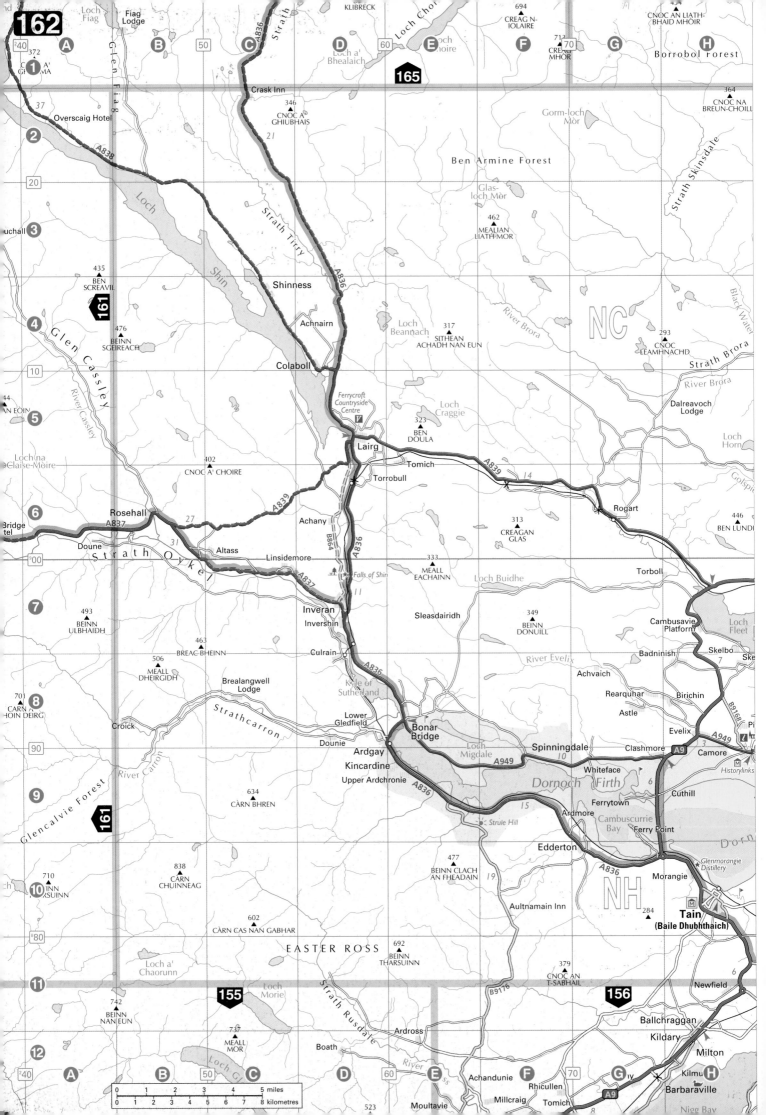

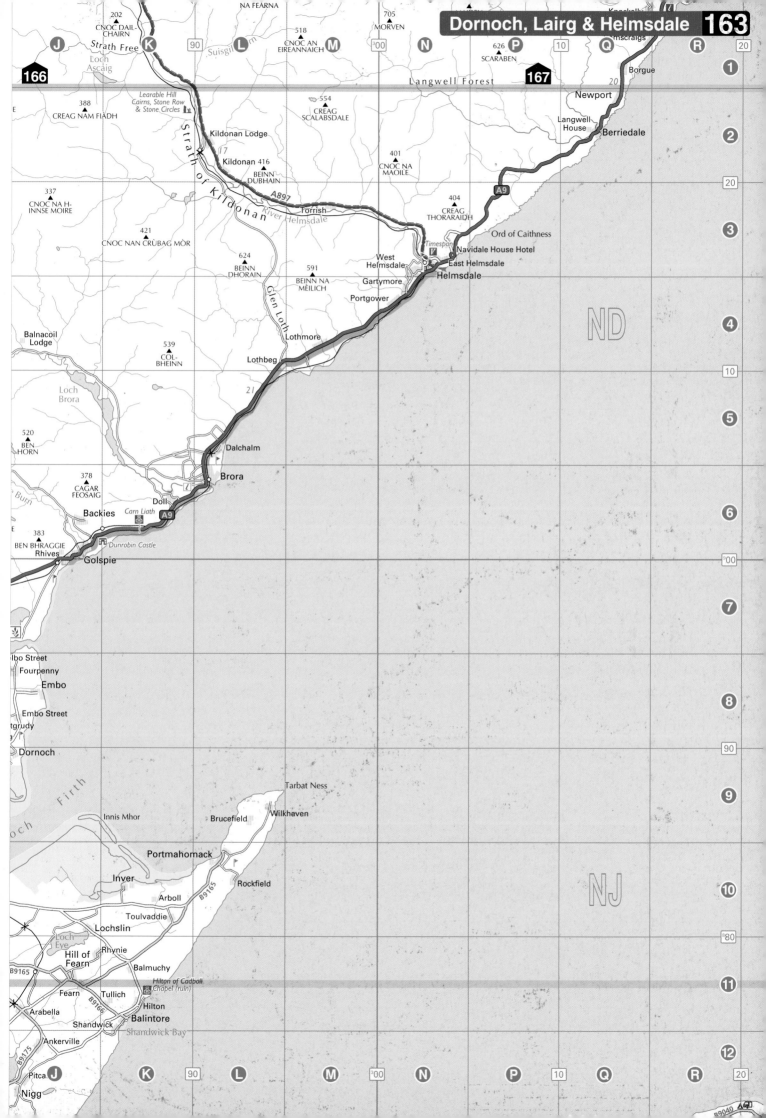

J **K** **L** **M** **N** **P** **Q** **R**

166
167

1
2
3
4
5
6
7
8
9
10
11
12

CNOC DAIL-CHAIRN 202

NA FEARNA

Strath Free
Loch Ascaig

Suisgill

518
CNOC AN EIREANNAICH

705
MORVEN

626
SCARABEN

Knockalty
Borgue

Newport

CREAG NAM FIADH 388

Learable Hill
Cairns, Stone Row
& Stone Circles

554
CREAG
SCALABSDALE

Langwell Forest

Langwell
House

Berriedale

Kildonan Lodge

Strath of Kildonan

Kildonan 416
BEINN
DUBHAIN

A897

401
CNOC NA
MAOILE

404
CREAG
THORARAIDH

A9

20

20

Ord of Caithness

CNOC NA H-INNSE MOIRE 337

Torrish

River Helmsdale

Timespan
Navidale House Hotel

CNOC NAN CRÙBAG MÒR 421

624
BEINN
DHORAIN

591
BEINN NA
MÈILICH

West
Helmsdale
Gartymore

East Helmsdale
Helmsdale

Portgower

Glen Loth

Lothmore

ND

Balnacoil
Lodge

539
COL-BHEINN

Lothbeg

Loch Brora

21

520
BEN
HORN

Dalchalm

CAGAR
FEOSAIG 378

Brora

Doll

Backies
Carn Liath
A9

Burn

BEN BHRAGGIE 383
Rhives

Dunrobin Castle

Golspie

lbo Street
Fourpenny
Embo

Embo Street
tgrudy

Dornoch

Firth

90

Tarbat Ness

Innis Mhor

Brucefield
Wilkhaven

NJ

Portmahomack

Inver
Rockfield

Arboll
B9165

Toulvaddie

Lochslin

Loch
Eye

Rhynie

Hill of
Fearn

Balmuchy

B9165

B80

Fearn
Tullich

Hilton of Cadboll
Chapel (ruin)

Arabella

Shandwick

Hilton
Balintore
Shandwick Bay

Ankerville

B9175

Pitca

Nigg

J **K** **L** **M** **N** **P** **Q** **R**

90
00
10
20

A9040

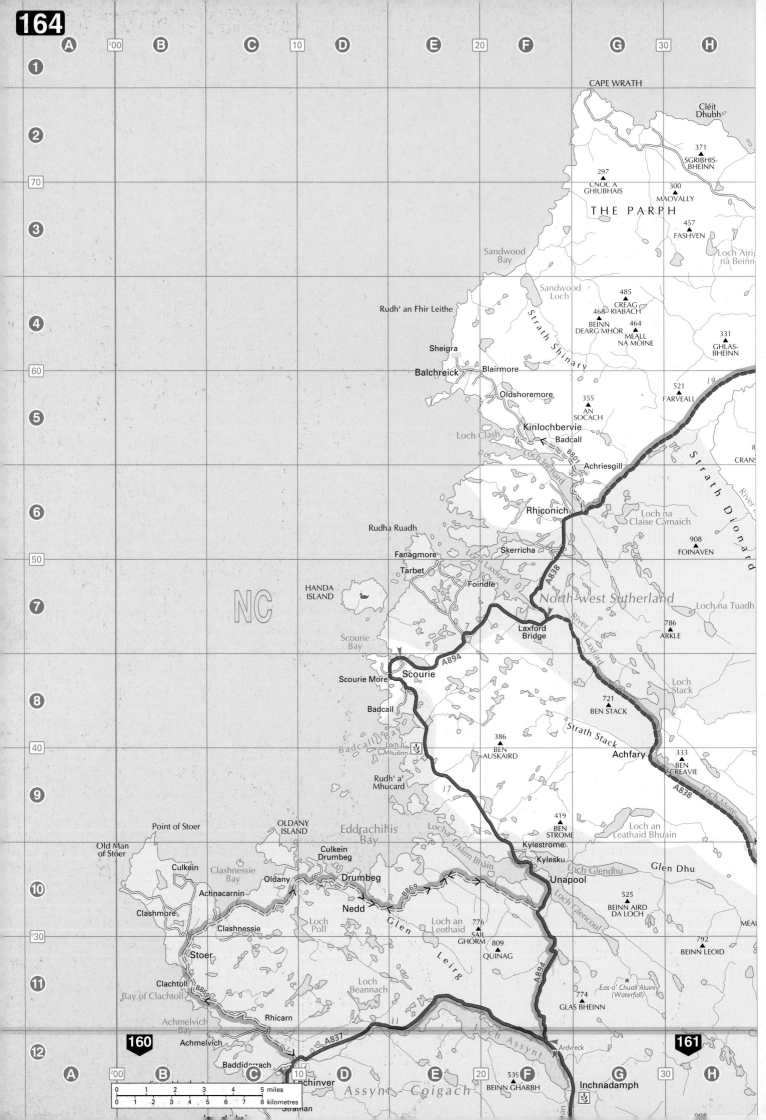

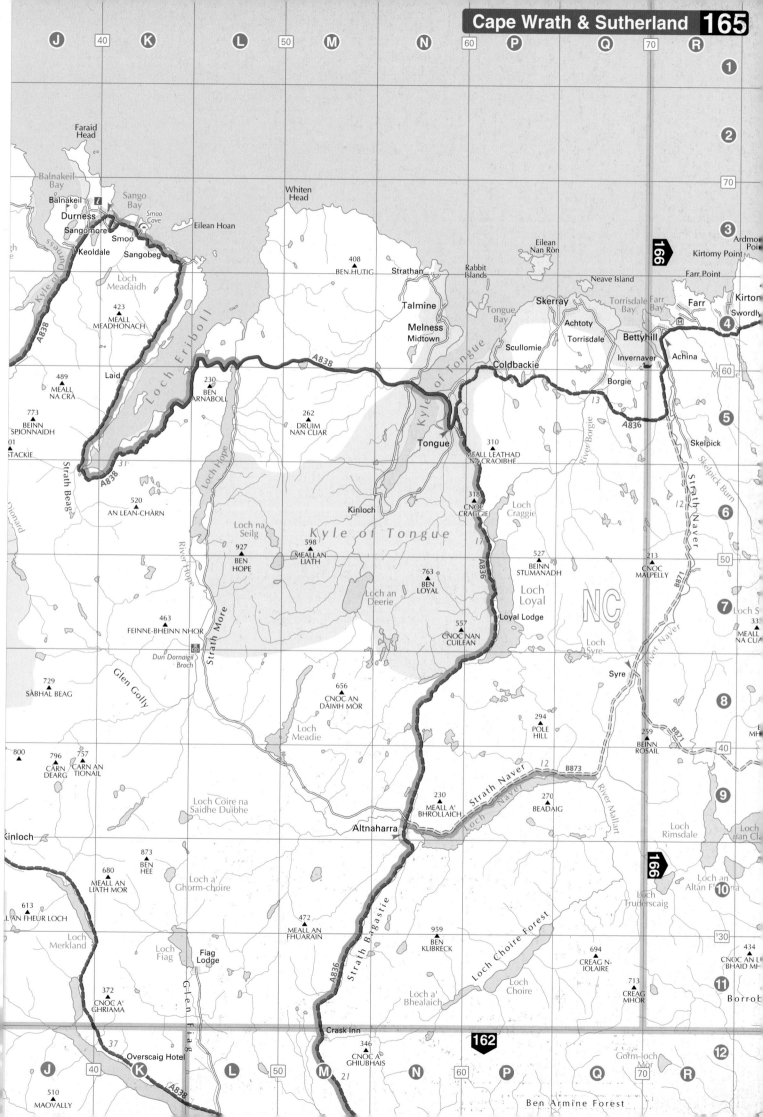

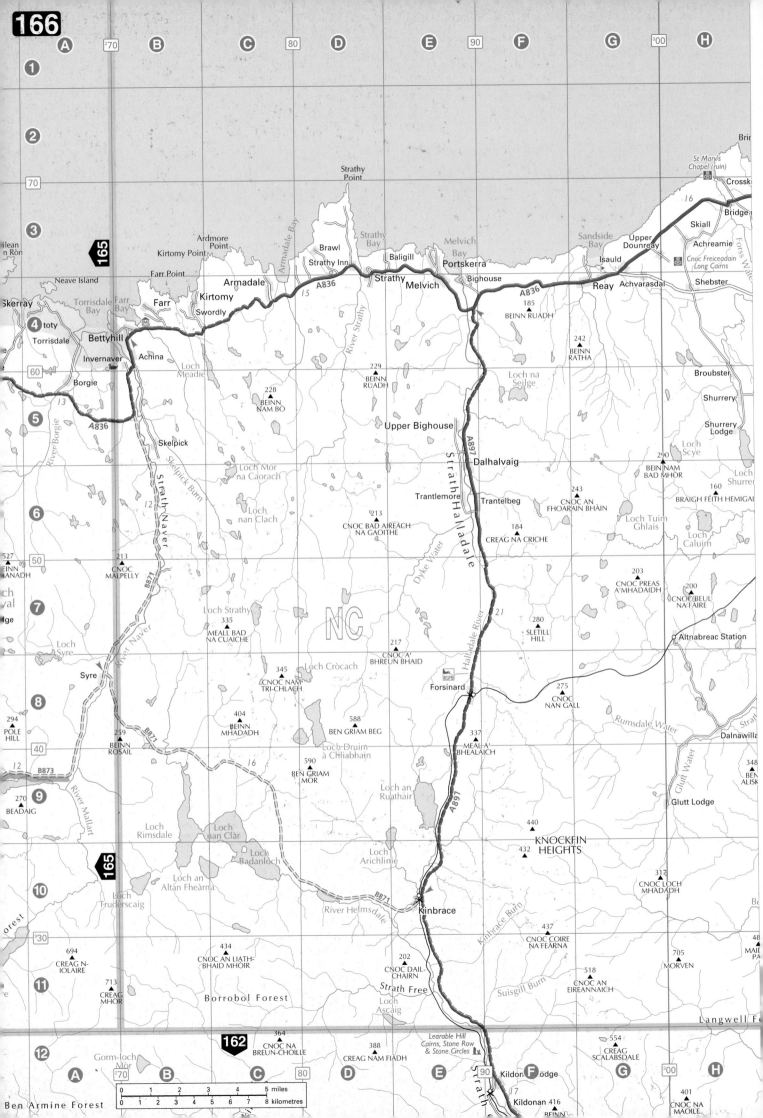

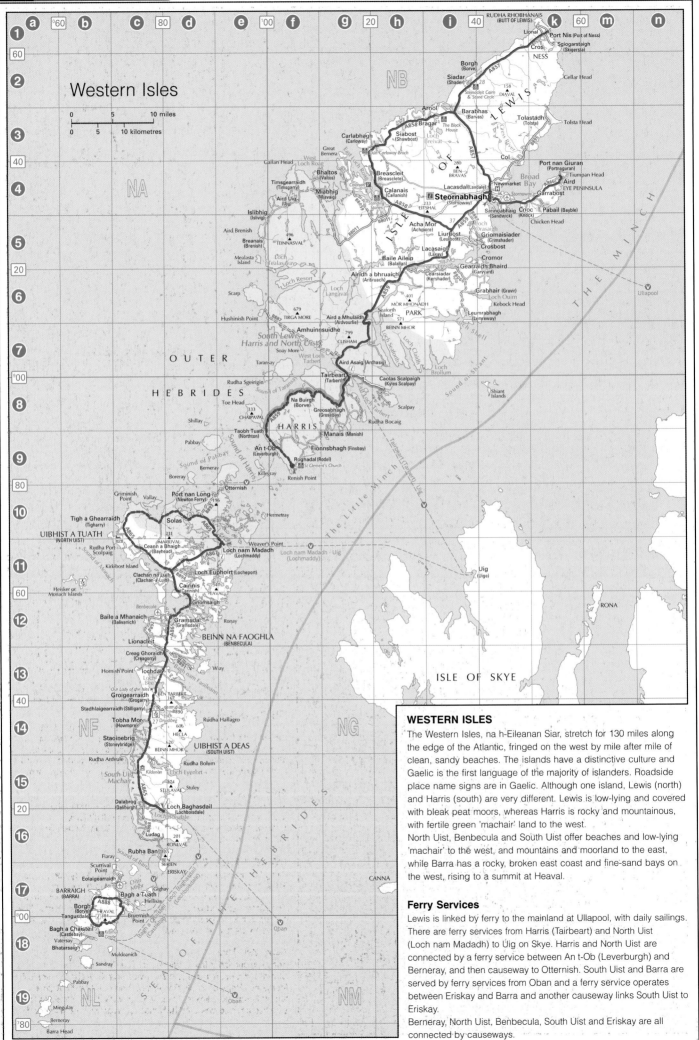

Western Isles

WESTERN ISLES

The Western Isles, na h-Eileanan Siar, stretch for 130 miles along the edge of the Atlantic, fringed on the west by mile after mile of clean, sandy beaches. The islands have a distinctive culture and Gaelic is the first language of the majority of islanders. Roadside place name signs are in Gaelic. Although one island, Lewis (north) and Harris (south) are very different. Lewis is low-lying and covered with bleak peat moors, whereas Harris is rocky and mountainous, with fertile green 'machair' land to the west.

North Uist, Benbecula and South Uist offer beaches and low-lying 'machair' to the west, and mountains and moorland to the east, while Barra has a rocky, broken east coast and fine-sand bays on the west, rising to a summit at Heaval.

Ferry Services

Lewis is linked by ferry to the mainland at Ullapool, with daily sailings. There are ferry services from Harris (Tairbeart) and North Uist (Loch nam Madadh) to Uig on Skye. Harris and North Uist are connected by a ferry service between An t-Ob (Leverburgh) and Berneray, and then causeway to Otternish. South Uist and Barra are served by ferry services from Oban and a ferry service operates between Eriskay and Barra and another causeway links South Uist to Eriskay.

Berneray, North Uist, Benbecula, South Uist and Eriskay are all connected by causeways.

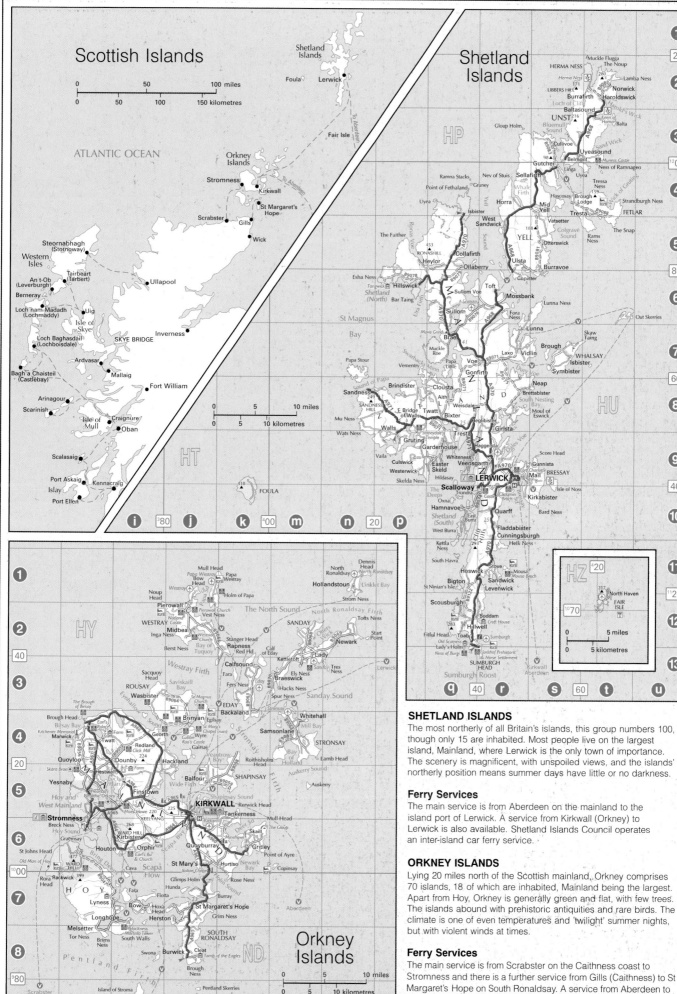

Scottish Islands

ATLANTIC OCEAN

Shetland Islands
Foula
Lerwick
Fair Isle

Orkney Islands
Stromness
Kirkwall
St Margaret's Hope
Scrabster
Gills
Wick

Steornabhagh (Stornoway)
Western Isles
Tairbeart (Tarbert)
An t-Ob (Leverburgh)
Berneray
Loch nam Madadh (Lochmaddy)
Uig
Isle of Skye
Ullapool
Inverness
Loch Baghasdail (Lochboisdale)
SKYE BRIDGE
Ardvasar
Mallaig
Bagh a Chaisteil (Castlebay)
Fort William
Arinagour
Scarinish
Craignure
Isle of Mull
Oban
Scalasaig
Port Askaig
Islay
Kennacraig
Port Ellen

Shetland Islands

Orkney Islands

KIRKWALL
Stromness

SHETLAND ISLANDS

The most northerly of all Britain's islands, this group numbers 100, though only 15 are inhabited. Most people live on the largest island, Mainland, where Lerwick is the only town of importance. The scenery is magnificent, with unspoiled views, and the islands' northerly position means summer days have little or no darkness.

Ferry Services

The main service is from Aberdeen on the mainland to the island port of Lerwick. A service from Kirkwall (Orkney) to Lerwick is also available. Shetland Islands Council operates an inter-island car ferry service.

ORKNEY ISLANDS

Lying 20 miles north of the Scottish mainland, Orkney comprises 70 islands, 18 of which are inhabited, Mainland being the largest. Apart from Hoy, Orkney is generally green and flat, with few trees. The islands abound with prehistoric antiquities and rare birds. The climate is one of even temperatures and 'twilight' summer nights, but with violent winds at times.

Ferry Services

The main service is from Scrabster on the Caithness coast to Stromness and there is a further service from Gills (Caithness) to St Margaret's Hope on South Ronaldsay. A service from Aberdeen to Kirkwall provides a link to Shetland at Lerwick. Inter-island car ferry services are also operated (advance reservations recommended).

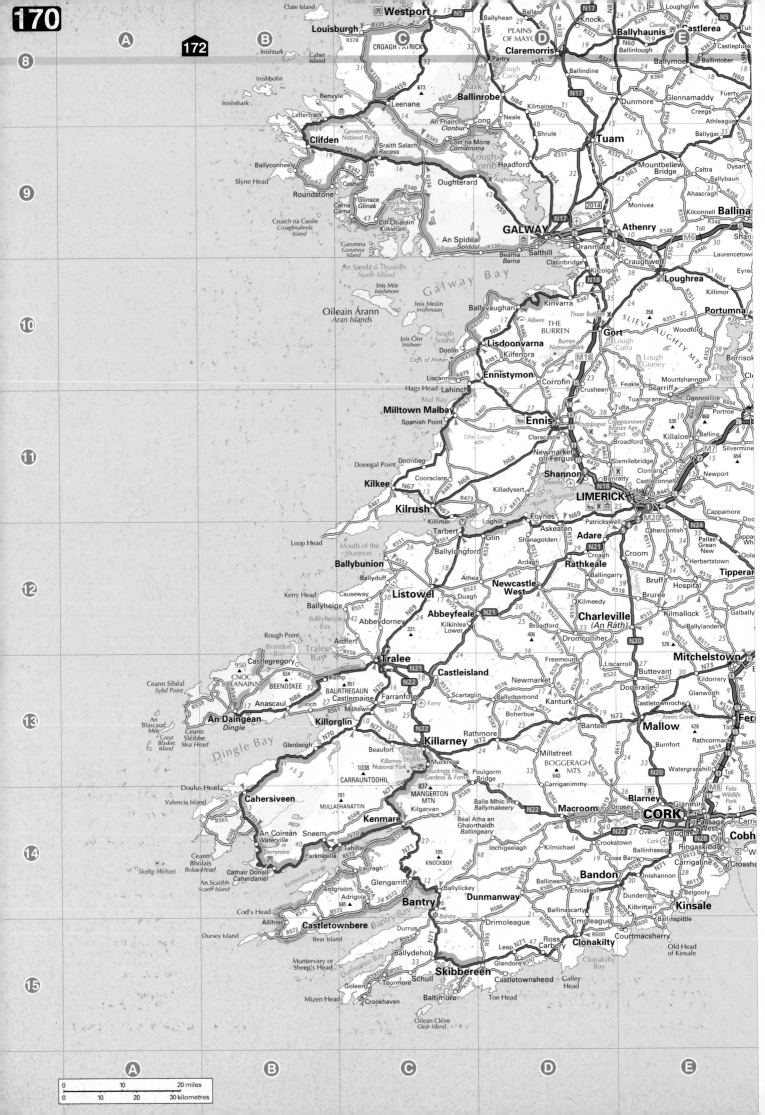

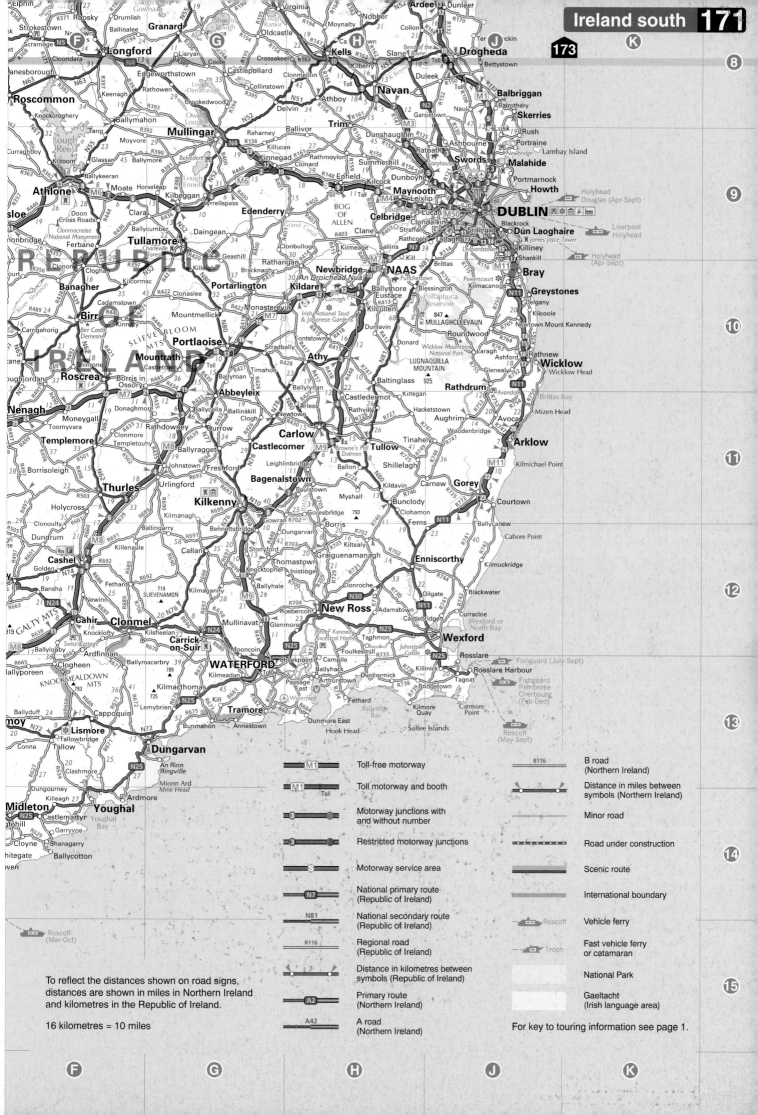

Ireland index

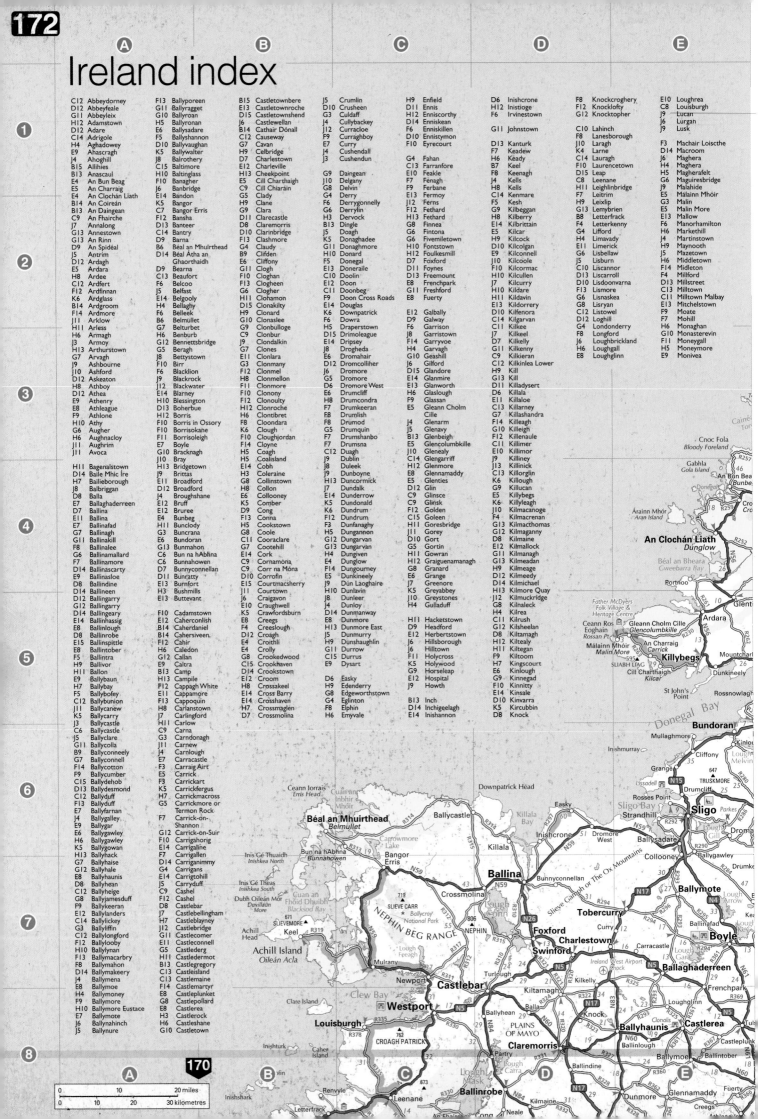

0   10   20 miles
0   10   20   30 kilometres

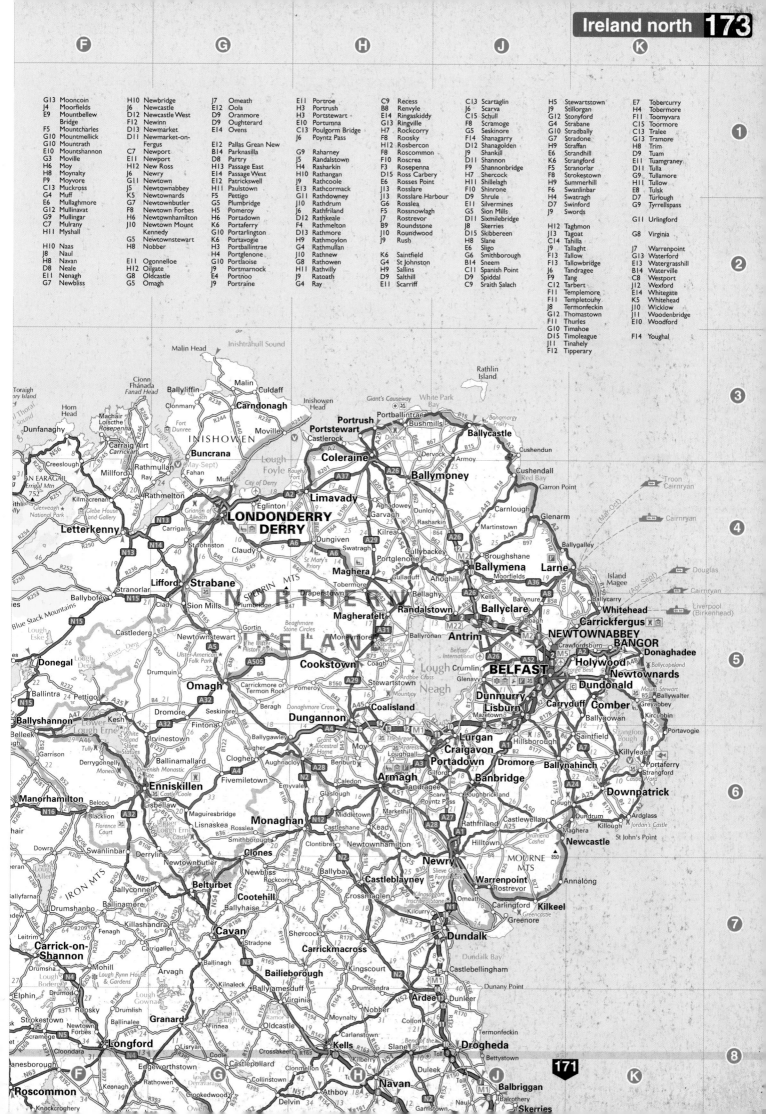

Restricted junctions

Motorway and Primary Route junctions which have access or exit restrictions are shown on the map pages thus:

M1 London - Leeds

Northbound
Access only from A1
(northbound)

Southbound
Exit only to A1
(southbound)

Northbound
Access only from A41
(northbound)

Southbound
Exit only to A41
(southbound)

Northbound
Access only from M25
(no link from A405)

Southbound
Exit only to M25 (no link
from A405)

Northbound
Access only from A414

Southbound
Exit only to A414

Northbound
Exit only to M45

Southbound
Access only from M45

Northbound
Exit only to M6
(northbound)

Southbound
Access only from M6

Northbound
Exit only, no access

Southbound
Access only, no exit

Northbound
Access only from A42

Southbound
No restriction

Northbound
No exit, access only

Southbound
Exit only, no access

Northbound
Exit only, no access

Southbound
Access only, no exit

Northbound
Exit only, no access

Southbound
Access only, no exit

Northbound
Exit only to M621

Southbound
Access only from M621

Northbound
Exit only to A1(M)
(northbound)

Southbound
Access only from A1(M)
(southbound)

M2 Rochester - Faversham

Westbound
No exit to A2
(eastbound)

Eastbound
No access from A2
(westbound)

M3 Sunbury - Southampton

Northeastbound
Access only from A303,
no exit

Southwestbound
Exit only to A303,
no access

Northbound
Exit only, no access

Southbound
Access only, no exit

Northeastbound
Access from M27 only.
No exit

Southwestbound
No access to M27
(westbound)

M4 London - South Wales

Westbound
Access only from A4
(westbound)

Eastbound
Exit only to A4
(eastbound)

Westbound
No exit to A4 (westbound)

Eastbound
No restriction

Westbound
Exit only to M48

Eastbound
Access only from M48

Westbound
Access only from M48

Eastbound
Exit only to M48

Westbound
Exit only, no access

Eastbound
Access only, no exit

Westbound
Exit only, no access

Eastbound
Access only, no exit

Westbound
Exit only to A48(M)

Eastbound
Access only from A48(M)

Westbound
Exit only, no access

Eastbound
No restriction

Westbound
Access only, no exit

Eastbound
No access or exit

M5 Birmingham - Exeter

Northeastbound
Access only, no exit

Southwestbound
Exit only, no access

Northeastbound
Access only from A417
(westbound)

Southwestbound
Exit only to A417
(eastbound)

Northeastbound
No access, exit only

Southwestbound
No exit, access only

Northeastbound
Exit only to M49

Southwestbound
Access only from M49

Northeastbound
No restriction

Southwestbound
Access only from A30
(westbound)

M6 Toll Motorway

See M6 Toll Motorway map on page 179

M6 Rugby - Carlisle

Northbound
Exit only to M6 Toll

Southbound
Access only from M6 Toll

Northbound
Access only from M42
(southbound)

Southbound
Exit only to M42

Northbound
Exit only, no access

Southbound
Access only, no exit

Northbound
Exit only to M54

Southbound
Access only from M54

Northbound
Access only from M6 Toll

Southbound
Exit only to M6 Toll

Northbound
No restriction

Southbound
Access only from M56
(eastbound)

Northbound
Access only, no exit

Southbound
No restriction

Northbound
Access only, no exit

Southbound
Exit only, no access

Northbound
Exit only, no access

Southbound
Access only, no exit

Northbound
No direct access, use adjacent slip road to jct 29A

Southbound
No direct exit, use adjacent slip road from jct 29A

Northbound
Access only, no exit

Southbound
Exit only, no access

Northbound
Access only from M61

Southbound
Exit only to M61

Northbound
Exit only, no access

Southbound
Access only, no exit

Northbound
Exit only, no access

Southbound
Access only, no exit

M8 Edinburgh - Bishopton

See Glasgow District map on pages 254-255

M9 Edinburgh - Dunblane

Northwestbound
Exit only to M9 spur

Southeastbound
Access only from M9 spur

Northwestbound
Access only, no exit

Southeastbound
Exit only, no access

Northwestbound
Exit only, no access

Southeastbound
Access only, no exit

Northwestbound
Access only, no exit

Southeastbound
Exit only to A905

Northwestbound
Exit only to M876 (southwestbound)

Southeastbound
Access only from M876 (northeastbound)

M11 London - Cambridge

Northbound
Access only from A406 (eastbound)

Southbound
Exit only to A406

Northbound
Exit only, no access

Southbound
Access only, no exit

Northbound
Exit only to A11

Southbound
Access only from A11

Northbound
Exit only, no access

Southbound
Access only, no exit

Northbound
Exit only, no access

Southbound
Access only, no exit

M20 Swanley - Folkestone

Northwestbound
Staggered junction; follow signs - access only

Southeastbound
Staggered junction; follow signs - exit only

Northwestbound
Exit only to M26 (westbound)

Southeastbound
Access only from M26 (eastbound)

Northwestbound
Access only from A20

Southeastbound
For access follow signs exit only to A20

Northwestbound
No restriction

Southeastbound
For exit follow signs

Northwestbound
Access only, no exit

Southeastbound
Exit only, no access

M23 Hooley - Crawley

Northbound
Exit only to A23 (northbound)

Southbound
Access only from A23 (southbound)

Northbound
Access only from A406 (eastbound)

Southbound
Exit only to A406

Northbound
Exit only, no access

Southbound
Access only, no exit

M25 London Orbital Motorway

See M25 London Orbital Motorway map on page 178

M26 Sevenoaks - Wrotham

Westbound
Exit only to clockwise M25 (westbound)

Eastbound
Access only from anti-clockwise M25 (eastbound)

Westbound
Access only from M20 (northwestbound)

Eastbound
Exit only to M20 (southeastbound)

M27 Cadnam - Portsmouth

Westbound
Staggered junction; follow signs - access only from M3 (southbound). Exit only to M3 (northbound)

Eastbound
Staggered junction; follow signs - access only from M3 (southbound). Exit only to M3 (northbound)

Westbound
Exit only, no access

Eastbound
Access only, no exit

Westbound
Staggered junction; follow signs - exit only to M275 (southbound)

Eastbound
Staggered junction; follow signs - access only from M275 (northbound)

M40 London - Birmingham

Northwestbound
Exit only, no access

Southeastbound
Access only, no exit

Northwestbound
Exit only, no access

Southeastbound
Access only, no exit

Northwestbound
Exit only to M40/A40

Southeastbound
Access only from M40/A40

(M40 continued)

Northwestbound
Access only, no exit

Southeastbound
Exit only, no access

Northwestbound
Access only, no exit

Southeastbound
Exit only, no access

Northwestbound
Access only, no exit

Southeastbound
Exit only, no access

M42 Bromsgrove - Measham

See Birmingham District map on pages 252-253

M45 Coventry - M1

Westbound
Access only from A45 (northbound)

Eastbound
Exit only, no access

Westbound
Access only from M1 (northbound)

Eastbound
Exit only to M1 (southbound)

M53 Mersey Tunnel - Chester

Northbound
Access only from M56 (westbound). Exit only to M56 (eastbound)

Southbound
Access only from M56 (westbound). Exit only to M56 (eastbound)

M54 Telford

Westbound
Access only from M6 (northbound)

Eastbound
Exit only to M6 (southbound)

M56 North Cheshire

For junctions 1,2,3,4 & 7 see Manchester District map on pages 256-257

Westbound
Access only, no exit

Eastbound
No access or exit

Westbound
Exit only to M53

Eastbound
Access only from M53

M57 Liverpool Outer Ring Road

Northwestbound
Access only, no exit

Southeastbound
Exit only, no access

Northwestbound
Access only from A580
(westbound)

Southeastbound
Exit only, no access

M58 Liverpool - Wigan

Westbound
Exit only, no access

Eastbound
Access only, no exit

M60 Manchester Orbital

See Manchester District map on pages 256-257

M61 Manchester - Preston

Northwestbound
No access or exit

Southeastbound
Exit only, no access

Northwestbound
Exit only to M6
(northbound)

Southeastbound
Access only from M6
(southbound)

M62 Liverpool - Kingston upon Hull

Westbound
Access only, no exit

Eastbound
Exit only, no access

Westbound
No access to A1(M)
(southbound)

Eastbound
No restriction

M65 Preston - Colne

Northeastbound
Exit only, no access

Southwestbound
Access only, no exit

Northeastbound
Access only, no exit

Southwestbound
Exit only, no access

M66 Bury

Northbound
Exit only to A56
(northbound)

Southbound
Access only from A56
(southbound)

Northbound
Exit only, no access

Southbound
Access only, no exit

M67 Hyde Bypass

Westbound
Access only, no exit

Eastbound
Exit only, no access

Westbound
Exit only, no access

Eastbound
Access only, no exit

Westbound
Exit only, no access

Eastbound
No restriction

M69 Coventry - Leicester

Northbound
Access only, no exit

Southbound
Exit only, no access

M73 East of Glasgow

Northbound
No access from or exit to A89. No access from M8 (eastbound)

Southbound
No access from or exit to A89. No exit to M8 (westbound)

M74 and A74(M) Glasgow - Gretna

Northbound
Exit only, no access

Southbound
Access only, no exit

Northbound
Access only, no exit

Southbound
Exit only, no access

Northbound
Access only, no exit

Southbound
Exit only, no access

M77 South of Glasgow

Northbound
No exit to M8 (westbound)

Southbound
No access from M8 (eastbound)

Northbound
Access only, no exit

Southbound
Exit only, no access

Northbound
Access only, no exit

Southbound
Exit only, no access

Northbound
Access only, no exit

Southbound
No restriction

M80 Glasgow - Stirling

Northbound
Exit only, no access

Southbound
Access only, no exit

Northbound
Access only, no exit

Southbound
Exit only, no access

Northbound
Access only, no exit

Southbound
Exit only, no access

Northbound
No access or exit

Southbound
Exit only, no access

Northbound
No restriction

Southbound
Access only, no exit

Northbound
Access only, no exit

Southbound
Exit only, no access

Northbound
Exit only, no access

Southbound
Access only, no exit

Northbound
Exit only, no access

Southbound
Access only, no exit

Northbound
Exit only, no access

Southbound
Access only, no exit

M90 Forth Road Bridge - Perth

Northbound
Exit only to A92
(eastbound)

Southbound
Access only from A92
(westbound)

Northbound
Access only, no exit

Southbound
Exit only, no access

Northbound
Exit only, no access

Southbound
Access only, no exit

Northbound
No access from A912
No exit to A912
(southbound)

Southbound
No access from A912
(northbound).
No exit to A912

M180 Doncaster - Grimsby

Westbound
Access only, no exit

Eastbound
Exit only, no access

M606 Bradford Spur

Northbound
Exit only, no access

Southbound
No restriction

M621 Leeds - M1

Clockwise
Access only, no exit

Anticlockwise
Exit only, no access

Clockwise
No exit or access

Anticlockwise
No restriction

Clockwise
Access only, no exit

Anticlockwise
Exit only, no access

Clockwise
Exit only, no access
Anticlockwise
Access only, no exit

Clockwise
Exit only to M1
(southbound)
Anticlockwise
Access only from M1
(northbound)

M876 Bonnybridge - Kincardine Bridge

Northeastbound
Access only from M80
(northbound)
Southwestbound
Exit only to M80
(southbound)

Northeastbound
Exit only to M9
(eastbound)
Southwestbound
Access only from M9
(westbound)

A1(M) South Mimms - Baldock

Northbound
Exit only, no access
Southbound
Access only, no exit

Northbound
No restriction
Southbound
Exit only, no access

Northbound
Access only, no exit
Southbound
No access or exit

A1(M) East of Leeds

Northbound
No access to M62
(eastbound)
Southbound
No restriction

Northbound
Access only from M1
(northbound)
Southbound
Exit only to M1
(southbound)

A1(M) Scotch Corner - Newcastle upon Tyne

Northbound
Exit only to A66(M)
(eastbound)
Southbound
Access only from A66(M)
(westbound)

Northbound
No access. Exit only to
A194(M) & A1
(northbound)
Southbound
No exit. Access only from
A194(M) & A1
(southbound)

A3(M) Horndean - Havant

Northbound
Access only from A3
Southbound
Exit only to A3

Northbound
Exit only, no access
Southbound
Access only, no exit

A48(M) Cardiff Spur

Westbound
Access only from M4
(westbound)
Eastbound
Exit only to M4
(eastbound)

Westbound
Exit only to A48
(westbound)
Eastbound
Access only from A48
(eastbound)

A66(M) Darlington Spur

Westbound
Exit only to A1(M)
(southbound)
Eastbound
Access only from A1(M)
(northbound)

A194(M) Newcastle upon Tyne

Northbound
Access only from A1(M)
(northbound)
Southbound
Exit only to A1(M)
(southbound)

A12 M25 - Ipswich

Northeastbound
Access only, no exit
Southwestbound
No restriction

Northeastbound
Exit only, no access
Southwestbound
Access only, no exit

Northeastbound
Exit only, no access
Southwestbound
Access only, no exit

Northeastbound
Access only, no exit
Southwestbound
Access only, no access

Northeastbound
No restriction
Southwestbound
Access only, no exit

Northeastbound
Exit only, no access
Southwestbound
Access only, no access

Northeastbound
Access only, no exit
Southwestbound
Exit only, no access

Northeastbound
Exit only, no access
Southwestbound
Access only, no exit

With A120
Northeastbound
Exit only, no access
Southwestbound
Access only, no exit

Northeastbound
Access only, no exit
Southwestbound
Exit only, no access

Northeastbound
Exit only (for Stratford
St Mary and Dedham)
Southwestbound
Access only

A14 M1 Felixstowe

Westbound
Exit only to M6 & M1
(northbound)
Eastbound
Access only from M6 &
M1 (southbound)

Westbound
Exit only, no access
Eastbound
Access only, no exit

Westbound
Access only from A1307
Eastbound
Exit only to A1307

Westbound
Access only, no exit
Eastbound
Exit only, no access

Westbound
Exit only to A11
Eastbound
Access only from A11

Westbound
Access only from A11
Eastbound
Exit only to A11

Westbound
Exit only, no access
Eastbound
Access only, no exit

Westbound
Access only, no exit
Eastbound
Exit only, no exit

A55 Holyhead - Chester

Westbound
Exit only, no access
Eastbound
Access only, no exit

Westbound
Access only, no exit
Eastbound
Exit only, no access

Westbound
Exit only, no access
Eastbound
No access or exit.

Westbound
Exit only, no access
Eastbound
No access or exit

Westbound
Exit only, no access
Eastbound
Access only, no exit

Westbound
Exit only to A5104
Eastbound
Access only from A5104

M25 London Orbital motorway

Refer also to atlas pages 36–37 and 50–51

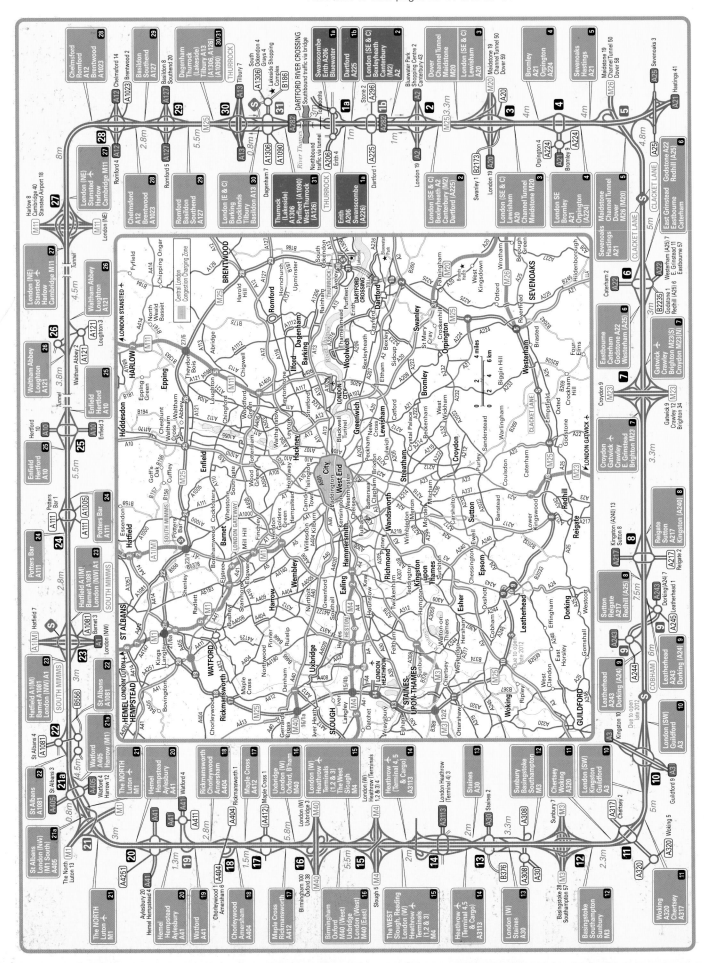

M6 Toll motorway

Refer also to atlas pages 58–59

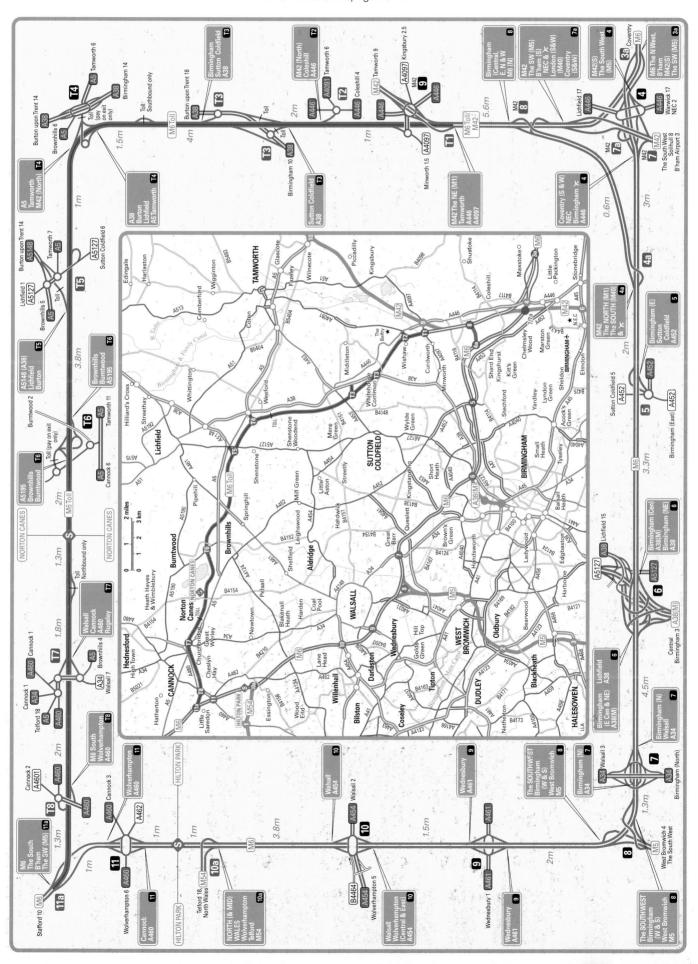

Street map symbols

Town, port and airport plans

Motorway and junction	One-way, gated/ closed road	Railway station	P Car park
Primary road single/dual carriageway	Restricted access road	o Light rapid transit system station	P+ Park and Ride (at least 6 days per week)
A road single/ dual carriageway	Pedestrian area	Level crossing	Bus/coach station
B road single/ dual carriageway	----- Footpath	Tramway	H Hospital
Local road single/ dual carriageway	- - - - Road under construction	Ferry route	H 24-hour Accident & Emergency hospital
Other road single/ dual carriageway, minor road	[------] Road tunnel	Airport, heliport	Petrol station, 24 hour Major suppliers only
Building of interest	M Museum	R Railair terminal	City wall
Ruined building	Castle	Theatre or performing arts centre	Escarpment
i Tourist Information Centre	Castle mound	Cinema	Cliff lift
V Visitor or heritage centre	• Monument, statue	† Abbey, chapel, church	River/canal, lake
World Heritage Site (UNESCO)	Post Office	Synagogue	Lock, weir
English Heritage site	Public library	Mosque	Park/sports ground
Historic Scotland site	Shopping centre	Golf Course	Cemetery
Cadw (Welsh heritage) site	Shopmobility	Racecourse	Woodland
National Trust site	Viewpoint	Nature reserve	Built-up area
National Trust Scotland site	Toilet, with facilities for the less able	Aquarium	Beach

Central London street map (see pages 232 - 241)

30 Speed camera site (fixed location) with speed limit in mph	London Underground station	Docklands Light Railway (DLR) station
40 Section of road with two or more fixed camera sites; speed limit in mph	London Overground station	Central London Congestion Charging Zone
50→ ←50 Average speed (SPECS™) camera system with speed limit in mph	Rail interchange	

Royal Parks (opening and closing times for traffic)

Green Park	Open 5am-midnight. Constitution Hill: closed Sundays
Hyde Park	Open 5am-midnight
Regent's Park	Open 5am-dusk. Most park roads closed midnight-7am
St James's Park	Open 5am-midnight. The Mall: closed Sundays

Traffic regulations in the City of London include security checkpoints and restrict the number of entry and exit points.

Note: Oxford Street is closed to through-traffic (except buses & taxis) 7am-7pm Monday-Saturday.

Central London Congestion Charging Zone

The daily charge for driving or parking a vehicle on public roads in the Congestion Charging Zone (CCZ), during operating hours, is £10 per vehicle per day in advance or on the day of travel. Alternatively you can pay £9 by registering with CC Auto Pay, an automated payment system. Drivers can also pay the next charging day after travelling in the zone but this will cost £12. Payment permits entry, travel within and exit from the CCZ by the vehicle as often as required on that day.

The CCZ operates between 7am and 6pm, Mon–Fri only. There is no charge at weekends, public holidays or betwen 25th Dec and 1st Jan inclusive.

For up to date information on the CCZ, exemptions, discounts or ways to pay, telephone 0845 900 1234, visit www.cclondon.com or write to Congestion Charging, P.O. Box 4782, Worthing BN11 9PS. Textphone users can call 020 7649 9123.

Towns, ports & airports

Central London

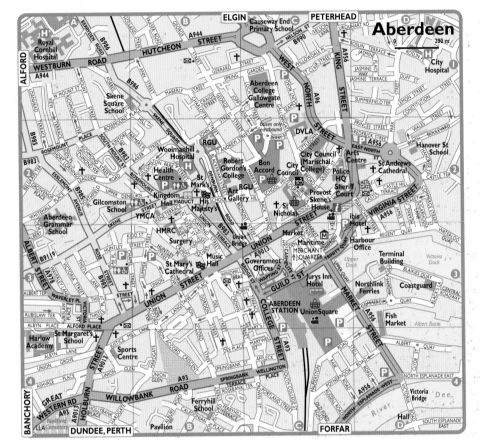

Aberdeen

Aberdeen is found on atlas page **151 N6**

C4	Affleck Street	B1	Maberly Street
A3	Albert Street	D2	Marischal Street
B4	Albury Road	C3	Market Street
A3	Alford Place	C1	Nelson Street
B1	Ann Street	C4	Palmerston Road
D2	Beach Boulevard	D1	Park Street
A2	Belgrave Terrace	C4	Portland Street
A1	Berryden Road	C4	Poynernook Road
B2	Blackfriars Street	D3	Regent Quay
D3	Blaikies Quay	A2	Richmond Street
B4	Bon Accord Crescent	A3	Rose Place
B3	Bon Accord Street	A3	Rose Street
C3	Bridge Street	A2	Rosemount Place
B4	Caledonian Place	A2	Rosemount Viaduct
C3	Carmelite Street	B2	St Andrew Street
A3	Chapel Street	C1	St Clair Street
B1	Charlotte Street	C2	School Hill
C3	College Street	B2	Skene Square
D1	Constitution Street	A3	Skene Street
B3	Crimon Place	B2	Skene Terrace
B3	Crown Street	C4	South College Street
B3	Dee Street	D4	South Esplanade East
B2	Denburn Road	A2	South Mount Street
B3	Diamond Street	B2	Spa Street
D2	East North Street	B4	Springbank Street
A2	Esslemont Avenue	B4	Springbank Terrace
C1	Gallowgate	B3	Summer Street
B1	George Street	D1	Summerfield Terrace
B2	Gilcomston Park	A3	Thistle Lane
B3	Golden Square	A3	Thistle Place
B3	Gordon Street	A3	Thistle Street
A4	Great Western Road	C3	Trinity Quay
C3	Guild Street	B3	Union Bridge
C3	Hadden Street	A4	Union Grove
D2	Hanover Street	B3	Union Street
B4	Hardgate	B2	Union Terrace
C2	Harriet Street	A2	Upper Denburn
A4	Holburn Street	D4	Victoria Road
A3	Huntley Street	A3	Victoria Street
B1	Hutcheon Street	A1	View Terrace
D1	Jasmine Terrace	D2	Virginia Street
B2	John Street	C3	Wapping Street
A4	Justice Mill Lane	A3	Waverley Place
C1	King Street	C4	Wellington Place
B3	Langstane Place	C1	West North Street
A2	Leadside Road	A1	Westburn Road
A1	Loanhead Terrace	A2	Whitehall Place
C1	Loch Street	A4	Willowbank Road

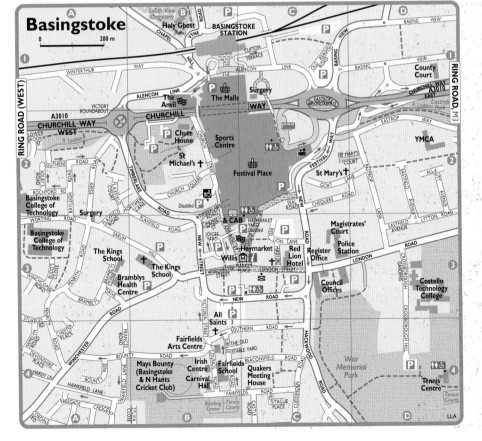

Basingstoke

Basingstoke is found on atlas page **22 H4**

C1	Alencon Link	C3	London Street
D2	Allnutt Avenue	A2	Lower Brook Street
C1	Basing View	D3	Lytton Road
C4	Beaconsfield Road	B3	Market Place
A4	Bounty Rise	C3	May Place
A4	Bounty Road	C4	Montague Place
A3	Bramblys Close	A2	Mortimer Lane
A3	Bramblys Drive	B3	New Road
A3	Budd's Close	C2	New Road
C4	Castle Road	B3	New Street
B1	Chapel Hill	C1	Old Reading Road
C2	Chequers Road	A3	Penrith Road
A4	Chester Place	A2	Rayleigh Road
B2	Churchill Way	C3	Red Lion Lane
D1	Churchill Way East	A2	Rochford Road
A2	Churchill Way West	C2	St Mary's Court
B2	Church Square	A3	Sarum Hill
B2	Church Street	C2	Seal Road
B3	Church Street	A2	Solby's Road
C4	Cliddesden Road	A2	Southend Road
C1	Clifton Terrace	B4	Southern Road
A4	Cordale Road	A3	Stukeley Road
B4	Council Road	B4	Sylvia Close
D3	Crossborough Gardens	B2	Timberlake Road
D3	Crossborough Hill	B3	Victoria Street
B3	Cross Street	A1	Victory Roundabout
A4	Devonshire Place	B1	Vyne Road
D2	Eastfield Avenue	A3	Winchcombe Road
D2	Eastrop Lane	A4	Winchester Road
C1	Eastrop Roundabout	B3	Winchester Street
D2	Eastrop Way	A1	Winterthur Way
A2	Essex Road	A3	Worting Road
B4	Fairfields Road	C3	Wote Street
C2	Festival Way		
A2	Flaxfield Court		
A3	Flaxfield Road		
B3	Flaxfield Road		
A4	Frances Road		
A4	Frescade Crescent		
C2	Goat Lane		
C4	Hackwood Road		
A4	Hamelyn Road		
A4	Hardy Lane		
A4	Hawkfield Lane		
C3	Haymarket Yard		
B3	Joices Yard		
B4	Jubilee Road		
D3	London Road		

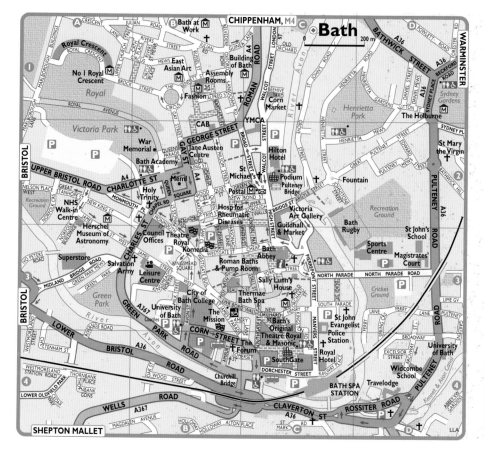

Bath

Bath is found on atlas page **20 D2**

D4	Archway Street	A3	Lower Bristol Road
C2	Argyle Street	A4	Lower Oldfield Park
B3	Avon Street	C3	Manvers Street
B1	Bartlett Street	A3	Midland Bridge Road
B2	Barton Street	B3	Milk Street
D1	Bathwick Street	B2	Milsom Street
B2	Beauford Square	A2	Monmouth Place
B3	Beau Street	B2	Monmouth Street
D1	Beckford Road	B2	New Bond Street
B1	Bennett Street	A2	New King Street
C2	Bridge Street	C3	New Orchard Street
C2	Broad Street	A3	Norfolk Buildings
D4	Broadway	C3	North Parade
A1	Brock Street	D3	North Parade Road
B2	Chapel Road	B2	Old King Street
A3	Charles Street	B1	Oxford Row
A2	Charlotte Street	C3	Pierrepont Street
C3	Cheap Street	B2	Princes Street
A4	Cheltenham Street	D2	Pulteney Road
B1	Circus Mews	B2	Queen Square
C4	Claverton Street	B2	Queen Street
B4	Corn Street	C4	Railway Place
D1	Daniel Street	B1	Rivers Street
C4	Dorchester Street	C1	Roman Road
D2	Edward Street	C4	Rossiter Road
B1	Gay Street	A1	Royal Avenue
B2	George Street	A1	Royal Crescent
C2	Great Pulteney Street	B3	St James's Parade
A2	Great Stanhope Street	C1	St John's Road
A3	Green Park Road	B3	Saw Close
B2	Green Street	C4	Southgate Street
C2	Grove Street	C3	South Parade
B1	Guinea Lane	D1	Stall Street
D1	Henrietta Gardens	D1	Sutton Street
C2	Henrietta Mews	D1	Sydney Place
C1	Henrietta Road	B1	The Circus
C2	Henrietta Street	A4	Thornbank Place
C3	Henry Street	B2	Union Street
C2	High Street	C2	Upper Borough Walls
B3	Hot Bath Street	A2	Upper Bristol Road
B3	James Street West	A1	Upper Church Street
B2	John Street	C2	Walcot Street
B1	Julian Road	A4	Wells Road
B3	Kingsmead North	B3	Westgate Buildings
C3	Kingston Road	B3	Westgate Street
B1	Lansdown Road	A4	Westmoreland Station
C1	London Street		Road
B3	Lower Borough Walls	C3	York Street

Blackpool

Blackpool is found on atlas page **88 C3**

B1	Abingdon Street	B3	Hornby Road
B3	Adelaide Street	D3	Hornby Road
B3	Albert Road	B3	Hull Road
C3	Albert Road	C4	Kay Street
C2	Alfred Street	C4	Kent Road
D4	Ashton Road	C2	King Street
B2	Bank Hey Street	C1	Larkhill Street
B1	Banks Street	D2	Leamington Road
C4	Belmont Avenue	D2	Leicester Road
D3	Bennett Avenue	C2	Leopold Grove
C4	Bethesda Road	D2	Lincoln Road
B2	Birley Street	C3	Livingstone Road
D4	Blenheim Avenue	B1	Lord Street
B4	Bonny Street	C4	Louise Street
C1	Buchanan Street	C1	Milbourne Street
C1	Butler Street	B3	New Bonny Street
D1	Caunce Street	C4	Palatine Road
C2	Cedar Square	D3	Palatine Road
C4	Central Drive	D2	Park Road
B4	Chapel Street	D4	Park Road
C1	Charles Street	D2	Peter Street
C3	Charnley Road	B4	Pier Street
B2	Cheapside	B1	Princess Parade
B2	Church Street	B1	Promenade
C2	Church Street	B1	Queen Street
D2	Church Street	D2	Raikes Parade
B2	Clifton Street	C3	Reads Avenue
D4	Clinton Avenue	D3	Reads Avenue
C2	Cookson Street	C2	Regent Road
B4	Coop Street	C4	Ribble Road
C3	Coronation Street	D3	Ripon Road
B2	Corporation Street	B4	Seasiders Way
B4	Dale Street	C1	Seed Street
B2	Deansgate	D1	Selbourne Road
B1	Dickson Road	C2	South King Street
D1	Edward Street	B1	Springfield Road
D1	Elizabeth Street	C3	Stanley Road
C1	Fisher Street	C1	Swainson Street
B4	Foxhall Road	B2	Talbot Road
D4	Freckleton Street	C1	Talbot Road
D1	General Street	C2	Topping Street
D1	George Street	B2	Tower Street
D1	Gorton Street	B3	Vance Road
D2	Granville Road	B2	Victoria Street
C1	Grosvenor Street	D1	Victory Road
D4	Harrison Street	B2	West Street
C4	Havelock Street	D4	Woolman Road
C1	High Street	B4	York Street

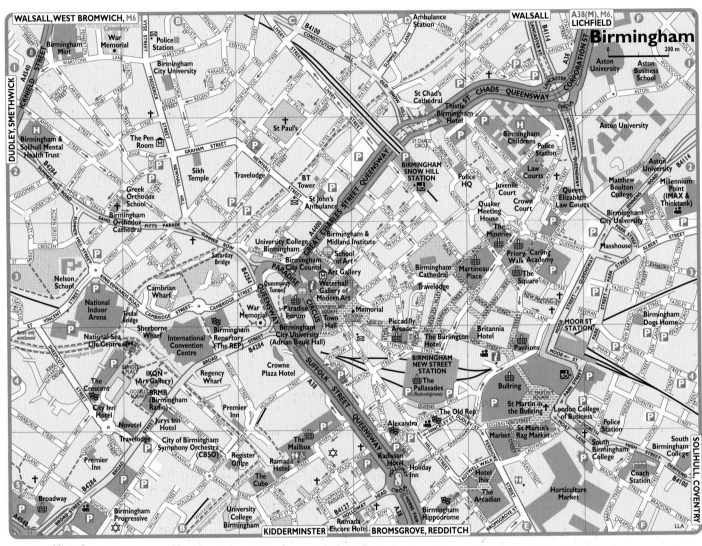

Birmingham

Birmingham is found on atlas page **58 G7**

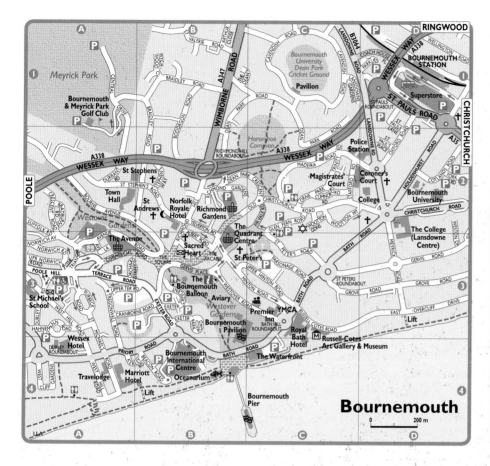

Bournemouth

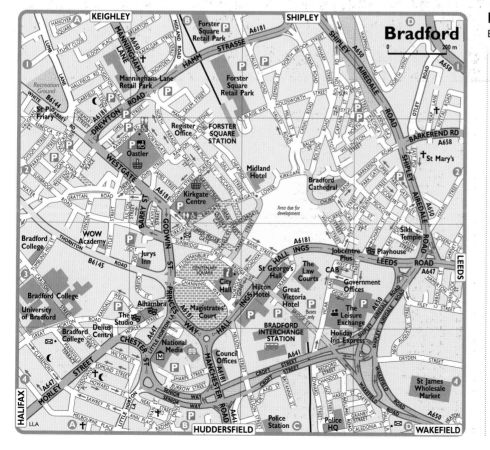

Bradford

Bournemouth

Bournemouth is found on atlas page **13 J6**

B3	Albert Road	A3	Poole Hill
B1	Arthur Close	A4	Priory Road
A3	Avenue Lane	A3	Purbeck Road
A3	Avenue Road	B2	Richmond Gardens
B4	Bath Road	B3	Richmond Hill
B4	Beacon Road	C3	Russell Cotes Road
B2	Bodorgon Road	A3	St Michael's Road
A2	Bourne Avenue	D1	St Pauls Lane
A2	Bradburne Road	D2	St Paul's Place
B1	Braidley Road	D1	St Pauls Road
C1	Cavendish Road	C3	St Peter's Road
A1	Central Drive	A2	St Stephen's Road
D2	Christchurch Road	B1	St Valerie Road
D1	Coach House Place	C2	Stafford Road
A3	Commercial Road	B2	Stephen's Way
D2	Cotlands Road	A2	Suffolk Road
A3	Cranborne Road	A3	Terrace Road
A2	Crescent Road	B3	The Arcade
C2	Cumnor Road	B1	The Deans
B2	Dean Park Crescent	B3	The Square
B2	Dean Park Road	A3	The Triangle
A3	Durley Road	A3	Tregonwell Road
A2	Durrant Road	C2	Trinity Road
D3	East Overcliff Drive	C3	Upper Hinton Road
B3	Exeter Crescent	A3	Upper Norwich Road
B3	Exeter Park Road	A3	Upper Terrace Road
B3	Exeter Road	D1	Wellington Road
C2	Fir Vale Road	A2	Wessex Way
B3	Gervis Place	A3	West Hill Road
D3	Gervis Road	D2	Weston Drive
C2	Glen Fern Road	B3	Westover Road
C3	Grove Road	B1	Wimborne Road
A3	Hahnemann Road	C2	Wootton Gardens
B3	Hinton Road	C2	Wootton Mount
D2	Holdenhurst Road	B1	Wychwood Close
A4	Kerley Road	B2	Yelverton Road
C1	Lansdowne Gardens	D2	York Road
C1	Lansdowne Road		
C2	Lorne Park Road		
C2	Madeira Road		
D3	Meyrick Road		
A3	Norwich Avenue		
A3	Norwich Road		
C2	Old Christchurch Road		
A3	Orchard Street		
D2	Oxford Road		
D1	Park Road		
C3	Parsonage Road		

Bradford

Bradford is found on atlas page **90 F4**

B3	Aldermanbury	A2	Longcroft Link
B2	Bank Street	C2	Lower Kirkgate
D2	Barkerend Road	A1	Lumb Lane
B2	Barry Street	B4	Manchester Road
C4	Bolling Road	A1	Manningham Lane
C2	Bolton Road	B1	Manor Row
C3	Bridge Street	B3	Market Street
C3	Broadway	B1	Midland Road
D2	Burnett Street	A4	Morley Street
C1	Canal Road	B4	Nelson Street
A3	Carlton Street	C1	North Brook Street
B3	Centenary Square	B2	Northgate
C4	Chandos Street	B1	North Parade
B3	Channing Way	C2	North Street
D3	Chapel Street	D1	North Wing
B2	Cheapside	D1	Otley Road
A4	Chester Street	A2	Paradise Street
C2	Church Bank	D2	Peckover Street
A4	Claremont	B2	Piccadilly
C4	Croft Street	C2	Pine Street
A1	Darfield Street	B3	Princes Way
B2	Darley Street	A3	Randall Well Street
A2	Drewton Road	A2	Rawson Road
D4	Dryden Street	B2	Rawson Square
B2	Duke Street	A2	Rebecca Street
D3	East Parade	A4	Sawrey Place
A4	Edmund Street	B4	Senior Way
C4	Edward Street	C1	Shipley Airedale Road
A1	Eldon Place	C2	Stott Hill
D3	Filey Street	A2	Sunbridge Road
C3	George Street	B3	Sunbridge Street
B2	Godwin Street	A3	Tetley Street
A2	Grattan Road	A3	Thornton Road
A4	Great Horton Road	B1	Trafalgar Street
A4	Grove Terrace	B3	Tyrell Street
A1	Hallfield Road	D2	Upper Park Gate
B4	Hall Ings	B2	Upper Piccadilly
B1	Hamm Strasse	C1	Valley Road
C1	Holdsworth Street	C3	Vicar Lane
A1	Houghton Place	D4	Wakefield Road
A4	Howard Street	D1	Wapping Road
B3	Hustlergate	A2	Water Lane
A1	Infirmary Street	C2	Wellington Street
B2	John Street	A2	Westgate
A4	Lansdowne Place	C1	Wharf Street
D3	Leeds Road	A1	White Abbey Road
A4	Little Horton	A2	Wigan Street
B4	Little Horton Lane	A4	Wilton Street

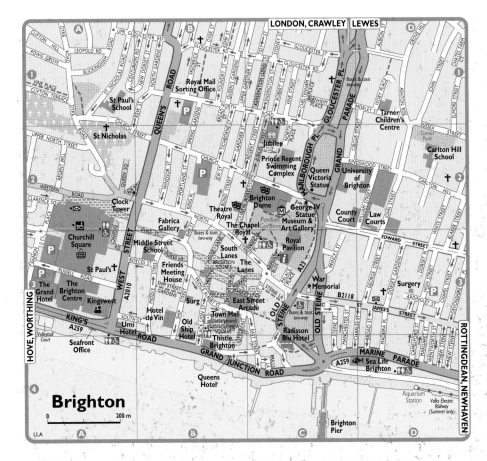

Brighton

Brighton is found on atlas page **24 H10**

D3	Ardingley Street	D4	Madeira Place
D1	Ashton Rise	C4	Manchester Street
B3	Bartholomew Square	D4	Margaret Street
B3	Black Lion Street	D4	Marine Parade
D3	Blaker Street	B3	Market Street
B2	Bond Street	C2	Marlborough Place
A3	Boyces Street	B3	Meeting House Lane
B3	Brighton Place	B3	Middle Street
D4	Broad Street	D1	Morley Street
A1	Buckingham Road	B1	New Dorset Street
D4	Camelford Street	B2	New Road
A3	Cannon Place	D4	New Steine
D2	Carlton Hill	B3	Nile Street
A1	Centurion Road	B1	North Gardens
D3	Chapel Street	C2	North Place
C4	Charles Street	B1	North Road
C1	Cheltenham Place	B2	North Street
A1	Church Road	C3	Old Steine
B2	Church Street	B2	Portland Street
C2	Circus Street	A1	Powis Grove
A1	Clifton Hill	B3	Prince Albert Street
A1	Clifton Terrace	C3	Prince's Street
D3	Devonshire Place	B1	Queen's Gardens
B3	Dukes Lane	A2	Queen Square
B2	Duke Street	B2	Queen's Road
C3	East Street	A2	Regency Road
C2	Edward Street	A2	Regent Hill
D1	Elmore Street	C2	Regent Street
B1	Foundry Street	C1	Robert Street
B1	Frederick Street	D3	St James's Street
B2	Gardner Street	A1	St Nicholas Road
D3	George Street	B3	Ship Street Gardens
C1	Gloucester Place	B1	Spring Gardens
B1	Gloucester Road	C4	Steine Street
C1	Gloucester Street	D2	Sussex Street
B4	Grand Junction Road	C1	Sydney Street
C2	Grand Parade	B2	Tichborne Street
D3	High Street	C1	Tidy Street
D1	Ivory Place	B1	Upper Gardner Street
D2	John Street	A1	Upper Gloucester Road
C2	Jubilee Street	A2	Upper North Street
C1	Kensington Gardens	C1	Vine Street
C1	Kensington Street	D4	Wentworth Street
B1	Kew Street	A2	Western Road
A3	King's Road	A3	West Street
C2	Kingswood Street	D3	White Street
A1	Leopold Road	D2	William Street
B4	Little East Street	B2	Windsor Street

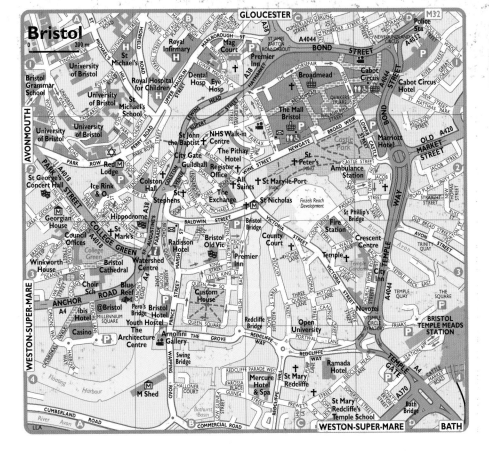

Bristol

Bristol is found on atlas page **31 Q10**

A3	Anchor Road	C2	Passage Street
D3	Avon Street	C1	Pembroke Street
B2	Baldwin Street	C1	Penn Street
D4	Bath Bridge	B3	Pero's Bridge
C1	Bond Street	A2	Perry Road
D2	Bond Street	C2	Philadelphia Street
C1	Broadmead	C4	Portwall Lane
D2	Broad Plain	C4	Prewett Street
B3	Broad Quay	B3	Prince Street
B2	Broad Street	B3	Queen Charlotte Street
C2	Broad Weir	B3	Queen Square
A3	Canons Way	C4	Redcliffe Hill
C3	Canynge Street	B4	Redcliffe Parade West
C2	Castle Street	C4	Redcliffe Way
A3	College Green	C4	Redcliff Mead Lane
B2	Colston Avenue	C3	Redcliff Street
B2	Colston Street	A1	Royal Fort Road
B4	Commercial Road	B2	Rupert Street
B2	Corn Street	B3	St Augustine's Parade
C3	Countership	A3	St George's Road
A4	Cumberland Road	D1	St Matthias Park
A3	Deanery Road	A1	St Michael's Hill
A3	Denmark Street	B2	St Stephen's Street
A3	Explore Lane	C3	St Thomas Street
C2	Fairfax Street	B2	Small Street
C3	Ferry Street	C4	Somerset Street
D3	Friary	A1	Southwell Street
A2	Frogmore Street	A1	Tankards Close
A3	Great George Street	B3	Telephone Avenue
D1	Great George Street	C3	Temple Back
B4	Guinea Street	D3	Temple Back East
C1	Haymarket	D4	Temple Gate
A2	Hill Street	C3	Temple Street
B1	Horfield Road	D3	Temple Way
D1	Houlton Street	B4	The Grove
D2	Jacob Street	C1	The Horsefair
B3	King Street	C2	The Pithay
B2	Lewins Mead	D2	Tower Hill
A2	Lodge Street	A2	Trenchard Street
D2	Lower Castle Street	A1	Tyndall Avenue
A2	Lower Church Lane	C1	Union Street
B1	Lower Maudlin Street	B1	Upper Maudlin Street
B1	Marlborough Hill	C2	Victoria Street
B1	Marlborough Street	B4	Wapping Road
B3	Marsh Street	B3	Welsh Back
C2	Newgate	B1	Whitson Street
D2	Old Market Street	C2	Wine Street
A2	Park Street	A1	Woodland Road

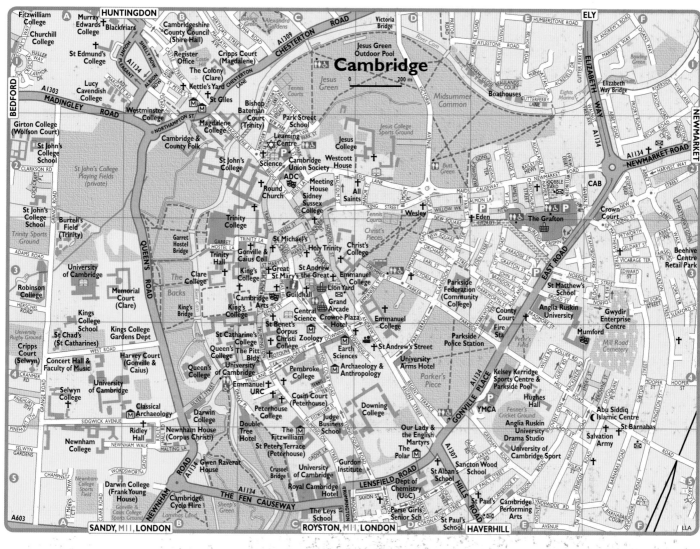

Cambridge

Cambridge is found on atlas page **62 G9**

University Colleges

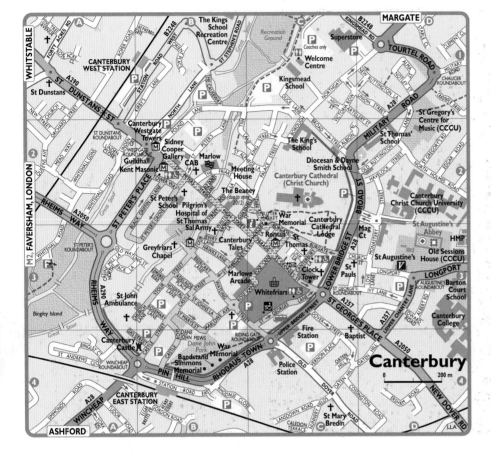

Canterbury

Canterbury is found on atlas page **39 K10**

B3	Adelaide Place	D1	Notley Street
D3	Albert Road	C4	Nunnery Fields
C2	Albion Place	C4	Oaten Hill
D1	Alma Street	C4	Old Dover Road
C1	Artillery Street	D2	Old Ruttington Lane
B3	Beercart Lane	A2	Orchard Street
B2	Best Lane	C2	Palace Street
A3	Black Griffin Lane	C3	Parade
C2	Borough	B4	Pin Hill
D2	Broad Street	B2	Pound Lane
C3	Burgate	A2	Queens Avenue
C2	Butter Market	A3	Rheims Way
C3	Canterbury Lane	B4	Rhodaus Town
B4	Castle Row	B3	Rose Lane
B3	Castle Street	B3	Rosemary Lane
C4	Cossington Road	B2	St Alphege Lane
C3	Dover Street	A1	St Dunstans Street
C1	Duck Lane	B3	St Edmunds Road
D2	Edgar Road	C3	St George's Lane
D3	Edward Road	C3	St George's Place
D4	Ersham Road	C3	St George's Street
A4	Gas Street	D2	St Gregory's Road
B4	Gordon Road	B3	St Johns Lane
B2	Guildhall Street	B3	St Margaret's Street
D2	Havelock Street	B3	St Marys Street
B3	Hawks Lane	B3	St Peter's Grove
B2	High Street	B2	St Peter's Lane
B3	Hospital Lane	A3	St Peter's Place
C3	Ivy Lane	B2	St Peters Street
B3	Jewry Lane	B4	Station Road East
C2	King Street	A1	Station Road West
B1	Kirby's Lane	B3	Stour Street
C4	Lansdown Road	D1	Sturry Road
A2	Linden Grove	C2	Sun Street
D3	Longport	B1	The Causeway
D3	Love Lane	B2	The Friars
C3	Lower Bridge Street	D1	Tourtel Road
D4	Lower Chantry Lane	B2	Tower Way
B3	Marlowe Avenue	A4	Tudor Road
A2	Mead Way	D1	Union Street
C3	Mercery Lane	C4	Upper Bridge Street
D2	Military Road	C4	Vernon Place
B1	Mill Lane	C1	Victoria Row
D3	Monastery Street	B3	Watling Street
D4	New Dover Road	A2	Whitehall Gardens
D1	New Ruttington Lane	A2	Whitehall Road
B1	North Lane	A4	Wincheap
C1	Northgate	A4	York Road

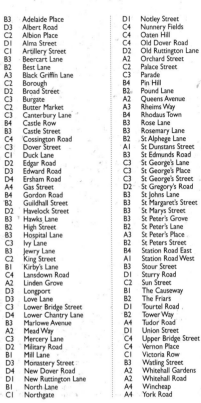

Cardiff

Cardiff is found on atlas page **30 G9**

D3	Adam Street	B1	Museum Avenue
D2	Adams Court	B1	Museum Place
D3	Adamscroft Place	D2	Newport Road Lane
D4	Atlantic Way	D2	North Luton Place
B2	Boulevard De Nantes	A1	North Road
C3	Bridge Street	D1	Oxford Lane
D4	Brigantine Place	D1	Oxford Street
C4	Bute Street	B1	Park Grove
C3	Bute Terrace	B1	Park Lane
B4	Callaghan Square	B1	Park Place
B3	Caroline Street	A3	Park Street
D1	Castle Lane	C3	Pellett Street
A2	Castle Street	A4	Pendyris Street
D3	Central Link	A3	Quay Street
B2	Charles Street	B2	Queen Street
C2	Churchill Way	C1	Richmond Crescent
A1	City Hall Road	C1	Richmond Road
D1	City Road	B1	St Andrew's Crescent
B2	Crockherbtown Lane	C1	St Andrew's Lane
B4	Custom House Street	B1	St Andrew's Place
C3	David Street	B2	St John Street
D3	Davis Street	B3	St Mary Street
C2	Dumfries Place	C1	St Peter's Street
D3	East Bay Close	C1	Salisbury Road
D1	East Grove	C3	Sandon Street
D4	Ellen Street	B4	Saunders Road
C2	Fford Churchill	D4	Schooner Way
D2	Fitzalan Place	C1	Senghennydd Road
D2	Fitzalan Road	B1	Stuttgarter Strasse
A4	Fitzhamon Embankment	B2	The Friary
D1	Glossop Road	B3	The Hayes
B2	Greyfriars Road	D1	The Parade
C3	Guildford Street	C1	The Walk
A3	Guildhall Place	B3	Trinity Street
A4	Havelock Street	A4	Tudor Street
B3	Hayes Bridge Road	D4	Tyndall Street
B2	Heol Siarl	D1	Vere Street
C4	Herbert Street	C2	Wesley Lane
B3	High Street	B4	West Canal Wharf
B2	High Street Arcade	C1	West Grove
B3	Hills Street	A3	Westgate Street
A1	King Edward VII Avenue	B3	Wharton Street
D2	Knox Road	C2	Windsor Lane
C4	Lloyd George Avenue	C1	Windsor Place
C3	Mary Ann Street	D3	Windsor Road
B4	Mill Lane	A3	Womanby Street
D2	Moira Place	A4	Wood Street
D2	Moira Terrace	B3	Working Street

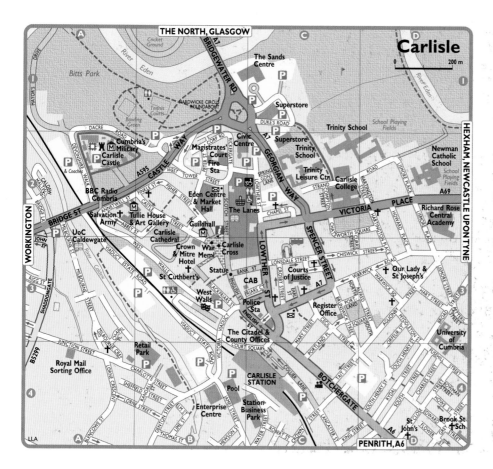

Carlisle

Carlisle is found on atlas page 110 G9

A2	Abbey Street	D2	Howard Place
D3	Aglionby Street	D4	Howe Street
A2	Annetwell Street	B4	James Street
B3	Bank Street	A3	John Street
B3	Blackfriars Street	A4	Junction Street
A4	Blencowe Street	C4	King Street
C4	Botchergate	C4	Lancaster Street
A2	Bridge Lane	B4	Lime Street
A2	Bridge Street	D2	Lismore Place
B1	Bridgewater Road	D3	Lismore Street
D3	Broad Street	C3	Lonsdale Street
C3	Brunswick Street	A4	Lorne Crescent
A2	Caldew Maltings	A4	Lorne Street
B2	Castle Street	C2	Lowther Street
B2	Castle Way	C3	Mary Street
C3	Cecil Street	A1	Mayor's Drive
A3	Chapel Place	A3	Milbourne Crescent
C2	Chapel Street	A3	Milbourne Street
D4	Charles Street	D3	Myddleton Street
A4	Charlotte Street	D3	North Alfred Street
C2	Chatsworth Square	D3	Orfeur Street
C3	Chiswick Street	D3	Petteril Street
D4	Close Street	B2	Peter Street
C4	Collier Lane	C4	Portland Place
C2	Compton Street	C3	Port-Land Square
B2	Corp Road	B4	Randall Street
B4	Court Square	B2	Rickergate
C3	Crosby Street	A3	Rigg Street
C4	Crown Street	C4	Robert Street
C3	Currie Street	D4	Rydal Street
A1	Dacre Road	B2	Scotch Street
B4	Denton Street	A3	Shaddongate
A2	Devonshire Walk	A4	Sheffield Street
C1	Duke's Road	D3	South Alfred Street
D4	Edward Street	D4	South Henry Street
B4	Elm Street	C2	Spencer Street
B3	English Street	C2	Spring Gardens Lane
B2	Finkle Street	C2	Strand Road
B2	Fisher Street	C4	Tait Street
D4	Flower Street	B4	Thomas Street
C3	Friars Court	A3	Viaduct Estate Road
D4	Fusehill Street	C2	Victoria Place
C2	Georgian Way	B4	Victoria Viaduct
D4	Grey Street	D3	Warwick Road
D2	Hartington Place	D3	Warwick Square
D2	Hartington Street	C4	Water Street
D3	Hart Street	B2	West Tower Street
B4	Hewson Street	B3	West Walls

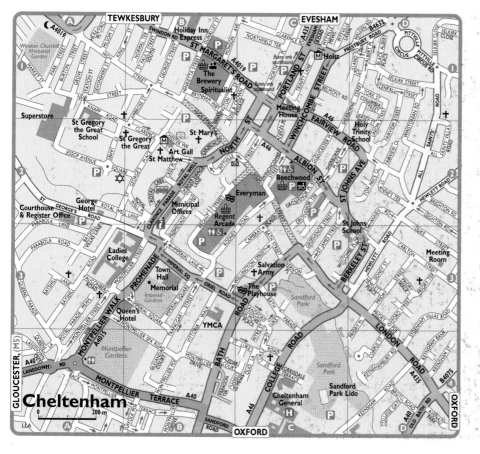

Cheltenham

Cheltenham is found on atlas page 46 H10

C2	Albion Street	B4	Montpellier Parade
D2	All Saints' Road	B4	Montpellier Spa Road
B1	Ambrose Street	A4	Montpellier Street
D4	Argyll Road	A4	Montpellier Terrace
A4	Back Montpellier Terrace	A4	Montpellier Walk
B4	Bath Road	A1	New Street
C3	Bath Street	B2	North Street
B1	Baynham Way	D4	Old Bath Road
A3	Bayshill Road	B3	Oriel Road
A3	Bayshill Villas Lane	A3	Parabola Lane
B1	Bennington Street	A3	Parabola Road
C3	Berkeley Street	A1	Park Street
A1	Burton Street	D1	Pittville Circus
D3	Carlton Street	D1	Pittville Circus Road
B2	Church Street	B2	Pittville Street
B2	Clarence Parade	C1	Portland Street
C1	Clarence Road	C1	Prestbury Road
B2	Clarence Street	D3	Priory Street
C4	College Road	B3	Promenade
B2	Crescent Terrace	A3	Queens Parade
A1	Devonshire Street	B2	Regent Street
D3	Duke Street	B3	Rodney Road
B1	Dunalley Street	B2	Royal Well
C1	Evesham Road	A2	Royal Well Lane
C2	Fairview Road	D2	St Anne's Road
D2	Fairview Street	D2	St Anne's Terrace
A3	Fauconberg Road	B2	St George's Place
D1	Glenfall Street	A2	St George's Road
C3	Grosvenor Street	B1	St George's Street
A1	Grove Street	A2	St James' Square
B1	Henrietta Street	C3	St James Street
D3	Hewlett Road	C2	St Johns Avenue
A1	High Street	B1	St Margaret's Road
C2	High Street	B1	St Paul's Street South
B3	Imperial Lane	C3	Sandford Street
B3	Imperial Square	D1	Selkirk Street
A2	Jessop Avenue	C2	Sherborne Street
D4	Keynsham Road	A1	Station Street
A1	King Street	B4	Suffolk Parade
A1	Knapp Road	B1	Swindon Road
A4	Lansdown Road	D3	Sydenham Villas Road
D2	Leighton Road	B4	Trafalgar Street
D3	London Road	D2	Union Street
D1	Malden Road	C3	Wellington Street
A1	Market Street	C2	Winchcombe Street
A1	Milsom Street	D2	Winstonian Road
B1	Monson Avenue	C3	Witcombe Place
B4	Montpellier Grove	D1	York Street

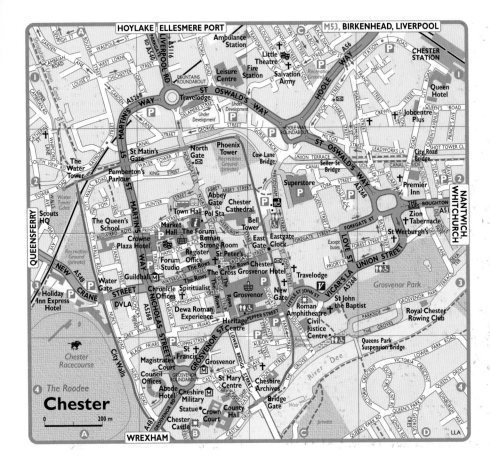

Chester

Chester is found on atlas page **81 N11**

C4	Albion Street	B3	Nicholas Street
D2	Bath Street	B2	Northgate Street
C1	Black Diamond Street	A3	Nun's Road
D2	Boughton	B1	Parkgate Road
A1	Bouverie Street	C3	Park Street
B3	Bridge Street	C3	Pepper Street
C1	Brook Street	B2	Princess Street
C2	Canal Side	C3	Priory Place
B4	Castle Street	C4	Queen's Park Road
C1	Charles Street	D1	Queen's Road
A1	Chichester Street	C2	Queen Street
D2	City Road	A2	Raymond Street
A2	City Walls Road	D2	Russell Street
B3	Commonhall Street	C1	St Anne Street
C1	Cornwall Street	D4	St John's Road
D1	Crewel Street	C3	St John Street
B4	Cuppin Street	A2	St Martin's Way
D2	Dee Hills Park	B4	St Mary's Hill
D2	Dee Lane	C4	St Olave Street
B1	Delamere Street	B1	St Oswald's Way
C4	Duke Street	B2	St Werburgh Street
B3	Eastgate Street	C2	Samuel Street
C1	Egerton Street	D2	Seller Street
C2	Foregate Street	B4	Shipgate Street
C3	Forest Street	C3	Souter's Lane
D1	Francis Street	A2	South View Road
C2	Frodsham Street	A3	Stanley Street
A1	Garden Lane	D1	Station Road
B2	George Street	D2	Steam Mill Street
C1	Gloucester Street	C4	Steele Street
C2	Gorse Stacks	C1	Talbot Street
D3	Grosvenor Park Terrace	A2	Tower Road
B4	Grosvenor Road	C1	Trafford Street
B4	Grosvenor Street	B3	Trinity Street
B3	Hamilton Place	D3	Union Street
C1	Hoole Way	C2	Union Terrace
B2	Hunter Street	A1	Upper Cambrian Road
B2	King Street	C3	Vicar's Lane
D2	Leadworks Lane	D4	Victoria Crescent
C3	Little St John Street	B1	Victoria Road
B1	Liverpool Road	C3	Volunteer Street
A1	Lorne Street	A1	Walpole Street
C3	Love Street	C1	Walter Street
B4	Lower Bridge Street	B3	Watergate Street
D4	Lower Park Road	B2	Water Tower Street
C2	Milton Street	B3	Weaver Street
A3	New Crane Street	B3	White Friars
C3	Newgate Street	C2	York Street

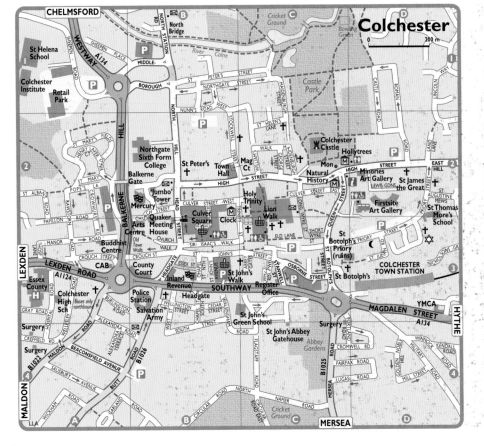

Colchester

Colchester is found on atlas page **52 G6**

C3	Abbey Gates	B1	Middleborough
A3	Alexandra Road	D4	Military Road
A4	Alexandra Terrace	D4	Mill Street
A3	Balkerne Hill	C4	Napier Road
A4	Beaconsfield Avenue	D3	Nicholsons Green
A3	Burlington Road	B1	North Bridge
A4	Butt Road	B1	Northgate Street
D1	Castle Road	B1	North Hill
B3	Cedar Street	B1	North Station Road
B3	Chapel Street North	B1	Nunn's Road
B3	Chapel Street South	C3	Osborne Street
B3	Church Street	A3	Papillon Road
B3	Church Walk	A2	Pope's Lane
C4	Circular Road East	C4	Portland Road
B4	Circular Road North	D3	Priory Street
A4	Creffield Road	C3	Queen Street
C4	Cromwell Road	A2	Rawstorn Road
A3	Crouch Street	D1	Roman Road
B3	Crouch Street	A2	St Alban's Road
A2	Crowhurst Road	D2	St Augustine Mews
C2	Culver Street East	C3	St Botolph's Street
B2	Culver Street West	C2	St Helen's Lane
D2	East Hill	B3	St John's Avenue
B3	Essex Street	B3	St John's Street
C4	Fairfax Road	D3	St Julian Road
C4	Flagstaff Road	A2	St Mary's Fields
A4	Garland Road	B1	St Peter's Street
C2	George Street	A4	Salisbury Avenue
D4	Golden Noble Hill	A1	Sheepen Place
A3	Gray Road	A1	Sheepen Road
B3	Headgate	C3	Short Wyre Street
B2	Head Street	B3	Sir Isaac's Walk
A2	Henry Laver Court	B4	South Street
B2	High Street	B3	Southway
A4	Hospital Road	C3	Stanwell Street
A3	Hospital Lane	B2	Trinity Street
D4	Kendall Road	B3	Walsingham Road
D2	Land Lane	A4	Wellesley Road
D2	Lewis Gardens	B3	Wellington Street
A3	Lexden Road	B1	West Stockwell Street
D1	Lincoln Way	B4	West Street
C2	Long Wyre Street	A1	Westway
C4	Lucas Road	C3	Whitewell Road
D3	Magdalen Street	A4	Wickham Road
C1	Maidenburgh Street	C2	William's Walk
A4	Maldon Road	D4	Winnock Road
A3	Manor Road		
C4	Mersea Road		

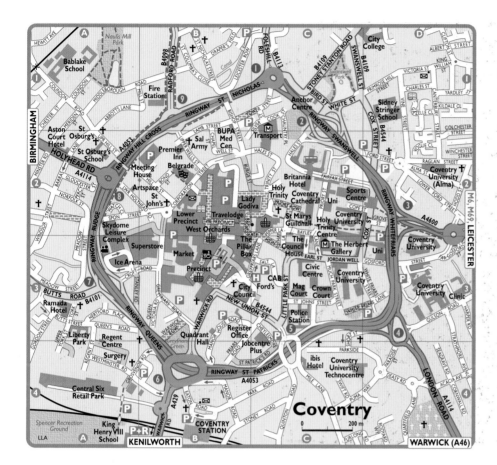

Coventry

Coventry is found on atlas page **59 M9**

A1	Abbotts Lane	A1	Mill Street
D4	Acacia Avenue	C3	Much Park Street
D2	Alma Street	B3	New Union Street
A2	Barras Lane	A2	Norfolk Street
C2	Bayley Lane	D4	Paradise Street
C1	Bird Street	B4	Park Road
B1	Bishop Street	C4	Parkside
B2	Broadgate	D1	Primrose Hill Street
B2	Burge Street	C2	Priory Row
A3	Butts Road	C2	Priory Street
A3	Butts Street	C4	Puma Way
D1	Canterbury Street	D4	Quaryfield Lane
A2	Chester Street	A3	Queen's Road
C3	Cheylesmore	B3	Queen Victoria Road
D4	Cornwall Road	C4	Quinton Road
B2	Corporation Street	B1	Radford Road
A1	Coundon Road	D2	Raglan Street
D1	Cox Street	A4	Regent Street
D2	Cox Street	A2	Ringway Hill Cross
A3	Croft Road	A3	Ringway Queens
C3	Earl Street	A3	Ringway Rudge
B4	Eaton Road	B1	Ringway St Nicholas
C2	Fairfax Street	B4	Ringway St Patricks
C1	Foleshill Road	C1	Ringway Swanswell
A2	Gloucester Street	D2	Ringway Whitefriars
D3	Gosford Street	C3	St Johns Street
B3	Greyfriars Lane	B1	St Nicholas Street
B3	Greyfriars Road	C3	Salt Lane
A4	Grosvenor Road	D4	Seagrave Road
D3	Gulson Road	A2	Spon Street
C2	Hales Street	A3	Stanley Road
A3	Hertford Place	B4	Stoney Road
C3	High Street	C1	Stoney Stanton Road
B2	Hill Street	D3	Strathmore Avenue
A2	Holyhead Road	C1	Swanswell Street
C3	Jordan Well	B1	Tower Street
B2	Lamb Street	C2	Trinity Street
B1	Leicester Row	B2	Upper Hill Street
C3	Little Park Street	A4	Upper Wells Street
D4	London Road	D1	Victoria Street
D2	Lower Ford Street	D1	Vine Street
A2	Lower Holyhead Road	B3	Warwick Road
B4	Manor House Road	B4	Warwick Road
B4	Manor Road	A4	Westminster Road
A3	Meadow Street	D3	White Friars Street
A1	Meriden Street	C1	White Street
A1	Middleborough Road	A3	Windsor Street
C4	Mile Lane	D1	Yardley Street

Darlington

Darlington is found on atlas page **103 Q8**

A3	Abbey Road	C2	Northgate
B1	Barningham Street	B2	North Lodge Terrace
B1	Bartlett Street	B4	Northumberland Street
B3	Beaumont Street	A4	Oakdene Avenue
C4	Bedford Street	A2	Outram Street
A4	Beechwood Avenue	D3	Parkgate
B3	Blackwellgate	D4	Park Lane
B3	Bondgate	C4	Park Place
D3	Borough Road	B1	Pendower Street
C3	Brunswick Street	D4	Pensbury Street
D4	Brunton Street	B4	Polam Lane
C1	Chestnut Street	A3	Portland Place
A4	Cleveland Terrace	B3	Powlett Street
C4	Clifton Road	C3	Priestgate
B2	Commercial Street	B3	Raby Terrace
A4	Coniscliffe Road	C2	Russell Street
B1	Corporation Road	B2	St Augustine's Way
C2	Crown Street	C2	St Cuthbert's Way
B1	Dodds Street	C4	St Cuthbert's Way
A3	Duke Street	D4	St James Place
B1	Easson Road	A1	Salisbury Terrace
D1	East Mount Road	B3	Salt Yard
B3	East Raby Street	A4	Scarth Street
C3	East Street	B3	Skinnergate
A2	Elms Road	B4	South Arden Street
C4	Feethams	A4	Southend Avenue
A3	Fife Road	A2	Stanhope Road North
B2	Four Riggs	A3	Stanhope Road South
C2	Freemans Place	C3	Stonebridge
B2	Gladstone Street	B2	Sun Street
B4	Grange Road	C4	Swan Street
A1	Greenbank Road	A3	Swinburne Road
B2	Greenbank Road	A2	Trinity Road
D3	Green Street	B3	Tubwell Row
C4	Hargreave Terrace	A4	Uplands Road
D2	Haughton Road	C2	Valley Street North
C1	High Northgate	A2	Vane Terrace
B3	High Row	C4	Victoria Embankment
A1	Hollyhurst Road	B4	Victoria Road
B3	Houndgate	C4	Victoria Road
D3	Jack Way Steeple	A2	West Crescent
C1	John Street	A3	West Powlett Street
B2	Kendrew Street	B3	West Row
B1	Kingston Street	B4	West Street
A4	Langholm Crescent	A2	Woodland Road
A3	Larchfield Street	D3	Yarm Road
A2	Maude Street		
D4	Neasham Road		

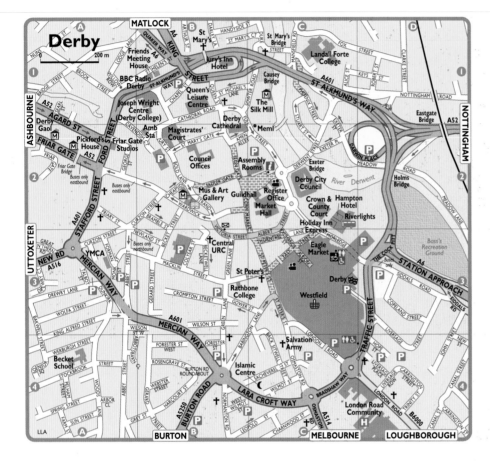

Derby

Derby is found on atlas page **72 B3**

A4	Abbey Street	A4	King Alfred Street
A1	Agard Street	B1	King Street
C3	Albert Street	B4	Lara Croft Way
B4	Babington Lane	B4	Leopold Street
C4	Back Sitwell Street	D4	Liversage Row
B3	Becket Street	D3	Liversage Street
B2	Bold Lane	A1	Lodge Lane
C4	Bradshaw Way	C3	London Road
B2	Bramble Street	B3	Macklin Street
A1	Bridge Street	C1	Mansfield Road
A1	Brook Street	D2	Meadow Lane
B4	Burton Road	D2	Meadow Road
D4	Canal Street	B3	Mercian Way
D4	Carrington Street	C3	Morledge
B1	Cathedral Road	A3	Newland Street
A2	Cavendish Court	A3	New Road
B1	Chapel Street	D4	New Street
D1	Clarke Street	D1	Nottingham Road
D3	Copeland Street	C4	Osmaston Road
B2	Corn Market	C1	Phoenix Street
B3	Crompton Street	B1	Queen Street
A2	Curzon Street	D1	Robert Street
A3	Curzon Street	B4	Rosengrave Street
C2	Darwin Place	C4	Sacheverel Street
C2	Derwent Street	B2	Sadler Gate
A3	Drewry Lane	C1	St Alkmund's Way
C1	Duke Street	B1	St Helen's Street
A3	Dunkirk	B2	St Mary's Gate
C3	East Street	C3	St Peter's Street
C3	Exchange Street	D3	Siddals Road
C2	Exeter Place	C1	Sowter Road
C2	Exeter Street	A4	Spring Street
A2	Ford Street	A3	Stafford Street
B4	Forester Street West	D3	Station Approach
A3	Forman Street	A4	Stockbrook Street
C1	Fox Street	B2	Strand
A2	Friary Street	C1	Stuart Street
B1	Full Street	A4	Sun Street
B3	Gerard Street	D3	The Cock Pitt
B3	Gower Street	C3	Thorntree Lane
B3	Green Lane	D4	Traffic Street
A4	Grey Street	D4	Trinity Street
B1	Handyside Street	B2	Victoria Street
B4	Harcourt Street	B2	Wardwick
B2	Iron Gate	A4	Werburgh Street
D4	John Street	C4	Wilmot Street
B2	Jury Street	A3	Wolfa Street
D1	Keys Street	A4	Woods Lane

Doncaster

Doncaster is found on atlas page **91 P10**

D3	Alderson Drive	B1	Montague Street
B3	Apley Road	B4	Nelson Street
A4	Balby Road Bridge	B1	Nether Hall Road
B3	Beechfield Road	A1	North Bridge Road
C1	Broxholme Lane	C4	North Street
C4	Carr House Road	D1	Osborne Road
B4	Carr Lane	C4	Palmer Street
C4	Chequer Avenue	B2	Park Road
C3	Chequer Road	B2	Park Terrace
C4	Childers Street	B2	Prince's Street
B1	Christ Church Road	A2	Priory Place
A1	Church View	B4	Prospect Place
B1	Church Way	C1	Queen's Road
C4	Clark Avenue	C4	Rainton Road
A4	Cleveland Street	C3	Ravensworth Road
B3	College Road	C1	Rectory Gardens
C4	Cooper Street	C2	Regent Square
B2	Coopers Terrace	D3	Roman Road
B1	Copley Road	C1	Royal Avenue
B3	Cunningham Road	B4	St James Street
D3	Danum Road	C1	St Mary's Road
B1	Dockin Hill Road	A2	St Sepulchre Gate
A2	Duke Street	A3	St Sepulchre Gate West
B2	East Laith Gate	C1	St Vincent Avenue
C3	Elmfield Road	C1	St Vincent Road
A4	Exchange Street	B2	Scot Lane
D3	Firbeck Road	B2	Silver Street
B2	Frances Street	B3	Somerset Road
B2	Georges Gate	C2	South Parade
C2	Glyn Avenue	C4	South Street
A4	Green Dyke Lane	A2	Spring Gardens
A1	Grey Friars' Road	A4	Stirling Street
C2	Hall Cross Hill	C4	Stockil Road
B2	Hall Gate	D4	Theobald Avenue
D4	Hamilton Road	C1	Thorne Road
B1	Hannington Street	C2	Thorne Road
A2	High Street	C2	Town Fields
C1	Highfield Road	D1	Town Moor Avenue
B4	Jarratt Street	A2	Trafford Way
C1	King's Road	C1	Vaughan Avenue
C2	Lawn Avenue	B3	Waterdale
C2	Lawn Road	D3	Welbeck Road
D4	Lime Tree Avenue	A2	West Laith Gate
D3	Manor Drive	A3	West Street
A2	Market Place	C3	Whitburn Road
B1	Market Road	B4	White Way
B1	Milbanke Street	D1	Windsor Road
B4	Milton Walk	B2	Wood Street

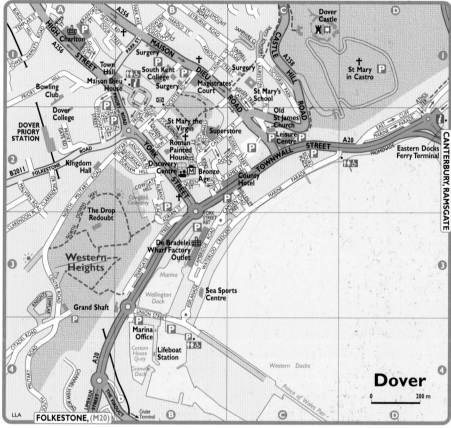

Dover

Dover is found on atlas page **27 P3**

B3	Adrian Street	B2	New Street
B2	Albany Place	A2	Norman Street
C1	Ashen Tree Lane	A3	North Downs Way
D1	Athol Terrace	A3	North Military Road
B2	Biggin Street	B1	Park Avenue
A1	Burgh Hill	B1	Park Street
B3	Cambridge Road	B2	Pencester Road
C2	Camden Crescent	A1	Peter Street
B2	Cannon Street	A2	Priory Gate Road
C1	Castle Hill Road	A1	Priory Hill
B1	Castlemount Road	A1	Priory Road
B2	Castle Street	B2	Priory Street
A3	Centre Road	D2	Promenade
A4	Channel View Road	B2	Queen's Gate
B2	Church Street	B2	Queen Street
A4	Citadel Road	B2	Russell Street
A3	Clarendon Place	B2	St James Street
A2	Clarendon Road	C1	Samphire Close
B2	Cowgate Hill	A2	Saxon Street
A1	Crafford Street	B3	Snargate Street
B2	Dolphin Lane	A4	South Military Road
C2	Douro Place	B2	Stembrook
A1	Dour Street	C1	Taswell Close
B2	Durham Close	B1	Taswell Street
B2	Durham Hill	A1	Templar Street
D2	East Cliff	A4	The Viaduct
A2	Effingham Street	A1	Tower Hamlets Road
B3	Esplanade	C2	Townwall Street
A2	Folkestone Road	B3	Union Street
B1	Godwyne Close	C1	Victoria Park
B1	Godwyne Road	B3	Waterloo Crescent
B1	Harold Street	C2	Wellesley Road
B1	Harold Street	A1	Wood Street
C1	Heritage Gardens	B2	York Street
A1	Hewitt Road	B3	York Street Roundabout
A1	High Street		
B2	King Street		
A3	Knights Templar		
B2	Lancaster Road		
C1	Laureston Place		
B1	Leyburne Road		
A4	Limekiln Street		
B1	Maison Dieu Road		
A2	Malvern Road		
C2	Marine Parade		
D2	Marine Parade		
B2	Military Road		
B2	Mill Lane		

Dundee

Dundee is found on atlas page **142 G11**

B2	Albert Square	C1	Ladywell Avenue
B2	Bank Street	B1	Laurel Bank
A1	Barrack Road	A1	Lochee Road
B2	Barrack Road	D1	Marketgait
B2	Bell Street	C1	Marketgait East
D1	Blackscroft	D2	McDonald Street
A1	Blinshall Street	B2	Meadowside
A2	Blinshall Street	A2	Miln Street
C1	Bonnybank Road	C2	Murraygate
A2	Brown Street	A4	Nethergate
C2	Candle Lane	B2	Nicoll Street
C2	Castle Street	C1	North Lindsay Street
C2	Chapel Street	B1	North Marketgait
C3	City Square	C1	North Victoria Road
C2	Commercial Street	A3	Old Hawkhill
D1	Constable Street	B2	Panmure Street
A1	Constitution Crescent	A3	Park Place
A1	Constitution Road	A4	Perth Road
B2	Constitution Road	D1	Princes Street
A2	Court House Square	B1	Prospect Place
C1	Cowgate	C1	Queen Street
D1	Cowgate	B2	Rattray Street
C3	Crighton Street	B2	Reform Street
D1	Dens Street	B4	Riverside Drive
C3	Dock Street	A4	Roseangle
A2	Douglas Street	C1	St Andrews Street
B1	Dudhope Street	A1	Scrimgeour Place
C3	Earl Grey Place	A4	Seabraes Lane
D2	East Dock Street	C2	Seagate
D1	East Whale Lane	A2	Session Street
B2	Euclid Crescent	C3	Shore Terrace
B2	Euclid Street	C3	South Marketgait
C1	Forebank Road	B3	South Tay Street
B2	Forester Street	C3	South Victoria Dock Road
D1	Foundry Lane	B2	South Ward Road
C2	Gellatly Street	C1	Sugarhouse Wynd
B4	Greenmarket	D3	Tay Road Bridge
A2	Guthrie Street	C2	Trades Lane
A3	Hawkhill	B3	Union Street
C3	High Street	B1	Union Terrace
B1	Hilltown	B2	Ward Road
B1	Hilltown Terrace	D1	Weavers Yard
A3	Hunter Street	A2	West Bell Street
A1	Infirmary Brae	A2	West Marketgait
B2	Johnston Street	A3	West Port
C1	King Street	D2	West Victoria Dock Road
C1	Kirk Lane	C3	Whitehall Place
A1	Laburn Street	C3	Whitehall Street

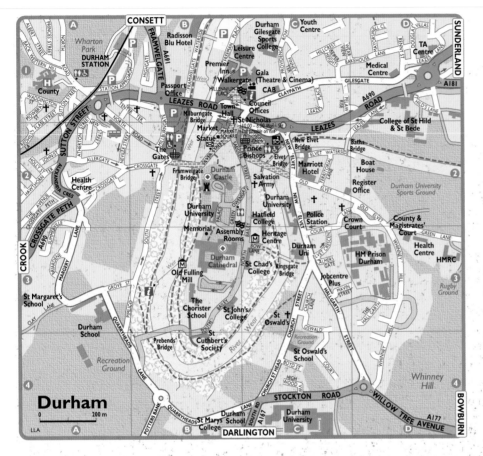

Durham

Durham is found on atlas page **103 Q2**

A1	Albert Street	D1	Mayorswell Close
A2	Alexandra Crescent	B1	Milburngate Bridge
A2	Allergate	B2	Millburngate
A2	Atherton Street	B1	Millennium Place
A1	Back Western Hill	A1	Mowbray Street
C1	Bakehouse Lane	A2	Neville Street
C2	Baths Bridge	C2	New Elvet
C3	Bow Lane	C2	New Elvet Bridge
C4	Boyd Street	A2	New Street
A3	Briardene	C3	North Bailey
C3	Church Lane	A1	North Road
C4	Church Street	C2	Old Elvet
C4	Church Street Head	C3	Oswald Court
A3	Clay Lane	B2	Owengate
C1	Claypath	B2	Palace Green
C3	Court Lane	C3	Palmers Gate
A2	Crossgate	C1	Pelaw Rise
A3	Crossgate Peth	A3	Pimlico
D1	Douglas Villas	B4	Potters Bank
C2	Elvet Bridge	B4	Prebends' Bridge
C3	Elvet Crescent	A1	Princes' Street
C2	Elvet Waterside	C1	Providence Row
C1	Finney Terrace	A3	Quarryheads Lane
A2	Flass Street	A2	Redhills Lane
B1	Framwelgate	D1	Renny Street
B2	Framwelgate Bridge	B2	Saddler Street
B1	Framwelgate Waterside	D1	St Hild's Lane
B1	Freeman Place	B2	Silver Street
C1	Gilesgate	B3	South Bailey
D3	Green Lane	C4	South Road
A3	Grove Street	B3	South Street
C3	Hallgarth Street	A1	Station Approach
A2	Hawthorn Terrace	C4	Stockton Road
B1	Highgate	A3	Summerville
C4	High Road View	A2	Sutton Street
C2	High Street	A1	Tenter Terrace
C1	Hillcrest	C2	Territorial Lane
A2	Holly Street	A2	The Avenue
A2	John Street	D3	The Hall Garth
C1	Keiper Heights	A1	Waddington Street
C3	Kingsgate Bridge	C1	Wear View
D1	Leazes Lane	D3	Whinney Hill
D2	Leazes Lane	D4	Willow Tree Avenue
C1	Leazes Place		
B1	Leazes Road		
A3	Margery Lane		
B2	Market Square		
C3	Mavin Street		

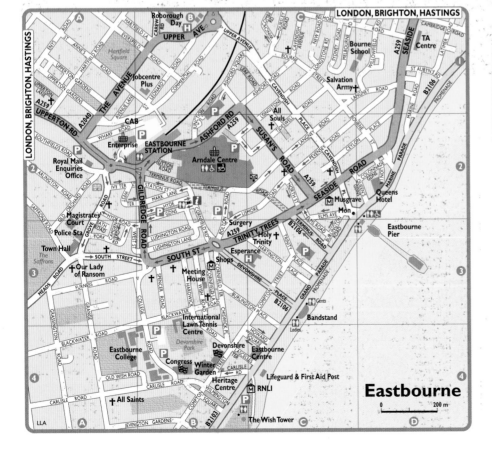

Eastbourne

Eastbourne is found on atlas page **25 P11**

A2	Arlington Road	D1	Langney Road
B2	Ashford Road	C2	Langney Road
C1	Ashford Road	B4	Lascelles Terrace
B1	Ashford Square	D1	Latimer Road
A1	Avenue Lane	B1	Leaf Road
C1	Belmore Road	B2	Lismore Road
A4	Blackwater Road	C1	Longstone Road
B3	Bolton Road	B3	Lushington Road
C1	Bourne Street	D2	Marine Parade
B3	Burlington Place	D1	Marine Road
C3	Burlington Road	B2	Mark Lane
A3	Camden Road	A3	Meads Road
B1	Carew Road	C1	Melbourne Road
A4	Carlisle Road	A2	Old Orchard Road
B4	Carlisle Road	A4	Old Wish Road
C1	Cavendish Avenue	C2	Pevensey Road
C1	Cavendish Place	C3	Promenade
C2	Ceylon Place	D2	Queen's Gardens
B3	Chiswick Place	A2	Saffrons Road
B3	College Road	A1	St Anne's Road
D2	Colonnade Gardens	D1	St Aubyn's Road
B1	Commercial Road	B1	St Leonard's Road
B4	Compton Street	D1	Seaside
C3	Compton Street	C2	Seaside Road
B3	Cornfield Lane	A2	Southfields Road
B2	Cornfield Road	A3	South Street
B3	Cornfield Terrace	B3	South Street
B3	Devonshire Place	B3	Spencer Road
C1	Dursley Road	B2	Station Street
C3	Elms Road	C2	Susan's Road
A1	Enys Road	B2	Sutton Road
A1	Eversfield Road	C1	Sydney Road
A3	Furness Road	B2	Terminus Road
B2	Gildredge Road	C3	Terminus Road
C3	Grand Parade	A1	The Avenue
A3	Grange Road	C2	Tideswell Road
A3	Grassington Road	C3	Trinity Place
A3	Grove Road	B3	Trinity Trees
B3	Hardwick Road	B1	Upper Avenue
A1	Hartfield Lane	A1	Upperton Gardens
A1	Hartfield Road	A1	Upperton Lane
C3	Hartington Place	A1	Upperton Road
C4	Howard Square	A3	West Street
B2	Hyde Gardens	A2	West Terrace
A2	Hyde Road	D1	Willowfield Road
A2	Ivy Terrace	B4	Wilmington Square
A4	Jevington Gardens	B3	Wish Road
B2	Junction Road	A3	York Road

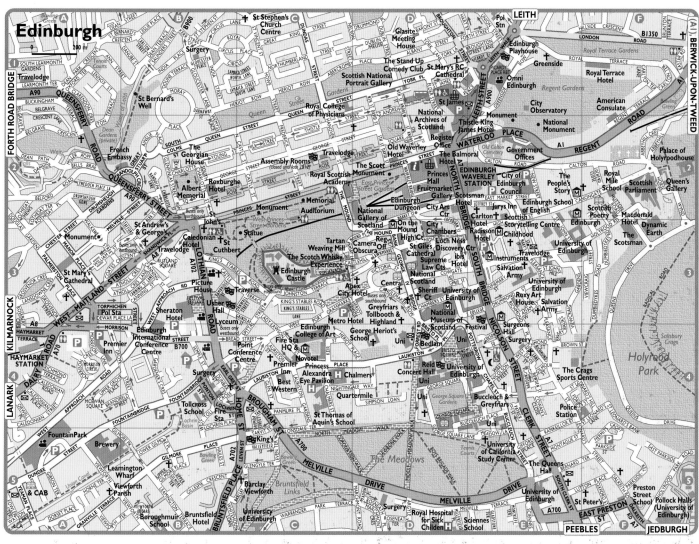

Edinburgh

Edinburgh is found on atlas page **127 P3**

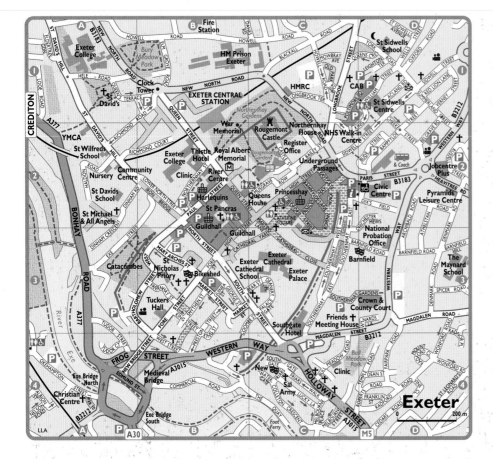

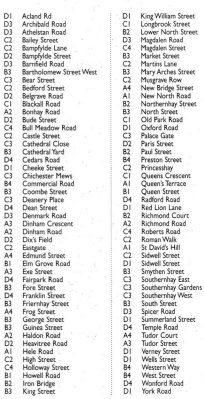

Exeter

Exeter is found on atlas page **9 M6**

D1	Acland Rd	D1	King William Street
D3	Archibald Road	C1	Longbrook Street
D3	Athelstan Road	B2	Lower North Street
C2	Bailey Street	D3	Magdalen Road
C2	Bampfylde Lane	C4	Magdalen Street
D2	Bampfylde Street	B3	Market Street
D3	Barnfield Road	C2	Martins Lane
B3	Bartholomew Street West	B3	Mary Arches Street
C3	Bear Street	C2	Musgrave Row
C2	Bedford Street	A4	New Bridge Street
D2	Belgrave Road	A1	New North Road
C1	Blackall Road	B2	Northernhay Street
A2	Bonhay Road	B3	North Street
D2	Bude Street	C1	Old Park Road
C4	Bull Meadow Road	D1	Oxford Road
C2	Castle Street	C3	Palace Gate
C3	Cathedral Close	D2	Paris Street
B3	Cathedral Yard	B2	Paul Street
D4	Cedars Road	B4	Preston Street
D1	Cheeke Street	C2	Princesshay
C3	Chichester Mews	C1	Queens Crescent
B4	Commercial Road	A1	Queen's Terrace
B3	Coombe Street	B1	Queen Street
C3	Deanery Place	D4	Radford Road
D4	Dean Street	D1	Red Lion Lane
D3	Denmark Road	B2	Richmond Court
A3	Dinham Crescent	A2	Richmond Road
A2	Dinham Road	C4	Roberts Road
D2	Dix's Field	C2	Roman Walk
C2	Eastgate	A1	St David's Hill
A4	Edmund Street	C2	Sidwell Street
B1	Elm Grove Road	D1	Sidwell Street
A3	Exe Street	B3	Smythen Street
D4	Fairpark Road	C3	Southernhay East
B3	Fore Street	C3	Southernhay Gardens
D4	Franklin Street	C3	Southernhay West
B3	Friernhay Street	B3	South Street
A4	Frog Street	D3	Spicer Road
B3	George Street	D1	Summerland Street
B3	Guinea Street	D4	Temple Road
A2	Haldon Road	A4	Tudor Court
D2	Heavitree Road	A3	Tudor Street
A1	Hele Road	D1	Verney Street
C2	High Street	D1	Wells Street
C4	Holloway Street	B4	Western Way
B1	Howell Road	B4	West Street
B2	Iron Bridge	D4	Wonford Road
B3	King Street	D1	York Road

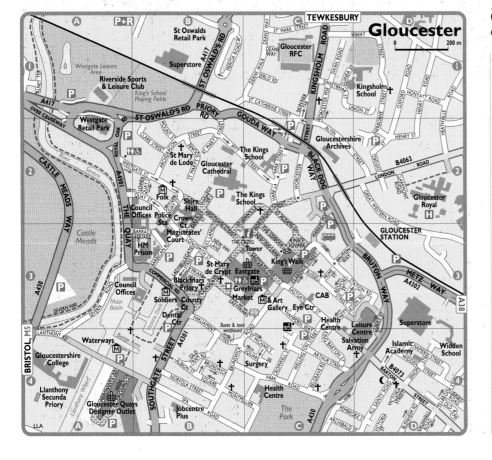

Gloucester

Gloucester is found on atlas page **46 F11**

D4	Albert Street	B4	Montpellier
B4	Albion Street	D4	Napier Street
D4	All Saints' Road	C3	Nettleton Road
C2	Alvin Street	B3	New Inn Lane
B2	Archdeacon Street	C3	New Inn Lane
C4	Archibald Street	B4	Norfolk Street
C4	Arthur Street	C3	Northgate Street
B3	Barbican Road	B4	Old Tram Road
B3	Barrack Square	A1	Over Causeway
D4	Barton Street	D1	Oxford Road
C3	Bedford Street	D2	Oxford Street
C4	Belgrave Road	C4	Park Road
B3	Berkeley Street	C2	Park Street
C2	Black Dog Way	B3	Parliament Street
D4	Blenheim Road	C4	Pembroke Street
B4	Brunswick Road	B2	Pitt Street
B4	Brunswick Square	B1	Priory Road
D3	Bruton Way	B2	Quay Street
B3	Bull Lane	A2	Royal Oak Road
A2	Castle Meads Way	C3	Russell Street
C3	Clarence Street	C2	St Aldate Street
B2	Clare Street	C1	St Catherine Street
B3	Commercial Road	B3	St John's Lane
C4	Cromwell Street	C1	St Mark Street
C1	Deans Walk	B2	St Mary's Square
C3	Eastgate Street	B2	St Mary's Street
B1	Gouda Way	C4	St Michael's Square
D2	Great Western Road	B1	St Oswald's Road
B3	Greyfriars	C1	Sebert Street
C3	Hampden Way	A3	Severn Road
B3	Hare Lane	D2	Sherborne Street
D2	Heathville Road	D4	Sinope Street
D1	Henry Road	B3	Southgate Street
D2	Henry Street	B4	Spa Road
A4	High Orchard Street	C3	Station Road
D1	Honyatt Road	C1	Swan Road
C4	King Barton Street	C1	Sweetbriar Street
C1	Kingsholm Road	B3	The Cross
C3	King's Square	C3	The Oxbode
B3	Ladybellegate Street	A2	The Quay
A4	Llanthony Road	C1	Union Street
D2	London Road	B2	Upper Quay Street
B3	Longsmith Street	D4	Vauxhall Road
C3	Market Parade	C4	Wellington Street
A4	Merchants' Road	A2	Westgate Street
B1	Mercia Road	D4	Widden Street
D3	Metz Way	C2	Worcester Parade
D4	Millbrook Street	C2	Worcester Street

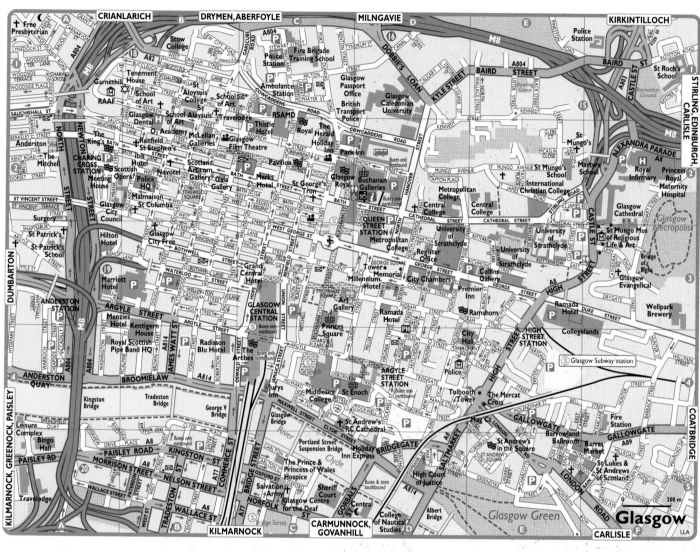

Glasgow

Glasgow is found on atlas page **125 P4**

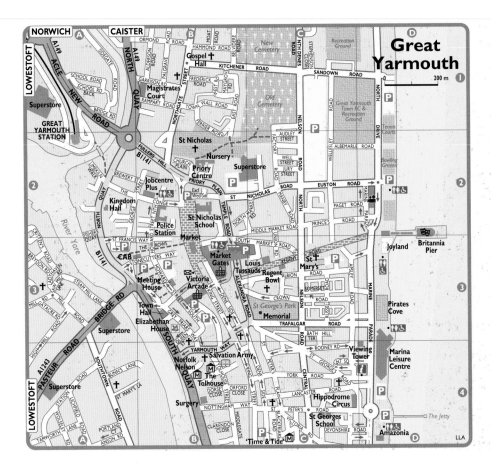

Great Yarmouth

Great Yarmouth is found on atlas page **77 Q10**

A1	Acle New Road	C1	North Denes Road
C2	Albemarle Road	D1	North Drive
C3	Albion Road	C2	North Market Road
B1	Alderson Road	A2	North Quay
B3	Alexandra Road	B1	Northgate Street
A4	Anson Road	B4	Nottingham Way
C3	Apsley Road	B1	Ormond Road
B1	Belvidere Road	C2	Paget Road
C4	Blackfriars Road	B1	Palgrave Road
A2	Brewery Street	A4	Pasteur Road
A3	Breydon Road	C2	Prince's Road
A1	Bridge Road	B2	Priory Plain
A3	Bridge Road	B4	Queen Street
A4	Bunn's Lane	B1	Rampart Road
B2	Church Plain	C3	Regent Road
A3	Critten's Road	C4	Rodney Road
C3	Crown Road	C3	Russell Road
B3	Dene Side	A3	St Francis Way
C4	Devonshire Road	C4	St George's Road
B1	East Road	B2	St Nicholas Road
C2	Euston Road	C4	St Peter's Plain
C2	Factory Road	C4	St Peter's Road
B1	Ferrier Road	C1	Sandown Road
A2	Fishers Quay	A3	Saw Mill Lane
B1	Frederick Road	A1	School Road
B2	Fullers Hill	A1	School Road Back
B1	Garrison Road	A1	Sidegate Road
A3	Gatacre Road	C3	South Market Road
A2	George Street	B3	South Quay
B3	Grey Friars Way	A4	Southtown Road
B1	Hammond Road	A4	Station Road
A3	High Mill Road	A3	Steam Mill Lane
B2	Howard Street North	C1	Stephenson Close
B3	Howard Street South	B3	Stonecutters Way
B3	King Street	A4	Tamworth Lane
B1	Kitchener Road	B2	Temple Road
A3	Ladyhaven Road	A2	The Conge
C4	Lancaster Road	B3	The Rows
A4	Lichfield Road	B4	Tolhouse Street
A2	Limekiln Walk	B1	Town Wall Road
C2	Manby Road	C3	Trafalgar Road
D3	Marine Parade	C3	Union Road
B1	Maygrove Road	C4	Victoria Road
C2	Middle Market Road	C2	Wellesley Road
B4	Middlegate	B1	West Road
B1	Moat Road	A4	Wolseley Road
C3	Nelson Road Central	B4	Yarmouth Way
C1	Nelson Road North	C4	York Road

Guildford

Guildford is found on atlas page **23 Q5**

C4	Abbot Road	B4	Millmead Terrace
B3	Angel Gate	A4	Mount Pleasant
B1	Artillery Road	D1	Nightingale Road
C1	Artillery Terrace	B3	North Street
A2	Bedford Road	C1	Onslow Road
A3	Bridge Street	B3	Onslow Street
C3	Bright Hill	C3	Oxford Road
D3	Brodie Road	C2	Pannells Court
B4	Bury Fields	B3	Park Street
B4	Bury Street	D3	Pewley Bank
C4	Castle Hill	D4	Pewley Fort Inner Court
C3	Castle Street	C3	Pewley Hill
B3	Chapel Street	D3	Pewley Way
C2	Chertsey Street	B3	Phoenix Court
D2	Cheselden Road	B4	Porridge Pot Alley
B1	Church Road	A4	Portsmouth Road
B2	College Road	D4	Poyle Road
B2	Commercial Road	B3	Quarry Street
D2	Dene Road	C2	Sandfield Terrace
D2	Denmark Road	D3	Semaphore Road
B1	Drummond Road	C3	South Hill
C1	Eagle Road	C1	Springfield Road
D2	Epsom Road	D1	Station Approach
C1	Falcon Road	C1	Stoke Fields
C4	Fort Road	C1	Stoke Road
D1	Foxenden Road	B3	Swan Lane
A3	Friary Bridge	C3	Sydenham Road
B3	Friary Street	A3	Testard Road
B1	George Road	C2	The Bars
A2	Guildford Park Road	A4	The Mount
D3	Harvey Road	B3	The Shambles
C2	Haydon Place	C3	Tunsgate
D4	High Pewley	A3	Upperton Road
B3	High Street	D1	Victoria Road
C2	Jeffries Passage	A1	Walnut Tree Close
D2	Jenner Road	C2	Ward Street
B2	Laundry Road	C4	Warwicks Bench
B2	Leapale Lane	B1	Wharf Road
B2	Leapale Road	A3	Wherwell Road
B1	Leas Road	B1	William Road
D2	London Road	A3	Wodeland Avenue
A4	Mareschal Road	B1	Woodbridge Road
C3	Market Street	B1	York Road
C2	Martyr Road		
A1	Mary Road		
B3	Millbrook		
B3	Mill Lane		
B3	Millmead		

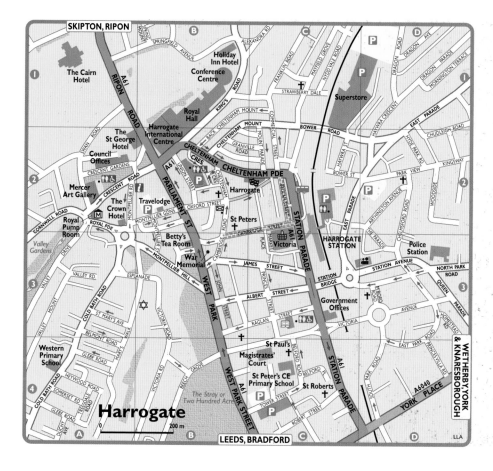

Harrogate

Harrogate is found on atlas page **97 M10**

C3	Albert Street	B2	Montpellier Street
B1	Alexandra Road	D1	Mornington Terrace
D2	Arthington Avenue	C2	Mount Parade
B2	Back Cheltenham Mount	D3	North Park Road
B4	Beech Grove	C1	Nydd Vale Road
C4	Belford Place	B2	Oxford Street
C4	Belford Road	D2	Park View
A3	Belmont Road	B2	Parliament Street
C2	Beulah Street	C3	Princes Street
C1	Bower Road	D4	Princes Villa Road
C2	Bower Street	D3	Queen Parade
B3	Cambridge Road	C3	Raglan Street
C2	Cambridge Street	A1	Ripon Road
D3	Chelmsford Road	C4	Robert Street
B2	Cheltenham Crescent	A2	Royal Parade
B2	Cheltenham Mount	A3	St Mary's Avenue
B2	Cheltenham Parade	A4	St Mary's Walk
D2	Chudleigh Road	A4	Somerset Road
A3	Cold Bath Road	D4	South Park Road
C1	Commercial Street	B1	Springfield Avenue
A2	Cornwall Road	B1	Spring Mount
A2	Crescent Gardens	D3	Station Avenue
A2	Crescent Road	C3	Station Bridge
D1	Dragon Avenue	C2	Station Parade
D1	Dragon Parade	C1	Strawberry Dale
D1	Dragon Road	A2	Swan Road
A4	Duchy Avenue	D2	The Parade
C2	East Parade	C4	Tower Street
D4	East Park Road	A4	Treesdale Road
A3	Esplanade	B2	Union Street
C1	Franklin Road	A3	Valley Drive
A4	Glebe Road	A3	Valley Mount
B2	Granville Road	A3	Valley Road
C2	Haywra Street	C3	Victoria Avenue
A4	Heywood Road	B3	Victoria Road
D3	Homestead Road	B3	West Park
D2	Hyde Park Road	B4	West Park Street
D2	Hywra Crescent	D2	Woodside
B3	James Street	D4	York Place
B3	John Street		
B1	King's Road		
D2	Kingsway		
C3	Market Place		
D3	Marlborough Road		
C1	Mayfield Grove		
B2	Montpellier Gardens		
B3	Montpellier Hill		
A2	Montpellier Road		

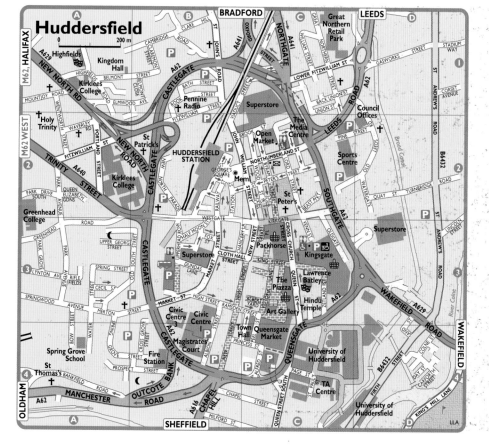

Huddersfield

Huddersfield is found on atlas page **90 E7**

B4	Albion Street	A2	New North Road
C4	Alfred Street	B4	New Street
C1	Back Union Street	C1	Northgate
A4	Bankfield Road	C2	Northumberland Street
B1	Bath Street	D2	Old Leeds Road
A1	Belmont Street	B3	Old South Street
C2	Brook Street	B4	Outcote Bank
C2	Byram Street	C1	Oxford Street
B1	Cambridge Road	A2	Park Avenue
D4	Carforth Street	A2	Park Drive South
B1	Castlegate	C4	Peel Street
B3	Chancery Lane	C2	Pine Street
B4	Chapel Hill	A2	Portland Street
B4	Chapel Street	B4	Princess Street
C2	Church Street	A4	Prospect Street
B1	Clare Hill	D2	Quay Street
B1	Claremont Street	C3	Queen Street
B3	Cloth Hall Street	C4	Queen Street South
C3	Cross Church Street	C4	Queensgate
B3	Dundas Lane	B2	Railway Street
A2	Elizabeth Queen Gardens	B3	Ramsden Street
A1	Elmwood Avenue	B1	Rook Street
D4	Firth Street	D2	St Andrew's Road
A2	Fitzwilliam Street	B2	St George's Square
B2	Fitzwilliam Street	B1	St John's Road
D1	Gasworks Street	C2	St Peter's Street
C1	Great Northern Street	C2	Southgate
A3	Greenhead Road	A4	Spring Grove Street
B3	Half Moon Street	A3	Spring Street
B3	High Street	A3	Springwood Avenue
A1	Highfields Road	D1	Stadium Way
B2	John William Street	B2	Station Street
C3	Kaye Street	A2	Trinity Street
D4	King's Mill Lane	D2	Turnbridge Road
C3	Kirkgate	C1	Union Street
C2	Leeds Road	A3	Upper George Street
D3	Lincoln Street	B3	Upperhead Row
C2	Lord Street	B2	Viaduct Street
C1	Lower Fitzwilliam Street	C3	Victoria Lane
A3	Lynton Avenue	D3	Wakefield Road
A4	Manchester Road	A3	Water Street
C3	Market Place	D2	Watergate
B3	Market Street	A2	Waverley Road
A3	Merton Street	A2	Wentworth Street
B4	Milford Street	B3	Westgate
A1	Mountjoy Road	C1	William Street
B2	New North Parade	C2	Wood Street
A1	New North Road	C3	Zetland Street

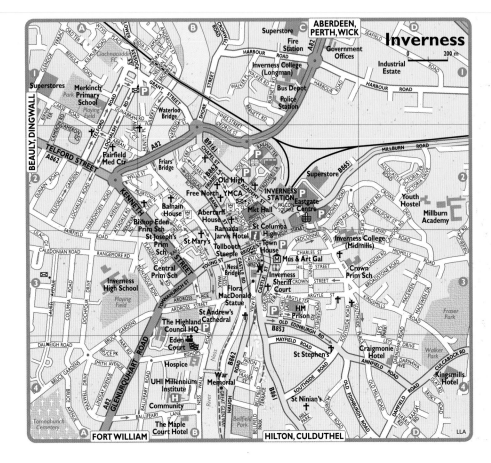

Inverness

Inverness is found on atlas page **156 B8**

D2	Abertaff Road	A1	Glendoe Terrace
B2	Academy Street	A4	Glenurquhart Road
B1	Anderson Street	C3	Gordon Terrace
D4	Annfield Road	B1	Grant Street
C3	Ardconnel Terrace	B4	Great Glen Way
B3	Ardross Street	C1	Harbour Road
C3	Argyle Street	D4	Harris Road
C3	Argyle Terrace	A2	Harrowden Road
A4	Ballifeary Lane	B4	Haugh Road
B4	Ballifeary Road	C3	High Street
B2	Bank Street	C4	Hill Park
C4	Bellfield Terrace	C3	Hill Street
A1	Benula Road	B2	Huntly Street
B1	Bernett Road	B1	Innes Street
A1	Birnie Terrace	D4	Islay Road
B4	Bishops Road	A2	Kenneth Street
B3	Bridge Street	B3	King Street
D3	Broadstone Road	D3	Kingsmills Road
A4	Bruce Avenue	A3	Laurel Avenue
A4	Bruce Gardens	A4	Lindsay Avenue
A4	Bruce Park	A2	Lochalsh Road
C1	Burnett Road	D3	Lovat Road
A3	Caledonian Road	A1	Lower Kessock Street
A2	Cameron Road	A4	Maxwell Drive
A2	Cameron Square	C4	Mayfield Road
A1	Carse Road	D3	Midmills Road
B3	Castle Road	D2	Millburn Road
C3	Castle Street	C3	Mitchell's Lane
B2	Chapel Street	C4	Muirfield Road
C3	Charles Street	C3	Old Edinburgh Road
A3	Columba Road	A4	Park Road
C2	Crown Circus	B3	Planefield Road
D2	Crown Drive	C3	Porterfield Road
C2	Crown Road	D4	Raasay Road
C3	Crown Street	A3	Rangemore Road
D4	Culcabock Road	A2	Ross Avenue
A4	Dalneigh Road	D1	Seafield Road
D4	Damfield Road	B1	Shore Street
D4	Darnaway Road	A4	Smith Avenue
C3	Denny Street	C3	Southside Place
A3	Dochfour Drive	C4	Southside Road
A1	Dunaban Road	A2	Telford Gardens
A2	Dunain Road	A2	Telford Road
B3	Duncraig Street	A2	Telford Street
D4	Erisky Road	B3	Tomnahurich Street
A3	Fairfield Road	D3	Union Road
C2	Falcon Square	C1	Walker Road
B2	Friars' Lane	B3	Young Street

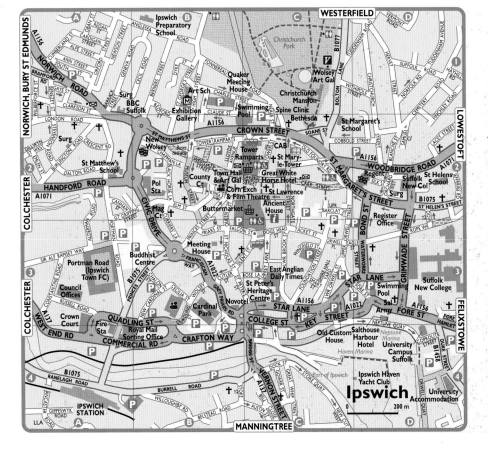

Ipswich

Ipswich is found on atlas page **53 L3**

A3	Alderman Road	A2	London Road
B1	Anglesea Road	C3	Lower Brook Street
A1	Barrack Street	C3	Lower Orwell Street
B4	Belstead Road	B2	Museum Street
B1	Berners Street	C1	Neale Street
B2	Black Horse Lane	D3	Neptune Quay
D2	Blanche Street	B3	New Cardinal Street
C1	Bolton Lane	A1	Newson Street
D3	Bond Street	C2	Northgate Street
A1	Bramford Road	A1	Norwich Road
C4	Bridge Street	C2	Old Foundry Road
A2	Burlington Road	D2	Orchard Street
B4	Burrell Road	A1	Orford Street
A1	Cardigan Street	C3	Orwell Place
C2	Carr Street	D4	Orwell Quay
B3	Cavern Street	A3	Portman Road
B1	Cecil Road	A3	Princes Street
D1	Cemetery Road	B3	Princes Street
B1	Charles Street	A3	Quadling Street
D1	Christchurch Street	B3	Quadling Street
B2	Civic Drive	B3	Queen Street
A1	Clarkson Street	A4	Ranelagh Road
C2	Cobbold Street	A1	Redan Street
C3	College Street	A3	Russell Road
A4	Commercial Road	B1	St George's Street
A3	Constantine Road	D2	St Helen's Street
B4	Crafton Way	C2	St Margaret's Street
B2	Crown Street	B2	St Matthews Street
A1	Cumberland Street	B3	St Nicholas Street
A2	Dalton Road	B3	St Peter's Street
C4	Dock Street	B3	Silent Street
D4	Duke Street	A3	Sir Alf Ramsey Way
C3	Eagle Street	A1	Soane Street
B2	Elm Street	A1	South Street
B3	Falcon Street	C3	Star Lane
B1	Fonnereau Road	C4	Stoke Quay
C3	Foundation Street	D1	Suffolk Road
B3	Franciscan Way	C3	Tacket Street
A1	Geneva Road	B2	Tower Ramparts
A2	Great Gripping Street	D1	Tuddenham Avenue
C4	Great Whip Street	C3	Turret Lane
B3	Grey Friars Road	C3	Upper Orwell Street
D3	Grimwade Street	C4	Vernon Street
A2	Handford Road	A3	West End Road
D1	Hervey Street	B2	Westgate Street
B1	High Street	B4	Willoughby Road
C3	Key Street	B3	Wolsey Street
B2	King Street	D2	Woodbridge Road

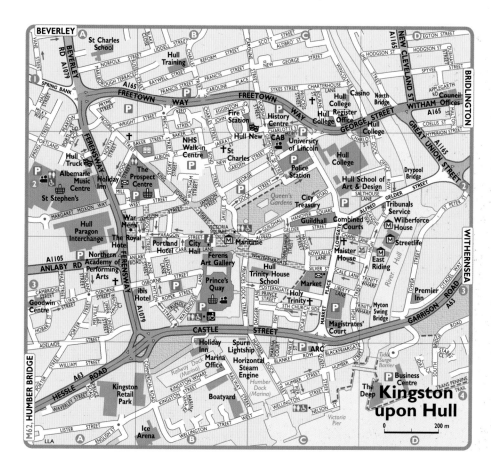

Kingston upon Hull

Kingston upon Hull is found on atlas page **93 J5**

A4	Adelaide Street	C3	Market Place
B2	Albion Street	A2	Mill Street
C2	Alfred Gelder Street	B3	Myton Street
A3	Anlaby Road	D1	New Cleveland Street
B2	Baker Street	B2	New Garden Street
A1	Beverley Road	C1	New George Street
C4	Blackfriargate	A1	Norfolk Street
C4	Blanket Row	B3	Osborne Street
B2	Bond Street	A3	Osborne Street
A2	Brook Street	B2	Paragon Street
B1	Caroline Street	A3	Pease Street
B3	Carr Lane	B1	Percy Street
B3	Castle Street	A3	Porter Street
C2	Chapel Lane	A2	Portland Place
B1	Charles Street	A2	Portland Street
C1	Charterhouse Lane	C3	Postergate
D3	Citadel Way	B3	Princes Dock Street
B4	Commercial Road	A1	Prospect Street
C3	Dagger Lane	C4	Queen Street
D2	Dock Office Row	B4	Railway Street
B2	Dock Street	B1	Raywell Street
D1	Durham Street	B1	Reform Street
B1	Egginton Street	A1	Russell Street
A2	Ferensway	A3	St Luke's Street
A1	Freetown Way	D2	St Peter Street
D2	Gandhi Way	B2	Saville Street
D3	Garrison Road	C3	Scale Lane
B2	George Street	C1	Scott Street
D1	George Street	C3	Silver Street
D1	Great Union Street	D4	South Bridge Road
C2	Grimston Street	C3	South Church Side
C2	Guildhall Road	B2	South Street
C2	Hanover Square	A1	Spring Bank
A4	Hessle Road	D1	Spyvee Street
C3	High Street	C1	Sykes Street
D1	Hodgson Street	D3	Tower Street
C4	Humber Dock Street	A3	Upper Union Street
C4	Humber Street	B2	Victoria Square
D1	Hyperion Street	B3	Waterhouse Lane
B2	Jameson Street	C4	Wellington Street
B2	Jarratt Street	B4	Wellington Street West
B2	King Edward Street	A2	West Street
B4	Kingston Street	C3	Whitefriargate
B1	Liddell Street	A4	William Street
C1	Lime Street	C1	Wincolmlee
A4	Lister Street	D1	Witham
C3	Lowgate	C1	Worship Street
A2	Margaret Moxon Way	A1	Wright Street

Lancaster

Lancaster is found on atlas page **95 K8**

D4	Aberdeen Road	A3	Lincoln Road
B4	Aldcliffe Road	B4	Lindow Street
C2	Alfred Street	C2	Lodge Street
D1	Ambleside Road	A2	Long Marsh Lane
D4	Balmoral Road	B1	Lune Street
D3	Bath Street	B3	Market Street
A3	Blades Street	A3	Meeting House Lane
D3	Bond Street	B3	Middle Street
D2	Borrowdale Road	D3	Moor Gate
C3	Brewery Lane	C3	Moor Lane
B2	Bridge Lane	B1	Morecambe Road
C3	Brock Street	C3	Nelson Street
D2	Bulk Road	C2	North Road
C3	Bulk Street	C1	Owen Road
B2	Cable Street	D3	Park Road
B3	Castle Hill	C2	Parliament Street
A3	Castle Park	D2	Patterdale Road
C2	Caton Road	B4	Penny Street
C3	Cheapside	B4	Portland Street
B3	China Street	D4	Primrose Street
B2	Church Street	D4	Prospect Street
B3	Common Garden Street	C4	Quarry Road
D4	Dale Street	B4	Queen Street
B3	Dallas Road	B4	Regent Street
D2	Dalton Road	D1	Ridge Lane
C3	Dalton Square	D1	Ridge Street
B2	Damside Street	C3	Robert Street
C1	Derby Road	C2	Rosemary Lane
C2	De Vitre Street	A1	St George's Quay
D4	Dumbarton Road	C2	St Leonard's Gate
D3	East Road	C4	St Peter's Road
C3	Edward Street	A3	Sibsey Street
A3	Fairfield Road	C4	South Road
B3	Fenton Street	A3	Station Road
C3	Gage Street	D4	Stirling Road
D2	Garnet Street	C3	Sulyard Street
C3	George Street	B3	Sun Street
D3	Grasmere Road	C4	Thurnham Street
C3	Great John Street	D2	Troutbeck Road
D4	Gregson Road	D3	Ulleswater Road
B1	Greyhound Bridge Road	A3	West Road
B4	High Street	A3	Westbourne Road
A3	Kelsey Street	A3	Wheatfield Street
D2	Kentmere Road	D3	Williamson Road
B3	King Street	A3	Wingate-Saul Road
C1	Kingsway	D2	Wolseley Street
D4	Kirkes Road	D3	Woodville Street
D1	Langdale Road	D3	Wyresdale Road

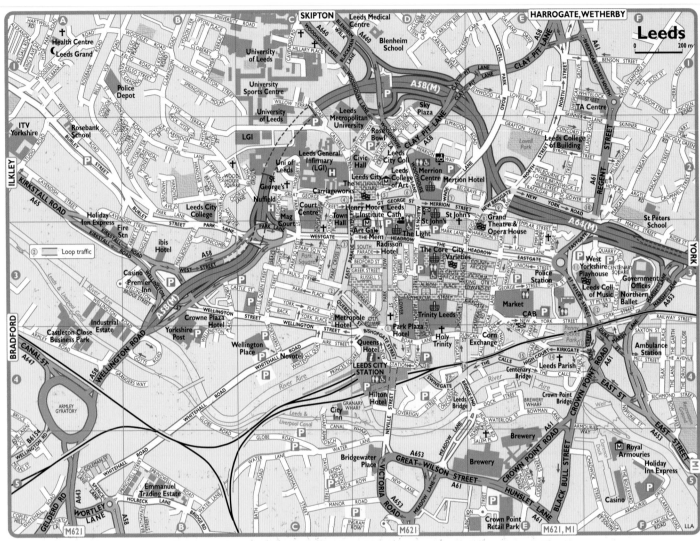

Leeds

Leeds is found on atlas page **90 H4**

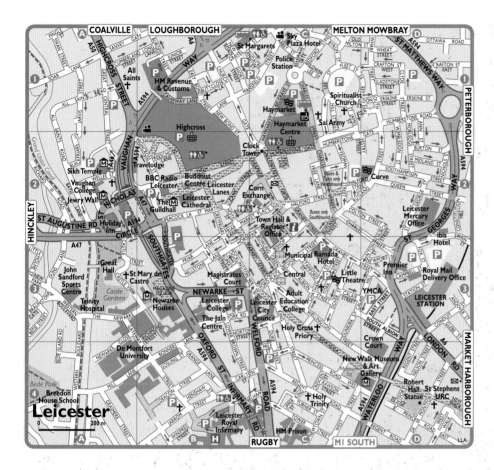

Leicester

Leicester is found on atlas page **72 F10**

C3	Albion Street	B4	Infirmary Road
A1	All Saints Road	B4	Jarrom Street
A2	Bath Lane	A1	Jarvis Street
C1	Bedford Street	C3	King Street
C1	Belgrave Gate	C1	Lee Street
C3	Belvoir Street	D3	London Road
C3	Bishop Street	B3	Lower Brown Street
B4	Bonners Lane	B3	Magazine Square
C3	Bowling Green Street	B1	Mansfield Street
B1	Burgess Street	B2	Market Place South
D2	Burton Street	C3	Market Street
C3	Calais Hill	A4	Mill Lane
D3	Campbell Street	D1	Morledge Street
B2	Cank Street	B3	Newarke Street
A3	Castle Street	C3	New Walk
C1	Charles Street	B3	Oxford Street
C3	Chatham Street	B2	Peacock Lane
C2	Cheapside	B3	Pocklington Walk
B1	Church Gate	D4	Princess Road East
D1	Clyde Street	C4	Princess Road West
C2	Colton Street	D2	Queen Street
D3	Conduit Street	C4	Regent Road
D1	Crafton Street West	D4	Regent Street
B4	Deacon Street	A2	Richard III Road
D4	De Montfort Street	C2	Rutland Street
C3	Dover Street	A2	St Augustine Road
C3	Duke Street	D2	St George Street
A3	Duns Lane	D2	St Georges Way
B1	East Bond Street Lane	C1	St James Street
D1	Erskine Street	D1	St Matthews Way
C1	Fleet Street	A2	St Nicholas Circle
B3	Friar Lane	A1	Sanvey Gate
C2	Gallowtree Gate	A1	Soar Lane
A3	Gateway Street	D3	South Albion Street
C2	Granby Street	D2	Southampton Street
A4	Grasmere Street	B3	Southgates
B1	Gravel Street	D3	Station Street
A1	Great Central Street	A3	The Newarke
B2	Greyfriars	C4	Tower Street
C2	Halford Street	A2	Vaughan Way
C2	Haymarket	D4	Waterloo Way
A1	Highcross Street	C3	Welford Road
B2	Highcross Street	A2	Welles Street
B2	High Street	C3	Wellington Street
C1	Hill Street	A4	Western Boulevard
B3	Horsefair Street	C4	West Street
C2	Humberstone Gate	D1	Wharf Street South
D1	Humberstone Road	C2	Yeoman Street

Lincoln

Lincoln is found on atlas page **86 C6**

B2	Alexandra Terrace	B2	Motherby Lane
D2	Arboretum Avenue	A2	Nelson Street
D3	Bagholme Road	B3	Newland
C1	Bailgate	A2	Newland Street West
C3	Bank Street	C4	Norman Street
B3	Beaumont Fee	C1	Northgate
A1	Belle Vue Terrace	B3	Orchard Street
A3	Brayford Way	C4	Oxford Street
B4	Brayford Wharf East	B3	Park Street
A3	Brayford Wharf North	C4	Pelham Street
C3	Broadgate	D2	Pottergate
B1	Burton Road	A1	Queen's Crescent
A2	Carholme Road	A1	Richmond Road
A1	Carline Road	A4	Rope Walk
C2	Cathedral Street	D3	Rosemary Lane
B1	Chapel Lane	A2	Rudgard Lane
A2	Charles Street West	D3	St Hugh Street
D2	Cheviot Street	B4	St Mark Street
C3	City Square	C2	St Martin's Street
C3	Clasketgate	B4	St Mary's Street
B4	Cornhill	C3	St Rumbold's Street
D3	Croft Street	C3	Saltergate
C2	Danesgate	C3	Silver Street
A3	Depot Street	C4	Sincil Street
B2	Drury Lane	B2	Spring Hill
C1	East Bight	C2	Steep Hill
C1	Eastgate	C3	Swan Street
C3	Free School Lane	B4	Tentercroft Street
C3	Friars Lane	A2	The Avenue
C2	Grantham Street	C3	Thorngate
D1	Greetwellgate	A4	Triton Road
A2	Gresham Street	B1	Union Road
B3	Guildhall Street	C3	Unity Square
A1	Hampton Street	B2	Victoria Street
B3	High Street	C3	Victoria Terrace
B3	Hungate	D2	Vine Street
D3	John Street	C3	Waterside North
D1	Langworthgate	C3	Waterside South
C2	Lindum Road	B1	Westgate
D2	Lindum Terrace	A2	West Parade
B3	Lucy Tower Street	A2	Whitehall Grove
A1	May Crescent	B3	Wigford Way
C4	Melville Street	D1	Winnow Sty Lane
C2	Michaelgate	D3	Winn Street
C2	Minster Yard	D2	Wragby Road
B3	Mint Lane	A1	Yarborough Road
B3	Mint Street	A1	York Avenue
D3	Monks Road		
D3	Montague Street		

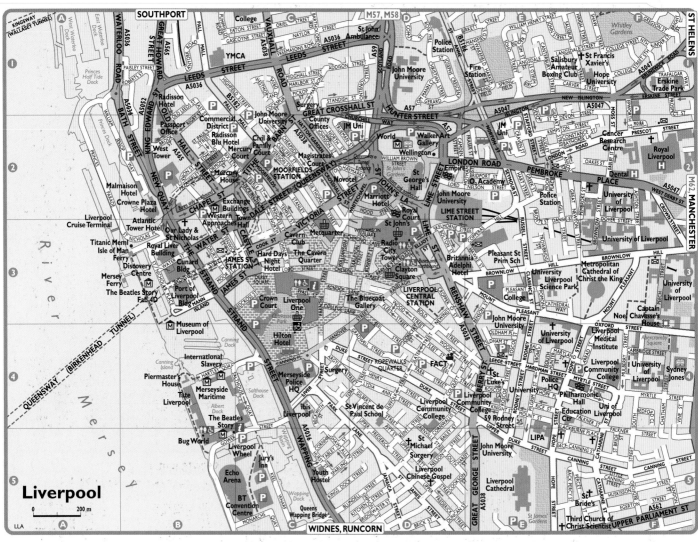

Liverpool

Liverpool is found on atlas page **81 L6**

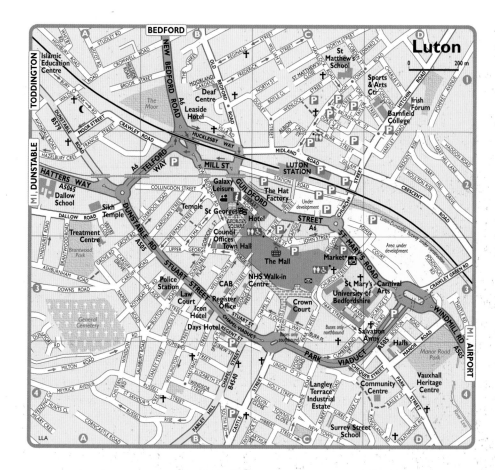

Luton

Luton is found on atlas page **50 C6**

B3	Adelaide Street	C4	Hibbert Street
C4	Albert Road	A1	Highbury Road
B2	Alma Street	C1	High Town Road
C4	Arthur Street	D1	Hitchin Road
A3	Ashburnham Road	C4	Holly Street
A1	Biscot Road	B2	Hucklesby Way
A3	Brantwood Road	B3	Inkerman Street
C1	Brunswick Street	C3	John Street
C2	Burr Street	B3	King Street
A1	Bury Park Road	C4	Latimer Road
B3	Buxton Road	B2	Liverpool Road
A3	Cardiff Road	D4	Manor Road
B2	Cardigan Street	A4	Meyrick Avenue
B4	Castle Street	C2	Midland Road
B4	Chapel Street	B2	Mill Street
B3	Chapel Viaduct	A4	Milton Road
D1	Charles Street	A1	Moor Street
C4	Chequer Street	A3	Napier Road
A4	Chiltern Road	B1	New Bedford Road
C2	Church Street	C4	New Town Street
C3	Church Street	B1	Old Bedford Road
C1	Cobden Street	C3	Park Street
B2	Collingdon Street	C3	Park Street West
D1	Concorde Street	C4	Park Viaduct
D3	Crawley Green Road	B3	Princess Street
A1	Crawley Road	B3	Regent Street
D2	Crescent Road	B1	Reginald Street
A1	Cromwell Road	A3	Rothesay Road
C4	Cumberland Street	A4	Russell Rise
A2	Dallow Road	B4	Russell Street
C1	Dudley Street	C3	St Mary's Road
B4	Dumfries Street	A4	Salisbury Road
A1	Dunstable Road	B4	Stanley Street
B4	Farley Hill	C2	Station Road
C3	Flowers Way	D4	Strathmore Ave
B1	Frederick Street	B3	Stuart Street
B3	George Street	C4	Surrey Street
B3	George Street West	B4	Tavistock Street
B3	Gordon Street	B2	Telford Way
A3	Grove Road	B3	Upper George Street
B2	Guildford Street	D3	Vicarage Street
D2	Hart Hill Drive	A1	Waldeck Road
D2	Hart Hill Lane	B4	Wellington Street
D2	Hartley Road	C1	Wenlock Street
B4	Hastings Street	D3	Windmill Road
A2	Hatters Way	B4	Windsor Street
C1	Havelock Road	A4	Winsdon Road
A2	Hazelbury Crescent	C1	York Street

Maidstone

Maidstone is found on atlas page **38 C10**

D1	Albany Street	B2	Market Buildings
D2	Albion Place	C2	Marsham Street
D1	Allen Street	D4	Meadow Walk
D3	Ashford Road	B3	Medway Street
B3	Bank Street	C4	Melville Road
B4	Barker Road	B3	Mill Street
A3	Bedford Place	D3	Mote Avenue
B3	Bishops Way	D3	Mote Road
C2	Brewer Street	D2	Old School Place
A3	Broadway	C4	Orchard Street
B3	Broadway	C3	Padsole Lane
C4	Brunswick Street	B3	Palace Avenue
A2	Buckland Hill	D1	Princes Street
A2	Buckland Road	C4	Priory Road
C1	Camden Street	B2	Pudding Lane
D3	Chancery Lane	D2	Queen Anne Road
A4	Charles Street	A4	Reginald Road
C2	Church Street	A3	Rocky Hill
B4	College Avenue	C3	Romney Place
C4	College Road	B2	Rose Yard
C1	County Road	A4	Rowland Close
D4	Crompton Gardens	A2	St Anne Court
D2	Cromwell Road	B2	St Faith's Street
A4	Douglas Road	D1	St Luke's Avenue
B2	Earl Street	D1	St Luke's Road
D4	Elm Grove	A2	St Peters Street
B1	Fairmeadow	B1	Sandling Road
A4	Florence Road	D1	Sittingbourne Road
D1	Foley Street	D3	Square Hill Road
C4	Foster Street	B1	Stacey Street
C3	Gabriel's Hill	B1	Station Road
C4	George Street	A3	Terrace Road
D4	Greenside	A4	Tonbridge Road
A4	Hart Street	C2	Tufton Street
D4	Hastings Road	C2	Union Street
C4	Hayle Road	C4	Upper Stone Street
D1	Heathorn Street	A3	Victoria Road
C1	Hedley Street	D2	Vinters Road
B3	High Street	C3	Wat Tyler Way
D1	Holland Road	B1	Week Street
C1	James Street	C1	Well Road
C1	Jeffrey Street	A4	Westree Road
C3	King Street	C1	Wheeler Street
D4	Kingsley Road	C1	Woollett Street
C4	Knightrider Street	C2	Wyatt Street
A1	Lesley Place		
A3	London Road		
C3	Lower Stone Street		

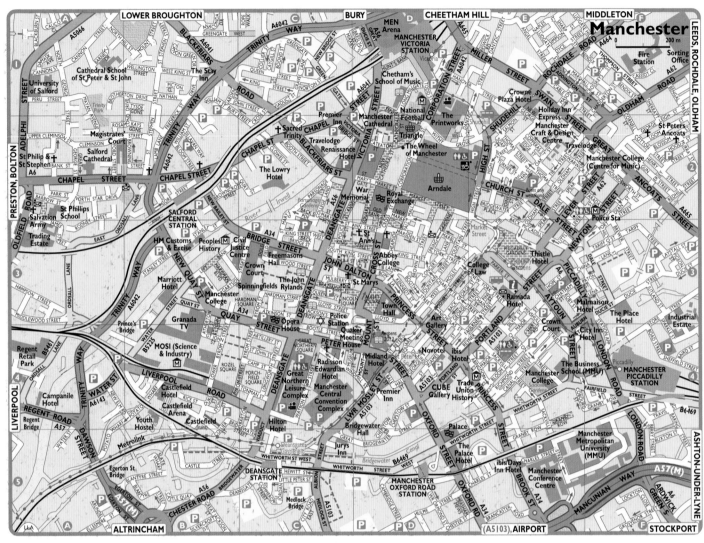

Manchester

Manchester is found on atlas page **82 H5**

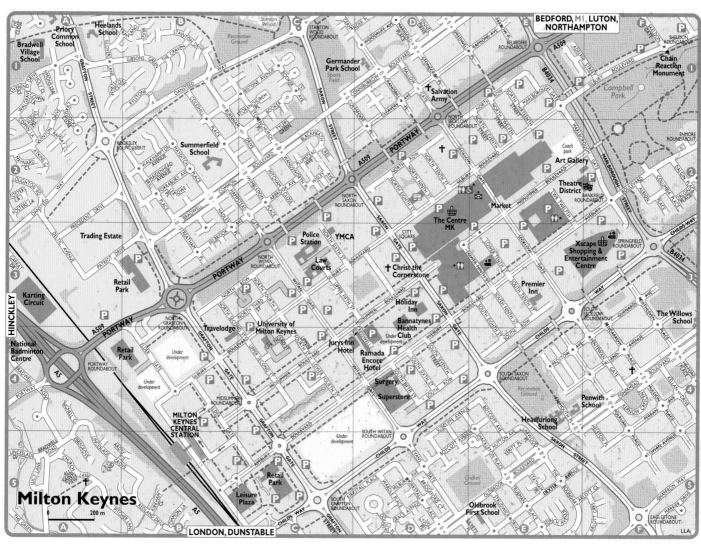

Milton Keynes

Milton Keynes is found on atlas page **49 N7**

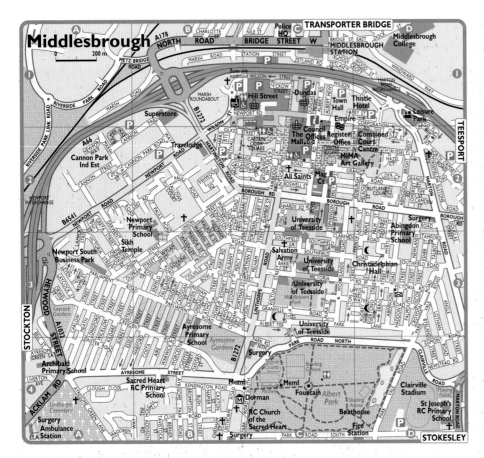

Middlesbrough

Middlesbrough is found on atlas page **104 E7**

Newport

Newport is found on atlas page **31 K7**

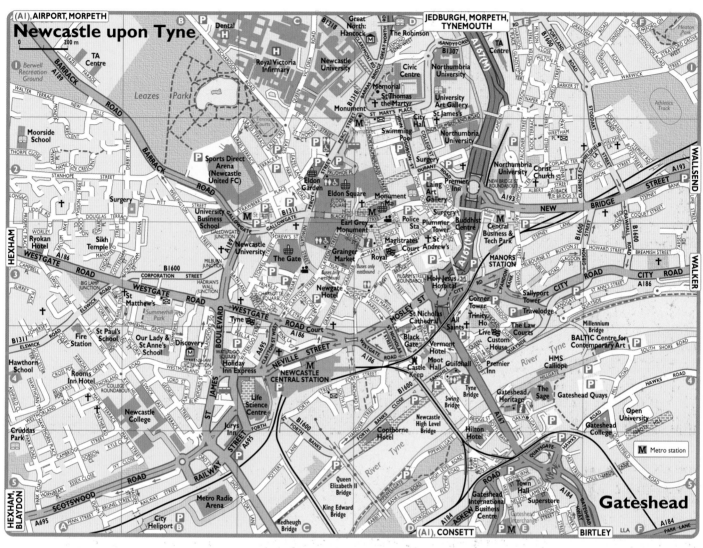

Newcastle upon Tyne

Newcastle upon Tyne is found on atlas page 113 **K8**

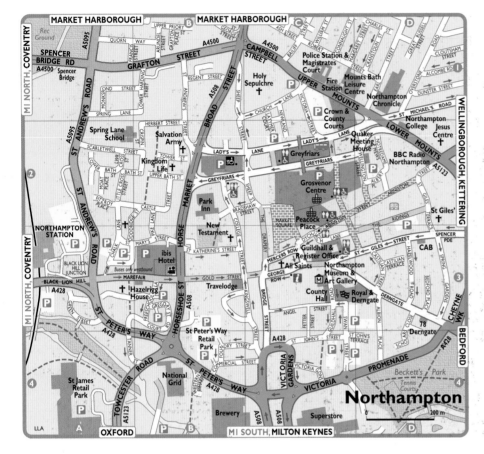

Northampton

Northampton is found on atlas page **60 G8**

C2	Abington Street
D2	Albert Place
D3	Albion Place
C3	Angel Street
B1	Arundel Street
C1	Ash Street
C1	Bailiff Street
A3	Black Lion Hill
B2	Bradshaw Street
C3	Bridge Street
B1	Broad Street
C1	Campbell Street
D3	Castilian Street
B2	Castle Street
A3	Chalk Lane
D3	Cheyne Walk
C1	Church Lane
B2	College Street
B4	Commercial Street
C1	Connaught Street
B3	Court Road
D1	Cranstoun Street
B2	Crispin Street
D3	Derngate
A3	Doddridge Street
D1	Dunster Street
D1	Dychurch Lane
D1	Earl Street
C3	Fetter Street
A2	Fitzroy Place
B4	Foundry Street
A1	Francis Street
B3	Freeschool Lane
C3	George Row
B3	Gold Street
A1	Grafton Street
D1	Great Russell Street
A3	Green Street
B3	Gregory Street
B2	Greyfriars
C3	Guildhall Road
D3	Hazelwood Road
B2	Herbert Street
B3	Horse Market
B3	Horseshoe Street
C3	Kingswell Street
B2	Lady's Lane
A2	Little Cross Street

A2	Lower Bath Street
A2	Lower Cross Street
B1	Lower Harding Street
D2	Lower Mounts
A3	Marefair
C1	Margaret Street
C2	Market Square
C3	Mercers Row
A2	Moat Place
A1	Monkspond Street
C1	Newland
D2	Notredame Mews
D1	Overstone Road
B3	Pike Lane
A1	Quorn Way
B1	Regent Street
C1	Robert Street
A2	St Andrew's Road
B1	St Andrew's Street
D3	St Giles Street
D2	St Giles' Terrace
C4	St John's Street
B3	St Katherine's Street
A3	St Mary's Street
D1	St Michael's Road
B4	St Peter's Way
A2	Scarletwell Street
D4	Scholars Close
B1	Sheep Street
C2	Sheep Street
A1	Spencer Bridge Road
D3	Spencer Parade
D3	Spring Gardens
A1	Spring Lane
C3	Swan Street
A4	Tanner Street
C2	The Drapery
D2	The Ridings
A4	Towcester Road
B2	Tower Street
B2	Upper Bath Street
C1	Upper Mounts
B1	Upper Priory Street
C4	Victoria Gardens
C4	Victoria Promenade
C1	Victoria Street
D2	Wellington Street
B4	Western Wharf

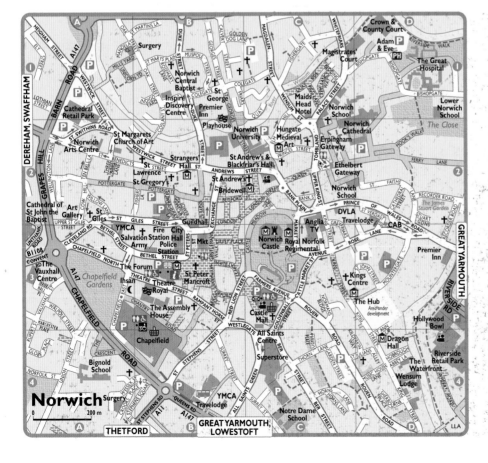

Norwich

Norwich is found on atlas page **77 J10**

B4	All Saints Green
C2	Bank Plain
A1	Barn Road
C1	Bedding Lane
B2	Bedford Street
C4	Ber Street
A3	Bethel Street
D1	Bishopgate
B3	Brigg Street
B1	Calvert Street
C3	Castle Meadow
D2	Cathedral Street
C3	Cattle Market Street
B3	Chantry Road
A3	Chapelfield East
A3	Chapelfield North
A3	Chapelfield Road
A3	Cleveland Road
B1	Colegate
A3	Convent Road
B2	Coslany Street
A2	Cow Hill
B3	Davey Place
B2	Dove Street
B1	Duke Street
C2	Elm Hill
B2	Exchange Street
C3	Farmers Avenue
D2	Ferry Lane
C1	Fishergate
B1	Friars Quay
B3	Gentlemans Walk
C3	Goldenball Street
A2	Grapes Hill
B3	Haymarket
A1	Heigham Street
C2	King Street
B2	London Street
B2	Lower Goat Lane
C1	Magdalen Street
C3	Market Avenue
A1	Mills Yard
D3	Mountergate
D4	Music House Lane
B2	Muspole Street
A4	Norfolk Street
A1	Oak Street
C1	Palace Street

A2	Pottergate
C2	Prince of Wales Road
C2	Princes Street
C1	Quay Side
B4	Queens Road
C2	Queen Street
B3	Rampant Horse Street
D2	Recorder Road
B3	Red Lion Street
D3	Riverside Road
D1	Riverside Walk
C3	Rose Lane
C3	Rouen Road
A4	Rupert Street
B2	St Andrews Street
A2	St Benedicts Street
D2	St Faiths Lane
B1	St Georges Street
A2	St Giles Street
C4	St Julians Alley
B1	St Marys Plain
B3	St Peters Street
B4	St Stephens Road
A4	St Stephens Square
B4	St Stephens Street
A2	St Swithins Road
D2	St Verdast Street
B4	Surrey Street
A2	Ten Bell Lane
B3	Theatre Street
C4	Thorn Lane
C2	Tombland
A1	Unicorn Yard
A4	Union Street
A3	Unthank Road
B2	Upper Goat Lane
C2	Upper King Street
A2	Upper St Giles Street
A3	Vauxhall Street
A3	Walpole Street
C1	Wensum Street
A4	Wessex Street
B3	Westlegate
A1	Westwick Street
D4	Wherry Road
C1	Whitefriars
B3	White Lion Street
A2	Willow Lane

Nottingham

Nottingham is found on atlas page **72 F3**

B3	Albert Street	A3	Lenton Road
D2	Barker Gate	C2	Lincoln Street
D1	Bath Street	B3	Lister Gate
D3	Bellar Gate	D4	London Road
D2	Belward Street	B2	Long Row
C2	Broad Street	C2	Lower Parliament Street
C3	Broadway	B3	Low Pavement
A2	Bromley Place	A2	Maid Marian Way
D1	Brook Street	B2	Market Street
B1	Burton Street	C3	Middle Hill
C4	Canal Street	B1	Milton Street
C2	Carlton Street	A3	Mount Street
C4	Carrington Street	B2	Norfolk Place
A4	Castle Boulevard	A2	North Circus Street
B3	Castle Gate	A3	Park Row
B3	Castle Road	D3	Parliament Street
B2	Chapel Bar	C2	Pelham Street
A1	Chaucer Street	A4	Peveril Drive
A1	Clarendon Street	C3	Pilcher Gate
C3	Cliff Road	C3	Popham Street
B4	Collin Street	B2	Poultry
D2	Cranbrook Street	B2	Queen Street
C2	Cumber Street	A2	Regent Street
C1	Curzon Place	D1	St Ann's Well Road
A2	Derby Road	A3	St James's Street
B2	Exchange Walk	C3	St Marks Gate
D3	Fisher Gate	C1	St Marks Street
C3	Fletcher Gate	C3	St Mary's Gate
B1	Forman Street	B3	St Peter's Gate
A3	Friar Lane	A1	Shakespeare Street
D2	Gedling Street	B2	Smithy Row
C2	George Street	B2	South Parade
C1	Glasshouse Street	B1	South Sherwood Street
A1	Goldsmith Street	B3	Spaniel Row
C2	Goose Gate	C4	Station Street
C3	Halifax Place	C2	Stoney Street
C2	Heathcote Street	A1	Talbot Street
C2	High Cross Street	C2	Thurland Street
C3	High Pavement	C4	Trent Street
D2	Hockley	A2	Upper Parliament Street
D3	Hollow Stone	C2	Victoria Street
A4	Hope Drive	C2	Warser Gate
B3	Hounds Gate	C3	Weekday Cross
C1	Howard Street	A2	Wellington Circus
C1	Huntingdon Street	B2	Wheeler Gate
C1	Kent Street	B4	Wilford Street
C1	King Edward Street	A1	Wollaton Street
B2	King Street	C2	Woolpack Lane

Oldham

Oldham is found on atlas page **83 K4**

B3	Ascroft Street	D1	Mortimer Street
B1	Bar Gap Road	A4	Napier Street East
D4	Barlow Street	A2	New Radcliffe Street
B3	Barn Street	A3	Oldham Way
D2	Beever Street	B4	Park Road
D2	Bell Street	A4	Park Street
B1	Belmont Street	B3	Peter Street
A3	Booth Street	C3	Queen Street
C3	Bow Street	B1	Radcliffe Street
D2	Brook Street	B1	Raleigh Close
B3	Brunswick Street	A1	Ramsden Street
C2	Cardinal Street	D2	Regent Street
A1	Chadderton Way	C3	Rhodes Bank
B3	Chaucer Street	C2	Rhodes Street
C3	Clegg Street	B1	Rifle Street
B1	Coldhurst Road	A1	Rochdale Road
B4	Cromwell Street	B2	Rock Street
B4	Crossbank Street	C3	Roscoe Street
B2	Curzon Street	A1	Ruskin Street
A1	Dunbar Street	A1	St Hilda's Drive
B2	Eden Street	B3	St Marys Street
C2	Egerton Street	B2	St Mary's Way
C3	Firth Street	D1	Shaw Road
B2	Fountain Street	C1	Shaw Street
B1	Franklin Street	C1	Siddall Street
D2	Gower Street	B3	Silver Street
A2	Grange Street	C3	Southgate Street
C3	Greaves Street	D4	South Hill Street
D4	Greengate Street	D3	Southlink
D3	Hamilton Street	D2	Spencer Street
D4	Hardy Street	B1	Sunfield Road
C4	Harmony Street	D1	Thames Street
D2	Henshaw Street	A1	Trafalgar Street
C1	Higginshaw Road	B1	Trinity Street
A2	Highfield Street	A1	Tulbury Street
B3	High Street	B3	Union Street
B3	Hobson Street	A4	Union Street West
D4	Hooper Street	B3	Union Street West
C1	Horsedge Street	D2	Wallshaw Street
A3	John Street	B4	Wall Street
B3	King Street	A1	Ward Street
D2	Lemnos Street	C3	Waterloo Street
C1	Malby Street	B4	Wellington Street
A4	Malton Street	A2	West End Street
A3	Manchester Street	B3	West Street
B3	Market Place	D2	Willow Street
C4	Marlborough Street	C4	Woodstock Street
A3	Middleton Road	C3	Yorkshire Street

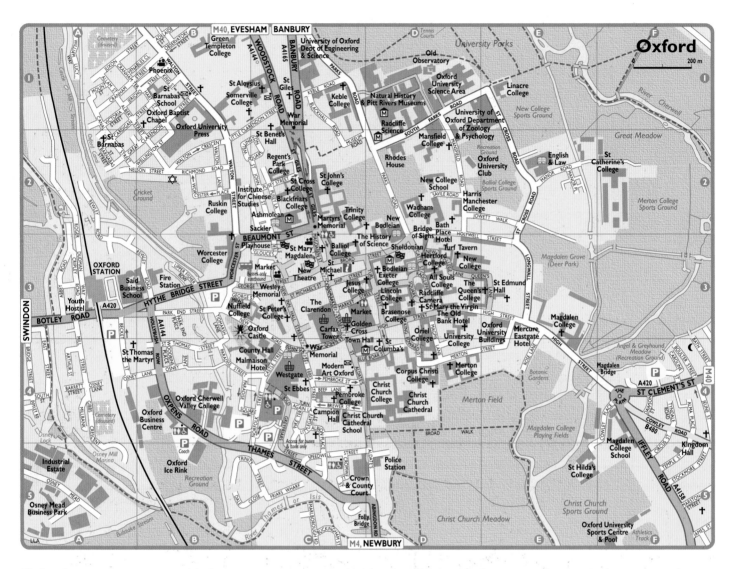

Oxford

Oxford is found on atlas page **34 F3**

University Colleges

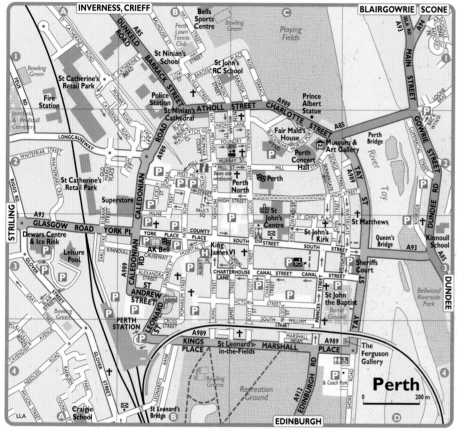

Perth

Perth is found on atlas page **134 E3**

B3	Albert Place	B1	Melville Street
B3	Alexandra Street	B2	Mill Street
D1	Ardchoille Park	C2	Mill Street
B1	Atholl Street	B2	Milne Street
D2	Back Wynd	A1	Monart Road
B1	Balhousie Street	B2	Murray Street
B1	Barossa Place	A4	Needless Road
B1	Barrack Street	B3	New Row
C2	Blackfriars Wynd	B2	North Methven Street
B2	Black Watch Garden	C2	North Port
B2	Caledonian Road	B2	North William Street
B3	Caledonian Road	A2	Old Market Place
C3	Canal Street	B2	Paul Street
A4	Cavendish Avenue	D2	Perth Bridge
C3	Charles Street	A4	Pickletullum Road
C2	Charlotte Street	B3	Pomarium Street
B3	Charterhouse Lane	C3	Princes Street
D2	Commercial Street	D3	Queen's Bridge
B3	County Place	A4	Raeburn Park
B4	Cross Street	A2	Riggs Road
D3	Dundee Road	D3	Riverside
B1	Dunkeld Road	C1	Rose Terrace
A3	Earls Dyke	B3	St Andrew Street
C4	Edinburgh Road	A1	St Catherine's Road
A1	Feus Road	C3	St John's Place
B2	Foundry Lane	C3	St John Street
C2	George Street	B4	St Leonard's Bank
A3	Glasgow Road	B2	St Paul's Square
A3	Glover Street	C2	Scott Street
A4	Glover Street	C3	Scott Street
D2	Gowrie Street	D4	Shore Road
A3	Gray Street	C2	Skinnergate
B1	Hay Street	B2	South Methven Street
B2	High Street	C3	South Street
C2	High Street	C4	South William Street
B3	Hospital Street	D3	Speygate
D1	Isla Road	B1	Stormont Street
C3	James Street	D2	Tay Street
C3	King Edward Street	D4	Tay Street
B4	Kings Place	B2	Union Lane
B3	King Street	C3	Victoria Street
A3	Kinnoull Causeway	D2	Watergate
C2	Kinnoull Street	B2	West Mill Wynd
B3	Leonard Street	A2	Whitefriars Crescent
D1	Lochie Brae	A2	Whitefriar Street
A2	Longcauseway	A4	Wilson Street
D1	Main Street	A3	York Place
C4	Marshall Place	B3	York Place

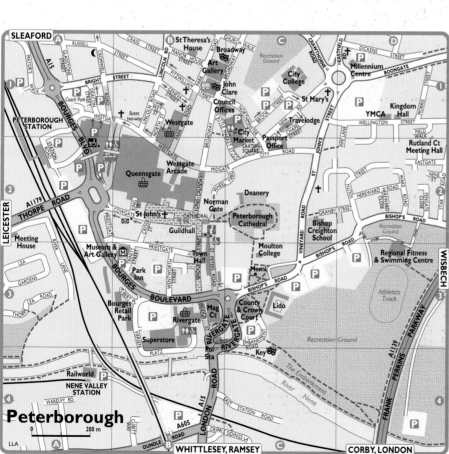

Peterborough

Peterborough is found on atlas page **74 C11**

B3	Albert Place	C1	New Road
C3	Bishop's Road	C1	Northminster
D1	Boongate	B1	North Street
A1	Bourges Boulevard	B4	Oundle Road
B3	Bridge Street	B1	Park Road
A1	Bright Street	B1	Peet Street
B2	Broadway	D2	Pipe Lane
C1	Brook Street	A2	Priestgate
B2	Cathedral Square	B3	Rivergate
B1	Cattle Market Street	A2	River Lane
C1	Chapel Street	A1	Russell Street
B2	Church Street	C2	St John's Street
C1	Church Walk	B3	St Peters Road
C2	City Road	D2	South Street
B2	Cowgate	D2	Star Road
B1	Craig Street	A2	Station Road
C1	Crawthorne Road	A3	Thorpe Lea Road
B4	Cripple Sidings Lane	A2	Thorpe Road
A1	Cromwell Road	B3	Trinity Street
B2	Cross Street	B3	Viersen Platz
B4	Cubitt Way	C3	Vineyard Road
A1	Deacon Street	D2	Wake Road
D1	Dickens Street	A4	Wareley Road
D1	Eastfield Road	D1	Wellington Street
D2	Eastgate	B3	Wentworth Street
C4	East Station Road	A1	Westgate
C3	Embankment Road		
B2	Exchange Street		
D2	Fengate Close		
D1	Field Walk		
B1	Fitzwilliam Street		
D4	Frank Perkins Parkway		
B1	Geneva Street		
A1	Gladstone Street		
C2	Granby Street		
D2	Hereward Close		
D2	Hereward Road		
B2	King Street		
C2	Laxton Square		
A3	Lea Gardens		
B1	Lincoln Road		
B4	London Road		
B2	Long Causeway		
B1	Manor House Street		
A1	Mayor's Walk		
B2	Midgate		
D1	Morris Street		
D2	Nene Street		

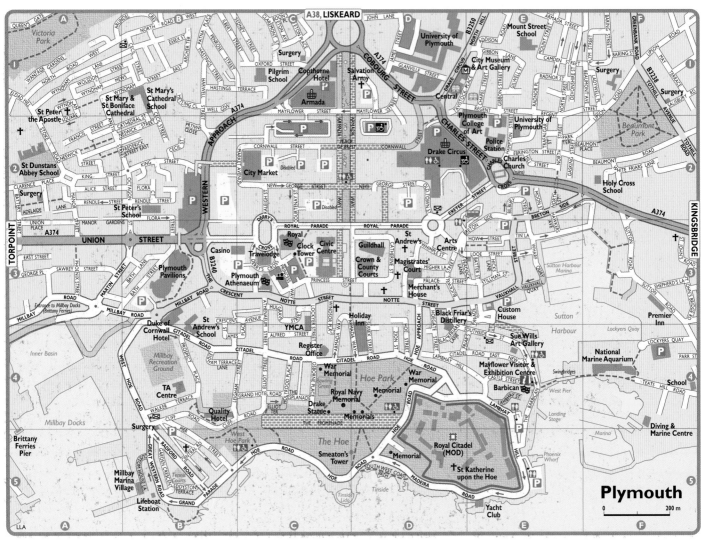

Plymouth

Plymouth is found on atlas page **6 D8**

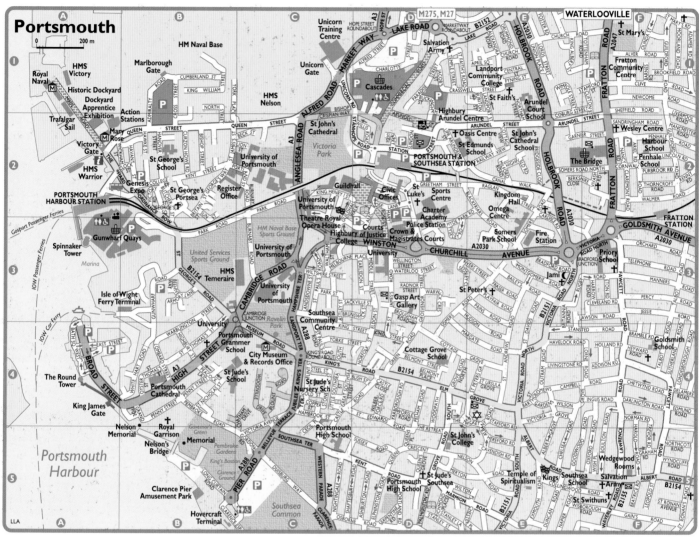

Portsmouth

Portsmouth is found on atlas page **14 H7**

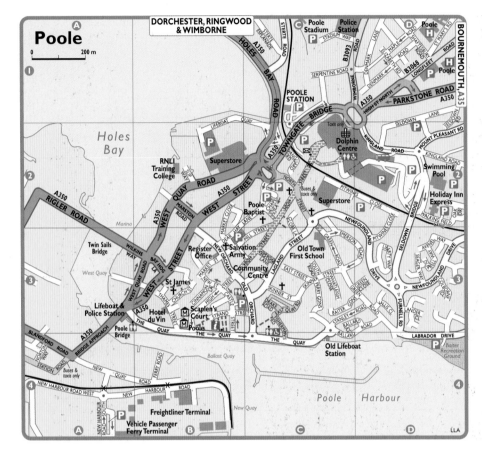

Poole

Poole is found on atlas page **12 H6**

D3	Avenel Way	A4	New Quay Road
C3	Baiter Gardens	B3	New Street
C3	Ballard Close	C2	North Street
C4	Ballard Road	A4	Norton Way
B3	Bay Hog Lane	D2	Oak Drive
A3	Blandford Road	B3	Old Orchard
A4	Bridge Approach	D1	Parkstone Road
B3	Castle Street	C3	Perry Gardens
C2	Chapel Lane	C2	Pitwines Close
B3	Church Street	A3	Poole Bridge
B3	Cinnamon Lane	A2	Rigler Road
D3	Colborne Close	D1	St Mary's Road
B3	Dear Hay Lane	D3	Seager Way
D1	Denmark Lane	D3	Seldown Bridge
D1	Denmark Road	D2	Seldown Lane
C3	Drake Road	D2	Seldown Road
D3	Durrell Way	C1	Serpentine Road
C3	East Quay Road	D1	Shaftesbury Road
C3	East Street	C3	Skinner Street
D1	Elizabeth Road	B2	Slip Way
C3	Emerson Road	C3	South Road
B4	Ferry Road	C1	Stadium Way
C3	Fisherman's Road	C3	Stanley Road
D3	Furnell Road	C1	Sterte Esplanade
C2	Globe Lane	C1	Sterte Road
D3	Green Close	B3	Strand Street
C3	Green Road	B3	Thames Street
B3	High Street	B3	The Quay
D1	High Street North	C2	Towngate Bridge
C3	Hill Street	A3	Twin Sails Bridge
C1	Holes Bay Road	D3	Vallis Close
D2	Kingland Road	C2	Vanguard Road
D4	Labrador Drive	D2	Walking Field Lane
C3	Lagland Street	C3	Westons Lane
D3	Lander Close	B3	West Quay Road
D3	Liberty Way	B3	West Street
B2	Lifeboat Quay	C3	Whatleigh Close
D1	Longfleet Road	A3	Wilkins Way
D1	Maple Road	D1	Wimborne Road
B2	Market Close		
B3	Market Street		
B2	Marston Road		
D2	Mount Pleasant Road		
C2	Newfoundland Drive		
A4	New Harbour Road		
A4	New Harbour Road South		
A4	New Harbour Road West		
B3	New Orchard		

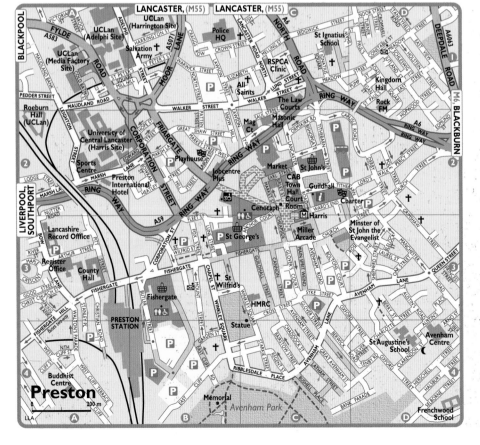

Preston

Preston is found on atlas page **88 G5**

A1	Adelphi Street	C2	Lancaster Road
A3	Arthur Street	C1	Lancaster Road North
C4	Avenham Lane	C4	Latham Street
C3	Avenham Road	B1	Lawson Street
C3	Avenham Street	A2	Leighton Street
C4	Berwick Road	C1	Lund Street
C2	Birley Street	B3	Lune Street
C3	Boltons Court	D3	Manchester Road
A3	Bow Lane	C2	Market Street
B3	Butler Street	B2	Market Street West
C2	Carlisle Road	A2	Marsh Lane
C4	Chaddock Street	A1	Maudland Bank
B3	Chapel Street	A1	Maudland Road
D4	Charlotte Street	C1	Meadow Street
C3	Cheapside	B1	Moor Lane
A3	Christ Church Street	B3	Mount Street
C3	Church Street	C1	North Road
D4	Clarendon Street	D3	Oak Street
B2	Corporation Street	C2	Ormskirk Road
B3	Corpration Street	C3	Oxford Street
B1	Craggs Row	A1	Pedder Street
C3	Cross Street	D2	Percy Street
B1	Crown Street	A3	Pitt Street
D1	Deepdale Road	D2	Pole Street
D2	Derby Street	D1	Pump Street
C2	Earl Street	D3	Queen Street
B4	East Cliff	B4	Ribblesdale Place
D1	East Street	B2	Ring Way
D2	Edmund Street	D3	Rose Street
A2	Edward Street	D3	St Austin's Road
B1	Elizabeth Street	D1	St Paul's Road
B3	Fishergate	D1	St Paul's Square
A4	Fishergate Hill	B1	St Peter's Street
B3	Fleet Street	C1	Sedgwick Street
B3	Fox Street	D3	Shepherd Street
B2	Friargate	B2	Snow Hill
A1	Fylde Road	D1	Stanleyfield Road
C3	Glover Street	C4	Starkie Street
C4	Great Avenham Street	C3	Syke Street
B2	Great Shaw Street	C2	Tithebarn Street
D2	Grimshaw Street	B1	Walker Street
C3	Guildhall Street	A3	Walton's Parade
B1	Harrington Street	C2	Ward's End
B2	Heatley Street	B1	Warwick Street
D4	Herschell Street	A4	West Cliff
D1	Holstein Street	A4	West Cliff Terrace
D2	Hopwood Street	B3	Winkley Square
D1	Jutland Street		

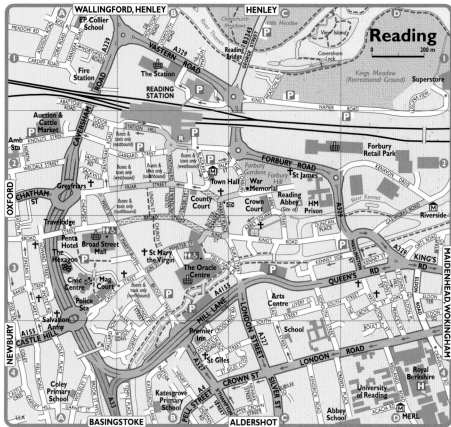

Reading

Reading is found on atlas page **35 K10**

C3	Abbey Square	D3	King's Road
C2	Abbey Street	B3	King Street
A1	Addison Road	A2	Knollys Street
A3	Anstey Road	C3	Livery Close
A3	Baker Street	C4	London Road
B2	Blagrave Street	C3	London Street
D4	Boult Street	A4	Mallard Row
B3	Bridge Street	B2	Market Place
A3	Broad Street	B4	Mill Lane
A4	Brook Street West	B3	Minster Street
B3	Buttermarket	C1	Napier Road
A1	Cardiff Road	C4	Newark Street
A3	Carey Street	A1	Northfield Road
A4	Castle Hill	B4	Parthia Close
A3	Castle Street	B4	Pell Street
A2	Caversham Road	D3	Prince's Street
A2	Chatham Street	C3	Queen's Road
A2	Cheapside	B2	Queen Victoria Street
B3	Church Street	D4	Redlands Road
B4	Church Street	A1	Ross Road
A4	Coley Place	A2	Sackville Street
D4	Craven Road	B4	St Giles Close
B4	Crossland Road	D3	St John's Road
B2	Cross Street	B3	St Mary's Butts
C4	Crown Street	C3	Sidmouth Street
B4	Deansgate Road	C4	Silver Street
C3	Duke Street	B3	Simmonds Street
C3	Duncan Place	B4	Southampton Street
C3	East Street	C3	South Street
D3	Eldon Road	B2	Station Hill
A4	Field Road	B2	Station Road
B4	Fobney Street	B3	Swan Place
C2	Forbury Road	A1	Swansea Road
B2	Friar Street	C2	The Forbury
A4	Garnet Street	A2	Tudor Road
B2	Garrard Street	B2	Union Street
D3	Gas Works Road	C4	Upper Crown Street
C1	George Street	A2	Vachel Road
A2	Greyfriars Road	B2	Valpy Street
B3	Gun Street	B1	Vastern Road
B4	Henry Street	B4	Waterside Gardens
A3	Howard Street	D3	Watlington Street
B4	Katesgrove Lane	A2	Weldale Street
D2	Kenavon Drive	A2	West Street
C4	Kendrick Road	A4	Wolseley Street
C3	Kennet Side	B3	Yield Hall Place
D3	Kennet Street	A1	York Road
C1	King's Meadow Road	A3	Zinzan Street

Salisbury

Salisbury is found on atlas page **21 M9**

C1	Albany Road	A1	Kingsland Road
A1	Ashley Road	C1	King's Road
B2	Avon Approach	D3	Laverstock Road
C2	Bedwin Street	B3	Malthouse Lane
C2	Belle Vue Road	D2	Manor Road
C4	Blackfriars Way	C1	Marlborough Road
C3	Blue Boar Row	A1	Meadow Road
D1	Bourne Avenue	A1	Middleton Road
C2	Bourne Hill	D3	Milford Hill
B3	Bridge Street	C3	Milford Street
C3	Brown Street	A3	Mill Road
D1	Campbell Road	C3	Minster Street
B1	Castle Street	B1	Nelson Road
C3	Catherine Street	B3	New Canal
C2	Chipper Lane	B3	New Street
A2	Churchfields Road	B3	North Street
D3	Churchill Way East	D1	Park Street
C1	Churchill Way North	C3	Pennyfarthing Street
C4	Churchill Way South	C1	Queen's Road
B2	Churchill Way West	C3	Queen Street
D2	Clarendon Road	D3	Rampart Road
A1	Clifton Road	A3	Rectory Road
A1	Coldharbour Lane	C2	Rollestone Street
C1	College Street	C4	St Ann Street
B3	Cranebridge Road	C2	St Edmund's Church Street
B3	Crane Street	D1	St Mark's Avenue
A1	Devizes Road	D1	St Mark's Road
A3	Dew's Road	B2	St Paul's Road
B3	East Street	C2	Salt Lane
D2	Elm Grove	C2	Scots Lane
D2	Elm Grove Road	A1	Sidney Street
C2	Endless Street	B3	Silver Street
D2	Estcourt Road	D4	Southampton Road
C4	Exeter Street	A3	South Street
D4	Eyres Way	A2	South Western Road
D2	Fairview Road	B2	Spire View
A2	Fisherton Street	B2	Summerlock Approach
D3	Fowler's Road	D4	Tollgate Road
C4	Friary Lane	C3	Trinity Street
A1	Gas Lane	D1	Wain-A-Long Road
A1	George Street	D2	Wessex Road
C3	Gigant Street	A3	West Street
C2	Greencroft Street	A2	Wilton Road
C3	Guilder Lane	C3	Winchester Street
C1	Hamilton Road	A2	Windsor Road
B3	High Street	C1	Woodstock Road
C3	Ivy Street	C1	Wyndham Road
D2	Kelsey Road	A2	York Road

Sheffield

Sheffield is found on atlas page **84 E3**

C2	Angel Street	C4	Howard Street
C3	Arundel Gate	A1	Hoyle Street
C4	Arundel Street	C2	King Street
B3	Backfields	B1	Lambert Street
A2	Bailey Street	B3	Leopold Street
B3	Balm Green	A3	Mappin Street
C2	Bank Street	B4	Matilda Street
B3	Barkers Pool	C2	Meetinghouse Lane
A2	Broad Lane	C2	Mulberry Street
D2	Broad Street	A2	Newcastle Street
C4	Brown Street	C2	New Street
B3	Cambridge Street	C3	Norfolk Street
B2	Campo Lane	B2	North Church Street
B3	Carver Street	B3	Orchard Street
C1	Castlegate	B2	Paradise Street
C2	Castle Street	B3	Pinstone Street
B4	Charles Street	C3	Pond Hill
A4	Charter Row	C3	Pond Street
B2	Church Street	A3	Portobello Street
C2	Commercial Street	B2	Queen Street
B1	Corporation Street	A2	Rockingham Street
B3	Cross Burgess Street	B2	St James Street
D1	Cutlers Gate	C2	Scargill Croft
D1	Derek Dooley Way	A1	Scotland Street
A3	Devonshire Street	B1	Shalesmoor
A3	Division Street	D4	Sheaf Street
C2	Dixon Lane	C4	Shoreham Street
D2	Duke Street	D4	Shrewsbury Road
D2	Exchange Street	B2	Silver Street
B4	Eyre Street	A1	Smithfield
C2	Fig Tree Lane	C2	Snig Hill
A4	Fitzwilliam Street	A2	Solly Street
C3	Flat Street	C4	Suffolk Road
B1	Furnace Hill	C3	Surrey Street
B4	Furnival Gate	D4	Talbot Street
D1	Furnival Road	B2	Tenter Street
C4	Furnival Street	B2	Townhead Street
A2	Garden Street	A4	Trafalgar Street
C2	George Street	B3	Trippet Lane
B1	Gibralter Street	B4	Union Street
C3	Harmer Lane	B2	Vicar Lane
C2	Harts Head	D1	Victoria Station Road
B2	Hawley Street	C2	Waingate
C2	Haymarket	A4	Wellington Street
C2	High Street	B2	West Bar
A3	Holland Street	A3	West Street
A2	Hollis Croft	A2	White Croft
B3	Holly Street	C2	York Street

Shrewsbury

Shrewsbury is found on atlas page **56 H2**

D3	Abbey Foregate	B1	Longner Street
D1	Albert Street	B4	Luciefelde Road
B1	Alma Street	B2	Mardol
C4	Back Lime Street	B3	Market Street
B2	Barker Street	C3	Milk Street
D1	Beacall's Lane	D4	Moreton Crescent
C3	Beeches Lane	B1	Mount Street
C4	Belle Vue Gardens	B3	Murivance
D4	Belle Vue Road	B1	Nettles Lane
B3	Belmont	D1	Newpark Road
C3	Belmont Bank	A2	New Street
D1	Benyon Street	D1	North Street
D4	Betton Street	D3	Old Coleham
B2	Bridge Street	D3	Old Potts Way
D1	Burton Street	A2	Park Avenue
C2	Butcher Row	C4	Pengrove
A4	Canonbury	D4	Pound Close
C1	Castle Foregate	C2	Pride Hill
C2	Castle Gates	B3	Princess Street
C2	Castle Street	A2	Priory Road
C1	Chester Street	B3	Quarry Place
B3	Claremont Bank	A2	Quarry View
B3	Claremont Hill	C4	Raby Crescent
B3	Claremont Street	B2	Raven Meadows
D3	Coleham Head	B2	Roushill
B3	College Hill	B3	St Chad's Terrace
A2	Copthorne Road	A1	St George's Street
C1	Coton Hill	B3	St Johns Hill
B4	Crescent Lane	C3	St Julians Friars
B3	Cross Hill	C2	St Mary's Place
A1	Darwin Gardens	C2	St Mary's Street
A1	Darwin Street	C2	St Mary's Water Lane
C3	Dogpole	D4	Salters Lane
A1	Drinkwater Street	D1	Severn Bank
C3	Fish Street	D1	Severn Street
A2	Frankwell	B3	Shop Latch
B2	Frankwell Quay	B2	Smithfield Road
A2	Greenhill Avenue	B3	Swan Hill
C4	Greyfriars Road	D1	The Dana
C3	High Street	A1	The Mount
B2	Hill's Lane	B3	The Square
C1	Howard Street	B3	Town Walls
B1	Hunter Street	A2	Victoria Avenue
B4	Kingsland Road	D1	Victoria Street
C4	Lime Street	A2	Water Lane
C4	Longden Coleham	D1	Water Street
C4	Longden Gardens	D1	West Street
C4	Longden Road	C3	Wyle Cop

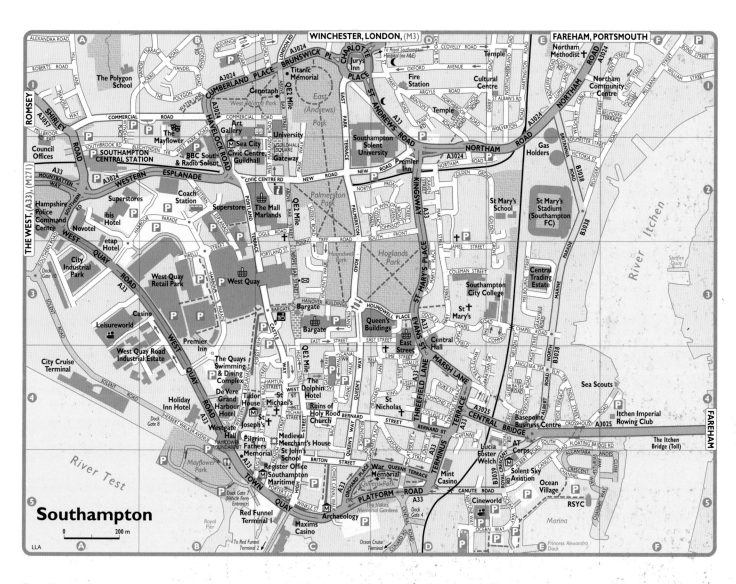

Southampton

Southampton is found on atlas page **14 D4**

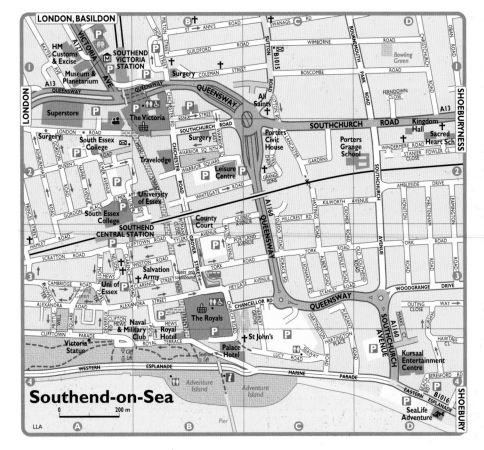

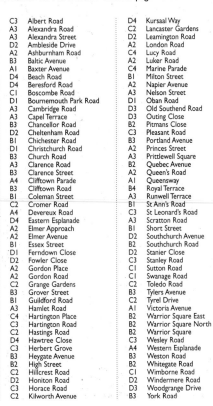

Southend-on-Sea

Southend-on-Sea is found on atlas page **38 E4**

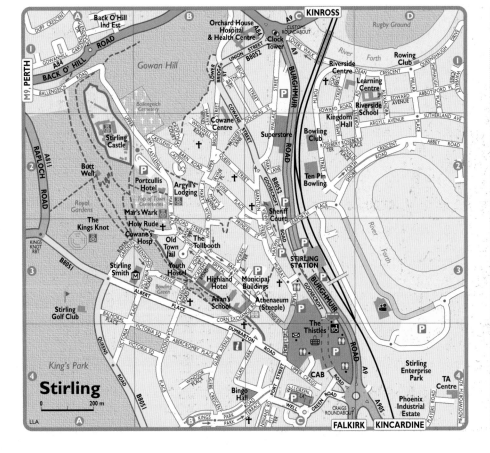

Stirling

Stirling is found on atlas page **133 M9**

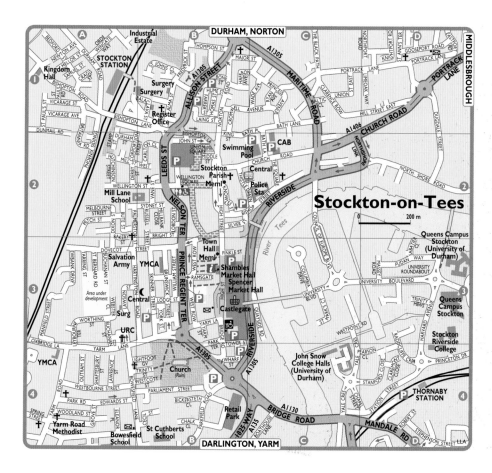

Stockton-on-Tees

Stockton-on-Tees is found on atlas page **104 D7**

Stoke-on-Trent (Hanley)

Stoke-on-Trent (Hanley) is found on atlas page **70 F5**

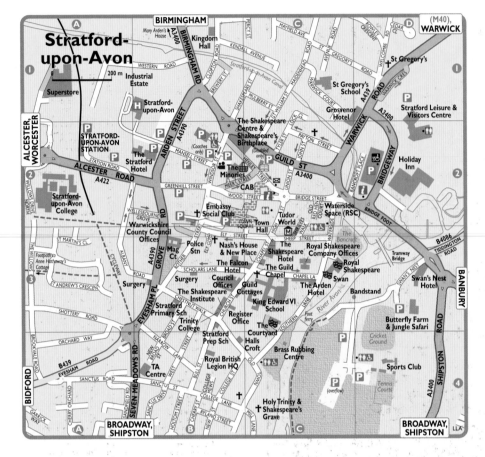

Stratford-upon-Avon

Stratford-upon-Avon is found on atlas page **47 P3**

A3	Albany Road	C2	Old Red Hen Court
A2	Alcester Road	C4	Old Town
B2	Arden Street	A4	Orchard Way
C1	Avenue Road	C2	Payton Street
C2	Bancroft Place	C1	Percy Street
B1	Birmingham Road	B3	Rother Street
B1	Brewery Street	D1	Rowley Crescent
D2	Bridge Foot	B4	Ryland Street
C2	Bridge Street	A3	St Andrew's Crescent
D2	Bridgeway	C1	St Gregory's Road
B4	Broad Street	A3	St Martin's Close
A4	Brookvale Road	B4	Sanctus Drive
B4	Bull Street	A4	Sanctus Road
D1	Cedar Close	B4	Sanctus Street
C3	Chapel Lane	A4	Sandfield Road
C3	Chapel Street	B3	Scholars Lane
A4	Cherry Orchard	A4	Seven Meadows Road
B4	Cherry Street	B1	Shakespeare Street
B3	Chestnut Walk	C3	Sheep Street
B3	Church Street	D4	Shipston Road
B1	Clopton Road	A3	Shottery Road
B4	College Lane	C3	Shrieves Walk
B4	College Mews	C3	Southern Lane
B4	College Street	A2	Station Road
B3	Ely Gardens	D3	Swan's Nest
B3	Ely Street	A3	The Willows
B3	Evesham Place	D3	Tiddington Road
A4	Evesham Road	B2	Town Square
A4	Garrick Way	D3	Tramway Bridge
C1	Great William Street	C2	Tyler Street
B2	Greenhill Street	C2	Union Street
B3	Grove Road	C1	Warwick Court
C2	Guild Street	D1	Warwick Crescent
B2	Henley Street	C2	Warwick Road
C3	High Street	C3	Waterside
B4	Holtom Street	D1	Welcombe Road
C2	John Street	B2	Wellesbourne Grove
B1	Kendall Avenue	B1	Western Road
C2	Lock Close	B4	West Street
C1	Maidenhead Road	A2	Willows Drive North
B2	Mansell Street	B2	Windsor Street
C1	Mayfield Avenue	B2	Wood Street
B2	Meer Street		
C4	Mill Lane		
C1	Mulberry Street		
B4	Narrow Lane		
B4	New Broad Street		
B4	New Street		

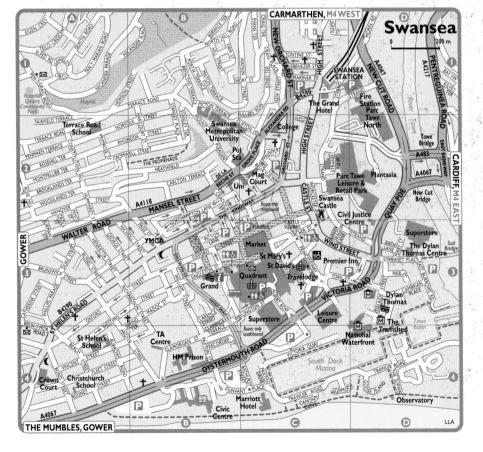

Swansea

Swansea is found on atlas page **29 J6**

D3	Adelaide Street	C1	New Orchard Street
C2	Alexandra Road	C1	New Street
A4	Argyle Street	A1	Nicander Parade
D3	Bath Lane	A3	Nicholl Street
A4	Beach Street	A2	Norfolk Street
A4	Bond Street	B1	North Hill Road
A3	Brunswick Street	B2	Northampton Lane
A4	Burrows Road	C2	Orchard Street
C3	Caer Street	A3	Oxford Street
B2	Carlton Terrace	B4	Oystermouth Road
C2	Castle Street	B3	Page Street
A3	Catherine Street	B3	Park Street
B3	Clarence Street	B4	Paxton Street
C2	Clifton Hill	D1	Pentreguinea Road
A2	Constituion Hill	A1	Pen-Y-Graig Road
B2	Cradock Street	B3	Picton Lane
C1	Craig Place	D3	Pier Street
A2	Cromwell Street	A2	Primrose Street
B2	De La Beche Street	C3	Princess Way
B3	Dillwyn Street	D2	Quay Parade
A3	Duke Street	B4	Recorder Street
B4	Dunvant Place	A2	Rhondda Street
D2	East Bank Way	A3	Richardson Street
D3	East Burrows Road	A4	Rodney Street
C1	Ebenezer Street	A2	Rose Hill
A1	Elfed Road	A3	Russel Street
D3	Ferry Street	A3	St Helen's Road
A4	Firm Street	B1	Short Street
A4	Fleet Street	B3	Singleton Street
A3	George Street	D3	Somerset Place
B4	Glamorgan Street	C1	Strand
C3	Green Lane Dragon	A1	Tan Y Marian Road
C3	Grove Place	A1	Teilo Crescent
A2	Hanover Street	A2	Terrace Road
B2	Harcourt Street	B2	The Kingsway
B2	Heathfield	C1	Tontine Street
A3	Henrietta Street	C4	Trawler Road
A1	Hewson Street	C4	Victoria Quay
C2	High Street	C3	Victoria Road
B1	Hill Street	A4	Vincent Street
A2	Humphrey Street	A3	Walter Road
A1	Islwyn Road	C1	Watkin Street
A1	Llewelyn Circle	A3	Wellington Street
B3	Madoc Street	B3	West Way
B2	Mansel Street	A4	Western Street
C1	Mariner Street	B3	William Street
B2	Mount Pleasant	C3	Wind Street
D1	New Cut Road	C3	York Street

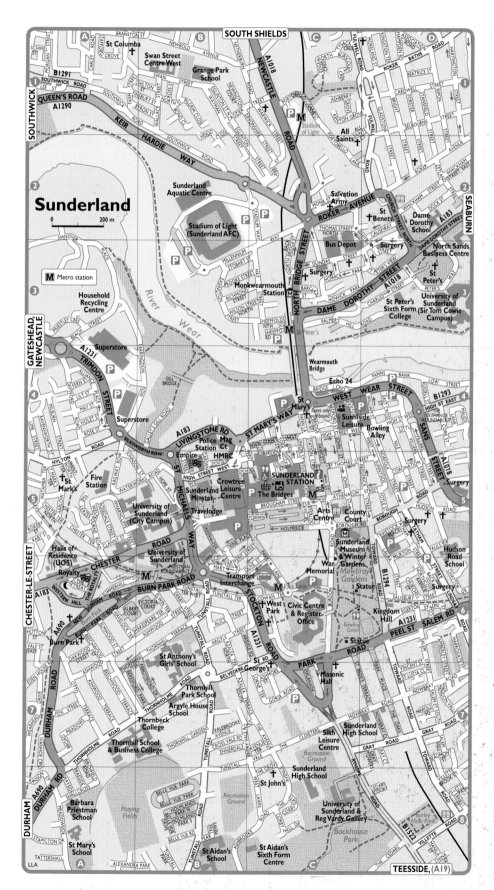

Sunderland

Sunderland is found on atlas page 113 **N9**

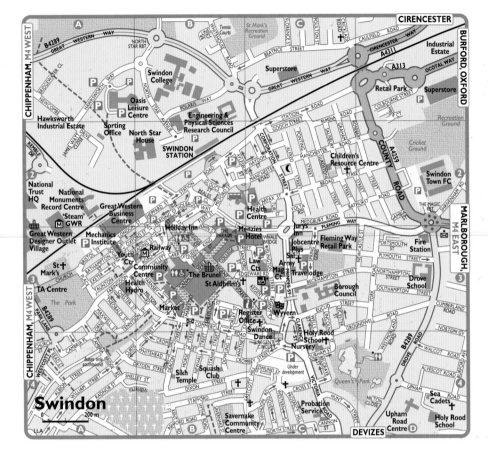

Swindon

Swindon is found on atlas page **33 M8**

A4	Albion Street	C3	Islington Street
C2	Alfred Street	B3	John Street
B4	Ashford Road	B3	King Street
B2	Aylesbury Street	A3	London Street
C2	Bathurst Road	C2	Manchester Road
C3	Beckhampton Street	B3	Market Street
B2	Bridge Street	A3	Maxwell Street
A3	Bristol Street	C2	Medgbury Road
C2	Broad Street	B2	Milford Street
A4	Cambria Bridge Road	B3	Milton Road
B3	Canal Walk	B3	Morley Street
C2	Carfax Street	B4	Morse Street
B3	Carr Street	D3	Newcastle Street
A3	Chester Street	A1	Newcombe Drive
A3	Church Place	B4	Newhall Street
D1	Cirencester Way	D3	Northampton Street
C3	Clarence Street	B1	North Star Avenue
B3	College Street	D1	Ocotal Way
B3	Commercial Road	A3	Park Lane
C2	Corporation Street	D3	Plymouth Street
D2	County Road	B1	Polaris Way
B4	Cromby Street	C2	Ponting Street
A4	Curtis Street	D3	Portsmouth Street
B4	Deacon Street	C3	Princes Street
B4	Dixon Street	C4	Prospect Hill
C4	Dover Street	B3	Queen Street
B4	Dowling Street	A4	Radnor Street
D4	Drove Road	C3	Regent Place
A4	Dryden Street	B3	Regent Street
C4	Eastcott Hill	C2	Rosebery Street
B2	East Street	C2	Salisbury Street
B3	Edgeware Road	B3	Sanford Street
C1	Elmina Road	B2	Sheppard Street
A3	Emlyn Square	D3	Southampton Street
C3	Euclid Street	B4	Stafford Street
A3	Faringdon Road	B4	Stanier Street
B3	Farnsby Street	B2	Station Road
B2	Fleet Street	C4	Swindon Road
C3	Fleming Way	A3	Tennyson Street
C2	Gladstone Street	A3	Theobald Street
C2	Gooch Street	C4	Victoria Road
C2	Graham Street	B3	Villett Street
A1	Great Western Way	A4	Westcott Place
C3	Groundwell Road	C4	Western Street
B3	Havelock Street	B4	Whitehead Street
A1	Hawksworth Way	B4	Whitney Street
C2	Haydon Street	A4	William Street
B2	Holbrook Way	D3	York Road

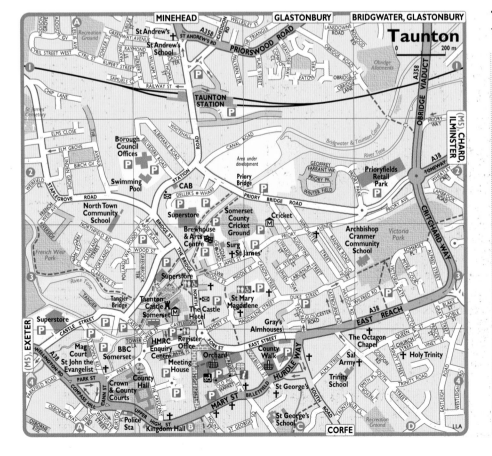

Taunton

Taunton is found on atlas page **18 H10**

B2	Albemarle Road	A3	Northfield Road
D3	Alfred Street	B3	North Street
C4	Alma Street	C1	Obridge Road
B2	Belvedere Road	D2	Obridge Viaduct
C4	Billetfield	B4	Old Pig Market
C4	Billet Street	A4	Parkfield Road
B2	Bridge Street	A4	Park Street
B2	Canal Road	B4	Paul Street
A4	Cann Street	C1	Plais Street
C3	Canon Street	A3	Portland Street
A4	Castle Street	B1	Priorswood Road
B1	Cheddon Road	C3	Priory Avenue
A1	Chip Lane	C2	Priory Bridge Road
D4	Church Street	D4	Queen Street
A3	Clarence Street	B1	Railway Street
A3	Cleveland Street	C3	Ranmer Road
A4	Compass Hill	A1	Raymond Street
D2	Critchard Way	A1	Rupert Street
A1	Cyril Street	B1	St Andrew's Road
B2	Deller's Wharf	C3	St Augustine Street
C3	Duke Street	B3	St James Street
C3	Eastbourne Road	A4	St John's Road
D4	Eastleigh Road	A1	Samuels Court
D3	East Reach	C4	South Road
C4	East Street	D4	South Street
B4	Fore Street	A2	Staplegrove Road
A1	Fowler Street	B2	Station Road
A2	French Weir Avenue	C3	Stephen Street
D3	Gloucester Road	C3	Stephen Way
C3	Grays Street	C3	Tancred Street
A1	Greenway Avenue	A2	The Avenue
C3	Gyffarde Street	B3	The Bridge
B4	Hammet Street	B4	The Crescent
C3	Haydon Road	C1	The Triangle
B1	Herbert Street	B1	Thomas Street
B4	High Street	D2	Toneway
C3	Hugo Street	B4	Tower Street
C4	Hurdle Way	D4	Trinity Road
C3	Laburnum Street	D4	Trinity Street
D2	Lambrook Way	B4	Upper High Street
C1	Lansdowne Road	D3	Victoria Gate
A1	Leslie Avenue	D3	Victoria Road
A2	Linden Grove	D4	Viney Street
B3	Lower Middle Street	A4	Wellington Road
B3	Magdalene Street	C3	Wilfred Road
B4	Mary Street	B1	William Street
A1	Maxwell Street	C2	Winchester Street
B3	Middle Street	B3	Wood Street

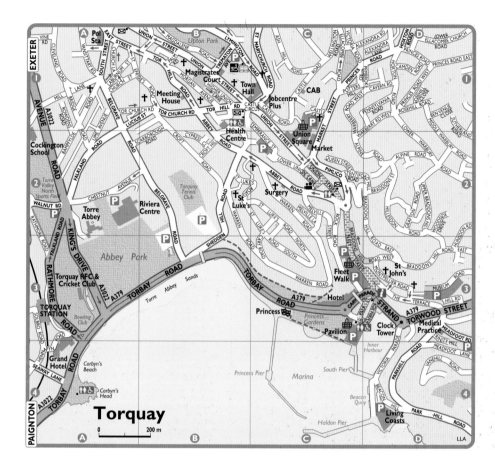

Torquay

Torquay is found on atlas page **7 N6**

B1	Abbey Road	D1	Middle Warbury Road
C1	Alexandra Road	A1	Mill Lane
C2	Alpine Road	D3	Montpellier Road
C1	Ash Hill Road	B1	Morgan Avenue
A1	Avenue Road	D3	Museum Road
A2	Bampfylde Road	B1	Palm Road
D4	Beacon Hill	D4	Parkhill Road
A1	Belgrave Road	C1	Pembroke Road
D3	Braddons Hill Road East	D1	Pennsylvania Road
C2	Braddons Hill Road West	C2	Pimlico
D2	Braddons Street	C1	Potters Hill
A1	Bridge Road	C1	Princes Road
D1	Camden Road	C2	Queen Street
C3	Cary Parade	A2	Rathmore Road
C3	Cary Road	C2	Rock Road
C1	Castle Lane	D1	Rosehill Road
C1	Castle Road	A1	St Efride's Road
D1	Cavern Road	B2	St Luke's Road
A2	Chestnut Avenue	C1	St Marychurch Road
A1	Church Lane	B2	Scarborough Road
A1	Church Street	A4	Seaway Lane
A1	Cleveland Road	B3	Shedden Hill Road
B2	Croft Hill	A3	Solbro Road
B2	Croft Road	D3	South Hill Road
A1	East Street	A1	South Street
C1	Ellacombe Road	C2	Stentiford Hill Road
A2	Falkland Road	D3	Strand
C3	Fleet Street	D1	Sutherland Road
D2	Grafton Road	C2	Temperance Street
A4	Hennapyn Road	D3	The Terrace
B1	Higher Union Lane	A4	Torbay Road
D2	Hillesdon Road	A1	Tor Church Road
D1	Hoxton Road	B1	Tor Hill Road
D3	Hunsdon Road	D3	Torwood Street
A3	King's Drive	B1	Trematon Ave
A1	Laburnum Street	D3	Trinity Hill
A2	Lime Avenue	B1	Union Street
D1	Lower Ellacombe Church Road	D2	Upper Braddons Hill
		D4	Vanehill Road
C2	Lower Union Lane	A1	Vansittart Road
D2	Lower Warbury Road	C3	Vaughan Parade
A1	Lucius Street	D4	Victoria Parade
B1	Lymington Road	C1	Victoria Road
B1	Magdalene Road	A1	Vine Road
C2	Market Street	A2	Walnut Road
D4	Meadfoot Lane	C1	Warberry Road West
C2	Melville Lane	B2	Warren Road
C2	Melville Street	C1	Wellington Road

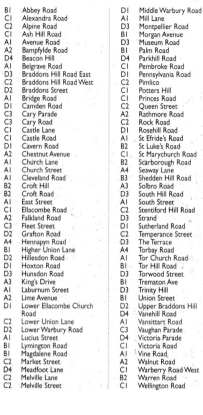

Tunbridge Wells

Tunbridge Wells is found on atlas page **25 N3**

C1	Albert Street	B4	High Street
C4	Arundel Road	C2	Lansdowne Road
D2	Bayhall Road	B1	Lime Hill Road
C1	Belgrave Road	A4	Linden Park Road
B4	Berkeley Road	B4	Little Mount Sion
A1	Boyne Park	A2	London Road
C4	Buckingham Road	B2	Lonsdale Gardens
C3	Calverley Gardens	B4	Madeira Park
C2	Calverley Park	A4	Major York's Road
D2	Calverley Park Gardens	A3	Mount Edgcumbe Road
C2	Calverley Road	B1	Meadow Road
C1	Calverley Street	A1	Molyneux Park Road
D4	Cambridge Gardens	C2	Monson Road
D3	Cambridge Street	B2	Monson Way
D3	Camden Hill	A3	Mount Edgcumbe Road
D3	Camden Park	A2	Mount Ephraim
C1	Camden Road	B1	Mount Ephraim Road
D2	Carlton Road	C3	Mountfield Gardens
A2	Castle Road	C3	Mountfield Road
B3	Castle Street	B2	Mount Pleasant Avenue
B4	Chapel Place	B2	Mount Pleasant Road
B3	Christchurch Avenue	B4	Mount Sion
A2	Church Road	B4	Nevill Street
B2	Civic Way	B1	Newton Road
C4	Claremont Gardens	C4	Norfolk Road
C4	Claremont Road	D2	North Street
B2	Clarence Road	D3	Oakfield Court Road
B2	Crescent Road	D3	Park Street
B1	Culverden Street	D2	Pembury Road
C1	Dale Street	C4	Poona Road
B1	Dudley Road	D3	Prince's Street
B4	Eden Road	D3	Prospect Road
A4	Eridge Road	B1	Rock Villa Road
C4	Farmcombe Lane	A1	Royal Chase
C4	Farmcombe Road	D1	St James' Road
D1	Ferndale	D1	Sandrock Road
A4	Frant Road	A1	Somerville Gardens
B4	Frog Lane	B3	South Green
C1	Garden Road	B3	Station Approach
C1	Garden Street	D1	Stone Street
D3	George Street	C3	Sutherland Road
B1	Goods Station Road	C1	Tunnel Road
C4	Grecian Road	B1	Upper Grosvenor Road
B1	Grosvenor Road	B3	Vale Avenue
C3	Grove Hill Gardens	B3	Vale Road
C3	Grove Hill Road	C1	Victoria Road
C3	Guildford Road	B4	Warwick Park
B1	Hanover Road	C1	Wood Street
		B2	York Road

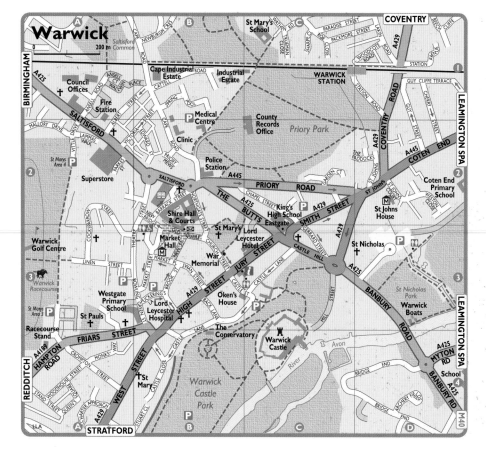

Warwick

Warwick is found on atlas page **59 L11**

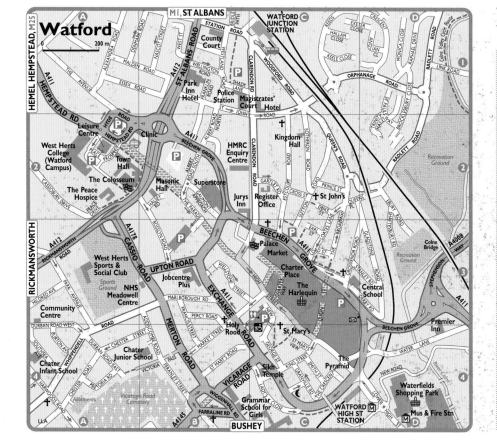

Watford

Watford is found on atlas page **50 D11**

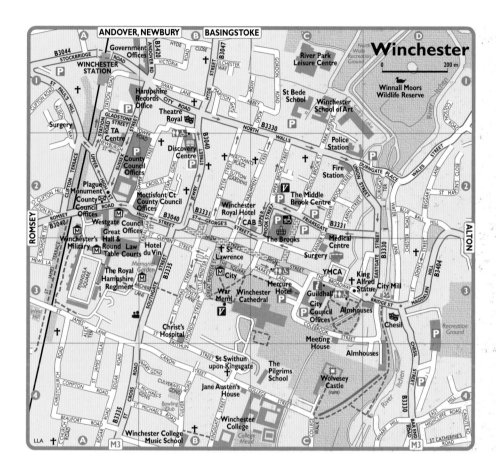

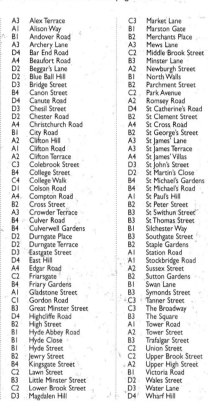

Winchester

Winchester is found on atlas page **22 E9**

A3	Alex Terrace	C3	Market Lane
A1	Alison Way	B1	Marston Gate
B1	Andover Road	B2	Merchants Place
A3	Archery Lane	A3	Mews Lane
D4	Bar End Road	C2	Middle Brook Street
A4	Beaufort Road	B3	Minster Lane
D2	Beggar's Lane	A2	Newburgh Street
D2	Blue Ball Hill	B1	North Walls
D3	Bridge Street	B2	Parchment Street
B4	Canon Street	C2	Park Avenue
D4	Canute Road	A2	Romsey Road
D3	Chesil Street	D4	St Catherine's Road
D2	Chester Road	B2	St Clement Street
A4	Christchurch Road	A4	St Cross Road
B1	City Road	B2	St George's Street
A2	Clifton Hill	A3	St James' Lane
A1	Clifton Road	A3	St James Terrace
A2	Clifton Terrace	A4	St James' Villas
C3	Colebrook Street	D3	St John's Street
B4	College Street	D2	St Martin's Close
C4	College Walk	B4	St Michael's Gardens
D1	Colson Road	B4	St Michael's Road
A4	Compton Road	A1	St Paul's Hill
B2	Cross Street	B2	St Peter Street
A3	Crowder Terrace	B3	St Swithun Street
B4	Culver Road	B3	St Thomas Street
B4	Culverwell Gardens	B1	Silchester Way
D2	Durngate Place	B3	Southgate Street
D2	Durngate Terrace	B2	Staple Gardens
D3	Eastgate Street	A1	Station Road
D4	East Hill	A1	Stockbridge Road
A4	Edgar Road	A2	Sussex Street
C2	Friarsgate	B2	Sutton Gardens
B4	Friary Gardens	B1	Swan Lane
A1	Gladstone Street	B3	Symonds Street
C1	Gordon Road	C3	Tanner Street
B3	Great Minster Street	C3	The Broadway
D4	Highcliffe Road	B3	The Square
B2	High Street	A1	Tower Road
B1	Hyde Abbey Road	A2	Tower Street
B1	Hyde Close	B3	Trafalgar Street
B1	Hyde Street	C2	Union Street
B2	Jewry Street	C2	Upper Brook Street
B4	Kingsgate Street	A2	Upper High Street
C2	Lawn Street	B1	Victoria Road
B3	Little Minster Street	D2	Wales Street
C2	Lower Brook Street	D3	Water Lane
D3	Magdalen Hill	D4	Wharf Hill

Wolverhampton

Wolverhampton is found on atlas page **58 D5**

A3	Alexander Street	B1	Park Road East
A1	Bath Avenue	A2	Park Road West
A2	Bath Road	B3	Peel Street
B3	Bell Street	B4	Penn Road
D3	Bilston Road	D2	Piper's Row
C3	Bilston Street	B3	Pitt Street
B2	Birch Street	D4	Powlett Street
C2	Broad Street	C2	Princess Street
C3	Castle Street	B2	Queen Square
A3	Chapel Ash	C2	Queen Street
B4	Church Lane	B2	Raby Street
B4	Church Street	A3	Raglan Street
B2	Clarence Road	D2	Railway Drive
B2	Clarence Street	B2	Red Lion Street
D4	Cleveland Road	A4	Retreat Street
B3	Cleveland Street	A2	Ring Road St Andrews
D2	Corn Hill	D2	Ring Road St Davids
D1	Culwell Street	C4	Ring Road St Georges
A4	Dale Street	B4	Ring Road St Johns
B3	Darlington Street	B3	Ring Road St Marks
C4	Dudley Road	C1	Ring Road St Patricks
C2	Dudley Street	B2	Ring Road St Peters
B3	Fold Street	A4	Russell Street
C2	Fryer Street	C4	St John's Square
C3	Garrick Street	A3	St Mark's Road
C3	George's Parade	A3	St Mark's Street
A4	Graiseley Street	B3	Salop Street
A4	Great Brickkiln Street	B3	School Street
C1	Great Western Street	B3	Skinner Street
D1	Grimstone Street	C3	Snow Hill
A3	Herrick Street	C1	Stafford Street
D2	Horseley Fields	A3	Stephenson Street
D4	Hospital Street	B4	Stewart Street
A1	Lansdown Road	B3	Summer Row
C4	Lever Street	D4	Sutherland Place
C2	Lichfield Street	B3	Temple Street
C1	Little's Lane	B4	Thomas Street
C2	Long Street	C3	Tower Street
A3	Lord Street	D4	Vicarage Road
A4	Mander Street	B3	Victoria Street
C3	Market Street	B1	Waterloo Road
A4	Merridale Street	D1	Wednesfield Road
D3	Middle Cross	C2	Westbury Street
B2	Mitre Fold	B1	Whitmore Hill
A1	Molineux Street	C2	Whitmore Street
B2	North Street	C2	Worcester Street
A1	Park Avenue	C2	Wulfruna Street
		A4	Zoar Street

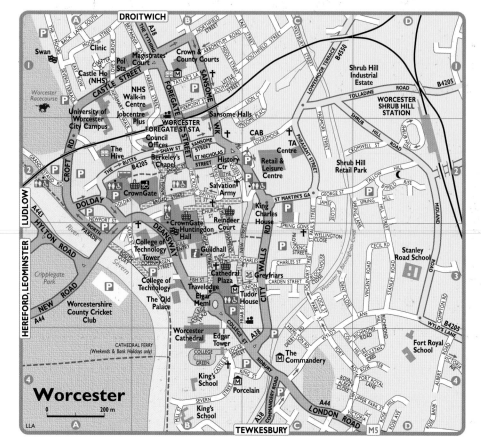

Worcester

Worcester is found on atlas page **46 G4**

D4	Albert Road		B1	Middle Street
B2	Angel Street		D2	Midland Road
B1	Arboretum Road		B4	Mill Street
A1	Back Lane South		A1	Moor Street
C3	Blockhouse Close		A2	Newport Street
A1	Britannia Road		A3	New Road
B2	Broad Street		C3	New Street
D2	Byfield Rise		B1	Northfield Street
C3	Carden Street		A3	North Parade
A1	Castle Street		C1	Padmore Street
A4	Cathedral Ferry		C3	Park Street
D3	Cecil Road		C2	Pheasant Street
C3	Charles Street		B1	Pierpoint Street
A1	Charter Place		C3	Providence Street
B2	Church Street		B3	Pump Street
C3	City Walls Road		A3	Quay Street
C4	Cole Hill		B2	Queen Street
B3	College Street		D4	Richmond Road
C4	Commandery Road		D4	Rose Hill
D3	Compton Road		D4	Rose Terrace
B3	Copenhagen Street		C2	St Martin's Gate
A2	Croft Road		B2	St Nicholas Street
D2	Cromwell Street		C3	St Paul's Street
B3	Deansway		B2	St Swithin Street
C3	Dent Close		B1	Sansome Walk
C4	Derby Road		B4	Severn Street
A2	Dolday		A1	Severn Terrace
B1	East Street		B2	Shaw Street
B4	Edgar Street		D2	Shrub Hill Road
B1	Farrier Street		C4	Sidbury
B3	Fish Street		C1	Southfield Street
B1	Foregate Street		D2	Spring Hill
C4	Fort Royal Hill		D3	Stanley Road
C3	Foundry Street		D2	Tallow Hill
C3	Friar Street		B1	Taylor's Lane
C2	George Street		A2	The Butts
A2	Grandstand Road		B2	The Cross
C3	Hamilton Road		A1	The Moors
B3	High Street		B2	The Shambles
D2	Hill Street		B1	The Tything
A3	Hylton Road		C1	Tolladine Road
B4	King Street		B2	Trinity Street
B1	Little Southfield Street		C3	Union Street
C3	Lock Street		D4	Upper Park Street
C4	London Road		D3	Vincent Road
A1	Love's Grove		C3	Wellington Close
C2	Lowesmoor		C1	Westbury Street
C1	Lowesmoor Terrace		C4	Wyld's Lane

York

York is found on atlas page **98 C10**

C2	Aldwark		C3	Lower Ousegate
D4	Barbican Road		B3	Lower Priory Street
B4	Bishopgate Street		C2	Low Petergate
B3	Bishophill Senior		D3	Margaret Street
D2	Black Horse Lane		C2	Market Street
B2	Blake Street		A3	Micklegate
A4	Blossom Street		B1	Minster Yard
B1	Bootham		C1	Monkgate
B3	Bridge Street		B2	Museum Street
B3	Buckingham Street		D3	Navigation Road
D4	Cemetery Road		B2	New Street
C2	Church Street		B2	North Street
C3	Clifford Street		A3	Nunnery Lane
C1	College Street		C1	Ogleforth
C2	Colliergate		D2	Palmer Lane
B2	Coney Street		D2	Palmer Street
C3	Coppergate		D4	Paragon Street
B4	Cromwell Road		C2	Parliament Street
B2	Davygate		C2	Pavement
C1	Deangate		D2	Peasholme Green
B4	Dove Street		D3	Percy's Lane
B2	Duncombe Place		C3	Piccadilly
D2	Dundas Street		B4	Price's Lane
B3	Fairfax Street		C3	Priory Street
D4	Fawcett Street		A3	Queen Street
C2	Feasegate		B2	Rougier Street
B3	Fetter Lane		C2	St Andrewgate
C2	Finkle Street		D3	St Denys' Road
C4	Fishergate		B1	St Leonard's Place
D1	Foss Bank		B3	St Martins Lane
C3	Fossgate		C1	St Maurice's Road
D2	Foss Islands Road		C2	St Saviourgate
D3	George Street		C2	St Saviours Place
B1	Gillygate		A4	Scarcroft Road
C2	Goodramgate		C2	Shambles
B4	Hampden Street		B3	Skeldergate
C3	High Ousegate		C2	Spen Lane
B1	High Petergate		B2	Spurriergate
A4	Holgate Road		A3	Station Road
D4	Hope Street		B2	Stonegate
D2	Hungate		C2	Swinegate
D1	Jewbury		C2	The Stonebow
D4	Kent Street		A3	Toft Green
C3	King Street		C3	Tower Street
B4	Kyme Street		B3	Trinity Lane
B2	Lendal		B4	Victor Street
D4	Long Close Lane		D3	Walmgate
C1	Lord Mayor's Walk		B2	Wellington Road

Major airports

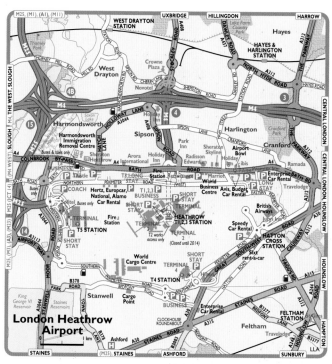

London Heathrow Airport – 16 miles west of London

Telephone: 0844 335 1801 or visit *www.heathrowairport.com*
Parking: short-stay, long-stay and business parking is available.
For booking and charges tel: 0844 335 1000
Public Transport: coach, bus, rail and London Underground.
There are several 4-star and 3-star hotels within easy reach of the airport.
Car hire facilities are available.

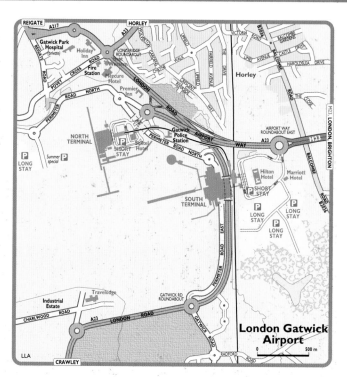

London Gatwick Airport – 35 miles south of London

Telephone: 0844 892 0322 or visit *www.gatwickairport.com*
Parking: short and long-stay parking is available at both the North and South terminals.
For booking and charges tel: 0844 811 8311.
Public Transport: coach, bus and rail.
There are several 4-star and 3-star hotels within easy reach of the airport.
Car hire facilities are available.

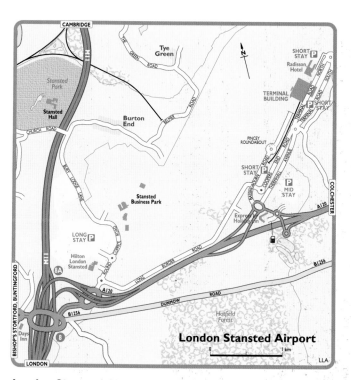

London Stansted Airport – 36 miles north east of London

Telephone: 0844 335 1803 or visit *www.stanstedairport.com*
Parking: short, mid and long-stay open-air parking is available.
For booking and charges tel: 0844 335 1000
Public Transport: coach, bus and direct rail link to London on the Stansted Express.
There are several hotels within easy reach of the airport.
Car hire facilities are available.

London Luton Airport – 33 miles north of London

Telephone: 01582 405100 or visit *www.london-luton.co.uk*
Parking: short-term, mid-term and long-stay parking is available.
For booking and charges tel: 01582 405 100
Public Transport: coach, bus and rail.
There are several hotels within easy reach of the airport.
Car hire facilities are available.

Major airports

London City Airport – 7 miles east of London

Telephone: 020 7646 0088 or visit *www.londoncityairport.com*
Parking: short and long-stay open-air parking is available.
For booking and charges tel: 0871 360 1390
Public Transport: easy access to the rail network, Docklands Light Railway and the London Underground.
There are 5-star, 4-star and 3-star hotels within easy reach of the airport.
Car hire facilities are available.

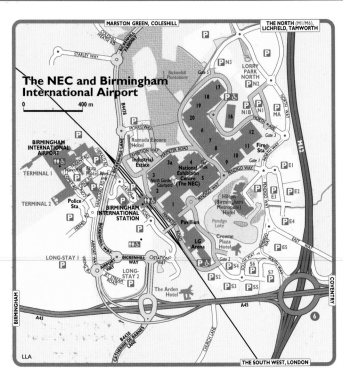

Birmingham International Airport – 8 miles east of Birmingham

Telephone: 0844 576 6000 or visit *www.birminghamairport.co.uk*
Parking: short, mid-term and long-stay parking is available.
For booking and charges tel: 0844 576 6000
Public Transport: Air-Rail Link service operates every 2 minutes to and from Birmingham International Railway Station & Interchange.
There is one 3-star hotel adjacent to the airport and several 4 and 3-star hotels within easy reach of the airport. Car hire facilities are available.

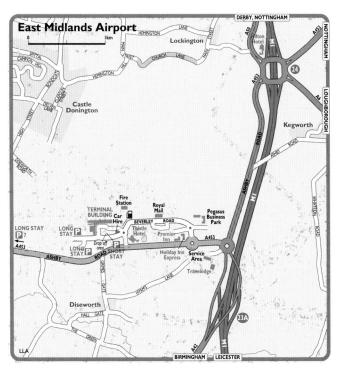

East Midlands Airport – 15 miles south west of Nottingham, next to the M1 at junctions 23A and 24

Telephone: 0871 919 9000 or visit *www.eastmidlandsairport.com*
Parking: short and long-stay parking is available.
For booking and charges tel: 0871 310 3300
Public Transport: bus and coach services to major towns and cities in the East Midlands.
Call 0870 608 2608 for information.
There are several 3-star hotels within easy reach of the airport.
Car hire facilities are available.

Manchester Airport – 10 miles south of Manchester

Telephone: 0871 271 0711 or visit *www.manchesterairport.co.uk*
Parking: short and long-stay parking is available.
For booking and charges tel: 0871 310 2200
Public Transport: bus, coach and rail.
There are several 4-star and 3-star hotels within easy reach of the airport.
Car hire facilities are available.

Major airports

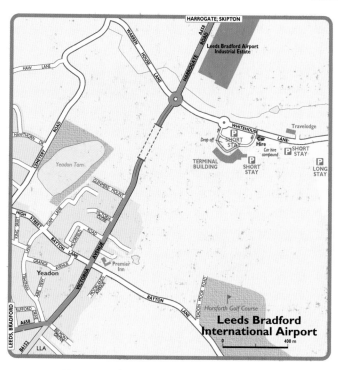

Leeds Bradford International Airport – 7 miles north east of Bradford and 9 miles north west of Leeds

Telephone: 0113 250 9696 or visit *www.leedsbradfordairport.co.uk*
Parking: short, mid-term and long-stay parking is available.
For booking and charges tel: 0113 250 9696
Public Transport: bus service operates every 30 minutes from Bradford, Leeds and Otley.
There are several 4-star and 3-star hotels within easy reach of the airport.
Car hire facilities are available.

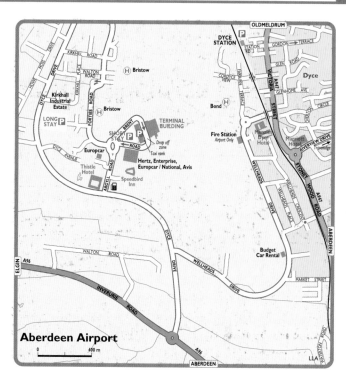

Aberdeen Airport – 7 miles north west of Aberdeen

Telephone: 0844 481 6666 or visit *www.aberdeenairport.com*
Parking: short and long-stay parking is available.
For booking and charges tel: 0844 335 1000
Public Transport: regular bus service to central Aberdeen.
There are several 4-star and 3-star hotels within easy reach of the airport.
Car hire facilities are available.

Edinburgh Airport – 7 miles west of Edinburgh

Telephone: 0844 481 8989 or visit *www.edinburghairport.com*
Parking: short and long-stay parking is available.
For booking and charges tel: 0844 335 1000
Public Transport: regular bus services to central Edinburgh.
There are several 4-star and 3-star hotels within easy reach of the airport.
Car hire facilities are available.

Glasgow Airport – 8 miles west of Glasgow

Telephone: 0844 481 5555 or visit *www.glasgowairport.com*
Parking: short and long-stay parking is available.
For booking and charges tel: 0844 335 1000
Public Transport: regular coach services operate direct to central Glasgow and Edinburgh.
There are several 3-star hotels within easy reach of the airport.
Car hire facilities are available.

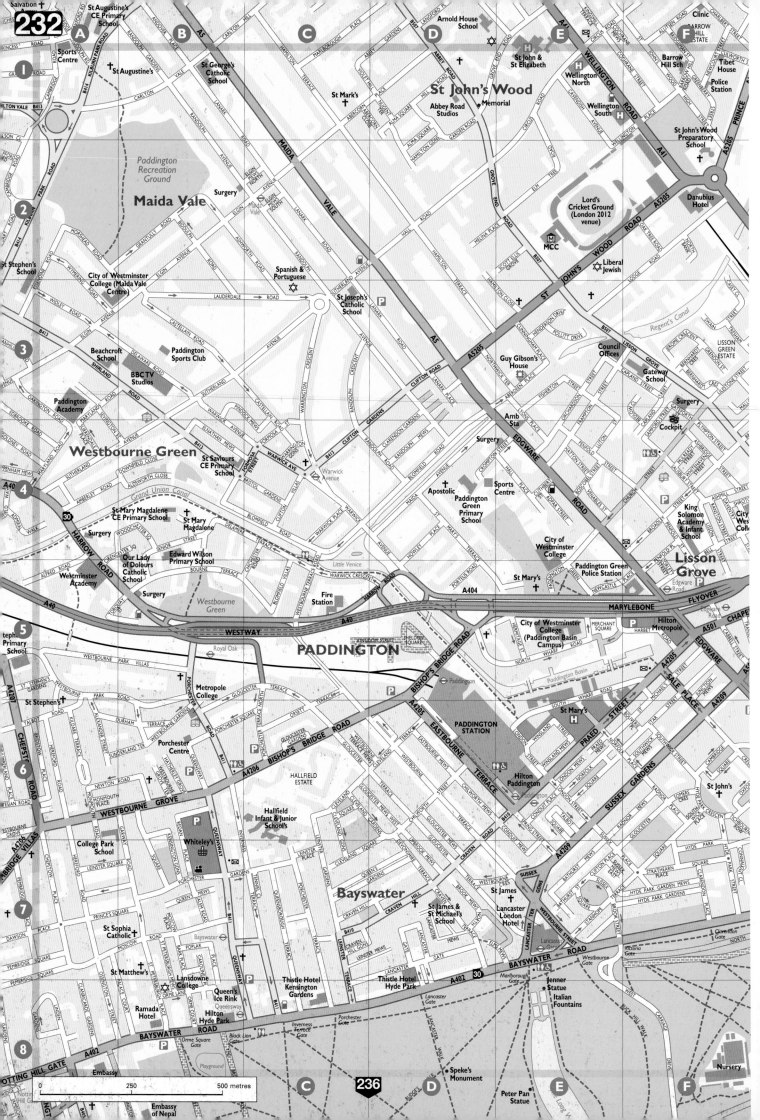

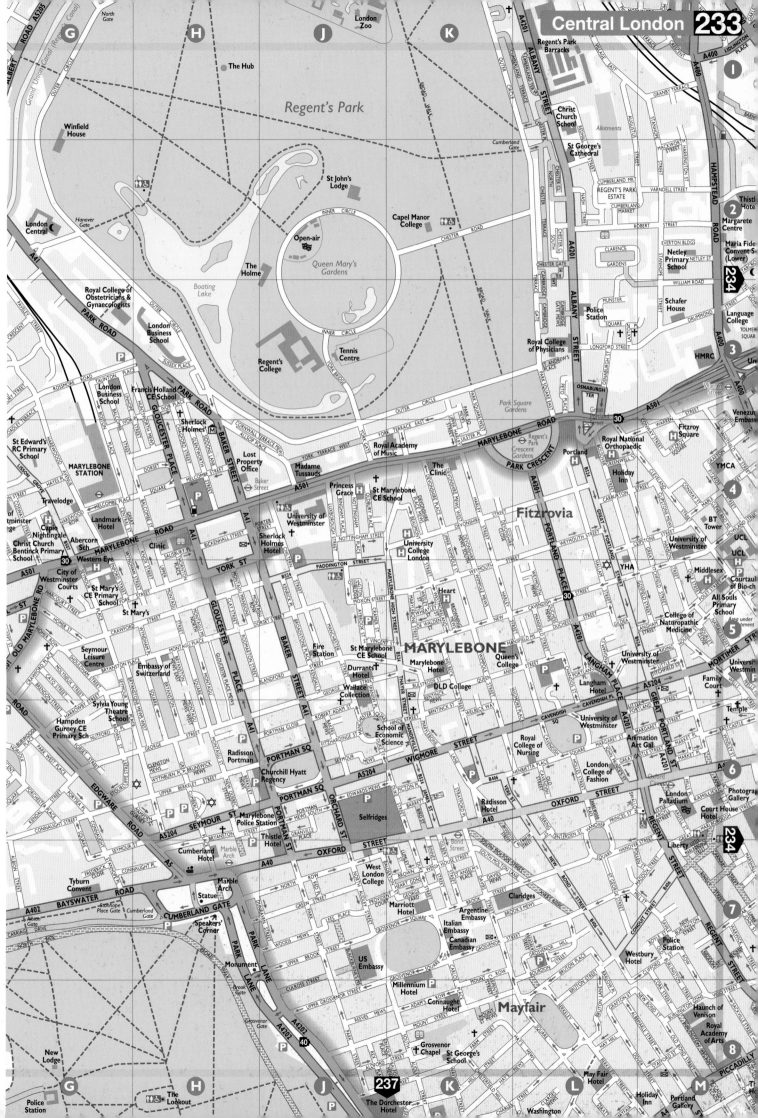

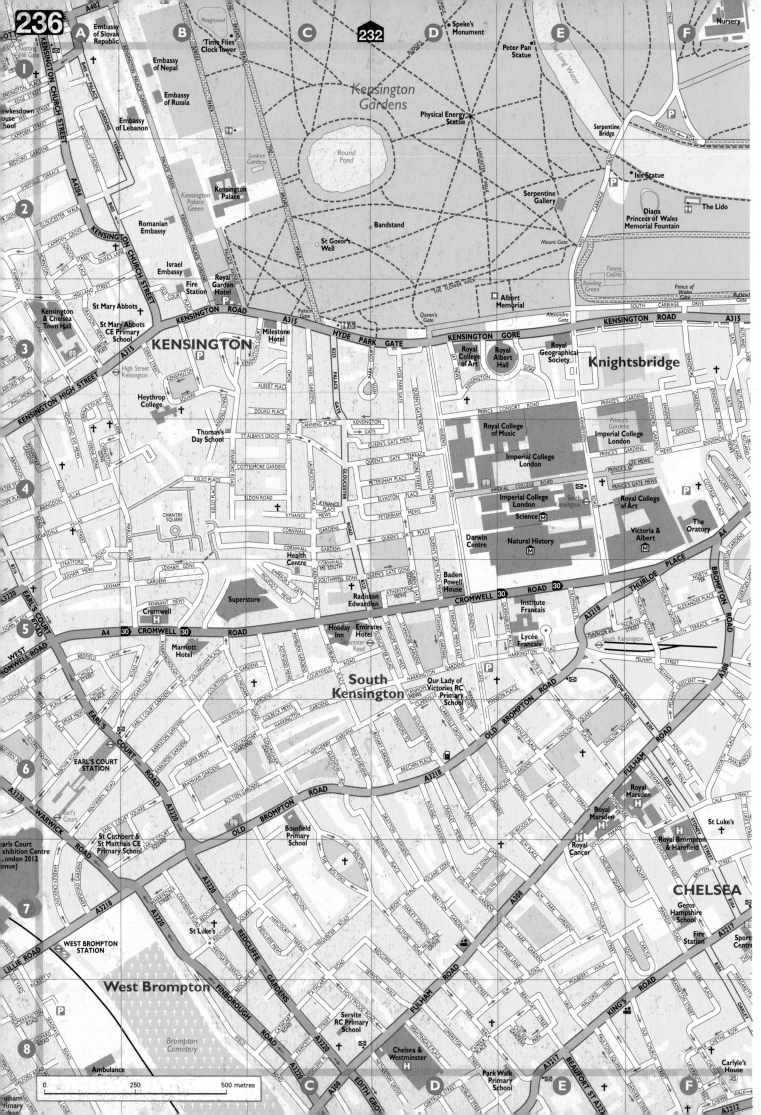

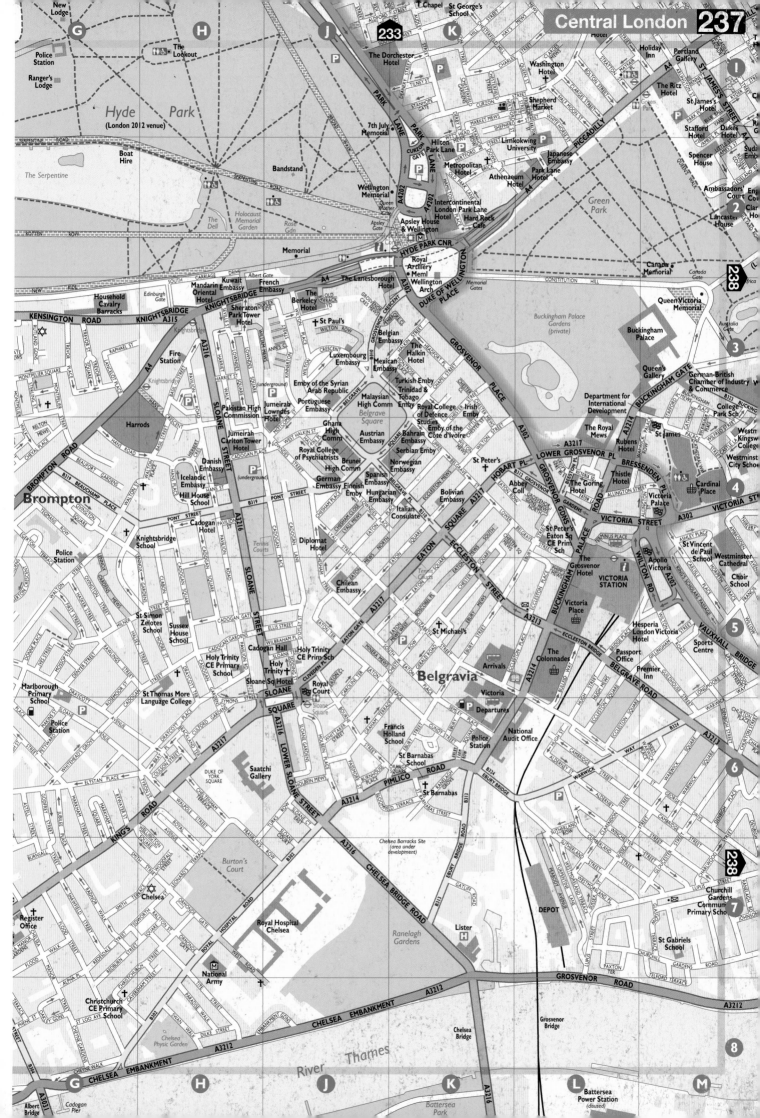

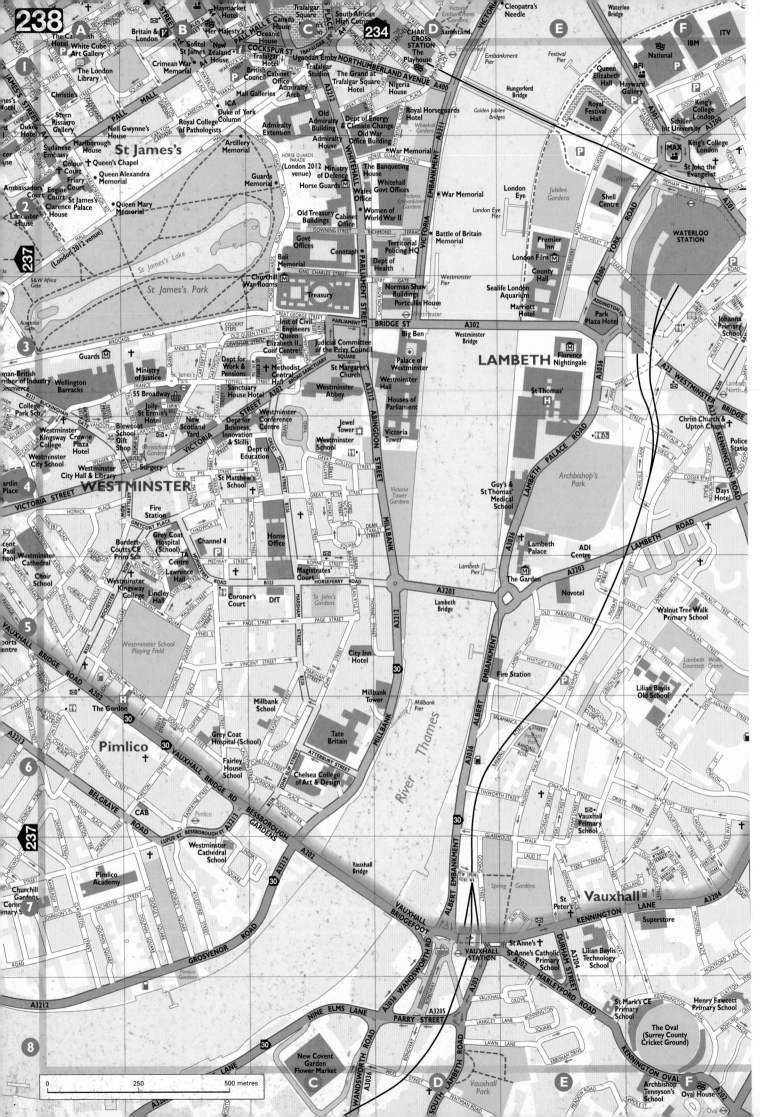

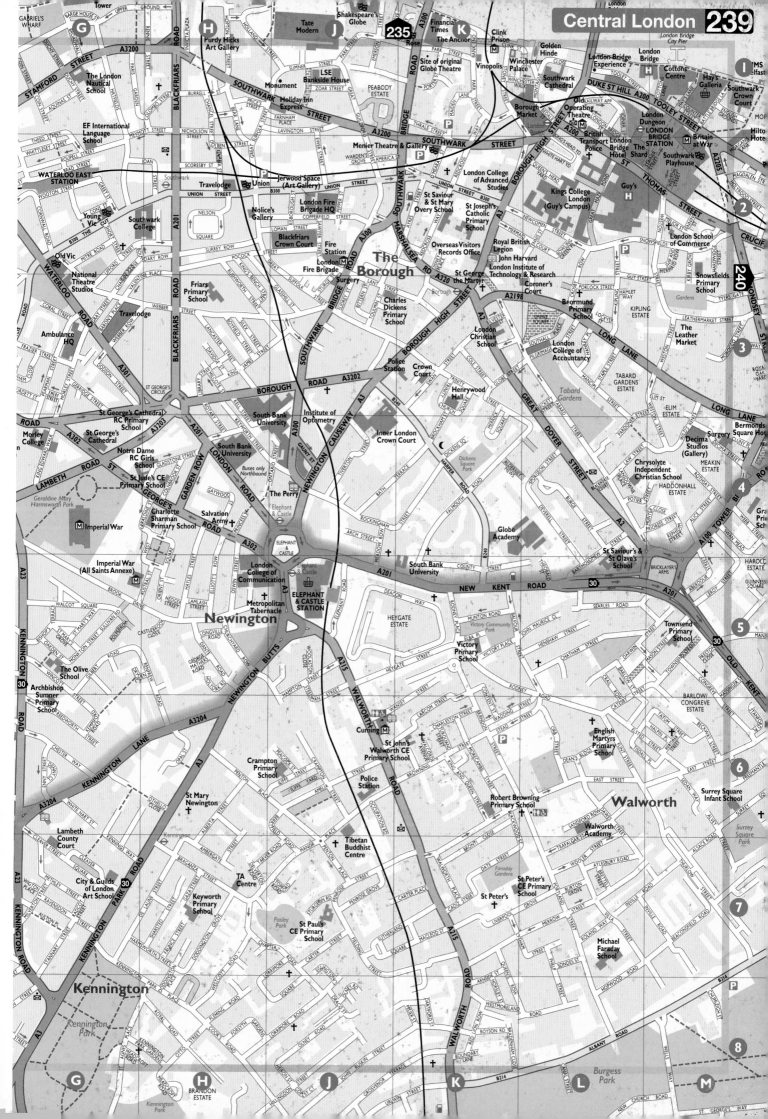

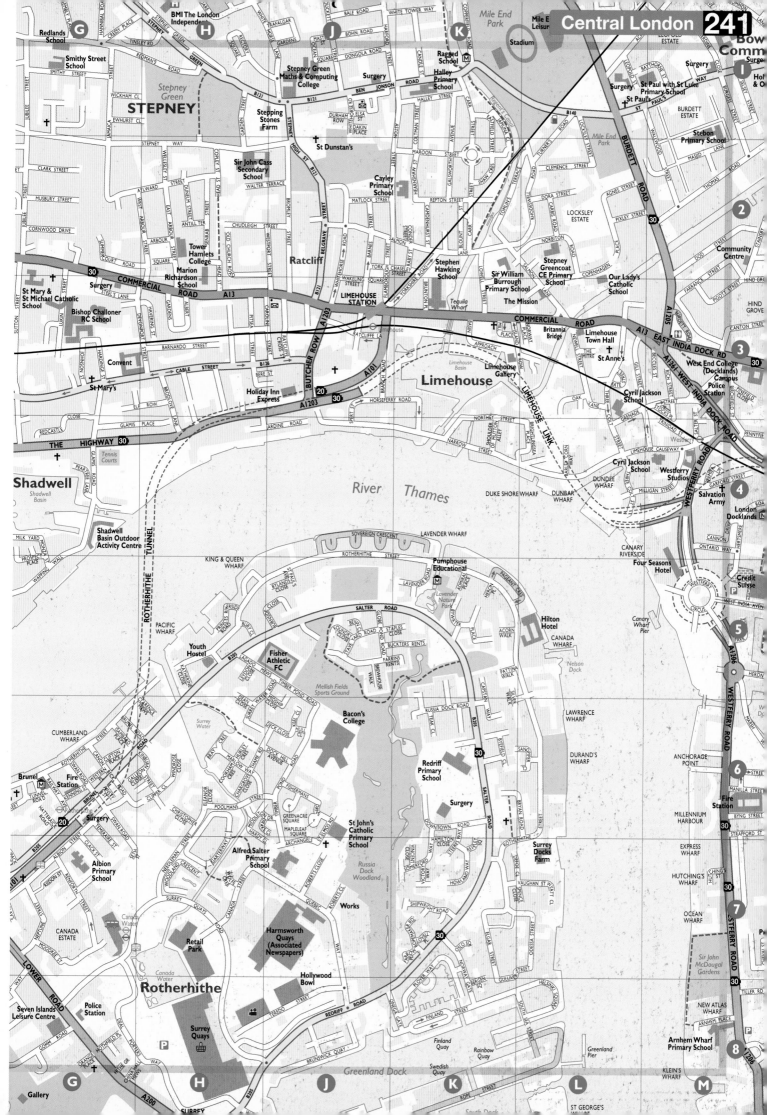

Central London street index

In this index, street and station names are listed in alphabetical order and written in full, but may be abbreviated on the map. Each entry is followed by its Postcode District and each street name is preceded by the page number and the grid reference to the square in which the name is found. Names are asterisked (*) in the index where there is insufficient space to show them on the map.

Carlisle Avenue - Eyre Sreet Hill 243

240 B3 Carlisle Avenue EC3N
238 F4 Carlisle Lane SE1
237 M5 Carlisle Place SW1P
234 B6 Carlisle Street W1D
233 K7 Carlos Place W1K
238 B2 Carlton Gardens SW1Y
232 B1 Carlton Hill NW6
238 B1 Carlton House Terrace SW1Y
237 L1 Carlton Street W1J
232 A1 Carlton Vale NW6
232 B1 Carlton Vale NW6
239 F7 Carlyle Square SW3
235 G7 Carmelite Street EC4Y
233 M7 Carnaby Street W1F
232 B7 Caroline Place W2
241 H3 Caroline Street E1
237 J5 Caroline Terrace SW1W
233 K7 Carpenter Street W1K
237 L1 Carrington Street W1J
241 K1 Carr Street E14
238 B3 Carteret Street SW1H
235 H7 Carter Lane EC4V
239 K7 Carter Place SE17
239 J7 Carter Street SE17
235 J4 Carthusian Street EC1M
234 D8 Carting Lane WC2R
234 C2 Cartwright Gardens WC1H
240 C4 Cartwright Street E1
232 F3 Casey Close NW8
240 C1 Casson Street E1
232 B3 Castellain Road W9
239 G5 Castlebrook Close SE11
237 M4 Castle Lane SW1E
239 L6 Catesby Street SE17
240 F7 Cathay Street SE16
236 C8 Cathcart Road SW10
237 M4 Cathedral Walk SW1E
237 M4 Catherine Place SW1E
234 D7 Catherine Street WC2E
233 G5 Cato Street W1H
238 B6 Causton Street SW1P
240 F1 Cavell Street E1
232 E1 Cavendish Avenue NW8
233 L6 Cavendish Place W1G
233 L6 Cavendish Square W1G
235 L1 Cavendish Street N1
237 G8 Caversham Street SW3
238 B4 Caxton Street SW1H
235 K2 Cayton Street EC1V
238 F4 Centaur Street SE1
235 J2 Central Street EC1V
235 G1 Chadwell Street EC1R
238 B4 Chadwick Street SW1P
233 H4 Chagford Street NW1
234 B1 Chalton Street NW1
240 D7 Chambers Street SE16
240 C3 Chamber Street E1
240 D6 Chambers Wharf SE16
239 H1 Chancel Street SE1
234 F5 Chancery Lane WC2A
234 F5 Chancery Lane ⊖ WC1V
234 C8 Chandos Place WC2N
233 L5 Chandos Street W1G
236 B4 Chantry Square W8
234 F1 Chapel Market N1
232 F5 Chapel Street NW1
237 K3 Chapel Street SW1X
239 G3 Chaplin Close SE1
240 E3 Chapman Street E1
239 H7 Chapter Road SE17
238 B6 Chapter Street SW1P
241 H6 Chargrove Close SE16
238 D1 Charing Cross ⇌ ⊖ WC2N
234 B6 Charing Cross Road WC2H
234 C8 Charing Cross Road WC2N
232 F1 Charlbert Street NW8
234 B8 Charles II Street SW1Y
235 M2 Charles Square N1
237 K1 Charles Street W1J
239 K6 Charleston Street SE17
235 M3 Charlotte Road EC2A
234 A4 Charlotte Street W1T
238 A6 Charlwood Place SW1V
237 M7 Charlwood Street SW1V
238 A6 Charlwood Street SW1V
234 B1 Charrington Street NW1
235 H4 Charterhouse Square EC1M
235 G5 Charterhouse Street EC1M
235 L2 Chart Street N1
241 J2 Chaseley Street E14
239 L5 Chatham Street SE17
235 K6 Cheapside EC2V
237 K8 Chelsea Bridge SW1W
237 J7 Chelsea Bridge Road SW1W
237 G8 Chelsea Embankment SW3
236 F7 Chelsea Manor Gardens SW3
237 G7 Chelsea Manor Street SW3
236 E8 Chelsea Park Gardens SW3
236 E7 Chelsea Square SW3
237 H6 Cheltenham Terrace SW3
234 B4 Chenies Mews WC1E
234 B4 Chenies Street WC1E
236 A4 Cheniston Gardens W8
232 A7 Chepstow Place W2
232 A6 Chepstow Road W2
235 K3 Chequer Street EC1Y
235 L1 Cherbury Street N1
240 E7 Cherry Garden Street SE16
237 J4 Chesham Close SW1X
237 J4 Chesham Place SW1X
237 J4 Chesham Street SW1X
237 K3 Chester Close SW1X
233 L2 Chester Close North NW1
233 L2 Chester Close South NW1
237 K1 Chesterfield Gardens W1J
233 K8 Chesterfield Hill W1J
237 K1 Chesterfield Street W1J
233 L2 Chester Gate NW1
237 K3 Chester Mews SW1X
233 L1 Chester Place NW1
233 K2 Chester Road NW1
237 K5 Chester Row SW1W
237 K5 Chester Square SW1W
237 K4 Chester Square Mews SW1W
237 K4 Chester Street SW1X
233 L2 Chester Terrace NW1
239 G6 Chester Way SE11
237 G4 Cheval Place SW7
241 M7 Cheval Street E14
237 G8 Cheyne Gardens SW3
236 F8 Cheyne Row SW3
236 F8 Cheyne Walk SW3
238 E2 Chicheley Street SE1
232 A1 Chichester Road NW6
232 C5 Chichester Road W2
238 A7 Chichester Street SW1V
240 C1 Chicksand Street E1
240 E4 Chigwell Hill E1W
236 A5 Child's Place SW5
236 A5 Child's Street SW5
233 J4 Chiltern Street W1U
232 D6 Chilworth Mews W2
232 D6 Chilworth Street W2
241 G8 China Hall Mews SE16
232 A4 Chippenham Mews W9
235 K4 Chiswell Street EC1Y
234 A4 Chitty Street W1T
237 G8 Christchurch Street SW3
240 D3 Christian Street E1
235 M3 Christina Street EC2A
241 H6 Christopher Close SE16
235 L4 Christopher Street EC2A
241 H2 Chudleigh Street E1
239 M8 Chumleigh Street SE5
237 L7 Churchill Gardens Road SW1V
232 F4 Church Street NW8
234 B2 Church Way NW1
239 H5 Churchyard Row SE1
238 A6 Churton Place SW1V
238 A6 Churton Street SW1V
232 E1 Circus Road NW8
232 A5 Cirencester Square W2
235 J1 City Garden Row N1
235 J1 City Road EC1V
235 L3 City Road EC1Y
235 H6 City Thameslink ⇌ EC4M
237 H5 Clabon Mews SW1X
241 G7 Clack Street SE16
232 A8 Clanricarde Gardens W2
234 F1 Claremont Square N1
233 L2 Clarence Gardens NW1
241 G6 Clarence Mews SE16
232 D4 Clarendon Gardens W9
232 F7 Clarendon Gate W2
232 F7 Clarendon Place W2
237 L6 Clarendon Street SW1V
236 D6 Clareville Grove SW7
236 D6 Clareville Street SW7
237 L1 Clarges Mews W1J
237 L1 Clarges Street W1J
240 F2 Clark Street E1
238 A7 Claverton Street SW1V
240 F5 Clave Street E1W
233 H5 Clay Street W1U
238 F8 Clayton Street SE11
239 G7 Cleaver Square SE11
239 G7 Cleaver Street SE11
240 F5 Clegg Street E1W
241 L2 Clemence Street E14
235 L7 Clements Lane EC4N
240 E8 Clement's Road SE16
233 H6 Clenston Mews W1H
235 L3 Clere Street EC2A
235 G4 Clerkenwell Close EC1R
235 G3 Clerkenwell Lane EC1R
235 G4 Clerkenwell Road EC1M
232 C6 Cleveland Gardens W2
233 M4 Cleveland Mews W1T
238 A1 Cleveland Place SW1Y
238 A2 Cleveland Row SW1A
232 C6 Cleveland Square W2
233 M4 Cleveland Street W1T
232 D6 Cleveland Terrace W2
233 M7 Clifford Street W1S
232 C4 Clifton Gardens W9
241 G6 Clifton Place SE16
232 E7 Clifton Place W2
232 D3 Clifton Road W9
235 M3 Clifton Street EC2A
232 C4 Clifton Villas W9
239 K1 Clink Street SE1
241 H6 Clipper Close SE16
233 M4 Clipstone Mews W1W
233 L4 Clipstone Street W1W
237 J5 Cliveden Place SW1W
235 K7 Cloak Lane EC4R
235 J5 Cloth Fair EC1A
235 J5 Cloth Street EC1A
240 A8 Cluny Place SE1
240 B2 Cobb Street E1
234 A2 Cobourg Street NW1
238 A5 Coburg Close SW1P
232 E1 Cochrane Mews NW8
232 E1 Cochrane Street NW8
235 H5 Cock Lane EC1A
238 C1 Cockspur Street SW1Y
240 D5 Codling Close * E1W
239 G1 Coin Street SE1
240 D2 Coke Street E1
236 C6 Colbeck Mews SW7
235 H1 Colebrook Row N1
236 B7 Coleherne Road SW10
235 L6 Coleman Street EC2R
239 K3 Cole Street SE1
234 F3 Coley Street WC1X
235 K7 College Hill EC4R
235 K7 College Street EC4R
240 D8 Collett Road SE16
234 E1 Collier Street N1
236 B6 Collingham Gardens SW5
236 B5 Collingham Place SW5
236 B5 Collingham Road SW5
239 H4 Colnbrook Street SE1
239 H1 Colombo Street SE1
234 D4 Colonnade WC1N
241 K2 Coltman Street E14
240 D2 Commercial Road E1
241 K3 Commercial Road E14
240 B1 Commercial Street E1
235 H3 Compton Street EC1V
238 E2 Concert Hall Approach SE1
241 K2 Conder Street E14
232 E6 Conduit Mews W2
232 E6 Conduit Place W2
233 L7 Conduit Street W1S
239 M5 Congreve Street SE17
232 F7 Connaught Close W2
233 G7 Connaught Place W2
233 G6 Connaught Square W2
233 G6 Connaught Street W2
239 G2 Cons Street SE1
237 L3 Constitution Hill SW1A
239 K5 Content Street SE17
233 M4 Conway Street W1T
241 H6 Cookham Crescent SE16
239 H8 Cook's Road SE17
235 J1 Coombs Street N1
234 B1 Cooper's Lane Estate NW1
240 B3 Cooper's Road EC3N
241 L2 Copenhagen Place E14
236 A4 Cope Place W8
239 J8 Copley Court SE17
241 H2 Copley Street E1
241 K1 Copperfield Road E3
239 J2 Copperfield Street SE1
235 L6 Copthall Avenue EC2R
234 C5 Coptic Street WC1A
239 G3 Coral Street SE1
234 C3 Coram Street WC1H
240 E5 Cork Square E1W
233 M8 Cork Street W1S
232 F4 Corlett Street NW1
235 L6 Cornhill EC3V
236 C4 Cornwall Gardens SW7
236 C5 Cornwall Mews South SW7
238 F1 Cornwall Road SE1
239 G2 Cornwall Road SE1
240 E3 Cornwall Street E1
233 H4 Cornwall Terrace Mews NW1
241 G2 Cornwood Drive E1
235 M2 Coronet Street N1
235 G3 Corporation Row EC1R
235 L2 Corsham Street N1
238 F4 Cosser Street SE1
233 G4 Cosway Street NW1
236 F4 Cottage Place SW3
236 B4 Cottesmore Gardens W8
239 M1 Cottons Lane SE1
237 H6 Coulson Street SW3
239 M1 Counter Street SE1
239 K5 County Street SE1
238 F7 Courtenay Square SE11
238 F6 Courtenay Street SE11
236 B5 Courtfield Gardens SW5
236 C5 Courtfield Road SW7
240 E1 Court Street E1
235 K8 Cousin Lane SE1
234 D7 Covent Garden WC2E
234 D7 Covent Garden ⊖ WC2E
234 B8 Coventry Street W1D
235 H4 Cowcross Street EC1M
235 L3 Cowper Street EC2A
239 L5 Crail Row SE17
233 J5 Cramer Street W1U
239 J6 Crampton Street SE17
234 C7 Cranbourn Street WC2H
234 A1 Cranleigh Street NW1
236 D6 Cranley Gardens SW7
236 D6 Cranley Mews SW7
236 E6 Cranley Place SW7
235 L1 Cranston Estate N1
235 L2 Cranwood Street EC1V
232 D7 Craven Hill W2
232 D7 Craven Hill W2
232 C7 Craven Hill Gardens W2
232 D7 Craven Road W2
238 D1 Craven Street WC2N
232 D7 Craven Terrace W2
235 G3 Crawford Passage EC1R
233 G5 Crawford Place W1H
233 G5 Crawford Street W1H
240 A3 Creechurch Lane EC3A
235 H7 Creed Lane EC4V
236 D6 Cresswell Place SW10
241 G1 Cressy Place E1
234 D2 Crestfield Street WC1H
240 A8 Crimscott Street SE1
240 B1 Crispin Street E1
234 D2 Cromer Street WC1H
232 D2 Crompton Street W2
236 E5 Cromwell Place SW7
236 B5 Cromwell Road SW5
236 E5 Cromwell Road SW7
235 M1 Crondall Court N1
235 L1 Crondall Street N1
235 H1 Cropley Street N1
239 L3 Crosby Row SE1
240 A4 Cross Lane EC3R
240 B3 Crosswall EC3N
240 E3 Crowder Street E1
240 A6 Crucifix Lane SE1
234 F1 Cruikshank Street WC1X
240 A3 Crutched Friars EC3N
241 M6 Cuba Street E14
234 E2 Cubitt Street WC1X
237 H6 Culford Gardens SW3
240 F7 Culling Road SE16
235 M7 Cullum Street EC3M
237 J8 Culross Street W1K
232 F1 Culworth Street NW8
234 F2 Cumberland Gardens WC1X
233 G7 Cumberland Gate W2
233 J2 Cumberland Market NW1
237 L6 Cumberland Street SW1V
233 K1 Cumberland Terrace NW1
233 L1 Cumberland Terrace Mews NW1
241 G6 Cumberland Wharf SE16
235 G1 Cumming Street N1
237 K6 Cundy Street SW1W
232 E3 Cunningham Place NW8
238 C6 Cureton Street SW1P
240 B6 Curlew Street SE1
234 F6 Cursitor Street EC4A
235 M3 Curtain Road EC2A
235 M4 Curtain Road EC2A
237 K2 Curzon Gate W2
237 K1 Curzon Street W1J
232 E4 Cuthbert Street W2
240 A2 Cutler Street EC3A
234 F1 Cynthia Street N1
234 A4 Cypress Place W1T
235 H3 Cyrus Street EC1V

D

238 B3 Dacre Street SW1H
241 J1 Dakin Place E1
235 H3 Dallington Street EC1V
240 F2 Damien Street E1
234 E5 Dane Street WC1R
234 B7 Dansey Place W1D
239 H5 Dante Road SE11
236 F8 Danvers Street SW3
234 A6 D'Arblay Street W1F
239 K8 Dartford Street SE17
238 B3 Dartmouth Street SW1H
239 L5 Darwin Street SE17
239 K7 Date Street SE17
240 D1 Davenant Street E1
232 F4 Daventry Street NW1
239 H3 Davidge Street SE1
233 K7 Davies Mews W1K
233 K7 Davies Street W1K
239 L6 Dawes Street SE17
232 A7 Dawson Place W2
239 J5 Deacon Way SE17
241 G8 Deal Porters Way SE16
240 D1 Deal Street E1
238 C5 Dean Bradley Street SW1P
241 H6 Dean Close SE16
238 E7 Deancross Street E1
237 K1 Deanery Street W1K
238 B3 Dean Farrar Street SW1H
238 C5 Dean Ryle Street SW1P
239 L6 Dean's Buildings SE17
238 C4 Dean Stanley Street SW1P
234 B6 Dean Street W1D
238 C4 Dean Yard SW1P
239 M4 Decima Street SE1
241 J6 Deck Close SE16
241 K7 Defoe Close SE16
232 B4 Delamere Terrace W2
239 H7 De Laune Street SE17
232 B3 Delaware Road W9
240 F3 Dellow Street E1
239 H7 Delverton Road SE17
237 M6 Denbigh Place SW1V
234 B7 Denman Street W1D
234 C6 Denmark Street WC2H
239 G6 Denny Close SE11
237 G5 Denyer Street SW3
238 D3 Derby Gate SW1A
237 K1 Derby Street W1J
233 L6 Dering Street W1S
236 B3 Derry Street W8
236 C3 De Vere Gardens W8
239 L4 Deverell Street SE1
241 G3 Devonport Street E1
233 K4 Devonshire Close W1G
233 K4 Devonshire Mews South W1G
233 K4 Devonshire Mews West W1G
233 K4 Devonshire Place W1G
233 K4 Devonshire Place Mews W1G
240 A2 Devonshire Row EC2M
240 A2 Devonshire Square EC2M
233 K4 Devonshire Street W1G
232 D7 Devonshire Terrace W2
233 K5 De Walden Street W1G
240 D7 Dickens Estate SE16
239 K4 Dickens Square SE1
237 H8 Dilke Street SW3
235 K2 Dingley Place EC1V
235 J2 Dingley Road EC1V
240 E5 Discovery Walk E1W
239 K2 Disney Place SE1
235 J7 Distaff Lane EC4V
238 F6 Distin Street SE11
240 C7 Dockhead SE1
240 D8 Dockley Road SE16
240 D4 Dock Street E1
239 H7 Doddington Grove SE17
239 H8 Doddington Place SE17
239 G3 Dodson Street SE1
241 M2 Dod Street E14
239 H2 Dolben Street SE1
238 E7 Dolland Street SE11
238 A7 Dolphin Square SW1V
238 B7 Dolphin Square SW1V
234 E4 Dombey Street WC1N
235 L5 Dominion Street EC2A
235 F1 Donegal Street N1
241 J1 Dongola Road E1
237 G5 Donne Place SW3
238 F1 Doon Street SE1
241 L2 Dora Street E14
234 B2 Doric Way NW1
235 G7 Dorset Rise EC4Y
233 H4 Dorset Square NW1
233 H5 Dorset Street W1U
234 E3 Doughty Mews WC1N
234 E3 Doughty Street WC1N
238 B6 Douglas Street SW1P
236 C3 Douro Place W8
240 D5 Douthwaite Square * E1W
236 E6 Dovehouse Street SW3
237 L1 Dover Street W1J
233 L8 Dover Street W1S
235 K7 Dowgate Hill EC4R
232 B4 Downfield Close W9
238 C2 Downing Street SW1A
237 K2 Down Street W1J
241 K6 Downtown Road SE16
237 J5 D'Oyley Street SW1X
239 J8 Draco Street SE17
241 H6 Drake Close SE16
237 G5 Draycott Avenue SW3
237 H6 Draycott Place SW3
237 H5 Draycott Terrace SW3
236 A3 Drayson Mews W8
236 D6 Drayton Gardens SW10
240 A6 Druid Street SE1
240 B6 Druid Street SE1
234 B2 Drummond Crescent NW1
240 E8 Drummond Road SE16
234 A3 Drummond Street NW1
234 D6 Drury Lane WC2B
239 G5 Dryden Court SE11
234 D6 Dryden Street WC2B
233 L5 Duchess Mews W1G
233 L5 Duchess Street W1B
239 G1 Duchy Street SE1
241 J1 Duckett Street E1
234 B6 Duck Lane W1F
235 K4 Dufferin Street EC1Y
237 K3 Duke of Wellington Place SW1W
237 H6 Duke of York Square SW3
234 A8 Duke of York Street SW1Y
241 K4 Duke Shore Wharf E14
236 A2 Duke's Lane W8
240 B2 Duke's Place EC3A
234 C2 Duke's Road WC1H
233 K7 Duke Street W1K
233 J6 Duke Street W1U
239 L1 Duke Street Hill SE1
238 A1 Duke Street St James's SW1Y
241 L4 Dunbar Wharf E14
234 C8 Duncannon Street WC2N
235 H1 Duncan Terrace N1
240 E5 Dundee Street E1W
241 L4 Dundee Wharf E14
241 H2 Dunelm Street E1
240 C8 Dunlop Place SE16
233 H7 Dunraven Street W1K
240 A3 Dunster Court EC3R
237 H3 Duplex Ride SW1X
241 L6 Durand's Wharf SE16
241 J1 Durham Row E1
238 E7 Durham Street SE11
232 A6 Durham Terrace W2
234 C6 Dyott Street WC1A
235 M4 Dysart Street EC2A

E

235 H4 Eagle Close EC1M
234 E5 Eagle Street WC1R
236 A7 Eardley Crescent SW5
234 C7 Earlham Street WC2H
236 A6 Earl's Court ⇌ ⊖ SW5
236 B6 Earl's Court Gardens SW5
236 A6 Earl's Court Road SW5
236 A6 Earl's Court Square SW5
235 H2 Earlstoke Street EC1V
235 M4 Earl Street EC2A
234 C6 Earnshaw Street WC2H
241 H2 East Arbour Street E1
232 D6 Eastbourne Mews W2
232 D6 Eastbourne Terrace W2
234 A6 Eastcastle Street W1W
235 M7 Eastcheap EC3M
241 K1 Eastfield Street E14
241 M3 East India Dock Road E14
240 D6 East Lane SE16
234 F3 Easton Street WC1X
235 H5 East Poultry Avenue EC1A
235 L2 East Road N1
240 C4 East Smithfield E1W
239 L6 East Street SE17
237 J5 Eaton Close SW1W
237 J5 Eaton Gate SW1W
237 L4 Eaton Lane SW1W
237 J5 Eaton Mews North SW1W
237 K5 Eaton Mews South SW1W
237 K5 Eaton Mews West SW1W
237 J4 Eaton Place SW1X
237 K4 Eaton Row SW1W
237 K5 Eaton Square SW1W
237 J5 Eaton Terrace SW1W
238 E8 Ebbisham Drive SW8
237 K6 Ebury Bridge SW1W
237 K7 Ebury Bridge Road SW1W
237 K5 Ebury Mews SW1W
237 K6 Ebury Square SW1W
237 K5 Ebury Street SW1W
237 L5 Eccleston Bridge SW1W
237 K4 Eccleston Mews SW1X
237 L5 Eccleston Place SW1W
237 L6 Eccleston Square SW1V
237 K4 Eccleston Street SW1X
232 A3 Edbrooke Road W9
236 A1 Edge Street W8
232 F5 Edgware Road W2
232 F5 Edgware Road ⊖ NW1
237 H3 Edinburgh Gate SW1X
236 C8 Edith Grove SW10
233 J6 Edwards Mews W1H
236 F5 Egerton Crescent SW3
236 F5 Egerton Gardens SW3
237 G4 Egerton Terrace SW3
239 J7 Eglington Court SE17
239 K5 Elba Place SE17
235 L5 Eldon Place EC2M
236 B4 Eldon Road W8
241 H6 Eleanor Close SE16
239 J4 Elephant & Castle SE1
239 J5 Elephant & Castle ⇌ ⊖ SE1
240 F6 Elephant Lane SE16
239 J5 Elephant Road SE17
241 G3 Elf Row E1W
241 K7 Elgar Street SE16
232 B2 Elgin Avenue W9
232 C2 Elgin Mews North W9
232 C2 Elgin Mews South W9
235 H1 Elia Mews N1
235 H1 Elia Street N1
239 M3 Elim Estate SE1
239 M3 Elim Street SE1
237 K5 Elizabeth Street SW1W
240 D3 Ellen Street E1
239 H5 Elliott's Row SE11
237 J5 Ellis Street SW1X
232 A4 Elmfield Way W9
236 E7 Elm Park Gardens SW10
236 E7 Elm Park Lane SW3
236 E8 Elm Park Road SW3
236 E7 Elm Place SW7
232 D7 Elms Mews W2
234 F4 Elm Street WC1X
232 E2 Elm Tree Road NW8
232 B4 Elnathan Mews W9
241 J1 Elsa Street E1
239 L6 Elsted Street SE17
236 D4 Elvaston Mews SW7
236 D4 Elvaston Place SW7
238 B5 Elverton Street SW1P
235 G5 Ely Place EC1N
237 G6 Elystan Place SW3
236 F6 Elystan Street SW3
238 D1 Embankment ⊖ WC2N
237 H8 Embankment Gardens SW3
238 D1 Embankment Place WC2N
240 D7 Emba Street SE16
234 E4 Emerald Street WC1N
239 J1 Emerson Street SE1
238 A5 Emery Hill Street SW1P
239 G3 Emery Street SE1
236 C5 Emperor's Gate SW7
239 L3 Empire Square SE1
236 A7 Empress Place SW6
234 C6 Endell Street WC2H
234 B3 Endsleigh Gardens WC1H
234 B3 Endsleigh Place WC1H
234 B3 Endsleigh Street WC1H
233 G5 Enford Street W1H
239 M1 English Grounds SE1
240 C8 Enid Street SE16
236 F3 Ennismore Gardens SW7
236 F3 Ennismore Gardens Mews SW7
236 F3 Ennismore Mews SW7
236 F4 Ennismore Street SW7
239 G6 Enny Street SE11
240 D4 Ensign Street E1
235 L3 Epworth Street EC2A
238 C6 Erasmus Street SW1P
235 K4 Errol Street EC1Y
232 A3 Essendine Road W9
234 F7 Essex Street WC2R
236 A3 Essex Villas W8
235 J2 Europa Place EC1V
234 B2 Euston ⇌ ⊖ NW1
234 B3 Euston Road NW1
234 B2 Euston Square NW1
234 A3 Euston Square ⊖ NW1
234 A3 Euston Street NW1
236 D7 Evelyn Gardens SW7
235 L1 Evelyn Way N1
234 A1 Eversholt Street NW1
233 M2 Everton Buildings NW1
239 J2 Ewer Street SE1
241 G1 Ewhurst Close E1
235 M4 Exchange Square EC2A
234 D7 Exeter Street WC2E
236 E3 Exhibition Road SW7
235 G3 Exmouth Market EC1R
239 M6 Exon Street SE17
238 F2 Exton Street SE1
234 F4 Eyre Street Hill EC1R

244 Fairclough Street - Kirby Street

F

240 D3 Fairclough Street E1
240 B6 Fair Street SE1
239 K4 Falmouth Road SE1
235 J4 Fann Street EC1M
235 M1 Fanshaw Street N1
234 B6 Fareham Street W1D
236 A1 Farmer Street W8
236 A8 Farm Lane SW6
233 K8 Farm Street W1K
239 J1 Farnham Place SE1
241 M3 Farrance Street E14
235 G4 Farringdon ⇌ ⊖ EC1M
235 G4 Farringdon Lane EC1R
234 F3 Farringdon Road EC1R
235 H5 Farringdon Street EC1M
241 J5 Farrins Rents SE16
241 K7 Farrow Place SE16
240 F5 Farthing Fields * E1W
240 B1 Fashion Street E1
239 H7 Faunce Street SE17
236 C8 Fawcett Street SW10
235 L3 Featherstone Street EC1Y
240 A3 Fenchurch Avenue EC3M
240 A3 Fenchurch Buildings EC3M
240 A3 Fenchurch Place EC3M
240 A3 Fenchurch Street EC3M
240 A3 Fenchurch Street ⇌ EC3M
240 B8 Fendall Street SE1
239 M2 Fenning Street SE1
238 D8 Fentiman Road SW8
234 F2 Fernsbury Street WC1X
235 G6 Fetter Lane EC4A
240 D2 Fieldgate Street E1
239 J7 Fielding Street SE17
234 E1 Field Street WC1X
236 B8 Finborough Road SW10
235 L6 Finch Lane EC3V
241 K8 Finland Street SE16
235 L5 Finsbury Circus EC2M
235 G3 Finsbury Estate EC1R
235 M4 Finsbury Market EC2A
235 L4 Finsbury Square EC2A
235 L4 Finsbury Street EC2Y
237 G5 First Street SW3
241 J6 Fishermans Drive SE16
234 D5 Fisher Street WC1R
232 E3 Fisherton Street NW8
235 L7 Fish Street Hill EC3R
238 F5 Fitzalan Street SE11
233 J6 Fitzhardinge Street W1H
233 M4 Fitzroy Square W1T
233 M4 Fitzroy Street W1T
241 J3 Flamborough Street E14
240 C4 Flank Street E1
234 C3 Flaxman Terrace WC1H
235 G6 Fleet Street EC4A
239 H8 Fleming Road SE17
240 D3 Fletcher Street E1
239 L6 Flint Street SE17
234 C6 Flitcroft Street WC2H
240 D7 Flockton Street SE16
237 G7 Flood Street SW3
237 G7 Flood Walk SW3
234 D7 Floral Street WC2E
233 M5 Foley Street W1W
240 D3 Forbes Street E1
240 D2 Fordham Street E1
240 F2 Ford Square E1
235 K5 Fore Street EC2Y
232 C4 Formosa Street W9
233 G6 Forset Street W1H
239 H8 Forsyth Gardens SE17
240 B1 Fort Street E1
235 K4 Fortune Street EC1Y
235 J6 Foster Lane EC2V
236 E6 Foulis Terrace SW7
241 J5 Foundry Close SE16
240 B1 Fournier Street E1
240 E5 Fowey Close E1W
232 E4 Frampton Street NW8
238 A5 Francis Street SW1P
240 F8 Frankland Close SE16
237 H6 Franklin's Row SW3
239 G3 Frazier Street SE1
240 C8 Frean Street SE16
233 G7 Frederick Close W2
234 E2 Frederick Street WC1X
237 J3 Frederic Mews * SW1X
239 M6 Freemantle Street SE17
235 H2 Friend Street EC1V
234 B6 Frith Street W1D
240 E1 Fulbourne Street E1
240 F7 Fulford Street SE16
236 D8 Fulham Road SW10
236 F6 Fulham Road SW3
234 F5 Furnival Street EC4A
238 B5 Fynes Street SW1P

G

239 G1 Gabriel's Wharf SE1
240 B6 Gainsford Street SE1
241 G6 Galleon Close SE16
241 K2 Galsworthy Avenue E14
235 K2 Galway Street EC1V
239 H2 Gambia Street SE1
232 D1 Garden Road NW8
239 H4 Garden Row SE1
241 H1 Garden Street E1
235 M3 Garden Walk EC2A
235 J2 Gard Street EC1V
241 M4 Garford Street E14
235 G3 Garnault Place EC1R
240 F4 Garnet Street E1W
235 K3 Garrett Street EC1Y
234 C7 Garrick Street WC2E
241 H7 Garterway SE16
232 B6 Garway Road W2
240 E8 Gataker Street * SE16
236 F3 Gate Mews SW7
232 F3 Gateforth Street NW8
233 L3 Gate Mews NW1
235 M3 Gatesborough Street * EC2A
234 E5 Gate Street WC2A
237 K7 Gatliff Road SW1W
239 J4 Gaunt Street SE1
238 C4 Gayfere Street SW1P
239 H4 Gaywood Street SE1
239 H7 Gaza Street SE17
240 C7 Gedling Place SE1
235 J3 Gee Street EC1V
239 H5 George Mathers Road SE11
240 C7 George Row SE16
233 H6 George Street W1H
233 K7 George Yard W1K
239 H4 Geraldine Street SE1
237 K5 Gerald Road SW1W
234 B7 Gerrard Street W1D
239 G3 Gerridge Street SE1
236 D8 Gertrude Street SW10
238 E5 Gibson Road SE11
234 C5 Gilbert Place WC1A
239 G5 Gilbert Road SE11
233 K7 Gilbert Street W1K
233 L5 Gildea Street W1W
237 M5 Gillingham Street SW1V
241 L3 Gill Street E14
236 D7 Gilston Road SW10
235 H5 Giltspur Street EC1A
239 H4 Gladstone Street SE1
241 G4 Glamis Place E1W
241 G4 Glamis Road E1W
237 M7 Glasgow Terrace SW1V
239 J3 Glasshill Street SE1
234 A7 Glasshouse Street W1B
238 D7 Glasshouse Walk SE11
236 F7 Glebe Place SW3
236 C6 Gledhow Road SW5
233 H4 Glentworth Street NW1
241 J5 Globe Pond Road SE16
239 K3 Globe Street SE1
240 A4 Gloucester Court * EC3R
232 C6 Gloucester Gardens W2
232 D6 Gloucester Mews W2
232 C6 Gloucester Mews West W2
233 H3 Gloucester Place NW1
233 H5 Gloucester Place W1U
233 H5 Gloucester Place Mews W1U
236 C4 Gloucester Road SW7
236 D6 Gloucester Road SW7
236 C5 Gloucester Road ⊖ SW7
232 F6 Gloucester Square W2
237 M7 Gloucester Street SW1V
232 B5 Gloucester Terrace W2
232 D6 Gloucester Terrace W2
236 A2 Gloucester Walk W8
235 G2 Gloucester Way EC1R
238 F7 Glyn Street SE11
237 G6 Godfrey Street SW3
238 D7 Goding Street SE11
235 J7 Godliman Street EC4V
235 K1 Godwin Close N1
238 D1 Golden Jubilee Bridge WC2N
235 J4 Golden Lane EC1Y
234 A7 Golden Square W1F
240 E3 Golding Street E1
232 A4 Goldney Road W9
235 K6 Goldsmith Street EC2V
241 G8 Gomm Road SE16
234 A5 Goodge Place W1T
234 A5 Goodge Street W1T
234 B5 Goodge Street ⊖ W1T
240 C8 Goodwin Close SE16
236 A2 Gordon Place W8
234 B3 Gordon Square WC1H
234 B3 Gordon Street WC1H
236 D4 Gore Street SW7
240 A2 Goring Street * EC3A
233 L5 Gosfield Street W1W
234 B6 Goslett Yard WC2H
235 H1 Goswell Road EC1V
234 F3 Gough Street WC1X
240 B2 Goulston Street E1
234 B5 Gower Mews WC1E
234 A3 Gower Place NW1
234 B3 Gower Street WC1E
240 D2 Gower's Walk E1
235 M7 Gracechurch Street EC3V
234 B2 Grafton Place NW1
233 L8 Grafton Street W1S
234 A4 Grafton Way W1T
235 J1 Graham Street N1
237 J6 Graham Terrace SW1W
233 M1 Granby Terrace NW1
235 H5 Grand Avenue EC1A
240 B8 Grange Road SE1
240 A8 Grange Walk SE1
240 B8 Grange Yard SE1
232 B2 Grantully Road W9
233 J6 Granville Place W1H
232 A1 Granville Road NW6
234 F2 Granville Square WC1X
234 C6 Grape Street WC2H
240 B2 Gravel Lane E1
234 D2 Gray's Inn Road WC1X
234 F5 Gray's Inn Square WC1R
239 G3 Gray Street SE1
233 L6 Great Castle Street W1G
233 G4 Great Central Street NW1
234 B6 Great Chapel Street W1D
238 C4 Great College Street SW1P
233 H6 Great Cumberland Place W1H
239 K3 Great Dover Street SE1
235 M3 Great Eastern Street EC2A
238 C3 Great George Street SW1P
239 J1 Great Guildford Street SE1
234 E4 Great James Street WC1N
233 M7 Great Marlborough Street W1F
239 L2 Great Maze Pond SE1
234 C7 Great New Portland Street WC2H
240 D1 Greatorex Street E1
234 D4 Great Ormond Street WC1N
234 F2 Great Percy Street WC1X
238 B4 Great Peter Street SW1P
233 L4 Great Portland Street W1W
233 L4 Great Portland Street ⊖ W1W
234 A7 Great Pulteney Street W1F
234 D6 Great Queen Street WC2B
234 C5 Great Russell Street WC1B
238 C1 Great Scotland Yard SW1A
238 C4 Great Smith Street SW1P
239 H2 Great Suffolk Street SE1
235 H4 Great Sutton Street EC1V
235 L6 Great Swan Alley EC2R
233 M4 Great Titchfield Street W1W
235 M7 Great Tower Street EC3M
240 A4 Great Tower Street EC3R
235 L6 Great Winchester Street EC2N
234 B7 Great Windmill Street W1D
234 B6 Greek Street W1D
241 J6 Greenacre Square SE16
240 E5 Green Bank E1W
232 F1 Greenberry Street NW8
238 A5 Greencoat Place SW1P
238 A4 Green Coat Row SW1P
240 D2 Greenfield Road E1
238 F3 Greenham Close SE1
237 M1 Green Park ⊖ W1J
233 J7 Green Street W1K
233 L4 Greenwell Street W1W
239 G2 Greet Street SE1
241 L4 Grenade Street E14
232 F3 Grendon Street NW8
236 C5 Grenville Place SW7
235 J6 Gresham Street EC2V
234 B5 Gresse Street W1T
235 G5 Greville Street EC1N
238 B4 Greycoat Place SW1P
238 B4 Greycoat Street SW1P
240 A8 Grigg's Place SE1
237 L8 Grosvenor Bridge SW8
237 J3 Grosvenor Crescent SW1X
237 J3 Grosvenor Crescent Mews SW1X
237 L4 Grosvenor Gardens SW1W
237 L4 Grosvenor Gardens Mews East SW1W
237 L4 Grosvenor Gardens Mews North SW1W
237 L4 Grosvenor Gardens Mews South * SW1W
233 H8 Grosvenor Gate W2
233 L7 Grosvenor Hill W1K
237 K3 Grosvenor Place SW1X
237 L8 Grosvenor Road SW1V
233 J7 Grosvenor Square W1K
233 K7 Grosvenor Street W1K
239 J8 Grosvenor Terrace SE5
232 D2 Grove End Road NW8
237 M5 Guildhouse Street SW1V
234 D4 Guilford Street WC1N
239 M5 Guinness Square SE1
241 K8 Gulliver Street SE16
235 G6 Gunpowder Square EC4A
240 B1 Gun Street E1
240 C2 Gunthorpe Street E1
235 J6 Gutter Lane EC2V
239 L3 Guy Street SE1

H

235 L2 Haberdasher Street N1
239 M4 Haddonhall Estate SE1
240 F3 Hainton Close E1
240 F2 Halcrow Street * E1
237 L1 Half Moon Street W1J
236 A8 Halford Road SW6
237 K4 Halkin Place SW1X
237 J3 Halkin Street SW1X
233 L5 Hallam Street W1W
241 K1 Halley Street E14
232 C6 Hallfield Estate W2
232 E4 Hall Place W2
232 D2 Hall Road NW8
235 H2 Hall Street EC1V
239 M6 Halpin Place SE17
237 G5 Halsey Street SW3
232 D2 Hamilton Close NW8
241 K7 Hamilton Close SE16
232 D2 Hamilton Gardens NW8
237 K2 Hamilton Place W1J
232 C1 Hamilton Terrace NW8
239 L3 Hamlet Way SE1
240 B4 Hammett Street EC3N
234 B1 Hampden Close NW1
233 H6 Hampden Gurney Street W2
233 M2 Hampstead Road NW1
239 J6 Hampton Street SE17
240 C1 Hanbury Street E1
234 E5 Hand Court WC1V
234 D3 Handel Street WC1N
239 L3 Hankey Place SE1
241 G1 Hannibal Road E1
233 L6 Hanover Square W1S
233 L7 Hanover Street W1S
237 H3 Hans Crescent SW3
233 M4 Hanson Street W1W
237 H4 Hans Place SW1X
237 G4 Hans Road SW3
237 H4 Hans Street SW1X
234 B6 Hanway Place W1T
234 B6 Hanway Street W1T
232 F5 Harbet Road W2
234 E4 Harbour Street WC1N
233 G5 Harcourt Street W1H
236 C7 Harcourt Terrace SW10
241 G3 Hardinge Street E1W
235 G2 Hardwick Street EC1R
239 M2 Hardwidge Street SE1
241 H6 Hardy Close SE16
233 L6 Harewood Place W1G
233 G4 Harewood Row NW1
233 G4 Harewood Avenue NW1
241 J1 Harford Street E1
238 E8 Harleyford Road SE11
236 D7 Harley Gardens SW10
233 K4 Harley Street W1G
239 G7 Harmsworth Street SE17
240 A8 Harold Estate SE1
239 K4 Harper Road SE1
237 H3 Harriet Street SW1X
237 H3 Harriet Walk SW1X
236 C6 Harrington Gardens SW7
236 E5 Harrington Road SW7
233 M1 Harrington Square NW1
233 M2 Harrington Street NW1
234 D2 Harrison Street WC1H
233 G6 Harrowby Street W1H
240 B2 Harrow Place E1
232 A4 Harrow Road W2
240 A3 Hart Street EC3R
237 G5 Hasker Street SW3
234 C2 Hastings Street WC1H
239 G1 Hatfields SE1
232 B6 Hatherley Grove W2
241 G6 Hatteraick Road SE16
235 G4 Hatton Garden EC1N
232 E4 Hatton Street W2
235 G4 Hatton Wall EC1N
241 H3 Havering Street E1
235 J1 Haverstock Street N1
241 H6 Hawke Place * SE16
240 B3 Haydon Street EC3N
233 G4 Hayes Place NW1
233 L8 Hay Hill W1J
239 H5 Hayles Street SE11
234 B8 Haymarket SW1Y
235 J4 Hayne Street EC1A
239 M1 Hay's Lane SE1
233 L8 Hay's Mews W1J
235 H3 Haywood Place EC1R
237 K3 Headfort Place SW1X
241 H2 Head Street E1
241 K2 Hearnshaw Street E14
235 M4 Hearn Street EC2A
234 E3 Heathcote Street WC1N
233 M7 Heddon Street W1B
234 A7 Heddon Street W1S
239 H5 Hedger Street SE11
239 J8 Heiron Street SE17
240 D5 Hellings Street E1W
235 K3 Helmet Row EC1V
241 L8 Helsinki Square SE16
232 E3 Henderson Drive NW8
240 A3 Heneage Lane EC3A
240 C1 Heneage Street E1
233 L6 Henrietta Place W1G
234 D7 Henrietta Street WC2E
240 D2 Henriques Street E1
239 L5 Henshaw Street SE17
235 G4 Herbal Hill EC1R
237 H4 Herbert Crescent SW1X
234 C3 Herbrand Street WC1H
238 F4 Hercules Road SE1
232 A6 Hereford Road W2
236 D6 Hereford Square SW7
232 E5 Hermitage Street W2
240 D5 Hermitage Wall E1W
235 H2 Hermit Street EC1V
241 K5 Heron Place SE16
241 M5 Heron Quay E14
238 C6 Herrick Street SW1P
237 K2 Hertford Street W1J
241 M4 Hertsmere Road E14
236 B6 Hesper Mews SW5
240 E3 Hessel Street E1
235 M3 Hewett Street EC2A
239 J5 Heygate Estate SE17
239 J5 Heygate Street SE17
238 B6 Hide Place SW1P
234 E5 High Holborn WC1V
236 A3 High Street Kensington ⊖ W8
236 A8 Hildyard Road SW6
240 F5 Hilliards Court E1W
239 J8 Hillingdon Street SE17
232 D1 Hill Road NW8
233 M6 Hills Place W1F
233 K8 Hill Street W1J
233 K6 Hinde Street W1U
241 M3 Hind Grove E14
241 M3 Hindgrove Area E14
241 G8 Hithe Grove SE16
237 K4 Hobart Place SW1W
236 D8 Hobury Street SW10
236 B6 Hogarth Road SW5
237 J6 Holbein Mews SW1W
237 J6 Holbein Place SW1W
235 G5 Holborn EC1N
234 E5 Holborn ⊖ WC2B
235 G5 Holborn Viaduct EC1A
234 F2 Holford Street WC1X
239 H1 Holland Street SE1
236 A3 Holland Street W8
234 A6 Hollen Street W1F
233 L6 Holles Street W1C
236 C8 Hollywood Road SW10
239 H5 Holyoak Road SE11
239 M2 Holyrood Street SE1
240 A6 Holyrood Street SE1
235 M4 Holywell Row EC2A
235 M1 Homefield Street * N1
233 G5 Homer Row W1H
233 G5 Homer Street W1H
240 D3 Hooper Street E1
240 C1 Hopetown Street E1
234 A7 Hopkins Street W1F
239 H1 Hopton Street SE1
239 L8 Hopwood Road SE17
236 A3 Hornton Place W8
236 A2 Hornton Street W8
234 B7 Horse & Dolphin Yard W1D
241 J3 Horseferry Road E14
238 B4 Horseferry Road SW1P
238 C2 Horse Guards Avenue SW1A
238 C2 Horse Guards Parade SW1A
238 C2 Horse Guards Road SW1A
240 B6 Horselydown Lane SE1
239 K8 Horsley Street SE17
235 H5 Hosier Lane EC1A
241 G8 Hothfield Place SE16
238 F6 Hotspur Street SE11
234 E6 Houghton Street WC2A
240 A2 Houndsditch EC3A
238 A4 Howick Place SW1E
234 A4 Howland Street W1T
241 K7 Howland Way SE16
232 D4 Howley Place W2
235 M2 Hoxton Square N1
235 M1 Hoxton Street N1
237 L6 Hugh Mews SW1V
237 L6 Hugh Street SW1V
237 L6 Hugh Street SW1V
241 J6 Hull Close SE16
235 J2 Hull Street EC1V
238 E1 Hungerford Bridge SE1
239 M4 Hunter Close SE1
234 D3 Hunter Street WC1N
234 A4 Huntley Street WC1E
239 M6 Huntsman Street SE17
233 H3 Huntsworth Mews NW1
241 H6 Hurley Crescent SE16
241 M7 Hutching's Street E14
235 G7 Hutton Street EC4Y
237 K2 Hyde Park Corner W1J
237 K2 Hyde Park Corner ⊖ W1J
236 D3 Hyde Park Court SW7
232 F6 Hyde Park Crescent W2
232 F7 Hyde Park Garden Mews W2
232 F7 Hyde Park Gardens W2
236 C3 Hyde Park Gate SW7
236 D3 Hyde Park Gate SW7
232 F7 Hyde Park Square W2
232 F7 Hyde Park Street W2

I

235 M7 Idol Lane EC3R
236 B8 Ifield Road SW10
239 J6 Iliffe Street SE17
239 J6 Iliffe Yard SE17
236 D4 Imperial College Road SW7
240 B3 India Street EC3N
234 A7 Ingestre Place W1F
234 F2 Inglebert Street EC1R
238 E5 Ingram Close SE11
233 J2 Inner Circle NW1
232 B6 Inverness Terrace W2
232 C8 Inverness Terrace Gate W2
239 H1 Invicta Plaza SE1
239 L7 Inville Road SE17
235 K6 Ironmonger Lane EC2V
235 K2 Ironmonger Row EC1V
234 C8 Irving Street WC2N
241 G6 Isambard Place SE16
241 K3 Island Row E14
236 A4 Iverna Court W8
236 A4 Iverna Gardens W8
237 G5 Ives Street SW3
233 G4 Ivor Place NW1
236 F6 Ixworth Place SW3

J

240 C6 Jacob Street SE1
240 F8 Jamaica Gate SE16
240 C7 Jamaica Road SE1
240 E7 Jamaica Road SE16
241 G2 Jamaica Street E1
240 C6 Jamaica Wharf SE1
233 K6 James Street W1U
234 D7 James Street WC2E
236 A1 Jameson Street W8
241 K1 Jamuna Close E14
240 D7 Janeway Street SE16
241 J4 Jardine Road E1W
240 C6 Java Wharf SE1
236 D3 Jay Mews SW7
234 A8 Jermyn Street SW1Y
232 F3 Jerome Crescent NW8
240 B3 Jewery Street EC3N
239 G2 Joan Street SE1
234 E4 Jockey's Fields WC1R
238 F3 Johanna Street SE1
234 D8 John Adam Street WC2N
235 G7 John Carpenter Street EC4Y
240 D7 John Felton Road SE16
240 C4 John Fisher Street E1
238 C5 John Islip Street SW1P
233 L6 John Prince's Street W1G
240 D7 John Roll Way SE16
239 J8 John Ruskin Street SE5
238 C6 John Slip Street SW1P
234 E4 John's Mews WC1N
238 A7 Johnson's Place SW1V
241 G3 Johnson Street E1
234 E4 John Street WC1N
239 L1 Joiner Street SE1
238 E6 Jonathan Street SE11
237 G6 Jubilee Place SW3
241 G2 Jubilee Street E1
236 B1 Jubilee Walk W8
234 C2 Judd Street WC1H
232 F5 Junction Mews W2
238 E5 Juxon Street SE11

K

241 H5 Katherine Close SE16
234 E6 Kean Street WC2B
241 J6 Keel Close SE16
234 E6 Keeley Street WC2B
240 E7 Keeton's Road SE16
239 H3 Kell Street SE1
236 B4 Kelso Place W8
234 E6 Kemble Street WC2B
236 A7 Kempsford Gardens SW5
239 G6 Kempsford Road SE11
233 J5 Kendall Place W1U
233 G6 Kendal Street W2
240 D5 Kennet Street E1W
241 G6 Kenning Street SE16
239 G7 Kennings Way SE11
239 H7 Kennington ⊖ SE11
238 E7 Kennington Lane SE11
238 E8 Kennington Oval SE11
239 G8 Kennington Park Gardens SE11
239 G7 Kennington Park Place SE11
239 G7 Kennington Park Road SE11
238 F4 Kennington Road SE1
239 G5 Kennington Road SE11
238 F8 Kennnington Oval SE11
233 J5 Kenrick Place W1U
236 A1 Kensington Church Street W8
236 B3 Kensington Court W8
232 B6 Kensington Gardens Square W2
236 C4 Kensington Gate W8
236 D3 Kensington Gore SW7
236 A4 Kensington High Street W8
236 B1 Kensington Palace Gardens W8
236 B2 Kensington Palace Gardens W8
236 A1 Kensington Place W8
237 G3 Kensington Road SW7
236 B3 Kensington Road W8
236 B3 Kensington Square W8
234 C3 Kenton Street WC1H
236 A6 Kenway Road SW5
234 D1 Keystone Close N1
239 H4 Keyworth Street SE1
232 A2 Kilburn Park Road NW6
232 A6 Kildare Terrace W2
234 E1 Killick Street N1
241 H6 Kinburn Street SE16
240 E2 Kinder Street E1
241 H5 King & Queen Wharf SE16
239 K6 King and Queen Street SE17
238 C2 King Charles Street SW1A
232 C5 Kingdom Street W2
235 J6 King Edward Street EC1A
239 G4 King Edward Walk SE1
239 H3 King James Street SE1
233 M7 Kingly Street W1F
235 L6 King's Arms Yard EC2R
239 H2 King's Bench Street SE1
235 H7 Kingscote Street EC4V
234 D1 King's Cross ⇌ N1C
234 E2 King's Cross Road WC1X
234 D1 King's Cross St Pancras ⊖ N1C
239 L1 King's Head Yard SE1
234 F4 King's Mews WC1N
232 E1 Kingsmill Terrace NW8
235 J2 King Square EC1V
236 E8 King's Road SW3
237 M5 King's Scholars Passage SW1P
240 F6 King's Stairs Close SE16
234 D7 King Street WC2E
238 A1 King Street SW1Y
235 K6 King Street EC2V
234 E6 Kingsway WC2B
235 L7 King William Street EC4N
237 J3 Kinnerton Place North * SW1X
237 J3 Kinnerton Place South * SW1X
237 J3 Kinnerton Street SW1X
237 J3 Kinnerton Yard * SW1X
239 L3 Kipling Estate SE1
239 L3 Kipling Street SE1
240 D7 Kirby Estate SE16
239 M3 Kirby Grove SE1
235 G4 Kirby Street EC1N

246 Parker's Row - Stopford Road

240 C7 Parker's Row SE1
234 D6 Parker Street WC2B
233 H7 Park Lane W1K
237 J1 Park Lane W2
237 M1 Park Place SW1A
233 H3 Park Road NW1
233 L3 Park Square East NW1
233 K3 Park Square Mews NW1
233 K3 Park Square West NW1
239 K1 Park Street SE1
233 J7 Park Street W1K
233 L1 Park Village East NW1
236 D8 Park Walk SW10
233 G6 Park West Place W2
238 C2 Parliament Street SW1A
238 D8 Parry Street SW8
237 J6 Passmore Street SW1W
235 J6 Paternoster Square EC1A
236 A4 Pater Street W8
241 K5 Pattina Walk SE16
235 M3 Paul Street EC2A
236 E8 Paultons Square SW3
233 G3 Paveley Street NW1
237 H3 Pavilion Road SW1X
237 H4 Pavilion Street SW1X
237 L7 Paxton Terrace SW1V
237 L7 Peabody Avenue SW1V
239 J1 Peabody Estate SE1
239 J6 Peacock Street SE17
240 F5 Pearl Street E1W
239 G3 Pearman Street SE1
235 G3 Pear Tree Court EC1R
241 G4 Peartree Lane E1W
235 J3 Pear Tree Street EC1V
236 A1 Peel Street W8
235 K2 Peerless Street EC1V
236 F6 Pelham Crescent SW7
236 F5 Pelham Place SW7
236 F5 Pelham Street SW7
239 K8 Pelier Street SE17
235 G6 Pemberton Row EC4A
232 A8 Pembridge Gardens W2
232 A7 Pembridge Place W2
232 A7 Pembridge Square W2
232 A7 Pembridge Villas W11
237 J3 Pembroke Close SW1X
240 F5 Penang Street E1W
232 F5 Penfold Place NW8
232 E4 Penfold Street NW8
236 B5 Pennant Mews W8
240 D4 Pennington Street E1W
241 M4 Pennyfields E14
239 J7 Penrose Grove SE17
239 J7 Penrose Street SE17
240 E7 Penryn Road SE16
239 H6 Penton Place SE17
234 E2 Penton Rise WC1X
234 F1 Penton Street N1
234 E1 Pentonville Road N1
236 A6 Penywern Road SW5
239 J2 Pepper Street SE1
240 A4 Pepys Street EC3N
235 H3 Percival Street EC1V
234 F2 Percy Circus WC1X
234 B5 Percy Street W1T
238 B4 Perkin's Rent SW1P
236 D4 Petersham Mews SW7
236 C4 Petersham Place SW7
234 B7 Peter Street W1F
233 L3 Peto Place NW1
240 B2 Petticoat Lane E1
238 A3 Petty France SW1H
240 A4 Petty Wales EC3R
237 G6 Petyward SW3
239 L7 Phelp Street SE17
237 G8 Phene Street SW3
236 A3 Phillimore Walk W8
235 M7 Philpot Lane EC3M
240 E2 Philpot Street E1
237 L5 Phipp's Mews SW1W
235 M3 Phipp Street EC2A
234 F3 Phoenix Place WC1X
234 B1 Phoenix Road NW1
234 C6 Phoenix Street WC2H
234 A8 Piccadilly W1J
237 L2 Piccadilly W1J
237 M1 Piccadilly Arcade SW1Y
234 A8 Piccadilly Circus W1B
234 B8 Piccadilly Circus ⊖ W1J
235 J2 Pickard Street EC1V
233 K6 Picton Place W1U
240 E6 Pier Head E1W
241 M3 Pigott Street E14
239 L3 Pilgrimage Street SE1
238 B6 Pimlico ⊖ SW1V
237 J6 Pimlico Road SW1W
240 D3 Pinchin Street E1
235 M4 Pindar Street EC2A
232 B3 Pindock Mews W9
234 F3 Pine Street EC1R
235 M1 Pitfield Street N1
241 H3 Pitsea Street E1
237 K2 Pitt's Head Mews W1J
236 A2 Pitt Street W8
241 L2 Pixley Street E14
235 L3 Platina Street * EC2A
241 K8 Plover Way SE16
240 D2 Plumbers Row E1
235 G5 Plumtree Court EC4A
232 F4 Plympton Street NW8
239 H2 Pocock Street SE1
234 A6 Poland Street W1F
233 L7 Pollen Street W1S
232 E3 Pollitt Drive NW8
239 G5 Polperrom SE11
234 B1 Polygon Road NW1
236 F6 Pond Place SW3
240 E3 Ponler Street E1
238 C6 Ponsonby Place SW1P
238 C6 Ponsonby Terrace SW1P
238 B8 Ponton Road SW1V
237 H4 Pont Street SW1X
241 H6 Poolmans Street SE16
240 B7 Pope Street SE1
232 B7 Poplar Place W2
235 H6 Poppin's Court EC4A
232 B7 Porchester Gardens W2
232 C8 Porchester Gate W2
233 G6 Porchester Place W2
232 B5 Porchester Road W2
232 B6 Porchester Square W2
232 C7 Porchester Terrace W2
232 C6 Porchester Terrace North W2
239 L3 Porlock Street SE1
233 H4 Porter Street NW1
232 D5 Porteus Road W2
233 L4 Portland Place W1B
233 L5 Portland Place W1B
240 E5 Portland Square E1W
239 L7 Portland Street SE17
233 J6 Portman Close W1H
233 J6 Portman Mews South W1H
233 J6 Portman Square W1H
233 J6 Portman Street W1H
234 F4 Portpool Lane EC1N
233 G6 Portsea Place W2
234 E6 Portsmouth Street WC2A
240 B3 Portsoken Street E1
234 E6 Portugal Street WC2A
239 L4 Potier Street SE1
240 B6 Potters Fields SE1
240 E7 Pottery Street SE16
235 K6 Poultry EC2V
234 D4 Powis Place WC1N
232 E6 Praed Mews W2
232 E6 Praed Street W2
238 E5 Pratt Walk SE1
241 M4 Premier Place E14
240 C3 Prescot Street E1
239 M5 Preston Close SE1
239 H1 Price's Street SE1
234 F2 Prideaux Place WC1X
240 A1 Primrose Street EC2A
232 F1 Prince Albert Road NW8
236 D3 Prince Consort Road SW7
240 C1 Princelet Street E1
236 F3 Prince of Wales Gate SW7
234 A8 Princes Arcade SW1Y
236 E3 Prince's Gardens SW7
236 E4 Prince's Gate Mews SW7
241 H5 Princes Riverside Road SE16
232 A7 Prince's Square W2
232 A1 Princess Road NW6
239 H4 Princess Street SE1
233 L6 Princes Street W1B
235 L6 Prince's Street EC2R
234 E5 Princeton Street WC1R
239 L4 Prioress Street SE1
234 E1 Priory Green Estate N1
236 D7 Priory Walk SW10
234 E5 Proctor Street WC1V
241 G5 Prospect Place E1W
240 E7 Prospect Street SE16
233 J7 Provident Court W1K
235 L1 Provost Street N1
240 F5 Prusom Street E1W
235 M7 Pudding Lane EC3R
240 D3 Pumphouse Mews E1
240 A7 Purbrook Street SE1
235 M1 Purcell Street N1
234 B1 Purchese Street NW1

Q

241 J7 Quebec Way SE16
238 B3 Queen Anne's Gate SW1H
233 K5 Queen Ann Street W1G
240 B6 Queen Elizabeth Street SE1
237 J2 Queen Mother Gate W2
232 C7 Queensborough Terrace W2
236 E5 Queensbury Place SW7
232 C7 Queen's Gardens W2
236 D3 Queen's Gate SW7
236 D4 Queen's Gate SW7
236 D5 Queen's Gate Gardens SW7
236 D4 Queen's Gate Mews SW7
236 D4 Queen's Gate Place SW7
236 D4 Queen's Gate Place Mews SW7
236 C4 Queen's Gate Terrace SW7
239 L2 Queen's Head Yard SE1
232 B7 Queen's Mews W2
234 D4 Queen Square WC1N
239 K7 Queen's Row SE17
235 K7 Queen Street EC4N
237 L1 Queen Street W1J
235 K7 Queen Street Place EC4R
240 A5 Queen's Walk SE1
237 M2 Queen's Walk SW1A
232 B6 Queensway W2
232 B8 Queensway ⊖ W2
235 J7 Queen Victoria Street EC4V
235 H1 Quick Street N1

R

241 K2 Raby Street E14
240 B8 Radcliffe Road SE1
239 G7 Radcot Street SE11
232 E6 Radnor Mews W2
232 F6 Radnor Place W2
235 K3 Radnor Street EC1V
237 G7 Radnor Walk SW3
239 L1 Railway Approach SE1
241 G6 Railway Avenue SE16
234 D1 Railway Street N1
240 F5 Raine Street E1W
237 H7 Ralston Street SW3
233 M6 Ramillies Place W1F
233 M6 Ramillies Street W1F
240 E2 Rampart Street E1
238 B6 Rampayne Street SW1V
238 D6 Randall Road SE11
238 E6 Randall Row SE11
232 B1 Randolph Avenue W9
232 C3 Randolph Crescent W9
232 B1 Randolph Gardens NW6
232 D4 Randolph Mews W9
232 C4 Randolph Road W9
237 K6 Ranelagh Grove SW1W
238 A7 Ranelagh Road SW1V
240 B3 Rangoon Street * EC3N
232 F4 Ranston Street NW8
237 G3 Raphael Street SW7
241 J3 Ratcliffe Cross Street E1W
241 J3 Ratcliffe Lane E14
234 B5 Rathbone Place W1T
234 A5 Rathbone Street W1T
240 F1 Raven Row E1
239 G7 Ravensdon Street SE11
235 M3 Ravey Street EC2A
237 G5 Rawlings Street SW3
235 H2 Rawstone Street EC1V
235 G4 Ray Street EC1R
240 E5 Reardon Place E1W
240 E5 Reardon Street E1W
241 H1 Rectory Square E1
232 B6 Redan Place W2
237 G7 Redburn Street SW3
241 G4 Redcastle Close E1W
236 B7 Redcliffe Gardens SW10
236 C7 Redcliffe Mews SW10
236 C8 Redcliffe Place SW10
236 D7 Redcliffe Road SW10
236 B7 Redcliffe Square SW10
236 B8 Redcliffe Street SW10
239 K2 Redcross Way SE1
237 G7 Redesdale Street SW3
236 A5 Redfield Lane SW5
233 L1 Redhill Street NW1
239 K8 Red Lion Row SE5
234 E5 Red Lion Square WC1R
234 E5 Red Lion Street WC2B
241 G1 Redman's Road E1
233 J7 Red Place W1K
241 J8 Redriff Road SE16
239 G6 Reedworth Street SE11
233 J8 Reeves Mews W1K
240 D1 Regal Close E1
235 M1 Regan Way N1
238 B5 Regency Street SW1P
234 A7 Regent Place W1B
233 L4 Regent's Park ⊖ W1B
233 L2 Regent's Park Estate NW1
234 D2 Regent Square WC1H
234 B8 Regent Street SW1Y
233 M7 Regent Street W1S
237 G4 Relton Mews SW7
235 H1 Remington Street N1
234 E6 Remnant Street WC2A
241 G7 Renforth Street SE16
239 H5 Renfrew Road SE11
239 H1 Rennie Street SE1
239 M4 Rephidim Street SE1
241 K2 Repton Street E14
241 K7 Reveley Square SE16
233 J8 Rex Place W1K
241 L2 Rhodeswell Road E14
241 M3 Rich Street E14
236 A8 Rickett Street SW6
234 B4 Ridgemount Street WC1E
234 B4 Ridgemount Gardens WC1E
233 M5 Riding House Street W1W
240 B7 Riley Road SE1
239 J2 Risborough Street SE1
241 G7 Risdon Street SE16
234 F1 Rissinghill Street N1
234 F2 River Street EC1R
235 M3 Rivington Street EC2A
233 J6 Robert Adam Street W1U
241 J7 Roberts Close SE16
233 L2 Robert Street NW1
238 A5 Rochester Row SW1P
238 B5 Rochester Street SW1P
239 J4 Rockingham Street SE1
235 H1 Rocliffe Street N1
240 D5 Roding Mews E1W
233 H5 Rodmarton Street W1U
239 K5 Rodney Place SE17
239 K5 Rodney Road SE17
234 E1 Rodney Street N1
234 E4 Roger Street WC1N
236 D6 Roland Gardens SW7
239 L7 Roland Way SE17
240 E2 Romford Street E1
234 B7 Romilly Street W1D
238 C5 Romney Street SW1P
235 M7 Rood Lane EC3M
241 K7 Ropemaker Road SE16
235 L4 Ropemaker Street EC2Y
240 B7 Roper Lane SE1
241 K8 Rope Street SE16
240 E2 Rope Walk Gardens E1
236 D6 Rosary Gardens SW7
235 K3 Roscoe Street EC1Y
235 K8 Rose Alley SE1
234 F3 Rosebery Avenue EC1R
237 G6 Rosemoor Street SW3
234 C7 Rose Street WC2E
233 G3 Rossmore Road NW1
239 H3 Rotary Street SE1
241 G6 Rotherhithe ⊖ SE16
241 G6 Rotherhithe Street SE16
241 J4 Rotherhithe Street SE16
241 H5 Rotherhithe Tunnel SE16
239 M4 Rothsay Street SE1
236 F2 Rotten Row W2
240 C8 Rouel Road SE16
239 G2 Roupell Street SE1
237 H6 Royal Avenue SW3
237 H7 Royal Hospital Road SW3
240 C4 Royal Mint Street E1
232 B5 Royal Oak ⊖ W2
240 A7 Royal Oak Yard SE1
239 H8 Royal Road SE17
238 E3 Royal Street SE1
232 A1 Rudolph Road NW6
234 E4 Rugby Street WC1N
240 F4 Rum Close E1W
240 F7 Rupack Street SE16
234 B7 Rupert Street W1D
239 H2 Rushworth Street SE1
238 A2 Russell Court SW1A
234 C4 Russell Square WC1B
234 D4 Russell Square ⊖ WC1N
234 D7 Russell Street WC2B
241 K6 Russia Dock Road SE16
238 B5 Rutherford Street SW1P
237 G3 Rutland Gardens SW7
236 F3 Rutland Gate SW7
236 F4 Rutland Mews SW7
236 F4 Rutland Street SW7
238 A1 Ryder Street SW1Y

S

234 A8 Sackville Street W1S
235 G4 Saffron Hill EC1N
235 G4 Saffron Street EC1N
238 F5 Sail Street SE11
239 G8 St Agnes Place SE11
236 B4 St Alban's Grove W8
234 B8 St Alban's Street SW1Y
235 K5 St Alphage Garden EC2Y
235 H7 St Andrews Hill EC4V
233 L3 St Andrew's Place NW1
235 G5 St Andrew Street EC4A
234 B6 St Anne's Court W1F
238 C4 St Ann's Street SW1P
233 K7 St Anselm's Place W1K
237 K6 St Barnabas Street SW1W
240 B2 St Botolph Street EC3N
235 G6 St Bride Street EC4A
234 D2 St Chad's Street WC1H
240 B3 St Clare Street EC3N
234 E6 St Clements Lane WC2A
235 G4 St Cross Street EC1N
235 M8 St Dunstan's Hill EC3R
235 M7 St Dunstan's Lane EC3R
241 J7 St Elmos Road SE16
238 B3 St Ermin's Hill SW1H
239 H3 St George's Circus SE1
237 M6 St George's Drive SW1V
240 D3 St George's Estate E1
235 M7 St George's Lane * EC3R
239 G4 St George's Road SE1
238 B7 St George's Square SW1V
233 L7 St George Street W1S
234 C6 St Giles High Street WC2H
235 M6 St Helen's Place EC3A
234 B8 St James Market * SW1Y
238 B3 St James's Park ⊖ SW1H
237 M2 St James's Place SW1A
240 D8 St James's Road SE16
238 A1 St James's Square SW1Y
237 M1 St James's Street SW1A
235 G3 St James Way EC1R
235 H4 St John's Lane EC1M
235 H4 St John's Place EC1M
235 H4 St John's Square EC1V
235 H2 St John Street EC1V
232 F1 St John's Wood High Street NW8
232 E3 St John's Wood Road NW8
240 C5 St Katharine's Way E1W
237 H7 St Leonard's Terrace SW3
237 G8 St Loo Avenue SW3
235 K3 St Luke's Close EC1V
236 F6 St Luke's Street SW3
240 C2 St Manningtree E1
240 C3 St Mark Street E1
234 C7 St Martin's Lane WC2N
235 J6 St Martin's le Grand EC1A
235 M8 St Mary at Hill EC3R
240 A3 St Mary Axe EC3A
240 F7 St Mary Church Street SE16
239 G5 St Mary's Grove SE11
232 D4 St Mary's Terrace W2
239 G5 St Mary's Way SE11
238 B4 St Matthew Street SW1P
232 F6 St Michael's Street W2
240 F7 St Olav's Square SE16
238 E7 St Oswald's Place SE11
234 C1 St Pancras International ⇌ N1C
235 J6 St Paul's ⊖ EC1A
241 J5 St Paul's Avenue SE16
235 J6 St Paul's Churchyard EC4M
241 L1 St Paul's Way E3
232 B7 St Petersburgh Mews W2
232 B7 St Petersburgh Place W2
240 C6 St Saviours Wharf SE1
232 A5 St Stephen's Gardens W2
235 L7 St Swithin's Lane EC4N
239 L2 St Thomas Street SE1
233 J5 St Vincent Street W1U
238 D6 Salamanca Street SE1
232 B7 Salem Road W2
232 F5 Sale Place W2
235 G6 Salisbury Court EC4Y
233 H4 Salisbury Place W1H
232 F4 Salisbury Street NW8
241 J2 Salmon Lane E14
241 J5 Salter Road SE16
241 M4 Salter Street E14
232 F4 Samford Street NW8
240 D5 Sampson Street E1W
238 F6 Sancroft Street SE11
239 L6 Sandford Row SE17
234 E5 Sandland Street WC1R
241 L6 Sandpiper Close SE16
234 C2 Sandwich Street WC1H
240 B1 Sandy's Row E1
235 G3 Sans Walk EC1R
234 E6 Sardinia Street WC2A
240 B3 Savage Gardens EC3N
233 M7 Savile Row W1S
234 E8 Savoy Hill WC2R
234 D8 Savoy Place WC2R
234 E7 Savoy Street WC2E
239 J2 Sawyer Street SE1
234 A5 Scala Street W1T
240 E5 Scandrett Street E1W
240 C3 Scarborough Street E1
236 A4 Scarsdale Villas W8
241 H6 Schooner Close * SE16
239 H2 Scoresby Street SE1
237 H3 Scotch House Junction SW1X
238 C1 Scotland Place SW1A
232 E2 Scott Ellis Grove NW8
240 D7 Scott Lidgett Crescent SE16
235 M3 Scrutton Street EC2A
234 D2 Seaford Street WC1H
236 A8 Seagrave Road SW6
239 L5 Searles Road SE1
235 H2 Sebastian Street EC1V
238 F2 Secker Street SE1
239 M6 Sedan Way SE17
237 J5 Sedding Street SW1X
234 E3 Seddon Street WC1X
240 A4 Seething Lane EC3N
235 H3 Sekforde Street EC1R
241 M1 Selsey Street E14
236 E6 Selwood Place SW7
237 K6 Semley Place SW1W
232 B4 Senior Street W2
241 H2 Senrab Street E1
234 F6 Serle Street WC2A
236 E1 Serpentine Bridge W2
236 F2 Serpentine Road W2
241 G7 Seth Street SE16
240 D2 Settles Street E1
234 C6 Seven Dials WC2H
237 H3 Seville Street SW1X
232 A3 Sevington Street W9
235 J3 Seward Street EC1V
233 J6 Seymour Mews W1H
233 G5 Seymour Place W1H
233 H6 Seymour Street W1H
233 G7 Seymour Street W2
236 C7 Seymour Walk SW10
240 B6 Shad Thames SE1
240 C6 Shad Thames SE1
240 F3 Shadwell ⊖ ⊖ E1
240 F3 Shadwell Gardens E1
234 B7 Shaftesbury Avenue W1D
234 C6 Shaftesbury Avenue WC2H
235 K1 Shaftesbury Street N1
240 A6 Shand Street SE1
239 H7 Sharsted Street SE17
241 K2 Shaw Crescent E14
237 G7 Shawfield Street SW3
236 A2 Sheffield Terrace W8
232 D5 Sheldon Square W2
241 M1 Shelmerdine Close E3
234 D6 Shelton Street WC2H
235 K1 Shepherdess Walk N1
237 K1 Shepherd Street W1J
234 B6 Sheraton Street W1F
235 L7 Sherborne Lane EC4N
239 M2 Ship and Mermaid Row SE1
241 K7 Shipwright Road SE16
232 A3 Shirland Road W9
235 G5 Shoe Lane EC4A
240 B4 Shorter Street EC3N
234 C6 Shorts Gardens WC2H
239 G2 Short Street SE1
241 K4 Shoulder of Mutton Alley E14
233 G5 Shouldham Street W1H
232 F4 Shroton Street NW1
233 H4 Siddons Lane W1H
234 D3 Sidmouth Street WC1N
240 F2 Sidney Square E1
240 F1 Sidney Street E1
239 H3 Silex Street SE1
235 K4 Silk Street EC2Y
241 K5 Silver Walk SE16
239 K3 Silvester Street SE1
235 L3 Singer Street EC2A
237 J6 Skinner Place * SW1W
235 K7 Skinners Lane EC4V
235 G3 Skinner Street EC1R
240 F8 Slippers Place SE16
237 G6 Sloane Avenue SW3
237 J6 Sloane Court SW3
237 J6 Sloane Court East SW3
237 J6 Sloane Gardens SW1W
237 J5 Sloane Square SW1W
237 J6 Sloane Square ⊖ SW1W
237 H3 Sloane Street SW1X
237 J5 Sloane Terrace SW1X
240 E5 Smeaton Street E1W
235 H5 Smithfield Street EC1A
238 C4 Smith Square SW1P
237 G7 Smith Street SW3
237 G7 Smith Terrace SW3
241 G1 Smithy Street E1
235 M4 Snowden Street EC2A
235 H5 Snow Hill EC1A
239 L2 Snowsfields SE1
234 B6 Soho Square W1D
234 B6 Soho Street W1D
241 K7 Somerford Way SE16
232 F6 Somers Crescent W2
234 A1 Somerstown Estate NW1
239 L7 Sondes Street SE17
238 A3 South & West Africa Gate SW1A
239 L3 Southall Place SE1
234 F5 Southampton Buildings WC2A
234 D5 Southampton Place WC1A
234 D4 Southampton Row WC1B
234 D7 Southampton Street WC2E
233 K8 South Audley Street W1K
237 H3 South Carriage Drive SW1X
236 F3 South Carriage Drive SW7
237 J5 South Eaton Place SW1W
234 E1 Southern Street N1
236 E4 South Kensington ⊖ SW7
236 E5 South Kensington ⊖ SW7
238 D8 South Lambeth Road SW8
233 K7 South Molton Lane W1K
233 K7 South Molton Street W1K
236 E7 South Parade SW3
235 L5 South Place EC2M
241 L8 South Sea Street SE16
234 F5 South Square WC1R
237 J1 South Street W1K
240 C3 South Tenter Street E1
236 F5 South Terrace SW7
239 H2 Southwark ⊖ SE1
235 K8 Southwark Bridge SE1
239 J3 Southwark Bridge Road SE1
240 E8 Southwark Park Road SE16
239 H1 Southwark Street SE1
236 C5 Southwell Gardens SW7
232 E6 South Wharf Road W2
232 F6 Southwick Mews W2
232 F6 Southwick Place W2
232 F6 Southwick Street W2
240 F4 Sovereign Close E1W
241 J4 Sovereign Crescent SE16
233 J5 Spanish Place W1U
240 C8 Spa Road SE16
236 A6 Spear Mews SW5
240 C1 Spelman Street E1
241 K7 Spence Close SE16
235 H2 Spencer Street EC1V
238 A4 Spenser Street SW1E
241 J4 Spert Street E14
240 A1 Spital Square E1
238 C1 Spring Gardens SW1A
232 E6 Spring Street W2
239 L4 Spurgeon Street SE1
238 F3 Spur Road SE1
238 F7 Stables Way SE11
238 A2 Stable Yard Road SW1A
234 C6 Stacey Street WC2H
237 M3 Stafford Place SW1E
232 A2 Stafford Road NW6
233 M8 Stafford Street W1S
236 A3 Stafford Terrace W8
239 L2 Stainer Street SE1
241 M2 Stainsby Road E14
240 F8 Stalham Street SE16
239 G1 Stamford Street SE1
239 M6 Stanford Place SE1
236 B4 Stanford Road W8
241 H6 Stanhope Close * SE16
236 D5 Stanhope Gardens SW7
237 K1 Stanhope Gate W1K
236 D5 Stanhope Mews SW7
236 D5 Stanhope Mews East SW7
236 D5 Stanhope Mews West SW7
233 G7 Stanhope Place W2
233 G7 Stanhope Place Gate W2
237 K1 Stanhope Row W1J
233 M1 Stanhope Street NW1
232 E7 Stanhope Terrace W2
239 G7 Stannary Street SE11
241 J5 Staples Close SE16
239 L3 Staple Street SE1
234 A2 Starcross Street NW1
232 F6 Star Street W2
241 J5 Stave Yard Road SE16
239 K6 Stead Street SE17
239 J5 Steedman Street SE17
241 G3 Steel's Lane E1
241 K7 Steeres Way SE16
234 A3 Stephenson Way NW1
234 B5 Stephen Street W1T
241 H1 Stepney Green E1
241 J1 Stepney High Street E1
240 E1 Stepney Way E1
237 G3 Sterling Street SW7
240 E5 Stevedore Street E1W
240 A7 Stevens Street SE1
240 B1 Steward Street * E1
236 F6 Stewart's Grove SW3
235 J7 Stew Lane EC4V
238 A5 Stillington Street SW1P
240 D5 Stockholm Way E1W
241 M3 Stocks Place E14
234 F5 Stone Buildings WC2A
235 G6 Stonecutter Street EC4A
240 B2 Stoney Lane E1
239 K1 Stoney Street SE1
239 J7 Stopford Road SE17

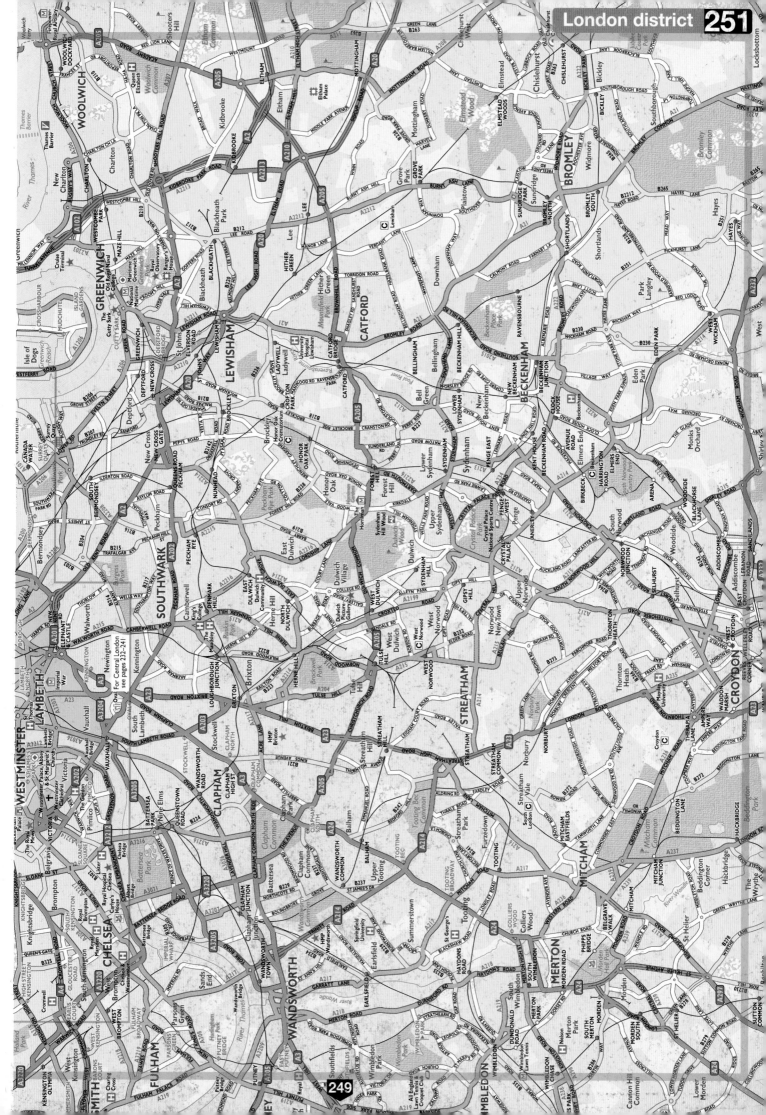

For Central London see pages 232–241

Newington For Central London see pages 232–241

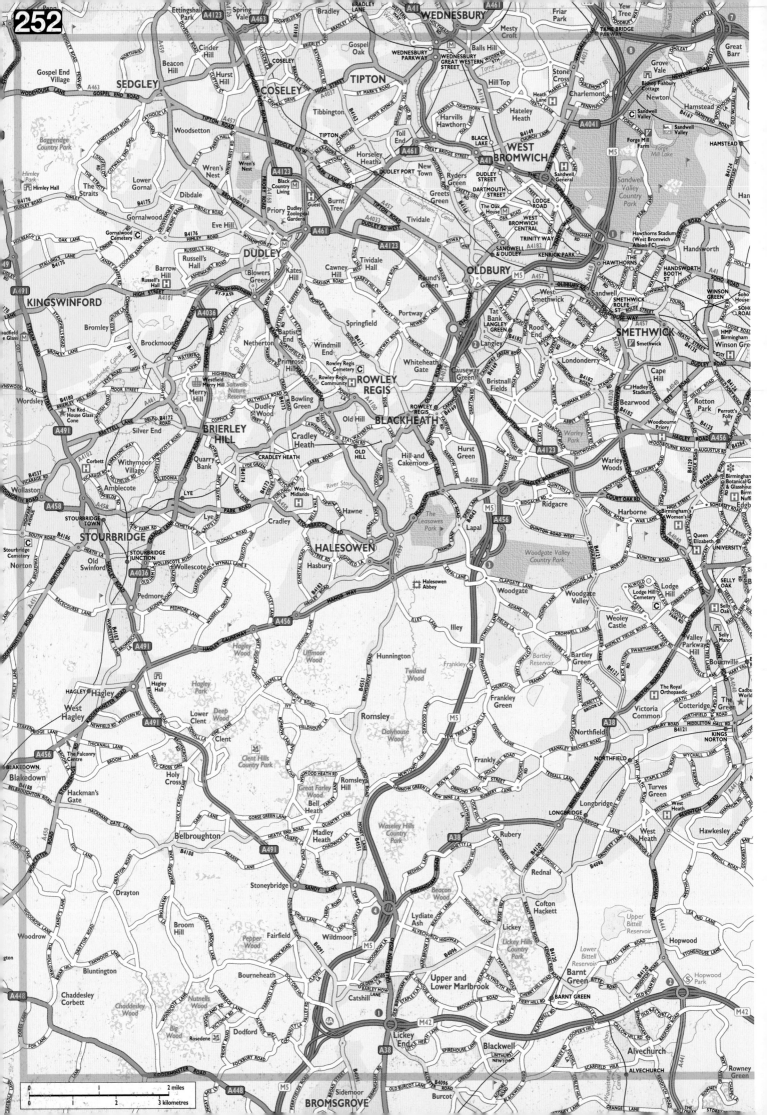

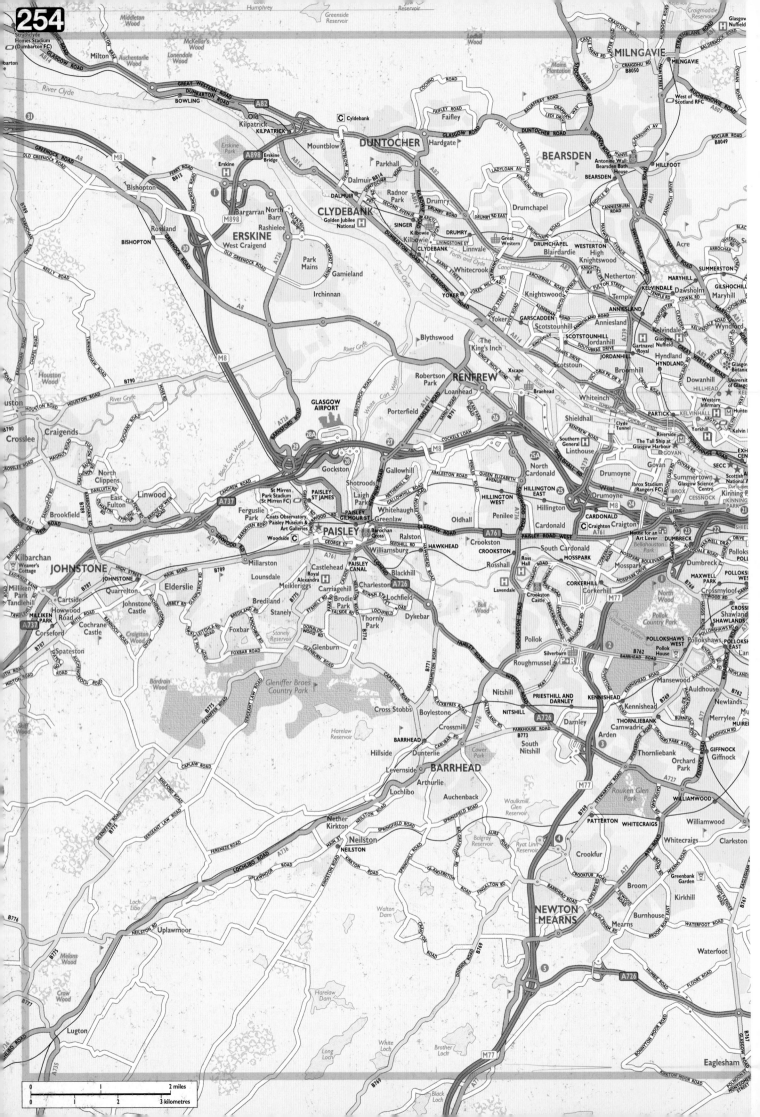

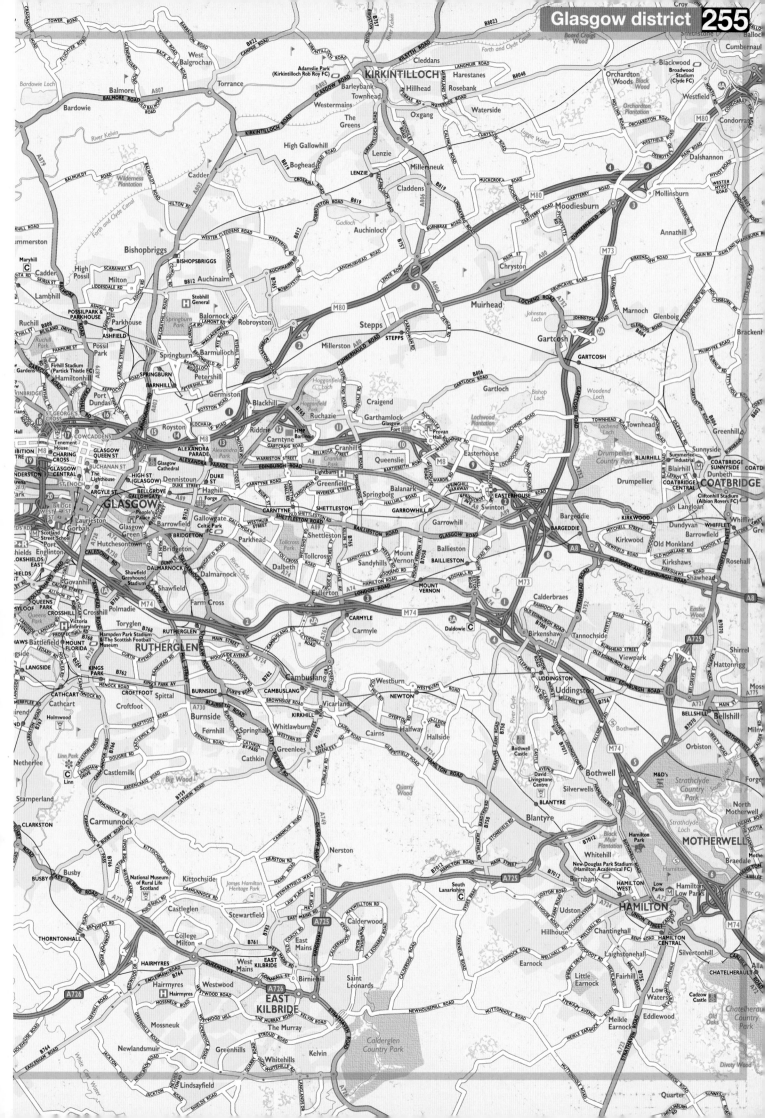

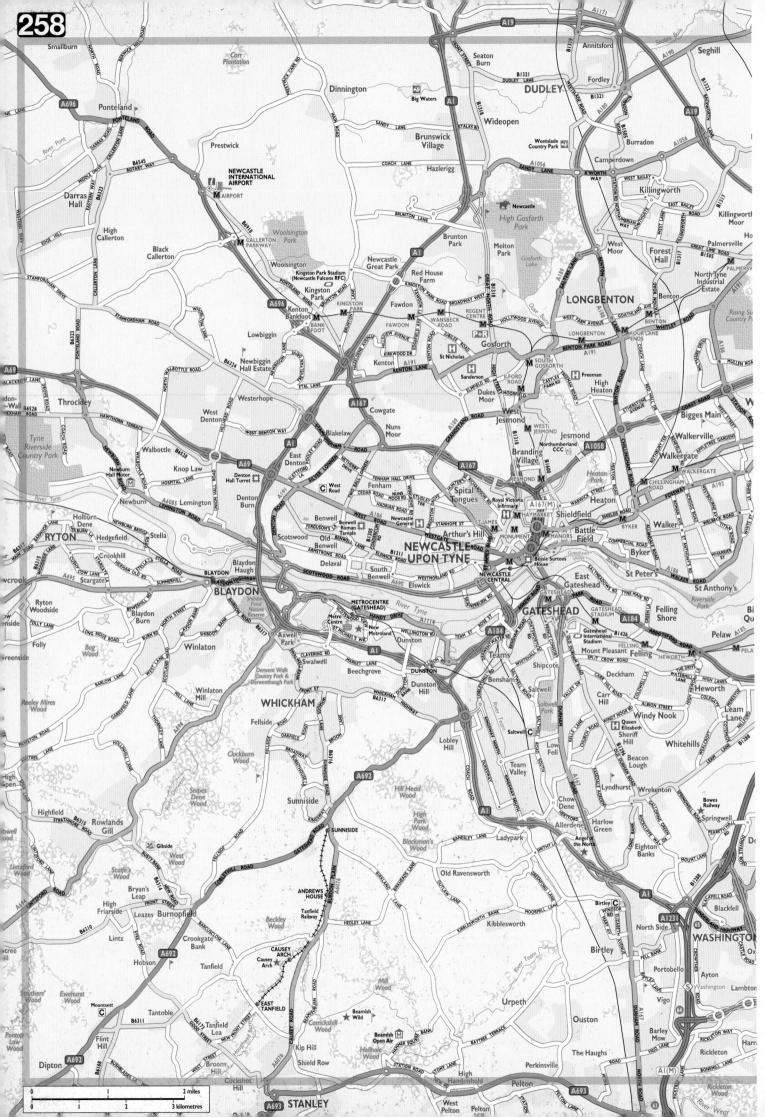

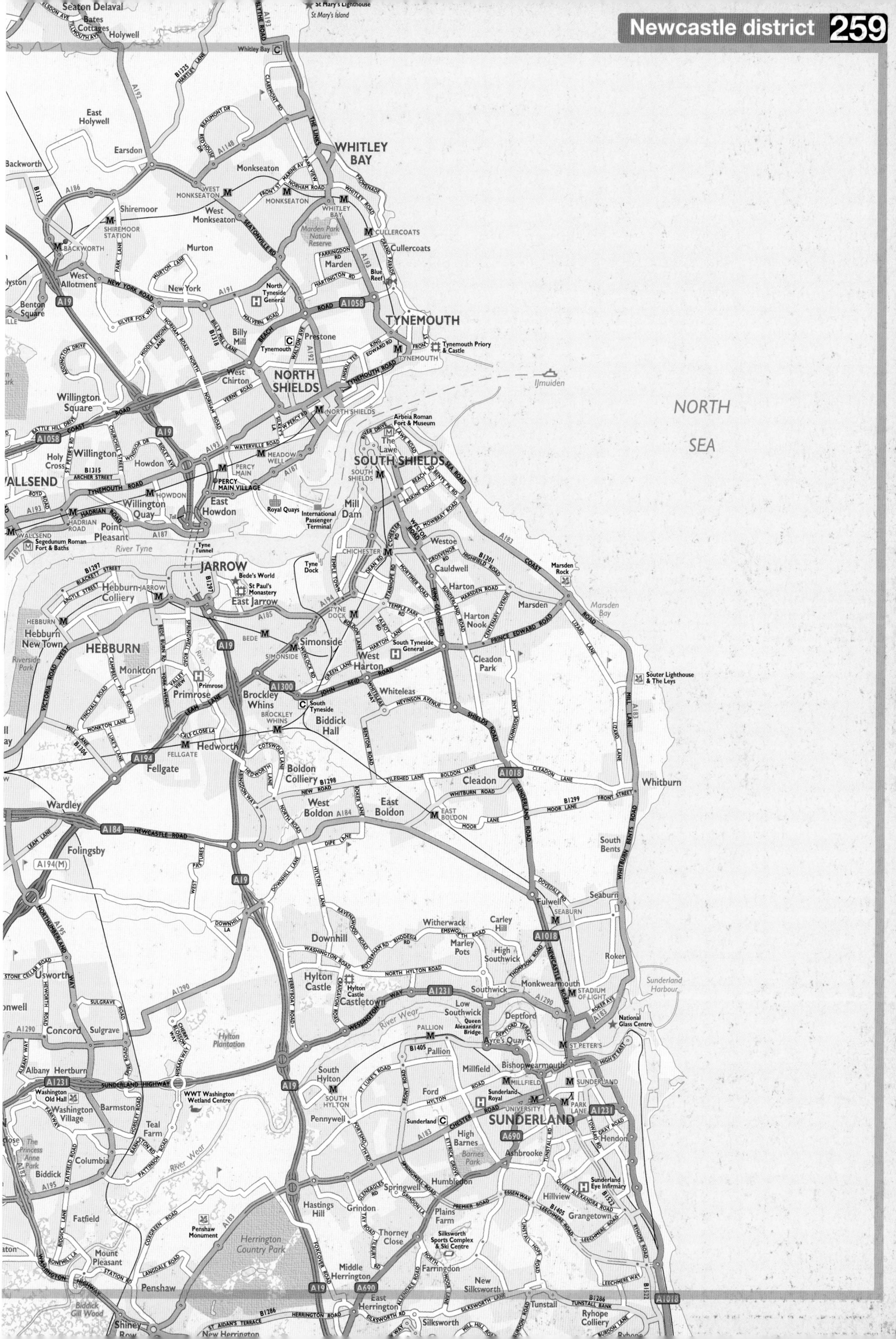

NORTH

SEA

Towns and places

St Mary's Lighthouse
St Mary's Island
Seaton Delaval
Bates Cottages
Holywell
East Holywell
Earsdon
Backworth
West Allotment
Shiremoor
SHIREMOOR STATION
BACKWORTH
Benton Square
Murton
New York
WHITLEY BAY
West Monkseaton
Monkseaton
MONKSEATON
WHITLEY BAY
Marden Park Nature Reserve
Marden
CULLERCOATS
Cullercoats
Blue Reef
North Tyneside General
Billy Mill
Prestone
TYNEMOUTH
Tynemouth
Tynemouth Priory & Castle
TYNEMOUTH
West Chirton
NORTH SHIELDS
NORTH SHIELDS
IJmuiden
Willington Square
Howdon
Waterville Road
Meadow Well
Arbeia Roman Fort & Museum
The Lawe
SOUTH SHIELDS
SOUTH SHIELDS
Holy Cross
Willington
Percy Main
PERCY MAIN VILLAGE
Royal Quays
International Passenger Terminal
Mill Dam
Westoe
WALLSEND
Howdon
Willington Quay
East Howdon
CHICHESTER
Cauldwell
Harton
Harton Nook
Marsden Rock
Point Pleasant
Tyne Tunnel
Segedunum Roman Fort & Baths
River Tyne
Tyne Dock
Marsden
Marsden Bay
JARROW
Bede's World
St Paul's Monastery
East Jarrow
Tyne Dock
South Tyneside General
Cleadon Park
Hebburn Colliery
BEDE
Simonside
SIMONSIDE
West Harton
Souter Lighthouse & The Leys
HEBBURN
Hebburn New Town
Monkton
Primrose
Brockley Whins
Whiteleas
Riverside Park
Primrose
Brockley Whins
Biddick Hall
Cleadon
Hedworth
FELLGATE
Boldon Colliery
Whitburn
Fellgate
Cleadon
Wardley
West Boldon
East Boldon
EAST BOLDON
South Bents
Folingsby
Downhill
Seaburn
Witherwack
Carley Hill
SEABURN
Roker
Usworth
Downhill
Marley Pots
High Southwick
Hylton Castle
Castletown
Monkwearmouth
STADIUM OF LIGHT
Sunderland Harbour
Concord
Sulgrave
Hylton Plantation
River Wear
Southwick
National Glass Centre
Low Southwick
Queen Alexandra Bridge
Deptford
Deptford Terrace
ST PETER'S
Albany
Hertburn
SUNDERLAND HIGHWAY
WWT Washington Wetland Centre
PALLION
Ayre's Quay
Washington Old Hall
Washington Village
South Hylton
SOUTH HYLTON
Pallion
Millfield
MILLFIELD
Bishopwearmouth
SUNDERLAND
Teal Farm
Ford
Sunderland Royal
UNIVERSITY
PARK LANE
Barmston
Pennywell
Sunderland
High Barnes
SUNDERLAND
Ashbrooke
Hendon
Columbia
Barnes Park
Biddick
Springwell
Humbledon
Sunderland Eye Infirmary
Hillview
Fatfield
Hastings Hill
Grindon
Plains Farm
Essen Way
Grangetown
Mount Pleasant
Penshaw Monument
Herrington Country Park
Thorney Close
Silksworth Sports Complex & Ski Centre
Middle Herrington
New Silksworth
Farringdon
Penshaw
Biddick Gill Wood
Shiney Row
New Herrington
East Herrington
Silksworth
Tunstall
Ryhope Colliery

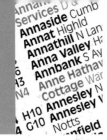

Index to place names

This index lists places appearing in the main-map section of the atlas in alphabetical order. The reference before each name gives the atlas page number and grid reference of the square in which the place appears. The map shows counties, unitary authorities and administrative areas, together with a list of the abbreviated name forms used in the index.

The top 100 places of tourist interest are indexed in **red** (or **green** if a World Heritage site), motorway service areas in **blue** and airports in blue *italic*.

Scotland

Abers	**Aberdeenshire**
Ag & B	**Argyll and Bute**
Angus	**Angus**
Border	**Scottish Borders**
C Aber	**City of Aberdeen**
C Dund	**City of Dundee**
C Edin	**City of Edinburgh**
C Glas	**City of Glasgow**
Clacks	**Clackmannanshire (1)**
D & G	**Dumfries & Galloway**
E Ayrs	**East Ayrshire**
E Duns	**East Dunbartonshire (2)**
E Loth	**East Lothian**
E Rens	**East Renfrewshire (3)**
Falk	**Falkirk**
Fife	**Fife**
Highld	**Highland**
Inver	**Inverclyde (4)**
Mdloth	**Midlothian (5)**
Moray	**Moray**
N Ayrs	**North Ayrshire**
N Lans	**North Lanarkshire (6)**
Ork	**Orkney Islands**
P & K	**Perth & Kinross**
Rens	**Renfrewshire (7)**
S Ayrs	**South Ayrshire**
Shet	**Shetland Islands**
S Lans	**South Lanarkshire**
Stirlg	**Stirling**
W Duns	**West Dunbartonshire (8)**
W Isls	**Western Isles (Na h-Eileanan an Iar)**
W Loth	**West Lothian**

Wales

Blae G	**Blaenau Gwent (9)**
Brdgnd	**Bridgend (10)**
Caerph	**Caerphilly (11)**
Cardif	**Cardiff**
Carmth	**Carmarthenshire**
Cerdgn	**Ceredigion**
Conwy	**Conwy**
Denbgs	**Denbighshire**
Flints	**Flintshire**
Gwynd	**Gwynedd**
IoA	**Isle of Anglesey**
Mons	**Monmouthshire**
Myr Td	**Merthyr Tydfil (12)**
Neath	**Neath Port Talbot (13)**
Newpt	**Newport (14)**
Pembks	**Pembrokeshire**
Powys	**Powys**
Rhondd	**Rhondda Cynon Taff (15)**
Swans	**Swansea**
Torfn	**Torfaen (16)**
V Glam	**Vale of Glamorgan (17)**
Wrexhm	**Wrexham**

Channel Islands & Isle of Man

Guern	**Guernsey**
Jersey	**Jersey**
IoM	**Isle of Man**

England

BaNES	**Bath & N E Somerset (18)**
Barns	**Barnsley (19)**
Bed	**Bedford**
Birm	**Birmingham**
Bl w D	**Blackburn with Darwen (20)**
Bmouth	**Bournemouth**
Bolton	**Bolton (21)**
Bpool	**Blackpool**
Br & H	**Brighton & Hove (22)**
Br For	**Bracknell Forest (23)**
Bristl	**City of Bristol**
Bucks	**Buckinghamshire**
Bury	**Bury (24)**
C Beds	**Central Bedfordshire**
C Brad	**City of Bradford**
C Derb	**City of Derby**
C KuH	**City of Kingston upon Hull**
C Leic	**City of Leicester**
C Nott	**City of Nottingham**
C Pete	**City of Peterborough**
C Plym	**City of Plymouth**
C Port	**City of Portsmouth**
C Soton	**City of Southampton**
C Stke	**City of Stoke-on-Trent**
C York	**City of York**
Calder	**Calderdale (25)**
Cambs	**Cambridgeshire**
Ches E	**Cheshire East**
Ches W	**Cheshire West and Chester**
Cnwll	**Cornwall**
Covtry	**Coventry**
Cumb	**Cumbria**
Darltn	**Darlington (26)**
Derbys	**Derbyshire**
Devon	**Devon**
Donc	**Doncaster (27)**
Dorset	**Dorset**
Dudley	**Dudley (28)**
Dur	**Durham**
E R Yk	**East Riding of Yorkshire**
E Susx	**East Sussex**
Essex	**Essex**
Gatesd	**Gateshead (29)**
Gloucs	**Gloucestershire**
Gt Lon	**Greater London**
Halton	**Halton (30)**
Hants	**Hampshire**
Hartpl	**Hartlepool (31)**
Herefs	**Herefordshire**
Herts	**Hertfordshire**
IoS	**Isles of Scilly**
IoW	**Isle of Wight**
Kent	**Kent**
Kirk	**Kirklees (32)**
Knows	**Knowsley (33)**
Lancs	**Lancashire**
Leeds	**Leeds**
Leics	**Leicestershire**
Lincs	**Lincolnshire**
Lpool	**Liverpool**
Luton	**Luton**
M Keyn	**Milton Keynes**
Manch	**Manchester**
Medway	**Medway**
Middsb	**Middlesbrough**
NE Lin	**North East Lincolnshire**
N Linc	**North Lincolnshire**
N Som	**North Somerset (34)**
N Tyne	**North Tyneside (35)**
N u Ty	**Newcastle upon Tyne**
N York	**North Yorkshire**
Nhants	**Northamptonshire**
Norfk	**Norfolk**
Notts	**Nottinghamshire**
Nthumb	**Northumberland**
Oldham	**Oldham (36)**
Oxon	**Oxfordshire**
Poole	**Poole**
R & Cl	**Redcar & Cleveland**
Readg	**Reading**
Rochdl	**Rochdale (37)**
Rothm	**Rotherham (38)**
Rutlnd	**Rutland**
S Glos	**South Gloucestershire (39)**
S on T	**Stockton-on-Tees (40)**
S Tyne	**South Tyneside (41)**
Salfd	**Salford (42)**
Sandw	**Sandwell (43)**
Sefton	**Sefton (44)**
Sheff	**Sheffield**
Shrops	**Shropshire**
Slough	**Slough (45)**
Solhll	**Solihull (46)**
Somset	**Somerset**
St Hel	**St Helens (47)**
Staffs	**Staffordshire**
Sthend	**Southend-on-Sea**
Stockp	**Stockport (48)**
Suffk	**Suffolk**
Sundld	**Sunderland**
Surrey	**Surrey**
Swindn	**Swindon**
Tamesd	**Tameside (49)**
Thurr	**Thurrock (50)**
Torbay	**Torbay**
Traffd	**Trafford (51)**
W & M	**Windsor and Maidenhead (52)**
W Berk	**West Berkshire**
W Susx	**West Sussex**
Wakefd	**Wakefield (53)**
Warrtn	**Warrington (54)**
Warwks	**Warwickshire**
Wigan	**Wigan (55)**
Wilts	**Wiltshire**
Wirral	**Wirral (56)**
Wokham	**Wokingham (57)**
Wolves	**Wolverhampton (58)**
Worcs	**Worcestershire**
Wrekin	**Telford & Wrekin (59)**
Wsall	**Walsall (60)**

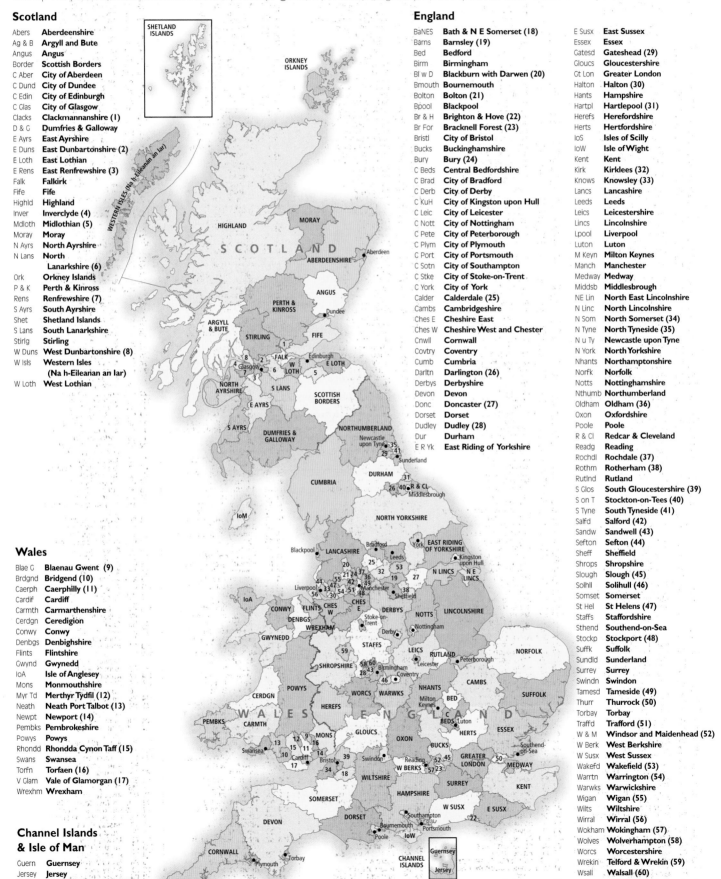

Abbas Combe - Anthonys 261

A

20 D10 **Abbas Combe** Somset
57 P11 **Abberley** Worcs
57 N11 **Abberley Common** Worcs
52 H8 **Abberton** Essex
47 J4 **Abberton** Worcs
119 M8 **Abberwick** Nthumb
51 N8 **Abbess Roding** Essex
10 C2 **Abbey** Devon
55 P10 **Abbey-Cwm-Hir** Powys
84 D4 **Abbeydale** Sheff
45 M8 **Abbey Dore** Herefs
70 H3 **Abbey Green** Staffs
19 J11 **Abbey Hill** Somset
129 K7 **Abbey St Bathans** Border
95 M10 **Abbeystead** Lancs
110 C10 **Abbey Town** Cumb
89 J6 **Abbey Village** Lancs
37 L5 **Abbey Wood** Gt Lon
118 B8 **Abbotrule** Border
16 F9 **Abbots Bickington** Devon
71 K10 **Abbots Bromley** Staffs
11 M7 **Abbotsbury** Dorset
83 M6 **Abbot's Chair** Derbys
134 E5 **Abbots Deuglie** P & K
16 G6 **Abbotsham** Devon
7 M5 **Abbotskerswell** Devon
50 C10 **Abbots Langley** Herts
7 L9 **Abbotsleigh** Devon
31 P10 **Abbots Leigh** N Som
62 B9 **Abbotsley** Cambs
47 K3 **Abbots Morton** Worcs
62 B5 **Abbots Ripton** Cambs
47 L4 **Abbot's Salford** Warwks
22 G8 **Abbotstone** Hants
22 C10 **Abbotswood** Hants
22 B5 **Abbots Worthy** Hants
22 B6 **Abbotts Ann** Hants
12 G4 **Abbott Street** Dorset
56 F9 **Abcott** Shrops
57 K7 **Abdon** Shrops
46 C11 **Abenhall** Gloucs
43 J2 **Aberaeron** Cerdgn
30 D4 **Aberaman** Rhondd
55 J2 **Aberangell** Gwynd
42 F6 **Aber-arad** Carmth
147 Q2 **Aberarder** Highld
134 F4 **Aberargie** P & K
43 J2 **Aberarth** Cerdgn
29 K7 **Aberavon** Neath
42 G6 **Aber-banc** Cerdgn
30 G4 **Aberbargoed** Caerph
30 H4 **Aberbeeg** Blae G
30 E4 **Abercanaid** Myr Td
30 H5 **Abercarn** Caerph
40 G4 **Abercastle** Pembks
55 J4 **Abercegir** Powys
147 J7 **Aberchalder Lodge** Highld
158 F7 **Aberchirder** Abers
44 G10 **Aber Clydach** Powys
29 M2 **Abercraf** Powys
29 M5 **Abercregan** Neath
30 D5 **Abercwmboi** Rhondd
41 P2 **Abercych** Pembks
30 E6 **Abercynon** Rhondd
134 D3 **Aberdalgie** P & K
30 D4 **Aberdare** Rhondd
66 B9 **Aberdaron** Gwynd
151 N6 **Aberdeen** C Aber
151 M5 *Aberdeen Airport* C Aber
151 M6 **Aberdeen Crematorium** C Aber
66 G4 **Aberdesach** Gwynd
134 F10 **Aberdour** Fife
29 L5 **Aberdulais** Neath
54 E5 **Aberdyfi** Gwynd
44 F5 **Aberedw** Powys
40 E4 **Abereiddy** Pembks
66 F7 **Abererch** Gwynd
30 E4 **Aberfan** Myr Td
141 L8 **Aberfeldy** P & K
78 F11 **Aberffraw** IoA
54 F9 **Aberffrwd** Cerdgn
91 L3 **Aberford** Leeds
132 G7 **Aberfoyle** Stirlg
29 P8 **Abergarw** Brdgnd
29 M4 **Abergarwed** Neath
31 J2 **Abergavenny** Mons
80 C9 **Abergele** Conwy
43 K6 **Aber-giar** Carmth
43 L8 **Abergorlech** Carmth
44 B4 **Abergwesyn** Powys
42 H10 **Abergwili** Carmth
54 H4 **Abergwydol** Powys
29 N5 **Abergwynfi** Neath
79 M10 **Abergwyngregyn** Gwynd
54 F3 **Abergynolwyn** Gwynd
55 P6 **Aberhafesp** Powys
55 J5 **Aberhosan** Powys
29 N8 **Aberkenfig** Brdgnd
128 D4 **Aberlady** E Loth
143 J6 **Aberlemno** Angus
54 H3 **Aberllefenni** Gwynd
44 H7 **Aberllynfi** Powys
157 P9 **Aberlour** Moray
54 F10 **Aber-Magwr** Cerdgn
43 L3 **Aber-meurig** Cerdgn
69 K3 **Abermorddu** Flints
56 B6 **Abermule** Powys
42 F10 **Abernant** Carmth
30 D4 **Aber-nant** Rhondd
134 F4 **Abernethy** P & K
142 D11 **Abernyte** P & K
42 E4 **Aberporth** Cerdgn
66 E9 **Abersoch** Gwynd
31 J4 **Abersychan** Torfn
30 D10 **Aberthin** V Glam
30 H4 **Abertillery** Blae G
30 F7 **Abertridwr** Caerph
68 D11 **Abertridwr** Powys
30 F3 **Abertysswg** Caerph
134 B4 **Aberuthven** P & K
44 D9 **Aberyscir** Powys
54 D8 **Aberystwyth** Cerdgn
54 E8 **Aberystwyth Crematorium** Cerdgn
34 E5 **Abingdon-on-Thames** Oxon
36 D11 **Abinger Common** Surrey
36 C11 **Abinger Hammer** Surrey
60 G8 **Abington** Nhants
116 C6 **Abington** S Lans
50 H2 **Abington Pigotts** Cambs
116 C6 *Abington Services* S Lans
24 D7 **Abingworth** W Susx
73 J6 **Ab Kettleby** Leics
47 K4 **Ab Lench** Worcs
33 M3 **Ablington** Gloucs
21 N5 **Ablington** Wilts
83 Q8 **Abney** Derbys
71 J4 **Above Church** Staffs
150 E8 **Aboyne** Abers
82 D4 **Abram** Wigan
155 Q10 **Abriachan** Highld
51 L11 **Abridge** Essex
126 D2 **Abronhill** N Lans
32 D10 **Abson** S Glos
48 H5 **Abthorpe** Nhants
87 M5 **Aby** Lincs
98 B11 **Acaster Malbis** C York
91 P2 **Acaster Selby** N York
89 M5 **Accrington** Lancs
89 M5 **Accrington Crematorium** Lancs
136 F5 **Acha** Ag & B
123 N4 **Achahoish** Ag & B
141 R8 **Achalader** P & K
138 G11 **Achaleven** Ag & B
168 i5 **Acha Mor** W Isls
155 J5 **Achanalt** Highld
156 A3 **Achandunie** Highld
162 D6 **Achany** Highld
138 B4 **Acharacle** Highld
138 C7 **Acharn** Highld
141 J9 **Acharn** P & K
167 L8 **Achavanich** Highld
160 G6 **Achduart** Highld
164 G9 **Achfary** Highld
144 C6 **A'Chill** Highld
160 G5 **Achiltibuie** Highld
166 B4 **Achina** Highld
120 E8 **Achinhoan** Ag & B
154 B9 **Achintee** Highld
153 Q10 **Achintraid** Highld
160 H2 **Achmelvich** Highld
153 R11 **Achmore** Highld
168 i5 **Achmore** W Isls
164 B10 **Achnacarnin** Highld
146 F10 **Achnacarry** Highld
145 J6 **Achnacloich** Highld
147 L4 **Achnaconeran** Highld
138 F9 **Achnacroish** Ag & B
137 M5 **Achnadrish House** Ag & B
141 L10 **Achnafauld** P & K
156 B3 **Achnagarron** Highld
137 M2 **Achnaha** Highld
160 G4 **Achnahaird** Highld
162 D4 **Achnairn** Highld
138 F5 **Achnalea** Highld
130 F10 **Achnamara** Ag & B
154 G6 **Achnasheen** Highld
154 D8 **Achnashellach Lodge** Highld
157 P11 **Achnastank** Moray
137 L2 **Achosnich** Highld
138 C8 **Achranich** Highld
166 H3 **Achreamie** Highld
139 L4 **Achriabhach** Highld
164 G6 **Achriesgill** Highld
165 Q4 **Achtoty** Highld
61 M4 **Achurch** Nhants
162 G8 **Achvaich** Highld
166 G4 **Achvarasdal** Highld
167 Q6 **Ackergill** Highld
104 E7 **Acklam** Middsb
98 F8 **Acklam** N York
57 P5 **Ackleton** Shrops
119 P10 **Acklington** Nthumb
91 L6 **Ackton** Wakefd
91 L7 **Ackworth Moor Top** Wakefd
77 N9 **Acle** Norfk
58 H8 **Acock's Green** Birm
39 P8 **Acol** Kent
98 B10 **Acomb** C York
112 D7 **Acomb** Nthumb
10 D2 **Acombe** Somset
45 Q8 **Aconbury** Herefs
89 M6 **Acre** Lancs
69 J6 **Acrefair** Wrexhm
70 A4 **Acton** Ches E
12 G9 **Acton** Dorset
36 F4 **Acton** Gt Lon
56 E8 **Acton** Shrops
70 E6 **Acton** Staffs
52 E2 **Acton** Suffk
58 B11 **Acton** Worcs
46 C4 **Acton Beauchamp** Herefs
82 C9 **Acton Bridge** Ches W
57 J4 **Acton Burnell** Shrops
46 C4 **Acton Green** Herefs
69 K4 **Acton Park** Wrexhm
57 J4 **Acton Pigott** Shrops
57 L5 **Acton Round** Shrops
56 H7 **Acton Scott** Shrops
70 G11 **Acton Trussell** Staffs
32 F8 **Acton Turville** S Glos
70 D9 **Adbaston** Staffs
19 Q10 **Adber** Dorset
72 F3 **Adbolton** Notts
48 E7 **Adderbury** Oxon
70 B7 **Adderley** Shrops
119 M4 **Adderstone** Nthumb
126 H5 **Addiewell** W Loth
96 G11 **Addingham** C Brad
49 K9 **Addington** Bucks
37 J8 **Addington** Gt Lon
37 Q9 **Addington** Kent
36 H7 **Addiscombe** Gt Lon
36 C8 **Addlestone** Surrey
36 C7 **Addlestonemoor** Surrey
87 P7 **Addlethorpe** Lincs
70 B11 **Adeney** Wrekin
50 C9 **Adeyfield** Herts
55 P4 **Adfa** Powys
56 G10 **Adforton** Herefs
39 M11 **Adisham** Kent
47 P9 **Adlestrop** Gloucs
92 D6 **Adlingfleet** E R Yk
83 K8 **Adlington** Ches E
89 J8 **Adlington** Lancs
71 J10 **Admaston** Staffs
57 L2 **Admaston** Wrekin
47 P5 **Admington** Warwks
42 F6 **Adpar** Cerdgn
19 J9 **Adsborough** Somset
18 G7 **Adscombe** Somset
49 K9 **Adstock** Bucks
48 G4 **Adstone** Nhants
83 J7 **Adswood** Stockp
24 C6 **Adversane** W Susx
157 L11 **Advie** Highld
90 G5 **Adwalton** Leeds
35 J5 **Adwell** Oxon
91 N9 **Adwick Le Street** Donc
91 M10 **Adwick upon Dearne** Donc
109 L3 **Ae** D & G
109 M3 **Ae Bridgend** D & G
29 N5 **Afan Forest Park** Neath
89 M8 **Affetside** Bury
158 E9 **Affleck** Abers
12 D6 **Affpuddle** Dorset
146 F3 **Affric Lodge** Highld
80 G10 **Afon-wen** Flints
7 L6 **Afton** Devon
13 P7 **Afton** IoW
82 H4 **Agecroft Crematorium** Salfd
96 G3 **Agglethorpe** N York
81 M7 **Aigburth** Lpool
99 L11 **Aike** E R Yk
111 J11 **Aiketgate** Cumb
110 D11 **Aikhead** Cumb
110 E10 **Aikton** Cumb
87 M5 **Ailby** Lincs
45 L5 **Ailey** Herefs
74 B11 **Ailsworth** C Pete
97 M4 **Ainderby Quernhow** N York
97 M2 **Ainderby Steeple** N York
53 K7 **Aingers Green** Essex
88 C8 **Ainsdale** Sefton
88 B8 **Ainsdale-on-Sea** Sefton
111 K11 **Ainstable** Cumb
89 M8 **Ainsworth** Bury
105 K9 **Ainthorpe** N York
81 M5 **Aintree** Sefton
127 L5 **Ainville** W Loth
130 F7 **Aird** Ag & B
106 E5 **Aird** D & G
168 k4 **Aird** W Isls
168 g6 **Aird a Mhulaidh** W Isls
168 g7 **Aird Asaig** W Isls
153 N9 **Aird Dhubh** Highld
131 K2 **Airdeny** Ag & B
137 N10 **Aird of Kinloch** Ag & B
145 J7 **Aird of Sleat** Highld
126 D4 **Airdrie** N Lans
126 D4 **Airdriehill** N Lans
108 E6 **Airds of Kells** D & G
168 f4 **Aird Uig** W Isls
168 h6 **Airidh a bhruaich** W Isls
108 G9 **Airieland** D & G
142 E7 **Airlie** Angus
92 B6 **Airmyn** E R Yk
141 Q10 **Airntully** P & K
145 M6 **Airor** Highld
133 Q10 **Airth** Falk
96 D9 **Airton** N York
73 Q3 **Aisby** Lincs
85 Q2 **Aisby** Lincs
102 E11 **Aisgill** Cumb
6 H6 **Aish** Devon
7 L7 **Aish** Devon
18 G7 **Aisholt** Somset
97 L3 **Aiskew** N York
98 F3 **Aislaby** N York
105 N9 **Aislaby** N York
104 D8 **Aislaby** S on T
86 B4 **Aisthorpe** Lincs
169 q8 **Aith** Shet
119 J5 **Akeld** Nthumb
49 K7 **Akeley** Bucks
53 K2 **Akenham** Suffk
5 Q7 **Albaston** Cnwll
56 F2 **Alberbury** Shrops
24 G7 **Albourne** W Susx
24 G7 **Albourne Green** W Susx
57 Q4 **Albrighton** Shrops
69 N11 **Albrighton** Shrops
65 K4 **Alburgh** Norfk
51 K6 **Albury** Herts
35 J3 **Albury** Oxon
36 B11 **Albury** Surrey
51 K6 **Albury End** Herts
36 C11 **Albury Heath** Surrey
76 H5 **Alby Hill** Norfk
155 Q6 **Alcaig** Highld
56 H7 **Alcaston** Shrops
47 L3 **Alcester** Warwks
58 G8 **Alcester Lane End** Birm
25 M9 **Alciston** E Susx
18 C5 **Alcombe** Somset
32 F11 **Alcombe** Wilts
61 Q5 **Alconbury** Cambs
61 Q5 **Alconbury Weston** Cambs
97 P7 **Aldborough** N York
76 H5 **Aldborough** Norfk
33 Q9 **Aldbourne** Wilts
93 M3 **Aldbrough** E R Yk
103 P8 **Aldbrough St John** N York
35 Q2 **Aldbury** Herts
95 K8 **Aldcliffe** Lancs
141 L5 **Aldclune** P & K
65 P10 **Aldeburgh** Suffk
65 N3 **Aldeby** Norfk
50 D11 **Aldenham** Herts
21 N9 **Alderbury** Wilts
84 F11 **Aldercar** Derbys
76 G8 **Alderford** Norfk
13 K2 **Alderholt** Dorset
32 E6 **Alderley** Gloucs
82 H9 **Alderley Edge** Ches E
59 N8 **Aldermans Green** Covtry
34 G11 **Aldermaston** W Berk
47 P5 **Alderminster** Warwks
71 N9 **Alder Moor** Staffs
69 N3 **Aldersey Green** Ches W
23 N4 **Aldershot** Hants
47 K8 **Alderton** Gloucs
49 K5 **Alderton** Nhants
69 N10 **Alderton** Shrops
53 P3 **Alderton** Suffk
32 F8 **Alderton** Wilts
71 Q4 **Alderwasley** Derbys
97 L7 **Aldfield** N York
69 M3 **Aldford** Ches W
73 P10 **Aldgate** Rutlnd
52 F6 **Aldham** Essex
52 J2 **Aldham** Suffk
15 P5 **Aldingbourne** W Susx
94 F6 **Aldingham** Cumb
27 J4 **Aldington** Kent
47 L6 **Aldington** Worcs
27 J4 **Aldington Corner** Kent
150 B2 **Aldivalloch** Moray
132 D9 **Aldochlay** Ag & B
56 G9 **Aldon** Shrops
109 P11 **Aldoth** Cumb
62 F6 **Aldreth** Cambs
58 G4 **Aldridge** Wsall
65 N9 **Aldringham** Suffk
98 G8 **Aldro** N York
33 N3 **Aldsworth** Gloucs
15 L5 **Aldsworth** W Susx
150 B2 **Aldunie** Moray
84 B9 **Aldwark** Derbys
97 Q8 **Aldwark** N York
15 P7 **Aldwick** W Susx
61 M4 **Aldwincle** Nhants
34 G9 **Aldworth** W Berk
125 K2 **Alexandria** W Duns
18 G7 **Aley** Somset
16 D9 **Alfardisworthy** Devon
10 C5 **Alfington** Devon
24 B4 **Alfold** Surrey
24 B4 **Alfold Bars** W Susx
24 B3 **Alfold Crossways** Surrey
150 F4 **Alford** Abers
87 N5 **Alford** Lincs
20 B8 **Alford** Somset
87 M5 **Alford Crematorium** Lincs
84 F9 **Alfreton** Derbys
46 D4 **Alfrick** Worcs
46 D4 **Alfrick Pound** Worcs
25 M10 **Alfriston** E Susx
74 E3 **Algarkirk** Lincs
20 B8 **Alhampton** Somset
92 E6 **Alkborough** N Linc
32 E3 **Alkerton** Gloucs
48 C6 **Alkerton** Oxon
27 N3 **Alkham** Kent
69 P7 **Alkington** Shrops
71 M7 **Alkmonton** Derbys
7 L8 **Allaleigh** Devon
149 L9 **Allanaquoich** Abers
126 E6 **Allanbank** N Lans
129 M9 **Allanton** Border
126 E6 **Allanton** N Lans
126 C7 **Allanton** S Lans
32 B4 **Allaston** Gloucs
22 E10 **Allbrook** Hants
21 L2 **All Cannings** Wilts
112 B9 **Allendale** Nthumb
59 J5 **Allen End** Warwks
112 C11 **Allenheads** Nthumb
112 G10 **Allensford** Dur
51 L7 **Allen's Green** Herts
45 P7 **Allensmore** Herefs
72 B4 **Allenton** C Derb
17 P6 **Aller** Devon
19 M9 **Aller** Somset
100 E3 **Allerby** Cumb
9 P6 **Allercombe** Devon
18 B5 **Allerford** Somset
98 H4 **Allerston** N York
98 F11 **Allerthorpe** E R Yk
90 E4 **Allerton** C Brad
156 D4 **Allerton** Highld
81 M7 **Allerton** Lpool
91 L5 **Allerton Bywater** Leeds
97 P9 **Allerton Mauleverer** N York
59 M8 **Allesley** Covtry
72 A3 **Allestree** C Derb
3 K4 **Allet Common** Cnwll
73 L10 **Allexton** Leics
83 L11 **Allgreave** Ches E
38 D6 **Allhallows** Medway
38 D6 **Allhallows-on-Sea** Medway
153 Q6 **Alligin Shuas** Highld
70 F11 **Allimore Green** Staffs
11 K6 **Allington** Dorset
38 C10 **Allington** Kent
73 M2 **Allington** Lincs
21 L2 **Allington** Wilts
21 P7 **Allington** Wilts
32 G9 **Allington** Wilts
94 H5 **Allithwaite** Cumb
133 P9 **Alloa** Clacks
100 E2 **Allonby** Cumb
82 F10 **Allostock** Ches W
114 F4 **Alloway** S Ayrs
10 H2 **Allowenshay** Somset
65 L5 **All Saints South Elmham** Suffk
57 N5 **Allscott** Shrops
57 L2 **Allscott** Wrekin
56 H5 **All Stretton** Shrops
81 K11 **Alltami** Flints
139 M7 **Alltchaorunn** Highld
44 F5 **Alltmawr** Powys
42 H8 **Alltwalis** Carmth
29 K4 **Alltwen** Neath
43 K5 **Alltyblaca** Cerdgn
11 P2 **Allweston** Dorset
64 E7 **Allwood Green** Suffk
45 L4 **Almeley** Herefs
45 L4 **Almeley Wooton** Herefs
12 F5 **Almer** Dorset
91 P9 **Almholme** Donc
70 C8 **Almington** Staffs
15 M7 **Almodington** W Susx
134 D2 **Almondbank** P & K
90 F8 **Almondbury** Kirk
32 B8 **Almondsbury** S Glos
97 Q7 **Alne** N York
156 B4 **Alness** Highld
119 J8 **Alnham** Nthumb
119 P8 **Alnmouth** Nthumb
119 N8 **Alnwick** Nthumb
36 E4 **Alperton** Gt Lon
52 E4 **Alphamstone** Essex
64 B11 **Alpheton** Suffk
9 M6 **Alphington** Devon
77 K11 **Alpington** Norfk
84 B8 **Alport** Derbys
69 Q3 **Alpraham** Ches E
53 J7 **Alresford** Essex
59 J2 **Alrewas** Staffs
70 D3 **Alsager** Ches E
70 D5 **Alsagers Bank** Staffs
71 M4 **Alsop en le Dale** Derbys
111 P11 **Alston** Cumb
10 G4 **Alston** Devon
47 J8 **Alstone** Gloucs
19 K5 **Alstone** Somset
71 L3 **Alstonefield** Staffs
19 M4 **Alston Sutton** Somset
17 N7 **Alswear** Devon
83 K4 **Alt** Oldham
160 F4 **Altandhu** Highld
5 L5 **Altarnun** Cnwll
162 C6 **Altass** Highld
138 B10 **Altcreich** Ag & B
124 C3 **Altgaltraig** Ag & B
89 M4 **Altham** Lancs
38 F2 **Althorne** Essex
92 D9 **Althorpe** N Linc
166 H7 **Altnabreac Station** Highld
165 N9 **Altnaharra** Highld
91 K6 **Altofts** Wakefd
84 E8 **Alton** Derbys
23 K7 **Alton** Hants
71 K6 **Alton** Staffs
21 N5 **Alton** Wilts
21 M2 **Alton Barnes** Wilts
11 Q4 **Alton Pancras** Dorset
21 M2 **Alton Priors** Wilts
71 K6 *Alton Towers* Staffs
82 G7 **Altrincham** Traffd
82 F7 **Altrincham Crematorium** Traffd
132 F7 **Altskeith Hotel** Stirlg
133 P8 **Alva** Clacks
81 P10 **Alvanley** Ches W
72 B4 **Alvaston** C Derb
58 F10 **Alvechurch** Worcs
59 K4 **Alvecote** Warwks
21 J10 **Alvediston** Wilts
57 P8 **Alveley** Shrops
17 J6 **Alverdiscott** Devon
14 H7 **Alverstoke** Hants
14 G9 **Alverstone** IoW
91 J6 **Alverthorpe** Wakefd
73 K2 **Alverton** Notts
157 L5 **Alves** Moray
33 Q4 **Alvescot** Oxon
32 B7 **Alveston** S Glos
47 P3 **Alveston** Warwks
87 L2 **Alvingham** Lincs
32 B4 **Alvington** Gloucs
74 B11 **Alwalton** C Pete
118 H9 **Alwinton** Nthumb
90 H2 **Alwoodley** Leeds
91 J2 **Alwoodley Gates** Leeds
142 C8 **Alyth** P & K
84 D10 **Ambergate** Derbys
86 H11 **Amber Hill** Lincs
32 G4 **Amberley** Gloucs
24 B8 **Amberley** W Susx
84 E9 **Amber Row** Derbys
25 N8 **Amberstone** E Susx
119 Q10 **Amble** Nthumb
58 C7 **Amblecote** Dudley
90 D5 **Ambler Thorn** C Brad
101 L10 **Ambleside** Cumb
41 K5 **Ambleston** Pembks
48 H11 **Ambrosden** Oxon
92 E8 **Amcotts** N Linc
62 F5 **America** Cambs
35 Q5 **Amersham** Bucks
35 Q5 **Amersham Common** Bucks
35 Q5 **Amersham Old Town** Bucks
35 Q5 **Amersham on the Hill** Bucks
70 H9 **Amerton** Staffs
21 N6 **Amesbury** Wilts
168 f7 **Amhuinnsuidhe** W Isls
59 K4 **Amington** Staffs
109 M4 **Amisfield Town** D & G
78 G6 **Amlwch** IoA
28 H2 **Ammanford** Carmth
98 E6 **Amotherby** N York
22 D10 **Ampfield** Hants
98 B5 **Ampleforth** N York
33 L4 **Ampney Crucis** Gloucs
33 L4 **Ampney St Mary** Gloucs
33 L4 **Ampney St Peter** Gloucs
22 B6 **Amport** Hants
50 B3 **Ampthill** C Beds
64 B7 **Ampton** Suffk
41 N9 **Amroth** Pembks
141 L10 **Amulree** P & K
50 E8 **Amwell** Herts
138 E5 **Anaheilt** Highld
73 P2 **Ancaster** Lincs
56 B7 **Anchor** Shrops
129 P11 **Ancroft** Nthumb
118 B6 **Ancrum** Border
15 Q6 **Ancton** W Susx
87 P5 **Anderby** Lincs
19 K8 **Andersea** Somset
18 H8 **Andersfield** Somset
12 E5 **Anderson** Dorset
82 D9 **Anderton** Ches W
6 C8 **Anderton** Cnwll
22 C5 **Andover** Hants
47 K11 **Andoversford** Gloucs
80 f2 **Andreas** IoM
66 B9 **Anelog** Gwynd
36 H7 **Anerley** Gt Lon
81 M6 **Anfield** Lpool
81 M6 **Anfield Crematorium** Lpool
2 F6 **Angarrack** Cnwll
3 K6 **Angarrick** Cnwll
57 K9 **Angelbank** Shrops
18 G11 **Angersleigh** Somset
110 D9 **Angerton** Cumb
40 G10 **Angle** Pembks
78 G8 **Anglesey** IoA
24 C10 **Angmering** W Susx
97 R11 **Angram** N York
102 G11 **Angram** N York
2 H10 **Angrouse** Cnwll
112 D7 **Anick** Nthumb
156 E3 **Ankerville** Highld
73 K7 **Ankle Hill** Leics
92 H5 **Anlaby** E R Yk
75 P5 **Anmer** Norfk
15 J4 **Anmore** Hants
110 C7 **Annan** D & G
109 P2 *Annandale Water Services* D & G
94 B3 **Annaside** Cumb
154 A7 **Annat** Highld
126 C3 **Annathill** N Lans
22 C6 **Anna Valley** Hants
114 H3 **Annbank** S Ayrs
47 N4 *Anne Hathaway's Cottage* Warwks
84 H10 **Annesley** Notts
84 G10 **Annesley Woodhouse** Notts
113 J10 **Annfield Plain** Dur
125 N4 **Anniesland** C Glas
113 L6 **Annitsford** N Tyne
56 H3 **Annscroft** Shrops
88 C5 **Ansdell** Lancs
20 B8 **Ansford** Somset
59 M6 **Ansley** Warwks
71 N9 **Anslow** Staffs
71 M10 **Anslow Gate** Staffs
71 N10 **Anslow Lees** Staffs
23 P8 **Ansteadbrook** Surrey
23 K6 **Anstey** Hants
51 K4 **Anstey** Herts
72 F9 **Anstey** Leics
135 P7 **Anstruther** Fife
24 G6 **Ansty** W Susx
59 P8 **Ansty** Warwks
21 J9 **Ansty** Wilts
12 C4 **Ansty Cross** Dorset
14 H4 **Anthill Common** Hants
36 B8 **Anthonys** Surrey

262 Anthorn - Badcaul

110 C9 Anthorn Cumb
77 K5 Antingham Norfk
168 f9 An t-Ob W Isls
87 K11 Anton's Gowt Lincs
5 Q11 Antony Cnwll
82 D9 Antrobus Ches W
16 F11 Anvil Corner Devon
27 K2 Anvil Green Kent
86 F10 Anwick Lincs
108 C9 Anwoth D & G
37 K9 Aperfield Gt Lon
58 E10 Apes Dale Worcs
73 Q11 Apethorpe Nhants
70 F11 Apeton Staffs
86 F5 Apley Lincs
84 E5 Apperknowle Derbys
46 G9 Apperley Gloucs
90 F3 Apperley Bridge C Brad
112 G9 Apperley Dene Nthumb
96 C2 Appersett N York
138 G8 Appin Ag & B
92 G8 Appleby N Linc
102 C6 Appleby-in-Westmorland Cumb
59 M3 Appleby Magna Leics
59 M3 Appleby Parva Leics
50 H10 Appleby Street Herts
153 N9 Applecross Highld
9 Q2 Appledore Devon
16 H5 Appledore Devon
26 G6 Appledore Kent
26 G5 Appledore Heath Kent
34 F6 Appleford Oxon
109 P4 Applegarth Town D & G
91 K8 Applehaigh Wakefd
22 B5 Appleshaw Hants
101 J5 Applethwaite Cumb
81 Q7 Appleton Halton
34 D4 Appleton Oxon
82 D8 Appleton Warrtn
98 E3 Appleton-le-Moors N York
98 E6 Appleton-le-Street N York
91 P2 Appleton Roebuck N York
82 D8 Appleton Thorn Warrtn
104 C10 Appleton Wiske N York
117 Q7 Appletreehall Border
96 G8 Appletreewick N York
18 E10 Appley Somset
88 G9 Appley Bridge Lancs
14 G10 Apse Heath IoW
50 D4 Apsley End C Beds
15 M6 Apuldram W Susx
156 E2 Arabella Highld
143 L9 Arbirlot Angus
163 K10 Arboll Highld
35 L11 Arborfield Wokham
35 L11 Arborfield Cross Wokham
84 E3 Arbourthorne Sheff
143 L9 Arbroath Angus
143 P2 Arbuthnott Abers
26 E4 Arcadia Kent
28 D4 Archddu Carmth
103 Q7 Archdeacon Newton Darltn
132 E11 Archencarroch W Duns
157 N9 Archiestown Moray
11 c1 Archirondel Jersey
70 D2 Arclid Green Ches E
159 P10 Ardallie Abers
131 M3 Ardanaiseig Hotel Ag & B
153 Q10 Ardaneaskan Highld
153 Q10 Ardarroch Highld
122 F10 Ardbeg Ag & B
124 D4 Ardbeg Ag & B
131 P11 Ardbeg Ag & B
161 K9 Ardcharnich Highld
137 K12 Ardchiavaig Ag & B
131 K5 Ardchonnel Ag & B
132 H5 Ardchullarie More Stirlg
131 Q9 Arddarroch Ag & B
69 J11 Arddleen Powys
146 E9 Ardechive Highld
124 H9 Ardeer N Ayrs
50 H5 Ardeley Herts
145 Q2 Ardelve Highld
132 D11 Arden Ag & B
47 M4 Ardens Grafton Warwks
130 G3 Ardentallen Ag & B
131 P10 Ardentinny Ag & B
124 C3 Ardentraive Ag & B
140 G10 Ardeonaig Stirlg
156 D7 Ardersier Highld
160 H9 Ardessie Highld
130 G7 Ardfern Ag & B
123 J5 Ardfernal Ag & B
162 D8 Ardgay Highld
139 J5 Ardgour Highld
124 G3 Ardgowan Inver
124 F3 Ardhallow Ag & B
168 g7 Ardhasig W Isls
153 P6 Ardheslaig Highld
161 K9 Ardindrean Highld
24 H5 Ardingly W Susx
34 D7 Ardington Oxon
34 D7 Ardington Wick Oxon
124 B4 Ardlamont Ag & B
53 J6 Ardleigh Essex
52 H5 Ardleigh Heath Essex
142 D9 Ardler P & K
48 F9 Ardley Oxon
51 M8 Ardley End Essex
132 C4 Ardlui Ag & B
130 C10 Ardlussa Ag & B
161 J7 Ardmair Highld
124 D4 Ardmaleish Ag & B
123 K10 Ardminish Ag & B
138 C3 Ardmolich Highld
125 J2 Ardmore Ag & B
162 G9 Ardmore Highld
131 P11 Ardnadam Ag & B
155 P8 Ardnagrask Highld
154 A10 Ardnarff Highld
138 E5 Ardnastang Highld
123 N8 Ardpatrick Ag & B
130 H10 Ardrishaig Ag & B
155 R3 Ardross Highld
124 G9 Ardrossan N Ayrs
91 K9 Ardsley Barns
91 J5 Ardsley East Leeds
137 P3 Ardslignish Highld
122 G9 Ardtalla Ag & B
138 A3 Ardtoe Highld
130 F5 Arduaine Ag & B
155 Q5 Ardullie Highld
145 K7 Ardvasar Highld
133 J3 Ardvorlich P & K
168 g6 Ardvourlie W Isls
106 F8 Ardwell D & G
83 J5 Ardwick Manch
57 P10 Areley Kings Worcs
138 B4 Arevegaig Highld
23 M7 Arford Hants
30 G5 Argoed Caerph
69 K10 Argoed Shrops
44 D2 Argoed Mill Powys
25 N5 Argos Hill E Susx
131 Q7 Argyll Forest Park Ag & B
168 h6 Aribruach W Isls
137 J11 Aridhglas Ag & B
136 F5 Arileod Ag & B
136 G4 Arinagour Ag & B
130 H2 Ariogan Ag & B
145 L10 Arisaig Highld
145 L11 Arisaig House Highld
97 N8 Arkendale N York
51 L4 Arkesden Essex
95 M6 Arkholme Lancs
100 F3 Arkleby Cumb
110 G2 Arkleton D & G
103 K10 Arkle Town N York
50 F11 Arkley Gt Lon
91 P9 Arksey Donc
84 F6 Arkwright Town Derbys
46 H10 Arle Gloucs
100 D7 Arlecdon Cumb
48 C5 Arlescote Warwks
50 E3 Arlesey C Beds
57 M2 Arleston Wrekin
82 E8 Arley Ches E
59 L6 Arley Warwks
32 D2 Arlingham Gloucs
17 L3 Arlington Devon
25 M9 Arlington E Susx
33 M3 Arlington Gloucs
17 L3 Arlington Beccott Devon
145 K7 Armadale Highld
166 C4 Armadale Highld
126 G4 Armadale W Loth
100 G5 Armaside Cumb
111 K11 Armathwaite Cumb
77 K11 Arminghall Norfk
71 K11 Armitage Staffs
90 E8 Armitage Bridge Kirk
90 H4 Armley Leeds
47 P6 Armscote Warwks
70 G5 Armshead Staffs
61 N3 Armston Nhants
91 Q10 Armthorpe Donc
136 G3 Arnabost Ag & B
94 D4 Arnaby Cumb
96 D6 Arncliffe N York
96 D6 Arncliffe Cote N York
135 N6 Arncroach Fife
157 P8 Arndilly House Moray
12 G7 Arne Dorset
60 D2 Arnesby Leics
134 E5 Arngask P & K
145 P5 Arnisdale Highld
153 K8 Arnish Highld
127 Q5 Arniston Mdloth
168 i3 Arnol W Isls
93 K2 Arnold E R Yk
85 J11 Arnold Notts
133 J9 Arnprior Stirlg
95 K5 Arnside Cumb
137 P6 Aros Ag & B
69 N7 Arowry Wrexhm
94 G4 Arrad Foot Cumb
92 H2 Arram E R Yk
120 H4 Arran N Ayrs
97 K2 Arrathorne N York
14 F9 Arreton IoW
153 N6 Arrina Highld
62 D10 Arrington Cambs
132 B7 Arrochar Ag & B
47 L3 Arrow Warwks
58 F10 Arrowfield Top Worcs
56 G3 Arscott Shrops
156 A8 Artafallie Highld
90 H2 Arthington Leeds
60 G4 Arthingworth Nhants
54 E2 Arthog Gwynd
159 N10 Arthrath Abers
91 K3 Arthursdale Leeds
159 P11 Artrochie Abers
24 B9 Arundel W Susx
100 E6 Asby Cumb
124 E5 Ascog Ag & B
35 P11 Ascot W & M
48 B8 Ascott Warwks
48 B11 Ascott Earl Oxon
48 B11 Ascott-under-Wychwood Oxon
97 N5 Asenby N York
73 J7 Asfordby Leics
73 J7 Asfordby Hill Leics
86 F11 Asgarby Lincs
87 K7 Asgarby Lincs
7 L9 Ash Devon
17 J10 Ash Devon
12 E2 Ash Dorset
37 P8 Ash Kent
39 N10 Ash Kent
19 J10 Ash Somset
19 N10 Ash Somset
23 P4 Ash Surrey
34 G9 Ashampstead W Berk
34 G9 Ashampstead Green W Berk
64 H11 Ashbocking Suffk
71 M5 Ashbourne Derbys
18 E10 Ashbrittle Somset
25 Q8 Ashburnham Place E Susx
7 K4 Ashburton Devon
8 D5 Ashbury Devon
33 Q7 Ashbury Oxon
92 E9 Ashby N Linc
87 M7 Ashby by Partney Lincs
93 N10 Ashby cum Fenby NE Lin
86 E9 Ashby de la Launde Lincs
72 B7 Ashby-de-la-Zouch Leics
73 J8 Ashby Folville Leics
60 C2 Ashby Magna Leics
60 B3 Ashby Parva Leics
87 K6 Ashby Puerorum Lincs
60 C7 Ashby St Ledgers Nhants
77 L11 Ashby St Mary Norfk
46 H8 Ashchurch Gloucs
9 M9 Ashcombe Devon
19 K2 Ashcombe N Som
19 M7 Ashcott Somset
51 N2 Ashdon Essex
22 F4 Ashe Hants
52 G11 Asheldham Essex
52 B3 Ashen Essex
35 K2 Ashendon Bucks
35 P4 Asheridge Bucks
22 C11 Ashfield Hants
46 A10 Ashfield Herefs
133 M7 Ashfield Stirlg
65 J9 Ashfield cum Thorpe Suffk
63 N9 Ashfield Green Suffk
65 K7 Ashfield Green Suffk
24 F5 Ashfold Crossways W Susx
6 H9 Ashford Devon
17 J4 Ashford Devon
26 H3 Ashford Kent
36 C6 Ashford Surrey
57 J10 Ashford Bowdler Shrops
57 J10 Ashford Carbonell Shrops
22 G2 Ashford Hill Hants
83 Q11 Ashford in the Water Derbys
126 D7 Ashgill S Lans
23 P5 Ash Green Surrey
59 M8 Ash Green Warwks
10 B2 Ashill Devon
76 B11 Ashill Norfk
19 K11 Ashill Somset
38 E3 Ashingdon Essex
113 L3 Ashington Nthumb
12 H5 Ashington Poole
19 Q10 Ashington Somset
24 D7 Ashington W Susx
117 P6 Ashkirk Border
14 E6 Ashlett Hants
46 F9 Ashleworth Gloucs
46 F9 Ashleworth Quay Gloucs
63 L8 Ashley Cambs
82 G8 Ashley Ches E
17 M9 Ashley Devon
13 K4 Ashley Dorset
32 H6 Ashley Gloucs
13 N5 Ashley Hants
22 C8 Ashley Hants
27 P2 Ashley Kent
60 G2 Ashley Nhants
70 D7 Ashley Staffs
32 F11 Ashley Wilts
35 Q3 Ashley Green Bucks
71 P4 Ashleyhay Derbys
13 K4 Ashley Heath Dorset
56 H11 Ashley Moor Herefs
69 Q7 Ash Magna Shrops
22 D3 Ashmansworth Hants
16 E8 Ashmansworthy Devon
32 E5 Ashmead Green Gloucs
5 P2 Ashmill Devon
17 P7 Ash Mill Devon
20 H11 Ashmore Dorset
34 F11 Ashmore Green W Berk
48 B3 Ashorne Warwks
84 D8 Ashover Derbys
84 D8 Ashover Hay Derbys
59 M10 Ashow Warwks
69 Q7 Ash Parva Shrops
46 B6 Ashperton Herefs
7 L7 Ashprington Devon
18 G9 Ash Priors Somset
17 L9 Ashreigney Devon
52 H2 Ash Street Suffk
36 E9 Ashtead Surrey
9 P2 Ash Thomas Devon
74 B9 Ashton C Pete
81 Q11 Ashton Ches W
2 G8 Ashton Cnwll
9 L8 Ashton Devon
22 F11 Ashton Hants
45 Q2 Ashton Herefs
124 G2 Ashton Inver
49 L5 Ashton Nhants
61 N3 Ashton Nhants
19 M5 Ashton Somset
20 G3 Ashton Common Wilts
20 H3 Ashton Hill Wilts
82 C5 Ashton-in-Makerfield Wigan
33 K6 Ashton Keynes Wilts
47 J7 Ashton under Hill Worcs
83 K5 Ashton-under-Lyne Tamesd
82 G6 Ashton upon Mersey Traffd
13 P2 Ashurst Hants
25 M3 Ashurst Kent
88 F9 Ashurst Lancs
24 E7 Ashurst W Susx
25 K3 Ashurstwood W Susx
23 N4 Ash Vale Surrey
5 P2 Ashwater Devon
50 G3 Ashwell Herts
73 M8 Ashwell Rutlnd
19 L11 Ashwell Somset
50 G2 Ashwell End Herts
64 G2 Ashwellthorpe Norfk
20 B5 Ashwick Somset
75 P7 Ashwicken Norfk
58 C7 Ashwood Staffs
94 E5 Askam in Furness Cumb
91 P8 Askern Donc
11 L6 Askerswell Dorset
35 M3 Askett Bucks
101 P6 Askham Cumb
85 M6 Askham Notts
98 B11 Askham Bryan C York
98 A11 Askham Richard C York
131 J9 Asknish Ag & B
96 D2 Askrigg N York
97 J11 Askwith N York
74 A4 Aslackby Lincs
64 H3 Aslacton Norfk
73 J3 Aslockton Notts
19 N7 Asney Somset
64 H9 Aspall Suffk
100 F2 Aspatria Cumb
51 J5 Aspenden Herts
83 M7 Aspenshaw Derbys
74 E3 Asperton Lincs
70 E8 Aspley Staffs
49 P7 Aspley Guise C Beds
49 P8 Aspley Heath C Beds
58 G10 Aspley Heath Warwks
89 J9 Aspull Wigan
82 D5 Aspull Common Wigan
92 B5 Asselby E R Yk
87 N5 Asserby Lincs
87 N5 Asserby Turn Lincs
52 F4 Assington Suffk
63 N10 Assington Green Suffk
70 E2 Astbury Ches E
49 J4 Astcote Nhants
87 J5 Asterby Lincs
56 F3 Asterley Shrops
56 F6 Asterton Shrops
33 Q2 Asthall Oxon
34 B2 Asthall Leigh Oxon
162 G8 Astle Highld
69 P11 Astley Shrops
59 M7 Astley Warwks
82 F4 Astley Wigan
57 P11 Astley Worcs
57 N5 Astley Abbots Shrops
89 L8 Astley Bridge Bolton
57 Q11 Astley Cross Worcs
82 F5 Astley Green Wigan
58 G7 Aston Birm
69 R5 Aston Ches E
82 C9 Aston Ches W
83 Q8 Aston Derbys
81 L11 Aston Flints
45 P2 Aston Herefs
50 G6 Aston Herts
34 B4 Aston Oxon
84 G3 Aston Rothm
57 Q6 Aston Shrops
69 P9 Aston Shrops
70 D6 Aston Staffs
70 F10 Aston Staffs
35 L8 Aston Wokham
57 L3 Aston Wrekin
49 M10 Aston Abbotts Bucks
57 L8 Aston Botterell Shrops
70 G8 Aston-by-Stone Staffs
47 M2 Aston Cantlow Warwks
35 N2 Aston Clinton Bucks
46 C10 Aston Crews Herefs
46 H8 Aston Cross Gloucs
50 G6 Aston End Herts
57 M6 Aston-Eyre Shrops
58 E11 Aston Fields Worcs
59 Q6 Aston Flamville Leics
82 C9 Aston Heath Ches W
46 C10 Aston Ingham Herefs
70 A3 Aston juxta Mondrum Ches E
48 E4 Aston le Walls Nhants
47 N7 Aston Magna Gloucs
57 J7 Aston Munslow Shrops
56 F8 Aston on Clun Shrops
56 E3 Aston Pigott Shrops
56 E3 Aston Rogers Shrops
35 K5 Aston Rowant Oxon
35 L3 Aston Sandford Bucks
47 K7 Aston Somerville Worcs
47 M6 Aston-sub-Edge Gloucs
34 G7 Aston Tirrold Oxon
72 C5 Aston-upon-Trent Derbys
34 G7 Aston Upthorpe Oxon
48 F7 Astrop Nhants
35 N2 Astrope Herts
50 F3 Astwick C Beds
84 F8 Astwith Derbys
49 Q5 Astwood M Keyn
58 D11 Astwood Worcs
47 K2 Astwood Bank Worcs
46 G3 Astwood Crematorium Worcs
73 R3 Aswarby Lincs
87 L6 Aswardby Lincs
57 J3 Atcham Shrops
47 K4 Atch Lench Worcs
12 C6 Athelhampton Dorset
65 J7 Athelington Suffk
19 K9 Athelney Somset
128 E4 Athelstaneford E Loth
14 E11 Atherfield Green IoW
17 K7 Atherington Devon
24 B10 Atherington W Susx
19 L11 Atherstone Somset
59 M5 Atherstone Warwks
47 P4 Atherstone on Stour Warwks
82 E4 Atherton Wigan
103 Q10 Atley Hill N York
71 N5 Atlow Derbys
154 B10 Attadale Highld
72 E4 Attenborough Notts
86 C2 Atterby Lincs
84 E3 Attercliffe Sheff
57 L5 Atterley Shrops
72 B11 Atterton Leics
64 E2 Attleborough Norfk
59 N6 Attleborough Warwks
76 G8 Attlebridge Norfk
63 M10 Attleton Green Suffk
99 P10 Atwick E R Yk
32 G11 Atworth Wilts
45 P5 Auberrow Herefs
86 B8 Aubourn Lincs
149 N2 Auchbreck Moray
159 L11 Auchedly Abers
143 N2 Auchenblae Abers
133 M10 Auchenbowie Stirlg
108 G10 Auchencairn D & G
109 L4 Auchencairn D & G
121 K6 Auchencairn N Ayrs
129 M7 Auchencrow Border
127 P5 Auchendinny Mdloth
126 H7 Auchengray S Lans
157 R5 Auchenhalrig Moray
126 E9 Auchenheath S Lans
115 R8 Auchenhessnane D & G
124 B3 Auchenlochan Ag & B
125 K8 Auchenmade N Ayrs
106 H7 Auchenmalg D & G
125 K8 Auchentiber N Ayrs
131 L7 Auchindrain Ag & B
161 K10 Auchindrean Highld
158 G8 Auchininna Abers
115 L3 Auchinleck E Ayrs
126 B3 Auchinloch N Lans
126 C2 Auchinstarry N Lans
139 K3 Auchintore Highld
159 Q10 Auchiries Abers
148 F8 Auchlean Highld
151 M8 Auchlee Abers
150 G3 Auchleven Abers
126 E10 Auchlochan S Lans
150 F7 Auchlossan Abers
132 G2 Auchlyne Stirlg
115 K2 Auchmillan E Ayrs
143 M9 Auchmithie Angus
134 G7 Auchmuirbridge Fife
142 H5 Auchnacree Angus
159 M9 Auchnagatt Abers
149 N3 Auchnarrow Moray
106 C5 Auchnotteroch D & G
157 Q7 Auchroisk Moray
133 Q5 Auchterarder P & K
147 K6 Auchteraw Highld
148 G3 Auchterblair Highld
153 Q2 Auchtercairn Highld
134 G8 Auchterderran Fife
142 E10 Auchterhouse Angus
158 H9 Auchterless Abers
134 G5 Auchtermuchty Fife
155 N6 Auchterneed Highld
134 G9 Auchtertool Fife
145 P2 Auchtertyre Highld
132 H3 Auchtubh Stirlg
167 Q3 Auckengill Highld
91 Q10 Auckley Donc
83 K5 Audenshaw Tamesd
70 B6 Audlem Ches E
70 D4 Audley Staffs
51 M3 Audley End Essex
52 D4 Audley End Essex
64 B11 Audley End Suffk
51 M3 Audley End House Essex
70 E10 Audmore Staffs
58 C7 Audnam Dudley
101 J3 Aughertree Cumb
92 B3 Aughton E R Yk
88 D9 Aughton Lancs
95 M7 Aughton Lancs
84 G3 Aughton Rothm
21 P3 Aughton Wilts
88 E9 Aughton Park Lancs
156 G6 Auldearn Highld
45 P4 Aulden Herefs
109 K3 Auldgirth D & G
125 Q7 Auldhouse S Lans
146 A3 Ault a' chruinn Highld
160 D9 Aultbea Highld
160 A9 Aultgrishin Highld
155 L3 Aultguish Inn Highld
84 G7 Ault Hucknall Derbys
158 B7 Aultmore Moray
147 N3 Aultnagoire Highld
162 F10 Aultnamain Inn Highld
73 Q8 Aunby Lincs
9 P4 Aunk Devon
73 Q3 Aunsby Lincs
31 Q7 Aust S Glos
74 E6 Austendike Lincs
85 L2 Austerfield Donc
90 B9 Austerlands Oldham
91 K4 Austhorpe Leeds
90 E9 Austonley Kirk
59 L3 Austrey Warwks
95 R7 Austwick N York
87 L4 Authorpe Lincs
87 P6 Authorpe Row Lincs
33 M11 Avebury Wilts
33 L11 Avebury Trusloe Wilts
37 N4 Aveley Thurr
32 G5 Avening Gloucs
85 N10 Averham Notts
6 H9 Aveton Gifford Devon
148 F5 Aviemore Highld
34 C11 Avington W Berk
156 C6 Avoch Highld
13 K5 Avon Hants
126 G3 Avonbridge Falk
48 D4 Avon Dassett Warwks
31 P9 Avonmouth Bristl
7 J7 Avonwick Devon
22 B10 Awbridge Hants
31 Q7 Awkley S Glos
10 C4 Awliscombe Devon
32 D3 Awre Gloucs
72 D2 Awsworth Notts
58 C9 Axborough Worcs
19 M4 Axbridge Somset
22 H6 Axford Hants
33 P10 Axford Wilts
10 F5 Axminster Devon
10 F6 Axmouth Devon
80 G8 Axton Flints
103 Q6 Aycliffe Dur
112 F7 Aydon Nthumb
32 B4 Aylburton Gloucs
111 P11 Ayle Nthumb
9 P6 Aylesbeare Devon
35 M2 Aylesbury Bucks
93 M9 Aylesby NE Lin
38 B10 Aylesford Kent
39 M11 Aylesham Kent
72 F10 Aylestone C Leic
72 F10 Aylestone Park C Leic
76 H4 Aylmerton Norfk
76 H6 Aylsham Norfk
46 C7 Aylton Herefs
47 M10 Aylworth Gloucs
56 G11 Aymestrey Herefs
48 F8 Aynho Nhants
50 F8 Ayot Green Herts
50 E7 Ayot St Lawrence Herts
50 F7 Ayot St Peter Herts
114 F3 Ayr S Ayrs
96 F3 Aysgarth N York
18 D11 Ayshford Devon
94 H4 Ayside Cumb
73 M10 Ayston Rutlnd
51 N7 Aythorpe Roding Essex
129 N7 Ayton Border
97 L6 Azerley N York

B

7 N5 Babbacombe Torbay
72 D2 Babbington Notts
69 K9 Babbinswood Shrops
51 J7 Babbs Green Herts
19 Q9 Babcary Somset
44 A7 Babel Carmth
63 M11 Babel Green Suffk
80 H10 Babell Flints
8 G9 Babeny Devon
34 D4 Bablock Hythe Oxon
62 H10 Babraham Cambs
85 L4 Babworth Notts
78 G8 Bachau IoA
56 H8 Bache Shrops
56 C6 Bacheldre Powys
26 D9 Bachelor's Bump E Susx
169 e3 Backaland Ork
94 H4 Backbarrow Cumb
41 Q7 Backe Carmth
159 P7 Backfolds Abers
81 M10 Backford Ches W
81 M10 Backford Cross Ches W
163 J6 Backies Highld
145 L10 Back of Keppoch Highld
71 K4 Back o' th' Brook Staffs
63 M9 Back Street Suffk
31 N11 Backwell N Som
113 M6 Backworth N Tyne
59 J7 Bacon's End Solhll
76 G4 Baconsthorpe Norfk
45 M8 Bacton Herefs
77 L5 Bacton Norfk
64 F8 Bacton Suffk
64 E8 Bacton Green Suffk
89 P6 Bacup Lancs
153 P3 Badachro Highld
33 N8 Badbury Swindn
60 C9 Badby Nhants
164 E8 Badcall Highld
164 F5 Badcall Highld
160 G8 Badcaul Highld

Baddeley Edge - Beckfoot 263

70 G4 Baddeley Edge C Stke
70 G4 Baddeley Green C Stke
59 K10 Baddesley Clinton Warwks
59 L5 Baddesley Ensor Warwks
160 H2 Baddidarrach Highld
127 L7 Baddinsgill Border
158 G10 Badenscoth Abers
149 Q4 Badenyon Abers
5 L4 Badgall Cnwll
74 H11 Badgeney Cambs
57 P5 Badger Shrops
2 D7 Badger's Cross Cnwll
37 L8 Badgers Mount Kent
46 H11 Badgeworth Gloucs
19 L4 Badgworth Somset
5 M4 Badharlick Cnwll
145 N2 Badicaul Highld
65 L8 Badingham Suffk
38 H11 Badlesmere Kent
116 F7 Badlieu Border
167 M7 Badlipster Highld
160 F8 Badluachrach Highld
162 H8 Badninish Highld
160 H8 Badrallach Highld
47 L6 Badsey Worcs
23 N5 Badshot Lea Surrey
91 M8 Badsworth Wakefd
64 D8 Badwell Ash Suffk
64 E8 Badwell Green Suffk
12 C2 Bagber Dorset
97 Q4 Bagby N York
87 L6 Bag Enderby Lincs
33 K3 Bagendon Gloucs
37 M8 Bagginswood Shrops
100 G2 Baggrow Cumb
168 b18 Bagh a Chaisteil W Isls
39 J11 Bagham Kent
168 c17 Bagh a Tuath W Isls
81 J9 Bagillt Flints
59 M10 Baginton Warwks
29 K6 Baglan Neath
90 G3 Bagley Leeds
69 M9 Bagley Shrops
19 N5 Bagley Somset
23 J6 Bagmore Hants
70 G4 Bagnall Staffs
34 E11 Bagnor W Berk
57 K10 Bagot Shrops
23 P2 Bagshot Surrey
34 B11 Bagshot Wilts
32 C7 Bagstone S Glos
84 G10 Bagthorpe Notts
72 C9 Bagworth Leics
45 N9 Bagwy Llydiart Herefs
90 F3 Baildon C Brad
90 E3 Baildon Green C Brad
168 h5 Baile Ailein W Isls
168 c12 Baile a Mhanaich W Isls
136 H11 Baile Mor Ag & B
23 J9 Bailey Green Hants
111 K5 Baileyhead Cumb
90 E5 Bailiff Bridge Calder
126 B5 Baillieston C Glas
95 K9 Bailrigg Lancs
96 D2 Bainbridge N York
158 F10 Bainshole Abers
74 A9 Bainton C Pete
99 K10 Bainton E R Yk
48 G9 Bainton Oxon
135 K7 Baintown Fife
118 C7 Bairnkine Border
51 J7 Baker's End Herts
37 P4 Baker Street Thurr
84 B7 Bakewell Derbys
68 B7 Bala Gwynd
168 h5 Balallan W Isls
155 M11 Balbeg Highld
134 F2 Balbeggie P & K
155 P8 Balblair Highld
156 C4 Balblair Highld
91 P10 Balby Donc
108 H11 Balcary D & G
155 P9 Balchraggan Highld
164 E4 Balchreick Highld
24 H4 Balcombe W Susx
24 H4 Balcombe Lane W Susx
135 Q6 Balcomie Links Fife
97 N5 Baldersby N York
97 N5 Baldersby St James N York
89 J4 Balderstone Lancs
89 Q8 Balderstone Rochdl
85 P10 Balderton Notts
3 K5 Baldhu Cnwll
135 L5 Baldinnie Fife
134 C4 Baldinnies P & K
50 F4 Baldock Herts
50 F3 Baldock Services Herts
142 H11 Baldovie C Dund
80 f5 Baldrine IoM
26 D9 Baldslow E Susx
80 e5 Baldwin IoM
110 F10 Baldwinholme Cumb
70 D7 Baldwin's Gate Staffs
25 J3 Baldwin's Hill W Susx
76 E4 Bale Norfk
142 D11 Baledgarno P & K
136 B7 Balemartine Ag & B
127 M4 Balerno C Edin
134 H7 Balfarg Fife
143 J4 Balfield Angus
169 d5 Balfour Ork
132 G10 Balfron Stirlg
158 G9 Balgaveny Abers
134 C9 Balgonar Fife
106 F9 Balgowan D & G
147 Q9 Balgowan Highld
152 F4 Balgown Highld
106 C5 Balgracie D & G
116 B6 Balgray S Lans
36 G6 Balham Gt Lon
142 D8 Balhary P & K
142 A10 Balholmie P & K
166 E3 Baligill Highld
142 D6 Balintore Angus
156 F2 Balintore Highld
156 C3 Balintraid Highld
168 c12 Balivanich W Isls
97 Q4 Balk N York
142 E9 Balkeerie Angus
92 C5 Balkholme E R Yk
80 c7 Ballabeg IoM
139 K6 Ballachulish Highld
80 b7 Ballafesson IoM
80 g3 Ballajora IoM
80 b7 Ballakilpheric IoM
80 c7 Ballamodha IoM
124 C5 Ballanlay Ag & B
114 A11 Ballantrae S Ayrs
38 F3 Ballards Gore Essex
59 L6 Ballards Green Warwks
80 c7 Ballasalla IoM
150 B8 Ballater Abers
80 d3 Ballaugh IoM
156 D2 Ballchraggan Highld
128 D4 Ballencrieff E Loth
136 B6 Ballevullin Ag & B
70 F4 Ball Green C Stke
70 H3 Ball Haye Green Staffs
22 D2 Ball Hill Hants
71 N4 Ballidon Derbys
120 G4 Balliekine N Ayrs
131 N8 Balliemore Ag & B
114 D9 Balligmorrie S Ayrs
132 G4 Ballimore Stirlg
157 M10 Ballindalloch Moray
134 H2 Ballindean P & K
52 E3 Ballingdon Suffk
35 P4 Ballinger Common Bucks
46 A8 Ballingham Herefs
134 F8 Ballingry Fife
141 N7 Ballinluig P & K
142 G7 Ballinshoe Angus
141 R6 Ballintuim P & K
156 C8 Balloch Highld
126 C3 Balloch N Lans
133 N4 Balloch P & K
114 F8 Balloch S Ayrs
132 D11 Balloch W Duns
23 Q9 Balls Cross W Susx
25 L3 Balls Green E Susx
32 G5 Ball's Green Gloucs
137 L7 Ballygown Ag & B
122 E6 Ballygrant Ag & B
136 F4 Ballyhaugh Ag & B
145 P2 Balmacara Highld
108 E5 Balmaclellan D & G
108 E12 Balmae D & G
132 E9 Balmaha Stirlg
135 J6 Balmalcolm Fife
108 D11 Balmangan D & G
151 P4 Balmedie Abers
69 M8 Balmer Heath Shrops
135 K3 Balmerino Fife
13 P4 Balmerlawn Hants
120 H5 Balmichael N Ayrs
149 P9 Balmoral Castle Grounds Abers
125 P3 Balmore E Duns
163 K11 Balmuchy Highld
134 G10 Balmule Fife
135 L3 Balmullo Fife
163 J4 Balnacoil Lodge Highld
154 C8 Balnacra Highld
149 P9 Balnacroft Abers
156 B10 Balnafoich Highld
141 M7 Balnaguard P & K
136 c2 Balnahard Ag & B
137 M9 Balnahard Ag & B
155 M11 Balnain Highld
165 J3 Balnakeil Highld
91 P7 Balne N York
141 P10 Balquharn P & K
132 G3 Balquhidder Stirlg
59 K9 Balsall Common Solhll
58 G8 Balsall Heath Birm
59 K9 Balsall Street Solhll
48 C6 Balscote Oxon
63 J10 Balsham Cambs
169 t3 Baltasound Shet
70 D4 Balterley Staffs
70 D4 Balterley Green Staffs
70 C4 Balterley Heath Staffs
107 M5 Baltersan D & G
19 P8 Baltonsborough Somset
130 F4 Balvicar Ag & B
145 P4 Balvraid Highld
156 E11 Balvraid Highld
2 F7 Balwest Cnwll
88 H5 Bamber Bridge Lancs
51 N6 Bamber's Green Essex
119 N4 Bamburgh Nthumb
119 N3 Bamburgh Castle Nthumb
84 B4 Bamford Derbys
89 P8 Bamford Rochdl
101 P7 Bampton Cumb
18 C10 Bampton Devon
34 B4 Bampton Oxon
101 P7 Bampton Grange Cumb
139 L2 Banavie Highld
48 E6 Banbury Oxon
48 E6 Banbury Crematorium Oxon
28 E2 Bancffosfelen Carmth
150 H8 Banchory Abers
151 N7 Banchory-Devenick Abers
28 D2 Bancycapel Carmth
42 F11 Bancyfelin Carmth
42 H7 Banc-y-ffordd Carmth
142 C11 Bandirran P & K
94 G3 Bandrake Head Cumb
158 G5 Banff Abers
79 K10 Bangor Gwynd
79 K10 Bangor Crematorium Gwynd
69 L5 Bangor-is-y-coed Wrexhm
5 L2 Bangors Cnwll
88 D9 Bangor's Green Lancs
64 C7 Bangrove Suffk
64 F4 Banham Norfk
13 N3 Bank Hants
109 M7 Bankend D & G
141 Q10 Bankfoot P & K
115 L5 Bankglen E Ayrs
101 K11 Bank Ground Cumb
151 N6 Bankhead C Aber
116 D2 Bankhead S Lans
96 D10 Bank Newton N York
126 D2 Banknock Falk
111 L8 Banks Cumb
88 D6 Banks Lancs
58 E11 Banks Green Worcs
110 C4 Bankshill D & G
46 B2 Bank Street Worcs
90 E6 Bank Top Calder
88 G9 Bank Top Lancs
77 J6 Banningham Norfk
51 Q6 Bannister Green Essex
133 N9 Bannockburn Stirlg
36 G9 Banstead Surrey
6 H10 Bantham Devon
126 C2 Banton N Lans
19 L3 Banwell N Som
38 F9 Bapchild Kent
21 J7 Bapton Wilts
168 i3 Barabhas W Isls
125 J11 Barassie S Ayrs
156 C3 Barbaraville Highld
83 P8 Barber Booth Derbys
94 H4 Barber Green Cumb
114 H4 Barbieston S Ayrs
95 N4 Barbon Cumb
69 R3 Barbridge Ches E
17 N2 Barbrook Devon
60 B6 Barby Nhants
138 H9 Barcaldine Ag & B
47 Q7 Barcheston Warwks
110 H8 Barclose Cumb
25 K8 Barcombe E Susx
25 K7 Barcombe Cross E Susx
90 C3 Barcroft C Brad
96 H2 Barden N York
37 N11 Barden Park Kent
51 P4 Bardfield End Green Essex
51 Q5 Bardfield Saling Essex
86 F7 Bardney Lincs
72 C8 Bardon Leics
111 Q8 Bardon Mill Nthumb
125 P3 Bardowie E Duns
25 Q5 Bardown E Susx
125 J3 Bardrainney Inver
94 G6 Bardsea Cumb
91 K2 Bardsey Leeds
66 A10 Bardsey Island Gwynd
83 K4 Bardsley Oldham
64 C7 Bardwell Suffk
95 K8 Bare Lancs
3 K8 Bareppa Cnwll
107 K4 Barfad D & G
76 G10 Barford Norfk
47 Q2 Barford Warwks
48 D8 Barford St John Oxon
21 L8 Barford St Martin Wilts
48 D8 Barford St Michael Oxon
39 N11 Barfrestone Kent
84 E11 Bargate Derbys
126 B5 Bargeddie N Lans
30 G5 Bargoed Caerph
107 L2 Bargrennan D & G
61 P5 Barham Cambs
39 M11 Barham Kent
64 G11 Barham Suffk
27 M2 Barham Crematorium Kent
62 E8 Bar Hill Cambs
74 A8 Barholm Lincs
72 G9 Barkby Leics
72 G9 Barkby Thorpe Leics
69 P9 Barkers Green Shrops
73 K4 Barkestone-le-Vale Leics
35 L11 Barkham Wokham
37 K4 Barking Gt Lon
64 F11 Barking Suffk
37 K3 Barkingside Gt Lon
64 F11 Barking Tye Suffk
90 D7 Barkisland Calder
3 J3 Barkla Shop Cnwll
73 N2 Barkston Lincs
91 M3 Barkston Ash N York
51 J3 Barkway Herts
126 B5 Barlanark C Glas
70 F7 Barlaston Staffs
23 Q11 Barlavington W Susx
84 G5 Barlborough Derbys
91 Q4 Barlby N York
72 C9 Barlestone Leics
51 K3 Barley Herts
89 N2 Barley Lancs
51 K5 Barleycroft End Herts
91 K11 Barley Hole Rothm
73 L9 Barleythorpe Rutlnd
38 F4 Barling Essex
86 E6 Barlings Lincs
108 H9 Barlochan D & G
84 D6 Barlow Derbys
113 J8 Barlow Gatesd
91 Q5 Barlow N York
98 F11 Barmby Moor E R Yk
92 A5 Barmby on the Marsh E R Yk
75 R4 Barmer Norfk
38 B10 Barming Heath Kent
120 F3 Barmollack Ag & B
67 L11 Barmouth Gwynd
104 B7 Barmpton Darltn
99 P9 Barmston E R Yk
65 P5 Barnaby Green Suffk
131 L9 Barnacarry Ag & B
74 A9 Barnack C Pete
59 N8 Barnacle Warwks
103 L7 Barnard Castle Dur
34 D2 Barnard Gate Oxon
63 M11 Barnardiston Suffk
108 H9 Barnbarroch D & G
91 M10 Barnburgh Donc
65 P4 Barnby Suffk
91 Q9 Barnby Dun Donc
85 Q10 Barnby in the Willows Notts
85 L4 Barnby Moor Notts
106 E10 Barncorkrie D & G
37 L5 Barnehurst Gt Lon
36 F5 Barnes Gt Lon
37 P11 Barnes Street Kent
50 F11 Barnet Gt Lon
93 J9 Barnetby le Wold N Linc
50 F11 Barnet Gate Gt Lon
76 D5 Barney Norfk
64 B6 Barnham Suffk
15 Q6 Barnham W Susx
76 F10 Barnham Broom Norfk
143 M6 Barnhead Angus
142 H11 Barnhill C Dund
69 N4 Barnhill Ches W
157 L6 Barnhill Moray
106 C3 Barnhills D & G
103 L8 Barningham Dur
64 D6 Barningham Suffk
93 M10 Barnoldby le Beck NE Lin
96 C11 Barnoldswick Lancs
91 N8 Barnsdale Bar Donc
24 D5 Barns Green W Susx
91 J9 Barnsley Barns
33 L4 Barnsley Gloucs
91 K9 Barnsley Crematorium Barns
39 N10 Barnsole Kent
17 K5 Barnstaple Devon
51 P7 Barnston Essex
81 K8 Barnston Wirral
73 J3 Barnstone Notts
58 F10 Barnt Green Worcs
127 M3 Barnton C Edin
82 D10 Barnton Ches W
61 M4 Barnwell All Saints Nhants
61 N4 Barnwell St Andrew Nhants
46 G11 Barnwood Gloucs
45 P3 Baron's Cross Herefs
101 P2 Baronwood Cumb
114 E9 Barr S Ayrs
168 b17 Barra W Isls
168 c17 Barra Airport W Isls
107 L8 Barrachan D & G
168 b17 Barraigh W Isls
136 A7 Barrapoll Ag & B
102 F8 Barras Cumb
112 D6 Barrasford Nthumb
80 d4 Barregarrow IoM
69 Q3 Barrets Green Ches E
125 M6 Barrhead E Rens
114 D11 Barrhill S Ayrs
62 E11 Barrington Cambs
19 L11 Barrington Somset
2 G6 Barripper Cnwll
125 K7 Barrmill N Ayrs
167 N2 Barrock Highld
46 G10 Barrow Gloucs
89 L3 Barrow Lancs
73 M7 Barrow Rutlnd
57 M4 Barrow Shrops
20 D8 Barrow Somset
63 N8 Barrow Suffk
75 L10 Barroway Drove Norfk
89 K8 Barrow Bridge Bolton
118 G8 Barrow Burn Nthumb
73 M3 Barrowby Lincs
73 N10 Barrowden Rutlnd
89 P3 Barrowford Lancs
31 P11 Barrow Gurney N Som
93 J6 Barrow Haven N Linc
84 F5 Barrow Hill Derbys
94 E7 Barrow-in-Furness Cumb
94 D7 Barrow Island Cumb
81 N4 Barrow Nook Lancs
70 B3 Barrow's Green Ches E
20 F8 Barrow Street Wilts
93 J6 Barrow-upon-Humber N Linc
72 F7 Barrow upon Soar Leics
72 B5 Barrow upon Trent Derbys
20 B2 Barrow Vale BaNES
143 J11 Barry Angus
30 F11 Barry V Glam
30 F11 Barry Island V Glam
72 H8 Barsby Leics
65 M4 Barsham Suffk
59 K9 Barston Solhll
45 R6 Bartestree Herefs
159 K11 Barthol Chapel Abers
52 B7 Bartholomew Green Essex
70 D4 Barthomley Ches E
13 P2 Bartley Hants
58 F8 Bartley Green Birm
63 J11 Bartlow Cambs
62 F9 Barton Cambs
69 M4 Barton Ches W
47 L9 Barton Gloucs
45 K3 Barton Herefs
88 D9 Barton Lancs
88 G3 Barton Lancs
103 P9 Barton N York
34 G3 Barton Oxon
7 N5 Barton Torbay
47 M4 Barton Warwks
75 P9 Barton Bendish Norfk
32 F5 Barton End Gloucs
71 M11 Barton Green Staffs
48 H8 Barton Hartshorn Bucks
98 E8 Barton Hill N York
72 E4 Barton in Fabis Notts
72 B9 Barton in the Beans Leics
50 C4 Barton-le-Clay C Beds
98 E6 Barton-le-Street N York
98 E8 Barton-le-Willows N York
63 M6 Barton Mills Suffk
13 M6 Barton-on-Sea Hants
47 Q8 Barton-on-the-Heath Warwks
19 P8 Barton St David Somset
61 J5 Barton Seagrave Nhants
22 D6 Barton Stacey Hants
17 M3 Barton Town Devon
77 M7 Barton Turf Norfk
71 M11 Barton-under-Needwood Staffs
92 H6 Barton-upon-Humber N Linc
82 G5 Barton upon Irwell Salfd
92 H6 Barton Waterside N Linc
91 J9 Barugh Barns
91 J9 Barugh Green Barns
168 i3 Barvas W Isls
63 J5 Barway Cambs
72 C11 Barwell Leics
17 K10 Barwick Devon
51 J7 Barwick Herts
11 M2 Barwick Somset
91 L3 Barwick in Elmet Leeds
69 M10 Baschurch Shrops
48 D2 Bascote Warwks
48 C2 Bascote Heath Warwks
64 E9 Base Green Suffk
70 H4 Basford Green Staffs
89 K2 Bashall Eaves Lancs
89 L2 Bashall Town Lancs
13 M5 Bashley Hants
38 B4 Basildon Essex
38 C4 Basildon & District Crematorium Essex
22 H4 Basingstoke Hants
22 G5 Basingstoke Crematorium Hants
84 C6 Baslow Derbys
19 K5 Bason Bridge Somset
31 J7 Bassaleg Newpt
128 G10 Bassendean Border
100 H4 Bassenthwaite Cumb
22 D11 Bassett C Sotn
50 H2 Bassingbourn Cambs
72 G3 Bassingfield Notts
86 B9 Bassingham Lincs
73 P5 Bassingthorpe Lincs
50 H5 Bassus Green Herts
37 P9 Basted Kent
74 B8 Baston Lincs
77 N8 Bastwick Norfk
19 K3 Batch Somset
36 C2 Batchworth Herts
36 C2 Batchworth Heath Herts
11 N4 Batcombe Dorset
20 C7 Batcombe Somset
82 E9 Bate Heath Ches E
50 D7 Batford Herts
20 D2 Bath BaNES
32 E11 Bathampton BaNES
18 E10 Bathealton Somset
32 E11 Batheaston BaNES
32 E11 Bathford BaNES
126 H4 Bathgate W Loth
85 N9 Bathley Notts
5 M7 Bathpool Cnwll
19 J9 Bathpool Somset
53 N5 Bath Side Essex
126 G4 Bathville W Loth
19 Q4 Bathway Somset
90 G6 Batley Kirk
47 N8 Batsford Gloucs
7 J11 Batson Devon
104 G9 Battersby N York
36 G5 Battersea Gt Lon
6 F9 Battisborough Cross Devon
64 F11 Battisford Suffk
64 E11 Battisford Tye Suffk
26 C8 Battle E Susx
44 E8 Battle Powys
19 K4 Battleborough Somset
47 J10 Battledown Gloucs
142 H6 Battledykes Angus
69 P11 Battlefield Shrops
86 H9 Battle of Britain Memorial Flight Lincs
38 C3 Battlesbridge Essex
49 Q9 Battlesden C Beds
18 B9 Battleton Somset
64 C9 Battlies Green Suffk
13 P5 Battramsley Cross Hants
23 M6 Batt's Corner Hants
46 G6 Baughton Worcs
22 G2 Baughurst Hants
150 G9 Baulds Abers
34 B6 Baulking Oxon
86 H6 Baumber Lincs
33 K4 Baunton Gloucs
57 M9 Baveney Wood Shrops
21 K8 Baverstock Wilts
76 H10 Bawburgh Norfk
76 E7 Bawdeswell Norfk
19 K7 Bawdrip Somset
53 P3 Bawdsey Suffk
75 N6 Bawsey Norfk
85 K2 Bawtry Donc
89 M5 Baxenden Lancs
59 L5 Baxterley Warwks
63 N9 Baxter's Green Suffk
152 D7 Bay Highld
168 k4 Bayble W Isls
22 F10 Baybridge Hants
112 E10 Baybridge Nthumb
94 F6 Baycliff Cumb
33 Q9 Baydon Wilts
50 H9 Bayford Herts
20 D9 Bayford Somset
168 c11 Bayhead W Isls
95 K10 Bay Horse Lancs
37 M10 Bayley's Hill Kent
64 G11 Baylham Suffk
48 F9 Baynard's Green Oxon
104 H9 Baysdale Abbey N York
45 R9 Baysham Herefs
56 H3 Bayston Hill Shrops
52 B3 Baythorne End Essex
57 M10 Bayton Worcs
57 N10 Bayton Common Worcs
34 E4 Bayworth Oxon
32 D10 Beach S Glos
49 L7 Beachampton Bucks
75 Q9 Beachamwell Norfk
31 Q6 Beachley Gloucs
25 N11 Beachy Head E Susx
10 D3 Beacon Devon
52 G7 Beacon End Essex
25 M4 Beacon Hill E Susx
26 D5 Beacon Hill Kent
85 P10 Beacon Hill Notts
23 N7 Beacon Hill Surrey
35 L5 Beacon's Bottom Bucks
35 P6 Beaconsfield Bucks
35 Q7 Beaconsfield Services Bucks
98 D4 Beadlam N York
50 D3 Beadlow C Beds
119 P5 Beadnell Nthumb
17 K8 Beaford Devon
91 N5 Beal N York
119 L2 Beal Nthumb
5 P8 Bealbury Cnwll
5 P6 Bealsmill Cnwll
71 N9 Beam Hill Staffs
71 K7 Beamhurst Staffs
11 K4 Beaminster Dorset
113 K10 Beamish Dur
96 G10 Beamsley N York
37 N6 Bean Kent
32 H11 Beanacre Wilts
119 L7 Beanley Nthumb
8 D8 Beardon Devon
89 K5 Beardwood Bl w D
9 N4 Beare Devon
24 E2 Beare Green Surrey
47 N2 Bearley Warwks
47 N2 Bearley Cross Warwks
103 P2 Bearpark Dur
125 N3 Bearsden E Duns
38 D10 Bearsted Kent
70 C7 Bearstone Shrops
58 F7 Bearwood Birm
45 M3 Bearwood Herefs
12 H5 Bearwood Poole
116 F10 Beattock D & G
51 N9 Beauchamp Roding Essex
84 D4 Beauchief Sheff
59 J11 Beaudesert Warwks
30 G2 Beaufort Blae G
14 C6 Beaulieu Hants
14 C6 Beaulieu House Hants
13 P3 Beaulieu Road Station Hants
155 P8 Beauly Highld
79 L9 Beaumaris IoA
110 F9 Beaumont Cumb
53 L7 Beaumont Essex
11 b2 Beaumont Jersey
103 Q7 Beaumont Hill Darltn
59 K10 Beausale Warwks
22 G9 Beauworth Hants
8 C5 Beaworthy Devon
52 B6 Beazley End Essex
81 L8 Bebington Wirral
113 L4 Bebside Nthumb
65 N4 Beccles Suffk
88 F6 Becconsall Lancs
57 P4 Beckbury Shrops
37 J7 Beckenham Gt Lon
37 J7 Beckenham Crematorium Gt Lon
100 D9 Beckermet Cumb
75 Q11 Beckett End Norfk
94 D3 Beckfoot Cumb

264 Beckfoot - Blackley

100 G10 Beckfoot Cumb
102 B11 Beck Foot Cumb
109 N11 Beckfoot Cumb
47 J7 Beckford Worcs
33 L11 Beckhampton Wilts
105 M10 Beck Hole N York
85 Q10 Beckingham Lincs
85 N3 Beckingham Notts
20 F4 Beckington Somset
56 F9 Beckjay Shrops
26 E7 Beckley E Susx
13 M5 Beckley Hants
34 G2 Beckley Oxon
63 L5 Beck Row Suffk
96 F11 Becks C Brad
94 E4 Beck Side Cumb
94 H4 Beck Side Cumb
37 K4 Beckton Gt Lon
97 L10 Beckwithshaw N York
37 L3 Becontree Gt Lon
11 b1 Becquet Vincent Jersey
97 L3 Bedale N York
103 L4 Bedburn Dur
20 G11 Bedchester Dorset
30 E7 Beddau Rhondd
67 K5 Beddgelert Gwynd
25 K9 Beddingham E Susx
36 H7 Beddington Gt Lon
36 G7 Beddington Corner Gt Lon
65 J8 Bedfield Suffk
65 J8 Bedfield Little Green Suffk
61 M11 Bedford Bed
61 N10 Bedford Crematorium Bed
26 B5 Bedgebury Cross Kent
24 B6 Bedham W Susx
15 K5 Bedhampton Hants
64 H8 Bedingfield Suffk
64 H8 Bedingfield Green Suffk
97 L8 Bedlam N York
113 L4 Bedlington Nthumb
30 E4 Bedlinog Myr Td
31 Q10 Bedminster Bristl
31 Q10 Bedminster Down Bristl
50 C10 Bedmond Herts
70 H11 Bednall Staffs
118 B7 Bedrule Border
56 F9 Bedstone Shrops
30 G7 Bedwas Caerph
30 G4 Bedwellty Caerph
59 N7 Bedworth Warwks
59 M7 Bedworth Woodlands Warwks
72 H9 Beeby Leics
23 J7 Beech Hants
70 F7 Beech Staffs
23 J2 Beech Hill W Berk
21 L3 Beechingstoke Wilts
34 E9 Beedon W Berk
34 E9 Beedon Hill W Berk
99 N10 Beeford E R Yk
84 C7 Beeley Derbys
93 M10 Beelsby NE Lin
34 G11 Beenham W Berk
35 M9 Beenham's Heath W & M
5 J3 Beeny Cnwll
10 E7 Beer Devon
19 M8 Beer Somset
19 K10 Beercrocombe Somset
11 N2 Beer Hackett Dorset
7 L10 Beesands Devon
87 N4 Beesby Lincs
7 L10 Beeson Devon
61 Q11 Beeston C Beds
69 P3 Beeston Ches W
90 H4 Beeston Leeds
76 C8 Beeston Norfk
72 E3 Beeston Notts
76 H3 Beeston Regis Norfk
109 J7 Beeswing D & G
95 K5 Beetham Cumb
10 F2 Beetham Somset
76 D8 Beetley Norfk
30 H8 Began Cardif
34 E2 Begbroke Oxon
75 J9 Begdale Cambs
41 M9 Begelly Pembks
90 H6 Beggarington Hill Leeds
45 K2 Beggar's Bush Powys
56 B9 Beguildy Powys
77 M10 Beighton Norfk
84 F4 Beighton Sheff
168 d12 Beinn Na Faoghla W Isls
125 K7 Beith N Ayrs
39 L10 Bekesbourne Kent
39 L10 Bekesbourne Hill Kent
77 K8 Belaugh Norfk
58 D9 Belbroughton Worcs
12 C3 Belchalwell Dorset
12 C3 Belchalwell Street Dorset
52 D3 Belchamp Otten Essex
52 C3 Belchamp St Paul Essex
52 D3 Belchamp Walter Essex
87 J5 Belchford Lincs
119 M4 Belford Nthumb
72 F9 Belgrave C Leic
128 H4 Belhaven E Loth
151 N4 Belhelvie Abers
150 D2 Belhinnie Abers
150 B5 Bellabeg Abers
45 M6 Bellamore Herefs
130 F9 Bellanoch Ag & B
92 D5 Bellasize E R Yk
142 C6 Bellaty Angus
50 G9 Bell Bar Herts
96 D9 Bell Busk N York
87 M5 Belleau Lincs
58 D9 Bell End Worcs
96 H2 Bellerby N York
8 G9 Bellever Devon
110 G9 Belle Vue Cumb
91 J7 Belle Vue Wakefd
116 D6 Bellfield S Lans
126 E11 Bellfield S Lans
58 D9 Bell Heath Worcs
23 K10 Bell Hill Hants
35 P3 Bellingdon Bucks
112 B4 Bellingham Nthumb
120 C4 Belloch Ag & B
120 C5 Bellochantuy Ag & B
69 P5 Bell o' th' Hill Ches W
13 J2 Bellows Cross Dorset
64 H11 Bells Cross Suffk
126 C5 Bellshill N Lans
119 M4 Bellshill Nthumb
126 E6 Bellside N Lans
127 J4 Bellsquarry W Loth
25 P3 Bells Yew Green E Susx
20 B2 Belluton BaNES
156 A6 Belmaduthy Highld
73 Q8 Belmesthorpe Rutlnd
89 K7 Belmont Bl w D
36 G8 Belmont Gt Lon
114 F4 Belmont S Ayrs
169 s3 Belmont Shet
150 B4 Belnacraig Abers
4 F9 Belowda Cnwll
84 D11 Belper Derbys
84 D11 Belper Lane End Derbys
84 H5 Belph Derbys
112 G5 Belsay Nthumb
117 R5 Belses Border
7 K7 Belsford Devon
50 B10 Belsize Herts
53 K3 Belstead Suffk
8 F6 Belstone Devon
89 L6 Belthorn Lancs
39 L8 Beltinge Kent
111 Q8 Beltingham Nthumb
92 D9 Beltoft N Linc
72 C6 Belton Leics
73 N3 Belton Lincs
92 C9 Belton N Linc
77 P11 Belton Norfk
73 L10 Belton Rutlnd
37 Q11 Beltring Kent
37 L5 Belvedere Gt Lon
73 L4 Belvoir Leics
73 L4 Belvoir Castle Leics
14 H9 Bembridge IoW
21 M8 Bemerton Wilts
99 P6 Bempton E R Yk
65 Q5 Benacre Suffk
168 d12 Benbecula W Isls
168 c12 Benbecula Airport W Isls
115 P8 Benbuie D & G
138 G10 Benderloch Ag & B
26 D5 Benenden Kent
112 G10 Benfieldside Dur
77 L6 Bengates Norfk
50 H8 Bengeo Herts
47 K6 Bengeworth Worcs
65 M9 Benhall Green Suffk
65 M9 Benhall Street Suffk
143 Q4 Benholm Abers
98 A9 Beningbrough N York
50 G6 Benington Herts
87 L11 Benington Lincs
87 M11 Benington Sea End Lincs
79 J8 Benllech IoA
131 N10 Benmore Ag & B
5 M3 Bennacott Cnwll
121 J7 Bennan N Ayrs
101 M6 Bennet Head Cumb
92 D5 Bennetland E R Yk
35 L5 Bennett End Bucks
139 M3 Ben Nevis Highld
86 H4 Benniworth Lincs
26 B2 Benover Kent
96 H11 Ben Rhydding C Brad
125 J9 Benslie N Ayrs
34 H6 Benson Oxon
51 M5 Bentfield Green Essex
57 M4 Benthall Shrops
46 H11 Bentham Gloucs
151 L7 Benthoul C Aber
56 E4 Bentlawn Shrops
91 P9 Bentley Donc
92 H3 Bentley E R Yk
23 L6 Bentley Hants
53 K4 Bentley Suffk
59 L5 Bentley Warwks
51 N11 Bentley Crematorium Essex
50 G11 Bentley Heath Herts
59 J9 Bentley Heath Solhll
17 M4 Benton Devon
110 F2 Bentpath D & G
17 N5 Bentwichen Devon
23 J6 Bentworth Hants
142 E11 Benvie Angus
11 L4 Benville Dorset
62 D2 Benwick Cambs
58 G11 Beoley Worcs
145 L9 Beoraidbeg Highld
23 N11 Bepton W Susx
51 L5 Berden Essex
40 E4 Berea Pembks
6 C5 Bere Alston Devon
6 D6 Bere Ferrers Devon
2 H9 Berepper Cnwll
12 D6 Bere Regis Dorset
77 L11 Bergh Apton Norfk
19 M7 Berhill Somset
34 G5 Berinsfield Oxon
32 C5 Berkeley Gloucs
32 C5 Berkeley Heath Gloucs
32 D4 Berkeley Road Gloucs
35 Q3 Berkhamsted Herts
20 F5 Berkley Somset
59 K9 Berkswell Solhll
36 H5 Bermondsey Gt Lon
59 N7 Bermuda Warwks
145 P3 Bernera Highld
152 G7 Bernisdale Highld
34 H6 Berrick Prior Oxon
34 H6 Berrick Salome Oxon
163 Q2 Berriedale Highld
101 L5 Berrier Cumb
56 B4 Berriew Powys
119 K2 Berrington Nthumb
57 J3 Berrington Shrops
57 K11 Berrington Worcs
57 K11 Berrington Green Worcs
19 J4 Berrow Somset
46 E8 Berrow Worcs
46 D3 Berrow Green Worcs
90 E8 Berry Brow Kirk
16 H9 Berry Cross Devon
17 K3 Berry Down Cross Devon
31 Q2 Berry Hill Gloucs
41 L2 Berry Hill Pembks
158 D5 Berryhillock Moray
158 D7 Berryhillock Moray
17 K2 Berrynarbor Devon
7 L6 Berry Pomeroy Devon
37 K9 Berry's Green Gt Lon
69 K5 Bersham Wrexhm
80 G9 Berthengam Flints
25 M9 Berwick E Susx
33 L10 Berwick Bassett Wilts
113 J5 Berwick Hill Nthumb
21 L7 Berwick St James Wilts
20 H10 Berwick St John Wilts
20 H8 Berwick St Leonard Wilts
129 P9 Berwick-upon-Tweed Nthumb
73 L5 Bescaby Leics
88 D8 Bescar Lancs
69 Q9 Besford Shrops
46 H6 Besford Worcs
91 Q10 Bessacarr Donc
34 E4 Bessels Leigh Oxon
89 N9 Besses o' th' Barn Bury
99 P7 Bessingby E R Yk
76 H4 Bessingham Norfk
25 P4 Bestbeech Hill E Susx
64 F2 Besthorpe Norfk
85 P8 Besthorpe Notts
85 J11 Bestwood Village Notts
99 L11 Beswick E R Yk
56 G5 Betchcott Shrops
36 F10 Betchworth Surrey
43 L2 Bethania Cerdgn
67 N6 Bethania Gwynd
53 J7 Beth Chatto Garden Essex
68 C7 Bethel Gwynd
79 J11 Bethel Gwynd
78 F10 Bethel IoA
68 F10 Bethel Powys
26 F3 Bethersden Kent
79 L11 Bethesda Gwynd
41 L7 Bethesda Pembks
43 N9 Bethlehem Carmth
36 H4 Bethnal Green Gt Lon
70 D5 Betley Staffs
37 P6 Betsham Kent
39 P11 Betteshanger Kent
10 H4 Bettiscombe Dorset
69 N7 Bettisfield Wrexhm
70 B7 Betton Shrops
57 J3 Betton Strange Shrops
31 J6 Bettws Newpt
43 L4 Bettws Bledrws Cerdgn
55 Q5 Bettws Cedewain Powys
42 F5 Bettws Evan Cerdgn
31 L3 Bettws-Newydd Mons
166 B4 Bettyhill Highld
29 P7 Betws Brdgnd
28 H2 Betws Carmth
67 J3 Betws Garmon Gwynd
68 D5 Betws Gwerfil Goch Denbgs
67 P3 Betws-y-Coed Conwy
80 C10 Betws-yn-Rhos Conwy
42 E5 Beulah Cerdgn
44 C4 Beulah Powys
24 H9 Bevendean Br & H
85 L6 Bevercotes Notts
92 H3 Beverley E R Yk
32 G6 Beverston Gloucs
32 C5 Bevington Gloucs
100 H4 Bewaldeth Cumb
111 L6 Bewcastle Cumb
57 P9 Bewdley Worcs
97 J7 Bewerley N York
99 P11 Bewholme E R Yk
25 Q4 Bewlbridge Kent
26 B10 Bexhill E Susx
37 L6 Bexley Gt Lon
37 L5 Bexleyheath Gt Lon
23 P9 Bexleyhill W Susx
38 E10 Bexon Kent
75 M10 Bexwell Norfk
64 C9 Beyton Suffk
64 C9 Beyton Green Suffk
168 f4 Bhaltos W Isls
168 b18 Bhatarsaigh W Isls
32 C6 Bibstone S Glos
33 M3 Bibury Gloucs
48 G10 Bicester Oxon
59 J8 Bickenhill Solhll
74 D3 Bicker Lincs
74 D3 Bicker Bar Lincs
74 D3 Bicker Gauntlet Lincs
82 D4 Bickershaw Wigan
81 N4 Bickerstaffe Lancs
69 P4 Bickerton Ches E
7 L11 Bickerton Devon
97 Q10 Bickerton N York
119 J10 Bickerton Nthumb
58 C2 Bickford Staffs
7 L4 Bickington Devon
17 J5 Bickington Devon
6 E6 Bickleigh Devon
9 M3 Bickleigh Devon
17 J5 Bickleton Devon
69 P5 Bickley Ches W
37 K7 Bickley Gt Lon
99 J2 Bickley N York
57 L10 Bickley Worcs
69 P5 Bickley Moss Ches W
52 C11 Bicknacre Essex
18 F7 Bicknoller Somset
38 E10 Bicknor Kent
13 K2 Bickton Hants
45 P2 Bicton Herefs
56 D8 Bicton Shrops
69 M11 Bicton Shrops
25 N2 Bidborough Kent
23 K5 Bidden Hants
26 E4 Biddenden Kent
26 E3 Biddenden Green Kent
61 M10 Biddenham Bed
32 G10 Biddestone Wilts
19 L4 Biddisham Somset
48 H7 Biddlesden Bucks
119 J9 Biddlestone Nthumb
70 F3 Biddulph Staffs
70 G3 Biddulph Moor Staffs
16 H6 Bideford Devon
47 M4 Bidford-on-Avon Warwks
81 K6 Bidston Wirral
92 C2 Bielby E R Yk
151 M7 Bieldside C Aber
14 F11 Bierley IoW
49 M11 Bierton Bucks
107 L9 Big Balcraig D & G
6 H9 Bigbury Devon
6 H10 Bigbury-on-Sea Devon
93 J9 Bigby Lincs
115 N8 Big Carlae D & G
94 D7 Biggar Cumb
116 E3 Biggar S Lans
71 M3 Biggin Derbys
71 P5 Biggin Derbys
91 N4 Biggin N York
37 K9 Biggin Hill Gt Lon
37 K8 Biggin Hill Airport Gt Lon
50 E2 Biggleswade C Beds
110 F4 Bigholms D & G
166 E4 Bighouse Highld
22 H8 Bighton Hants
110 E10 Biglands Cumb
15 Q4 Bignor W Susx
30 H3 Big Pit Blaenavon Torfn
100 D8 Bigrigg Cumb
160 B11 Big Sand Highld
169 q11 Bigton Shet
72 E2 Bilborough C Nott
18 D6 Bilbrook Somset
58 C4 Bilbrook Staffs
98 A11 Bilbrough N York
167 N6 Bilbster Highld
103 P6 Bildershaw Dur
52 G2 Bildeston Suffk
5 M3 Billacott Cnwll
37 Q2 Billericay Essex
73 J10 Billesdon Leics
47 M3 Billesley Warwks
74 B4 Billingborough Lincs
82 B4 Billinge St Hel
64 H6 Billingford Norfk
76 E7 Billingford Norfk
104 E6 Billingham S on T
86 G10 Billinghay Lincs
91 L10 Billingley Barns
24 C5 Billingshurst W Susx
57 N8 Billingsley Shrops
49 P10 Billington C Beds
89 L3 Billington Lancs
70 F10 Billington Staffs
77 N9 Billockby Norfk
103 N3 Billy Row Dur
88 G3 Bilsborrow Lancs
87 N5 Bilsby Lincs
15 Q6 Bilsham W Susx
26 H5 Bilsington Kent
85 K8 Bilsthorpe Notts
85 L8 Bilsthorpe Moor Notts
127 P5 Bilston Mdloth
58 E5 Bilston Wolves
72 B9 Bilstone Leics
27 J2 Bilting Kent
93 L4 Bilton E R Yk
97 M9 Bilton N York
97 Q11 Bilton N York
119 P8 Bilton Nthumb
59 Q10 Bilton Warwks
119 P8 Bilton Banks Nthumb
86 H2 Binbrook Lincs
103 P4 Binchester Blocks Dur
11 P8 Bincombe Dorset
20 B5 Binegar Somset
24 E7 Bines Green W Susx
35 M10 Binfield Br For
35 K9 Binfield Heath Oxon
112 E6 Bingfield Nthumb
73 J3 Bingham Notts
12 C4 Bingham's Melcombe Dorset
90 E3 Bingley C Brad
69 P11 Bings Shrops
76 D4 Binham Norfk
59 N9 Binley Covtry
22 D4 Binley Hants
59 N9 Binley Woods Warwks
12 E7 Binnegar Dorset
126 F3 Binniehill Falk
23 Q5 Binscombe Surrey
34 E3 Binsey Oxon
14 G8 Binstead IoW
23 L6 Binsted Hants
15 Q5 Binsted W Susx
47 M4 Binton Warwks
76 E7 Bintree Norfk
56 E4 Binweston Shrops
52 F8 Birch Essex
89 P9 Birch Rochdl
75 Q4 Bircham Newton Norfk
75 Q4 Bircham Tofts Norfk
51 M6 Birchanger Essex
51 M6 Birchanger Green Services Essex
71 L8 Birch Cross Staffs
90 E7 Birchencliffe Kirk
56 H11 Bircher Herefs
58 G6 Birchfield Birm
52 F8 Birch Green Essex
50 G8 Birch Green Herts
46 G5 Birch Green Worcs
30 G9 Birchgrove Cardif
29 K5 Birchgrove Swans
25 K5 Birchgrove W Susx
69 P2 Birch Heath Ches W
81 Q10 Birch Hill Ches W
39 P8 Birchington Kent
59 L6 Birchley Heath Warwks
59 L4 Birchmoor Warwks
49 Q8 Birchmoor Green C Beds
84 B8 Birchover Derbys
89 N9 Birch Services Rochdl
83 M7 Birch Vale Derbys
86 B7 Birchwood Lincs
10 E2 Birch Wood Somset
82 E6 Birchwood Warrtn
85 K2 Bircotes Notts
52 B3 Birdbrook Essex
97 Q5 Birdforth N York
15 M6 Birdham W Susx
59 P11 Birdingbury Warwks
32 H2 Birdlip Gloucs
111 M7 Birdoswald Cumb
98 G7 Birdsall N York
90 G9 Birds Edge Kirk
51 N9 Birds Green Essex
57 P7 Birdsgreen Shrops
10 H4 Birdsmoorgate Dorset
64 E11 Bird Street Suffk
91 J10 Birdwell Barns
46 D11 Birdwood Gloucs
118 E3 Birgham Border
162 H8 Birichin Highld
88 H8 Birkacre Lancs
104 B10 Birkby N York
88 C8 Birkdale Sefton
158 D4 Birkenbog Abers
81 L7 Birkenhead Wirral
158 H8 Birkenhills Abers
90 G5 Birkenshaw Kirk
149 Q9 Birkhall Abers
142 F11 Birkhill Angus
117 J7 Birkhill D & G
73 P6 Birkholme Lincs
91 N5 Birkin N York
90 H5 Birks Leeds
111 Q7 Birkshaw Nthumb
45 P4 Birley Herefs
84 D2 Birley Carr Sheff
37 Q8 Birling Kent
119 P9 Birling Nthumb
25 N11 Birling Gap E Susx
46 H6 Birlingham Worcs
58 G7 Birmingham Birm
59 J8 Birmingham Airport Solhll
141 P9 Birnam P & K
159 N11 Birness Abers
150 F8 Birse Abers
150 E8 Birsemore Abers
90 G5 Birstall Kirk
72 F9 Birstall Leics
97 K9 Birstwith N York
74 B4 Birthorpe Lincs
113 L9 Birtley Gatesd
56 F11 Birtley Herefs
112 C5 Birtley Nthumb
113 L9 Birtley Crematorium Gatesd
46 E7 Birts Street Worcs
73 M11 Bisbrooke Rutlnd
86 H4 Biscathorpe Lincs
3 R3 Biscovey Cnwll
35 M7 Bisham W & M
47 J4 Bishampton Worcs
17 N6 Bish Mill Devon
103 P5 Bishop Auckland Dur
86 D2 Bishopbridge Lincs
125 Q3 Bishopbriggs E Duns
92 G3 Bishop Burton E R Yk
104 B4 Bishop Middleham Dur
157 N5 Bishopmill Moray
97 M7 Bishop Monkton N York
86 C2 Bishop Norton Lincs
39 L11 Bishopsbourne Kent
21 K2 Bishops Cannings Wilts
56 E7 Bishop's Castle Shrops
11 P2 Bishop's Caundle Dorset
47 J9 Bishop's Cleeve Gloucs
46 C5 Bishop's Frome Herefs
35 Q10 Bishops Gate Surrey
51 P7 Bishop's Green Essex
22 F2 Bishop's Green Hants
18 H10 Bishops Hull Somset
48 C3 Bishop's Itchington Warwks
18 G9 Bishops Lydeard Somset
46 F10 Bishop's Norton Gloucs
17 P7 Bishop's Nympton Devon
70 D9 Bishop's Offley Staffs
51 L6 Bishop's Stortford Herts
22 H8 Bishop's Sutton Hants
48 B2 Bishop's Tachbrook Warwks
17 K6 Bishop's Tawton Devon
7 N4 Bishopsteignton Devon
22 E11 Bishopstoke Hants
28 G7 Bishopston Swans
35 M2 Bishopstone Bucks
25 L10 Bishopstone E Susx
45 N6 Bishopstone Herefs
39 M8 Bishopstone Kent
33 P8 Bishopstone Swindn
21 L9 Bishopstone Wilts
20 G6 Bishopstrow Wilts
19 Q3 Bishop Sutton BaNES
22 G11 Bishop's Waltham Hants
10 F2 Bishopswood Somset
58 B3 Bishop's Wood Staffs
31 Q11 Bishopsworth Bristl
97 L8 Bishop Thornton N York
98 B11 Bishopthorpe C York
104 C6 Bishopton Darltn
125 L3 Bishopton Rens
47 N3 Bishopton Warwks
98 F9 Bishop Wilton E R Yk
31 L7 Bishton Newpt
71 J10 Bishton Staffs
32 H3 Bisley Gloucs
23 Q3 Bisley Surrey
23 P3 Bisley Camp Surrey
88 C2 Bispham Bpool
88 F8 Bispham Green Lancs
3 K5 Bissoe Cnwll
13 K4 Bisterne Hants
37 N10 Bitchet Green Kent
73 P5 Bitchfield Lincs
17 J3 Bittadon Devon
6 H7 Bittaford Devon
76 C8 Bittering Norfk
57 K9 Bitterley Shrops
14 E4 Bitterne C Sotn
60 B3 Bitteswell Leics
32 C11 Bitton S Glos
35 K8 Bix Oxon
169 q8 Bixter Shet
72 F11 Blaby Leics
129 L9 Blackadder Border
7 L8 Blackawton Devon
100 D9 Blackbeck Cumb
10 B3 Blackborough Devon
75 N7 Blackborough End Norfk
33 Q4 Black Bourton Oxon
25 M6 Blackboys E Susx
84 D11 Blackbrook Derbys
82 B5 Blackbrook St Hel
70 D7 Blackbrook Staffs
36 E11 Blackbrook Surrey
151 L5 Blackburn Abers
89 K5 Blackburn Bl w D
84 E2 Blackburn Rothm
126 H4 Blackburn W Loth
89 K6 Blackburn with Darwen Services Bl w D
113 J7 Black Callerton N u Ty
64 F2 Black Car Norfk
24 G3 Black Corner W Susx
115 M6 Blackcraig E Ayrs
138 G11 Black Crofts Ag & B
4 E9 Black Cross Cnwll
82 G10 Blackden Heath Ches E
151 P5 Blackdog Abers
9 K3 Black Dog Devon
8 D9 Blackdown Devon
10 H4 Blackdown Dorset
109 P10 Blackdyke Cumb
91 J9 Blacker Barns
91 K10 Blacker Hill Barns
37 L6 Blackfen Gt Lon
14 D6 Blackfield Hants
110 G8 Blackford Cumb
133 P6 Blackford P & K
19 M5 Blackford Somset
20 C9 Blackford Somset
72 A7 Blackfordby Leics
14 E11 Blackgang IoW
127 M2 Blackhall C Edin
104 E3 Blackhall Dur
104 E3 Blackhall Colliery Dur
112 H9 Blackhall Mill Gatesd
117 N3 Blackhaugh Border
52 H7 Blackheath Essex
37 J5 Blackheath Gt Lon
58 E7 Blackheath Sandw
65 N7 Blackheath Suffk
36 B11 Blackheath Surrey
112 G5 Black Heddon Nthumb
159 Q6 Blackhill Abers
159 Q9 Blackhill Abers
112 G10 Blackhill Dur
159 M8 Blackhill of Clackriach Abers
9 N6 Blackhorse Devon
74 E3 Blackjack Lincs
33 K11 Blackland Wilts
89 Q2 Black Lane Ends Lancs
116 E9 Blacklaw D & G
83 J4 Blackley Manch

Blackley Crematorium - Bradley 265

82 H4 Blackley Crematorium Manch
142 A5 Blacklunans P & K
45 Q7 Blackmarstone Herefs
29 P7 Blackmill Brdgnd
23 L8 Blackmoor Hants
90 H3 Black Moor Leeds
19 N2 Blackmoor N Som
90 D8 Blackmoorfoot Kirk
51 P10 Blackmore Essex
52 B5 Blackmore End Essex
50 E7 Blackmore End Herts
127 K2 Blackness Falk
23 L6 Blacknest Hants
35 Q11 Blacknest W & M
52 C7 Black Notley Essex
89 P2 Blacko Lancs
28 H6 Black Pill Swans
88 C3 Blackpool Bpool
7 L4 Blackpool Devon
7 M9 Blackpool Devon
88 C4 Blackpool Airport Lancs
111 K5 Blackpool Gate Cumb
126 F4 Blackridge W Loth
2 H7 Blackrock Cnwll
30 H2 Blackrock Mons
89 J8 Blackrod Bolton
157 M10 Blacksboat Moray
109 M7 Blackshaw D & G
90 B5 Blackshaw Head Calder
64 G8 Blacksmith's Green Suffk
16 L6 Blacksnape Bl w D
24 F7 Blackstone W Susx
65 Q4 Black Street Suffk
41 J9 Black Tar Pembks
48 H11 Blackthorn Oxon
64 C9 Blackthorpe Suffk
92 D6 Blacktoft E R Yk
151 M7 Blacktop C Aber
8 C3 Black Torrington Devon
71 P5 Blackwall Derbys
3 J4 Blackwater Cnwll
23 M3 Blackwater Hants
14 F9 Blackwater IoW
19 J11 Blackwater Somset
120 H6 Blackwaterfoot N Ayrs
110 H10 Blackwell Cumb
103 Q8 Blackwell Darltn
83 P10 Blackwell Derbys
84 F9 Blackwell Derbys
47 P6 Blackwell Warwks
58 E10 Blackwell Worcs
46 E9 Blackwellsend Green Gloucs
30 G5 Blackwood Caerph
109 K3 Blackwood D & G
126 D9 Blackwood S Lans
70 G3 Blackwood Hill Staffs
81 M11 Blacon Ches W
27 L2 Bladbean Kent
107 M7 Bladnoch D & G
34 E2 Bladon Oxon
19 M10 Bladon Somset
42 D5 Blaenannerch Cerdgn
67 N5 Blaenau Ffestiniog Gwynd
31 J3 Blaenavon Torfn
44 C7 Blaen Dyryn Powys
41 N3 Blaenffos Pembks
29 P6 Blaengarw Brdgnd
54 E8 Blaengeuffordd Cerdgn
29 N3 Blaengwrach Neath
29 N5 Blaengwynfi Neath
30 D5 Blaenllechau Rhondd
43 M2 Blaenpennal Cerdgn
54 D9 Blaenplwyf Cerdgn
42 E5 Blaenporth Cerdgn
29 P5 Blaenrhondda Rhondd
135 P5 Blaenwaun Carmth
42 F9 Blaen-y-Coed Carmth
30 F2 Blaen-y-cwm Blae G
55 J9 Blaenycwm Cerdgn
29 P5 Blaen-y-cwm Rhondd
19 P3 Blagdon N Som
18 H11 Blagdon Somset
7 M6 Blagdon Torbay
18 H11 Blagdon Hill Somset
111 P11 Blagill Cumb
88 F9 Blaguegate Lancs
139 J2 Blaich Highld
138 B4 Blain Highld
30 H3 Blaina Blae G
141 L4 Blair Atholl P & K
133 L8 Blair Drummond Stirlg
142 B8 Blairgowrie P & K
134 B10 Blairhall Fife
134 B8 Blairingone P & K
133 N8 Blairlogie Stirlg
131 P11 Blairmore Ag & B
164 E5 Blairmore Highld
124 B4 Blair's Ferry Ag & B
46 D11 Blaisdon Gloucs
57 Q9 Blakebrook Worcs
58 C9 Blakedown Worcs
52 B7 Blake End Essex
70 H5 Blakeley Lane Staffs
82 C10 Blakemere Ches W
45 M6 Blakemere Herefs
7 K6 Blakemore Devon
58 F4 Blakenall Heath Wsall
32 C3 Blakeney Gloucs
76 E3 Blakeney Norfk
70 C5 Blakenhall Ches E
58 D5 Blakenhall Wolves
58 B8 Blakeshall Worcs
48 H4 Blakesley Nhants
112 E10 Blanchland Nthumb
12 F3 Blandford Camp Dorset
12 E3 Blandford Forum Dorset
12 E3 Blandford St Mary Dorset
97 K10 Bland Hill N York
125 N2 Blanefield Stirlg
86 E8 Blankney Lincs
126 B6 Blantyre S Lans
139 L4 Blar a' Chaorainn Highld
147 Q9 Blargie Highld
139 K4 Blarmachfoldach Highld
13 L3 Blashford Hants
73 L11 Blaston Leics
73 P11 Blatherwycke Nhants
94 F3 Blawith Cumb
108 D4 Blawquhairn D & G
65 M10 Blaxhall Suffk
91 R10 Blaxton Donc
113 J8 Blaydon Gatesd
19 N5 Bleadney Somset
19 K3 Bleadon N Som
20 E8 Bleak Street Somset
39 K9 Blean Kent
86 F4 Bleasby Lincs
85 M11 Bleasby Notts
95 M11 Bleasdale Lancs
102 D8 Bleatarn Cumb
57 K10 Bleathwood Herefs
135 L4 Blebocraigs Fife
56 C11 Bleddfa Powys
47 P10 Bledington Gloucs
35 L4 Bledlow Bucks
35 L5 Bledlow Ridge Bucks
20 G3 Bleet Wilts
128 D7 Blegbie E Loth
102 B4 Blencarn Cumb
110 C11 Blencogo Cumb
15 K4 Blendworth Hants
100 G2 Blennerhasset Cumb
48 F11 Bletchingdon Oxon
36 H10 Bletchingley Surrey
49 N8 Bletchley M Keyn
69 R8 Bletchley Shrops
41 L6 Bletherston Pembks
61 M9 Bletsoe Bed
34 F7 Blewbury Oxon
76 H6 Blickling Norfk
85 J9 Blidworth Notts
85 J10 Blidworth Bottoms Notts
118 F8 Blindburn Nthumb
100 F4 Blindcrake Cumb
37 J11 Blindley Heath Surrey
5 J7 Blisland Cnwll
13 L2 Blissford Hants
57 N10 Bliss Gate Worcs
49 K4 Blisworth Nhants
71 K11 Blithbury Staffs
109 P10 Blitterlees Cumb
47 N8 Blockley Gloucs
77 L10 Blofield Norfk
77 L9 Blofield Heath Norfk
64 E6 Blo Norton Norfk
118 A6 Bloomfield Border
70 C8 Blore Staffs
71 L5 Blore Staffs
23 K5 Blounce Hants
71 K8 Blounts Green Staffs
88 D7 Blowick Sefton
48 D7 Bloxham Oxon
86 E10 Bloxholm Lincs
58 E4 Bloxwich Wsall
12 E6 Bloxworth Dorset
97 J9 Blubberhouses N York
4 E10 Blue Anchor Cnwll
18 D6 Blue Anchor Somset
38 B9 Blue Bell Hill Kent
83 P8 Blue John Cavern Derbys
81 L5 Blundellsands Sefton
65 Q2 Blundeston Suffk
61 Q10 Blunham C Beds
33 M7 Blunsdon St Andrew Swindn
58 D10 Bluntington Worcs
62 E6 Bluntisham Cambs
5 N9 Blunts Cnwll
58 H11 Blunts Green Warwks
70 F6 Blurton C Stke
86 B2 Blyborough Lincs
65 N6 Blyford Suffk
57 Q2 Blymhill Staffs
57 Q2 Blymhill Lawn Staffs
85 K3 Blyth Notts
113 M4 Blyth Nthumb
127 L8 Blyth Bridge Border
65 N6 Blythburgh Suffk
113 M4 Blyth Crematorium Nthumb
128 F10 Blythe Border
70 H6 Blythe Bridge Staffs
59 K6 Blythe End Warwks
70 H6 Blythe Marsh Staffs
85 Q2 Blyton Lincs
135 P5 Boarhills Fife
14 H5 Boarhunt Hants
38 C10 Boarley Kent
89 N6 Boarsgreave Lancs
25 M4 Boarshead E Susx
88 H9 Boar's Head Wigan
34 F3 Boars Hill Oxon
34 H2 Boarstall Bucks
8 D6 Boasley Cross Devon
155 Q3 Boath Highld
148 G4 Boat of Garten Highld
38 E8 Bobbing Kent
57 Q6 Bobbington Staffs
51 M9 Bobbingworth Essex
5 K10 Bocaddon Cnwll
52 C7 Bocking Essex
52 C6 Bocking Churchstreet Essex
46 A2 Bockleton Worcs
5 J9 Boconnoc Cnwll
159 R9 Boddam Abers
169 q12 Boddam Shet
46 G9 Boddington Gloucs
78 E8 Bodedern IoA
80 E9 Bodelwyddan Denbgs
45 Q4 Bodenham Herefs
21 N9 Bodenham Wilts
45 Q4 Bodenham Moor Herefs
78 G6 Bodewryd IoA
80 F10 Bodfari Denbgs
78 G9 Bodffordd IoA
66 E7 Bodfuan Gwynd
76 G3 Bodham Norfk
26 C6 Bodiam E Susx
26 C6 Bodiam Castle E Susx
48 E7 Bodicote Oxon
4 F7 Bodieve Cnwll
5 J11 Bodinnick Cnwll
25 Q8 Bodle Street Green E Susx
4 H8 Bodmin Cnwll
5 K6 Bodmin Moor Cnwll
79 Q10 Bodnant Garden Conwy
64 A2 Bodney Norfk
78 F11 Bodorgan IoA
27 K2 Bodsham Kent
4 G9 Bodwen Cnwll
59 J5 Bodymoor Heath Warwks
156 A7 Bogallan Highld
159 P10 Bogbrae Abers
125 L11 Bogend S Ayrs
128 C5 Boggs Holdings E Loth
127 N4 Boghall Mdloth
126 H4 Boghall W Loth
126 D9 Boghead S Lans
157 R5 Bogmoor Moray
149 M3 Bogmuir Abers
158 E8 Bogniebrae Abers
15 P7 Bognor Regis W Susx
148 G3 Bogroy Highld
108 D4 Bogue D & G
5 Q8 Bohetherick Cnwll
3 M7 Bohortha Cnwll
146 H11 Bohuntine Highld
2 B7 Bojewyan Cnwll
4 H9 Bokiddick Cnwll
103 N6 Bolam Dur
112 H4 Bolam Nthumb
6 H11 Bolberry Devon
82 B7 Bold Heath St Hel
58 H6 Boldmere Birm
113 M8 Boldon Colliery S Tyne
13 P5 Boldre Hants
103 K8 Boldron Dur
85 N3 Bole Notts
84 C9 Bolehill Derbys
84 D6 Bole Hill Derbys
2 H6 Bolenowe Cnwll
18 C11 Bolham Devon
10 D2 Bolham Water Devon
3 K3 Bolingey Cnwll
83 K9 Bollington Ches E
83 K9 Bollington Cross Ches E
32 D2 Bollow Gloucs
24 G6 Bolney W Susx
61 N9 Bolnhurst Bed
143 L7 Bolshan Angus
84 G6 Bolsover Derbys
90 D7 Bolster Moor Kirk
90 H11 Bolsterstone Sheff
97 Q3 Boltby N York
150 C5 Boltenstone Abers
35 L6 Bolter End Bucks
89 L9 Bolton Bolton
102 B6 Bolton Cumb
128 E6 Bolton E Loth
98 F10 Bolton E R Yk
119 M8 Bolton Nthumb
96 G10 Bolton Abbey N York
96 G10 Bolton Bridge N York
96 A11 Bolton by Bowland Lancs
111 J7 Boltonfellend Cumb
100 H2 Boltongate Cumb
95 K7 Bolton le Sands Lancs
100 H2 Bolton Low Houses Cumb
100 H2 Bolton New Houses Cumb
103 Q11 Bolton-on-Swale N York
91 N2 Bolton Percy N York
95 K7 Bolton Town End Lancs
91 M10 Bolton Upon Dearne Barns
89 J8 Bolton West Services Lancs
5 K6 Bolventor Cnwll
113 L4 Bomarsund Nthumb
69 N11 Bomere Heath Shrops
162 E8 Bonar Bridge Highld
139 J11 Bonawe Ag & B
92 H7 Bonby N Linc
41 P3 Boncath Pembks
118 A8 Bonchester Bridge Border
14 G11 Bonchurch IoW
8 G4 Bondleigh Devon
88 F2 Bonds Lancs
8 H9 Bonehill Devon
59 J4 Bonehill Staffs
134 C11 Bo'ness Falk
58 F2 Boney Hay Staffs
125 K2 Bonhill W Duns
57 Q4 Boningale Shrops
118 C6 Bonjedward Border
126 E6 Bonkle N Lans
143 K10 Bonnington Angus
27 J4 Bonnington Kent
135 K7 Bonnybank Fife
126 E2 Bonnybridge Falk
159 L7 Bonnykelly Abers
127 Q4 Bonnyrigg Mdloth
142 E10 Bonnyton Angus
84 C9 Bonsall Derbys
110 D6 Bonshaw Tower D & G
45 M11 Bont Mons
67 M11 Bontddu Gwynd
55 K4 Bont-Dolgadfan Powys
54 F7 Bont-goch or Elerch Cerdgn
87 N6 Bonthorpe Lincs
54 E11 Bontnewydd Cerdgn
66 H3 Bontnewydd Gwynd
68 E3 Bontuchel Denbgs
30 E10 Bonvilston V Glam
68 F6 Bonwm Denbgs
29 J5 Bon-y-maen Swans
17 J4 Boode Devon
35 M6 Booker Bucks
69 Q9 Booley Shrops
128 F10 Boon Border
70 E4 Boon Hill Staffs
14 F4 Boorley Green Hants
105 J7 Boosbeck R & Cl
52 D5 Boose's Green Essex
100 G10 Boot Cumb
90 C5 Booth Calder
86 C9 Boothby Graffoe Lincs
73 P4 Boothby Pagnell Lincs
92 B5 Boothferry E R Yk
83 K8 Booth Green Ches E
82 F4 Boothstown Salfd
90 D5 Booth Town Calder
60 G8 Boothville Nhants
94 C3 Bootle Cumb
81 L5 Bootle Sefton
82 G10 Boots Green Ches W
53 M2 Boot Street Suffk
103 K10 Booze N York
57 L11 Boraston Shrops
10 c1 Bordeaux Guern
38 E9 Borden Kent
23 M10 Borden W Susx
110 C10 Border Cumb
111 M4 Border Forest Park
117 R4 Borders Crematorium Border
96 D7 Bordley N York
23 L7 Bordon Camp Hants
52 C10 Boreham Essex
20 G6 Boreham Wilts
25 Q8 Boreham Street E Susx
50 E11 Borehamwood Herts
110 C2 Boreland D & G
152 B7 Boreraig Highld
57 J3 Boreton Shrops
168 b17 Borgh W Isls
168 j2 Borgh W Isls
165 Q5 Borgie Highld
108 D11 Borgue D & G
167 K11 Borgue Highld
52 D3 Borley Essex
52 D3 Borley Green Essex
64 D9 Borley Green Suffk
152 F3 Borneskitaig Highld
108 D11 Borness D & G
97 N7 Boroughbridge N York
37 P9 Borough Green Kent
69 L4 Borras Head Wrexhm
72 C4 Borrowash Derbys
97 P3 Borrowby N York
105 L7 Borrowby N York
134 B11 Borrowstoun Falk
38 B8 Borstal Medway
54 E6 Borth Cerdgn
117 N8 Borthwickbrae Border
117 N7 Borthwickshiels Border
67 K7 Borth-y-Gest Gwynd
152 G8 Borve Highld
168 b17 Borve W Isls
168 f8 Borve W Isls
168 j2 Borve W Isls
95 L6 Borwick Lancs
101 K11 Borwick Lodge Cumb
94 D5 Borwick Rails Cumb
2 B7 Bosavern Cnwll
46 C6 Bosbury Herefs
4 G8 Boscarne Cnwll
4 H3 Boscastle Cnwll
13 K6 Boscombe Bmouth
21 P7 Boscombe Wilts
3 Q3 Boscoppa Cnwll
15 M6 Bosham W Susx
15 M6 Bosham Hoe W Susx
41 J12 Bosherston Pembks
2 C7 Boskednan Cnwll
2 C9 Boskenna Cnwll
83 K11 Bosley Ches E
4 D9 Bosoughan Cnwll
98 E8 Bossall N York
4 H4 Bossiney Cnwll
27 L2 Bossingham Kent
18 A5 Bossington Somset
82 E11 Bostock Green Ches W
74 F2 Boston Lincs
87 K11 Boston Crematorium Lincs
97 P11 Boston Spa Leeds
2 C7 Boswarthan Cnwll
3 P5 Boswinger Cnwll
2 B7 Botallack Cnwll
50 G11 Botany Bay Gt Lon
72 D10 Botcheston Leics
64 E6 Botesdale Suffk
113 K3 Bothal Nthumb
34 F9 Bothampstead W Berk
85 L6 Bothamsall Notts
100 G3 Bothel Cumb
11 K6 Bothenhampton Dorset
126 C6 Bothwell S Lans
126 C6 Bothwell Services S Lans
35 Q4 Botley Bucks
14 F4 Botley Hants
34 E3 Botley Oxon
49 K10 Botolph Claydon Bucks
24 E9 Botolphs W Susx
27 K5 Botolph's Bridge Kent
73 L3 Bottesford Leics
92 E9 Bottesford N Linc
62 H8 Bottisham Cambs
135 K3 Bottomcraig Fife
88 F5 Bottom of Hutton Lancs
89 K8 Bottom o' th' Moor Bolton
89 Q6 Bottoms Calder
2 B9 Bottoms Cnwll
59 K6 Botts Green Warwks
5 Q9 Botusfleming Cnwll
66 D8 Botwnnog Gwynd
37 L11 Bough Beech Kent
44 G7 Boughrood Powys
31 Q5 Boughspring Gloucs
60 G7 Boughton Nhants
75 P10 Boughton Norfk
85 L7 Boughton Notts
26 H2 Boughton Aluph Kent
49 Q7 Boughton End C Beds
38 C11 Boughton Green Kent
26 E2 Boughton Malherbe Kent
38 C11 Boughton Monchelsea Kent
39 J10 Boughton Street Kent
105 L7 Boulby R & Cl
90 C6 Boulder Clough Calder
14 C9 Bouldnor IoW
57 J7 Bouldon Shrops
119 Q8 Boulmer Nthumb
41 J8 Boulston Pembks
86 C7 Boultham Lincs
62 D9 Bourn Cambs
74 A6 Bourne Lincs
37 M2 Bournebridge Essex
58 F8 Bournebrook Birm
61 M8 Bourne End Bed
35 N7 Bourne End Bucks
49 Q6 Bourne End C Beds
50 B9 Bourne End Herts
13 J6 Bournemouth Bmouth
13 K5 Bournemouth Airport Dorset
13 K6 Bournemouth Crematorium Bmouth
32 H4 Bournes Green Gloucs
38 F4 Bournes Green Sthend
58 E10 Bournheath Worcs
113 M10 Bournmoor Dur
32 D6 Bournstream Gloucs
58 F8 Bournville Birm
20 E8 Bourton Dorset
19 L2 Bourton N Som
33 P7 Bourton Oxon
57 K5 Bourton Shrops
21 K2 Bourton Wilts
59 P10 Bourton on Dunsmore Warwks
47 N8 Bourton-on-the-Hill Gloucs
47 N10 Bourton-on-the-Water Gloucs
136 H3 Bousd Ag & B
110 E9 Boustead Hill Cumb
94 G3 Bouth Cumb
96 H6 Bouthwaite N York
47 K3 Bouts Worcs
35 P9 Boveney Bucks
13 J2 Boveridge Dorset
9 K9 Bovey Tracey Devon
50 B10 Bovingdon Herts
35 M7 Bovingdon Green Bucks
51 M9 Bovinger Essex
12 D7 Bovington Dorset
12 D7 Bovington Camp Dorset
12 D7 Bovington Tank Museum Dorset
110 F9 Bow Cumb
7 L7 Bow Devon
8 H4 Bow Devon
37 J4 Bow Gt Lon
169 c7 Bow Ork
102 H6 Bowbank Dur
49 P8 Bow Brickhill M Keyn
32 G3 Bowbridge Gloucs
104 B3 Bowburn Dur
14 E9 Bowcombe IoW
10 C6 Bowd Devon
117 R4 Bowden Border
7 L9 Bowden Devon
32 H11 Bowden Hill Wilts
82 G7 Bowdon Traffd
167 M4 Bower Highld
31 Q10 Bower Ashton Bristl
21 K10 Bowerchalke Wilts
20 H2 Bowerhill Wilts
19 N11 Bower Hinton Somset
52 G3 Bower House Tye Suffk
167 M4 Bowermadden Highld
70 E7 Bowers Staffs
38 C4 Bowers Gifford Essex
134 D9 Bowershall Fife
91 L5 Bower's Row Leeds
103 J8 Bowes Dur
88 F2 Bowgreave Lancs
109 M7 Bowhouse D & G
5 K5 Bowithick Cnwll
81 N4 Bowker's Green Lancs
117 P2 Bowland Border
95 J3 Bowland Bridge Cumb
45 Q4 Bowley Herefs
45 Q4 Bowley Town Herefs
23 P7 Bowlhead Green Surrey
90 F4 Bowling C Brad
125 L3 Bowling W Duns
69 L5 Bowling Bank Wrexhm
46 F4 Bowling Green Worcs
101 K11 Bowmanstead Cumb
122 D8 Bowmore Ag & B
110 D8 Bowness-on-Solway Cumb
101 M11 Bowness-on-Windermere Cumb
135 J5 Bow of Fife Fife
143 J8 Bowriefauld Angus
101 L4 Bowscale Cumb
119 J2 Bowsden Nthumb
101 N11 Bowston Cumb
54 E7 Bow Street Cerdgn
64 E2 Bow Street Norfk
76 H10 Bowthorpe Norfk
32 G4 Box Gloucs
32 F11 Box Wilts
32 D2 Boxbush Gloucs
46 C10 Boxbush Gloucs
61 M11 Box End Bed
52 G3 Boxford Suffk
34 D10 Boxford W Berk
15 P5 Boxgrove W Susx
36 E10 Box Hill Surrey
38 C10 Boxley Kent
50 B9 Boxmoor Herts
16 C11 Box's Shop Cnwll
52 G5 Boxted Essex
52 H5 Boxted Essex
64 A11 Boxted Suffk
52 H5 Boxted Cross Essex
32 F6 Boxwell Gloucs
62 D8 Boxworth Cambs
62 E7 Boxworth End Cambs
63 M9 Boyden End Suffk
39 M8 Boyden Gate Kent
71 M7 Boylestone Derbys
158 F5 Boyndie Abers
159 M5 Boyndlie Abers
99 N7 Boynton E R Yk
143 L8 Boysack Angus
11 P2 Boys Hill Dorset
84 E7 Boythorpe Derbys
5 N3 Boyton Cnwll
53 Q2 Boyton Suffk
21 J7 Boyton Wilts
51 P9 Boyton Cross Essex
52 B3 Boyton End Suffk
61 K9 Bozeat Nhants
80 d6 Braaid IoM
65 K9 Brabling Green Suffk
27 K3 Brabourne Kent
27 J3 Brabourne Lees Kent
167 P3 Brabstermire Highld
152 F10 Bracadale Highld
74 A8 Braceborough Lincs
86 C7 Bracebridge Heath Lincs
86 C7 Bracebridge Low Fields Lincs
73 Q3 Braceby Lincs
96 C11 Bracewell Lancs
84 E9 Brackenfield Derbys
126 C4 Brackenhirst N Lans
110 E11 Brackenthwaite Cumb
97 L10 Brackenthwaite N York
15 M7 Bracklesham W Susx
146 F11 Brackletter Highld
48 G7 Brackley Nhants
48 H6 Brackley Hatch Nhants
35 N11 Bracknell Br For
133 N6 Braco P & K
158 D7 Bracobrae Moray
64 H2 Bracon Ash Norfk
145 M9 Bracora Highld
145 M9 Bracorina Highld
5 P3 Bradaford Devon
71 N4 Bradbourne Derbys
104 B5 Bradbury Dur
48 H5 Bradden Nhants
5 K9 Braddock Cnwll
70 F4 Bradeley C Stke
35 M5 Bradenham Bucks
33 K9 Bradenstoke Wilts
9 Q3 Bradfield Devon
53 K5 Bradfield Essex
77 K5 Bradfield Norfk
84 C2 Bradfield Sheff
34 H10 Bradfield W Berk
64 B10 Bradfield Combust Suffk
70 B3 Bradfield Green Ches E
53 K5 Bradfield Heath Essex
64 C10 Bradfield St Clare Suffk
64 C10 Bradfield St George Suffk
90 F4 Bradford C Brad
5 J6 Bradford Cnwll
16 G10 Bradford Devon
112 G5 Bradford Nthumb
119 N4 Bradford Nthumb
11 M2 Bradford Abbas Dorset
20 F2 Bradford Leigh Wilts
20 F2 Bradford-on-Avon Wilts
18 G10 Bradford-on-Tone Somset
11 P6 Bradford Peverell Dorset
17 K5 Bradiford Devon
14 H9 Brading IoW
71 N5 Bradley Derbys

266 Bradley - Broomhaugh

22 H6 Bradley Hants
90 F6 Bradley Kirk
96 F4 Bradley N York
93 M9 Bradley NE Lin
70 F11 Bradley Staffs
58 E5 Bradley Wolves
47 J2 Bradley Worcs
69 K4 Bradley Wrexhm
69 P5 Bradley Common Ches W
19 J7 Bradley Green Somset
59 L4 Bradley Green Warwks
47 J2 Bradley Green Worcs
71 K6 Bradley in the Moors Staffs
32 B8 Bradley Stoke S Glos
72 F4 Bradmore Notts
19 K7 Bradney Somset
9 N4 Bradninch Devon
17 L5 Bradninch Devon
71 J3 Bradnop Staffs
45 K3 Bradnor Green Herefs
11 K6 Bradpole Dorset
89 L8 Bradshaw Bolton
90 D5 Bradshaw Calder
90 D8 Bradshaw Kirk
5 P5 Bradstone Devon
70 D2 Bradwall Green Ches E
83 Q8 Bradwell Derbys
17 J3 Bradwell Devon
52 D7 Bradwell Essex
49 M6 Bradwell M Keyn
77 Q11 Bradwell Norfk
70 F5 Bradwell Crematorium Staffs
52 H10 Bradwell-on-Sea Essex
52 G10 Bradwell Waterside Essex
16 E9 Bradworthy Devon
156 B5 Brae Highld
169 q7 Brae Shet
133 M11 Braeface Falk
143 M7 Braehead Angus
107 M7 Braehead D & G
126 H7 Braehead S Lans
149 M9 Braemar Abers
161 K11 Braemore Highld
167 J11 Braemore Highld
147 J9 Brae Roy Lodge Highld
124 G3 Braeside Inver
142 D6 Braes of Coul Angus
158 A6 Braes of Enzie Moray
169 f3 Braeswick Ork
131 K6 Braevallich Ag & B
103 Q6 Brafferton Darltn
97 P6 Brafferton N York
60 H9 Brafield-on-the-Green Nhants
168 h3 Bragar W Isls
50 G6 Bragbury End Herts
126 E8 Braidwood S Lans
71 P6 Brailsford Derbys
71 P6 Brailsford Green Derbys
32 C3 Brain's Green Gloucs
52 C7 Braintree Essex
64 G7 Braiseworth Suffk
22 C9 Braishfield Hants
90 C2 Braithwaite C Brad
100 H6 Braithwaite Cumb
84 H2 Braithwell Donc
91 L7 Braken Hill Wakefd
24 E8 Bramber W Susx
22 E10 Brambridge Hants
72 E3 Bramcote Notts
59 P7 Bramcote Warwks
72 E3 Bramcote Crematorium Notts
22 H9 Bramdean Hants
77 K11 Bramerton Norfk
50 G7 Bramfield Herts
65 M7 Bramfield Suffk
53 K2 Bramford Suffk
83 J8 Bramhall Stockp
91 L2 Bramham Leeds
90 H2 Bramhope Leeds
23 J3 Bramley Hants
90 G3 Bramley Leeds
84 G2 Bramley Rothm
24 B2 Bramley Surrey
22 H3 Bramley Corner Hants
23 J3 Bramley Green Hants
96 H9 Bramley Head N York
39 M10 Bramling Kent
9 M5 Brampford Speke Devon
62 B6 Brampton Cambs
102 C6 Brampton Cumb
111 K8 Brampton Cumb
85 P5 Brampton Lincs
77 J7 Brampton Norfk
91 L10 Brampton Rothm
65 N5 Brampton Suffk
46 B9 Brampton Abbotts Herefs
60 G3 Brampton Ash Nhants
56 F10 Brampton Bryan Herefs
84 G3 Brampton-en-le-Morthen Rothm
71 K8 Bramshall Staffs
21 Q11 Bramshaw Hants
23 K2 Bramshill Hants
23 M8 Bramshott Hants
19 M9 Bramwell Somset
137 N2 Branault Highld
75 Q2 Brancaster Norfk
75 Q2 Brancaster Staithe Norfk
103 P3 Brancepeth Dur
157 K7 Branchill Moray
87 L11 Brand End Lincs
157 N3 Branderburgh Moray
99 N11 Brandesburton E R Yk
65 J9 Brandeston Suffk
46 D9 Brand Green Gloucs
16 G11 Brandis Corner Devon
76 G7 Brandiston Norfk
103 P2 Brandon Dur
86 B11 Brandon Lincs
119 K7 Brandon Nthumb
63 N3 Brandon Suffk
59 P9 Brandon Warwks
63 K3 Brandon Bank Norfk
63 K2 Brandon Creek Norfk
76 F10 Brandon Parva Norfk
98 B6 Brandsby N York
92 H11 Brandy Wharf Lincs
2 C8 Brane Cnwll
51 Q5 Bran End Essex
12 H6 Branksome Poole
13 J6 Branksome Park Poole
22 D6 Bransbury Hants
85 Q5 Bransby Lincs
10 D7 Branscombe Devon
46 E4 Bransford Worcs
13 L5 Bransgore Hants
93 K4 Bransholme C KuH
57 M9 Bransley Shrops
58 G10 Branson's Cross Worcs
73 L5 Branston Leics
86 D7 Branston Lincs
71 N10 Branston Staffs
86 E7 Branston Booths Lincs
14 G10 Branstone IoW
86 B10 Brant Broughton Lincs
53 K5 Brantham Suffk
100 E6 Branthwaite Cumb
101 J3 Branthwaite Cumb
92 F5 Brantingham E R Yk
91 Q10 Branton Donc
119 K7 Branton Nthumb
97 P8 Branton Green N York
118 G3 Branxton Nthumb
69 P2 Brassey Green Ches W
71 N4 Brassington Derbys
37 L9 Brasted Kent
37 L10 Brasted Chart Kent
150 H8 Brathens Abers
87 N8 Bratoft Lincs
86 B4 Brattleby Lincs
18 B5 Bratton Somset
20 H4 Bratton Wilts
57 L2 Bratton Wrekin
8 C6 Bratton Clovelly Devon
17 L4 Bratton Fleming Devon
20 C9 Bratton Seymour Somset
51 J5 Braughing Herts
51 K6 Braughing Friars Herts
60 B7 Braunston Nhants
73 L9 Braunston Rutlnd
72 F10 Braunstone Leics
16 H4 Braunton Devon
98 E5 Brawby N York
166 D3 Brawl Highld
104 F9 Braworth N York
35 P9 Bray W & M
60 G4 Braybrooke Nhants
33 K7 Braydon Wilts
33 J6 Braydon Brook Wilts
33 K7 Braydon Side Wilts
17 M5 Brayford Devon
25 Q8 Bray's Hill E Susx
5 N7 Bray Shop Cnwll
100 D9 Braystones Cumb
97 K11 Braythorn N York
91 Q4 Brayton N York
35 N9 Braywick W & M
35 N9 Braywoodside W & M
5 M3 Brazacott Cnwll
27 L2 Breach Kent
38 D8 Breach Kent
50 E6 Breachwood Green Herts
69 M7 Breaden Heath Shrops
72 B3 Breadsall Derbys
32 D4 Breadstone Gloucs
45 K4 Breadward Herefs
2 G8 Breage Cnwll
155 N9 Breakachy Highld
36 C3 Breakspear Crematorium Gt Lon
162 C8 Brealangwell Lodge Highld
32 B3 Bream Gloucs
21 N11 Breamore Hants
19 J3 Brean Somset
168 e5 Breanais W Isls
90 C5 Brearley Calder
97 M8 Brearton N York
168 h4 Breascleit W Isls
168 h4 Breasclete W Isls
72 D4 Breaston Derbys
43 K8 Brechfa Carmth
143 L5 Brechin Angus
64 D3 Breckles Norfk
44 E9 Brecon Powys
44 E10 Brecon Beacons National Park
83 K6 Bredbury Stockp
26 D8 Brede E Susx
46 B3 Bredenbury Herefs
65 K11 Bredfield Suffk
38 E9 Bredgar Kent
38 C9 Bredhurst Kent
46 H7 Bredon Worcs
46 H7 Bredon's Hardwick Worcs
46 H7 Bredon's Norton Worcs
45 L6 Bredwardine Herefs
72 C6 Breedon on the Hill Leics
126 H5 Breich W Loth
89 L9 Breightmet Bolton
92 B4 Breighton E R Yk
45 P7 Breinton Herefs
33 J10 Bremhill Wilts
17 M6 Bremridge Devon
25 Q2 Brenchley Kent
16 F10 Brendon Devon
17 P2 Brendon Devon
18 D8 Brendon Hill Somset
123 P3 Brenfield Ag & B
168 e5 Brenish W Isls
113 K5 Brenkley N u Ty
52 F2 Brent Eleigh Suffk
36 E5 Brentford Gt Lon
73 K7 Brentingby Leics
19 K4 Brent Knoll Somset
6 H7 Brent Mill Devon
51 K4 Brent Pelham Herts
37 N2 Brentwood Essex
26 H6 Brenzett Kent
26 H6 Brenzett Green Kent
71 K11 Brereton Staffs
70 D2 Brereton Green Ches E
82 H11 Brereton Heath Ches E
71 K11 Brereton Hill Staffs
169 s9 Bressay Shet
64 F5 Bressingham Norfk
64 F5 Bressingham Common Norfk
71 P10 Bretby Derbys
71 P10 Bretby Crematorium Derbys
59 P9 Bretford Warwks
47 L6 Bretforton Worcs
88 F6 Bretherton Lancs
169 r8 Brettabister Shet
64 C5 Brettenham Norfk
64 D11 Brettenham Suffk
84 B5 Bretton Derbys
69 L2 Bretton Flints
51 N6 Brewers End Essex
36 H10 Brewer Street Surrey
58 C3 Brewood Staffs
12 D6 Briantspuddle Dorset
51 N5 Brick End Essex
50 H9 Brickendon Herts
50 D10 Bricket Wood Herts
84 D4 Brick Houses Sheff
52 B5 Brickkiln Green Essex
47 J6 Bricklehampton Worcs
80 f1 Bride IoM
100 F4 Bridekirk Cumb
41 N2 Bridell Pembks
8 D7 Bridestowe Devon
158 E10 Brideswell Abers
9 K7 Bridford Devon
39 L11 Bridge Kent
94 D4 Bridge End Cumb
110 G11 Bridge End Cumb
6 H9 Bridge End Devon
103 K3 Bridge End Dur
51 Q4 Bridge End Essex
74 B3 Bridge End Lincs
100 E5 Bridgefoot Cumb
51 L3 Bridge Green Essex
19 Q10 Bridgehampton Somset
97 M6 Bridge Hewick N York
112 G10 Bridgehill Dur
97 J7 Bridgehouse Gate N York
14 G6 Bridgemary Hants
70 C5 Bridgemere Ches E
158 D10 Bridgend Abers
120 E4 Bridgend Ag & B
122 D7 Bridgend Ag & B
143 J4 Bridgend Angus
29 P9 Bridgend Brdgnd
42 C5 Bridgend Cerdgn
101 M8 Bridgend Cumb
116 F9 Bridgend D & G
6 F9 Bridgend Devon
135 K5 Bridgend Fife
158 A11 Bridgend Moray
134 E3 Bridgend P & K
127 J2 Bridgend W Loth
142 D7 Bridgend of Lintrathen Angus
150 F4 Bridge of Alford Abers
133 M8 Bridge of Allan Stirlg
149 M3 Bridge of Avon Moray
157 M10 Bridge of Avon Moray
140 E8 Bridge of Balgie P & K
142 B5 Bridge of Brewlands Angus
149 L3 Bridge of Brown Highld
142 A7 Bridge of Cally P & K
150 H8 Bridge of Canny Abers
142 D7 Bridge of Craigisla Angus
108 F9 Bridge of Dee D & G
151 N6 Bridge of Don C Aber
156 G9 Bridge of Dulsie Highld
150 H10 Bridge of Dye Abers
134 E4 Bridge of Earn P & K
140 D6 Bridge of Ericht P & K
151 J9 Bridge of Feugh Abers
166 H3 Bridge of Forss Highld
150 B8 Bridge of Gairn Abers
140 D6 Bridge of Gaur P & K
158 E7 Bridge of Marnoch Abers
139 P10 Bridge of Orchy Ag & B
141 L4 Bridge of Tilt P & K
158 A5 Bridge of Tynet Moray
169 p8 Bridge of Walls Shet
125 K4 Bridge of Weir Rens
17 M9 Bridge Reeve Devon
16 D11 Bridgerule Devon
56 F5 Bridges Shrops
45 N6 Bridge Sollers Herefs
52 E2 Bridge Street Suffk
5 N4 Bridgetown Cnwll
18 B8 Bridgetown Somset
81 P10 Bridge Trafford Ches W
32 C10 Bridge Yate S Glos
64 D4 Bridgham Norfk
57 N6 Bridgnorth Shrops
19 J7 Bridgwater Somset
19 K8 Bridgwater Services Somset
99 P7 Bridlington E R Yk
11 K6 Bridport Dorset
46 A10 Bridstow Herefs
89 N3 Brierfield Lancs
91 L8 Brierley Barns
46 B11 Brierley Gloucs
45 P3 Brierley Herefs
58 D7 Brierley Hill Dudley
104 E4 Brierton Hartpl
101 J6 Briery Cumb
92 H9 Brigg N Linc
77 L6 Briggate Norfk
105 N9 Briggswath N York
100 E4 Brigham Cumb
101 J6 Brigham Cumb
99 M10 Brigham E R Yk
90 E6 Brighouse Calder
14 D10 Brighstone IoW
84 C9 Brightgate Derbys
34 C4 Brighthampton Oxon
90 H11 Brightholmlee Sheff
8 F5 Brightley Devon
25 Q6 Brightling E Susx
53 J8 Brightlingsea Essex
24 H10 Brighton Br & H
3 N3 Brighton Cnwll
81 L5 Brighton le Sands Sefton
126 G2 Brightons Falk
34 D9 Brightwalton W Berk
34 D9 Brightwalton Green W Berk
34 D9 Brightwalton Holt W Berk
53 N3 Brightwell Suffk
35 J5 Brightwell Baldwin Oxon
34 G6 Brightwell-cum-Sotwell Oxon
35 J6 Brightwell Upperton Oxon
103 L8 Brignall Dur
132 G6 Brig o'Turk Stirlg
93 N10 Brigsley NE Lin
95 K3 Brigsteer Cumb
61 K3 Brigstock Nhants
35 J2 Brill Bucks
3 J8 Brill Cnwll
45 K5 Brilley Herefs
57 J11 Brimfield Herefs
57 J11 Brimfield Cross Herefs
84 F6 Brimington Derbys
9 K9 Brimley Devon
32 H2 Brimpsfield Gloucs
22 G2 Brimpton W Berk
22 G2 Brimpton Common W Berk
32 G4 Brimscombe Gloucs
81 L8 Brimstage Wirral
84 D4 Brincliffe Sheff
92 B4 Brind E R Yk
19 P7 Brindham Somset
169 p8 Brindister Shet
88 H6 Brindle Lancs
57 Q2 Brineton Staffs
60 H2 Bringhurst Leics
46 D3 Bringsty Common Herefs
61 N5 Brington Cambs
76 E5 Brininghamn Norfk
85 M10 Brinkely Notts
87 L6 Brinkhill Lincs
63 K10 Brinkley Cambs
59 P9 Brinklow Warwks
33 K8 Brinkworth Wilts
89 J6 Brinscall Lancs
19 M4 Brinscombe Somset
19 M2 Brinsea N Som
84 G11 Brinsley Notts
45 N6 Brinsop Herefs
84 F3 Brinsworth Rothm
76 E4 Brinton Norfk
169 d4 Brinyan Ork
110 H10 Brisco Cumb
76 C7 Brisley Norfk
32 B10 Brislington Bristl
26 F4 Brissenden Green Kent
31 Q10 Bristol Bristl
31 P11 Bristol Airport N Som
31 Q10 Bristol Zoo Bristl
76 F5 Briston Norfk
6 F5 Brisworthy Devon
89 P6 Britannia Lancs
21 N9 Britford Wilts
30 F4 Brithdir Caerph
67 P11 Brithdir Gwynd
38 B10 British Legion Village Kent
29 K6 Briton Ferry Neath
35 J6 Britwell Salome Oxon
7 N7 Brixham Torbay
6 F8 Brixton Devon
36 H5 Brixton Gt Lon
20 G7 Brixton Deverill Wilts
60 F6 Brixworth Nhants
33 Q3 Brize Norton Oxon
33 Q3 Brize Norton Airport Oxon
58 C11 Broad Alley Worcs
33 M6 Broad Blunsdon Swindn
83 L6 Broadbottom Tamesd
15 M5 Broadbridge W Susx
24 D4 Broadbridge Heath W Susx
47 N7 Broad Campden Gloucs
90 D7 Broad Carr Calder
21 K9 Broad Chalke Wilts
89 P6 Broad Clough Lancs
9 N5 Broadclyst Devon
125 J3 Broadfield Inver
41 M10 Broadfield Pembks
145 K3 Broadford Highld
26 B4 Broad Ford Kent
24 C6 Broadford Bridge W Susx
117 J8 Broadgairhill Border
64 D9 Broadgrass Green Suffk
63 L8 Broad Green Cambs
52 E7 Broad Green Essex
46 E3 Broad Green Worcs
58 E10 Broad Green Worcs
129 M9 Broadhaugh Border
40 G8 Broad Haven Pembks
82 G7 Broadheath Traffd
57 M11 Broadheath Worcs
10 C4 Broadhembury Devon
7 L5 Broadhempston Devon
63 J5 Broad Hill Cambs
33 M9 Broad Hinton Wilts
85 Q6 Broadholme Lincs
26 D8 Broadland Row E Susx
28 C3 Broadlay Carmth
22 D2 Broad Layings Hants
51 K9 Broadley Essex
89 P7 Broadley Lancs
158 A5 Broadley Moray
51 K9 Broadley Common Essex
47 M5 Broad Marston Worcs
12 B7 Broadmayne Dorset
70 E5 Broad Meadow Staffs
22 H5 Broadmere Hants
46 B11 Broadmoor Gloucs
41 L9 Broadmoor Pembks
8 H4 Broadnymett Devon
94 C2 Broad Oak Cumb
11 J5 Broadoak Dorset
25 P6 Broad Oak E Susx
26 D8 Broad Oak E Susx
32 C2 Broadoak Gloucs
23 L4 Broad Oak Hants
45 P10 Broad Oak Herefs
39 L9 Broad Oak Kent
82 B5 Broad Oak St Hel
69 L3 Broadoak Wrexhm
65 K6 Broad Road Suffk
51 Q8 Broad's Green Essex
39 Q8 Broadstairs Kent
31 P4 Broadstone Mons
12 H5 Broadstone Poole
57 J7 Broadstone Shrops
26 E8 Broad Street E Susx
51 N7 Broad Street Essex
27 K3 Broad Street Kent
38 D10 Broad Street Kent
38 C7 Broad Street Medway
21 M3 Broad Street Wilts
52 E10 Broad Street Green Essex
33 L9 Broad Town Wilts
46 E3 Broadwas Worcs
50 F6 Broadwater Herts
24 D10 Broadwater W Susx
58 B9 Broadwaters Worcs
28 C3 Broadway Carmth
41 Q8 Broadway Carmth
40 G8 Broadway Pembks
19 K11 Broadway Somset
65 M6 Broadway Suffk
47 L7 Broadway Worcs
31 Q2 Broadwell Gloucs
47 P9 Broadwell Gloucs
33 Q4 Broadwell Oxon
59 Q11 Broadwell Warwks
11 P8 Broadwey Dorset
11 J4 Broadwindsor Dorset
8 F3 Broadwood Kelly Devon
5 Q4 Broadwoodwidger Devon
45 L6 Brobury Herefs
153 K8 Brochel Highld
139 J11 Brochroy Ag & B
88 G2 Brock Lancs
46 E4 Brockamin Worcs
22 H11 Brockbridge Hants
65 J6 Brockdish Norfk
58 C10 Brockencote Worcs
13 P4 Brockenhurst Hants
126 E10 Brocketsbrae S Lans
64 G8 Brockford Green Suffk
64 G8 Brockford Street Suffk
60 D8 Brockhall Nhants
36 E11 Brockham Surrey
46 H9 Brockhampton Gloucs
47 K10 Brockhampton Gloucs
15 K5 Brockhampton Hants
46 A8 Brockhampton Herefs
46 C3 Brockhampton Estate Herefs
11 Q3 Brockhampton Green Dorset
90 F8 Brockholes Kirk
84 D8 Brockhurst Derbys
59 Q8 Brockhurst Warwks
101 K2 Brocklebank Cumb
93 K8 Brocklesby Lincs
31 N11 Brockley N Som
64 A7 Brockley Suffk
63 M11 Brockley Green Suffk
64 A11 Brockley Green Suffk
101 N3 Brockleymoor Cumb
58 D7 Brockmoor Dudley
8 C5 Brockscombe Devon
22 F11 Brock's Green Hants
56 E4 Brockton Shrops
56 E7 Brockton Shrops
57 K6 Brockton Shrops
57 N4 Brockton Shrops
70 E8 Brockton Staffs
31 P4 Brockweir Gloucs
22 H9 Brockwood Park Hants
46 G11 Brockworth Gloucs
4 G8 Brocton Cnwll
70 H11 Brocton Staffs
121 K4 Brodick N Ayrs
156 H6 Brodie Moray
91 N9 Brodsworth Donc
152 H4 Brogaig Highld
49 Q7 Brogborough C Beds
32 H7 Brokenborough Wilts
83 J10 Broken Cross Ches E
82 E10 Broken Cross Ches W
20 F4 Brokerswood Wilts
81 M8 Bromborough Wirral
64 G6 Brome Suffk
64 H6 Brome Street Suffk
65 L11 Bromeswell Suffk
110 C11 Bromfield Cumb
56 H9 Bromfield Shrops
61 M10 Bromham Bed
33 J11 Bromham Wilts
91 J11 Bromley Barns
58 D7 Bromley Dudley
37 K7 Bromley Gt Lon
57 N5 Bromley Shrops
37 K7 Bromley Common Gt Lon
53 J6 Bromley Cross Essex
26 G4 Bromley Green Kent
56 E4 Bromlow Shrops
38 C8 Brompton Medway
104 C11 Brompton N York
99 J4 Brompton-by-Sawdon N York
103 P11 Brompton-on-Swale N York
18 E8 Brompton Ralph Somset
18 C8 Brompton Regis Somset
46 C10 Bromsash Herefs
46 D8 Bromsberrow Gloucs
46 D8 Bromsberrow Heath Gloucs
58 E10 Bromsgrove Worcs
70 D11 Bromstead Heath Staffs
46 C4 Bromyard Herefs
46 C3 Bromyard Downs Herefs
67 N8 Bronaber Gwynd
54 E11 Bronant Cerdgn
57 J7 Broncroft Shrops
42 F5 Brongest Cerdgn
69 N7 Bronington Wrexhm
44 G8 Bronllys Powys
42 H10 Bronwydd Carmth
45 J5 Bronydd Powys
69 J7 Bronygarth Shrops
79 Q9 Bron-y-Nant Crematorium Conwy
41 Q9 Brook Carmth
13 N2 Brook Hants
22 B9 Brook Hants
14 C10 Brook IoW
27 J3 Brook Kent
23 P7 Brook Surrey
36 C11 Brook Surrey
65 K2 Brooke Norfk
73 L9 Brooke Rutlnd
93 M11 Brookenby Lincs
61 N8 Brook End Bed
61 Q11 Brook End C Beds
61 N6 Brook End Cambs
49 P6 Brook End M Keyn
125 L5 Brookfield Rens
34 H5 Brookhampton Oxon
20 B9 Brookhampton Somset
13 N2 Brook Hill Hants
80 F11 Brook House Denbgs
95 L8 Brookhouse Lancs
84 H3 Brookhouse Rothm
70 E2 Brookhouse Green Ches E
83 M7 Brookhouses Derbys
26 G6 Brookland Kent
82 G6 Brooklands Traffd
50 F10 Brookmans Park Herts
55 Q5 Brooks Powys
72 H7 Brooksby Leics
39 N8 Brooks End Kent
24 D6 Brooks Green W Susx
37 N2 Brook Street Essex
26 F5 Brook Street Kent
52 D2 Brook Street Suffk
24 H5 Brook Street W Susx
32 F2 Brookthorpe Gloucs
75 P11 Brookville Norfk
23 Q3 Brookwood Surrey
50 E2 Broom C Beds
84 F2 Broom Rothm
47 L4 Broom Warwks
65 M3 Broome Norfk
56 G8 Broome Shrops
58 D9 Broome Worcs
82 F7 Broomedge Warrtn
119 M8 Broome Park Nthumb
24 D6 Broomer's Corner W Susx
24 C7 Broomershill W Susx
52 B9 Broomfield Essex
38 D11 Broomfield Kent
39 L8 Broomfield Kent
18 H8 Broomfield Somset
69 M11 Broomfields Shrops
92 E5 Broomfleet E R Yk
76 D7 Broom Green Norfk
35 Q11 Broomhall W & M
112 F8 Broomhaugh Nthumb

Broom Hill - Caerwedros 267

91 L10 Broom Hill Barns
12 H4 Broom Hill Dorset
84 H11 Broom Hill Notts
119 P10 Broomhill Nthumb
58 D9 Broom Hill Worcs
70 A5 Broomhill Green Ches E
112 F8 Broomley Nthumb
103 P2 Broompark Dur
46 D8 Broom's Green Gloucs
76 A6 Broomsthorpe Norfk
38 H9 Broom Street Kent
163 L6 Brora Highld
57 M4 Broseley Shrops
74 E8 Brotherhouse Bar Lincs
102 H3 Brotherlee Dur
87 J11 Brothertoft Lincs
91 M5 Brotherton N York
105 J7 Brotton R & Cl
166 H5 Broubster Highld
102 E8 Brough Cumb
83 Q8 Brough Derbys
92 F5 Brough E R Yk
167 M2 Brough Highld
85 P9 Brough Notts
169 s7 Brough Shet
69 Q6 Broughall Shrops
169 s4 Brough Lodge Shet
102 E8 Brough Sowerby Cumb
116 G3 Broughton Border
35 M2 Broughton Bucks
62 C5 Broughton Cambs
69 K2 Broughton Flints
22 B8 Broughton Hants
88 G4 Broughton Lancs
49 N7 Broughton M Keyn
92 G9 Broughton N Linc
96 D10 Broughton N York
98 F6 Broughton N York
60 H5 Broughton Nhants
48 D7 Broughton Oxon
82 H4 Broughton Salfd
70 D8 Broughton Staffs
29 P10 Broughton V Glam
60 B2 Broughton Astley Leics
94 F4 Broughton Beck Cumb
20 G2 Broughton Gifford Wilts
47 J2 Broughton Green Worcs
46 H4 Broughton Hackett Worcs
94 E3 Broughton-in-Furness Cumb
107 N8 Broughton Mains D & G
94 E2 Broughton Mills Cumb
100 E4 Broughton Moor Cumb
33 P4 Broughton Poggs Oxon
94 E3 Broughton Tower Cumb
142 H11 Broughty Ferry C Dund
94 F6 Brow End Cumb
102 D9 Brownber Cumb
22 G7 Brown Candover Hants
88 D8 Brown Edge Lancs
70 G4 Brown Edge Staffs
69 N2 Brown Heath Ches W
69 N9 Brownheath Shrops
159 L9 Brownhill Abers
135 N4 Brownhills Fife
58 F3 Brownhills Wsall
119 N6 Brownieside Nthumb
22 G3 Browninghill Green Hants
70 F3 Brown Lees Staffs
70 E2 Brownlow Heath Ches E
100 D6 Brownrigg Cumb
110 C10 Brownrigg Cumb
12 H7 Brownsea Island Dorset
58 G6 Brown's Green Birm
16 D6 Brownsham Devon
32 G4 Browns Hill Gloucs
60 B5 Brownsover Warwks
6 H8 Brownston Devon
64 F9 Brown Street Suffk
75 N7 Brow-of-the-Hill Norfk
77 P11 Browston Green Norfk
99 J2 Broxa N York
51 J9 Broxbourne Herts
128 H4 Broxburn E Loth
127 K3 Broxburn W Loth
119 P7 Broxfield Nthumb
51 N5 Broxted Essex
69 N4 Broxton Ches W
25 L8 Broyle Side E Susx
167 P9 Bruan Highld
141 K4 Bruar P & K
163 L9 Brucefield Highld
124 E6 Bruchag Ag & B
69 M2 Bruera Ches W
47 Q10 Bruern Abbey Oxon
122 C7 Bruichladdich Ag & B
65 L8 Bruisyard Suffk
65 L8 Bruisyard Street Suffk
92 E9 Brumby N Linc
71 L2 Brund Staffs
77 L10 Brundall Norfk
65 K8 Brundish Suffk
65 K7 Brundish Street Suffk
138 C3 Brunery Highld
2 E6 Brunnion Cnwll
56 F8 Brunslow Shrops
113 K6 Brunswick Village N u Ty
90 H5 Bruntcliffe Leeds
96 G11 Brunthwaite C Brad
60 D3 Bruntingthorpe Leics
135 J3 Brunton Fife
119 P6 Brunton Nthumb
21 P3 Brunton Wilts
17 M10 Brushford Devon
18 B9 Brushford Somset
20 C7 Bruton Somset
58 C11 Bryan's Green Worcs
12 E3 Bryanston Dorset
35 N5 Bryant's Bottom Bucks
110 C6 Brydekirk D & G
2 b2 Bryher IoS
69 J4 Brymbo Wrexhm
19 P11 Brympton Somset
28 F4 Bryn Carmth
82 D10 Bryn Ches W
29 M6 Bryn Neath
56 D7 Bryn Shrops
82 C4 Bryn Wigan
29 K2 Brynamman Carmth
41 M3 Brynberian Pembks
29 L6 Brynbryddan Neath
67 L7 Bryn-bwbach Gwynd
30 C8 Bryncae Rhondd
29 P8 Bryncethin Brdgnd
66 H6 Bryncir Gwynd
29 K5 Bryn-coch Neath
66 C8 Bryncroes Gwynd
54 E4 Bryncrug Gwynd
78 E10 Bryn Du IoA
67 N9 Bryn-Eden Gwynd
68 F5 Bryneglwys Denbgs
69 K6 Brynfields Wrexhm
80 H10 Brynford Flints
82 C4 Bryn Gates Wigan
30 D7 Bryn Golau Rhondd
78 F9 Bryngwran IoA
31 L3 Bryngwyn Mons
44 H5 Bryngwyn Powys
41 K3 Bryn-Henllan Pembks
42 F4 Brynhoffnant Cerdgn
88 E5 Bryning Lancs
30 H4 Brynithel Blae G
30 G2 Brynmawr Blae G
66 C8 Bryn-mawr Gwynd
29 P8 Brynmenyn Brdgnd
28 H6 Brynmill Swans
30 C8 Brynna Rhondd
55 Q4 Bryn-penarth Powys
67 K2 Brynrefail Gwynd
78 H7 Brynrefail IoA
30 D8 Brynsadler Rhondd
68 E4 Bryn Saith Marchog Denbgs
78 H11 Brynsiencyn IoA
78 H8 Brynteg IoA
69 J2 Bryn-y-bal Flints
79 Q9 Bryn-y-Maen Conwy
69 J6 Bryn-yr-Eos Wrexhm
144 F3 Bualintur Highld
80 H9 Buarth-draw Flints
59 N10 Bubbenhall Warwks
92 B3 Bubwith E R Yk
117 L8 Buccleuch Border
132 F10 Buchanan Smithy Stirlg
159 R8 Buchanhaven Abers
133 Q2 Buchanty P & K
133 L7 Buchany Stirlg
132 H9 Buchlyvie Stirlg
110 G11 Buckabank Cumb
61 Q7 Buckden Cambs
96 D5 Buckden N York
77 M10 Buckenham Norfk
10 C4 Buckerell Devon
7 J5 Buckfast Devon
7 J5 Buckfastleigh Devon
135 K8 Buckhaven Fife
45 Q11 Buckholt Mons
5 P2 Buckhorn Devon
20 E10 Buckhorn Weston Dorset
37 K2 Buckhurst Hill Essex
158 B4 Buckie Moray
49 J8 Buckingham Bucks
35 N2 Buckland Bucks
6 H10 Buckland Devon
47 L7 Buckland Gloucs
13 P5 Buckland Hants
51 J4 Buckland Herts
27 P3 Buckland Kent
34 B5 Buckland Oxon
36 F10 Buckland Surrey
16 G7 Buckland Brewer Devon
35 P3 Buckland Common Bucks
20 E4 Buckland Dinham Somset
16 H10 Buckland Filleigh Devon
7 J4 Buckland in the Moor Devon
6 D5 Buckland Monachorum Devon
11 P3 Buckland Newton Dorset
11 P8 Buckland Ripers Dorset
10 F2 Buckland St Mary Somset
7 K9 Buckland-Tout-Saints Devon
34 G10 Bucklebury W Berk
14 D6 Bucklers Hard Hants
53 M3 Bucklesham Suffk
69 J2 Buckley Flints
59 J11 Buckley Green Warwks
82 F8 Bucklow Hill Ches E
73 M6 Buckminster Leics
70 G5 Bucknall C Stke
86 G7 Bucknall Lincs
48 G9 Bucknell Oxon
56 F10 Bucknell Shrops
158 B4 Buckpool Moray
151 M6 Bucksburn C Aber
16 F7 Buck's Cross Devon
24 C4 Bucks Green W Susx
88 H6 Buckshaw Village Lancs
50 C10 Bucks Hill Herts
23 M6 Bucks Horn Oak Hants
16 F7 Buck's Mills Devon
99 P6 Buckton E R Yk
56 F10 Buckton Herefs
119 L3 Buckton Nthumb
61 P5 Buckworth Cambs
85 K7 Budby Notts
70 C5 Buddileigh Staffs
16 C10 Bude Cnwll
5 N10 Budge's Shop Cnwll
9 N4 Budlake Devon
119 N3 Budle Nthumb
9 Q8 Budleigh Salterton Devon
25 L6 Budlett's Common E Susx
3 K7 Budock Water Cnwll
70 B6 Buerton Ches E
60 E9 Bugbrooke Nhants
7 L8 Bugford Devon
70 F2 Buglawton Ches E
4 G10 Bugle Cnwll
20 E10 Bugley Dorset
98 F9 Bugthorpe E R Yk
57 L4 Buildwas Shrops
44 E4 Builth Road Powys
44 E4 Builth Wells Powys
35 P2 Bulbourne Herts
21 L8 Bulbridge Wilts
73 R5 Bulby Lincs
21 N6 Bulford Wilts
21 N6 Bulford Camp Wilts
69 P4 Bulkeley Ches E
59 N7 Bulkington Warwks
20 H3 Bulkington Wilts
16 F9 Bulkworthy Devon
97 N2 Bullamoor N York
78 G6 Bull Bay IoA
84 E10 Bullbridge Derbys
35 N11 Bullbrook Br For
50 F9 Bullen's Green Herts
46 E11 Bulley Gloucs
100 E3 Bullgill Cumb
45 Q7 Bullinghope Herefs
22 E6 Bullington Hants
86 E5 Bullington Lincs
39 L8 Bullockstone Kent
50 G7 Bull's Green Herts
65 N3 Bull's Green Norfk
52 D3 Bulmer Essex
98 D7 Bulmer N York
52 D4 Bulmer Tye Essex
37 P3 Bulphan Thurr
10 D7 Bulstone Devon
50 B10 Bulstrode Herts
26 C10 Bulverhythe E Susx
159 M8 Bulwark Abers
72 E2 Bulwell C Nott
61 L2 Bulwick Nhants
51 K9 Bumble's Green Essex
145 L10 Bunacaimb Highld
146 F10 Bunarkaig Highld
69 Q3 Bunbury Ches E
69 Q3 Bunbury Heath Ches E
155 R8 Bunchrew Highld
24 D8 Buncton W Susx
145 Q2 Bundalloch Highld
137 K11 Bunessan Ag & B
65 L4 Bungay Suffk
87 J10 Bunker's Hill Lincs
122 F5 Bunnahabhain Ag & B
72 F5 Bunny Notts
155 M11 Buntait Highld
51 J5 Buntingford Herts
64 G3 Bunwell Norfk
64 G3 Bunwell Hill Norfk
71 N7 Bupton Derbys
83 M10 Burbage Derbys
59 P6 Burbage Leics
21 P2 Burbage Wilts
45 L2 Burcher Herefs
25 Q4 Burchett's Green E Susx
35 M8 Burchett's Green W & M
21 L8 Burcombe Wilts
34 G5 Burcot Oxon
58 E10 Burcot Worcs
57 N5 Burcote Shrops
49 M11 Burcott Bucks
49 N10 Burcott Bucks
98 H8 Burdale N York
52 F5 Bures Essex
33 Q2 Burford Oxon
57 K11 Burford Shrops
137 K6 Burg Ag & B
64 F6 Burgate Suffk
23 L9 Burgates Hants
50 D4 Burge End Herts
24 H7 Burgess Hill W Susx
65 J11 Burgh Suffk
110 F9 Burgh by Sands Cumb
77 P10 Burgh Castle Norfk
22 E2 Burghclere Hants
157 L4 Burghead Moray
35 J11 Burghfield W Berk
35 J11 Burghfield Common W Berk
36 F9 Burgh Heath Surrey
26 B8 Burgh Hill E Susx
45 P6 Burghill Herefs
6 G10 Burgh Island Devon
87 P7 Burgh le Marsh Lincs
77 J6 Burgh next Aylsham Norfk
86 H3 Burgh on Bain Lincs
77 N9 Burgh St Margaret Norfk
65 P3 Burgh St Peter Norfk
91 N8 Burghwallis Donc
38 B9 Burham Kent
23 K11 Buriton Hants
69 R4 Burland Ches E
4 F7 Burlawn Cnwll
32 G4 Burleigh Gloucs
18 E11 Burlescombe Devon
12 C6 Burleston Dorset
7 L9 Burlestone Devon
13 M4 Burley Hants
73 M8 Burley Rutlnd
56 H8 Burley Shrops
69 R6 Burleydam Ches E
46 A5 Burley Gate Herefs
97 J11 Burley in Wharfedale C Brad
13 M4 Burley Lawn Hants
13 M4 Burley Street Hants
90 F2 Burley Wood Head C Brad
77 M9 Burlingham Green Norfk
45 K3 Burlingjobb Powys
57 P2 Burlington Shrops
69 N9 Burlton Shrops
27 K5 Burmarsh Kent
47 Q7 Burmington Warwks
91 P5 Burn N York
83 J6 Burnage Manch
71 P8 Burnaston Derbys
101 P7 Burnbanks Cumb
126 F6 Burnbrae N Lans
98 G11 Burnby E R Yk
91 J11 Burn Cross Sheff
15 Q6 Burndell W Susx
89 L9 Burnden Bolton
89 Q8 Burnedge Rochdl
101 P11 Burneside Cumb
97 M4 Burneston N York
32 C11 Burnett BaNES
117 N8 Burnfoot Border
117 Q7 Burnfoot Border
109 L2 Burnfoot D & G
110 F3 Burnfoot D & G
117 M11 Burnfoot D & G
134 B7 Burnfoot P & K
35 P8 Burnham Bucks
93 J7 Burnham N Linc
75 R2 Burnham Deepdale Norfk
50 G7 Burnham Green Herts
76 A3 Burnham Market Norfk
76 A3 Burnham Norton Norfk
38 F2 Burnham-on-Crouch Essex
19 K5 Burnham-on-Sea Somset
76 A3 Burnham Overy Norfk
76 A3 Burnham Overy Staithe Norfk
76 B3 Burnham Thorpe Norfk
159 R9 Burnhaven Abers
116 B11 Burnhead D & G
151 J4 Burnhervie Abers
57 P4 Burnhill Green Staffs
113 J11 Burnhope Dur
125 K7 Burnhouse N Ayrs
99 L2 Burniston N York
89 N4 Burnley Lancs
89 N4 Burnley Crematorium Lancs
129 P7 Burnmouth Border
88 C2 Burn Naze Lancs
133 L7 Burn of Cambus Stirlg
113 J9 Burnopfield Dur
111 J9 Burnrigg Cumb
96 F8 Burnsall N York
142 G6 Burnside Angus
143 J7 Burnside Angus
134 F6 Burnside Fife
157 M4 Burnside Moray
127 K3 Burnside W Loth
142 G11 Burnside of Duntrune Angus
36 B10 Burntcommon Surrey
71 N8 Burntheath Derbys
53 J6 Burnt Heath Essex
34 G10 Burnt Hill W Berk
3 K6 Burnthouse Cnwll
103 M6 Burnt Houses Dur
134 G10 Burntisland Fife
25 M5 Burnt Oak E Susx
58 G3 Burntwood Staffs
58 G3 Burntwood Green Staffs
97 L8 Burnt Yates N York
18 G11 Burnworthy Somset
36 B10 Burpham Surrey
24 B9 Burpham W Susx
113 L6 Burradon N Tyne
119 J9 Burradon Nthumb
169 t2 Burrafirth Shet
2 H7 Burras Cnwll
5 Q8 Burraton Cnwll
169 s5 Burravoe Shet
102 C7 Burrells Cumb
142 C10 Burrelton P & K
10 G3 Burridge Devon
17 K4 Burridge Devon
14 F4 Burridge Hants
97 K3 Burrill N York
92 D9 Burringham N Linc
17 L8 Burrington Devon
56 G10 Burrington Herefs
19 N3 Burrington N Som
63 K9 Burrough End Cambs
63 K9 Burrough Green Cambs
73 K8 Burrough on the Hill Leics
95 N6 Burrow Lancs
18 B6 Burrow Somset
19 L8 Burrow Bridge Somset
23 Q2 Burrowhill Surrey
36 C11 Burrows Cross Surrey
28 E6 Burry Swans
28 E6 Burry Green Swans
28 D4 Burry Port Carmth
88 E8 Burscough Lancs
88 E8 Burscough Bridge Lancs
92 D4 Bursea E R Yk
99 M11 Burshill E R Yk
14 E5 Bursledon Hants
70 F5 Burslem C Stke
53 J3 Burstall Suffk
11 J4 Burstock Dorset
64 G5 Burston Norfk
70 G8 Burston Staffs
24 H2 Burstow Surrey
93 M5 Burstwick E R Yk
96 C3 Burtersett N York
111 K8 Burtholme Cumb
63 N8 Burthorpe Green Suffk
110 H11 Burthwaite Cumb
4 E10 Burthy Cnwll
19 L6 Burtle Hill Somset
74 E3 Burtoft Lincs
69 P2 Burton Ches W
81 L10 Burton Ches W
11 P6 Burton Dorset
13 L6 Burton Dorset
86 C6 Burton Lincs
119 N4 Burton Nthumb
41 J9 Burton Pembks
11 L2 Burton Somset
18 G6 Burton Somset
20 F8 Burton Wilts
32 F9 Burton Wilts
99 N8 Burton Agnes E R Yk
11 K7 Burton Bradstock Dorset
73 P5 Burton Coggles Lincs
93 L3 Burton Constable Hall E R Yk
48 C4 Burton Dassett Warwks
51 M6 Burton End Essex
63 L11 Burton End Suffk
99 M6 Burton Fleming E R Yk
59 L9 Burton Green Warwks
69 K3 Burton Green Wrexhm
59 P7 Burton Hastings Warwks
95 L5 Burton-in-Kendal Cumb
95 L5 Burton-in-Kendal Services Cumb
95 P6 Burton in Lonsdale N York
72 G2 Burton Joyce Notts
61 K6 Burton Latimer Nhants
73 K7 Burton Lazars Leics
97 M8 Burton Leonard N York
72 F6 Burton on the Wolds Leics
72 H11 Burton Overy Leics
74 B2 Burton Pedwardine Lincs
93 M4 Burton Pidsea E R Yk
91 M5 Burton Salmon N York
52 D6 Burton's Green Essex
92 E7 Burton upon Stather N Linc
71 N10 Burton upon Trent Staffs
86 B6 Burton Waters Lincs
82 C6 Burtonwood Warrtn
82 C6 Burtonwood Services Warrtn
69 P3 Burwardsley Ches W
57 L7 Burwarton Shrops
25 Q6 Burwash E Susx
25 P6 Burwash Common E Susx
25 Q6 Burwash Weald E Susx
63 J7 Burwell Cambs
87 L5 Burwell Lincs
78 G6 Burwen IoA
169 d8 Burwick Ork
89 N8 Bury Bury
62 C4 Bury Cambs
18 B9 Bury Somset
24 B8 Bury W Susx
50 D3 Bury End C Beds
51 L6 Bury Green Herts
64 B9 Bury St Edmunds Suffk
98 F8 Burythorpe N York
125 P6 Busby E Rens
97 N4 Busby Stoop N York
33 P5 Buscot Oxon
143 P4 Bush Abers
16 C10 Bush Cnwll
45 P4 Bush Bank Herefs
58 D4 Bushbury Wolves
58 D4 Bushbury Crematorium Wolves
72 H10 Bushby Leics
50 D11 Bushey Herts
36 D2 Bushey Heath Herts
65 J4 Bush Green Norfk
64 C10 Bush Green Suffk
50 H11 Bush Hill Park Gt Lon
46 G8 Bushley Worcs
46 G8 Bushley Green Worcs
61 P8 Bushmead Bed
56 G7 Bushmoor Shrops
33 L9 Bushton Wilts
102 B2 Busk Cumb
86 E3 Buslingthorpe Lincs
32 G4 Bussage Gloucs
19 L7 Bussex Somset
25 N5 Butcher's Cross E Susx
19 P2 Butcombe N Som
124 C4 Bute Ag & B
19 P8 Butleigh Somset
19 P7 Butleigh Wootton Somset
35 M3 Butler's Cross Bucks
84 H11 Butler's Hill Notts
48 B4 Butlers Marston Warwks
65 M11 Butley Suffk
53 Q2 Butley High Corner Suffk
98 E9 Buttercrambe N York
129 K7 Butterdean Border
103 M5 Butterknowle Dur
9 N3 Butterleigh Devon
84 F10 Butterley Derbys
100 G7 Buttermere Cumb
22 B2 Buttermere Wilts
70 E4 Butters Green Staffs
90 E5 Buttershaw C Brad
141 Q8 Butterstone P & K
70 E6 Butterton Staffs
71 K3 Butterton Staffs
104 C4 Butterwick Dur
87 L11 Butterwick Lincs
98 E5 Butterwick N York
99 K6 Butterwick N York
70 B4 Butt Green Ches E
56 C3 Buttington Powys
57 N9 Buttonbridge Shrops
57 P9 Buttonoak Shrops
14 D5 Buttsash Hants
16 D11 Buttsbear Cross Cnwll
52 C11 Butt's Green Essex
64 E10 Buxhall Suffk
64 E10 Buxhall Fen Street Suffk
25 L6 Buxted E Susx
83 N10 Buxton Derbys
77 J7 Buxton Norfk
76 H7 Buxton Heath Norfk
44 H10 Bwlch Powys
69 J4 Bwlchgwyn Wrexhm
43 L3 Bwlchllan Cerdgn
42 G10 Bwlchnewydd Carmth
66 E9 Bwlchtocyn Gwynd
68 G11 Bwlch-y-cibau Powys
68 G10 Bwlch-y-Ddar Powys
42 H5 Bwlchyfadfa Cerdgn
55 P5 Bwlch-y-ffridd Powys
41 P3 Bwlch-y-groes Pembks
28 G5 Bwlchymyrdd Swans
55 N10 Bwlch-y-sarnau Powys
113 J9 Byermoor Gatesd
103 P4 Byers Green Dur
48 F4 Byfield Nhants
36 C8 Byfleet Surrey
45 M6 Byford Herefs
50 G3 Bygrave Herts
113 L8 Byker N u Ty
98 A5 Byland Abbey N York
68 C2 Bylchau Conwy
82 F11 Byley Ches W
28 F5 Bynea Carmth
118 E10 Byrness Nthumb
9 P8 Bystock Devon
61 N5 Bythorn Cambs
45 M2 Byton Herefs
112 F8 Bywell Nthumb
23 Q10 Byworth W Susx

C

16 G7 Cabbacott Devon
93 K10 Cabourne Lincs
122 G7 Cabrach Ag & B
150 B2 Cabrach Moray
95 K11 Cabus Lancs
25 L5 Cackle Street E Susx
25 Q7 Cackle Street E Susx
26 D8 Cackle Street E Susx
9 M3 Cadbury Devon
17 M8 Cadbury Barton Devon
125 Q3 Cadder E Duns
50 C7 Caddington C Beds
117 P3 Caddonfoot Border
91 N10 Cadeby Donc
72 C10 Cadeby Leics
9 M3 Cadeleigh Devon
25 P6 Cade Street E Susx
3 J11 Cadgwith Cnwll
134 H7 Cadham Fife
82 F6 Cadishead Salfd
28 H5 Cadle Swans
88 G4 Cadley Lancs
21 P4 Cadley Wilts
33 P11 Cadley Wilts
35 L6 Cadmore End Bucks
13 P2 Cadnam Hants
92 H10 Cadney N Linc
68 H2 Cadole Flints
30 F11 Cadoxton V Glam
29 L5 Cadoxton Juxta-Neath Neath
68 D7 Cadwst Denbgs
67 J2 Caeathro Gwynd
29 M2 Caehopkin Powys
86 C3 Caenby Lincs
43 N6 Caeo Carmth
29 N6 Caerau Brdgnd
30 F9 Caerau Cardif
29 M2 Cae'r-bont Powys
28 G2 Cae'r bryn Carmth
67 M11 Caerdeon Gwynd
40 E5 Caer Farchell Pembks
78 E9 Caergeiliog IoA
69 K3 Caergwrle Flints
79 P10 Caerhun Conwy
117 M10 Caerlanrig Border
31 K6 Caerleon Newpt
31 K6 Caerleon Roman Amphitheatre Newpt
66 H2 Caernarfon Gwynd
66 H2 Caernarfon Castle Gwynd
30 G7 Caerphilly Caerph
55 N6 Caersws Powys
42 G3 Caerwedros Cerdgn

270 Claonaig - Coombe

123 Q8 Claonaig Ag & B
12 H4 Clapgate Dorset
51 K6 Clapgate Herts
61 M10 Clapham Bed
9 L7 Clapham Devon
36 G5 Clapham Gt Lon
95 Q7 Clapham N York
24 C9 Clapham W Susx
61 M10 Clapham Green Bed
27 J4 Clap Hill Kent
101 L10 Clappersgate Cumb
11 J3 Clapton Somset
20 B4 Clapton Somset
31 N10 Clapton-in-Gordano N Som
47 N11 Clapton-on-the-Hill Gloucs
17 M7 Clapworthy Devon
54 E8 Clarach Cerdgn
112 H8 Claravale Gatesd
41 L6 Clarbeston Pembks
41 K6 Clarbeston Road Pembks
85 M4 Clarborough Notts
63 N11 Clare Suffk
108 G7 Clarebrand D & G
109 N7 Clarencefield D & G
112 F7 Clarewood Nthumb
117 Q7 Clarilaw Border
22 G4 Clarken Green Hants
24 E3 Clark's Green Surrey
125 P6 Clarkston E Rens
162 G5 Clashmore Highld
164 B10 Clashmore Highld
164 C10 Clashnessie Highld
149 N3 Clashnoir Moray
134 B3 Clathy P & K
134 C3 Clathymore P & K
150 E2 Clatt Abers
55 M6 Clatter Powys
51 P8 Clatterford End Essex
18 E8 Clatworthy Somset
88 G2 Claughton Lancs
95 M7 Claughton Lancs
81 L7 Claughton Wirral
19 J8 Clavelshay Somset
59 J11 Claverdon Warwks
31 N11 Claverham N Som
51 L4 Clavering Essex
57 P6 Claverley Shrops
20 E2 Claverton BaNES
20 E2 Claverton Down BaNES
30 E9 Clawdd-coch V Glam
68 E4 Clawdd-newydd Denbgs
95 L5 Clawthorpe Cumb
5 P2 Clawton Devon
86 F2 Claxby Lincs
87 N6 Claxby Lincs
98 D9 Claxton N York
77 L11 Claxton Norfk
59 Q7 Claybrooke Magna Leics
65 P5 Clay Common Suffk
60 C5 Clay Coton Nhants
84 E8 Clay Cross Derbys
48 E5 Claydon Oxon
53 K2 Claydon Suffk
50 H6 Clay End Herts
110 G5 Claygate D & G
26 B3 Claygate Kent
36 E8 Claygate Surrey
37 P9 Claygate Cross Kent
37 K2 Clayhall Gt Lon
18 D10 Clayhanger Devon
58 F4 Clayhanger Wsall
18 G11 Clayhidon Devon
26 D7 Clayhill E Susx
13 P3 Clayhill Hants
62 H8 Clayhithe Cambs
167 L5 Clayock Highld
62 E10 Claypit Hill Cambs
32 E3 Claypits Gloucs
85 P11 Claypole Lincs
87 M5 Claythorpe Lincs
90 E4 Clayton C Brad
91 M9 Clayton Donc
24 G8 Clayton W Susx
88 H6 Clayton Green Lancs
89 M4 Clayton-le-Moors Lancs
88 H6 Clayton-le-Woods Lancs
90 H8 Clayton West Kirk
85 M3 Clayworth Notts
144 G10 Cleadale Highld
113 N8 Cleadon S Tyne
6 E5 Clearbrook Devon
31 Q3 Clearwell Gloucs
31 Q3 Clearwell Meend Gloucs
103 Q8 Cleasby N York
169 d8 Cleat Ork
103 M7 Cleatlam Dur
100 D8 Cleator Cumb
100 D7 Cleator Moor Cumb
90 F5 Cleckheaton Kirk
57 K8 Cleedownton Shrops
57 K9 Cleehill Shrops
126 D6 Cleekhimin N Lans
57 K8 Clee St Margaret Shrops
57 K9 Cleestanton Shrops
93 P9 Cleethorpes NE Lin
57 L9 Cleeton St Mary Shrops
31 N11 Cleeve N Som
34 H8 Cleeve Oxon
47 J9 Cleeve Hill Gloucs
47 L5 Cleeve Prior Worcs
128 F3 Cleghornie E Loth
45 N7 Clehonger Herefs
134 D8 Cleish P & K
126 D6 Cleland N Lans
50 B8 Clement's End C Beds
37 M6 Clement Street Kent
131 J2 Clenamacrie Ag & B
33 N11 Clench Common Wilts
75 L6 Clenchwarton Norfk
159 J5 Clenerty Abers
58 D9 Clent Worcs
57 M9 Cleobury Mortimer Shrops
57 L7 Cleobury North Shrops
120 C5 Cleongart Ag & B
156 E7 Clephanton Highld
117 K11 Clerkhill D & G
115 R7 Cleuch-head D & G
33 L9 Clevancy Wilts
31 M10 Clevedon N Som
48 C10 Cleveley Oxon
88 C2 Cleveleys Lancs
33 J7 Cleverton Wilts
19 M4 Clewer Somset
76 E3 Cley next the Sea Norfk
101 Q6 Cliburn Cumb
22 H5 Cliddesden Hants
59 K5 Cliff Warwks
89 L4 Cliffe Lancs
38 B6 Cliffe Medway
91 R4 Cliffe N York
103 P7 Cliffe N York
26 E9 Cliff End E Susx
38 B7 Cliffe Woods Medway
45 J5 Clifford Herefs
91 L2 Clifford Leeds
47 N4 Clifford Chambers Warwks
46 D10 Clifford's Mesne Gloucs
39 P9 Cliffsend Kent
31 Q10 Clifton Bristl
50 E3 Clifton C Beds
72 E4 Clifton C Nott
98 B10 Clifton C York
90 F6 Clifton Calder
101 P5 Clifton Cumb
71 M6 Clifton Derbys
17 L3 Clifton Devon
91 N11 Clifton Donc
88 F4 Clifton Lancs
97 J11 Clifton N York
113 K4 Clifton Nthumb
48 E8 Clifton Oxon
82 G4 Clifton Salfd
46 F5 Clifton Worcs
59 L2 Clifton Campville Staffs
34 F5 Clifton Hampden Oxon
49 P4 Clifton Reynes M Keyn
60 B5 Clifton upon Dunsmore Warwks
46 D2 Clifton upon Teme Worcs
39 Q7 Cliftonville Kent
15 Q6 Climping W Susx
20 E5 Clink Somset
97 L9 Clint N York
151 L5 Clinterty C Aber
76 E9 Clint Green Norfk
118 B4 Clintmains Border
55 J2 Clipiau Gwynd
77 N9 Clippesby Norfk
73 P7 Clipsham Rutlnd
60 F4 Clipston Nhants
72 G4 Clipston Notts
49 P9 Clipstone C Beds
85 J8 Clipstone Notts
89 L2 Clitheroe Lancs
69 P10 Clive Shrops
93 J10 Clixby Lincs
33 J6 Cloatley Wilts
68 E4 Clocaenog Denbgs
158 B5 Clochan Moray
82 B6 Clock Face St Hel
56 C3 Cloddiau Powys
45 L9 Clodock Herefs
20 D6 Cloford Somset
159 P9 Clola Abers
50 C3 Clophill C Beds
61 N4 Clopton Nhants
65 J11 Clopton Suffk
65 J11 Clopton Corner Suffk
63 N10 Clopton Green Suffk
64 D10 Clopton Green Suffk
10 c1 Clos du Valle Guern
109 J2 Closeburn D & G
109 K2 Closeburnmill D & G
80 c6 Closeclark IoM
11 M2 Closworth Somset
50 G4 Clothall Herts
69 P2 Clotton Ches W
59 Q7 Cloudesley Bush Warwks
46 A7 Clouds Herefs
89 Q9 Clough Oldham
89 Q6 Clough Foot Calder
90 D7 Clough Head Calder
99 L2 Cloughton N York
105 R11 Cloughton Newlands N York
169 q8 Clousta Shet
142 E3 Clova Angus
16 E7 Clovelly Devon
117 P3 Clovenfords Border
139 J5 Clovulin Highld
89 N5 Clow Bridge Lancs
84 G5 Clowne Derbys
57 N10 Clows Top Worcs
69 L6 Cloy Wrexhm
146 D5 Cluanie Inn Highld
146 D5 Cluanie Lodge Highld
5 M3 Clubworthy Cnwll
107 L6 Clugston D & G
56 E8 Clun Shrops
156 F8 Clunas Highld
56 F8 Clunbury Shrops
41 M7 Clunderwen Carmth
148 D2 Clune Highld
146 F10 Clunes Highld
56 F9 Clungunford Shrops
141 R9 Clunie P & K
56 E8 Clunton Shrops
134 G8 Cluny Fife
20 B3 Clutton BaNES
69 N4 Clutton Ches W
20 B3 Clutton Hill BaNES
67 K2 Clwt-y-bont Gwynd
30 H2 Clydach Mons
29 J4 Clydach Swans
30 C6 Clydach Vale Rhondd
125 M3 Clydebank W Duns
125 M3 Clydebank Crematorium W Duns
41 Q3 Clydey Pembks
33 L9 Clyffe Pypard Wilts
131 Q11 Clynder Ag & B
29 M4 Clyne Neath
66 G5 Clynnog-fawr Gwynd
45 J6 Clyro Powys
9 N6 Clyst Honiton Devon
9 P4 Clyst Hydon Devon
9 N7 Clyst St George Devon
9 P4 Clyst St Lawrence Devon
9 N6 Clyst St Mary Devon
168 j4 Cnoc W Isls
54 F10 Cnwch Coch Cerdgn
5 M6 Coad's Green Cnwll
84 E5 Coal Aston Derbys
30 G3 Coalbrookvale Blae G
126 E11 Coalburn S Lans
112 H8 Coalburns Gatesd
32 E4 Coaley Gloucs
38 C2 Coalhill Essex
57 M3 Coalmoor Wrekin
32 C8 Coalpit Heath S Glos
58 F5 Coal Pool Wsall
57 M4 Coalport Wrekin
133 Q8 Coalsnaughton Clacks
65 J7 Coal Street Suffk
134 H8 Coaltown of Balgonie Fife
135 J8 Coaltown of Wemyss Fife
72 C8 Coalville Leics
111 N9 Coanwood Nthumb
19 N10 Coat Somset
126 C4 Coatbridge N Lans
126 C4 Coatdyke N Lans
33 N8 Coate Swindn
21 K2 Coate Wilts
74 F11 Coates Cambs
33 J4 Coates Gloucs
86 B4 Coates Lincs
85 P4 Coates Notts
23 Q11 Coates W Susx
104 G5 Coatham R & Cl
103 Q6 Coatham Mundeville Darltn
17 L6 Cobbaton Devon
47 J11 Coberley Gloucs
45 P7 Cobhall Common Herefs
37 Q7 Cobham Kent
36 D8 Cobham Surrey
36 D9 Cobham Services Surrey
51 Q7 Coblers Green Essex
21 K10 Cobley Dorset
45 P2 Cobnash Herefs
10 b1 Cobo Guern
70 F5 Cobridge C Stke
159 M5 Coburby Abers
84 F6 Cock Alley Derbys
104 H11 Cockayne N York
62 C11 Cockayne Hatley C Beds
69 L5 Cock Bank Wrexhm
47 L4 Cock Bevington Warwks
149 P6 Cock Bridge Abers
129 K5 Cockburnspath Border
52 D11 Cock Clarks Essex
63 M10 Cock & End Suffk
128 C4 Cockenzie and Port Seton E Loth
88 G4 Cocker Bar Lancs
89 L5 Cocker Brook Lancs
95 K10 Cockerham Lancs
100 F4 Cockermouth Cumb
50 D6 Cockernhoe Herts
90 G5 Cockersdale Leeds
28 H6 Cockett Swans
103 M6 Cockfield Dur
64 C11 Cockfield Suffk
50 G11 Cockfosters Gt Lon
51 Q7 Cock Green Essex
23 N11 Cocking W Susx
23 N11 Cocking Causeway W Susx
7 M6 Cockington Torbay
19 M5 Cocklake Somset
100 H10 Cockley Beck Cumb
75 Q10 Cockley Cley Norfk
26 E8 Cock Marling E Susx
35 L8 Cockpole Green Wokham
3 K3 Cocks Cnwll
57 K7 Cockshutford Shrops
69 M9 Cockshutt Shrops
38 C11 Cock Street Kent
76 D3 Cockthorpe Norfk
2 E7 Cockwells Cnwll
9 N8 Cockwood Devon
18 H6 Cockwood Somset
83 M9 Cockyard Derbys
45 N8 Cockyard Herefs
64 G11 Coddenham Suffk
69 N3 Coddington Ches W
46 D6 Coddington Herefs
85 P10 Coddington Notts
21 J7 Codford St Mary Wilts
21 J7 Codford St Peter Wilts
50 F7 Codicote Herts
24 C6 Codmore Hill W Susx
84 F11 Codnor Derbys
32 D9 Codrington S Glos
58 C4 Codsall Staffs
58 B4 Codsall Wood Staffs
30 D7 Coedely Rhondd
31 J8 Coedkernew Newpt
31 L2 Coed Morgan Mons
69 J3 Coedpoeth Wrexhm
69 J3 Coed Talon Flints
69 K11 Coedway Powys
42 G5 Coed-y-Bryn Cerdgn
31 L6 Coed-y-caerau Newpt
31 K5 Coed-y-paen Mons
44 H10 Coed-yr-ynys Powys
67 K10 Coed Ystumgwern Gwynd
29 N2 Coelbren Powys
7 M5 Coffinswell Devon
61 M9 Coffle End Bed
9 N8 Cofton Devon
58 F9 Cofton Hackett Worcs
30 G10 Cogan V Glam
60 H8 Cogenhoe Nhants
34 C3 Cogges Oxon
52 E7 Coggeshall Essex
25 N5 Coggin's Mill E Susx
148 C4 Coignafearn Highld
149 Q8 Coilacriech Abers
132 H6 Coilantogle Stirlg
152 F10 Coillore Highld
29 P8 Coity Brdgnd
168 j4 Col W Isls
162 D4 Colaboll Highld
4 D9 Colan Cnwll
10 B7 Colaton Raleigh Devon
152 C8 Colbost Highld
103 N11 Colburn N York
102 C6 Colby Cumb
80 b7 Colby IoM
77 J5 Colby Norfk
52 G6 Colchester Essex
52 G7 Colchester Crematorium Essex
34 F11 Cold Ash W Berk
60 E5 Cold Ashby Nhants
32 E10 Cold Ashton S Glos
47 M11 Cold Aston Gloucs
165 P4 Coldbackie Highld
102 D10 Coldbeck Cumb
41 M8 Cold Blow Pembks
49 P4 Cold Brayfield M Keyn
95 Q6 Cold Cotes N York
24 H9 Coldean Br & H
7 L4 Coldeast Devon
90 B5 Colden Calder
22 E10 Colden Common Hants
65 N9 Coldfair Green Suffk
74 H10 Coldham Cambs
86 D4 Cold Hanworth Lincs
3 K4 Coldharbour Cnwll
9 Q2 Coldharbour Devon
31 Q4 Coldharbour Gloucs
50 D7 Cold Harbour Herts
34 H9 Cold Harbour Oxon
24 D2 Coldharbour Surrey
20 G5 Cold Harbour Wilts
70 A10 Cold Hatton Wrekin
70 A10 Cold Hatton Heath Wrekin
113 P11 Cold Hesledon Dur
91 K8 Cold Hiendley Wakefd
49 J4 Cold Higham Nhants
129 N6 Coldingham Border
98 A4 Cold Kirby N York
70 F8 Coldmeece Staffs
73 J9 Cold Newton Leics
5 L4 Cold Northcott Cnwll
52 E11 Cold Norton Essex
73 L8 Cold Overton Leics
27 N2 Coldred Kent
17 M10 Coldridge Devon
118 F3 Coldstream Border
24 B7 Coldwaltham W Susx
45 N7 Coldwell Herefs
159 N10 Coldwells Abers
57 K8 Cold Weston Shrops
20 C8 Cole Somset
56 E7 Colebatch Shrops
6 E7 Colebrook C Plym
9 P3 Colebrook Devon
9 J5 Colebrooke Devon
86 C8 Coleby Lincs
92 E7 Coleby N Linc
59 K7 Cole End Warwks
9 J4 Coleford Devon
31 Q2 Coleford Gloucs
20 C5 Coleford Somset
18 F8 Coleford Water Somset
64 H4 Colegate End Norfk
50 G8 Cole Green Herts
51 K4 Cole Green Herts
22 E4 Cole Henley Hants
12 H4 Colehill Dorset
50 E8 Coleman Green Herts
25 K4 Coleman's Hatch E Susx
69 M8 Colemere Shrops
23 K8 Colemore Hants
57 N5 Colemore Green Shrops
134 E2 Colenden P & K
72 C7 Coleorton Leics
32 F10 Colerne Wilts
33 K2 Colesbourne Gloucs
7 K9 Cole's Cross Devon
10 H4 Coles Cross Dorset
61 P9 Colesden Bed
53 K3 Coles Green Suffk
35 P5 Coleshill Bucks
33 P6 Coleshill Oxon
59 K7 Coleshill Warwks
10 B4 Colestocks Devon
19 Q3 Coley BaNES
24 F4 Colgate W Susx
135 M7 Colinsburgh Fife
127 N4 Colinton C Edin
124 C3 Colintraive Ag & B
76 C6 Colkirk Norfk
136 G4 Coll Ag & B
142 C11 Collace P & K
169 q5 Collafirth Shet
136 F4 Coll Airport Ag & B
7 J11 Collaton Devon
7 M6 Collaton St Mary Torbay
157 L4 College of Roseisle Moray
23 N2 College Town Br For
134 H5 Collessie Fife
17 M8 Colleton Mills Devon
37 M2 Collier Row Gt Lon
51 J6 Collier's End Herts
26 C7 Collier's Green E Susx
26 C4 Colliers Green Kent
26 B2 Collier Street Kent
113 M11 Colliery Row Sundld
151 Q2 Collieston Abers
109 M5 Collin D & G
21 P4 Collingbourne Ducis Wilts
21 P3 Collingbourne Kingston Wilts
97 N11 Collingham Leeds
85 P8 Collingham Notts
46 B2 Collington Herefs
60 G9 Collingtree Nhants
82 C6 Collins Green Warrtn
46 D3 Collins Green Worcs
143 L8 Colliston Angus
10 B4 Colliton Devon
73 P10 Collyweston Nhants
114 B10 Colmonell S Ayrs
61 P9 Colmworth Bed
36 B5 Colnbrook Slough
62 E5 Colne Cambs
89 P3 Colne Lancs
90 F6 Colne Bridge Kirk
89 P2 Colne Edge Lancs
52 D5 Colne Engaine Essex
76 H10 Colney Norfk
50 F9 Colney Heath Herts
50 E10 Colney Street Herts
33 L3 Coln Rogers Gloucs
33 M3 Coln St Aldwyns Gloucs
33 L2 Coln St Dennis Gloucs
136 b2 Colonsay Ag & B
136 b3 Colonsay Airport Ag & B
158 F11 Colpy Abers
117 L2 Colquhar Border
4 H7 Colquite Cnwll
16 F9 Colscott Devon
96 H4 Colsterdale N York
73 N6 Colsterworth Lincs
73 J4 Colston Bassett Notts
157 L5 Coltfield Moray
23 L4 Colt Hill Hants
77 K8 Coltishall Norfk
94 G3 Colton Cumb
91 K4 Colton Leeds
91 N2 Colton N York
76 G10 Colton Norfk
71 J10 Colton Staffs
25 P2 Colt's Hill Kent
9 N5 Columbjohn Devon
44 H4 Colva Powys
109 J10 Colvend D & G
46 E6 Colwall Herefs
112 E5 Colwell Nthumb
71 J10 Colwich Staffs
72 G2 Colwick Notts
29 P9 Colwinston V Glam
15 P6 Colworth W Susx
80 B9 Colwyn Bay Conwy
10 F6 Colyford Devon
10 E6 Colyton Devon
7 J11 Combe Devon
45 L2 Combe Herefs
48 D11 Combe Oxon
22 C2 Combe W Berk
12 G5 Combe Almer Dorset
23 P7 Combe Common Surrey
20 E2 Combe Down BaNES
7 L5 Combe Fishacre Devon
18 G8 Combe Florey Somset
20 D3 Combe Hay BaNES
7 N4 Combeinteignhead Devon
17 K2 Combe Martin Devon
10 D4 Combe Raleigh Devon
82 D9 Comberbach Ches W
59 J3 Comberford Staffs
62 E9 Comberton Cambs
56 H11 Comberton Herefs
10 G2 Combe St Nicholas Somset
10 F6 Combpyne Devon
71 K7 Combridge Staffs
48 B4 Combrook Warwks
83 M9 Combs Derbys
64 E10 Combs Suffk
64 E10 Combs Ford Suffk
19 J6 Combwich Somset
150 H6 Comers Abers
58 B11 Comhampton Worcs
63 J8 Commercial End Cambs
55 J4 Commins Coch Powys
105 J8 Commondale N York
88 C4 Common Edge Bpool
100 D6 Common End Cumb
5 L8 Common Moor Cnwll
33 M7 Common Platt Wilts
82 B10 Commonside Ches W
71 N6 Commonside Derbys
84 D5 Common Side Derbys
69 N9 Commonwood Shrops
69 L4 Commonwood Wrexhm
19 J8 Compass Somset
83 L6 Compstall Stockp
108 E10 Compstonend D & G
7 M6 Compton Devon
22 B9 Compton Hants
22 E9 Compton Hants
57 Q8 Compton Staffs
23 Q5 Compton Surrey
34 F8 Compton W Berk
15 L4 Compton W Susx
21 M4 Compton Wilts
20 G11 Compton Abbas Dorset
47 L11 Compton Abdale Gloucs
33 K10 Compton Bassett Wilts
33 Q7 Compton Beauchamp Oxon
19 L3 Compton Bishop Somset
21 K9 Compton Chamberlayne Wilts
20 B2 Compton Dando BaNES
19 N8 Compton Dundon Somset
19 M11 Compton Durville Somset
31 Q8 Compton Greenfield S Glos
19 P3 Compton Martin BaNES
20 B9 Compton Pauncefoot Somset
11 M6 Compton Valence Dorset
48 B4 Compton Verney Warwks
134 C10 Comrie Fife
133 M3 Comrie P & K
139 J4 Conaglen House Highld
145 Q2 Conchra Highld
141 Q9 Concraigie P & K
95 K9 Conder Green Lancs
47 J7 Conderton Worcs
47 N9 Condicote Gloucs
126 C3 Condorrat N Lans
56 H3 Condover Shrops
46 G11 Coney Hill Gloucs
24 D6 Coneyhurst Common W Susx
98 E6 Coneysthorpe N York
97 N9 Coneythorpe N York
64 D6 Coney Weston Suffk
23 M8 Conford Hants
5 M6 Congdon's Shop Cnwll
72 B9 Congerstone Leics
75 P6 Congham Norfk
70 F2 Congleton Ches E
67 N6 Congl-y-wal Gwynd
19 M2 Congresbury N Som
58 D2 Congreve Staffs
109 L7 Conheath D & G
156 H7 Conicavel Moray
86 H9 Coningsby Lincs
61 Q3 Conington Cambs
62 D7 Conington Cambs
91 N11 Conisbrough Donc
93 R11 Conisholme Lincs
101 K11 Coniston Cumb
93 L3 Coniston E R Yk
96 D10 Coniston Cold N York
96 E7 Conistone N York
81 K11 Connah's Quay Flints
138 G11 Connel Ag & B
115 M5 Connel Park E Ayrs
2 F6 Connor Downs Cnwll
155 P6 Conon Bridge Highld
96 E11 Cononley N York
70 H5 Consall Staffs
112 H10 Consett Dur
97 J2 Constable Burton N York
89 N6 Constable Lee Lancs
3 J8 Constantine Cnwll
4 D7 Constantine Bay Cnwll
155 N6 Contin Highld
79 P9 Conwy Conwy
38 G9 Conyer Kent
64 B8 Conyer's Green Suffk
26 B10 Cooden E Susx
16 G10 Cookbury Devon
16 F10 Cookbury Wick Devon
35 N7 Cookham W & M
35 N7 Cookham Dean W & M
35 N7 Cookham Rise W & M
47 L3 Cookhill Worcs
65 L6 Cookley Suffk
58 B8 Cookley Worcs
35 J6 Cookley Green Oxon
151 M9 Cookney Abers
25 K8 Cooksbridge E Susx
58 D11 Cooksey Green Worcs
53 L8 Cook's Green Essex
64 D11 Cooks Green Suffk
70 G6 Cookshill Staffs
4 H8 Cooksland Cnwll
51 P9 Cooksmill Green Essex
82 C10 Cookson Green Ches W
24 D6 Coolham W Susx
38 C6 Cooling Medway
38 B7 Cooling Street Medway
2 G5 Coombe Cnwll
3 L5 Coombe Cnwll
3 N3 Coombe Cnwll
7 N4 Coombe Devon

Coombe - Cross Lanes 271

9 K8 **Coombe** Devon
10 C6 **Coombe** Devon
32 E6 **Coombe** Gloucs
23 J10 **Coombe** Hants
21 M4 **Coombe** Wilts
21 M9 **Coombe Bissett** Wilts
7 N4 **Coombe Cellars** Devon
23 J10 **Coombe Cross** Hants
46 G9 **Coombe Hill** Gloucs
12 D8 **Coombe Keynes** Dorset
7 N5 **Coombe Pafford** Torbay
24 E9 **Coombes** W Susx
45 M2 **Coombes-Moor** Herefs
20 E8 **Coombe Street** Somset
58 E7 **Coombeswood** Dudley
51 L10 **Coopersale Common** Essex
51 L10 **Coopersale Street** Essex
37 L11 **Cooper's Corner** Kent
25 L6 **Coopers Green** E Susx
50 E9 **Coopers Green** Herts
39 P9 **Cooper Street** Kent
89 J9 **Cooper Turning** Bolton
24 C8 **Cootham** W Susx
53 K3 **Copdock** Suffk
52 F7 **Copford Green** Essex
97 M8 **Copgrove** N York
169 r6 **Copister** Shet
61 P11 **Cople** Bed
90 D6 **Copley** Calder
103 L5 **Copley** Dur
83 L5 **Copley** Tamesd
83 Q9 **Coplow Dale** Derbys
98 B11 **Copmanthorpe** C York
70 E9 **Copmere End** Staffs
88 E3 **Copp** Lancs
16 C11 **Coppathorne** Cnwll
70 G11 **Coppenhall** Staffs
70 C3 **Coppenhall Moss** Ches E
2 F6 **Copperhouse** Cnwll
57 N8 **Coppicegate** Shrops
61 Q5 **Coppingford** Cambs
26 F2 **Coppins Corner** Kent
9 J4 **Copplestone** Devon
88 H8 **Coppull** Lancs
88 H8 **Coppull Moor** Lancs
24 E6 **Copsale** W Susx
89 K4 **Copster Green** Lancs
59 Q7 **Copston Magna** Warwks
39 N9 **Cop Street** Kent
51 K10 **Copthall Green** Essex
59 J9 **Copt Heath** Solhll
97 M6 **Copt Hewick** N York
5 M3 **Copthorne** Cnwll
24 H3 **Copthorne** W Susx
72 D8 **Copt Oak** Leics
76 C4 **Copy's Green** Norfk
13 P2 **Copythorne** Hants
52 H3 **Coram Street** Suffk
37 N3 **Corbets Tey** Gt Lon
11 a2 **Corbiere** Jersey
112 E8 **Corbridge** Nthumb
61 J3 **Corby** Nhants
73 Q6 **Corby Glen** Lincs
111 J9 **Corby Hill** Cumb
121 K5 **Cordon** N Ayrs
84 D5 **Cordwell** Derbys
57 L10 **Coreley** Shrops
35 P7 **Cores End** Bucks
18 H11 **Corfe** Somset
12 G8 **Corfe Castle** Dorset
12 G5 **Corfe Mullen** Dorset
56 H7 **Corfton** Shrops
149 P6 **Corgarff** Abers
22 H10 **Corhampton** Hants
25 Q2 **Corks Pond** Kent
59 M7 **Corley** Warwks
59 L7 **Corley Ash** Warwks
59 L8 **Corley Moor** Warwks
59 M7 **Corley Services** Warwks
142 E4 **Cormuir** Angus
52 F3 **Cornard Tye** Suffk
8 G7 **Corndon** Devon
88 E4 **Corner Row** Lancs
94 C2 **Corney** Cumb
104 B4 **Cornforth** Dur
158 E6 **Cornhill** Abers
118 G3 **Cornhill-on-Tweed** Nthumb
89 Q5 **Cornholme** Calder
51 Q3 **Cornish Hall End** Essex
136 B6 **Cornoigmore** Ag & B
102 F2 **Cornriggs** Dur
103 M2 **Cornsay** Dur
103 N2 **Cornsay Colliery** Dur
155 Q6 **Corntown** Highld
29 P9 **Corntown** V Glam
47 Q9 **Cornwell** Oxon
6 G7 **Cornwood** Devon
7 L7 **Cornworthy** Devon
139 K2 **Corpach** Highld
76 G6 **Corpusty** Norfk
150 D7 **Corrachree** Abers
139 J5 **Corran** Highld
145 P6 **Corran** Highld
80 g4 **Corrany** IoM
110 D3 **Corrie** D & G
121 K3 **Corrie** N Ayrs
120 H7 **Corriecravie** N Ayrs
121 K4 **Corriegills** N Ayrs
146 H9 **Corriegour Lodge Hotel** Highld
155 L5 **Corriemoille** Highld
155 L11 **Corrimony** Highld
85 Q2 **Corringham** Lincs
38 B5 **Corringham** Thurr
54 H3 **Corris** Gwynd
54 G3 **Corris Uchaf** Gwynd
131 Q5 **Corrow** Ag & B
145 K3 **Corry** Highld
8 F5 **Corscombe** Devon
11 L3 **Corscombe** Dorset
46 E9 **Corse** Gloucs
46 F8 **Corse Lawn** Gloucs
32 G10 **Corsham** Wilts
150 H6 **Corsindae** Abers
20 F5 **Corsley** Wilts
20 F5 **Corsley Heath** Wilts
108 G5 **Corsock** D & G
32 C11 **Corston** BaNES
32 H8 **Corston** Wilts
127 M3 **Corstorphine** C Edin
67 L10 **Cors-y-Gedol** Gwynd
142 F6 **Cortachy** Angus
65 Q2 **Corton** Suffk
20 H6 **Corton** Wilts
20 B10 **Corton Denham** Somset
139 K4 **Coruanan** Highld
68 E6 **Corwen** Denbgs
11 N7 **Coryates** Dorset
8 C8 **Coryton** Devon
38 B5 **Coryton** Thurr
72 E11 **Cosby** Leics
58 D6 **Coseley** Dudley
57 Q3 **Cosford** Shrops
49 L6 **Cosgrove** Nhants
15 J5 **Cosham** C Port
41 K10 **Cosheston** Pembks
141 J8 **Coshieville** P & K
72 D2 **Cossall** Notts
72 D2 **Cossall Marsh** Notts
72 G8 **Cossington** Leics
19 L6 **Cossington** Somset
76 H9 **Costessey** Norfk
72 F5 **Costock** Notts
73 L6 **Coston** Leics
76 F10 **Coston** Norfk
34 C4 **Cote** Oxon
19 K6 **Cote** Somset
82 C11 **Cotebrook** Ches W
111 J10 **Cotehill** Cumb
95 K3 **Cotes** Cumb
72 F6 **Cotes** Leics
70 E8 **Cotes** Staffs
60 B4 **Cotesbach** Leics
70 E8 **Cotes Heath** Staffs
18 G9 **Cotford St Luke** Somset
72 G3 **Cotgrave** Notts
151 M4 **Cothal** Abers
85 N11 **Cotham** Notts
18 G8 **Cothelstone** Somset
103 K7 **Cotherstone** Dur
34 E5 **Cothill** Oxon
10 E4 **Cotleigh** Devon
72 D2 **Cotmanhay** Derbys
62 F9 **Coton** Cambs
60 E6 **Coton** Nhants
69 P8 **Coton** Shrops
59 J4 **Coton** Staffs
70 E10 **Coton** Staffs
70 H8 **Coton** Staffs
70 F10 **Coton Clanford** Staffs
70 H8 **Coton Hayes** Staffs
56 H2 **Coton Hill** Shrops
71 M9 **Coton in the Clay** Staffs
71 N11 **Coton in the Elms** Derbys
71 P11 **Coton Park** Derbys
33 J3 **Cotswolds**
7 K6 **Cott** Devon
22 D6 **Cottage End** Hants
88 G4 **Cottam** Lancs
85 P5 **Cottam** Notts
62 F7 **Cottenham** Cambs
96 B2 **Cotterdale** N York
50 H5 **Cottered** Herts
58 F8 **Cotteridge** Birm
61 M2 **Cotterstock** Nhants
60 F6 **Cottesbrooke** Nhants
73 N8 **Cottesmore** Rutlnd
92 H4 **Cottingham** E R Yk
60 H2 **Cottingham** Nhants
90 E3 **Cottingley** C Brad
90 H4 **Cottingley Hall Crematorium** Leeds
48 G8 **Cottisford** Oxon
64 F8 **Cotton** Suffk
61 N11 **Cotton End** Bed
89 Q3 **Cotton Tree** Lancs
150 E2 **Cottown** Abers
151 K4 **Cottown** Abers
159 K9 **Cottown of Gight** Abers
6 C5 **Cotts** Devon
69 R11 **Cotwall** Wrekin
70 G8 **Cotwalton** Staffs
5 J10 **Couch's Mill** Cnwll
46 A10 **Coughton** Herefs
47 L2 **Coughton** Warwks
123 M6 **Coulaghailtro** Ag & B
154 C9 **Coulags** Highld
100 C9 **Coulderton** Cumb
150 E7 **Coull** Abers
131 Q10 **Coulport** Ag & B
36 G9 **Coulsdon** Gt Lon
21 J4 **Coulston** Wilts
116 E4 **Coulter** S Lans
23 Q11 **Coultershaw Bridge** W Susx
18 H6 **Coultings** Somset
98 C6 **Coulton** N York
135 K3 **Coultra** Fife
57 K3 **Cound** Shrops
57 K4 **Coundlane** Shrops
103 P5 **Coundon** Dur
103 P5 **Coundon Grange** Dur
96 D3 **Countersett** N York
21 N6 **Countess** Wilts
52 E5 **Countess Cross** Essex
9 M7 **Countess Wear** Devon
72 F11 **Countesthorpe** Leics
17 N2 **Countisbury** Devon
142 C10 **Coupar Angus** P & K
88 H5 **Coup Green** Lancs
102 D7 **Coupland** Cumb
118 H4 **Coupland** Nthumb
123 P10 **Cour** Ag & B
27 J4 **Court-at-Street** Kent
145 L8 **Courteachan** Highld
49 L4 **Courteenhall** Nhants
43 L10 **Court Henry** Carmth
38 H3 **Courtsend** Essex
18 H8 **Courtway** Somset
128 B6 **Cousland** Mdloth
25 Q4 **Cousley Wood** E Susx
131 Q11 **Cove** Ag & B
129 K5 **Cove** Border
18 C11 **Cove** Devon
23 N3 **Cove** Hants
160 C8 **Cove** Highld
151 P7 **Cove Bay** C Aber
65 P6 **Cove Bottom** Suffk
65 Q5 **Covehithe** Suffk
58 D3 **Coven** Staffs
62 G4 **Coveney** Cambs
87 K2 **Covenham St Bartholomew** Lincs
87 K2 **Covenham St Mary** Lincs
58 D3 **Coven Heath** Staffs
59 M9 **Coventry** Covtry
59 N10 *Coventry Airport* Warwks
3 K10 **Coverack** Cnwll
2 H7 **Coverack Bridges** Cnwll
96 H3 **Coverham** N York
61 N6 **Covington** Cambs
116 D3 **Covington** S Lans
95 N5 **Cowan Bridge** Lancs
25 P8 **Cowbeech** E Susx
74 E7 **Cowbit** Lincs
30 C10 **Cowbridge** V Glam
83 N10 **Cowdale** Derbys
25 L2 **Cowden** Kent
134 F9 **Cowdenbeath** Fife
25 L2 **Cowden Pound** Kent
25 L2 **Cowden Station** Kent
71 Q5 **Cowers Lane** Derbys
14 E7 **Cowes** IoW
97 Q3 **Cowesby** N York
21 Q10 **Cowesfield Green** Wilts
24 F6 **Cowfold** W Susx
95 R3 **Cowgill** Cumb
64 F8 **Cow Green** Suffk
32 B6 **Cowhill** S Glos
133 N10 **Cowie** Stirlg
99 K7 **Cowlam** E R Yk
9 M5 **Cowley** Devon
33 J2 **Cowley** Gloucs
36 C4 **Cowley** Gt Lon
34 F4 **Cowley** Oxon
88 H7 **Cowling** Lancs
90 B2 **Cowling** N York
97 K3 **Cowling** N York
63 M10 **Cowlinge** Suffk
90 F7 **Cowmes** Kirk
89 N6 **Cowpe** Lancs
113 L4 **Cowpen** Nthumb
104 E6 **Cowpen Bewley** S on T
15 J4 **Cowplain** Hants
102 G2 **Cowshill** Dur
19 N2 **Cowslip Green** N Som
97 P10 **Cowthorpe** N York
56 F10 **Coxall** Herefs
70 B6 **Coxbank** Ches E
72 B2 **Coxbench** Derbys
19 P7 **Coxbridge** Somset
65 N5 **Cox Common** Suffk
5 K2 **Coxford** Cnwll
76 B6 **Coxford** Norfk
57 Q7 **Coxgreen** Staffs
38 B11 **Coxheath** Kent
104 B3 **Coxhoe** Dur
19 P6 **Coxley** Somset
90 H7 **Coxley** Wakefd
19 P6 **Coxley Wick** Somset
5 Q7 **Coxpark** Cnwll
51 N11 **Coxtie Green** Essex
98 A5 **Coxwold** N York
29 P9 **Coychurch** Brdgnd
29 P8 **Coychurch Crematorium** Brdgnd
114 H4 **Coylton** S Ayrs
148 G5 **Coylumbridge** Highld
29 N7 **Coytrahen** Brdgnd
58 F11 **Crabbs Cross** Worcs
13 J3 **Crab Orchard** Dorset
24 F5 **Crabtree** W Susx
69 K6 **Crabtree Green** Wrexhm
102 C6 **Crackenthorpe** Cumb
5 J2 **Crackington Haven** Cnwll
70 E4 **Crackley** Staffs
59 L10 **Crackley** Warwks
57 P2 **Crackleybank** Shrops
103 J11 **Crackpot** N York
96 E8 **Cracoe** N York
10 B2 **Craddock** Devon
51 L6 **Cradle End** Herts
58 D7 **Cradley** Dudley
46 D5 **Cradley** Herefs
58 D7 **Cradley Heath** Sandw
44 E8 **Cradoc** Powys
5 P11 **Crafthole** Cnwll
49 N11 **Crafton** Bucks
95 K6 **Crag Foot** Lancs
149 J2 **Craggan** Highld
90 G3 **Cragg Hill** Leeds
113 K10 **Craghead** Dur
44 B10 **Crai** Powys
158 C6 **Craibstone** Moray
143 J8 **Craichie** Angus
143 M6 **Craig** Angus
154 D8 **Craig** Highld
115 L5 **Craigbank** E Ayrs
127 N7 **Craigburn** Border
29 J4 **Craigcefnparc** Swans
110 F3 **Craigcleuch** D & G
159 K11 **Craigdam** Abers
130 G6 **Craigdhu** Ag & B
151 J5 **Craigearn** Abers
157 P9 **Craigellachie** Moray
134 E3 **Craigend** P & K
125 M3 **Craigend** Rens
132 C11 **Craigendoran** Ag & B
125 L4 **Craigends** Rens
107 K5 **Craighlaw** D & G
122 H6 **Craighouse** Ag & B
141 R9 **Craigie** P & K
125 L11 **Craigie** S Ayrs
159 M4 **Craigiefold** Abers
108 G9 **Craigley** D & G
29 K4 **Craig Llangiwg** Neath
127 N3 **Craiglockhart** C Edin
127 Q3 **Craigmillar** C Edin
69 J7 **Craignant** Shrops
115 Q10 **Craigneston** D & G
126 D4 **Craigneuk** N Lans
126 D6 **Craigneuk** N Lans
138 C10 **Craignure** Ag & B
143 M5 **Craigo** Angus
30 C9 **Craig Penllyn** V Glam
135 K5 **Craigrothie** Fife
132 F3 **Craigruie** Stirlg
52 B4 **Craig's End** Essex
143 J10 **Craigton** Angus
151 L7 **Craigton** C Aber
125 M7 **Craigton** E Rens
125 N5 **Craigton Crematorium** C Glas
142 E7 **Craigton of Airlie** Angus
29 K4 **Craig-y-Duke** Neath
44 A11 **Craig-y-nos** Powys
135 Q6 **Crail** Fife
118 C6 **Crailing** Border
92 C11 **Craiselound** N Linc
97 K3 **Crakehall** N York
97 P6 **Crakehill** N York
71 K7 **Crakemarsh** Staffs
98 E8 **Crambe** N York
113 L5 **Cramlington** Nthumb
127 M2 **Cramond** C Edin
127 M2 **Cramond Bridge** C Edin
22 C10 **Crampmoor** Hants
82 G11 **Cranage** Ches E
70 E7 **Cranberry** Staffs
13 J2 **Cranborne** Dorset
35 P10 **Cranbourne** Br For
26 C4 **Cranbrook** Kent
26 C4 **Cranbrook Common** Kent
91 J10 **Crane Moor** Barns
76 C9 **Crane's Corner** Norfk
49 Q6 **Cranfield** C Beds
16 E7 **Cranford** Devon
36 D5 **Cranford** Gt Lon
61 K5 **Cranford St Andrew** Nhants
61 K5 **Cranford St John** Nhants
32 G2 **Cranham** Gloucs
37 N3 **Cranham** Gt Lon
47 M4 **Cranhill** Warwks
81 Q5 **Crank** St Hel
24 C3 **Cranleigh** Surrey
64 E7 **Cranmer Green** Suffk
14 C8 **Cranmore** IoW
20 C6 **Cranmore** Somset
73 K11 **Cranoe** Leics
65 L9 **Cransford** Suffk
128 H7 **Cranshaws** Border
80 g1 **Cranstal** IoM
99 L10 **Cranswick** E R Yk
4 B9 **Crantock** Cnwll
86 D11 **Cranwell** Lincs
63 N2 **Cranwich** Norfk
76 D11 **Cranworth** Norfk
130 F6 **Craobh Haven** Ag & B
6 E5 **Crapstone** Devon
131 K8 **Crarae** Ag & B
162 C2 **Crask Inn** Highld
155 N9 **Crask of Aigas** Highld
119 Q7 **Craster** Nthumb
45 K7 **Craswall** Herefs
58 D3 **Crateford** Staffs
65 L6 **Cratfield** Suffk
151 K8 **Crathes** Abers
151 J8 **Crathes Castle** Abers
149 P8 **Crathie** Abers
147 P9 **Crathie** Highld
104 D9 **Crathorne** N York
56 G8 **Craven Arms** Shrops
112 H8 **Crawcrook** Gatesd
81 P4 **Crawford** Lancs
116 D6 **Crawford** S Lans
116 B6 **Crawfordjohn** S Lans
22 D8 **Crawley** Hants
34 B2 **Crawley** Oxon
24 G3 **Crawley** W Susx
24 H3 **Crawley Down** W Susx
103 J2 **Crawleyside** Dur
89 N5 **Crawshawbooth** Lancs
143 R2 **Crawton** Abers
52 F8 **Craxe's Green** Essex
96 D5 **Cray** N York
37 M5 **Crayford** Gt Lon
98 B6 **Crayke** N York
76 F5 **Craymere Beck** Norfk
38 B3 **Crays Hill** Essex
34 H8 **Cray's Pond** Oxon
71 N9 **Craythorne** Staffs
9 N2 **Craze Lowman** Devon
35 L8 **Crazies Hill** Wokham
17 Q8 **Creacombe** Devon
138 H9 **Creagan Inn** Ag & B
168 c13 **Creag Ghoraidh** W Isls
168 c13 **Creagorry** W Isls
139 Q4 **Creaguaineach Lodge** Highld
69 P8 **Creamore Bank** Shrops
60 F6 **Creaton** Nhants
110 D6 **Creca** D & G
45 P6 **Credenhill** Herefs
9 K4 **Crediton** Devon
107 K2 **Creebank** D & G
107 M4 **Creebridge** D & G
12 F8 **Creech** Dorset
19 J9 **Creech Heathfield** Somset
19 J9 **Creech St Michael** Somset
3 N4 **Creed** Cnwll
37 L4 **Creekmouth** Gt Lon
38 F2 **Creeksea** Essex
64 F10 **Creeting St Mary** Suffk
73 Q6 **Creeton** Lincs
107 N6 **Creetown** D & G
80 a8 **Cregneash** IoM
80 e5 **Cregny Baa** IoM
44 G4 **Cregrina** Powys
135 J3 **Creich** Fife
30 E8 **Creigiau** Cardif
6 D8 **Cremyll** Cnwll
57 K4 **Cressage** Shrops
83 Q10 **Cressbrook** Derbys
41 L9 **Cresselly** Pembks
35 M6 **Cressex** Bucks
52 C7 **Cressing** Essex
113 L2 **Cresswell** Nthumb
41 L9 **Cresswell** Pembks
70 H7 **Cresswell** Staffs
84 H6 **Creswell** Derbys
58 G2 **Creswell Green** Staffs
65 J9 **Cretingham** Suffk
123 M8 **Cretshengan** Ag & B
70 C3 **Crewe** Ches E
69 M4 **Crewe** Ches W
70 C3 **Crewe Crematorium** Ches E
70 C3 **Crewe Green** Ches E
69 K11 **Crew Green** Powys
11 J3 **Crewkerne** Somset
50 H10 **Crews Hill Station** Gt Lon
72 B4 **Crewton** C Derb
132 D2 **Crianlarich** Stirlg
43 K4 **Cribyn** Cerdgn
66 H7 **Criccieth** Gwynd
84 D10 **Crich** Derbys
84 D10 **Crich Carr** Derbys
128 B7 **Crichton** Mdloth
31 N6 **Crick** Mons
60 C6 **Crick** Nhants
44 F6 **Crickadarn** Powys
10 H3 **Cricket St Thomas** Somset
69 J10 **Crickheath** Shrops
45 J11 **Crickhowell** Powys
33 L6 **Cricklade** Wilts
36 F3 **Cricklewood** Gt Lon
91 N6 **Cridling Stubbs** N York
133 P3 **Crieff** P & K
4 G9 **Criggan** Cnwll
69 J11 **Criggion** Powys
91 J7 **Crigglestone** Wakefd
89 P8 **Crimble** Rochdl
159 Q6 **Crimond** Abers
75 N10 **Crimplesham** Norfk
47 P5 **Crimscote** Warwks
155 M9 **Crinaglack** Highld
130 F9 **Crinan** Ag & B
126 E6 **Crindledyke** N Lans
76 H10 **Cringleford** Norfk
96 F11 **Cringles** C Brad
41 M8 **Crinow** Pembks
2 E6 **Cripplesease** Cnwll
13 J2 **Cripplestyle** Dorset
26 C7 **Cripp's Corner** E Susx
148 B2 **Croachy** Highld
4 G7 **Croanford** Cnwll
37 M7 **Crockenhill** Kent
35 K7 **Crocker End** Oxon
15 P5 **Crockerhill** W Susx
9 J6 **Crockernwell** Devon
45 Q11 **Crocker's Ash** Herefs
20 G6 **Crockerton** Wilts
108 H6 **Crocketford** D & G
98 C11 **Crockey Hill** C York
37 K10 **Crockham Hill** Kent
37 P11 **Crockhurst Street** Kent
52 H6 **Crockleford Heath** Essex
10 G2 **Crock Street** Somset
29 N5 **Croeserw** Neath
40 F4 **Croes-goch** Pembks
42 G6 **Croes-lan** Cerdgn
67 L6 **Croesor** Gwynd
42 H11 **Croesyceiliog** Carmth
31 K5 **Croesyceiliog** Torfn
31 K6 **Croes-y-mwyalch** Torfn
31 K4 **Croes-y-pant** Mons
72 E11 **Croft** Leics
87 P8 **Croft** Lincs
82 D6 **Croft** Warrtn
132 F10 **Croftamie** Stirlg
2 H6 **Croft Mitchell** Cnwll
110 F10 **Crofton** Cumb
91 K7 **Crofton** Wakefd
21 Q2 **Crofton** Wilts
103 Q9 **Croft-on-Tees** N York
161 K10 **Croftown** Highld
157 P7 **Crofts** Moray
82 G5 **Crofts Bank** Traffd
157 P5 **Crofts of Dipple** Moray
159 P5 **Crofts of Savoch** Abers
28 F6 **Crofty** Swans
68 D7 **Crogen** Gwynd
130 E2 **Croggan** Ag & B
111 L11 **Croglin** Cumb
162 B8 **Croick** Highld
156 D4 **Cromarty** Highld
134 D11 **Crombie** Fife
149 K2 **Cromdale** Highld
50 G5 **Cromer** Herts
77 J3 **Cromer** Norfk
84 C9 **Cromford** Derbys
32 C6 **Cromhall** S Glos
32 C7 **Cromhall Common** S Glos
168 j5 **Cromor** W Isls
89 Q9 **Crompton Fold** Oldham
85 N8 **Cromwell** Notts
115 M3 **Cronberry** E Ayrs
23 L5 **Crondall** Hants
80 e6 **Cronkbourne** IoM
80 d4 **Cronk-y-Voddy** IoM
81 P7 **Cronton** Knows
101 N11 **Crook** Cumb
103 N3 **Crook** Dur
100 G2 **Crookdake** Cumb
88 H9 **Crooke** Wigan
46 B11 **Crooked End** Gloucs
125 M10 **Crookedholm** E Ayrs
34 B10 **Crooked Soley** Wilts
84 D3 **Crookes** Sheff
112 H10 **Crookhall** Dur
118 H3 **Crookham** Nthumb
22 F2 **Crookham** W Berk
23 L4 **Crookham Village** Hants
116 G5 **Crook Inn** Border
95 L4 **Crooklands** Cumb
134 C7 **Crook of Devon** P & K
71 N7 **Cropper** Derbys
48 E5 **Cropredy** Oxon
72 F8 **Cropston** Leics
47 J5 **Cropthorne** Worcs
98 F3 **Cropton** N York
72 H3 **Cropwell Bishop** Notts
72 H3 **Cropwell Butler** Notts
168 k1 **Cros** W Isls
168 i5 **Crosbost** W Isls
100 E3 **Crosby** Cumb
80 d6 **Crosby** IoM
92 E8 **Crosby** N Linc
81 L5 **Crosby** Sefton
102 D9 **Crosby Garret** Cumb
102 B8 **Crosby Ravensworth** Cumb
100 E3 **Crosby Villa** Cumb
19 Q6 **Croscombe** Somset
69 M9 **Crosemere** Shrops
90 E8 **Crosland Edge** Kirk
90 E8 **Crosland Hill** Kirk
19 M4 **Cross** Somset
123 P9 **Crossaig** Ag & B
136 B7 **Crossapoll** Ag & B
45 N11 **Cross Ash** Mons
26 C2 **Cross-at-Hand** Kent
24 B9 **Crossbush** W Susx
100 E3 **Crosscanonby** Cumb
3 J3 **Cross Coombe** Cnwll
77 J4 **Crossdale Street** Norfk
61 N9 **Cross End** Bed
52 E5 **Cross End** Essex
88 D6 **Crossens** Sefton
90 E2 **Cross Flatts** C Brad
134 D10 **Crossford** Fife
126 E8 **Crossford** S Lans
5 N4 **Crossgate** Cnwll
74 D5 **Crossgate** Lincs
70 G7 **Crossgate** Staffs
128 B6 **Crossgatehall** E Loth
125 K9 **Crossgates** E Ayrs
134 E10 **Crossgates** Fife
91 K4 **Cross Gates** Leeds
99 L4 **Crossgates** N York
44 F2 **Crossgates** Powys
95 M8 **Crossgill** Lancs
5 P4 **Cross Green** Devon
91 J4 **Cross Green** Leeds
58 D3 **Cross Green** Staffs
64 A11 **Cross Green** Suffk
64 B10 **Cross Green** Suffk
64 D11 **Cross Green** Suffk
28 G2 **Cross Hands** Carmth
41 N6 **Crosshands** Carmth
125 M11 **Crosshands** E Ayrs
41 L8 **Cross Hands** Pembks
84 F11 **Cross Hill** Derbys
134 F8 **Crosshill** Fife
114 F6 **Crosshill** S Ayrs
96 F11 **Cross Hills** N York
125 K10 **Crosshouse** E Ayrs
57 J3 **Cross Houses** Shrops
57 M6 **Cross Houses** Shrops
25 N6 **Cross in Hand** E Susx
42 G3 **Cross Inn** Cerdgn
43 K2 **Cross Inn** Cerdgn
41 M9 **Cross Inn** Pembks
30 E8 **Cross Inn** Rhondd
132 C10 **Cross Keys** Ag & B
30 H6 **Crosskeys** Caerph
32 G10 **Cross Keys** Wilts
166 H3 **Crosskirk** Highld
94 G3 **Crosslands** Cumb
14 F9 **Cross Lane** IoW
57 N5 **Cross Lane Head** Shrops
2 H9 **Cross Lanes** Cnwll
3 K5 **Cross Lanes** Cnwll

272 Cross Lanes - Detchant

98 A8 **Cross Lanes** N York
69 K11 **Crosslanes** Shrops
69 L5 **Cross Lanes** Wrexhm
125 L4 **Crosslee** Rens
90 G6 **Crossley** Kirk
108 F7 **Crossmichael** D & G
44 G10 **Cross Oak** Powys
158 H11 **Cross of Jackston** Abers
71 P5 **Cross o' th' hands** Derbys
24 G6 **Crosspost** W Susx
150 F6 **Crossroads** Abers
151 K9 **Crossroads** Abers
64 H6 **Cross Street** Suffk
143 J6 **Crosston** Angus
82 G9 **Cross Town** Ches E
45 N11 **Crossway** Mons
44 F3 **Crossway** Powys
31 P6 **Crossway Green** Mons
58 B11 **Crossway Green** Worcs
12 C7 **Crossways** Dorset
41 M3 **Crosswell** Pembks
95 J2 **Crosthwaite** Cumb
88 F7 **Croston** Lancs
77 K8 **Crostwick** Norfk
77 L6 **Crostwight** Norfk
37 P9 **Crouch** Kent
39 J10 **Crouch** Kent
36 H3 **Crouch End** Gt Lon
21 L9 **Croucheston** Wilts
11 Q2 **Crouch Hill** Dorset
37 K11 **Crough House Green** Kent
48 F8 **Croughton** Nhants
159 K4 **Crovie** Abers
13 L4 **Crow** Hants
2 G7 **Crowan** Cnwll
25 M4 **Crowborough** E Susx
25 M4 **Crowborough Town** E Susx
18 F7 **Crowcombe** Somset
83 P11 **Crowdecote** Derbys
83 N5 **Crowden** Derbys
8 C5 **Crowden** Devon
22 E10 **Crowdhill** Hants
37 N9 **Crowdleham** Kent
83 Q4 **Crow Edge** Barns
35 K5 **Crowell** Oxon
62 D9 **Crow End** Cambs
48 H6 **Crowfield** Nhants
64 G10 **Crowfield** Suffk
64 G10 **Crowfield Green** Suffk
77 L7 **Crowgate Street** Norfk
51 N11 **Crow Green** Essex
129 J5 **Crowhill** E Loth
46 B9 **Crow Hill** Herefs
84 D5 **Crowhole** Derbys
26 C9 **Crowhurst** E Susx
37 J11 **Crowhurst** Surrey
37 J11 **Crowhurst Lane End** Surrey
74 D8 **Crowland** Lincs
64 E7 **Crowland** Suffk
2 E7 **Crowlas** Cnwll
92 C8 **Crowle** N Linc
46 H3 **Crowle** Worcs
46 H3 **Crowle Green** Worcs
34 H7 **Crowmarsh Gifford** Oxon
65 K7 **Crown Corner** Suffk
6 D7 **Crownhill** C Plym
49 M7 **Crownhill Crematorium** M Keyn
23 Q6 **Crownpits** Surrey
76 F11 **Crownthorpe** Norfk
2 G7 **Crowntown** Cnwll
2 B8 **Crows-an-Wra** Cnwll
51 Q5 **Crow's Green** Essex
76 D10 **Crowshill** Norfk
5 M8 **Crow's Nest** Cnwll
56 F4 **Crowsnest** Shrops
23 M2 **Crowthorne** Wokham
82 C10 **Crowton** Ches W
59 J2 **Croxall** Staffs
93 L11 **Croxby** Lincs
103 Q3 **Croxdale** Dur
71 K7 **Croxden** Staffs
50 C11 **Croxley Green** Herts
81 N5 **Croxteth** Lpool
62 B8 **Croxton** Cambs
93 J8 **Croxton** N Linc
64 B4 **Croxton** Norfk
76 D5 **Croxton** Norfk
70 D8 **Croxton** Staffs
70 D8 **Croxtonbank** Staffs
69 Q4 **Croxton Green** Ches E
73 L5 **Croxton Kerrial** Leics
156 D8 **Croy** Highld
126 C2 **Croy** N Lans
16 G4 **Croyde** Devon
16 G4 **Croyde Bay** Devon
62 D11 **Croydon** Cambs
36 H7 **Croydon** Gt Lon
36 H7 **Croydon Crematorium** Gt Lon
148 B9 **Crubenmore** Highld
56 G3 **Cruckmeole** Shrops
56 G2 **Cruckton** Shrops
159 Q10 **Cruden Bay** Abers
70 A11 **Crudgington** Wrekin
33 J6 **Crudwell** Wilts
8 D5 **Cruft** Devon
56 B10 **Crug** Powys
4 E6 **Crugmeer** Cnwll
43 N7 **Crugybar** Carmth
56 B8 **Crug-y-byddar** Powys
30 H5 **Crumlin** Caerph
5 L11 **Crumplehorn** Cnwll
82 H4 **Crumpsall** Manch
27 J2 **Crundale** Kent
41 J7 **Crundale** Pembks
41 N8 **Crunwear** Pembks
9 L2 **Cruwys Morchard** Devon
22 D3 **Crux Easton** Hants
11 N5 **Cruxton** Dorset
28 E2 **Crwbin** Carmth
35 N5 **Cryers Hill** Bucks
41 N4 **Crymmych** Pembks
29 L4 **Crynant** Neath
36 H6 **Crystal Palace** Gt Lon
153 N6 **Cuaig** Highld
130 F5 **Cuan** Ag & B
59 M11 **Cubbington** Warwks
4 B10 **Cubert** Cnwll
90 G10 **Cubley** Barns
49 M10 **Cublington** Bucks
45 N7 **Cublington** Herefs
24 H5 **Cuckfield** W Susx
20 E9 **Cucklington** Somset
85 J6 **Cuckney** Notts
74 D6 **Cuckoo Bridge** Lincs
23 K6 **Cuckoo's Corner** Hants
69 L2 **Cuckoo's Nest** Ches W
34 G4 **Cuddesdon** Oxon
35 K2 **Cuddington** Bucks
82 C10 **Cuddington** Ches W
69 N5 **Cuddington Heath** Ches W
88 F3 **Cuddy Hill** Lancs
37 K9 **Cudham** Gt Lon
8 D9 **Cudliptown** Devon
13 J5 **Cudnell** Bmouth
91 K9 **Cudworth** Barns
10 H2 **Cudworth** Somset
82 B7 **Cuerdley Cross** Warrtn
23 J3 **Cufaude** Hants
50 H10 **Cuffley** Herts
138 H6 **Cuil** Highld
155 R6 **Culbokie** Highld
17 Q2 **Culbone** Somset
155 N9 **Culburnie** Highld
156 B9 **Culcabock** Highld
156 F7 **Culcharry** Highld
82 E6 **Culcheth** Warrtn
158 D11 **Culdrain** Abers
153 N9 **Culduie** Highld
64 A7 **Culford** Suffk
102 B5 **Culgaith** Cumb
34 F5 **Culham** Oxon
164 B10 **Culkein** Highld
164 D10 **Culkein Drumbeg** Highld
32 H5 **Culkerton** Gloucs
158 D4 **Cullen** Moray
113 N6 **Cullercoats** N Tyne
151 K7 **Cullerlie** Abers
156 A5 **Cullicudden** Highld
90 D3 **Cullingworth** C Brad
144 G3 **Cuillin Hills** Highld
130 E5 **Cullipool** Ag & B
169 s3 **Cullivoe** Shet
156 C8 **Culloden** Highld
9 P3 **Cullompton** Devon
9 P3 **Cullompton Services** Devon
18 F11 **Culm Davy** Devon
56 H8 **Culmington** Shrops
10 C2 **Culmstock** Devon
160 H6 **Culnacraig** Highld
108 G10 **Culnaightrie** D & G
153 J5 **Culnaknock** Highld
53 M2 **Culpho** Suffk
162 D8 **Culrain** Highld
134 B10 **Culross** Fife
114 F5 **Culroy** S Ayrs
158 G11 **Culsalmond** Abers
107 N8 **Culscadden** D & G
107 K7 **Culshabbin** D & G
169 p9 **Culswick** Shet
151 N3 **Cultercullen** Abers
151 M7 **Cults** C Aber
37 P8 **Culverstone Green** Kent
73 Q2 **Culverthorpe** Lincs
48 F5 **Culworth** Nhants
114 D5 **Culzean Castle & Country Park** S Ayrs
126 D3 **Cumbernauld** N Lans
126 D2 **Cumbernauld Village** N Lans
87 P6 **Cumberworth** Lincs
110 F11 **Cumdivock** Cumb
159 K7 **Cuminestown** Abers
129 K8 **Cumledge** Border
110 G10 **Cummersdale** Cumb
109 P7 **Cummertrees** D & G
157 L4 **Cummingston** Moray
115 L3 **Cumnock** E Ayrs
34 E4 **Cumnor** Oxon
111 L10 **Cumrew** Cumb
109 N3 **Cumrue** D & G
111 J10 **Cumwhinton** Cumb
111 K10 **Cumwhitton** Cumb
97 P6 **Cundall** N York
125 K9 **Cunninghamhead** N Ayrs
169 r10 **Cunningsburgh** Shet
135 K5 **Cupar** Fife
135 K5 **Cupar Muir** Fife
84 C6 **Curbar** Derbys
14 F4 **Curbridge** Hants
34 B3 **Curbridge** Oxon
14 F4 **Curdridge** Hants
59 J6 **Curdworth** Warwks
19 J11 **Curland** Somset
34 E10 **Curridge** W Berk
127 M4 **Currie** C Edin
19 K10 **Curry Mallet** Somset
19 L9 **Curry Rivel** Somset
26 E4 **Curteis Corner** Kent
26 B3 **Curtisden Green** Kent
7 J8 **Curtisknowle** Devon
2 H9 **Cury** Cnwll
150 E5 **Cushnie** Abers
18 G8 **Cushuish** Somset
45 J6 **Cusop** Herefs
107 N11 **Cutcloy** D & G
18 B7 **Cutcombe** Somset
89 P8 **Cutgate** Rochdl
162 H9 **Cuthill** Highld
67 L11 **Cutiau** Gwynd
51 N4 **Cutler's Green** Essex
4 H9 **Cutmadoc** Cnwll
5 N9 **Cutmere** Cnwll
58 C11 **Cutnall Green** Worcs
47 L8 **Cutsdean** Gloucs
91 L6 **Cutsyke** Wakefd
84 D6 **Cutthorpe** Derbys
5 P9 **Cuttivett** Cnwll
35 J5 **Cuxham** Oxon
38 B8 **Cuxton** Medway
93 L10 **Cuxwold** Lincs
30 G3 **Cwm** Blae G
80 F9 **Cwm** Denbgs
29 L6 **Cwmafan** Neath
30 D5 **Cwmaman** Rhondd
43 L5 **Cwmann** Carmth
31 J3 **Cwmavon** Torfn
28 E4 **Cwm-bach** Carmth
41 Q5 **Cwmbach** Carmth
44 H7 **Cwmbach** Powys
30 D4 **Cwmbach** Rhondd
44 E4 **Cwmbach Llechrhyd** Powys
55 L8 **Cwmbelan** Powys
31 J6 **Cwmbran** Torfn
54 G8 **Cwmbrwyno** Cerdgn
28 E4 **Cwm Capel** Carmth
30 H6 **Cwmcarn** Caerph
31 N3 **Cwmcarvan** Mons
30 H3 **Cwm-celyn** Blae G
55 K2 **Cwm-Cewydd** Gwynd
41 Q2 **Cwm-cou** Cerdgn
44 G11 **Cwm Crawnon** Powys
30 C4 **Cwmdare** Rhondd
43 M8 **Cwmdu** Carmth
44 H10 **Cwmdu** Powys
28 H6 **Cwmdu** Swans
42 G8 **Cwmduad** Carmth
28 H4 **Cwm Dulais** Swans
43 P8 **Cwmdwr** Carmth
29 N7 **Cwmfelin** Brdgnd
30 E4 **Cwmfelin** Myr Td
41 N7 **Cwmfelin Boeth** Carmth
30 G6 **Cwmfelinfach** Caerph
41 P6 **Cwmfelin Mynach** Carmth
42 H11 **Cwmffrwd** Carmth
29 L2 **Cwmgiedd** Powys
29 K2 **Cwmgorse** Carmth
28 G2 **Cwmgwili** Carmth
29 N4 **Cwmgwrach** Neath
42 F7 **Cwmhiraeth** Carmth
43 N9 **Cwm-Ifor** Carmth
44 B5 **Cwm Irfon** Powys
43 J11 **Cwmisfael** Carmth
55 J3 **Cwm Llinau** Powys
29 K2 **Cwmllynfell** Neath
28 F2 **Cwmmawr** Carmth
41 Q4 **Cwm Morgan** Carmth
29 P5 **Cwmparc** Rhondd
42 G7 **Cwmpengraig** Carmth
67 P5 **Cwm Penmachno** Conwy
30 D4 **Cwmpennar** Rhondd
44 H10 **Cwmrhos** Powys
29 J5 **Cwmrhydyceirw** Swans
43 J5 **Cwmsychbant** Cerdgn
30 H3 **Cwmtillery** Blae G
29 L2 **Cwm-twrch Isaf** Powys
29 L2 **Cwm-twrch Uchaf** Powys
28 G2 **Cwm-y-glo** Carmth
67 K2 **Cwm-y-glo** Gwynd
45 K10 **Cwmyoy** Mons
54 H10 **Cwmystwyth** Cerdgn
54 F5 **Cwrt** Gwynd
43 J5 **Cwrt-newydd** Cerdgn
45 J11 **Cwrt-y-gollen** Powys
55 Q3 **Cyfronydd** Powys
29 K4 **Cylibebyll** Neath
29 N5 **Cymer** Neath
30 D6 **Cymmer** Rhondd
43 R6 **Cynghordy** Carmth
28 E3 **Cynheidre** Carmth
29 M5 **Cynonville** Neath
68 E6 **Cynwyd** Denbgs
42 G9 **Cynwyl Elfed** Carmth

D

7 N5 **Daccombe** Devon
101 N5 **Dacre** Cumb
97 J8 **Dacre** N York
97 J8 **Dacre Banks** N York
102 G3 **Daddry Shield** Dur
49 J7 **Dadford** Bucks
72 C11 **Dadlington** Leics
28 F4 **Dafen** Carmth
76 D10 **Daffy Green** Norfk
37 M4 **Dagenham** Gt Lon
33 J3 **Daglingworth** Gloucs
49 Q11 **Dagnall** Bucks
64 E9 **Dagworth** Suffk
114 E7 **Dailly** S Ayrs
7 M5 **Dainton** Devon
135 L4 **Dairsie** Fife
82 E4 **Daisy Hill** Bolton
90 H5 **Daisy Hill** Leeds
168 c15 **Dalabrog** W Isls
131 K5 **Dalavich** Ag & B
108 H8 **Dalbeattie** D & G
71 P8 **Dalbury** Derbys
80 b6 **Dalby** IoM
87 M7 **Dalby** Lincs
98 C6 **Dalby** N York
141 N7 **Dalcapon** P & K
163 L5 **Dalchalm** Highld
146 H5 **Dalchreichart** Highld
133 L4 **Dalchruin** P & K
134 C2 **Dalcrue** P & K
87 J7 **Dalderby** Lincs
9 P8 **Dalditch** Devon
126 B5 **Daldowie Crematorium** C Glas
101 P2 **Dale** Cumb
72 C3 **Dale** Derbys
40 F9 **Dale** Pembks
101 J6 **Dale Bottom** Cumb
84 B8 **Dale End** Derbys
96 E11 **Dale End** N York
26 B5 **Dale Hill** E Susx
105 L7 **Dalehouse** N York
138 C4 **Dalelia** Highld
124 H8 **Dalgarven** N Ayrs
134 F11 **Dalgety Bay** Fife
115 L5 **Dalgig** E Ayrs
133 M3 **Dalginross** P & K
141 N8 **Dalguise** P & K
166 E6 **Dalhalvaig** Highld
63 M8 **Dalham** Suffk
168 c15 **Daliburgh** W Isls
127 Q4 **Dalkeith** Mdloth
157 L7 **Dallas** Moray
65 K10 **Dallinghoo** Suffk
25 Q7 **Dallington** E Susx
60 F8 **Dallington** Nhants
97 J6 **Dallow** N York
131 P2 **Dalmally** Ag & B
132 G8 **Dalmary** Stirlg
115 J6 **Dalmellington** E Ayrs
127 L2 **Dalmeny** C Edin
156 B4 **Dalmore** Highld
125 M3 **Dalmuir** W Duns
138 C4 **Dalnabreck** Highld
140 H3 **Dalnacardoch** P & K
148 F4 **Dalnahaitnach** Highld
140 F3 **Dalnaspidal** P & K
166 H8 **Dalnawillan Lodge** Highld
141 J6 **Daloist** P & K
134 D7 **Dalqueich** P & K
114 F8 **Dalquhairn** S Ayrs
162 H5 **Dalreavoch Lodge** Highld
124 H8 **Dalry** N Ayrs
114 G5 **Dalrymple** E Ayrs
126 D7 **Dalserf** S Lans
120 B9 **Dalsmeran** Ag & B
110 G10 **Dalston** Cumb
36 H4 **Dalston** Gt Lon
109 K3 **Dalswinton** D & G
95 L5 **Dalton** Cumb
109 P6 **Dalton** D & G
88 F9 **Dalton** Lancs
97 P5 **Dalton** N York
103 M9 **Dalton** N York
112 H6 **Dalton** Nthumb
84 G2 **Dalton** Rothm
94 E6 **Dalton-in-Furness** Cumb
113 P11 **Dalton-le-Dale** Dur
84 G2 **Dalton Magna** Rothm
103 Q9 **Dalton-on-Tees** N York
84 G2 **Dalton Parva** Rothm
104 E4 **Dalton Piercy** Hartpl
133 J3 **Dalveich** Stirlg
147 Q11 **Dalwhinnie** Highld
10 E4 **Dalwood** Devon
50 G5 **Damask Green** Herts
21 M11 **Damerham** Hants
77 N10 **Damgate** Norfk
64 E4 **Dam Green** Norfk
38 E9 **Danaway** Kent
52 C10 **Danbury** Essex
105 K9 **Danby** N York
105 J10 **Danby Bottom** N York
104 B11 **Danby Wiske** N York
157 P8 **Dandaleith** Moray
127 Q4 **Danderhall** Mdloth
83 L11 **Danebridge** Ches E
50 H6 **Dane End** Herts
25 N4 **Danegate** E Susx
25 K5 **Danehill** E Susx
72 F10 **Dane Hills** C Leic
76 F10 **Danemoor Green** Norfk
57 N6 **Danesford** Shrops
84 F8 **Danesmoor** Derbys
39 J11 **Dane Street** Kent
26 G3 **Daniel's Water** Kent
158 H6 **Danshillock** Abers
128 F6 **Danskine** E Loth
93 N4 **Danthorpe** E R Yk
58 H11 **Danzey Green** Warwks
71 J9 **Dapple Heath** Staffs
23 M2 **Darby Green** Hants
89 L9 **Darcy Lever** Bolton
45 J11 **Dardy** Powys
30 H2 **Daren-felen** Mons
37 N6 **Darenth** Kent
82 C8 **Daresbury** Halton
91 L10 **Darfield** Barns
85 J5 **Darfoulds** Notts
39 J9 **Dargate** Kent
5 M8 **Darite** Cnwll
38 C8 **Darland** Medway
69 L3 **Darland** Wrexhm
58 E5 **Darlaston** Wsall
58 E5 **Darlaston Green** Wsall
97 K9 **Darley** N York
72 B3 **Darley Abbey** C Derb
84 C8 **Darley Bridge** Derbys
84 C8 **Darley Dale** Derbys
59 J10 **Darley Green** Solhll
50 D6 **Darleyhall** Herts
97 J9 **Darley Head** N York
47 P6 **Darlingscott** Warwks
103 Q8 **Darlington** Darltn
103 Q8 **Darlington Crematorium** Darltn
69 Q8 **Darliston** Shrops
85 N6 **Darlton** Notts
58 H3 **Darnford** Staffs
117 Q4 **Darnick** Border
55 J4 **Darowen** Powys
158 H8 **Darra** Abers
16 C8 **Darracott** Devon
16 H4 **Darracott** Devon
113 J6 **Darras Hall** Nthumb
91 M7 **Darrington** Wakefd
65 N8 **Darsham** Suffk
20 B6 **Darshill** Somset
37 M6 **Dartford** Kent
7 K6 **Dartington** Devon
6 H4 **Dartmeet** Devon
8 G9 **Dartmoor National Park** Devon
7 M8 **Dartmouth** Devon
91 J8 **Darton** Barns
125 P10 **Darvel** E Ayrs
25 Q7 **Darwell Hole** E Susx
89 K6 **Darwen** Bl w D
35 Q9 **Datchet** W & M
50 G7 **Datchworth** Herts
50 G7 **Datchworth Green** Herts
89 L9 **Daubhill** Bolton
157 N9 **Daugh of Kinermony** Moray
33 J8 **Dauntsey** Wilts
157 J10 **Dava** Highld
82 E10 **Davenham** Ches W
83 K7 **Davenport** Stockp
82 H9 **Davenport Green** Ches E
82 H7 **Davenport Green** Traffd
60 C8 **Daventry** Nhants
127 N2 **Davidson's Mains** C Edin
5 K4 **Davidstow** Cnwll
37 P8 **David Street** Kent
117 J10 **Davington** D & G
38 H9 **Davington Hill** Kent
151 J2 **Daviot** Abers
156 C10 **Daviot** Highld
156 C9 **Daviot House** Highld
25 M7 **Davis's Town** E Susx
158 C7 **Davoch of Grange** Moray
82 G5 **Davyhulme** Traffd
58 F4 **Daw End** Wsall
36 F11 **Dawesgreen** Surrey
57 M3 **Dawley** Wrekin
9 N9 **Dawlish** Devon
9 N9 **Dawlish Warren** Devon
80 B10 **Dawn** Conwy
18 G10 **Daws Green** Somset
38 D4 **Daws Heath** Essex
5 N5 **Daw's House** Cnwll
74 H4 **Dawsmere** Lincs
85 J11 **Daybrook** Notts
70 D3 **Day Green** Ches E
70 H8 **Dayhills** Staffs
58 E9 **Dayhouse Bank** Worcs
47 P9 **Daylesford** Gloucs
80 G10 **Ddol** Flints
68 D11 **Ddol-Cownwy** Powys
39 Q11 **Deal** Kent
100 E5 **Dean** Cumb
7 J6 **Dean** Devon
17 L2 **Dean** Devon
17 N2 **Dean** Devon
21 J11 **Dean** Dorset
22 D8 **Dean** Hants
22 G11 **Dean** Hants
89 P5 **Dean** Lancs
48 B10 **Dean** Oxon
20 C6 **Dean** Somset
37 N7 **Dean Bottom** Kent
117 M8 **Deanburnhaugh** Border
7 J6 **Deancombe** Devon
34 E3 **Dean Court** Oxon
89 K9 **Deane** Bolton
22 F4 **Deane** Hants
21 J11 **Dean End** Dorset
90 H10 **Dean Head** Barns
90 C7 **Deanhead** Kirk
21 J11 **Deanland** Dorset
15 K4 **Deanlane End** W Susx
7 J6 **Dean Prior** Devon
112 B8 **Deanraw** Nthumb
83 J8 **Dean Row** Ches E
127 J4 **Deans** W Loth
100 E5 **Deanscales** Cumb
49 L7 **Deanshanger** Nhants
157 R7 **Deanshaugh** Moray
133 L7 **Deanston** Stirlg
38 B11 **Dean Street** Kent
100 E3 **Dearham** Cumb
89 Q7 **Dearnley** Rochdl
65 J11 **Debach** Suffk
51 K11 **Debden** Essex
51 N4 **Debden** Essex
51 N4 **Debden Green** Essex
64 H9 **Debenham** Suffk
46 F5 **Deblin's Green** Worcs
127 J3 **Dechmont** W Loth
127 J4 **Dechmont Road** W Loth
48 E8 **Deddington** Oxon
53 J5 **Dedham** Essex
53 J5 **Dedham Heath** Essex
35 P9 **Dedworth** W & M
61 K2 **Deene** Nhants
61 L2 **Deenethorpe** Nhants
90 H11 **Deepcar** Sheff
23 P3 **Deepcut** Surrey
95 Q4 **Deepdale** Cumb
96 C5 **Deepdale** N York
74 B9 **Deeping Gate** C Pete
74 C9 **Deeping St James** Lincs
74 D7 **Deeping St Nicholas** Lincs
46 G8 **Deerhurst** Gloucs
46 G9 **Deerhurst Walton** Gloucs
38 G9 **Deerton Street** Kent
46 H6 **Defford** Worcs
44 C9 **Defynnog** Powys
79 P9 **Deganwy** Conwy
130 F5 **Degnish** Ag & B
91 Q2 **Deighton** C York
104 C10 **Deighton** N York
67 K2 **Deiniolen** Gwynd
4 H5 **Delabole** Cnwll
82 C11 **Delamere** Ches W
151 P3 **Delfrigs** Abers
17 J7 **Delley** Devon
157 K11 **Delliefure** Highld
15 M6 **Dell Quay** W Susx
34 C2 **Delly End** Oxon
149 M4 **Delnabo** Moray
157 M10 **Delnashaugh Inn** Moray
156 C3 **Delny** Highld
90 B9 **Delph** Oldham
112 H11 **Delves** Dur
52 C4 **Delvin End** Essex
73 Q3 **Dembleby** Lincs
4 F9 **Demelza** Cnwll
91 M11 **Denaby** Donc
91 M11 **Denaby Main** Donc
36 D10 **Denbies** Surrey
80 F11 **Denbigh** Denbgs
135 K4 **Denbrae** Fife
7 L5 **Denbury** Devon
84 E11 **Denby** Derbys
84 E11 **Denby Bottles** Derbys
90 G9 **Denby Dale** Kirk
34 C6 **Denchworth** Oxon
94 E6 **Dendron** Cumb
50 B3 **Denel End** C Beds
134 B4 **Denfield** P & K
61 L5 **Denford** Nhants
52 G11 **Dengie** Essex
36 B3 **Denham** Bucks
63 N8 **Denham** Suffk
64 H7 **Denham** Suffk
63 N8 **Denham End** Suffk
36 B3 **Denham Green** Bucks
64 H7 **Denham Green** Suffk
159 N7 **Denhead** Abers
135 M5 **Denhead** Fife
142 F11 **Denhead of Gray** C Dund
117 R7 **Denholm** Border
90 D4 **Denholme** C Brad
90 D4 **Denholme Clough** C Brad
66 F7 **Denio** Gwynd
15 J4 **Denmead** Hants
151 N5 **Denmore** C Aber
24 E5 **Denne Park** W Susx
65 K8 **Dennington** Suffk
133 N11 **Denny** Falk
133 N11 **Dennyloanhead** Falk
134 H4 **Den of Lindores** Fife
90 B8 **Denshaw** Oldham
151 L8 **Denside** Abers
27 M3 **Densole** Kent
63 N10 **Denston** Suffk
71 K6 **Denstone** Staffs
39 K9 **Denstroude** Kent
95 Q3 **Dent** Cumb
61 Q3 **Denton** Cambs
103 P7 **Denton** Darltn
25 L10 **Denton** E Susx
27 M2 **Denton** Kent
37 Q6 **Denton** Kent
73 M4 **Denton** Lincs
96 H11 **Denton** N York
60 H9 **Denton** Nhants
65 K4 **Denton** Norfk
34 G4 **Denton** Oxon
83 K5 **Denton** Tamesd
75 M10 **Denver** Norfk
119 P8 **Denwick** Nthumb
76 E11 **Deopham** Norfk
64 E2 **Deopham Green** Norfk
63 N9 **Depden** Suffk
63 N9 **Depden Green** Suffk
37 J5 **Deptford** Gt Lon
21 K7 **Deptford** Wilts
72 B3 **Derby** C Derb
17 K5 **Derby** Devon
80 c8 **Derbyhaven** IoM
141 L7 **Derculich** P & K
76 D9 **Dereham** Norfk
30 F4 **Deri** Caerph
16 E11 **Derril** Devon
27 M2 **Derringstone** Kent
70 F10 **Derrington** Staffs
16 E11 **Derriton** Devon
33 J10 **Derry Hill** Wilts
92 D9 **Derrythorpe** N Linc
75 N4 **Dersingham** Norfk
137 L5 **Dervaig** Ag & B
68 E4 **Derwen** Denbgs
43 L10 **Derwen Fawr** Carmth
54 G5 **Derwenlas** Powys
101 J6 **Derwent Water** Cumb
43 M11 **Derwydd** Carmth
60 H4 **Desborough** Nhants
72 D10 **Desford** Leics
158 D5 **Deskford** Moray
119 L3 **Detchant** Nthumb

Detling - Dyffryn 273

38 C10 **Detling** Kent
57 M7 **Deuxhill** Shrops
31 N5 **Devauden** Mons
54 G9 **Devil's Bridge** Cerdgn
59 L6 **Devitts Green** Warwks
21 K2 **Devizes** Wilts
6 D8 **Devonport** C Plym
133 Q8 **Devonside** Clacks
3 K6 **Devoran** Cnwll
128 B7 **Dewarton** Mdloth
12 C5 **Dewlish** Dorset
90 G6 **Dewsbury** Kirk
90 G6 **Dewsbury Moor** Kirk
90 G6 **Dewsbury Moor Crematorium** Kirk
68 H11 **Deytheur** Powys
31 P11 **Dial** N Som
23 P9 **Dial Green** W Susx
24 E7 **Dial Post** W Susx
11 K4 **Dibberford** Dorset
14 D5 **Dibden** Hants
14 D5 **Dibden Purlieu** Hants
58 H9 **Dickens Heath** Solhll
64 H5 **Dickleburgh** Norfk
47 L8 **Didbrook** Gloucs
34 F6 **Didcot** Oxon
34 F6 **Didcot Railway Centre** Oxon
61 Q7 **Diddington** Cambs
57 J7 **Diddlebury** Shrops
45 P8 **Didley** Herefs
23 M11 **Didling** W Susx
32 F7 **Didmarton** Gloucs
82 H6 **Didsbury** Manch
6 H6 **Didworthy** Devon
86 E10 **Digby** Lincs
152 H4 **Digg** Highld
90 C9 **Diggle** Oldham
88 F9 **Digmoor** Lancs
50 F7 **Digswell** Herts
50 G8 **Digswell Water** Herts
43 J3 **Dihewyd** Cerdgn
77 L6 **Dilham** Norfk
70 H6 **Dilhorne** Staffs
89 M5 **Dill Hall** Lancs
61 P7 **Dillington** Cambs
112 E8 **Dilston** Nthumb
20 G5 **Dilton** Wilts
20 F5 **Dilton Marsh** Wilts
45 N4 **Dilwyn** Herefs
89 L7 **Dimple** Bolton
84 C8 **Dimple** Derbys
41 Q4 **Dinas** Carmth
4 E7 **Dinas** Cnwll
66 D7 **Dinas** Gwynd
41 K3 **Dinas** Pembks
30 D6 **Dinas** Rhondd
66 G3 **Dinas Dinlle** Gwynd
67 R11 **Dinas-Mawddwy** Gwynd
30 G10 **Dinas Powys** V Glam
19 Q6 **Dinder** Somset
45 Q7 **Dinedor** Herefs
31 N2 **Dingestow** Mons
81 M7 **Dingle** Lpool
26 D5 **Dingleden** Kent
60 G3 **Dingley** Nhants
155 P6 **Dingwall** Highld
68 D6 **Dinmael** Conwy
150 D8 **Dinnet** Abers
113 K6 **Dinnington** N u Ty
84 H3 **Dinnington** Rothm
11 J2 **Dinnington** Somset
67 K2 **Dinorwic** Gwynd
35 L2 **Dinton** Bucks
21 K8 **Dinton** Wilts
109 P2 **Dinwoodie** D & G
16 E8 **Dinworthy** Devon
18 H10 **Dipford** Somset
23 K3 **Dipley** Hants
120 F4 **Dippen** Ag & B
121 K7 **Dippen** N Ayrs
23 M5 **Dippenhall** Surrey
8 B3 **Dippermill** Devon
8 B8 **Dippertown** Devon
157 Q6 **Dipple** Moray
114 D7 **Dipple** S Ayrs
7 J7 **Diptford** Devon
113 J10 **Dipton** Dur
112 D8 **Diptonmill** Nthumb
128 E3 **Dirleton** E Loth
112 C11 **Dirt Pot** Nthumb
45 K2 **Discoed** Powys
72 D6 **Diseworth** Leics
97 N6 **Dishforth** N York
83 L8 **Disley** Ches E
64 G5 **Diss** Norfk
44 E3 **Disserth** Powys
100 D6 **Distington** Cumb
100 D6 **Distington Hall Crematorium** Cumb
21 L8 **Ditchampton** Wilts
20 B7 **Ditcheat** Somset
65 L3 **Ditchingham** Norfk
24 H7 **Ditchling** E Susx
57 J2 **Ditherington** Shrops
32 F11 **Ditteridge** Wilts
7 M7 **Dittisham** Devon
38 B10 **Ditton** Kent
63 L9 **Ditton Green** Cambs
57 L7 **Ditton Priors** Shrops
47 J8 **Dixton** Gloucs
31 P2 **Dixton** Mons
5 K2 **Dizzard** Cnwll
90 B9 **Dobcross** Oldham
5 L8 **Dobwalls** Cnwll
9 J7 **Doccombe** Devon
155 R9 **Dochgarroch** Highld
23 M6 **Dockenfield** Surrey
95 M6 **Docker** Lancs
75 Q3 **Docking** Norfk
45 R3 **Docklow** Herefs
101 L6 **Dockray** Cumb
110 E11 **Dockray** Cumb
7 J10 **Dodbrooke** Devon
51 N11 **Doddinghurst** Essex
62 F2 **Doddington** Cambs
38 F10 **Doddington** Kent
85 Q6 **Doddington** Lincs
119 J4 **Doddington** Nthumb
57 L9 **Doddington** Shrops
9 L7 **Doddiscombsleigh** Devon
69 R6 **Dodd's Green** Ches E
75 N4 **Doddshill** Norfk
5 N9 **Doddy Cross** Cnwll
60 D8 **Dodford** Nhants
58 D10 **Dodford** Worcs
32 E8 **Dodington** S Glos
18 G6 **Dodington** Somset
69 L2 **Dodleston** Ches W
17 J8 **Dodscott** Devon
125 N7 **Dodside** E Rens
71 J8 **Dod's Leigh** Staffs
91 J9 **Dodworth** Barns
91 J10 **Dodworth Bottom** Barns
91 J10 **Dodworth Green** Barns
58 H5 **Doe Bank** Birm
84 G7 **Doe Lea** Derbys
86 H9 **Dogdyke** Lincs
90 F8 **Dogley Lane** Kirk
23 L4 **Dogmersfield** Hants
33 L7 **Dogridge** Wilts
74 C10 **Dogsthorpe** C Pete
9 N5 **Dog Village** Devon
55 P2 **Dolanog** Powys
55 Q11 **Dolau** Powys
43 N6 **Dolaucothi** Carmth
67 J6 **Dolbenmaen** Gwynd
70 C9 **Doley** Staffs
55 L4 **Dolfach** Powys
55 J3 **Dol-for** Powys
55 Q7 **Dolfor** Powys
79 P11 **Dolgarrog** Conwy
67 N11 **Dolgellau** Gwynd
54 F4 **Dolgoch** Gwynd
42 H8 **Dol-gran** Carmth
163 K6 **Doll** Highld
134 B8 **Dollar** Clacks
134 B8 **Dollarfield** Clacks
56 D11 **Dolley Green** Powys
54 F8 **Dollwen** Cerdgn
80 H10 **Dolphin** Flints
95 L10 **Dolphinholme** Lancs
127 L8 **Dolphinton** S Lans
17 K9 **Dolton** Devon
80 B10 **Dolwen** Conwy
67 N4 **Dolwyddelan** Conwy
54 E7 **Dolybont** Cerdgn
45 J3 **Dolyhir** Powys
69 J11 **Domgay** Powys
118 G2 **Donaldson's Lodge** Nthumb
91 P10 **Doncaster** Donc
91 P10 **Doncaster Carr** Donc
91 R8 **Doncaster North Services** Donc
20 H10 **Donhead St Andrew** Wilts
20 H10 **Donhead St Mary** Wilts
134 F10 **Donibristle** Fife
18 E6 **Doniford** Somset
74 D3 **Donington** Lincs
86 H4 **Donington on Bain** Lincs
72 D5 **Donington Park Services** Leics
74 D4 **Donington Southing** Lincs
59 M2 **Donisthorpe** Leics
27 K5 **Donkey Street** Kent
23 P2 **Donkey Town** Surrey
47 N9 **Donnington** Gloucs
46 D8 **Donnington** Herefs
57 K3 **Donnington** Shrops
34 E11 **Donnington** W Berk
15 N6 **Donnington** W Susx
57 N2 **Donnington** Wrekin
57 N2 **Donnington Wood** Wrekin
10 G2 **Donyatt** Somset
24 E5 **Doomsday Green** W Susx
114 F4 **Doonfoot** S Ayrs
149 K4 **Dorback Lodge** Highld
11 P6 **Dorchester** Dorset
34 G6 **Dorchester** Oxon
59 L4 **Dordon** Warwks
84 D4 **Dore** Sheff
155 Q11 **Dores** Highld
36 E11 **Dorking** Surrey
52 F4 **Dorking Tye** Suffk
25 K2 **Dormans Land** Surrey
25 J2 **Dormans Park** Surrey
46 A6 **Dormington** Herefs
47 J3 **Dormston** Worcs
47 P8 **Dorn** Gloucs
35 P9 **Dorney** Bucks
145 Q2 **Dornie** Highld
162 H9 **Dornoch** Highld
110 D7 **Dornock** D & G
167 J6 **Dorrery** Highld
59 J10 **Dorridge** Solhll
86 E10 **Dorrington** Lincs
56 H4 **Dorrington** Shrops
70 C6 **Dorrington** Shrops
47 M5 **Dorsington** Warwks
45 L6 **Dorstone** Herefs
35 J2 **Dorton** Bucks
59 K5 **Dosthill** Staffs
78 F10 **Dothan** IoA
11 K5 **Dottery** Dorset
5 K9 **Doublebois** Cnwll
32 G6 **Doughton** Gloucs
80 e6 **Douglas** IoM
116 A4 **Douglas** S Lans
142 G11 **Douglas and Angus** C Dund
80 e6 **Douglas Borough Crematorium** IoM
131 P8 **Douglas Pier** Ag & B
142 G8 **Douglastown** Angus
116 B3 **Douglas Water** S Lans
126 E11 **Douglas West** S Lans
20 B6 **Doulting** Somset
169 D4 **Dounby** Ork
161 Q6 **Doune** Highld
133 L7 **Doune** Stirlg
114 C8 **Dounepark** S Ayrs
162 D8 **Dounie** Highld
6 E5 **Dousland** Devon
69 L10 **Dovaston** Shrops
84 G10 **Dove Green** Notts
83 N9 **Dove Holes** Derbys
100 E4 **Dovenby** Cumb
27 P3 **Dover** Kent
82 D4 **Dover** Wigan
27 P3 **Dover Castle** Kent
53 M5 **Dovercourt** Essex
58 C11 **Doverdale** Worcs
71 L8 **Doveridge** Derbys
36 G11 **Doversgreen** Surrey
141 P8 **Dowally** P & K
88 E4 **Dowbridge** Lancs
47 K11 **Dowdeswell** Gloucs
30 E3 **Dowlais** Myr Td
17 K9 **Dowland** Devon
10 H2 **Dowlish Ford** Somset
10 H2 **Dowlish Wake** Somset
33 L5 **Down Ampney** Gloucs
5 N11 **Downderry** Cnwll
37 K8 **Downe** Gt Lon
32 F5 **Downend** Gloucs
14 F9 **Downend** IoW
32 C9 **Downend** S Glos
34 E9 **Downend** W Berk
142 F11 **Downfield** C Dund
5 M7 **Downgate** Cnwll
5 P7 **Downgate** Cnwll
38 B2 **Downham** Essex
37 J6 **Downham** Gt Lon
89 M2 **Downham** Lancs
75 M10 **Downham Market** Norfk
46 G10 **Down Hatherley** Gloucs
19 Q9 **Downhead** Somset
20 C5 **Downhead** Somset
4 D8 **Downhill** Cnwll
134 D2 **Downhill** P & K
88 D9 **Downholland Cross** Lancs
103 M11 **Downholme** N York
5 P3 **Downicarey** Devon
151 N9 **Downies** Abers
80 H9 **Downing** Flints
35 M5 **Downley** Bucks
8 H4 **Down St Mary** Devon
24 H9 **Downs Crematorium** Br & H
20 B4 **Downside** Somset
20 B6 **Downside** Somset
36 D9 **Downside** Surrey
6 E8 **Down Thomas** Devon
13 N6 **Downton** Hants
21 N10 **Downton** Wilts
74 B5 **Dowsby** Lincs
74 E8 **Dowsdale** Lincs
70 F10 **Doxey** Staffs
119 N6 **Doxford** Nthumb
32 D10 **Doynton** S Glos
30 H7 **Draethen** Caerph
126 D8 **Draffan** S Lans
92 F8 **Dragonby** N Linc
24 D6 **Dragons Green** W Susx
85 M2 **Drakeholes** Notts
57 Q8 **Drakelow** Worcs
124 H7 **Drakemyre** N Ayrs
46 H5 **Drakes Broughton** Worcs
6 C4 **Drakewalls** Cnwll
96 F10 **Draughton** N York
60 G5 **Draughton** Nhants
92 A5 **Drax** N York
91 R5 **Drax Hales** N York
59 P10 **Draycote** Warwks
33 N9 **Draycot Foliat** Swindn
72 C4 **Draycott** Derbys
47 N7 **Draycott** Gloucs
57 Q6 **Draycott** Shrops
19 N4 **Draycott** Somset
19 Q10 **Draycott** Somset
46 G5 **Draycott** Worcs
71 M9 **Draycott in the Clay** Staffs
70 H6 **Draycott in the Moors** Staffs
9 J2 **Drayford** Devon
15 J5 **Drayton** C Port
60 H2 **Drayton** Leics
74 D3 **Drayton** Lincs
76 H9 **Drayton** Norfk
34 E6 **Drayton** Oxon
48 D6 **Drayton** Oxon
19 M10 **Drayton** Somset
58 D9 **Drayton** Worcs
59 J4 **Drayton Bassett** Staffs
35 P2 **Drayton Beauchamp** Bucks
59 J4 **Drayton Manor Park** Staffs
49 M9 **Drayton Parslow** Bucks
34 G5 **Drayton St Leonard** Oxon
96 G9 **Drebley** N York
80 g3 **Dreemskerry** IoM
40 H8 **Dreen Hill** Pembks
28 F2 **Drefach** Carmth
42 G7 **Drefach** Carmth
43 J5 **Drefach** Cerdgn
42 G7 **Drefelin** Carmth
125 K10 **Dreghorn** N Ayrs
27 M3 **Drellingore** Kent
128 E4 **Drem** E Loth
70 G6 **Dresden** C Stke
8 H6 **Drewsteignton** Devon
87 L6 **Driby** Lincs
99 L9 **Driffield** E R Yk
33 L5 **Driffield** Gloucs
33 L5 **Driffield Cross Roads** Gloucs
2 C8 **Drift** Cnwll
100 E11 **Drigg** Cumb
90 G5 **Drighlington** Leeds
137 P5 **Drimnin** Highld
11 J4 **Drimpton** Dorset
138 H2 **Drimsallie** Highld
98 B11 **Dringhouses** C York
64 D9 **Drinkstone** Suffk
64 D9 **Drinkstone Green** Suffk
11 M3 **Drive End** Dorset
50 F6 **Driver's End** Herts
71 J9 **Drointon** Staffs
46 G2 **Droitwich** Worcs
134 E4 **Dron** P & K
84 E5 **Dronfield** Derbys
84 D5 **Dronfield Woodhouse** Derbys
114 H4 **Drongan** E Ayrs
142 E10 **Dronley** Angus
12 C3 **Droop** Dorset
84 E2 **Dropping Well** Rothm
22 H11 **Droxford** Hants
83 K5 **Droylsden** Tamesd
68 D6 **Druid** Denbgs
40 G7 **Druidston** Pembks
139 K3 **Druimarbin** Highld
139 J8 **Druimavuic** Ag & B
123 M5 **Druimdrishaig** Ag & B
145 L11 **Druimindarroch** Highld
124 A2 **Drum** Ag & B
134 C7 **Drum** P & K
116 C3 **Drumalbin** S Lans
164 D10 **Drumbeg** Highld
158 E9 **Drumblade** Abers
106 E9 **Drumbreddon** D & G
153 P11 **Drumbuie** Highld
110 E9 **Drumburgh** Cumb
109 J10 **Drumburn** D & G
125 N3 **Drumchapel** C Glas
140 G6 **Drumchastle** P & K
125 Q10 **Drumclog** S Lans
135 L7 **Drumeldrie** Fife
116 G4 **Drumelzier** Border
145 L4 **Drumfearn** Highld
151 J8 **Drumfrennie** Abers
142 G7 **Drumgley** Angus
148 D7 **Drumguish** Highld
157 M11 **Drumin** Moray
115 K8 **Drumjohn** D & G
107 J2 **Drumlamford** S Ayrs
150 G6 **Drumlasie** Abers
110 E10 **Drumleaning** Cumb
120 C8 **Drumlemble** Ag & B
151 K11 **Drumlithie** Abers
107 L8 **Drummoddie** D & G
106 F10 **Drummore** D & G
158 A9 **Drummuir** Moray
155 P11 **Drumnadrochit** Highld
106 F10 **Drumnaglaur** D & G
158 D7 **Drumnagorrach** Moray
109 J5 **Drumpark** D & G
161 K6 **Drumrunie Lodge** Highld
114 E5 **Drumshang** S Ayrs
152 H8 **Drumuie** Highld
148 G3 **Drumuillie** Highld
133 K7 **Drumvaich** Stirlg
134 E6 **Drunzie** P & K
119 Q11 **Druridge** Nthumb
69 J2 **Drury** Flints
102 C7 **Drybeck** Cumb
158 B5 **Drybridge** Moray
125 K10 **Drybridge** N Ayrs
46 B11 **Drybrook** Gloucs
118 A4 **Dryburgh** Border
85 Q11 **Dry Doddington** Lincs
62 E8 **Dry Drayton** Cambs
132 F10 **Drymen** Stirlg
159 M8 **Drymuir** Abers
152 G11 **Drynoch** Highld
34 E4 **Dry Sandford** Oxon
43 L10 **Dryslwyn** Carmth
37 Q3 **Dry Street** Essex
57 K3 **Dryton** Shrops
159 J5 **Dubford** Abers
64 H8 **Dublin** Suffk
161 P3 **Duchally** Highld
50 C2 **Duck End** Bed
62 B8 **Duck End** Cambs
51 Q4 **Duck End** Essex
51 Q5 **Duck End** Essex
52 B7 **Duckend Green** Essex
69 N4 **Duckington** Ches W
34 C3 **Ducklington** Oxon
61 P9 **Duck's Cross** Bed
51 L3 **Duddenhoe End** Essex
127 P3 **Duddingston** C Edin
73 P10 **Duddington** Nhants
18 H10 **Duddlestone** Somset
25 L5 **Duddleswell** E Susx
57 M8 **Duddlewick** Shrops
118 H2 **Duddo** Nthumb
69 P2 **Duddon** Ches W
94 D3 **Duddon Bridge** Cumb
81 Q11 **Duddon Common** Ches W
69 K7 **Dudleston** Shrops
69 L7 **Dudleston Heath** Shrops
58 D6 **Dudley** Dudley
113 L6 **Dudley** N Tyne
90 F4 **Dudley Hill** C Brad
58 E6 **Dudley Port** Sandw
57 L10 **Dudnill** Shrops
13 J5 **Dudsbury** Dorset
35 Q3 **Dudswell** Herts
72 A2 **Duffield** Derbys
29 M5 **Duffryn** Neath
157 Q9 **Dufftown** Moray
157 M4 **Duffus** Moray
102 C5 **Dufton** Cumb
98 H7 **Duggleby** N York
153 P11 **Duirinish** Highld
145 M5 **Duisdalemore** Highld
139 J2 **Duisky** Highld
30 F2 **Dukestown** Blae G
53 J3 **Duke Street** Suffk
83 K5 **Dukinfield** Tamesd
83 K5 **Dukinfield Crematorium** Tamesd
78 H7 **Dulas** IoA
19 Q6 **Dulcote** Somset
9 Q3 **Dulford** Devon
141 K8 **Dull** P & K
126 C2 **Dullatur** N Lans
63 K9 **Dullingham** Cambs
63 K9 **Dullingham Ley** Cambs
148 H3 **Dulnain Bridge** Highld
61 Q8 **Duloe** Bed
5 L10 **Duloe** Cnwll
18 B9 **Dulverton** Somset
36 H6 **Dulwich** Gt Lon
125 K2 **Dumbarton** W Duns
47 K7 **Dumbleton** Gloucs
109 L5 **Dumfries** D & G
132 G11 **Dumgoyne** Stirlg
22 G5 **Dummer** Hants
39 Q8 **Dumpton** Kent
143 M6 **Dun** Angus
140 H6 **Dunalastair** P & K
124 F3 **Dunan** Ag & B
145 J2 **Dunan** Highld
140 C6 **Dunan** P & K
120 C10 **Dunaverty** Ag & B
19 K6 **Dunball** Somset
128 H4 **Dunbar** E Loth
167 L11 **Dunbeath** Highld
138 F11 **Dunbeg** Ag & B
133 M7 **Dunblane** Stirlg
134 H4 **Dunbog** Fife
22 B9 **Dunbridge** Hants
155 Q6 **Duncanston** Highld
150 F2 **Duncanstone** Abers
9 L7 **Dunchideock** Devon
59 Q10 **Dunchurch** Warwks
49 J4 **Duncote** Nhants
109 L4 **Duncow** D & G
134 E6 **Duncrievie** P & K
23 Q11 **Duncton** W Susx
142 G11 **Dundee** C Dund
135 K2 **Dundee Airport** C Dund
142 F11 **Dundee Crematorium** C Dund
19 N8 **Dundon** Somset
125 K11 **Dundonald** S Ayrs
160 H9 **Dundonnell** Highld
110 D11 **Dundraw** Cumb
147 J5 **Dundreggan** Highld
108 F11 **Dundrennan** D & G
31 Q11 **Dundry** N Som
151 K6 **Dunecht** Abers
134 D10 **Dunfermline** Fife
134 E10 **Dunfermline Crematorium** Fife
33 M5 **Dunfield** Gloucs
83 Q4 **Dunford Bridge** Barns
38 F10 **Dungate** Kent
126 B10 **Dungavel** S Lans
20 G4 **Dunge** Wilts
27 J8 **Dungeness** Kent
84 C3 **Dungworth** Sheff
85 P6 **Dunham** Notts
81 P10 **Dunham-on-the-Hill** Ches W
46 H2 **Dunhampstead** Worcs
58 B11 **Dunhampton** Worcs
82 F7 **Dunham Town** Traffd
82 F7 **Dunham Woodhouses** Traffd
86 D5 **Dunholme** Lincs
135 N5 **Dunino** Fife
133 N11 **Dunipace** Falk
141 P9 **Dunkeld** P & K
20 D3 **Dunkerton** BaNES
10 C3 **Dunkeswell** Devon
97 M11 **Dunkeswick** N York
81 M10 **Dunkirk** Ches W
39 J10 **Dunkirk** Kent
32 E7 **Dunkirk** S Glos
21 J2 **Dunkirk** Wilts
37 P10 **Dunk's Green** Kent
143 K4 **Dunlappie** Angus
22 E4 **Dunley** Hants
57 P11 **Dunley** Worcs
125 L8 **Dunlop** E Ayrs
147 P3 **Dunmaglass** Highld
4 G8 **Dunmere** Cnwll
133 P10 **Dunmore** Falk
167 M2 **Dunnet** Highld
143 J8 **Dunnichen** Angus
134 C5 **Dunning** P & K
98 D10 **Dunnington** C York
99 P10 **Dunnington** E R Yk
47 L4 **Dunnington** Warwks
89 N5 **Dunnockshaw** Lancs
38 C9 **Dunn Street** Kent
124 F2 **Dunoon** Ag & B
157 J8 **Dunphail** Moray
106 G6 **Dunragit** D & G
129 K9 **Duns** Border
84 B6 **Dunsa** Derbys
74 B5 **Dunsby** Lincs
89 L8 **Dunscar** Bolton
109 J4 **Dunscore** D & G
91 Q9 **Dunscroft** Donc
104 H7 **Dunsdale** R & Cl
35 K9 **Dunsden Green** Oxon
16 E10 **Dunsdon** Devon
24 B3 **Dunsfold** Surrey
9 K7 **Dunsford** Devon
134 G5 **Dunshalt** Fife
159 N8 **Dunshillock** Abers
84 G8 **Dunsill** Notts
105 N8 **Dunsley** N York
58 C8 **Dunsley** Staffs
35 N3 **Dunsmore** Bucks
95 P11 **Dunsop Bridge** Lancs
50 B6 **Dunstable** C Beds
71 M10 **Dunstall** Staffs
46 G6 **Dunstall Common** Worcs
63 M8 **Dunstall Green** Suffk
119 P7 **Dunstan** Nthumb
119 P6 **Dunstan Steads** Nthumb
18 C6 **Dunster** Somset
48 E9 **Duns Tew** Oxon
113 K8 **Dunston** Gatesd
86 E8 **Dunston** Lincs
77 J11 **Dunston** Norfk
70 G11 **Dunston** Staffs
6 F8 **Dunstone** Devon
8 H9 **Dunstone** Devon
70 G11 **Dunston Heath** Staffs
91 Q9 **Dunsville** Donc
93 J3 **Dunswell** E R Yk
127 K8 **Dunsyre** S Lans
5 P6 **Dunterton** Devon
48 C9 **Dunthrop** Oxon
33 J3 **Duntisbourne Abbots** Gloucs
33 J3 **Duntisbourne Leer** Gloucs
33 J3 **Duntisbourne Rouse** Gloucs
11 P3 **Duntish** Dorset
125 M3 **Duntocher** W Duns
49 M10 **Dunton** Bucks
50 F2 **Dunton** C Beds
76 B5 **Dunton** Norfk
60 B2 **Dunton Bassett** Leics
37 M9 **Dunton Green** Kent
37 Q2 **Dunton Wayletts** Essex
152 G3 **Duntulm** Highld
114 E4 **Dunure** S Ayrs
28 G6 **Dunvant** Swans
152 D8 **Dunvegan** Highld
65 P7 **Dunwich** Suffk
70 G3 **Dunwood** Staffs
110 H10 **Durdar** Cumb
3 K8 **Durgan** Cnwll
103 Q2 **Durham** Dur
103 Q2 **Durham Cathedral** Dur
103 Q2 **Durham Crematorium** Dur
104 B3 **Durham Services** Dur
104 C8 **Durham Tees Valley Airport** S on T
116 B10 **Durisdeer** D & G
116 B10 **Durisdeermill** D & G
91 J7 **Durkar** Wakefd
19 J7 **Durleigh** Somset
22 F11 **Durley** Hants
21 P2 **Durley** Wilts
22 F11 **Durley Street** Hants
39 N10 **Durlock** Kent
39 P9 **Durlock** Kent
46 B7 **Durlow Common** Herefs
89 Q7 **Durn** Rochdl
165 K3 **Durness** Highld
151 J2 **Durno** Abers
138 H6 **Duror** Highld
131 K6 **Durran** Ag & B
24 D9 **Durrington** W Susx
21 N6 **Durrington** Wilts
151 K8 **Durris** Abers
32 E5 **Dursley** Gloucs
46 C10 **Dursley Cross** Gloucs
19 J9 **Durston** Somset
12 E3 **Durweston** Dorset
60 F8 **Duston** Nhants
148 G3 **Duthil** Highld
56 C9 **Dutlas** Powys
51 P5 **Duton Hill** Essex
5 N4 **Dutson** Cnwll
82 C9 **Dutton** Ches W
62 G11 **Duxford** Cambs
34 C5 **Duxford** Oxon
62 G11 **Duxford Aircraft Museum** Cambs
79 N9 **Dwygyfylchi** Conwy
78 G11 **Dwyran** IoA
151 M5 **Dyce** C Aber
52 B4 **Dyer's End** Essex
28 E4 **Dyfatty** Carmth
54 F2 **Dyffrydan** Gwynd
29 N6 **Dyffryn** Brdgnd
30 E4 **Dyffryn** Myr Td
30 E10 **Dyffryn** V Glam

274 Dyffryn Ardudwy - Ellesmere

67 K10 Dyffryn Ardudwy Gwynd
54 H8 Dyffryn Castell Cerdgn
29 N2 Dyffryn Cellwen Neath
74 B6 Dyke Lincs
156 H6 Dyke Moray
142 C7 Dykehead Angus
142 F6 Dykehead Angus
126 F6 Dykehead N Lans
132 H8 Dykehead Stirlg
143 N4 Dykelands Abers
142 D6 Dykends Angus
158 H9 Dykeside Abers
55 K6 Dylife Powys
27 K6 Dymchurch Kent
46 D8 Dymock Gloucs
32 D9 Dyrham S Glos
135 J9 Dysart Fife
80 F9 Dyserth Denbgs

E

58 E9 Eachway Worcs
112 H6 Eachwick Nthumb
95 J11 Eagland Hill Lancs
85 Q7 Eagle Lincs
85 Q7 Eagle Barnsdale Lincs
85 Q7 Eagle Moor Lincs
104 D7 Eaglescliffe S on T
100 E5 Eaglesfield Cumb
110 D6 Eaglesfield D & G
125 P7 Eaglesham E Rens
89 L8 Eagley Bolton
80 c6 Eairy IoM
85 L8 Eakring Notts
92 C8 Ealand N Linc
36 E4 Ealing Gt Lon
111 N9 Eals Nthumb
101 P5 Eamont Bridge Cumb
96 D11 Earby Lancs
89 K6 Earcroft Bl w D
57 N6 Eardington Shrops
45 N3 Eardisland Herefs
45 L5 Eardisley Herefs
69 L9 Eardiston Shrops
57 M11 Eardiston Worcs
62 E5 Earith Cambs
119 J5 Earle Nthumb
82 C5 Earlestown St Hel
35 K10 Earley Wokham
76 H10 Earlham Norfk
77 J10 Earlham Crematorium Norfk
152 F5 Earlish Highld
61 J8 Earls Barton Nhants
52 E6 Earls Colne Essex
47 J3 Earls Common Worcs
46 G6 Earl's Croome Worcs
57 L9 Earlsditton Shrops
59 M9 Earlsdon Covtry
25 P7 Earl's Down E Susx
135 M7 Earlsferry Fife
36 G6 Earlsfield Gt Lon
159 K11 Earlsford Abers
64 E8 Earl's Green Suffk
90 H6 Earlsheaton Kirk
72 D11 Earl Shilton Leics
65 J9 Earl Soham Suffk
83 N11 Earl Sterndale Derbys
117 R3 Earlston Border
125 L10 Earlston E Ayrs
64 G10 Earl Stonham Suffk
36 G11 Earlswood Surrey
58 H10 Earlswood Warwks
31 N6 Earlswood Common Mons
15 M7 Earnley W Susx
88 G6 Earnshaw Bridge Lancs
113 M6 Earsdon N Tyne
113 J2 Earsdon Nthumb
65 L4 Earsham Norfk
98 C9 Earswick C York
15 P5 Eartham W Susx
32 C7 Earthcott S Glos
104 G9 Easby N York
130 E4 Easdale Ag & B
23 P10 Easebourne W Susx
59 Q9 Easenhall Warwks
23 P6 Eashing Surrey
35 J2 Easington Bucks
104 D2 Easington Dur
93 Q7 Easington E R Yk
119 M4 Easington Nthumb
35 J5 Easington Oxon
105 K7 Easington R & Cl
104 D2 Easington Colliery Dur
113 N11 Easington Lane Sundld
98 A7 Easingwold N York
39 N11 Easole Street Kent
142 E9 Eassie and Nevay Angus
30 D11 East Aberthaw V Glam
7 K9 East Allington Devon
17 R6 East Anstey Devon
22 C5 East Anton Hants
103 P11 East Appleton N York
14 G9 East Ashey IoW
15 M5 East Ashling W Susx
22 D5 East Aston Hants
99 K3 East Ayton N York
5 M2 East Balsdon Cnwll
30 H3 East Bank Blae G
86 G4 East Barkwith Lincs
38 B11 East Barming Kent
105 M8 East Barnby N York
50 G11 East Barnet Gt Lon
129 J4 East Barns E Loth
76 C5 East Barsham Norfk
76 H4 East Beckham Norfk
36 C6 East Bedfont Gt Lon
53 J5 East Bergholt Suffk
90 F5 East Bierley Kirk
76 D8 East Bilney Norfk
25 L10 East Blatchington E Susx
12 E6 East Bloxworth Dorset
113 N8 East Boldon S Tyne
14 C6 East Boldre Hants
119 M7 East Bolton Nthumb
104 B8 Eastbourne Darltn
25 P11 Eastbourne E Susx
25 P10 Eastbourne Crematorium E Susx
19 K7 East Bower Somset
76 C10 East Bradenham Norfk
19 K4 East Brent Somset
65 P8 Eastbridge Suffk
72 H2 East Bridgford Notts
103 J7 East Briscoe Dur
30 G10 Eastbrook V Glam
17 M5 East Buckland Devon
9 Q8 East Budleigh Devon
90 C2 Eastburn C Brad
99 K9 Eastburn E R Yk
35 Q8 East Burnham Bucks
12 D7 East Burton Dorset
36 D2 Eastbury Herts
34 B9 Eastbury W Berk
112 H11 East Butsfield Dur
92 D9 East Butterwick N Linc
96 F10 Eastby N York
127 K4 East Calder W Loth
76 H11 East Carleton Norfk
90 G2 East Carlton Leeds
60 H3 East Carlton Nhants
12 C8 East Chaldon (Chaldon Herring) Dorset
34 C7 East Challow Oxon
7 K10 East Charleton Devon
11 M3 East Chelborough Dorset
25 J7 East Chiltington E Susx
11 K2 East Chinnock Somset
21 M4 East Chisenbury Wilts
21 Q5 East Cholderton Hants
38 G7 Eastchurch Kent
36 C10 East Clandon Surrey
49 K9 East Claydon Bucks
31 M10 East Clevedon N Som
11 L2 East Coker Somset
32 G4 Eastcombe Gloucs
18 G8 Eastcombe Somset
20 B6 East Compton Somset
7 L7 East Cornworthy Devon
109 P9 East Cote Cumb
36 D3 Eastcote Gt Lon
49 J4 Eastcote Nhants
59 J9 Eastcote Solhll
16 D8 Eastcott Cnwll
21 K3 Eastcott Wilts
92 B2 East Cottingwith E R Yk
21 P2 Eastcourt Wilts
33 J6 Eastcourt Wilts
14 F7 East Cowes IoW
91 R6 East Cowick E R Yk
104 B10 East Cowton N York
113 L5 East Cramlington Nthumb
20 C6 East Cranmore Somset
12 F8 East Creech Dorset
110 F11 East Curthwaite Cumb
25 N11 East Dean E Susx
46 C10 East Dean Gloucs
21 Q9 East Dean Hants
15 P4 East Dean W Susx
9 Q5 East Devon Crematorium Devon
7 L9 Eastdown Devon
17 L3 East Down Devon
85 N5 East Drayton Notts
36 H5 East Dulwich Gt Lon
31 Q11 East Dundry N Som
93 J5 East Ella C KuH
61 P9 East End Bed
49 Q6 East End C Beds
93 L4 East End E R Yk
93 N5 East End E R Yk
38 F3 Eastend Essex
51 K8 East End Essex
14 C7 East End Hants
22 D2 East End Hants
51 L5 East End Herts
26 D4 East End Kent
38 G7 East End Kent
49 P6 East End M Keyn
31 N10 East End N Som
48 C11 East End Oxon
20 C5 East End Somset
53 K4 East End Suffk
149 P9 Easter Balmoral Abers
31 Q8 Easter Compton S Glos
156 D7 Easter Dalziel Highld
15 P5 Eastergate W Susx
126 B4 Easterhouse C Glas
127 N5 Easter Howgate Mdloth
155 Q6 Easter Kinkell Highld
155 Q9 Easter Moniack Highld
59 L9 Eastern Green Covtry
151 L7 Easter Ord Abers
135 P6 Easter Pitkierie Fife
169 q9 Easter Skeld Shet
118 E4 Easter Softlaw Border
21 K4 Easterton Wilts
19 K4 Eastertown Somset
21 P4 East Everleigh Wilts
38 B11 East Farleigh Kent
60 F4 East Farndon Nhants
92 D11 East Ferry Lincs
126 F5 Eastfield N Lans
99 L4 Eastfield N York
86 D3 East Firsby Lincs
128 E4 East Fortune E Loth
91 L4 East Garforth Leeds
34 C9 East Garston W Berk
103 J3 Eastgate Dur
74 B7 Eastgate Lincs
76 G7 Eastgate Norfk
34 D7 East Ginge Oxon
72 G8 East Goscote Leics
21 Q2 East Grafton Wilts
65 N8 East Green Suffk
21 P9 East Grimstead Wilts
25 J3 East Grinstead W Susx
26 F7 East Guldeford E Susx
60 E7 East Haddon Nhants
34 F7 East Hagbourne Oxon
93 K7 East Halton N Linc
37 K4 East Ham Gt Lon
81 M8 Eastham Wirral
81 M8 Eastham Ferry Wirral
35 M11 Easthampstead Park Crematorium Br For
45 N2 Easthampton Herefs
34 D6 East Hanney Oxon
52 C11 East Hanningfield Essex
91 M7 East Hardwick Wakefd
64 D4 East Harling Norfk
104 D11 East Harlsey N York
21 M9 East Harnham Wilts
19 Q3 East Harptree BaNES
104 D7 East Hartburn S on T
113 L5 East Hartford Nthumb
23 L11 East Harting W Susx
20 H9 East Hatch Wilts
62 C10 East Hatley Cambs
97 J2 East Hauxwell N York
143 K10 East Haven Angus
35 L11 Eastheath Wokham
74 C2 East Heckington Lincs
103 N2 East Hedleyhope Dur
163 N3 East Helmsdale Highld
34 E7 East Hendred Oxon
99 J5 East Heslerton N York
19 M2 East Hewish N Som
25 M7 East Hoathly E Susx
12 E7 East Holme Dorset
57 K5 Easthope Shrops
52 F7 Easthorpe Essex
85 M10 Easthorpe Notts
19 Q5 East Horrington Somset
36 C10 East Horsley Surrey
119 K4 East Horton Nthumb
13 J5 East Howe Bmouth
98 C9 East Huntington C York
19 K5 East Huntspill Somset
50 D7 East Hyde C Beds
17 N2 East Ilkerton Devon
34 E8 East Ilsley W Berk
8 H3 Eastington Devon
32 E3 Eastington Gloucs
33 M2 Eastington Gloucs
87 L8 East Keal Lincs
33 M11 East Kennett Wilts
91 K2 East Keswick Leeds
125 Q7 East Kilbride S Lans
8 C5 East Kimber Devon
87 K8 East Kirkby Lincs
12 D7 East Knighton Dorset
17 Q7 East Knowstone Devon
20 G8 East Knoyle Wilts
19 M11 East Lambrook Somset
89 M9 East Lancashire Crematorium Bury
108 H6 Eastlands D & G
27 P2 East Langdon Kent
60 F2 East Langton Leics
15 N5 East Lavant W Susx
23 P11 East Lavington W Susx
103 N9 East Layton N York
33 P4 Eastleach Martin Gloucs
33 N3 Eastleach Turville Gloucs
72 F5 East Leake Notts
118 G3 East Learmouth Nthumb
6 H8 East Leigh Devon
7 K7 East Leigh Devon
8 G3 East Leigh Devon
16 H6 Eastleigh Devon
22 E11 Eastleigh Hants
76 B8 East Lexham Norfk
38 G10 Eastling Kent
128 F4 East Linton E Loth
23 L9 East Liss Hants
34 D7 East Lockinge Oxon
37 J4 East London Crematorium Gt Lon
92 C11 East Lound N Linc
12 E8 East Lulworth Dorset
99 J7 East Lutton N York
18 G9 East Lydeard Somset
19 Q8 East Lydford Somset
38 B10 East Malling Kent
37 Q9 East Malling Heath Kent
15 M4 East Marden W Susx
85 M6 East Markham Notts
21 L11 East Martin Hants
96 D10 East Marton N York
23 J10 East Meon Hants
18 C11 East Mere Devon
52 H9 East Mersea Essex
72 D5 East Midlands Airport Leics
36 D7 East Molesey Surrey
75 P10 Eastmoor Norfk
12 F6 East Morden Dorset
90 D2 East Morton C Brad
116 B10 East Morton D & G
98 D5 East Ness N York
93 N3 East Newton E R Yk
15 J7 Eastney C Port
46 D7 Eastnor Herefs
73 K10 East Norton Leics
92 D7 Eastoft N Linc
7 L4 East Ogwell Devon
61 P6 Easton Cambs
110 E9 Easton Cumb
8 H7 Easton Devon
11 P10 Easton Dorset
22 F8 Easton Hants
73 N5 Easton Lincs
76 G9 Easton Norfk
19 P5 Easton Somset
65 K10 Easton Suffk
34 D10 Easton W Berk
32 G10 Easton Wilts
32 G7 Easton Grey Wilts
31 P9 Easton-in-Gordano N Som
61 J9 Easton Maudit Nhants
73 Q10 Easton-on-the-Hill Nhants
21 P2 Easton Royal Wilts
20 F11 East Orchard Dorset
129 P9 East Ord Nthumb
5 P3 East Panson Devon
13 J5 East Parley Dorset
37 Q11 East Peckham Kent
41 J10 East Pennar Pembks
19 Q7 East Pennard Somset
61 Q7 East Perry Cambs
7 K11 East Portlemouth Devon
7 K11 East Prawle Devon
24 C10 East Preston W Susx
11 Q3 East Pulham Dorset
16 F8 East Putford Devon
18 F6 East Quantoxhead Somset
38 D8 East Rainham Medway
113 M11 East Rainton Sundld
93 M11 East Ravendale NE Lin
76 B6 East Raynham Norfk
74 E11 Eastrea Cambs
99 L7 East Riding Crematorium E R Yk
110 D7 Eastriggs D & G
91 K2 East Rigton Leeds
92 C5 Eastrington E R Yk
19 L2 East Rolstone N Som
33 P6 Eastrop Swindn
104 D10 East Rounton N York
76 A6 East Rudham Norfk
76 H3 East Runton Norfk
77 L6 East Ruston Norfk
39 P11 Eastry Kent
128 D6 East Saltoun E Loth
23 N10 Eastshaw W Susx
36 F6 East Sheen Gt Lon
34 C10 East Shefford W Berk
113 L4 East Sleekburn Nthumb
77 P8 East Somerton Norfk
85 N2 East Stockwith Lincs
12 E7 East Stoke Dorset
85 N11 East Stoke Notts
20 F10 East Stour Dorset
39 N9 East Stourmouth Kent
17 L6 East Stowford Devon
22 F6 East Stratton Hants
27 P2 East Studdal Kent
26 D2 East Sutton Kent
5 K9 East Taphouse Cnwll
16 H6 East-the-Water Devon
119 N10 East Thirston Nthumb
37 Q5 East Tilbury Thurr
23 K8 East Tisted Hants
86 F4 East Torrington Lincs
76 F9 East Tuddenham Norfk
21 Q9 East Tytherley Hants
33 J10 East Tytherton Wilts
9 K3 East Village Devon
32 B10 Eastville Bristl
87 M9 Eastville Lincs
57 J6 East Wall Shrops
75 P7 East Walton Norfk
19 P4 East Water Somset
8 G6 East Week Devon
73 K5 Eastwell Leics
22 B10 East Wellow Hants
135 J8 East Wemyss Fife
126 H4 East Whitburn W Loth
51 K8 Eastwick Herts
37 L5 East Wickham Gt Lon
41 L10 East Williamston Pembks
75 N7 East Winch Norfk
21 P8 East Winterslow Wilts
15 L7 East Wittering W Susx
96 H3 East Witton N York
84 G11 Eastwood Notts
38 D4 Eastwood Sthend
112 D3 East Woodburn Nthumb
62 F2 Eastwood End Cambs
22 D2 East Woodhay Hants
20 E6 East Woodlands Somset
23 L7 East Worldham Hants
64 C3 East Wretham Norfk
16 D8 East Youlstone Devon
59 N11 Eathorpe Warwks
83 J11 Eaton Ches E
69 Q2 Eaton Ches W
73 K5 Eaton Leics
77 J10 Eaton Norfk
85 M5 Eaton Notts
34 D4 Eaton Oxon
56 F7 Eaton Shrops
57 J7 Eaton Shrops
45 N7 Eaton Bishop Herefs
49 Q10 Eaton Bray C Beds
57 K3 Eaton Constantine Shrops
61 Q9 Eaton Ford Cambs
49 Q10 Eaton Green C Beds
33 Q5 Eaton Hastings Oxon
57 J3 Eaton Mascott Shrops
61 Q9 Eaton Socon Cambs
70 B10 Eaton upon Tern Shrops
82 D6 Eaves Brow Warrtn
59 L8 Eaves Green Solhll
98 H4 Ebberston N York
21 J10 Ebbesborne Wake Wilts
30 G3 Ebbw Vale Blae G
112 H9 Ebchester Dur
19 L2 Ebdon N Som
9 N7 Ebford Devon
32 F3 Ebley Gloucs
69 N5 Ebnal Ches W
45 P3 Ebnall Herefs
47 N6 Ebrington Gloucs
8 D6 Ebsworthy Devon
22 E3 Ecchinswell Hants
129 K6 Ecclaw Border
110 C6 Ecclefechan D & G
118 E2 Eccles Border
38 B9 Eccles Kent
82 G5 Eccles Salfd
84 D4 Ecclesall Sheff
82 F5 Eccles Crematorium Salfd
84 E2 Ecclesfield Sheff
45 M5 Eccles Green Herefs
70 E9 Eccleshall Staffs
90 F3 Eccleshill C Brad
127 K3 Ecclesmachan W Loth
77 N6 Eccles on Sea Norfk
64 E4 Eccles Road Norfk
69 M2 Eccleston Ches W
88 G7 Eccleston Lancs
81 P5 Eccleston St Hel
88 G7 Eccleston Green Lancs
151 J6 Echt Abers
118 D5 Eckford Border
84 F5 Eckington Derbys
46 H6 Eckington Worcs
60 H8 Ecton Nhants
71 K3 Ecton Staffs
83 P7 Edale Derbys
169 e3 Eday Ork
169 e3 Eday Airport Ork
24 F8 Edburton W Susx
109 P11 Edderside Cumb
162 G10 Edderton Highld
39 L8 Eddington Kent
127 N8 Eddleston Border
126 C7 Eddlewood S Lans
37 K11 Edenbridge Kent
89 N7 Edenfield Lancs
101 Q4 Edenhall Cumb
73 R6 Edenham Lincs
95 J5 Eden Mount Cumb
37 J7 Eden Park Gt Lon
3 Q3 Eden Project Cnwll
84 B7 Edensor Derbys
132 C9 Edentaggart Ag & B
91 Q9 Edenthorpe Donc
66 D7 Edern Gwynd
19 P7 Edgarley Somset
58 G8 Edgbaston Birm
3 J7 Edgcombe Cnwll
49 J10 Edgcott Bucks
17 Q4 Edgcott Somset
32 F3 Edge Gloucs
56 F3 Edge Shrops
69 Q10 Edgebolton Shrops
31 Q2 Edge End Gloucs
76 F5 Edgefield Norfk
76 F5 Edgefield Green Norfk
89 L9 Edgefold Bolton
69 N4 Edge Green Ches W
48 C5 Edgehill Warwks
69 L11 Edgerley Shrops
90 E7 Edgerton Kirk
89 N6 Edgeside Lancs
32 H3 Edgeworth Gloucs
9 K2 Edgeworthy Devon
7 M5 Edginswell Torbay
47 K2 Edgiock Worcs
70 C11 Edgmond Wrekin
70 C10 Edgmond Marsh Wrekin
56 F7 Edgton Shrops
36 E2 Edgware Gt Lon
89 L7 Edgworth Bl w D
152 E7 Edinbane Highld
127 P3 Edinburgh C Edin
127 L3 Edinburgh Airport C Edin
127 P3 Edinburgh Castle C Edin
127 N2 Edinburgh Royal Botanic Gardens C Edin
127 N3 Edinburgh Zoo C Edin
59 K2 Edingale Staffs
108 H8 Edingham D & G
85 L9 Edingley Notts
77 L5 Edingthorpe Norfk
77 L5 Edingthorpe Green Norfk
129 M9 Edington Border
113 J4 Edington Nthumb
19 L7 Edington Somset
20 H4 Edington Wilts
19 L6 Edington Burtle Somset
19 L4 Edingworth Somset
16 D7 Edistone Devon
19 K5 Edithmead Somset
73 N9 Edith Weston Rutlnd
49 Q11 Edlesborough Bucks
119 M9 Edlingham Nthumb
86 H6 Edlington Lincs
111 J9 Edmond Castle Cumb
13 J2 Edmondsham Dorset
113 K11 Edmondsley Dur
73 M7 Edmondthorpe Leics
4 F7 Edmonton Cnwll
36 H2 Edmonton Gt Lon
112 F10 Edmundbyers Dur
118 D3 Ednam Border
71 N6 Ednaston Derbys
141 L7 Edradynate P & K
129 L8 Edrom Border
69 P8 Edstaston Shrops
47 N2 Edstone Warwks
46 C3 Edvin Loach Herefs
72 F3 Edwalton Notts
52 F3 Edwardstone Suffk
30 E5 Edwardsville Myr Td
43 M8 Edwinsford Carmth
85 K7 Edwinstowe Notts
50 F2 Edworth C Beds
46 B3 Edwyn Ralph Herefs
143 L4 Edzell Angus
143 L4 Edzell Woods Abers
29 L5 Efail-fach Neath
30 E8 Efail Isaf Rhondd
66 F7 Efailnewydd Gwynd
68 G9 Efail-Rhyd Powys
41 M5 Efailwen Carmth
68 F3 Efenechtyd Denbgs
110 F2 Effgill D & G
36 D10 Effingham Surrey
71 M11 Efflinch Staffs
9 L4 Efford Devon
6 E7 Efford Crematorium C Plym
22 D4 Egbury Hants
23 Q10 Egdean W Susx
89 L8 Egerton Bolton
26 F2 Egerton Kent
26 E2 Egerton Forstal Kent
91 P6 Eggborough N York
6 E7 Eggbuckland C Plym
17 M9 Eggesford Devon
49 Q9 Eggington C Beds
71 P9 Egginton Derbys
104 D8 Egglescliffe S on T
103 J6 Eggleston Dur
36 B6 Egham Surrey
35 Q10 Egham Wick Surrey
73 M9 Egleton Rutlnd
119 M7 Eglingham Nthumb
4 G7 Egloshayle Cnwll
5 M4 Egloskerry Cnwll
79 Q10 Eglwysbach Conwy
30 D11 Eglwys-Brewis V Glam
69 N6 Eglwys Cross Wrexhm
54 F5 Eglwys Fach Cerdgn
41 M3 Eglwyswrw Pembks
85 M7 Egmanton Notts
100 D8 Egremont Cumb
81 L6 Egremont Wirral
105 M9 Egton N York
105 M10 Egton Bridge N York
35 Q7 Egypt Bucks
22 E6 Egypt Hants
144 G10 Eigg Highld
52 F6 Eight Ash Green Essex
145 P4 Eilanreach Highld
54 H8 Eisteddfa Gurig Cerdgn
44 B2 Elan Valley Powys
44 C2 Elan Village Powys
32 B7 Elberton S Glos
15 P6 Elbridge W Susx
6 E8 Elburton C Plym
33 M8 Elcombe Swindn
34 C11 Elcot W Berk
74 F11 Eldernell Cambs
46 E8 Eldersfield Worcs
125 L5 Elderslie Rens
51 N4 Elder Street Essex
103 P5 Eldon Dur
90 E2 Eldwick C Brad
151 L10 Elfhill Abers
119 N4 Elford Nthumb
59 J2 Elford Staffs
157 N5 Elgin Moray
144 H5 Elgol Highld
27 L3 Elham Kent
135 M7 Elie Fife
119 J9 Elilaw Nthumb
78 F8 Elim IoA
14 C4 Eling Hants
85 L5 Elkesley Notts
33 J2 Elkstone Gloucs
158 F6 Ella Abers
7 N6 Ellacombe Torbay
90 E6 Elland Calder
90 E6 Elland Lower Edge Calder
123 M4 Ellary Ag & B
71 L6 Ellastone Staffs
95 K9 Ellel Lancs
129 J7 Ellemford Border
130 E4 Ellenabeich Ag & B
100 D3 Ellenborough Cumb
82 F4 Ellenbrook Salfd
70 E9 Ellenhall Staffs
24 C3 Ellen's Green Surrey
104 D11 Ellerbeck N York
105 L8 Ellerby N York
69 R10 Ellerdine Heath Wrekin
9 N4 Ellerhayes Devon
139 J8 Elleric Ag & B
92 F5 Ellerker E R Yk
92 C2 Ellers N York
92 B3 Ellerton E R Yk
103 Q11 Ellerton N York
70 C9 Ellerton Shrops
35 M3 Ellesborough Bucks
69 L8 Ellesmere Shrops

Ellesmere Port - Fifehead Neville 275

81 N9 **Ellesmere Port** Ches W
13 K3 **Ellingham** Hants
65 M3 **Ellingham** Norfk
119 N5 **Ellingham** Nthumb
97 J4 **Ellingstring** N York
61 Q6 **Ellington** Cambs
113 L2 **Ellington** Nthumb
61 Q6 **Ellington Thorpe** Cambs
20 E5 **Elliots Green** Somset
22 H5 **Ellisfield** Hants
153 J4 **Ellishader** Highld
72 C8 **Ellistown** Leics
159 N11 **Ellon** Abers
101 M3 **Ellonby** Cumb
65 N4 **Ellough** Suffk
92 F5 **Elloughton** E R Yk
31 Q3 **Ellwood** Gloucs
75 J9 **Elm** Cambs
58 D11 **Elmbridge** Worcs
51 L3 **Elmdon** Essex
59 J8 **Elmdon** Solhll
59 J8 **Elmdon Heath** Solhll
15 Q6 **Elmer** W Susx
37 J7 **Elmers End** Gt Lon
88 G9 **Elmer's Green** Lancs
72 D11 **Elmesthorpe** Leics
52 C10 **Elm Green** Essex
18 H2 **Elmhurst** Staffs
47 J6 **Elmley Castle** Worcs
58 C11 **Elmley Lovett** Worcs
46 E11 **Elmore** Gloucs
46 E11 **Elmore Back** Gloucs
37 M3 **Elm Park** Gt Lon
16 C7 **Elmscott** Devon
53 J2 **Elmsett** Suffk
57 N11 **Elms Green** Worcs
53 J7 **Elmstead Heath** Essex
53 J7 **Elmstead Market** Essex
53 J7 **Elmstead Row** Essex
27 K3 **Elmsted** Kent
39 N9 **Elmstone** Kent
46 H9 **Elmstone Hardwicke** Gloucs
99 K3 **Elmswell** E R Yk
64 D9 **Elmswell** Suffk
84 H6 **Elmton** Derbys
161 L4 **Elphin** Highld
128 B6 **Elphinstone** E Loth
151 L6 **Elrick** Abers
107 K8 **Elrig** D & G
112 C8 **Elrington** Nthumb
112 D2 **Elsdon** Nthumb
91 K11 **Elsecar** Barns
51 M5 **Elsenham** Essex
34 F2 **Elsfield** Oxon
92 H8 **Elsham** N Linc
76 F8 **Elsing** Norfk
96 D11 **Elslack** N York
14 H6 **Elson** Hants
69 L7 **Elson** Shrops
116 F2 **Elsrickle** S Lans
23 P6 **Elstead** Surrey
23 M11 **Elsted** W Susx
73 R6 **Elsthorpe** Lincs
104 B6 **Elstob** Dur
88 H4 **Elston** Lancs
85 N11 **Elston** Notts
21 L6 **Elston** Wilts
17 M8 **Elstone** Devon
61 N11 **Elstow** Bed
50 E11 **Elstree** Herts
93 M4 **Elstronwick** E R Yk
88 E3 **Elswick** Lancs
113 K8 **Elswick** N u Ty
62 D8 **Elsworth** Cambs
101 K10 **Elterwater** Cumb
37 K6 **Eltham** Gt Lon
37 K6 **Eltham Crematorium** Gt Lon
62 C9 **Eltisley** Cambs
89 M8 **Elton** Bury
61 N2 **Elton** Cambs
81 P9 **Elton** Ches W
84 B8 **Elton** Derbys
32 D2 **Elton** Gloucs
56 H10 **Elton** Herefs
73 K3 **Elton** Notts
104 D7 **Elton** S on T
81 P10 **Elton Green** Ches W
112 G8 **Eltringham** Nthumb
116 D7 **Elvanfoot** S Lans
72 C4 **Elvaston** Derbys
63 P4 **Elveden** Suffk
23 M3 **Elvetham Heath** Hants
128 D5 **Elvingston** E Loth
98 E11 **Elvington** C York
39 N11 **Elvington** Kent
17 M5 **Elwell** Devon
104 E4 **Elwick** Hartpl
119 M3 **Elwick** Nthumb
70 C2 **Elworth** Ches E
18 E8 **Elworthy** Somset
62 H4 **Ely** Cambs
30 F9 **Ely** Cardif
49 N5 **Emberton** M Keyn
100 G4 **Embleton** Cumb
104 D5 **Embleton** Dur
119 P6 **Embleton** Nthumb
163 J8 **Embo** Highld
20 B4 **Emborough** Somset
163 J8 **Embo Street** Highld
96 F10 **Embsay** N York
13 N3 **Emery Down** Hants
90 G8 **Emley** Kirk
90 G8 **Emley Moor** Kirk
35 M11 **Emmbrook** Wokham
35 K9 **Emmer Green** Readg
84 G5 **Emmett Carr** Derbys
35 K4 **Emmington** Oxon
75 J9 **Emneth** Norfk
75 K9 **Emneth Hungate** Norfk
73 N9 **Empingham** Rutlnd
23 L8 **Empshott** Hants
23 K8 **Empshott Green** Hants
57 J2 **Emstrey Crematorium** Shrops
15 K5 **Emsworth** Hants
34 D11 **Enborne** W Berk
22 D2 **Enborne Row** W Berk
57 J5 **Enchmarsh** Shrops
72 E11 **Enderby** Leics
95 L4 **Endmoor** Cumb
70 G4 **Endon** Staffs
70 G4 **Endon Bank** Staffs
51 J11 **Enfield** Gt Lon
50 H11 **Enfield Crematorium** Gt Lon
51 J11 **Enfield Lock** Gt Lon
51 J11 **Enfield Wash** Gt Lon
21 M4 **Enford** Wilts
32 C8 **Engine Common** S Glos
45 Q4 **England's Gate** Herefs
34 H10 **Englefield** W Berk
35 Q10 **Englefield Green** Surrey
70 D4 **Engleseabrook** Ches E
46 A11 **English Bicknor** Gloucs
20 D2 **Englishcombe** BaNES
69 N9 **English Frankton** Shrops
4 D7 **Engollan** Cnwll
22 C5 **Enham-Alamein** Hants
18 H7 **Enmore** Somset
20 G10 **Enmore Green** Dorset
100 E7 **Ennerdale Bridge** Cumb
4 F10 **Enniscaven** Cnwll
141 Q5 **Enochdhu** P & K
137 K6 **Ensay** Ag & B
13 J5 **Ensbury** Bmouth
69 M11 **Ensdon** Shrops
17 K6 **Ensis** Devon
70 G9 **Enson** Staffs
48 C10 **Enstone** Oxon
116 B10 **Enterkinfoot** D & G
104 E9 **Enterpen** N York
58 B7 **Enville** Staffs
168 c17 **Eolaigearraidh** W Isls
32 E2 **Epney** Gloucs
85 L11 **Epperstone** Notts
51 L10 **Epping** Essex
51 K9 **Epping Green** Essex
50 G9 **Epping Green** Herts
51 K10 **Epping Upland** Essex
103 N8 **Eppleby** N York
92 H4 **Eppleworth** E R Yk
36 F8 **Epsom** Surrey
48 C6 **Epwell** Oxon
92 C10 **Epworth** N Linc
92 C10 **Epworth Turbary** N Linc
69 L6 **Erbistock** Wrexhm
58 H6 **Erdington** Birm
25 N3 **Eridge Green** E Susx
25 M4 **Eridge Station** E Susx
123 Q4 **Erines** Ag & B
138 G9 **Eriska** Ag & B
168 c17 **Eriskay** W Isls
63 M5 **Eriswell** Suffk
37 M5 **Erith** Gt Lon
21 J4 **Erlestoke** Wilts
6 G8 **Ermington** Devon
76 H5 **Erpingham** Norfk
38 F10 **Erriottwood** Kent
147 P3 **Errogie** Highld
134 G3 **Errol** P & K
125 M3 **Erskine** Rens
106 D4 **Ervie** D & G
53 M5 **Erwarton** Suffk
44 F6 **Erwood** Powys
104 B9 **Eryholme** N York
68 H3 **Eryrys** Denbgs
2 B8 **Escalls** Cnwll
103 N4 **Escomb** Dur
18 E7 **Escott** Somset
91 Q2 **Escrick** N York
42 G9 **Esgair** Carmth
54 D11 **Esgair** Cerdgn
54 H3 **Esgairgeiliog** Powys
43 M6 **Esgerdawe** Carmth
79 Q9 **Esgyryn** Conwy
103 N2 **Esh** Dur
36 D8 **Esher** Surrey
90 F2 **Esholt** C Brad
119 P11 **Eshott** Nthumb
96 D9 **Eshton** N York
103 N2 **Esh Winning** Dur
155 N9 **Eskadale** Highld
127 Q4 **Eskbank** Mdloth
100 F10 **Eskdale Green** Cumb
117 K11 **Eskdalemuir** D & G
93 Q11 **Eskham** Lincs
91 Q7 **Eskholme** Donc
103 M6 **Esperley Lane Ends** Dur
88 E3 **Esprick** Lancs
73 Q8 **Essendine** Rutlnd
50 G9 **Essendon** Herts
156 A10 **Essich** Highld
58 E4 **Essington** Staffs
151 N2 **Esslemont** Abers
104 F7 **Eston** R & Cl
118 H3 **Etal** Nthumb
21 K2 **Etchilhampton** Wilts
26 B6 **Etchingham** E Susx
27 L4 **Etchinghill** Kent
71 J11 **Etchinghill** Staffs
25 M6 **Etchingwood** E Susx
76 E9 **Etling Green** Norfk
32 C3 **Etloe** Gloucs
35 Q9 **Eton** W & M
35 P9 **Eton Wick** W & M
70 F5 **Etruria** C Stke
148 B9 **Etteridge** Highld
102 G5 **Ettersgill** Dur
70 C2 **Ettiley Heath** Ches E
58 D5 **Ettingshall** Wolves
47 Q5 **Ettington** Warwks
74 B9 **Etton** C Pete
92 G2 **Etton** E R Yk
117 K8 **Ettrick** Border
117 M6 **Ettrickbridge** Border
117 K8 **Ettrickhill** Border
71 P8 **Etwall** Derbys
57 M7 **Eudon George** Shrops
64 B6 **Euston** Suffk
75 J11 **Euximoor Drove** Cambs
88 H7 **Euxton** Lancs
45 K2 **Evancoyd** Powys
155 R4 **Evanton** Highld
86 E11 **Evedon** Lincs
57 N3 **Evelith** Shrops
162 H8 **Evelix** Highld
45 K2 **Evenjobb** Powys
48 G8 **Evenley** Nhants
47 P9 **Evenlode** Gloucs
103 N6 **Evenwood** Dur
103 N6 **Evenwood Gate** Dur
20 B7 **Evercreech** Somset
92 D2 **Everingham** E R Yk
21 P4 **Everleigh** Wilts
99 K3 **Everley** N York
49 Q8 **Eversholt** C Beds
11 M4 **Evershot** Dorset
23 L2 **Eversley** Hants
23 L2 **Eversley Cross** Hants
92 F4 **Everthorpe** E R Yk
62 B10 **Everton** C Beds
13 N6 **Everton** Hants
81 L6 **Everton** Lpool
85 L2 **Everton** Notts
110 G5 **Evertown** D & G
46 C5 **Evesbatch** Herefs
47 K6 **Evesham** Worcs
72 G10 **Evington** C Leic
90 H11 **Ewden Village** Sheff
36 F8 **Ewell** Surrey
27 N3 **Ewell Minnis** Kent
34 H6 **Ewelme** Oxon
33 K5 **Ewen** Gloucs
29 P9 **Ewenny** V Glam
86 F11 **Ewerby** Lincs
86 F11 **Ewerby Thorpe** Lincs
24 C2 **Ewhurst** Surrey
26 C7 **Ewhurst Green** E Susx
24 C3 **Ewhurst Green** Surrey
81 L11 **Ewloe** Flints
81 K11 **Ewloe Green** Flints
89 K5 **Ewood** Bl w D
89 M6 **Ewood Bridge** Lancs
8 B5 **Eworthy** Devon
23 M5 **Ewshot** Hants
45 M9 **Ewyas Harold** Herefs
8 F4 **Exbourne** Devon
18 B10 **Exbridge** Somset
14 D6 **Exbury** Hants
25 M11 **Exceat** E Susx
97 L3 **Exelby** N York
9 M6 **Exeter** Devon
9 N6 *Exeter Airport* Devon
9 M6 **Exeter & Devon Crematorium** Devon
9 N6 **Exeter Services** Devon
17 R4 **Exford** Somset
56 H3 **Exfordsgreen** Shrops
47 M3 **Exhall** Warwks
59 N7 **Exhall** Warwks
35 J8 **Exlade Street** Oxon
90 C2 **Exley Head** C Brad
9 M7 **Exminster** Devon
17 R4 **Exmoor National Park**
9 P8 **Exmouth** Devon
63 K7 **Exning** Suffk
27 L3 **Exted** Kent
9 N7 **Exton** Devon
22 H10 **Exton** Hants
73 N8 **Exton** Rutlnd
18 B8 **Exton** Somset
9 M6 **Exwick** Devon
84 B5 **Eyam** Derbys
48 F5 **Eydon** Nhants
74 D10 **Eye** C Pete
45 P2 **Eye** Herefs
64 G7 **Eye** Suffk
74 D10 **Eye Green** C Pete
73 J7 **Eye Kettleby** Leics
129 N7 **Eyemouth** Border
62 C11 **Eyeworth** C Beds
38 D11 **Eyhorne Street** Kent
65 L11 **Eyke** Suffk
61 Q9 **Eynesbury** Cambs
37 M7 **Eynsford** Kent
34 D3 **Eynsham** Oxon
11 J6 **Eype** Dorset
152 G7 **Eyre** Highld
27 N2 **Eythorne** Kent
45 P2 **Eyton** Herefs
56 F2 **Eyton** Shrops
56 F7 **Eyton** Shrops
69 M10 **Eyton** Shrops
69 L6 **Eyton** Wrexhm
57 K3 **Eyton on Severn** Shrops
57 M2 **Eyton upon the Weald Moors** Wrekin

F

22 C3 **Faccombe** Hants
104 E10 **Faceby** N York
68 D11 **Fachwen** Powys
89 P7 **Facit** Lancs
84 G8 **Fackley** Notts
69 Q4 **Faddiley** Ches E
98 D3 **Fadmoor** N York
29 J4 **Faerdre** Swans
29 J4 **Fagwyr** Swans
125 M3 **Faifley** W Duns
31 P10 **Failand** N Som
115 J2 **Failford** S Ayrs
83 J4 **Failsworth** Oldham
54 E2 **Fairbourne** Gwynd
91 M5 **Fairburn** N York
83 N10 **Fairfield** Derbys
26 G6 **Fairfield** Kent
58 D9 **Fairfield** Worcs
33 N4 **Fairford** Gloucs
33 N4 **Fairford Park** Gloucs
109 J9 **Fairgirth** D & G
75 N7 **Fair Green** Norfk
88 C5 **Fairhaven** Lancs
169 t11 **Fair Isle** Shet
23 Q4 **Fairlands** Surrey
124 G7 **Fairlie** N Ayrs
26 E9 **Fairlight** E Susx
10 B5 **Fairmile** Devon
36 D8 **Fairmile** Surrey
117 P4 **Fairnilee** Border
22 E11 **Fair Oak** Hants
70 D8 **Fairoak** Staffs
23 J2 **Fair Oak Green** Hants
37 P8 **Fairseat** Kent
52 C8 **Fairstead** Essex
75 M6 **Fairstead** Norfk
77 K7 **Fairstead** Norfk
25 L5 **Fairwarp** E Susx
30 F9 **Fairwater** Cardif
16 G7 **Fairy Cross** Devon
76 C6 **Fakenham** Norfk
64 C6 **Fakenham Magna** Suffk
128 C7 **Fala** Mdloth
128 C7 **Fala Dam** Mdloth
48 G6 **Falcut** Nhants
86 E4 **Faldingworth** Lincs
11 c2 **Faldouet** Jersey
32 C6 **Falfield** S Glos
53 N4 **Falkenham** Suffk
133 P11 **Falkirk** Falk
133 P11 **Falkirk Crematorium** Falk
134 H6 **Falkland** Fife
116 D3 **Fallburn** S Lans
84 E8 **Fallgate** Derbys
133 N9 **Fallin** Stirlg
119 N6 **Fallodon** Nthumb
83 J6 **Fallowfield** Manch
112 D7 **Fallowfield** Nthumb
131 K5 **Falls of Blarghour** Ag & B
25 J9 **Falmer** E Susx
3 L7 **Falmouth** Cnwll
117 M9 **Falnash** Border
99 L3 **Falsgrave** N York
111 P3 **Falstone** Nthumb
164 E7 **Fanagmore** Highld
50 B5 **Fancott** C Beds
155 N9 **Fanellan** Highld
98 B2 **Fangdale Beck** N York
98 F10 **Fangfoss** E R Yk
137 L7 **Fanmore** Ag & B
154 H4 **Fannich Lodge** Highld
118 B2 **Fans** Border
49 N8 **Far Bletchley** M Keyn
62 B2 **Farcet** Cambs
60 G9 **Far Cotton** Nhants
57 K9 **Farden** Shrops
14 G5 **Fareham** Hants
101 K11 **Far End** Cumb
58 G2 **Farewell** Staffs
57 N9 **Far Forest** Worcs
87 K5 **Farforth** Lincs
32 E4 **Far Green** Gloucs
33 Q5 **Faringdon** Oxon
88 G5 **Farington** Lancs
111 L9 **Farlam** Cumb
31 P11 **Farleigh** N Som
37 J8 **Farleigh** Surrey
20 F3 **Farleigh Hungerford** Somset
22 H5 **Farleigh Wallop** Hants
87 N6 **Farlesthorpe** Lincs
95 L4 **Farleton** Cumb
95 M7 **Farleton** Lancs
84 C8 **Farley** Derbys
71 K6 **Farley** Staffs
21 P9 **Farley** Wilts
63 M10 **Farley Green** Suffk
36 C11 **Farley Green** Surrey
23 K2 **Farley Hill** Wokham
32 E2 **Farleys End** Gloucs
15 J5 **Farlington** C Port
98 C7 **Farlington** N York
57 L8 **Farlow** Shrops
20 C2 **Farmborough** BaNES
51 P8 **Farmbridge End** Essex
47 L9 **Farmcote** Gloucs
57 P6 **Farmcote** Shrops
43 M6 **Farmers** Carmth
47 M11 **Farmington** Gloucs
34 E3 **Farmoor** Oxon
82 B4 **Far Moor** Wigan
2 H7 **Farms Common** Cnwll
72 B7 **Farm Town** Leics
158 D7 **Farmtown** Moray
84 D11 **Farnah Green** Derbys
37 K8 **Farnborough** Gt Lon
23 N4 **Farnborough** Hants
34 D8 **Farnborough** W Berk
48 D5 **Farnborough** Warwks
23 N3 **Farnborough Park** Hants
23 N3 **Farnborough Street** Hants
23 Q6 **Farncombe** Surrey
61 K8 **Farndish** Bed
69 M4 **Farndon** Ches W
85 N10 **Farndon** Notts
119 Q3 **Farne Islands** Nthumb
143 L6 **Farnell** Angus
21 J11 **Farnham** Dorset
51 L6 **Farnham** Essex
97 M8 **Farnham** N York
65 M9 **Farnham** Suffk
23 M5 **Farnham** Surrey
35 Q7 **Farnham Common** Bucks
51 L5 **Farnham Green** Essex
35 Q8 **Farnham Royal** Bucks
37 M7 **Farningham** Kent
90 H4 **Farnley** Leeds
97 K11 **Farnley** N York
90 F8 **Farnley Tyas** Kirk
85 K9 **Farnsfield** Notts
89 L9 **Farnworth** Bolton
81 Q7 **Farnworth** Halton
32 H4 **Far Oakridge** Gloucs
148 E7 **Farr** Highld
156 B11 **Farr** Highld
166 B4 **Farr** Highld
147 P3 **Farraline** Highld
9 P6 **Farringdon** Devon
20 B3 **Farrington Gurney** BaNES
101 L11 **Far Sawrey** Cumb
90 G3 **Farsley** Leeds
52 D11 **Farther Howegreen** Essex
26 D2 **Farthing Green** Kent
48 F7 **Farthinghoe** Nhants
27 N3 **Farthingloe** Kent
48 H4 **Farthingstone** Nhants
37 K8 **Farthing Street** Gt Lon
90 F7 **Fartown** Kirk
90 G4 **Fartown** Leeds
10 D5 **Farway** Devon
139 J8 **Fasnacloich** Ag & B
147 J2 **Fasnakyle** Highld
139 J2 **Fassfern** Highld
113 L10 **Fatfield** Sundld
111 K10 **Faugh** Cumb
71 M9 **Fauld** Staffs
126 G5 **Fauldhouse** W Loth
52 C8 **Faulkbourne** Essex
20 D4 **Faulkland** Somset
69 Q8 **Fauls** Shrops
38 H9 **Faversham** Kent
97 P6 **Fawdington** N York
113 K7 **Fawdon** N u Ty
119 K7 **Fawdon** Nthumb
71 K2 **Fawfieldhead** Staffs
37 N7 **Fawkham Green** Kent
48 C11 **Fawler** Oxon
35 L7 **Fawley** Bucks
14 E6 **Fawley** Hants
34 C8 **Fawley** W Berk
46 A9 **Fawley Chapel** Herefs
81 J11 **Fawnog** Flints
60 C9 **Fawsley** Nhants
92 E6 **Faxfleet** E R Yk
24 F4 **Faygate** W Susx
81 M5 **Fazakerley** Lpool
59 K4 **Fazeley** Staffs
97 J4 **Fearby** N York
156 E2 **Fearn** Highld
140 H9 **Fearnan** P & K
153 N6 **Fearnbeg** Highld
82 D6 **Fearnhead** Warrtn
153 N5 **Fearnmore** Highld
124 A2 **Fearnoch** Ag & B
58 D3 **Featherstone** Staffs
91 L6 **Featherstone** Wakefd
47 K2 **Feckenham** Worcs
52 E7 **Feering** Essex
103 J11 **Feetham** N York
96 A7 **Feizor** N York
25 J3 **Felbridge** Surrey
77 J4 **Felbrigg** Norfk
25 J2 **Felcourt** Surrey
50 B10 **Felden** Herts
42 G7 **Felindre** Carmth
43 L10 **Felindre** Carmth
43 P9 **Felindre** Carmth
43 L3 **Felindre** Cerdgn
44 H10 **Felindre** Powys
56 B8 **Felindre** Powys
28 H4 **Felindre** Swans
41 M3 **Felindre Farchog** Pembks
43 K3 **Felin Fach** Cerdgn
44 F8 **Felinfach** Powys
28 F4 **Felinfoel** Carmth
43 K10 **Felingwm Isaf** Carmth
43 K10 **Felingwm Uchaf** Carmth
44 G7 **Felin-newydd** Powys
97 Q4 **Felixkirk** N York
53 P5 **Felixstowe** Suffk
53 P4 **Felixstowe Ferry** Suffk
118 H2 **Felkington** Nthumb
91 K8 **Felkirk** Wakefd
113 L8 **Felling** Gatesd
90 C2 **Fell Lane** C Brad
101 K3 **Fell Side** Cumb
61 L9 **Felmersham** Bed
77 K6 **Felmingham** Norfk
15 P7 **Felpham** W Susx
64 C10 **Felsham** Suffk
51 Q6 **Felsted** Essex
36 D6 **Feltham** Gt Lon
36 C6 **Felthamhill** Surrey
76 H8 **Felthorpe** Norfk
46 A5 **Felton** Herefs
31 P11 **Felton** N Som
119 N10 **Felton** Nthumb
69 L11 **Felton Butler** Shrops
63 M2 **Feltwell** Norfk
90 F7 **Fenay Bridge** Kirk
89 N3 **Fence** Lancs
84 F3 **Fence** Rothm
113 M11 **Fence Houses** Sundld
48 G11 **Fencott** Oxon
87 N8 **Fendike Corner** Lincs
62 G8 **Fen Ditton** Cambs
62 D7 **Fen Drayton** Cambs
74 D6 **Fen End** Lincs
59 K10 **Fen End** Solhll
119 L2 **Fenham** Nthumb
89 K5 **Feniscliffe** Bl w D
89 J5 **Feniscowles** Bl w D
10 C5 **Feniton** Devon
62 F2 **Fenland Crematorium** Cambs
57 P8 **Fenn Green** Shrops
38 C6 **Fenn Street** Medway
71 M5 **Fenny Bentley** Derbys
10 C5 **Fenny Bridges** Devon
48 D4 **Fenny Compton** Warwks
72 B11 **Fenny Drayton** Leics
49 N8 **Fenny Stratford** M Keyn
113 J2 **Fenrother** Nthumb
62 D7 **Fenstanton** Cambs
63 P10 **Fenstead End** Suffk
64 D2 **Fen Street** Norfk
64 H9 **Fen Street** Suffk
70 F6 **Fenton** C Stke
62 D5 **Fenton** Cambs
111 K9 **Fenton** Cumb
85 P5 **Fenton** Lincs
85 Q10 **Fenton** Lincs
85 N4 **Fenton** Notts
119 J4 **Fenton** Nthumb
128 E3 **Fenton Barns** E Loth
91 P7 **Fenwick** Donc
125 M9 **Fenwick** E Ayrs
112 G6 **Fenwick** Nthumb
119 L2 **Fenwick** Nthumb
3 L6 **Feock** Cnwll
122 F6 **Feolin Ferry** Ag & B
125 J9 **Fergushill** N Ayrs
152 B7 **Feriniquarrie** Highld
10 c2 **Fermain Bay** Guern
142 H5 **Fern** Angus
30 C5 **Ferndale** Rhondd
13 J4 **Ferndown** Dorset
156 H8 **Ferness** Highld
33 Q6 **Fernham** Oxon
46 G3 **Fernhill Heath** Worcs
23 N9 **Fernhurst** W Susx
135 J4 **Fernie** Fife
126 C7 **Ferniegair** S Lans
152 F11 **Fernilea** Highld
83 M9 **Fernilee** Derbys
85 P10 **Fernwood** Notts
97 N8 **Ferrensby** N York
92 G6 **Ferriby Sluice** N Linc
145 L6 **Ferrindonald** Highld
24 C10 **Ferring** W Susx
91 M6 **Ferrybridge** Wakefd
91 M6 **Ferrybridge Services** Wakefd
143 N6 **Ferryden** Angus
103 Q4 **Ferryhill** Dur
162 G9 **Ferry Point** Highld
28 C2 **Ferryside** Carmth
162 G9 **Ferrytown** Highld
64 F5 **Fersfield** Norfk
139 R2 **Fersit** Highld
148 F7 **Feshiebridge** Highld
36 D9 **Fetcham** Surrey
169 t4 **Fetlar** Shet
159 N7 **Fetterangus** Abers
143 M3 **Fettercairn** Abers
48 F9 **Fewcott** Oxon
97 J10 **Fewston** N York
43 M10 **Ffairfach** Carmth
54 G11 **Ffair Rhos** Cerdgn
43 M6 **Ffald-y-Brenin** Carmth
45 J11 **Ffawyddog** Powys
67 N6 **Ffestiniog** Gwynd
67 M6 **Ffestiniog Railway** Gwynd
68 F2 **Ffordd-las** Denbgs
28 G4 **Fforest** Carmth
45 K10 **Fforest** Mons
28 H5 **Fforest Fach** Swans
29 K4 **Fforest Goch** Neath
42 G5 **Ffostrasol** Cerdgn
69 J3 **Ffrith** Flints
42 G4 **Ffynnonddewi** Cerdgn
80 G8 **Ffynnongroyw** Flints
43 K4 **Ffynnon-Oer** Cerdgn
165 L11 **Fiag Lodge** Highld
37 J8 **Fickleshole** Surrey
46 H8 **Fiddington** Gloucs
18 H6 **Fiddington** Somset
12 D2 **Fiddleford** Dorset
4 C10 **Fiddlers Green** Cnwll
51 L10 **Fiddlers Hamlet** Essex
71 J8 **Field** Staffs
94 H4 **Field Broughton** Cumb
76 E4 **Field Dalling** Norfk
101 N3 **Fieldhead** Cumb
72 D9 **Field Head** Leics
20 E10 **Fifehead Magdalen** Dorset
12 C2 **Fifehead Neville** Dorset

276 Fifehead St Quintin - Gamlingay

12 C2 Fifehead St Quintin Dorset
158 B7 Fife Keith Moray
47 P11 Fifield Oxon
35 P9 Fifield W & M
21 M4 Fifield Wilts
21 N5 Figheldean Wilts
32 H7 Filands Wilts
77 P9 Filby Norfk
99 N4 Filey N York
49 N5 Filgrave M Keyn
33 P4 Filkins Oxon
8 H2 Filleigh Devon
17 M6 Filleigh Devon
86 B3 Fillingham Lincs
59 L7 Fillongley Warwks
23 J9 Filmore Hill Hants
32 B9 Filton S Glos
98 H8 Fimber E R Yk
142 H6 Finavon Angus
75 N9 Fincham Norfk
23 L2 Finchampstead Wokham
131 J7 Fincharn Ag & B
15 K4 Finchdean Hants
51 Q4 Finchingfield Essex
36 G2 Finchley Gt Lon
71 Q8 Findern Derbys
157 J5 Findhorn Moray
148 E2 Findhorn Bridge Highld
158 C4 Findochty Moray
134 C4 Findo Gask P & K
151 N8 Findon Abers
24 D9 Findon W Susx
155 R5 Findon Mains Highld
150 G7 Findrack House Abers
61 K6 Finedon Nhants
73 P11 Fineshade Nhants
65 J8 Fingal Street Suffk
134 F4 Fingask P & K
35 L6 Fingest Bucks
97 J3 Finghall N York
110 E9 Fingland Cumb
115 Q4 Fingland D & G
39 P11 Finglesham Kent
52 H7 Fingringhoe Essex
52 B3 Finkle Green Essex
91 J11 Finkle Street Barns
140 E11 Finlarig Stirlg
48 H8 Finmere Oxon
140 D6 Finnart P & K
64 F8 Finningham Suffk
91 R11 Finningley Donc
168 f9 Finsbay W Isls
58 E10 Finstall Worcs
94 H3 Finsthwaite Cumb
48 C11 Finstock Oxon
169 c5 Finstown Ork
159 J7 Fintry Abers
133 J10 Fintry Stirlg
150 G9 Finzean Abers
137 J11 Fionnphort Ag & B
168 f9 Fionnsbhagh W Isls
95 N2 Firbank Cumb
85 J3 Firbeck Rothm
97 L3 Firby N York
98 E7 Firby N York
89 Q8 Firgrove Rochdl
25 L9 Firle E Susx
87 N8 Firsby Lincs
21 P8 Firsdown Wilts
103 M4 Fir Tree Dur
14 G8 Fishbourne IoW
15 M5 Fishbourne W Susx
15 M5 Fishbourne Roman Palace W Susx
104 C4 Fishburn Dur
133 P8 Fishcross Clacks
15 N6 Fisher W Susx
158 G10 Fisherford Abers
127 Q3 Fisherrow E Loth
22 E10 Fisher's Pond Hants
95 J11 Fisher's Row Lancs
23 P8 Fisherstreet W Susx
156 C7 Fisherton Highld
114 E4 Fisherton S Ayrs
21 K7 Fisherton de la Mere Wilts
59 J3 Fisherwick Staffs
35 N8 Fishery Estate W & M
41 J3 Fishguard Pembks
91 R8 Fishlake Donc
8 D3 Fishleigh Devon
74 E3 Fishmere End Lincs
138 B9 Fishnish Pier Ag & B
10 H5 Fishpond Bottom Dorset
32 B9 Fishponds Bristl
74 G2 Fishtoft Lincs
87 K11 Fishtoft Drove Lincs
88 H5 Fishwick Lancs
152 E11 Fiskavaig Highld
86 D6 Fiskerton Lincs
85 M10 Fiskerton Notts
93 N4 Fitling E R Yk
21 M5 Fittleton Wilts
24 B7 Fittleworth W Susx
74 H8 Fitton End Cambs
69 M11 Fitz Shrops
18 F9 Fitzhead Somset
18 G9 Fitzroy Somset
91 L7 Fitzwilliam Wakefd
25 L6 Five Ash Down E Susx
25 N5 Five Ashes E Susx
18 E6 Five Bells Somset
46 B5 Five Bridges Herefs
82 B9 Fivecrosses Ches W
19 L10 Fivehead Somset
5 L5 Fivelanes Cnwll
31 M6 Five Lanes Mons
37 P11 Five Oak Green Kent
11 c2 Five Oaks Jersey
24 C5 Five Oaks W Susx
28 E3 Five Roads Carmth
38 D11 Five Wents Kent
52 C9 Flack's Green Essex
35 N7 Flackwell Heath Bucks
47 J5 Fladbury Worcs
169 r10 Fladdabister Shet
83 P11 Flagg Derbys
99 Q6 Flamborough E R Yk
99 R6 Flamborough Head E R Yk
98 F5 Flamingo Land Theme Park N York
50 C8 Flamstead Herts
15 Q6 Flansham W Susx
91 J6 Flanshaw Wakefd
90 D3 Flappit Spring C Brad
96 D9 Flasby N York
83 M11 Flash Staffs
152 E7 Flashader Highld
50 B10 Flaunden Herts
73 K2 Flawborough Notts
97 Q7 Flawith N York
31 P11 Flax Bourton N Som
97 N9 Flaxby N York
46 C11 Flaxley Gloucs
82 C10 Flaxmere Ches W
18 F7 Flaxpool Somset
98 D8 Flaxton N York
60 D2 Fleckney Leics
60 B8 Flecknoe Warwks
85 P6 Fledborough Notts
11 N8 Fleet Dorset
15 K6 Fleet Hants
23 M4 Fleet Hants
74 G6 Fleet Lincs
14 F5 Fleetend Hants
74 G6 Fleet Hargate Lincs
23 L3 Fleet Services Hants
94 G11 Fleetwood Lancs
30 D11 Flemingston V Glam
126 B6 Flemington S Lans
63 P7 Flempton Suffk
37 M11 Fletcher Green Kent
5 J8 Fletchersbridge Cnwll
100 H2 Fletchertown Cumb
25 K6 Fletching E Susx
30 G5 Fleur-de-lis Caerph
16 C10 Flexbury Cnwll
23 P4 Flexford Surrey
100 D4 Flimby Cumb
26 B5 Flimwell E Susx
81 J10 Flint Flints
85 M11 Flintham Notts
81 J10 Flint Mountain Flints
93 M3 Flinton E R Yk
59 L8 Flint's Green Solhll
26 C4 Flishinghurst Kent
75 P5 Flitcham Norfk
50 C3 Flitton C Beds
50 B4 Flitwick C Beds
92 E8 Flixborough N Linc
92 E8 Flixborough Stather N Linc
99 L5 Flixton N York
65 L4 Flixton Suffk
82 F6 Flixton Traffd
90 G8 Flockton Kirk
90 H7 Flockton Green Kirk
118 H3 Flodden Nthumb
152 H3 Flodigarry Highld
94 H5 Flookburgh Cumb
64 H2 Flordon Norfk
60 D8 Flore Nhants
119 J10 Flotterton Nthumb
25 P8 Flowers Green E Susx
53 J2 Flowton Suffk
90 H6 Flushdyke Wakefd
3 L7 Flushing Cnwll
10 B6 Fluxton Devon
47 J3 Flyford Flavell Worcs
38 B5 Fobbing Thurr
157 Q6 Fochabers Moray
30 F3 Fochriw Caerph
92 E7 Fockerby N Linc
19 Q9 Foddington Somset
55 M2 Foel Powys
28 F2 Foelgastell Carmth
29 N6 Foel y Dyffryn Brdgnd
92 C3 Foggathorpe E R Yk
129 K10 Fogo Border
157 N6 Fogwatt Moray
164 E7 Foindle Highld
142 B5 Folda Angus
71 J7 Fole Staffs
59 N8 Foleshill Covtry
11 P2 Folke Dorset
27 M4 Folkestone Kent
73 R4 Folkingham Lincs
25 N10 Folkington E Susx
61 P3 Folksworth Cambs
99 M5 Folkton N York
158 H11 Folla Rule Abers
97 M10 Follifoot N York
8 E5 Folly Gate Devon
23 M5 Folly Hill Surrey
30 D11 Fonmon V Glam
20 H8 Fonthill Bishop Wilts
20 H8 Fonthill Gifford Wilts
20 G11 Fontmell Magna Dorset
12 D2 Fontmell Parva Dorset
15 P5 Fontwell W Susx
30 E11 Font-y-gary V Glam
83 Q9 Foolow Derbys
37 L6 Footscray Gt Lon
150 B5 Forbestown Abers
103 N8 Forcett N York
130 H7 Ford Ag & B
35 L3 Ford Bucks
84 F4 Ford Derbys
6 G8 Ford Devon
7 K10 Ford Devon
16 G7 Ford Devon
47 L9 Ford Gloucs
118 H3 Ford Nthumb
56 G2 Ford Shrops
18 E9 Ford Somset
19 Q4 Ford Somset
71 K4 Ford Staffs
15 Q6 Ford W Susx
21 N8 Ford Wilts
32 F9 Ford Wilts
8 D6 Forda Devon
25 M2 Fordcombe Kent
134 F10 Fordell Fife
56 C4 Forden Powys
51 Q7 Ford End Essex
7 K5 Forder Green Devon
95 K11 Ford Green Lancs
63 K6 Fordham Cambs
52 F6 Fordham Essex
75 M11 Fordham Norfk
52 F6 Fordham Heath Essex
56 G2 Ford Heath Shrops
13 K2 Fordingbridge Hants
99 L5 Fordon E R Yk
143 N2 Fordoun Abers
64 F8 Ford's Green Suffk
52 F6 Fordstreet Essex
18 G11 Ford Street Somset
9 K5 Fordton Devon
34 B2 Fordwells Oxon
39 L10 Fordwich Kent
158 E5 Fordyce Abers
70 G10 Forebridge Staffs
72 A5 Foremark Derbys
10 b2 Forest Guern
103 Q10 Forest N York
96 A10 Forest Becks Lancs
119 L11 Forestburn Gate Nthumb
83 L10 Forest Chapel Ches E
37 K3 Forest Gate Gt Lon
24 D2 Forest Green Surrey
113 L7 Forest Hall N Tyne
111 L9 Forest Head Cumb
37 J6 Forest Hill Gt Lon
34 G3 Forest Hill Oxon
102 G4 Forest-in-Teesdale Dur
97 M9 Forest Lane Head N York
134 B9 Forest Mill Clacks
32 B2 Forest of Dean Gloucs
37 L2 Forest Park Crematorium Gt Lon
25 K4 Forest Row E Susx
14 E9 Forest Side IoW
15 L4 Forestside W Susx
85 J8 Forest Town Notts
142 H7 Forfar Angus
134 D4 Forgandenny P & K
54 H5 Forge Powys
31 J5 Forge Hammer Torfn
30 H3 Forge Side Torfn
158 A7 Forgie Moray
158 B7 Forgieside Moray
158 F8 Forgue Abers
58 G9 Forhill Worcs
88 C9 Formby Sefton
64 G3 Forncett End Norfk
64 H3 Forncett St Mary Norfk
64 H3 Forncett St Peter Norfk
64 A8 Fornham All Saints Suffk
64 B8 Fornham St Martin Suffk
156 G7 Fornighty Highld
157 J6 Forres Moray
70 H6 Forsbrook Staffs
167 M10 Forse Highld
58 G10 Forshaw Heath Warwks
166 E8 Forsinard Highld
11 P5 Forston Dorset
147 K6 Fort Augustus Highld
134 D4 Forteviot P & K
126 G7 Forth S Lans
46 G8 Forthampton Gloucs
10 b1 Fort Hommet Guern
140 H8 Fortingall P & K
10 c1 Fort le Marchant Guern
22 D6 Forton Hants
95 K10 Forton Lancs
69 M11 Forton Shrops
10 G3 Forton Somset
70 D10 Forton Staffs
158 G8 Fortrie Abers
156 C6 Fortrose Highld
11 P10 Fortuneswell Dorset
139 L3 Fort William Highld
35 P6 Forty Green Bucks
50 H11 Forty Hill Gt Lon
64 G10 Forward Green Suffk
22 B3 Fosbury Wilts
47 P10 Foscot Oxon
49 J5 Foscote Nhants
74 F4 Fosdyke Lincs
74 F4 Fosdyke Bridge Lincs
141 J6 Foss P & K
33 L2 Fossebridge Gloucs
42 H2 Foss-y-ffin Cerdgn
91 R8 Fosterhouses Donc
51 L9 Foster Street Essex
71 M8 Foston Derbys
60 D2 Foston Leics
73 M2 Foston Lincs
98 D7 Foston N York
99 N9 Foston on the Wolds E R Yk
87 K2 Fotherby Lincs
100 D4 Fothergill Cumb
61 N2 Fotheringhay Nhants
169 k10 Foula Shet
110 H11 Foulbridge Cumb
91 K7 Foulby Wakefd
129 N8 Foulden Border
75 Q11 Foulden Norfk
59 K6 Foul End Warwks
25 P7 Foul Mile E Susx
38 G3 Foulness Island Essex
10 b2 Foulon Vale Crematorium Guern
89 P2 Foulridge Lancs
76 E7 Foulsham Norfk
128 C10 Fountainhall Border
59 J9 Four Ashes Solhll
57 Q7 Four Ashes Staffs
58 D3 Four Ashes Staffs
64 E7 Four Ashes Suffk
10 b2 Four Cabots Guern
69 J11 Four Crosses Powys
58 E3 Four Crosses Staffs
37 L11 Four Elms Kent
19 Q8 Four Foot Somset
18 H7 Four Forks Somset
89 J9 Four Gates Bolton
75 J7 Four Gotes Cambs
90 H10 Four Lane End Barns
69 Q2 Four Lane Ends Ches W
2 H6 Four Lanes Cnwll
70 E3 Fourlanes End Ches E
23 J7 Four Marks Hants
78 D9 Four Mile Bridge IoA
58 H5 Four Oaks Birm
26 E7 Four Oaks E Susx
46 C9 Four Oaks Gloucs
59 K8 Four Oaks Solhll
163 J8 Fourpenny Highld
34 G9 Four Points W Berk
28 D3 Four Roads Carmth
47 P8 Four Shire Stone Warwks
112 C7 Fourstones Nthumb
26 C6 Four Throws Kent
37 P10 Four Wents Kent
21 K9 Fovant Wilts
151 P3 Foveran Abers
5 J11 Fowey Cnwll
82 E5 Fowley Common Warrtn
37 Q11 Fowlhall Kent
142 E11 Fowlis Angus
133 Q3 Fowlis Wester P & K
62 F11 Fowlmere Cambs
46 A8 Fownhope Herefs
125 M5 Foxbar Rens
8 C7 Foxcombe Devon
23 Q4 Fox Corner Surrey
47 K11 Foxcote Gloucs
20 D3 Foxcote Somset
80 c6 Foxdale IoM
52 D3 Foxearth Essex
37 P7 Foxendown Kent
94 E3 Foxfield Cumb
33 J9 Foxham Wilts
51 N11 Fox Hatch Essex
13 P2 Foxhills Hants
3 P3 Foxhole Cnwll
99 L6 Foxholes N York
25 M7 Foxhunt Green E Susx
48 H4 Foxley Nhants
76 E7 Foxley Norfk
32 G7 Foxley Wilts
58 F11 Foxlydiate Worcs
52 H6 Fox Street Essex
71 J5 Foxt Staffs
62 F11 Foxton Cambs
104 C6 Foxton Dur
60 F3 Foxton Leics
104 D11 Foxton N York
96 C5 Foxup N York
82 D11 Foxwist Green Ches W
57 L9 Foxwood Shrops
46 A9 Foy Herefs
147 M3 Foyers Highld
156 F7 Foynesfield Highld
2 F7 Fraddam Cnwll
4 E10 Fraddon Cnwll
59 J2 Fradley Staffs
70 H8 Fradswell Staffs
99 P8 Fraisthorpe E R Yk
25 L6 Framfield E Susx
77 K11 Framingham Earl Norfk
77 K11 Framingham Pigot Norfk
65 K9 Framlingham Suffk
11 N5 Frampton Dorset
74 F3 Frampton Lincs
32 C8 Frampton Cotterell S Glos
32 H4 Frampton Mansell Gloucs
32 D3 Frampton on Severn Gloucs
74 F2 Frampton West End Lincs
64 H10 Framsden Suffk
103 Q2 Framwellgate Moor Dur
57 Q9 Franche Worcs
82 D9 Frandley Ches W
5 P3 Frankaborough Devon
81 J7 Frankby Wirral
77 L7 Frankfort Norfk
45 Q5 Franklands Gate Herefs
58 E8 Frankley Worcs
58 E8 Frankley Services Worcs
44 G3 Franksbridge Powys
59 P10 Frankton Warwks
25 N3 Frant E Susx
159 N4 Fraserburgh Abers
53 J7 Frating Essex
53 J7 Frating Green Essex
15 J6 Fratton C Port
5 P11 Freathy Cnwll
63 L6 Freckenham Suffk
88 E5 Freckleton Lancs
84 D6 Freebirch Derbys
73 L6 Freeby Leics
22 E5 Freefolk Hants
71 J6 Freehay Staffs
34 D2 Freeland Oxon
77 N10 Freethorpe Norfk
77 N11 Freethorpe Common Norfk
74 G2 Freiston Lincs
17 J5 Fremington Devon
103 K11 Fremington N York
32 B9 Frenchay S Glos
8 G7 Frenchbeer Devon
37 L10 French Street Kent
141 K6 Frenich P & K
23 M6 Frensham Surrey
88 B9 Freshfield Sefton
20 E2 Freshford Wilts
13 P7 Freshwater IoW
13 P7 Freshwater Bay IoW
41 K11 Freshwater East Pembks
65 K6 Fressingfield Suffk
53 L4 Freston Suffk
167 Q3 Freswick Highld
32 D2 Fretherne Gloucs
77 J8 Frettenham Norfk
134 H6 Freuchie Fife
41 J8 Freystrop Pembks
58 F6 Friar Park Sandw
25 L4 Friar's Gate E Susx
98 E3 Friars' Hill N York
11 N7 Friar Waddon Dorset
75 J10 Friday Bridge Cambs
65 J10 Friday Street Suffk
65 L11 Friday Street Suffk
65 M9 Friday Street Suffk
36 D11 Friday Street Surrey
98 H9 Fridaythorpe E R Yk
71 M2 Friden Derbys
90 D6 Friendly Calder
36 G2 Friern Barnet Gt Lon
86 E4 Friesthorpe Lincs
86 B11 Frieston Lincs
35 L6 Frieth Bucks
84 G10 Friezeland Notts
34 D5 Frilford Oxon
34 F10 Frilsham W Berk
23 N3 Frimley Surrey
23 N3 Frimley Green Surrey
38 B8 Frindsbury Medway
75 P4 Fring Norfk
48 H9 Fringford Oxon
38 E10 Frinsted Kent
53 M7 Frinton-on-Sea Essex
143 K8 Friockheim Angus
54 E2 Friog Gwynd
72 H7 Frisby on the Wreake Leics
87 N9 Friskney Lincs
87 N9 Friskney Eaudike Lincs
25 N11 Friston E Susx
65 N9 Friston Suffk
84 E10 Fritchley Derbys
13 M2 Fritham Hants
87 K11 Frith Bank Lincs
57 M11 Frith Common Worcs
16 H8 Frithelstock Devon
16 H8 Frithelstock Stone Devon
23 M7 Frithend Hants
50 B9 Frithsden Herts
87 K10 Frithville Lincs
26 D3 Frittenden Kent
7 L10 Frittiscombe Devon
65 J3 Fritton Norfk
77 P11 Fritton Norfk
48 F9 Fritwell Oxon
90 E3 Frizinghall C Brad
100 D7 Frizington Cumb
32 E4 Frocester Gloucs
57 J4 Frodesley Shrops
81 Q9 Frodsham Ches W
118 E5 Frogden Border
62 E11 Frog End Cambs
62 H9 Frog End Cambs
84 B5 Froggatt Derbys
71 J5 Froghall Staffs
13 L2 Frogham Hants
39 N11 Frogham Kent
7 K10 Frogmore Devon
74 C8 Frognall Lincs
3 K5 Frogpool Cnwll
57 Q11 Frog Pool Worcs
5 N8 Frogwell Cnwll
60 B2 Frolesworth Leics
20 E5 Frome Somset
11 M4 Frome St Quintin Dorset
46 C5 Fromes Hill Herefs
80 F11 Fron Denbgs
66 F7 Fron Gwynd
67 J4 Fron Gwynd
56 B5 Fron Powys
56 C4 Fron Powys
69 J6 Froncysyllte Denbgs
68 B7 Fron-goch Gwynd
69 J6 Fron Isaf Wrexhm
65 P5 Frostenden Suffk
103 K3 Frosterley Dur
49 Q8 Froxfield C Beds
33 Q11 Froxfield Wilts
23 K9 Froxfield Green Hants
22 D10 Fryern Hill Hants
51 P10 Fryerning Essex
98 D6 Fryton N York
137 Q6 Fuinary Highld
86 B10 Fulbeck Lincs
62 H9 Fulbourn Cambs
33 Q2 Fulbrook Oxon
22 E8 Fulflood Hants
98 C11 Fulford C York
18 H9 Fulford Somset
70 H7 Fulford Staffs
36 G5 Fulham Gt Lon
24 F8 Fulking W Susx
17 M4 Fullaford Devon
125 J10 Fullarton N Ayrs
51 M5 Fuller's End Essex
69 N4 Fuller's Moor Ches W
52 B8 Fuller Street Essex
37 N9 Fuller Street Kent
22 C7 Fullerton Hants
87 J6 Fulletby Lincs
47 Q5 Fullready Warwks
98 E9 Full Sutton E R Yk
125 L7 Fullwood E Ayrs
35 Q7 Fulmer Bucks
76 D5 Fulmodeston Norfk
86 E5 Fulnetby Lincs
74 E6 Fulney Lincs
90 F9 Fulstone Kirk
93 P11 Fulstow Lincs
48 C10 Fulwell Oxon
113 N9 Fulwell Sundld
88 G4 Fulwood Lancs
84 G9 Fulwood Notts
84 D3 Fulwood Sheff
18 H10 Fulwood Somset
64 H2 Fundenhall Norfk
15 M5 Funtington W Susx
14 G5 Funtley Hants
133 M2 Funtullich P & K
10 F4 Furley Devon
131 L7 Furnace Ag & B
28 F4 Furnace Carmth
54 F5 Furnace Cerdgn
59 K6 Furnace End Warwks
25 K5 Furner's Green E Susx
83 M8 Furness Vale Derbys
51 K5 Furneux Pelham Herts
26 E4 Further Quarter Kent
49 L6 Furtho Nhants
17 N2 Furzehill Devon
12 H4 Furzehill Dorset
87 J6 Furzehills Lincs
15 J4 Furzeley Corner Hants
35 N8 Furze Platt W & M
21 Q11 Furzley Hants
10 E2 Fyfett Somset
51 N9 Fyfield Essex
21 Q5 Fyfield Hants
34 D5 Fyfield Oxon
21 N2 Fyfield Wilts
33 M11 Fyfield Wilts
21 K9 Fyfield Bavant Wilts
105 P10 Fylingthorpe N York
23 M10 Fyning W Susx
159 J10 Fyvie Abers

G

125 M7 Gabroc Hill E Ayrs
72 H8 Gaddesby Leics
50 C8 Gaddesden Row Herts
78 H7 Gadfa IoA
114 H3 Gadgirth S Ayrs
69 L7 Gadlas Shrops
44 H10 Gaer Powys
31 M5 Gaer-llwyd Mons
78 H10 Gaerwen IoA
48 D9 Gagingwell Oxon
125 J10 Gailes N Ayrs
58 D2 Gailey Staffs
103 N7 Gainford Dur
85 P3 Gainsborough Lincs
52 B4 Gainsford End Essex
153 Q2 Gairloch Highld
146 F11 Gairlochy Highld
134 E8 Gairneybridge P & K
102 B9 Gaisgill Cumb
110 G11 Gaitsgill Cumb
117 P3 Galashiels Border
95 K9 Galgate Lancs
20 B9 Galhampton Somset
130 G2 Gallanachbeg Ag & B
130 G2 Gallanachmore Ag & B
69 P4 Gallantry Bank Ches E
134 H9 Gallatown Fife
59 M6 Galley Common Warwks
52 B11 Galleywood Essex
147 P10 Gallovie Highld
114 H10 Galloway Forest Park
142 G9 Gallowfauld Angus
142 B10 Gallowhill P & K
52 F6 Gallows Green Essex
46 H2 Gallows Green Worcs
35 J8 Gallowstree Common Oxon
145 P3 Galltair Highld
67 K2 Gallt-y-foel Gwynd
23 M4 Gally Hill Hants
25 L3 Gallypot Street E Susx
6 H10 Galmpton Devon
7 M7 Galmpton Torbay
97 L6 Galphay N York
125 N10 Galston E Ayrs
83 M11 Gamballs Green Staffs
102 B3 Gamblesby Cumb
52 C9 Gambles Green Essex
110 E10 Gamelsby Cumb
83 M6 Gamesley Derbys
62 B10 Gamlingay Cambs

278 Grangetown - Hainford

104 F6 Grangetown R & Cl
113 P10 Grangetown Sundld
113 K10 Grange Villa Dur
99 N9 Gransmoor E R Yk
51 Q6 Gransmore Green Essex
40 G4 Granston Pembks
62 F9 Grantchester Cambs
73 N3 Grantham Lincs
73 N3 Grantham Crematorium Lincs
127 N2 Granton C Edin
149 J2 Grantown-on-Spey Highld
45 Q2 Grantsfield Herefs
129 L6 Grantshouse Border
82 D7 Grappenhall Warrtn
93 J10 Grasby Lincs
101 K9 Grasmere Cumb
83 L4 Grasscroft Oldham
81 M7 Grassendale Lpool
101 K2 Grassgarth Cumb
52 B4 Grass Green Essex
96 F8 Grassington N York
84 F7 Grassmoor Derbys
85 N7 Grassthorpe Notts
21 Q6 Grateley Hants
71 J8 Gratwich Staffs
62 C8 Graveley Cambs
50 F5 Graveley Herts
58 H6 Gravelly Hill Birm
56 E4 Gravelsbank Shrops
39 J9 Graveney Kent
37 Q6 Gravesend Kent
168 i6 Gravir W Isls
92 F11 Grayingham Lincs
101 Q11 Grayrigg Cumb
37 P5 Grays Thurr
23 N7 Grayshott Hants
100 C5 Grayson Green Cumb
23 P8 Grayswood Surrey
104 F5 Graythorpe Hartpl
35 J11 Grazeley Wokham
91 L11 Greasbrough Rothm
81 K7 Greasby Wirral
84 G11 Greasley Notts
62 H11 Great Abington Cambs
61 L5 Great Addington Nhants
47 M3 Great Alne Warwks
88 C9 Great Altcar Lancs
51 J8 Great Amwell Herts
102 C8 Great Asby Cumb
64 D8 Great Ashfield Suffk
104 G8 Great Ayton N York
52 B11 Great Baddow Essex
32 F8 Great Badminton S Glos
51 Q4 Great Bardfield Essex
61 P10 Great Barford Bed
58 F5 Great Barr Sandw
33 P2 Great Barrington Gloucs
81 P11 Great Barrow Ches W
64 B8 Great Barton Suffk
98 E5 Great Barugh N York
112 E4 Great Bavington Nthumb
53 M2 Great Bealings Suffk
21 Q2 Great Bedwyn Wilts
53 K7 Great Bentley Essex
60 H8 Great Billing Nhants
75 Q4 Great Bircham Norfk
64 G11 Great Blakenham Suffk
101 N4 Great Blencow Cumb
70 A10 Great Bolas Wrekin
36 D10 Great Bookham Surrey
2 C7 Great Bosullow Cnwll
48 E5 Great Bourton Oxon
60 F3 Great Bowden Leics
63 L10 Great Bradley Suffk
52 E9 Great Braxted Essex
64 E11 Great Bricett Suffk
49 P8 Great Brickhill Bucks
70 F9 Great Bridgeford Staffs
60 E7 Great Brington Nhants
53 J6 Great Bromley Essex
100 E4 Great Broughton Cumb
104 F9 Great Broughton N York
82 E9 Great Budworth Ches W
104 B7 Great Burdon Darltn
37 Q2 Great Burstead Essex
104 F9 Great Busby N York
51 N7 Great Canfield Essex
87 M3 Great Carlton Lincs
73 Q9 Great Casterton Rutlnd
20 G2 Great Chalfield Wilts
26 G3 Great Chart Kent
57 P2 Great Chatwell Staffs
70 F4 Great Chell C Stke
51 M2 Great Chesterford Essex
21 J4 Great Cheverell Wilts
51 K3 Great Chishill Cambs
53 L8 Great Clacton Essex
91 J7 Great Cliffe Wakefd
100 D5 Great Clifton Cumb
93 M9 Great Coates NE Lin
47 J6 Great Comberton Worcs
37 P9 Great Comp Kent
111 J10 Great Corby Cumb
52 E3 Great Cornard Suffk
93 M2 Great Cowden E R Yk
33 Q6 Great Coxwell Oxon
60 H5 Great Cransley Nhants
76 B11 Great Cressingham Norfk
101 J6 Great Crosthwaite Cumb
71 M7 Great Cubley Derbys
124 F6 Great Cumbrae Island N Ayrs
73 J8 Great Dalby Leics
61 J8 Great Doddington Nhants
45 Q11 Great Doward Herefs
76 B9 Great Dunham Norfk
51 P6 Great Dunmow Essex
21 M7 Great Durnford Wilts
51 P5 Great Easton Essex
60 H2 Great Easton Leics
88 E2 Great Eccleston Lancs
98 E4 Great Edstone N York
64 E2 Great Ellingham Norfk
20 D5 Great Elm Somset
60 C9 Great Everdon Nhants
62 E10 Great Eversden Cambs
97 L2 Great Fencote N York
33 L7 Greatfield Wilts
64 E10 Great Finborough Suffk
74 A8 Greatford Lincs
76 B9 Great Fransham Norfk
50 B8 Great Gaddesden Herts
71 K7 Greatgate Staffs
61 P4 Great Gidding Cambs
98 G10 Great Givendale E R Yk
65 L9 Great Glemham Suffk
72 H11 Great Glen Leics
73 M3 Great Gonerby Lincs
62 C9 Great Gransden Cambs
50 G2 Great Green Cambs
65 K4 Great Green Norfk
64 C10 Great Green Suffk
64 C8 Great Green Suffk
98 F5 Great Habton N York
74 B2 Great Hale Lincs
51 M7 Great Hallingbury Essex
23 L8 Greatham Hants
104 E5 Greatham Hartpl
24 B7 Greatham W Susx
35 M4 Great Hampden Bucks
61 J6 Great Harrowden Nhants
89 L4 Great Harwood Lancs
34 H4 Great Haseley Oxon
93 L2 Great Hatfield E R Yk
70 H10 Great Haywood Staffs
91 P6 Great Heck N York
52 E4 Great Henny Essex
20 H3 Great Hinton Wilts
64 D3 Great Hockham Norfk
53 M8 Great Holland Essex
35 N11 Great Hollands Br For
52 G5 Great Horkesley Essex
51 K5 Great Hormead Herts
90 E4 Great Horton C Brad
49 L8 Great Horwood Bucks
91 L9 Great Houghton Barns
60 G9 Great Houghton Nhants
83 Q9 Great Hucklow Derbys
99 N9 Great Kelk E R Yk
35 M3 Great Kimble Bucks
35 N5 Great Kingshill Bucks
101 J9 Great Langdale Cumb
103 Q11 Great Langton N York
52 B8 Great Leighs Essex
93 K9 Great Limber Lincs
49 N6 Great Linford M Keyn
64 B7 Great Livermere Suffk
84 B6 Great Longstone Derbys
113 L11 Great Lumley Dur
56 H3 Great Lyth Shrops
46 E5 Great Malvern Worcs
52 D5 Great Maplestead Essex
88 C3 Great Marton Bpool
75 Q6 Great Massingham Norfk
76 G10 Great Melton Norfk
81 J6 Great Meols Wirral
34 H4 Great Milton Oxon
35 N4 Great Missenden Bucks
89 L3 Great Mitton Lancs
39 Q11 Great Mongeham Kent
64 H3 Great Moulton Norfk
51 J6 Great Munden Herts
102 E8 Great Musgrave Cumb
69 L11 Great Ness Shrops
52 B7 Great Notley Essex
31 L2 Great Oak Mons
53 L6 Great Oakley Essex
61 J3 Great Oakley Nhants
50 D5 Great Offley Herts
102 D7 Great Ormside Cumb
110 F10 Great Orton Cumb
97 P8 Great Ouseburn N York
60 F4 Great Oxendon Nhants
51 Q9 Great Oxney Green Essex
76 A9 Great Palgrave Norfk
26 B3 Great Pattenden Kent
62 B8 Great Paxton Cambs
88 D4 Great Plumpton Lancs
77 L9 Great Plumstead Norfk
73 N4 Great Ponton Lincs
17 J9 Great Potheridge Devon
91 L5 Great Preston Leeds
48 F7 Great Purston Nhants
62 C4 Great Raveley Cambs
47 N11 Great Rissington Gloucs
48 B8 Great Rollright Oxon
41 J6 Great Rudbaxton Pembks
76 D6 Great Ryburgh Norfk
119 K8 Great Ryle Nthumb
56 H4 Great Ryton Shrops
51 Q5 Great Saling Essex
101 Q3 Great Salkeld Cumb
51 P3 Great Sampford Essex
58 E3 Great Saredon Staffs
81 M11 Great Saughall Ches W
63 N8 Great Saxham Suffk
34 C9 Great Shefford W Berk
62 G10 Great Shelford Cambs
104 B10 Great Smeaton N York
76 C5 Great Snoring Norfk
33 J8 Great Somerford Wilts
70 C9 Great Soudley Shrops
104 B6 Great Stainton Darltn
38 E3 Great Stambridge Essex
61 P8 Great Staughton Cambs
87 M8 Great Steeping Lincs
32 B8 Great Stoke S Glos
39 P10 Great Stonar Kent
27 J7 Greatstone-on-Sea Kent
101 Q6 Great Strickland Cumb
62 B6 Great Stukeley Cambs
86 H5 Great Sturton Lincs
81 M9 Great Sutton Ches W
57 J8 Great Sutton Shrops
112 D5 Great Swinburne Nthumb
48 D9 Great Tew Oxon
52 E6 Great Tey Essex
63 L10 Great Thurlow Suffk
16 H8 Great Torrington Devon
119 K10 Great Tosson Nthumb
52 E9 Great Totham Essex
52 E9 Great Totham Essex
86 H2 Great Tows Lincs
94 F6 Great Urswick Cumb
38 F4 Great Wakering Essex
52 F3 Great Waldingfield Suffk
76 C4 Great Walsingham Norfk
51 Q8 Great Waltham Essex
82 H9 Great Warford Ches E
37 N2 Great Warley Essex
47 J8 Great Washbourne Gloucs
8 H7 Great Weeke Devon
61 K3 Great Weldon Nhants
64 B10 Great Welnetham Suffk
53 J4 Great Wenham Suffk
112 F6 Great Whittington Nthumb
52 G8 Great Wigborough Essex
63 J9 Great Wilbraham Cambs
21 L7 Great Wishford Wilts
76 G7 Great Witchingham Norfk
32 H2 Great Witcombe Gloucs
57 P11 Great Witley Worcs
47 Q8 Great Wolford Warwks
48 G6 Greatworth Nhants
63 L11 Great Wratting Suffk
50 F5 Great Wymondley Herts
58 E3 Great Wyrley Staffs
69 Q11 Great Wytheford Shrops
77 Q10 Great Yarmouth Norfk
77 Q11 Great Yarmouth Crematorium Norfk
52 C4 Great Yeldham Essex
87 M7 Grebby Lincs
80 d5 Greeba IoM
80 F11 Green Denbgs
94 H4 Green Bank Cumb
126 G5 Greenburn W Loth
113 J11 Greencroft Hall Dur
23 N7 Green Cross Surrey
19 Q4 Green Down Somset
61 M11 Green End Bed
61 N8 Green End Bed
61 P10 Green End Bed
61 P8 Green End Bed
61 Q4 Green End Cambs
62 B6 Green End Cambs
62 E9 Green End Cambs
62 G7 Green End Cambs
62 G8 Green End Cambs
50 G4 Green End Herts
50 H4 Green End Herts
50 H6 Green End Herts
48 B10 Greenend Oxon
59 L7 Green End Warwks
131 Q9 Greenfield Ag & B
50 C4 Greenfield C Beds
80 H9 Greenfield Flints
146 G7 Greenfield Highld
83 L4 Greenfield Oldham
35 K6 Greenfield Oxon
36 D4 Greenford Gt Lon
126 D3 Greengairs N Lans
90 F3 Greengates C Brad
100 F3 Greengill Cumb
88 E3 Greenhalgh Lancs
18 E10 Greenham Somset
34 E11 Greenham W Berk
97 Q9 Green Hammerton N York
111 Q3 Greenhaugh Nthumb
110 G11 Green Head Cumb
111 N7 Greenhead Nthumb
58 E2 Green Heath Staffs
82 F4 Greenheys Salfd
109 P5 Greenhill D & G
126 E2 Greenhill Falk
46 D5 Greenhill Herefs
39 L8 Greenhill Kent
116 C4 Greenhill S Lans
33 L7 Green Hill Wilts
84 F11 Greenhillocks Derbys
37 N5 Greenhithe Kent
125 N10 Greenholm E Ayrs
101 Q9 Greenholme Cumb
117 R6 Greenhouse Border
96 H8 Greenhow Hill N York
167 M3 Greenland Highld
84 E3 Greenland Sheff
35 L7 Greenlands Bucks
9 J9 Green Lane Devon
47 L2 Green Lane Worcs
129 J10 Greenlaw Border
109 M5 Greenlea D & G
133 N6 Greenloaning P & K
90 H11 Green Moor Barns
89 M8 Greenmount Bury
92 D5 Green Oak E R Yk
124 H2 Greenock Inver
124 H2 Greenock Crematorium Inver
94 G4 Greenodd Cumb
19 Q4 Green Ore Somset
101 N10 Green Quarter Cumb
76 G8 Greensgate Norfk
116 E2 Greenshields S Lans
112 H8 Greenside Gatesd
90 F7 Greenside Kirk
49 J5 Greens Norton Nhants
52 H6 Greenstead Essex
52 D6 Greenstead Green Essex
51 M10 Greensted Essex
26 C9 Green Street E Susx
46 G11 Green Street Gloucs
50 E11 Green Street Herts
51 L6 Green Street Herts
46 G5 Green Street Worcs
37 L8 Green Street Green Gt Lon
37 N6 Green Street Green Kent
52 H2 Greenstreet Green Suffk
51 K7 Green Tye Herts
46 D8 Greenway Gloucs
19 K10 Greenway Somset
30 E10 Greenway V Glam
57 N10 Greenway Worcs
37 J5 Greenwich Gt Lon
47 K8 Greet Gloucs
57 K10 Greete Shrops
87 K6 Greetham Lincs
73 N8 Greetham Rutlnd
90 D6 Greetland Calder
88 H5 Gregson Lane Lancs
19 M7 Greinton Somset
80 c7 Grenaby IoM
61 J8 Grendon Nhants
59 L5 Grendon Warwks
46 A3 Grendon Green Herefs
49 J10 Grendon Underwood Bucks
6 D4 Grenofen Devon
84 D2 Grenoside Sheff
84 D2 Grenoside Crematorium Sheff
168 g8 Greosabhagh W Isls
69 K4 Gresford Wrexhm
76 H4 Gresham Norfk
152 E7 Greshornish House Hotel Highld
76 D8 Gressenhall Norfk
76 D8 Gressenhall Green Norfk
95 M7 Gressingham Lancs
70 C4 Gresty Green Ches E
103 L8 Greta Bridge Dur
110 F7 Gretna D & G
110 F7 Gretna Green D & G
110 F7 Gretna Services D & G
47 K8 Gretton Gloucs
61 J2 Gretton Nhants
57 J5 Gretton Shrops
97 K5 Grewelthorpe N York
65 P7 Grey Friars Suffk
97 J6 Greygarth N York
92 C9 Grey Green N Linc
19 L8 Greylake Somset
109 N3 Greyrigg D & G
35 K8 Greys Green Oxon
100 E5 Greysouthen Cumb
101 M4 Greystoke Cumb
143 J9 Greystone Angus
23 K4 Greywell Hants
10 H4 Gribb Dorset
92 C3 Gribthorpe E R Yk
59 N7 Griff Warwks
31 J5 Griffithstown Torfn
72 C7 Griffydam Leics
23 M8 Griggs Green Hants
89 J8 Grimeford Village Lancs
84 E3 Grimesthorpe Sheff
91 L9 Grimethorpe Barns
46 F2 Grimley Worcs
114 F5 Grimmet S Ayrs
87 L3 Grimoldby Lincs
69 L9 Grimpo Shrops
88 H4 Grimsargh Lancs
93 N8 Grimsby NE Lin
93 N9 Grimsby Crematorium NE Lin
49 J4 Grimscote Nhants
16 D10 Grimscott Cnwll
168 j5 Grimshader W Isls
89 L6 Grimshaw Bl w D
88 F8 Grimshaw Green Lancs
73 Q6 Grimsthorpe Lincs
93 N3 Grimston E R Yk
72 H6 Grimston Leics
75 P6 Grimston Norfk
11 N6 Grimstone Dorset
64 C8 Grimstone End Suffk
5 Q3 Grinacombe Moor Devon
99 N6 Grindale E R Yk
57 P4 Grindle Shrops
84 B5 Grindleford Derbys
95 R11 Grindleton Lancs
69 P6 Grindley Brook Shrops
83 Q9 Grindlow Derbys
118 H2 Grindon Nthumb
104 C5 Grindon S on T
71 K4 Grindon Staffs
112 B7 Grindon Hill Nthumb
118 H2 Grindonrigg Nthumb
85 M2 Gringley on the Hill Notts
110 G9 Grinsdale Cumb
69 P10 Grinshill Shrops
103 K11 Grinton N York
168 j5 Griomaisiader W Isls
168 d12 Griomsaigh W Isls
136 F4 Grishipoll Ag & B
25 K6 Grisling Common E Susx
99 M4 Gristhorpe N York
64 C2 Griston Norfk
169 e6 Gritley Ork
33 K8 Grittenham Wilts
32 G8 Grittleton Wilts
94 E4 Grizebeck Cumb
94 G2 Grizedale Cumb
72 E9 Groby Leics
68 D2 Groes Conwy
30 E8 Groes-faen Rhondd
66 D7 Groesffordd Gwynd
80 E10 Groesffordd Marli Denbgs
56 C2 Groesllwyd Powys
66 H3 Groeslon Gwynd
67 J2 Groeslon Gwynd
30 F7 Groes-Wen Caerph
168 c14 Grogarry W Isls
120 F3 Grogport Ag & B
168 c14 Groigearraidh W Isls
65 M10 Gromford Suffk
80 F8 Gronant Flints
25 M3 Groombridge E Susx
168 g8 Grosebay W Isls
45 N10 Grosmont Mons
105 M9 Grosmont N York
52 G3 Groton Suffk
83 L4 Grotton Oldham
11 c2 Grouville Jersey
49 P10 Grove Bucks
11 P10 Grove Dorset
39 M9 Grove Kent
85 M5 Grove Notts
34 D6 Grove Oxon
41 J10 Grove Pembks
38 C10 Grove Green Kent
26 B3 Grovenhurst Kent
37 K6 Grove Park Gt Lon
32 C7 Grovesend S Glos
28 G4 Grovesend Swans
37 N7 Grubb Street Kent
160 E9 Gruinard Highld
122 C6 Gruinart Ag & B
144 E2 Grula Highld
137 N7 Gruline Ag & B
2 C8 Grumbla Cnwll
65 J11 Grundisburgh Suffk
169 p9 Gruting Shet
139 L8 Gualachulain Highld
74 G8 Guanockgate Lincs
135 M4 Guardbridge Fife
46 F5 Guarlford Worcs
141 P8 Guay P & K
10 b2 Guernsey Airport Guern
26 E9 Guestling Green E Susx
26 E8 Guestling Thorn E Susx
76 F6 Guestwick Norfk
83 K5 Guide Bridge Tamesd
113 L3 Guide Post Nthumb
62 G2 Guilden Morden Cambs
81 N11 Guilden Sutton Ches W
23 Q5 Guildford Surrey
23 Q5 Guildford Crematorium Surrey
38 D9 Guildstead Kent
142 A11 Guildtown P & K
60 E6 Guilsborough Nhants
56 C2 Guilsfield Powys
39 N10 Guilton Kent
114 G5 Guiltreehill S Ayrs
17 K4 Guineaford Devon
104 H7 Guisborough R & Cl
90 F2 Guiseley Leeds
76 E6 Guist Norfk
47 L10 Guiting Power Gloucs
128 D3 Gullane E Loth
64 A10 Gulling Green Suffk
2 D7 Gulval Cnwll
6 D4 Gulworthy Devon
41 M10 Gumfreston Pembks
60 E3 Gumley Leics
4 D10 Gummow's Shop Cnwll
92 B3 Gunby E R Yk
73 N6 Gunby Lincs
87 N7 Gunby Lincs
22 H8 Gundleton Hants
26 C5 Gun Green Kent
25 N8 Gun Hill E Susx
59 L7 Gun Hill Warwks
17 L5 Gunn Devon
103 J11 Gunnerside N York
112 D6 Gunnerton Nthumb
92 D8 Gunness N Linc
6 C4 Gunnislake Cnwll
169 s9 Gunnista Shet
74 C10 Gunthorpe C Pete
92 D11 Gunthorpe N Linc
76 E5 Gunthorpe Norfk
72 H2 Gunthorpe Notts
65 Q2 Gunton Suffk
2 H9 Gunwalloe Cnwll
18 C8 Gupworthy Somset
14 E7 Gurnard IoW
83 K10 Gurnett Ches E
20 B5 Gurney Slade Somset
29 L3 Gurnos Powys
38 H10 Gushmere Kent
12 H2 Gussage All Saints Dorset
12 G2 Gussage St Andrew Dorset
12 G2 Gussage St Michael Dorset
27 P3 Guston Kent
169 s4 Gutcher Shet
143 K7 Guthrie Angus
74 H10 Guyhirn Cambs
74 G10 Guyhirn Gull Cambs
20 F10 Guy's Marsh Dorset
119 P10 Guyzance Nthumb
80 F8 Gwaenysgor Flints
78 F9 Gwalchmai IoA
67 L3 Gwastadnant Gwynd
29 J2 Gwaun-Cae-Gurwen Carmth
42 C4 Gwbert on Sea Cerdgn
2 G5 Gwealavellan Cnwll
3 J8 Gweek Cnwll
31 L4 Gwehelog Mons
44 F6 Gwenddwr Powys
3 J5 Gwennap Cnwll
31 K5 Gwent Crematorium Mons
3 J10 Gwenter Cnwll
81 J11 Gwernaffield Flints
31 M4 Gwernesney Mons
43 K8 Gwernogle Carmth
68 H2 Gwernymynydd Flints
69 K4 Gwersyllt Wrexhm
80 G8 Gwespyr Flints
3 P3 Gwindra Cnwll
2 F6 Gwinear Cnwll
2 F5 Gwithian Cnwll
78 G7 Gwredog IoA
30 G5 Gwrhay Caerph
68 E5 Gwyddelwern Denbgs
43 J7 Gwyddgrug Carmth
69 J4 Gwynfryn Wrexhm
55 P11 Gwystre Powys
68 A2 Gwytherin Conwy
69 K5 Gyfelia Wrexhm
66 G5 Gyrn-goch Gwynd

H

56 F4 Habberley Shrops
57 Q9 Habberley Worcs
89 N4 Habergham Lancs
87 P7 Habertoft Lincs
23 M10 Habin W Susx
93 K8 Habrough NE Lin
74 B5 Hacconby Lincs
73 Q3 Haceby Lincs
65 L10 Hacheston Suffk
36 G7 Hackbridge Gt Lon
84 F4 Hackenthorpe Sheff
76 F11 Hackford Norfk
97 K2 Hackforth N York
70 A5 Hack Green Ches E
169 c4 Hackland Ork
60 H9 Hackleton Nhants
39 P11 Hacklinge Kent
58 C9 Hackman's Gate Worcs
99 K2 Hackness N York
19 K5 Hackness Somset
36 H4 Hackney Gt Lon
86 C4 Hackthorn Lincs
101 P6 Hackthorpe Cumb
37 N3 Hacton Gt Lon
118 E3 Hadden Border
35 K3 Haddenham Bucks
62 G5 Haddenham Cambs
128 E5 Haddington E Loth
86 B8 Haddington Lincs
65 N2 Haddiscoe Norfk
159 K10 Haddo Abers
61 P2 Haddon Cambs
83 P4 Hade Edge Kirk
83 M5 Hadfield Derbys
51 K7 Hadham Cross Herts
51 K6 Hadham Ford Herts
38 D4 Hadleigh Essex
52 H3 Hadleigh Suffk
52 G3 Hadleigh Heath Suffk
46 G2 Hadley Worcs
57 M2 Hadley Wrekin
71 L10 Hadley End Staffs
50 G11 Hadley Wood Gt Lon
37 P10 Hadlow Kent
25 M6 Hadlow Down E Susx
69 P10 Hadnall Shrops
112 E7 Hadrian's Wall Nthumb
51 N2 Hadstock Essex
46 H2 Hadzor Worcs
26 E3 Haffenden Quarter Kent
80 B11 Hafodunos Conwy
69 K5 Hafod-y-bwch Wrexhm
30 H4 Hafod-y-coed Blae G
30 H5 Hafodyrynys Caerph
89 P3 Haggate Lancs
111 J6 Haggbeck Cumb
169 q9 Haggersta Shet
119 K2 Haggerston Nthumb
17 K2 Haggington Hill Devon
126 D2 Haggs Falk
45 R6 Hagley Herefs
58 D8 Hagley Worcs
52 G4 Hagmore Green Suffk
87 K8 Hagnaby Lincs
87 N5 Hagnaby Lincs
87 K7 Hagworthingham Lincs
89 J9 Haigh Wigan
88 H4 Haighton Green Lancs
100 D9 Haile Cumb
47 K8 Hailes Gloucs
51 J8 Hailey Herts
34 C2 Hailey Oxon
34 H7 Hailey Oxon
25 N9 Hailsham E Susx
61 Q8 Hail Weston Cambs
37 L2 Hainault Gt Lon
39 Q8 Haine Kent
77 J8 Hainford Norfk

Hainton - Hay Street 279

86 G4 Hainton Lincs
90 D3 Hainworth C Brad
99 N8 Haisthorpe E R Yk
40 G9 Hakin Pembks
85 L10 Halam Notts
134 E10 Halbeath Fife
9 P2 Halberton Devon
167 M4 Halcro Highld
95 L5 Hale Cumb
81 P8 Hale Halton
21 N11 Hale Hants
20 D9 Hale Somset
23 M5 Hale Surrey
82 G7 Hale Traffd
81 P8 Hale Bank Halton
82 G7 Halebarns Traffd
25 N8 Hale Green E Susx
88 D2 Hale Nook Lancs
65 M2 Hales Norfk
70 C8 Hales Staffs
74 F5 Halesgate Lincs
71 M6 Hales Green Derbys
58 E8 Halesowen Dudley
39 K10 Hales Place Kent
37 Q11 Hale Street Kent
38 F3 Halesville Essex
65 M6 Halesworth Suffk
81 P7 Halewood Knows
7 L4 Halford Devon
56 G8 Halford Shrops
47 Q5 Halford Warwks
95 L3 Halfpenny Cumb
58 B6 Halfpenny Green Staffs
97 K4 Halfpenny Houses N York
43 M8 Halfway Carmth
44 A8 Halfway Carmth
84 F4 Halfway Sheff
34 D11 Halfway W Berk
23 P10 Halfway Bridge W Susx
56 E2 Halfway House Shrops
38 F7 Halfway Houses Kent
90 D5 Halifax Calder
125 L7 Halket E Ayrs
167 K5 Halkirk Highld
81 J10 Halkyn Flints
125 L7 Hall E Rens
72 D3 Hallam Fields Derbys
25 C7 Halland E Susx
73 K11 Hallaton Leics
20 B3 Hallatrow BaNES
111 L9 Hallbankgate Cumb
95 N3 Hallbeck Cumb
90 H7 Hall Cliffe Wakefd
88 E4 Hall Cross Lancs
100 H11 Hall Dunnerdale Cumb
31 Q8 Hallen S Glos
61 M11 Hall End Bed
50 C3 Hall End C Beds
84 E9 Hallfield Gate Derbys
104 B2 Hallgarth Dur
126 F2 Hall Glen Falk
58 H8 Hall Green Birm
152 D6 Hallin Highld
38 B9 Halling Medway
87 K3 Hallington Lincs
112 E5 Hallington Nthumb
89 K8 Halliwell Bolton
85 L10 Halloughton Notts
46 F3 Hallow Worcs
46 F3 Hallow Heath Worcs
7 L11 Hallsands Devon
51 K9 Hall's Green Essex
50 G5 Hall's Green Herts
94 D3 Hallthwaites Cumb
5 K4 Hallworthy Cnwll
116 H2 Hallyne Border
70 D5 Halmer End Staffs
46 C5 Halmond's Frome Herefs
32 D4 Halmore Gloucs
15 P5 Halnaker W Susx
88 D8 Halsall Lancs
48 G6 Halse Nhants
18 F9 Halse Somset
2 E6 Halsetown Cnwll
93 N5 Halsham E R Yk
17 J4 Halsinger Devon
52 D5 Halstead Essex
37 L8 Halstead Kent
73 K9 Halstead Leics
11 L3 Halstock Dorset
18 F7 Halsway Somset
101 L3 Haltcliff Bridge Cumb
92 H4 Haltemprice Crematorium E R Yk
86 H8 Haltham Lincs
87 L11 Haltoft End Lincs
35 N3 Halton Bucks
82 B8 Halton Halton
95 L8 Halton Lancs
91 K4 Halton Leeds
112 E7 Halton Nthumb
69 K7 Halton Wrexhm
96 F10 Halton East N York
87 M8 Halton Fenside Lincs
96 C5 Halton Gill N York
95 L7 Halton Green Lancs
87 M7 Halton Holegate Lincs
111 M9 Halton Lea Gate Nthumb
5 Q8 Halton Quay Cnwll
112 F7 Halton Shields Nthumb
96 B10 Halton West N York
111 P8 Haltwhistle Nthumb
77 N10 Halvergate Norfk
7 K8 Halwell Devon
8 B5 Halwill Devon
8 B4 Halwill Junction Devon
10 E4 Ham Devon
32 C5 Ham Gloucs
47 J10 Ham Gloucs
36 E6 Ham Gt Lon
39 P11 Ham Kent
19 J9 Ham Somset
20 C5 Ham Somset
22 B2 Ham Wilts
35 L7 Hambleden Bucks
14 H4 Hambledon Hants
23 Q7 Hambledon Surrey
14 E5 Hamble-le-Rice Hants
88 D2 Hambleton Lancs
91 P4 Hambleton N York
88 D2 Hambleton Moss Side Lancs
19 L10 Hambridge Somset
32 B9 Hambrook S Glos
15 L5 Hambrook W Susx
20 F9 Ham Common Dorset
87 K7 Hameringham Lincs
61 P5 Hamerton Cambs
46 E6 Ham Green Herefs
26 E6 Ham Green Kent
38 D8 Ham Green Kent
31 P9 Ham Green N Som
47 K2 Ham Green Worcs
37 Q8 Ham Hill Kent
126 C6 Hamilton S Lans
126 C6 Hamilton Services S Lans
11 M3 Hamlet Dorset
25 N9 Hamlins E Susx
24 C9 Hammerpot W Susx
36 F5 Hammersmith Gt Lon
58 G3 Hammerwich Staffs
25 K3 Hammerwood E Susx
50 H10 Hammond Street Herts
12 D2 Hammoon Dorset
169 q10 Hamnavoe Shet
25 P10 Hampden Park E Susx
51 N4 Hamperden End Essex
47 L11 Hampnett Gloucs
91 N8 Hampole Donc
13 J5 Hampreston Dorset
95 J4 Hampsfield Cumb
95 K10 Hampson Green Lancs
36 G3 Hampstead Gt Lon
34 F9 Hampstead Norreys W Berk
97 L9 Hampsthwaite N York
61 Q2 Hampton C Pete
10 F5 Hampton Devon
36 D7 Hampton Gt Lon
39 L8 Hampton Kent
57 N7 Hampton Shrops
33 N6 Hampton Swindn
47 K6 Hampton Worcs
45 R7 Hampton Bishop Herefs
36 E7 Hampton Court Palace & Gardens Gt Lon
32 G5 Hampton Fields Gloucs
69 P5 Hampton Green Ches W
69 P5 Hampton Heath Ches W
59 K8 Hampton in Arden Solhll
57 N7 Hampton Loade Shrops
58 C11 Hampton Lovett Worcs
47 Q3 Hampton Lucy Warwks
59 L11 Hampton Magna Warwks
47 Q2 Hampton on the Hill Warwks
48 F11 Hampton Poyle Oxon
36 E7 Hampton Wick Gt Lon
21 P11 Hamptworth Wilts
76 C7 Hamrow Norfk
25 K8 Hamsey E Susx
37 J9 Hamsey Green Surrey
71 L11 Hamstall Ridware Staffs
58 G6 Hamstead Birm
14 D8 Hamstead IoW
34 D11 Hamstead Marshall W Berk
103 M4 Hamsterley Dur
112 H9 Hamsterley Dur
26 H5 Hamstreet Kent
19 Q8 Ham Street Somset
19 L3 Hamwood N Som
12 G6 Hamworthy Poole
71 M9 Hanbury Staffs
47 J2 Hanbury Worcs
73 Q4 Hanby Lincs
63 K11 Hanchet End Suffk
70 E6 Hanchurch Staffs
164 D7 Handa Island Highld
105 K7 Handale R & Cl
9 P5 Hand and Pen Devon
81 N11 Handbridge Ches W
24 G5 Handcross W Susx
83 J8 Handforth Ches E
69 P2 Hand Green Ches W
69 N3 Handley Ches W
84 E8 Handley Derbys
51 Q10 Handley Green Essex
71 K11 Handsacre Staffs
58 F7 Handsworth Birm
84 F3 Handsworth Sheff
35 N6 Handy Cross Bucks
70 F6 Hanford C Stke
12 D2 Hanford Dorset
90 H6 Hanging Heaton Kirk
60 G6 Hanging Houghton Nhants
21 K7 Hanging Langford Wilts
24 G9 Hangleton Br & H
24 C10 Hangleton W Susx
32 B10 Hanham S Glos
70 B5 Hankelow Ches E
33 J6 Hankerton Wilts
25 P9 Hankham E Susx
70 F5 Hanley C Stke
46 F6 Hanley Castle Worcs
57 M11 Hanley Child Worcs
46 F6 Hanley Swan Worcs
57 M11 Hanley William Worcs
96 C8 Hanlith N York
69 N7 Hanmer Wrexhm
17 L6 Hannaford Devon
87 N5 Hannah Lincs
22 F3 Hannington Hants
60 H6 Hannington Nhants
33 N6 Hannington Swindn
33 N5 Hannington Wick Swindn
50 D4 Hanscombe End C Beds
49 M5 Hanslope M Keyn
74 A6 Hanthorpe Lincs
36 E5 Hanwell Gt Lon
48 D6 Hanwell Oxon
56 G3 Hanwood Shrops
36 D6 Hanworth Gt Lon
76 H4 Hanworth Norfk
116 B4 Happendon S Lans
77 M5 Happisburgh Norfk
77 M6 Happisburgh Common Norfk
81 P10 Hapsford Ches W
89 M4 Hapton Lancs
64 H2 Hapton Norfk
7 K7 Harberton Devon
7 K7 Harbertonford Devon
39 K10 Harbledown Kent
58 F8 Harborne Birm
59 Q9 Harborough Magna Warwks
118 H10 Harbottle Nthumb
7 J6 Harbourneford Devon
58 E11 Harbours Hill Worcs
13 K2 Harbridge Hants
13 K2 Harbridge Green Hants
48 C3 Harbury Warwks
73 J4 Harby Leics
85 Q6 Harby Notts
9 L8 Harcombe Devon
10 D6 Harcombe Devon
10 G5 Harcombe Bottom Devon
90 D3 Harden C Brad
58 F4 Harden Wsall
32 H10 Hardenhuish Wilts
151 K7 Hardgate Abers
108 H7 Hardgate D & G
97 L8 Hardgate N York
125 N3 Hardgate W Duns
24 B7 Hardham W Susx
88 D3 Hardhorn Lancs
76 E11 Hardingham Norfk
60 G9 Hardingstone Nhants
20 D4 Hardington Somset
11 L2 Hardington Mandeville Somset
11 L3 Hardington Marsh Somset
11 L2 Hardington Moor Somset
16 C7 Hardisworthy Devon
14 D5 Hardley Hants
77 M11 Hardley Street Norfk
49 P5 Hardmead M Keyn
96 C2 Hardraw N York
89 M6 Hardsough Lancs
84 F8 Hardstoft Derbys
14 H6 Hardway Hants
20 D8 Hardway Somset
49 M11 Hardwick Bucks
62 E9 Hardwick Cambs
60 H7 Hardwick Nhants
65 J4 Hardwick Norfk
34 C3 Hardwick Oxon
48 G9 Hardwick Oxon
84 G3 Hardwick Rothm
58 G5 Hardwick Wsall
32 E2 Hardwicke Gloucs
46 H9 Hardwicke Gloucs
52 F7 Hardy's Green Essex
25 N8 Harebeating E Susx
87 K7 Hareby Lincs
90 D3 Hare Croft C Brad
36 C2 Harefield Gt Lon
53 K6 Hare Green Essex
35 M9 Hare Hatch Wokham
71 M7 Harehill Derbys
91 J4 Harehills Leeds
119 L6 Harehope Nthumb
117 Q6 Harelaw Border
110 H5 Harelaw D & G
113 J10 Harelaw Dur
26 D4 Hareplain Kent
102 B2 Haresceugh Cumb
32 F2 Harescombe Gloucs
32 F2 Haresfield Gloucs
22 E8 Harestock Hants
51 K9 Hare Street Essex
51 M10 Hare Street Essex
51 J5 Hare Street Herts
97 M11 Harewood Leeds
45 Q9 Harewood End Herefs
6 G7 Harford Devon
64 G3 Hargate Norfk
83 P9 Hargatewall Derbys
69 N2 Hargrave Ches W
61 M6 Hargrave Nhants
63 N9 Hargrave Suffk
110 G8 Harker Cumb
53 L5 Harkstead Suffk
59 K2 Harlaston Staffs
73 M4 Harlaxton Lincs
67 K8 Harlech Gwynd
69 N11 Harlescott Shrops
36 F4 Harlesden Gt Lon
84 G5 Harlesthorpe Derbys
7 K9 Harleston Devon
65 J5 Harleston Norfk
64 E9 Harleston Suffk
60 F8 Harlestone Nhants
89 P3 Harle Syke Lancs
91 K11 Harley Rothm
57 K4 Harley Shrops
50 B4 Harlington C Beds
91 M10 Harlington Donc
36 C5 Harlington Gt Lon
152 D9 Harlosh Highld
51 K8 Harlow Essex
112 G7 Harlow Hill Nthumb
92 B3 Harlthorpe E R Yk
62 E10 Harlton Cambs
4 D6 Harlyn Cnwll
12 G8 Harman's Cross Dorset
96 H3 Harmby N York
50 G7 Harmer Green Herts
69 N10 Harmer Hill Shrops
36 C5 Harmondsworth Gt Lon
86 C8 Harmston Lincs
57 K4 Harnage Shrops
112 G4 Harnham Nthumb
33 L4 Harnhill Gloucs
37 M2 Harold Hill Gt Lon
40 G7 Haroldston West Pembks
169 t2 Haroldswick Shet
37 N2 Harold Wood Gt Lon
98 C4 Harome N York
50 D8 Harpenden Herts
10 B6 Harpford Devon
99 M8 Harpham E R Yk
75 Q5 Harpley Norfk
46 C2 Harpley Worcs
60 E8 Harpole Nhants
167 K5 Harpsdale Highld
35 L8 Harpsden Oxon
86 B3 Harpswell Lincs
83 J4 Harpurhey Manch
83 N10 Harpur Hill Derbys
110 H10 Harraby Cumb
17 K6 Harracott Devon
145 L3 Harrapool Highld
134 B2 Harrietfield P & K
38 E11 Harrietsham Kent
36 H3 Harringay Gt Lon
100 C5 Harrington Cumb
87 L6 Harrington Lincs
60 G4 Harrington Nhants
73 N11 Harringworth Nhants
168 f8 Harris W Isls
70 F3 Harriseahead Staffs
100 G2 Harriston Cumb
97 M10 Harrogate N York
97 M10 Harrogate Crematorium N York
61 K9 Harrold Bed
90 C9 Harrop Dale Oldham
36 E3 Harrow Gt Lon
5 Q7 Harrowbarrow Cnwll
61 N11 Harrowden Bed
103 Q7 Harrowgate Village Darltn
64 B11 Harrow Green Suffk
36 E3 Harrow on the Hill Gt Lon
36 E2 Harrow Weald Gt Lon
62 F10 Harston Cambs
73 L4 Harston Leics
92 D2 Harswell E R Yk
104 E4 Hart Hartpl
112 G3 Hartburn Nthumb
64 A11 Hartest Suffk
25 L3 Hartfield E Susx
62 C6 Hartford Cambs
82 D10 Hartford Ches W
18 C9 Hartford Somset
23 L3 Hartfordbridge Hants
51 Q7 Hartford End Essex
103 N9 Hartforth N York
20 F11 Hartgrove Dorset
69 N3 Harthill Ches W
126 G5 Harthill N Lans
84 G4 Harthill Rothm
71 L2 Hartington Derbys
112 F3 Hartington Nthumb
16 D7 Hartland Devon
16 C7 Hartland Quay Devon
58 B10 Hartlebury Worcs
104 F4 Hartlepool Hartpl
104 F4 Hartlepool Crematorium Hartpl
102 E9 Hartley Cumb
26 C5 Hartley Kent
37 P7 Hartley Kent
113 M5 Hartley Nthumb
37 P7 Hartley Green Kent
70 H9 Hartley Green Staffs
23 J3 Hartley Wespall Hants
23 L3 Hartley Wintney Hants
38 D9 Hartlip Kent
98 E2 Hartoft End N York
98 E8 Harton N York
113 N7 Harton S Tyne
56 H7 Harton Shrops
46 F10 Hartpury Gloucs
90 F6 Hartshead Kirk
90 F6 Hartshead Moor Services Calder
70 F5 Hartshill C Stke
59 M6 Hartshill Warwks
71 Q10 Hartshorne Derbys
119 J7 Hartside Nthumb
101 M8 Hartsop Cumb
104 E3 Hart Station Hartpl
18 E9 Hartswell Somset
49 L4 Hartwell Nhants
97 K8 Hartwith N York
126 E6 Hartwood N Lans
117 N6 Hartwoodmyres Border
37 Q8 Harvel Kent
47 L5 Harvington Worcs
58 C10 Harvington Worcs
85 L2 Harwell Notts
34 E7 Harwell Oxon
53 N5 Harwich Essex
89 L8 Harwood Bolton
102 F4 Harwood Dur
105 Q11 Harwood Dale N York
89 L8 Harwood Lee Bolton
50 G6 Harwood Park Crematorium Herts
85 K2 Harworth Notts
58 E8 Hasbury Dudley
24 B3 Hascombe Surrey
60 F5 Haselbech Nhants
11 K2 Haselbury Plucknett Somset
59 K11 Haseley Warwks
59 K11 Haseley Green Warwks
59 K10 Haseley Knob Warwks
47 M3 Haselor Warwks
46 F9 Hasfield Gloucs
40 G9 Hasguard Pembks
88 D9 Haskayne Lancs
65 J11 Hasketon Suffk
84 E7 Hasland Derbys
23 P8 Haslemere Surrey
89 M6 Haslingden Lancs
62 F10 Haslingfield Cambs
70 C3 Haslington Ches E
70 D3 Hassall Ches E
70 D3 Hassall Green Ches E
27 J2 Hassell Street Kent
77 M10 Hassingham Norfk
100 G7 Hassness Cumb
24 H7 Hassocks W Susx
84 B6 Hassop Derbys
23 P8 Haste Hill Surrey
167 P6 Haster Highld
87 N7 Hasthorpe Lincs
27 J2 Hastingleigh Kent
26 D10 Hastings E Susx
19 K11 Hastings Somset
26 D9 Hastings Borough Crematorium E Susx
51 L9 Hastingwood Essex
35 P3 Hastoe Herts
104 C2 Haswell Dur
104 C2 Haswell Plough Dur
61 Q11 Hatch C Beds
19 K10 Hatch Beauchamp Somset
61 N8 Hatch End Bed
36 D2 Hatch End Gt Lon
14 C6 Hatchet Gate Hants
50 D8 Hatching Green Herts
82 C10 Hatchmere Ches W
93 M10 Hatcliffe NE Lin
91 R9 Hatfield Donc
46 A3 Hatfield Herefs
50 F9 Hatfield Herts
46 G4 Hatfield Worcs
51 M7 Hatfield Broad Oak Essex
51 M7 Hatfield Heath Essex
52 C9 Hatfield Peverel Essex
92 A9 Hatfield Woodhouse Donc
34 B6 Hatford Oxon
22 B4 Hatherden Hants
8 D4 Hatherleigh Devon
72 E6 Hathern Leics
33 N3 Hatherop Gloucs
84 B4 Hathersage Derbys
84 B4 Hathersage Booths Derbys
70 B5 Hatherton Ches E
58 E2 Hatherton Staffs
62 C10 Hatley St George Cambs
5 Q9 Hatt Cnwll
83 L6 Hattersley Tamesd
22 H7 Hattingley Hants
159 Q10 Hatton Abers
142 H9 Hatton Angus
71 N8 Hatton Derbys
36 C5 Hatton Gt Lon
86 G5 Hatton Lincs
56 H6 Hatton Shrops
82 C8 Hatton Warrtn
59 K11 Hatton Warwks
69 N2 Hatton Heath Ches W
151 L4 Hatton of Fintray Abers
115 J2 Haugh E Ayrs
87 M5 Haugh Lincs
89 Q8 Haugh Rochdl
87 K4 Haugham Lincs
125 Q2 Haughhead E Duns
119 K5 Haugh Head Nthumb
64 E9 Haughley Suffk
64 E9 Haughley Green Suffk
158 B10 Haugh of Glass Moray
108 H7 Haugh of Urr D & G
143 L6 Haughs of Kinnaird Angus
85 L6 Haughton Notts
69 K11 Haughton Powys
57 M5 Haughton Shrops
57 N3 Haughton Shrops
69 L9 Haughton Shrops
69 Q11 Haughton Shrops
70 F10 Haughton Staffs
83 K6 Haughton Green Tamesd
104 B7 Haughton le Skerne Darltn
69 Q3 Haughton Moss Ches E
50 H6 Haultwick Herts
59 K2 Haunton Staffs
11 b1 Hautes Croix Jersey
62 F10 Hauxton Cambs
70 F2 Havannah Ches E
15 K5 Havant Hants
45 N4 Haven Herefs
86 H10 Haven Bank Lincs
93 L5 Haven Side E R Yk
14 G8 Havenstreet IoW
91 K8 Havercroft Wakefd
41 J7 Haverfordwest Pembks
63 L11 Haverhill Suffk
94 D5 Haverigg Cumb
37 M2 Havering-atte-Bower Gt Lon
49 M6 Haversham M Keyn
94 G4 Haverthwaite Cumb
104 E6 Haverton Hill S on T
19 N2 Havyat N Som
19 P7 Havyatt Somset
81 L11 Hawarden Flints
46 H5 Hawbridge Worcs
52 C7 Hawbush Green Essex
94 E6 Hawcoat Cumb
42 F5 Hawen Cerdgn
96 C3 Hawes N York
65 J2 Hawe's Green Norfk
46 F2 Hawford Worcs
117 Q8 Hawick Border
10 G4 Hawkchurch Devon
63 N10 Hawkedon Suffk
26 D2 Hawkenbury Kent
20 G4 Hawkeridge Wilts
9 Q7 Hawkerland Devon
32 E7 Hawkesbury S Glos
59 N8 Hawkesbury Warwks
32 E7 Hawkesbury Upton S Glos
59 L8 Hawkes End Covtry
83 L7 Hawk Green Stockp
119 P8 Hawkhill Nthumb
26 C5 Hawkhurst Kent
25 M7 Hawkhurst Common E Susx
27 M4 Hawkinge Kent
27 M3 Hawkinge Crematorium Kent
23 K9 Hawkley Hants
82 C4 Hawkley Wigan
17 R5 Hawkridge Somset
110 G11 Hawksdale Cumb
89 M7 Hawkshaw Bury
101 L11 Hawkshead Cumb
101 K11 Hawkshead Hill Cumb
116 A3 Hawksland S Lans
51 Q4 Hawkspur Green Essex
69 Q8 Hawkstone Shrops
96 E6 Hawkswick N York
90 F2 Hawksworth Leeds
73 K2 Hawksworth Notts
38 E3 Hawkwell Essex
112 G6 Hawkwell Nthumb
23 N3 Hawley Hants
37 M6 Hawley Kent
47 L10 Hawling Gloucs
98 A3 Hawnby N York
90 C3 Haworth C Brad
35 P3 Hawridge Bucks
64 B10 Hawstead Suffk
64 B10 Hawstead Green Suffk
113 P11 Hawthorn Dur
23 J8 Hawthorn Hants
30 E7 Hawthorn Rhondd
35 N10 Hawthorn Hill Br For
86 H9 Hawthorn Hill Lincs
73 Q5 Hawthorpe Lincs
85 N10 Hawton Notts
98 C9 Haxby C York
98 C9 Haxby Gates C York
92 C11 Haxey N Linc
92 C10 Haxey Carr N Linc
37 K11 Haxted Surrey
21 M5 Haxton Wilts
3 P3 Hay Cnwll
4 F7 Hay Cnwll
20 D2 Haycombe Crematorium BaNES
82 C5 Haydock St Hel
20 C4 Haydon BaNES
20 C11 Haydon Dorset
19 J10 Haydon Somset
112 B8 Haydon Bridge Nthumb
33 M7 Haydon Wick Swindn
5 P7 Haye Cnwll
36 C4 Hayes Gt Lon
37 K7 Hayes Gt Lon
36 C4 Hayes End Gt Lon
131 M3 Hayfield Ag & B
83 M7 Hayfield Derbys
57 L2 Haygate Wrekin
75 K7 Hay Green Norfk
143 J9 Hayhillock Angus
2 F6 Hayle Cnwll
58 E8 Hayley Green Dudley
15 K6 Hayling Island Hants
70 B4 Haymoor Green Ches E
9 J7 Hayne Devon
18 C11 Hayne Devon
50 C2 Haynes (Church End) C Beds
50 C2 Haynes (Northwood End) C Beds
50 D2 Haynes (Silver End) C Beds
50 C2 Haynes (West End) C Beds
45 J6 Hay-on-Wye Powys
40 G5 Hayscastle Pembks
40 H5 Hayscastle Cross Pembks
37 N11 Haysden Kent
51 J5 Hay Street Herts

Lendalfoot - Llanddeiniol 285

114 B9 Lendalfoot S Ayrs
132 H6 Lendrick Stirlg
159 R9 Lendrum Terrace Abers
38 E11 Lenham Kent
26 F2 Lenham Heath Kent
147 N2 Lenie Highld
118 G2 Lennel Border
108 D10 Lennox Plunton D & G
125 Q2 Lennoxtown E Duns
35 P8 Lent Bucks
72 F3 Lenton C Nott
73 Q4 Lenton Lincs
76 F8 Lenwade Norfk
126 B3 Lenzie E Duns
150 E5 Leochel-Cushnie Abers
58 H3 Leomansley Staffs
45 P3 Leominster Herefs
32 F4 Leonard Stanley Gloucs
11 a1 Leoville Jersey
14 D7 Lepe Hants
152 B8 Lephin Highld
98 F8 Leppington N York
90 G7 Lepton Kirk
130 H2 Lerags Ag & B
10 a2 L'Eree Guern
5 J10 Lerryn Cnwll
169 r9 Lerwick Shet
10 b2 Les Arquets Guern
119 P8 Lesbury Nthumb
10 c2 Les Hubits Guern
150 F3 Leslie Abers
134 H7 Leslie Fife
10 b2 Les Lohiers Guern
126 E10 Lesmahagow S Lans
10 b2 Les Murchez Guern
5 J3 Lesnewth Cnwll
10 b2 Les Nicolles Guern
10 c1 Les Quartiers Guern
11 a2 Les Quennevais Jersey
10 b2 Les Sages Guern
77 M6 Lessingham Norfk
110 D10 Lessonhall Cumb
3 K9 Lestowder Cnwll
10 b2 Les Villets Guern
106 D5 Leswalt D & G
11 a1 L'Etacq Jersey
50 E11 Letchmore Heath Herts
50 F4 Letchworth Garden City Herts
34 C8 Letcombe Bassett Oxon
34 C7 Letcombe Regis Oxon
143 J8 Letham Angus
118 C9 Letham Border
133 P10 Letham Falk
135 J5 Letham Fife
143 L8 Letham Grange Angus
142 A9 Lethendy P & K
150 F3 Lethenty Abers
159 K9 Lethenty Abers
65 K10 Letheringham Suffk
76 F4 Letheringsett Norfk
8 H8 Lettaford Devon
154 C3 Letterewe Highld
145 Q3 Letterfearn Highld
146 H9 Letterfinlay Lodge Hotel Highld
145 M10 Lettermorar Highld
161 K9 Letters Highld
116 B6 Lettershaw S Lans
40 H5 Letterston Pembks
149 J4 Lettoch Highld
157 L11 Lettoch Highld
45 L5 Letton Herefs
56 F10 Letton Herefs
37 L9 Lett's Green Kent
50 G8 Letty Green Herts
85 J3 Letwell Rothm
135 M3 Leuchars Fife
168 i6 Leumrabhagh W Isls
168 i5 Leurbost W Isls
3 Q4 Levalsa Meor Cnwll
70 F11 Levedale Staffs
51 L6 Level's Green Essex
99 N11 Leven E R Yk
135 K7 Leven Fife
95 K3 Levens Cumb
51 J6 Levens Green Herts
83 J6 Levenshulme Manch
169 r11 Levenwick Shet
168 f9 Leverburgh W Isls
74 H8 Leverington Cambs
50 C9 Leverstock Green Herts
87 M11 Leverton Lincs
10 b1 Le Villocq Guern
53 M4 Levington Suffk
98 G2 Levisham N York
34 B3 Lew Oxon
5 M5 Lewannick Cnwll
8 C7 Lewdown Devon
25 K8 Lewes E Susx
40 H6 Leweston Pembks
37 J6 Lewisham Gt Lon
37 J6 Lewisham Crematorium Gt Lon
147 N2 Lewiston Highld
29 P7 Lewistown Brdgnd
45 L3 Lewis Wych Herefs
35 K5 Lewknor Oxon
16 E11 Leworthy Devon
17 M4 Leworthy Devon
38 G9 Lewson Street Kent
88 F3 Lewth Lancs
8 C7 Lewtrenchard Devon
52 G6 Lexden Essex
19 J7 Lexworthy Somset
5 K8 Ley Cnwll
37 Q9 Leybourne Kent
96 H2 Leyburn N York
70 D5 Leycett Staffs
50 E6 Leygreen Herts
35 Q4 Ley Hill Bucks
88 G6 Leyland Lancs
82 C4 Leyland Green St Hel
151 K5 Leylodge Abers
159 P7 Leys Abers
142 D10 Leys P & K
39 H7 Leysdown-on-Sea Kent
143 L8 Leysmill Angus
142 F8 Leys of Cossans Angus
45 R2 Leysters Herefs
37 J3 Leyton Gt Lon
37 J3 Leytonstone Gt Lon
5 N6 Lezant Cnwll
2 H7 Lezerea Cnwll
157 P5 Lhanbryde Moray
44 D9 Libanus Powys
116 D2 Libberton S Lans
127 P4 Liberton C Edin
58 H3 Lichfield Staffs
58 E9 Lickey Worcs
58 E10 Lickey End Worcs
58 E10 Lickey Rock Worcs
23 P9 Lickfold W Susx
8 C8 Liddaton Green Devon
138 D6 Liddesdale Highld
33 P8 Liddington Swindn
84 D5 Lidgate Derbys
63 M9 Lidgate Suffk
91 R10 Lidget Donc
85 K7 Lidgett Notts
26 D8 Lidham Hill E Susx
49 Q7 Lidlington C Beds
38 C9 Lidsing Kent
142 E11 Liff Angus
58 G8 Lifford Birm
5 P4 Lifton Devon
5 P4 Liftondown Devon
48 B3 Lighthorne Warwks
48 C3 Lighthorne Heath Warwks
23 P2 Lightwater Surrey
70 G6 Lightwood C Stke
70 A6 Lightwood Green Ches E
69 L6 Lightwood Green Wrexhm
60 C5 Lilbourne Nhants
119 K6 Lilburn Tower Nthumb
70 C11 Lilleshall Wrekin
50 D5 Lilley Herts
34 D9 Lilley W Berk
117 Q5 Lilliesleaf Border
49 K7 Lillingstone Dayrell Bucks
49 K6 Lillingstone Lovell Bucks
11 N2 Lillington Dorset
12 H7 Lilliput Poole
18 G5 Lilstock Somset
57 N2 Lilyhurst Shrops
89 J7 Limbrick Lancs
50 C6 Limbury Luton
56 F11 Limebrook Herefs
89 N8 Limefield Bury
126 C7 Limekilnburn S Lans
134 D11 Limekilns Fife
126 F3 Limerigg Falk
14 D10 Limerstone IoW
111 Q11 Limestone Brae Nthumb
46 F8 Lime Street Worcs
19 P10 Limington Somset
115 M2 Limmerhaugh E Ayrs
77 M11 Limpenhoe Norfk
20 E2 Limpley Stoke Wilts
37 K10 Limpsfield Surrey
37 K10 Limpsfield Chart Surrey
84 H10 Linby Notts
23 N8 Linchmere W Susx
109 L5 Lincluden D & G
86 C6 Lincoln Lincs
86 C6 Lincoln Crematorium Lincs
57 Q11 Lincomb Worcs
7 J10 Lincombe Devon
16 H2 Lincombe Devon
95 J4 Lindale Cumb
94 E5 Lindal in Furness Cumb
24 H5 Lindfield W Susx
23 M7 Lindford Hants
90 E7 Lindley Kirk
97 K11 Lindley N York
82 H9 Lindow End Ches E
57 M11 Lindridge Worcs
51 P5 Lindsell Essex
52 G2 Lindsey Suffk
52 G2 Lindsey Tye Suffk
19 L7 Liney Somset
13 L3 Linford Hants
37 Q5 Linford Thurr
90 D3 Lingbob C Brad
105 J7 Lingdale R & Cl
56 F11 Lingen Herefs
25 J2 Lingfield Surrey
77 M10 Lingwood Norfk
152 F4 Linicro Highld
46 F8 Linkend Worcs
22 C3 Linkenholt Hants
26 D6 Linkhill Kent
5 N7 Linkinhorne Cnwll
134 H9 Linktown Fife
157 N5 Linkwood Moray
56 F6 Linley Shrops
46 C4 Linley Green Herefs
57 M5 Linleygreen Shrops
126 H2 Linlithgow W Loth
118 G9 Linshiels Nthumb
162 C7 Linsidemore Highld
49 P9 Linslade C Beds
65 L6 Linstead Parva Suffk
110 H9 Linstock Cumb
58 E10 Linthurst Worcs
90 E8 Linthwaite Kirk
129 L8 Lintlaw Border
158 D4 Lintmill Moray
118 E5 Linton Border
63 J11 Linton Cambs
71 P11 Linton Derbys
46 C9 Linton Herefs
38 C11 Linton Kent
97 N11 Linton Leeds
96 E8 Linton N York
113 L2 Linton Nthumb
71 P11 Linton Heath Derbys
46 C10 Linton Hill Herefs
97 Q8 Linton-on-Ouse N York
13 L3 Linwood Hants
86 F3 Linwood Lincs
125 L5 Linwood Rens
168 c13 Lionacleit W Isls
168 k1 Lional W Isls
25 N7 Lions Green E Susx
23 M8 Liphook Hants
70 C8 Lipley Shrops
81 K6 Liscard Wirral
18 A8 Liscombe Somset
5 M9 Liskeard Cnwll
138 E9 Lismore Ag & B
23 L9 Liss Hants
99 N9 Lissett E R Yk
23 L9 Liss Forest Hants
86 F4 Lissington Lincs
52 E3 Liston Essex
30 G8 Lisvane Cardif
31 K7 Liswerry Newpt
76 B8 Litcham Norfk
29 P8 Litchard Brdgnd
48 H4 Litchborough Nhants
22 E4 Litchfield Hants
81 L5 Litherland Sefton
50 H2 Litlington Cambs
25 M10 Litlington E Susx
62 H11 Little Abington Cambs
61 L6 Little Addington Nhants
107 M8 Little Airies D & G
50 F5 Little Almshoe Herts
47 M2 Little Alne Warwks
88 C9 Little Altcar Sefton
51 J8 Little Amwell Herts
102 C9 Little Asby Cumb
58 G5 Little Aston Staffs
14 E11 Little Atherfield IoW
104 G8 Little Ayton N York
52 C10 Little Baddow Essex
32 F8 Little Badminton S Glos
110 E9 Little Bampton Cumb
51 Q4 Little Bardfield Essex
61 Q9 Little Barford Bed
76 G5 Little Barningham Norfk
33 P2 Little Barrington Gloucs
81 P11 Little Barrow Ches W
98 F5 Little Barugh N York
112 E5 Little Bavington Nthumb
53 M2 Little Bealings Suffk
105 N10 Littlebeck N York
33 Q11 Little Bedwyn Wilts
53 K6 Little Bentley Essex
50 G9 Little Berkhamsted Herts
60 H8 Little Billing Nhants
49 P10 Little Billington C Beds
45 Q8 Little Birch Herefs
88 C2 Little Bispham Bpool
53 K2 Little Blakenham Suffk
101 N4 Little Blencow Cumb
58 F4 Little Bloxwich Wsall
24 B6 Little Bognor W Susx
71 P4 Little Bolehill Derbys
82 F7 Little Bollington Ches E
36 D10 Little Bookham Surrey
9 K2 Littleborough Devon
85 P4 Littleborough Notts
89 Q7 Littleborough Rochdl
39 M10 Littlebourne Kent
48 E6 Little Bourton Oxon
60 F3 Little Bowden Leics
63 L10 Little Bradley Suffk
45 L2 Little Brampton Herefs
56 F8 Little Brampton Shrops
52 D9 Little Braxted Essex
143 K5 Little Brechin Angus
11 M7 Littlebredy Dorset
49 P8 Little Brickhill M Keyn
70 F9 Little Bridgeford Staffs
60 E8 Little Brington Nhants
53 J6 Little Bromley Essex
100 E4 Little Broughton Cumb
82 C11 Little Budworth Ches W
156 A7 Littleburn Highld
37 Q2 Little Burstead Essex
51 M3 Littlebury Essex
51 L3 Littlebury Green Essex
73 Q7 Little Bytham Lincs
51 N6 Little Canfield Essex
87 L3 Little Carlton Lincs
85 N9 Little Carlton Notts
73 Q9 Little Casterton Rutlnd
93 K2 Little Catwick E R Yk
61 P6 Little Catworth Cambs
87 L4 Little Cawthorpe Lincs
35 Q5 Little Chalfont Bucks
26 F2 Little Chart Kent
51 M2 Little Chesterford Essex
26 B3 Little Cheveney Kent
21 J4 Little Cheverell Wilts
51 K3 Little Chishill Cambs
53 L8 Little Clacton Essex
33 Q4 Little Clanfield Oxon
100 E5 Little Clifton Cumb
93 M9 Little Coates NE Lin
47 J6 Little Comberton Worcs
26 B10 Little Common E Susx
37 P9 Little Comp Kent
47 Q8 Little Compton Warwks
111 J9 Little Corby Cumb
52 F4 Little Cornard Suffk
21 M4 Littlecott Wilts
46 B4 Little Cowarne Herefs
33 Q6 Little Coxwell Oxon
97 K2 Little Crakehall N York
60 H5 Little Cransley Nhants
76 B11 Little Cressingham Norfk
81 L4 Little Crosby Sefton
100 H5 Little Crosthwaite Cumb
71 M7 Little Cubley Derbys
73 K8 Little Dalby Leics
32 C2 Littledean Gloucs
45 Q8 Little Dewchurch Herefs
63 L9 Little Ditton Cambs
45 Q11 Little Doward Herefs
22 B3 Littledown Hants
62 H4 Little Downham Cambs
99 L9 Little Driffield E R Yk
76 B9 Little Dunham Norfk
141 P9 Little Dunkeld P & K
51 Q6 Little Dunmow Essex
21 M8 Little Durnford Wilts
51 P6 Little Easton Essex
72 B2 Little Eaton Derbys
64 E2 Little Ellingham Norfk
20 D5 Little Elm Somset
60 C9 Little Everdon Nhants
62 E10 Little Eversden Cambs
33 P4 Little Faringdon Oxon
97 L2 Little Fencote N York
91 N3 Little Fenton N York
76 C9 Little Fransham Norfk
35 Q2 Little Gaddesden Herts
45 N10 Little Garway Herefs
61 P4 Little Gidding Cambs
65 L10 Little Glemham Suffk
46 C10 Little Gorsley Herefs
62 C9 Little Gransden Cambs
73 J2 Little Green Notts
20 D5 Little Green Somset
87 K2 Little Grimsby Lincs
85 M4 Little Gringley Notts
98 E5 Little Habton N York
51 K6 Little Hadham Herts
74 B2 Little Hale Lincs
72 D2 Little Hallam Derbys
51 M7 Little Hallingbury Essex
9 P8 Littleham Devon
16 G7 Littleham Devon
35 N4 Little Hampden Bucks
24 B10 Littlehampton W Susx
12 D2 Little Hanford Dorset
61 J6 Little Harrowden Nhants
34 H4 Little Haseley Oxon
93 L2 Little Hatfield E R Yk
77 K7 Little Hautbois Norfk
40 G8 Little Haven Pembks
24 E4 Littlehaven W Susx
58 H4 Little Hay Staffs
83 M7 Little Hayfield Derbys
71 J10 Little Haywood Staffs
70 F11 Little Heath Staffs
35 J10 Little Heath W Berk
7 L6 Littlehempston Devon
57 K11 Little Hereford Herefs
52 G5 Little Horkesley Essex
51 K5 Little Hormead Herts
25 L7 Little Horsted E Susx
90 F4 Little Horton C Brad
21 K2 Little Horton Wilts
49 L8 Little Horwood Bucks
91 L9 Little Houghton Barns
60 H9 Little Houghton Nhants
119 P7 Littlehoughton Nthumb
83 Q9 Little Hucklow Derbys
82 F4 Little Hulton Salfd
34 F10 Little Hungerford W Berk
97 Q5 Little Hutton N York
61 K7 Little Irchester Nhants
99 M9 Little Kelk E R Yk
20 E5 Little Keyford Somset
35 M3 Little Kimble Bucks
48 B4 Little Kineton Warwks
35 N5 Little Kingshill Bucks
108 H8 Little Knox D & G
101 K10 Little Langdale Cumb
21 K7 Little Langford Wilts
51 M9 Little Laver Essex
82 D9 Little Leigh Ches W
52 B8 Little Leighs Essex
89 M9 Little Lever Bolton
49 M6 Little Linford M Keyn
19 N10 Little Load Somset
34 H2 Little London Bucks
74 H11 Little London Cambs
25 N6 Little London E Susx
51 L5 Little London Essex
51 Q3 Little London Essex
46 D11 Little London Gloucs
22 C5 Little London Hants
22 H3 Little London Hants
90 G3 Little London Leeds
74 D6 Little London Lincs
74 H6 Little London Lincs
87 K6 Little London Lincs
75 L6 Little London Norfk
55 N7 Little London Powys
83 Q10 Little Longstone Derbys
70 D5 Little Madeley Staffs
46 E6 Little Malvern Worcs
81 L11 Little Mancot Flints
52 D5 Little Maplestead Essex
46 C7 Little Marcle Herefs
17 J9 Little Marland Devon
35 N7 Little Marlow Bucks
75 Q6 Little Massingham Norfk
76 H10 Little Melton Norfk
149 Q8 Littlemill Abers
156 G7 Littlemill Highld
31 K4 Little Mill Mons
34 H4 Little Milton Oxon
35 P5 Little Missenden Bucks
39 P11 Little Mongeham Kent
84 E8 Littlemoor Derbys
19 K8 Little Moor Somset
34 F4 Littlemore Oxon
102 E8 Little Musgrave Cumb
69 M11 Little Ness Shrops
81 K9 Little Neston Ches W
41 J5 Little Newcastle Pembks
103 M7 Little Newsham Dur
19 N11 Little Norton Somset
53 M6 Little Oakley Essex
61 J3 Little Oakley Nhants
61 L9 Little Odell Bed
50 D5 Little Offley Herts
102 D7 Little Ormside Cumb
110 G9 Little Orton Cumb
63 K3 Little Ouse Cambs
97 P8 Little Ouseburn N York
72 A4 Littleover C Derb
60 F4 Little Oxendon Nhants
59 K8 Little Packington Warwks
26 B2 Little Pattenden Kent
61 Q8 Little Paxton Cambs
4 E7 Little Petherick Cnwll
88 D4 Little Plumpton Lancs
77 L9 Little Plumstead Norfk
73 N4 Little Ponton Lincs
63 J3 Littleport Cambs
63 J3 Littleport Bridge Cambs
14 F6 Little Posbrook Hants
17 J9 Little Potheridge Devon
91 K4 Little Preston Leeds
48 G4 Little Preston Nhants
82 D11 Littler Ches W
62 C5 Little Raveley Cambs
92 D6 Little Reedness E R Yk
97 N10 Little Ribston N York
47 N11 Little Rissington Gloucs
47 Q8 Little Rollright Oxon
84 C7 Little Rowsley Derbys
76 D6 Little Ryburgh Norfk
119 K8 Little Ryle Nthumb
56 H4 Little Ryton Shrops
101 Q3 Little Salkeld Cumb
51 Q4 Little Sampford Essex
23 M2 Little Sandhurst Br For
58 D3 Little Saredon Staffs
81 M11 Little Saughall Ches W
63 P8 Little Saxham Suffk
155 L6 Little Scatwell Highld
62 G10 Little Shelford Cambs
59 K11 Little Shrewley Warwks
9 M3 Little Silver Devon
88 D3 Little Singleton Lancs
91 R3 Little Skipwith N York
91 N7 Little Smeaton N York
76 D5 Little Snoring Norfk
32 E8 Little Sodbury S Glos
32 D8 Little Sodbury End S Glos
22 C8 Little Somborne Hants
33 J8 Little Somerford Wilts
70 C9 Little Soudley Shrops
96 B7 Little Stainforth N York
104 B6 Little Stainton Darltn
81 N10 Little Stanney Ches W
61 P8 Little Staughton Bed
87 M8 Little Steeping Lincs
70 G8 Little Stoke Staffs
27 J7 Littlestone-on-Sea Kent
64 G9 Little Stonham Suffk
72 H10 Little Stretton Leics
56 G6 Little Stretton Shrops
101 Q7 Little Strickland Cumb
62 B5 Little Stukeley Cambs
70 E8 Little Sugnall Staffs
81 M9 Little Sutton Ches W
57 J8 Little Sutton Shrops
112 D5 Little Swinburne Nthumb
108 F10 Little Sypland D & G
48 C9 Little Tew Oxon
52 E7 Little Tey Essex
62 H5 Little Thetford Cambs
97 Q5 Little Thirkleby N York
76 F4 Little Thornage Norfk
88 D2 Little Thornton Lancs
104 D2 Little Thorpe Dur
72 E11 Littlethorpe Leics
97 M7 Littlethorpe N York
63 L10 Little Thurlow Suffk
63 L10 Little Thurlow Green Suffk
37 P5 Little Thurrock Thurr
142 E7 Littleton Angus
19 Q2 Littleton BaNES
81 N11 Littleton Ches W
108 D9 Littleton D & G
12 E4 Littleton Dorset
22 E8 Littleton Hants
19 N8 Littleton Somset
23 Q5 Littleton Surrey
36 C7 Littleton Surrey
32 F8 Littleton Drew Wilts
31 Q7 Littleton-on-Severn S Glos
21 K4 Littleton Pannell Wilts
16 H8 Little Torrington Devon
52 E9 Little Totham Essex
100 H7 Little Town Cumb
104 B2 Littletown Dur
89 K3 Little Town Lancs
82 D6 Little Town Warrtn
72 A9 Little Twycross Leics
94 F6 Little Urswick Cumb
38 F4 Little Wakering Essex
51 M2 Little Walden Essex
52 F2 Little Waldingfield Suffk
76 C4 Little Walsingham Norfk
52 B9 Little Waltham Essex
37 P2 Little Warley Essex
47 J8 Little Washbourne Gloucs
92 G4 Little Weighton E R Yk
61 K3 Little Weldon Nhants
64 B10 Little Welnetham Suffk
87 K3 Little Welton Lincs
53 J4 Little Wenham Suffk
57 L3 Little Wenlock Wrekin
20 B9 Little Weston Somset
14 G9 Little Whitefield IoW
65 K6 Little Whittingham Green Suffk
112 E7 Little Whittington Nthumb
35 M9 Littlewick Green W & M
62 H9 Little Wilbraham Cambs
11 J4 Littlewindsor Dorset
46 H11 Little Witcombe Gloucs
46 E2 Little Witley Worcs
34 G6 Little Wittenham Oxon
47 Q7 Little Wolford Warwks
58 E3 Littlewood Staffs
36 G8 Little Woodcote Gt Lon
49 N10 Littleworth Bucks
34 B5 Littleworth Oxon
58 F2 Littleworth Staffs
70 G10 Littleworth Staffs
24 E6 Littleworth W Susx
46 G4 Littleworth Worcs
47 J2 Littleworth Worcs
35 P7 Littleworth Common Bucks
63 L11 Little Wratting Suffk
61 L8 Little Wymington Bed
50 F5 Little Wymondley Herts
58 F3 Little Wyrley Staffs
69 Q11 Little Wytheford Shrops
52 C4 Little Yeldham Essex
51 Q7 Littley Green Essex
83 Q9 Litton Derbys
96 D6 Litton N York
19 Q4 Litton Somset
11 L6 Litton Cheney Dorset
168 i5 Liurbost W Isls
81 L6 Liverpool Lpool
90 F6 Liversedge Kirk
9 K9 Liverton Devon
105 K7 Liverton R & Cl
105 K7 Liverton Mines R & Cl
38 E11 Liverton Street Kent
127 K4 Livingston W Loth
127 J4 Livingston Village W Loth
80 H10 Lixwm Flints
3 J11 Lizard Cnwll
78 C8 Llaingoch IoA
55 P8 Llaithddu Powys
55 K4 Llan Powys
67 L11 Llanaber Gwynd
66 F6 Llanaelhaearn Gwynd
54 F10 Llanafan Cerdgn
44 D3 Llanafan-Fawr Powys
44 D4 Llanafan-fechan Powys
79 J7 Llanallgo IoA
66 G7 Llanarmon Gwynd
68 G8 Llanarmon Dyffryn Ceiriog Wrexhm
68 G3 Llanarmon-yn-Ial Denbgs
42 H3 Llanarth Cerdgn
31 L2 Llanarth Mons
43 K11 Llanarthne Carmth
80 G8 Llanasa Flints
78 F7 Llanbabo IoA
54 E8 Llanbadarn Fawr Cerdgn
55 P9 Llanbadarn Fynydd Powys
44 G5 Llanbadarn-y-garreg Powys
31 L5 Llanbadoc Mons
78 F6 Llanbadrig IoA
31 L6 Llanbeder Newpt
67 K9 Llanbedr Gwynd
44 G5 Llanbedr Powys
45 J10 Llanbedr Powys
68 F3 Llanbedr-Dyffryn-Clwyd Denbgs
79 J8 Llanbedrgoch IoA
66 E8 Llanbedrog Gwynd
79 P11 Llanbedr-y-Cennin Conwy
67 K2 Llanberis Gwynd
30 D11 Llanbethery V Glam
55 Q10 Llanbister Powys
30 C10 Llanblethian V Glam
41 P6 Llanboidy Carmth
30 F6 Llanbradach Caerph
55 K4 Llanbrynmair Powys
30 D11 Llancadle V Glam
30 D10 Llancarfan V Glam
31 L4 Llancayo Mons
45 P10 Llancloudy Herefs
54 E6 Llancynfelyn Cerdgn
30 G9 Llandaff Cardif
67 K9 Llandanwg Gwynd
29 K5 Llandarcy Neath
41 Q8 Llandawke Carmth
78 H10 Llanddaniel Fab IoA
43 K11 Llanddarog Carmth
54 D10 Llanddeiniol Cerdgn

Low Barlings - Mappowder 287

86 E6 **Low Barlings** Lincs
105 K11 **Low Bell End** N York
95 N7 **Low Bentham** N York
95 N5 **Low Biggins** Cumb
102 B10 **Low Borrowbridge** Cumb
84 C2 **Low Bradfield** Sheff
96 F11 **Low Bradley** N York
101 M2 **Low Braithwaite** Cumb
92 C10 **Low Burnham** N Linc
119 P9 **Low Buston** Nthumb
100 C6 **Lowca** Cumb
98 E10 **Low Catton** E R Yk
103 Q8 **Low Coniscliffe** Darltn
110 H9 **Low Crosby** Cumb
85 L11 **Lowdham** Notts
104 B8 **Low Dinsdale** Darltn
69 N8 **Lowe** Shrops
70 H3 **Lowe Hill** Staffs
97 K4 **Low Ellington** N York
18 H7 **Lower Aisholt** Somset
12 C4 **Lower Ansty** Dorset
46 G9 **Lower Apperley** Gloucs
48 H11 **Lower Arncott** Oxon
9 K8 **Lower Ashton** Devon
35 K8 **Lower Assendon** Oxon
88 D4 **Lower Ballam** Lancs
88 F4 **Lower Bartle** Lancs
34 H9 **Lower Basildon** W Berk
45 M3 **Lower Bearwood** Herefs
24 F5 **Lower Beeding** W Susx
61 L3 **Lower Benefield** Nhants
58 E11 **Lower Bentley** Worcs
57 P6 **Lower Beobridge** Shrops
84 F10 **Lower Birchwood** Derbys
48 E4 **Lower Boddington** Nhants
2 B7 **Lower Boscaswell** Cnwll
23 M6 **Lower Bourne** Surrey
48 B7 **Lower Brailes** Warwks
145 L3 **Lower Breakish** Highld
83 K6 **Lower Bredbury** Stockp
46 F3 **Lower Broadheath** Worcs
45 M4 **Lower Broxwood** Herefs
46 B8 **Lower Buckenhill** Herefs
45 Q7 **Lower Bullingham** Herefs
21 N11 **Lower Burgate** Hants
9 P5 **Lower Burrowton** Devon
45 N3 **Lower Burton** Herefs
61 Q11 **Lower Caldecote** C Beds
32 D4 **Lower Cam** Gloucs
19 L3 **Lower Canada** N Som
60 B9 **Lower Catesby** Nhants
44 E7 **Lower Chapel** Powys
21 J9 **Lower Chicksgrove** Wilts
22 B4 **Lower Chute** Wilts
36 H3 **Lower Clapton** Gt Lon
58 D9 **Lower Clent** Worcs
9 K4 **Lower Creedy** Devon
83 M8 **Lower Crossings** Derbys
90 G9 **Lower Cumberworth** Kirk
89 K5 **Lower Darwen** Bl w D
61 N7 **Lower Dean** Bed
90 G9 **Lower Denby** Kirk
153 P5 **Lower Diabaig** Highld
25 N8 **Lower Dicker** E Susx
56 H8 **Lower Dinchope** Shrops
56 E8 **Lower Down** Shrops
97 P8 **Lower Dunsforth** N York
46 B5 **Lower Egleton** Herefs
71 K3 **Lower Elkstone** Staffs
71 L6 **Lower Ellastone** Staffs
35 J3 **Lower End** Bucks
49 P7 **Lower End** M Keyn
60 H9 **Lower End** Nhants
61 J8 **Lower End** Nhants
21 N4 **Lower Everleigh** Wilts
14 D7 **Lower Exbury** Hants
27 N2 **Lower Eythorne** Kent
31 P10 **Lower Failand** N Som
23 K7 **Lower Farringdon** Hants
36 C6 **Lower Feltham** Gt Lon
24 B7 **Lower Fittleworth** W Susx
80 c6 **Lower Foxdale** IoM
69 L8 **Lower Frankton** Shrops
41 J8 **Lower Freystrop** Pembks
23 L6 **Lower Froyle** Hants
7 N5 **Lower Gabwell** Devon
162 D8 **Lower Gledfield** Highld
19 N6 **Lower Godney** Somset
58 D6 **Lower Gornal** Dudley
50 D3 **Lower Gravenhurst** C Beds
50 E4 **Lower Green** Herts
51 K4 **Lower Green** Herts
25 N2 **Lower Green** Kent
25 P2 **Lower Green** Kent
76 D4 **Lower Green** Norfk
58 D3 **Lower Green** Staffs
63 M7 **Lower Green** Suffk
65 L10 **Lower Hacheston** Suffk
36 C7 **Lower Halliford** Surrey
11 L3 **Lower Halstock Leigh** Dorset
38 E8 **Lower Halstow** Kent
12 G6 **Lower Hamworthy** Poole
39 L11 **Lower Hardres** Kent
45 K2 **Lower Harpton** Herefs
38 D9 **Lower Hartlip** Kent
84 E10 **Lower Hartshay** Derbys
35 L2 **Lower Hartwell** Bucks
70 E7 **Lower Hatton** Staffs
94 E3 **Lower Hawthwaite** Cumb
45 K3 **Lower Hergest** Herefs
48 E10 **Lower Heyford** Oxon
95 J8 **Lower Heysham** Lancs
38 B7 **Lower Higham** Kent
53 L4 **Lower Holbrook** Suffk
69 L9 **Lower Hordley** Shrops
24 B7 **Lower Horncroft** W Susx
89 N4 **Lowerhouse** Lancs
90 F7 **Lower Houses** Kirk
46 E5 **Lower Howsell** Worcs
82 F6 **Lower Irlam** Salfd
72 B2 **Lower Kilburn** Derbys
32 E7 **Lower Kilcott** Gloucs
122 C11 **Lower Killeyan** Ag & B
11 M5 **Lower Kingcombe** Dorset
36 F10 **Lower Kingswood** Surrey
69 K2 **Lower Kinnerton** Ches W
19 N2 **Lower Langford** N Som
135 L7 **Lower Largo** Fife
71 J7 **Lower Leigh** Staffs
47 P8 **Lower Lemington** Gloucs
55 M11 **Lower Llanfadog** Powys
17 J6 **Lower Lovacott** Devon
17 L4 **Lower Loxhore** Devon
46 A11 **Lower Lydbrook** Gloucs
56 G11 **Lower Lye** Herefs
30 H7 **Lower Machen** Newpt
45 L8 **Lower Maes-coed** Herefs
13 J4 **Lower Mannington** Dorset
20 E6 **Lower Marston** Somset
31 Q4 **Lower Meend** Gloucs
18 H8 **Lower Merridge** Somset
48 F6 **Lower Middleton Cheney** Nhants
19 P5 **Lower Milton** Somset
47 J5 **Lower Moor** Worcs
32 B6 **Lower Morton** S Glos
51 J9 **Lower Nazeing** Essex
47 P2 **Lower Norton** Warwks
20 E10 **Lower Nyland** Dorset
30 G11 **Lower Penarth** V Glam
58 C5 **Lower Penn** Staffs
13 P6 **Lower Pennington** Hants
88 G5 **Lower Penwortham** Lancs
82 F10 **Lower Peover** Ches E
89 Q8 **Lower Place** Rochdl
35 K2 **Lower Pollicott** Bucks
47 N5 **Lower Quinton** Warwks
38 D8 **Lower Rainham** Medway
52 H4 **Lower Raydon** Suffk
18 D7 **Lower Roadwater** Somset
95 N8 **Lower Salter** Lancs
33 J8 **Lower Seagry** Wilts
51 L8 **Lower Sheering** Essex
49 Q6 **Lower Shelton** C Beds
35 L9 **Lower Shiplake** Oxon
48 E2 **Lower Shuckburgh** Warwks
47 N10 **Lower Slaughter** Gloucs
90 H6 **Lower Soothill** Kirk
32 C3 **Lower Soudley** Gloucs
27 M3 **Lower Standen** Kent
32 H8 **Lower Stanton St Quintin** Wilts
38 D6 **Lower Stoke** Medway
32 C6 **Lower Stone** Gloucs
58 G4 **Lower Stonnall** Staffs
64 D3 **Lower Stow Bedon** Norfk
12 D5 **Lower Street** Dorset
26 B9 **Lower Street** E Susx
77 K4 **Lower Street** Norfk
63 N10 **Lower Street** Suffk
64 G11 **Lower Street** Suffk
82 D8 **Lower Stretton** Warrtn
11 K5 **Lower Stroud** Dorset
50 C5 **Lower Sundon** C Beds
14 E5 **Lower Swanwick** Hants
47 N9 **Lower Swell** Gloucs
48 D7 **Lower Tadmarton** Oxon
9 Q4 **Lower Tale** Devon
71 J7 **Lower Tean** Staffs
65 N2 **Lower Thurlton** Norfk
2 H8 **Lower Town** Cnwll
7 J4 **Lower Town** Devon
46 B6 **Lower Town** Herefs
41 J3 **Lower Town** Pembks
5 N6 **Lower Trebullett** Cnwll
3 K6 **Lower Treluswell** Cnwll
48 B5 **Lower Tysoe** Warwks
65 K11 **Lower Ufford** Suffk
9 L8 **Lower Upcott** Devon
22 F11 **Lower Upham** Hants
38 C7 **Lower Upnor** Medway
18 F7 **Lower Vexford** Somset
82 D7 **Lower Walton** Warrtn
12 B5 **Lower Waterston** Dorset
19 M4 **Lower Weare** Somset
60 D9 **Lower Weedon** Nhants
45 K4 **Lower Welson** Herefs
46 H7 **Lower Westmancote** Worcs
12 D4 **Lower Whatcombe** Dorset
20 D5 **Lower Whatley** Somset
82 D9 **Lower Whitley** Ches W
32 D5 **Lower Wick** Gloucs
46 F4 **Lower Wick** Worcs
22 H6 **Lower Wield** Hants
25 N10 **Lower Willingdon** E Susx
82 H11 **Lower Withington** Ches E
35 M7 **Lower Woodend** Bucks
21 M7 **Lower Woodford** Wilts
11 M4 **Lower Wraxhall** Dorset
46 E6 **Lower Wyche** Worcs
90 F5 **Lower Wyke** C Brad
73 J9 **Lowesby** Leics
65 Q3 **Lowestoft** Suffk
100 F6 **Loweswater** Cumb
113 L9 **Low Fell** Gatesd
24 G3 **Lowfield Heath** W Susx
132 F10 **Low Gartachorrans** Stirlg
112 D8 **Low Gate** Nthumb
111 K9 **Low Gettbridge** Cumb
102 B11 **Lowgill** Cumb
95 P8 **Lowgill** Lancs
97 K6 **Low Grantley** N York
97 K9 **Low Green** N York
57 Q9 **Low Habberley** Worcs
19 M9 **Low Ham** Somset
97 L9 **Low Harrogate** N York
105 P9 **Low Hawsker** N York
111 J11 **Low Hesket** Cumb
98 F7 **Low Hutton** N York
94 F3 **Lowick** Cumb
61 L4 **Lowick** Nhants
119 K3 **Lowick** Nthumb
94 F3 **Lowick Bridge** Cumb
94 F3 **Lowick Green** Cumb
101 P7 **Low Knipe** Cumb
97 J8 **Low Laithe** N York
103 M5 **Lowlands** Dur
31 J5 **Lowlands** Torfn
86 G5 **Low Langton** Lincs
83 M7 **Low Leighton** Derbys
100 G5 **Low Lorton** Cumb
98 G5 **Low Marishes** N York
85 P7 **Low Marnham** Notts
119 M3 **Low Middleton** Nthumb
105 J11 **Low Mill** N York
90 F5 **Low Moor** C Brad
113 M11 **Low Moorsley** Sundld
100 C6 **Low Moresby** Cumb
95 J4 **Low Newton** Cumb
100 G2 **Low Row** Cumb
101 L3 **Low Row** Cumb
111 L8 **Low Row** Cumb
103 J11 **Low Row** N York
106 D4 **Low Salchrie** D & G
92 F8 **Low Santon** N Linc
59 J11 **Lowsonford** Warwks
77 L7 **Low Street** Norfk
37 Q5 **Low Street** Thurr
64 H2 **Low Tharston** Norfk
101 P6 **Lowther** Cumb
101 P6 **Lowther Castle** Cumb
99 M8 **Lowthorpe** E R Yk
8 G4 **Lowton** Devon
18 G11 **Lowton** Somset
82 D5 **Lowton** Wigan
82 D5 **Lowton Common** Wigan
82 D5 **Lowton St Mary's** Wigan
134 C10 **Low Torry** Fife
87 J6 **Low Toynton** Lincs
91 L10 **Low Valley** Barns
94 G4 **Low Wood** Cumb
104 C9 **Low Worsall** N York
101 L10 **Low Wray** Cumb
18 B11 **Loxbeare** Devon
24 B3 **Loxhill** Surrey
17 L4 **Loxhore** Devon
17 L4 **Loxhore Cott** Devon
47 Q4 **Loxley** Warwks
71 K8 **Loxley Green** Staffs
46 D6 **Loxter** Herefs
19 L3 **Loxton** N Som
24 B4 **Loxwood** W Susx
165 P7 **Loyal Lodge** Highld
60 F3 **Lubenham** Leics
87 M11 **Lucasgate** Lincs
23 P2 **Lucas Green** Surrey
18 B6 **Luccombe** Somset
14 G11 **Luccombe Village** IoW
119 N4 **Lucker** Nthumb
5 P7 **Luckett** Cnwll
52 D5 **Lucking Street** Essex
32 F8 **Luckington** Wilts
135 L3 **Lucklawhill** Fife
32 F10 **Lucknam** Wilts
18 B7 **Luckwell Bridge** Somset
45 N2 **Lucton** Herefs
103 P8 **Lucy Cross** N York
168 c16 **Ludag** W Isls
93 N11 **Ludborough** Lincs
6 H8 **Ludbrook** Devon
41 M8 **Ludchurch** Pembks
90 C5 **Luddenden** Calder
90 C5 **Luddenden Foot** Calder
38 G9 **Luddenham Court** Kent
37 Q7 **Luddesdown** Kent
92 D7 **Luddington** N Linc
47 N4 **Luddington** Warwks
61 P4 **Luddington in the Brook** Nhants
86 G3 **Ludford** Lincs
57 J10 **Ludford** Shrops
49 J11 **Ludgershall** Bucks
21 Q4 **Ludgershall** Wilts
2 E7 **Ludgvan** Cnwll
77 M8 **Ludham** Norfk
57 J9 **Ludlow** Shrops
10 H2 **Ludney** Somset
20 H10 **Ludwell** Wilts
104 C2 **Ludworth** Dur
50 G5 **Luffenhall** Herts
5 N3 **Luffincott** Devon
128 D4 **Luffness** E Loth
115 L3 **Lugar** E Ayrs
128 F5 **Luggate Burn** E Loth
45 N2 **Lugg Green** Herefs
126 D3 **Luggiebank** N Lans
125 L7 **Lugton** E Ayrs
45 R6 **Lugwardine** Herefs
145 J2 **Luib** Highld
130 E5 **Luing** Ag & B
45 N6 **Lulham** Herefs
59 K2 **Lullington** Derbys
25 M10 **Lullington** E Susx
20 E4 **Lullington** Somset
31 P11 **Lulsgate Bottom** N Som
46 D3 **Lulsley** Worcs
12 D8 **Lulworth Camp** Dorset
90 C6 **Lumb** Calder
89 N6 **Lumb** Lancs
90 B6 **Lumbutts** Calder
91 M4 **Lumby** N York
125 Q3 **Lumloch** E Duns
150 F7 **Lumphanan** Abers
134 F9 **Lumphinnans** Fife
150 D3 **Lumsden** Abers
143 M7 **Lunan** Angus
142 H7 **Lunanhead** Angus
134 D2 **Luncarty** P & K
99 K11 **Lund** E R Yk
91 R4 **Lund** N York
142 D10 **Lundie** Angus
135 L7 **Lundin Links** Fife
135 L7 **Lundin Mill** Fife
16 A2 **Lundy** Devon
65 J3 **Lundy Green** Norfk
130 E6 **Lunga** Ag & B
169 r7 **Lunna** Shet
37 Q9 **Lunsford** Kent
26 B9 **Lunsford's Cross** E Susx
81 L4 **Lunt** Sefton
45 M3 **Luntley** Herefs
10 D3 **Luppitt** Devon
7 J8 **Lupridge** Devon
91 J7 **Lupset** Wakefd
95 M4 **Lupton** Cumb
23 P9 **Lurgashall** W Susx
18 B11 **Lurley** Devon
87 K7 **Lusby** Lincs
7 K7 **Luscombe** Devon
6 G8 **Luson** Devon
132 D9 **Luss** Ag & B
130 C10 **Lussagiven** Ag & B
152 D6 **Lusta** Highld
9 J8 **Lustleigh** Devon
45 P2 **Luston** Herefs
143 M4 **Luthermuir** Abers
135 J4 **Luthrie** Fife
58 D8 **Lutley** Dudley
9 M9 **Luton** Devon
10 B4 **Luton** Devon
50 C6 **Luton** Luton
38 C8 **Luton** Medway
50 D6 *Luton Airport* Luton
60 B4 **Lutterworth** Leics
6 F7 **Lutton** Devon
6 H6 **Lutton** Devon
74 H5 **Lutton** Lincs
61 P3 **Lutton** Nhants
18 C7 **Luxborough** Somset
4 H10 **Luxulyan** Cnwll
83 L4 **Luzley** Tamesd
167 M9 **Lybster** Highld
56 E7 **Lydbury North** Shrops
17 M4 **Lydcott** Devon
26 H7 **Lydd** Kent
27 J7 *Lydd Airport* Kent
27 N2 **Lydden** Kent
39 Q8 **Lydden** Kent
73 M11 **Lyddington** Rutlnd
18 F8 **Lydeard St Lawrence** Somset
23 K3 **Lyde Green** Hants
8 D7 **Lydford** Devon
19 Q8 **Lydford on Fosse** Somset
89 Q5 **Lydgate** Calder
90 B7 **Lydgate** Rochdl
56 E6 **Lydham** Shrops
33 L7 **Lydiard Green** Wilts
33 L7 **Lydiard Millicent** Wilts
33 M8 **Lydiard Tregoze** Swindn
81 M4 **Lydiate** Sefton
58 E9 **Lydiate Ash** Worcs
12 B2 **Lydlinch** Dorset
32 B4 **Lydney** Gloucs
41 L11 **Lydstep** Pembks
58 D8 **Lye** Dudley
19 N2 **Lye Cross** N Som
35 Q4 **Lye Green** Bucks
25 M4 **Lye Green** E Susx
59 J11 **Lye Green** Warwks
57 P10 **Lye Head** Worcs
20 F5 **Lye's Green** Wilts
34 C6 **Lyford** Oxon
27 K3 **Lymbridge Green** Kent
10 G6 **Lyme Regis** Dorset
27 L3 **Lyminge** Kent
13 P5 **Lymington** Hants
24 B10 **Lyminster** W Susx
82 E7 **Lymm** Warrtn
27 K4 **Lympne** Kent
19 K4 **Lympsham** Somset
9 N8 **Lympstone** Devon
17 N2 **Lynbridge** Devon
148 D7 **Lynchat** Highld
76 H10 **Lynch Green** Norfk
13 P3 **Lyndhurst** Hants
73 N10 **Lyndon** Rutlnd
58 H7 **Lyndon Green** Birm
117 J2 **Lyne** Border
36 B7 **Lyne** Surrey
69 M8 **Lyneal** Shrops
46 B8 **Lyne Down** Herefs
9 L9 **Lyneham** Devon
47 Q10 **Lyneham** Oxon
33 K9 **Lyneham** Wilts
33 K9 *Lyneham Airport* Wilts
111 K6 **Lyneholmford** Cumb
113 L2 **Lynemouth** Nthumb
151 K5 **Lyne of Skene** Abers
103 L5 **Lynesack** Dur
169 c7 **Lyness** Ork
76 F8 **Lyng** Norfk
19 K9 **Lyng** Somset
17 N2 **Lynmouth** Devon
58 G4 **Lynn** Staffs
70 D11 **Lynn** Wrekin
38 F9 **Lynsted** Kent
16 C10 **Lynstone** Cnwll
17 N2 **Lynton** Devon
11 P3 **Lyon's Gate** Dorset
45 L3 **Lyonshall** Herefs
12 F5 **Lytchett Matravers** Dorset
12 G6 **Lytchett Minster** Dorset
167 N4 **Lyth** Highld
88 D5 **Lytham** Lancs
88 C5 **Lytham St Anne's** Lancs
56 H3 **Lythbank** Shrops
105 M8 **Lythe** N York
167 J3 **Lythmore** Highld

M

3 K7 **Mabe Burnthouse** Cnwll
87 P4 **Mablethorpe** Lincs
83 K10 **Macclesfield** Ches E
83 K10 **Macclesfield Crematorium** Ches E
158 H5 **Macduff** Abers
120 D10 **Macharioch** Ag & B
30 H7 **Machen** Caerph
120 G5 **Machrie** N Ayrs
120 B7 **Machrihanish** Ag & B
136 b3 **Machrins** Ag & B
54 G4 **Machynlleth** Powys
28 F5 **Machynys** Carmth
71 Q7 **Mackworth** Derbys
128 C5 **Macmerry** E Loth
8 D6 **Maddaford** Devon
134 B3 **Madderty** P & K
21 L6 **Maddington** Wilts
126 G2 **Maddiston** Falk
15 Q4 **Madehurst** W Susx
70 D6 **Madeley** Staffs
57 M4 **Madeley** Wrekin
70 D5 **Madeley Heath** Staffs
10 C2 **Madford** Devon
62 E8 **Madingley** Cambs
45 N7 **Madley** Herefs
46 F5 **Madresfield** Worcs
2 D7 **Madron** Cnwll
78 H8 **Maenaddwyn** IoA
79 P11 **Maenan** Conwy
41 L5 **Maenclochog** Pembks
30 D9 **Maendy** V Glam
3 K8 **Maenporth** Cnwll
67 M6 **Maentwrog** Gwynd
42 G3 **Maen-y-groes** Cerdgn
16 C10 **Maer** Cnwll
70 D7 **Maer** Staffs
43 N9 **Maerdy** Carmth
30 C5 **Maerdy** Rhondd
69 K10 **Maesbrook** Shrops
69 K9 **Maesbury** Shrops
69 K9 **Maesbury Marsh** Shrops
31 J7 **Maes-glas** Newpt
41 P6 **Maesgwynne** Carmth
68 H2 **Maeshafn** Denbgs
42 G6 **Maesllyn** Cerdgn
44 E5 **Maesmynis** Powys
44 E5 **Maesmynis** Powys
29 N6 **Maesteg** Brdgnd
43 L11 **Maesybont** Carmth
30 G6 **Maesycwmmer** Caerph
51 M9 **Magdalen Laver** Essex
157 Q8 **Maggieknockater** Moray
51 L5 **Maggots End** Essex
25 P8 **Magham Down** E Susx
81 M4 **Maghull** Sefton
60 B4 **Magna Park** Leics
31 M7 **Magor** Mons
31 M7 *Magor Services* Mons
24 G3 **Maidenbower** W Susx
20 F7 **Maiden Bradley** Wilts
7 N5 **Maidencombe** Torbay
10 F5 **Maidenhayne** Devon
31 Q11 **Maiden Head** N Som
35 N8 **Maidenhead** W & M
113 J11 **Maiden Law** Dur
11 M5 **Maiden Newton** Dorset
114 D6 **Maidens** S Ayrs
35 P10 **Maiden's Green** Br For
87 K5 **Maidenwell** Lincs
41 J11 **Maiden Wells** Pembks
48 H4 **Maidford** Nhants
49 K7 **Maids Moreton** Bucks
38 C10 **Maidstone** Kent
38 D10 *Maidstone Services* Kent
60 F5 **Maidwell** Nhants
169 r9 **Mail** Shet
31 K7 **Maindee** Newpt
169 d6 **Mainland** Ork
169 r8 **Mainland** Shet
104 B4 **Mainsforth** Dur
143 J5 **Mains of Balhall** Angus
143 L3 **Mains of Balnakettle** Abers
157 L11 **Mains of Dalvey** Highld
143 N3 **Mains of Haulkerton** Abers
150 D2 **Mains of Lesmoir** Abers
143 J6 **Mains of Melgunds** Angus
109 K9 **Mainsriddle** D & G
56 D7 **Mainstone** Shrops
46 F10 **Maisemore** Gloucs
58 H9 **Major's Green** Worcs
72 B2 **Makeney** Derbys
7 J11 **Malborough** Devon
83 N8 **Malcoff** Derbys
36 E8 **Malden Rushett** Gt Lon
52 E10 **Maldon** Essex
96 D8 **Malham** N York
152 H5 **Maligar** Highld
145 L8 **Mallaig** Highld
145 L8 **Mallaigvaig** Highld
127 M4 **Malleny Mills** C Edin
51 L5 **Mallows Green** Essex
78 G11 **Malltraeth** IoA
55 K2 **Mallwyd** Gwynd
32 H7 **Malmesbury** Wilts
17 P2 **Malmsmead** Devon
69 N5 **Malpas** Ches W
3 L5 **Malpas** Cnwll
31 K6 **Malpas** Newpt
46 D10 **Malswick** Gloucs
87 K4 **Maltby** Lincs
84 H2 **Maltby** Rothm
104 E8 **Maltby** S on T
87 N4 **Maltby le Marsh** Lincs
52 G7 **Malting Green** Essex
26 F3 **Maltman's Hill** Kent
98 F6 **Malton** N York
46 E6 **Malvern Hills**
46 E5 **Malvern Link** Worcs
46 E6 **Malvern Wells** Worcs
57 M10 **Mamble** Worcs
31 K4 **Mamhilad** Mons
3 K9 **Manaccan** Cnwll
55 Q4 **Manafon** Powys
168 g9 **Manais** W Isls
9 J8 **Manaton** Devon
87 L3 **Manby** Lincs
59 M5 **Mancetter** Warwks
82 H5 **Manchester** Manch
82 H8 *Manchester Airport* Manch
81 L11 **Mancot** Flints
146 H7 **Mandally** Highld
129 L9 **Manderston House** Border
62 G3 **Manea** Cambs
58 H5 **Maney** Birm
103 P8 **Manfield** N York
11 K5 **Mangerton** Dorset
32 C9 **Mangotsfield** S Glos
50 D6 **Mangrove Green** Herts
2 H7 **Manhay** Cnwll
168 g9 **Manish** W Isls
90 B6 **Mankinholes** Calder
81 Q10 **Manley** Ches W
30 G4 **Manmoel** Caerph
136 B7 **Mannel** Ag & B
21 M3 **Manningford Bohune** Wilts
21 M3 **Manningford Bruce** Wilts
90 E3 **Manningham** C Brad
24 F5 **Manning's Heath** W Susx
13 J3 **Mannington** Dorset
53 K5 **Manningtree** Essex
151 N7 **Mannofield** C Aber
41 L11 **Manorbier** Pembks
41 K10 **Manorbier Newton** Pembks
43 N9 **Manordeilo** Carmth
118 C4 **Manorhill** Border
40 H3 **Manorowen** Pembks
37 K3 **Manor Park** Gt Lon
37 K3 **Manor Park Crematorium** Gt Lon
45 M6 **Mansell Gamage** Herefs
45 N5 **Mansell Lacy** Herefs
95 N4 **Mansergh** Cumb
115 M5 **Mansfield** E Ayrs
84 H8 **Mansfield** Notts
84 H9 **Mansfield & District Crematorium** Notts
84 H8 **Mansfield Woodhouse** Notts
94 F4 **Mansriggs** Cumb
20 F11 **Manston** Dorset
39 P8 **Manston** Kent
91 K4 **Manston** Leeds
12 G3 **Manswood** Dorset
73 N3 **Manthorpe** Lincs
73 R7 **Manthorpe** Lincs
92 F10 **Manton** N Linc
85 K5 **Manton** Notts
73 M10 **Manton** Rutlnd
33 N11 **Manton** Wilts
51 L5 **Manuden** Essex
51 M8 **Manwood Green** Essex
20 C9 **Maperton** Somset
85 M8 **Maplebeck** Notts
36 B2 **Maple Cross** Herts
35 J9 **Mapledurham** Oxon
23 J4 **Mapledurwell** Hants
24 E6 **Maplehurst** W Susx
37 N8 **Maplescombe** Kent
71 M5 **Mapleton** Derbys
37 L11 **Mapleton** Kent
72 C2 **Mapperley** Derbys
72 F2 **Mapperley Park** C Nott
11 L5 **Mapperton** Dorset
58 G11 **Mappleborough Green** Warwks
93 M2 **Mappleton** E R Yk
91 J8 **Mapplewell** Barns
12 B3 **Mappowder** Dorset

Miles Hope - Mynydd Isa 289

45 R2 Miles Hope Herefs
134 D10 Milesmark Fife
83 J5 Miles Platting Manch
38 F7 Mile Town Kent
118 H4 Milfield Nthumb
84 E11 Milford Derbys
16 C7 Milford Devon
55 P6 Milford Powys
70 H10 Milford Staffs
23 P6 Milford Surrey
40 H9 Milford Haven Pembks
13 N6 Milford on Sea Hants
31 Q3 Milkwall Gloucs
11 a1 Millais Jersey
23 M9 Milland W Susx
23 M9 Milland Marsh W Susx
90 C6 Mill Bank Calder
101 J5 Millbeck Cumb
159 P9 Millbreck Abers
23 M6 Millbridge Surrey
50 B3 Millbrook C Beds
14 C4 Millbrook C Sotn
6 C8 Millbrook Cnwll
11 b2 Millbrook Jersey
83 L5 Millbrook Tamesd
83 L7 Mill Brow Stockp
151 K6 Millbuie Abers
155 Q7 Millbuie Highld
7 L9 Millcombe Devon
77 L11 Mill Common Norfk
65 N5 Mill Common Suffk
26 D7 Millcorner E Susx
156 B3 Millcraig Highld
7 J6 Mill Cross Devon
71 L4 Milldale Staffs
35 L7 Mill End Bucks
62 D4 Mill End Cambs
32 D5 Millend Gloucs
50 H4 Mill End Herts
127 Q4 Millerhill Mdloth
83 P10 Miller's Dale Derbys
71 P4 Millers Green Derbys
51 N9 Miller's Green Essex
125 Q4 Millerston C Glas
89 P7 Millgate Lancs
63 K11 Mill Green Cambs
51 P10 Mill Green Essex
50 F8 Mill Green Herts
74 D6 Mill Green Lincs
64 G5 Mill Green Norfk
70 B9 Millgreen Shrops
58 G4 Mill Green Staffs
71 K10 Mill Green Staffs
52 G3 Mill Green Suffk
64 D10 Mill Green Suffk
64 G9 Mill Green Suffk
65 L9 Mill Green Suffk
45 K5 Millhalf Herefs
10 E4 Millhayes Devon
95 K6 Millhead Lancs
126 C7 Millheugh S Lans
25 P9 Mill Hill E Susx
36 F2 Mill Hill Gt Lon
124 B3 Millhouse Ag & B
101 L3 Millhouse Cumb
109 P3 Millhousebridge D & G
90 G10 Millhouse Green Barns
91 L10 Millhouses Barns
84 D4 Millhouses Sheff
125 L5 Milliken Park Rens
41 J8 Millin Cross Pembks
98 G10 Millington E R Yk
70 E8 Millmeece Staffs
95 L4 Millness Cumb
133 N4 Mill of Drummond P & K
132 D11 Mill of Haldane W Duns
94 D4 Millom Cumb
5 K2 Millook Cnwll
2 F7 Millpool Cnwll
5 J7 Millpool Cnwll
124 F7 Millport N Ayrs
95 J4 Mill Side Cumb
37 Q9 Mill Street Kent
76 F8 Mill Street Norfk
64 F7 Mill Street Suffk
84 D5 Millthorpe Derbys
95 P2 Millthrop Cumb
151 M7 Milltimber C Aber
149 P6 Milltown Abers
150 D4 Milltown Abers
5 J10 Milltown Cnwll
110 F5 Milltown D & G
84 E8 Milltown Derbys
17 K4 Milltown Devon
150 H7 Milltown of Campfield Abers
157 P9 Milltown of Edinvillie Moray
150 G7 Milltown of Learney Abers
134 E7 Milnathort P & K
125 P3 Milngavie E Duns
89 Q8 Milnrow Rochdl
95 K4 Milnthorpe Cumb
91 J7 Milnthorpe Wakefd
152 B8 Milovaig Highld
57 L10 Milson Shrops
38 F10 Milstead Kent
21 N5 Milston Wilts
74 B4 Milthorpe Lincs
48 G5 Milthorpe Nhants
70 G4 Milton C Stke
62 G8 Milton Cambs
111 L8 Milton Cumb
106 H7 Milton D & G
108 H6 Milton D & G
71 Q9 Milton Derbys
153 N9 Milton Highld
155 N11 Milton Highld
155 Q8 Milton Highld
156 D3 Milton Highld
167 P6 Milton Highld
125 K4 Milton Inver
37 Q6 Milton Kent
149 M4 Milton Moray
158 D5 Milton Moray
19 K3 Milton N Som
31 L7 Milton Newpt
85 M6 Milton Notts
34 E6 Milton Oxon
48 E7 Milton Oxon
141 Q5 Milton P & K
41 K10 Milton Pembks
19 N10 Milton Somset
132 G7 Milton Stirlg
125 L3 Milton W Duns
12 D4 Milton Abbas Dorset
5 Q6 Milton Abbot Devon
127 P5 Milton Bridge Mdloth
49 Q8 Milton Bryan C Beds
20 C7 Milton Clevedon Somset
6 D5 Milton Combe Devon
35 J4 Milton Common Oxon
16 F9 Milton Damerel Devon
32 D2 Milton End Gloucs
33 M4 Milton End Gloucs
61 M9 Milton Ernest Bed
69 N3 Milton Green Ches W
34 E6 Milton Hill Oxon
49 N7 Milton Keynes M Keyn
21 N2 Milton Lilbourne Wilts
60 F9 Milton Malsor Nhants
140 F10 Milton Morenish P & K
150 F7 Milton of Auchinhove Abers
135 J7 Milton of Balgonie Fife
132 E9 Milton of Buchanan Stirlg
126 B2 Milton of Campsie E Duns
156 B9 Milton of Leys Highld
151 M7 Milton of Murtle C Aber
150 B8 Milton of Tullich Abers
20 E9 Milton on Stour Dorset
38 F9 Milton Regis Kent
25 M10 Milton Street E Susx
47 Q11 Milton-under-Wychwood Oxon
18 F9 Milverton Somset
59 M11 Milverton Warwks
70 H8 Milwich Staffs
80 H10 Milwr Flints
131 K8 Minard Ag & B
12 G2 Minchington Dorset
32 G4 Minchinhampton Gloucs
118 F4 Mindrum Nthumb
18 C5 Minehead Somset
69 J4 Minera Wrexhm
33 K6 Minety Wilts
67 K7 Minffordd Gwynd
138 B4 Mingarrypark Highld
87 K8 Miningsby Lincs
5 M7 Minions Cnwll
114 F5 Minishant S Ayrs
55 K2 Minllyn Gwynd
107 M4 Minnigaff D & G
39 N8 Minnis Bay Kent
159 J5 Minnonie Abers
70 B2 Minshull Vernon Ches E
97 N8 Minskip N York
13 N2 Minstead Hants
23 N10 Minsted W Susx
38 G7 Minster Kent
39 P9 Minster Kent
56 F3 Minsterley Shrops
34 B2 Minster Lovell Oxon
46 E11 Minsterworth Gloucs
11 P4 Minterne Magna Dorset
11 P4 Minterne Parva Dorset
86 G6 Minting Lincs
159 N8 Mintlaw Abers
75 N7 Mintlyn Crematorium Norfk
117 R6 Minto Border
56 G6 Minton Shrops
41 K8 Minwear Pembks
59 J6 Minworth Birm
100 C7 Mirehouse Cumb
167 P4 Mireland Highld
90 G7 Mirfield Kirk
32 H3 Miserden Gloucs
30 D5 Miskin Rhondd
30 D8 Miskin Rhondd
85 L2 Misson Notts
60 C4 Misterton Leics
85 N2 Misterton Notts
11 K3 Misterton Somset
53 K5 Mistley Essex
53 K5 Mistley Heath Essex
36 G7 Mitcham Gt Lon
46 C11 Mitcheldean Gloucs
3 M3 Mitchell Cnwll
116 D11 Mitchellslacks D & G
31 N2 Mitchel Troy Mons
113 J3 Mitford Nthumb
3 J3 Mithian Cnwll
70 F11 Mitton Staffs
48 H8 Mixbury Oxon
90 D5 Mixenden Calder
64 E10 Moats Tye Suffk
82 G9 Mobberley Ches E
71 J6 Mobberley Staffs
45 M6 Moccas Herefs
79 Q9 Mochdre Conwy
55 P7 Mochdre Powys
107 K8 Mochrum D & G
13 L3 Mockbeggar Hants
26 B2 Mockbeggar Kent
100 E6 Mockerkin Cumb
6 H8 Modbury Devon
70 G7 Moddershall Staffs
79 J7 Moelfre IoA
68 G9 Moelfre Powys
67 J3 Moel Tryfan Gwynd
116 F9 Moffat D & G
61 P11 Moggerhanger C Beds
71 Q11 Moira Leics
38 H11 Molash Kent
144 G5 Mol-chlach Highld
68 H2 Mold Flints
90 F7 Moldgreen Kirk
51 N6 Molehill Green Essex
52 B7 Molehill Green Essex
92 H2 Molescroft E R Yk
112 H4 Molesden Nthumb
61 N5 Molesworth Cambs
17 Q6 Molland Devon
81 M10 Mollington Ches W
48 D5 Mollington Oxon
126 C3 Mollinsburn N Lans
43 K2 Monachty Cerdgn
143 P2 Mondynes Abers
65 J10 Monewden Suffk
134 D2 Moneydie P & K
35 N9 Moneyrow Green W & M
115 Q9 Moniaive D & G
142 H11 Monifieth Angus
142 H10 Monikie Angus
134 H5 Monimail Fife
41 M2 Monington Pembks
91 K9 Monk Bretton Barns
50 F11 Monken Hadley Gt Lon
91 N5 Monk Fryston N York
46 B6 Monkhide Herefs
110 F9 Monkhill Cumb
57 L6 Monkhopton Shrops
45 P3 Monkland Herefs
16 H7 Monkleigh Devon
29 P10 Monknash V Glam
8 E3 Monkokehampton Devon
113 M6 Monkseaton N Tyne
52 G2 Monks Eleigh Suffk
24 F5 Monk's Gate W Susx
82 H10 Monks Heath Ches E
22 H3 Monk Sherborne Hants
27 K3 Monks Horton Kent
18 E7 Monksilver Somset
59 Q8 Monks Kirby Warwks
65 J8 Monk Soham Suffk
58 H9 Monkspath Solhll
35 M4 Monks Risborough Bucks
87 M7 Monksthorpe Lincs
51 P5 Monk Street Essex
31 K4 Monkswood Mons
10 D4 Monkton Devon
39 N9 Monkton Kent
114 G2 Monkton S Ayrs
113 M8 Monkton S Tyne
29 P10 Monkton V Glam
20 E2 Monkton Combe BaNES
20 G7 Monkton Deverill Wilts
32 F11 Monkton Farleigh Wilts
19 J9 Monkton Heathfield Somset
12 H2 Monkton Up Wimborne Dorset
10 G5 Monkton Wyld Dorset
113 N9 Monkwearmouth Sundld
23 J8 Monkwood Hants
58 D5 Monmore Green Wolves
31 P2 Monmouth Mons
45 M6 Monnington on Wye Herefs
107 L9 Monreith D & G
19 N11 Montacute Somset
89 K8 Montcliffe Bolton
56 G2 Montford Shrops
69 M11 Montford Bridge Shrops
150 F4 Montgarrie Abers
56 C5 Montgomery Powys
82 G5 Monton Salfd
143 N6 Montrose Angus
10 b2 Mont Saint Guern
22 B6 Monxton Hants
83 Q11 Monyash Derbys
150 H4 Monymusk Abers
133 P2 Monzie P & K
126 B3 Moodiesburn N Lans
135 J4 Moonzie Fife
91 J3 Moor Allerton Leeds
11 J5 Moorbath Dorset
87 J8 Moorby Lincs
45 M3 Moorcot Herefs
12 G3 Moor Crichel Dorset
13 J6 Moordown Bmouth
82 C8 Moore Halton
49 Q10 Moor End C Beds
90 D5 Moor End Calder
17 M10 Moor End Devon
32 D4 Moorend Gloucs
88 D2 Moor End Lancs
91 Q3 Moor End N York
92 A7 Moorends Donc
22 E11 Moorgreen Hants
50 H5 Moor Green Herts
84 G11 Moorgreen Notts
84 D6 Moorhall Derbys
45 M5 Moorhampton Herefs
90 E3 Moorhead C Brad
90 G5 Moor Head Leeds
110 E10 Moorhouse Cumb
110 F9 Moorhouse Cumb
91 M8 Moorhouse Donc
85 N7 Moorhouse Notts
37 K10 Moorhouse Bank Surrey
19 K8 Moorland Somset
19 L7 Moorlinch Somset
97 R9 Moor Monkton N York
100 D8 Moor Row Cumb
110 D11 Moor Row Cumb
105 J8 Moorsholm R & Cl
20 E11 Moorside Dorset
88 E4 Moor Side Lancs
88 F3 Moor Side Lancs
90 G3 Moorside Leeds
87 J9 Moor Side Lincs
89 Q9 Moorside Oldham
27 K4 Moorstock Kent
58 E8 Moor Street Birm
38 D8 Moor Street Medway
5 L9 Moorswater Cnwll
91 M8 Moorthorpe Wakefd
6 E4 Moortown Devon
13 L4 Moortown Hants
14 D10 Moortown IoW
90 H3 Moortown Leeds
93 J11 Moortown Lincs
69 R11 Moortown Wrekin
162 H10 Morangie Highld
145 L9 Morar Highld
158 A5 Moray Crematorium Moray
61 P2 Morborne Cambs
9 J3 Morchard Bishop Devon
11 J6 Morcombelake Dorset
73 N10 Morcott Rutlnd
69 J9 Morda Shrops
12 F5 Morden Dorset
36 G7 Morden Gt Lon
45 R7 Mordiford Herefs
104 B5 Mordon Dur
56 E6 More Shrops
18 C9 Morebath Devon
118 E6 Morebattle Border
95 J8 Morecambe Lancs
33 M7 Moredon Swindn
161 J7 Morefield Highld
27 M4 Morehall Kent
7 K8 Moreleigh Devon
140 F10 Morenish P & K
100 C7 Moresby Parks Cumb
22 F9 Morestead Hants
12 D7 Moreton Dorset
51 M9 Moreton Essex
45 Q2 Moreton Herefs
35 J4 Moreton Oxon
70 D11 Moreton Staffs
71 L9 Moreton Staffs
81 K7 Moreton Wirral
69 Q10 Moreton Corbet Shrops
9 J7 Moretonhampstead Devon
47 P8 Moreton-in-Marsh Gloucs
46 B5 Moreton Jeffries Herefs
69 Q10 Moretonmill Shrops
48 B3 Moreton Morrell Warwks
45 Q5 Moreton on Lugg Herefs
48 B4 Moreton Paddox Warwks
48 G5 Moreton Pinkney Nhants
70 A8 Moreton Say Shrops
32 E3 Moreton Valence Gloucs
42 F4 Morfa Cerdgn
67 J7 Morfa Bychan Gwynd
66 G3 Morfa Dinlle Gwynd
29 N3 Morfa Glas Neath
66 D6 Morfa Nefyn Gwynd
30 F8 Morganstown Cardif
21 N10 Morgan's Vale Wilts
128 F5 Morham E Loth
54 E9 Moriah Cerdgn
102 B6 Morland Cumb
82 H8 Morley Ches E
72 B2 Morley Derbys
103 M5 Morley Dur
90 H5 Morley Leeds
82 H8 Morley Green Ches E
64 F2 Morley St Botolph Norfk
5 N7 Mornick Cnwll
127 N3 Morningside C Edin
126 E6 Morningside N Lans
65 J3 Morningthorpe Norfk
113 J3 Morpeth Nthumb
143 N5 Morphie Abers
71 L11 Morrey Staffs
71 J4 Morridge Side Staffs
29 J5 Morriston Swans
76 E3 Morston Norfk
16 H2 Mortehoe Devon
84 G3 Morthen Rothm
23 J2 Mortimer W Berk
35 J11 Mortimer Common W Berk
45 N2 Mortimer's Cross Herefs
22 H2 Mortimer West End Hants
36 F5 Mortlake Gt Lon
36 E5 Mortlake Crematorium Gt Lon
101 N3 Morton Cumb
110 G10 Morton Cumb
84 F8 Morton Derbys
14 H9 Morton IoW
74 A6 Morton Lincs
85 P2 Morton Lincs
85 M10 Morton Notts
69 J10 Morton Shrops
85 Q8 Morton Hall Lincs
127 P4 Mortonhall Crematorium C Edin
97 M2 Morton-on-Swale N York
76 G8 Morton on the Hill Norfk
103 N6 Morton Tinmouth Dur
2 C6 Morvah Cnwll
5 M10 Morval Cnwll
146 B3 Morvich Highld
57 M6 Morville Shrops
57 M6 Morville Heath Shrops
6 C5 Morwellham Quay Devon
16 C8 Morwenstow Cnwll
84 F4 Mosborough Sheff
125 M9 Moscow E Ayrs
57 P6 Mose Shrops
101 L4 Mosedale Cumb
58 G8 Moseley Birm
58 D5 Moseley Wolves
46 F3 Moseley Worcs
89 L9 Moses Gate Bolton
136 B7 Moss Ag & B
91 P8 Moss Donc
69 K4 Moss Wrexhm
150 D4 Mossat Abers
169 r6 Mossbank Shet
81 Q5 Moss Bank St Hel
100 C5 Mossbay Cumb
114 H3 Mossblown S Ayrs
82 F7 Mossbrow Traffd
118 C7 Mossburnford Border
108 E6 Mossdale D & G
115 J7 Mossdale E Ayrs
88 E2 Moss Edge Lancs
82 E9 Moss End Ches E
126 C5 Mossend N Lans
100 F5 Mosser Mains Cumb
70 F2 Mossley Ches E
83 L4 Mossley Tamesd
117 M11 Mosspaul Hotel Border
110 C10 Moss Side Cumb
156 F6 Moss-side Highld
88 D4 Moss Side Lancs
81 M4 Moss Side Sefton
157 Q6 Mosstodloch Moray
107 P7 Mossyard D & G
88 G8 Mossy Lea Lancs
11 K3 Mosterton Dorset
83 J4 Moston Manch
69 Q9 Moston Shrops
70 C2 Moston Green Ches E
80 H8 Mostyn Flints
20 G9 Motcombe Dorset
6 G9 Mothecombe Devon
101 M5 Motherby Cumb
126 C6 Motherwell N Lans
36 F7 Motspur Park Gt Lon
37 K6 Mottingham Gt Lon
22 B9 Mottisfont Hants
14 D10 Mottistone IoW
83 L5 Mottram in Longdendale Tamesd
83 J9 Mottram St Andrew Ches E
10 b2 Mouilpied Guern
81 Q10 Mouldsworth Ches W
141 M6 Moulin P & K
24 H9 Moulsecoomb Br & H
34 G8 Moulsford Oxon
49 P6 Moulsoe M Keyn
156 A3 Moultavie Highld
82 E11 Moulton Ches W
74 F6 Moulton Lincs
103 P10 Moulton N York
60 G7 Moulton Nhants
63 L8 Moulton Suffk
30 E11 Moulton V Glam
74 E7 Moulton Chapel Lincs
77 M10 Moulton St Mary Norfk
74 F5 Moulton Seas End Lincs
4 B10 Mount Cnwll
5 J8 Mount Cnwll
90 D7 Mount Kirk
90 D4 Mountain C Brad
30 D5 Mountain Ash Rhondd
127 M8 Mountain Cross Border
39 J11 Mountain Street Kent
3 J5 Mount Ambrose Cnwll
52 F5 Mount Bures Essex
26 B7 Mountfield E Susx
155 Q5 Mountgerald House Highld
3 J4 Mount Hawke Cnwll
2 H10 Mount Hermon Cnwll
4 D9 Mountjoy Cnwll
127 P6 Mount Lothian Mdloth
51 P11 Mountnessing Essex
31 P6 Mounton Mons
70 E3 Mount Pleasant Ches E
71 P11 Mount Pleasant Derbys
84 D11 Mount Pleasant Derbys
103 Q4 Mount Pleasant Dur
93 N3 Mount Pleasant E R Yk
25 K7 Mount Pleasant E Susx
64 D3 Mount Pleasant Norfk
63 M11 Mount Pleasant Suffk
47 K2 Mount Pleasant Worcs
113 J10 Mountsett Crematorium Dur
72 F8 Mountsorrel Leics
21 K10 Mount Sorrel Wilts
90 D5 Mount Tabor Calder
23 P6 Mousehill Surrey
2 D8 Mousehole Cnwll
109 N6 Mouswald D & G
70 F3 Mow Cop Ches E
118 F6 Mowhaugh Border
72 F9 Mowmacre Hill C Leic
60 D3 Mowsley Leics
147 L11 Moy Highld
156 D11 Moy Highld
145 Q4 Moyle Highld
41 M2 Moylegrove Pembks
120 C3 Muasdale Ag & B
151 N9 Muchalls Abers
45 Q8 Much Birch Herefs
46 B5 Much Cowarne Herefs
45 P8 Much Dewchurch Herefs
19 M10 Muchelney Somset
19 M10 Muchelney Ham Somset
51 K7 Much Hadham Herts
88 F6 Much Hoole Lancs
88 F6 Much Hoole Town Lancs
5 L10 Muchlarnick Cnwll
46 C8 Much Marcle Herefs
57 L5 Much Wenlock Shrops
144 F12 Muck Highld
37 Q4 Mucking Thurr
37 Q5 Muckingford Thurr
76 G3 Muckleburgh Collection Norfk
11 N6 Muckleford Dorset
70 C7 Mucklestone Staffs
57 L5 Muckley Shrops
87 L4 Muckton Lincs
17 K4 Muddiford Devon
25 M8 Muddles Green E Susx
13 L6 Mudeford Dorset
19 Q11 Mudford Somset
19 Q11 Mudford Sock Somset
19 N5 Mudgley Somset
38 H7 Mud Row Kent
125 P2 Mugdock Stirlg
152 G10 Mugeary Highld
71 P6 Mugginton Derbys
71 P6 Muggintonlane End Derbys
112 F11 Muggleswick Dur
158 H7 Muirden Abers
143 K10 Muirdrum Angus
158 G8 Muiresk Abers
142 E11 Muirhead Angus
134 H6 Muirhead Fife
126 B4 Muirhead N Lans
115 N2 Muirkirk E Ayrs
133 L11 Muirmill Stirlg
150 F5 Muir of Fowlis Abers
157 M6 Muir of Miltonduff Moray
155 P7 Muir of Ord Highld
146 E11 Muirshearlich Highld
159 N10 Muirtack Abers
133 Q5 Muirton P & K
155 N7 Muirton Mains Highld
142 B9 Muirton of Ardblair P & K
102 H11 Muker N York
76 H11 Mulbarton Norfk
157 R7 Mulben Moray
2 D7 Mulfra Cnwll
137 Q9 Mull Ag & B
17 J3 Mullacott Cross Devon
2 H10 Mullion Cnwll
2 H10 Mullion Cove Cnwll
87 P6 Mumby Lincs
46 B4 Munderfield Row Herefs
46 C4 Munderfield Stocks Herefs
77 L4 Mundesley Norfk
63 P2 Mundford Norfk
65 L2 Mundham Norfk
52 E11 Mundon Hill Essex
26 F2 Mundy Bois Kent
101 L4 Mungrisdale Cumb
156 A7 Munlochy Highld
124 H8 Munnoch N Ayrs
46 C6 Munsley Herefs
57 J7 Munslow Shrops
8 G7 Murchington Devon
47 L6 Murcot Worcs
48 G11 Murcott Oxon
33 J6 Murcott Wilts
167 L3 Murkle Highld
146 C9 Murlaggan Highld
23 K3 Murrell Green Hants
142 H10 Murroes Angus
74 G9 Murrow Cambs
49 M9 Mursley Bucks
38 F9 Murston Kent
142 H6 Murthill Angus
141 R10 Murthly P & K
98 C10 Murton C York
102 D6 Murton Cumb
113 N11 Murton Dur
113 M6 Murton N Tyne
129 P10 Murton Nthumb
10 F6 Musbury Devon
98 D5 Muscoates N York
127 Q3 Musselburgh E Loth
73 L3 Muston Leics
99 M5 Muston N York
58 C10 Mustow Green Worcs
36 G3 Muswell Hill Gt Lon
108 E11 Mutehill D & G
65 P4 Mutford Suffk
133 P4 Muthill P & K
9 P3 Mutterton Devon
57 N2 Muxton Wrekin
167 L6 Mybster Highld
43 Q8 Myddfai Carmth
69 N10 Myddle Shrops
43 J3 Mydroilyn Cerdgn
88 F3 Myerscough Lancs
3 L6 Mylor Cnwll
3 L6 Mylor Bridge Cnwll
41 M4 Mynachlog ddu Pembks
80 H10 Mynydd-llan Flints
56 F7 Myndtown Shrops
31 N6 Mynydd-bach Mons
29 J5 Mynydd-Bach Swans
54 G9 Mynydd Buch Cerdgn
28 D3 Mynyddgarreg Carmth
69 J2 Mynydd Isa Flints

290 Mynydd Llandygai - Newton Valence

79 L11 Mynydd Llandygai Gwynd
66 E8 Mynytho Gwynd
151 J8 Myrebird Abers
118 A11 Myredykes Border
23 N3 Mytchett Surrey
90 B5 Mytholm Calder
90 C5 Mytholmroyd Calder
88 D4 Mythop Lancs
97 P7 Myton-on-Swale N York

N

160 C10 Naast Highld
89 J5 Nab's Head Lancs
168 f8 Na Buirgh W Isls
98 B11 Naburn C York
90 E3 Nab Wood Crematorium C Brad
27 J3 Naccolt Kent
39 L11 Nackington Kent
53 M3 Nacton Suffk
99 M9 Nafferton E R Yk
32 G5 Nag's Head Gloucs
46 B11 Nailbridge Gloucs
18 H9 Nailsbourne Somset
31 N10 Nailsea N Som
72 C9 Nailstone Leics
32 F5 Nailsworth Gloucs
156 F6 Nairn Highld
36 F11 Nalderswood Surrey
2 G7 Nancegollan Cnwll
2 D6 Nancledra Cnwll
66 D8 Nanhoron Gwynd
80 H11 Nannerch Flints
72 E7 Nanpantan Leics
4 F10 Nanpean Cnwll
2 B8 Nanquidno Cnwll
4 G8 Nanstallon Cnwll
30 D2 Nant-ddu Powys
42 G3 Nanternis Cerdgn
43 J10 Nantgaredig Carmth
30 F7 Nantgarw Rhondd
55 M11 Nant-glas Powys
68 D2 Nantglyn Denbgs
55 M9 Nantgwyn Powys
67 L4 Nant Gwynant Gwynd
67 J4 Nantile Gwynd
69 J10 Nantmawr Shrops
55 N11 Nantmel Powys
67 L5 Nantmor Gwynd
67 L3 Nant Peris Gwynd
70 B4 Nantwich Ches E
30 F2 Nant-y-Bwch Blae G
43 J11 Nant-y-caws Carmth
31 K3 Nant-y-derry Mons
29 M6 Nantyffyllon Brdgnd
30 G2 Nantyglo Blae G
68 H9 Nant-y-gollen Shrops
29 P6 Nant-y-moel Brdgnd
79 M10 Nant-y-pandy Conwy
35 M5 Naphill Bucks
46 G5 Napleton Worcs
96 C10 Nappa N York
48 E2 Napton on the Hill Warwks
41 M8 Narberth Pembks
72 E11 Narborough Leics
75 P8 Narborough Norfk
5 N10 Narkurs Cnwll
66 H5 Nasareth Gwynd
60 E5 Naseby Nhants
49 L8 Nash Bucks
37 K8 Nash Gt Lon
45 L2 Nash Herefs
31 K8 Nash Newpt
57 L10 Nash Shrops
57 P8 Nash End Worcs
35 M3 Nash Lee Bucks
23 J5 Nash's Green Hants
37 P7 Nash Street Kent
73 R11 Nassington Nhants
32 E3 Nastend Gloucs
51 J6 Nasty Herts
102 E9 Nateby Cumb
88 F2 Nateby Lancs
59 J2 National Memorial Arboretum Staffs
72 F9 National Space Science Centre C Leic
95 L3 Natland Cumb
52 H2 Naughton Suffk
47 M10 Naunton Gloucs
46 G7 Naunton Worcs
47 J4 Naunton Beauchamp Worcs
86 C9 Navenby Lincs
51 M11 Navestock Essex
51 N11 Navestock Side Essex
163 N3 Navidale House Hotel Highld
156 D5 Navity Highld
98 D4 Nawton N York
52 G5 Nayland Suffk
51 K9 Nazeing Essex
51 K9 Nazeing Gate Essex
13 L5 Neacroft Hants
59 M8 Neal's Green Warwks
169 s8 Neap Shet
71 K5 Near Cotton Staffs
101 L11 Near Sawrey Cumb
36 F3 Neasden Gt Lon
104 B8 Neasham Darltn
29 L5 Neath Neath
23 K6 Neatham Hants
77 L7 Neatishead Norfk
54 C11 Nebo Cerdgn
67 Q3 Nebo Conwy
66 H4 Nebo Gwynd
78 H6 Nebo IoA
76 B10 Necton Norfk
164 D10 Nedd Highld
113 K4 Nedderton Nthumb
52 G2 Nedging Suffk
52 H2 Nedging Tye Suffk
65 J5 Needham Norfk
64 F10 Needham Market Suffk
63 M7 Needham Street Suffk
62 D6 Needingworth Cambs
57 M9 Neen Savage Shrops
57 M10 Neen Sollars Shrops
57 L7 Neenton Shrops
66 E6 Nefyn Gwynd
125 M6 Neilston E Rens
30 F5 Nelson Caerph
89 P3 Nelson Lancs
116 B2 Nemphlar S Lans
19 P2 Nempnett Thrubwell BaNES
111 Q11 Nenthall Cumb
102 E2 Nenthead Cumb
118 C3 Nenthorn Border
9 J5 Neopardy Devon
24 F7 Nep Town W Susx
68 H2 Nercwys Flints
122 B8 Nereabolls Ag & B
125 Q6 Nerston S Lans
119 J4 Nesbit Nthumb
96 G11 Nesfield N York
81 L9 Ness Ches W
81 L9 Ness Botanic Gardens Ches W
69 L11 Nesscliffe Shrops
81 K9 Neston Ches W
32 G11 Neston Wilts
57 L6 Netchwood Shrops
82 H9 Nether Alderley Ches E
21 M5 Netheravon Wilts
117 Q2 Nether Blainslie Border
159 J6 Netherbrae Abers
72 H5 Nether Broughton Leics
126 D8 Netherburn S Lans
11 K5 Netherbury Dorset
110 G6 Netherby Cumb
97 M11 Netherby N York
11 P5 Nether Cerne Dorset
109 P3 Nethercleuch D & G
19 Q11 Nether Compton Dorset
60 B8 Nethercote Warwks
5 P2 Nethercott Devon
16 H4 Nethercott Devon
151 L3 Nether Crimond Abers
157 R5 Nether Dallachy Moray
31 Q4 Netherend Gloucs
9 M4 Nether Exe Devon
26 B8 Netherfield E Susx
72 F7 Netherfield Leics
72 G2 Netherfield Notts
116 C8 Nether Fingland S Lans
92 C11 Nethergate N Linc
76 F6 Nethergate Norfk
21 M9 Netherhampton Wilts
84 F5 Nether Handley Derbys
142 F9 Nether Handwick Angus
91 L11 Nether Haugh Rothm
11 J3 Netherhay Dorset
85 M5 Nether Headon Notts
84 E10 Nether Heage Derbys
60 E9 Nether Heyford Nhants
116 E8 Nether Howcleugh S Lans
95 L7 Nether Kellet Lancs
159 Q9 Nether Kinmundy Abers
71 L8 Netherland Green Staffs
84 H6 Nether Langwith Notts
108 F12 Netherlaw D & G
151 M9 Netherley Abers
109 M3 Nethermill D & G
159 M9 Nethermuir Abers
36 G9 Netherne-on-the-Hill Surrey
90 E7 Netheroyd Hill Kirk
84 B5 Nether Padley Derbys
125 N6 Netherplace E Rens
98 B10 Nether Poppleton C York
101 K3 Nether Row Cumb
59 L2 Netherseal Derbys
97 Q2 Nether Silton N York
56 D10 Nether Skyborry Shrops
18 G7 Nether Stowey Somset
51 N8 Nether Street Essex
21 J2 Netherstreet Wilts
90 E9 Netherthong Kirk
84 F6 Netherthorpe Derbys
143 J6 Netherton Angus
7 M4 Netherton Devon
58 D7 Netherton Dudley
22 C3 Netherton Hants
45 Q9 Netherton Herefs
90 E8 Netherton Kirk
126 D7 Netherton N Lans
119 J9 Netherton Nthumb
34 D5 Netherton Oxon
142 A7 Netherton P & K
57 N8 Netherton Shrops
125 P2 Netherton Stirlg
90 H7 Netherton Wakefd
47 J6 Netherton Worcs
100 C9 Nethertown Cumb
167 Q1 Nethertown Highld
89 L3 Nethertown Lancs
71 L11 Nethertown Staffs
116 G2 Netherurd Border
22 B7 Nether Wallop Hants
100 F10 Nether Wasdale Cumb
110 G11 Nether Welton Cumb
47 P10 Nether Westcote Gloucs
59 K6 Nether Whitacre Warwks
116 A7 Nether Whitecleuch S Lans
35 K2 Nether Winchendon Bucks
112 G2 Netherwitton Nthumb
149 J3 Nethy Bridge Highld
14 E5 Netley Hants
13 P2 Netley Marsh Hants
35 J7 Nettlebed Oxon
20 B5 Nettlebridge Somset
11 L5 Nettlecombe Dorset
14 F11 Nettlecombe IoW
50 B8 Nettleden Herts
86 D5 Nettleham Lincs
37 Q10 Nettlestead Kent
37 Q10 Nettlestead Green Kent
14 H8 Nettlestone IoW
113 L11 Nettlesworth Dur
93 K10 Nettleton Lincs
32 F9 Nettleton Wilts
32 F9 Nettleton Shrub Wilts
6 F9 Netton Devon
21 M7 Netton Wilts
43 P10 Neuadd Carmth
55 L9 Neuadd-ddu Powys
38 C3 Nevendon Essex
41 L2 Nevern Pembks
60 H2 Nevill Holt Leics
109 L7 New Abbey D & G
159 L5 New Aberdour Abers
37 J8 New Addington Gt Lon
97 J11 Newall Leeds
22 G8 New Alresford Hants
142 C8 New Alyth P & K
74 D10 Newark C Pete
169 g2 Newark Ork
85 N10 Newark-on-Trent Notts
92 H2 New Arram E R Yk
126 D6 Newarthill N Lans
37 P7 New Ash Green Kent
85 P10 New Balderton Notts
27 L3 Newbarn Kent
37 P7 New Barn Kent
50 G11 New Barnet Gt Lon
61 J8 New Barton Nhants
127 Q4 Newbattle Mdloth
119 L6 New Bewick Nthumb
110 C7 Newbie D & G
94 B2 Newbiggin Cumb
94 F7 Newbiggin Cumb
101 N5 Newbiggin Cumb
102 B5 Newbiggin Cumb
111 L11 Newbiggin Cumb
102 H5 Newbiggin Dur
112 H11 Newbiggin Dur
96 E2 Newbiggin N York
96 F3 Newbiggin N York
113 M3 Newbiggin-by-the-Sea Nthumb
142 D9 Newbigging Angus
142 G10 Newbigging Angus
142 H10 Newbigging Angus
127 J8 Newbigging S Lans
102 D10 Newbiggin-on-Lune Cumb
59 Q9 New Bilton Warwks
84 E6 Newbold Derbys
72 C7 Newbold Leics
59 Q9 Newbold on Avon Warwks
47 P5 Newbold on Stour Warwks
47 Q3 Newbold Pacey Warwks
59 Q8 Newbold Revel Warwks
72 C10 Newbold Verdon Leics
87 K9 New Bolingbroke Lincs
74 D9 Newborough C Pete
78 G11 Newborough IoA
71 L9 Newborough Staffs
48 F7 Newbottle Nhants
113 M10 Newbottle Sundld
86 C6 New Boultham Lincs
53 N3 Newbourne Suffk
49 M6 New Bradwell M Keyn
84 E6 New Brampton Derbys
103 P2 New Brancepeth Dur
127 L3 Newbridge C Edin
30 H5 Newbridge Caerph
43 K3 Newbridge Cerdgn
2 C7 Newbridge Cnwll
3 K5 Newbridge Cnwll
109 K5 Newbridge D & G
21 Q11 Newbridge Hants
14 D9 Newbridge IoW
98 G3 New Bridge N York
34 D4 Newbridge Oxon
69 J6 Newbridge Wrexhm
46 F7 Newbridge Green Worcs
31 L6 Newbridge-on-Usk Mons
44 E3 Newbridge on Wye Powys
81 K11 New Brighton Flints
81 L6 New Brighton Wirral
84 G10 New Brinsley Notts
105 J6 New Brotton R & Cl
112 C7 Newbrough Nthumb
69 K4 New Broughton Wrexhm
64 F3 New Buckenham Norfk
9 J4 Newbuildings Devon
151 P2 Newburgh Abers
159 N6 Newburgh Abers
134 G4 Newburgh Fife
88 F8 Newburgh Lancs
98 A5 Newburgh Priory N York
113 J7 Newburn N u Ty
82 F4 New Bury Bolton
20 C5 Newbury Somset
34 E11 Newbury W Berk
20 F6 Newbury Wilts
37 K3 Newbury Park Gt Lon
101 Q6 Newby Cumb
96 B11 Newby Lancs
95 Q7 Newby N York
99 L2 Newby N York
104 F8 Newby N York
94 H3 Newby Bridge Cumb
110 G10 Newby Cross Cumb
111 J9 Newby East Cumb
101 Q6 Newby Head Cumb
159 K7 New Byth Abers
110 G10 Newby West Cumb
97 N3 Newby Wiske N York
45 N11 Newcastle Mons
56 D8 Newcastle Shrops
113 J6 Newcastle Airport Nthumb
42 F6 Newcastle Emlyn Carmth
111 J3 Newcastleton Border
70 E5 Newcastle-under-Lyme Staffs
113 K8 Newcastle upon Tyne N u Ty
41 P3 Newchapel Pembks
70 F4 Newchapel Staffs
25 J2 Newchapel Surrey
30 G2 Newchurch Blae G
45 M4 Newchurch Herefs
14 G9 Newchurch IoW
27 J5 Newchurch Kent
31 N5 Newchurch Mons
45 J4 Newchurch Powys
71 L10 Newchurch Staffs
89 N3 Newchurch in Pendle Lancs
76 H9 New Costessey Norfk
109 P11 New Cowper Cumb
127 Q3 Newcraighall C Edin
91 K7 New Crofton Wakefd
54 E9 New Cross Cerdgn
37 J5 New Cross Gt Lon
19 M11 New Cross Somset
115 M5 New Cumnock E Ayrs
26 D8 New Cut E Susx
159 L8 New Deer Abers
113 L5 New Delaval Nthumb
90 B9 New Delph Oldham
36 B4 New Denham Bucks
24 E2 Newdigate Surrey
60 F8 New Duston Nhants
98 C9 New Earswick C York
84 G11 New Eastwood Notts
91 N11 New Edlington Donc
157 N5 New Elgin Moray
93 L3 New Ellerby E R Yk
35 N10 Newell Green Br For
37 K6 New Eltham Gt Lon
47 L2 New End Worcs
26 D6 Newenden Kent
74 C10 New England C Pete
52 B3 New England Essex
46 D9 Newent Gloucs
90 H4 New Farnley Leeds
81 L7 New Ferry Wirral
103 P4 Newfield Dur
113 K10 Newfield Dur
156 D2 Newfield Highld
74 C11 New Fletton C Pete
13 N3 New Forest National Park
22 G4 Newfound Hants
91 M5 New Fryston Wakefd
40 G6 Newgale Pembks
108 D5 New Galloway D & G
76 E3 Newgate Norfk
50 H9 Newgate Street Herts
135 L6 New Gilston Fife
2 b1 New Grimsby IoS
69 R5 Newhall Ches E
71 P10 Newhall Derbys
119 N5 Newham Nthumb
113 M5 New Hartley Nthumb
127 P2 Newhaven C Edin
71 M2 Newhaven Derbys
25 K10 Newhaven E Susx
36 C8 New Haw Surrey
41 M10 New Hedges Pembks
113 M10 New Herrington Sundld
89 Q8 Newhey Rochdl
76 B4 New Holkham Norfk
93 J6 New Holland N Linc
105 N8 Newholm N York
84 G7 New Houghton Derbys
75 Q5 New Houghton Norfk
126 D5 Newhouse N Lans
96 B6 New Houses N York
82 C4 New Houses Wigan
95 M2 New Hutton Cumb
38 B10 New Hythe Kent
25 K6 Newick E Susx
27 K4 Newingreen Kent
27 L4 Newington Kent
38 E9 Newington Kent
34 H5 Newington Oxon
56 G8 Newington Shrops
32 F6 Newington Bagpath Gloucs
43 J7 New Inn Carmth
31 K5 New Inn Torfn
56 D9 New Invention Shrops
77 J10 New Lakenham Norfk
116 B2 New Lanark S Lans
93 J4 Newland C KuH
94 G5 Newland Cumb
92 D5 Newland E R Yk
31 Q3 Newland Gloucs
92 A6 Newland N York
34 C3 Newland Oxon
17 Q4 Newland Somset
46 E5 Newland Worcs
128 B7 Newlandrig Mdloth
111 K2 Newlands Border
101 K3 Newlands Cumb
112 G9 Newlands Nthumb
157 P7 Newlands of Dundurcas Moray
88 E8 New Lane Lancs
82 D6 New Lane End Warrtn
110 G4 New Langholm D & G
87 M9 New Leake Lincs
159 N7 New Leeds Abers
91 K9 New Lodge Barns
88 G5 New Longton Lancs
106 G5 New Luce D & G
2 D8 Newlyn Cnwll
4 C10 Newlyn East Cnwll
151 M4 Newmachar Abers
126 E6 Newmains N Lans
36 F7 New Malden Gt Lon
51 M8 Newman's End Essex
52 E3 Newman's Green Suffk
63 K8 Newmarket Suffk
168 j4 Newmarket W Isls
104 H6 New Marske R & Cl
34 F3 New Marston Oxon
69 K8 New Marton Shrops
151 K11 New Mill Abers
117 P8 Newmill Border
2 D7 New Mill Cnwll
35 P2 New Mill Herts
90 F9 New Mill Kirk
158 B7 Newmill Moray
91 J7 Newmillerdam Wakefd
142 G5 Newmill of Inshewan Angus
127 M4 Newmills C Edin
3 M3 New Mills Cnwll
83 M7 New Mills Derbys
134 C10 Newmills Fife
31 P3 Newmills Mons
55 P4 New Mills Powys
142 A11 Newmiln P & K
125 N10 Newmilns E Ayrs
13 M5 New Milton Hants
53 K5 New Mistley Essex
41 L5 New Moat Pembks
69 L8 Newnes Shrops
51 Q9 Newney Green Essex
32 C2 Newnham Gloucs
23 K4 Newnham Hants
50 F3 Newnham Herts
38 G10 Newnham Kent
60 C9 Newnham Nhants
57 L11 Newnham Worcs
85 L7 New Ollerton Notts
58 G6 New Oscott Birm
159 L6 New Pitsligo Abers
4 E6 New Polzeath Cnwll
5 N4 Newport Cnwll
12 E5 Newport Dorset
92 E4 Newport E R Yk
51 M4 Newport Essex
32 D5 Newport Gloucs
163 Q2 Newport Highld
14 F9 Newport IoW
31 K7 Newport Newpt
77 Q8 Newport Norfk
41 L3 Newport Pembks
70 C11 Newport Wrekin
135 L2 Newport-on-Tay Fife
49 N6 Newport Pagnell M Keyn
49 N6 Newport Pagnell Services M Keyn
24 C5 Newpound Common W Susx
114 F3 New Prestwick S Ayrs
42 G3 New Quay Cerdgn
4 C9 Newquay Cnwll
52 H7 New Quay Essex
4 D9 Newquay Airport Cnwll
77 K9 New Rackheath Norfk
45 J2 New Radnor Powys
101 N3 New Rent Cumb
112 G9 New Ridley Nthumb
90 B2 New Road Side N York
27 J7 New Romney Kent
91 Q11 New Rossington Donc
54 G10 New Row Cerdgn
89 J3 New Row Lancs
133 P9 New Sauchie Clacks
82 H11 Newsbank Ches E
158 H11 Newseat Abers
88 G3 Newsham Lancs
97 N4 Newsham N York
103 M8 Newsham N York
113 M5 Newsham Nthumb
91 K7 New Sharlston Wakefd
92 B5 Newsholme E R Yk
96 B10 Newsholme Lancs
119 N4 New Shoreston Nthumb
113 N10 New Silksworth Sundld
105 J7 New Skelton R & Cl
90 F8 Newsome Kirk
73 N3 New Somerby Lincs
36 G2 New Southgate Crematorium Gt Lon
88 H9 New Springs Wigan
117 R4 Newstead Border
84 H10 Newstead Notts
119 N5 Newstead Nthumb
126 D6 New Stevenston N Lans
45 L3 New Street Herefs
72 C7 New Swannington Leics
91 M4 Newthorpe N York
84 G11 Newthorpe Notts
38 C4 New Thundersley Essex
24 G8 Newtimber W Susx
86 D3 Newtoft Lincs
131 L8 Newton Ag & B
118 B6 Newton Border
29 M9 Newton Brdgnd
50 F2 Newton C Beds
62 F11 Newton Cambs
74 H8 Newton Cambs
30 H9 Newton Cardif
69 P3 Newton Ches W
81 N11 Newton Ches W
82 B9 Newton Ches W
94 E6 Newton Cumb
84 F9 Newton Derbys
45 L8 Newton Herefs
45 Q4 Newton Herefs
56 F11 Newton Herefs
155 Q7 Newton Highld
156 C8 Newton Highld
156 D4 Newton Highld
167 P7 Newton Highld
88 C3 Newton Lancs
95 M6 Newton Lancs
73 Q3 Newton Lincs
127 Q4 Newton Mdloth
157 M5 Newton Moray
157 Q5 Newton Moray
98 H6 Newton N York
61 J4 Newton Nhants
76 A8 Newton Norfk
72 H2 Newton Notts
112 F8 Newton Nthumb
118 H9 Newton Nthumb
116 C4 Newton S Lans
126 B5 Newton S Lans
58 F6 Newton Sandw
69 M8 Newton Shrops
18 F7 Newton Somset
71 J9 Newton Staffs
52 F3 Newton Suffk
127 K2 Newton W Loth
60 B5 Newton Warwks
21 P10 Newton Wilts
7 M4 Newton Abbot Devon
110 D9 Newton Arlosh Cumb
103 Q6 Newton Aycliffe Dur
104 E5 Newton Bewley Hartpl
49 P4 Newton Blossomville M Keyn
61 L7 Newton Bromswold Nhants
72 B9 Newton Burgoland Leics
119 P5 Newton-by-the-Sea Nthumb
86 D3 Newton by Toft Lincs
5 N8 Newton Ferrers Cnwll
6 F9 Newton Ferrers Devon
168 d10 Newton Ferry W Isls
65 J2 Newton Flotman Norfk
127 Q5 Newtongrange Mdloth
31 P6 Newton Green Mons
72 G11 Newton Harcourt Leics
83 J4 Newton Heath Manch
151 N9 Newtonhill Abers
91 J6 Newton Hill Wakefd
95 P10 Newton-in-Bowland Lancs
91 M2 Newton Kyme N York
97 K3 Newton-le-Willows N York
82 C5 Newton-le-Willows St Hel
127 Q5 Newtonloan Mdloth
49 M8 Newton Longville Bucks
125 N6 Newton Mearns E Rens
143 L5 Newtonmill Angus
148 C8 Newtonmore Highld
103 P9 Newton Morrell N York
41 J9 Newton Mountain Pembks
105 L7 Newton Mulgrave N York
134 F5 Newton of Balcanquhal P & K
135 N7 Newton of Balcormo Fife
97 R9 Newton on Ouse N York
98 G2 Newton-on-Rawcliffe N York
69 N10 Newton on the Hill Shrops
119 N9 Newton-on-the-Moor Nthumb
85 P6 Newton on Trent Lincs
10 B7 Newton Poppleford Devon
48 H8 Newton Purcell Oxon
59 L3 Newton Regis Warwks
101 N4 Newton Reigny Cumb
9 L5 Newton St Cyres Devon
77 J8 Newton St Faith Norfk
20 D2 Newton St Loe BaNES
16 G9 Newton St Petrock Devon
71 P9 Newton Solney Derbys
22 D6 Newton Stacey Hants
107 M4 Newton Stewart D & G
21 P6 Newton Tony Wilts
17 J6 Newton Tracey Devon
104 G8 Newton under Roseberry R & Cl
112 H3 Newton Underwood Nthumb
98 E11 Newton upon Derwent E R Yk
23 K8 Newton Valence Hants

Newton Wamphray - Ogbourne Maizey 291

109 P2 **Newton Wamphray** D & G
88 F4 **Newton with Scales** Lancs
30 G3 **Newtown** Blae G
82 B9 **Newtown** Ches W
2 F8 **Newtown** Cnwll
5 M6 **Newtown** Cnwll
101 P6 **Newtown** Cumb
109 P11 **Newtown** Cumb
110 G8 **Newtown** Cumb
111 K8 **Newtown** Cumb
115 Q5 **Newtown** D & G
83 L8 **Newtown** Derbys
9 Q5 **Newtown** Devon
17 P6 **Newtown** Devon
11 K4 **Newtown** Dorset
12 G3 **New Town** Dorset
21 J11 **New Town** Dorset
21 J11 **New Town** Dorset
25 L6 **New Town** E Susx
32 C4 **Newtown** Gloucs
13 N2 **Newtown** Hants
14 H4 **Newtown** Hants
22 E2 **Newtown** Hants
45 P3 **Newtown** Herefs
45 Q8 **Newtown** Herefs
46 B5 **Newtown** Herefs
46 D7 **Newtown** Herefs
147 K7 **Newtown** Highld
14 D8 **Newtown** IoW
88 G7 **Newtown** Lancs
61 L5 **New Town** Nhants
119 J4 **Newtown** Nthumb
119 K10 **Newtown** Nthumb
119 K5 **Newtown** Nthumb
12 H6 **Newtown** Poole
55 Q6 **Newtown** Powys
30 E5 **Newtown** Rhondd
69 M10 **Newtown** Shrops
69 N8 **Newtown** Shrops
10 F2 **Newtown** Somset
58 E4 **Newtown** Staffs
70 G2 **Newtown** Staffs
82 C4 **Newtown** Wigan
20 H9 **Newtown** Wilts
21 Q2 **Newtown** Wilts
33 Q10 **New Town** Wilts
46 G3 **Newtown** Worcs
58 D9 **Newtown** Worcs
3 J9 **Newtown-in-St Martin** Cnwll
72 E9 **Newtown Linford** Leics
125 K6 **Newtown of Beltrees** Rens
117 R4 **Newtown St Boswells** Border
72 D10 **Newtown Unthank** Leics
30 F4 **New Tredegar** Caerph
126 E10 **New Trows** S Lans
84 E7 **New Tupton** Derbys
142 D9 **Newtyle** Angus
75 J9 **New Walsoken** Cambs
93 N10 **New Waltham** NE Lin
84 E5 **New Whittington** Derbys
128 C5 **New Winton** E Loth
34 C2 **New Yatt** Oxon
36 C3 **Newyears Green** Gt Lon
131 K5 **Newyork** Ag & B
86 H9 **New York** Lincs
113 M6 **New York** N Tyne
97 J8 **New York** N York
15 K3 **Nextend** Herefs
41 J9 **Neyland** Pembks
80 b6 **Niarbyl** IoM
32 C3 **Nibley** Gloucs
32 C8 **Nibley** S Glos
32 D5 **Nibley Green** Gloucs
18 F11 **Nicholashayne** Devon
28 F7 **Nicholaston** Swans
111 K7 **Nickies Hill** Cumb
97 M8 **Nidd** N York
151 N7 **Nigg** C Aber
156 E3 **Nigg** Highld
156 D4 **Nigg Ferry** Highld
32 D10 **Nimlet** BaNES
111 Q10 **Ninebanks** Nthumb
33 M7 **Nine Elms** Swindn
40 E6 **Nine Wells** Pembks
26 B9 **Ninfield** E Susx
14 C9 **Ningwood** IoW
118 C5 **Nisbet** Border
129 K9 **Nisbet Hill** Border
14 F11 **Niton** IoW
125 N5 **Nitshill** C Glas
37 N9 **Noah's Ark** Kent
37 Q2 **Noak Bridge** Essex
37 M2 **Noak Hill** Gt Lon
90 H9 **Noblethorpe** Barns
56 H2 **Nobold** Shrops
60 E8 **Nobottle** Nhants
86 E8 **Nocton** Lincs
77 M11 **Nogdam End** Norfk
34 F2 **Noke** Oxon
40 G7 **Nolton** Pembks
40 G7 **Nolton Haven** Pembks
69 P5 **No Man's Heath** Ches W
59 L3 **No Man's Heath** Warwks
5 M10 **No Man's Land** Cnwll
9 K2 **Nomansland** Devon
21 Q11 **Nomansland** Wilts
69 N9 **Noneley** Shrops
39 N11 **Nonington** Kent
95 L4 **Nook** Cumb
111 J5 **Nook** Cumb
36 E7 **Norbiton** Gt Lon
88 C2 **Norbreck** Bpool
46 D6 **Norbridge** Herefs
69 Q5 **Norbury** Ches E
71 L6 **Norbury** Derbys
36 H7 **Norbury** Gt Lon
56 F6 **Norbury** Shrops
70 D10 **Norbury** Staffs
69 Q5 **Norbury Common** Ches E
70 D10 **Norbury Junction** Staffs
58 B11 **Norchard** Worcs
82 D8 **Norcott Brook** Ches W
88 C2 **Norcross** Lancs
15 L10 **Nordelph** Norfk
89 P8 **Norden** Rochdl
57 M5 **Nordley** Shrops
77 P10 **Norfolk Broads** Norfk
129 N10 **Norham** Nthumb
90 D6 **Norland Town** Calder
82 C10 **Norley** Ches W
14 C7 **Norleywood** Hants
25 K8 **Norlington** E Susx
86 C3 **Normanby** Lincs
92 E7 **Normanby** N Linc
98 E4 **Normanby** N York
104 F7 **Normanby** R & Cl
93 K11 **Normanby le Wold** Lincs
61 Q2 **Norman Cross** Cambs
23 P4 **Normandy** Surrey
25 Q9 **Norman's Bay** E Susx
9 Q4 **Norman's Green** Devon
72 A4 **Normanton** C Derb
73 L2 **Normanton** Leics
86 B11 **Normanton** Lincs
85 M10 **Normanton** Notts
73 N9 **Normanton** Rutlnd
91 K6 **Normanton** Wakefd
21 M6 **Normanton** Wilts
72 B8 **Normanton le Heath** Leics
72 E6 **Normanton on Soar** Notts
72 G4 **Normanton on the Wolds** Notts
85 N7 **Normanton on Trent** Notts
88 C3 **Normoss** Lancs
23 P6 **Norney** Surrey
20 G2 **Norrington Common** Wilts
5 Q8 **Norris Green** Cnwll
81 M6 **Norris Green** Lpool
72 A7 **Norris Hill** Leics
90 G6 **Norristhorpe** Kirk
64 D2 **Northacre** Norfk
49 Q10 **Northall** Bucks
97 N2 **Northallerton** N York
76 D9 **Northall Green** Norfk
14 D4 **Northam** C Sotn
16 H6 **Northam** Devon
60 G8 **Northampton** Nhants
58 B11 **Northampton** Worcs
84 H4 **North Anston** Rothm
35 P11 **North Ascot** Br For
48 E9 **North Aston** Oxon
50 G10 **Northaw** Herts
10 F2 **Northay** Somset
22 C10 **North Baddesley** Hants
139 K5 **North Ballachulish** Highld
20 B9 **North Barrow** Somset
76 C4 **North Barsham** Norfk
38 C4 **North Benfleet** Essex
15 P6 **North Bersted** W Susx
128 E3 **North Berwick** E Loth
103 N4 **North Bitchburn** Dur
113 M4 **North Blyth** Nthumb
14 H4 **North Boarhunt** Hants
13 L5 **North Bockhampton** Dorset
74 C9 **Northborough** C Pete
39 P11 **Northbourne** Kent
8 H8 **North Bovey** Devon
20 G3 **North Bradley** Wilts
8 C8 **North Brentor** Devon
20 D7 **North Brewham** Somset
23 Q7 **North Bridge** Surrey
26 B7 **Northbridge Street** E Susx
22 F7 **Northbrook** Hants
48 E10 **Northbrook** Oxon
50 G2 **North Brook End** Cambs
16 H3 **North Buckland** Devon
77 M10 **North Burlingham** Norfk
20 B9 **North Cadbury** Somset
86 B5 **North Carlton** Lincs
85 J4 **North Carlton** Notts
92 E4 **North Cave** E R Yk
33 K3 **North Cerney** Gloucs
25 J6 **North Chailey** E Susx
23 Q9 **Northchapel** W Susx
21 N11 **North Charford** Hants
119 N6 **North Charlton** Nthumb
36 F7 **North Cheam** Gt Lon
20 C9 **North Cheriton** Somset
11 J6 **North Chideock** Dorset
35 Q3 **Northchurch** Herts
92 E3 **North Cliffe** E R Yk
85 P6 **North Clifton** Notts
103 Q4 **North Close** Dur
87 L2 **North Cockerington** Lincs
138 G11 **North Connel** Ag & B
29 M8 **North Cornelly** Brdgnd
3 K10 **North Corner** Cnwll
93 P10 **North Cotes** Lincs
5 N3 **Northcott** Devon
10 B2 **Northcott** Devon
10 C3 **Northcott** Devon
2 H5 **North Country** Cnwll
34 E5 **Northcourt** Oxon
65 P4 **North Cove** Suffk
103 Q10 **North Cowton** N York
49 P6 **North Crawley** M Keyn
37 L6 **North Cray** Gt Lon
76 B4 **North Creake** Norfk
19 K9 **North Curry** Somset
99 J10 **North Dalton** E R Yk
97 N10 **North Deighton** N York
17 J5 **North Devon Crematorium** Devon
39 Q7 **Northdown** Kent
38 F10 **North Downs**
92 A3 **North Duffield** N York
152 G3 **North Duntulm** Highld
36 F7 **North East Surrey Crematorium** Gt Lon
84 E7 **Northedge** Derbys
27 L3 **North Elham** Kent
87 J2 **North Elkington** Lincs
76 D7 **North Elmham** Norfk
91 M8 **North Elmsall** Wakefd
35 K6 **Northend** Bucks
15 J6 **North End** C Port
110 F9 **North End** Cumb
20 F9 **North End** Dorset
93 L2 **North End** E R Yk
93 N4 **North End** E R Yk
51 Q7 **North End** Essex
21 M11 **North End** Hants
22 G9 **North End** Hants
72 F7 **North End** Leics
74 D2 **North End** Lincs
87 M3 **North End** Lincs
92 H11 **North End** Lincs
93 P10 **North End** Lincs
93 K6 **North End** N Linc
31 M11 **North End** N Som
61 L7 **North End** Nhants
64 D3 **North End** Norfk
119 M10 **North End** Nthumb
81 L4 **North End** Sefton
15 Q6 **North End** W Susx
24 D9 **North End** W Susx
48 C4 **Northend** Warwks
82 H7 **Northenden** Manch
35 P7 **Northend Woods** Bucks
160 A10 **North Erradale** Highld
72 G10 **North Evington** C Leic
38 E2 **North Fambridge** Essex
92 G5 **North Ferriby** E R Yk
58 F9 **Northfield** Birm
151 N6 **Northfield** C Aber
93 H5 **Northfield** E R Yk
73 Q9 **Northfields** Lincs
37 P6 **Northfleet** Kent
99 N10 **North Frodingham** E R Yk
13 L2 **North Gorley** Hants
65 J4 **North Green** Norfk
65 L9 **North Green** Suffk
65 M8 **North Green** Suffk
86 D6 **North Greetwell** Lincs
98 G7 **North Grimston** N York
38 B8 **North Halling** Medway
15 K6 **North Hayling** Hants
119 L4 **North Hazelrigg** Nthumb
17 N5 **North Heasley** Devon
24 C6 **North Heath** W Susx
18 D10 **North Hele** Devon
5 M6 **North Hill** Cnwll
36 C4 **North Hillingdon** Gt Lon
34 E3 **North Hinksey Village** Oxon
36 E11 **North Holmwood** Surrey
7 J7 **North Huish** Devon
86 B7 **North Hykeham** Lincs
26 D7 **Northiam** E Susx
61 P11 **Northill** C Beds
32 D3 **Northington** Gloucs
22 G7 **Northington** Hants
92 H10 **North Kelsey** Lincs
156 B8 **North Kessock** Highld
93 K7 **North Killingholme** N Linc
97 P3 **North Kilvington** N York
60 D4 **North Kilworth** Leics
13 L4 **North Kingston** Hants
86 G10 **North Kyme** Lincs
99 Q6 **North Landing** E R Yk
87 K10 **Northlands** Lincs
33 M2 **Northleach** Gloucs
35 M3 **North Lee** Bucks
97 L6 **North Lees** N York
10 D5 **Northleigh** Devon
17 L5 **Northleigh** Devon
27 K2 **North Leigh** Kent
34 C2 **North Leigh** Oxon
85 N4 **North Leverton with Habblesthorpe** Notts
8 D5 **Northlew** Devon
47 L5 **North Littleton** Worcs
19 N7 **Northload Bridge** Somset
64 E5 **North Lopham** Norfk
73 N10 **North Luffenham** Rutlnd
23 M11 **North Marden** W Susx
49 L10 **North Marston** Bucks
128 B8 **North Middleton** Mdloth
119 J6 **North Middleton** Nthumb
159 K9 **North Millbrex** Abers
106 E7 **North Milmain** D & G
17 N6 **North Molton** Devon
34 D4 **Northmoor** Oxon
34 G7 **North Moreton** Oxon
142 F7 **Northmuir** Angus
15 N6 **North Mundham** W Susx
85 N9 **North Muskham** Notts
92 F3 **North Newbald** E R Yk
48 D6 **North Newington** Oxon
21 M3 **North Newnton** Wilts
19 K8 **North Newton** Somset
15 K6 **Northney** Hants
32 D5 **North Nibley** Gloucs
22 F4 **North Oakley** Hants
37 N3 **North Ockendon** Gt Lon
36 D4 **Northolt** Gt Lon
81 J11 **Northop** Flints
81 K11 **Northop Hall** Flints
104 F7 **North Ormesby** Middsb
87 J2 **North Ormsby** Lincs
90 G6 **Northorpe** Kirk
74 A7 **Northorpe** Lincs
74 D3 **Northorpe** Lincs
92 E11 **Northorpe** Lincs
97 N3 **North Otterington** N York
19 N7 **Northover** Somset
19 P10 **Northover** Somset
86 E2 **North Owersby** Lincs
90 E5 **Northowram** Calder
11 K3 **North Perrott** Somset
19 J8 **North Petherton** Somset
5 M4 **North Petherwin** Cnwll
76 B10 **North Pickenham** Norfk
47 J4 **North Piddle** Worcs
11 L5 **North Poorton** Dorset
12 F7 **Northport** Dorset
13 L3 **North Poulner** Hants
134 E11 **North Queensferry** Fife
17 P5 **North Radworthy** Devon
86 D11 **North Rauceby** Lincs
77 J4 **Northrepps** Norfk
87 L4 **North Reston** Lincs
97 L11 **North Rigton** N York
13 L5 **North Ripley** Hants
83 J11 **North Rode** Ches E
169 g1 **North Ronaldsay** Ork
169 g1 *North Ronaldsay Airport* Ork
100 H4 **North Row** Cumb
75 M7 **North Runcton** Norfk
94 D7 **North Scale** Cumb
85 P7 **North Scarle** Lincs
113 L3 **North Seaton** Nthumb
113 L3 **North Seaton Colliery** Nthumb
138 G9 **North Shian** Ag & B
113 N7 **North Shields** N Tyne
38 F4 **North Shoebury** Sthend
88 C3 **North Shore** Bpool
74 E11 **North Side** C Pete
100 C5 **North Side** Cumb
105 J7 **North Skelton** R & Cl
93 R11 **North Somercotes** Lincs
97 L5 **North Stainley** N York
102 F8 **North Stainmore** Cumb
37 P4 **North Stifford** Thurr
32 D11 **North Stoke** BaNES
34 H7 **North Stoke** Oxon
24 B8 **North Stoke** W Susx
63 J7 **North Street** Cambs
21 N11 **North Street** Hants
22 H8 **North Street** Hants
38 H10 **North Street** Kent
38 D7 **North Street** Medway
34 H10 **North Street** W Berk
119 P4 **North Sunderland** Nthumb
5 N2 **North Tamerton** Cnwll
8 G4 **North Tawton** Devon
133 M10 **North Third** Stirlg
93 N11 **North Thoresby** Lincs
119 P10 **North Togston** Nthumb
168 e9 **Northton** W Isls
17 J10 **North Town** Devon
19 Q6 **North Town** Somset
35 N8 **North Town** W & M
76 E9 **North Tuddenham** Norfk
168 c10 **North Uist** W Isls
118 G10 **Northumberland National Park** Nthumb
113 J7 **North Walbottle** N u Ty
77 K5 **North Walsham** Norfk
22 G5 **North Waltham** Hants
23 K4 **North Warnborough** Hants
18 F9 **Northway** Somset
28 G7 **Northway** Swans
51 L10 **North Weald Bassett** Essex
85 N3 **North Wheatley** Notts
7 M5 **North Whilborough** Devon
82 E10 **Northwich** Ches W
31 Q11 **North Wick** BaNES
31 Q7 **Northwick** S Glos
19 L5 **Northwick** Somset
46 F3 **Northwick** Worcs
19 Q3 **North Widcombe** BaNES
86 G3 **North Willingham** Lincs
84 F7 **North Wingfield** Derbys
73 N6 **North Witham** Lincs
75 Q11 **Northwold** Norfk
70 F5 **Northwood** C Stke
84 C8 **Northwood** Derbys
36 C2 **Northwood** Gt Lon
14 E8 **Northwood** IoW
69 N8 **Northwood** Shrops
46 D11 **Northwood Green** Gloucs
11 P2 **North Wootton** Dorset
75 M6 **North Wootton** Norfk
19 Q6 **North Wootton** Somset
32 F9 **North Wraxall** Wilts
33 M8 **North Wroughton** Swindn
105 K10 **North York Moors National Park**
91 N7 **Norton** Donc
25 L10 **Norton** E Susx
46 G10 **Norton** Gloucs
82 C8 **Norton** Halton
50 F4 **Norton** Herts
13 P7 **Norton** IoW
45 N10 **Norton** Mons
19 K2 **Norton** N Som
98 F6 **Norton** N York
60 C8 **Norton** Nhants
85 J6 **Norton** Notts
56 E11 **Norton** Powys
104 D6 **Norton** S on T
84 E4 **Norton** Sheff
56 H8 **Norton** Shrops
57 K3 **Norton** Shrops
57 L8 **Norton** Shrops
57 N4 **Norton** Shrops
64 D8 **Norton** Suffk
28 H7 **Norton** Swans
15 P5 **Norton** W Susx
32 G8 **Norton** Wilts
46 G4 **Norton** Worcs
47 K5 **Norton** Worcs
20 H6 **Norton Bavant** Wilts
70 F8 **Norton Bridge** Staffs
58 F3 **Norton Canes** Staffs
58 F3 **Norton Canes Services** Staffs
45 M5 **Norton Canon** Herefs
76 F6 **Norton Corner** Norfk
85 Q9 **Norton Disney** Lincs
20 E7 **Norton Ferris** Wilts
18 G9 **Norton Fitzwarren** Somset
13 P7 **Norton Green** IoW
19 Q2 **Norton Hawkfield** BaNES
51 P10 **Norton Heath** Essex
70 C7 **Norton in Hales** Shrops
70 F4 **Norton in the Moors** C Stke
59 M3 **Norton-Juxta-Twycross** Leics
97 P6 **Norton-le-Clay** N York
47 P2 **Norton Lindsey** Warwks
64 D8 **Norton Little Green** Suffk
20 B2 **Norton Malreward** BaNES
51 N10 **Norton Mandeville** Essex
20 E3 **Norton St Philip** Somset
65 N2 **Norton Subcourse** Norfk
19 N11 **Norton sub Hamdon** Somset
45 M5 **Norton Wood** Herefs
85 N8 **Norwell** Notts
85 M8 **Norwell Woodhouse** Notts
77 J10 **Norwich** Norfk
77 J9 *Norwich Airport* Norfk
77 J10 **Norwich Cathedral** Norfk
77 J8 **Norwich (St Faith) Crematorium** Norfk
169 t2 **Norwick** Shet
133 P9 **Norwood** Clacks
84 G4 **Norwood** Derbys
27 J5 **Norwood** Kent
51 N9 **Norwood End** Essex
90 E5 **Norwood Green** Calder
36 D5 **Norwood Green** Gt Lon
24 F2 **Norwood Hill** Surrey
74 H11 **Norwoodside** Cambs
73 J11 **Noseley** Leics
6 F9 **Noss Mayo** Devon
97 L4 **Nosterfield** N York
51 P2 **Nosterfield End** Cambs
145 Q2 **Nostie** Highld
47 M10 **Notgrove** Gloucs
29 M9 **Nottage** Brdgnd
5 P9 **Notter** Cnwll
72 F3 **Nottingham** C Nott
11 P8 **Nottington** Dorset
91 J8 **Notton** Wakefd
32 H11 **Notton** Wilts
52 C9 **Nounsley** Essex
57 Q11 **Noutard's Green** Worcs
64 B9 **Nowton** Suffk
56 G2 **Nox** Shrops
35 J7 **Nuffield** Oxon
98 G11 **Nunburnholme** E R Yk
84 H10 **Nuncargate** Notts
111 J11 **Nunclose** Cumb
59 N6 **Nuneaton** Warwks
34 G5 **Nuneham Courtenay** Oxon
36 H5 **Nunhead** Gt Lon
99 N11 **Nunkeeling** E R Yk
97 R9 **Nun Monkton** N York
20 D5 **Nunney** Somset
20 D6 **Nunney Catch** Somset
45 R6 **Nunnington** Herefs
98 D5 **Nunnington** N York
93 N9 **Nunsthorpe** NE Lin
98 C10 **Nunthorpe** C York
104 F8 **Nunthorpe** Middsb
104 F8 **Nunthorpe Village** Middsb
21 N9 **Nunton** Wilts
97 M6 **Nunwick** N York
112 C6 **Nunwick** Nthumb
32 B5 **Nupdown** S Glos
49 N11 **Nup End** Bucks
32 E3 **Nupend** Gloucs
35 N10 **Nuptown** Br For
22 C11 **Nursling** Hants
23 L10 **Nursted** Hants
21 K2 **Nursteed** Wilts
58 B5 **Nurton** Staffs
15 L5 **Nutbourne** W Susx
24 C7 **Nutbourne** W Susx
36 H10 **Nutfield** Surrey
72 E2 **Nuthall** Notts
51 K4 **Nuthampstead** Herts
24 E5 **Nuthurst** W Susx
25 K5 **Nutley** E Susx
22 H6 **Nutley** Hants
89 M7 **Nuttall** Bury
91 Q10 **Nutwell** Donc
167 Q4 **Nybster** Highld
15 N7 **Nyetimber** W Susx
23 M10 **Nyewood** W Susx
17 N10 **Nymet Rowland** Devon
8 H4 **Nymet Tracey** Devon
32 F4 **Nympsfield** Gloucs
18 F10 **Nynehead** Somset
19 M8 **Nythe** Somset
15 P5 **Nyton** W Susx

O

72 G10 **Oadby** Leics
38 E9 **Oad Street** Kent
46 F2 **Oakall Green** Worcs
71 J6 **Oakamoor** Staffs
127 K4 **Oakbank** W Loth
8 D5 **Oak Cross** Devon
30 G5 **Oakdale** Caerph
18 G9 **Oake** Somset
58 C4 **Oaken** Staffs
95 L11 **Oakenclough** Lancs
57 N2 **Oakengates** Wrekin
81 K10 **Oakenholt** Flints
103 N3 **Oakenshaw** Dur
90 F5 **Oakenshaw** Kirk
84 E10 **Oakerthorpe** Derbys
43 J3 **Oakford** Cerdgn
18 B10 **Oakford** Devon
18 B10 **Oakfordbridge** Devon
83 K11 **Oakgrove** Ches E
73 M9 **Oakham** Rutlnd
70 D4 **Oakhanger** Ches E
23 L7 **Oakhanger** Hants
20 B5 **Oakhill** Somset
37 N10 **Oakhurst** Kent
62 F8 **Oakington** Cambs
44 E4 **Oaklands** Powys
46 E11 **Oakle Street** Gloucs
61 M10 **Oakley** Bed
34 H2 **Oakley** Bucks
134 C10 **Oakley** Fife
22 G4 **Oakley** Hants
35 L4 **Oakley** Oxon
12 H5 **Oakley** Poole
64 H6 **Oakley** Suffk
35 P9 **Oakley Green** W & M
55 M7 **Oakley Park** Powys
32 H4 **Oakridge** Gloucs
89 K4 **Oaks** Lancs
56 G4 **Oaks** Shrops
33 J6 **Oaksey** Wilts
71 M8 **Oaks Green** Derbys
111 K5 **Oakshaw Ford** Cumb
23 K9 **Oakshott** Hants
59 M2 **Oakthorpe** Leics
104 C8 **Oak Tree** Darltn
72 B3 **Oakwood** C Derb
112 D7 **Oakwood** Nthumb
90 C3 **Oakworth** C Brad
38 H9 **Oare** Kent
17 P2 **Oare** Somset
21 N2 **Oare** Wilts
73 Q3 **Oasby** Lincs
19 L9 **Oath** Somset
142 H6 **Oathlaw** Angus
36 C7 **Oatlands Park** Surrey
130 H2 **Oban** Ag & B
138 G10 *Oban Airport* Ag & B
56 E9 **Obley** Shrops
141 P10 **Obney** P & K
20 C11 **Oborne** Dorset
74 A8 **Obthorpe** Lincs
64 H7 **Occold** Suffk
167 N9 **Occumster** Highld
115 K3 **Ochiltree** E Ayrs
72 C3 **Ockbrook** Derbys
58 E6 **Ocker Hill** Sandw
46 E2 **Ockeridge** Worcs
36 C9 **Ockham** Surrey
137 P1 **Ockle** Highld
24 D2 **Ockley** Surrey
46 A5 **Ocle Pychard** Herefs
99 L7 **Octon** E R Yk
19 P11 **Odcombe** Somset
20 D2 **Odd Down** BaNES
46 H3 **Oddingley** Worcs
47 P9 **Oddington** Gloucs
48 G11 **Oddington** Oxon
61 L9 **Odell** Bed
8 C4 **Odham** Devon
23 K4 **Odiham** Hants
90 F5 **Odsal** C Brad
50 G3 **Odsey** Cambs
21 M9 **Odstock** Wilts
72 B9 **Odstone** Leics
59 N11 **Offchurch** Warwks
47 L5 **Offenham** Worcs
83 K7 **Offerton** Stockp
113 M9 **Offerton** Sundld
25 K8 **Offham** E Susx
37 Q9 **Offham** Kent
24 B9 **Offham** W Susx
70 D9 **Offleymarsh** Staffs
62 B7 **Offord Cluny** Cambs
62 B7 **Offord D'Arcy** Cambs
53 J2 **Offton** Suffk
10 D5 **Offwell** Devon
33 N10 **Ogbourne Maizey** Wilts

Pedlinge - Pontarddulais 293

27 K4 Pedlinge Kent
58 D8 Pedmore Dudley
19 M7 Pedwell Somset
117 K2 Peebles Border
80 b5 Peel IoM
88 D4 Peel Lancs
14 G6 Peel Common Hants
27 L4 Peene Kent
26 E6 Peening Quarter Kent
72 C7 Peggs Green Leics
50 D4 Pegsdon C Beds
113 K3 Pegswood Nthumb
39 Q9 Pegwell Kent
153 J11 Peinchorran Highld
152 G6 Peinlich Highld
40 H7 Pelcomb Pembks
40 H7 Pelcomb Bridge Pembks
40 H7 Pelcomb Cross Pembks
52 G8 Peldon Essex
25 P4 Pell Green E Susx
58 F4 Pelsall Wsall
58 F4 Pelsall Wood Wsall
113 L10 Pelton Dur
113 L10 Pelton Fell Dur
109 P11 Pelutho Cumb
5 L10 Pelynt Cnwll
28 F4 Pemberton Carmth
82 C4 Pemberton Wigan
26 E2 Pembles Cross Kent
28 D4 Pembrey Carmth
45 M3 Pembridge Herefs
41 J10 Pembroke Pembks
41 J10 Pembroke Dock Pembks
40 F6 Pembrokeshire Coast National Park Pembks
25 P2 Pembury Kent
45 R9 Pen-allt Herefs
31 P2 Penallt Mons
41 M11 Penally Pembks
3 P5 Penare Cnwll
30 G10 Penarth V Glam
41 M7 Penblewin Pembks
54 F8 Pen-bont Rhydybeddau Cerdgn
42 E4 Penbryn Cerdgn
42 H7 Pencader Carmth
66 G6 Pencaenewydd Gwynd
128 C6 Pencaitland E Loth
78 F10 Pencarnisiog IoA
43 K5 Pencarreg Carmth
5 J5 Pencarrow Cnwll
44 F9 Pencelli Powys
28 F5 Penclawdd Swans
30 C8 Pencoed Brdgnd
46 A4 Pencombe Herefs
45 Q9 Pencoyd Herefs
45 R10 Pencraig Herefs
68 D9 Pencraig Powys
2 B7 Pendeen Cnwll
29 P3 Penderyn Rhondd
41 P9 Pendine Carmth
82 G4 Pendlebury Salfd
89 M3 Pendleton Lancs
46 E8 Pendock Worcs
4 G6 Pendoggett Cnwll
11 L2 Pendomer Somset
30 E9 Pendoylan V Glam
29 P8 Pendre Brdgnd
54 H4 Penegoes Powys
3 L5 Penelewey Cnwll
41 L6 Pen-ffordd Pembks
30 G5 Pengam Caerph
30 H9 Pengam Cardif
37 J6 Penge Gt Lon
4 H5 Pengelly Cnwll
78 H6 Pengorffwysfa IoA
5 M8 Pengover Green Cnwll
31 K3 Pen-groes-oped Mons
80 E9 Pengwern Denbgs
2 H10 Penhale Cnwll
4 E10 Penhale Cnwll
4 H9 Penhale Cnwll
5 Q11 Penhale Cnwll
3 K3 Penhallow Cnwll
3 J6 Penhalurick Cnwll
3 J6 Penhalvean Cnwll
33 N7 Penhill Swindn
31 M6 Penhow Newpt
25 Q7 Penhurst E Susx
54 E3 Peniarth Gwynd
127 N6 Penicuik Mdloth
42 H10 Peniel Carmth
68 D2 Peniel Denbgs
152 H9 Penifiler Highld
120 E7 Peninver Ag & B
67 K2 Penisarwaun Gwynd
90 G10 Penistone Barns
3 K7 Penjerrick Cnwll
82 C7 Penketh Warrtn
114 D8 Penkill S Ayrs
58 D2 Penkridge Staffs
5 L2 Penlean Cnwll
20 G4 Penleigh Wilts
69 M6 Penley Wrexhm
28 H5 Penllergaer Swans
78 F8 Pen-llyn IoA
30 C9 Penllyn V Glam
78 G11 Pen-lon IoA
67 P4 Penmachno Conwy
30 G5 Penmaen Caerph
28 F7 Penmaen Swans
79 N9 Penmaenan Conwy
79 N9 Penmaenmawr Conwy
67 M11 Penmaenpool Gwynd
30 E11 Penmark V Glam
79 L8 Penmon IoA
67 J6 Penmorfa Gwynd
3 L4 Penmount Crematorium Cnwll
79 J10 Penmynydd IoA
35 P6 Penn Bucks
58 C5 Penn Wolves
54 F4 Pennal Gwynd
159 K4 Pennan Abers
43 K2 Pennant Cerdgn
68 D8 Pennant Denbgs
55 K5 Pennant Powys
68 D9 Pennant-Melangell Powys
28 G7 Pennard Swans
56 F5 Pennerley Shrops
9 L4 Pennicott Devon
90 B3 Pennines
94 F5 Pennington Cumb
13 P5 Pennington Hants
89 J9 Pennington Green Wigan
44 G9 Pennorth Powys
35 P5 Penn Street Bucks
32 D10 Pennsylvania S Glos
94 G4 Penny Bridge Cumb
137 N10 Pennycross Ag & B
77 L7 Pennygate Norfk
137 N10 Pennyghael Ag & B
114 E5 Pennyglen S Ayrs
84 H5 Penny Green Derbys
74 G5 Penny Hill Lincs
9 L2 Pennymoor Devon
113 N9 Pennywell Sundld
42 D5 Penparc Cerdgn
54 D8 Penparcau Cerdgn
30 F5 Penpedairheol Caerph
31 K4 Penpedairheol Mons
31 K4 Penperlleni Mons
4 H4 Penpethy Cnwll
4 H10 Penpillick Cnwll
3 L6 Penpol Cnwll
5 J11 Penpoll Cnwll
2 G6 Penponds Cnwll
4 H7 Penpont Cnwll
108 H2 Penpont D & G
44 D9 Penpont Powys
6 G8 Penquit Devon
5 N6 Penrest Cnwll
41 Q3 Penrherber Carmth
41 P2 Pen-rhiw Pembks
30 E5 Penrhiwceiber Rhondd
29 K2 Pen Rhiwfawr Neath
42 G6 Penrhiw-llan Cerdgn
42 F5 Penrhiw-pal Cerdgn
66 E8 Penrhos Gwynd
78 D8 Penrhos IoA
31 M2 Penrhos Mons
29 M2 Penrhos Powys
79 K10 Penrhos garnedd Gwynd
79 Q8 Penrhyn Bay Conwy
79 L10 Penrhyn Castle Gwynd
54 E8 Penrhyncoch Cerdgn
67 L7 Penrhyndeudraeth Gwynd
79 Q8 Penrhyn-side Conwy
28 E7 Penrice Swans
120 G3 Penrioch N Ayrs
101 P4 Penrith Cumb
4 D7 Penrose Cnwll
101 M5 Penruddock Cumb
3 K7 Penryn Cnwll
80 D9 Pensarn Conwy
57 N11 Pensax Worcs
81 K8 Pensby Wirral
20 E8 Penselwood Somset
20 B2 Pensford BaNES
46 H6 Pensham Worcs
113 M10 Penshaw Sundld
25 M2 Penshurst Kent
37 M11 Penshurst Station Kent
5 M7 Pensilva Cnwll
58 D7 Pensnett Dudley
9 J4 Penstone Devon
55 P6 Penstrowed Powys
3 Q4 Pentewan Cnwll
79 K11 Pentir Gwynd
4 B9 Pentire Cnwll
41 M9 Pentlepoir Pembks
63 P11 Pentlow Essex
63 P11 Pentlow Street Essex
75 P8 Pentney Norfk
110 H5 Pentonbridge Cumb
22 B5 Penton Grafton Hants
22 B5 Penton Mewsey Hants
79 J9 Pentraeth IoA
68 E2 Pentre Denbgs
81 L11 Pentre Flints
31 K3 Pentre Mons
31 M4 Pentre Mons
55 P7 Pentre Powys
56 B7 Pentre Powys
56 D6 Pentre Powys
30 C5 Pentre Rhondd
69 L11 Pentre Shrops
69 J6 Pentre Wrexhm
43 L5 Pentre bach Cerdgn
81 J9 Pentre Bach Flints
30 E4 Pentrebach Myr Td
44 C8 Pentre-bach Powys
56 B2 Pentrebeirdd Powys
78 H10 Pentre Berw IoA
67 N4 Pentre-bont Conwy
69 K5 Pentrebychan Crematorium Wrexhm
42 F6 Pentre-cagel Carmth
68 F4 Pentre-celyn Denbgs
55 K3 Pentre-celyn Powys
29 J6 Pentre-chwyth Swans
69 J8 Pentre-clawdd Shrops
42 G7 Pentre-cwrt Carmth
68 G5 Pentredwr Denbgs
67 J7 Pentrefelin Gwynd
78 G6 Pentrefelin IoA
81 K10 Pentre Ffwrndan Flints
67 R4 Pentrefoelas Conwy
41 N4 Pentregalar Pembks
42 G4 Pentregat Cerdgn
43 M11 Pentre-Gwenlais Carmth
67 K9 Pentre Gwynfryn Gwynd
81 J10 Pentre Halkyn Flints
56 E9 Pentre Hodrey Shrops
80 D10 Pentre Isaf Conwy
68 E2 Pentre Llanrhaeadr Denbgs
56 B5 Pentre Llifior Powys
44 D4 Pentre-llwyn-llwyd Powys
54 E9 Pentre-llyn Cerdgn
68 C4 Pentre-llyn-cymmer Conwy
55 K4 Pentre-Maw Powys
30 C9 Pentre Meyrick V Glam
31 J4 Pentre-piod Torfn
31 J7 Pentre-poeth Newpt
42 G4 Pentre'rbryn Cerdgn
43 M5 Pentre'r-felin Cerdgn
79 Q11 Pentre'r Felin Conwy
44 C8 Pentre'r-felin Powys
68 D2 Pentre Saron Denbgs
67 Q2 Pentre-tafarn-y-fedw Conwy
43 R7 Pentre ty gwyn Carmth
84 E10 Pentrich Derbys
21 K11 Pentridge Dorset
30 H4 Pen-twyn Caerph
31 P3 Pen-twyn Mons
31 J4 Pen-twyn Torfn
30 G5 Pentwynmaur Caerph
30 F8 Pentyrch Cardif
4 G10 Penwithick Cnwll
22 D2 Penwood Hants
44 B11 Penwyllt Powys
43 M10 Penybanc Carmth
44 G2 Penybont Powys
68 H10 Pen-y-bont Powys
68 E10 Pen-y-bont-fawr Powys
41 N2 Pen-y-bryn Pembks
29 M2 Pen-y-cae Powys
69 J5 Penycae Wrexhm
31 M5 Pen-y-cae-mawr Mons
66 B9 Penycaerau Gwynd
80 G9 Pen-y-cefn Flints
31 N3 Pen-y-clawdd Mons
30 E7 Pen-y-coedcae Rhondd
40 G6 Pen-y-cwn Pembks
29 N8 Pen-y-fai Brdgnd
80 H11 Pen-y-felin Flints
69 K2 Penyffordd Flints
67 J3 Penyffridd Gwynd
54 E7 Pen-y-garn Cerdgn
68 F10 Pen-y-Garnedd Powys
44 H9 Pen-y-genffordd Powys
66 C8 Pen-y-graig Gwynd
30 D6 Penygraig Rhondd
28 G2 Penygroes Carmth
66 H4 Penygroes Gwynd
67 M3 Pen-y-Gwryd Gwynd
30 C9 Pen-y-lan V Glam
28 E4 Pen-y-Mynydd Carmth
69 K2 Penymynydd Flints
67 L3 Pen-y-pass Gwynd
31 M2 Pen-yr-Heol Mons
30 D3 Pen-yr-Heolgerrig Myr Td
78 H6 Penysarn IoA
68 H4 Pen-y-stryt Denbgs
30 C4 Penywaun Rhondd
2 D7 Penzance Cnwll
2 D7 Penzance Heliport Cnwll
46 H4 Peopleton Worcs
82 G10 Peover Heath Ches E
23 P6 Peper Harow Surrey
70 A10 Peplow Shrops
51 P8 Pepper's Green Essex
50 C7 Pepperstock C Beds
125 K9 Perceton N Ayrs
159 N4 Percyhorner Abers
10 b2 Perelle Guern
21 Q5 Perham Down Wilts
18 C5 Periton Somset
36 E4 Perivale Gt Lon
9 P6 Perkins Village Devon
113 L10 Perkinsville Dur
85 K6 Perlethorpe Notts
3 K6 Perranarworthal Cnwll
3 K3 Perranporth Cnwll
2 E8 Perranuthnoe Cnwll
3 K3 Perranwell Cnwll
3 K6 Perranwell Cnwll
3 K6 Perran Wharf Cnwll
3 K3 Perranzabuloe Cnwll
33 K3 Perrott's Brook Gloucs
58 G6 Perry Birm
58 G6 Perry Barr Birm
58 G6 Perry Barr Crematorium Birm
52 D7 Perry Green Essex
51 K7 Perry Green Herts
33 J7 Perry Green Wilts
45 R9 Perrystone Hill Herefs
10 G3 Perry Street Somset
70 E9 Pershall Staffs
46 H5 Pershore Worcs
61 N7 Pertenhall Bed
134 E3 Perth P & K
134 D2 Perth Crematorium P & K
69 L8 Perthy Shrops
45 A6 Perton Herefs
58 C5 Perton Staffs
20 G7 Pertwood Wilts
74 C11 Peterborough C Pete
74 C10 Peterborough Crematorium C Pete
61 P2 Peterborough Services Cambs
45 L7 Peterchurch Herefs
151 L7 Peterculter C Aber
159 R8 Peterhead Abers
104 D2 Peterlee Dur
23 K10 Petersfield Hants
50 D7 Peter's Green Herts
36 E6 Petersham Gt Lon
16 H10 Peters Marland Devon
31 J9 Peterstone Wentlooge Newpt
30 E9 Peterston-super-Ely V Glam
45 R10 Peterstow Herefs
8 D9 Peter Tavy Devon
39 K11 Petham Kent
5 M4 Petherwin Gate Cnwll
17 J10 Petrockstow Devon
49 N5 Petsoe End M Keyn
27 J2 Pet Street Kent
26 E9 Pett E Susx
64 H10 Pettaugh Suffk
39 L11 Pett Bottom Kent
142 G9 Petterden Angus
116 D2 Pettinain S Lans
65 L10 Pettistree Suffk
18 D10 Petton Devon
69 M9 Petton Shrops
37 L7 Petts Wood Gt Lon
134 H10 Pettycur Fife
32 E7 Petty France S Glos
151 N3 Pettymuk Abers
23 Q10 Petworth W Susx
25 P9 Pevensey E Susx
25 Q10 Pevensey Bay E Susx
21 N2 Pewsey Wilts
35 L7 Pheasant's Hill Bucks
46 H3 Phepson Worcs
113 M10 Philadelphia Sundld
16 D7 Philham Devon
117 N5 Philiphaugh Border
2 F6 Phillack Cnwll
3 M6 Philleigh Cnwll
51 P7 Philpot End Essex
127 K2 Philpstoun W Loth
46 B9 Phocle Green Herefs
23 L3 Phoenix Green Hants
148 C9 Phones Highld
19 M9 Pibsbury Somset
100 D6 Pica Cumb
59 K5 Piccadilly Warwks
50 B9 Piccotts End Herts
91 N9 Pickburn Donc
98 F4 Pickering N York
22 C5 Picket Piece Hants
13 L3 Picket Post Hants
59 L8 Pickford Covtry
59 L8 Pickford Green Covtry
97 M4 Pickhill N York
56 G5 Picklescott Shrops
82 E9 Pickmere Ches E
18 G9 Pickney Somset
70 C10 Pickstock Wrekin
89 L6 Pickup Bank Bl w D
16 H3 Pickwell Devon
73 K8 Pickwell Leics
32 G10 Pickwick Wilts
73 Q4 Pickworth Lincs
73 P8 Pickworth RutInd
81 N10 Picton Ches W
80 G8 Picton Flints
104 D9 Picton N York
25 K10 Piddinghoe E Susx
35 M6 Piddington Bucks
49 M4 Piddington Nhants
48 H11 Piddington Oxon
11 Q5 Piddlehinton Dorset
11 Q5 Piddletrenthide Dorset
62 D5 Pidley Cambs
103 P7 Piercebridge Darltn
169 d2 Pierowall Ork
46 H9 Piff's Elm Gloucs
113 J3 Pigdon Nthumb
47 P2 Pigeon Green Warwks
12 H4 Pig Oak Dorset
45 M5 Pig Street Herefs
71 M3 Pikehall Derbys
12 H4 Pilford Dorset
51 N11 Pilgrims Hatch Essex
85 Q2 Pilham Lincs
31 P9 Pill N Som
5 P9 Pillaton Cnwll
5 P9 Pillatonmill Cnwll
47 Q5 Pillerton Hersey Warwks
47 Q5 Pillerton Priors Warwks
56 D11 Pilleth Powys
91 J10 Pilley Barns
13 P5 Pilley Hants
13 P5 Pilley Bailey Hants
31 K7 Pillgwenlly Newpt
16 H6 Pillhead Devon
95 J11 Pilling Lancs
94 H11 Pilling Lane Lancs
31 Q7 Pilning S Glos
27 J8 Pilot Inn Kent
71 L2 Pilsbury Derbys
11 J5 Pilsdon Dorset
73 R9 Pilsgate C Pete
84 B6 Pilsley Derbys
84 F8 Pilsley Derbys
77 M9 Pilson Green Norfk
25 K6 Piltdown E Susx
17 K5 Pilton Devon
61 M4 Pilton Nhants
73 N10 Pilton RutInd
19 Q6 Pilton Somset
28 D7 Pilton Green Swans
89 L2 Pimlico Lancs
48 H6 Pimlico Nhants
12 F3 Pimperne Dorset
74 D5 Pinchbeck Lincs
74 C5 Pinchbeck Bars Lincs
74 D6 Pinchbeck West Lincs
91 R7 Pincheon Green Donc
104 G8 Pinchinthorpe R & Cl
88 G7 Pincock Lancs
88 D8 Pinfold Lancs
64 A10 Pinford End Suffk
28 D4 Pinged Carmth
35 J11 Pingewood W Berk
50 G5 Pin Green Herts
9 N6 Pinhoe Devon
59 L8 Pinkett's Booth Covtry
32 G7 Pinkney Wilts
59 N9 Pinley Covtry
59 K11 Pinley Green Warwks
53 M4 Pin Mill Suffk
114 C9 Pinminnoch S Ayrs
114 D9 Pinmore S Ayrs
10 C7 Pinn Devon
36 D3 Pinner Gt Lon
36 D3 Pinner Green Gt Lon
69 Q5 Pinsley Green Ches E
47 J5 Pinvin Worcs
114 D10 Pinwherry S Ayrs
84 G10 Pinxton Derbys
45 Q6 Pipe and Lyde Herefs
56 H10 Pipe Aston Herefs
70 C6 Pipe Gate Shrops
58 G3 Pipehill Staffs
156 F7 Piperhill Highld
5 M5 Pipers Pool Cnwll
60 H3 Pipewell Nhants
17 J4 Pippacott Devon
88 H6 Pippin Street Lancs
44 H7 Pipton Powys
23 P3 Pirbright Surrey
23 P3 Pirbright Camp Surrey
118 C5 Pirnie Border
120 G3 Pirnmill N Ayrs
50 D4 Pirton Herts
46 G5 Pirton Worcs
54 F9 Pisgah Cerdgn
35 K7 Pishill Oxon
66 E6 Pistyll Gwynd
141 K4 Pitagowan P & K
159 N5 Pitblae Abers
134 D2 Pitcairngreen P & K
156 E3 Pitcalnie Highld
151 J2 Pitcaple Abers
142 E4 Pitcarity Angus
32 G3 Pitchcombe Gloucs
49 L10 Pitchcott Bucks
74 E4 Pitcher Row Lincs
57 J4 Pitchford Shrops
35 L4 Pitch Green Bucks
23 N7 Pitch Place Surrey
23 Q4 Pitch Place Surrey
157 M10 Pitchroy Moray
20 C8 Pitcombe Somset
29 N10 Pitcot V Glam
128 G5 Pitcox E Loth
150 H4 Pitfichie Abers
158 G9 Pitglassie Abers
162 H8 Pitgrudy Highld
135 J6 Pitlessie Fife
141 M6 Pitlochry P & K
150 H2 Pitmachie Abers
148 C7 Pitmain Highld
151 M2 Pitmedden Abers
151 M2 Pitmedden Garden Abers
18 H11 Pitminster Somset
143 K8 Pitmuies Angus
150 H5 Pitmunie Abers
19 N9 Pitney Somset
134 G2 Pitroddie P & K
135 L5 Pitscottie Fife
38 B4 Pitsea Essex
83 K4 Pitses Oldham
60 G7 Pitsford Nhants
49 P11 Pitstone Bucks
18 D11 Pitt Devon
22 E9 Pitt Hants
143 N3 Pittarrow Abers
32 D5 Pitt Court Gloucs
135 P7 Pittenweem Fife
134 H8 Pitteuchar Fife
104 B2 Pittington Dur
150 H3 Pittodrie House Hotel Abers
21 P8 Pitton Wilts
37 P11 Pitt's Wood Kent
159 N4 Pittulie Abers
4 F6 Pityme Cnwll
113 L11 Pity Me Dur
26 F2 Pivington Kent
65 J6 Pixey Green Suffk
36 E10 Pixham Surrey
126 D4 Plains N Lans
4 F6 Plain Street Cnwll
57 J5 Plaish Shrops
37 K4 Plaistow Gt Lon
24 B4 Plaistow W Susx
21 Q11 Plaitford Hants
82 D5 Plank Lane Wigan
78 D9 Plas Cymyran IoA
22 F2 Plastow Green Hants
37 P9 Platt Kent
82 D4 Platt Bridge Wigan
69 P7 Platt Lane Shrops
38 E11 Platts Heath Kent
113 L11 Plawsworth Dur
37 P10 Plaxtol Kent
26 F7 Playden E Susx
53 M2 Playford Suffk
35 K9 Play Hatch Oxon
3 L5 Playing Place Cnwll
46 E8 Playley Green Gloucs
56 G3 Plealey Shrops
133 N10 Plean Stirlg
134 G5 Pleasance Fife
89 J5 Pleasington Bl w D
89 J5 Pleasington Crematorium Bl w D
84 H8 Pleasley Derbys
84 H8 Pleasleyhill Notts
11 Q2 Pleck Dorset
51 N5 Pledgdon Green Essex
91 J7 Pledwick Wakefd
10 b1 Pleinheaume Guern
11 a1 Plemont Jersey
81 P10 Plemstall Ches W
111 P8 Plenmeller Nthumb
51 Q8 Pleshey Essex
153 Q11 Plockton Highld
56 F7 Plowden Shrops
56 F4 Plox Green Shrops
26 F2 Pluckley Kent
26 F3 Pluckley Station Kent
26 F3 Pluckley Thorne Kent
39 N9 Plucks Gutter Kent
100 G3 Plumbland Cumb
95 K2 Plumgarths Cumb
82 F10 Plumley Ches E
94 G5 Plumpton Cumb
101 N3 Plumpton Cumb
25 J8 Plumpton E Susx
48 G5 Plumpton Nhants
49 K6 Plumpton End Nhants
25 J7 Plumpton Green E Susx
101 P3 Plumpton Head Cumb
37 K5 Plumstead Gt Lon
76 G5 Plumstead Norfk
76 G4 Plumstead Green Norfk
72 G4 Plumtree Notts
26 D2 Plumtree Green Kent
73 K4 Plungar Leics
26 F4 Plurenden Kent
11 Q4 Plush Dorset
5 M5 Plusha Cnwll
5 N7 Plushabridge Cnwll
42 G4 Plwmp Cerdgn
6 D8 Plymouth C Plym
6 E6 Plymouth Airport C Plym
6 E7 Plympton C Plym
6 E8 Plymstock C Plym
9 Q4 Plymtree Devon
98 C3 Pockley N York
98 G11 Pocklington E R Yk
74 D6 Pode Hole Lincs
19 P10 Podimore Somset
61 K8 Podington Bed
70 D7 Podmore Staffs
53 K9 Point Clear Essex
74 B4 Pointon Lincs
13 K6 Pokesdown Bmouth
160 F4 Polbain Highld
5 N10 Polbathic Cnwll
127 J5 Polbeth W Loth
4 G8 Polbrock Cnwll
2 H7 Poldark Mine Cnwll
61 N3 Polebrook Nhants
46 F4 Pole Elm Worcs
25 N10 Polegate E Susx
90 D7 Pole Moor Kirk
59 L4 Polesworth Warwks
2 B9 Polgigga Cnwll
160 G5 Polglass Highld
3 P3 Polgooth Cnwll
115 P7 Polgown D & G
24 B10 Poling W Susx
24 B9 Poling Corner W Susx
4 H11 Polkerris Cnwll
77 L5 Pollard Street Norfk
91 Q7 Pollington E R Yk
138 D4 Polloch Highld
125 P5 Pollokshaws C Glas
125 P5 Pollokshields C Glas
3 P4 Polmassick Cnwll
4 H11 Polmear Cnwll
126 G2 Polmont Falk
145 N11 Polnish Highld
5 L11 Polperro Cnwll
5 J11 Polruan Cnwll
19 P6 Polsham Somset
52 G4 Polstead Suffk
52 G3 Polstead Heath Suffk
130 G8 Poltalloch Ag & B
3 J10 Poltescoe Cnwll
9 N5 Poltimore Devon
127 P5 Polton Mdloth
129 J9 Polwarth Border
5 M5 Polyphant Cnwll
4 E6 Polzeath Cnwll
127 N6 Pomathorn Mdloth
83 P11 Pomeroy Derbys
44 G7 Ponde Powys
62 C2 Pondersbridge Cambs
51 J11 Ponders End Gt Lon
3 K6 Ponsanooth Cnwll
100 E9 Ponsonby Cumb
3 K10 Ponsongath Cnwll
7 J4 Ponsworthy Devon
28 G3 Pont Abraham Services Carmth
11 c2 Pontac Jersey
28 H2 Pontamman Carmth
28 D2 Pontantwn Carmth
29 K4 Pontardawe Neath
28 G4 Pontarddulais Swans

294 Pont-ar-gothi - Ranton

43 K10 Pont-ar-gothi Carmth
44 B9 Pont-ar-Hydfer Powys
43 P10 Pont-ar-llechau Carmth
42 H9 Pontarsais Carmth
69 J2 Pontblyddyn Flints
67 N3 Pont Cyfyng Conwy
79 P11 Pont Dolgarrog Conwy
55 N6 Pontdolgoch Powys
31 J7 Pont-Ebbw Newpt
91 M6 Pontefract Wakefd
91 L6 Pontefract Crematorium Wakefd
113 J6 Ponteland Nthumb
54 G8 Ponterwyd Cerdgn
56 F3 Pontesbury Shrops
56 F3 Pontesbury Hill Shrops
56 G3 Pontesford Shrops
68 H7 Pontfadog Wrexhm
41 K4 Pontfaen Pembks
44 D8 Pont-faen Powys
42 F4 Pontgarreg Cerdgn
41 M2 Pontgarreg Pembks
28 E3 Ponthenry Carmth
31 K6 Ponthir Torfn
42 E5 Ponthirwaun Cerdgn
30 G5 Pontllanfraith Caerph
28 H5 Pontlliw Swans
31 P3 Pontlottyn Caerph
66 G4 Pontlyfni Gwynd
28 F3 Pont Morlais Carmth
29 P3 Pontneddfechan Neath
31 J5 Pontnewydd Torfn
31 J4 Pontnewynydd Torfn
67 M2 Pont Pen-y-benglog Gwynd
54 G11 Pontrhydfendigaid Cerdgn
67 R9 Pont Rhyd-sarn Gwynd
29 N7 Pont Rhyd-y-cyff Brdgnd
29 L6 Pont-rhyd-y-fen Neath
54 G10 Pontrhydygroes Cerdgn
31 J5 Pontrhydyrun Torfn
45 M9 Pontrilas Herefs
55 Q2 Pont Robert Powys
67 J2 Pont-rug Gwynd
25 Q7 Ponts Green E Susx
42 H5 Pontshaen Cerdgn
46 B10 Pontshill Herefs
30 E2 Pontsticill Myr Td
29 N3 Pont Walby Neath
42 H6 Pontwelly Carmth
28 E3 Pontyates Carmth
28 F2 Pontyberem Carmth
69 K7 Pont-y-blew Wrexhm
69 J3 Pontybodkin Flints
30 D8 Pontyclun Rhondd
29 P6 Pontycymer Brdgnd
41 M3 Pontyglasier Pembks
30 D6 Pontygwaith Rhondd
41 M3 Pontygynon Pembks
67 P4 Pont-y-pant Conwy
31 J4 Pontypool Torfn
31 K5 Pontypool Road Torfn
30 E7 Pontypridd Rhondd
40 H5 Pont-yr-hafod Pembks
29 P7 Pont-yr-Rhyl Brdgnd
30 H6 Pontywaun Caerph
2 H5 Pool Cnwll
2 b2 Pool IoS
97 K11 Pool Leeds
12 H6 Poole Poole
12 H5 Poole Crematorium Poole
33 J5 Poole Keynes Gloucs
160 D10 Poolewe Highld
101 N6 Pooley Bridge Cumb
64 F5 Pooley Street Norfk
70 F3 Poolfold Staffs
45 R4 Pool Head Herefs
46 D9 Poolhill Gloucs
134 C7 Pool of Muckhart Clacks
56 D2 Pool Quay Powys
52 C4 Pool Street Essex
37 L11 Pooting's Kent
22 G6 Popham Hants
37 J4 Poplar Gt Lon
65 N8 Poplar Street Suffk
14 D8 Porchfield IoW
77 K11 Poringland Norfk
2 H7 Porkellis Cnwll
18 A5 Porlock Somset
17 R2 Porlock Weir Somset
123 N8 Portachoillan Ag & B
153 P11 Port-an-Eorna Highld
138 G8 Port Appin Ag & B
122 F6 Port Askaig Ag & B
124 A4 Portavadie Ag & B
124 D4 Port Bannatyne Ag & B
31 P9 Portbury N Som
110 D8 Port Carlisle Cumb
122 C8 Port Charlotte Ag & B
14 H5 Portchester Hants
14 H5 Portchester Crematorium Hants
104 E6 Port Clarence S on T
124 B3 Port Driseach Ag & B
122 E10 Port Ellen Ag & B
151 K3 Port Elphinstone Abers
106 D3 Portencalzie D & G
124 F8 Portencross N Ayrs
80 a8 Port Erin IoM
11 N7 Portesham Dorset
158 B4 Portessie Moray
80 g3 Port e Vullen IoM
28 E7 Port Eynon Swans
40 H7 Portfield Gate Pembks
5 Q4 Portgate Devon
4 G5 Port Gaverne Cnwll
125 J3 Port Glasgow Inver
158 A5 Portgordon Moray
163 N4 Portgower Highld
4 C9 Porth Cnwll
30 D6 Porth Rhondd
3 K9 Porthallow Cnwll
5 L11 Porthallow Cnwll
29 M9 Porthcawl Brdgnd
4 D7 Porthcothan Cnwll
2 B9 Porthcurno Cnwll
66 D6 Porth Dinllaen Gwynd
153 P3 Port Henderson Highld
40 F4 Porthgain Pembks
2 B9 Porthgwarra Cnwll
70 E5 Porthill Staffs
3 L5 Porthkea Cnwll
30 E11 Porthkerry V Glam
2 G8 Porthleven Cnwll
67 K7 Porthmadog Gwynd
2 C6 Porthmeor Cnwll
3 K8 Porth Navas Cnwll
3 P5 Portholland Cnwll
3 L9 Porthoustock Cnwll
3 Q3 Porthpean Cnwll
2 H4 Porthtowan Cnwll
69 L5 Porthwgan Wrexhm
43 K11 Porthyrhyd Carmth
69 J10 Porth-y-Waen Shrops
131 Q9 Portincaple Ag & B
11 a1 Portinfer Jersey
92 C4 Portington E R Yk
131 K5 Portinnisherrich Ag & B
101 J6 Portinscale Cumb
4 F5 Port Isaac Cnwll
31 N9 Portishead N Som
158 C4 Portknockie Moray
11 P10 Portland Dorset
151 N8 Portlethen Abers
109 J10 Portling D & G
3 N6 Portloe Cnwll
106 E9 Port Logan D & G
5 L11 Portlooe Cnwll
163 L10 Portmahomack Highld
67 K7 Portmeirion Gwynd
3 Q5 Portmellon Cnwll
144 F12 Port Mor Highld
13 P5 Portmore Hants
105 L7 Port Mulgrave N York
138 G8 Portnacroish Ag & B
168 k4 Portnaguran W Isls
122 A9 Portnahaven Ag & B
152 E11 Portnalong Highld
168 k4 Port nan Giuran W Isls
168 d10 Port nan Long W Isls
168 k1 Port Nis W Isls
127 Q3 Portobello C Edin
113 L9 Portobello Gatesd
58 E5 Portobello Wolves
132 H7 Port of Menteith Stirlg
168 k1 Port of Ness W Isls
21 N7 Porton Wilts
5 Q6 Portontown Devon
106 C7 Portpatrick D & G
4 F5 Port Quin Cnwll
138 F8 Port Ramsay Ag & B
2 H4 Portreath Cnwll
152 H9 Portree Highld
80 b8 Port St Mary IoM
3 M6 Portscatho Cnwll
14 H6 Portsea C Port
166 E3 Portskerra Highld
31 N7 Portskewett Mons
24 G9 Portslade Br & H
24 G9 Portslade-by-Sea Br & H
106 C6 Portslogan D & G
14 H7 Portsmouth C Port
89 Q5 Portsmouth Calder
80 d7 Port Soderick IoM
14 H5 Port Solent C Port
131 L3 Portsonachan Hotel Ag & B
158 E4 Portsoy Abers
81 L8 Port Sunlight Wirral
14 D4 Portswood C Sotn
29 L7 Port Talbot Neath
29 J6 Port Tennant Swans
137 L2 Portuairk Highld
45 P6 Portway Herefs
45 P7 Portway Herefs
58 E7 Portway Sandw
58 G10 Portway Worcs
122 A9 Port Wemyss Ag & B
107 K9 Port William D & G
5 P11 Portwrinkle Cnwll
107 N10 Portyerrock D & G
9 K5 Posbury Devon
57 M4 Posenhall Shrops
63 N11 Poslingford Suffk
117 J4 Posso Border
8 G9 Postbridge Devon
35 K4 Postcombe Oxon
12 G6 Post Green Dorset
27 K4 Postling Kent
77 K10 Postwick Norfk
150 G8 Potarch Abers
49 Q8 Potsgrove C Beds
50 B9 Potten End Herts
39 N8 Potten Street Kent
99 K5 Potter Brompton N York
64 H3 Pottergate Street Norfk
86 E7 Potterhanworth Lincs
86 E7 Potterhanworth Booths Lincs
77 N8 Potter Heigham Norfk
21 J3 Potterne Wilts
21 J3 Potterne Wick Wilts
35 P4 Potter Row Bucks
50 F10 Potters Bar Herts
95 K10 Potters Brook Lancs
58 B8 Potter's Cross Staffs
50 D9 Potters Crouch Herts
26 E2 Potter's Forstal Kent
59 N8 Potters Green Covtry
25 M6 Potter's Green E Susx
51 J6 Potter's Green Herts
50 F7 Pottersheath Herts
72 D11 Potters Marston Leics
71 L7 Potter Somersal Derbys
49 L6 Potterspury Nhants
151 N4 Potterton Abers
91 L3 Potterton Leeds
76 C7 Potthorpe Norfk
20 F6 Pottle Street Wilts
104 E10 Potto N York
62 B11 Potton C Beds
75 P6 Pott Row Norfk
52 F7 Pott's Green Essex
83 K9 Pott Shrigley Ches E
16 C10 Poughill Cnwll
9 L3 Poughill Devon
13 L3 Poulner Hants
21 J3 Poulshot Wilts
33 L4 Poulton Gloucs
81 L6 Poulton Wirral
88 C3 Poulton-le-Fylde Lancs
33 L5 Poulton Priory Gloucs
57 N10 Pound Bank Worcs
11 P6 Poundbury Dorset
28 G6 Poundffald Swans
25 L5 Poundgate E Susx
25 M6 Pound Green E Susx
63 M10 Pound Green Suffk
57 P9 Pound Green Worcs
24 G3 Pound Hill W Susx
48 H9 Poundon Bucks
25 M2 Poundsbridge Kent
7 J4 Poundsgate Devon
5 L2 Poundstock Cnwll
22 E3 Pound Street Hants
25 M6 Pounsley E Susx
107 N8 Pouton D & G
65 M7 Pouy Street Suffk
24 G2 Povey Cross Surrey
119 L7 Powburn Nthumb
9 N8 Powderham Devon
11 L5 Powerstock Dorset
109 P7 Powfoot D & G
46 D6 Pow Green Herefs
110 D9 Powhill Cumb
46 F4 Powick Worcs
134 C8 Powmill P & K
12 B8 Poxwell Dorset
36 B5 Poyle Slough
24 G8 Poynings W Susx
20 C10 Poyntington Dorset
83 K8 Poynton Ches E
69 Q11 Poynton Wrekin
69 Q11 Poynton Green Wrekin
41 J7 Poyston Cross Pembks
64 D10 Poystreet Green Suffk
2 F8 Praa Sands Cnwll
37 L8 Pratt's Bottom Gt Lon
2 G6 Praze-an-Beeble Cnwll
2 H10 Predannack Wollas Cnwll
69 Q8 Prees Shrops
94 H11 Preesall Lancs
69 Q8 Prees Green Shrops
69 J7 Preesgweene Shrops
69 Q7 Prees Heath Shrops
69 Q7 Prees Higher Heath Shrops
69 Q8 Prees Lower Heath Shrops
119 K8 Prendwick Nthumb
42 H6 Pren-gwyn Cerdgn
67 K6 Prenteg Gwynd
81 L7 Prenton Wirral
81 P6 Prescot Knows
10 B2 Prescott Devon
57 M8 Prescott Shrops
69 M10 Prescott Shrops
142 B4 Presnerb Angus
118 F3 Pressen Nthumb
80 F8 Prestatyn Denbgs
83 J9 Prestbury Ches E
47 J10 Prestbury Gloucs
45 L2 Presteigne Powys
20 B6 Prestleigh Somset
89 M9 Prestolee Bolton
129 K8 Preston Border
24 H9 Preston Br & H
7 M4 Preston Devon
11 Q8 Preston Dorset
93 L4 Preston E R Yk
33 K4 Preston Gloucs
50 E6 Preston Herts
38 H9 Preston Kent
39 M9 Preston Kent
88 G5 Preston Lancs
119 N5 Preston Nthumb
73 M10 Preston Rutlnd
57 J2 Preston Shrops
18 E7 Preston Somset
64 C11 Preston Suffk
7 M6 Preston Torbay
33 K9 Preston Wilts
33 Q10 Preston Wilts
59 J11 Preston Bagot Warwks
49 J9 Preston Bissett Bucks
18 F9 Preston Bowyer Somset
69 P10 Preston Brockhurst Shrops
82 C8 Preston Brook Halton
22 H6 Preston Candover Hants
48 G4 Preston Capes Nhants
88 H4 Preston Crematorium Lancs
34 H6 Preston Crowmarsh Oxon
60 G9 Preston Deanery Nhants
59 J11 Preston Green Warwks
69 N11 Preston Gubbals Shrops
56 G2 Preston Montford Shrops
47 P5 Preston on Stour Warwks
104 D7 Preston on Tees S on T
82 C8 Preston on the Hill Halton
45 M6 Preston on Wye Herefs
128 B5 Prestonpans E Loth
95 L4 Preston Patrick Cumb
19 P11 Preston Plucknett Somset
39 N9 Preston Street Kent
96 G2 Preston-under-Scar N York
70 B11 Preston upon the Weald Moors Wrekin
45 R5 Preston Wynne Herefs
82 H4 Prestwich Bury
113 J6 Prestwick Nthumb
114 G2 Prestwick S Ayrs
114 G2 *Prestwick Airport S Ayrs*
35 N4 Prestwood Bucks
58 C7 Prestwood Staffs
29 P6 Price Town Brdgnd
63 J4 Prickwillow Cambs
19 P4 Priddy Somset
8 B3 Priestacott Devon
83 P10 Priestcliffe Derbys
83 P10 Priestcliffe Ditch Derbys
95 L6 Priest Hutton Lancs
125 P10 Priestland E Ayrs
90 E5 Priestley Green Calder
56 D5 Priest Weston Shrops
37 Q8 Priestwood Green Kent
60 B2 Primethorpe Leics
76 F8 Primrose Green Norfk
129 K8 Primrosehill Border
62 E3 Primrose Hill Cambs
84 F9 Primrose Hill Derbys
58 D7 Primrose Hill Dudley
88 D9 Primrose Hill Lancs
118 F5 Primsidemill Border
41 M8 Princes Gate Pembks
35 M4 Princes Risborough Bucks
59 P10 Princethorpe Warwks
6 F4 Princetown Devon
15 L5 Prinsted W Susx
68 E2 Prion Denbgs
111 J7 Prior Rigg Cumb
56 H9 Priors Halton Shrops
48 E3 Priors Hardwick Warwks
57 N2 Priorslee Wrekin
48 E3 Priors Marston Warwks
46 G10 Priors Norton Gloucs
33 M7 Priory Vale Swindn
45 K5 Priory Wood Herefs
30 D9 Prisk V Glam
20 C2 Priston BaNES
64 G4 Pristow Green Norfk
38 E4 Prittlewell Sthend
23 J9 Privett Hants
17 K4 Prixford Devon
3 M4 Probus Cnwll
128 E4 Prora E Loth
100 F2 Prospect Cumb
2 G7 Prospidnick Cnwll
159 K5 Protstonhill Abers
112 G8 Prudhoe Nthumb
2 F8 Prussia Cove Cnwll
20 B2 Publow BaNES
51 J6 Puckeridge Herts
19 L11 Puckington Somset
32 C9 Pucklechurch S Glos
46 G7 Puckrup Gloucs
82 F11 Puddinglake Ches W
81 L10 Puddington Ches W
9 K2 Puddington Devon
64 F3 Puddledock Norfk
12 C6 Puddletown Dorset
45 R3 Pudleston Herefs
90 G4 Pudsey Leeds
24 B7 Pulborough W Susx
70 C10 Puleston Wrekin
69 L3 Pulford Ches W
11 Q3 Pulham Dorset
64 H4 Pulham Market Norfk
65 J4 Pulham St Mary Norfk
32 B6 Pullens Green S Glos
50 C4 Pulloxhill C Beds
127 K4 Pumpherston W Loth
43 N6 Pumsaint Carmth
41 K5 Puncheston Pembks
11 L7 Puncknowle Dorset
25 P6 Punnett's Town E Susx
15 J5 Purbrook Hants
37 N5 Purfleet Thurr
19 K6 Puriton Somset
52 D11 Purleigh Essex
36 H8 Purley Gt Lon
35 J9 Purley W Berk
56 D9 Purlogue Shrops
32 G11 Purlpit Wilts
62 G3 Purls Bridge Cambs
20 C11 Purse Caundle Dorset
58 C10 Purshull Green Worcs
56 F8 Purslow Shrops
91 L7 Purston Jaglin Wakefd
10 H3 Purtington Somset
32 C3 Purton Gloucs
32 C4 Purton Gloucs
33 L7 Purton Wilts
33 L6 Purton Stoke Wilts
49 K5 Pury End Nhants
34 C5 Pusey Oxon
46 B7 Putley Herefs
46 B7 Putley Green Herefs
32 E3 Putloe Gloucs
36 F6 Putney Gt Lon
36 F6 Putney Vale Crematorium Gt Lon
16 G3 Putsborough Devon
35 N2 Puttenham Herts
23 P5 Puttenham Surrey
52 D3 Puttock End Essex
11 N8 Putton Dorset
49 L6 Puxley Nhants
19 M2 Puxton N Som
28 E4 Pwll Carmth
40 H10 Pwllcrochan Pembks
30 H2 Pwll-du Mons
68 F4 Pwll-glas Denbgs
44 E8 Pwllgloyw Powys
66 F7 Pwllheli Gwynd
31 P6 Pwllmeyric Mons
41 Q7 Pwll Trap Carmth
29 L6 Pwll-y-glaw Neath
79 Q9 Pydew Conwy
84 F10 Pye Bridge Derbys
24 G8 Pyecombe W Susx
31 K7 Pye Corner Newpt
58 E2 Pye Green Staffs
29 M8 Pyle Brdgnd
18 F8 Pyleigh Somset
20 B7 Pylle Somset
62 G3 Pymoor Cambs
11 K6 Pymore Dorset
36 B9 Pyrford Surrey
35 J5 Pyrton Oxon
61 J6 Pytchley Nhants
16 E11 Pyworthy Devon

Q

56 C8 Quabbs Shrops
74 D4 Quadring Lincs
74 D4 Quadring Eaudike Lincs
49 K10 Quainton Bucks
30 E5 Quaker's Yard Myr Td
113 J10 Quaking Houses Dur
18 G7 Quantock Hills Somset
169 r10 Quarff Shet
21 Q6 Quarley Hants
72 A2 Quarndon Derbys
14 G8 Quarr Hill IoW
125 K4 Quarrier's Village Inver
73 R2 Quarrington Lincs
104 B3 Quarrington Hill Dur
82 C11 Quarrybank Ches W
58 D7 Quarry Bank Dudley
157 M5 Quarrywood Moray
124 F5 Quarter N Ayrs
126 C7 Quarter S Lans
57 N6 Quatford Shrops
57 P7 Quatt Shrops
103 N2 Quebec Dur
32 F2 Quedgeley Gloucs
63 J4 Queen Adelaide Cambs
38 F7 Queenborough Kent
19 Q10 Queen Camel Somset
32 B11 Queen Charlton BaNES
17 Q8 Queen Dart Devon
132 G7 Queen Elizabeth Forest Park Stirlg
46 G7 Queenhill Worcs
20 E8 Queen Oak Dorset
14 G10 Queen's Bower IoW
90 E4 Queensbury C Brad
81 L11 Queensferry Flints
69 K9 Queen's Head Shrops
126 B4 Queenslie C Glas
61 M11 Queen's Park Bed
60 G8 Queen's Park Nhants
37 Q11 Queen Street Kent
33 K7 Queen Street Wilts
126 B2 Queenzieburn N Lans
51 M4 Quendon Essex
72 G8 Queniborough Leics
33 M4 Quenington Gloucs
95 L8 Quernmore Lancs
58 G6 Queslett Birm
5 N9 Quethiock Cnwll
34 G9 Quick's Green W Berk
64 E4 Quidenham Norfk
22 F4 Quidhampton Hants
21 M8 Quidhampton Wilts
69 P8 Quina Brook Shrops
48 H4 Quinbury End Nhants
58 E8 Quinton Dudley
49 L4 Quinton Nhants
49 L4 Quinton Green Nhants
4 C9 Quintrell Downs Cnwll
71 L6 Quixhall Staffs
129 K7 Quixwood Border
5 Q2 Quoditch Devon
133 N3 Quoig P & K
72 F7 Quorn Leics
116 D3 Quothquan S Lans
169 e6 Quoyburray Ork
169 b4 Quoyloo Ork

R

153 K9 Raasay Highld
26 C2 Rabbit's Cross Kent
50 F7 Rableyheath Herts
110 C10 Raby Cumb
81 L9 Raby Wirral
116 G4 Rachan Mill Border
79 L11 Rachub Gwynd
17 R8 Rackenford Devon
24 B8 Rackham W Susx
77 K9 Rackheath Norfk
109 M6 Racks D & G
169 b7 Rackwick Ork
71 P7 Radbourne Derbys
89 M9 Radcliffe Bury
119 Q10 Radcliffe Nthumb
72 G3 Radcliffe on Trent Notts
49 J8 Radclive Bucks
33 Q5 Radcot Oxon
156 C6 Raddery Highld
18 D9 Raddington Somset
135 M6 Radernie Fife
59 M8 Radford Covtry
48 B2 Radford Semele Warwks
18 H7 Radlet Somset
50 E10 Radlett Herts
17 N7 Radley Devon
34 F5 Radley Oxon
51 P9 Radley Green Essex
69 Q3 Radmore Green Ches E
35 L5 Radnage Bucks
20 C4 Radstock BaNES
48 G6 Radstone Nhants
48 C5 Radway Warwks
61 M9 Radwell Bed
50 F3 Radwell Herts
51 P3 Radwinter Essex
51 P3 Radwinter End Essex
30 F8 Radyr Cardif
86 D11 RAF College (Cranwell) Lincs
157 K6 Rafford Moray
72 H7 Ragdale Leics
56 H6 Ragdon Shrops
2 D8 Raginnis Cnwll
31 M3 Raglan Mons
85 P6 Ragnall Notts
148 E2 Raigbeg Highld
46 G3 Rainbow Hill Worcs
81 P4 Rainford St Hel
37 M4 Rainham Gt Lon
38 D8 Rainham Medway
81 P6 Rainhill St Hel
81 Q6 Rainhill Stoops St Hel
83 K9 Rainow Ches E
82 H4 Rainsough Bury
97 N5 Rainton N York
85 J9 Rainworth Notts
102 B9 Raisbeck Cumb
111 P11 Raise Cumb
98 H8 Raisthorpe N York
134 G2 Rait P & K
87 K4 Raithby Lincs
87 L7 Raithby Lincs
105 N8 Raithwaite N York
23 M9 Rake Hants
89 Q8 Rakewood Rochdl
148 C8 Ralia Highld
43 L5 Ram Carmth
152 B9 Ramasaig Highld
3 J7 Rame Cnwll
6 C9 Rame Cnwll
32 C9 Ram Hill S Glos
26 G2 Ram Lane Kent
11 M4 Rampisham Dorset
94 E7 Rampside Cumb
62 F7 Rampton Cambs
85 P5 Rampton Notts
89 M7 Ramsbottom Bury
33 Q10 Ramsbury Wilts
167 K11 Ramscraigs Highld
23 K10 Ramsdean Hants
22 G3 Ramsdell Hants
48 C11 Ramsden Oxon
46 H5 Ramsden Worcs
38 B3 Ramsden Bellhouse Essex
38 B2 Ramsden Heath Essex
62 C3 Ramsey Cambs
53 M5 Ramsey Essex
80 g3 Ramsey IoM
62 D3 Ramsey Forty Foot Cambs
62 B4 Ramsey Heights Cambs
52 F10 Ramsey Island Essex
40 D6 Ramsey Island Pembks
62 C3 Ramsey Mereside Cambs
62 C3 Ramsey St Mary's Cambs
39 Q8 Ramsgate Kent
96 H6 Ramsgill N York
103 M5 Ramshaw Dur
112 E11 Ramshaw Dur
53 P3 Ramsholt Suffk
118 D10 Ramshope Nthumb
71 K5 Ramshorn Staffs
8 G6 Ramsley Devon
23 P8 Ramsnest Common Surrey
86 H5 Ranby Lincs
85 L4 Ranby Notts
86 F5 Rand Lincs
36 E9 Randalls Park Crematorium Surrey
32 F3 Randwick Gloucs
125 K4 Ranfurly Rens
71 M10 Rangemore Staffs
32 C7 Rangeworthy S Glos
115 J5 Rankinston E Ayrs
73 L8 Ranksborough Rutlnd
52 B8 Rank's Green Essex
140 B6 Rannoch Station P & K
18 B6 Ranscombe Somset
85 L3 Ranskill Notts
70 F10 Ranton Staffs

Ranton Green - Roucan 295

70 E10 Ranton Green Staffs
77 M9 Ranworth Norfk
133 M9 Raploch Stirlg
169 e2 Rapness Ork
19 K11 Rapps Somset
108 G11 Rascarrel D & G
131 N11 Rashfield Ag & B
58 D11 Rashwood Worcs
97 Q6 Raskelf N York
30 G2 Rassau Blae G
90 E6 Rastrick Calder
145 R4 Ratagan Highld
72 E9 Ratby Leics
72 A11 Ratcliffe Culey Leics
72 D5 Ratcliffe on Soar Notts
72 G8 Ratcliffe on the Wreake Leics
21 N6 Ratfyn Wilts
159 N5 Rathen Abers
135 K3 Rathillet Fife
96 B9 Rathmell N York
127 L3 Ratho C Edin
127 L3 Ratho Station C Edin
158 B4 Rathven Moray
22 D10 Ratlake Hants
48 C5 Ratley Warwks
39 M11 Ratling Kent
56 G5 Ratlinghope Shrops
75 K8 Rattan Row Norfk
167 N2 Rattar Highld
101 K2 Ratten Row Cumb
110 G11 Ratten Row Cumb
88 E2 Ratten Row Lancs
7 J6 Rattery Devon
64 D10 Rattlesden Suffk
25 N10 Ratton Village E Susx
142 B8 Rattray P & K
110 G11 Raughton Cumb
110 G11 Raughton Head Cumb
61 L6 Raunds Nhants
91 M11 Ravenfield Rothm
100 E11 Ravenglass Cumb
46 D4 Ravenhills Green Worcs
65 M2 Raveningham Norfk
105 Q10 Ravenscar N York
126 D6 Ravenscraig N Lans
80 e3 Ravensdale IoM
61 N10 Ravensden Bed
102 G10 Ravenseat N York
85 J10 Ravenshead Notts
69 R4 Ravensmoor Ches E
90 G6 Ravensthorpe Kirk
60 E6 Ravensthorpe Nhants
72 C8 Ravenstone Leics
49 M4 Ravenstone M Keyn
102 D10 Ravenstonedale Cumb
126 G8 Ravenstruther S Lans
103 M9 Ravensworth N York
105 P9 Raw N York
98 B10 Rawcliffe C York
92 A6 Rawcliffe E R Yk
92 A6 Rawcliffe Bridge E R Yk
90 G3 Rawdon Leeds
90 G3 Rawdon Crematorium Leeds
38 F10 Rawling Street Kent
91 L11 Rawmarsh Rothm
58 F2 Rawnsley Staffs
38 C3 Rawreth Essex
10 E3 Rawridge Devon
89 N6 Rawtenstall Lancs
52 H4 Raydon Suffk
112 D2 Raylees Nthumb
38 D3 Rayleigh Essex
10 G5 Raymond's Hill Devon
52 B7 Rayne Essex
36 F7 Raynes Park Gt Lon
63 J7 Reach Cambs
89 M4 Read Lancs
35 K10 Reading Readg
35 K9 Reading Crematorium Readg
35 J11 Reading Services W Berk
26 F5 Reading Street Kent
39 Q8 Reading Street Kent
102 B7 Reagill Cumb
2 G6 Realwa Cnwll
162 G8 Rearquhar Highld
72 H8 Rearsby Leics
70 A4 Rease Heath Ches E
166 G4 Reay Highld
39 M8 Reculver Kent
18 E11 Red Ball Devon
41 L10 Redberth Pembks
50 D8 Redbourn Herts
92 G11 Redbourne N Linc
31 P3 Redbrook Gloucs
69 P6 Redbrook Wrexhm
26 F4 Redbrook Street Kent
156 G8 Redburn Highld
111 Q8 Redburn Nthumb
104 H6 Redcar R & Cl
108 H7 Redcastle D & G
155 Q8 Redcastle Highld
110 E11 Red Dial Cumb
126 G2 Redding Falk
126 G2 Reddingmuirhead Falk
83 J6 Reddish Stockp
58 F11 Redditch Worcs
58 F11 Redditch Crematorium Worcs
63 P9 Rede Suffk
65 K5 Redenhall Norfk
22 B5 Redenham Hants
112 C4 Redesmouth Nthumb
143 P3 Redford Abers
143 K9 Redford Angus
23 N9 Redford W Susx
117 M7 Redfordgreen Border
30 D7 Redgate Rhondd
134 D2 Redgorton P & K
64 E6 Redgrave Suffk
151 K7 Redhill Abers
13 J5 Red Hill Bmouth
50 H4 Redhill Herts
19 N2 Redhill N Som
36 G10 Redhill Surrey
47 M3 Red Hill Warwks
65 N5 Redisham Suffk
31 Q9 Redland Bristl
169 C4 Redland Ork
64 H7 Redlingfield Suffk
64 H7 Redlingfield Green Suffk
63 L6 Red Lodge Suffk
89 N7 Red Lumb Rochdl
20 D8 Redlynch Somset
21 P10 Redlynch Wilts
100 F4 Redmain Cumb
57 P11 Redmarley Worcs
46 E8 Redmarley D'Abitot Gloucs
104 C6 Redmarshall S on T
73 K3 Redmile Leics
96 F2 Redmire N York
143 P2 Redmyre Abers
58 F9 Rednal Birm
69 L9 Rednal Shrops
118 A3 Redpath Border
153 N4 Redpoint Highld
16 D10 Red Post Cnwll
88 H9 Red Rock Wigan
41 P8 Red Roses Carmth
119 Q11 Red Row Nthumb
2 H5 Redruth Cnwll
20 H2 Redstocks Wilts
142 B11 Redstone P & K
41 M7 Redstone Cross Pembks
70 E4 Red Street Staffs
89 N9 Redvales Bury
79 J8 Red Wharf Bay IoA
31 M8 Redwick Newpt
31 P7 Redwick S Glos
103 P6 Redworth Darltn
51 J3 Reed Herts
77 N11 Reedham Norfk
92 C6 Reedness E R Yk
86 H7 Reeds Beck Lincs
89 N6 Reeds Holme Lancs
86 D6 Reepham Lincs
76 G7 Reepham Norfk
103 K11 Reeth N York
59 L9 Reeves Green Solhll
80 f2 Regaby IoM
19 F2 Regil N Som
160 F4 Reiff Highld
36 G10 Reigate Surrey
99 N5 Reighton N York
151 M4 Reisque Abers
167 P6 Reiss Highld
4 B10 Rejerrah Cnwll
2 H7 Releath Cnwll
2 F7 Relubbus Cnwll
156 H8 Relugas Moray
35 L8 Remenham Wokham
35 L8 Remenham Hill Wokham
72 F6 Rempstone Notts
33 K3 Rendcomb Gloucs
65 L9 Rendham Suffk
65 L11 Rendlesham Suffk
125 N4 Renfrew Rens
61 N10 Renhold Bed
84 G5 Renishaw Derbys
119 P7 Rennington Nthumb
125 K2 Renton W Duns
101 Q2 Renwick Cumb
77 N8 Repps Norfk
71 Q9 Repton Derbys
156 C8 Resaurie Highld
3 P5 Rescassa Cnwll
3 P4 Rescorla Cnwll
138 C5 Resipole Highld
2 G5 Reskadinnick Cnwll
156 B4 Resolis Highld
29 M4 Resolven Neath
131 Q6 Rest and be thankful Ag & B
129 M7 Reston Border
3 L6 Restronguet Cnwll
143 J7 Reswallie Angus
4 E9 Reterth Cnwll
85 M4 Retford Notts
4 G9 Retire Cnwll
38 C2 Rettendon Essex
4 D10 Retyn Cnwll
87 J8 Revesby Lincs
7 J11 Rew Devon
7 K4 Rew Devon
9 M5 Rewe Devon
14 E8 Rew Street IoW
5 Q4 Rexon Devon
65 P6 Reydon Suffk
76 E10 Reymerston Norfk
41 L9 Reynalton Pembks
28 E7 Reynoldston Swans
5 P6 Rezare Cnwll
31 L4 Rhadyr Mons
43 Q6 Rhandirmwyn Carmth
55 M11 Rhayader Powys
155 P8 Rheindown Highld
80 H10 Rhes-y-cae Flints
68 F2 Rhewl Denbgs
68 G6 Rhewl Denbgs
80 G8 Rhewl-fawr Flints
80 H8 Rhewl Mostyn Flints
164 C11 Rhicarn Highld
164 G6 Rhiconich Highld
156 B3 Rhicullen Highld
29 P3 Rhigos Rhondd
160 G7 Rhireavach Highld
163 J6 Rhives Highld
30 G8 Rhiwbina Cardif
67 M5 Rhiwbryfdir Gwynd
31 J7 Rhiwderyn Newpt
67 K2 Rhiwen Gwynd
30 D7 Rhiwinder Rhondd
68 B7 Rhiwlas Gwynd
79 K11 Rhiwlas Gwynd
68 G8 Rhiwlas Powys
30 E8 Rhiwsaeson Rhondd
19 J8 Rhode Somset
37 Q11 Rhoden Green Kent
85 J5 Rhodesia Notts
27 L3 Rhodes Minnis Kent
40 E5 Rhodiad-y-brenin Pembks
108 F9 Rhonehouse D & G
30 E11 Rhoose V Glam
42 G7 Rhos Carmth
68 F2 Rhos Denbgs
29 K4 Rhos Neath
78 F6 Rhosbeirio IoA
79 J9 Rhoscefnhir IoA
78 D9 Rhoscolyn IoA
40 H10 Rhoscrowther Pembks
81 J11 Rhosesmor Flints
66 F7 Rhos-fawr Gwynd
67 J3 Rhosgadfan Gwynd
78 G7 Rhosgoch IoA
44 H5 Rhosgoch Powys
43 K2 Rhos Haminiog Cerdgn
41 N2 Rhoshill Pembks
66 C9 Rhoshirwaun Gwynd
66 H6 Rhoslan Gwynd
54 D3 Rhoslefain Gwynd
69 J5 Rhosllanerchrugog Wrexhm
78 H7 Rhos Lligwy IoA
43 M10 Rhosmaen Carmth
78 H9 Rhosmeirch IoA
78 E10 Rhosneigr IoA
69 L4 Rhosnesni Wrexhm
79 Q8 Rhôs-on-Sea Conwy
69 K4 Rhosrobin Wrexhm
28 D7 Rhossili Swans
66 H3 Rhostryfan Gwynd
69 K5 Rhostyllen Wrexhm
78 G7 Rhosybol IoA
68 F10 Rhos y-brithdir Powys
69 K8 Rhosygadfa Shrops
54 E10 Rhos-y-garth Cerdgn
68 B8 Rhos-y-gwaliau Gwynd
66 C7 Rhos-y-llan Gwynd
69 J6 Rhosymedre Wrexhm
56 D11 Rhos-y-meirch Powys
132 B11 Rhu Ag & B
80 F9 Rhualit Denbgs
124 C3 Rhubodach Ag & B
69 Q2 Rhuddall Heath Ches W
43 J6 Rhuddlan Cerdgn
80 E9 Rhuddlan Denbgs
44 G5 Rhulen Powys
123 M10 Rhunahaorine Ag & B
67 L6 Rhyd Gwynd
42 H9 Rhydargaeau Carmth
43 L7 Rhydcymerau Carmth
46 F5 Rhydd Worcs
67 K4 Rhyd-Ddu Gwynd
29 K5 Rhydding Neath
68 C2 Rhydgaled Conwy
67 Q4 Rhydlanfair Conwy
42 F5 Rhydlewis Cerdgn
66 B9 Rhydlios Gwynd
68 A4 Rhyd-lydan Conwy
42 H5 Rhydowen Cerdgn
54 D11 Rhydrosser Cerdgn
45 J5 Rhydspence Herefs
68 H4 Rhydtalog Flints
68 B7 Rhyd-uchaf Gwynd
66 E8 Rhyd-y-clafdy Gwynd
68 H8 Rhydycroesau Shrops
54 D9 Rhydyfelin Cerdgn
30 E7 Rhydyfelin Rhondd
80 C9 Rhyd-y-foel Conwy
29 K3 Rhydyfro Neath
79 K11 Rhyd-y-groes Gwynd
67 Q10 Rhydymain Gwynd
31 K3 Rhyd-y-meirch Mons
81 J11 Rhydymwyn Flints
54 E7 Rhyd-y pennau Cerdgn
54 E4 Rhyd-yr-onnen Gwynd
67 M6 Rhyd-y-sarn Gwynd
80 E8 Rhyl Denbgs
30 F3 Rhymney Caerph
134 F3 Rhynd P & K
150 D2 Rhynie Abers
163 J11 Rhynie Highld
57 P10 Ribbesford Worcs
88 H4 Ribbleton Lancs
88 E4 Ribby Lancs
89 K3 Ribchester Lancs
84 D9 Riber Derbys
93 L9 Riby Lincs
91 Q3 Riccall N York
111 K2 Riccarton Border
125 L10 Riccarton E Ayrs
56 H11 Richards Castle Herefs
36 B5 Richings Park Bucks
36 E6 Richmond Gt Lon
103 N10 Richmond N York
84 F3 Richmond Sheff
10 b2 Richmond Fort Guern
18 F8 Rich's Holford Somset
70 G10 Rickerscote Staffs
19 N3 Rickford N Som
7 K11 Rickham Devon
64 E6 Rickinghall Suffk
51 L4 Rickling Essex
51 M5 Rickling Green Essex
36 C2 Rickmansworth Herts
117 Q6 Riddell Border
84 F10 Riddings Derbys
17 L9 Riddlecombe Devon
90 D2 Riddlesden C Brad
19 Q3 Ridge BaNES
12 F7 Ridge Dorset
50 F10 Ridge Herts
21 J8 Ridge Wilts
44 F2 Ridgebourne Powys
36 H11 Ridge Green Surrey
59 L6 Ridge Lane Warwks
27 M3 Ridge Row Kent
84 F4 Ridgeway Derbys
47 K2 Ridgeway Worcs
46 D5 Ridgeway Cross Herefs
52 B3 Ridgewell Essex
25 L7 Ridgewood E Susx
49 Q7 Ridgmont C Beds
112 F8 Riding Mill Nthumb
37 P8 Ridley Kent
111 Q8 Ridley Nthumb
69 Q4 Ridley Green Ches E
77 L5 Ridlington Norfk
73 L10 Ridlington Rutlnd
77 L5 Ridlington Street Norfk
112 D4 Ridsdale Nthumb
98 B3 Rievaulx N York
98 B4 Rievaulx Abbey N York
110 E7 Rigg D & G
126 D3 Riggend N Lans
156 F7 Rigghoul Highld
95 N4 Rigmadon Park Cumb
87 M5 Rigsby Lincs
116 B3 Rigside S Lans
89 J5 Riley Green Lancs
58 H2 Rileyhill Staffs
5 M7 Rilla Mill Cnwll
5 M7 Rillaton Cnwll
98 H6 Rillington N York
96 B11 Rimington Lancs
20 B10 Rimpton Somset
93 P5 Rimswell E R Yk
41 J5 Rinaston Pembks
57 N5 Rindleford Shrops
108 E9 Ringford D & G
84 C4 Ringinglow Sheff
76 G9 Ringland Norfk
25 L6 Ringles Cross E Susx
38 E10 Ringlestone Kent
89 M9 Ringley Bolton
25 K8 Ringmer E Susx
6 H9 Ringmore Devon
7 N4 Ringmore Devon
88 F8 Ring o'Bells Lancs
157 P9 Ringorm Moray
74 G10 Ring's End Cambs
65 N4 Ringsfield Suffk
65 N4 Ringsfield Corner Suffk
35 Q2 Ringshall Herts
64 E11 Ringshall Suffk
64 F11 Ringshall Stocks Suffk
61 L5 Ringstead Nhants
75 P2 Ringstead Norfk
13 L3 Ringwood Hants
27 Q2 Ringwould Kent
2 F8 Rinsey Cnwll
2 G8 Rinsey Croft Cnwll
25 M8 Ripe E Susx
84 E10 Ripley Derbys
13 L5 Ripley Hants
97 L8 Ripley N York
36 C9 Ripley Surrey
92 G4 Riplingham E R Yk
23 J10 Riplington Hants
97 M6 Ripon N York
74 A5 Rippingale Lincs
39 Q11 Ripple Kent
46 G7 Ripple Worcs
90 C7 Ripponden Calder
122 D11 Risabus Ag & B
45 Q4 Risbury Herefs
92 F8 Risby N Linc
63 P7 Risby Suffk
30 H6 Risca Caerph
93 L2 Rise E R Yk
25 P4 Riseden E Susx
26 B4 Riseden Kent
74 D5 Risegate Lincs
86 C5 Riseholme Lincs
100 D4 Risehow Cumb
61 M8 Riseley Bed
23 K2 Riseley Wokham
64 H8 Rishangles Suffk
89 L4 Rishton Lancs
90 C7 Rishworth Calder
89 M5 Rising Bridge Lancs
72 D3 Risley Derbys
82 E6 Risley Warrtn
97 K7 Risplith N York
22 B2 Rivar Wilts
52 D8 Rivenhall End Essex
27 N3 River Kent
23 P10 River W Susx
62 H7 River Bank Cambs
155 P7 Riverford Highld
37 M9 Riverhead Kent
12 C2 Rivers Corner Dorset
89 J8 Rivington Lancs
17 R7 Roachill Devon
49 L4 Roade Nhants
65 K3 Road Green Norfk
111 K6 Roadhead Cumb
126 F8 Roadmeetings S Lans
115 L4 Roadside E Ayrs
167 L4 Roadside Highld
18 D7 Roadwater Somset
152 D9 Roag Highld
94 E7 Roa Island Cumb
114 E7 Roan of Craigoch S Ayrs
51 L4 Roast Green Essex
30 G9 Roath Cardif
117 N8 Roberton Border
116 C5 Roberton S Lans
26 B7 Robertsbridge E Susx
90 F6 Roberttown Kirk
41 L7 Robeston Wathen Pembks
110 D6 Robgill Tower D & G
70 G3 Robin Hill Staffs
88 G8 Robin Hood Lancs
91 J5 Robin Hood Leeds
58 H8 Robin Hood Crematorium Solhll
91 R11 Robin Hood Doncaster Sheffield Airport Donc
52 B4 Robinhood End Essex
105 Q9 Robin Hood's Bay N York
6 E6 Roborough Devon
17 K8 Roborough Devon
81 N6 Roby Knows
88 G9 Roby Mill Lancs
71 L7 Rocester Staffs
40 G6 Roch Pembks
89 P8 Rochdale Rochdl
89 P8 Rochdale Crematorium Rochdl
4 F9 Roche Cnwll
38 B8 Rochester Medway
118 F11 Rochester Nthumb
38 E3 Rochford Essex
57 L11 Rochford Worcs
40 G6 Roch Gate Pembks
4 E6 Rock Cnwll
29 L6 Rock Neath
119 P6 Rock Nthumb
24 D8 Rock W Susx
57 N10 Rock Worcs
9 P6 Rockbeare Devon
21 M11 Rockbourne Hants
110 G8 Rockcliffe Cumb
108 H10 Rockcliffe D & G
110 F8 Rockcliffe Cross Cumb
70 F3 Rock End Staffs
7 N6 Rockend Torbay
81 L7 Rock Ferry Wirral
163 L10 Rockfield Highld
31 N2 Rockfield Mons
17 P2 Rockford Devon
13 L3 Rockford Hants
57 J9 Rockgreen Shrops
32 C6 Rockhampton S Glos
4 H5 Rockhead Cnwll
56 D9 Rockhill Shrops
58 E11 Rock Hill Worcs
61 J2 Rockingham Nhants
64 D2 Rockland All Saints Norfk
77 L11 Rockland St Mary Norfk
64 D2 Rockland St Peter Norfk
85 M6 Rockley Notts
33 N10 Rockley Wilts
89 P6 Rockliffe Lancs
131 Q9 Rockville Ag & B
35 L7 Rockwell End Bucks
18 F10 Rockwell Green Somset
32 F6 Rodborough Gloucs
33 M7 Rodbourne Swindn
32 H8 Rodbourne Wilts
45 L2 Rodd Herefs
119 K6 Roddam Nthumb
11 N8 Rodden Dorset
103 N3 Roddymoor Dur
20 F4 Rode Somset
70 E3 Rode Heath Ches E
83 J11 Rode Heath Ches E
168 f9 Rodel W Isls
69 Q11 Roden Wrekin
18 D7 Rodhuish Somset
57 K2 Rodington Wrekin
57 K2 Rodington Heath Wrekin
32 D2 Rodley Gloucs
90 G3 Rodley Leeds
32 H5 Rodmarton Gloucs
25 K9 Rodmell E Susx
38 F9 Rodmersham Kent
38 F9 Rodmersham Green Kent
19 N5 Rodney Stoke Somset
71 N6 Rodsley Derbys
19 J6 Rodway Somset
97 N7 Roecliffe N York
83 L5 Roe Cross Tamesd
50 F9 Roe Green Herts
50 H4 Roe Green Herts
82 G4 Roe Green Salfd
36 F6 Roehampton Gt Lon
24 E4 Roffey W Susx
162 G6 Rogart Highld
23 M10 Rogate W Susx
101 L11 Roger Ground Cumb
31 J7 Rogerstone Newpt
168 f9 Roghadal W Isls
31 N7 Rogiet Mons
34 H6 Roke Oxon
113 P9 Roker Sundld
77 N8 Rollesby Norfk
73 J10 Rolleston Leics
85 M10 Rolleston Notts
71 N9 Rolleston on Dove Staffs
93 M2 Rolston E R Yk
19 L2 Rolstone N Som
26 D5 Rolvenden Kent
26 E5 Rolvenden Layne Kent
103 J6 Romaldkirk Dur
20 E2 Roman Baths & Pump Room BaNES
97 N2 Romanby N York
127 M8 Romanno Bridge Border
17 N7 Romansleigh Devon
26 E3 Romden Castle Kent
152 G7 Romesdal Highld
13 J3 Romford Dorset
37 M3 Romford Gt Lon
83 K6 Romiley Stockp
37 N8 Romney Street Kent
22 C10 Romsey Hants
57 P8 Romsley Shrops
58 E8 Romsley Worcs
153 L6 Rona Highld
123 M9 Ronachan Ag & B
20 G3 Rood Ashton Wilts
102 H2 Rookhope Dur
14 F10 Rookley IoW
14 F10 Rookley Green IoW
19 L4 Rooks Bridge Somset
18 E8 Rooks Nest Somset
97 K3 Rookwith N York
93 N4 Roos E R Yk
94 E7 Roose Cumb
94 F7 Roosebeck Cumb
61 N9 Roothams Green Bed
22 H8 Ropley Hants
22 H8 Ropley Dean Hants
23 J8 Ropley Soke Hants
73 P4 Ropsley Lincs
159 Q7 Rora Abers
56 E4 Rorrington Shrops
158 A7 Rosarie Moray
3 K3 Rose Cnwll
88 E3 Roseacre Lancs
17 P7 Rose Ash Devon
126 E8 Rosebank S Lans
41 L5 Rosebush Pembks
5 K2 Rosecare Cnwll
4 C10 Rosecliston Cnwll
105 K11 Rosedale Abbey N York
52 F6 Rose Green Essex
52 F4 Rose Green Suffk
52 G3 Rose Green Suffk
15 P7 Rose Green W Susx
162 B6 Rosehall Highld
159 M4 Rosehearty Abers
25 L7 Rose Hill E Susx
89 N4 Rose Hill Lancs
69 N11 Rosehill Shrops
157 L4 Roseisle Moray
25 P10 Roselands E Susx
41 J9 Rosemarket Pembks
156 C6 Rosemarkie Highld
10 D2 Rosemary Lane Devon
142 B9 Rosemount P & K
4 F8 Rosenannon Cnwll
3 L9 Rosenithon Cnwll
25 M6 Roser's Cross E Susx
4 G10 Rosevean Cnwll
3 M6 Rosevine Cnwll
2 G6 Rosewarne Cnwll
127 P5 Rosewell Mdloth
104 D6 Roseworth S on T
2 G6 Roseworthy Cnwll
101 P7 Rosgill Cumb
2 B9 Roskestal Cnwll
152 D9 Roskhill Highld
3 K9 Roskorwell Cnwll
110 F11 Rosley Cumb
127 P5 Roslin Mdloth
71 N11 Rosliston Derbys
132 B11 Rosneath Ag & B
108 D12 Ross D & G
119 M3 Ross Nthumb
69 L3 Rossett Wrexhm
97 L10 Rossett Green N York
91 Q11 Rossington Donc
125 L3 Rossland Rens
46 A10 Ross-on-Wye Herefs
167 N9 Roster Highld
82 F8 Rostherne Ches E
101 J8 Rosthwaite Cumb
71 L6 Roston Derbys
2 F8 Rosudgeon Cnwll
134 E11 Rosyth Fife
119 L10 Rothbury Nthumb
72 H7 Rotherby Leics
25 N5 Rotherfield E Susx
35 K8 Rotherfield Greys Oxon
35 K8 Rotherfield Peppard Oxon
84 F2 Rotherham Rothm
84 G2 Rotherham Crematorium Rothm
60 F9 Rothersthorpe Nhants
60 F9 Rothersthorpe Services Nhants
23 K3 Rotherwick Hants
157 P8 Rothes Moray
124 D5 Rothesay Ag & B
158 H10 Rothiebrisbane Abers
158 E8 Rothiemay Moray
148 H6 Rothiemurchus Lodge Highld
158 H10 Rothienorman Abers
72 F8 Rothley Leics
112 F3 Rothley Nthumb
158 G11 Rothmaise Abers
91 J5 Rothwell Leeds
93 K11 Rothwell Lincs
60 H4 Rothwell Nhants
99 M10 Rotsea E R Yk
142 F4 Rottal Lodge Angus
25 J10 Rottingdean Br & H
100 C8 Rottington Cumb
109 M5 Roucan D & G

296 Roucan Loch Crematorium - Sandysike

109 M5 Roucan Loch Crematorium D & G
14 F10 Roud IoW
76 A7 Rougham Norfk
64 C9 Rougham Green Suffk
70 G7 Rough Close Staffs
39 K10 Rough Common Kent
89 N2 Roughlee Lancs
149 Q5 Roughpark Abers
86 H8 Roughton Lincs
77 J4 Roughton Norfk
57 P6 Roughton Shrops
37 P10 Roughway Kent
52 E11 Roundbush Essex
50 F11 Round Bush Herts
51 N8 Roundbush Green Essex
50 D6 Round Green Luton
11 J3 Roundham Somset
91 J3 Roundhay Leeds
58 E7 Rounds Green Sandw
37 Q7 Round Street Kent
24 C5 Roundstreet Common W Susx
21 K2 Roundway Wilts
142 F7 Roundyhill Angus
169 c3 Rousay Ork
10 F6 Rousdon Devon
48 E10 Rousham Oxon
47 K4 Rous Lench Worcs
124 F5 Routenburn N Ayrs
93 J2 Routh E R Yk
35 L5 Rout's Green Bucks
4 H6 Row Cnwll
95 K3 Row Cumb
102 B4 Row Cumb
110 H5 Rowanburn D & G
132 D8 Rowardennan Stirlg
83 M7 Rowarth Derbys
14 F4 Row Ash Hants
19 N3 Rowberrow Somset
14 E10 Rowborough IoW
21 J2 Rowde Wilts
8 F5 Rowden Devon
79 P10 Rowen Conwy
71 M5 Rowfield Derbys
111 N8 Rowfoot Nthumb
18 H9 Rowford Somset
52 B7 Row Green Essex
52 H7 Rowhedge Essex
24 D4 Rowhook W Susx
59 K11 Rowington Warwks
84 B6 Rowland Derbys
15 K4 Rowland's Castle Hants
113 J9 Rowland's Gill Gatesd
23 M6 Rowledge Surrey
112 G11 Rowley Dur
92 G4 Rowley E R Yk
56 E3 Rowley Shrops
90 F8 Rowley Hill Kirk
58 E7 Rowley Regis Sandw
58 E7 Rowley Regis Crematorium Sandw
45 M9 Rowlstone Herefs
24 B2 Rowly Surrey
14 G6 Rowner Hants
58 F10 Rowney Green Worcs
22 C11 Rownhams Hants
22 C11 Rownhams Services Hants
100 E7 Rowrah Cumb
49 M11 Rowsham Bucks
84 C7 Rowsley Derbys
82 H9 Rows of Trees Ches E
34 E7 Rowstock Oxon
86 E9 Rowston Lincs
84 G8 Rowthorne Derbys
69 M2 Rowton Ches W
56 F2 Rowton Shrops
56 G8 Rowton Shrops
69 R11 Rowton Wrekin
36 B8 Row Town Surrey
118 C4 Roxburgh Border
92 F7 Roxby N Linc
105 L7 Roxby N York
61 Q10 Roxton Bed
51 P9 Roxwell Essex
36 E5 Royal Botanic Gardens Gt Lon
103 P6 Royal Oak Darltn
81 N4 Royal Oak Lancs
69 R6 Royal's Green Ches E
146 H11 Roy Bridge Highld
90 G8 Roydhouse Kirk
51 K8 Roydon Essex
64 G5 Roydon Norfk
75 P6 Roydon Norfk
51 K9 Roydon Hamlet Essex
91 K8 Royston Barns
51 J2 Royston Herts
89 Q9 Royton Oldham
11 c1 Rozel Jersey
69 K6 Ruabon Wrexhm
136 D6 Ruaig Ag & B
3 N6 Ruan High Lanes Cnwll
3 M5 Ruan Lanihorne Cnwll
3 J10 Ruan Major Cnwll
3 J10 Ruan Minor Cnwll
46 B11 Ruardean Gloucs
46 B11 Ruardean Hill Gloucs
46 B11 Ruardean Woodside Gloucs
58 E9 Rubery Birm
168 c16 Rubha Ban W Isls
101 P2 Ruckcroft Cumb
45 P7 Ruckhall Herefs
26 H5 Ruckinge Kent
87 K5 Ruckland Lincs
57 J4 Ruckley Shrops
104 E9 Rudby N York
112 H7 Rudchester Nthumb
72 F4 Ruddington Notts
32 C2 Ruddle Gloucs
3 Q3 Ruddlemoor Cnwll
46 E10 Rudford Gloucs
20 F4 Rudge Somset
32 B7 Rudgeway S Glos
24 C4 Rudgwick W Susx
46 B9 Rudhall Herefs
82 E10 Rudheath Ches W
82 F10 Rudheath Woods Ches E
52 D11 Rudley Green Essex
32 F10 Rudloe Wilts
30 H7 Rudry Caerph
99 M7 Rudston E R Yk
70 H3 Rudyard Staffs
118 B6 Ruecastle Border
88 F7 Rufford Lancs
98 A10 Rufforth C York
68 E6 Rug Denbgs
60 B5 Rugby Warwks
71 J11 Rugeley Staffs
19 J9 Ruishton Somset
36 C3 Ruislip Gt Lon
144 E8 Rum Highld
158 A7 Rumbach Moray
134 C8 Rumbling Bridge P & K
65 L5 Rumburgh Suffk
103 N4 Rumby Hill Dur
4 D7 Rumford Cnwll
126 G2 Rumford Falk
30 H9 Rumney Cardif
18 G10 Rumwell Somset
81 Q8 Runcorn Halton
15 N6 Runcton W Susx
75 M9 Runcton Holme Norfk
23 N5 Runfold Surrey
76 F10 Runhall Norfk
77 P9 Runham Norfk
77 Q10 Runham Norfk
18 F10 Runnington Somset
52 C10 Runsell Green Essex
88 G7 Runshaw Moor Lancs
105 M7 Runswick N York
142 D4 Runtaleave Angus
38 C3 Runwell Essex
35 L9 Ruscombe Wokham
46 B7 Rushall Herefs
64 H5 Rushall Norfk
21 M3 Rushall Wilts
58 F4 Rushall Wsall
64 B9 Rushbrooke Suffk
57 J6 Rushbury Shrops
50 H4 Rushden Herts
61 L7 Rushden Nhants
38 F7 Rushenden Kent
25 P5 Rusher's Cross E Susx
9 C9 Rushford Devon
64 C5 Rushford Norfk
53 L8 Rush Green Essex
37 M3 Rush Green Gt Lon
50 F6 Rush Green Herts
82 E7 Rush Green Warrtn
25 P7 Rushlake Green E Susx
65 P4 Rushmere Suffk
53 L2 Rushmere St Andrew Suffk
23 N6 Rushmoor Surrey
45 L3 Rushock Herefs
58 C10 Rushock Worcs
83 J6 Rusholme Manch
69 Q2 Rushton Ches W
60 H4 Rushton Nhants
57 L3 Rushton Shrops
70 G2 Rushton Spencer Staffs
46 F4 Rushwick Worcs
103 P5 Rushyford Dur
133 J7 Ruskie Stirlg
86 E10 Ruskington Lincs
94 G3 Rusland Cross Cumb
24 F3 Rusper W Susx
32 C2 Ruspidge Gloucs
52 B9 Russell Green Essex
35 K7 Russell's Water Oxon
65 K7 Russel's Green Suffk
24 F2 Russ Hill Surrey
25 N3 Rusthall Kent
24 B10 Rustington W Susx
99 K4 Ruston N York
99 M8 Ruston Parva E R Yk
105 N9 Ruswarp N York
57 K6 Ruthall Shrops
118 B4 Rutherford Border
125 Q5 Rutherglen S Lans
4 G8 Ruthernbridge Cnwll
68 F3 Ruthin Denbgs
151 N7 Ruthrieston C Aber
158 D8 Ruthven Abers
142 D8 Ruthven Angus
148 D8 Ruthven Highld
4 E9 Ruthvoes Cnwll
100 H3 Ruthwaite Cumb
109 N7 Ruthwell D & G
37 L6 Ruxley Corner Gt Lon
45 Q11 Ruxton Green Herefs
69 L10 Ruyton-XI-Towns Shrops
112 F6 Ryal Nthumb
11 J5 Ryall Dorset
46 G6 Ryall Worcs
37 Q8 Ryarsh Kent
35 J3 Rycote Oxon
101 L9 Rydal Cumb
14 G8 Ryde IoW
26 F7 Rye E Susx
69 P8 Ryebank Shrops
46 B10 Ryeford Herefs
26 F7 Rye Foreign E Susx
26 F8 Rye Harbour E Susx
93 M5 Ryehill E R Yk
35 K11 Ryeish Green Wokham
46 E7 Rye Street Worcs
73 Q8 Ryhall Rutlnd
91 K8 Ryhill Wakefd
113 P10 Ryhope Sundld
84 G7 Rylah Derbys
86 D5 Ryland Lincs
72 E3 Rylands Notts
96 E9 Rylstone N York
11 M2 Ryme Intrinseca Dorset
91 P3 Ryther N York
113 J8 Ryton Gatesd
98 F5 Ryton N York
57 P4 Ryton Shrops
59 P7 Ryton Warwks
59 N10 Ryton-on-Dunsmore Warwks
112 H8 Ryton Woodside Gatesd

S

89 M3 Sabden Lancs
51 M11 Sabine's Green Essex
50 H7 Sacombe Herts
50 H7 Sacombe Green Herts
113 K11 Sacriston Dur
104 B7 Sadberge Darltn
120 E5 Saddell Ag & B
60 E2 Saddington Leics
75 M7 Saddle Bow Norfk
24 G8 Saddlescombe W Susx
101 N9 Sadgill Cumb
51 M3 Saffron Walden Essex
41 L10 Sageston Pembks
76 C11 Saham Hills Norfk
76 B11 Saham Toney Norfk
69 M2 Saighton Ches W
129 N6 St Abbs Border
128 H7 St Agnes Border
3 J3 St Agnes Cnwll
2 b3 St Agnes IoS
50 D9 St Albans Herts
3 L3 St Allen Cnwll
10 b2 St Andrew Guern
135 N4 St Andrews Fife
135 N4 St Andrews Botanic Garden Fife
30 F10 St Andrew's Major V Glam
11 K6 St Andrews Well Dorset
88 C5 St Anne's Lancs
109 N2 St Ann's D & G
5 Q7 St Ann's Chapel Cnwll
6 H9 St Ann's Chapel Devon
3 K8 St Anthony Cnwll
25 P10 St Anthony's Hill E Susx
31 P5 St Arvans Mons
80 E10 St Asaph Denbgs
30 D11 St Athan V Glam
11 b2 St Aubin Jersey
3 Q3 St Austell Cnwll
100 C8 St Bees Cumb
3 R3 St Blazey Cnwll
3 R3 St Blazey Gate Cnwll
118 A4 St Boswells Border
11 a2 St Brelade Jersey
11 a2 St Brelade's Bay Jersey
4 F7 St Breock Cnwll
4 H6 St Breward Cnwll
31 Q4 St Briavels Gloucs
40 F8 St Brides Pembks
29 N10 St Bride's Major V Glam
31 M7 St Brides Netherwent Mons
30 E9 St Brides super-Ely V Glam
31 J8 St Brides Wentlooge Newpt
6 D7 St Budeaux C Plym
47 M7 Saintbury Gloucs
2 C8 St Buryan Cnwll
32 E11 St Catherine BaNES
131 N6 St Catherines Ag & B
32 F4 St Chloe Gloucs
41 Q7 St Clears Carmth
5 L8 St Cleer Cnwll
3 M5 St Clement Cnwll
11 c2 St Clement Jersey
5 L5 St Clether Cnwll
124 C4 St Colmac Ag & B
4 E9 St Columb Major Cnwll
4 C9 St Columb Minor Cnwll
4 E10 St Columb Road Cnwll
159 Q5 St Combs Abers
65 K5 St Cross South Elmham Suffk
143 N5 St Cyrus Abers
133 Q3 St David's P & K
40 E5 St David's Pembks
3 J5 St Day Cnwll
18 E6 St Decumans Somset
4 F10 St Dennis Cnwll
45 N8 St Devereux Herefs
42 C5 St Dogmaels Pembks
41 J5 St Dogwells Pembks
5 Q8 St Dominick Cnwll
29 P11 St Donats V Glam
21 J2 St Edith's Marsh Wilts
4 F6 St Endellion Cnwll
4 D10 St Enoder Cnwll
3 L4 St Erme Cnwll
5 P10 St Erney Cnwll
2 F6 St Erth Cnwll
2 F6 St Erth Praze Cnwll
4 D7 St Ervan Cnwll
4 D8 St Eval Cnwll
3 P4 St Ewe Cnwll
30 F9 St Fagans Cardif
30 F9 St Fagans Welsh Life Museum Cardif
159 Q7 St Fergus Abers
133 K3 St Fillans P & K
41 L10 St Florence Pembks
5 J2 St Gennys Cnwll
80 D9 St George Conwy
19 L2 St Georges N Som
30 F9 St George's V Glam
36 C8 St George's Hill Surrey
5 P10 St Germans Cnwll
17 J8 St Giles in the Wood Devon
5 P3 St Giles-on-the-Heath Devon
3 K7 St Gluvia's Cnwll
55 M10 St Harmon Powys
103 N5 St Helen Auckland Dur
100 D4 St Helens Cumb
26 D9 St Helens E Susx
14 H9 St Helens IoW
81 Q5 St Helens St Hel
81 P5 St Helens Crematorium St Hel
36 G7 St Helier Gt Lon
11 b2 St Helier Jersey
2 E7 St Hilary Cnwll
30 D10 St Hilary V Glam
10 B3 Saint Hill Devon
25 J3 Saint Hill W Susx
30 H4 St Illtyd Blae G
50 E5 St Ippollitts Herts
40 F9 St Ishmael's Pembks
4 E7 St Issey Cnwll
5 N8 St Ive Cnwll
5 N8 St Ive Cross Cnwll
62 D6 St Ives Cambs
2 E5 St Ives Cnwll
13 K4 St Ives Dorset
77 K7 St James Norfk
60 F8 St James's End Nhants
65 L5 St James South Elmham Suffk
4 E8 St Jidgey Cnwll
5 Q11 St John Cnwll
11 b1 St John Jersey
103 L4 St Johns Dur
80 c5 St Johns IoM
37 M9 St Johns Kent
23 Q3 St Johns Surrey
46 F4 St Johns Worcs
17 J6 St John's Chapel Devon
102 G3 St John's Chapel Dur
75 K8 St John's Fen End Norfk
75 K8 St John's Highway Norfk
116 D3 St John's Kirk S Lans
108 D4 St John's Town of Dalry D & G
36 G4 St John's Wood Gt Lon
80 e2 St Jude's IoM
2 B7 St Just Cnwll
3 L6 St Just-in-Roseland Cnwll
159 J11 St Katherines Abers
3 K9 St Keverne Cnwll
4 G6 St Kew Cnwll
4 G6 St Kew Highway Cnwll
5 L9 St Keyne Cnwll
4 G8 St Lawrence Cnwll
52 G11 St Lawrence Essex
14 F11 St Lawrence IoW
11 b1 St Lawrence Jersey
39 Q8 St Lawrence Kent
35 P3 St Leonards Bucks
13 K4 St Leonards Dorset
26 D10 St Leonards E Susx
37 Q9 St Leonard's Street Kent
2 B9 St Levan Cnwll
30 F10 St Lythans V Glam
4 G7 St Mabyn Cnwll
134 F3 St Madoes P & K
45 M8 St Margarets Herefs
51 J8 St Margarets Herts
27 Q3 St Margaret's at Cliffe Kent
169 d7 St Margaret's Hope Ork
65 L5 St Margaret South Elmham Suffk
80 c7 St Marks IoM
3 J9 St Martin Cnwll
5 M10 St Martin Cnwll
10 b2 St Martin Guern
11 c1 St Martin Jersey
2 c1 St Martin's IoS
142 B11 St Martin's P & K
69 K7 St Martins Shrops
69 K7 St Martin's Moor Shrops
11 a1 St Mary Jersey
22 D4 St Mary Bourne Hants
7 N5 St Marychurch Torbay
30 D10 St Mary Church V Glam
37 L7 St Mary Cray Gt Lon
30 C9 St Mary Hill V Glam
27 J6 St Mary in the Marsh Kent
36 G3 St Marylebone Crematorium Gt Lon
2 c2 St Mary's IoS
169 d6 St Mary's Ork
27 J6 St Mary's Bay Kent
31 N11 St Mary's Grove N Som
38 D6 St Mary's Hoo Medway
45 P11 St Maughans Mons
45 P11 St Maughans Green Mons
3 L7 St Mawes Cnwll
4 D8 St Mawgan Cnwll
5 P8 St Mellion Cnwll
30 H8 St Mellons Cardif
4 D7 St Merryn Cnwll
3 P3 St Mewan Cnwll
3 P5 St Michael Caerhays Cnwll
19 K8 St Michael Church Somset
3 M5 St Michael Penkevil Cnwll
26 E4 St Michaels Kent
57 K11 St Michaels Worcs
88 F2 St Michael's on Wyre Lancs
65 L5 St Michael South Elmham Suffk
4 F6 St Minver Cnwll
135 N7 St Monans Fife
5 K8 St Neot Cnwll
61 Q8 St Neots Cambs
40 H3 St Nicholas Pembks
30 E10 St Nicholas V Glam
39 N8 St Nicholas at Wade Kent
133 M9 St Ninians Stirlg
65 P2 St Olaves Norfk
53 K8 St Osyth Essex
11 a1 St Ouen Jersey
45 Q10 St Owens Cross Herefs
37 L7 St Pauls Cray Gt Lon
50 E6 St Paul's Walden Herts
11 a1 St Peter Jersey
10 c2 St Peter Port Guern
10 b2 St Peter's Guern
39 Q8 St Peter's Kent
62 B6 St Peter's Hill Cambs
41 J11 St Petrox Pembks
5 L9 St Pinnock Cnwll
114 G3 St Quivox S Ayrs
3 J10 St Ruan Cnwll
10 c1 St Sampson Guern
10 b2 St Saviour Guern
11 b2 St Saviour Jersey
3 N3 St Stephen Cnwll
5 N4 St Stephens Cnwll
5 Q10 St Stephens Cnwll
4 H5 St Teath Cnwll
4 H6 St Tudy Cnwll
41 J11 St Twynnells Pembks
5 J10 St Veep Cnwll
143 L9 St Vigeans Angus
4 F9 St Wenn Cnwll
45 P10 St Weonards Herefs
30 E9 St y-Nyll V Glam
7 J11 Salcombe Devon
10 D7 Salcombe Regis Devon
52 F9 Salcott-cum-Virley Essex
82 G6 Sale Traffd
87 N5 Saleby Lincs
46 H3 Sale Green Worcs
26 C7 Salehurst E Susx
43 M9 Salem Carmth
54 F8 Salem Cerdgn
137 P7 Salen Ag & B
138 B5 Salen Highld
89 K4 Salesbury Lancs
49 P7 Salford C Beds
47 Q9 Salford Oxon
82 H5 Salford Salfd
47 L4 Salford Priors Warwks
36 G11 Salfords Surrey
77 L9 Salhouse Norfk
134 C9 Saline Fife
21 M9 Salisbury Wilts
21 M9 Salisbury Cathedral Wilts
21 N8 Salisbury Crematorium Wilts
21 L6 Salisbury Plain Wilts
101 P3 Salkeld Dykes Cumb
76 G7 Salle Norfk
87 K6 Salmonby Lincs
47 L10 Salperton Gloucs
61 N10 Salph End Bed
126 E5 Salsburgh N Lans
70 H9 Salt Staffs
109 N11 Salta Cumb
90 E3 Saltaire C Brad
6 C7 Saltash Cnwll
156 C3 Saltburn Highld
105 J6 Saltburn-by-the-Sea R & Cl
73 M5 Saltby Leics
110 C10 Salt Coates Cumb
100 E11 Saltcoats Cumb
124 G9 Saltcoats N Ayrs
88 D5 Saltcotes Lancs
25 J10 Saltdean Br & H
100 C5 Salterbeck Cumb
96 C11 Salterforth Lancs
82 D11 Salterswall Ches W
21 M7 Salterton Wilts
87 N2 Saltfleet Lincs
87 N2 Saltfleetby All Saints Lincs
87 N2 Saltfleetby St Clement Lincs
87 M3 Saltfleetby St Peter Lincs
32 C11 Saltford BaNES
76 F3 Salthouse Norfk
58 H7 Saltley Birm
31 K8 Saltmarsh Newpt
92 C6 Saltmarshe E R Yk
69 L2 Saltney Flints
98 E5 Salton N York
16 H7 Saltrens Devon
113 L8 Saltwell Crematorium Gatesd
113 J4 Saltwick Nthumb
27 L4 Saltwood Kent
24 D9 Salvington W Susx
46 G2 Salwarpe Worcs
11 K5 Salway Ash Dorset
47 L2 Sambourne Warwks
70 C10 Sambrook Wrekin
88 H4 Samlesbury Lancs
89 J5 Samlesbury Bottoms Lancs
18 F11 Sampford Arundel Somset
18 E6 Sampford Brett Somset
8 F4 Sampford Courtenay Devon
18 F11 Sampford Moor Somset
9 P2 Sampford Peverell Devon
6 E4 Sampford Spiney Devon
169 f4 Samsonlane Ork
53 J8 Samson's Corner Essex
128 D5 Samuelston E Loth
122 B5 Sanaigmore Ag & B
2 C8 Sancreed Cnwll
92 E3 Sancton E R Yk
19 M5 Sand Somset
145 M7 Sandaig Highld
100 H2 Sandale Cumb
91 J7 Sandal Magna Wakefd
144 G11 Sandavore Highld
169 f2 Sanday Ork
169 f2 Sanday Airport Ork
70 D2 Sandbach Ches E
70 D2 Sandbach Services Ches E
131 P11 Sandbank Ag & B
12 H7 Sandbanks Poole
158 E4 Sandend Abers
36 H8 Sanderstead Gt Lon
102 D7 Sandford Cumb
9 K4 Sandford Devon
12 F7 Sandford Dorset
13 L4 Sandford Hants
14 F10 Sandford IoW
19 M3 Sandford N Som
126 C9 Sandford S Lans
69 K10 Sandford Shrops
69 Q8 Sandford Shrops
34 F4 Sandford-on-Thames Oxon
20 B10 Sandford Orcas Dorset
48 D9 Sandford St Martin Oxon
27 M4 Sandgate Kent
159 N4 Sandhaven Abers
106 E8 Sandhead D & G
91 L11 Sandhill Rothm
11 M4 Sandhills Dorset
11 P2 Sandhills Dorset
91 K3 Sand Hills Leeds
34 G3 Sandhills Oxon
23 P7 Sandhills Surrey
112 E7 Sandhoe Nthumb
131 L8 Sandhole Ag & B
92 D3 Sand Hole E R Yk
92 D4 Sandholme E R Yk
74 F3 Sandholme Lincs
23 M2 Sandhurst Br For
46 F10 Sandhurst Gloucs
26 D6 Sandhurst Kent
26 C6 Sandhurst Cross Kent
97 N4 Sandhutton N York
98 D9 Sand Hutton N York
72 D3 Sandiacre Derbys
87 P4 Sandilands Lincs
82 D10 Sandiway Ches W
21 M11 Sandleheath Hants
34 E4 Sandleigh Oxon
20 E10 Sandley Dorset
38 C10 Sandling Kent
82 G11 Sandlow Green Ches E
169 n8 Sandness Shet
52 B11 Sandon Essex
50 H4 Sandon Herts
70 G9 Sandon Staffs
70 G9 Sandon Bank Staffs
14 G10 Sandown IoW
5 M10 Sandplace Cnwll
50 E8 Sandridge Herts
32 H11 Sandridge Wilts
75 N5 Sandringham Norfk
35 M6 Sands Bucks
105 N8 Sandsend N York
94 E4 Sand Side Cumb
95 K4 Sandside Cumb
92 B9 Sandtoft N Linc
38 E11 Sandway Kent
39 P10 Sandwich Kent
101 M7 Sandwick Cumb
169 r11 Sandwick Shet
168 j4 Sandwick W Isls
100 C8 Sandwith Cumb
100 C8 Sandwith Newtown Cumb
61 Q11 Sandy C Beds
87 J9 Sandy Bank Lincs
81 L11 Sandycroft Flints
25 N6 Sandy Cross E Susx
46 C3 Sandy Cross Herefs
110 D2 Sandyford D & G
7 M4 Sandygate Devon
80 e2 Sandygate IoM
40 G9 Sandy Haven Pembks
109 J9 Sandyhills D & G
95 J8 Sandylands Lancs
90 E3 Sandy Lane C Brad
78 C7 Sandylane Staffs
28 G7 Sandylane Swans
33 J11 Sandy Lane Wilts
69 M6 Sandy Lane Wrexhm
8 H7 Sandy Park Devon
110 G7 Sandysike Cumb

Sandyway - Shoreditch 297

45 P9 Sandyway Herefs
165 K3 Sangobeg Highld
165 K3 Sangomore Highld
82 C7 Sankey Bridges Warrtn
57 P11 Sankyn's Green Worcs
137 L2 Sanna Bay Highld
168 j4 Sanndabhaig W Isls
124 C8 Sannox N Ayrs
115 Q6 Sanquhar D & G
100 F10 Santon Cumb
80 d7 Santon IoM
100 F10 Santon Bridge Cumb
63 P3 Santon Downham Suffk
59 Q6 Sapcote Leics
46 D2 Sapey Common Herefs
64 C6 Sapiston Suffk
62 B6 Sapley Cambs
71 M8 Sapperton Derbys
32 H4 Sapperton Gloucs
73 Q4 Sapperton Lincs
74 F5 Saracen's Head Lincs
167 P8 Sarclet Highld
14 F5 Sarisbury Hants
29 P8 Sarn Brdgnd
66 C8 Sarn Gwynd
55 M5 Sarn Powys
56 C6 Sarn Powys
42 F11 Sarnau Carmth
42 F4 Sarnau Cerdgn
68 C7 Sarnau Gwynd
44 E8 Sarnau Powys
68 H11 Sarnau Powys
66 E9 Sarn Bach Gwynd
45 M4 Sarnesfield Herefs
29 P8 Sarn Park Services Brdgnd
69 J11 Sarn-wen Powys
28 H2 Saron Carmth
42 G7 Saron Carmth
66 H3 Saron Gwynd
79 J11 Saron Gwynd
50 B11 Sarratt Herts
39 N8 Sarre Kent
47 Q10 Sarsden Oxon
22 B6 Sarson Hants
103 M2 Satley Dur
27 N4 Satmar Kent
102 H11 Satron N York
17 M7 Satterleigh Devon
94 G2 Satterthwaite Cumb
35 K8 Satwell Oxon
151 J5 Sauchen Abers
142 B11 Saucher P & K
143 M4 Sauchieburn Abers
32 D3 Saul Gloucs
85 N3 Saundby Notts
41 M10 Saundersfoot Pembks
35 L4 Saunderton Bucks
16 H4 Saunton Devon
87 L7 Sausthorpe Lincs
3 K4 Saveock Cnwll
70 H7 Saverley Green Staffs
90 G6 Savile Town Kirk
60 B7 Sawbridge Warwks
51 L8 Sawbridgeworth Herts
99 J4 Sawdon N York
72 D4 Sawley Derbys
96 A11 Sawley Lancs
97 K7 Sawley N York
62 G11 Sawston Cambs
61 Q4 Sawtry Cambs
73 L7 Saxby Leics
86 D3 Saxby Lincs
92 G7 Saxby All Saints N Linc
72 H6 Saxelbye Leics
64 F9 Saxham Street Suffk
85 Q5 Saxilby Lincs
76 E4 Saxlingham Norfk
65 J2 Saxlingham Green Norfk
65 J2 Saxlingham Nethergate Norfk
65 J2 Saxlingham Thorpe Norfk
65 M9 Saxmundham Suffk
72 H3 Saxondale Notts
63 L9 Saxon Street Cambs
65 K8 Saxtead Suffk
65 K9 Saxtead Green Suffk
65 J8 Saxtead Little Green Suffk
76 G5 Saxthorpe Norfk
91 M3 Saxton N York
24 G7 Sayers Common W Susx
98 C6 Scackleton N York
100 H9 Scafell Pike Cumb
85 L2 Scaftworth Notts
98 G6 Scagglethorpe N York
136 b3 Scalasaig Ag & B
92 D5 Scalby E R Yk
99 L2 Scalby N York
61 M9 Scald End Bed
60 G6 Scaldwell Nhants
110 H8 Scaleby Cumb
110 H8 Scalebyhill Cumb
111 L11 Scale Houses Cumb
94 F6 Scales Cumb
101 K5 Scales Cumb
110 H11 Scalesceugh Cumb
73 K6 Scalford Leics
105 K8 Scaling N York
105 K8 Scaling Dam R & Cl
169 r10 Scalloway Shet
153 L11 Scalpay Highld
87 J5 Scamblesby Lincs
90 D7 Scammonden Kirk
138 E3 Scamodale Highld
98 H5 Scampston N York
86 C5 Scampton Lincs
156 A10 Scaniport Highld
90 D7 Scapegoat Hill Kirk
130 D7 Scarba Ag & B
99 L3 Scarborough N York
3 N3 Scarcewater Cnwll
84 G7 Scarcliffe Derbys
91 K2 Scarcroft Leeds
167 N2 Scarfskerry Highld
103 L8 Scargill Dur
136 C7 Scarinish Ag & B
88 D8 Scarisbrick Lancs
100 H4 Scarness Cumb
76 D9 Scarning Norfk
73 J2 Scarrington Notts
88 E9 Scarth Hill Lancs
91 M3 Scarthingwell N York
93 N9 Scartho NE Lin
169 q6 Scatsta Airport Shet
92 G9 Scawby N Linc
91 N10 Scawsby Donc
91 P9 Scawthorpe Donc
98 A4 Scawton N York
25 J6 Scayne's Hill W Susx
44 G9 Scethrog Powys
70 E3 Scholar Green Ches E
90 E4 Scholemoor Crematorium C Brad
90 F5 Scholes Kirk
90 F9 Scholes Kirk
91 K3 Scholes Leeds
91 K11 Scholes Rothm
88 H9 Scholes Wigan
103 Q6 School Aycliffe Dur
90 E4 School Green C Brad
70 A2 School Green Ches W
35 K11 Schoolgreen Wokham
10 H4 School House Dorset
90 G8 Scissett Kirk
40 H4 Scleddau Pembks
85 K4 Scofton Notts
64 H6 Scole Norfk
134 E2 Scone P & K
153 J11 Sconser Highld
135 K7 Scoonie Fife
86 E9 Scopwick Lincs
160 G7 Scoraig Highld
99 L11 Scorborough E R Yk
3 J5 Scorrier Cnwll
7 J5 Scorriton Devon
95 L11 Scorton Lancs
103 Q10 Scorton N York
77 K7 Sco Ruston Norfk
110 H9 Scotby Cumb
103 P9 Scotch Corner N York
95 K9 Scotforth Lancs
70 D5 Scot Hay Staffs
86 D5 Scothern Lincs
73 Q4 Scotland Lincs
113 L4 Scotland Gate Nthumb
134 F7 Scotlandwell P & K
89 J9 Scot Lane End Bolton
167 J5 Scotscalder Station Highld
110 G6 Scotsdike Cumb
112 F3 Scot's Gap Nthumb
150 F4 Scotsmill Abers
125 N4 Scotstoun C Glas
113 K8 Scotswood N u Ty
92 E10 Scotter Lincs
92 E10 Scotterthorpe Lincs
73 R6 Scottlethorpe Lincs
92 E11 Scotton Lincs
97 M9 Scotton N York
103 N11 Scotton N York
77 K7 Scottow Norfk
73 R3 Scott Willoughby Lincs
76 D11 Scoulton Norfk
71 K9 Scounslow Green Staffs
164 E8 Scourie Highld
164 D8 Scourie More Highld
169 q12 Scousburgh Shet
90 B9 Scouthead Oldham
167 K2 Scrabster Highld
118 C7 Scraesburgh Border
87 K7 Scrafield Lincs
119 J9 Scrainwood Nthumb
74 G2 Scrane End Lincs
72 G9 Scraptoft Leics
77 Q8 Scratby Norfk
98 E9 Scrayingham N York
26 C8 Scrays E Susx
74 A2 Scredington Lincs
87 M7 Scremby Lincs
129 Q10 Scremerston Nthumb
72 J2 Screveton Notts
87 J7 Scrivelsby Lincs
97 M9 Scriven N York
85 L2 Scrooby Notts
71 M8 Scropton Derbys
86 H9 Scrub Hill Lincs
97 L2 Scruton N York
110 H6 Scuggate Cumb
165 P4 Scullomie Highld
76 B5 Sculthorpe Norfk
92 E8 Scunthorpe N Linc
28 E7 Scurlage Swans
10 G2 Sea Somset
11 J3 Seaborough Dorset
70 E6 Seabridge Staffs
27 L4 Seabrook Kent
113 P9 Seaburn Sundld
81 L6 Seacombe Wirral
91 K3 Seacroft Leeds
87 Q8 Seacroft Lincs
74 F3 Seadyke Lincs
152 H9 Seafield Highld
127 J4 Seafield W Loth
127 P2 Seafield Crematorium C Edin
25 L11 Seaford E Susx
81 L5 Seaforth Sefton
72 G7 Seagrave Leics
33 J8 Seagry Heath Wilts
113 P11 Seaham Dur
119 P4 Seahouses Nthumb
37 N9 Seal Kent
23 N5 Seale Surrey
99 L4 Seamer N York
104 E8 Seamer N York
124 G8 Seamill N Ayrs
77 N6 Sea Palling Norfk
93 J9 Searby Lincs
39 J9 Seasalter Kent
100 D10 Seascale Cumb
100 H11 Seathwaite Cumb
100 H8 Seathwaite Cumb
94 H4 Seatle Cumb
100 H8 Seatoller Cumb
5 N11 Seaton Cnwll
100 D4 Seaton Cumb
10 E6 Seaton Devon
113 N11 Seaton Dur
99 P11 Seaton E R Yk
39 M10 Seaton Kent
113 M5 Seaton Nthumb
73 N11 Seaton Rutlnd
113 K6 Seaton Burn N Tyne
104 F5 Seaton Carew Hartpl
113 M5 Seaton Delaval Nthumb
92 C2 Seaton Ross E R Yk
113 M5 Seaton Sluice Nthumb
11 J6 Seatown Dorset
104 G10 Seave Green N York
14 H8 Seaview IoW
110 C10 Seaville Cumb
11 J2 Seavington St Mary Somset
19 M11 Seavington St Michael Somset
31 J5 Sebastopol Torfn
101 L2 Sebergham Cumb
59 L3 Seckington Warwks
95 P2 Sedbergh Cumb
31 P6 Sedbury Gloucs
96 C2 Sedbusk N York
47 K7 Sedgeberrow Worcs
73 M3 Sedgebrook Lincs
63 L4 Sedge Fen Suffk
104 C5 Sedgefield Dur
75 P3 Sedgeford Norfk
20 G9 Sedgehill Wilts
19 L4 Sedgemoor Services Somset
58 D6 Sedgley Dudley
82 H4 Sedgley Park Bury
95 L3 Sedgwick Cumb
26 C8 Sedlescombe E Susx
35 M2 Sedrup Bucks
38 F10 Seed Kent
20 H2 Seend Wilts
20 H2 Seend Cleeve Wilts
35 Q6 Seer Green Bucks
65 L2 Seething Norfk
81 M4 Sefton Sefton
81 L4 Sefton Town Sefton
113 L6 Seghill Nthumb
70 F9 Seighford Staffs
79 J11 Seion Gwynd
58 B5 Seisdon Staffs
69 J8 Selattyn Shrops
23 K8 Selborne Hants
91 Q4 Selby N York
23 P10 Selham W Susx
36 H7 Selhurst Gt Lon
117 P5 Selkirk Border
45 R9 Sellack Herefs
169 s4 Sellafirth Shet
2 C7 Sellan Cnwll
18 H11 Sellick's Green Somset
27 J4 Sellindge Kent
38 H10 Selling Kent
20 H2 Sells Green Wilts
58 F8 Selly Oak Birm
25 M9 Selmeston E Susx
37 J8 Selsdon Gt Lon
32 F4 Selsey Gloucs
15 N8 Selsey W Susx
24 H4 Selsfield Common W Susx
101 P11 Selside Cumb
96 A5 Selside N York
27 M3 Selsted Kent
84 G10 Selston Notts
18 B5 Selworthy Somset
52 G2 Semer Suffk
20 G2 Semington Wilts
20 G9 Semley Wilts
74 B4 Sempringham Lincs
36 B9 Send Surrey
36 B9 Send Marsh Surrey
30 F6 Senghenydd Caerph
2 B8 Sennen Cnwll
2 B8 Sennen Cove Cnwll
44 C9 Sennybridge Powys
85 K3 Serlby Notts
97 Q5 Sessay N York
75 M8 Setchey Norfk
13 P4 Setley Hants
128 C4 Seton Mains E Loth
96 B8 Settle N York
98 G6 Settrington N York
18 G8 Seven Ash Somset
47 K10 Sevenhampton Gloucs
33 P6 Sevenhampton Swindn
53 M3 Seven Hills Crematorium Suffk
37 L3 Seven Kings Gt Lon
37 M9 Sevenoaks Kent
37 M10 Sevenoaks Weald Kent
29 M3 Seven Sisters Neath
47 J11 Seven Springs Gloucs
52 F6 Seven Star Green Essex
31 P8 Severn Beach S Glos
46 G6 Severn Stoke Worcs
31 Q7 Severn View Services S Glos
61 N10 Sevick End Bed
26 H3 Sevington Kent
51 N3 Sewards End Essex
51 J11 Sewardstonebury Essex
49 Q10 Sewell C Beds
99 P7 Sewerby E R Yk
3 J7 Seworgan Cnwll
73 M6 Sewstern Leics
104 E9 Sexhow N York
47 N8 Sezincote Gloucs
168 k1 Sgiogarstaigh W Isls
35 J3 Shabbington Bucks
57 Q3 Shackerley Shrops
72 B9 Shackerstone Leics
72 C4 Shacklecross Derbys
23 P5 Shackleford Surrey
89 Q6 Shade Calder
168 i2 Shader W Isls
104 B2 Shadforth Dur
65 N5 Shadingfield Suffk
26 G4 Shadoxhurst Kent
91 J3 Shadwell Leeds
64 C5 Shadwell Norfk
51 K3 Shaftenhoe End Herts
20 G10 Shaftesbury Dorset
91 P9 Shaftholme Donc
91 K8 Shafton Barns
91 K8 Shafton Two Gates Barns
82 E4 Shakerley Wigan
22 B2 Shalbourne Wilts
14 C9 Shalcombe IoW
23 J6 Shalden Hants
23 K6 Shalden Green Hants
7 N4 Shaldon Devon
14 D9 Shalfleet IoW
52 B6 Shalford Essex
36 B11 Shalford Surrey
52 B6 Shalford Green Essex
70 F9 Shallowford Staffs
39 J11 Shalmsford Street Kent
48 H7 Shalstone Bucks
24 B2 Shamley Green Surrey
142 H5 Shandford Angus
132 B10 Shandon Ag & B
156 F2 Shandwick Highld
73 J11 Shangton Leics
113 L5 Shankhouse Nthumb
14 G10 Shanklin IoW
101 Q7 Shap Cumb
169 e5 Shapinsay Ork
12 F4 Shapwick Dorset
19 M7 Shapwick Somset
59 J7 Shard End Birm
72 C4 Shardlow Derbys
58 D3 Shareshill Staffs
91 K7 Sharlston Wakefd
91 K7 Sharlston Common Wakefd
58 H9 Sharman's Cross Solhll
38 C7 Sharnal Street Medway
61 L9 Sharnbrook Bed
89 P6 Sharneyford Lancs
59 Q6 Sharnford Leics
11 Q3 Sharnhill Green Dorset
88 G4 Sharoe Green Lancs
97 M6 Sharow N York
50 C4 Sharpenhoe C Beds
119 J10 Sharperton Nthumb
77 M7 Sharp Green Norfk
32 C4 Sharpness Gloucs
25 J4 Sharpthorne W Susx
5 M7 Sharptor Cnwll
58 E11 Sharpway Gate Worcs
76 E4 Sharrington Norfk
57 P8 Shatterford Worcs
39 N10 Shatterling Kent
84 B4 Shatton Derbys
6 E6 Shaugh Prior Devon
11 J5 Shave Cross Dorset
70 B4 Shavington Ches E
90 C3 Shaw C Brad
89 Q9 Shaw Oldham
33 M7 Shaw Swindn
34 E11 Shaw W Berk
32 G11 Shaw Wilts
57 L2 Shawbirch Wrekin
168 h3 Shawbost W Isls
69 Q10 Shawbury Shrops
89 P8 Shawclough Rochdl
46 C9 Shaw Common Gloucs
119 L8 Shawdon Hill Nthumb
60 B4 Shawell Leics
22 E9 Shawford Hants
89 P6 Shawforth Lancs
50 H4 Shaw Green Herts
88 G7 Shaw Green Lancs
97 L10 Shaw Green N York
109 J5 Shawhead D & G
97 L8 Shaw Mills N York
126 D7 Shawsburn S Lans
20 G6 Shear Cross Wilts
109 M7 Shearington D & G
60 D2 Shearsby Leics
19 J8 Shearston Somset
16 G10 Shebbear Devon
70 D9 Shebdon Staffs
166 H4 Shebster Highld
125 P6 Sheddens E Rens
14 G4 Shedfield Hants
71 L2 Sheen Staffs
84 E6 Sheepbridge Derbys
113 J9 Sheep Hill Dur
90 F7 Sheepridge Kirk
91 J4 Sheepscar Leeds
32 G2 Sheepscombe Gloucs
6 F5 Sheepstor Devon
8 C3 Sheepwash Devon
113 L3 Sheepwash Nthumb
31 N9 Sheepway N Som
72 A10 Sheepy Magna Leics
72 A10 Sheepy Parva Leics
51 M8 Sheering Essex
38 F7 Sheerness Kent
36 B8 Sheerwater Surrey
23 L10 Sheet Hants
2 D8 Sheffield Cnwll
84 E3 Sheffield Sheff
34 H11 Sheffield Bottom W Berk
84 E3 Sheffield City Road Crematorium Sheff
25 K5 Sheffield Green E Susx
50 D3 Shefford C Beds
164 E4 Sheigra Highld
57 L4 Sheinton Shrops
56 G9 Shelderton Shrops
58 J8 Sheldon Birm
83 Q11 Sheldon Derbys
10 C3 Sheldon Devon
38 H10 Sheldwich Kent
38 H10 Sheldwich Lees Kent
90 E5 Shelf Calder
64 G5 Shelfanger Norfk
47 M2 Shelfield Warwks
58 F4 Shelfield Wsall
47 M2 Shelfield Green Warwks
72 H2 Shelford Notts
59 P7 Shelford Warwks
118 G2 Shellacres Nthumb
51 N9 Shelley Essex
90 G8 Shelley Kirk
52 H4 Shelley Suffk
90 G8 Shelley Far Bank Kirk
34 B6 Shellingford Oxon
51 P9 Shellow Bowells Essex
46 D2 Shelsley Beauchamp Worcs
46 D2 Shelsley Walsh Worcs
61 M7 Shelton Bed
65 J3 Shelton Norfk
73 K2 Shelton Notts
56 H2 Shelton Shrops
65 J3 Shelton Green Norfk
72 B4 Shelton Lock C Derb
70 E7 Shelton Under Harley Staffs
56 E5 Shelve Shrops
45 Q6 Shelwick Herefs
51 P11 Shenfield Essex
48 C6 Shenington Oxon
50 E10 Shenley Herts
49 M7 Shenley Brook End M Keyn
50 E10 Shenleybury Herts
49 M7 Shenley Church End M Keyn
45 M7 Shenmore Herefs
107 K5 Shennanton D & G
58 H4 Shenstone Staffs
58 C10 Shenstone Worcs
58 H4 Shenstone Woodend Staffs
72 B11 Shenton Leics
149 N2 Shenval Moray
74 F8 Shepeau Stow Lincs
50 G6 Shephall Herts
36 F4 Shepherd's Bush Gt Lon
35 K8 Shepherd's Green Oxon
32 D4 Shepherds Patch Gloucs
27 N2 Shepherdswell Kent
90 F9 Shepley Kirk
32 B5 Shepperdine S Glos
36 C7 Shepperton Surrey
36 C7 Shepperton Green Surrey
62 E11 Shepreth Cambs
72 D7 Shepshed Leics
19 M11 Shepton Beauchamp Somset
20 B6 Shepton Mallet Somset
20 C8 Shepton Montague Somset
38 C11 Shepway Kent
104 D3 Sheraton Dur
20 B11 Sherborne Dorset
33 N2 Sherborne Gloucs
19 Q3 Sherborne Somset
22 H3 Sherborne St John Hants
47 Q2 Sherbourne Warwks
104 B2 Sherburn Dur
99 K5 Sherburn N York
104 B2 Sherburn Hill Dur
91 M4 Sherburn in Elmet N York
36 C11 Shere Surrey
76 B6 Shereford Norfk
21 Q10 Sherfield English Hants
23 J3 Sherfield on Loddon Hants
89 M5 Sherfin Lancs
7 K10 Sherford Devon
12 F6 Sherford Dorset
57 P2 Sheriffhales Shrops
98 D7 Sheriff Hutton N York
76 H3 Sheringham Norfk
49 N5 Sherington M Keyn
24 F7 Shermanbury W Susx
75 P4 Shernborne Norfk
21 J7 Sherrington Wilts
32 G7 Sherston Wilts
72 F2 Sherwood C Nott
85 K9 Sherwood Forest Notts
85 L7 Sherwood Forest Crematorium Notts
125 Q5 Shettleston C Glas
88 G9 Shevington Wigan
88 G8 Shevington Moor Wigan
88 G9 Shevington Vale Wigan
5 P10 Sheviock Cnwll
90 D5 Shibden Head C Brad
14 F9 Shide IoW
118 F3 Shidlaw Nthumb
146 A4 Shiel Bridge Highld
153 Q7 Shieldaig Highld
109 M3 Shieldhill D & G
126 F2 Shieldhill Falk
116 E2 Shieldhill House Hotel S Lans
126 D6 Shields N Lans
138 B3 Shielfoot Highld
142 G6 Shielhill Angus
124 G3 Shielhill Inver
34 C4 Shifford Oxon
57 N3 Shifnal Shrops
119 N9 Shilbottle Nthumb
103 P5 Shildon Dur
125 M6 Shillford E Rens
18 C10 Shillingford Devon
34 G6 Shillingford Oxon
9 M7 Shillingford Abbot Devon
9 M7 Shillingford St George Devon
12 D2 Shillingstone Dorset
50 D4 Shillington C Beds
118 G9 Shillmoor Nthumb
33 Q3 Shilton Oxon
59 P8 Shilton Warwks
64 H5 Shimpling Norfk
64 B11 Shimpling Suffk
64 B11 Shimpling Street Suffk
103 Q2 Shincliffe Dur
113 M10 Shiney Row Sundld
35 K11 Shinfield Wokham
62 D11 Shingay Cambs
53 Q3 Shingle Street Suffk
7 K6 Shinnersbridge Devon
162 C4 Shinness Highld
37 N10 Shipbourne Kent
76 D10 Shipdham Norfk
19 M3 Shipham Somset
7 M5 Shiphay Torbay
35 L9 Shiplake Oxon
35 K9 Shiplake Row Oxon
19 L3 Shiplate N Som
90 F3 Shipley C Brad
72 C2 Shipley Derbys
57 Q5 Shipley Shrops
24 D6 Shipley W Susx
24 H2 Shipley Bridge Surrey
26 H4 Shipley Hatch Kent
65 M3 Shipmeadow Suffk
63 K4 Shippea Hill Station Cambs
34 E5 Shippon Oxon
47 Q6 Shipston on Stour Warwks
49 L9 Shipton Bucks
47 K11 Shipton Gloucs
98 B9 Shipton N York
57 K6 Shipton Shrops
21 P5 Shipton Bellinger Hants
11 K6 Shipton Gorge Dorset
15 M7 Shipton Green W Susx
32 G7 Shipton Moyne Gloucs
48 E11 Shipton-on-Cherwell Oxon
92 E2 Shiptonthorpe E R Yk
47 Q11 Shipton-under-Wychwood Oxon
35 J5 Shirburn Oxon
88 D8 Shirdley Hill Lancs
102 B3 Shire Cumb
84 H7 Shirebrook Derbys
84 E2 Shiregreen Sheff
31 P9 Shirehampton Bristl
113 M6 Shiremoor N Tyne
31 N6 Shirenewton Mons
58 G4 Shire Oak Wsall
85 J4 Shireoaks Notts
26 F4 Shirkoak Kent
84 F9 Shirland Derbys
57 L5 Shirlett Shrops
14 D4 Shirley C Sotn
71 N6 Shirley Derbys
37 J7 Shirley Gt Lon
58 H9 Shirley Solhll
45 N3 Shirl Heath Herefs
14 G4 Shirrell Heath Hants
123 Q3 Shirvan Ag & B
17 L4 Shirwell Devon
120 H6 Shiskine N Ayrs
103 K3 Shittlehope Dur
45 N2 Shobdon Herefs
13 L3 Shobley Hants
9 L4 Shobrooke Devon
72 H6 Shoby Leics
69 M5 Shocklach Ches W
69 M5 Shocklach Green Ches W
38 F4 Shoeburyness Sthend
39 Q11 Sholden Kent
14 E4 Sholing C Sotn
56 G2 Shoot Hill Shrops
4 D7 Shop Cnwll
16 C9 Shop Cnwll
15 N5 Shopwyke W Susx
89 Q7 Shore Rochdl
36 H4 Shoreditch Gt Lon
18 H10 Shoreditch Somset

298 Shoreham - Southowram

37 M8 **Shoreham** Kent
24 F9 *Shoreham Airport* W Susx
24 F9 **Shoreham-by-Sea** W Susx
129 N10 **Shoreswood** Nthumb
22 G9 **Shorley** Hants
33 K5 **Shorncote** Gloucs
37 Q6 **Shorne** Kent
5 M10 **Shorta Cross** Cnwll
25 L6 **Shortbridge** E Susx
23 M6 **Shortfield Common** Surrey
25 L7 **Shortgate** E Susx
58 G6 **Short Heath** Birm
23 L7 **Shortheath** Hants
58 E4 **Short Heath** Wsall
3 L4 **Shortlanesend** Cnwll
125 L10 **Shortlees** E Ayrs
61 N11 **Shortstown** Bed
14 E10 **Shorwell** IoW
20 D3 **Shoscombe** BaNES
65 J2 **Shotesham** Norfk
38 C3 **Shotgate** Essex
53 M4 **Shotley** Suffk
112 G10 **Shotley Bridge** Dur
112 G10 **Shotleyfield** Nthumb
53 M5 **Shotley Gate** Suffk
53 M4 **Shotley Street** Suffk
38 H11 **Shottenden** Kent
23 N8 **Shottermill** Surrey
47 N4 **Shottery** Warwks
48 D5 **Shotteswell** Warwks
53 P3 **Shottisham** Suffk
71 Q5 **Shottle** Derbys
71 Q5 **Shottlegate** Derbys
104 C5 **Shotton** Dur
104 D3 **Shotton** Dur
81 L11 **Shotton** Flints
113 K5 **Shotton** Nthumb
118 F4 **Shotton** Nthumb
104 C2 **Shotton Colliery** Dur
126 F6 **Shotts** N Lans
81 L10 **Shotwick** Ches W
157 N6 **Shougle** Moray
75 N9 **Shouldham** Norfk
75 N9 **Shouldham Thorpe** Norfk
46 F3 **Shoulton** Worcs
25 Q4 **Shover's Green** E Susx
70 D5 **Shraleybrook** Staffs
69 L11 **Shrawardine** Shrops
57 Q11 **Shrawley** Worcs
36 B4 **Shreding Green** Bucks
59 K11 **Shrewley** Warwks
56 H2 **Shrewsbury** Shrops
21 L6 **Shrewton** Wilts
15 P6 **Shripney** W Susx
33 P7 **Shrivenham** Oxon
64 D3 **Shropham** Norfk
52 G7 **Shrub End** Essex
46 A6 **Shucknall** Herefs
51 P2 **Shudy Camps** Cambs
130 F6 **Shuna** Ag & B
46 H11 **Shurdington** Gloucs
35 M10 **Shurlock Row** W & M
47 K2 **Shurnock** Worcs
166 H5 **Shurrery** Highld
166 H5 **Shurrery Lodge** Highld
18 H6 **Shurton** Somset
59 K6 **Shustoke** Warwks
9 L4 **Shute** Devon
10 F5 **Shute** Devon
48 C6 **Shutford** Oxon
70 F10 **Shut Heath** Staffs
46 G7 **Shuthonger** Gloucs
49 K5 **Shutlanger** Nhants
9 N9 **Shutterton** Devon
58 C3 **Shutt Green** Staffs
59 L3 **Shuttington** Warwks
84 G6 **Shuttlewood** Derbys
89 N7 **Shuttleworth** Bury
168 h3 **Siabost** W Isls
168 i2 **Siadar** W Isls
60 E4 **Sibbertoft** Nhants
56 G8 **Sibdon Carwood** Shrops
48 C7 **Sibford Ferris** Oxon
48 C7 **Sibford Gower** Oxon
52 C5 **Sible Hedingham** Essex
51 P5 **Sibley's Green** Essex
5 L7 **Siblyback** Cnwll
87 L10 **Sibsey** Lincs
87 K10 **Sibsey Fenside** Lincs
74 A11 **Sibson** Cambs
72 B10 **Sibson** Leics
167 P6 **Sibster** Highld
85 M6 **Sibthorpe** Notts
85 N11 **Sibthorpe** Notts
65 M8 **Sibton** Suffk
64 B9 **Sicklesmere** Suffk
97 N11 **Sicklinghall** N York
19 J9 **Sidbrook** Somset
10 C6 **Sidbury** Devon
57 M7 **Sidbury** Shrops
91 K9 **Sid Cop** Barns
19 M3 **Sidcot** N Som
37 L6 **Sidcup** Gt Lon
100 D4 **Siddick** Cumb
82 H10 **Siddington** Ches E
33 K5 **Siddington** Gloucs
58 E10 **Sidemoor** Worcs
77 K4 **Sidestrand** Norfk
10 C6 **Sidford** Devon
15 N7 **Sidlesham** W Susx
15 N7 **Sidlesham Common** W Susx
26 B10 **Sidley** E Susx
10 C7 **Sidmouth** Devon
56 H8 **Siefton** Shrops
7 K4 **Sigford** Devon
99 P11 **Sigglesthorne** E R Yk
30 C10 **Sigingstone** V Glam
33 P2 **Signet** Oxon
22 H2 **Silchester** Hants
72 G7 **Sileby** Leics
94 C4 **Silecroft** Cumb
64 G2 **Silfield** Norfk
43 L4 **Silian** Cerdgn
22 D10 **Silkstead** Hants
90 H9 **Silkstone** Barns
90 H10 **Silkstone Common** Barns
73 R2 **Silk Willoughby** Lincs
109 P10 **Silloth** Cumb
99 K2 **Silpho** N York
96 F11 **Silsden** C Brad
50 C3 **Silsoe** C Beds
20 E9 **Silton** Dorset
127 N5 **Silverburn** Mdloth
95 K6 **Silverdale** Lancs
70 E5 **Silverdale** Staffs
52 D8 **Silver End** Essex
159 J5 **Silverford** Abers
76 H6 **Silvergate** Norfk
65 L9 **Silverlace Green** Suffk
65 K6 **Silverley's Green** Suffk
49 J6 **Silverstone** Nhants
38 E6 **Silver Street** Kent
19 P8 **Silver Street** Somset
9 N4 **Silverton** Devon
3 J4 **Silverwell** Cnwll
57 L9 **Silvington** Shrops
89 N9 **Simister** Bury
83 M6 **Simmondley** Derbys
112 C6 **Simonburn** Nthumb
17 P4 **Simonsbath** Somset
18 F11 **Simonsburrow** Devon
89 M4 **Simonstone** Lancs
96 C2 **Simonstone** N York
129 L11 **Simprim** Border
49 N7 **Simpson** M Keyn
40 G7 **Simpson Cross** Pembks
129 L9 **Sinclair's Hill** Border
115 J4 **Sinclairston** E Ayrs
97 M4 **Sinderby** N York
112 B10 **Sinderhope** Nthumb
82 F7 **Sinderland Green** Traffd
35 L11 **Sindlesham** Wokham
72 A4 **Sinfin** C Derb
49 L8 **Singleborough** Bucks
37 K9 **Single Street** Gt Lon
26 H3 **Singleton** Kent
88 D3 **Singleton** Lancs
15 N4 **Singleton** W Susx
37 Q6 **Singlewell** Kent
26 D3 **Sinkhurst Green** Kent
150 D5 **Sinnarhard** Abers
98 E3 **Sinnington** N York
46 F2 **Sinton** Worcs
46 F2 **Sinton** Worcs
46 F2 **Sinton Green** Worcs
36 C5 **Sipson** Gt Lon
30 F2 **Sirhowy** Blae G
26 C4 **Sissinghurst** Kent
32 C9 **Siston** S Glos
5 P3 **Sitcott** Devon
2 G8 **Sithney** Cnwll
2 G8 **Sithney Common** Cnwll
2 G8 **Sithney Green** Cnwll
38 F9 **Sittingbourne** Kent
57 P7 **Six Ashes** Shrops
30 H4 **Six Bells** Blae G
86 G3 **Sixhills** Lincs
63 J9 **Six Mile Bottom** Cambs
27 K3 **Sixmile Cottages** Kent
21 J11 **Sixpenny Handley** Dorset
11 b1 **Six Rues** Jersey
95 K3 *Sizergh Castle* Cumb
65 P9 **Sizewell** Suffk
169 e6 **Skaill** Ork
115 K4 **Skares** E Ayrs
151 N9 **Skateraw** Abers
129 J5 **Skateraw** E Loth
152 G8 **Skeabost** Highld
103 N10 **Skeeby** N York
73 J10 **Skeffington** Leics
93 Q7 **Skeffling** E R Yk
84 G8 **Skegby** Notts
85 N7 **Skegby** Notts
87 Q8 **Skegness** Lincs
162 H7 **Skelbo** Highld
162 H8 **Skelbo Street** Highld
91 N8 **Skelbrooke** Donc
74 F3 **Skeldyke** Lincs
86 B6 **Skellingthorpe** Lincs
83 K8 **Skellorn Green** Ches E
91 N8 **Skellow** Donc
90 G8 **Skelmanthorpe** Kirk
88 F9 **Skelmersdale** Lancs
124 F4 **Skelmorlie** N Ayrs
166 B5 **Skelpick** Highld
108 H3 **Skelston** D & G
98 B9 **Skelton** C York
101 M3 **Skelton** Cumb
92 C5 **Skelton** E R Yk
97 N7 **Skelton** N York
103 L10 **Skelton** N York
105 J7 **Skelton** R & Cl
101 K10 **Skelwith Bridge** Cumb
87 M7 **Skendleby** Lincs
151 K5 **Skene House** Abers
45 P10 **Skenfrith** Mons
99 L9 **Skerne** E R Yk
165 Q4 **Skerray** Highld
164 F6 **Skerricha** Highld
95 K8 **Skerton** Lancs
59 P6 **Sketchley** Leics
28 H6 **Sketty** Swans
29 K5 **Skewen** Neath
98 C6 **Skewsby** N York
77 J6 **Skeyton** Norfk
77 K6 **Skeyton Corner** Norfk
166 H3 **Skiall** Highld
87 M2 **Skidbrooke** Lincs
93 R11 **Skidbrooke North End** Lincs
92 H4 **Skidby** E R Yk
168 k1 **Skigersta** W Isls
18 C9 **Skilgate** Somset
73 M5 **Skillington** Lincs
109 P9 **Skinburness** Cumb
133 Q11 **Skinflats** Falk
152 C8 **Skinidin** Highld
34 D11 **Skinners Green** W Berk
105 K7 **Skinningrove** R & Cl
123 R8 **Skipness** Ag & B
110 G4 **Skipper's Bridge** D & G
110 G11 **Skiprigg** Cumb
99 P10 **Skipsea** E R Yk
99 P10 **Skipsea Brough** E R Yk
96 E10 **Skipton** N York
97 N5 **Skipton-on-Swale** N York
91 R3 **Skipwith** N York
93 K3 **Skirlaugh** E R Yk
116 F3 **Skirling** Border
35 L6 **Skirmett** Bucks
88 E9 **Skirpenbeck** E R Yk
102 B4 **Skirwith** Cumb
95 Q6 **Skirwith** N York
167 Q3 **Skirza** Highld
110 H7 **Skitby** Cumb
35 L4 **Skittle Green** Bucks
40 D10 **Skokholm Island** Pembks
40 D9 **Skomer Island** Pembks
145 L3 **Skulamus** Highld
56 D10 **Skyborry Green** Shrops
52 F7 **Skye Green** Essex
148 H3 **Skye of Curr** Highld
96 G8 **Skyreholme** N York
90 B5 **Slack** Calder
90 B9 **Slackcote** Oldham
95 K5 **Slack Head** Cumb
87 P6 **Slackholme End** Lincs
159 K8 **Slacks of Cairnbanno** Abers
32 G3 **Slad** Gloucs
10 C3 **Slade** Devon
17 J2 **Slade** Devon
17 Q6 **Slade** Devon
34 G6 **Slade End** Oxon
37 M5 **Slade Green** Gt Lon
58 D3 **Slade Heath** Staffs
84 H3 **Slade Hooton** Rothm
4 G7 **Sladesbridge** Cnwll
46 F8 **Slades Green** Worcs
111 N10 **Slaggyford** Nthumb
95 Q10 **Slaidburn** Lancs
90 D8 **Slaithwaite** Kirk
84 C9 **Slaley** Derbys
112 E9 **Slaley** Nthumb
126 F3 **Slamannan** Falk
49 P10 **Slapton** Bucks
7 L9 **Slapton** Devon
48 H5 **Slapton** Nhants
89 P9 **Slattocks** Rochdl
24 G5 **Slaugham** W Susx
32 F10 **Slaughterford** Wilts
60 F3 **Slawston** Leics
23 M7 **Sleaford** Hants
86 E11 **Sleaford** Lincs
101 Q7 **Sleagill** Cumb
69 N9 **Sleap** Shrops
70 A11 **Sleapford** Wrekin
50 E9 **Sleapshyde** Herts
162 E7 **Sleasdairidh** Highld
41 K7 **Slebech** Pembks
46 F8 **Sledge Green** Worcs
99 J8 **Sledmere** E R Yk
111 K5 **Sleetbeck** Cumb
12 G5 **Sleight** Dorset
103 J8 **Sleightholme** Dur
105 N9 **Sleights** N York
12 F6 **Slepe** Dorset
167 N3 **Slickly** Highld
120 H7 **Sliddery** N Ayrs
144 G2 **Sligachan** Highld
131 P9 **Sligrachan** Ag & B
32 D4 **Slimbridge** Gloucs
70 E8 **Slindon** Staffs
15 Q5 **Slindon** W Susx
24 D4 **Slinfold** W Susx
79 L11 **Sling** Gwynd
98 D6 **Slingsby** N York
50 C7 **Slip End** C Beds
50 G3 **Slip End** Herts
61 L5 **Slipton** Nhants
71 J11 **Slitting Mill** Staffs
130 G8 **Slockavullin** Ag & B
77 K7 **Sloley** Norfk
8 H7 **Sloncombe** Devon
87 N6 **Sloothby** Lincs
35 Q9 **Slough** Slough
35 Q8 **Slough Crematorium** Bucks
19 J11 **Slough Green** Somset
24 G5 **Slough Green** W Susx
154 A10 **Slumbay** Highld
23 Q4 **Slyfield Green** Surrey
95 K7 **Slyne** Lancs
118 B3 **Smailholm** Border
89 Q7 **Smallbridge** Rochdl
9 L5 **Smallbrook** Devon
31 Q4 **Smallbrook** Gloucs
77 L7 **Smallburgh** Norfk
83 N9 **Smalldale** Derbys
83 Q8 **Smalldale** Derbys
24 F8 **Small Dole** W Susx
72 C2 **Smalley** Derbys
72 C2 **Smalley Common** Derbys
72 C2 **Smalley Green** Derbys
24 H2 **Smallfield** Surrey
58 H7 **Small Heath** Birm
26 E5 **Small Hythe** Kent
10 G4 **Smallridge** Devon
70 F4 **Smallthorne** C Stke
103 M8 **Smallways** N York
70 E2 **Smallwood** Ches E
94 H11 **Small Wood Hey** Lancs
64 E5 **Smallworth** Norfk
22 C5 **Smannell** Hants
102 D9 **Smardale** Cumb
26 E3 **Smarden** Kent
26 E3 **Smarden Bell** Kent
25 M2 **Smart's Hill** Kent
119 L3 **Smeafield** Nthumb
138 A2 **Smearisary** Highld
10 D2 **Smeatharpe** Devon
27 J4 **Smeeth** Kent
60 E2 **Smeeton Westerby** Leics
97 J8 **Smelthouses** N York
167 L10 **Smerral** Highld
58 C6 **Smestow** Staffs
58 F7 **Smethwick** Sandw
70 E2 **Smethwick Green** Ches E
72 A7 **Smisby** Derbys
14 F8 **Smitheclose** IoW
46 E4 **Smith End Green** Worcs
110 H7 **Smithfield** Cumb
95 K9 **Smith Green** Lancs
91 K9 **Smithies** Barns
9 Q2 **Smithincott** Devon
51 K3 **Smith's End** Herts
51 N6 **Smith's Green** Essex
51 Q2 **Smith's Green** Essex
160 B11 **Smithstown** Highld
156 C8 **Smithton** Highld
89 Q7 **Smithy Bridge** Rochdl
82 F10 **Smithy Green** Ches E
83 J7 **Smithy Green** Stockp
84 E11 **Smithy Houses** Derbys
59 Q7 **Smockington** Leics
165 K3 **Smoo** Highld
52 F8 **Smythe's Green** Essex
108 H3 **Snade** D & G
56 F4 **Snailbeach** Shrops
63 K7 **Snailwell** Cambs
99 J4 **Snainton** N York
91 Q6 **Snaith** E R Yk
83 P6 **Snake Pass Inn** Derbys
97 L4 **Snape** N York
65 M10 **Snape** Suffk
88 D8 **Snape Green** Lancs
65 M10 **Snape Street** Suffk
37 K3 **Snaresbrook** Gt Lon
72 A9 **Snarestone** Leics
86 D4 **Snarford** Lincs
26 G6 **Snargate** Kent
26 H6 **Snave** Kent
46 H4 **Sneachill** Worcs
56 E6 **Snead** Powys
64 H4 **Sneath Common** Norfk
105 N9 **Sneaton** N York
105 P9 **Sneatonthorpe** N York
86 E4 **Snelland** Lincs
82 H10 **Snelson** Ches E
71 M6 **Snelston** Derbys
64 D3 **Snetterton** Norfk
75 N4 **Snettisham** Norfk
72 C8 **Snibston** Leics
46 E9 **Snig's End** Gloucs
119 K10 **Snitter** Nthumb
86 C2 **Snitterby** Lincs
47 P3 **Snitterfield** Warwks
84 C8 **Snitterton** Derbys
57 K9 **Snitton** Shrops
26 F3 **Snoadhill** Kent
45 L6 **Snodhill** Herefs
38 B9 **Snodland** Kent
37 Q11 **Snoll Hatch** Kent
90 H10 **Snowden Hill** Barns
67 L4 **Snowdon** Gwynd
67 Q9 **Snowdonia National Park**
51 K4 **Snow End** Herts
47 L8 **Snowshill** Gloucs
64 F5 **Snow Street** Norfk
15 J4 **Soake** Hants
30 E8 **Soar** Cardif
7 J11 **Soar** Devon
44 D8 **Soar** Powys
144 F5 **Soay** Highld
22 H11 **Soberton** Hants
14 H4 **Soberton Heath** Hants
101 N5 **Sockbridge** Cumb
104 B9 **Sockburn** Darltn
80 F10 **Sodom** Denbgs
69 K7 **Sodylt Bank** Shrops
63 J6 **Soham** Cambs
63 J5 **Soham Cotes** Cambs
168 d10 **Solas** W Isls
40 G8 **Solbury** Pembks
16 E9 **Soldon** Devon
16 E9 **Soldon Cross** Devon
23 J7 **Soldridge** Hants
27 J2 **Sole Street** Kent
37 Q7 **Sole Street** Kent
59 J9 **Solihull** Solhll
45 N3 **Sollers Dilwyn** Herefs
46 B8 **Sollers Hope** Herefs
88 F7 **Sollom** Lancs
40 F6 **Solva** Pembks
110 F5 **Solwaybank** D & G
73 K8 **Somerby** Leics
93 J9 **Somerby** Lincs
84 F10 **Somercotes** Derbys
13 L6 **Somerford** Dorset
33 K5 **Somerford Keynes** Gloucs
15 M7 **Somerley** W Susx
65 P2 **Somerleyton** Suffk
71 L7 **Somersal Herbert** Derbys
87 K6 **Somersby** Lincs
62 E5 **Somersham** Cambs
53 J2 **Somersham** Suffk
48 E9 **Somerton** Oxon
19 N9 **Somerton** Somset
63 P10 **Somerton** Suffk
57 K2 **Somerwood** Shrops
24 E9 **Sompting** W Susx
35 L9 **Sonning** Wokham
35 K8 **Sonning Common** Oxon
35 K9 **Sonning Eye** Oxon
69 K5 **Sontley** Wrexhm
13 L5 **Sopley** Hants
32 F7 **Sopworth** Wilts
107 M8 **Sorbie** D & G
167 K4 **Sordale** Highld
136 H3 **Sorisdale** Ag & B
115 L2 **Sorn** E Ayrs
167 N4 **Sortat** Highld
86 H5 **Sotby** Lincs
86 F8 **Sots Hole** Lincs
65 N5 **Sotterley** Suffk
81 J11 **Soughton** Flints
49 N9 **Soulbury** Bucks
101 N5 **Soulby** Cumb
102 D8 **Soulby** Cumb
48 F8 **Souldern** Oxon
61 L8 **Souldrop** Bed
70 A5 **Sound** Ches E
157 R7 **Sound Muir** Moray
32 C9 **Soundwell** S Glos
8 D6 **Sourton** Devon
94 E4 **Soutergate** Cumb
75 R8 **South Acre** Norfk
27 M3 **South Alkham** Kent
36 D5 **Southall** Gt Lon
7 K11 **South Allington** Devon
133 P9 **South Alloa** Falk
47 J9 **Southam** Gloucs
48 D2 **Southam** Warwks
23 P10 **South Ambersham** W Susx
14 D4 **Southampton** C Sotn
22 E11 *Southampton Airport* Hants
22 D11 **Southampton Crematorium** Hants
84 H4 **South Anston** Rothm
35 P11 **South Ascot** W & M
26 H3 **South Ashford** Kent
14 C7 **South Baddesley** Hants
139 K6 **South Ballachulish** Highld
98 B10 **South Bank** C York
104 F6 **South Bank** R & Cl
20 B9 **South Barrow** Somset
36 G8 **South Beddington** Gt Lon
5 N3 **South Beer** Cnwll
38 C4 **South Benfleet** Essex
15 P6 **South Bersted** W Susx
13 L5 **South Bockhampton** Dorset
37 K7 **Southborough** Gt Lon
25 N2 **Southborough** Kent
13 K6 **Southbourne** Bmouth
15 L5 **Southbourne** W Susx
11 J5 **South Bowood** Dorset
91 Q8 **South Bramwith** Donc
6 H6 **South Brent** Devon
20 D7 **South Brewham** Somset
31 Q11 **South Bristol Crematorium** Bristl
119 P11 **South Broomhill** Nthumb
76 E10 **Southburgh** Norfk
77 M10 **South Burlingham** Norfk
99 K10 **Southburn** E R Yk
20 B9 **South Cadbury** Somset
86 B5 **South Carlton** Lincs
85 J4 **South Carlton** Notts
92 F4 **South Cave** E R Yk
33 K5 **South Cerney** Gloucs
25 J7 **South Chailey** E Susx
10 G3 **South Chard** Somset
119 N6 **South Charlton** Nthumb
20 C10 **South Cheriton** Somset
103 P5 **South Church** Dur
38 F4 **Southchurch** Sthend
103 M7 **South Cleatlam** Dur
92 E3 **South Cliffe** E R Yk
85 P6 **South Clifton** Notts
87 L3 **South Cockerington** Lincs
29 M8 **South Cornelly** Brdgnd
5 K2 **Southcott** Cnwll
8 D5 **Southcott** Devon
9 J8 **Southcott** Devon
16 G8 **Southcott** Devon
21 N3 **Southcott** Wilts
35 M2 **Southcourt** Bucks
65 P5 **South Cove** Suffk
76 B4 **South Creake** Norfk
90 E8 **South Crosland** Kirk
72 H8 **South Croxton** Leics
99 K11 **South Dalton** E R Yk
37 N7 **South Darenth** Kent
25 J9 **South Downs National Park**
92 A4 **South Duffield** N York
25 K9 **Southease** E Susx
87 J3 **South Elkington** Lincs
91 M8 **South Elmsall** Wakefd
120 C10 **Southend** Ag & B
93 Q7 **South End** E R Yk
21 M11 **South End** Hants
46 D6 **South End** Herefs
93 K6 **South End** N Linc
64 D3 **South End** Norfk
33 N10 **Southend** Wilts
38 E4 *Southend Airport* Essex
38 E4 **Southend Crematorium** Sthend
38 E4 **Southend-on-Sea** Sthend
101 L3 **Southernby** Cumb
26 E2 **Southernden** Kent
29 N10 **Southerndown** V Glam
109 L10 **Southerness** D & G
153 N3 **South Erradale** Highld
10 B6 **Southerton** Devon
63 K2 **Southery** Norfk
37 N3 **South Essex Crematorium** Gt Lon
38 E3 **South Fambridge** Essex
34 C8 **South Fawley** W Berk
92 G6 **South Ferriby** N Linc
92 H5 **South Field** E R Yk
126 E3 **Southfield** Falk
37 P6 **Southfleet** Kent
14 F11 **Southford** IoW
36 G2 **Southgate** Gt Lon
75 N4 **Southgate** Norfk
76 B4 **Southgate** Norfk
76 G7 **Southgate** Norfk
28 G7 **Southgate** Swans
37 J11 **South Godstone** Surrey
13 L2 **South Gorley** Hants
113 K7 **South Gosforth** N u Ty
37 Q2 **South Green** Essex
52 H8 **South Green** Essex
38 E9 **South Green** Kent
76 F9 **South Green** Norfk
64 H6 **South Green** Suffk
127 M3 **South Gyle** C Edin
38 B2 **South Hanningfield** Essex
23 L11 **South Harting** W Susx
15 K7 **South Hayling** Hants
119 L4 **South Hazelrigg** Nthumb
35 P4 **South Heath** Bucks
25 K10 **South Heighton** E Susx
113 N11 **South Hetton** Dur
91 K8 **South Hiendley** Wakefd
5 N7 **South Hill** Cnwll
19 N9 **South Hill** Somset
34 F4 **South Hinksey** Oxon
16 C7 **South Hole** Devon
24 E2 **South Holmwood** Surrey
37 M4 **South Hornchurch** Gt Lon
19 Q5 **South Horrington** Somset
6 H10 **South Huish** Devon
86 B8 **South Hykeham** Lincs
113 N9 **South Hylton** Sundld
50 E2 **Southill** C Beds
22 F5 **Southington** Hants
92 H11 **South Kelsey** Lincs
156 B8 **South Kessock** Highld
93 K7 **South Killingholme** N Linc
97 P4 **South Kilvington** N York
60 D4 **South Kilworth** Leics
91 L8 **South Kirkby** Wakefd
7 L4 **South Knighton** Devon
86 G11 **South Kyme** Lincs
126 B6 **South Lanarkshire Crematorium** S Lans
10 E6 **Southleigh** Devon
34 C3 **South Leigh** Oxon
85 N4 **South Leverton** Notts
47 L5 **South Littleton** Worcs
36 G7 **South London Crematorium** Gt Lon
64 E5 **South Lopham** Norfk
73 N10 **South Luffenham** Rutlnd
25 K8 **South Malling** E Susx
33 N7 **South Marston** Swindn
36 G10 **South Merstham** Surrey
119 J6 **South Middleton** Nthumb
91 M4 **South Milford** N York
6 J10 **South Milton** Devon
50 F10 **South Mimms** Herts
50 F10 *South Mimms Services* Herts
38 G2 **Southminster** Essex
17 N6 **South Molton** Devon
113 J10 **South Moor** Dur
34 C5 **Southmoor** Oxon
34 G7 **South Moreton** Oxon
142 F7 **Southmuir** Angus
15 N6 **South Mundham** W Susx
85 N9 **South Muskham** Notts
92 F3 **South Newbald** E R Yk
48 D8 **South Newington** Oxon
21 L8 **South Newton** Wilts
84 F9 **South Normanton** Derbys
36 H7 **South Norwood** Gt Lon
36 H11 **South Nutfield** Surrey
37 N4 **South Ockendon** Thurr
61 Q8 **Southoe** Cambs
64 H8 **Southolt** Suffk
87 L5 **South Ormsby** Lincs
74 A10 **Southorpe** C Pete
90 H7 **South Ossett** Wakefd
97 N3 **South Otterington** N York
11 N6 **Southover** Dorset
25 Q5 **Southover** E Susx
86 E2 **South Owersby** Lincs
90 E6 **Southowram** Calder

Tabley Hill - Thurston Planch 301

T

82 F9 Tabley Hill Ches E
48 E11 Tackley Oxon
64 G2 Tacolneston Norfk
91 M2 Tadcaster N York
83 P10 Taddington Derbys
47 L8 Taddington Gloucs
16 H8 Taddiport Devon
22 H2 Tadley Hants
62 C11 Tadlow Cambs
48 C7 Tadmarton Oxon
32 D10 Tadwick BaNES
36 F9 Tadworth Surrey
30 F2 Tafarnaubach Blae G
41 L4 Tafarn-y-bwlch Pembks
68 G2 Tafarn-y-Gelyn Denbgs
30 F8 Taff's Well Rhondd
55 K4 Tafolwern Powys
29 L7 Taibach Neath
162 H10 Tain Highld
167 M3 Tain Highld
66 G4 Tai'n Lôn Gwynd
168 g7 Tairbeart W Isls
44 D9 Tai'r Bull Powys
51 N6 Takeley Essex
51 M6 Takeley Street Essex
44 F8 Talachddu Powys
80 G8 Talacre Flints
9 Q5 Talaton Devon
40 F8 Talbenny Pembks
30 D8 Talbot Green Rhondd
13 J6 Talbot Village Bmouth
10 B5 Taleford Devon
55 L4 Talerddig Powys
42 H4 Talgarreg Cerdgn
44 H8 Talgarth Powys
152 E11 Talisker Highld
70 E4 Talke Staffs
70 E4 Talke Pits Staffs
111 L9 Talkin Cumb
154 B3 Talladale Highld
116 G6 Talla Linnfoots Border
114 H8 Tallaminnock S Ayrs
69 M6 Tallarn Green Wrexhm
100 F3 Tallentire Cumb
43 M8 Talley Carmth
74 A9 Tallington Lincs
69 J5 Tallwrn Wrexhm
165 N4 Talmine Highld
42 F9 Talog Carmth
43 K3 Talsarn Cerdgn
67 L7 Talsarnau Gwynd
4 E8 Talskiddy Cnwll
78 H9 Talwrn IoA
69 L5 Talwrn Wrexhm
54 F7 Tal-y-bont Cerdgn
79 P11 Tal-y-Bont Conwy
67 K10 Tal-y-bont Gwynd
79 L10 Tal-y-bont Gwynd
44 G10 Talybont-on-Usk Powys
79 P10 Tal-y-Cafn Conwy
45 N11 Tal-y-coed Mons
30 D9 Tal-y-garn Rhondd
54 G3 Tal-y-llyn Gwynd
66 H4 Talysarn Gwynd
31 J4 Tal-y-Waun Torfn
55 J4 Talywern Powys
89 D4 Tamer Lane End Wigan
6 D6 Tamerton Foliot C Plym
59 K4 Tamworth Staffs
74 G2 Tamworth Green Lincs
59 K4 Tamworth Services Warwks
97 Q9 Tancred N York
40 G5 Tancredston Pembks
37 J10 Tandridge Surrey
113 J9 Tanfield Dur
113 J10 Tanfield Lea Dur
41 J7 Tangiers Pembks
22 B4 Tangley Hants
15 P5 Tangmere W Susx
168 b17 Tangusdale W Isls
102 G9 Tan Hill N York
169 e6 Tankerness Ork
91 J11 Tankersley Barns
39 K8 Tankerton Kent
167 P7 Tannach Highld
151 K11 Tannachie Abers
142 H6 Tannadice Angus
58 G10 Tanner's Green Worcs
65 J8 Tannington Suffk
126 C5 Tannochside N Lans
84 D9 Tansley Derbys
61 N2 Tansor Nhants
113 J10 Tantobie Dur
104 F8 Tanton N York
58 D10 Tanwood Worcs
58 H10 Tanworth in Arden Warwks
67 M6 Tan-y-Bwlch Gwynd
68 C2 Tan-y-fron Conwy
69 J4 Tan-y-fron Wrexhm
67 M5 Tan-y-grisiau Gwynd
42 E5 Tan-y-groes Cerdgn
168 e9 Taobh Tuath W Isls
35 P8 Taplow Bucks
123 L9 Tarbert Ag & B
123 Q6 Tarbert Ag & B
168 g7 Tarbert W Isls
132 C7 Tarbet Ag & B
145 N9 Tarbet Highld
164 E7 Tarbet Highld
81 P7 Tarbock Green Knows
114 H2 Tarbolton S Ayrs
127 J6 Tarbrax S Lans
58 E11 Tardebigge Worcs
142 H2 Tarfside Angus
150 D7 Tarland Abers
88 F6 Tarleton Lancs
88 E8 Tarlscough Lancs
33 J5 Tarlton Gloucs
19 L4 Tarnock Somset
109 P11 Tarns Cumb
95 J2 Tarnside Cumb
69 Q2 Tarporley Ches W
17 R5 Tarr Somset
12 F4 Tarrant Crawford Dorset
12 F2 Tarrant Gunville Dorset
12 F2 Tarrant Hinton Dorset
12 F4 Tarrant Keyneston Dorset
12 F3 Tarrant Launceston Dorset
12 F3 Tarrant Monkton Dorset
12 F3 Tarrant Rawston Dorset
12 F3 Tarrant Rushton Dorset
25 K10 Tarring Neville E Susx
46 B6 Tarrington Herefs
145 J5 Tarskavaig Highld
159 L11 Tarves Abers
81 P11 Tarvin Ches W
81 P11 Tarvin Sands Ches W
64 H2 Tasburgh Norfk
57 M6 Tasley Shrops
48 C10 Taston Oxon
71 N10 Tatenhill Staffs
49 M5 Tathall End M Keyn
95 N7 Tatham Lancs
87 K4 Tathwell Lincs
37 K9 Tatsfield Surrey
69 N3 Tattenhall Ches W
76 B6 Tatterford Norfk
76 A6 Tattersett Norfk
86 H9 Tattershall Lincs
86 G9 Tattershall Bridge Lincs
86 H9 Tattershall Thorpe Lincs
53 K4 Tattingstone Suffk
53 K4 Tattingstone White Horse Suffk
10 G3 Tatworth Somset
157 R8 Tauchers Moray
18 H10 Taunton Somset
18 H10 Taunton Deane Crematorium Somset
18 G10 Taunton Deane Services Somset
76 H9 Taverham Norfk
51 N7 Taverners Green Essex
41 N8 Tavernspite Pembks
6 D4 Tavistock Devon
8 G5 Taw Green Devon
17 K6 Tawstock Devon
83 M9 Taxal Derbys
131 L3 Taychreggan Hotel Ag & B
141 J5 Tay Forest Park P & K
123 L10 Tayinloan Ag & B
46 D10 Taynton Gloucs
33 P2 Taynton Oxon
139 J11 Taynuilt Ag & B
135 M2 Tayport Fife
130 E10 Tayvallich Ag & B
86 G2 Tealby Lincs
142 G10 Tealing Angus
113 K9 Team Valley Gatesd
145 L6 Teangue Highld
155 Q5 Teanord Highld
102 B10 Tebay Cumb
102 B9 Tebay Services Cumb
49 Q9 Tebworth C Beds
9 K6 Tedburn St Mary Devon
47 J8 Teddington Gloucs
36 E6 Teddington Gt Lon
46 C3 Tedstone Delamere Herefs
46 C3 Tedstone Wafer Herefs
104 F6 Teesport R & Cl
104 E7 Teesside Crematorium Middsb
104 E7 Teesside Park S on T
60 E6 Teeton Nhants
21 J8 Teffont Evias Wilts
21 J8 Teffont Magna Wilts
41 P4 Tegryn Pembks
73 M7 Teigh Rutlnd
8 G7 Teigncombe Devon
7 M4 Teigngrace Devon
7 N4 Teignmouth Devon
117 N9 Teindside Border
57 M3 Telford Wrekin
57 N2 Telford Crematorium Wrekin
57 N3 Telford Services Shrops
20 F3 Tellisford Somset
25 K10 Telscombe E Susx
25 K10 Telscombe Cliffs E Susx
140 G6 Tempar P & K
109 N3 Templand D & G
5 J7 Temple Cnwll
127 Q6 Temple Mdloth
59 K9 Temple Balsall Solhll
43 K4 Temple Bar Cerdgn
20 B3 Temple Cloud BaNES
20 D10 Templecombe Somset
63 L10 Temple End Suffk
27 N3 Temple Ewell Kent
47 M3 Temple Grafton Warwks
47 L9 Temple Guiting Gloucs
91 Q6 Temple Hirst N York
84 F7 Temple Normanton Derbys
151 L11 Temple of Fiddes Abers
102 B5 Temple Sowerby Cumb
9 L2 Templeton Devon
41 M8 Templeton Pembks
112 H10 Templetown Dur
61 Q10 Tempsford C Beds
57 K11 Tenbury Wells Worcs
41 M10 Tenby Pembks
53 K7 Tendring Essex
53 K6 Tendring Green Essex
53 K6 Tendring Heath Essex
75 L11 Ten Mile Bank Norfk
53 J7 Tenpenny Heath Essex
26 E5 Tenterden Kent
52 C8 Terling Essex
69 R11 Tern Wrekin
70 A8 Ternhill Shrops
109 K5 Terregles D & G
98 D6 Terrington N York
75 L6 Terrington St Clement Norfk
75 K8 Terrington St John Norfk
58 H10 Terry's Green Warwks
38 B11 Teston Kent
14 C4 Testwood Hants
32 G6 Tetbury Gloucs
32 G5 Tetbury Upton Gloucs
69 L8 Tetchill Shrops
5 N2 Tetcott Devon
87 K6 Tetford Lincs
93 P10 Tetney Lincs
93 P10 Tetney Lock Lincs
35 J4 Tetsworth Oxon
58 C4 Tettenhall Wolves
58 C5 Tettenhall Wood Wolves
84 G8 Teversal Notts
62 G9 Teversham Cambs
117 N9 Teviothead Border
50 G8 Tewin Herts
50 G7 Tewin Wood Herts
46 G8 Tewkesbury Gloucs
38 G9 Teynham Kent
90 F3 Thackley C Brad
100 F6 Thackthwaite Cumb
101 M5 Thackthwaite Cumb
24 D7 Thakeham W Susx
35 K3 Thame Oxon
36 E7 Thames Ditton Surrey
37 L4 Thamesmead Gt Lon
39 Q8 Thanet Crematorium Kent
39 K10 Thanington Kent
116 D3 Thankerton S Lans
64 H3 Tharston Norfk
34 F11 Thatcham W Berk
81 Q6 Thatto Heath St Hel
51 P4 Thaxted Essex
97 M3 Theakston N York
92 E7 Thealby N Linc
19 N5 Theale Somset
34 H10 Theale W Berk
93 J3 Thearne E R Yk
70 E3 The Bank Ches E
57 L5 The Bank Shrops
33 K4 The Beeches Gloucs
65 N8 Theberton Suffk
71 J9 The Blythe Staffs
56 F5 The Bog Shrops
47 J3 The Bourne Worcs
153 J11 The Braes Highld
58 C6 The Bratch Staffs
45 P2 The Broad Herefs
128 H5 The Brunt E Loth
80 e4 The Bungalow IoM
57 Q11 The Burf Worcs
46 G11 The Butts Gloucs
32 H3 The Camp Gloucs
69 N6 The Chequer Wrexhm
61 P9 The City Bed
35 L5 The City Bucks
47 Q9 The Common Oxon
21 P8 The Common Wilts
33 K7 The Common Wilts
26 B3 The Corner Kent
60 F9 The Counties Crematorium Nhants
80 d2 The Cronk IoM
60 E3 Theddingworth Leics
87 N3 Theddlethorpe All Saints Lincs
87 N3 Theddlethorpe St Helen Lincs
125 J7 The Den N Ayrs
32 B2 The Forest of Dean Crematorium Gloucs
45 L3 The Forge Herefs
26 H4 The Forstal Kent
70 B8 The Fouralls Shrops
38 E8 The Garden of England Crematorium Kent
94 D4 The Green Cumb
52 C8 The Green Essex
105 L9 The Green N York
20 G8 The Green Wilts
46 G6 The Grove Worcs
24 C4 The Haven W Susx
46 F9 The Haw Gloucs
104 F4 The Headland Hartpl
94 D4 The Hill Cumb
35 M9 The Holt Wokham
45 Q2 The Hundred Herefs
9 J2 Thelbridge Cross Devon
26 G5 The Leacon Kent
35 P4 The Lee Bucks
80 e1 The Lhen IoM
125 P6 The Linn Crematorium E Rens
64 E6 Thelnetham Suffk
157 Q5 The Lochs Moray
64 H5 Thelveton Norfk
82 E7 Thelwall Warrtn
82 H6 The Manchester Crematorium Manch
56 E5 The Marsh Powys
76 F7 Themelthorpe Norfk
113 K10 The Middles Dur
26 C6 The Moor Kent
28 H7 The Mumbles Swans
125 Q7 The Murray S Lans
46 G8 The Mythe Gloucs
31 P3 The Narth Mons
151 J8 The Neuk Abers
48 F6 Thenford Nhants
33 K11 Theobald's Green Wilts
23 N5 The Park Crematorium Hants
32 D5 The Quarry Gloucs
26 E3 The Quarter Kent
46 H10 The Reddings Gloucs
50 H3 Therfield Herts
44 H8 The Rhôs Powys
91 Q10 The Rose Hill Crematorium Donc
133 M3 The Ross P & K
23 N5 The Sands Surrey
32 F10 The Shoe Wilts
57 M5 The Smithies Shrops
62 G11 The Spike Cambs
59 L10 The Spring Warwks
31 J5 The Square Torfn
37 P11 The Stair Kent
26 F6 The Stocks Kent
23 L7 The Straits Hants
20 H3 The Strand Wilts
64 B5 Thetford Norfk
63 P3 Thetford Forest Park
101 L2 Thethwaite Cumb
2 F6 The Towans Cnwll
50 D6 The Vale Crematorium Luton
45 Q5 The Vauld Herefs
57 N3 The Wyke Shrops
51 K11 Theydon Bois Essex
92 A2 Thicket Priory N York
32 F10 Thickwood Wilts
86 H6 Thimbleby Lincs
104 D11 Thimbleby N York
81 K8 Thingwall Wirral
97 Q5 Thirkleby N York
97 Q4 Thirlby N York
128 F10 Thirlestane Border
97 K3 Thirn N York
97 P4 Thirsk N York
93 L4 Thirtleby E R Yk
88 E3 Thistleton Lancs
73 N7 Thistleton Rutlnd
63 L5 Thistley Green Suffk
98 G8 Thixendale N York
112 E5 Thockrington Nthumb
74 H9 Tholomas Drove Cambs
97 Q7 Tholthorpe N York
41 M9 Thomas Chapel Pembks
101 M2 Thomas Close Cumb
158 E10 Thomastown Abers
47 L2 Thomas Town Warwks
64 C2 Thompson Norfk
37 Q6 Thong Kent
96 F3 Thoralby N York
85 K6 Thoresby Notts
87 N5 Thoresthorpe Lincs
93 L11 Thoresway Lincs
93 M11 Thorganby Lincs
92 A2 Thorganby N York
105 K11 Thorgill N York
65 N7 Thorington Suffk
52 H4 Thorington Street Suffk
96 E10 Thorlby N York
51 L7 Thorley Herts
14 C9 Thorley IoW
51 L6 Thorley Houses Herts
14 C9 Thorley Street IoW
97 Q6 Thormanby N York
104 E7 Thornaby-on-Tees S on T
76 F4 Thornage Norfk
49 K8 Thornborough Bucks
97 L5 Thornborough N York
90 F4 Thornbury C Brad
16 G10 Thornbury Devon
46 B3 Thornbury Herefs
32 B6 Thornbury S Glos
110 E10 Thornby Cumb
60 E5 Thornby Nhants
71 J3 Thorncliff Staffs
94 D6 Thorncliffe Crematorium Cumb
10 H4 Thorncombe Dorset
23 Q6 Thorncombe Street Surrey
61 Q11 Thorncott Green C Beds
14 D10 Thorncross IoW
64 G8 Thorndon Suffk
8 D6 Thorndon Cross Devon
92 A8 Thorne Donc
19 P11 Thorne Coffin Somset
7 K5 Thornecroft Devon
16 G8 Thornehillhead Devon
91 K2 Thorner Leeds
58 G4 Thornes Staffs
91 J7 Thornes Wakefd
18 F10 Thorne St Margaret Somset
36 B5 Thorney Bucks
74 E10 Thorney C Pete
85 Q6 Thorney Notts
19 M10 Thorney Somset
13 M5 Thorney Hill Hants
15 L6 Thorney Island W Susx
74 F10 Thorney Toll Cambs
19 J10 Thornfalcon Somset
11 N2 Thornford Dorset
111 Q7 Thorngrafton Nthumb
19 L8 Thorngrove Somset
93 M5 Thorngumbald E R Yk
75 P2 Thornham Norfk
64 G7 Thornham Magna Suffk
64 G7 Thornham Parva Suffk
73 R10 Thornhaugh C Pete
14 E4 Thornhill C Sotn
30 G8 Thornhill Caerph
100 D9 Thornhill Cumb
116 B11 Thornhill D & G
83 Q8 Thornhill Derbys
90 H7 Thornhill Kirk
133 K7 Thornhill Stirlg
30 G8 Thornhill Crematorium Cardif
90 G7 Thornhill Lees Kirk
90 F6 Thornhills Calder
99 N8 Thornholme E R Yk
12 E4 Thornicombe Dorset
118 G4 Thornington Nthumb
103 M3 Thornley Dur
104 C3 Thornley Dur
112 B9 Thornley Gate Nthumb
125 P6 Thornliebank E Rens
63 M9 Thorns Suffk
83 M7 Thornsett Derbys
82 G8 Thorns Green Ches E
100 H5 Thornthwaite Cumb
97 J9 Thornthwaite N York
142 F8 Thornton Angus
49 K7 Thornton Bucks
90 D4 Thornton C Brad
98 F11 Thornton E R Yk
134 H8 Thornton Fife
88 C2 Thornton Lancs
72 D9 Thornton Leics
86 H7 Thornton Lincs
104 E8 Thornton Middsb
129 P10 Thornton Nthumb
40 H9 Thornton Pembks
81 L4 Thornton Sefton
93 J7 Thornton Curtis N Linc
81 L4 Thornton Garden of Rest Crematorium Sefton
125 P6 Thorntonhall S Lans
36 H7 Thornton Heath Gt Lon
81 L8 Thornton Hough Wirral
96 D11 Thornton-in-Craven N York
95 P6 Thornton in Lonsdale N York
97 N2 Thornton-le-Beans N York
98 D7 Thornton-le-Clay N York
98 G4 Thornton le Dale N York
92 H11 Thornton le Moor Lincs
97 N3 Thornton-le-Moor N York
81 N10 Thornton-le-Moors Ches W
97 P3 Thornton-le-Street N York
129 K5 Thorntonloch E Loth
96 E3 Thornton Rust N York
97 J3 Thornton Steward N York
97 K3 Thornton Watlass N York
51 L10 Thornwood Common Essex
128 G10 Thornydykes Border
101 L6 Thornythwaite Cumb
73 K2 Thoroton Notts
97 P11 Thorp Arch Leeds
71 M4 Thorpe Derbys
99 K11 Thorpe E R Yk
87 N4 Thorpe Lincs
96 F8 Thorpe N York
65 N2 Thorpe Norfk
85 N11 Thorpe Notts
36 B7 Thorpe Surrey
64 H6 Thorpe Abbotts Norfk
72 E7 Thorpe Acre Leics
73 K6 Thorpe Arnold Leics
91 M7 Thorpe Audlin Wakefd
98 H6 Thorpe Bassett N York
38 F4 Thorpe Bay Sthend
73 M11 Thorpe by Water Rutlnd
91 K11 Thorpe Common Rothm
59 L3 Thorpe Constantine Staffs
77 K9 Thorpe End Norfk
53 L7 Thorpe Green Essex
88 H6 Thorpe Green Lancs
64 C11 Thorpe Green Suffk
91 K11 Thorpe Hesley Rothm
91 P8 Thorpe in Balne Donc
60 F2 Thorpe Langton Leics
104 C5 Thorpe Larches Dur
36 B6 Thorpe Lea Surrey
86 B4 Thorpe le Fallows Lincs
53 L7 Thorpe-le-Soken Essex
92 D2 Thorpe le Street E R Yk
60 H5 Thorpe Malsor Nhants
48 F6 Thorpe Mandeville Nhants
77 J4 Thorpe Market Norfk
76 H8 Thorpe Marriot Norfk
64 C11 Thorpe Morieux Suffk
65 P10 Thorpeness Suffk
91 J5 Thorpe on the Hill Leeds
86 B7 Thorpe on the Hill Lincs
36 B7 Thorpe Park Surrey
77 K10 Thorpe St Andrew Norfk
87 N8 Thorpe St Peter Lincs
84 H4 Thorpe Salvin Rothm
73 J8 Thorpe Satchville Leics
104 C6 Thorpe Thewles S on T
86 F9 Thorpe Tilney Lincs
97 Q9 Thorpe Underwood N York
60 G4 Thorpe Underwood Nhants
61 M4 Thorpe Waterville Nhants
91 P4 Thorpe Willoughby N York
75 M9 Thorpland Norfk
53 J8 Thorrington Essex
9 M4 Thorverton Devon
50 D7 Thrales End C Beds
64 G6 Thrandeston Suffk
61 L5 Thrapston Nhants
100 G3 Threapland Cumb
96 E8 Threapland N York
69 M6 Threapwood Ches W
71 J6 Threapwood Staffs
71 J6 Threapwood Head Staffs
114 F6 Threave S Ayrs
108 F8 Threave Castle D & G
45 Q10 Three Ashes Herefs
24 G3 Three Bridges W Susx
3 J4 Three Burrows Cnwll
26 D4 Three Chimneys Kent
44 H7 Three Cocks Powys
52 C6 Three Counties Crematorium Essex
28 G6 Three Crosses Swans
25 P6 Three Cups Corner E Susx
46 C2 Three Gates Worcs
77 L8 Threehammer Common Norfk
5 L4 Three Hammers Cnwll
75 K10 Three Holes Norfk
74 A3 Threekingham Lincs
25 Q4 Three Leg Cross E Susx
13 J3 Three Legged Cross Dorset
35 K11 Three Mile Cross Wokham
3 K4 Threemilestone Cnwll
127 K2 Three Miletown W Loth
26 D9 Three Oaks E Susx
101 K5 Threlkeld Cumb
51 L9 Threshers Bush Essex
96 E8 Threshfield N York
77 P9 Thrigby Norfk
102 H6 Thringarth Dur
72 C7 Thringstone Leics
97 M2 Thrintoft N York
62 F11 Thriplow Cambs
84 H3 Throapham Rothm
74 G9 Throckenhalt Lincs
50 H4 Throcking Herts
113 J7 Throckley N u Ty
47 J4 Throckmorton Worcs
13 K5 Throop Bmouth
12 D6 Throop Dorset
112 H3 Throphill Nthumb
119 K10 Thropton Nthumb
133 P9 Throsk Stirlg
32 H3 Througham Gloucs
109 J4 Throughgate D & G
8 G6 Throwleigh Devon
38 G10 Throwley Kent
38 G11 Throwley Forstal Kent
72 E4 Thrumpton Notts
85 M4 Thrumpton Notts
167 P7 Thrumster Highld
93 P9 Thrunscoe NE Lin
119 L8 Thrunton Nthumb
33 Q5 Thrup Oxon
32 G4 Thrupp Gloucs
48 E11 Thrupp Oxon
8 B7 Thrushelton Devon
72 H7 Thrussington Leics
21 Q5 Thruxton Hants
45 N8 Thruxton Herefs
91 M11 Thrybergh Rothm
72 C4 Thulston Derbys
38 C4 Thundersley Essex
72 F8 Thurcaston Leics
84 G3 Thurcroft Rothm
16 D9 Thurdon Cnwll
76 H5 Thurgarton Norfk
85 L11 Thurgarton Notts
90 H10 Thurgoland Barns
72 E11 Thurlaston Leics
59 Q10 Thurlaston Warwks
19 J10 Thurlbear Somset
74 A7 Thurlby Lincs
86 B8 Thurlby Lincs
87 N5 Thurlby Lincs
61 N9 Thurleigh Bed
6 H10 Thurlestone Devon
19 J8 Thurloxton Somset
90 G10 Thurlstone Barns
65 N2 Thurlton Norfk
70 E3 Thurlwood Ches E
72 G9 Thurmaston Leics
72 G10 Thurnby Leics
77 N8 Thurne Norfk
38 D10 Thurnham Kent
61 N4 Thurning Nhants
76 F6 Thurning Norfk
91 M9 Thurnscoe Barns
37 N5 Thurrock Services Thurr
110 F10 Thursby Cumb
89 Q4 Thursden Lancs
76 D5 Thursford Norfk
23 P7 Thursley Surrey
167 K3 Thurso Highld
81 J8 Thurstaston Wirral
64 C8 Thurston Suffk
90 B9 Thurston Clough Oldham
110 F9 Thurstonfield Cumb
90 F8 Thurstonland Kirk
64 C9 Thurston Planch Suffk

302 Thurton - Trillacott

77 L11 Thurton Norfk
71 N7 Thurvaston Derbys
76 E10 Thuxton Norfk
102 G11 Thwaite N York
64 G8 Thwaite Suffk
94 G2 Thwaite Head Cumb
90 D2 Thwaites C Brad
65 L2 Thwaite St Mary Norfk
90 D2 Thwaites Brow C Brad
99 L6 Thwing E R Yk
134 C3 Tibbermore P & K
116 B11 Tibbers D & G
46 E10 Tibberton Gloucs
46 H3 Tibberton Worcs
70 B10 Tibberton Wrekin
117 J6 Tibbie Shiels Inn Border
64 G4 Tibenham Norfk
84 F8 Tibshelf Derbys
99 K9 Tibthorpe E R Yk
25 Q4 Ticehurst E Susx
22 G8 Tichborne Hants
73 P9 Tickencote Rutlnd
31 N10 Tickenham N Som
49 N6 Tickford End M Keyn
85 J2 Tickhill Donc
56 H6 Ticklerton Shrops
72 B6 Ticknall Derbys
93 J2 Tickton E R Yk
58 H9 Tidbury Green Solhll
21 Q3 Tidcombe Wilts
34 H4 Tiddington Oxon
47 P3 Tiddington Warwks
32 G9 Tiddleywink Wilts
25 P4 Tidebrook E Susx
5 P10 Tideford Cnwll
5 N9 Tideford Cross Cnwll
31 Q5 Tidenham Gloucs
83 Q9 Tideswell Derbys
34 H10 Tidmarsh W Berk
47 Q7 Tidmington Warwks
21 L11 Tidpit Hants
21 P5 Tidworth Wilts
40 H8 Tiers Cross Pembks
49 K4 Tiffield Nhants
143 J5 Tigerton Angus
168 c10 Tigh a Ghearraidh W Isls
168 c10 Tigharry W Isls
124 B3 Tighnabruaich Ag & B
7 K6 Tigley Devon
61 N7 Tilbrook Cambs
37 P5 Tilbury Thurr
52 B3 Tilbury Green Essex
52 C3 Tilbury Juxta Clare Essex
59 J7 Tile Cross Birm
59 L9 Tile Hill Covtry
59 J9 Tilehouse Green Solhll
35 J10 Tilehurst Readg
23 N6 Tilford Surrey
24 G4 Tilgate W Susx
24 G4 Tilgate Forest Row W Susx
19 Q7 Tilham Street Somset
46 C8 Tillers Green Gloucs
133 Q8 Tillicoultry Clacks
126 E8 Tillietudlem S Lans
52 G11 Tillingham Essex
45 P6 Tillington Herefs
23 Q10 Tillington W Susx
45 P5 Tillington Common Herefs
150 H6 Tillybirloch Abers
150 G5 Tillyfourie Abers
151 M3 Tillygreig Abers
134 E6 Tillyrie P & K
39 P11 Tilmanstone Kent
75 L7 Tilney All Saints Norfk
75 L7 Tilney High End Norfk
75 K8 Tilney St Lawrence Norfk
21 K5 Tilshead Wilts
69 P7 Tilstock Shrops
69 N4 Tilston Ches W
69 Q3 Tilstone Bank Ches W
69 Q2 Tilstone Fearnall Ches W
49 Q10 Tilsworth C Beds
73 J9 Tilton on the Hill Leics
32 F5 Tiltups End Gloucs
51 N5 Tilty Essex
86 F9 Timberland Lincs
70 F2 Timbersbrook Ches E
18 C6 Timberscombe Somset
97 J10 Timble N York
18 C9 Timewell Devon
110 F6 Timpanheck D & G
82 G7 Timperley Traffd
20 C3 Timsbury BaNES
22 B10 Timsbury Hants
168 f4 Timsgarry W Isls
168 f4 Timsgearraidh W Isls
64 B8 Timworth Suffk
64 B8 Timworth Green Suffk
12 C6 Tincleton Dorset
111 M9 Tindale Cumb
103 N5 Tindale Crescent Dur
49 J8 Tingewick Bucks
90 H5 Tingley Leeds
50 B4 Tingrith C Beds
169 r9 *Tingwall Airport Shet*
5 P4 Tinhay Devon
22 D5 Tinker's Hill Hants
84 C8 Tinkersley Derbys
84 F2 Tinsley Sheff
24 G3 Tinsley Green W Susx
4 H4 Tintagel Cnwll
4 G4 Tintagel Castle Cnwll
31 P4 Tintern Abbey Mons
31 P4 Tintern Parva Mons
19 N11 Tintinhull Somset
83 M5 Tintwistle Derbys
109 M4 Tinwald D & G
73 Q9 Tinwell Rutlnd
17 P2 Tippacott Devon
75 K11 Tipp's End Norfk
13 N5 Tiptoe Hants
58 E6 Tipton Sandw
58 E6 Tipton Green Sandw
10 B6 Tipton St John Devon
52 E8 Tiptree Essex
52 E8 Tiptree Heath Essex
44 B6 Tirabad Powys
136 C7 Tiree Ag & B
136 C7 *Tiree Airport Ag & B*
123 M7 Tiretigan Ag & B
46 F9 Tirley Gloucs
30 F4 Tirphil Caerph
101 P5 Tirril Cumb
69 J3 Tir-y-fron Flints
20 H9 Tisbury Wilts
24 C4 Tisman's Common W Susx
71 M4 Tissington Derbys
16 C6 Titchberry Devon
14 F5 Titchfield Hants
14 F5 Titchfield Common Hants
61 M5 Titchmarsh Nhants
75 Q2 Titchwell Norfk
72 H3 Tithby Notts
45 L2 Titley Herefs
50 F5 Titmore Green Herts
37 K10 Titsey Surrey
16 C11 Titson Cnwll
70 F7 Tittensor Staffs
76 B7 Tittleshall Norfk
57 B11 Titton Worcs
69 Q2 Tiverton Ches W
9 N2 Tiverton Devon
64 H4 Tivetshall St Margaret Norfk
64 H4 Tivetshall St Mary Norfk
18 B5 Tivington Somset
90 H9 Tivy Dale Barns
70 H10 Tixall Staffs
73 P10 Tixover Rutlnd
169 q12 Toab Shet
84 E9 Toadhole Derbys
84 D10 Toadmoor Derbys
137 N4 Tobermory Ag & B
130 E6 Toberonochy Ag & B
168 c14 Tobha Mor W Isls
158 G11 Tocher Abers
158 D4 Tochieneal Moray
33 K9 Tockenham Wilts
33 K8 Tockenham Wick Wilts
104 H7 Tocketts R & Cl
89 K6 Tockholes Bl w D
32 B7 Tockington S Glos
97 Q10 Tockwith N York
20 E11 Todber Dorset
119 M11 Todburn Nthumb
50 B5 Toddington C Beds
47 K8 Toddington Gloucs
50 B5 Toddington Services C Beds
50 F5 Todds Green Herts
47 P7 Todenham Gloucs
142 G10 Todhills Angus
110 G8 Todhills Cumb
103 P4 Todhills Dur
110 G8 Todhills Services Cumb
89 Q6 Todmorden Calder
84 G4 Todwick Rothm
62 E9 Toft Cambs
82 G9 Toft Ches E
73 R7 Toft Lincs
169 r6 Toft Shet
59 Q10 Toft Warwks
103 N5 Toft Hill Dur
86 H8 Toft Hill Lincs
65 N3 Toft Monks Norfk
86 D3 Toft next Newton Lincs
76 B6 Toftrees Norfk
76 D9 Toftwood Norfk
119 P10 Togston Nthumb
145 K5 Tokavaig Highld
35 K9 Tokers Green Oxon
168 k3 Tolastadh W Isls
4 E10 Toldish Cnwll
18 F8 Tolland Somset
21 J11 Tollard Farnham Dorset
20 H11 Tollard Royal Wilts
91 P9 Toll Bar Donc
59 N9 Tollbar End Covtry
11 M5 Toller Fratrum Dorset
11 M5 Toller Porcorum Dorset
97 R8 Tollerton N York
72 G4 Tollerton Notts
11 L4 Toller Whelme Dorset
52 G9 Tollesbury Essex
52 F9 Tolleshunt D'Arcy Essex
52 F9 Tolleshunt Knights Essex
52 F9 Tolleshunt Major Essex
12 C6 Tolpuddle Dorset
168 k3 Tolsta W Isls
36 E7 Tolworth Gt Lon
148 E2 Tomatin Highld
146 H5 Tomchrasky Highld
146 F7 Tomdoun Highld
147 J2 Tomich Highld
155 P8 Tomich Highld
156 B3 Tomich Highld
162 E5 Tomich Highld
149 M4 Tomintoul Moray
48 E2 Tomlow Warwks
155 P9 Tomnacross Highld
149 N2 Tomnavoulin Moray
70 G4 Tompkin Staffs
31 K4 Ton Mons
31 L5 Ton Mons
37 N11 Tonbridge Kent
29 N8 Tondu Brdgnd
18 F10 Tonedale Somset
54 D4 Ton fanau Gwynd
90 G4 Tong C Brad
38 G10 Tong Kent
57 P3 Tong Shrops
72 C6 Tonge Leics
38 G11 Tong Green Kent
23 N5 Tongham Surrey
108 E10 Tongland D & G
57 P3 Tong Norton Shrops
165 N5 Tongue Highld
74 C7 Tongue End Lincs
30 F8 Tongwynlais Cardif
29 M5 Tonmawr Neath
29 L5 Tonna Neath
30 E7 Ton-teg Rhondd
50 H7 Tonwell Herts
30 C6 Tonypandy Rhondd
30 D7 Tonyrefail Rhondd
34 G4 Toot Baldon Oxon
51 M10 Toot Hill Essex
22 C11 Toothill Hants
33 M8 Toothill Swindn
36 G6 Tooting Gt Lon
36 G6 Tooting Bec Gt Lon
97 N5 Topcliffe N York
65 K3 Topcroft Norfk
65 K3 Topcroft Street Norfk
61 M8 Top End Bed
91 Q7 Topham Donc
89 P9 Top of Hebers Rochdl
52 B4 Toppesfield Essex
89 L8 Toppings Bolton
64 H2 Toprow Norfk
9 N7 Topsham Devon
69 J3 Top-y-rhos Flints
120 G6 Torbeg N Ayrs
162 H7 Torboll Highld
156 A9 Torbreck Highld
7 L5 Torbryan Devon
139 L2 Torcastle Highld
7 L10 Torcross Devon
155 R7 Tore Highld
5 J11 Torfrey Cnwll
123 P7 Torinturk Ag & B
85 P5 Torksey Lincs
32 E9 Tormarton S Glos
120 G5 Tormore N Ayrs
156 D7 Tornagrain Highld
150 G6 Tornaveen Abers
147 P2 Torness Highld
103 N4 Toronto Dur
100 H3 Torpenhow Cumb
126 H3 Torphichen W Loth
150 G7 Torphins Abers
6 C7 Torpoint Cnwll
7 N6 Torquay Torbay
7 N5 Torquay Crematorium Torbay
128 C10 Torquhan Border
6 F8 Torr Devon
153 K8 Torran Highld
125 Q3 Torrance E Duns
125 K9 Torranyard N Ayrs
18 D7 Torre Somset
154 B6 Torridon Highld
153 R6 Torridon House Highld
145 J3 Torrin Highld
120 E4 Torrisdale Ag & B
165 Q4 Torrisdale Highld
163 M3 Torrish Highld
95 K8 Torrisholme Lancs
162 D6 Torrobull Highld
151 N6 Torry C Aber
134 C10 Torryburn Fife
10 a2 Torteval Guern
109 M5 Torthorwald D & G
24 B10 Tortington W Susx
58 B10 Torton Worcs
32 D6 Tortworth S Glos
152 H9 Torvaig Highld
94 F2 Torver Cumb
133 N10 Torwood Falk
117 P3 Torwoodlee Border
85 L3 Torworth Notts
16 D7 Tosberry Devon
153 N10 Toscaig Highld
62 B8 Toseland Cambs
95 R9 Tosside Lancs
64 D9 Tostock Suffk
152 C7 Totaig Highld
152 G8 Tote Highld
153 J5 Tote Highld
23 N10 Tote Hill W Susx
22 G7 Totford Hants
87 M4 Tothill Lincs
13 P7 Totland IoW
84 D5 Totley Sheff
84 D4 Totley Brook Sheff
7 L6 Totnes Devon
72 E4 Toton Notts
136 F4 Totronald Ag & B
152 F4 Totscore Highld
36 H2 Tottenham Gt Lon
75 M8 Tottenhill Norfk
36 F2 Totteridge Gt Lon
49 Q10 Totternhoe C Beds
89 M8 Tottington Bury
89 L4 Tottleworth Lancs
14 C4 Totton Hants
35 N9 Touchen End W & M
91 M2 Toulston N York
18 G8 Toulton Somset
163 K10 Toulvaddie Highld
38 C11 Tovil Kent
3 Q4 Towan Cnwll
4 D7 Towan Cnwll
124 E4 Toward Ag & B
124 E4 Toward Quay Ag & B
49 J5 Towcester Nhants
2 D6 Towednack Cnwll
35 K3 Towersey Oxon
150 C5 Towie Abers
103 M3 Tow Law Dur
74 H11 Town End Cambs
95 J4 Town End Cumb
101 K9 Town End Cumb
102 B5 Town End Cumb
125 K2 Townend W Duns
111 K11 Towngate Cumb
74 B8 Towngate Lincs
88 E9 Town Green Lancs
77 M9 Town Green Norfk
83 Q4 Townhead Barns
100 E3 Townhead Cumb
101 M10 Town Head Cumb
102 B4 Townhead Cumb
109 M3 Townhead D & G
96 B9 Town Head N York
108 F8 Townhead of Greenlaw D & G
134 E10 Townhill Fife
104 C3 Town Kelloe Dur
5 Q7 Townlake Devon
82 E5 Town Lane Wigan
25 K7 Town Littleworth E Susx
82 D5 Town of Lowton Wigan
25 N4 Town Row E Susx
22 G3 Towns End Hants
10 H2 Townsend Somset
2 F7 Townshend Cnwll
63 N3 Town Street Suffk
32 D6 Townwell S Glos
118 F5 Town Yetholm Border
98 C9 Towthorpe C York
98 H8 Towthorpe E R Yk
91 M3 Towton N York
80 D9 Towyn Conwy
81 M7 Toxteth Lpool
87 L8 Toynton All Saints Lincs
87 L8 Toynton Fen Side Lincs
87 M8 Toynton St Peter Lincs
37 L10 Toy's Hill Kent
114 H3 Trabboch E Ayrs
115 J3 Trabbochburn E Ayrs
3 J9 Traboe Cnwll
18 E10 Tracebridge Somset
156 F6 Tradespark Highld
44 D9 Trallong Powys
84 D9 Tramway Museum Derbys
128 C5 Tranent E Loth
81 L7 Tranmere Wirral
166 E6 Trantelbeg Highld
166 E6 Trantlemore Highld
113 J4 Tranwell Nthumb
43 N11 Trapp Carmth
128 F4 Traprain E Loth
58 H11 Trap's Green Warwks
22 C2 Trapshill W Berk
117 L4 Traquair Border
35 J11 Trash Green W Berk
89 Q3 Trawden Lancs
54 F10 Trawscoed Cerdgn
67 N7 Trawsfynydd Gwynd
30 D6 Trealaw Rhondd
88 E4 Treales Lancs
78 D9 Trearddur Bay IoA
152 F7 Treaslane Highld
4 E6 Treator Cnwll
30 D10 Tre Aubrey V Glam
30 D6 Trebanog Rhondd
29 K4 Trebanos Neath
5 M6 Trebartha Cnwll
4 H4 Trebarwith Cnwll
5 M4 Trebeath Cnwll
4 E6 Trebetherick Cnwll
18 D7 Treborough Somset
4 D9 Trebudannon Cnwll
5 N6 Trebullett Cnwll
4 H6 Treburgett Cnwll
5 P6 Treburley Cnwll
4 D7 Treburrick Cnwll
4 H9 Trebyan Cnwll
44 B9 Trecastle Powys
5 N5 Trecogo Cnwll
8 F4 Trecott Devon
41 J4 Trecwn Pembks
30 C4 Trecynon Rhondd
5 L5 Tredaule Cnwll
2 D8 Tredavoe Cnwll
30 F3 Tredegar Blae G
4 H7 Tredethy Cnwll
46 H9 Tredington Gloucs
47 Q6 Tredington Warwks
4 E7 Tredinnick Cnwll
4 G10 Tredinnick Cnwll
5 K8 Tredinnick Cnwll
5 L10 Tredinnick Cnwll
5 M10 Tredinnick Cnwll
44 G8 Tredomen Powys
41 L2 Tredrissi Pembks
4 F6 Tredrizzick Cnwll
31 L6 Tredunnock Mons
44 G8 Tredustan Powys
2 B9 Treen Cnwll
2 C6 Treen Cnwll
4 H10 Treesmill Cnwll
84 F3 Treeton Rothm
40 G3 Trefasser Pembks
78 G10 Trefdraeth IoA
44 G8 Trefecca Powys
55 M6 Trefeglwys Powys
54 E11 Trefenter Cerdgn
41 J6 Treffgarne Pembks
40 G5 Treffgarne Owen Pembks
30 E7 Trefforest Rhondd
40 G5 Treffynnon Pembks
30 F2 Trefil Blae G
43 K3 Trefilan Cerdgn
40 F4 Trefin Pembks
69 J9 Treflach Wood Shrops
68 H11 Trefnannau Powys
80 F10 Trefnant Denbgs
69 J9 Trefonen Shrops
66 F5 Trefor Gwynd
78 F8 Trefor IoA
5 J5 Trefrew Cnwll
67 P2 Trefriw Conwy
5 M5 Tregadillett Cnwll
31 P3 Tre-gagle Mons
78 H8 Tregaian IoA
31 M2 Tregare Mons
3 K9 Tregarne Cnwll
43 N3 Tregaron Cerdgn
79 L11 Tregarth Gwynd
4 D9 Tregaswith Cnwll
4 H4 Tregatta Cnwll
4 G8 Tregawne Cnwll
5 L4 Tregeare Cnwll
68 G8 Tregeiriog Wrexhm
78 F6 Tregele IoA
4 G6 Tregellist Cnwll
3 M5 Tregenna Cnwll
2 B7 Tregeseal Cnwll
3 L7 Tregew Cnwll
30 C3 Tre-Gibbon Rhondd
3 K9 Tregidden Cnwll
3 Q4 Tregiskey Cnwll
40 F5 Treglemais Pembks
5 K2 Tregole Cnwll
3 J6 Tregolls Cnwll
4 E7 Tregonce Cnwll
4 F9 Tregonetha Cnwll
3 N5 Tregony Cnwll
5 J5 Tregoodwell Cnwll
3 Q3 Tregorrick Cnwll
4 F9 Tregoss Cnwll
44 H7 Tregoyd Powys
3 Q3 Tregrehan Mills Cnwll
42 H6 Tre-groes Cerdgn
4 H9 Tregullon Cnwll
4 F7 Tregunna Cnwll
5 L5 Tregunnon Cnwll
4 D8 Tregurrian Cnwll
55 P5 Tregynon Powys
42 H11 Tre-gynwr Carmth
30 D6 Trehafod Rhondd
5 Q10 Trehan Cnwll
30 E5 Treharris Myr Td
4 G6 Treharrock Cnwll
4 D7 Trehemborne Cnwll
43 L5 Treherbert Carmth
29 P5 Treherbert Rhondd
5 N9 Trehunist Cnwll
5 N6 Trekenner Cnwll
4 H4 Treknow Cnwll
3 J10 Trelan Cnwll
5 K3 Trelash Cnwll
3 M3 Trelassick Cnwll
5 L11 Trelawne Cnwll
80 F9 Trelawnyd Flints
3 K9 Treleague Cnwll
3 K10 Treleaver Cnwll
41 Q4 Trelech Carmth
42 F9 Trelech a'r Betws Carmth
40 E5 Treleddyd-fawr Pembks
3 L6 Trelew Cnwll
30 F5 Trelewis Myr Td
4 G5 Treligga Cnwll
4 F6 Trelights Cnwll
4 G6 Trelill Cnwll
5 N5 Trelinnoe Cnwll
3 N3 Trelion Cnwll
3 L6 Trelissick Cnwll
3 L6 Trelissick Garden Cnwll
31 P3 Trellech Mons
31 N4 Trelleck Grange Mons
80 G8 Trelogan Flints
4 E8 Trelow Cnwll
3 J9 Trelowarren Cnwll
5 M10 Trelowia Cnwll
3 M6 Treluggan Cnwll
56 D4 Trelystan Powys
67 K7 Tremadog Gwynd
5 K4 Tremail Cnwll
42 D5 Tremain Cerdgn
5 L4 Tremaine Cnwll
5 M8 Tremar Cnwll
5 P10 Trematon Cnwll
5 M8 Trembraze Cnwll
80 F10 Tremeirchion Denbgs
2 C7 Tremethick Cross Cnwll
4 G9 Tremore Cnwll
80 G9 Tre-Mostyn Flints
3 L9 Trenance Cnwll
4 D8 Trenance Cnwll
4 E7 Trenance Cnwll
3 Q4 Trenarren Cnwll
57 M2 Trench Wrekin
35 J9 Trench Green Oxon
3 M3 Trendeal Cnwll
2 D6 Trendrine Cnwll
4 F7 Treneague Cnwll
2 H7 Trenear Cnwll
5 L4 Treneglos Cnwll
2 G6 Trenerth Cnwll
5 K11 Trenewan Cnwll
4 H6 Trenewth Cnwll
5 K3 Trengune Cnwll
4 C9 Treninnick Cnwll
4 B10 Trenowah Cnwll
3 K7 Trenoweth Cnwll
19 Q11 Trent Dorset
70 F6 Trentham C Stke
17 L2 Trentishoe Devon
72 D4 Trentlock Derbys
85 P4 Trent Port Lincs
70 F6 Trent Vale C Stke
2 G7 Trenwheal Cnwll
29 P9 Treoes V Glam
30 C5 Treorchy Rhondd
4 G6 Trequite Cnwll
54 F6 Tre'r-ddol Cerdgn
30 D9 Trerhyngyll V Glam
5 N10 Trerulefoot Cnwll
42 E4 Tresaith Cerdgn
3 M4 Tresawle Cnwll
2 b2 Tresco IoS
2 b2 *Tresco Heliport IoS*
58 C5 Trescott Staffs
2 F7 Trescowe Cnwll
4 B10 Tresean Cnwll
32 E6 Tresham Gloucs
136 G7 Treshnish Isles Ag & B
3 M4 Tresillian Cnwll
5 J5 Tresinney Cnwll
5 L2 Treskinnick Cross Cnwll
5 L4 Tresmeer Cnwll
5 J3 Tresparrett Cnwll
141 K5 Tressait P & K
169 q8 Tresta Shet
169 t4 Tresta Shet
85 N5 Treswell Notts
2 G5 Treswithian Cnwll
2 G5 Treswithian Downs Crematorium Cnwll
54 F6 Tre Taliesin Cerdgn
4 H4 Trethevey Cnwll
2 B9 Trethewey Cnwll
30 G7 Trethomas Caerph
3 N3 Trethosa Cnwll
4 G10 Trethurgy Cnwll
40 E5 Tretio Pembks
45 Q10 Tretire Herefs
44 H10 Tretower Powys
69 J3 Treuddyn Flints
5 M6 Trevadlock Cnwll
4 H3 Trevalga Cnwll
69 L3 Trevalyn Wrexhm
4 F6 Trevanger Cnwll
4 F7 Trevanson Cnwll
2 D7 Trevarrack Cnwll
4 E9 Trevarren Cnwll
4 D8 Trevarrian Cnwll
3 P5 Trevarrick Cnwll
3 J5 Trevarth Cnwll
41 P7 Trevaughan Carmth
42 G10 Tre-Vaughan Carmth
2 D5 Treveal Cnwll
4 B10 Treveal Cnwll
4 H6 Treveighan Cnwll
3 J3 Trevellas Downs Cnwll
5 L9 Trevelmond Cnwll
4 C10 Trevemper Cnwll
3 P5 Treveor Cnwll
3 M4 Treverbyn Cnwll
4 G10 Treverbyn Cnwll
3 K7 Treverva Cnwll
2 B9 Trevescan Cnwll
31 J4 Trevethin Torfn
4 H5 Trevia Cnwll
5 N8 Trevigro Cnwll
3 L6 Trevilla Cnwll
4 C10 Trevilson Cnwll
4 E10 Treviscoe Cnwll
3 N5 Treviskey Cnwll
3 P4 Trevithick Cnwll
4 D9 Trevithick Cnwll
4 C10 Trevoll Cnwll
4 D6 Trevone Cnwll
69 J6 Trevor Wrexhm
2 C8 Trevorgans Cnwll
4 E7 Trevorrick Cnwll
4 D6 Trevose Cnwll
2 G8 Trew Cnwll
4 H5 Trewalder Cnwll
44 H8 Trewalkin Powys
4 H4 Trewarmett Cnwll
5 J4 Trewassa Cnwll
2 F8 Trewavas Cnwll
5 L5 Treween Cnwll
2 B7 Trewellard Cnwll
5 M5 Trewen Cnwll
2 H8 Trewennack Cnwll
41 K11 Trewent Pembks
56 D2 Trewern Powys
4 G5 Trewetha Cnwll
4 G6 Trewethern Cnwll
5 M10 Trewidland Cnwll
3 K10 Trewillis Cnwll
5 L5 Trewint Cnwll
5 M9 Trewint Cnwll
3 M6 Trewithian Cnwll
5 N7 Trewoodloe Cnwll
2 H10 Trewoon Cnwll
3 P3 Trewoon Cnwll
3 M5 Treworga Cnwll
3 L4 Treworgan Cnwll
3 M6 Treworlas Cnwll
5 J3 Treworld Cnwll
3 M6 Treworthal Cnwll
45 L10 Tre-wyn Mons
4 D7 Treyarnon Cnwll
23 M11 Treyford W Susx
13 J4 Trickett's Cross Dorset
111 L7 Triermain Cumb
41 J6 Triffleton Pembks
5 M4 Trillacott Cnwll

West Bradford - Whitekirk 305

89 L2 West Bradford Lancs
19 Q7 West Bradley Somset
90 H8 West Bretton Wakefd
72 F3 West Bridgford Notts
103 J7 West Briscoe Dur
58 F6 West Bromwich Sandw
58 F6 West Bromwich Crematorium Sandw
39 P7 Westbrook Kent
34 D10 Westbrook W Berk
33 J11 Westbrook Wilts
17 M5 West Buckland Devon
18 G10 West Buckland Somset
96 F3 West Burton N York
15 Q4 West Burton W Susx
48 H7 Westbury Bucks
56 F3 Westbury Shrops
20 G4 Westbury Wilts
20 G5 Westbury Leigh Wilts
32 D2 Westbury on Severn Gloucs
31 Q9 Westbury-on-Trym Bristl
19 P5 Westbury-sub-Mendip Somset
103 M2 West Butsfield Dur
92 D9 West Butterwick N Linc
88 D4 Westby Lancs
36 B8 West Byfleet Surrey
106 F11 West Cairngaan D & G
77 Q9 West Caister Norfk
127 J5 West Calder W Loth
19 Q10 West Camel Somset
12 C8 West Chaldon Dorset
34 C7 West Challow Oxon
7 K10 West Charleton Devon
11 L3 West Chelborough Dorset
119 P11 West Chevington Nthumb
24 C7 West Chiltington W Susx
12 K2 West Chinnock Somset
21 M4 West Chisenbury Wilts
36 B10 West Clandon Surrey
27 P3 West Cliffe Kent
34 E6 Westcliff-on-Sea Sthend
11 L2 West Coker Somset
7 K6 West Combe Devon
20 C7 Westcombe Somset
19 Q6 West Compton Somset
11 M6 West Compton Abbas Dorset
47 P10 Westcote Gloucs
48 D9 Westcote Barton Oxon
49 K11 Westcott Bucks
9 P4 Westcott Devon
36 D11 Westcott Surrey
92 A2 West Cottingwith N York
21 P2 Westcourt Wilts
91 Q6 West Cowick E R Yk
28 H7 West Cross Swans
5 M3 West Curry Cnwll
110 F11 West Curthwaite Cumb
25 M11 Westdean E Susx
15 N4 West Dean W Susx
20 J10 West Dean Wilts
74 B9 West Deeping Lincs
81 M6 West Derby Lpool
75 N10 West Dereham Norfk
119 M6 West Ditchburn Nthumb
17 J3 West Down Devon
21 K5 Westdown Camp Wilts
4 H5 Westdowns Cnwll
36 C5 West Drayton Gt Lon
85 M6 West Drayton Notts
167 M2 West Dunnet Highld
37 M7 Wested Kent
92 H5 West Ella E R Yk
49 Q4 West End Bed
35 N10 West End Br For
30 H5 West End Caerph
62 D7 West End Cambs
110 F9 West End Cumb
92 F4 West End E R Yk
93 L4 West End E R Yk
93 N5 West End E R Yk
32 E3 Westend Gloucs
14 E4 West End Hants
21 K2 West End Hants
50 G9 West End Herts
50 H9 West End Herts
89 L5 West End Lancs
90 G3 West End Leeds
93 Q11 West End Lincs
31 N11 West End N Som
91 N2 West End N York
76 C10 West End Norfk
77 Q9 West End Norfk
34 G7 West End Oxon
32 D7 West End S Glos
20 C8 West End Somset
23 P2 West End Surrey
36 D8 West End Surrey
36 F9 West End W & M
24 F7 West End W Susx
20 H10 West End Wilts
21 J10 West End Wilts
33 J9 West End Wilts
23 J2 West End Green Hants
111 Q7 Westend Town Nthumb
27 K4 Westenhanger Kent
167 K6 Westerdale Highld
105 J9 Westerdale N York
53 L2 Westerfield Suffk
15 P5 Westergate W Susx
37 K10 Westerham Kent
113 J7 Westerhope N u Ty
7 M6 Westerland Devon
32 C9 Westerleigh S Glos
32 D9 Westerleigh Crematorium S Glos
127 J3 Wester Ochiltree W Loth
135 P6 Wester Pitkierie Fife
160 F11 Wester Ross Highld
15 N5 Westerton W Susx
143 M7 Westerton of Rossie Angus
169 p9 Westerwick Shet
36 F8 West Ewell Surrey
38 B11 West Farleigh Kent
48 F4 West Farndon Nhants
69 K9 West Felton Shrops
20 C4 Westfield BaNES
100 C5 Westfield Cumb
26 D8 Westfield E Susx
167 J4 Westfield Highld
126 C3 Westfield N Lans
76 D10 Westfield Norfk
126 G3 Westfield W Loth
12 B3 Westfields Dorset
45 P6 Westfields Herefs
142 B8 Westfields of Rattray P & K
38 C9 Westfield Sole Kent
99 M5 West Flotmanby N York
18 F10 Westford Somset
102 H3 Westgate Dur
92 C9 Westgate N Linc
76 D3 Westgate Norfk
90 G5 Westgate Hill C Brad
39 P7 Westgate on Sea Kent
76 H7 Westgate Street Norfk
34 D7 West Ginge Oxon
21 P2 West Grafton Wilts
23 K3 West Green Hants
21 P9 West Grimstead Wilts
24 E6 West Grinstead W Susx
91 P5 West Haddlesey N York
60 D6 West Haddon Nhants
34 F7 West Hagbourne Oxon
58 D8 West Hagley Worcs
65 N5 Westhall Suffk
72 C2 West Hallam Derbys
72 C2 West Hallam Common Derbys
92 F6 West Halton N Linc
11 P9 Westham Dorset
25 P10 Westham E Susx
37 J4 West Ham Gt Lon
19 M5 Westham Somset
15 N5 Westhampnett W Susx
84 E5 West Handley Derbys
34 D6 West Hanney Oxon
38 B2 West Hanningfield Essex
21 M9 West Harnham Wilts
19 Q3 West Harptree BaNES
23 L10 West Harting W Susx
19 J10 West Hatch Somset
20 H9 West Hatch Wilts
143 K10 West Haven Angus
19 M6 Westhay Somset
88 E9 Westhead Lancs
75 L9 West Head Norfk
58 F9 West Heath Birm
22 G3 West Heath Hants
163 N3 West Helmsdale Highld
34 D7 West Hendred Oxon
50 D10 West Hertfordshire Crematorium Herts
99 J5 West Heslerton N York
19 L2 West Hewish N Som
46 A6 Westhide Herefs
151 L6 Westhill Abers
9 Q6 West Hill Devon
25 J4 West Hoathly W Susx
12 E7 West Holme Dorset
19 Q6 Westholme Somset
45 P4 Westhope Herefs
56 H7 Westhope Shrops
37 P3 West Horndon Essex
48 F4 Westhorp Nhants
74 D4 Westhorpe Lincs
64 E8 Westhorpe Suffk
19 Q5 West Horrington Somset
36 C10 West Horsley Surrey
119 K4 West Horton Nthumb
27 N3 West Hougham Kent
89 K9 Westhoughton Bolton
95 P6 Westhouse N York
84 F9 Westhouses Derbys
13 J5 West Howe Bmouth
18 B8 West Howetown Somset
36 E10 Westhumble Surrey
134 D3 West Huntingtower P & K
19 K6 West Huntspill Somset
50 D7 West Hyde C Beds
36 B2 West Hyde Herts
27 K5 West Hythe Kent
17 N2 West Ilkerton Devon
34 E8 West Ilsley W Berk
15 L6 West Itchenor W Susx
87 L8 West Keal Lincs
33 M11 West Kennett Wilts
124 G8 West Kilbride N Ayrs
37 N8 West Kingsdown Kent
32 F9 West Kington Wilts
81 J7 West Kirby Wirral
98 H5 West Knapton N York
12 B7 West Knighton Dorset
20 G8 West Knoyle Wilts
119 L2 West Kyloe Nthumb
6 G8 Westlake Devon
19 M11 West Lambrook Somset
51 K6 Westland Green Herts
27 P2 West Langdon Kent
23 N10 West Lavington W Susx
21 K4 West Lavington Wilts
103 M8 West Layton N York
72 E5 West Leake Notts
118 F3 West Learmouth Nthumb
104 E10 West Lees N York
8 G3 West Leigh Devon
16 H6 Westleigh Devon
18 E11 Westleigh Devon
18 F8 West Leigh Somset
65 N8 Westleton Suffk
76 A8 West Lexham Norfk
56 F3 Westley Shrops
63 P8 Westley Suffk
63 K9 Westley Waterless Cambs
98 C8 West Lilling N York
35 L2 Westlington Bucks
127 M7 West Linton Border
110 G8 Westlinton Cumb
32 E9 West Littleton S Glos
34 D7 West Lockinge Oxon
36 F4 West London Crematorium Gt Lon
12 D8 West Lulworth Dorset
99 J7 West Lutton N York
19 Q8 West Lydford Somset
17 N2 West Lyn Devon
19 K9 West Lyng Somset
75 M6 West Lynn Norfk
37 Q9 West Malling Kent
46 E5 West Malvern Worcs
15 L4 West Marden W Susx
85 M6 West Markham Notts
39 N9 Westmarsh Kent
93 N9 West Marsh NE Lin
96 C10 West Marton N York
20 G10 West Melbury Dorset
91 L10 West Melton Rothm
22 H10 West Meon Hants
23 J9 West Meon Hut Hants
22 H9 West Meon Woodlands Hants
52 H9 West Mersea Essex
24 H8 Westmeston E Susx
112 G8 West Mickley Nthumb
57 Q9 West Midland Safari Park Worcs
50 H7 Westmill Herts
51 J5 Westmill Herts
11 L5 West Milton Dorset
36 G5 Westminster Gt Lon
38 F7 West Minster Kent
36 D7 West Molesey Surrey
19 J9 West Monkton Somset
13 J4 West Moors Dorset
12 F5 West Morden Dorset
118 B2 West Morriston Border
90 D2 West Morton C Brad
19 Q10 West Mudford Somset
142 F7 Westmuir Angus
98 D5 West Ness N York
104 C7 West Newbiggin Darltn
100 F2 Westnewton Cumb
93 M3 West Newton E R Yk
75 N5 West Newton Norfk
19 J9 West Newton Somset
36 H6 West Norwood Gt Lon
36 H6 West Norwood Crematorium Gt Lon
113 N7 Westoe S Tyne
7 L4 West Ogwell Devon
32 D11 Weston BaNES
70 C4 Weston Ches E
10 C4 Weston Devon
10 D7 Weston Devon
11 P10 Weston Dorset
81 Q8 Weston Halton
23 K10 Weston Hants
45 M3 Weston Herefs
50 G4 Weston Herts
74 E6 Weston Lincs
97 J11 Weston N York
48 G5 Weston Nhants
85 N7 Weston Notts
56 E10 Weston Shrops
57 L6 Weston Shrops
69 J9 Weston Shrops
70 H9 Weston Staffs
34 C10 Weston W Berk
46 A6 Weston Beggard Herefs
32 G7 Westonbirt Gloucs
60 G2 Weston by Welland Nhants
22 F7 Weston Colley Hants
63 K10 Weston Colville Cambs
23 J5 Weston Corbett Hants
70 G6 Weston Coyney C Stke
60 G8 Weston Favell Nhants
63 K10 Weston Green Cambs
57 P2 Weston Heath Shrops
74 E6 Weston Hills Lincs
59 N7 Weston in Arden Warwks
50 B4 Westoning C Beds
31 M10 Weston-in-Gordano N Som
50 B4 Westoning Woodend C Beds
70 D10 Weston Jones Staffs
76 G8 Weston Longville Norfk
69 M10 Weston Lullingfields Shrops
6 D7 Weston Mill Crematorium C Plym
47 N4 Weston-on-Avon Warwks
48 F11 Weston-on-the-Green Oxon
23 J5 Weston Patrick Hants
69 J7 Weston Rhyn Shrops
47 M6 Weston-sub-Edge Gloucs
19 K2 Weston-super-Mare N Som
19 L2 Weston-super-Mare Crematorium N Som
35 N2 Weston Turville Bucks
57 Q2 Weston-under-Lizard Staffs
46 B10 Weston under Penyard Herefs
69 Q9 Weston-under-Redcastle Shrops
59 N11 Weston under Wetherley Warwks
71 P6 Weston Underwood Derbys
49 N4 Weston Underwood M Keyn
72 C5 Weston-upon-Trent Derbys
19 L8 Westonzoyland Somset
20 F11 West Orchard Dorset
33 M11 West Overton Wilts
98 F7 Westow N York
5 N3 West Panson Devon
151 K8 West Park Abers
13 J5 West Parley Dorset
37 P10 West Peckham Kent
5 N3 West Peeke Devon
113 K10 West Pelton Dur
19 P7 West Pennard Somset
4 B9 West Pentire Cnwll
61 P7 West Perry Cambs
17 R2 West Porlock Somset
19 L10 Westport Somset
11 Q3 West Pulham Dorset
16 F8 West Putford Devon
18 E6 West Quantoxhead Somset
126 G2 Westquarter Falk
30 F10 Westra V Glam
9 L4 West Raddon Devon
113 M11 West Rainton Dur
86 E3 West Rasen Lincs
93 M11 West Ravendale NE Lin
169 d2 Westray Ork
169 d1 Westray Airport Ork
76 B6 West Raynham Norfk
85 L4 West Retford Notts
34 G9 Westridge Green W Berk
126 G4 Westrigg W Loth
113 K7 West Road Crematorium N u Ty
33 P6 Westrop Swindn
104 D10 West Rounton N York
63 L5 West Row Suffk
75 R5 West Rudham Norfk
76 H3 West Runton Norfk
128 G10 Westruther Border
74 H11 Westry Cambs
128 D6 West Saltoun E Loth
9 K4 West Sandford Devon
169 r5 West Sandwick Shet
96 G4 West Scrafton N York
113 L4 West Sleekburn Nthumb
77 P7 West Somerton Norfk
11 Q7 West Stafford Dorset
92 C11 West Stockwith Notts
15 M5 West Stoke W Susx
102 G10 West Stonesdale N York
19 M5 West Stoughton Somset
20 E10 West Stour Dorset
39 N9 West Stourmouth Kent
63 P6 West Stow Suffk
21 M2 West Stowell Wilts
22 F6 West Stratton Hants
38 F11 West Street Kent
39 P11 West Street Kent
38 B6 West Street Medway
64 D7 West Street Suffk
63 P7 West Suffolk Crematorium Suffk
97 L5 West Tanfield N York
5 J9 West Taphouse Cnwll
123 P6 West Tarbert Ag & B
24 D10 West Tarring W Susx
119 N11 West Thirston Nthumb
15 L6 West Thorney W Susx
84 G5 Westthorpe Derbys
72 G5 West Thorpe Notts
37 N5 West Thurrock Thurr
37 Q5 West Tilbury Thurr
23 J9 West Tisted Hants
86 F4 West Torrington Lincs
19 P2 West Town BaNES
15 K7 West Town Hants
45 N2 West Town Herefs
31 N11 West Town N Som
19 P7 West Town Somset
20 D6 West Town Somset
21 Q9 West Tytherley Hants
75 J8 West Walton Norfk
75 J8 West Walton Highway Norfk
101 J2 Westward Cumb
16 G6 Westward Ho! Devon
26 G2 Westwell Kent
33 P3 Westwell Oxon
26 G2 Westwell Leacon Kent
21 Q11 West Wellow Hants
6 E9 West Wembury Devon
135 J9 West Wemyss Fife
62 F7 Westwick Cambs
103 L7 Westwick Dur
19 L2 West Wick N Som
77 K6 Westwick Norfk
63 K11 West Wickham Cambs
37 J7 West Wickham Gt Lon
41 K9 West Williamston Pembks
20 H3 West Wiltshire Crematorium Wilts
75 M7 West Winch Norfk
21 P8 West Winterslow Wilts
15 L7 West Wittering W Susx
96 G3 West Witton N York
9 P5 Westwood Devon
37 P6 Westwood Kent
39 Q8 Westwood Kent
84 G10 Westwood Notts
111 Q7 Westwood Nthumb
20 F3 Westwood Wilts
112 C3 West Woodburn Nthumb
22 C2 West Woodhay W Berk
59 L9 Westwood Heath Covtry
20 E6 West Woodlands Somset
92 B10 Westwoodside N Linc
23 K7 West Worldham Hants
24 D10 West Worthing W Susx
63 K10 West Wratting Cambs
35 M6 West Wycombe Bucks
112 H8 West Wylam Nthumb
32 G9 West Yatton Wilts
37 P7 West Yoke Kent
16 D8 West Youlstone Cnwll
38 D8 Wetham Green Kent
111 J10 Wetheral Cumb
97 P11 Wetherby Leeds
97 P10 Wetherby Services N York
64 E9 Wetherden Suffk
64 G8 Wetheringsett Suffk
52 B5 Wethersfield Essex
64 G9 Wetherup Street Suffk
70 H5 Wetley Rocks Staffs
69 R2 Wettenhall Ches E
71 L3 Wetton Staffs
99 J9 Wetwang E R Yk
70 D8 Wetwood Staffs
21 Q3 Wexcombe Wilts
35 Q8 Wexham Slough
35 Q8 Wexham Street Bucks
76 G3 Weybourne Norfk
23 N5 Weybourne Surrey
65 J5 Weybread Suffk
65 J6 Weybread Street Suffk
36 C8 Weybridge Surrey
10 G5 Weycroft Devon
167 L4 Weydale Highld
22 B5 Weyhill Hants
11 P9 Weymouth Dorset
11 P9 Weymouth Crematorium Dorset
49 M8 Whaddon Bucks
62 E11 Whaddon Cambs
32 F2 Whaddon Gloucs
20 G2 Whaddon Wilts
21 N9 Whaddon Wilts
101 P6 Whale Cumb
84 H6 Whaley Derbys
83 M8 Whaley Bridge Derbys
84 H6 Whaley Thorns Derbys
167 P8 Whaligoe Highld
89 L3 Whalley Lancs
89 L3 Whalley Banks Lancs
169 s7 Whalsay Shet
112 H4 Whalton Nthumb
74 F6 Whaplode Lincs
74 F8 Whaplode Drove Lincs
48 D4 Wharf Warwks
96 A7 Wharfe N York
88 E3 Wharles Lancs
49 P6 Wharley End C Beds
84 C2 Wharncliffe Side Sheff
98 H7 Wharram-le-Street N York
82 E11 Wharton Ches W
45 Q3 Wharton Herefs
103 N9 Whashton N York
95 L4 Whasset Cumb
47 Q6 Whatcote Warwks
59 K5 Whateley Warwks
52 H2 Whatfield Suffk
10 H3 Whatley Somset
20 D5 Whatley Somset
32 C8 Whatley's End S Glos
26 C8 Whatlington E Susx
27 K3 Whatsole Street Kent
84 D10 Whatstandwell Derbys
73 J3 Whatton Notts
107 M8 Whauphill D & G
103 J10 Whaw N York
3 J5 Wheal Rose Cnwll
65 P3 Wheatacre Norfk
35 J5 Wheatfield Oxon
50 E8 Wheathampstead Herts
57 L8 Wheathill Shrops
19 Q8 Wheathill Somset
90 D5 Wheatley Calder
23 L6 Wheatley Hants
34 G3 Wheatley Oxon
104 C3 Wheatley Hill Dur
91 P10 Wheatley Hills Donc
89 N3 Wheatley Lane Lancs
58 C2 Wheaton Aston Staffs
69 K4 Wheatsheaf Wrexhm
18 B7 Wheddon Cross Somset
27 K2 Wheelbarrow Town Kent
35 M6 Wheeler End Bucks
35 L10 Wheeler's Green Wokham
26 D3 Wheeler's Street Kent
23 P6 Wheelerstreet Surrey
70 D3 Wheelock Ches E
70 D3 Wheelock Heath Ches E
89 J6 Wheelton Lancs
91 M5 Wheldale Wakefd
92 A2 Wheldrake C York
33 N5 Whelford Gloucs
35 Q4 Whelpley Hill Bucks
101 K3 Whelpo Cumb
81 J9 Whelston Flints
50 H6 Whempstead Herts
98 C7 Whenby N York
64 A10 Whepstead Suffk
53 L3 Wherstead Suffk
22 C6 Wherwell Hants
83 P9 Wheston Derbys
37 Q11 Whetsted Kent
36 G2 Whetstone Gt Lon
72 F11 Whetstone Leics
110 C11 Wheyrigg Cumb
94 C4 Whicham Cumb
48 B8 Whichford Warwks
113 K8 Whickham Gatesd
8 C5 Whiddon Devon
8 G6 Whiddon Down Devon
53 K3 Whight's Corner Suffk
142 H9 Whigstreet Angus
60 D8 Whilton Nhants
16 F11 Whimble Devon
9 P5 Whimple Devon
77 M6 Whimpwell Green Norfk
76 E10 Whinburgh Norfk
88 D2 Whin Lane End Lancs
108 F10 Whinnie Liggate D & G
110 F10 Whinnow Cumb
159 Q11 Whinnyfold Abers
104 C7 Whinny Hill S on T
14 F8 Whippingham IoW
50 B7 Whipsnade C Beds
9 M6 Whipton Devon
84 D4 Whirlow Sheff
86 B7 Whisby Lincs
73 L8 Whissendine Rutlnd
76 C7 Whissonsett Norfk
131 Q9 Whistlefield Ag & B
131 N9 Whistlefield Inn Ag & B
35 L10 Whistley Green Wokham
81 P6 Whiston Knows
60 H8 Whiston Nhants
84 F3 Whiston Rothm
58 C2 Whiston Staffs
71 J5 Whiston Staffs
57 P4 Whiston Cross Shrops
71 J5 Whiston Eaves Staffs
59 L6 Whitacre Fields Warwks
94 C4 Whitbeck Cumb
46 D3 Whitbourne Herefs
113 P8 Whitburn S Tyne
126 G5 Whitburn W Loth
81 M9 Whitby Ches W
105 N8 Whitby N York
81 M10 Whitbyheath Ches W
129 J8 Whitchester Border
32 B11 Whitchurch BaNES
49 M10 Whitchurch Bucks
30 G9 Whitchurch Cardif
6 D4 Whitchurch Devon
22 E5 Whitchurch Hants
45 R11 Whitchurch Herefs
34 H9 Whitchurch Oxon
40 F5 Whitchurch Pembks
69 P6 Whitchurch Shrops
10 H5 Whitchurch Canonicorum Dorset
34 H9 Whitchurch Hill Oxon
11 Q7 Whitcombe Dorset
56 F6 Whitcot Shrops
56 D8 Whitcott Keysett Shrops
27 K2 Whiteacre Kent
59 K6 Whiteacre Heath Warwks
52 C5 Whiteash Green Essex
18 F11 White Ball Somset
147 M4 Whitebridge Highld
31 P3 Whitebrook Mons
151 N4 Whitecairns Abers
36 H4 Whitechapel Gt Lon
88 H2 White Chapel Lancs
41 N3 Whitechurch Pembks
31 Q3 Whitecliffe Gloucs
52 E6 White Colne Essex
89 J7 White Coppice Lancs
127 Q3 Whitecraig E Loth
32 B3 Whitecroft Gloucs
106 G6 Whitecrook D & G
2 E7 Whitecross Cnwll
2 H9 White Cross Cnwll
4 F7 Whitecross Cnwll
126 H2 Whitecross Falk
46 E8 White End Worcs
162 G9 Whiteface Highld
120 G3 Whitefarland N Ayrs
114 E6 Whitefaulds S Ayrs
89 N9 Whitefield Bury
17 N4 Whitefield Devon
18 E9 Whitefield Somset
81 P7 Whitefield Lane End Knows
151 J2 Whiteford Abers
82 D11 Whitegate Ches W
23 K4 Whitehall Hants
169 f4 Whitehall Ork
24 D6 Whitehall W Susx
100 C7 Whitehaven Cumb
38 H10 Whitehill Kent
72 C8 Whitehill Leics
23 L8 Whitehill and Bordon Hants
158 G4 Whitehills Abers
150 G5 Whitehouse Abers
123 P7 Whitehouse Ag & B
58 H5 Whitehouse Common Birm
128 F3 Whitekirk E Loth

Be prepared on your journey... just in case

AA Road Safety Kit
Exclusively available at **theAA.com/shop/safety**

Only £25*
NORMALLY £50 AT
theAA.com/shop
Includes free P&P**

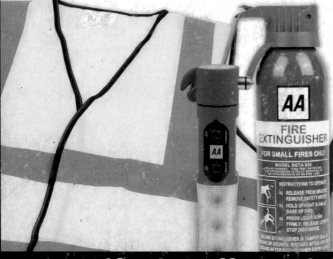

Half price offer, only with AA Atlases

Durable Zipped Bag
Neatly keeps the safety equipment altogether and ready for any breakdown or emergency.

Hazard Warning Triangle
Alert oncoming traffic in hazardous situations. RRP £9.99.

Reflective Emergency Jacket
For maximum visibility in emergencies. RRP £7.99.

First Aid Kit
Contains: plasters, dressings, foil blanket, microporous adhesive tape, wipes, gloves and scissors. RRP £7.99.

Fire Extinguisher
(950g) Lightweight and easy to operate. RRP £14.99.

3-in-One Emergency Beacon
360 degree flashing beacon, seat belt cutter and an emergency glass hammer all in one. RRP £11.99.

How to buy:
To buy this kit for only £25*, simply visit **theAA.com/shop/safety** add to your basket, then enter promotion code **SAFETY**

AA Car Essentials